FREE AFRI

NORTH
VIRGINIA, AND
SOUTH CAROLINA

From the Colonial Period to About 1820

VOLUME II

Winner:
North Carolina Genealogical Society
Award of Excellence in Publishing
and
The American Society of Genealogists'
Donald Lines Jacobus Award

Fifth Edition
by
Paul Heinegg

CLEARFIELD

First Edition, 1992
Second Edition, 1994
Third Edition, 1997
Fourth Edition, 2001
Fifth Edition, 2005

Printed for
Clearfield Company, Inc. by
Genealogical Publishing Co., Inc.
Baltimore, Maryland
2005

International Standard Book Number Volume II: 0-8063-5282-5
Set Number: 0-8063-5280-9

Made in the United States of America

VOLUME II

JACKSON FAMILY

1. Thomas Jackson, born say 1685, was a "Free Negro" who was "Old and infirm" by 18 April 1746 when the Amelia County court exempted him from paying taxes. Perhaps his wife was Eliza Jackson, a "mulatto" taxable in Amelia County in Charles Irby's District in 1747. On 24 August 1758 the court ordered the churchwardens of Raleigh Parish to bind out his children: Will, Tom, and Hannah Jackson [Orders 1735-46, fol. 362; List of Tithables, 1747; Orders 1757-60, 135]. His children were
    - i.   Will.
    - ii.   Tom.
2   - iii. Hannah, born say 1745.

2. Hannah Jackson, born say 1745, may have been the Hannah Jackson whose son Peter (no race indicated) was ordered bound out by the churchwardens of Raleigh Parish in Amelia County on 22 March 1764 [Orders 1764-5, 46]. She may have been the mother of
    - i.   Peter, born say 1763, taxable in Charlotte County in 1795, and from 1800 to 1806: a "f. negroe" from 1800 to 1806, a ditcher listed with wife Rachel in 1805 [PPTL 1782-1813, frames 317, 468, 580, 607, 642, 675, 682] and head of a Jefferson County household of 8 "other free" in 1810 [VA:67].
    - ii.   Edy, born about 1771, registered in Amelia County on 26 September 1816: *a Negroe woman of a light complection, aged about forty five years, five feet high, born free as appears by a certificate from Obedience Hammm with whom she served her apprenticeship* [Register of Free Negroes 1804-35, no. 113].

Hanover, Prince Edward, Lunenburg, and Charlotte counties
1. Dorcas[1] Jackson, born say 1730, petitioned the Prince Edward County court in November 1756 for release from her indenture to Samuel Wallace. The case was dismissed after hearing witnesses, and in August 1757 the court bound her daughter Abby to her master. Dorcas petitioned the court again in August 1758, and this time the court ordered her release because her indenture was not legal. She had been bound out by the churchwardens of St. Paul's Parish, Hanover County, to one Edward Wade, and there was no record of his having transferred the indenture to Wallace. John Coldwell, Letitia Coldwell and William Crocket were witnesses for Dorcas [Orders 1754-8, fols. 97, 104, 121, 159, 163]. She was living in Lunenburg County (no race indicated) when the court ordered the churchwardens of Cornwall Parish to bind her daughter Susannah to Godfrey Jones on 13 October 1763 and her daughter Hannah to William Rivers on 14 February 1765 [Orders 1763-4, 257; 1764-5, 203]. In April 1769 (her children) Dorcas and Isaac Jackson complained to the Prince Edward County court about Wallace, and (her daughter) Nancy Jackson brought complaint against him in May 1769. The complaints were dismissed in March 1770 [Orders 1767-70, 195, 204, 263, 270]. Her children were
2   - i.   Isaac, born about 1748.
3   - ii.   Abby[1], born say 1755.
    - iii. Dorcas[2], born say 1757.
    - iv.   Nancy, born say 1756, brought complaint about Samuel Wallace in 1769. Her son Samuel was bound to Wallace on 19 October 1772 [Orders 1771-81, pt.1, 174].
    - v.   Susannah, born say 1760, bound to Godfrey Jones in Lunenburg County in on 13 October 1763.
    - vi.   Hannah, born say 1762, bound to William Rivers in Lunenburg County on 14 February 1765.
4   - vii. ?Burwell, born say 1768.

5   viii.   ?Berryman, born about 1769.

2.   Isaac Jackson, born about 1748, complained to the Prince Edward County court against his master Samuel Wallace in April 1769. He married Catherine **Byrd**, 22 September 1797 Lunenburg County bond. He was taxable in Stephen Bedford's list for Charlotte County from 1806 to 1812: called "Isaac Jackson, Sr., fn" in 1807 when he was listed as a carpenter with his wife Caty, a male child and 3 female children, levy free in 1809 [PPTL 1782-1813, frames 675, 711, 717, 745, 751, 783, 814, 846]. He was a "free Negro" head of a Charlotte County household of 7 "other free" in 1810 [VA:68]. He registered in Charlotte County on 18 August 1815: *son of Darcas Jackson, a free Mulatto, Black looking complexion, aged 67, born free.* (His widow) Catherine registered on 16 October 1819: *Catherine Jackson, formerly the wife of Isaac Jackson, daughter of Mary Bird, a free woman, Mulatto complexion, aged 50* [Ailsworth, *Charlotte County--Rich Indeed*, 486]. They were the parents of
     i.   Nancy **Chavous**, born about 1796, registered in Charlotte County on 21 October 1831: *wife of Isaac Chavous & daughter of Caty Jackson, Bright complexion, aged 35, born free* [Ailsworth, *Charlotte County-- Rich Indeed*, 489-90].
     ii.   Melchijah, born about 1812, registered in Charlotte County on 21 October 1831: *son of Caty Jackson, Bright, nearly white complexion, born free* [Ailsworth, *Charlotte County--Rich Indeed*, 490].

3.   Abby[1] Jackson, born say 1755, was bound to Samuel Wallace by the Prince Edward County court in 1757. She may have been the mother of Nutly(?) and Berryman Jackson whose indentures were voluntarily delivered to the Prince Edward County court by John Gilcrist on 19 June 1780. The court cancelled the indentures and ordered the churchwardens to bind Nutly to John Davison and Berryman to William Ewing [Orders 1771-81, part 2, 79]. She was the mother of
     i.   Dorcas[3], bound to Samuel Wallace by the Prince Edward County court on 19 October 1772 [Orders 1771-81, pt.1, 174].
     ii.   ?Nutly, bound to John Davison on 19 June 1780. She may have been the Nettie Jackson who married Joseph **Byrd**, 20 August 1790 Charlotte County bond, Burwell Jackson surety.
     iii. Abby[2], born about 1791, listed in Charlotte County as a planter in the same household as Joshua **Gallimore** in 1811, listed in her own household in 1812, a spinner with a male child in 1812 [PPTL 1782- 1813, frames 814, 846]. She registered in Charlotte County on 2 May 1831: *Dark complexion, aged 40, born free* [Ailsworth, *Charlotte County--Rich Indeed*, 488].
     iv.   William, born about 1807, son of Abby Jackson, bound apprentice to Richard Stone by the Mecklenburg County, Virginia court on 12 February 1810 [Orders 1809-10, 127], registered in Charlotte County on 6 June 1831: *son of Abby Jackson, Dark complexion, aged 24, born free* [Ailsworth, *Charlotte County--Rich Indeed*, 488].

4.   Burwell Jackson, born say 1768, was surety for the 20 August 1790 Charlotte County marriage of Nettie Jackson and Joseph **Byrd**. He was head of a Nelson County household of 6 "other free" in 1810 [VA:705]. He and his wife Alley were the parents of
     i.   Nancy **Cousins**, born about 1794, registered in Charlotte County on 15 December 1814: *daughter of Burwell Jackson and Alley his wife, free persons of Colour, Mulatto complexion, aged 24, born free* [Ailsworth, *Charlotte County--Rich Indeed*, 486].

5.   Berry Jackson, born about 1769, was called Berryman Jackson on 19 June 1780 when the Prince Edward County court cancelled his indenture to John

Gilcrist and bound him instead to William Ewing [Orders 1771-81, part 2, 79]. He was taxable in Charlotte County in 1791, 1792 and a "f. Mulattoe" taxable from 1800 to 1806: a ditcher living with wife Clary and son Booker in 1802 [PPTL 1782-1813, frames 230, 279, 468, 505, 538, 542, 580, 607, 648, 675, 682]. He registered in Charlotte County on 6 June 1831: *Bright complexion, aged 62, born free*. He died before 2 June 1834 when his widow Betsy Jackson, daughter of Sally **Gash**, registered in Charlotte County [Ailsworth, *Charlotte County--Rich Indeed*, 488]. Berry was the father of

    i.   Booker, born about 1801, registered in Charlotte County on 7 January 1823: *son of Berry Jackson and Clarissa his wife, free persons, Bright yellow complexion, aged 22, born free* [Ailsworth, *Charlotte County--Rich Indeed*, 486].

    ii.   Preston, born about 1803, registered in Charlotte County on 5 January 1829 and 24 October 1831: *son of Berry Jackson and Clarissa his wife, Bright complexion, aged 28, born free* [Ailsworth, *Charlotte County--Rich Indeed*, 490].

    iii.   Walker, registered in Charlotte County on 6 October 1828: *son of Berry Jackson and Clara his wife free people of Colour, Dark complexion, no age, born free* [Ailsworth, *Charlotte County--Rich Indeed*, 487].

    iv.   George, born about 1805, registered in Charlotte County on 6 October 1828: *son of Berry Jackson and Betsy his wife, free people of Colour, Bright complexion, aged 23, born free* [Ailsworth, *Charlotte County--Rich Indeed*, 487].

Other members of a Jackson family in Virginia were

    i.   Henry, born say 1669, was called "Harry a Maletto," the servant of William Sterling, in March 1689/90 when Francis Betteley deposed to the Northampton County, Virginia court that he had been harrowing wheat in company with Harry when Harry told him where Mr. John Baron stored cloth and other goods (which Betteley later stole). Harry was called Henry Jackson, "maletto servant to William Sterling," on 29 September 1690 when he sued for his freedom. The case was resolved by the parties agreeing that Henry would serve one year and then be discharged from service with reasonable clothing. On 28 May 1697 he, called "the maletto," was presented for driving a cart on Sunday. He was discharged from the presentment on payment of the court fees [Wills, Orders, 1689-98, 46, 62, 64-5; 1698-1710, 427, 451].

    ii.   Stephen born say 1760, a "mulatto" (no age mentioned) who was bound as an apprentice hatter to Moses Doolittle in Spotsylvania County on 17 March 1774 [Deeds 1771-4].

    iii.   William, a man of color from Amherst County who served in the Revolution and lived in Bedford County [National Archives pension file W7877 cited by NSDAR, *African American Patriots*, 150].

    iv.   Charles, born about 1770, head of a York County household of 9 "other free" and a slave in 1810 [VA:876]. He registered in York County on 17 September 1810: *a bright mulato about 40 years of age...long straight hair - Born free* [Free Negro Register 1798-1831, no. 53].

    v.   Davis, head of an Amelia County household of 6 "other free" in 1810 [VA:237].

    vi.   Ned, "free Black" head of a Nottoway County household of 11 "other free" in 1810 [VA:1017].

    vii.   Edward, head of a Goochland County household of 9 "other free" in 1810 [VA:699].

    viii.   John, head of a Nelson County household of 5 "other free" in 1810 [VA:705].

ix. Edward, head of a Norfolk County household of 4 "other free" in 1810 [VA:927].
x. Prissy, head of a Norfolk County household of 7 "other free" in 1810 [VA:906].
xi. Holley, head of a Chesterfield County household of 6 "other free" in 1810 [VA:1062].
xii. Jordan, head of a Rockingham County household of 6 "other free" in 1810 [VA:11].
xiii. John, head of a Richmond City household of 5 "other free" and a slave in 1810 [VA:332].

Members of a Jackson family in North Carolina were
i. Daniel, head of a Richmond County household of 8 "other free" in 1790 [NC:45].
ii. Gabriel, head of a Burke County household of 11 "other free" and a white woman in 1800 [NC:763].
iii. Frederick, born say 1775, a "Mulatto" head of an Edgecombe County household of 2 "other free" and one white woman in 1800 [NC:212] and 9 "free colored" in 1820 [NC:127].
iv. Chloe, head of a Martin County household of 5 "other free" in 1800 [NC:388].
v. Matthew, head of a New Hanover County household of 2 "other free" and a slave in 1800 [NC:308].
vi. Mourning, head of a Tyrrell County household of 1 "other free" in 1810 [NC:796].

Members of a Jackson family in South Carolina were
i. John, head of a Charleston District, St. Bartholomew's Parish household of 8 "other free" in 1790 [SC:36] and a Beaufort County household of 8 in 1800 [SC:98].
ii. Stephen, head of a St. Bartholomew's Parish, Charleston District, South Carolina household of 6 "other free" in 1790 [SC:36] and 8 in 1800 [SC:98].
iii. Thomas, head of a St. Bartholomew's Parish household of 3 "other free" in 1790 [SC:36].
iv. James, head of a Union District household of 6 "other free" in 1800 [SC:244].

JACOB FAMILY

1. Tabitha Jacob, born say 1732, an "Indian," was sued by Bartholomew Pettit for a 1 pound, 7 shillings debt in Northampton County, Virginia, on 15 April 1752 [Orders 1751-3, 89]. She may have been the ancestor of
i. Tinsey, married Solomon **Jeffrey**, 16 January 1788 Northampton County bond, William Satchell security. Tinsey may have been identical to Tiney Jacob who was presented for bastard bearing in Northampton County on 13 May 1772 [Minutes 1771-7, 58].
ii. Polly, married William **Francis**, 30 December 1791 Northampton County bond, Abraham **Lang** security.
iii. James, married Patience **Only**, 23 December 1809 Northampton County bond, Cudjo **Stephens** security.

JACOBS FAMILY

1. Gabriel Jacobs, born say 1650, and (his wife?) Bab, called "Gabriel and Bab," were "Negroes" tithable from 1664 to 1667 in the Northampton County, Virginia household of Captain John Custis [Orders 1657-64, fol. 198; 1664-74, p.15, fol.42]. In 1668 he was called "Gabriell Jacob," and in 1677 Gabriel and

Bab Jacob, Daniel Webb, Isbell Webb, and Fred Tucker were "Negroes" taxed
in John Custis' household [Orders 1674-79, 191]. John Custis made a
Northampton County will, proved 10 February 1695/6, by which he gave his
slave Gabriel Jacob to his wife Tabitha for four years to work on their
"sloope" and then to be free. Custis also gave slaves young Daniel and Bab to
his grandson John Custis [OW 1689-98, 357]. Gabriel was the father of

2   i.   Daniel, born say 1670.
     ii.   Jenny, "Gabriel's daughter," a slave John Custis gave his wife Tabitha
           Custis by his will [OW 1689-98, 355-60].

2.   Daniel Jacob, born say 1670, may have been identical to a "Negro man named
     Daniel" who was freed by the will of Thomas Harmonson, Sr., which was
     proved in Northampton County on 28 November 1702, after the death of his
     widow Elizabeth, on condition he pay 200 pounds of tobacco annually to
     someone whom his wife would assign payment or to his son-in-law William
     Waterson. He was called Daniel Jacob "Negro" on 30 May 1704 when a white
     woman named Joan Dauly was given twenty lashes for stealing goods from
     him [OW&c 1698-1710, 112, 205-206]. Edward **Carter** "Mullator" chose him
     as his guardian in 1707. He was called "Daniell Jacob Negro" on 28 July 1709
     when he agreed to pay Jean Grimes's fine for bastard bearing [OW&c 1698-
     1710, 320, 485]. He sued Thomas **Carter** for a debt of 1,100 pounds of
     tobacco on 20 June 1716 and sued Edward **Harmon** for a debt of 600 pounds
     of tobacco in August 1727 [Orders 1710-16, 255-6; 1722-9, 299]. In
     September 1729 he was sued for planting corn and fencing-in an area which
     blocked Daniel Call's bridle path [Mihalyka, *Loose Papers 1628-1731*, 150],
     206]. He was a Northampton County taxable in his own household from 1720
     to 1723 and was a "negro" taxable head of a household from 1724 to 1731
     with (his wife) Elizabeth, and (children) Isaac, Frances, Abigail, and Elizabeth
     Jacob [Bell, *Northampton County Tithables*, 2, 24, 36, 53, 75, 115, 129, 146,
     161, 171, 190, 229]. He sued the estate of John Clay, deceased, for 100
     pounds of tobacco and a side of sole leather on 10 January 1732/3. His suit
     against Ezekiel Warriner for trespass and assault was dismissed on 13
     February 1732/3 due to Warriner's death. Daniel died before 10 April 1733
     when his widow Elizabeth Jacob declared in court that he had died without
     making a will. His greatest creditor, Gertrude Harmonson, was granted
     administration on the estate. Harmonson accused Elizabeth Jacob and Isaac
     Jacob, "Negroes," of converting part of the estate to their own use. The jury
     found in favor of Harmonson for 2 pounds, 5 shillings. However, Elizabeth
     and Isaac won on appeal, arguing that the administrator was not entitled to the
     wheat in the estate since Daniel died before the first of March [Orders 1732-
     42, 38, 42, 45, 64, 67, 71, 76, 97, 120]. Daniel was probably the father of

3   i.   Isaac[1], born say 1705.
     ii.   Frances, born say 1706, married Daniel **Webb** about 1731 when he
           was taxable in her father's household and she was called Frances
           Webb.
    iii.   Abigail[1], born say 1708, presented for bastard bearing on 11 May
           1731. (Her father) Daniel Jacob paid her fine and indemnified the
           parish [Orders 1729-32, 84, 95].
     iv.   Elizabeth, born say 1710, taxable in her father's household from 1727
           to 1731.

Their probable descendants in North Carolina were
4   i.   Abraham, born say 1730.
     ii.   Matthew[1], born say 1735, received a patent for 160 acres on Hickey
           Branch of Long Creek in New Hanover County on 23 October 1761
           [Hoffman, *Land Patents*, I:417]. He was head of a New Hanover
           County household of 8 "other free" in 1790 [NC:194]. His 13
           September 1786 New Hanover County will was proved on 4 October

1791 [WB C:198; Minutes 1779-92, 428]. He mentioned his wife Margaret; brother John[1] Jacobs; and Zachariah and Primus Jacobs, sons of his unnamed sister.

5   iii.   an unnamed sister of Matthew[1], born say 1736.

      iv.   Zachariah[1], born say 1740, patented 100 acres on the east side of Black River in New Hanover County on 19 December 1763. On 3 December 1767 he appeared in New Hanover County court upon recognizance returned by Hezekiah Doane, Esq., and was discharged from court because no complainant appeared [Minutes 1738-69, 327].

      v.   John[1], born say 1745, brother of Matthew[1] Jacobs. He was living in New Hanover County on the east side of Ryley's Creek on 13 September 1779 when Thomas Carter entered land bordering his [Pruitt, *Land Entries: New Hanover County*, 19] and was mentioned in the 13 September 1786 New Hanover County will of his brother Matthew[1] Jacobs [WB C:198]. He was head of a New Hanover County household of 9 "other free in 1790 [NC:194] and 5 in Bladen County in 1800. He sold land by deed proved in New Hanover County in September Court 1795 [Minutes 1792-98, 152] and sold 50 acres in New Hanover County on the east side of Rileys Creek on 10 December 1799 [DB N:217].

      vi.   Abigail[2], born say 1750, a "Molattow" taxable in the Bertie County household of Benjamin **James** in the 1769 tax list of Josiah Harrell and the 1774 list of Samuel Granberry [CR 10.702.1, box 2]. She may have been Benjamin's common-law wife.

3.   Isaac[1] Jacobs, born say 1705, was taxable in the Northampton County, Virginia household of (his father) Daniel Jacobs from 1724 to 1731. He was called "Isaac Jacob Negro" in the March 1745 session of the Chowan County, North Carolina General Court in which Francis Pugh's executor had a case against him for debt [Chowan County General Court Dockets, 1742-45, March 1745 Reference Docket #4]. He or his son was probably the Isaac Jacobs who was counted as white in Camden District, Richland County, South Carolina, in 1790, head of a household of 4 males over 16, 4 under 16, and a female, living nearby Benjamin Jacobs, Henry **Bunch**, and Barney **Sweat** who were also counted as white [SC:26].[119] Mary Jacobs, Sarah Jacobs, and female members of the **Harris, Rawlinson, Sweat, Wilson, Bottom, Grooms, Jeffers** and **Portie** families were residents of Richland District who petitioned the South Carolina legislature in 1806 asking to be exempted from the tax on free Negro women [S.C. Archives series S.165015, item 01885]. Isaac's descendants were most likely:

      i.   Benjamin[1], head of a household of 2 whites and a slave in Camden District, Richland County, in 1790 [SC:26], perhaps the Benjamin Jacobs who sold land by deed proved in South Carolina in 1770 [Lucas, *Index to Deeds of South Carolina*, Q-3:306].

      ii.   Nancy, head of a Richland District household of 7 "other free" in 1810, counted near John **Webb** [SC:176].

      iii.   Benjamin[2], head of a household of 3 "whites" in Camden District, Richland County in 1790 [SC:26] and 6 "other free" in Richland District in 1810 [SC:175a].

---

[119]Henry **Bunch** was head of a Newberry District household of 2 "other free" in 1800 [SC:66]. Neighbors of the Jacobs family who were counted as white in Camden District, Richland County in 1790 [SC:26] and "other free" in Richland District in 1810 were Moses **Harris** [SC:180], William, Nathaniel, Catherine, Benjamin, John, James, and Sam **Rawlinson** [SC:171, 175a, 177a, 178, 179], Berry **Jeffers/ Jeffries** [SC:176], and Arthur and Benjamin **Neal** [SC:174, 177]. William **Neal** was a "mulatto" taxable in New Hanover County in 1763 [SS 837] and taxable in Brunswick County in 1769 [*NCGSJ* V:242].

    iv.   William, head of a Richland District household of 4 "other free" in 1810 [SC:176].

    v.   John^2, head of a Newberry District, South Carolina household of 6 "other free" in 1800 [SC:80] and a Richland District household of 8 "other free" in 1810 [SC:175a].

    vi.   Isaac^2, head of a Richland District household of 6 "other free" in 1810 [SC:175a]. He was living in New Hanover County on 11 April 1818 when he sold lot number 5 which ran parallel to Chestnut Street on the eastern boundary of the town of Wilmington. He sold two more lots in Wilmington on both sides of Chestnut Street near Fifth Street on 8 May 1820. According to the deed, this land was part of 33 acres patented by Isaac in 1809 and recorded in book O:305 [DB Q:191; R:104].

4.   Abraham Jacobs, born say 1730, patented 125 acres in Duplin County on the west side of "Six Run on the marsh branch of Rown" on 21 April 1764 [Hoffman, *Land Patents*, I:59]. Five months later on 18 September 1764 he bought 200 acres on the south side of Rowan Swamp [Duplin DB 1:474], and five years later he patented a further 60 acres in the same area of Duplin County [Hoffman, *Land Patents*, II:160]. This part of Duplin became Sampson County in 1784 and he was taxed there on 385 acres and one black poll in 1784 [L.P. 64.1 by *N.C. Genealogy* XIV: 2169]. He received a lease and release for land proved in South Carolina between 1767 and 1768 [Lucas, *Index to Deeds of South Carolina*, G-3:557]. On 18 August 1791 he bought a further 36 acres near his land in Sampson County [DB 9:132]. He was head of a Sampson County household of 3 "other free" in 1790 [NC:52] and 5 in 1800 [NC:515]. His 13 February 1807 Sampson County will left all to his executrix Susanna **Carter** [WB A:49]. His children may have been

    i.   Thomas, born say 1752, patented 200 acres next to Abraham Jacobs' Duplin County land on 22 January 1773 [Hoffman, *Land Patents*, II:310] and was taxed on this land in Sampson County in 1784 [L.P. 64.1 by *N.C. Genealogy* XIV:2169]. He was head of a Sampson County household of 7 "other free" in 1790 [NC:53], 10 in 1800 [NC:515], and 8 "free colored" in 1820 [NC:278]. He may have been the father of Thomas Jacobs, Jr., head of a Sampson County household of 8 "free colored" in 1820 [NC:278].

    ii.   Susanna **Carter**, executrix of Abraham's will, perhaps the wife of Moses^2 **Carter** who also owned land near Rowan Swamp.

    iii.   Matthew^2, head of a Sampson County household of 4 "free colored" in 1820 [NC:278].

    iv.   Peter^2, head of a Sampson County household of 5 "free colored" in 1820 [NC:278]. He sold 150 acres in New Hanover County on Poplar Branch adjoining Brian Buxton on 27 May 1817 [DB Q:175].

5.   An unnamed sister of Matthew^1 Jacobs, born say 1736, was mentioned in Matthew's 13 September 1786 New Hanover County will. Her children were

6   i.   Zachariah^2, born on 4 October 1753.

    ii.   ?Peter^1, not counted in the 1790 census, deceased by 21 May 1792 when John Jacobs proved to the New Hanover County court that Zachariah Jacobs was his heir [Minutes 1792-98, 8].

7   iii.   Primus, born about 1760.

8   iv.   ?Shadrack, born say 1762.

    v.   ?Ezekiah, head of a Brunswick County household of 4 "other free" in 1800 [NC:13], and 8 in 1810 [NC:236]. He recorded a certificate of his discharge from his service as a soldier in the North Carolina Line on 18 February 1788 in New Hanover County [*NCGSJ* XI:114]. He entered 100 acres in Brunswick County on Gum Swamp on 3 November 1800, 100 acres near Livingston's Creek including his settlement on 14 December 1804 (called Zedekiah Jacobs), 200 acres on the north side of Gum Swamp on 4 January 1811, 100 acres in the fork of Mill Branch on 16 June 1815, 200 acres on the north side of Gum Swamp where he formerly lived on 28 January 1820, and 75 acres in the fork of Mill Branch and Town Creek on 28 January 1820 [Pruitt, *Land Entries, Brunswick County*, 67, 91, 122, 138, 159].

vi. ?Josiah, perhaps the J. Jacobs, Sr., who was head of a Brunswick County household of 4 "other free" in 1810 [NC:234]. He entered 100 acres on the south side of Lewis Branch in Brunswick County on 12 November 1798 [Pruitt, *Land Entries, Brunswick County*, 52].

6. Zachariah[2] Jacobs was born on 4 October 1753 according to his Revolutionary War pension application in New Hanover County on 13 December 1832 [M805-466, frame 0444]. He was a "Black" taxable in Brunswick County in 1772 [GA 11.1] and was head of a New Hanover County household of 6 "other free" in 1790 [NC:194], 10 in 1800 [NC:313], and 5 in Richland District, South Carolina, in 1810 [SC:175a]. He enlisted in October 1781 from Brunswick County, North Carolina, and left the service about a year later. He was in a skirmish near Dorchester, South Carolina, and was wounded in the leg at Guilford Courthouse. He married Sally Jacobs in New Hanover County in October 1791 according to her application for a pension as his surviving widow [M805-466, frame 0444]. He assigned his right to his final pay for twelve months service in the Continental Line to Isaac Cole in New Hanover County on 6 December 1791 [*NCGSJ* XI:114]. He received 80 acres in New Hanover by the will of his uncle Matthew[1] Jacobs [WB C:198]. He entered 200 acres in New Hanover County on the west side of Long Creek joining Matthew Jacobs on 7 April 1794 [Pruitt, *Land Entries: New Hanover County*, 59]. He may have been the Zachariah Jacobs who appeared in New Hanover County court on 21 May 1792 and was proved by John Jacobs to be the heir of Peter Jacobs [Minutes 1792-98, 8]. He was living in Brunswick County on 18 October 1815 when he sold 80 acres in New Hanover County on a branch of Long Creek which was willed to him by his uncle Matthew Jacobs (called his father in the deed) [DB P:595-6]. He died 10 April 1847 on Moore's Creek in New Hanover County according to his pension papers. His children were

i. William, born about 1791, sixty-six years old on 12 May 1857 when he testified on his mother's behalf in her application to obtain a widow's pension [M805-466, frame 0444]. He may have been the William Jacobs who was head of a New Hanover County household of 2 "other free" in 1800 [NC:308] and a Richland District household of 4 "other free" in 1810 [SC:176].

ii. John[4], born about 1805, fifty-two years old on 12 May 1857 [M805-466, frame 0444].

7. Primus Jacobs, born about 1760 according to his Revolutionary War pension application, received 80 acres by the 13 September 1786 New Hanover County will of his uncle Matthew[1] Jacobs and was executor of the will [WB C:198]. He was head of a New Hanover County household of 4 "other free" in 1790 [NC:194] and 7 "other free," one white woman, and one white boy 5-15 years old in 1800 [NC:314]. Perhaps the boy was James Futch. The 26 August 1794 New Hanover County court ordered Primus to show cause why James Futch should not be bound out by the court [Minutes 1792-98, 105]. He patented 100 acres in New Hanover County on the west side of Long Creek on 17 July 1801. On 25 November 1811 he sold 80 acres on the south side of a branch of Long Creek which was willed to him by his uncle Matthew Jacobs (called his father in the deed), and on 22 January 1817 sold 351 acres in New Hanover County on Poplar Branch adjoining Isaac Lamb [DB O:263; U:23]. He was about sixty years old on 11 November 1819 when he appeared in New Hanover County court and declared that he enlisted in the Revolution in New Hanover County in August 1782. He was about the same age on 15 August

1820 when he made a further declaration, stating that he was a cooper, but because of a broken shoulder he had difficulty supporting his family which consisted of his fifty-five-year old wife and four unnamed children aged twenty-four, twenty-two, twenty, and sixteen [M804-1403, frame 0193]. By order of the September 1827 term of the New Hanover County court the sheriff sold 200 acres of his land on the west side of Cypress adjoining Isaac Lamb for a debt he and (his son?) Matthew Jacobs owed [DB T:96-7]. His wife Ann Jacobs appeared in Cumberland County court on 6 December 1834 and proved to the satisfaction of the court that he was a pensioner and that he died in New Hanover County on 23 July 1834 [Minutes 1831-35]. Perhaps their children were

    i.   Matthew[3], a codefendant with Primus in a suit in New Hanover County court in September 1827.

    ii.   John[3], head of a Cumberland County household of 9 "free colored" in District 9 in 1820 [NC:169].

    iii.   Levi, an insolvent Cumberland County taxpayer for the year 1825 listed in court on 9 September 1826 [Minutes 1823-27]. On 4 March 1835 the Cumberland County court ordered that he be sold or hired out if he did not pay a fine [Minutes 1831-35].

    iv.   Thomas, a resident of New Hanover County on 10 September 1840 when he sold 175 acres on the west side of Cypress joining Isaac Lamb to (his brother?) Matthew Jacobs [DB Y:288].

8.   Shadrack Jacobs, born say 1762, bought 75 acres in Bladen County near the Brunswick County line on 6 February 1798 [DB 7:142]. He was head of a Bladen County household of 6 "other free" in 1800, 6 in 1810 [NC:203], and 7 "free colored" in Columbus County in 1820 [NC:50]. He called himself Shadrack Jacob of Columbus County in his 27 April 1818 Bladen County will, naming his wife Mary and children Arthur and Peggy.

JAMES FAMILY

1.   Andrew[1] James, born say 1650, was a "Negro Boy" named Andrew who was left by John Griggs, Sr., deceased, to his son John Griggs before 27 March 1655. Andrew was listed in the account of the estate of John Griggs (Sr.) on 8 September 1659 [DWO 1:264; 3:64]. John Griggs called him Andrew James "Negroe" on 23 December 1673 when they made an agreement that he was to be free when Griggs died. And on 22 October 1677 they signed an agreement whereby Andrew would work for himself as a carpenter for one year, in exchange for which, Andrew was to pay Griggs 500 pounds of tobacco at the start of the year, plant 3,000 corn husks, and pay 2,000 pounds of tobacco at the end of the year. Griggs was not to hinder him from working at his trade of carpenter during that year except for planting the corn. Griggs died before the completion of the year, and Andrew was a free man. On 26 August 1678 the court examined the accounts between him and Richard Savoy and ordered him to pay Savoy 640 pounds of tobacco. On 24 January 1678/9 the executor of Griggs estate, Thomas Nutton, sued Andrew for the 2,000 pounds of tobacco which he was supposed to have delivered to Griggs at the completion of their agreement, but Andrew answered that he had not been able to pay that amount because he had been assigned other work by Griggs. Andrew was reported to have left the county by 24 October 1682 when the sheriff attached his estate worth about 2,800 pounds of tobacco for debts he owed Thomas Nutton/ Nutting, Samuel Singnell, John Travellion, and William Wise [DOW 6:47, 59, 67, 94, 113, 117, 434, 463]. He was probably the Andrew James who received nine shillings by the 11 September 1696 North Carolina will of James Lankston. Lankston also left "Negro Betty" a sow. There was no location mentioned in the will, but it was probably in what is now Bertie County since the executor, William Duckinfield, was a resident of Bertie

County [SS vol. 849]. James Langston may have been related to Christopher Langston, a resident of York County on 10 October 1679 [DWO 6:126]. Andrew was probably the grandfather of

2   i.   Andrew[2], born say 1710.
3   ii.   David[1], born say 1720.
4   iii.   Solomon[1], born say 1725.

2.   Andrew[2] James, born say 1710, was taxable on two tithes in the 1757 Bertie summary list, was a delinquent taxpayer in the 1758 Bertie tax list of Edward Rasor, and was a "Mulatto" taxable on one tithe in the list of John Brickell in 1759 [CR 10.702.1]. He may have been out of the county in 1751 when his wife Ann James "fr: nego" was taxable in James Weston's household [CCR 190]. She may have been the Ann James, "free negro," who was a taxable head of her own household in Norfolk County, Virginia, near Tanners Bridge between 1752 and 1761. In 1754 Ann **Page** was in her household, and in 1757 Hannah **Williams** was in her household [Wingo, *Norfolk County Tithables, 1751-65*, 30, 92, 120, 143, 166]. Andrew and his unnamed wife were "free Mulatto" taxables in the 1761 Bertie County list of John Hill, and he was head of a "free Mulatto" household in John Hill's 1763 list with Ann James and (their daughter?) Mary James. Andrew died about 1764, and Ann was called a widow in the 1764 Bertie summary list. He must have been a very poor man as the May 1764 session of the Bertie court assigned administration of his estate to John Pearson on security of only twenty pounds [Haun, *Bertie County Court Minutes*, III:668]. Ann was taxable in her own household in 1772 in the list of Humphrey Nichols [CR 10.702.1]. Their children were

     i.   Elizabeth[1], born say 1735, called "daughter of Ann" in the 1772 list of Humphrey Nichols. There was also an Elizabeth James, "free negro" taxable in David[1] James' household in 1751, who was called David's wife in the 1759 list of John Brickell. Since it is not possible to differentiate the two Elizabeths in the Bertie records, all information about the two has been listed under Elizabeth, wife of David.
5   ii.   ?Hester, born about 1739.
6   iii.   ?Mary[1], born say 1741.
7   iv.   Benjamin[1], born about 1749.
     v.   Sophia, born about 1751, "daughter of Ann" bound to John Pearson on 28 April 1757.
8   vi.   Rebecca/Beck, born about 1752.
   vii.   Sarah[1], born about 1753, a taxable "free Mulatto" in John Moore's 1768 household and in her brother Benjamin's household from 1768 to 1773.
  viii.   Isaac, born about 1753, "child of Ann" bound to Edward Rasor to be a cordwainer on 29 July 1757 [CR 10.101]. He was taxable in Edward Rasor's household in an untitled 1765 Bertie list and in Rasor's household in Rasor's 1772 list. He was a private in Pearson's 7th North Carolina Regiment in the Revolutionary War. He was head of a Hertford County household of one "other free" in 1800.
9   ix.   Elisha, born about 1755.
     x.   Punch, born about 1758, called "Bastard Mulatoe of Ann James aged about Seventeen" when she was ordered bound to Samuel Moore by the May 1775 Bertie court [Haun, *Bertie County Court Minutes*, IV:157].
10   xi.   Jeremiah[2], born about 1758.
11   xii.   Frederick[1], born about 1751.

3.   David[1] James, born say 1720, and his wife Elizabeth James were taxable "free negros" in the 1751 Bertie County Tax Summary List filed with the central government [CCR 190]. He may have been the same David James who was bound as an apprentice gunsmith to James Isedel on 5 July 1727 in Princess Anne County, Virginia [Orders 1717-28, 288a]. Elizabeth was listed alone in

the 1756 tax list of Constable John Redditt. In December 1757 David was in Beaufort County court, called "free negro" when he was sued by the administrators of Thomas Ryan's estate [Beaufort County court Minutes, Appearance Prosecution, and Trial Dockets, 1756-61, 1:43b]. He had returned to Bertie County by 1759 when he and Elizabeth were taxables in the list of John Brickell [CR 10.702.1, Box 1]. David probably died or left the county about 1762 since he was not listed in the tax records after 1761 and Elizabeth's children were bound out beginning 27 February 1763.

There were two Elizabeth Jameses in the early Bertie tax records; one was called the wife of David in the 1759 list of John Brickell, and the other was called the daughter of Andrew in the 1772 list of Humphrey Nichols. It is not possible to distinguish between the two, so they are counted as the same person in this history.

Elizabeth bought 250 acres near the "Downyeterry Swamp" in Bertie County on 7 June 1761 [DB K:72] and recorded her livestock mark in Bertie court on 14 July 1761 and in April 1762 [Haun, *Bertie County Court Minutes*, II:544]. That year Elizabeth, David, and Jesse were taxable in their own household in the list of John Hill. Elizabeth seems to have sold or lost her land since she was not head of her own household in the tax lists for 1763 and thereafter, and five of her children were bound out in 1763. However, there was no deed of sale recorded for the land. Elizabeth was taxable in Arthur Williams' household in the tax lists from 1763 to 1772, and two of her children were taxed in his household when they reached twelve years of age: William in 1765 and Mary in 1767. In 1772 she was taxed in her own household, called "daughter of Andrew," in the list of Humphrey Nichols, perhaps living on the 75 acres which her son William purchased on 5 September 1772. She witnessed the 10 January 1777 Bertie will of John Harrell [WB B:92].[120] She married John Gardner, a white man, 9 February 1780 Bertie County bond, Martin Gardner bondsman. Her children were

12	i.	Jesse[1], born about 1749.
13	ii.	William[1], born about 1751.
	iii.	Nanny/ Nancy, born about 1753, "Nanny the Daughter of Betty James a Free Mulattoe about the age of Ten Years," ordered bound to Ephraim Weston by the May 1763 Bertie court [Haun, *Bertie County Court Minutes*, III:615]. She was called "Nancy," a taxable in his household in 1767 in the list of John Crickett.
	iv.	Mary[2], born about 1754.
	v.	Pattey[1], born about 1755, "Daughter of Betty James a Free Mulatoe," ordered bound to Richard Bell in May 1763 [Haun, *Bertie County Court Minutes*, III:615].
	vi.	Ann, born about 1756, a seven-year-old child of Elizabeth ordered bound to Arthur Williams in May 1763 [Haun, *Bertie County Court Minutes*, III:621].
	vii.	Thomas[1], born about 1757, the six-year-old son of Betty James, "Free Mulatoe," ordered bound to John Moore in May 1763. Humphrey Hardy was granted administration on his estate on 6 August 1792 with 500 pounds security [Haun, *Bertie County Court Minutes*, VI:957]. The administrator had a certificate from the Board of Army Accounts that wages due were settled at Halifax in the amount of 69 pounds [Bertie Estate Papers].
14	viii.	Catherine, born about 1759.
15	ix.	David[2], born about 1761.

---

[120]A Thomas Herrill, born about 1693, was a "Mulatto" living in Northampton County, Virginia, in April 1723 [Northampton County L.P. 5, Thomas Herrill's Petition].

x. Sophia, born about 1762, a "Mulatoe orphan aged about III years," no last name stated, ordered bound to Solomon Cherry on 28 March 1765 [CR 10.101.7]. She was taxable as Saphira James in Solomon's household in the 1767 list of William Cherry. She was ordered bound to Solomon Cherry again at the age of fifteen years by the August 1777 Bertie court, "the Mulato Daughter of Elizabeth James."

xi. Andrew⁴, born about 1765, "the Bastard Child of Betty aged about five Years," ordered bound to Charles Sowell in June 1770 [Haun, *Bertie County Court Minutes*, III:914]. The Northampton County estate of John Bridgers received money from him between 3 February 1797 and 3 September 1799 [Gammon, *Records of Estates Northampton County*, I:105]. He was in Halifax County by 26 March 1813 when Whitmell Cotton of Halifax County for 1 shilling gave him a lifetime lease on 600 acres [DB 23:31].

xii. Benjamin², born about 1766, "the Bastard Child of Betty James aged about four years," ordered bound to Charles Sowell by the June 1770 Bertie court [Haun, *Bertie County Court Minutes*, III:914]. He may have been the Benjamin James who was head of a Martin County household of 4 "other free" in 1790 [NC:68], 7 in 1800 [NC:398], and 7 "other free" in Halifax County in 1810 [NC:28].

xiii. Elizabeth³, born about 1769, six-year-old "Mulato Bastard of Elizabeth James," ordered bound to Hardy Weston by the May 1775 Bertie court [Haun, *Bertie County Court Minutes*, IV:147].

4. Solomon¹ James, born say 1725, and James Willsford (alias Howl) of unnamed county sold 340 acres on "Guys Hall" Swamp in Bertie County in 1759. This was half of a tract of 680 acres, the other half sold by Absolem /Abraham James of Pitt County on 23 June 1763 [DB I:402; K:470]. He may have been the Solomon James who was number 19 in the Payroll of the First Troop of Georgia Rangers from 18 August 1759 to 18 November 1759 [Clark, *Colonial Soldiers of the South*, 985]. On 26 October 1767 he recorded a patent for 100 acres in Bladen County on the northeast side of Drowning Creek [Hoffman, *Land Patents*, II:461] and sold this land two years later on 10 March 1769 [DB 23:23]. He was a "Mulato" taxable in Bladen County between 1768 and 1776, called Solomon James, Senr., in 1769, taxable with his son Solomon from 1772 to 1776 and head of a Bladen County household of one male under 21 or over 60 years old in 1786 [Byrd, *Bladen County Tax Lists*, I:7, 16, 45, 81, 110; II:67, 82, 183]. He was the father of

i. Solomon², Jr., born say 1755, a taxable "Mulato" in his father's Bladen County household in 1772, "Molato" head of his own household in 1776 and head of a household of two white males from 21 to 60, two under 21 or over 60, and five white females in 1786 [Byrd, *Bladen County Tax Lists*, I:81; II:67, 183]. He purchased 150 acres in Bladen County on the south side of Drowning Creek near the mouth of Raft Swamp in 1783 [DB 1:314]. He entered 150 acres on the west side of Drowning Creek on 29 September 1787 [Pruitt, *Robeson County Land Entries, 1787-1795*, 9]. He was called Saul James on 7 November 1784 when he received a patent for 150 acres in Bladen County on the east side of Drowning Creek below the mouth of Jacks Branch [DB 1:24]. He was head of a Robeson County household of 9 "other free" and one white woman in 1790 [NC:49].

5. Hester James, born about 1739, was a taxable "free Mulatto" in Samuel Moore's Bertie County household in the 1757 list of Joseph Jordan [CR 10.702.1]. She was taxable in John Moore's household in the list of John Hill from 1761 until 1774. Her children were

i. John¹, born about 1756, "7 year old orphan of Easter," bound to John Moore on 30 August 1763 [CR 10.101]. He purchased 157 acres on

Conoho Creek in Martin County from Lot Harrell on 3 February 1776
[DB A:167], and he was taxable in Martin County in 1779 on 542
pounds valuation in District 7 [GA 30.1]. He was head of a Bertie
County household of 8 "other free" in 1790 [NC:13], 11 in 1800
[NC:56], and 7 in 1810 [NC:149]. His Bertie County estate,
administered by William Green on 13 August 1817, mentioned his
widow Polly and buyers: Mary, John, Right, and Reuben James.

    ii.   ?William², born about 1760, taxable with Hester in John Moore's
household in 1772, 1773, and 1774. He was not indentured. He
witnessed a 9 March 1779 Martin County deed [DB A:225].

6.   Mary¹ James, born say 1741, was taxable in Andrew James' Bertie County
household in the 1763 list of John Hill. In the undated (1772?) list of
Humphrey Hardy she was a "Molatto" head of her own household, taxed on
herself and "husband Jim" [CR 10.702.1, box 13]. Her children were

    i.   Andrew³, born about 1756, "son of Poll James (and Base Born),"
ordered bound to John Pearson by the July 1761 Bertie court [Haun,
Bertie County Court Minutes, II:538]. He was taxable in Ephraim
Weston's household in the 1768 list of Humphrey Nichols as "Andrew
J___ free." He married Janey **Drury**, 24 February 1784 Bertie County
bond with his uncle Benjamin James bondsman. Andrew was head of
a Bertie County household of 4 "other free" in 1790 [NC:13], 6 in
1800 [NC:56], and 6 in 1810 [NC:166].

    ii.   James¹, born say 1759, "son of Poll," ordered bound to John Pearson
by the July 1761 Bertie court [Haun, *Bertie County Court Minutes*,
II:538].

16   iii.   Dorcas, born about 1760.

    iv.   Elizabeth²/ Bett, born about 1762, "Mulattoe...of Mary," ordered
bound to John Pearson by the May 1764 Bertie court. She was fifteen
years old when she was bound to Mrs. Pearson in August 1777 [Haun,
Bertie County Court Minutes, III:668; IV:241].

7.   Benjamin¹ James, born about 1749, "son of Ann," was bound by the Bertie
County court to John Pearson to learn husbandry on 28 April 1757 [CR
10.101]. He was taxable in Samuel Moore's household in the 1761 list of John
Hill. He was head of his own household in 1768 and 1769 in the list of Josiah
Harrell, taxable on himself, his sister Sarah James, and Abigail **Jacobs**,
perhaps his common-law wife. He and Abigail were taxable in the 1774 list
of Samuel Granberry. He was taxable in Bertie County on 3 horses and 4
cattle in 1778 [CR 10.702.1, box 3]. On 8 March 1779 he married Lucy
Murray, Bertie County bond. He and his brother Jeremiah gave Seth Peebles
of Northampton County power of attorney to obtain settlement of their
Revolutionary War service pay [*NCGSJ* XI:114]. He was taxable on two polls
in District 14 of Halifax County in 1784 and 1785, and one poll in 1787,
1788, and 1790. On 8 January 1792 he purchased 200 acres on the west side
of Little Swamp in Halifax County near the Northampton County line and 109
acres on both sides of the new road on 25 January 1803 [DB 18:832; 19:288].
On 8 June 1796 Thomas **Dempsey** was bound an apprentice to him by the
Northampton County court [Minutes 1792-96, 250]. He was head of a Halifax
County household of 6 "other free" in 1790 [NC:68], 7 in 1800 [NC:322], 7
in 1810 [NC:29], and 5 "free colored" in 1820 [NC:153]. He and (his son?)
Hardy James sold 237 acres on Little Swamp on 23 March 1818 [DB 24:298].
His children were probably

    i.   Hardy, born about 1775, married Mary James, 18 February 1801
Bertie County bond with Frederick James bondsman. He was head of
a Halifax County household of 2 "other free" in 1800 [NC:320], and
8 "free colored" in 1820 [NC:152].

ii. Willis, purchased 29 acres in Halifax County on 29 September 1804 [DB 19:493].

8. Rebecca/Beck James, born about 1752, "Daughter of Ann James," no age stated, was bound by the Bertie County court to John Pearson on 28 April 1757 [CR 10.101]. On 26 June 1765 the Bertie court again ordered her bound to John Pearson, stating her age as thirteen years, no parent named [Haun, *Bertie County Court Minutes*, III:710]. She was taxable in John Pearson's household in the 1767 list of Humphrey Nichols. Her child was
   i. Peggy[1], born about 1776, "a Bastard Child of Beck James aged three years," bound to William and Ann Virgin to be a weaver [Haun, *Bertie County Court Minutes*, IV:303].

9. Elisha James, born about 1755, "son of Ann," was bound by the Bertie County court to Samuel Moore to be a cordwainer on 29 July 1757 [CR 10.101]. He was taxable in Samuel Moore's household in 1767 in the list of John Crickett and was still in Moore's household in 1774 in the list of Samuel Granberry. He was listed among the militiamen from Northampton County who were paroled by Lord Cornwallis in Halifax in 1781, probably captured during the events surrounding the Battle of Guilford Courthouse on 15 March 1781 [*NCGSJ* IV:149]. He was head of a Northampton County household of 2 males and 3 females in Captain Winborne's District for the state census in 1786. In 1788, 1790, 1800, and 1802 he was a Halifax County taxable on one free poll in District 14 which bordered Northampton County. He was head of a Halifax County household of 6 "other free" in 1790 [NC:65], 7 in 1800 [NC:320], 4 in 1810 [NC:29], 6 "free colored" in 1820 [NC:152], and 9 "free colored" in 1830. He made a declaration in Halifax County court to obtain a Revolutionary War pension on 16 November 1824 stating that he was sixty-five years old and that his children then living at home were Franky, Emma, and Sally. His children were

17 i. ?Benjamin[3], born about 1790.
    ii. Franky, born 1816.
    iii. Emma, born 1822.
    iv. Sally, born 1823.

10. Jeremiah[2] James, born about 1758, the "orphan of Nann James aged about Six years," was bound by the Bertie County court to John Norwood to be a weaver on 1 June 1764 [CR 10.101.7]. He was a "free Mulatto" taxable in John Norwood's household in the undated (1772?) list of Humphrey Nichols [CR 10.702.1, box 13]. He was counted in the 1787 state census for Bertie County in H. H. Hardy's list, head of a household of 4 males and 3 females. He leased land in Northampton County on the east side of Urahaw Swamp on 1 January 1798 [DB 10:372] and was head of a Northampton County household of 3 "other free" in 1790 [NC:73] and 6 in 1800 [NC:453]. His estate, administered in Northampton County on 3 December 1805, mentioned Rebecca James. She was his wife who provided the following information when she applied for and was granted his Revolutionary War pension from Maury County, Tennessee:

He entered the service in Bertie County in Captain Blount's Company of the 10th Regiment for nine months on 20 July 1778 and again as a private in Captain Raiford's Company from 17 May 1781 to 15 April 1782. She was born in Virginia in May 1758 and married Jeremiah in Northampton County about February or March 1790. Jeremiah died on 1 October 1805, and she married Isham **Scott** about a year later. After **Scott** died, she moved to Maury County, Tennessee. She named her children in her pension application and gave evidence of their birth and her marriage to Jeremiah in a book published in 1792, entitled, *Baxter's Call to the Unconverted*:

> *Jeremiah James Son of Ann James was born March 11, 1762*
> *"   "   "   "   his book 1793*
> *Axom James Son of Jeremiah & Rebecca James born Nov. 27, 1790*
> *Uriah James   "   "   "   "   "   Aug. 25, 1794*
> *Asa James   "   "   "   "   "   Feb. 22, 1805*

Rebecca was living in the household of her son Exum in the 1850 census for District 19 of Maury County, Tennessee: a ninety-three-year-old woman born in Virginia [TN:220]. She named the following children in her application:

   i.   Exum, born 27 November 1790 according to the family "bible." He married Nancy **Hawkins**, 18 January 1826 Halifax County bond. She was mentioned in the Halifax County will of her father Solomon **Hawkins**, proved August 1816 [WB 3:589]. Exum was head of a Halifax County household of 4 "free colored" in 1820 [NC:306]. He and Nancy were living in Williamson County, Tennessee, on 3 December 1832 when they gave power of attorney to Jeremiah James of the same to sell their rights to land of Solomon **Hawkins** in Halifax County [DB 29:6, 7]. They were counted with their children in District 19 of Maury County, Tennessee, in 1850 [TN:220].

   ii.   Delilah.

   iii.   Uriah, born 25 August 1794.

   iv.   Jeremiah[4], born about 1800, counted in Maury County, Tennessee, in 1850.

   v.   Trusty.

   vi.   Kesiah, married James **Keemer**, 21 November 1817 Halifax County bond.

11. Frederick[1] James, born about 1764, was called "natural son of Ann James" when he was bound by the Bertie County court to John Norwood on 26 September 1768 [CR 10.101.7 by *NCGSJ* XIV:33]. He was listed among the Militiamen from Bertie County who were paroled by Lord Cornwallis in 1781 in Halifax, probably captured during the events surrounding the Battle of Guilford Courthouse on 15 March 1781 [*NCGSJ* IV:150]. He purchased 63 acres near a place commonly called "Tound Pocosin" in Bertie County on 21 August 1795 and leased for ten years on 24 August 1797 land in Bertie which he was to take possession at the end of the lease [DB R:29, 468]. He was head of a Bertie County household of 9 "other free" in 1790 [NC:13], 5 in 1800 [NC:54], and 3 "other free" and 3 slaves in 1810 [NC:148]. He wrote his own Bertie County will in rather good handwriting on 25 February 1817, proved February 1818.[121] He named his "Worthy friend" William Lee Gray his sole executor. In his inventory of the estate Gray wrote that there were "Sundry Book accts (the amt. unknown) all of which are Extremely doubtful - as the Testator was a colored man & there is no legal way to prove them." Frederick mentioned his wife Dicey and sons [WB G:45]. Dicey was head of a Bertie County household of 2 "free colored" women and one slave in 1820 [NC:82]. Their children were

   i.   Jonathan, born 1776-94, head of a Bertie County household of 2 "other free" and one slave in 1810 [NC:149] and 7 "free colored" in 1820 [NC:84].

   ii.   Allen, married Nancy **Smith**, 25 May 1808 Bertie County bond with Fred R. James bondsman. He was head of a Bertie County household of 3 "other free" in 1810 [NC:149].

   iii.   James[2].

---

[121]Solomon Cherry, William H. Green, and James Bognell proved the will in the February 1818 session of the Bertie County Court of Pleas and Quarter Sessions declaring "that they were acquainted with the hand writing of Frederick James."

    iv. Frederick[2].
    v. Jeremiah[3], whose Bertie County estate was administered on 10 February 1817.

12. Jesse[1] James, born about 1749, was taxable in David and Elizabeth James' Bertie County household in the 1761 list of John Hill. He was called Jesse Andrews, son of Elizabeth James, and was fourteen years old when he was apprenticed to John Perry on 23 February 1763 [CR 10.101.7]. He was taxed in Perry's household in the 1767 tax list of William Nichols. By 1780 he was a Northampton County taxable [LP 46.1]. He had 8 free persons in his Northampton County household in the 1786 state census and was head of a Northampton County household of 9 "other free" in 1790 [NC:73]. On 3 December 1792 administration on his Northampton County estate was granted to Matthew Griffin on 500 pounds security, his unnamed widow having relinquished her right [Minutes 1792-96, 40]. Perhaps she was Sarah James, a buyer at the sale of the estate of David James, who made a deed of gift of two cows and a mare to her daughters: Patty, Rachel, and Peggy James, on 7 November 1796 [DB 11:68]. Their children may have been
    i. Patty[2].
    ii. John[2], "a free mulatto" murdered in Northampton County. His murderer escaped from the Halifax County jail according to the 20 March 1793 issue of the *North Carolina Journal*: *Last night Harris Allen, who was committed for the murder of John James, a free mulatto, of Northampton County, made his escape from the gaol of this town. He is a remarkable tall man, and had on a short round jacket* [Fouts, *North Carolina Journal*, I:205].
    iii. Thomas[2], ordered bound by the Northampton County court as an apprentice on 3 February 1794. He bought land in Northampton County by deed proved in court on 7 March 1814, and he and his wife sold this land two years later by deed proved in court on 4 March 1816 [Minutes 1792-96, 93; 1813-21, n.p.].
    iv. Rachel.
    v. Peggy[2].

13. William[1] James, born about 1751, "12 year old son of Elizabeth James," was ordered bound to Arthur Williams by the 2 June 1763 Bertie court [Haun, *Bertie County Court Minutes*, III:621]. He was taxable in Arthur Williams' household with Elizabeth James in the 1766 list of John Crickett. On 5 September 1772 he purchased 75 acres near George Dempsey on Sams Branch and sold this land on 8 December 1777 [DB L:349; N:243]. In an undated (1772?) list of Humphrey Hardy he was taxable in his own household with his "wife Ann." He died before May 1788 when the Bertie court ordered his children bound as apprentices. Ann Gardner was granted administration on his Bertie County estate on 6 August 1792 [Haun, *Bertie County Court Minutes*, VI:697; VI:969]. His children were
    i. Piety, born about 1780, daughter of William, ordered bound to Mary Weston by the May 1788 Bertie court [Haun, *Bertie County Court Minutes*, VI:700].
    ii. William[3], born about 1784, "Mulatto son of William, decd," ordered bound to William Edwards to be a blacksmith.

14. Catherine James, born about 1759, a four-year-old child of Elizabeth James, was ordered bound an apprentice to Arthur Williams by the May 1763 Bertie court. She was taxable in the household of Elizabeth James, "daughter of Andrew," in the 1772 list of Humphrey Nichols. Her child was
    i. Frederick[3], born July 1783, "son of Catey James," ordered bound to Andrew James to be a cooper by the 28 February 1789 Bertie court [Haun, *Bertie County Court Minutes*, III:621, VI:742].

15. David[2] James, born about 1761, the "2 year old son of Elizabeth James," was ordered bound as an apprentice to Arthur Williams by the Bertie County court on 2 June 1763. He was a taxable in Thomas Perry's household in the 1774 Bertie County list of William Cherry. In August 1783 the Bertie court bound Thomas **Dempsey** to him to learn the trade of blacksmith [Haun, *Bertie County Court Minutes* III:621; V:458]. On 1 January 1784 he leased 99 acres on Urahaw Swamp in Northampton County [DB 9:101]. He was in Captain Winborne's District of Northampton County for the 1786 State Census where he had 7 persons in his household, and he was head of a Northampton County household of 3 "other free" and 2 slaves in 1790 [NC:73]. He purchased 185 acres on the south side of Urahaw Swamp on 28 February 1791 and 100 acres on the north side of the swamp on 3 March 1791. About a week later on 9 March 1791 he mortgaged both these tracts and his property, including 32 hogs, 7 cattle, and 3 horses [DB 11:350-1, 356]. His Northampton County estate was settled on 3 December 1792, the same day that Jesse James' estate was settled. David's widow Fanny James petitioned the court saying that he died intestate leaving 185 acres on Urahaw Swamp and two orphaned children, Milly and Jesse James. John **Walden** was security for her petition [Minutes 1792-96, 41]. His children were

    i.   Jesse[2], who sold his father's land by a deed proved on 6 June 1814 [Minutes 1813-21, n.p.].
    ii. Milly.

16. Dorcas James, born about 1760, "3 year old orphan of Mary," was bound to Arthur Williams in 1763. The February 1777 Bertie court ordered her bound to Mrs. Pearson, she having had a child while in servitude [Haun, *Bertie County Court Minutes*, IV:241]. Her daughter was

    i.   Sarah[2]/ Sall, born about 1777, bound to Sarah Clark on 21 August 1786 [Haun, *Bertie County Court Minutes*, V:598].

17. Benjamin[3] James, born about 1790 in Halifax County, was head of a Halifax County household of 7 "other free" in 1810 [NC:29], 11 "free colored" in 1820 [NC:152] and 9 in 1830 [NC:344]. He purchased 141 acres in Halifax County on Little Quankey Creek on 16 May 1818 and sold this land on 20 May 1832 [DB 24:269; 28:366]. He was counted in the 1850 and 1860 Halifax census, a cooper born in 1790. One of his children may have been

    i.   Temperance, married Squire **Walden**, 28 March 1832 Halifax County bond.

Some of the James families counted as "other free" in Virginia in 1810 may have also been the descendants of Andrew[1] James:

    i.   Silviah, head of a Surry County household of 7 "other free."
    ii. William, head of a Henrico County household of 6 "other free" [VA:1001].
    iii. Billey, head of a Henrico County household of 5 "other free" [VA:1012].
    iv. Polly, head of a Petersburg Town household of 2 "other free" and 2 slaves [VA:334b].

JAMESON FAMILY

1. James Jameson, born say 1758, was taxable in James City County from 1782 to 1814: taxable on a free tithe and 2 cattle in 1782, a horse and 3 cattle in 1785, called a "mulatto" in 1805, taxable on 2 free tithes in 1809 and 1810, called a "mulatto" from 1811 to 1813 and "cold." in 1814 [PPTL, 1782-99; 1800-15]. He and his wife Jane, "Free mulattoes," baptized their daughter Nancy in Bruton Parish, James City County, on 26 February 1785 [Bruton Parish Register, 36]. He and Jane were the parents of

    i.   ?Thomas, born say 1779, taxable in James City County from 1800 to 1814: a "mulatto" head of a household of 2 "Free Persons of Colour above 16 years" in 1813 [PPTL, 1800-15].

    ii. Nancy, baptized 26 February 1785.

    iii. ?William, born say 1788, a "mulatto" taxable in James City County from 1811 to 1814 [PPTL, 1800-15].

JARVIS FAMILY

1. Susan Jarvis, born say 1727, was a "Poor Mulatto" woman living in York County on 17 December 1759 when the court ordered the churchwardens of Yorkhampton Parish to bind out her children because she was unable to provide for them [Judgments & Orders 1759-63, 103]. She was head of a York County household of 2 "other free" in 1810 [VA:876]. She was called Susanna **Parrott** alias Susanna Jarvis when she was sued by Thomas Fauntleroy in a case heard in York County court between May 1801 and May 1802. James Trice, Thomas Trice (of King and Queen County) and John Bowden (of James City County), and Thomas Drewry were witnesses. The case was discontinued with each party paying their own costs [Orders 1795-1803, 457, 482, 483, 498, 516-8, 522]. She may have been the ancestor of

2   i.   Thomas¹, born say 1748.

2. Thomas¹ Jarvis, born say 1748, was living in the household of James Burwell on 19 November 1770 when the York County court presented Burwell for not listing him as a tithable [Judgments & Orders 1770-2, 104]. He left a 2 February 1781 York County will, proved 17 September 1782, by which he gave his estate to his "Mulatto Boy" Billy Jarvis who he expected to be freed by the next session of the Assembly. He asked that Billy be bound to James Horrey of Williamsburg to learn a trade and that his executors purchase Billy's brother and sister Franky and Johnny, two "Mulatto children," who were the property of Nathaniel Burwell of King's Creek [W&I 22:537]. He was the father of

    i.   William, born about 1769, registered in York County on 17 December 1810: *a bright Mulatto about 41 years of age...Emancipated by the will of Thomas Jarvis decd. recorded in York Ct. on the ___ day of 177_* [Free Negro Register, 1798-1831, no. 59]. He was called an orphan and apprentice of Stephen Mitchell, cabinet maker, on 18 January 1790 when he was discharged from his apprenticeship on his complaint that his master was not providing him sufficient clothing and was neglecting to instruct him in his trade [Orders 1788-95, 199]. He was taxable in York County on a tithe in 1791, taxable on 3 slaves from 1793 to 1812, and head of a household of 4 "free Negroes & mulattoes over 16" and 4 slaves in 1813 [PPTL, 1782-1841, frames 172, 193, 211, 230, 307, 340, 365, 391]. He was head of a York County household of 9 "other free" and 7 slaves in 1810 [VA:876].

Other members of the Jarvis family were

    i.   Charles, born about 1793, registered in York County on 18 April 1814: *abt. 21 years of age...light complexion, rather yellowish...Born free* [Free Negro Register, 1798-1831, no. 81].

    ii. Thomas², born about 1801, registered in York County on 18 November 1822: *a bright Mulatto about 21 years of age...has long bushy hair...born free* [Free Negro Register, 1798-1831, no. 81].

JASPER/ JESPER FAMILY

1. Margaret Jesper, born say 1690, was a "Molatto" presented by the York
    County court on 17 November 1735 and 15 May 1738 for failing to list herself
    as a tithable. On 21 August 1738 she was exempted from paying tax on her
    son because he was a cripple. Administration of her York County estate was
    granted to Anthony **Roberts** on 18 November 1751. The inventory was
    returned on 20 July 1752 and included furniture, household items and a
    breeding mare and two cows [Judgments & Orders 1749-53, 483; W&I
    18:237, 245, 414, 440; 20:266]. She may have been the mother of
    - i.   John, born say 1709, granted leave by the York County court to
           prosecute a suit against Anna Maria Timson on 15 February 1730/1.
           He was presented by the York County court on 15 November 1735 for
           failing to list his "Molatto" wife Anne as a tithable. On 13 May 1736
           he was charged by the court with stealing a cow [OW 17:154; W&I
           18:237, 244, 322].

2   ii. Elizabeth born say 1710.
3   iii. Mary, born say 1720.

2. Elizabeth Jasper, born say 1710, was living in Charles City County in
    February 1743/4 when the churchwardens of Westover Parish were ordered
    to bind out her children: Anthony, Robert, and Lucy (no race indicated) to
    Joseph Day [Orders 1737-51, 287]. She was the mother of
    - i.   ?Hannah[1], born say 1727, presented by the York County court on 20
           November 1749 for failing to list herself as a tithable [Judgments &
           Orders 1746-52, 256, 277, 284]. She was granted administration on the
           York County estate of Lucy Jasper on 19 June 1780 [Orders 1774-84,
           267].
    - ii. Anthony[1], born say 1728, father of Johnny **Peters** who was baptized in
           Bruton Parish, James City County, on 4 June 1748 [Bruton Parish
           Register, 8]. He was probably related to Anthony and Jasper **Peters** of
           York County. Francis **Morris** brought a suit against him which was
           dismissed by the Chesterfield County court in September 1760 [Orders
           1759-67, 85].
    - iii. Robert, born say 1730, taxable in Henrico County in 1786 [PPTL
           1782-1814, frame 86], taxable in Chesterfield County in 1788 [PPTL
           1786-1811, frame 41]. He may have been identical to "Jasper a
           Mulattoe" who was presented by the Henrico County court on 3 May
           1785 for failing to list his tithables [Orders 1784-7, 170].
    - iv. Lucy, born say 1732, died before 19 June 1780 when Hannah Jasper
           was granted administration on her York County estate. It was returned
           to court on 14 July 1780 and included a mare, two cows, a bed,
           furniture, and a spinning wheel [Orders 1774-84, 267; W&I 22:494].

3. Mary Jasper, born say 1720, "a Mulatto," was living in Charles City County
    in May 1746 when her children Sarah and Henry were ordered bound out by
    the churchwardens [Orders 1737-51, 410]. She was the mother of
    - i.   Sarah, born say 1737, agreed with her master Joseph Hix to give up
           her freedom dues in exchange for early release from her indenture in
           Charles City County on 1 December 1756 [Orders 1751-7, 441].

4   ii. Henry[1], born say 1740.
    iii. ?Martha, a "poor orphan" living in Bruton Parish on 17 August 1752
           when the York County court ordered the churchwardens to bind her out
           [Judgments & Orders 1752-4, 105].

4. Henry[1] Jasper, born say 1740, was bound apprentice in Charles City County
    in May 1746 and was a "mulatto" bound out in Chesterfield County on 3
    September 1756, no parent named [Orders 1754-59, 222]. He was a "Mullato"

taxable in Chesterfield County in 1776 [Tax List 1747-1821, frame 105], head of a Chesterfield County household of 7 persons in 1783 [VA:49] and was taxable in Chesterfield County on a tithe and a horse in 1786 [PPTL 1786-1811, frame 13]. He may have been the father of

i. Hannah[2], born about 1764, registered in Petersburg on August 19, 1794: *a brown Mulatto woman, five feet five inches high, thirty years old, born free and raised in Chesterfield County* [Register of Free Negroes 1794-1819, no. 62].

ii. Elizabeth[1], born about 1769, obtained a certificate of freedom in Chesterfield County on 9 January 1809 (and 18 July 1822): *forty years old, yellow complexion, born free* [Register of Free Negroes 1804-53, nos. 96, 457].

iii. Henry[2], born about 1772-4, obtained a certificate of freedom in Chesterfield County on 9 October 1826 (and 10 November 1828): *fifty two years old, Mulatto complexion, born free* [Register of Free Negroes 1804-53, nos. 551, 612]. He was taxable on 2 tithes in Chesterfield County from 1786 to 1795 and taxable on 1 tithe until 1811 when he was living with his wife and six children on William Bracket's land [PPTL 1786-1811, 202, 234, 268, 450, 525, 738, 782, 824]. He was head of a Chesterfield County household of 8 "other free" in 1810 [VA:70/1062].

iv. Wiley, born about 1774, obtained a certificate of freedom in Chesterfield County on 13 February 1809: *thirty five years old, yellow complexion, born free* [Register of Free Negroes 1804-53, no. 107]. He was taxable in Chesterfield County from 1794 to 1811, a "Mulatto" living in the Hundred in 1809 and a laborer living on Maria Stratton's land in 1811 [PPTL 1786-1811, frames 202, 301, 601, 689, 738, 782, 824]. He was head of a Chesterfield County household of 4 "other free" in 1810 [VA:70/1062].

v. Archer, born about 1779, obtained a certificate of freedom in Chesterfield County on 9 January 1809: *thirty years old, bright yellow complexion, born free* [Register of Free Negroes 1804-53, no. 79]. He was taxable in Chesterfield County from 1796 to 1811, a "Mulatto" living in the Hundred in 1809 and a laborer living with his wife on Maria Stratton's land in 1811 [frames 268, 374, 450, 689, 738, 824]. He was head of a Chesterfield County household of 6 "other free" in 1810 [VA:70/1062].

vi. Moses, born about 1787, obtained a certificate of freedom in Chesterfield County on 10 May 1813: *twenty six years old, yellow complexion, born free* [Register of Free Negroes 1804-53, no. 184]. He was taxable in Chesterfield County from 1801 to 1811 when he was living with his wife, mother (or wife['s] mother?) and four children on William Bracket's land [PPTL 1786-1811, 450, 488, 525, 782, 824].

Their descendants were

5　i. Nancy Kemp, born about 1765.

ii. Henry[3], born about 1781-2, obtained a certificate of freedom in Chesterfield County on 9 January 1809 (and 11 September 1815): *twenty seven years old, yellow complexion, born free* [Register of Free Negroes 1804-53, no. 80, 247].

iii. Elizabeth[2]/ Betsy, born about 1783, obtained a certificate of freedom in Chesterfield County on 9 October 1826: *forty three years old, Mulatto complexion, born free* [Register of Free Negroes 1804-53, no. 552].

iv. Anthony[2], taxable in James City County in 1796 and 1797 [PPTL, 1782-99], head of a York County household of 2 "other free" in 1810 [VA:890]. Perhaps his widow was Peggy Jasper, head of a York

County household of 2 "free Negroes & mulattoes over 16" in 1813 [PPTL, 1782-1841, frame 390].

v. Peter, "FB" head of a Princess Anne County household of 4 "other free" in 1810 [VA:459].

5. Nancy Kemp Jasper, born about 1765, registered in Petersburg on 16 August 1794: *a small, light col'd Mulatto woman, about five feet & half inches high, about twenty nine years old, Born free in Charles City & raised in County of Prince George* [Register of Free Negroes 1794-1819, no. 17]. She was the mother of

i. William Kemp **Cary**, born about 1786, registered in Petersburg on 13 September 1805: *a light brown Mulatto lad, son of Nancy Kemp Jasper, a free woman, five feet one inches high, nineteen years old, strait black hair* [Register of Free Negroes 1794-1819, no. 364].

Members of the Jasper family in North Carolina were

i. Sally, born 1776-1794, head of a Cumberland County household of 5 "free colored" in 1820 [NC:264].

ii. Henry, an insolvent taxpayer in the Upper Little River District of Cumberland County, North Carolina, on 6 September 1834. He may have been the father of Julia Jasper, a four-year-old "free girl of colour" bound to Archibald Graham by the Cumberland County court on the previous day. She was ten years old on 3 June 1840 when the court bound her to her grandfather Abram **Scott** [Minutes 1831-5, 1838-40].

JEFFERY FAMILY

Members of the Jeffery family were

i. Elizabeth, born say 1700, an Indian living in Northampton County, Virginia, on 12 January 1730/1 when she petitioned the court to order her former husband Thomas Fisherman, also an Indian, to return a mare and horse which were her property before their marriage [Orders 1729-32, 68; Mihalyka, *Loose Papers I:*237].

ii. Thomas, born say 1710, an Indian sued on 14 July 1736 in Northampton County, Virginia, by William Satchell for a debt of 500 pounds of tobacco [Orders 1732-42, 224]. He was tithable in Northampton County in 1744 adjoining Joseph Jeffery [Bell, *Northampton County Tithables*, 357]. He was allowed 200 pounds of tobacco from the county levy on 2 November 1747 [Orders 1742-8].

1   iii. Mary, born say 1710.

1. Mary Jeffery, born say 1710, died before 9 March 1773 when Daniel Eshon was granted administration on her Northampton County estate [Minutes 1771-7, 192]. Her inventory totaled 177 pounds, and included 45 pounds cash on hand, butter, hog fat, good pewter, knives and forks, 10 hoes, 3 plows, 30 cattle, 18 pigs, 22 hogs, 2 sheep, 22 barrels of corn, 3 horses, 6 ducks, 3 geese, 4 turkeys, and potato seed. Solomon Jeffery, Rachel Jeffery, Mary Jeffery, Thomas Fisherman, Mary Fisherman, Thomas Pool, and Abraham **Lang** were buyers at the sale of the estate. The account of the sales totaled 196 pounds and included a cart and wheels, beds, furniture and linen wheels. About 23 pounds was distributed to seven unnamed children [W&I 25:167-9, 262-6]. Mary was probably farming land on the Gingaskin reservation. She may have been the mother of

i. Stephen, born say 1729, an Indian sued by an Indian named John Daniel in a suit that was agreed in Northampton County on 11 March 1755 [Orders 1753-8, 199].

ii. Solomon[1], born say 1731, sued by William Teague on 15 December 1752 for trespass, assault and battery. He was called an Indian when he was sued for trespass, assault and battery by another Indian named John Daniel on 8 March 1757. George Powell sued him for a 1 pound, 7 shilling debt on 15 February 1758. On 14 July 1762 his wife Mary Jeffery ("Indian") took the oath of the peace against him and he was ordered to post 20 pounds security for his good behavior towards her [Orders 1751-3, 210; 1753-8, 400, 406, 482; Minutes 1761-5, 35]. He bought twenty-three items at the 8 February 1774 sale of Mary Jeffery's estate, including pigs and three harrow hoes.

iii. Rachel, taxable on a horse in Northampton County from 1800 to 1802 [PPTL 1782-1823, frames 310, 331].

iv. Joseph, tithable in Northampton County in 1744 [Bell, *Northampton County Tithables*, 357]. He was sued by Peter Hogg for debt on 11 September 1750 [Orders 1748-51, 270]. The court bound out his son Jesse Jeffery to Adiah Milby to be a marriner on 11 August 1773 [Minutes 1771-7, 156].

v. Thomas[2], bound to William Wood on 10 August 1773 [Minutes 1771-7, 151].

They were the ancestors of

i. Solomon[2], born say 1767, married Tinsey **Jacob**, 16 January 1788 Northampton County bond, William Satchell, Jr., security. Tincy Jeffery was a "N"(egro) counted in Northampton County in 1813 [PPTL, 1782-1823, frame 539].

ii. William, married Polly **Bingham**, 26 January 1803 Northampton County bond, Samuel **Beavans** security.

iii. Littleton, married Nancy **Collins**, 18 September 1810 Northampton County bond, James Jacob security. He was an "Indian" taxable on a horse in the Indian Town (the former Gingaskin reservation land) from 1811 to 1813, living with a "free negro" woman in his household in 1813 [PPTL 1782-1823, frames 492, 513, 539].

iv. Sophia, married Thomas **Carter**, 7 December 1803 Northampton County bond, Peter **Toyer** security. Sophia **Carter** was a "Negro" living in Indian Town in 1813 [PPTL, 1782-1823, frame 531].

v. Polly, married Nathan **Drighouse** (**Driggers**), 24 July 1810 Northampton County bond, Abraham **Lang** security.

JEFFRIES FAMILY

1. John[1] Jeffries, born say 1670, was a "Negroe man" belonging to Captain Robert Randall on 5 July 1698 when Randall brought him before the Surry County court to declare him a free man [DW 5:157; Haun, *Surry County Court Records*, V:211]. He was probably the "John Negroe" for whom Captain Randall was taxable in 1698. He was taxable in his own household in Surry County from 1699 to 1703 near William **Sweat** [*Magazine of Virginia Genealogy* vol.24, no.2, 69, 75, 83; no.3, 69, 72; DW 5:289]. He and William **Sweat** produced accounts against the public for fifty pounds of tobacco in Surry County court on 21 October 1713 [Orders 1713-18, 14]. On 18 February 1722 he received a patent for 100 acres in Surry County on the south side of Blackwater Swamp and north side of Seacock Swamp and another 70 acres adjoining this land and Richard Fitzpatrick on 30 August 1743 [Patents 11:188; 21:508]. He was called John Jeffries, Sr., in his 3 November 1746 Albemarle Parish, Surry County, will, recorded 16 June 1752, which named his daughter Martha Jeffries as executrix and gave her his land on Seacock Swamp. He also mentioned his daughter Mary **Powell**, left a gun to his grandson John Jeffreys and left his clothes to his grandson Benjamin **Tan**. If his daughter Martha died without heirs, the land was to pass to his grandson John Jeffrys [DW&c 1738-54, 798]. His children were

i. Martha.

2   ii.   John², Jr., born say 1690.
         iii.   Mary **Powell** (wife of Stephen **Powell**).
         iv.   a daughter, wife of Anthony **Tann** whose son Benjamin **Tann** was
                called an orphan on 20 February 1744 when the Surry County court
                ordered the churchwardens of Albemarle Parish to bind him out
                [Orders 1744-49, 11, 22].

2.   John² Jeffries, Jr., born say 1690, was called John Jeffries "the Younger" on
     14 December 1712 when he purchased 128 acres on the south side of
     Blackwater Swamp bounded by the College Line in Surry County [DW&c
     6:127]. (His wife?) Elizabeth Jeffers died 16 August 1745, and he died on 14
     January 1745/6 (informant John Jeffers) [Albemarle Parish, Surry and Sussex
     County, Parish Register 1739-1778, 161]. By his 24 December 1745 Surry
     County will, proved 19 March 1745/6, he left all his land on the north east
     side of Clift and Tar Kiln Branches and the College Plantation to his son
     Joseph and named his other children: Richard, John, Lucy, and Rebecca.
     Joseph was to care for his brother Richard until he reached twenty-one years
     of age. He allowed his unnamed father the use of the land he was living on
     until his death when it was to pass to his son John [DW&c 1738-54, 523]. His
     children were
3   i.   Joseph, born say 1715.
         ii.   Lucy.
4   iii. John⁴, born say 1720.
         iv.   Rebecca, born 13 March 1728/9, daughter of John Jeffries, Jr., and
               Eliza. his wife.
         v.   Richard, born 26 August 1732, son of John Jeffries, Jr., and his wife
               Eliza.
         vi.   ___ne (Anne), born 6 May 1738, daughter of John Jeffries, Jr., and
               Eliza his wife [Albemarle Parish, Surry and Sussex County Parish
               Register 1739-1778, part 1, 7, 38].

3.   Joseph Jeffries, born say 1715, received land on the northeast side of Clift and
     Tar Kiln Branches as well as the "College Plantation" by his father's 19 March
     1745/6 Surry County will. He was also to care for his younger brother Richard
     who was not yet twenty-one years old [DW&c 1738-54, 798]. He sold 100
     acres on the south side of Blackwater Swamp in Surry County, Virginia, on
     10 September 1747 [DB 5:124]. He returned an account of his father's estate
     to November 1747 Surry County court, but in March 1747/8 Thomas
     Alsobrook and John Anderson, his securities, complained to the court of his
     "ill conduct" and the court ordered him to deliver up the estate to them or
     provide the security bond himself [Orders 1744-9, 233-4]. He may have been
     the Joseph Jeffries who was sued in Brunswick County, Virginia court by
     Peter **Cumbo** in June 1749. The suit was dismissed when both parties failed
     to appear [Orders 1743-49, 523]. In July 1749 the Surry County court awarded
     him four pounds damages in his suit for trespass against James Winkles
     [Orders 1749-51, 597]. He was called "Joseph Jeffries a mullatto" in
     Southampton County when the court ordered the churchwardens of Nottoway
     Parish to bind out his children [Orders 1749-54, 388]. He was a taxable head
     of household with (his brother?) John Jeffries in Granville County, North
     Carolina, in the summary list for 1755 [CR 44.701.23], and he and his wife
     Ruth were "mulatto" taxables in the Cross Road District of Granville County
     in James Paine's list in Robert Collier's household in 1761 and in Thomas
     Hawtorn's household in 1762 [CR 44.701]. He mortgaged his livestock and
     furniture in Bute County to Charles Johnson on 19 November 1764 [Wills &
     Inventories 3:12, by Kerr, *Warren County Records*, 2]. He and John Jeffreys
     were insolvent taxpayers in Bute County in 1769 [Miscellaneous Tax Records
     in *N.C. Genealogy*, 2431]. Joseph was taxable in Warren County on an
     assessment of 59 pounds in 1779 and taxable in Captain Colclough's district

from 1781 to 1785: 610 pounds assessment in 1781, 83 pounds in 1782, taxable on 140 acres and poll tax in 1784, 2 polls in 1785, perhaps identical to Joseph Jefferson who was taxable on 196 acres and no polls in 1788 [1779 Assessments, p.2; Tax List 1781-1801, 17, 27, 63, 81, 97, 156; L.P. 64.1, p.19].

4. John[4] Jeffries, born say 1720, son of John[2] Jeffries, received a gun by the 3 November 1746 Surry County will of his grandfather John[1] Jeffries [D&W 1738-54, 798]. Sussex County was formed from the part of Surry County where the Jeffries lived. John sued William Bryan(t) in Sussex County court in April 1754, and he was sued by Howell Briggs and Arthur Richardson for a total of about 10 pounds currency in December 1754. He was not found by the sheriff so his estate (including nine cattle, a bed and furniture, a chest and gun and dishes) was attached and sold [Haun, *Sussex County Records*, 100, 114, 194]. On 12 February 1755 he sold 140 acres in Sussex County on the south side of Blackwater Swamp adjoining the College Line which was the land his grandfather John[1] Jeffries patented, part of a "Survey made by John Jeffries Deceased" on 13 August 1743 [Sussex County DB A:84]. He was taxable in Granville County, North Carolina, in the household of his brother Joseph Jeffries in 1755, and he and his wife Mary were "mulatto" taxables in the Cross Road District of Granville County, North Carolina, in James Paine's list in 1761 and 1762 [CR 44.701]. This part of Granville County became Bute County in 1769, and he and Joseph Jeffreys were insolvent taxpayers in Bute County in 1769 [Miscellaneous Tax Records in *N.C. Genealogy*, 2431]. He was taxable on only his own poll in Bute County in 1771 [Tax List CR.015.70001, p.12 of pamphlet] and taxable in Warren County on an assessment of 20 pounds in Captain Shearing's District in 1782 [Tax List 1781-1801, 46].

Perhaps Joseph and John Jeffries were the ancestors of some of those members of the Jeffries family counted as "other free" and "free colored" in Orange and Caswell Counties, North Carolina:
  i.   Jacob, born say 1760, taxable in Orange County in 1790 [NC:95] and head of an Orange County household of 9 "other free" in 1800 [NC:514]. He recorded a certificate in Orange County on 24 July 1791 that he was the "Mulatto Jacob" who received a discharge for twelve months service as a soldier in the Revolution [*NCGSJ* XI:115].
  ii. John[6], born about 1759, listed as a volunteer Continental soldier from Bute County in 1779: *born about 1759 in North Carolina, 5'6" tall, dark hair and dark eyes* [*NCGSJ* XV:109].
  iii. Reuben, married Kissiah **Hawly**, 30 May 1808 Caswell County bond, Miles **Scott** bondsman. Reuben was head of an Orange County, North Carolina household of 2 "free colored" in 1820 [NC:354]. Miles **Scott** was head of an Orange County household of 3 "other free" in 1810 [NC:817].
  iv. Elias, born 1776-1794, head of an Orange County, North Carolina household of 4 "free colored" in 1820 [NC:406].

Other Members of the Jeffries family in Virginia were
  i.   Margaret, born say 1690, paid 3 shillings, 9 pence on 16 September 1719 by the Surry County estate of Charles Savidge for her attendance at his funeral. The December 1722 account of the Surry County estate of Samuel Thompson included a 17 shillings payment to her, a 9 shillings payment to William **Sweat**, and William **Sweat**'s payment of his rent [Deeds, Wills 1715-30, 219, 456-7]. She and her daughter Margaret Jeffries, her husband William **Sweat**, and Francis **Locus** and his wife Hannah lost their right to 190 acres on the north side of the Meherrin River in Southampton County in a dispute with Arthur Taylor

heard at the Council of Virginia on 8 November 1753. Taylor received a patent for this land bordering Turraroe Creek on 24 January 1756 [Hall, *Executive Journals of the Council,* V:448; Patents 32:667]. She was called Margaret **Sweat** in Southampton County on 12 June 1755 when the court ordered that she be exempt from paying levies [Orders 1754-9, 94].

5   ii.   John³, born say 1718.

5.   John³ Jeffries, born say 1718, was called John Jefferson when he was granted 84 acres on Cattail Swamp in Brunswick County adjoining John Persons on 12 March 1739 [Patents 18:553-4]. He was called Jefferson in the early land records but called John Jeffres/ Jefferis when he voted in Brunswick County in June 1748 [DB 3:508, 510]. And he and his family were called Jeffries when they voted in Greensville County in 1792 and in the land records in the late 1790s and thereafter. On 26 May 1748 he purchased 228 acres in Brunswick County bounded by the north side of Cattail Creek from John Person of Isle of Wight County, heir to John Person of Surry County who was granted the land in 1726 [DB 3:447; Greensville DB 1:450]. He was among the freeholders of Brunswick County ordered to work on a road under Littleberry Robertson on 27 March 1759 [Orders 1757-9, 314]. His land on Cattail Creek was on the west side of Fountain Creek in the part of Brunswick County which became Greensville County in 1781. He was taxable in Meherrin Parish, Brunswick County, on 2 persons over the age of twenty-one and 1 person under the age of twenty-one in 1785 and free from personal tax in 1786 [PPTL 1782-98, frames 135, 159]. He was called John Jeffries on 28 June 1787 when the Greensville County court discharged him from paying taxes (due to old age) starting from the year 1786 [Orders 1781-9, 332]. He was taxable in Meherrin Parish, Greensville County, from 1787 to 1796: taxable on (his son) Nathan Jeffries and 3 horses in 1789, taxable on a horse in 1796 [PPTL 1782-1850, frames 43, 65, 84, 109, 138, 189, 202]. John and his wife Judy Jefferson made a deed of gift of 55 acres to their son Simon in 1796 and made deeds of sale to (their sons?) Andrew, Simon, Nathan, and John in Greensville County between 1789 and 1798. They sold 50 acres of land adjoining their land in Greensville County to Andrew Jeffers on 4 February 1789, sold 45 acres on Person's Branch adjoining William Robinson to John Jeffers, Junior, for 3 pounds on 25 April 1792, and sold 40 acres to Nathan Jeffries for 20 pounds on 23 January 1798. By the terms of the deed Nathan was not to take possession of the land until the death of John Jeffries. On 27 December 1798 John and his wife Judy Jeffries also sold two parcels of land adjoining theirs to Andrew Jeffries, one of 40 acres for 9 pounds and another of 84 acres for 50 pounds [DB 2:487, 498, 505-6, 520, 524]. He may have been the Jefferson who was paid as a witness on 24 August 1799 for William Lanier in the Greensville County suit of William Stewart [Orders 1790-9, 635]. John Jeffries' wife Judy was identified as Judy **Lane** by their great grandson Parker Jeffries (son of Sally Jeffries) in a Greene County, Ohio court suit in 1841 [Parker Jeffries v. Ankeny].¹²² Judy was probably the

---

¹²²The trustees of Zenia Township denied Parker Jeffries the right to vote because he was a "person of color." He sued them in court and provided depositions from witnesses who had been neighbors of the Jeffries family in Greensville County in order to prove that he was white and Indian. Sally Robinson deposed that Sally Jeffries "claimed to be of White and Indian and I never heard anything to the contrary." Henry Wyche deposed that he believed Andrew Jeffries was "of Indian and White" (blood). Susan **Wooten** deposed that she grew up near the family where they lived in Greensville County. (She was probably married to or a member of the mixed-race **Wooten** family who lived just across the state line in Northampton County, North Carolina). Parker lost his case in the local court but won his appeal to the supreme court of Ohio which ruled that: *There have been, even in this state, since its organization,*

granddaughter of Elizabeth Lane who confessed in Surry County, Virginia court on 7 January 1690/1 that she had two "Molato" children by "Nicholas Sessums his Negro Man" [Surry Orders 1682-91, 771, 777]. John's children were

6   i.   John⁵, born say 1745.
7   ii.   Andrew/ Drury¹, born say 1750.
     iii.   Shadrack, born say 1754, taxable in Meherrin Parish, Brunswick County, from 1784 to 1787 [PPTL 1782-98, frames 91, 136, 170, 204]. He voted in Greensville County on 26 April 1792 [DB 1:450]. He was surety for the 24 July 1794 Greensville County, Virginia marriage bond of (his niece) Grief Jeffries. He was taxable in Meherrin Parish, Greensville County, from 1788 to 1812: [PPTL 1782-1850, frames 64, 109, 138, 179, 202, 232, 260, 288, 322, 354, 387, 416, 433]. His 12 May 1812 Greensville County will was proved 12 October the same year. He left all his lands to his wife Sarah and at her death to Mary Jefferson (Jeffries). And he left his property to his wife and at her death to his brother Nathan with one-twelfth to go to Sarah **Wadkins (Watkins)**. His wife Sarah and brother Nathan were executors [WB 2:267-8].
8   iv.   Simon, born say 1756.
     v.   ?Jacob, born say 1758, taxable on 2 horses and 3 cattle in Meherrin Parish, Brunswick County, in 1783 and 1784 [PPTL 1782-98, frames 62, 91].
     vi.   Nathan, born say 1762, taxable on a horse and 3 cattle in Meherrin Parish, Brunswick County, in 1784 [PPTL 1782-98, frame 91], married Clary **Norton**, 23 June 1791 Greensville County bond, Repts **Steward** surety. He was a taxable in Meherrin Parish, Greensville County, from 1787 to 1827: listed in his father's household in 1787 and 1789, listed as a "Mulatto" in 1813, listed with son Nathan from 1818 to 1820, listed with son Shade in 1822 and 1823, listed with (son?) John in 1825, with William Jeffers in 1827 [PPTL 1799-1850, frames 43, 65, 84, 109, 127, 138, 162, 180, 189, 202, 219, 232, 245, 260, 274, 288, 303, 322, 337, 354, 372, 387, 416, 433, 447, 557, 581, 605, 653, 678, 705, 731, 804] and head of a Greensville County household of 9 "free colored" in 1820 [VA:263].

6.   John⁵ Jeffries, born say 1745, was taxable in Meherrin Parish, Brunswick County, Virginia, from 1782 to 1787: taxable on Isaac Jefferson's tithe in 1783, taxable on sons Isaac and Harris in 1784, called "John Jeffers, Junr." in 1785 [PPTL 1782-98, frames 23, 62, 136, 159, 204]. On 23 July 1787 and 25 November 1788 the Brunswick County court exempted him from payment of taxes charged on two persons listed by mistake [Orders 1784-8, 525; 1788-92, 95]. He was called John Jeffers, Jr., on 25 April 1792 when he purchased 45 acres in Greensville County on Person's Branch adjoining William Robinson's line from (his father?) John Jeffers, Sr. [DB 2:520]. He was taxable in Meherrin Parish, Greensville County, from 1789 to 1810: taxable

many persons of the precise breed of this plaintiff, I mean the offspring of whites and half-breed Indians, who have exercised political privileges and filled offices, and worthily discharged the duties of officers. One such is now a clerk of this court, and two are now members of this bar. In 1831 in the case of Polly Gray v. State of Ohio, 4 Ohio, 354, and in 1833, in the case of Williamson v. School Directors, etc., Wright, 178, it was held that, in the constitution, and the laws on this subject, there were enumerated three descriptions of persons--whites, blacks and mulattoes--upon the two last of whom disabilities rested; that the mulatto was the middle term between the extremes, or the offspring of white and black; that all nearer white than black, or of the grade between the mulattoes and the whites, were entitled to enjoy every political and social privilege of the white citizen [Edwin M. Stanton, Reporter, Reports of Cases Argued and Determined in the Supreme Court of Ohio (1873), XI:318-21].

on a free male tithable aged 16-21 and 2 horses in 1788 and 1789, taxable on (his sons) Harris and Isaac Jeffries' tithes in 1790, taxable on Harris Jeffries and a free male tithable aged 16-21 in 1793 [PPTL 1782-1850, frames 65, 109, 138, 180, 274, 402]. His son Thomas appeared in Orange County, North Carolina court on 26 May 1837 to obtain a pension for his father's services in the Revolution. He stated that his father was born in Halifax County, Virginia, in 1733 (perhaps date in error and place meant to be Halifax County, North Carolina), was drafted in the fall of the years 1780 and 1781, that his father was very infirm and blind in December 1832 when he moved him to Orange County, and that his father died 4 December 1834 leaving no widow [M804-1409, frames 350-1]. John was the father of

i. Isaac, born say 1766, under the age of twenty-one in 1783 when he was listed in his father's Brunswick County household [PPTL 1799-1815, frames 62, 91, 135, 170], taxable in his own Greensville County household in 1789, listed in his father's Greensville County household in 1792 [PPTL 1782-1850, frames 84, 138].

ii. Harris, born say 1768, under the age of twenty-one in 1784 when he was listed in his father's Brunswick County household [PPTL 1782-98, frame 91], charged with his own tax in Greensville County in 1788 and 1789, listed in his father's Greensville County household from 1790 to 1793 [PPTL 1782-1850, frames 65, 84, 109, 127, 138, 162].

iii. Thomas, born say 1770, married Silvey **Hathcock**, 8 October 1789 Greensville County bond, by Rev. William Garner [Ministers Returns p.147]. He was taxable in Greensville County from 1791 to 1798 and from 1804 to 1806 [PPTL 1782-1850, frames 127, 137, 162, 180, 189, 219, 245, 322, 337, 354]. He was head of an Orange County household of 9 "other free" in 1810 [NC:817] and 7 "free colored" in 1820 [NC:406].

iv. Lewis, taxable in Meherrin Parish, Greensville County, from 1794 to 1814: listed in John Jefferson's household in 1794, listed in Joel Prince's household in 1798, listed in Benjamin Woodroofe's household in 1807, listed as a "Mulatto" in 1813 and 1814 [PPTL 1782-1850, frames 180, 189, 218, 234, 322, 337, 354, 387, 402, 416, 433, 447, 463] and bondsman for the 5 February 1821 Orange County marriage bond of Tempe Jeffers and Dixon **Corn**. He was head of an Orange County household of 6 "free colored in 1820 [NC:412].

7. Andrew[1] Jeffries, born say 1750 (before 1776), was taxable in Meherrin Parish, Brunswick County, Virginia, from 1782 to 1787: taxable on a 4 horses and 4 cattle in 1782, taxable on John Jeffries' tithe in 1783 [PPTL 1782-98, frames 23, 62, 91, 136, 159, 203]. He purchased 50 acres in Meherrin Parish, Greensville County, adjoining Shadrack, Simon, and John Jeffers from John Jeffers on 4 February 1789, purchased 30 acres on the southside of Jordan's Road adjoining the land of John Jefferson (Jeffries) on 20 April 1790 and another 30 acres on the southside of Jordan's Road on 28 April 1796. And he purchased two parcels of land from John Jeffries and his wife Judy on 27 December 1798: one for 9 pounds and another of 84 acres for 50 pounds. He voted in Greensville County on 26 April 1792. He and his wife Mary sold 12-1/4 acres adjoining their land for $61 on 24 July 1815 [DB 1:292, 449; 2:359, 524; 4:520]. He was taxable in Meherrin Parish, Greensville County, from 1788 to 1812: listed with 2 tithables aged 16-21 in 1793 and 1794 [PPTL 1782-1850, frames 65, 84, 109, 127, 137, 162, 179, 189, 202, 219, 232, 260, 274, 288, 303, 322, 337, 354, 372, 387, 402, 416, 433]. He was called Andrew Jeffers when he was discharged from paying taxes in Greensville County in 1812 [Orders 1810-15, 253]. His 16 February 1821 Greensville County will was proved in October 1821. He left the part of his land adjoining David Robinson to his daughter Sally and the remainder on the southside to his daughters Linch and Morning. He named his surviving children: John, Drury,

Littleton, Linch, Jancy, Grief, Morning, and Sally. Maclin Jeffries, Sally Jeffries and Grief **Hathcock** were buyers at the sale of his estate [WB 3:240, 299]. Andrew's wife was identified as Mary **Dole** in the Greene County, Ohio court suit of his grandson Parker Jeffries (son of Sally Jeffries) in 1841 [Parker Jeffries v. Ankeny]. Mary may have been the daughter of William **Dale(s)**, head of a Northampton County, North Carolina household of 10 "other free" in 1790 [NC:76]. Andrew was the father of

  i.   John[7], born about 1765, taxable in Andrew Jeffries' Brunswick County household in 1783 [PPTL 1782-98], charged with his own tax in Meherrin Parish, Greensville County, from 1788 to 1807 [PPTL 1782-1850, frames 65, 84, 108, 127, 138, 218, 245, 260, 274, 288, 303, 322, 337, 372]. He was head of an Orange County, North Carolina household of 5 "free colored" in 1820 [NC:342]. He married Dilly **Ballard**, 8 December 1824 Orange County bond, Andrew and Eaton Jeffers bondsmen. He was about sixty-seven years old and living in Orange County on 26 November 1832 when he applied for a pension for his services in the Revolution. He stated that he enlisted in Brunswick County, Virginia, in 1780 and resided there until 1808 when he moved to Orange County. He made a second declaration in Orange County on 19 October 1837 that he had served in the place of his father Andrew Jeffreys. His widow Delilah was a resident of Alamance County on 19 November 1853 when she applied for a survivor's pension, testifying that they were married in 1822 and that her husband died on 15 April 1845. She was said to have been about eighty years old when she testified again in Alamance County on 11 April 1855 [M804-1409, frame 0363].
  ii. Andrew/Drury[2], born about 1768, married Silvia **Scott**, 28 January 1790 Greensville County bond, Andrew Jeffries surety. They were married by Rev. William Garner whose return was dated 10 Nov. 1789 [Minister's Returns, p.19]. He was taxable in Meherrin Parish, Greensville County, from 1788 to 1812: taxable in his father's household in 1788 and 1789 [PPTL 1782-1850, frames 65, 109, 137, 180, 202, 245, 303, 337, 372, 402, 433]. He was head of an Orange County, North Carolina household of 13 "free colored" in 1820 [NC:342]. He purchased 110 acres on Jordans Creek in Orange County from Robert Scott on 8 November 1832 [DB pp.254-5]. He made a deposition in Orange County on 10 November 1832 that he lived in Brunswick County when (his brother) John Jeffries left home to serve in the Revolution. He made a similar deposition in 1833 that he was born in Brunswick County about 1766, resided there until 1813 when he moved to North Carolina, and that he recollected that his brother returned home from service in 1781. He was deposed again on 19 October 1837 when he stated that he was about sixty-nine years old and the brother of John Jeffries. On 19 November 1853 he made a deposition for the survivor's pension application of John's widow Delilah Jeffries, stating that John and Delilah were married in 1822 [M804-1409, frames 375, 382, 425].
  iii. Littleton, born before 1776, taxable in Greensville County in Andrew Jeffries' household from 1797 to 1802, listed in his own household in 1803 [PPTL 1782-1850, frames 219, 232, 245, 260, 274, 288, 303]. He was head of an Orange County, North Carolina household of 4 "other free" in 1810 [NC:835] and 8 "free colored" in 1820 [NC:342].
  iv. Grief, born say 1772, daughter of Andrew Jeffries, married Colby **Hathcock**, 24 July 1794 Greensville County bond, Shadrach Jeffries surety [Minister's Returns p.30]. Colby was head of a Greensville County household of 8 whites in 1810 [VA:738]. Grief **Haithcock** was apparently a widow when she was head of a Greensville County household of 8 "free colored" in 1820 [VA:262].

    v.   Jancy/Ginsy[1], born before 1774, "over 21 years of age," married Robert Brooks **Corn**, 26 March 1795 Greensville County bond, Drury **Going** surety.

    vi.   Linchey Jeffers, born before 1776, head of a Greensville County household of 3 "free colored" in 1820 [VA:263].

    vii.   Mourning, born 1776-94, taxable in Greensville County on McLin Jeffries' tithe in 1822 and 1823 [PPTL 1782-1850, frames 653, 679], head of a Greensville County household of 4 "free colored" in 1820 [VA:263]. On 11 May 1807 Henry Avent, a white man, was charged in Greensville County court with begetting an illegitimate child by her, but the case was dismissed [Orders 1806-10, 100].

9   viii.   Sally, born say 1780.

8.   Simon Jeffries, born say 1756, was taxable in Meherrin Parish, Brunswick County, from 1783 to 1786 [PPTL 1782-98, frames 62, 91, 135, 159]. He received 55 acres in Greensville County, on which he was then living, from his father John Jeffers by deed of gift in 1796 [DB 1:487]. Simon was taxable in Greensville County from 1789 to 1807: taxable on 2 free male tithables and 3 horses in 1788, taxable on Surrell **Jones** Jeffries' tithe in 1789, taxable on a free male tithable aged 16-21 in 1790, 1792, 1794 and 1797, taxable on (his son?) Hudson Jeffries in 1798, taxable on a free male tithable 16-21 in 1801 [PPTL 1782-1850, frames 65, 84, 127, 138, 162, 180, 189, 202, 219, 232, 245, 260, 274, 303, 322, 337, 354, 372].[123] On 8 December 1807 he and his wife Silvey sold 51 acres in Greensville County to David Robinson [DB 4:73]. He was head of an Orange County, North Carolina household of 6 "free colored" in 1820 [NC:410]. He may have been the father of

    i.   Hudson, born say 1777, taxable in Greensville County from 1797 to 1805 [PPTL 1782-1850, frames 219, 232, 245, 260, 274, 303, 321, 337], head of a Caswell County, North Carolina household of 10 "free colored" in 1820 [NC:67].

9.   Sally Jeffries, born say 1780, was left land adjoining Robinson by her father's October 1821 Greensville County will. She had a child named Augustus by her Greensville County neighbor, Darius Robinson (a white man), according to her son's Greene County, Ohio petition to change his name to Robinson. Sally, Mourning, and Linchey Jeffers were listed together as "Mulatto" in the same Greensville County household in 1813. Sally was taxable on her son Wyatt Jeffries' tithe in 1823 [PPTL 1782-1850, frames 447, 679]. Her children were

    i.   Parker.

    ii.   Wyatt, head of a Whitley County, Indiana household of 4 "free colored" in 1840.

    iii.   Augustus, petitioned the Greene County, Ohio court to change his name to Augustus Wyche Robinson. The petition was filed on 8 May 1843 and recorded 29 May 1843.

Other Jeffries descendants were

    i.   Middy, head of a Northampton County, North Carolina household of 3 "other free" in 1810 [NC:731].

    ii.   Eady, born before 1776, head of a Greensville County household of 3 "free colored" in 1820 [VA:263].

    iii.   Jinncy[2], born before 1776, head of an Orange County, North Carolina household of 7 "free colored" in 1820 [NC:344].

    iv.   Martha, married Charles **Evans**, 17 August 1796 Mecklenburg County, Virginia bond, Kinchen **Chavous** security.

---

[123]Surrel Jones was head of an Orange County, North Carolina household of 5 "free colored" in 1820 [NC:410].

v.   Elizabeth, married Vines **Guy**, 8 January 1805 Orange County bond, Jesse **Blalock** bondsman. Vines was head of an Orange County household of 5 "other free" in 1810 [NC:795].
vi. Herbert, born 1776-94, taxable in Greensville County from 1809 to 1820: a "Mulatto" taxable in 1813 and 1814, a "F.N." in 1815 [PPTL 1782-1850, frames 387, 402, 433, 463, 557, 581, 605] and head of a Greensville County household of 4 "free colored" in 1820 [VA:263].
vii. Nancy, born 1776-1794, head of a Halifax County, North Carolina household of 4 "free colored" in 1830.
viii. Joshua, born 1776-1794, taxable in Greensville County from 1802 to 1806 [PPTL 1782-1850, frames 288, 303, 337, 354], head of an Orange County, North Carolina household of 7 "free colored" in 1820 [NC:344].
ix. John[8], born 1776-1794, head of an Orange County, North Carolina household of 10 "free colored" in 1820 [NC:340].
x.   Willis, born 1776-1794, head of an Orange County household of 4 "free colored" in 1820 [NC:340], perhaps the William Jeffries who married Penelope **Evans**, 21 February 1800 Orange County bond, Rept **Stewart** bondsman. Rape was head of an Orange County household of 2 "other free" in 1800 [NC:530].

South Carolina:
Members of the family in Richland District, South Carolina, were
i.   Berry, counted as white in 1790, head of household of 2 males over 16, 1 under 16, and 3 females [SC:26] and head of household of 10 "other free" in 1810 [SC:176]. He was probably related to Mary and Sarah Jeffers who were residents of Richland District in 1806 when they petitioned the South Carolina legislature to be exempted from the tax on free Negro women [S.C. Archives series S.165015, item 01885].
ii. Allen, counted as white in 1790, head of a household of 1 male over 16 and 2 females [SC:26].
iii. Betsy, head of a Richland District household of 3 "other free" in 1810 [SC:176].
iv. John[9], head of a Richland District household of 2 "other free" in 1810 [SC:176].

JENKINS FAMILY

1.   Annakin Jenkins, born say 1720, was a "Moll. girl" born in Captain Henry Randolph's house in Bristol Parish, Virginia, and bound to him on 9 October 1724 [Chamberlayne, *Register of Bristol Parish*, 19]. She was living in Chesterfield County on 5 December 1755 when the court ordered the churchwardens to bind out her daughter Patt Jenkins [Orders 1754-59, 150]. She was the mother of
2   i.   ?Francis[1], born say 1740.
3   ii. Pat, born say 1750.
4   iii. ?Doll, born say 1752.
     iv. ?Ann, born say 1756, mother of a "mulato" bastard child bound by the Augusta County court on 21 May 1777 [Orders 1774-9, 198].

2.   Francis[1] Jenkins, born say 1740, purchased 325 acres in Edgecombe County, North Carolina, on Compass Creek on 11 February 1762. He witnessed the 10 September 1765 Edgecombe County deed of John Jenkins, Sr., to Jesse Jenkins [DB 1:186; D:540]. On 12 October 1765 Elisha Battle called him a "mustee" when he reported to the Edgecombe County court that Francis had not listed his wife as a tithable [Minutes 1764-72, 42]. He was called Francis Jenkins alias Rogers on 4 August 1768 when he sold his land on Compass

Creek [DB D:79]. He may have been the Rogers Jenkins who purchased 300 acres in Nash County on the south side of Beach Run from James Cain on 10 October 1778. He and his wife Fanny sold this land on 5 April 1779 [DB 1:50]. He may have been the Francis Jenkins, Sr., who was taxable in Surry County, North Carolina, in 1820 on 158 acres, adjoining 87.5 acres on Falls Creek said to border land of "Free Jenkins." His widow may have been the Frances Jenkins who was head of a Surry County household of 6 "free colored" in 1830. They may have been the parents of

  i.   Jesse, head of a Nash County household of 9 "other free" in 1800 [NC:106], perhaps the Jesse Jenkins who purchased 235 acres in Edgecombe County from John Jenkins, Sr., on 10 September 1765, and perhaps the husband of Keddy Jenkins who was mentioned in the 10 November 1794 Edgecombe County will of William **Morgan**.
  ii. James, head of a Bertie County household of 6 "other free" in 1800 [NC:54], and 8 "other free" in Franklin County in 1810 [NC:826].
  iii. Benjamin, head of a Cumberland County, North Carolina household of 3 "other free" in 1800.
  iv. Thomas, head of a Northampton County, North Carolina household of 7 "other free" in 1810 [VA:730], and 9 "free colored" in 1820 [NC:238].

3. Pat Jenkins, born say 1750, was bound out in Chesterfield County on 5 December 1755. She may have been the mother of

  i.   Winney, born about 1771, obtained a certificate of freedom in Chesterfield County on 14 August 1819: *forty eight years old, brown complexion, born free* [Register of Free Negroes 1804-53, no. 390].
  ii. George, born in July 1779, registered in Petersburg on 21 January 1802: *a brown Mulatto man, born free & raised at Bermuda Hundred in the County of Chesterfield, five feet five inches high, short bushy hair, twenty two July last* [Register of Free Negroes 1794-1819, no. 223].
  iii. Anna, mother of Nancy Jenkins who married Archibald **Batts**, "free persons of color," 1 March 1815 Chesterfield County bond. Archibald was a "F.N." taxable on himself and a woman in Prince George County in 1813 [Waldrep, *1813 Tax List*].

4. Doll Jenkins, born say 1752, was living in Chesterfield County on 4 November 1774 when the court ordered the churchwardens of Dale Parish to bind out her daughter Martha [Orders 1774-84, 62]. She was the mother of

  i.   Martha, born say 1774, was ordered to be bound out on 4 November 1774, perhaps identical to Pat Jenkins who was ordered to be bound out in Chesterfield County on 7 August 1777 [Orders 1774-84, 180]. She registered in Petersburg on 9 July 1805: *Patty Ginkins, a dark brown Negro woman, five feet one inches high, thirty years old, born free and raised in the County of Chesterfield* [Register of Free Negroes 1794-1819, no. 309]. She was called Patsey Jenkins in 1810, head of a Petersburg Town household of 5 "other free" [VA:118a].
  ii. ?William, ordered bound out by the churchwardens of Manchester Parish in Chesterfield County on 1 March 1782, no race indicated [Orders 1774-84, 344].

Other members of the Jenkins family in Virginia were

  i.   Francis², married Nancy **Jackson**, 23 February 1786 Campbell County bond, Francis and Joseph Jenkins bondsmen. He was taxable in Campbell County from 1787 to 1790: his tax charged to James Robison in 1787 [PPTL, 1785-1814, frames 57, 85, 118, 152], taxable in Henry County from 1793 to 1795, listed with 2 tithables in 1795 [PPTL, 1782-1830, frames 392, 403, 417]. He and his wife Nancy sold property by deed proved in Henry County on 31 August 1795 [Orders 1792-7, 216].

   ii.   William, Sr., taxable in the northern district of Campbell County from 1787 to 1794 [PPTL, 1785-1814, frames 54, 86, 118, 191, 234, 304], levy free in Henry County in 1800, called "William Jinkins, Sr." in the list of "free Negroes & Mulattoes" in 1813 [PPTL, 1782-1830, frames 480, 579, 641].

   iii.   Joseph, Sr., taxable in the northern district of Campbell County in 1787 [PPTL, 1785-1814, frame 54].

   iv.   William, taxable in the northern district of Campbell County from 1789 to 1794, called "son of Ned." [PPTL, 1785-1814, frame 118, 152, 303], perhaps the one who married Elizabeth **Brown**, 10 September 1789 Campbell County bond.

   v.   John, taxable in the northern district of Campbell County from to 1792 [PPTL, 1785-1814, frames 235].

   vi.   Oliver, born say 1774, taxable Campbell County in 1791 and 1792 [PPTL, 1785-1814, frames 191, 234]. He, a "Mulattoe," married Fanny Jenkins, a "Mulattoe," 27 April 1792 Campbell County bond. He was taxable in Henry County from 1794 to 1815: in the list of "free Negroes & Mulattoes" in 1813 and 1814, listed with son William in 1814 [PPTL, 1782-1830, frames 403, 417, 439, 480, 579, 605, 641, 656, 692].

   vii.   Joseph, Jr., married Mary Jenkins, daughter of William and Anney Jenkins, 30 January 1786 Campbell County bond, Joseph and Francis Jenkins bondsmen. He was taxable in the northern district of Campbell County from 1787 to 1793 [PPTL, 1785-1814, frames 54, 118, 191, 234, 271], taxable in Henry County from 1794 to 1813, in the list of "free Negroes & Mulattoes" in 1813 [PPTL, 1782-1830, frames 403, 453, 505, 554, 592, 641].

   viii.   Hannah, head of a Richmond County household of 7 "other free" in 1810 [VA:401].

   ix.   Isham, head of a Buckingham County household of 3 "other free" in 1810 [VA:811].

   x.   Polly, a "free mulatto" baptized in Saint Marks Parish, Culpeper County on 19 March 1795 [*Virginia Genealogist*, vol.3, no.3, p.100]. On 22 March 1814 Francis Slaughter certified to the Amherst County court that she was bound to him by the overseers of the poor in Culpeper County until the age of eighteen, had served her time, and was then a free woman aged twenty-three [Orders 1811-4].

JOHNS FAMILY

1.   William[1] John, born say 1703, was leasing 76 acres in Charles Parish, York County, Virginia, near the border with Warwick County, from William Ferguson in September 1724 when Ferguson sold the land [Deeds & Bonds Book, Vol. III, 1713-39, 437; Richter, *A Community and its Neighborhoods,* 375]. He may have been related to John Johns who sued Major Lewis Burwell in York County court for his freedom dues on 24 June 1699 [DWO 11:150]. He was living in York County on 17 November 1740 when he was presented for failing to list his wife as a tithable, "she being a Mulatto." The court excused him from paying a fine but ordered that he pay her taxes that year and list her as a tithable in the future [W&I 18:652, 667]. They may have been the parents of

2   i.   Thomas, born say 1730.

3   ii.   James[1], born say 1742.

4   iii.   Mallory, born say 1752.

2. Thomas Johns, born say 1730, was living on a lot at Lowpoint, Surry County, Virginia, on 16 February 1773 when Archibald Dunlop sold this land [Hopkins, *Surry County Virginia Deeds and Estate Accounts, 1756-87*, 61]. He may have been the father of

5   i.   Joshua[1], born say 1753.
6   ii. John[1], born about 1762.

3. James[1] Johns, born say 1742, was a Revolutionary War soldier from Goochland County. In 1778 the Goochland County court provided his wife "needy relief" while he was serving in the Revolution [Jackson, *Virginia Negro Soldiers*, 37]. He may have been the father of

    i.   Sally, born say 1769, married John **Cockran**, 30 April 1790 Goochland County bond. Jacob **Banks** testified that Sally was of lawful age [DB 15:386].
    ii. John[2], born about 1777, registered as a free Negro in Goochland County on 5 May 1806: *a free man of color about twenty eight or thirty years of age, five feet ten inches and three quarters high, dark yellow complexion...straight black hair and was free born* [Register of Free Negroes, p.13, no.29]. He was a "Mulatto" taxable in Goochland County from 1804 to 1815 [PPTL, 1782-1809, frames 690, 743, 784, 869; 1810-32, frames 10, 76, 101, 169, 197, 263].
    iii. Nancy, born say 1778, married Riley **Scott**, 18 October 1799 Goochland County bond, Joseph **Scott** surety, 19 October marriage.
    iv. Susanna, born say 1785, married Edward **Morris**, 24 May 1806 Goochland County bond.
    v.   Lindsay, born about 1786, registered as a Free Negro in Goochland County in April 1807: *about twenty one years of age, five feet six and a quarter inches high...yellow complexion, Bushy hair* [Register of Free Negroes, p.16, no.35]. He was head of a Campbell County household of 1 "other free" in 1810 [VA:849].

4. Mallory Johns, born say 1752, was a "mulato" taxable in Tillotson Parish, Buckingham County, in 1773 [Woodson, *Virginia Tithables from Burned Counties*, 62]. On 6 October 1785 the Campbell County court ordered that he be added to the hands who worked on a road. He won a suit against Jesse Ewton for 600 pounds of inspected tobacco on 4 August 1786 [Orders 1785-6, 158]. He was taxable in Campbell County from 1786 to 1791: charged with a 16-21 year-old tithable in 1789, charged with Mallory Johns, Jr.'s tithe in 1790 [PPTL, 1785-1814, frames 22, 100, 134, 173]. He was granted 220 acres on the Main Ireland Creek, a branch of the Fluvanna River, in Buckingham County on 24 March 1790 [Grants 23:116]. He was taxable in Amherst County from 1797 to 1799. He may have been identical to or the father of "Jeffrey Johns or Patterson" who was taxable in Amherst County in 1806, called Mallory Johns or Patterson in 1807, 1809 and 1810, "Malory Johns or Patterson a man of color" in 1811, called "Jefrey Mallory Johns, M of C" in 1812, Malory Johns a "Mulatto" in 1813, Mallory Johns in a list of "Free Mulattoes & Negroes" in 1814, a "M.C." in 1815, working as a mechanic when he was in a list of "Free Negros and Mulattors" in 1816, a planter over the age of forty-five when he was in a list of "Free Negroes & Mulattoes" in 1818 [PPTL 1782-1803, frames 395, 453; 1804-23, frames 148, 170, 192, 214, 235, 256, 284, 336, 403]. He sued Caleb Watts for slander in Amherst County court on 22 July 1800. The suit was dismissed on 21 May 1802 because he failed to prosecute [Orders 1799-1801, 244, 281, 444; 1801-2, 145]. He was head of an Amherst County household of 1 "other free" in 1810 [VA:286]. He may have been identical to Jeffery Johns who was a 55-100 year-old head of an Amherst County household of 7 "free colored" and a white female 40-50 years old in 1830. He was the father of

i. ?John, born say 1770, a "melatto" taxable in the northern district of Campbell County in 1788 and 1789 [PPTL, 1785-1814, frames 85, 118].

ii. Mallory[2], born say 1772, listed in Mallory Johns, Sr.'s Campbell County household in 1790 then crossed off [PPTL, 1785-1814, frame 134].

iii. Sarah, born say 1774, a "mulatto," "daughter of Mallory Johns, Sr.," who consents," married Richard **Moss**, a "Negro," 14 May 1791 Campbell County bond, Henry **Moss** witness.

7   iv. ?William[2], born about 1777.

v. ?James[2], born about 1780, called "James Johns or Patterson" when he was taxable in Amherst County from 1809 to 1818: a "man of color" in 1811 and 1812, a "Mulatto" in 1813, a "M.C." in 1815, counted in a list of "Free Negroes & Mulattoes" in 1814 and 1818 [PPTL 1804-23, frames 169, 192, 214, 235, 256, 284, 303, 489]. He was head of an Amherst County household of 4 "other free" in 1810 [VA:282]. He registered as a "Free Negro" in Amherst County on 20 November 1843: *about 63 years of age, Bright mulatto, 5 feet 3 1/2 inches high...born free* [Register 1822-64, no.118]. On the same day his children born by Betsy **Terry** registered [Register, nos. 121-126], and Betsy **Terry** registered: *about 40 years of age, Bright mulatto, 5 feet 1 3/4 Inches high...born free* [Register, no.119]. Betsy was probably the daughter of William **Terry**, head of an Amherst County household of 7 "other free" in 1810 [VA:287].

vi. ?Charles, born about 1781, of Bedford County, married Louisa **Clark**, widow, by 1805 Amherst County bond. Charles was a "Blackman" taxable in Bedford County in 1800 and a "Negr." taxable on 2 tithes in 1813 [PPTL 1800A, p.13; Waldrep, *1813 Tax List*]. He registered in Bedford County on 24 October 1831: *five feet five inches high, Bright Mulatto, aged 50 years, Born free*. Louisa was called Lavisa Ann when she registered the same day: *five feet three inches high, Bright Mulatto, aged 52 years, Born free* [Register of Free Negroes 1820-60, p.16].

vii. ?Patterson, born about 1784, taxable in Amherst County from to 1818: a "Mulatto" in 1813, a "M.C." in 1815, in a list of "Free Negroes & Mulattoes" in 1814 and 1818 [PPTL 1804-23, frames 256, 284, 303, 489]. He registered on 16 November 1844: *bright mulatto, 5 feet 8 inches high about 60 years of age cock eyed born free* [Register, no.141]. He was married to Judy Johns when his children registered the same day [Register, nos. 142-3 by McLeRoy, *Strangers in Their Midst*, 68].

viii. ?Jesse, born about 1787, registered in Bedford County on 24 September 1832: *yellow complexion, 5 feet 4-1/2 inches, Bald head, Free born* [Register of Free Negroes 1820-60, p.19].

ix. ?Thomas, born about 1790, a "Mulatto" taxable in Amherst County in 1813 [PPTL 1804-23, frame 256]. He was counted as a seventy-year-old "Mulatto" farmer in the 1860 Amherst County census with "Mulatto" wife Catherine.

5. Joshua Johns, born say 1753, was taxable in Prince George County on 6 horses in 1782, a horse and 2 cattle in 1783, 2 horses and 3 cattle in 1784, on 2 tithables in 1799, 4 tithables in 1796 and 1797, 2 in 1799, a "Mulatto" taxable in 1801 and 1802 and a "free Negro" taxable in 1804, taxable on 4 tithables in 1809, 3 "free" tithables in 1810 and 2 in 1811 [PPTL, 1782-1811, frames 167, 184, 228, 287, 329, 428, 471, 704, 725, 746]. And he was taxable on 50 acres in 1799 [Land Tax List 1799, p.13]. He was head of a Prince George County household of 7 "other free" in 1810 [VA:533]. He may have been the father of

    i.   David, born say 1775, taxable in Prince George County from 1801 to 1811 [PPTL, 1782-1811, frames 535, 558, 582, 600, 606, 630, 655, 704, 746]. He married Polly **Scott**, daughter of Nicholas **Scott**, 23 January 1802 Surry County bond. He was head of a Prince George County household of 5 "other free" in 1810 [VA:546].

    ii.   Willis, born before 1776, a "free Negro" taxable in Prince George County in 1805 and 1806 [PPTL, 1782-1811, frames 630, 655]. He was taxable in Surry County from 1810 to 1816: taxable on 2 slaves in 1810 but not subject to personal tax; taxable on his own tithe in 1811; listed with 2 "free Negroes & Mulattoes above the age of 16" in 1813; taxable on a slave in 1816 [PPTL, 1791-1816, frames 671, 692, 710, 744, 821, 858]. He was head of a Surry County household of 6 "free colored" in 1830.

    iii.   Patsy, born say 1780, head of a Petersburg Town household of 8 "other free" and 4 slaves in 1810 [VA:119a].

    iv.   Maze, born say 1785, head of a Prince George County household of 2 "other free" in 1810 [VA:546].

6.   John^2 Johns, born about 1762, was taxable in Surry County in 1787, taxable on slaves Daniel, Once and Liza in 1793, taxable on his own tithe from 1795 to 1806, taxable on 4 slaves in 1807 [PPTL, 1782-90, frames 424; 1791-1816, 137, 216, 296, 335, 375, 490, 531, 595, 633]. He registered as a "Free Negro" in Surry County on 27 October 1796: *a mulatto man, of a bright cast, stout made, about 5'4" high, about 34 years old, born free* [Back of Guardian Accounts Book, 1783-1804, no.10]. He died before 1809 when the inventory of his estate was taken [Wills, Etc. 2:301]. He may have been the father of

    i.   Reuben, born say 1782, taxable in Surry County on a slave named Betty in 1803 and 1804, taxable on 2 slaves in 1806 [PPTL, 1791-1816, frames 533, 568, 614], a "free" taxable in Prince George County in 1809 and 1810 [PPTL, 1782-1811, frames 703, 725]. He married Rebecca **Walden**, 8 February 1818 Surry County bond, John **Walden** surety. She had married a member of the **Elliott** family by 9 September 1828 when she was mentioned in the Surry County will of her mother Priscilla **Walden** [WB 6:196].

7.   William^2 Johns, born about 1777, was taxable in Amherst County from 1799 to 1820: called "William Johns or Patterson" from 1800 to 1810, taxable on 3 tithes in 1810, called a "man of color" in 1811 and 1815, a "Mulatto" in 1813 [PPTL 1782-1803, frames 169, 192, 214, 453, 483, 519, 556, 590; 1804-23, frames 26, 68, 108, 256, 336, 539, 553]. He was head of an Amherst County household of 8 "other free" in 1810 [VA:271] and a seventy-three-year-old "Mulatto" farmer counted in the 1850 Amherst County census [VA:87].[124] He purchased 57 acres in Amherst County on Tobacco Row Mountain on 19 November 1807 and sold it on 15 October 1810 [DB L:348, 402]. He was called a "free man of color" when he purchased 400 acres on Bear Mountain in Amherst County on 13 December 1833 [DB U:317]. On 31 December 1856 he conveyed all his property on Bear Mountain to his children: 95 acres to Richard Johns, 109 acres to Thomas B. Johns, 96 acres and a

---

[124]Houck's *Indian Island in Amherst County* claims that William^2 Johns was the son of Robert Johns, a white man, and an Indian woman named Mary. However, the William Johns who was a son of Robert Johns was born before 1755 since he purchased land in Amherst County on 28 July 1775 [DB D:300]. He died about 1777 when Thomas Johns was granted administration on his estate [WB 1:323, 324]. According to Robert Johns' 1 March 1779 Amherst County estate papers, Amherst County marriage bonds, and census records, all Robert Johns' children were white and married whites [WB 1:456-458, 481-482; *Amherst County, Virginia, in the Revolution, Including Extracts from the "Lost Order Book" 1773-1782*, 86].

house to Tarleton Johns, 75 acres to Edith (widow of Joshua Johns) and 75 acres to Edmund **Branham** [DB DD:334-341]. His 7 February 1861 Amherst County will, proved 20 April 1863, left his estate to his granddaughter Judith **Branham** and named Edward **Branham** as his executor [WB 16:307]. He was the father of

    i.   Polly, born say 1799, mother of Richard Johns who registered in Amherst County on 10 November 1845: *Son of Polly Johns, very bright mulatto, 5 feet 10 inches 3/4 of an inch high, 32 years old in June 1846...Stout made Quick spoken free born* [Register, no. 170]. Polly married Edmund **Branham**, 1825 Amherst County bond. Richard was a thirty-six-year-old "Mulatto" farmer counted in the 1850 Amherst County census with thirty-six-year-old Creasy **Branham** [VA:87].

    ii.   William B., born about 1803, registered in Amherst County on 25 July 1860: *a free man of color, brown complexion, 57 years of age, 5 feet 9 1/2 inches high...born in Amherst County* [Register, no. 352 by McLeRoy, *Strangers in Their Midst*, 102]. On 17 February 1840 he made a deed of trust for his interest in the lands of his father William Johns to secure debts owed by Tarleton Johns [DB X:236-7].

    iii.   Joshua[2], born say 1807, married Edith **Terry**, daughter of Dicey **Terry**, 1828 Amherst County bond. Eady was a thirty-seven-year-old "Mulatto" counted in the 1850 Amherst County census [VA:87].

    iv.   Tarleton, born about 1812, a thirty-eight-year-old "Mulatto" counted in the 1850 Amherst County census [VA:88b]. He registered in Amherst County on 23 July 1860: *a free man of colour, bright complexion, 50 years of age* [Register, no.344 by McLeRoy, *Strangers in Their Midst*, 101].

JOHNSON FAMILY

1.   Anthony[1] Johnson "Negro," probably born about 1600, was free before 10 January 1647 when he purchased a calf from James Berry by deed proved in Northampton County, Virginia [ODW 1651-54, 123]. He patented 250 acres in Northampton County at "great Naswattock Creek" for the transportation of five persons, including his son Richard Johnson, on 24 July 1651 [Patents 1643-51, 326]. His wife Mary and their two daughters were excused from paying taxes by the Northampton County, Virginia court on 28 February 1652:

> ... *they have been Inhabitants in Virginia above thirty years...ordered that from the day of the date hearof (during their natural lives) the sd Mary Johnson & two daughters of Anthony Johnson Negro be disengaged and freed from payment of Taxes...*[ODW 1651-54, fol.161].

His "Negro servant," John Casor, attempted to gain his freedom by claiming he had been imported as an indentured servant. In 1653 Casor appealed to Captain Samuel Goldsmith who tried to intervene in his behalf, but Johnson insisted that

> *hee had ye Negro for his life* [ODW 1651-54, 226].

Johnson's wife and children tried to persuade him to release Casor, and his neighbor, Robert Parker, apparently allowed Casor to stay on his property. However, Anthony Johnson bought suit in Northampton County court against Robert Parker in 1654 for detaining his "Negro servant, John Casor," and the court upheld Johnson's right to hold Casor as a slave [Orders 1655-58, 10].

In 1665 he and his wife Mary, his son John and his wife Susanna, and their slave John Casor moved to Somerset County, Maryland, with Randall Revell and Ann Toft, who claimed them and many whites as head rights for 2,350 acres of land [Patents 8:495-6]. Anthony and his wife sold 250 acres of their own land, left 50 acres to their son Richard, and took fourteen head of cattle, a mare, and eighteen sheep with them [Accomack DW 1664-71, fol.10; p.12-fol.12]. On 10 September 1666 he leased 300 acres in Somerset County on the south side of Wicomico Creek in Wicomico Hundred, called "Tonies Vinyard," for two hundred years [Land Records O-1:32-33].

Anthony apparently died before August 1670 when "a jury of white men" in Accomack County decided that his land should be escheated since "he was a Negroe and by consequence an alien" [*Virginia Genealogist* 2:20, 109-113]. His lease in Somerset County, Maryland, was renegotiated by his widow Mary for ninety-nine years with the provision that her sons John and Richard would assume the lease after her death [Land Records O-2, 20-21]. Her slave, John Casor, recorded his livestock brand in court with her consent on 3 September 1672, and she recorded her mark a few weeks later on 26 September 1672 [*Archives of Maryland* 54:760-1]. He was called "John Cazara Negro" when he was a witness (signing) to a power of attorney by which she assigned her son John authority over her property and authority to sue for some debts in Virginia, and he was also witness on 3 September 1672 to her deed of gift to her grandchildren. She called herself "Mary Johnson...Negro (the relict of Anthony Johnson...Negro deceased)" in the deed by which she gave cattle to her three grandchildren: Anthony, Richard, and Francis [Somerset County Judicial Record 1671-75, 159-62]. She was called "Mary Johnson of Wiccocomoco...widow" in July 1676 when she purchased a mare and assigned it to John Corsala (her slave) [Somerset County Judicial Records 1675-7, 95]. She was called executor of Anthony Johnson deceased on 17 January 1690 when Edward Revell acted as her attorney in a suit she brought in Accomack County court [WDO 1678-82, 154]. She was living in Sussex County, Delaware, in March 1693/4 when Mary Okey appeared in court to support her complaint that her son John was not maintaining her as he had promised [Court Records 1680-99, 646, 655]. The children of Anthony and Mary Johnson were

2   i.   John[1], say 1631.
3   ii.   Richard[1], born about 1632.
      iii. a daughter, excused from paying tax by the February 1652 Northampton County court, perhaps the Joan[1] Johnson who in 1657 received 100 acres in Northampton County from "Deabendanba, Kinge of nusangs," being land next to her brother John [Whitelaw, *Virginia's Eastern Shore*, 671].
      iv. a daughter, excused from paying tax by the February 1652 Northampton County court.

2. John[1] Johnson, born say 1631, received a grant for 550 acres in Northampton County on 10 May 1652 "at great Naswattock Cr. adjacent to 200 acres granted Anthony Johnson" for the importation of eleven persons including Mary Johnson [Patents 3:101]. He received this patent after suing a white resident of the county, also named John Johnson, who tried to illegally take possession of the land [DW 1657-66, 57-58, 103; DW 1651-54, fol.200]. In 1660 he was head of a household of two tithables in Northampton County, called John Johnson Negro. He and his wife Susanna sold their land in 1664 [Whitelaw, *Virginia's Eastern Shore*, 671]. In November 1654 he and Mary **Gersheene**, an African American servant of his father, were punished for fornication [ODW 1654-55, fol.35, ODW 1651-54 p.226-fol.226]. On 17 January 1664/5 his wife Susannah petitioned the Northampton County court to release him from jail where he was held for begetting a child by Hannah Leach

who was probably white [Orders 1664-74, fol.92]. In 1665 he moved to Somerset County, Maryland, with his parents.

He was called "John Johnson Negro" on 11 March 1667/8 when he and two white men, Alexander King and John Richards, were charged in Somerset County court with stealing corn from an Indian named Katackcuweiticks. They confessed their guilt and were ordered to deliver two barrels of corn to the King of the Manoakin at Manoakin Town. John was sued by Randall Revell in Somerset County court for a minor debt on 13 January 1674/5 and appeared as a witness in a court case against Revell. The justices were at first doubtful about admitting the testimony of an African American against a white person. However, his testimony was allowed after he assured the court that he was a Christian and "did rightly understand the taking of an oath." He gave his age as thirty-seven in his deposition in 1670. He testified again in 1676 and was witness to several deeds. Edward Surman appointed him as guardian ("assistant") to his children by his will which was proved in Somerset County court on 10 January 1676/7 [*Archives of Maryland*, 54:675, 707, 712; Judicial Records 1670-1, 10, 15, 6, 205; 1671-5, 41, 260, 267-8, 429, 457-8; 1675-7, 47, 78]. He moved to Sussex County, Delaware, where he received a patent for 400 acres on Rehoboth Bay in September 1677. He purchased 200 acres in Sussex County and sold this land by deed which he acknowledged in court in April 1683. In August 1683 he was accused of murdering his wife Susan. The court took depositions from John Okey and Jeffry Summerford, and released him because they saw "no sign of murder." He appeared in Sussex County court as a witness on seven occasions between March 1680/81 and February 1688. He sued John Okey for debt in May 1685. And he was a defendant on sixteen occasions, mainly for debts. The court postponed action on one of these cases because he was in Virginia between December 1684 and May 1685. He was identified as a "Negro" on only three of these occasions, one a case in which he had the estate of Nathaniel Bradford in his custody. In August 1704 he was called "John Johnson, Free Nigroe, Aged Eighty Years and Poor and Past his Labour" when the Sussex County court agreed to maintain him for his lifetime on public funds. He was apparently still living in November 1707 when Walter Groombridge had a suit against him for a debt of three pounds [Horle, *Records of the Sussex County Court*, 103, 110, 144, 166, 190, 193, 204, 214, 216, 229, 235, 251, 253, 299, 315, 342, 356, 365, 384, 447, 462, 516, 540, 635, 797, 857, 919, 1201, 1314]. John[1]'s children were

4   i.   John[2], born say 1650.

     ii.   Anthony[2], born say 1655, devised a cow and a calf by the will of his grandmother Mary Johnson. He was sued in Sussex County, Delaware court on 7 May 1706 and was a witness in a Sussex County case in November 1709 [Horle, *Records of the Sussex County Court*, 1227, 1291].

    iii. ?Joan[2], a "Negro," married John Puckham, a baptized Monie tribesman, on 25 February 1682/3 in Somerset County, Maryland [Register of Liber IKL, Somerset Courthouse by Torrence, *Old Somerset*, 143]. See the **Puckham** history.

    iv. an unnamed son, born say 1667. William Futcher claimed in February 1689 Sussex County court that Johnson's son had been bound to serve him for nine years. The suit was canceled because of Futcher's death [Court Records 1680-99, 294, 322, 342].

    v. ?Elizabeth, born say 1670, living in Accomack County on 2 February 1702/3 when the court dismissed a case brought against her by William Yeo [Orders 1697-1703, 135a].

    vi. ?Comfort, born say 1680, "free Nigrene," presented by the Sussex County, Delaware court for having a bastard child in 1699. James Walker of Rehoboth Bay agreed to pay her fine and give her a three-year-old heifer in exchange for her serving him an additional thirteen months, and she bound her two-year-old son to him until the age of twenty-one years [Court Records 1680-99, 768, 774, 775]. In February 1706 she confessed to having a bastard child by Justice William Bagwell's servant, Patrick Delany, and in May 1706 she admitted to having a child by Rice Morgan [Horle, *Records of the Sussex County Court*, 1218, 1219, 1276, 1281].[125]

3. Richard[1] Johnson, born about 1632, was one of the five persons his father claimed head rights for in 1651. On 8 February 1653 Governor Richard Bennett instructed Nathaniel Littleton to deliver a black cow to him. On 28 September 1652 he claimed two headrights, and on 21 November 1654 he received a patent for 100 acres in Northampton County adjoining his father and his brother John [ODW 1651-54, fol.103, p.133; Patents 1652-55, 296]. On 19 January 1663/4 he brought suit in Accomack County court against Richard Buckland:

> *The Difference depending betweene Richard Johnson negro plt. & Richard Buckland defdt. concerning a house to bee built by ye sd Johnson for ye sd Buckland...*[DW 1663-66, 54].

He remained in Accomack County on 50 acres left to him by his father when his father took the rest of the family to Maryland [Accomack DW 1664-71, p.12-fol.12]. He purchased 590 acres near Matomkin from Christopher Tompson in December 1675 and conveyed half this land to his son Francis in 1678 [WD 1676-90, 14; *Virginia's Eastern Shore*, 1088]. He was taxable in Accomack County on two tithes from 1676 to 168? (called Richard Johnson, Sen.) [Orders 1676-8, 34, 57; WDO 1678-82, 18, 100]. He was sued for debt by Christopher Thompson on 14 September 1677 in Accomack County court [Orders 1676-8, 66, 84]. On 17 November 1681 his suit in Accomack County court against (his son) Richard Johnson, Jr., was dismissed. On 18 October 1682 he admitted to the Accomack County court that he owed William Parker 682 pounds of tobacco. On 3 December 1684, he admitted that he owed Walter Harges 1,000 pounds of tobacco, and he was sued by John Cole for 5,978 pounds of tobacco. He died before 19 March 1689 when his wife Susan Johnson, called a widow, was sued by Hendrick Johnson for some cooper's work he had performed for her after her husband's death [WDO 1678-82, 55, 155, 268, 322]. She came into court to give account of the estate of William Silverthorne which included several yards of linen lent to "Richard Johnson Negro Since deceased" [W&Co 1682-97, 142, 155, 157]. She may have been white since their son Richard was called a "Mulatto." Their children were

  i. Francis, born say 1655, received a calf by his grandmother's 3 September 1672 Somerset County deed of gift. He apprenticed himself to George Phebus in Somerset County for three years to be a cooper in November 1673 [Judicial Records 1671-75, 161-2, 336-7]. He moved to Sussex County, Delaware, with his uncle John[1] Johnson by 8 September 1685 when he was summoned as a witness in a court case between William Futcher and John Crew [Court Records 1680-99, 99]. He sued Henry Stretcher in Sussex court in November 1686, and he was called "Francis Johnson, the Negro" in June 1687 when the court ordered William Orion to pay him 20 shillings for taking up his

---

[125]Patrick Delaney's age was adjudged at thirteen years by the Accomack County, Virginia Court on 7 February 1700 [Orders 1697-1703, 84].

runaway servant, John Martin.[126] He testified in court for Henry Stretcher in October 1687. He was in Accomack County about February 1689 (called "Francis Johnson Mollatto" and "Brother" of Richard Johnson) when he agreed to complete a fence which Richard contracted to build for Colonel John West. In 1689 he sold the land in Accomack County which his father had conveyed to him in 1678 in order to pay a debt of 6,000 pounds of tobacco [WD 1676-90, 507a, 508; W&Co 1682-97, 155a, 156, 187-187a]. He was living on land adjoining William Futcher in Rehoboth Bay, Sussex County, in December 1690 and testified in Sussex County in March 1693 in a case between John Barker and Aminadab **Handsor** [Horle, *Records of the Sussex County Court*, 757; Court Records 1680-99, 600]. On 4 November 1707 Hill Drummond brought suit against him in Accomack County court for uttering scandalous words [Orders 1703-9, 103-103a]. On 8 April 1713 he paid Comfort **Driggers'** fine of 500 pounds of tobacco for the illegitimate child she had in Accomack County earlier that year. Perhaps Elizabeth Johnson, who gave evidence against Comfort, was a relation of his [Orders 1710-4, 56a, 58]. He was security in Accomack County court for Edward Winslow and his wife Anne who failed to appear to answer Thomas Dashiell and Ephraim Heather of Somerset County [Orders 1714-7, 19].[127] He may have been the Fran. Johnson who William **Driggus** appointed as one of the executors of his 7 June 1720 Somerset County will [WB 17:285].

ii. Richard[2], born say 1660, received a calf by his grandmother's 3 September 1672 Somerset County deed of gift [Judicial Records 1671-75, 161-162]. He and his wife Anne Johnson were servants of John Cole of Accomack County in 1680. She was required to serve her former master, William Whittington, an additional four years for having two illegitimate children while in his service [Northampton Orders 1678-83, 34; Accomack WDO 1678-82, 288-9]. On 3 September 1679 he was called Richard Johnson, Jr., when John Cole and his wife sued him in Accomack County court for kicking Mrs. Cole. On 5 August 1681 he deposed that about Christmas of 1680 he was the servant of John Cole of Motamkin [WDO 1678-82, 108, 288]. On 3 April 1688 Adam Michael sued him for 5,000 pounds of tobacco as a penalty for his nonperformance of a bond, and on 20 December 1688 Colonel John West sued him for failure to build a fence consisting of 400 wood panels for his cornfield (called "Richard Johnson Mollatto"). Richard completed only forty or fifty of the panels before turning the work over to "his Brother Francis Johnson" in exchange for a gun and several other items. On 16 June 1689 Captain William Custis won a suit for about one pound against Maximillian Gore who acted as his security. He was a tithable head of an Accomack County household in 1692. Esther Pharis identified him as the father of her illegitimate child who was born on 4 June 1695 [W&cO 1682-97, 129a, 132a, 150a, 155a, 156, 160, 258a; Orders 1690-9, 153, 173]. He was called "Richard Johnson, Mollattoe" in September 1699 when the Sussex County, Delaware court presented him for stealing a mare belonging to William Faucett of Somerset County. He was excused after explaining that he had already returned the mare, "taking of the Mare

---

[126]Francis Johnson was identified by race in only one of the seven times he was named in Sussex County Court [Horle, *Records of the Sussex County Court*, 356, 425, 468, 481, 720, 757, 863].

[127]Edward Winslow provided security for William **Driggers** in Somerset County Court when he was convicted of having an illegitimate child by Mary Winslow [Somerset County Judicial Records 1707-11, 95-6].

threw mistake, being so like his mare" [Court Records 1680-99, 780].
On 8 October 1707 he was called Richard Johnson "Mulatta" in
Accomack County court when Hill Drummond brought a suit against
him for debt [Orders 1703-9, 103-103a]. He may have been the
Richard Johnson of Carteret County, North Carolina, who purchased
130 acres on Core Sound on the east side of North River from George
Cogdell and sold this land on 2 October 1724 to (his nephew?) Jacob
Johnson and (his niece's husband?) Theophilus Norwood. The deed was
proved by John Simpson and Enoch Ward, who also proved the will of
(his brother?) William[1] Johnson [DB C:113-4].

   iii.   ?Morris, born say 1662, a "mulatto" who bound himself to work for
John Cole of Accomack County for four years in return for 3,569
pounds of tobacco as well as food, clothes and lodging in September
1690. He registered his cattle mark in Accomack County on 23 March
1694 [WD 1676-90, 531: W&cO 1682-97, 268].

5   iv.   ?William[1], born say 1668.

   v.   ?Abel, born say 1680, tithable head of an Accomack County household
in 1692 [W&cO 1682-97, 258a]. He registered his cattle mark in
Accomack County on 23 February 1694 and was called "Abel Johnson
Molatto" when Ester Rose (born about 1681) identified him as the
father of her illegitimate child in Accomack County court on 6 August
1700 [WO 1682-97, 268; Orders 1690-07, 126b; 1697-1703, 97]. On
7 September 1732 the Carteret County, North Carolina court reported
that he was (illegally) living together as man and wife with Ann
Witnell, and he produced a certificate to prove they were lawfully
married [Minutes 1723-47, fol.43b-c].[128]

4.   John[2] Johnson, born say 1650, was named as John Sr.'s son in 1670 when they
recorded their livestock brand in Somerset County, Maryland [*Archives of
Maryland* 54:757]. On 29 August 1677 he purchased a 44 acre lot on the east
side of the Chesapeake Bay and south side of the Wicomico River called
"Angola." This land probably adjoined "Tonys Vineyard" where his
grandmother was then living [Maryland Provincial Patents, Liber 20:224-5;
Davidson, *Free Blacks*, 29]. The land was escheated in 1706 with the notation,
"no heirs as I understand" [Maryland Provincial Rent Roll, Vol. no. 1, 34].
He was in Sussex County, Delaware, in December 1680 when he was fined
for singing "a scurlous disgracfull song" about Samuel Gray and his wife and
would have been whipped if William Futcher had not posted security for him.
He married Elizabeth Lowe (an English woman) in Sussex County, Delaware,
on 13 March 1680/1 [Court Records 1680-99, 2, 23]. She was probably the
Elizabeth Johnson who was twenty years old on 14 August 1683 when she
appeared as a witness in court. He apparently left the county sometime before
February 1683/4 when he was accused of killing a sow belonging to Andrew
Depree and taking the meat to John Okey's house [Horle, *Records of the
Sussex County Court*, 228, 260]. On 5 March 1699/1700 the Kent County,
Delaware court referred to him and his wife as "John Johnson, a free Negroe,
and Elizabeth his wife (an English woman)" when they were accused of
running away and leaving their seven-year-old daughter Susannah in the
custody of Thomas Nicholls. The court bound her to Nicholls until the age of
eighteen [Court Records 1699-1703, 14]. They were the parents of

   i.   ?John, born say 1682, a "Malattoe" servant boy ordered by the Sussex
County, Delaware court in September 1698 to serve his master, Justice
John Hill, another seven months for running away for a month [Court
Records 1680-99, 744].

---

[128]There was also an Abel Johnson in colonial New Hanover County, presented by the 11 March
1740 court for "working Constantly on the Lord's Day [Minutes 1738-69, 115].

ii. Susannah, born about 1693.

5. William[1] Johnston, born say 1668 in Accomack County, Virginia, was probably a son of Richard[1] Johnson since he also lived in Matomkin. He was a hired servant to John and Gertrude Cropper of Matomkin. He was a taxable head of a household in Major Bowman's Precinct in 1690. He was called a "Mullatto" on 8 November 1690 when he and two white men were accused of stealing goods from the cabin of a Matomkin Indian named Blincks. He won a suit against his employer, Gertrude Cropper, for 150 pounds of tobacco on 21 December 1692, and he won a suit against James Atkinson for a barrel of corn and a pair of "French Falls" shoes. In 1698 he was fined for fiddling and dancing on the Lord's day [Orders 1690-97, 2a-3, 86, 99a, 103, 191; 1697-1703, p.43a]. He purchased 150 acres near the Deep Creek and Hunting Creek in Matomkin from Christopher Tompson on 4 April 1699 [W&c 1692-1715, 368-9]. This was probably the land (his father?) Richard[1] Johnson purchased from Christopher Tompson in 1675. He and his wife Sarah sold this land in 1708 [Whitelaw, *Virginia's Eastern Shore*, 990, 993]. He may have moved to North Carolina soon afterwards since he was not mentioned again in the Accomack County records. His 5 November 1726 Carteret County, North Carolina will, proved March 1727/8, named his sons and daughter, and mentioned his son-in-law Theophilus Norwood, and grandson William **Norwood**. His wife Sarah was executor and was to keep all his land until her death [SS Wills 1722-35, 140]. The 5 March 1727/8 court mentioned a road on the east side of the North River from Wellses to the widow Johnston. At the June 1730 Carteret court she paid a debt of about 9 pounds to Joseph Richards, a New England merchant [Minutes 1723-46, fol.12a, fol.14a]. She probably died before 27 April 1739 when her sons Ezekiel and Stephen sold their land [DB D:216-9]. William[1]'s children mentioned in his will were

i. Thomas, born say 1700, taxable in Craven County, North Carolina, in 1720:

> *Thomas Johnson & Jacob* }
> *Johnson & Stephen Johnson* } *3*
> *Mulats* ----------------- [SS 837].

ii. Jacob[1], born say 1701, taxable in Craven County in 1720. He and his brother-in-law, Theophilus Norwood, purchased 130 acres in Carteret County on Core Sound and the east side of North River from (Jacob's uncle?) Richard[2] Johnson on 2 October 1724, and Theophilus sold him his half of this land on 6 June 1727 [DB C:171, 113]. Joseph Wicker, Esqr., informed the 5 March 1727/8 Carteret County court that he was living together in adultery with Ann Johnston. The court warned them that they would be fined 50 pounds if they continued to live together. James Shackleford sued him for a 17 pound debt in the June 1730 Carteret County court. The sheriff, Daniel Rees, had a case against him in the 7 December 1736 court, but the jury found in favor of Jacob [Minutes 1723-47, fol.10a, fol.14a, fol.32d]. He sold 130 acres in Carteret on 16 April 1740 [DB D:236-7].

iii. Stephen[1], born say 1703, taxable in Craven County in 1720. On 7 September 1732 the Carteret County court received information from Robert Wade that Stephen Johnson was living together as man and wife with Jane Jones, alias Jane Bruton, and also that (Stephen's uncle?) Abel Johnson was living together as man and wife with Ann Witnell. Both couples produced certificates to prove they were lawfully married [Minutes 1723-47, fol.43b-c]. He and his brother Ezekiel sold a 320 acre tract in Carteret County on the east side of North River for 225 pounds on 27 April 1739 [DB D:216-9]. This was land which they received by their father's will. Stephen moved to New Hanover County with Ezekiel/ Hezekiah, the Stephen Johnston who was listed there in the Muster Roll of Captain George Merrick's Wilmington Company on

27 November 1752 in the same list as Stephen Johnston, Jr., who was listed next to Joshua **Pavey** [Clark, *Colonial Soldiers of the South*, 683]. Stephen made oath on 7 July 1772 in New Hanover County court that he was unable to work on roads [Minutes, 1771-79, 52].

    iv. Elizabeth, born say 1705, married Theophilus Norwood, the Deputy Marshall and ferry-keeper on North River who was mentioned in her father's will. See the **Norwood** Family History.

6   v. John[4], born say 1710.

7   vi. Ezekiel/ Hezekiah, born say 1712.

8   vii. Solomon[1], born say 1714.

6. John[4] Johnson, born say 1710, received a warrant for 200 acres in Beaufort County, North Carolina, on 19 November 1744 [Saunders, *Colonial Records of North Carolina*, IV:703]. He purchased 50 acres on the north side of Bay River in the fork of Chapel Creek beginning at Whitehouse Creek in Beaufort County on 31 May 1748 and made a deed of gift of this land to his son William[4] on 5 December 1765 [DB 2:531; 4:99]. He was head of a Beaufort County household of 3 black tithables in 1755: "Johnson, Jno & son & wife" [SS 837]. He entered 100 acres in Bladen County on the southwest side of the Northwest Branch of Cape Fear River on 26 March 1753 and 100 acres adjoining this land on Pugh's Marsh Swamp on 27 August the same year when he was called John Johnson, Sr. [Philbeck, *Bladen County Land Entries*, nos. 701, 804]. John[4] Johnson's children were

    i. John[5], Jr., born say 1728, entered 100 acres in Bladen County on the north side of Pugh's marsh whereon John **Oxendine** was then living on 27 August 1753, the same day (his father?) John Johnson, Sr., entered land in this area [Philbeck, *Bladen County Land Entries*, no.805]. He was taxable with his unnamed wife in Bladen County in 1763, taxable on 3 "Mulatto" tithes in Cumberland County in 1767, and taxable with his wife in Bladen County from 1769 to 1774 ("Molatoes") [Byrd, *Bladen County Tax Lists*, I:20, 32, 66, 89, 123]. He and his wife were mentioned in the 19 September 1792 Cumberland County deed of Titus **Overton** who was a "black" Bladen County tithable in 1763 and a "Mulatto" taxable in 1767 [*N.C. Genealogy* XXI:3132, 3136]. According to the deed, John Johnson and his wife purchased 100 acres on the northeast side of the Northwest River near Beaverdam Pond on 27 April 1767, and they were buried there [DB 12:326].

9   ii. ?Abram[1], born say 1730.

    iii. ?Isaac, born say 1732, taxable on two black tithes in Beaufort County on himself and his wife in 1755 [SS 837]. He purchased 150 acres on the north side of Bay River at the mouth of a small creek in Craven County on 17 March 1770 and sold this land two years later on 20 August 1772 [DB 4:368]. He was a taxable "Molato" in Bladen County in 1768 [Byrd, *Bladen County Tax Lists*, I:7] and head of a Robeson County household of 1 "other free" in 1790 [NC:48].

    iv. ?Jesse, born say 1735, taxable on two black tithes in Beaufort County on himself and his wife in 1755 and 1764 [SS 837].

10   v. William[4], born say 1737.

7. Ezekiel/Hezekiah Johnson, born say 1712, received land by the February 1728/9 Carteret County will of his father William[1] Johnson [SS Wills 1722-35, 140].[129] He was in Onslow County on 1 February 1734/5 when the Onslow County court ordered John Arther's wife Elizabeth taken from him and returned to her husband on Core Sound [Minutes 1734-78, vol. I, fol.2c]. He

---

[129]He was called Ezekiel in Onslow and New Hanover Counties and Ezekiah/ Hezekiah in Craven County.

received an Onslow County patent for 400 acres on the west side of Turkey Point Creek adjoining (his brother) Jacob Johnson on 16 November 1738 and received a further 400 acres on the same date [Hoffman, *Land Patents*, I:122]. He and his brother Stephen sold their 320 acre tract in Carteret County on the east side of North River for 225 pounds on 27 April 1739 [DB D:216-9]. This was land they received by their father's will. Ezekiah purchased four hundred acres in Craven County on the north side of Neuse River at the mouth of Peter Ecles' upper gut in August 1743 and another 25 acres in this same area on 31 May 1750 [DB 1:401, 566]. On 10 September 1747 he sold his Onslow County land "known as Ezekiel Johnston Plantation" [DB C:1]. He was called Hezekiah Johnson when he recorded his mark in Hyde County court in September 1744 [Haun, *Hyde County Court Minutes*, I:47] and was in Craven County in June 1751 when he was fined by the County court

> *Hezekiah Johnston a Mollatto...for Concealing his Taxable_for the year 1750* [Haun, *Craven County Court Minutes*, IV:46].

He sold 100 acres of his land in Craven County on the north side of Neuse River on 8 October 1752 [DB 9-10:259] and was taxable on 345 acres in Craven in 1756 [Wills, Deeds, Bonds, Inventories, Accounts of Sales, 316]. As Ezekiel Johnson he was a taxable head of a New Hanover County household of two "Negro Males" in 1755 [T&C, box 1]. On 7 December 1759 he was allowed two pounds and eleven shillings by the General Assembly for the use of a horse impressed from him on an express from Wilmington to Virginia [Saunders, *Colonial Records of North Carolina*, VI:101]. He was awarded 30 shillings by the Craven County court in his issue on assault against Benjamin Price on 6 July 1763, and he was called Kiah Johnson on 9 April 1767 when he was ordered to pay Clifford Howe 15 pounds [Minutes 1762-4, 24c; 1767-75, n.p., Thursday court]. He purchased 100 acres in Craven County on the north side of the Neuse River joining Thomas Little, "running a mile back," on 9 March 1771 and sold this same land on 25 December 1774 [DB 19:180; 22:162]. His will (which has not survived) was proved in Craven County court by Gideon Tingle on 8 March 1784 [Minutes 1779-84, 66c]. The account of sales of his estate, returned in June court 1784, included buyers Thomas and Levy **Muckelroy**. There was a letter remaining in the New Bern Post Office for Hezekiah Johnson in 1788 [Fouts, *NC Gazette of New Bern*, I:5]. His wife may have been Ann Johnston, head of a Craven County household of 2 "other free" in 1790 [NC:134]. His children were

    i.   Jacob[2], born 17 November 1735, if he was the "Mulatto boy named Jacob" (no surname mentioned) who was bound to John Todd of Onslow County in July 1742 [Minutes 1734-49, fol.19a]. He purchased seven acres in Craven County adjoining his house and the land of David Roach on 9 March 1768 [DB 15:14] and was called the son of Hezekiah Johnston by the Craven County court on 11 June 1771 when the court recommended that he be exempt from taxes since he was an infirm person with no estate whatsoever [Minutes 1767-75, 178].

11   ii.   ?Jeremiah, born say 1755.

    iii.   ?Stephen, head of an Onslow County household of 9 "free colored" in 1820 [NC:334].

    iv.   ?Elizabeth, head of a New Hanover County household of 3 "Molatto" females and one "Molatto" male under 21 or over 60 in 1786 for the state census.

    v.   ?Keziah, born say 1765, married George **Curtis**, 20 May 1783 Craven County bond with George **Ransom** bondsman.

    vi.   Solomon[3], born 1 August 1771, ordered bound to James Carr as a house carpenter by the 14 September 1774 Craven County court [Minutes 1779-84, 77a]. He was called "Son of Hesekiah Johnson Dcd" when he was bound to John Allen to be a millwright by the 18 March

1785 Craven County court [Minutes 1784-86, 13c]. And on 15 June 1786 he was fifteen years old when he was ordered bound to Thomas Wilson as an apprentice blacksmith [Minutes 1786-87, 3b].

8. Solomon[1] Johnson, born say 1714, was taxable in Bladen County, North Carolina, with his wife and Jacob **Braveboy** in 1769 and taxable with his wife in 1770 and 1771 ("Molatoes") [Byrd, *Bladen County Tax Lists*, I:17, 45, 61]. He was granted land in Bladen County on Green Swamp east of Drowning Creek adjoining William **Driggers** on 22 December 1768 and sold this land on 22 July 1769. He purchased 200 acres on the south side of Raft Swamp from Solomon Johnston, Jr., on 1 January 1770 and was living in St. Matthew Parish, Georgia, on 3 October 1771 when he sold this land [DB 23:91, 135]. He may have been the father of

    i.   Solomon[2], born say 1740, called "Solomon Johnston, Junr.," a taxable in Bladen County with his wife from 1768 to 1770 ("Molatoes") [Byrd, *Bladen County Tax Lists*, I:8, 14, 45]. He purchased 200 acres in Bladen County on the south side of Raft Swamp from James Oberry and sold this land to Solomon Johnston, Sr., on 1 January 1770 [DB 23:135, 503].

9. Abram[1] Johnson, born say 1730, was taxable in Beaufort County in 1755:

Johnson, Abram & wife free N. 2 black tithes [SS 837].

and he and his wife were tithable in Beaufort in 1764 [SS 837]. In 1774 he was living on the north side of Bay River on the head of Chapel Creek which was land that John Johnson purchased in 1748 [Hoffman, *Land Patents*, I:667]. He purchased 30 acres on the north side of Bay River and west side of Chapel Creek on 28 November 1786 and was called Abraham Johnson, Senr., when he was granted a further 100 acres adjoining this land on the north side of Whitehouse Creek on 9 March 1799 [DB 7:200; 1:154]. He sold 25 acres on the north side of Whitehouse Creek to David Johnson on 22 November 1800 [DB 2-3:338]. He was head of a Beaufort County household of 5 "other free" in 1790 [NC:125] and 8 "other free" in 1800 [NC:11]. He devised land to his children by his 4 October 1800 Beaufort County will (no probate date) [WB p.429]. His children were

    i.   John[6], who received 40 acres on the south side of Whitehouse Creek by his father's will.

12   ii. Abram[2], born say 1775.

    iii. Rebecca, married ___ **Linsey**, perhaps the wife of Joshua **Lindsey**, Sr., head of a Craven County household of 4 "other free" in 1790 [NC:134].

    iv. Patty Johnston.

10. William[4] Johnson, born about 1737, was a "black" taxable with his wife in Beaufort County in 1764 [SS 837]. As mentioned above he received 50 acres from his father John[3] Johnson on 5 December 1765. Perhaps he was the William Johnston who was head of a Beaufort County household of one "other free" in 1800 [NC:11]. His children may have been

    i.   Joshua, taxed on an assessment of 101 pounds and four polls in Beaufort County in 1779 [*NCGSJ* XV:143], head of a Beaufort County household of 6 "other free" in 1790 [NC:126].

    ii. Cuff Levi, head of a Beaufort County household of 2 "other free" and one white woman in 1800 [NC:11].

11. Jeremiah[1] Johnston, born say 1755, was granted 200 acres in Hyde County on the west side of the Pungo River and the fork of the Indian Run on 28 October 1782. He sold 100 acres of this land on 21 January 1784 and the remainder on

12 February 1798 [DB B:921; D&E:208; K:410]. He received a second grant for 100 acres in Hyde on the west side of the Pungo River and the Indian Run Bridge on 9 August 1786 and sold this land on 12 February 1798. And he received a third grant for 100 acres on the west side of the Pungo River on 17 December 1794 [DB D&E:460; K:409; I:400]. He was head of a Hyde County household of 5 "other free" in 1790 and 6 in 1810 [NC:118]. His children were

  i. Jeremiah², Jr., sold his household goods to his father for 20 pounds on 27 August 1798 [DB K:498].

  ii. ?Brutus, born say 1760, described by Charles **Wood** as a man of colour who died at Valley Forge while serving as a soldier in the North Carolina Line of the Continental Army [*N.C. Genealogy* XVI:2580]. His estate descended to his brother David Johnson [*NCGSJ* IV:173].

  iii. ?David, married Charity **Driggers**, 20 December 1796 Craven County bond with Joshua **Lindsey** bondsman. He purchased 25 acres on the north side of Whitehouse Creek from Abram Johnson on 22 November 1800 [DB 2-3:338] and was head of a Hyde County household of 10 "other free" in 1810 [NC:117].

12. Abraham² Johnston, born say 1765, was head of a household of 4 "other free" in New Hanover County in 1790 [NC:194]. By the 4 October 1800 Beaufort County will of his father Abraham¹ Johnson, he received his father's plantation and "all the land that's belonging to all the rest of my removable estate." He bought land in Duplin County on 17 January 1809 and sold it soon after on 18 May 1810 [DB 4A:191]. He was head of a Craven County household of 7 "free colored" in 1820 [NC:67]. His 11 October 1843 Craven County will, proved November 1844, left 150 acres to his children Jeremiah Johnston and Martha **Dove**, and mentioned his grandchild Betsy **Dove** [WB D, folio 106]. Two of his children were

  i. Jeremiah³, married Mary **George**, 8 January 1828 Craven County bond, William **Martin** bondsman.

  ii. Martha **Dove**, wife of Arnett **Dove** and mother of Betsy **Dove**. She received 100 acres by her father's will. Arnett **Dove**, born about 1806, was about twelve years old on 10 March 1818 when he was listed as one of "Sundry Free Born Colored persons...as needy of proper persons" (to be bound to) [CR 028.101.1]. He married Patsy Johnston, 4 March 1824 Craven County bond, John A. Smith bondsman.

Another Johnson family
1. Jane Johnson, born say 1735, was the servant of John Ford of Fairfax County on 17 August 1756 when the court ordered that she serve him an additional year for having a "base born child a Mulatto." She was apparently the mother of

  i. Joseph, born in June 1755, a seven-year-old "Mulatto" child bound by the Fairfax County court to John Ford on 19 October 1762 [Orders 1756-63, 790, 14 (at end of microfilm reel)].

JOINER FAMILY

Members of the Joiner family were
1   i. Amy, born about 1758.
  ii. John, a "free Negro" taxable in Henrico County on a slave over the age of 16 in 1790 [PPTL 1782-1814, frame 219].
  iii. Betty, born about 1767, registered in Petersburg on 3 August 1805: *a dark brown Mulatto woman, five feet high, thirty eight years old, born free and raised in the County of Chesterfield according to a register of that County* [Register of Free Negroes 1794-1819, no. 348].

iv. Polly, born about 1769, registered in Petersburg on 18 August 1794: *a stout well made dark brown Mulatto woman, five feet four inches high, twenty five years old, born free in Chesterfield County* [Register of Free Negroes 1794-1819, no. 36]. She was head of a Petersburg household of 3 "other free" in 1810 [VA:122a].

v. Anna, born about 1772, registered in Petersburg on 14 August 1800: *a dark brown Mulatto girl, five feet two inches high, eighteen years old, short bushy hair, well made and born free & raised by William Alvis in Chesterfield County.* Renewed 9 July 1805: *5'3" has holes in ears* [Register of Free Negroes 1794-1819, no. 158].

vi. Dolly, born about 1775, registered in Petersburg on 15 August 1800: *a dark brown Mulatto woman, four feet ten inches high, twenty five years old, short bushy hair & holes in her ears for rings, born free & raised in the Town of Petersburg* [Register of Free Negroes 1794-1819, no. 179]. She was head of an "other free" Petersburg Town household in 1810 [VA:123b].

1. Amy Joiner, born about 1758, registered in Petersburg on 18 August 1794: *a dark brown Mulatto woman, five feet two inches high, about thirty six years old, born free in Chesterfield County* [Register of Free Negroes 1794-1819, no. 35]. She was taxable on (her son?) John Joiner in Dinwiddie County in 1800 [PPTL 1800-9, B, p.8]. She may have been the mother of

i. John, born about 1780, registered in Petersburg on 8 December 1801: *a dark brown Mulatto man, twenty one years old, five feet four and a half inches high, short wooly hair, born free in Chesterfield County & raised in the Town of Petersburg* [Register of Free Negroes 1794-1819, no. 219]. He was head of a Dinwiddie County household of 6 "other free" in 1810 [VA:150].

ii. Eliza, born about 1782, registered in Petersburg on 15 August 1800: *a brown Mulatto woman, four feet eleven inches, eighteen years old, short bushy hair, born free & raised in the Town of Petersburg* [Register of Free Negroes 1794-1819, no. 180].

iii. Thomas, born about 1783, registered in Petersburg on 10 July 1805: *a dark brown Mulatto man, five feet five inches high, twenty two years old, born free & raised in the Town of Petersburg* [Register of Free Negroes 1794-1819, no. 322]. He was head of a Petersburg Town household of 4 "other free" in 1810 [VA:126a].

iv. Nancy, born in November 1785, registered in Petersburg on 10 July 1805: *a dark brown Negro woman, four feet and a half inches high, twenty years old Nov. next, born free & raised in the Town of Petersburg* [Register of Free Negroes 1794-1819, no. 323]. She was head of a Petersburg Town household of 3 "other free" in 1810 [VA:117a].

v. Billy, born about 1786, registered in Petersburg on 22 June 1807: *a dark brown Negro man, five feet four and a half inches high, twenty one years old Oct. last. a Blacksmith, born free & raised in the Town of Petersburg* [Register of Free Negroes 1794-1819, no. 410].

JONES FAMILY

1. Elizabeth Jones, born say 1665, was a taxable in Henry Hart's Surry County household in Lawnes Creek Parish in 1682 [*Magazine of Virginia Genealogy,* vol.22, 3:56]. She may have been the ancestor of

2   i. Margaret, born say 1715.

ii. James[1], born say 1716, a soldier who enlisted in the expedition against the Spaniards at Carthagena and died in Jamaica. His "Mulatto" widow Rebecca Jones petitioned the Virginia House of Burgesses for a pension and was granted an allowance of five pounds on 26 May 1742 [McIlwaine, *Journals of the House of Burgesses*, 21, 37].

iii. Peter, born say 1723, a "negro" head of household with his wife Elizabeth and James **Weaver** in John Campbell's 1758 list for Bertie County and in John Brickell's 1759 list [CR 10.702.1]. Hertford County was formed from this part of Bertie County in 1759.

3 iv. Mary[1], born say 1725.

4 v. John[1], born say 1731.

5 vi. Richard, born say 1732.

6 vii. Abraham[1], born about 1734.

7 viii. Abraham[2], born say 1735.

8 ix. Samuel[1], born say 1738.

9 x. Philip, born say 1740.

xi. Richard, born say 1742, taxable with his wife ("Mulatoes") in Bladen County from 1768 to 1770 [Byrd, *Bladen County Tax Lists*, I:8, 16, 45]. On 9 September 1783 he sold 100 acres in Bladen County on the south side of Drowning Creek, south of Ashpole Swamp, which was land he had been granted on 11 November 1779. Ishmael **Chavis** witnessed the deed [DB 1:29]. He was head of a Robeson County household of 3 "other free," one white woman and one white male under sixteen years of age in 1790 [NC:49], head of a Beaufort District, South Carolina household of 8 "other free" in 1790 and 11 in 1800 [SC:120]. He may have been the father of Dick Jones, head of a Beaufort County, South Carolina household of 5 "other free" in 1800 [SC:104].

xii. Francis, born say 1750, a "Black" member of Captain James Fason's colonial Northampton County, North Carolina Militia [N.C. Archives Troop Returns, 1-3]. He was head of a Wake County household of 5 "other free" in 1790 [NC:103] and 8 "free colored" in Caswell County in 1820 [NC:66]. On 6 June 1818 he testified on behalf of Allen **Sweat** in Wake County court that he had served with him in the Revolutionary War [M804-2332].

2. Margaret Jones, born say 1715, was head of a Beaufort County household of 5 "black" taxables in 1755 [SS 837]. In 1769 she was living alone in the adjacent county of Craven [SS 837]. She sold 320 acres in Craven County on the south side of Neuse River near Chinquapin Creek to Joseph McKennie on 11 March 1775 with the proviso that she have a lifetime right to live on one hundred acres of this land [DB 21:240]. This part of Craven County became Jones County in 1779. Her descendants may have been

10 i. James[2], born say 1738.

ii. Hardy, head of a Jones County household of 5 "other free" in 1790 [NC:144], 7 "other free" and a white woman over the age of 45 in Lenoir County in 1810 [NC:300] and 4 "free colored" in 1820 [NC:295].

iii. Bazzilla, born before 1776, a "free colored" woman who was head of a Jones County household of 7 in 1830 [NC:132].

iv. William, head of a Jones County household of 3 "other free" in 1810 (J___, ___iam) [NC:265] and 8 "free colored" in 1830 [NC:132]. On 23 December 1826 he and Bazel Jones purchased land on both sides of Chinquapin Creek from Elijah Jones which was land he had received by his father's will [DB 16:359].

3. Mary[1] Jones, born say 1725, was a taxable head of a household of herself and Thomas and Mary Jones in the 1761 Cross Roads District of Granville County in the tax list of James Price as "mulattos &c" [CR 44.701.19]. In 1763 Mary had 4 taxables in her household in a list of Granville County insolvent taxpayers. Her children may have been

      i.   Thomas¹, born say 1743.

      ii. Mary², born say 1745, taxable in Mary Jones' Cross Roads District household in 1761.

4. John¹ Jones, born say 1731, was a "Mulatto" who lost his right to 200 acres in Brunswick County, Virginia, in a case heard before the Council of Virginia on 13 June 1753 [McIlwaine, *Executive Journals of the Council*, V:433]. He may have been the John Jones who was head of a Halifax County, North Carolina household of 6 "other free" in 1790 [NC:62]. Perhaps his widow was Margaret Jones, head of a household of 2 "other free" in the neighboring county of Northampton in 1800 [NC:453]. He may have been the father of

11   i.   Thomas², born say 1750.
12   ii. Tempy, born say 1765.

5. Richard Jones, born say 1732, and his wife Barshaba were taxable as two black tithes in the 1764 Granville County list of Samuel Benton. In 1768 his wife was called Mary when he was taxed with her and his son Ephraim in John Pope's list. He was still in Granville County in 1780 where he had no property but was taxable as a "married man" in Goshen District, and taxable on one poll in 1785. He may have been the Richard Jones who was head of a Martin County household of 5 "other free" in 1790 [NC:68]. His child was

      i.   Ephraim, born about 1755, taxed in his father's household in 1768. His estate was sold in Granville County on 16 November 1781 [WB 1:326].

6. Abraham¹ Jones, born about 1734, was head of a household of one Black male and one Black female in the 1767 Granville County tax list of John Pope adjacent to Richard Jones. In 1768 he was listed in Pope's list with his wife Charity. In the 1778 Militia Returns for Granville County he was listed in Captain John Rust's Company as a "mulatto," about forty-four years old [*The North Carolinian* VI:726 (Mil TR 4-40)]. He bought 8-1/2 head of cattle at the estate sale of Ephraim Jones on 16 November 1781 [WB 1:326]. He was taxable in Granville County in 1782 on 3 horses and 5 cattle and taxable on one poll in 1785 through 1788. Perhaps one of his children was

      i.   Jonathan, born about 1761, a seventeen-year-old "mulatto" listed in Captain Rust's Granville County Militia Returns adjacent to Abraham Jones [*The North Carolinian* VI:726], probably the Jonathan Jones who was taxable on one poll in Nash District of Person County in 1793 [*N.C. Genealogy* XVII:2673], head of a Person County household of 7 "other free" in 1800 [NC:597] and 8 "free colored" in 1820 [NC:498].

7. Abraham² Jones, born say 1735, was a man of mixed blood who petitioned the North Carolina General Assembly in 1797 stating that he had purchased his wife Lydia about 1757 and had six grown children Isaac, Jacob, Thomas, Abraham, Lewis and one other. He was concerned that once he died his wife and children would revert to slavery, having not been formally freed. His petition was rejected [http://history.uncg.edu/slaverypetitions/documentary.html,PAR#11279701]. He was head of an Anson County household of 7 "other free" in 1800 [NC:225] and 7 in Hertford County in 1810 [NC:98]. He was the father of

13   i.   Isaac, born say 1760.
      ii. Jacob, head of an Anson County household of 7 "other free" in 1800 [NC:225].
      iii. Thomas, head of an Anson County household of 5 "other free" in 1810 [NC:48] and head of a Mill Creek, Anson County household of 8 "free colored" and 2 white women in 1820 [NC:12].
      iv. Abraham.
      v.   Lewis.

8. Samuel[1] Jones, born say 1738, was taxable in Granville County on 150 acres, 2 horses, and 7 cattle in Fishing Creek District in 1782. He may have been the Samuel Jones who married Ann **Harris**, 24 November 1780 Granville County bond with Edward **Harris** bondsman. In 1786 he was head of an Epping Forest District household of 5 males and 3 females for the state census, and he was taxable in Granville County on 50 acres and 2 free polls in 1786. In 1788 he was taxable on 200 acres but was not subject to poll tax so he was probably over fifty years old. He was head of a Granville County household of 5 "other free" in 1800. He was taxable on 80 acres in Beaver Dam District for the last time in 1805 [Tax List 1803-09, 110]. One of his children was most likely

  i. Emmanuel, born say 1768, called "Manuel Scot Jones" on 7 February 1788 when he purchased cattle and tools from (his father?) Samuel Jones in Granville County [WB 2:153]. He entered 100 acres in Granville County on Buckhorn Creek on 17 March 1795 [Pruitt, *Granville County Land Entries,* 61]. He was taxable on one poll in Granville County in 1789, was taxed on 97-1/2 acres in Beaverdam District in 1797 and was charged with Samuel Jones's tax in the Beaverdam District of Granville County in 1802 [Tax List 1796-1802, 67, 326]. He was head of a Granville County household of 2 "other free" in 1810 [NC:864]. In 1815 he was taxed on 79 acres in Beaver Dam District, and he and a woman over forty-five years of age were counted as "free colored" in the 1820 Granville County census for Beaver Dam District [NC:16].

  ii. Samuel[2], born say 1778, head of a Granville County household of 2 "other free" in 1800.

  iii. Lyford, born say 1779, head of a Granville County household of 3 "other free" in 1800.

  iv. Phereby, born say 1782, married Daniel **Evans**, 10 September 1800 Granville County bond, Emanuel Scott Jones bondsman. Daniel was head of a Granville County household of 2 "other free" in 1800.

  v. Major, born say 1786, head of a Beaver Dam District household of 4 "other free" in 1810 and 4 "free colored" in 1820 [NC:16]. He married Honor **Bass**, 25 August 1814 Granville County bond, Elijah **Valentine** bondsman.

9. Philip Jones, born say 1740, was head of a Halifax County household of 7 "other free" in 1790 [NC:65] and 2 in 1800 (called Philip, Senr.) [NC:322]. He made a deposition in Northampton County court on 26 March 1791 that he enlisted and served as a soldier in the Continental Army [*NCGSJ* XI:118]. He may have been the Philip Jones who sometime before 7 September 1787 sold bounty land in Davidson County, Tennessee, which he received for his services in the War [Franklin County DB 6:89]. He sold 10 acres in Halifax County on Hog Pen Branch on 11 July 1795 [DB 17:831]. The Halifax branch of the family may have been related to Barshaba Jones of Granville County since a child named Barshaby Jones (no race mentioned) was ordered bound an apprentice by the 16 February 1836 Halifax County court. Philip's children may have been

  i. James[3], head of a Halifax County household of 4 "other free" in 1790 [NC:65] and 12 in 1810 [NC:29]. On 19 May 1823 he testified for Isham **Scott** in Halifax County court that he was in the service with him in Colonel Ashe's regiment.

  ii. Philip, Jr., born before 1776, head of a Halifax County household of 3 "other free" in 1800 [NC:322], 2 in Hertford County in 1810 [NC:100], and 9 "free colored" in Hertford County in 1820 [NC:182]. He was one of the "Sundry persons of Colour of Hertford County" who petitioned the General Assembly in 1822 to repeal the act which declared slaves to be competent witnesses against free African Americans [*NCGSJ* XI:252].

10. James[2] Jones, born say 1738, may have been one of the "black" tithables in the Beaufort County household of (his mother?) Margaret Jones in 1755. He was a "black" taxable in Craven County in 1769 [SS 837]. On 26 April 1780 he purchased 67 acres adjoining his land on Chinqapin Creek in Jones County from Jacob Jones, being the land where Jacob Jones, deceased, formerly lived, for 18 pounds [DB 3:90]. He was counted as white in the North Carolina state census for Jones County, recorded on 30 September 1786: head of a household of 1 male, 5 males and 5 free females, listed next to William **Morgan**, John **Conner**, and Mark **Conner** who were also counted as white [Governor's Office Census of 1784-7, Jones County family nos. 181-5]. He was head of a Jones County household of 11 "other free" in 1790 [NC:144]. By his 15 January 1790 Jones County will, proved February 1802, he left his wife his house and a third of his lands which were to be divided between his sons James and Bazel at her death or marriage. He divided the remainder of his land amongst his sons James, Frederick, Ezekiel, Elijah, and Jacob and left furniture and livestock to his daughters Elizabeth, Sarah, and Mary. His wife Sarah and son James were executors.[130] James was the father of

    i.   Elizabeth, received a bed, furniture and two cows by her father's will.

    ii. James[4], executor of his father's will, head of a Jones County household of 4 "other free" in 1810 [NC:265].

    iii. Frederick, received a bed and furniture, the bed he made use of, and the seventeen head of hogs he had raised, two cows, a mare, and a gun by his father's will.

    iv. Sarah, received a mare and two cows by her father's will.

    v. Ezekiah/ Ezekiel, head of a Jones County household of 4 "other free" in 1810 [NC:264].

    vi. Mary[4], received two cows, eighteen hogs, and a chest by her father's will.

    vii. Elijah, head of a Jones County household of 6 "other free" in 1810 [NC:265] and 5 "free colored" in 1830 [NC:132]. On 23 December 1826 he sold to Bazel and William Jones all the land on both sides of Chinquapin Creek which he had received by his father's will [DB 16:359].

    viii. Bazel, received a young horse by his father's will. He was head of a Jones County household of one "other free" in 1810 [NC:265].

    ix. Jacob, head of a Jones County household of 2 "other free" in 1790 [NC:144] and one "free colored" man 55-100 years old in 1830 [NC:132].

11. Thomas[1] Jones, born say 1743, was head of a Greensville County, Virginia household of 6 persons in 1783 [VA:55]. He was taxable in Greensville County from 1783 to 1797 [PPTL 1782-1850, frames 13, 84, 138, 162, 180, 189, 203, 219]. He and his wife Rebecca were named in the 10 February 1796 Greensville County marriage bond of their daughter Nancy. Their children were

14   i. ?Britton, born say 1763.

---

[130]Bazel Pritchard, Job Ives and Joseph Treurt (Truett) were witnesses to the will [WB 2:250]. Bazel Pritchard was counted six households away from James Jones in the 1786 state census [family no. 188] and eleven households away in the 1790 census. Job Ives was head of a Dobbs County household of a white man in 1790 [NC:138]. He was probably related to Isaac Ives who was listed two households from James Jones in the 1790 census: head of a household of a white woman and an "other free" man [NC:144]. Isaac and Job Ives were counted as white in Lenoir County in 1800 [NC:15].

ii. ?Elizabeth, born say 1768, married Meshack **Haithcock**, 26 December 1789 Greensville County bond.

iii. ?Mary³, born say 1770, married Reuben **Haithcock**, 30 January 1788 Greensville County bond, Braxton Robinson surety [Marriage Bonds, 28].

iv. ?Jesse, born say 1772, taxable in Greensville County from 1789 to 1801: taxable on two 16-21 year-old tithables and a horse in 1795; charged with Nathaniel Jones's tithe in 1800 [PPTL 1782-1850, frames 92, 180, 189, 219, 245, 260, 275]. He purchased land in Greensville County near Hick's Ford and Caton's Ferry from John and Agnes Day for 25 pounds on 8 February 1797 [DB 4:283]. The inventory of his Greensville County estate totalled about 35 pounds on 2 February 1805 [WB 1:535, 543; 2:5]. On 20 December 1804 Nancy Jones sold to Henry **Stewart** all her rights to the Greensville County estate of Jesse Jones, with Rebecca **Stewart** as witness [DB 3:412]. Aaron **Newsom** and his wife Christian of Brunswick County, Virginia, sold their part of the Greensville County estate of Jesse Jones to Henry **Stewart** on 13 October 1806 [Greensville County DB 3:507].

v. Sarah, born say 1776, married Thomas **Going**, 24 July 1794, Greensville County bond, William **Dungill** surety, and on 29 September 1794, called "Daughter of Thomas Jones" when she married Mark **Going**, 29 September 1794 Greensville County bond, Robert Brooks **Corn** bondsman.

vi. ?Bryant, born 24 December 1777, registered in Greensville County on 12 December 1807: *born free of Yellowish Complexion...Aged twenty nine years the 24th day of December last, 5 feet Nine & 3/4 Inches high* [Register of Free Negroes, 1805-32, no.12]. He was taxable in Greensville County from 1800 to 1807 [PPTL 1782-1850, frames 260, 275, 303, 322, 337, 354, 372], head of a Caswell County, North Carolina household of 5 "other free" in 1810 [NC:483] and

vii. Nancy, born say 1780, daughter of Thomas and Rebecca Jones, married Robert **Watkins**, 10 February 1796 Greensville County bond, Abraham **Artis** surety [Marriage Bonds, 34].

viii. ?James⁶, born about 1784, registered in Greensville County on 27 February 1807: *born free of a yellowish Complexion, freckled...Aged 23 years, five feet six Inches high* [Register of Free Negroes, 1805-32, no.9].

ix. ?Surrel/ Cyril, born say 1772, taxable in Greensville County on the south side of the Meherrin River from 1789 to 1811: called Surrell Jones **Jeffries** when he was taxable in Simon **Jeffries**' household in 1789 [PPTL 1782-1850, frames 84, 138, 162, 179, 189, 203, 219, 232, 245, 275, 354, 372, 402, 416]. He was head of an Orange County, North Carolina household of 5 "free colored" in 1820 [NC:410].

x. ?Nathaniel, born before 1776, taxable in Greensville from 1796 to 1806: his tax charged to Jesse Jones in 1800 [PPTL 1782-1850, frames 203, 245, 260, 275, 337, 354]. He was head of a Caswell County, North Carolina household of 6 "other free" in 1810 and 9 "free colored" in 1820 [NC:66].

xi. ?Sally, born about 1782, registered in Greensville County on 7 April 1825: *free born of black Complexion, between forty & forty five years old, 5 feet 8-1/8 Inches high in Shoes...and her Daughter Jacky Viney between three and four years old* [Register, no.145].

xii. ?Elizabeth/ Lizzy, born about 1780-1785, registered in Greensville County on 2 February 1830: *free born, dark yellow complexion, between forty five and fifty years of age, four feet 10-1/4 inches high...by occupation a weaver* [Register of Free Negroes, 1805-1832, no.175].

12. Tempy Jones, born say 1765, was probably the mother of Willie, Sterling, and Montfort Jones, "base born children" who were bound by the Halifax County, North Carolina court to Ephraim Knight on 25 August 1797 [Minutes 1796-8, Friday]. She died before 25 March 1814 when her son Mumford Jones received a certificate of freedom in Halifax County: *Mumford Jones, the son of Tempy Jones, decd., the grandson of Margarett Jones all of the county of Halifax in the state of North Carolina, was born free, that his grandfather and mother were likewise a free color'd people and their freedom never disputed as I ever new and I have them and his mother lived in my fathers family Twenty or Thirty years past & the said Molatoe Boy Mumford has lived with me for near fourteen years past & that he is now something above twenty one years of age. A. Knight* [Randolph County, Illinois, Servitude and Emancipation Register, vol. 1, 120]. She was the mother of

    i.   ?Willie, born about 1783, fourteen years old on 25 August 1797 when he was bound by the Halifax County court to Ephraim Knight to learn carpentry [Minutes 1796-8, Friday]. He was probably the William Jones, Sr., who was head of a Halifax County household of 8 "free colored" in 1830.

    ii. ?Sterling, born about 1785, twelve years old on 25 August 1797 when he was bound by the Halifax County court to Ephraim Knight to learn carpentry [Minutes 1796-8, Friday]. He was head of a Halifax County household of 13 "free colored" in 1830.

    iii. Mumford, born about 1788, nine years old on 25 August 1797 when he was bound by the Halifax County court to Ephraim Knight to learn carpentry [Minutes 1796-8, Friday]. He obtained a certificate of freedom in Halifax County signed by A. Knight on 25 March 1814 which he registered in Pendleton District, South Carolina, on 8 November 1819 and later recorded in Randolph County, Illinois [Randolph County Servitude and Emancipation Register, vol. 1, 120]. A. Knight was apparently identical to Abner Knight, son of Ephraim Knight whose Halifax County will was proved in November 1800 [Halifax County Minutes 1799-1802, 145].

    iv. ?Grizza, born about February 1795, two years and five months old on 25 August 1797 when she was bound by the Halifax County court to Ephraim Knight [Minutes 1796-8, Friday].

    v. Peggy, born about November 1796, nine months old on 25 August 1797 when she was bound by the Halifax County court to Ephraim Knight [Minutes 1796-8, Friday]. She was head of a Halifax County household of 6 "free colored" in 1830.

13. Isaac Jones, born say 1760, was head of a Robeson County household of 5 "other free" in 1800 [NC:386]. Perhaps his widow was Priscilla Jones, born before 1776, head of a Robeson County household of 5 "free colored" in 1820 [NC:302]. Isaac may have been the father of

    i.   Nathan, born 1776-94, head of a Robeson County household of 4 "free colored" in 1820.

    ii. Willey, head of a Robeson County household of 5 "free colored" in 1820 [NC:293].

    iii. Abraham, born 1786-1804, head of a Robeson County household of 5 "free colored" in 1840, a "free man of Colour," granted a permit to carry a gun in Robeson County by the 22 November 1841 court [Minutes 1839-43, 240].

14. Britton Jones, born about 1763, was a Revolutionary soldier from Greensville County, Virginia [Jackson, *Virginia Negro Soldiers*, 38], head of a Greensville County household of 2 persons in 1783 [VA:55], and 4 "free colored" in 1820 [VA:262]. He was taxable in Greensville County from 1792 to 1818: taxable on Willie Jones's tithe in 1803 and taxable on Willie and Bryant Jones's tithe

in 1804, a "Mulatto" listed with his wife Lucy and their unnamed daughter in 1813 [PPTL 1782-1850, frames 137, 179, 189, 203, 232, 245, 260, 304, 322, 337, 345, 372, 387, 402, 416, 426, 433, 447, 463, 483, 557]. He registered as a "Free Negro" in Greensville County on 1 April 1825: *free born of a Yellowish Complexion about Sixty-two years old, 5 feet 10-1/4 inches high...a planter* [Register of Free Negroes, 1805-32, no. 140]. He was the father of

    i.   ?Sarah, born 15 August 1787, registered on 12 December 1807: *born free of yellowish Complexion aged Nineteen years the 15th last August, five feet two & 1/2 Inches high* [Register of Free Negroes, no. 13].

   ii.   ?Benjamin, born about 1788, taxable in Greensville County from 1807 to 1827: listed with his wife Winifred, "Mulattos," in 1813 [PPTL 1782-1850, frames 372, 416, 447, 484, 679, 830]. He registered there on 7 April 1825: *free born of yellowish Complexion between 35 & 40 years old, 5 feet 9-1/8 inches high in Shoes...a planter* [Register of Free Negroes, 1805-32, no. 143].

  iii.   Edmund, born about 1791, registered in Greensville County on 3 January 1826: *(Son of Britton Jones) free born of a Yellowish Complexion, about 35 years of age, Six feet, two inches high (in Shoes)...freckled face...a farmer* [Register of Free Negroes, no. 151].

   iv.   ?Winney, born about 1792, registered in Greensville County on 7 April 1825: *free born of yellowish Complexion between thirty and thirty five years Old, 5 feet 4-1/2 Inches high...a weaver & her 6 Children, viz., Lucinda about 14 years old...Eliza Jane, 9 years old...Sally Ann nearly 3 years old, and Britton Anderson 12 years Old next December, Peterson Douglas 7 years old next month, and Jack Anderson 5 years Old in June next* [Register of Free Negroes, 1805-32, no. 142].

    v.   ?Peggy, born about 1797, registered in Greensville County on 15 April 1825: *born free of a yellow complexion, about 28 years old, 5 feet 4-1/2 inches high in shoes...a weaver* [Register of Free Negroes, 1805-32, no. 146].

   vi.   Willie, born say 1786, taxable in Greensville County from 1803 to 1814: his tax charged to Britton Jones from 1803 to 1805, listed as a "Mulatto" in 1814 [PPTL 1782-1850, frames 304, 322, 337, 354, 382, 402, 416, 463]. He was head of a Caswell County, North Carolina household of 10 "free colored" in 1820 [NC:67].

York County
1.   Sarah Jones, born say 1700, was presented by the York County court on 15 May 1738 for not listing herself as a tithable. The court excused her from paying the fine but ordered that she and Nanny Jones pay their levies for that year and the future [OW 18:414, 427]. She may have been the ancestor of

    i.   Nanny, born say 1719, presented by the York County court on 19 June 1738 for not listing herself as a tithable [OW 18:427], perhaps the Nanny Jones who was a "free" head of a Williamsburg City household of 3 "black" persons in 1782 [VA:45].

   ii.   Humphrey, sued a number of people for debt in York County court between 1748 and 1754. In a suit which he brought in chancery against John **Rollison** (**Rawlinson**) on 17 August 1752 the parties by their counsel agreed that the plaintiff and a witness named Thomas **Carter** were "Mulattos." The court ruled that the lease involved in the suit was obtained fraudulently and was, therefore, cancelled. **Rawlinson** appealed to the General Court. Humphrey sued **Rawlinson** for a 93 pound, 16 shilling debt on 19 November 1753 [Judgments & Orders 1746-52, 101, 112, 153, 163, 182; 1752-4, 119, 153, 166, 168, 170-1, 178, 196, 285, 343-4, 353, 495].

2 iii.   George, born say 1725.

   iv.   John[1], born say 1725, living in York County on 20 November 1749 when his wife Mary was presented for not listing herself as a tithable.

The charges were dismissed when John paid her tax and costs of the suit. Mary was presented again on 19 November 1750 for not listing herself [Judgment & Orders 1746-52, 256, 277, 364, 384].

3   v.   Barshaba, born say 1727.

vi. William, a "free Negro," who died before 7 November 1769 when the vestry of Elizabeth City paid for his coffin. The vestry also paid Jane Allen for maintaining him for four weeks during his sickness [von Doenhoff, *Vestry Book of Elizabeth City Parish 1751-1784*, 101].

vii. Edward, presented by the York County court on 19 November 1750 for not listing his wife Betty and "Will a Negro" (a slave). The court fined him 1,000 pounds of tobacco [Judgment & Orders 1746-52, 364, 384].

4   viii. James, born say 1745.

ix. Disey, born about 1749, registered in York County on 18 December 1809: *a woman of yellowish complexion supposed to be about 60 years of age...thin visage & has fierce black Eyes for one of her age. Born of free parents in the parish of Bruton & county of York* [Free Negro Register 1798-1831, no. 39].

x.   Mary, born say 1755, a "free Negro" attending the "Negro School" in Williamsburg in September 1762.

xi. Elisha, born say 1757, a "free Negro" attending the "Negro School" in Williamsburg in September 1762 [Stephenson, *Notes on the Negro School in Williamsburg, 1760-1774*, Colonial Williamsburg Foundation (1963), Appendix no. 1, iii, citing Manuscripts of Dr. Bray's Associates, American Papers, 1735-1774, S.P.G. Archives, London].

xii. Anny, sister of Sally Delaney who married John **Comboe (Cumbo)**, 10 August 1797 York County bond.

xiii. Susanna, married Henry **Ashby**, 23 January 1796 York County bond. He was taxable in James City County from 1795 to 1801. Susanna **Ashby** was taxable there on a horse in 1807 and head of a household of one "Free Person of Colour above 16 years" in 1813 [PPTL 1782-99; 1800-15].

2.   George Jones, born say 1725, sued Joseph **Kennedy (Cannady)** for trespass, assault and battery in a case which was dismissed by the York County court on 19 May 1746 when neither party appeared [W&I 19:429]. On 19 September 1763 he sued Peter **Gillett** for 35 shillings due by account with John **Poe** as his witness [Judgments & Orders 1759-63, 325; 1763-5, 79]. The court ordered George to pay Sarah **Freeman** 40 shillings on 15 January 1770 in her suit against him for trespass, assault and battery. Peter and Sarah **Gillett** were witnesses against him [Orders 1768-70, 407]. He was living in Halifax County, Virginia, on 20 April 1775 when he appeared in court to answer the complaint of his servant Mary Scandling. The court released her from his service because he was a "free Mulatto" and had purchased her indenture. However, two years later on 20 February 1777 the court ordered the churchwardens to bind Mary's son Macklin Scandling to George. Mary died before 19 November 1778 when Lucretia **Macklin** (who was also from York County) was charged with her murder. At Lucretia's hearing, George deposed that

he was riding on the road with Mary Scandling the deceased person behind him and met the prisoner Lucretia Macklin who insulted him with opprobrious language and pick'd up a stick about the size of his arm, and offer'd to strike which this deponent endeavour'd to fend off with his arm, but doth not know whether she struck the deceas'd on which the stick broke, on which this deponent got off his horse and went to the prisoner, in which time the deceas'd was off the horse and walk'd about thirty yards and sat down and call'd to this deponent to come to her for she was dying. And this deponent went to the deceas'd and took hold of her and she appear'd to be fainting. This deponent ask'd her to go, she reply'd she was not able, and lay there until she dy'd [Pleas 1774-79, 109, 193, 379].

Lucretia **Maclin** was counted in the 1782 census for Richmond City [VA:111].

George was taxable in Halifax County from 1783 to 1793: listed with two 16-21-year-old tithables in 1787, listed with 2 unnamed sons in 1788 and 1789, listed with 2 tithables in 1791, called a "FN" in 1789 and 1792, an exempt "Mulº" in 1793 [PPTL, 1782-1799, frames 22, 49, 137, 197, 270, 305, 374, 419]. On 27 May 1789 he complained to the Halifax County court against George Fitch for a breach of the peace, and he sold property by deed proved in Halifax County on 28 June 1789 [Pleas 1789-90, 251, 258]. He was apparently the father of

    i.   Jonathan, born say 1771, a "FN" taxable in Halifax County from 1792 to 1812: listed next to George Jones in 1792, called a "Mulº" from 1793 [PPTL, 1782-1799, frames 419, 444, 540, 606, 822; 1800-12, frames 62, 630, 810, 856, 1033].

    ii. ?Chesley, a "Mulatto" taxable in Halifax County in 1804 [PPTL, 1800-12, frame 377]. An undated Granville County, North Carolina civil action case stated that free men of color Jnº A. Jones and Chesley Jones had moved from the state of Virginia to Granville County and settled on land of William Marshall in the fork of Island Creek and had not complied with the law in such cases [N.C. Archives file CR 044.289.19].

3.   Barshaba Jones, born say 1727, had a daughter Eleanor whose birth on 26 November 1748 was recorded in Bruton Parish, James City County [Bruton Parish Register, 8]. He was called Bash Jones on 19 December 1748 when he sued Thomas Smith for debt in York County court in a suit which was dismissed by agreement of both parties [Judgments & Orders 1746-52, 150]. He was called "Barshaba Jones Negro" in Lunenburg County, Virginia, in the 1750 and 1752 tax list of Hugh Lawson [Tax List 1748-52, Virginia State Library Accession no.20094, p.2]. By 19 September 1759 he had moved to Granville County, North Carolina, where he pleaded guilty to trespass [Minutes 1754-70, 57]. An undated Granville County court affidavit by Henry Edwards requested

news of Whereabouts of free Negro runaway who is in his debt Barshaba Jones 9pds. he was sometime ago in Granville?...[CR 44.928.25].

In 1761 he and his wife Ann were 2 black tithables in the Baptist District, Granville County tax list of David Harris [CR 44.701.19]. He was taxable in the 1763 Granville County tax list of insolvents with 5 taxables. The Baptist District of Granville County became Bute County in 1764. Barsheba sold 206 acres in Bute County on the north side of Fishing Creek on 6 January 1765, 80 acres between Fishing Creek and Reedy Creek on 8 January 1765, and 200 acres on Reedy Creek on 5 February 1765 [Warren County DB 1:8; 2:135; A:324]. He was sued for 2 pounds, 19 shillings debt by Zachariah Bullock in Granville County court on 11 August 1765 [Minutes 1754-70, 138]. He was in Bladen County on 12 September 1783 when he was witness to the deed of Braswell Hunt to John Cade for land on Ashpole Swamp [DB 1:28] and was head of a Robeson County household of 1 "other free" in 1800 [NC:387]. His children were

    i.   Eleanor, born 26 November 1748 [Bruton Parish Register, 8].

    ii. William, born circa 1750, first taxed in his fathers's Granville County household in 1762. He was a taxable "Mulato" in Bladen County in James **Lowry**'s household from 1768 to 1771 and a "Molato" head of his own household in 1776 [Byrd, *Bladen County Tax Lists*, I:5, 17, 45, 60; II:65]. He was head of a Beaufort District, South Carolina household of 8 "other free" in 1790 and 12 in 1800 [SC:106].

    iii.   John², born circa 1750, first taxed in his father's Granville County household in 1762.

    iv.   ?Lucy, born say 1753, mother of a "Negro" boy, Dick Jones, born 15 June 1771, ordered bound to Joseph Norris in Bute County in February 1772 [Minutes 1767-76, 194]. He may have been the Richard Jones who was head of a Cumberland County household of 4 "other free" in 1810 [NC:619].

    v.   ?Burwell, a man of color from Lunenburg County who served in the Revolution [National Archives pension file R67SO cited by NSDAR, *African American Patriots*, 150].

    vi.   ?Martin, taxable on one poll in Person County in 1793 in Nash District, head of a Person County household of 7 "other free" in 1800 [NC:597].

4.   James³ Jones, born say 1745, and his wife Margaret, "free mulattoes," registered the birth of their son John in Bruton Parish, James City County. Their children were

    i.   John³, born 28 March 1767 [Bruton Parish Register, 31]. He may have been the John Jones who died before 19 September 1803 when (his wife?) Nancy Jones was granted administration on his York County estate with Charles Carter and John W. **De Rozario** as securities [Orders 1795-1803, 606].

Isle of Wight and Sussex counties

1.   Thomas Jones, born say 1748, a "Mulatto," and his wife Mary had their daughter Rebecca baptized in Albemarle Parish, Surry and Sussex counties, Virginia, in February 1774 [Richards, *Albemarle Parish Register*, no. 243]. He may have been the Thomas Jones who was head of an Isle of Wight County household of 7 "white" (free) persons in 1782 [VA:30], taxable there from 1783 to 1809: taxable on a slave over the age of sixteen in 1783; taxable on Robin, "a freed Negroe," in 1786; taxable on 2 horses in 1788; taxable on a slave and 2 horses in 1789; listed as a "F.N." in 1790 and thereafter; taxable on a free male tithable aged 16-21 in 1792; a slave and 3 horses in 1797, 2 tithes and 5 horses in 1800; 3 free tithes and 5 horses in 1801; 2 free tithes and 3 horses in 1803 when he was called Thomas Jones, F.N., Sr., in 1802 and 1803; taxable on his unnamed son's tithe in 1804; 2 tithes in 1805, 1806 and 1809 [PPTL 1782-1810, frames 40, 79, 121, 167, 199, 216, 263, 365, 409, 447, 512, 545, 563, 622, 639, 698, 739, 815] and head of a Sussex County household of 8 "other free" in 1810. He was the father of

2   i.   ?William, born say 1763.

    ii.   ?Willis, born say 1769, taxable in Isle of Wight County from 1788 to 1803: a "Molato" taxable on a horse in 1788; listed as a "F.N." in 1789 and thereafter; taxable on a slave and a horse in 1792 and 1796; taxable on 2 free males and a horse in 1800; called Willis Jones F.N. Senr. in 1803 [PPTL 1782-1810, frames 122, 167, 199, 216, 262, 318, 365, 380, 409, 447, 512, 545, 563, 622, 639] and head of a Surry County household of 3 "other free" and a slave in 1810.

    iii.   Rebecca, born 12 July 1773, baptized 13 February 1774 [Richards, *Albemarle Parish Register*, no. 243].

    iv.   ?John², a "F.N." taxable in Isle of Wight County in 1800 and 1801 [PPTL 1782-1810, frames 512, 563], head of a Sussex County household of 4 "other free" in 1810. He married Sacky **Cypress** on 12 February 1807 in Sussex County.

    v.   ?Polly, married Edwin **Roberts**, 7 January 1796 Isle of Wight County bond, Thomas Jones surety.

    vi.   ?Davis, born say 1776, called David Jones when he was taxable in the Isle of Wight County household of (his father?) Thomas Jones. He was a "F.N." taxable in Isle of Wight County from 1798 to 1805 [PPTL

1782-1810, frames 447, 464, 512, 563, 639, 699]. He married Clara
Banks, 5 June 1795 Isle of Wight County bond, Francis Young surety,
6 June marriage. He was head of a Petersburg Town household of 4
"other free" in 1810 [VA:119a].

vii. ?Thomas, Jr., born say 1783, a "F.N." taxable in Isle of Wight County
      from 1802 to 1810 [PPTL 1782-1810, frames 563, 622, 698, 729, 776,
      797, 852].

viii. Betsy **Andrews**, "daughter of Thomas Jones," married Joseph **Byrd**,
      23 December 1816 Surry County bond, John **Charity** surety.

2. William Jones, born say 1763, was taxable in Isle of Wight County from 1786
    to 1810: taxable on a horse and 4 cattle in 1786; called a "M." in 1789; a
    "F.N." in 1791; taxable on a slave and a horse in 1797; taxable on 2 free
    tithes and a horse in 1801; called William Jones, F.N., Senr., in 1804; taxable
    on 2 tithes and a horse in 1809 [PPTL 1782-1810, frames 79, 166, 216, 262,
    365, 380, 409, 447, 563, 622, 639, 739, 757, 815, 833] and a "Free Negro"
    head of an Isle of Wight County household of 3 "other free" in 1810 [VA:34].
    He was the father of

    i. John, born say 1785, a "F.N." taxable in Isle of Wight County from
        1803 to 1810: called "son of Wm" from 1803 to 1806; taxable on a
        slave and a horse in 1810 [PPTL 1782-1810, frames 622, 639, 699,
        739, 757, 815, 834].

Richmond, Essex and Orange counties, Virginia

1. Margaret Jones, born say 1680, was the mother of Ann Jones who was
    indentured to Anne Fenner (daughter of John Fenner) for eleven years by the
    Richmond County court on 2 May 1705. She may have been identical to
    "Margaret, late Servant to Joseph Belfield, now living at John Fenner's" who
    was presented by the Richmond County court on 4 October 1705 for bearing
    a "Molatto bastard." She was called Margaret Chiswick in court on 5
    December 1705 when she acknowledged that she had a "mulato...begott by a
    Negro" [Orders 1704-8, 57, 61, 93, 97, 101]. She may have been the ancestor
    of

    i.   William[1], born say 1715, a "mulatto," who owned a white servant
         woman named Margaret Irwin. William sold her to Isaac Arnold before
         27 March 1755 when the Orange County, Virginia court ruled that she
         was a free woman because William had no right to keep or dispose of
         her [Orders 1754-63, 80].

    ii. William[2], born say 1730, a "Mulatto" runaway servant man belonging
         to Moore Fauntleroy of Richmond County in August 1754 when he was
         taken up in Essex County [Essex County Orders 1753-4, 226].

2   iii. Mary, born about 1750.

2. Mary Jones, born about 1750, registered as a free Negro in Essex County on
    7 December 1810: *born free, dark Mulattoe, about sixty years of age, five feet
    two inches high* [Register of Free Negroes, 1810-43, no.3, p.2]. She was the
    mother of

    i.   ?Chaney, born about 1777, registered on 7 December 1810: *born free
         by affirmation of Richard Banks, dark Mulattoe, about 33 years of age,
         five feet three inches and three quarters* [Register of Free Negroes
         1810-43, no.4, p.3].

    ii. Milly, born about 1785, registered in Essex County on 8 December
         1810: *daughter of Mary Jones, appearing by statement of Thomas
         Brockenbrough in person that she has always passed as a free born
         person, 25 years of age, a light black* [Register of Free Negroes 1810-
         43, no.25, p.12].

Princess Anne/ Norfolk County
Members of the Jones family in Princess Anne and Norfolk counties born about
1750 were

    i.   Nanny, born say 1743, a taxable "free negro" in Norfolk County on the
north side of Tanners Creek in Elizabeth Grant's household in 1765
and taxable in her own household in 1768 [Wingo, *Norfolk County
Tithables, 1751-65*, 209; 1766-80, 49].

1   ii.   Judy, born say 1745.
2   iii.   Sarah, born say 1752.

1.   Judy[1] Jones, born say 1745, was the mother of seven children who were bound
as apprentices by the Princess Anne County court in 1778 and 1779: James,
Caleb, Elijah, Betty, Nat, Dick and Tom [Minutes 1773-82, 275, 293, 445].
She may have been the mother of Judah and Tom Jones, "free Negroes," who
were living in adjoining Norfolk County on 15 February 1770 when the court
ordered the churchwardens to bind them out [Orders 1768-71, 150]. Her
children were

    i.   ?Judah[2], born say 1764, a "free Negro" living in Norfolk County on 15
February 1770 when the court ordered her bound to Nanny Grant
[Orders 1768-71, 150].

    ii.   Tom, born say 1766, a "free Negro" living in Norfolk County on 15
February 1770 when the court ordered him bound to James McCoy
[Orders 1768-71, 150], perhaps identical to Tom Jones, son of Judy
Jones, who was bound to William Wishert in Princess Anne County on
11 November 1779 [Minutes 1773-82, 445].

    iii.   James, born say 1768, son of Judy Jones, bound apprentice by the
Princess Anne County court to William Wishart, Gent., to be a planter
on 9 July 1778 [Minutes 1773-82, 275].

    iv.   Caleb, born say 1770, bound by the Princess Anne County court to
William ___ to be a planter on 10 July 1778 [Minutes 1773-82, 293].

    v.   Elijah, born say 1771, son of Judy Jones, bound by the Princess Anne
County court as an apprentice planter to William Wishart on 10 July
1778, a "Free Mulatto" bound to William Russell to be a cooper on 8
April 1784 [Minutes 1773-82, 293; 1782-4, 193].

    vi.   Betty, born say 1773, daughter of Judy Jones, bound apprentice by the
Princess Anne County court on 10 July 1778 [Minutes 1773-82, 293].

    vii.   Nat, born say 1775, "free Negro" son of Judy Jones bound to William
Wishert by the Princess Anne County court on 11 November 1779
[Minutes 1773-82, 445].

    viii.   Dick, born say 1776, "free Negro" son of Judy Jones bound to William
Wishert on 11 November 1779. He and Tom Jones were called "Free
born Mulattoes" on 10 June 1784 when the Princess Anne County court
bound them to Jonathan Park to be tanners [Minutes 1773-82, 445;
1782-4, 212].

2.   Sarah Jones, born say 1752, was the mother of four children who were bound
as apprentices by the Princess Anne County court. They were

    i.   Argyle, born say 1772, son of Sarah Jones, bound by the Princess
Anne County court to Hillary ___ to be a blacksmith on 13 April
1775 and bound to be a mariner on 10 July 1778 [Minutes 1773-82,
94, 293]. He was head of a Norfolk County household of 1 "other
free" in 1810 [VA:927].

    ii.   Robert, born say 1774, son of Sarah Jones, bound to ___ Martin to be
a shoemaker on 10 July 1778 [Minutes 1773-82, 293].

    iii.   Dinah, born say 1775, daughter of Sarah Jones, bound to ___ Kilgore
on 10 July 1778 [Minutes 1773-82, 293].

    iv.   Mary, born say 1777, daughter of Sarah Jones, bound to Mary ___ on
10 July 1778 [Minutes 1773-82, 293]. She was a "free Black" head of

a Princess Anne County household of 10 "other free" in 1810 [VA:459].

JORDAN FAMILY

1. Francis Jordan, born say 17, presented his manumission, written by the clerk of the Council of Virginia, to the Norfolk County court on 20 June 1771 [Orders 1771-3, 4]. He was taxable in the household of Joshua Miers in Portsmouth Parish, Norfolk County, in 1767 and taxable in his own household in the Borough of Norfolk on Thomas **Teemar** and "negro Hester" (a slave) in 1772 and taxable on "negroes" Hester and Thomas in 1773 [Wingo, *Norfolk County Tithables, 1766-1780*, 18, 162, 215]. He married Sarah **Boyles**, 24 February 1792 Norfolk County bond. He may have been the father of
   i. Moses, head of a Norfolk County household of 1 "other free" in 1810 [VA:801].

JUMPER FAMILY

The Jumper family was apparently related to Tom Jumper, one of six Tuscarora Indians accused by five other Tuscarora Indians of murdering Jeremiah Pate of New Kent County on 14 October 1707.[131] Tom and another of the Indians poisoned themselves before they were brought to trial [McIlwaine, *Journals of the Council*, II:158, 173].

1. Hagar Jumper, born about 1750, obtained her freedom from Stephen Dance of Dinwiddie County in a court case based on her descent from an Indian woman. She registered in Petersburg on 14 August 1800: *a dark brown Mulatto or Indian woman, five feet two inches high, fifty years old, short bushy hair, obtained her freedom from Stephen Dance of the County of Dinwiddie as being a descendant of an Indian.* Renewed 1805, 1810, 1813, 1817 [Register of Free Negroes 1794-1819, no. 159]. She was probably the mother of
   i. Rochester, born about 1764, registered in Petersburg on 4 August 1803: *a dark brown Mulatto man, five feet seven and a half inches high, thirty nine years old, born free & raised in Dinwiddie County* [Register of Free Negroes 1794-1819, no. 257]. He was a "free Negro" taxable who lived with Daniel Pegram and kept his still in Dinwiddie County in 1802 [PPTL, 1800-9, list B, p.20].
   ii. Samuel, born say 1766, taxable in Dinwiddie County in 1787, 1788, 1790, 1795 and 1797, listed as a "free Negro" who followed "cropping" and lived near Joseph Thweatt in 1801 [PPTL, 1782-90 (1787 B, p.7), (1788 A, p.8), (1790 B, p.17), (1795 B, p.10), (1797 B, p.10); 1800-9, list B, p.25].
2 iii. Altha, born say 1767.
   iv. Philip, born say 1774, taxable in Dinwiddie County in 1795 [PPTL, 1782-90 (1795 B, p.10)].
   v. Hannah, born about 1778, "daughter of C. Jumper," married Littleberry **Lawrence**, 7 March 1796 Charlotte County bond, John **Williamson** surety. She and her husband Berry registered in Pittsylvania County in 1816: *a fifty-year-old black man with "mulatto" wife Hannah (aged thirty-five) and four daughters.*

2. Altha Jumper, born say 1767, was called Otha Jumper on 26 April 1785 when her suit against Isham **Lawrence** and his wife for trespass, assault and battery was dismissed by the Brunswick County, Virginia court at the defendants'

---

[131]The other five involved in the murder were Charles, Stephen, George, Jack Mason, and Will Mason.

costs [Orders 1784-8, 78, 125]. She was apparently identical to Altha **Rouse**, a "free negroe" planter counted with her children William, Priscilla and Jency and taxable on a horse in Stephen Bedford's Charlotte County tax list for 1802. She was called Altha Jumper in his list from 1803 to 1813: a "fm" weaver with a male and 2 female children and taxable on 2 horses in 1803, taxable on a free male tithable in 1809, listed as a planter from 1807 to 1810, a spinner from 1811 to 1813 [PPTL 1782-1813, frames 539, 542, 574, 580, 608, 642, 648, 675, 682, 711, 717, 751, 783, 808, 841, 841, 846, 877, 886]. She was a "F.N." head of a Charlotte County household of 4 "other free" in 1810 [VA:54]. She was the mother of
- i.   Priscilla, born say 1791.
- ii. William, born say 1793, a "fm" taxable in Charlotte County with a male and female in his household in 1813 [PPTL 1782-1813, frame 877].
- iii. Jency, born say 1795.

KEE/ KEYS FAMILY

1.   ____ Kee, born say 1700, was a soldier who was slain in the expedition against the Spaniards at Carthagena. His widow Elizabeth Kee, a "Mulatto," petitioned the Virginia House of Burgesses for a pension and was granted an allowance of five pounds on 26 May 1742 [McIlwaine, *Journals of the House of Burgesses*, 20, 37]. They were probably the ancestors of
- 2   i.   Andrew, born say 1760.
- 3   ii. John, born about 1763.
- 4   iii. Betty, born say 1785.

2.   Andrew Kee, born say 1760, was living in Essex County on 17 May 1784 when he was presented for failing to list himself as a tithable. On 20 December 1785 he and Humphrey **Fortune** were sued in Essex County for a debt of 2,500 pounds of tobacco with interest from 15 October 1782 [Orders 1784-7, 9, 174]. He may have been the father of
- i.   Robert, born about 1780, taxable in St. Ann's Parish, Essex County, in 1802 and 1810, listed as a "free Negro" in 1813 and 1814 [PPTL, 1782-1819, frames 347, 441, 510, 543]. He registered as a free Negro in Essex County on 17 August 1829: *born free by certificate of John Micon, Sr., bright Mulattoe, 49 years of age, 5 feet 5-1/8 inches* [Essex County Register 1810-43, p.98, no.216].
- ii. Walker Key, born about 1789, registered as a free Negro in Essex County on 17 August 1829: *born free by certificate of John Micon, Sr., dark Mulattoe, 40 years of age, 5 feet 7-3/4 inches* [Essex County Register 1810-43, p.95, no.209]. He was a "free Negro" counted in St. Ann's Parish, Essex County, with a female over the age of sixteen in 1813 [PPTL, 1782-1819, frame 510].
- iii. Judith, married Thomas **Fortune**, 23 December 1813 Essex County bond.
- iv. Delphia, a "free Negro" over the age of sixteen who was counted in St. Ann's Parish, Essex County, in 1813 [PPTL, 1782-1819, frame 510].

3.   John[1] Key, born about 1763, was a Lunenburg County, Virginia soldier of dark complexion who was born free in King and Queen County in 1763. In 1853 his widow Faithy **Lester** Key began receiving a pension for his services in the Revolutionary War [Jackson, *Virginia Negro Soldiers*, 39]. They may have been the parents of
- i.   John[2], born about 1809, registered in Amherst County on 20 January 1851: *a free man of Colour born in the County of King and Queen, bright Mulatto 5 feet 6-3/4 Inches high...age 42 years...derives his freedom from ancestors free prior to the 1st of May 1806* [McLeroy,

Strangers in their Midst, 75]. Esix Key, a 95 year-old "Mulatto," was counted in his household in the 1850 census for Amherst County.

4. Betty Key, born say 1785, was the mother of at least two persons who registered as free Negroes in Amherst county:

    i. Frances, born about 1809, registered in Amherst County on 21 May 1851: *a free woman of Colour daughter of Betsey Key a dark mulatto about forty two years of age, long strait black hair, five feet four and 1/2 Inches high born in Nelson County of parents free prior to the 1st of May 1806.*

    ii. Sally, born about 1816, registered in Amherst County on 17 February 1851: *daughter of Betsey Key bright mulatto 5 feet 3-1/2 Inches high...about 35 years of age, born in Nelson County* [McLeroy, *Strangers in their Midst*, 82].

    iii. ?William, born about 1821, registered in Amherst County on 17 February 1851: *about thirty years of age a dark mulatto...born of ancestors free prior to the 1st of May 1806* [McLeroy, *Strangers in their Midst*, 75-6, 82].

Other members of the family were

    i. Milly Keys, head of a Petersburg Town household of 5 "other free" in 1810 [VA:334a].

    ii. Polly Keys, head of a Spotsylvania County household of 2 "other free" in 1810 [VA:113a].

    iii. Brener Keys, head of a Spotsylvania County household of 1 "other free" in 1810 [VA:112a].

    iv. Betty Key, a "free Negro" living in Middlesex County, Virginia, in 1813 [PPTL 1782-1850, frame 272].

Beaufort County, North Carolina
1. Milly Keys, born say 1765, was head of a Beaufort County, North Carolina household of 4 "other free" in 1790 [NC:126] and 6 "free colored" in 1820 [NC:23]. She may have been the mother of

    i. Clary, head of a Beaufort County household of 5 "other free" in 1810 [NC:114].

    ii. Silvy, head of a Beaufort County household of 4 "other free" in 1810 [NC:127].

    iii. Amy, head of a Beaufort County household of 2 "other free" in 1810 [NC:114].

    iv. Mary, born 1776-1794, head of a Beaufort County household of 4 "free colored" in 1820 [NC:23].

    v. Nancy, born 1776-1794, head of a Beaufort County household of 4 "free colored" in 1820 [NC:24].

    vi. Sally, born 1776-1794, head of a Beaufort County household in 1810 [NC:127] and 5 "free colored" in 1820 [NC:23].

    vii. Penny, born 1776-1794, head of a Beaufort County household of "free colored" in 1820 [NC:23].

KEEMER FAMILY

1. James[1] Keemer, born say 1740, was presented by the York County court on 15 November 1762 for failing to list himself as a tithable. The case was dismissed when he paid his tax. On 20 May 1765 the court presented him for not attending Charles Parish Church [Judgments & Orders 1759-63, 437, 453, 480; 1763-5, 374, 448]. He was taxable in York County in 1784 [PPTL, 1782-1841, frame 89] and taxable in Southampton County from 1782 to 1794: taxable on a horse and 4 cattle in 1783 and 1784, taxable in Nottoway Parish on 2 horses and 2 cattle in 1787, taxable on a horse from 1790 to 1794 [PPTL

1782-92, frames 522, 587, 689, 849; 1792-1806, frames 34, 107]. He was a buyer at the sale of the Northampton County, North Carolina estate of Jesse Goodson which was recorded in September court 1798 [Gammon, *Record of Estates Northampton County*, I:96] and was head of a Northampton County household of 11 "other free" in 1800 [NC:466] and 6 in 1810 [NC:731]. His descendants were probably:

    i.   Edward, born say 1761, the son of a "free Negro" who the York County court ordered bound by the churchwardens of Yorkhampton Parish to Elizabeth Crandall to learn the trade of weaver on 21 July 1766 [Orders 1765-8, 76].

    ii.   Betty, born about 1774, registered in Southampton County on 20 October 1797: *age 23, Mullatto girl, 5 feet 3 inches free born So.ton. 20 October 1797* [Register of Free Negroes 1794-1832, no. 118].

    iii.   William, head of a Halifax County, North Carolina household of 5 "other free" in 1810 [NC:31], 2 "free colored" in 1830, and 2 in Ripley Township, Indiana, in 1840.

    iv.   John, head of a Halifax County household of 6 "free colored" in 1820 and 3 "free colored" in 1830. He was bondsman for the 28 March 1832 Halifax County marriage of Tempy **James** and Squire **Walden**. Perhaps Patsey Keemer was his widow. She applied to the Halifax County court and was granted a year's provisions from an unnamed estate on 20 November 1835 [Minutes 1832-46].

    v.   Jeremiah, married Sally **Archer**, 27 March 1820 Halifax County bond, John Scaff bondsman. He was head of a Halifax County household of 5 "free colored" in 1830.

    vi.   James², married Keziah **James**, 21 November 1817 Halifax County bond, Jeremiah Keemer bondsman.

    vii.   Eli, married Keziah **Plumly**, 6 July 1815 Northampton County, North Carolina bond, Jesse **Ash** bondsman.

KELLY FAMILY

1.   Mary Kelly, born say 1700, servant of Moses Maccubbins, confessed to the Anne Arundel County, Maryland court in June 1719 that she had a "Mallato" child by her master's "Negroe Harry." In August 1721 she confessed to having another child by Harry. She was ordered to serve seven years for each offense. Her children were bound to her master until the age of thirty-one [Judgment Record 1717-9, 380; 1720-1, 411]. She may have been the ancestor of

2   i.   John¹, born say 1750.
3   ii.   Milley, born say 1754.
       iii.   Jesse, born say 1760, a soldier in the Revolution from King William County, Virginia, who served as an apprentice to Lewis Lee [Jackson, *Virginia Negro Soldiers*, 39]. John Crittendon and Luke Cannon, officers of the 15th Virginia Regiment, recruited Jesse Kelly to serve in the army. Kelly's master, Lewis Lee won a suit against them for 35 pounds for the loss of his servant. Their King William County petition to the General Assembly of Virginia for reimbursement was rejected [http://history.uncg.edu/slaverypetitions/documentary.html, PAR# 11679201]. Jesse was taxable in Surry County, Virginia, from 1784 to 1801: taxable on a slave named Charlotte in 1788; listed as James Kee's tithable in 1794 [PPTL, 1782-90, frames 379, 477; 1791-1816, frames 112, 164, 298, 455]. He registered in Surry County as a free Negro on 11 April 1799: *a free born - mulatto man of a bright complexion...has a bushy head of hair* [Hudgins, *Register of Free Negroes*, 6].

4   iv.   Joseph¹, born say 1768.

    v.   Henry, born about 1770, a seventeen-year-old "mulatto" who ran away from someone in Hanover County, Virginia, according to the 22 March 1787 issue of the *Virginia Gazette* [Headley, *18th Century Newspapers*, 191].

2.   John¹ Kelly, born say 1750, may have been the member of the Kelly family who married the daughter of Ann **Weaver**. Ann **Weaver** was married to Thomas **Nickens** on 22 April 1778 when he mentioned his wife's granddaughter Ann **Weaver** Kelly in his Northumberland County will [RB 10:375]. John Kelly died before 1778 when Elijah **Weaver** was granted administration of his Northumberland County estate [RB 10:375; Orders 1773-83, 362, 371, 374]. John Kelly may have been the father of

    i.   Ann **Weaver** Kelly, born say 1773, mentioned in the 22 April 1778 Northumberland County will of her grandfather Thomas **Nickens** [RB 10:375], perhaps identical to Ann Kelly **Weaver** who married Aaron **Pinn**, 3 March 1794 Lancaster County bond.

3.   Milly Kelly, born say 1754, was living in Brunswick County, Virginia, on 27 May 1776 when the court ordered the churchwardens of St. Andrew's Parish to bind out her "Mulattoe" child John Kelly as an apprentice. She was probably the mother of a "Mulatto girl" named Judith Kelly who the court ordered the churchwardens of St. Andrew's Parish to bind out on 28 March 1774 [Orders 1774-82, 115; 1772-4, 512]. She was head of a Dinwiddie County household of 4 "other free" in 1810 [VA:152], perhaps identical to the Milly Kelly who was head of a Petersburg Town household of 5 "other free" in 1810 [VA:126a]. She was the mother of

    i.   ?Judith, a "Mulatto" girl ordered bound out by the churchwardens of St. Andrew's Parish, Brunswick County, on 28 March 1774. Her complaint against (her master?) Moses Quarles was dismissed by the same court [Orders 1772-4, 512, 513].

    ii.   John², born before 27 May 1776, perhaps identical to John Kelly who purchased 100 acres, tools, furniture, cattle and hogs in Halifax County, North Carolina, jointly with John **Lantern** and Moses Matthews on 30 October 1795 from John **Harmon** [DB 17:920].

    iii.   ?Edward, head of a Halifax County, North Carolina household of 2 "other free" in 1810 [NC:31].

4.   Joseph¹ Kelly, was head of a Craven County, North Carolina household of 2 "other free" in 1790 [NC:130]. He may have been the father of

    i.   Sarah, married Makey **Driggers**, 24 December 1809 Craven County bond, Joshua **Lindsey** bondsman, perhaps the same Sarah Kelly who married George² **Carter**, 8 September 1818 Craven County bond, Peter **George** bondsman.

Other members of the family in Virginia were

    i.   Elisa, head of a Westmoreland County household of 4 "other free" in 1810.

    ii.   James, head of a Stafford County household of 2 "other free" and 2 slaves in 1810 [VA:126].

    iii.   ?Joseph², married Nancy **Day**, 18 December 1812 Northumberland County bond, Stephen **Day** security.

    iv.   Mary Ann, married Willis **Banks** (persons of colour) 28 May 1821 Norfolk County bond.

KENDALL FAMILY

Members of the Kendall family in Virginia were

i.   James, head of a Stafford County household of 11 "other free" in 1810 [VA:134], a "BM" listed with "Molatto" wife Sally, daughter Sally and son Joe in 1813 [Waldrep, *1813 Tax List*].

ii.   George, taxable in Prince William County from 1796 to 1810: called a "Free Molatto" in 1799, a "yellow" man in 1806 and 1809, taxable on 3 tithes in 1809 and 1810 [PPTL, 1782-1810, frames 313, 402, 462, 643, 707, 736].

iii. Jack, born about 1772, head of a King George County household of 9 "other free" in 1810 [VA:206]. He was a "Molatto" taxable in Stafford County in 1813 [Waldrep, *1813 Tax List*]. He registered as a free Negro in Washington, D.C., on 10 June 1830: *a bright mulatto man about fifty-eight years old...Kendall's mother was born free...his father was also free...Elizabeth Kendall, John's wife...was born free* [Provine, *District of Columbia Free Negro Registers*, 178].

iv.   Anthony, taxable in Prince William County in 1800 and 1801 [PPTL, 1782-1810, frames 441, 462], head of a King George County household of 5 "other free" in 1810 [VA:206].

v.   Rachel, head of a Stafford County household of 4 "other free" in 1810 [VA:137].

KENT FAMILY

1. Priscilla Kent, born say 1740, was a white servant woman living in Carteret County in March 1759 when her "Molato Child" David was bound apprentice to James Williams until the age of thirty-one years [Minutes 1747-64, 244]. She had five illegitimate children for which she was made to serve her master a total of five additional years [Minutes 1764-77, 373, 388, 391]. Her children "born of her body by a Negro" were

i.   David, born say 1758 [Minutes 1747-64, 244].

ii.   Shadrack, born about 1760, Priscilla's four-year-old son bound to James White to be a ship carpenter in May 1764 [Minutes 1747-64, 302].

iii. Abraham, born in October 1766, a three-year-old child of Priscilla's bound to Caleb Bell in September 1770 until the age of thirty-one years [Minutes 1764-77, 388].

iv.   Anthony, born say 1770, bound an apprentice cooper to Andrew Bell in March 1775 [Minutes 1764-77, 443].

v.   Rachel, born say 1772, bound to Robert Read in March 1775 [Minutes 1764-77, 447].

KERSEY FAMILY

Two members of the Kersey family, perhaps brother and sister, were called "Negroes" in seventeenth-century Virginia county court records. They were

1   i.   Susannah, born say 1640.
2   ii.   Peter, born say 1648.

1. Susannah Carsey, born say 1640, was called "Susannah a free Negro woman" in Charles City County court on 15 September 1677 when the court rejected her petition to be exempt from paying taxes. And she was called "Negro Sue" in December 1687 when the court confirmed the indenture of her orphan-son John to Daniel Massingal. Captain Richard Nyatt certified that she had approved the indenture. In August 1689 she was called "Susan Carsey" when Massingal's executor, John Harrison, agreed in Charles City County court to

assume the remainder of the indenture that she had agreed to on behalf of her son John [Orders 1677-79, 216; 1687-95, 90, 223]. Her son was

    i.   John², born say 1670.

2. Peter¹ Kersey, born say 1645, was apparently the husband of Ann Kersey (a white woman?) who bound her son John Kersey as an apprentice to Richard Parker, brassier, in Surry County, Virginia, until the age of twenty-one on 26 January 1675/6 with her son's approval. Ann was about 30 years old on 15 June 1677 when she made a deposition in Surry County court regarding what she had heard Robert Austin say while she had been at Mr. Tompson's house [Deeds, Wills, Etc. 2, 1671-84, 102, 129]. Peter was "a Negroe" living in Surry County, Virginia, on 4 March 1678 when the court ordered him to return his son John Kersy to the estate of Judith Parker, deceased. The following year on 5 May 1679 his son John was apprenticed to William Hunt who was ordered by the court to find John Kersy sufficient apparel or return him to his father Peter Kersy [Haun, *Surry County Court Records*, III:240, 250]. He was called "Peter a Negro" when he was taxable in Thomas Sidway's household in 1683, called Peter Kersey in 1684 and 1685 when he was a taxable in Mrs. Sidway's household in Upper Sunken Marsh, and called Peter Kersey in 1686 when his son John was a taxable with him in Mrs. Sidway's household [*Magazine of Virginia Genealogy*, vol.22, no.1, 40, 46-7; vol. 23, no.2, 60]. He owed 16 pounds of tobacco to the 30 June 1694 Surry County estate of Thomas Jordan, deceased [DW 5:11]. His children were

3   i.   ?Thomas¹, born about 1665.
4   ii. John¹, born say 1668.
    iii. ?Peter², born about 1685, about seven years old in 1692 when he was bound an apprentice to William Hunt [Haun, *Surry County Court Records*, V:55]. In 1703 he was a "Negroe" tithable in William Hunt's household in the Upper Southwark Parish [DW 5:288]. He and "Betty a Malatto" were ordered to be added to the list of tithables by the petition of Jones Williams in the May 1712 session of the Surry County court [Orders 1701-13, 398]. He may have been the Peter Hersey, "an ancient free Negro," who successfully petitioned the 5 December 1753 Granville County court that he be recommended to the General Assembly as a person to be exempt from taxes [Owen, *Granville County Notes*, vol. I].

3. Thomas¹ Kersey, born say 1665, was a taxable in Benjamin Harrison's Surry County household in 1681 [*Magazine of Virginia Genealogy*, vol.22, 4:50] and appeared in Surry County court in March 1700/1 on the suit of Nathaniel Harrison who failed to appear [Haun, *Surry County Court Records*, VI:4]. He was a Chowan County taxable in 1720 in Captain Patterson's Company from Meherrin Creek to Meherrin River in the northeast corner of present-day Northampton County, North Carolina. On 2 May 1726 he purchased 200 acres on the south side of the river in what was then Bertie County [DB B:171]. His 28 October 1730 Bertie County will, proved August court 1731 by Arthur Williams, named his wife and executrix, Susanna; children; and grandchildren William Kersey and James **Reynolds** [SS Wills 1730-33, Thomas Ceorsie, N.C. Archives]. His children were

5   i.   John⁴, born say 1705.
    ii. Mary Pohagon.
    iii. Margaret **Reynolds**, born say 1710, bound her "bastard Mulatto" son, James **Reynolds**, to her father, but after the death of her father the court ordered him bound to John Boude on 16 November 1732 [Haun, *Bertie County Court Minutes*, I:79].
6   iv. Thomas², born say 1712.
    v. William¹, born say 1715, who was to receive 100 acres by his father's will after his mother's death.

  vi.   James[1], born say 1715-20, received a young mare by his father's will.
7 vii.   Peter[3], born say 1720.

4.   John[1] Kersey, born say 1668, was an apprentice to William Hunt in 1679 and
     was a taxable in Mrs. Sidway's Surry County household with his father Peter
     Kersey in Sunken Marsh in 1686. He was head of his own household in 1694
     [*Magazine of Virginia Genealogy,* vol.23, 1:60; 4:69]. He and Howell
     Edmunds proved George Briggs' will in March 1698/9 court [Haun, *Surry
     County Court Records,* V:217]. He purchased 70 acres in Surry County in
     Southwarke Parish adjoining Richard Washington and Abraham Evans on 6
     March 1693/4, and he and his wife Mary Kersey were residents of the
     adjoining county of Prince George on 25 April 1718 when they sold this land
     for 1 shilling to Richard Shock by deeds acknowledged by John Kersey in
     Surry County court [DW 4:353; DW&c 7:120; Orders 1713-18, 139]. John
     may have been the ancestor of
     i.   John[3] Carsey, born say 1696, purchased 80 acres in Surry County on
           6 August 1750 [DB 6:116]. He was exempted from paying taxes in
           Surry County on 16 March 1756 (most likely because of old age)
           [Orders 1753-57, 367].
     ii.   Hannah, whose Surry County will was recorded November 1761. She
           named her sister Mary Kersey executor. The estate was settled by
           William Kersey on 19 October 1762 [WB 10:286, 306].
     iii. George[1], born say 1720, a defendant in a 20 October 1743 Surry
           County suit for debt [Orders 1741-44, 83] and an insolvent Sussex
           County taxpayer in 1754 [*Southside Virginian* 6:48]. He, John, and
           Thomas Kersey were sued for debt in Sussex County in 1755 [Haun,
           Sussex County Court Records, I:248, 264, 309, 462, 500, 528]. He was
           listed in Captain Hardy Cone's Company of Edgecombe County Militia
           in the 1750s adjacent to Thomas Kersey [Clark, *Colonial Soldiers of
           the South,* 667].
8   iv.   Thomas[3], born say 1735.

5.   John[4] Kersey, born say 1705, was sued for trespass by Richard Sanderson in
     the March 1729 General Court of North Carolina [Saunders, *Colonial Records
     of North Carolina* VI:563]. He received 100 acres near Cashie Swamp in
     Bertie County by his father's 28 October 1730 will. He entered 100 acres
     including his improvements on Bear Swamp in Bladen County on 20 February
     1754, entered 100 acres on the east side of Drowning Creek on Bear Swamp
     on 3 May 1760 [Philbeck, *Bladen County Land Entries,* nos. 976, 1159], and
     received a patent for 100 acres on the east side of Bear Swamp in Bladen
     County on 18 November 1760 [Hoffman, *Land Patents,* I:395]. He purchased
     another 200 acres in Bladen County on the south side of Drowning Creek on
     9 November 1773 [DB 23:444]. He was taxable on one white poll and one
     black poll in Bladen County in 1763 and a "Mulato" taxable with his son Jacob
     and a slave named Brunswick in 1776 [Byrd, *Bladen County Tax Lists,* II:62,
     95; Bladen County Tax List (1763)]. He was the father of
     i.   Jacob, taxable in his father's Bladen County household in 1776. He
           was apparently a loyalist since all the land which he owned in Bladen
           County before 4 July 1776 was confiscated [DB 1:424, 433, 436].

6.   Thomas[2] Kersey, born say 1712, received a patent for 400 acres in Edgecombe
     County on 1 March 1743/4 [Saunders, *Colonial Records of North Carolina,*
     IV:677]. He sold the 100 acres of land which he inherited from his father on
     the south side of the Meherrin River in Northampton County on 29 December
     1748 [DB 1:392]. He purchased 120 acres in Edgecombe County on Sapony
     Creek adjacent to Samuel **Cannady** on 12 February 1755 and an additional
     307 acres near the Sapony Creek on 4 August 1761 [DB OO:95, 354]. On 9
     November 1764 he received a patent for 100 acres in Bladen County on the

east side of Drowning Creek, and while a resident of Bladen on 16 January 1765 he sold 400 acres of his land in Edgecombe which he received by patent on 1 March 1743/4 [Hoffman, *Land Patents*, II:521; DB C:318]. By 25 July 1774 he had acquired a total of 900 acres of land in Bladen near Drowning Creek by patents of 26 October 1767 and 25 July 1774 [Hoffman, *Land Patents*, II:167, 450, 599, 600, 666] and deed of 22 March 1770 [DB 23:67]. While a resident of Bladen on 5 October 1774 he sold another 120 acres of his land in Edgecombe County [DB 2:181]. He was witness to a 1769 Bladen County deed from James Oberry for land which was part of 640 acres that had belonged to Henry Oberry [DB 23:503]. He was a "Molato" taxable with Jesse Moss in Bladen County in 1768 and a white taxable with slaves Dick and Quac(?) in 1772. He was taxable on two "Molatoes" (himself and William **Horn**) and two slaves (Dick and Quash) in 1776 [Byrd, *Bladen County Tax Lists*, I:9, 71, 83, 124, 135; II:66, 76]. He died before May court 1778 when administration on his Bladen County estate was granted William Truman and Benjamin Odom [*NCGSJ* XIII:224]. Perhaps his wife was Mary Kersey who received a Bladen County grant for 200 acres on the west side of Drowning Creek south of Ash Pole Swamp on 12 November 1779 [DB 37:287] and was taxable on 400 acres in Bladen County in 1784. She sold 200 acres of this land to America Kersey on 10 May 1788 [DB C:370]. She was head of a Bladen County household of one white male under 21 or over 60 and two white females in 1786 [Byrd, *Bladen County Tax Lists*, II:184]. Administration on her estate was granted David Braswell in Robeson County court on 3 July 1799 on a bond of 100 pounds [Minutes I:78]. Thomas' children may have been

i. Ester Cairsey who was listed as a harborer of the "free Negors and Mullatus" who were living in what was then Bladen County on 13 October 1773 [G.A. 1773, Box 7].

ii. Sarah/Sally, born say 1750, supposed to have married Thomas **Lowry** in Franklin County before 1769 when **Lowry** moved to Robeson County. She was said to have been a "half-breed Tuscarora Indian woman" [Blu, *The Lowrie History*, 5].

iii. Thomas[4], a taxable "Molato" in Bladen County from 1768 to 1774 (called Thomas Cairsey, Junr.) [Byrd, *Bladen County Tax Lists*, I:4, 61, 81, 135].

iv. William[2], born say 1760, head of a Robeson County household of 4 "other free" in 1790 [NC:50]. He entered 50 acres on the west side of Peter's Swamp in Robeson County on 28 October 1789 [Pruitt, *Land Entries: Robeson County*, I:29] and purchased land in Robeson by deed proved on 6 January 1806 [Minutes I:348].

v. George[2], born before 1776, head of a Robeson County household of 5 "free colored" in 1820 [NC:310].

vi. Elizabeth, head of a Robeson County household of 3 "other free" in 1790 [NC:50] and 3 in 1800 [NC:388].

vii. James[2], born about 1764 according to the 1782 Militia Returns for Bladen County [*The North Carolinian* VI:751]. He entered 100 acres in Robeson County including his spring on 20 April 1787 [Pruitt, *Land Entries: Robeson County*, I:3]. On 11 September 1792 while a resident of Robeson County he sold 200 acres of land on the south side of Sapony Creek which had been owned by Thomas Kersey [Nash DB 6:118]. He was living alone in Robeson County, counted as white in 1790 [NC:48] and "other free" in 1800 [NC:388]. He purchased land in Robeson by deed proved 8 January 1799 and 26 February 1810 [Minutes I:58, 192]. He sold 108 acres in Robeson on the southeast side of the head of Jacob Swamp to Ninty Kersey on 21 August 1818 [DB S:38]. On 24 February 1834 he made a declaration in Robeson County court to obtain a pension for his services in the Revolution. He stated that he was born in 1762, volunteered in a company of militia on

1 August 1782 in what was then Bladen County in the town of Elizabeth. He marched to Charleston, South Carolina, to James Island, and received his discharge in Wilmington on 1 August 1783. He was never in any engagement "but once which was with a body of negroes above Charleston at a place called as he thinks the Quarter House." He was inscribed in the Roll of North Carolina on 4 March 1831 [M804-1477, S-8788].

viii.   Solomon, who purchased 200 acres in Bladen County adjoining John Rowland on 29 March 1785 [DB 25:240 & 1:299]. He was living alone in Robeson County, counted as white in 1790 [NC:49] and "other free" in 1800 [NC:388]. He sold land in Robeson by deed proved on 9 January 1799 [Minutes I:61].

ix.   Job, head of a Robeson County household of 4 "other free" and one white woman in Bladen County in 1800 and 5 "free colored" and one white woman in 1820 [NC:154].

x.   Abraham, head of a Liberty County, South Carolina household of 7 "other free" in 1800 [SC:785].

7.   Peter³ Kersey, born say 1720, received a mare by the 28 October 1730 Bertie County will of his father Thomas¹ Kersey. He was taxable on one "white" tithe in Bladen County in 1763 and a "Molato taxable with his son David from 1768 to 1772 [Byrd, *Bladen County Tax Lists*, I:8, 44, 79]. He received a patent for 100 acres on the northwest side of Drowning Creek on 16 December 1769 and sold this land on 19 November 1779 for 500 pounds [Hoffman, *Land Patents*, II:167; DB 37:185]. He was taxable on 150 acres and one poll in Captain Regan's district of Bladen County in 1784 and was head of a Robeson County household of 7 "other free" in 1790 [NC:50]. He was the father of

i.   David, born say 1750, a "Molato" taxable in Bladen County from 1768 to 1772.

ii.   ?Redding, a "Mix Blood" taxable in Jacob **Locklear**'s Bladen County household in 1774 [Byrd, *Bladen County Tax Lists*, I:135]. He entered 50 acres between Drowning Creek and Gum Swamp in Bladen County on 20 January 1789 [Pruitt, *Robeson County Land Entries, 1787-1795*, 21]. He was head of a Robeson County household of one white man in 1790 [NC:48].

8.   Thomas³ Kersey, born say 1735, received a patent for 104 acres in Sussex County on the southside of the Nottoway River and the fork of Ploughman Swamp on 16 August 1756 [*Magazine of Virginia Genealogy* 32:178 (Patents 33:302)] and sold this land on 6 January 1759 [DB A:349]. He purchased 175 acres in Southampton County on the north side of Three Creeks adjoining Thomas Wiggins and McLemore on 13 April 1760 [DB 2:357-8] and sold property by deed proved in Southampton County court on 12 April 1781 [Orders 1778-84, 149]. He may have been the father of

9   i.   William³, born about 1761.
10   ii.   Agatha, born say 1762.

iii.   Thomas⁵, born before 1767, taxable in Southampton County from 1787 to 1790, taxable in 1807 [PPTL 1782-1792, frames 641, 664, 713, 763; 1807-21, frame 70] and head of a Southampton County household of 5 "other free" in 1810 [VA:71].

iv.   Walden, born before 1767, taxable in St. Luke's Parish, Southampton County, from 1787 to 1795 [PPTL 1782-92, frames 641, 664, 713, 763, 878; 1792-1806, frames 56, 84, 164]. The Southampton County court fined him 500 pounds of tobacco on 14 August 1789 [Minutes 1786-90]. His house in Southampton County was mentioned in the 3 April 1793 Southampton County will of John Claud [WB 4:608]. He was taxable in Smith Creek District, Warren County, North Carolina, in 1801 [Tax List 1781-1801, 419], taxable in Mecklenburg County,

Virginia, in 1806 and 1807, and a "Mulatto" taxable in Mecklenburg County in 1818 and 1820 [PPTL 1806-28, 39, 66, 167, 656, 705]. He married Betsey **Hawley**, 1817 Granville County, North Carolina bond.

v. Willis, taxable in Southampton County in 1792, taxable in James Caulthorpe's household in 1793, taxable in his own household on a horse in 1794 and 1795 [PPTL 1782-92, frame 878; 1792-1806, frames 49, 84, 164].

vi. Delilah, born say 1778, married Cordall **Reed**, 19 November 1798 Southampton County bond, James **Sweat** surety.

vii. Loudoun, taxable in St. Luke's Parish, Southampton County, from 1801 to 1811, called a "M"(ulatto) in 1806 [PPTL 1792-1806, frames 512, 550, 688, 839; 1807-21, frames 47, 70, 189].

9. William[3] Kersey, born about 1761, was presented by the Southampton County court on 11 May 1780 for concealing a tithable [Orders 1778-84, 111]. He was taxable in Southampton County on a horse in 1782, taxable in John Claud's household in 1784, taxable from 1787 to 1792, charged with Willis Kersey's tithe in 1790 and 1791 but not listed as a tithable himself in 1791, taxable on his own tithe and a horse from 1793 to 1797, a "M"(ulatto) taxable in 1806 and 1807 [PPTL 1782-92, frames 504, 545, 641, 713, 820, 878; 1792-1806, frames 56, 164, 194, 267]. He was taxable in the Mecklenburg County, Virginia household of John **Chavis Walden** in 1786 [Personal Tax List, frame 149]. He married Polly **Evans**, 23 December 1786 Mecklenburg County bond, Kinchen **Chavous** surety. She was mentioned in the 22 May 1787 Mecklenburg County, Virginia will of her father Thomas **Evans**, Senior [WB 2:250]. He purchased 150 acres in Mecklenburg County on the Warren County line in 1804 and was taxable on 184 acres in 1813 and 274 acres in 1820 with the initials "C.S." after his name [Land Tax List 1782-1811A, 1811B-1824A]. He was head of a Warren County household of a white male over 16, two under 16, and three white females in 1790 (called William Corsey) [NC:76], 10 "other free" in 1800 [NC:814], 11 in 1810 [NC:765], and 7 "free colored" in 1820 [NC:798]. His 26 June 1829 Warren County will was proved in August 1836 (called William Cursey). He was called William Carsey in his pension application in which he stated that he was born in Southampton County in 1761, lived there and in Bute County, North Carolina, during the war, and married Polly **Evans** in Mecklenburg County in 1786. He died 26 June 1836 and his widow Mary died 14 September 1840. His children were named in his will, pension file, and in a Mecklenburg County chancery case [M804-481; Chancery suit 1841-010, LVA; Estate file CR 100.508.30, N.C. Archives]. He was the father of

i. Thomas[6], born about 1785, married Sally **Kersey**, 22 December 1813 Mecklenburg County bond, surety Hardaway **Drew**. He was sixty-five years old and Sally was fifty-five when they were counted in the 1850 Mecklenburg County census [VA:90].

ii. Elizabeth Carsey, born say 1787, married John **Chavous**, 6 July 1803 Warren County bond, Hutchings **Mayo** bondsman. John was head of a Carroll County, Tennessee household of 14 "free colored" in 1830. Elizabeth received land in Carroll County by her father's will.

iii. Peggy, born say 1790.

iv. Sally, born about 1798, married John **Stewart**.

v. Nancy, born say 1799, married Anderson **Drew**.

vi. Babby, married Martin **Anderson**.

vii. William H., born say 1800, married Margaret **Ivey**, 5 December 1822 Mecklenburg County bond. He was probably the Hill Kearsey who married Martha **Stewart**, 20 December 1821 Warren County bond, William Kearsey bondsman.

viii. Edmund, born say 1805.

10. Agatha Kersey, born say 1762, received a plantation of 150 acres by the 31 January 1791 Southampton County will of James Calthorpe, proved 12 December the same year and witnessed by John Claud. The land and money from the sale of his four slaves were to be used to raise and school three children: Mary Black, Agatha's son Joshua Cursey, and the child Agatha was pregnant with. If Agatha died or married, Mary Black was to have the land and Agatha's children were to have the plantation utilities [WB 4:600]. Agatha was taxable in St. Luke's Parish, Southampton County, on 3 free male tithables and a horse in 1794, 2 male tithables in 1796, taxable on a horse in 1803 and 1804, a free male tithable from 1807 to 1811, was a "M"(ulatto) taxable on a horse in 1813, and was living with her son Miles in 1814 [PPTL 1792-1806, frames 84, 196, 321, 384, 619, 688; 1807-21, frames 70, 167, 189, 321, 415]. She was head of a Southampton County, Virginia household of 6 "other free" in 1810 [VA:71]. She was the mother of

   i.   Joshua, born say 1784, named in the 31 January 1791 Southampton County will of James Calthorpe. The court appointed Joel McClemonds as his guardian on 12 July 1800 [Minutes 1799-1803, 103]. He was a "M"(ulatto) taxable in Southampton County from 1812 to 1814 [PPTL 1807-21, frames 288, 321, 415].

   ii. Miles, born say 1791, married Nancy **Bass**, 12 November 1810 Southampton County bond, Cordall **Reed** surety. He was taxable in Southampton County from 1802 to 1815: called a "Mulatto" from 1801 to 1806, taxable with his wife Viney **Bass** on Littleton Mason's land in 1812, living on land owned by his "Mother Aggy" in 1814 and 1815 [PPTL 1792-1806, frames 511, 549, 618, 687, 802, 838; 1807-21, frames 70, 166, 288, 415, 440].

KEYTON FAMILY

1. William[1] Keyton, born say 1716, was a "Mulatto Man" presented by the Westmoreland County, Virginia court on 26 May 1741 for cohabiting with a white woman named Sarah Heath and having several children by her. He was probably the brother of Bridget Keyton who was presented two months later on 29 July for cohabiting with Aaron Rose and having several children by him [Orders 1739-43, 99a, 114a].

KING FAMILY

1. Mary King, born say 1722, was presented by the Prince George's County, Maryland court on 22 March 1742/3 for having an illegitimate child on information of the constable for King George Hundred. She was not found by the sheriff, so the case was struck off the docket on 27 November 1744. She may have been the mother of Margaret King, a four-month-old child who the Prince George's County court sold to William Cheshire on 23 November 1742 until the age of thirty-one. (She was called Mary King in the court record and Margaret King in the index) [Court Record 1742-3, 215, 340, 612]. She may have been the ancestor of members of the King family who were counted in the 1810 census for nearby Prince William County, Virginia:

   i.   Samuel, head of a Prince William County household of 5 "other free" and 4 slaves in 1810 [VA:513].

   ii. Sarah, head of a Prince William County household of 4 "other free" in 1810 [VA:518].

Other members of the King family in Virginia were

1 i.   Francis, born say 1752.
2 ii.   Samuel, born say 1755.
   iii. Ann, born say 1760, a "mulatto" taxable on one free male tithable in Gloucester County in 1803 [PPTL, 1800-20].

  iv. Milly, head of a Petersburg household of 9 "other free" in 1810 [VA:123a].

  v. George, head of a Charles City County household of 2 "other free" in 1810 [VA:939]. On 1 June 1808 the Charles City County court bound William King to him as an apprentice cooper [WB 2:27].

  vi. Mason, born about 1784, registered in Petersburg on 31 May 1808: *a dark brown Negro woman, five feet two inches high, twenty four years old, born free & raised in the County of Prince George* [Register of Free Negroes 1794-1819, no. 422]. She was head of a Petersburg household of 2 "other free" in 1810 [VA:123a].

  vii. Susannah, born about 1785, registered in Petersburg on 16 January 1809: *a dark brown Negroe woman, five feet five and a half inches high, twenty three, strait made, born free & raised in the County of Prince George* [Register of Free Negroes 1794-1819, no. 454].

  viii. Edy, born about 1786, registered in Petersburg on 25 March 1809: *a dark brown, near black Negro woman, five feet one and half inches high, twenty three years old, born free & raised in the County of Prince George* [Register of Free Negroes 1794-1819, no. 459].

  ix. Anna, born about 1787, registered in Petersburg on 31 May 1808: *a very dark brown, near black Negro woman, five feet five inches high, straight made, twenty one years old, born free & raised in the County of Prince George* [Register of Free Negroes 1794-1819, no. 423].

  x. Polly, born about 1788, registered in Petersburg on 31 May 1808: *a dark brown Negro woman, five feet six inches high, twenty years old, straight made, born free & raised in the County of Prince George* [Register of Free Negroes 1794-1819, no. 424]. She was head of a Petersburg household of 2 "other free" and a slave in 1810 [VA:122b].

1. Francis King, born say 1752, was head of an Abingdon Parish, Gloucester County household of 7 free persons in 1784 [VA:68]. He was taxable in Gloucester County from 1783 to 1812: taxable on a slave, 4 horses and 8 cattle in 1783; taxable in Ware Parish in 1785; taxable on a horse and 5 cattle but his personal tax paid by Thomas Lewis in 1788; taxable on his own tithe and a horse in 1789, taxable on his own tithe in 1799 and 1800, a "mulatto" taxable in 1801 [PPTL, 1782-1799; 1800-20]. He was the father of

  i. John, born about 1771, registered in Petersburg on 11 September 1800: *a dark brown Mulatto man, five feet four inches high, twenty nine years old, born free & raised in Gloster County* [Register of Free Negroes 1794-1819, no. 206]. He was head of a Gloucester County household of 6 "other free" in 1810 [VA:407A]. He was called the "mulattoe son of Francis King" when he was taxable in Gloucester County in 1813 [PPTL, 1800-20].

  ii. ?Ellick, a "mulattoe" taxable in Gloucester County in 1813 [PPTL, 1800-20].

  iii. ?Sally, a "mul°" living at Robert **Meggs**' in Gloucester County in 1813 [PPTL, 1800-20].

  iv. ?Ruth, a "mul°" living at Robert **Meggs**' in Gloucester County 1813 [PPTL, 1800-20].

2. Samuel King, born say 1755, was head of a Petsworth Parish, Gloucester County household of 1 free person in 1783 [VA:53] and was taxable in Gloucester County from 1785 to 1799: taxable in Petsworth Parish on 2 cattle in 1785, taxable on a horse and 3 cattle in 1786, and taxable on a horse in 1797 [PPTL, 1782-99]. He was head of a Gloucester County household of 9 "other free" in 1810 [VA:407A]. He and his unnamed wife were "mulattoes" living at Hill Neck in Gloucester County in 1813 [PPTL, 1800-20]. He may have been the father of

     i.   Isaac, born say 1777, listed himself as a tithable the same day as Samuel King in Gloucester County in 1798 [PPTL, 1782-99].

    ii.   Lewis, born about 1778, a "mulattoe" bricklayer taxable in Gloucester County from 1804 to 1813 [PPTL, 1800-20]. He obtained free papers in Gloucester County in February 1827 and registered in York County on 6 June 1832: *a free tawney coloured man about forty nine years of age, five feet four and a half inches high...born free...appears from the above is about fifty four years of age* [Free Negroes Register 1831-50, no.338].

   iii. Ruth, a "mul°" living at "H.N." in Gloucester County in 1813 [PPTL, 1800-20].

   iv. Fanny, Sr., a "mul°" living on Matthew Kemp's land in Gloucester County in 1813 [PPTL, 1800-20].

    v.   Catey, a "mul°" living on Matthew Kemp's land in Gloucester County in 1813 [PPTL, 1800-20].

   vi. Martha, a "mul°" living on Matthew Kemp's land in Gloucester County in 1813 [PPTL, 1800-20].

KENNEY/ KINNEY FAMILY

The Kinney family were slaves of the Johnson family of Amelia and Louisa counties in 1798 when they won their freedom based on testimony from William Denton that they descended from an Indian woman named Joan Kenny who was an elderly woman in 1729 and came from the Indian Town on Pamunkey [LVA, Albemarle County Free Negro Papers, April 1798]. Patrick Belches named members of the family in his 29 December 1763 will which was proved in Louisa County on 10 April 1764: *to my wife Judy Belshches all my land in Louisa and following Negroes to wit Cuffy, Cupid, Sue, Sarah, Lewis, Liddy, Dilse, Phillis (at present in Spotsylvania) also Nell and her three children Jane, Lucy and Moll also Anna a daughter of Beck Kinny's also two old Negroes named Harry and Judy-- these last mentioned seven Negroes being in Louisa...also following Negroes to wit Indian Ben and wife Beck Kinney and their son Thom, also Moses Hoomes for the time he has to serve...unto my Daughter Margaret after my wife's decease the following slaves to wit Indian Ben and his wife Beck Kinny and her increase and their son Thom and old Jane...to my daughter Mary, Robin and Rachell children of Beck Kinny's* [WB 1:59-62]. Other members of the family born during the colonial period were

    i.   Isaac[1], born say 1745, an outlawed "Mulatto Fellow" who belonged to the estate of Colonel Richard Johnson on 20 July 1772 when he ran away. W. Johnson placed an ad in the 10 September 1772 issue of the *Virginia Gazette* offering 20 pounds to anyone who would kill him or 3 pounds for his capture. The ad described Isaac as: *Height five Feet nine or ten Inches, wears his own Hair, which is remarkably black, and curls well.* The ad went on to say that it was supposed he was harboured by Colonel John Snelson's Negroes, near this Place, among whom he has a Wife, or by his Brother, John Kenney, a Mulatto Slave belonging to Mr. Thomas Johnson of Louisa [Windley, *Runaway Slave Advertisements* 1:120].

    ii.   John[1] Kenney, brother of Isaac, a "Mulatto" slave who belonged to Thomas Johnson of Amelia County on 20 July 1772, perhaps identical to John Kenney, "Free Negro" taxable in St. Paul's Parish, Hanover County, on 3 slaves and 2 horses in 1803 [Cocke, *Hanover County Taxables*, 74].

   iii. Littleberry Mkinny, a "yellow" complexioned man from Louisa County who enlisted in the Revolution [NSDAR, *African American Patriots*, 151].

1   iv. ____ (torn), born say 1765.

2   v.   Amy, born say 1770.

3   vi.   Betsey, born say 1770.

     vii.   Wilson, born say 1772, a "free Mulatto" shoemaker living on Eppa Fielding's land in Louisa County about 1802 [Abercrombie, *Free Blacks of Louisa County*, 20]. He may have been identical to slave Wilson who was taxable in the Louisa County household of Thomas Johnson (Minor) from 1782 to 1786 [PPTL, 1782-1814].

1.   _____ (torn) Kenny, was a "free Mulatto" tailoress living with (her brother?) Wilson in Louisa County with her four children John, Betsey, Jane and Phillis about 1802 [Abercrombie, *Free Blacks of Louisa County*, 20]. She was the mother of

     i.   John[3].

     ii.   Betsy.

     iii.   Jane, born about 1779, registered in Louisa County on 9 July 1849: *a woman of colour who was born free, 5'4-1/2" high, believed to be 70 years old...dark copper colour* [Abercrombie, *Free Blacks of Louisa County*, 75].

     iv.   Phillis, born about 1791, registered in Louisa County on 5 September 1831: *a free woman of colour, about 40 years old...rather yellowish complexion.* Her son William (born about 1805) registered on 29 May 1826: *son of Phillis Kinney who was born free, bright mulatto, 5'4-1/2" high, hair inclined to be straight* [Abercrombie, *Free Blacks of Louisa County*, 37].

2.   Amy Kenny, born say 1770, was counted in a list of "free Mulattoes" at "Captain Johnson's old place" in Louisa County about 1802 with her children Sally, James, Daniel, Mary and Lucy [Abercrombie, *Free Blacks of Louisa County*, 20]. She was the mother of

     i.   Sally.

     ii.   James.

     iii.   Daniel.

     iv.   Mary.

     v.   Lucy.

     vi.   John[4], born about 1802, registered in Louisa County on 13 August 1827: *son of Amy Kinney a man of colour who was born free, dark complexion* [Abercrombie, *Free Blacks of Louisa County*, 32].

     vii.   David[2], registered in Louisa County on 10 January 1831: *son of Amey Kinney who was born free, dark complected about 5'6" high* [Abercrombie, *Free Blacks of Louisa County*, 36].

     viii.   Isaac[3], born about 1805, registered on 14 September 1829: *son of Amey Kinney born free, dark complexion about 5'9-3/4" high, 24 years old* [Abercrombie, *Free Blacks of Louisa County*, 34].

3.   Betsey Kinney, born say 1770, was called the housemaid of Thomas Johnson (minor) in his 13 March 1795 Louisa County will, proved 14 September 1795, by which he set her and her youngest daughter Rebecca free. He also gave Rebecca a slave named "Nancy's child Nanny." And he allowed Betty the use of 50 acres of land during her lifetime, a horse, two cows, four sheep, two sows and pigs and eight pounds annually [WB 3:605; Abercrombie, *Free Blacks of Louisa County*, 130-2]. She was living with (her brother?) Wilson in Louisa County with her two unnamed children about 1802 [Abercrombie, *Free Blacks of Louisa County*, 20]. She was the mother of

     i.   Jane, born about 1789, registered in Louisa County on 8 February 1839: *(daughter of Betsey Kinney) who was free born, darkish complexion about 50 years of age, about 5'3-1/2" high, lame in left leg which occasions a hopping in walking* [Abercrombie, *Free Blacks of Louisa County*, 56].

     ii.   Rebecca, set free in 1795.

Other members of the Kinney family were

4   i.   Milly, born about 1777.
   ii.   Isaac[2], born about 1784, counted as a "free Mulatto" blacksmith living with Cob at the Green Springs in Louisa County about 1802, registered there on 25 June 1817: *a free man of colour, born in sd. county, 33 years old, 5'6" high, rather light complexion* [Abercrombie, *Free Blacks of Louisa County*, 20, 24].
   iii.   Abraham, a free male taxable in Louisa County from 1795 to 1813 when he was included in a "List of Free Negroes & Mulattoes." He may have been identical to slave Abram who was taxable in Thomas Johnson (Minor)'s Louisa County household in 1782 [PPTL, 1782-1814]. He was a "free Mulatto" living near Trinity Church in Louisa County about 1802 [Abercrombie, *Free Blacks of Louisa County*, 20]. He made a deed of trust on 11 March 1817 for a horse, cart, two cows, a bed and all his property as payment for $150 lent to him by William C. **Ailstock** [DB N:192].
   iv.   Benjamin, a "F.N." taxable in Isle of Wight County from 1792 to 1800 [PPTL 1782-1810, frames 248, 337, 478].
   v.   David[1], born about 1794 in Fredericksville Parish, lived with William Morris at the Green Springs in Louisa County about 1802, registered in Louisa County on 30 December 1817: *bright mulatto, 23 years of age, 5'10" high* [Abercrombie, *Free Blacks of Louisa County*, 24, 28].
   vi.   John[2], a "free Mulatto" living with William B. Graves in Louisa County about 1802 [Abercrombie, *Free Blacks of Louisa County*, 20].

4. Milly Kinney, born about 1777, registered as a "free Negro" in Augusta County on 26 February 1822: *a dark coloured negroe...aged about Forty five years...Born free.* She also registered her children the same day. They were
   i.   Elizabeth, born about 1799, "black complexion."
   ii.   Jane, born about 1802, "dark complexion."
   iii. Sally, born about 1804, "yellow complexion."
   iv.   Mary, born about 1807, "dark complexion."
   v.   William, born about 1010, "dark complexion".
   vi.   Macy, born about 1813, "dark complexion."
   vii. Esther, born about 1815, "yellow complexion" [Register of Augusta County, no. 38, http://jefferson.village.virginia.edu/vshadow2/].

KNIGHT FAMILY

1. William[1] Knight, born say 1710, received a patent for 320 acres in Bertie County on 29 March 1743/4 [Saunders, *Colonial Records of North Carolina*, IV:632]. He purchased two tracts of land in Bertie County on 20 February 1746/7, one for 50 acres and the other for 350 acres on the north side of Potecasi Creek and land of Thomas Bonners. He sold 125 acres of this land on the same day to William Conner and made further sales of 100 acres on 7 August 1747 and 140 acres on 5 August 1749 [DB G:18, 19, 45, 204]. William Conner was taxed in his household in 1751 [CCR 190]. His 3 December 1751 Bertie County will was proved in February 1752. He mentioned his wife Martha, three of his children, and other unnamed children. Martha was taxed on one tithe in the 1753 list [CCR 190]. His children were
   i.   John.
   ii.   William[2], born say 1735, taxed on 1 tithe in Bertie County in 1753 and 9 tithes in 1754 [CCR 190]. He was a taxable "free Mulatto Male" in the 1761 list of William Gray and was in Henry Wood's household in an untitled 1765 fragment [CR 10.702.1]. Perhaps he was the William Knight who was taxed in Hertford County in 1779 on 165 acres and 5 slaves in district 2 [GA 30.1] and was head of a Hertford County household of 5 whites and 2 slaves in 1790 [NC:25].

iii. Nehemiah.
iv. ?James, a taxable "free Mulatto Male" in the 1761 Bertie Summary list.

2. Benjamin Knight, born say 1740, was listed in the muster roll of Colonel Richard Richardson's Battalion of South Carolina Militia in the 1759 Cherokee Expedition from 18 October 1759 to 10 January 1760 [Clark, *Colonial Soldiers of the South*, 898]. He was called Ben Night, "Mulatto," head of a 96 District, South Carolina household of 1 "other free" in 1790. Perhaps his children were
    i.   Dick, "Mulatto" head of a Cheraw District household of 7 "other free" in 1790 [SC:49] and a Chesterfield County, South Carolina household of 1 "other free" in 1800 [SC:103] and 15 in 1810 [SC:557].
    ii. Alexander, head of a Chesterfield County household of 9 "other free" in 1800 [SC:103].
    iii. Moses, born say 1760, a man of color who served in the Revolution from South Carolina [National Archives file W10182 cited by NSDAR, *African American Patriots*, 182].

3. George Night, born say 1745, was a taxable "mulatto" in Richard **Acock**'s household in Daniel Harris' list for Baptist District, Granville County, in 1761 [CR 44.701.1]. He was probably the husband of Martha **Acock** who was mentioned in Richard **Acock**'s 5 May 1788 Warren County will [WB 5:99].

Another member of the Knight family was
    i.   Lotty, head of a Gates County household of 7 "free colored" in 1820 [NC:161], perhaps the mother of Mary Knight who married Smith **Cuff**, 24 October 1799 Gates County bond.

LAMB FAMILY

1. Mary Lamb, born say 1705, was granted land in Bladen County in 1735 and entered 100 acres in Bladen County on Hogg Swamp, including the place she was then living, on 17 March 1756 [DB 1:288; Philbeck, *Bladen County Land Entries, 1743-61*, #254]. Her 11 November 1769 Bladen County will named the following legatees: Jacob Lamb, Isaac Lamb, Thomas Clark, Hardy Inman, Joshua Lamb, Rachel Davis, and Patience **Carter**. Jacob and Isaac Lamb were executors. Needham Lamb was a witness [Campbell, *Bladen County Abstracts of Wills*, 47]. She was probably the mother of
    i.   Jacob.
2   ii. Isaac, born say 1725.
    iii. Joshua.
    iv. Patience **Carter**.

2. Isaac Lamb, born say 1725, entered 250 acres on the north side of Hogg Swamp in Bladen County on 16 Mary 1754 [Philbeck, *Bladen County Land Entries, 1743-61*, #1004]. He was a Bladen County taxable in 1763. On 1 August 1770 he purchased 130 acres on Hogg Swamp which had been granted to Abram Lamb on 26 November 1757 and sold this land on 6 March 1775. And on 6 March 1775 he sold 130 acres on Hogg Swamp which had been granted to Abram Lamb on 26 November 1757 and conveyed to Isaac on 20 October 1758. He sold 200 acres on Old Field Swamp northeast of Tadpole on 26 April 1775 [DB 23:478, 520]. He was a taxable "Mulato" in Bladen County in 1768 (with his son Needham), in 1770 (with his son Needham and a white man named Shadrack Huit), in 1772 (with sons Needham and Ephraim), and taxable on 3 polls in 1774 [Byrd, *Bladen County Tax Lists*, I:7, 35, 111, 130]. He was living in South Carolina on 3 April 1786 when he sold 100 acres on the south side of Drowning Creek which was land he had been granted on 1 October 1758, and the same day he sold another 100 acres on the

west side of Drowning Creek on Hog Swamp which had been granted to Mary Lamb in 1735 [DB 1:132]. He was the father of

    i.   ?Arthur, born say 1745, taxable in Thomas Odam's Bladen County household in 1763, a "Mulato" taxable in Bladen County from 1768 to 1774, taxable with Meedy (Needham?) Lamb in 1776, and taxable on one male from 21 to 60 years old, two males under 21 or over 60, and seven females in 1786 [Byrd, *Bladen County Tax Lists*, I:4, 15, 35, 81, 111, 130; II:68, 84, 182]. He was counted as white in Robeson County in 1790, head of a household two males over 16 and five females [NC:49], and was counted as "other free" in Robeson County in 1800, head of a household of 5 persons [NC:389a].

    ii. Needham, born say 1748, taxable in his father's Bladen County household from 1768 to 1774, perhaps identical to Meedy Lamb who was living in the household of (his brother?) Arthur Lamb in 1776. Meedy was counted in the 1786 state census with one male 21 to 60 years old, two males under 21 or over 60, and five females [Byrd, *Bladen County Tax Lists*, I:7, 35, 111, 130; II:68, 185]. He was counted as white in Robeson County in 1790, head of a household of one male over 16, two under 16, and six females [NC:49]. He entered 100 acres in Robeson County in the fork of Big and Little Hog Swamp on 6 September 1787 [Pruitt, *Robeson County Land Entries, 1787-1795*, 7].

    iii. ?Barnabas, taxable in Bladen County in Thomas Odam's household in 1772 [Byrd, *Bladen County Tax Lists*, II:I:78]. He was counted as white in Robeson County in 1790, head of a household of one male over 16 and one female [NC:49], and counted as "other free" in Robeson County in 1810, head of a household of 7 persons [NC:155].

    iv. Ephraim, born say 1760, taxable in his father's Bladen County household in 1772.

Other members of the Lamb family in North Carolina and Virginia were

    i.   Stephney, born say 1743, "free negro" head of a Norfolk County, Virginia household in 1766.

    ii. Peggy, born say 1745, taxable head of a Norfolk County household in 1766 [Wingo, *Norfolk County Tithables 1766-80*, 8].

    iii. Lemon /Lamentation, called Lemon Land in 1790 when he was head of Northampton County, North Carolina household of 6 "other free" and 1 white woman [NC:72], called Lamentation Land in 1800 when he was head of a Northampton County household of 8 "other free" [NC:459], called Lemuel Land in 1810, head of a Halifax County household of 6 "other free" [NC:32] and called Lemon Lamb in 1820, head of a Halifax County household of 5 "free colored" [NC:156].

    iv. Rachel, born after 1794, head of a Gates County, North Carolina household of 1 "free colored" in 1820 [NC:161].

LANDUM/ LANDRUM FAMILY

1.   Jane **Driggers**, born in 1644, was one year old on 27 May 1645 when Emmanuel **Driggers** bound her to Captain Francis Pott to serve him until the age of thirty-one. On 24 May 1652 when she was eight years old, **Driggers** paid Captain Pott for her freedom [DW 1651-54, 82]. In 1663 she had an illegitimate daughter, Sarah **Landum**, by an Irish freeman, Dennam Olandum [Orders 1657-64, fol.179]. Jane married first, John **Gussal**, about 1665. He died shortly afterwards and in April 1666 she was charged in court with failing to prove his will. She had married William **Harman** by June 1666 when he submitted letters of administration on her first husband's estate [Orders 1664-7, fol.24, p.24]. Dennam and Jane's child was

2   i.   Sarah, born about 1663.

2. Sarah Landum/ Landrum, born about 1663, was living in Northampton County in 1689 (called Sarah Landrun) when she and (her aunt) Sarah **Driggers**, "free Negroes," were given twenty-five lashes on their bare backs for stealing some yarn from "a free Negro woman commonly called Black Nanny" [Orders 1679-89, 463]. A suit brought against her (called Sarah Landman, alias Driggus Negro") by Honorable John Custis, Esq., was dismissed by the Northampton County court on 29 December 1702 because he was not ready to prosecute. Frances **Driggers** and Samuel **George** were her witnesses. She was probably the mother of Thomas Landum, a one-year-old "Negro" bound to Richard Jacob in Northampton County in 1710 [OW&c 1698-1710, 123, 182-3, 504]. Her son was most likely

    i.   Thomas Landman, born about 1709, tithable in John **Driggers'** Northampton County household in 1729 [L.P. 1729].

LANG FAMILY

1. Elizabeth[1] Lang, born say 1653, was presented by the Accomack County court in 1671 for having an illegitimate child by an Indian named Kitt. Her child was bound as an apprentice to William Custis until the age of twenty-four, and she was ordered to serve an additional three years. She petitioned the court:

> *that the Indyan may not have the bringing up of my child, nor anything to doe with itt...It being the humble desire of your petitioner that a pagan may not have my child* [Deal, *Race and Class*, 54-5].

Her child was apparently the parent of

2   i.   Elizabeth[2], born say 1705.

2. Elizabeth[2] Lang, born say 1705, was presented by the grand jury of Northampton County, Virginia, for fornication on 11 May 1725. In February 1726/7 she complained to the court that her master Thomas Dell, a minister, was not supplying her with sufficient apparel. He called her "an Indian servant bought the last of Oct." when he replied that she tore her clothes when "she went romping with Negroes." On 12 September 1727 Dell proved to the court that she had absented herself from his service for sixty-seven days and asked that she be listed as a tithable in his household [Orders 1722-9, 181, 252, 295; Mihalyka, *Loose Papers 1628-1731*, 101, 140, 141]. On 12 February 1729/30 she acknowledged an indenture binding herself to John Satchell for three years and seven months from 11 April 1729 [Orders 1729-32, 8]. Her children were most likely

3   i.   Rachel, born say 1724.
    ii. Daniel, born say 1726, bound apprentice by the Northampton County court to John Floyd on 13 September 1732 to learn the trade of weaver [Orders 1732-42, 23].

3. Rachel Lang, born say 1724, was the mother of Jacob Lang, a six-year-old "Negro" boy who was bound by the Northampton County court to Captain Holloway Bunting on 9 June 1747 [Orders 1742-8, 148, 414-5]. Her petition against Addison Nottingham was dismissed on 10 September 1751. Sarah Etheridge was her witness. She may have been the Rachel Lang who sued Thomas Stripes on 10 October 1780 [Orders 1751-3, 11, 13; Minutes 1777-83, 278]. She was the mother of

    i.   Jacob, born on 19 February 1740/1, a "Negro Boy" bound to Halloway Bunting on 13 March 1743/4, called the son of Rachel on 9 June 1747 when he was again ordered bound to Captain Holloway Bunting [Orders 1742-8, 148, 414-5]. He was a "Mulatto" or "Negro" taxable in Northampton County from 1787 to 1813 [PPTL, 1782-1823, frames 74, 81, 179, 413, 540].

ii.   ?Abraham, born say 1750, a "free Negro" accused of murdering
Thomas Fisherman "Indian," in Northampton County on 10 May 1774
and sent for trial at the General Court of Virginia [Minutes 1771-7,
269]. He and his wife and others sued Devorax Godwin in
Northampton County on 12 May 1778. He and William **Roberts** were
sued in Northampton County court by John Daniel (an Indian) in a case
which was decided in their favor [Minutes 1777-83, 54, 188]. He was
tending crops on the Gingaskin Indian reservation, married to an Indian
woman and also living with another woman off the reservation
according to a report filed by the commissioners of the reservation in
January 1785 [L.P. cited by Rountree, *Eastern Shore Indians*, 186,
299-300]. He was security for the 30 December 1791 Northampton
County marriage of William **Francis** and Polly **Jacob**. He was taxable
in Northampton County in 1784, 1794 and from 1800 to 1811: a
"Negro" free from taxation starting in 1809. Perhaps his widow was
Betsy Lang who was a "N"(egro) listed in the Indian Town of
Northampton County in 1812 and 1813 [PPTL, 1782-1823, frames 31,
174, 289, 473, 492, 514, 540].

iii. ?Nancy, born say 1758, married Samuel **Stevens**, 16 July 1779
Northampton County bond, Abraham Lang security.

iv.   ?Ann, born say 1780, head of a Norfolk County household of 5 "other
free" and a slave in 1810 [VA:908].

LANSFORD FAMILY

1.   Ann[1] Lansford, born say 1695, the indentured servant of John Redford,
confessed to the Henrico County court in July 1713 that she had an illegitimate
child by a "Negro" [Orders 1710-4, 198, 247]. She was the ancestor of

i.   Hanna "Glansford," born say 1718, petitioned the Henrico County
court for freedom from her master John Redford in June 1739. The
court ruled that she had to serve until the age of thirty-one [Orders
1737-46, 81].

ii.   Ann[2], born say 1734, petitioned the Goochland County court against
William Pledge for her freedom and freedom dues on 18 February
1755 [Orders 1750-7, 499].

2   iii.   William, born say 1740.

2.   William Lansford, born say 1740, was ordered bound apprentice to William
Radford by the churchwardens of St. James Northam Parish, Goochland
County, in December 1750 (no race mentioned) and then bound to Mary
Radford in February 1752 [Orders 1750-57, 47, 120]. William married
Elizabeth **Scott** in Goochland County on 24 December 1761: *Mulattoes, he in
this parish and she in Hanover* [Jones, *The Douglas Register*, 347]. He may
have been the William Lansford who was head of an Amherst County
household of 10 free persons in 1783 [VA:48]. His children were

i.   Milley, born 28 May 1762, baptized 8 August 1762: *daughter of
William Lansford & Eliz: Scott Mulattoes* [Jones, *The Douglas Register*,
348].

ii.   ?Zachariah Lankford, born say 1763, a "free Negro" taxable on a horse
in St. Paul's Parish, Hanover County, in 1784, a "Mulatto" taxable in
1788, 1789, and 1792 [PPTL, 1782-91, pp. 211, 222, 265; 1792-1803,
p. 14]. He was a "F.N." taxable in the upper district of Henrico
County from 1801 to 1814: listed with his unnamed son in 1811 and
1812, listed with son and 2 unnamed daughters in 1813 [PPTL 1782-
1814, frames 448, 490, 536, 666, 725, 759, 824; Land Tax List, 1799-
1816]. He was head of a Henrico County household of 13 "other free"
in 1810 [VA:986].

iii. ?John Langford, a "FN" taxable in the upper district of Henrico County in 1801 and in 1811 with no race indicated. He was probably related to John Langford **Scott** who was taxable in the lower district of Henrico County in 1797 and 1799 [PPTL 1782-1814, frames 375, 391, 448, 666].

iv. ?Joseph, head of a Person County, North Carolina household of 6 "other free" in 1810 [NC:681].

LANTOR/ LANTERN FAMILY

Members of the Lantor/ Lantern family were

1   i.   Thomas[1], born say 1700.
2   ii.   Peter[1], born say 1705.

1. Thomas[1] Lantor, born say 1700, was paid 30 pounds of tobacco in King George County, Virginia, on 8 December 1722 for helping to guard a prisoner in the county jail. He was involved in several minor suits in King George County between 2 February 1722/3 and 6 March 1724/5 [Orders 1721-3, 74, 101; 1723-5, 166, 186, 208, 220, 236]. And he was involved in a number of lawsuits, mostly for debt, in Caroline County court as plaintiff and defendant between 11 May 1732 and 13 June 1746 [Orders 1732-40, 9, 11, 62, 63, 83, 91, 125, 129, 137, 149, 165, 166, 384; 1740-6, 139, 464, 561, 590]. He was the father of Elizabeth Saunders' "mulatto" child born before 12 September 1735 when Elizabeth identified him as the father in Caroline County court. The court ordered Elizabeth to serve her master Samuel Coleman additional time and ordered the child bound to Coleman. On 12 May 1738 Thomas sued Richard Buckner, Gentleman, for work he had done building two sheds adjoining John Buckner's house. The court ordered Buckner to pay him 40 shillings [Orders 1732-40, 307, 378, 481, 491, 503, 520]. On 10 February 1745/6 he produced a certificate in court for taking up two white servants belonging to John Glanton of Caroline County. That same day he was ordered to be placed in the stocks for half an hour, no explanation being given for the punishment [Orders 1740-6, 563, 565]. He was taxable in Orange County, Virginia, on 1 tithe, 4 horses and 5 cattle in 1782 [Little, *Orange County Tithables*, 144] and taxable on 2 tithes, 4 horses, and 6 cattle in 1787 [Schreiner-Yantis, *1787 Census*, 735]. He was head of an Orange County household of 5 "whites" in 1782 [VA:39] and 7 in 1785 [VA:97]. He may have been the father of

3   i.   Elizabeth, born say 1730.
4   ii.   Peter[2], born say 1732.
      iii.   Reuben, born say 1734, charged in Orange County court along with (his brother?) Peter Lantor, "Mulattos of St. Thomas's Parish...Planters," on 11 October 1755 for assaulting and beating John Lynch who they mistook for a runaway servant. He sued Henry Bourn on 26 May 1757 and was awarded 1 pound, 8 shillings. In October 1757 the court ordered the sheriff to sell a horse of his for a debt he owed Hugh Jones [Orders 1754-63, 178-9, 331, 355, 379, 413]. The Goochland County court granted Thomas Pleasants an attachment on his estate for 7 pounds, 17 shillings in August 1760. The garnishee, Richard Curd, testified that he owed Reuben money for building a house, but "he thinks the same not to be worth any thing being badly done." The court appointed a commission to view the house and decided it was worth 4 pounds, 11 shillings [Orders 1757-61, 347-8, 374-5]. He was sued for a debt 18 pounds in Amherst County on 7 July 1767 [Orders 1766-9, 172, 210].

2. Peter[1] Lantor, born say 1705, was required to post bond for his good behavior in King George County court on 4 February 1725/6 for abetting Richard

Haines to assault Thomas Farmer [Orders 1725-8, 298]. He was special bail for Thomas Lantor in a Caroline County court suit on 11 May 1732. He sued Thomas in court about a year later on 8 March 1732/3, but the case was dismissed. He owned land in Caroline County before 8 August 1734 when the court ordered that a road be cleared from Caroline Courthouse to his property. And on 12 September 1734 he was one of the freeholders ordered to clear a road from Bee Tree to the Spotsylvania County line. He purchased land from John Thomas by deed proved in Caroline County on 14 September 1739 [Orders 1732-40, 9, 54, 152, 157, 558]. On 20 April 1742 he and Thomas Powell entered a claim in Spotsylvania County court for taking up a runaway servant named Vincent Mills who belonged to William Covington of Essex County [Orders 1740-2, 165]. And on 24 August 1744 he made a claim in Caroline County court for taking up a runaway Negro slave named Jeffery who belonged to Captain James Garnett of Essex County. On 8 November 1745 the Caroline County court allocated 2,400 pounds of tobacco for his building Ginings Bridge [Orders 1740-6, 312, 540]. He may have been the father of

    i.   Jacob, born say 1740, sued for debt in King George County court on 3 June 1762 [Orders 1751-65, pt.4, 1013, 1015, 1071]. He married Polly Webb, 20 December 1787 Orange County, Virginia bond, Henry Clayton surety.

3.   Elizabeth Lantern, born say 1730, testified in Kent County, Delaware, on 22 November 1769 that (her son?) Peter Lantorn, who was assessed as a tithable the previous year, was born on 8 April 1750 and therefore should not have been tithable [Kent County Levy Assessments, 1768-84, Reel no.3, frame 38]. She married Robert **Game** before September 1782 when Robert named her (called Elizabeth Lanthorn) and her daughters Mary and Sarah in his Murderkill Hundred, Kent County, Delaware will [WB L-1, fol. 267-8]. She was the mother of

    i.   Peter[3], born 8 April 1750, tithable in Little Creek Hundred, Kent County, Delaware in 1772 and 1773, in Dover Hundred in 1778, in Little Creek in 1779 and 1780, and a delinquent Duck Creek Hundred taxable in 1781 and 1782 (called Peter Lantern/ Lanthron). He was head of a Murderkill Hundred household of 3 "other free" in 1800 (called Peter Lanteron) [DE:126].

5   ii.   ?Joseph[1] Lantern, born say 1756.
    iii.   Mary.
    iv.   Sarah.

4.   Peter[2] Lantor, born say 1732, was a witness for John Morgan in his suit against William Sisson in Orange County, Virginia court in May 1753, and on 28 September 1753 he sued Jeremiah Morton for a "Dary" he had built for Morton. He and William Sisson were sued for debt by Charles and Peter Copland on 25 July 1755 [Orders 1747-54, 447, 469, 501; 1754-63, 152, 169]. He was a tithable head of an Orange County household from 1755 to 1769, taxable on one tithe in 1755 and 4 tithes in 1759 [Little, *Orange County Tithables*, 42, 59]. On 11 October 1755 he and (his brother?) Reubin Lantor, "Mulattos of St. Thomas's Parish...Planters," were charged in Orange County court with assaulting and beating John Lynch who they mistook for a runaway servant. On 24 March 1757 he sued Andrew Mannen for trespass, assault and battery, and on 27 April 1758 Andrew Bourn, administrator of the estate of Robert Bourn, brought suit against him. On 24 November 1757 he and Sarah Bourn were indicted by the grand jury for fornication on the information of Andrew Bourn and Andrew Mannen. This indictment was titled "Peter Lantor and his wife" when it was dismissed on 23 June 1758. On 28 February 1760 he recorded his livestock mark, and on 2 November 1765 he was paid for building the bridge over the Mountain Run. On 24 November 1768 the grand

jury presented Peter for concealing his tithable-wife Sarah Lantor but was excused by the court on the following day [Orders 1754-63, 178-9, 357, 368, 388, 392, 411, 443, 511; 1763-9, 366, 535, 538]. He was taxable in Orange County from 1756 to 1769 - called Lanthorn, Lanter, Lantor, Lanton [Little, *Orange County Tithables*, 42, 46, 58, 59, 65, 82, 97, 101, 109]. On 29 September 1769 Alexander Waugh won two suits of ejectment against him, one for 156 acres and the other for 100 acres. On 2 October 1769 John Booth was charged with feloniously shooting and killing him. The court ordered Booth sent to the General Court for trial. (Booth was a co-defendant with Peter in a suit for debt on 24 August 1764) [Orders 1769-77, 35, 90; 1763-9, 190]. Sarah received 4 pounds annually for five years by the 21 June 1771 Orange County will of Caleb Sesson, proved 22 August 1771 [WB 2:436-7]. Her plantation was located near a new road which was ordered to be opened on 23 June 1774 from Chestnut Mountain over the Mountain Run [Orders 1769-77, 319, 340]. Peter may have been the father of

    i.   Thomas² Lanton, born say 1758, married to Mary Walker on 28 August 1783 by Rev. Aaron Bledsoe in Orange County [Ministers' Returns, 13].

    ii.   Peter⁴, born say 1766, married Hannah Webb, 31 May 1787 Orange County, Virginia bond.

    iii. Mildred, born say 1769, married John Webb, Jr., 20 January 1790 Orange County, Virginia bond, Jacob Lantor surety, 20 January marriage.

5.   Joseph¹ Lantern, born say 1756, was tithable in Dover Hundred, Kent County, Delaware from 1776 to 1785. He married Elizabeth **Harmon**, widow and administrator of Daniel **Harmon**'s 10 May 1774 Kent County estate [de Valinger, *Kent County, Delaware Probate Records*, 289]. He purchased 6 acres in Halifax County, North Carolina, for 44 pounds on 23 December 1789. On 30 October 1795 he, Moses Matthews, and John **Kelly** purchased 100 acres, tools, furniture, cattle, and hogs from John **Harmon**, and he purchased 100 acres near the road from Halifax Town to Enfield old courthouse from John **Harmon** on 3 December 1795 [DB 17:231, 920; 18:130]. Joseph was head of a Halifax County household of 7 "other free" and 7 slaves in 1800 [NC:324]. Perhaps his widow was Charity Lantern, head of a Halifax County household of 4 "other free" in 1810 [NC:34]. Joseph may have been the father of

    i.   Joseph², Jr., born say 1778, head of a Halifax County household of 3 "other free" in 1800 [NC:324].

    ii.   James, born say 1780, head of a Halifax County household of 2 "other free" in 1810 [NC:33] and 7 "free colored" in 1820 [NC:155].

LAWRENCE FAMILY

1.   Elizabeth Leurance, born say 1657, the servant of Thomas Townsend, confessed to the Middlesex County court on 3 September 1677 that she had a child by Ananias. Her master paid her fine and posted bond for maintenance of the child, so Ananias may have been a slave or an Indian [Orders 1673-77, 76]. She may have been the ancestor of

    i.   Alice, presented by the Prince George County court on 13 May 1718 for having an illegitimate child, no race indicated [Orders 1714-20, 186].

2   ii.   Martha¹, born say 1730.

    iii. Drury¹, born say 1734, petitioned the Amelia County court on 26 June 1755 asking to be discharged from his indenture to Charles Irby [Orders 1754-8, n.p.]. On 9 November 1769 the Lunenburg County court presented Richard Claiborne, Gentleman, for not listing him as a tithable [Orders 1769-77, 5]. He was apparently identical to Jury

Larrance, an "Indian" taxable in Cumberland Parish, Lunenburg County, in Henry Blagrave's list for 1772. A Drurey Larrance was taxable the same year in Richard Claiborne's list for Cumberland Parish; a Drurey Larrance was taxable in the compiled list for 1774, and a Jerry Laurance was taxable in the compiled list for 1775 [Bell, *Sunlight on the Southside*, 291, 293, 339, 361].

3   iv.   Robin, born say 1735.

2. Martha[1] Lawrence, born say 1728, was living in Brunswick County, Virginia, on 25 September 1751 when the court ordered the churchwardens of St. Andrew's Parish to bind out her poor infant son Richard Littlepage Lawrence. On 23 May 1753 the court bound out her son Isham Lawrence [Orders 1751-3, 55, 501]. She was the mother of

4   i.   Richard[1], born say 1747.
5   ii.   Isham, born say 1745.
      iii. ?Frances, born say 1752, mother of a "Mulatto" child ordered bound out to Elizabeth Woodward in Sussex County on 17 July 1777 [Orders 1777-82, 18].
6   iv.   ?Martha[2]/ Patty, born about 1754.

3. Robin Lawrence, born say 1735, died before 14 October 1786 when his widow Sarah married John **Thomas**, Brunswick County, Virginia bond. He was called "Indian" Robin Lawrence when his son Woody registered as a "free Negro" in Charlotte County on 15 April 1811 [Ailsworth, *Charlotte County--Rich Indeed*, 485]. Sarah was called Sarah **Thomas** on the 7 March 1796 Charlotte County marriage bond of her daughter Mason Lawrence. She was called Sarah Lawrence when she was taxable on a horse in Charlotte County from 1792 to 1795 [PPTL 1782-1813, frames 255, 279, 329]. Robin and Sarah were the parents of

      i.   Wood, born about 1767, taxable in the middle district of St. Andrew's Parish, Brunswick County, from 1782 to 1787: taxable on 2 horses and 4 cattle in 1782, taxable on a slave and 2 horses in 1788 [PPTL 1782-1798, frames 11, 42, 189, 218]. He was bondsman for his mother's 14 October 1786 Brunswick County marriage. On 30 November 1786 he sued Charles **Brandum** in Brunswick County court for a debt of 8 pounds [Orders 1784-8, 432, 475]. He was taxable on a horse in Charlotte County from 1791 to 1810 [PPTL 1782-1813, frames 231, 279, 329, 386, 451, 519, 657, 726, 792] and was a "Free Negro" head of a Charlotte County household of 6 "other free" in 1810 [VA:969]. He registered as a free Negro in Charlotte County on 15 April 1811: *Mulatto complexion, aged 44, born free* [Ailsworth, *Charlotte County--Rich Indeed*, 485].
      ii.   Sarah, born say 1767, "daughter of Robert Lawrence, deceased," married Peter **Rouse**, 19 October 1786 Brunswick County bond, Wood Lawrence bondsman.
      iii. ?Levina, born about 1768, married Alexander **Flood**, 4 April 1792 Charlotte County bond. She registered in Charlotte County on 26 November 1806: *Mulatto complexion, aged 38, born free* [Ailsworth, *Charlotte County--Rich Indeed*, 485].
      iv.   ?Berry/ Littleberry, born about 1769, taxable on a horse in Charlotte County from 1791 to 1799 [PPTL 1782-1813, frames 231, 279, 329, 386, 451]. He married Hannah **Jumper** (daughter of C. **Jumper**), 7 March 1796 Charlotte County bond, John **Williamson** surety. He registered as a "free Negro" in Charlotte County on 21 October 1799: *Black complexion, aged 30, born free* [Ailsworth, *Charlotte County-- Rich Indeed*, 485]. Berry registered again in Pittsylvania County using his Charlotte County papers: *a fifty-year-old black man with "mulatto"*

wife Hannah (aged thirty-five) and four daughters [Register of Free Negroes, pp. 6-7, nos. 16-20].

7   v. Nanny, born say 1770.

    vi. Mason, born say 1775, married John **Williamson**, 7 March 1796 Charlotte County bond, Littleberry Lawrence surety. John **Williamson** was a "Mulatto" taxable in Charlotte County from 1798 to 1806 [PPTL 1782-1813, frames 425, 456, 697].

    vii. ?Ferguson, taxable in Charlotte County in 1798 and 1799 [PPTL 1782-1813, frames 420, 451].

4. Richard[1] Lawrence, born say 1747, infant son of Martha Lawrence, was living in Brunswick County, Virginia, on 25 September 1751, when the court ordered the churchwardens of St. Andrew's Parish to bind him to Drury Stith, Gentleman. Richard was called an "Indian" on 26 September 1758 when the court again ordered the churchwardens to bind him out [Orders 1751-3, 55; 1757-9, 244]. On 28 October 1771 the court ordered the sheriff, Thomas Stith, Gentleman, to pay him 1 pound, 4 shillings for repairing the bridge over Sturgeon Run at Drury Stith's [Orders 1768-72, 423]. He was called Richard Littlepage Lawrence (signing) on 25 September 1775 when he and his wife Tabitha sold 100 acres in St. Andrew's Parish, Brunswick County, on Loyd's Run which he had been devised by the 26 July 1765 will of Drury Stith [DB 11:491]. He was taxable in the middle district of St. Andrew's Parish from 1784 to 1796: called Richard Littlepage Lawrence when he was listed with his son Miles in 1785 [PPTL 1782-1798, frames 77, 109, 189, 217, 251, 286, 339, 516]. On 26 July 1784 the Brunswick County court ordered the churchwardens of St. Andrew's Parish to bind out his children, "it appearing he does not take proper steps in bringing them up," and on 24 September 1787 the court ordered the overseers of the poor to bind out his son Zachariah. On 25 August 1788 he was presented for living in adultery with Nancy **Chavous**. This was probably the case against him which was dismissed on 24 March 1790 [Orders 1760-84, 471; 1784-8, 572; 1788-92, 60]. He was the father of

    i. Miles, born say 1767, taxable in the middle district of St. Andrew's Parish, Brunswick County, from 1784 to 1804: under the age of twenty-one when he was taxable in Richard Lawrence's household in 1784, called Richard's son in 1785, a "M"(ulatto) taxable from 1804 to 1807, crossed off the list in 1809 [PPTL 1782-1798, frames 77, 109, 339, 414, 448, 615; 1799-1815, frames 16, 168, 275, 371, 418, 457].

    ii. ?Sterling, born say 1769, taxable in St. Andrew's Parish, Brunswick County from 1799 to 1814: a "M"(ulatto) taxable from 1804 to 1809, perhaps married to Tabitha Lawrence who was listed with him in 1813. He was listed as a "FN" in 1814 [PPTL 1782-1798, frames 516, 565, 615; 1799-1815, frames 16, 66, 168, 275, 418, 494, 622, 652]. Sterling was head of a Brunswick County, Virginia household of 4 "other free" in 1810 [VA:721].

8   iii. Winny, born say 1771.

    iv. Zachariah, son of Richard Lawrence ordered bound out by the overseers of the poor on 24 September 1787 [1784-8, 572], perhaps identical to Sack Lawrence who was taxable in St. Andrew's Parish from 1796 to 1798.

5. Isham Lawrence, born say 1745, son of Martha Lawrence, was ordered bound out in Brunswick County, Virginia, on 23 May 1753 [Orders 1751-3, 501]. He was taxable in Brunswick County from 1782 to 1794: taxable on a horse and 2 cattle in 1782 [PPTL 1782-1798, frames 11, 109, 217, 251, 286, 360, 448]. He and Daniel Duggar were sued for debt of 6 pounds in Brunswick County court on 28 March 1785. Otha **Jumper** sued him and his unnamed wife for trespass, assault and battery. The suit was dismissed at the defendant's cost on 26 April 1785. He purchased property by deed proved in Brunswick County

on 24 April 1786 [Orders 1784-8, 78, 93, 119, 125, 326]. He was taxable in Lunenburg County from 1795 to 1804, taxable on 2 tithes and a slave in 1801 [PPTL 1782-1806]. He was counted in a "List of all free Negroes & Mulattoes in the lower District of Lunenburg" with his wife Letitia and children: Richard, Polly, Sally, and Griffin in 1802 and 1803 [LVA, Free Negro & Slave Records, 1802-1803 p.1]. Lettence was head of a Surry County, North Carolina household of 7 "free colored" in 1820. Isham's children were

 i. Richard[2], married Sally **Barber**, 23 September 1817 Surry County, North Carolina bond. He was head of a Surry County household of 5 "free colored" in 1830.

 ii. Polly.

 iii. Sally.

 iv. Griffin.

6. Martha[2]/ Patty Lawrence, born about 1754, registered in Petersburg on 18 August 1794: *a dark brown woman with long black hair, five feet high, about forty years old, born free & raised in Dinwiddie County* [Register of Free Negroes 1794-1819, no. 41]. She was the mother of

 i. Stith, born about 1775, ordered to be bound apprentice in Dale Parish, Chesterfield County, on 7 November 1783 and in June 1784 [Orders 1774-84, 496, 541]. He registered in Petersburg on 16 November 1796: *a dark brown Mulatto man, pitted with the small pox, short knotty hair, stout & well made, five feet nine inches high, Twenty one years old, born free & son of Patty Lawrence a free Mulatto woman & raised in County of Prince George* [Register of Free Negroes 1794-1819, no. 117].

 ii. ?Rhody, born about 1779, registered in Petersburg on 14 August 1800: *a dark brown Mulatto woman, five feet three inches high, twenty one years old, short bushy hair, holes in her ears for rings, born free & raised in the Town of Petersburg* [Register of Free Negroes 1794-1819, no. 160].

 iii. Peter[2], born about 1784, registered in Petersburg on 19 January 1802: *(son of Patty Lawrance, a free Mulatto woman) a dark brown Mulatto boy, seventeen to eighteen years old, five feet three and a half inches high, pitted with the small pox* [Register of Free Negroes 1794-1819, no. 222].

 iv. ?Fanny, born about 1774, registered in Petersburg on 14 August 1800: *a dark brown Mulatto woman, five feet one half inches high, twenty six years old, with bushy hair, born free & raised in the County of Prince George. Renewed 15 July 1805* [Register of Free Negroes 1794-1819, no. 161]. She was head of a Petersburg Town household of 1 "other free" and a slave in 1810 [VA:119a].

7. Nanny Lawrence, born say 1770, was living in Brunswick County, Virginia, on 20 March 1808 when her son Willie registered as a "free Negro" [Wynn, *Registry of Free Negroes*, 8]. Her children were

 i. Willie[1], born about 1787, "a base born Child of Colour," bound to Edward Murden of Halifax County, North Carolina. On 16 September 1796 the court charged Murden and John Harrison with having sold him (into slavery) and removed him from the state. He was apparently recovered because he registered as a "free Negro" in Brunswick County on 20 March 1808: *a mulatto man abt 21 years of age near 6 feet high is reputed to be the son of Nany Lawrence a free woman residing in this county.*

 ii. ?Thomas, born about 1792, registered in Brunswick County on 25 May 1813: *a mulatto man about twenty one years of age five feet ten inches high of a bright complection... born free in this county as appears by the certificate of John Elliott* [Wynn, *Registry of Free Negroes*, 16].

iii. Sarah, born about 1785, a base born child, no race mentioned, bound apprentice to Mascoff(?) Daley, spinster, by the 18 February 1800 Halifax County, North Carolina court.
iv. Pheba, born say 1790, head of a Halifax County, North Carolina household of 3 "other free" in 1810 [NC:33].

8. Winny Lawrence, born say 1771, was the "free Mulatto" mother of Francis Littlepage Lawrence who was baptized in Bristol Parish, Virginia, on 26 August 1792 [Chamberlayne, *Register of Bristol Parish*, 334]. She was the mother of

9   i. Francis, born 20 June 1791.

9. Francis Lawrence, born 20 June 1791, was baptized in Bristol Parish, Virginia, on 26 August 1792 [Chamberlayne, *Register of Bristol Parish*, 334]. He was living in Greensville County on 23 January 1794 when the court ordered the churchwardens to bind him to Edmund Branscomb [Orders 1790-9, 237]. He was taxable in St. Andrew's Parish, Brunswick County, Virginia, in 1811 [PPTL 1799-1815, frame 535]. He registered as a "Free Negro" in Brunswick County on 28 March 1820: *about twenty eight years of age five feet five & 1/4 inches high and of a yellow complexion...by occupation a carpenter who it appears by the evidence of Thomas Lanier was born free* [Wynne, *Register of Free Negroes*, 31]. He was head of a Halifax County, North Carolina household of 6 "free colored" in 1830 and was probably the father of

i. Willie[2], born about 1821, a fifteen-year-old boy of color ordered bound apprentice to John Sumerville by the Halifax County court on 15 August 1836 [Minutes 1832-46].

Other members of the Lawrence family were

i. Moses, born say 1760, a "Mulatto" head of household in Buxton's list for the 1784 census of Nansemond County [VA:74] and a "Free Negro" taxable on 4 horses and two slaves in Nansemond County in 1815 [Yantis, *A Supplement to the 1810 Census of Virginia*, S-14].
ii. Drury[2], born say 1760, a "yellow" complexioned soldier born in Prince George County who lived in Dinwiddie County when he was listed as a substitute who served in the Revolution [NSDAR, *African American Patriots*, 151].
iii. John, married Pheribe **Darden**, 10 January 1793 Southampton County bond. He was head of a Southampton County household of 7 "other free" in 1810 [VA:92].
iv. Peter[1], born about 1772, registered in Petersburg on 13 October 1794: *a dark brown Mulatto man, five feet eight and a half inches high, twenty two years old, born free & raised in County of Prince George* [Register of Free Negroes 1794-1819, no. 92].
v. Bilcey, head of a Washington County, Virginia household of 1 "other free" in 1810.
vi. Fed, born say 1780, a "mulatto lad" who ran away from Edward Harrison of Prince George County according to an ad placed in a Virginia newspaper on 18 August 1792 [Headley, *18th Century Newspapers*, 201].

Members of the Lawrence family in Essex and Westmoreland counties were

i. John, a "free Mulatto" overseer living on Ronand's land in Westmoreland County in 1801 [*Virginia Genealogist* 31:40].
ii. Cornelius, born about 1797, obtained a certificate of freedom in St. Mary's County, Maryland, on 28 November 1816: *aged nineteen years...light complexion...born free* [Certificates of Freedom 1806-64, 37]. He registered in Essex County, Virginia, on 21 June 1824: *born*

> *free by certificate of St. Mary's County, Maryland, 27 years of age* [Register of Free Negroes 1810-43, p.46, no. 115].

LAWS FAMILY

1. Martha Laws, born say 1740, was the mother of unnamed "Mulatto children" bound by the Lancaster County, Virginia court to Thomas B. Griffin, Gent., on 16 February 1767 until the age of thirty-one [Orders 1764-7, 234]. She was apparently the mother of

    i.   Chris, born about 1760, registered in Lancaster County on 16 June 1806: *Age 46, Color dark...emancipated by Doodridge P. Chichester* [Burkett, *Lancaster County Register of Free Negroes*, 2], head of a Lancaster County household of 4 "other free" in 1810 [VA:352].

    ii. Amine/ Ammala, born about 1764, registered in Lancaster County on 21 October 1816: *Age 52, Color tawny .. born free* [Burkett, *Lancaster County Register of Free Negroes*, 7], head of a Lancaster County household of 6 "other free" in 1810 [VA:352].

    iii. Leroy, born about 1772, registered in Lancaster County on 18 April 1808: *Age 36, Color yellow...born free in this county.*

    iv. Lindsay, born about 1774, registered in Lancaster County on 19 May 1803: *Age 29, Color mulatto...born free* [Burkett, *Lancaster County Register of Free Negroes*, 1, 2].

    v.   Eliza, born say 1775, married Thomas **Weaver**, 7 July 1794 Lancaster County bond.

LAWSON FAMILY

1. Margaret Lawson, born say 1668, was the servant of John Jones on 17 April 1689 when she won a suit for her freedom in Northumberland County court. Anne Farmer testified on Margaret's behalf that her husband William Farmer had imported Margaret into the country and sold her to Thomas Hobson for four years. She was one of the headrights for which Thomas Hobson was granted land in January 1701/2. On 16 July 1701 she was called the covenanted servant to Mrs. Sarah Howson when she confessed in Northumberland County court that she had had a child by a "Negro called Daniell Webb." The court ordered the churchwardens to dispose of her according to law at the expiration of her service [Orders 1678-98, part 2, 462; 1699-1713, part 1, 167, 195]. She was probably the mother of

2   i.   Robert[1], born say 1701.

2. Robert[1] Lason, born say 1701, was the "Mulatto" father of John Lason who was born in St. Stephen's Parish, Northumberland County, Virginia, on 10 December 1722 [Fleet, *Northumberland County Record of Births, 1661-1810*, 100]. He was the father of

    i.   John, born 10 December 1722.

They may have been the ancestors of the following members of the Lawson family:

    i.   Charles, born say 1770, head of a Cecil County, Maryland household of 6 "other free" in 1800 [MD:223] and 10 "other free" in Loudoun County, Virginia, in 1810 [VA:296].

    ii. Polly, head of a Spotsylvania County, Virginia household of 3 "other free" in 1810 [VA:108a].

    iii. George, head of a Stafford County, Virginia household of 7 "other free" and 2 slaves in 1810 [VA:128].

    iv. Thomas, "Mulatto" taxable in St. Paul's Parish, Hanover County, Virginia, from 1793 to 1801 [PPTL 1792-1803, pp. 47, 97, 152, 192, 213].

   v.   Charles, "Free Negro" taxable in St. Paul's Parish, Hanover County, from 1805 to 1815: taxable on 2 slaves from 1809 to 1812 [PPTL, 1804-24].

   vi. Robert[2], "Free Negro" taxable in St. Paul's Parish, Hanover County, in 1812 [PPTL 1804-24].

LEE FAMILY

1. Frances Lee, born say 1696, was living in York County on 17 September 1716 when she was presented for having a "Mulatto" child on the information of Edmund Curtis [OW 15:27, 38]. She may have been the ancestor of

   i.   Peggy, a "F.M." living in Richmond City in 1782 [VA:111].

   ii. William, head of a York County household of 6 "other free" in 1810.

   iii. John, head of a York County household of 2 "other free" in 1810.

   iv. Nancy, head of a Richmond City household of 8 "other free" in 1810 [VA:338].

   v.   Benjamin, head of a Hertford County, North Carolina household of 5 "other free" in 1810 [NC:107].

LEMON FAMILY

Members of the Lemon family in Gloucester County were

1   i.   Ambrose, born say 1725.

2   ii. Richard[1], born say 1730.

   iii. James[1], born say 1733, taxable in Gloucester County from 1769 to 1771 [Tax List 1770-1, 88], taxable in Ware Parish, Gloucester County, on his own free tithe, a slave, 3 horses and 15 cattle in 1782 [PPTL 1782-99], head of a Gloucester County household of 6 free persons in 1784 [VA:69], called James Lemon, Sr., in 1792 when he was taxable on a free tithe and 2 cattle and in 1793 when he was taxable on 3 horses but free from personal tax [PPTL 1782-99].

3   iv. Joshua, born say 1735.

4   v.   William[1], born say 1745.

   vi. William[2], born say 1750, called William Lemon, Jr., when he was tithable in Gloucester County from 1769 to 1770 [Tax List 1770-1, 207], perhaps identical to the William Lemon who was tithable in 1796, called "William (Teagle) Lemon" when he was tithable in 1797, 1806 and 1812. He, John and Richard Lemon were living at "Dr." (Dragon) Quarter of Gloucester County in 1800 [PPTL, 1782-99; 1800-20].

1. Ambrose Lemon, born say 1725, was taxable on 3 tithes in Gloucester County in 1770 and 1771. He paid James Lemon's personal tax in 1770 [Tax List 1770-1, 30, 51, 161, 172, 179]. He was not listed as a taxable in 1782 or the years following [PPTL, 1782-99]. Mary Lemon may have been his widow. She was taxable in Ware Parish, Gloucester County, on 2 horses and 3 cattle in 1782, taxable on 1 free male tithe, 9 slaves, 4 horses and 23 cattle in 1783, but taxable on only a horse and 2 cattle in 1784. Perhaps some of her slaves were transferred to Dixon Lemon who was taxable on 4 slaves in 1784 [PPTL, 1782-99]. He may have been the father of

5   i.   John[1], born say 1746.

6   ii. Lucy, born say 1760.

   iii. Dixon, born say 1762, head of a Petsworth Parish, Gloucester County household of 6 free persons in 1784 [VA:69], taxable in Petsworth Parish on his own free tithe, 3 slaves over the age of 16, a slave over the age of 12, 3 horses and 8 cattle in 1784 [PPTL 1782-99]. He was taxable in the lower district of King and Queen County on 2-3 slaves from 1790 to 1802, taxable on 2 free males in 1801 and 1802. His estate was taxable on a free male, a slave and a horse in 1803 and 1804. Ann Lemon (his widow?) was taxable on the same in 1805 and 1806. They were probably the parents of James Lemon who was taxable there on a horse from 1807 to 1813. Ann may have been identical to Nancy Lemon was taxable on a slave and a horse from 1809 to 1814. Dixon Lemon was a free male taxable in 1813. They were considered white in 1813 and later King and Queen County lists which identify all "free Negroes & Mulattoes above the age of 16" [PPTL, 1782-1803; 1804-16].

2.   Richard[1] Lemon, born say 1730, was taxable in Gloucester County on 2 tithes in 1770 [Tax List 1770-1, 88] and head of a Petsworth Parish, Gloucester County household of 9 free persons in 1783 and 8 free persons in 1784 [VA:53, 69]. He was taxable in Petsworth Parish on a free tithe, a slave over the age of 16 and 3 horses in 1789, free from personal tax in 1790, called Richard Lemon, Sr., in 1793 [PPTL 1782-99]. He was taxable on 76 acres from 1782 to 1794. His estate was taxable on the land in 1795 and 1796. By 1797 the land was divided among James, Robert, John, Susanna, Ann and Richard Lemon who were apparently his children [Land Tax List, 1782-1820]. He was the father of

   i.   Robert[1], born say 1750, listed in 1770 in the tax accounts of the clerk of Gloucester County. Mary Taylor paid him 100 pounds of tobacco in 1771 [Tax List 1770-1, 159, 184]. He was taxable in Ware Parish, Gloucester County, on a slave and 4 horses in 1785, taxable on a horse in 1789 and taxable on a slave in 1798 [PPTL 1782-99]. He was taxable on 12-4/5 acres from 1797 to 1806 and called "son of Richd., Mul°" when he was taxable on 36 acres from 1807 to 1817. He was listed as deceased in 1818 [Land Tax 1782-1820]. He was called Robert Lemon, Sr., from 1804 to 1812 [PPTL, 1800-20], perhaps the Ro. Lemon who was head of a household of 2 "other free," a white woman 26-45 years of age, and 2 slaves in 1810 [VA:407b]. He was called "son of Rich[d]" when he was tithable in Gloucester County in 1814 and 1815 [PPTL, 1800-20].

   ii. Richard[2], born say 1752, perhaps identical to Richard Lemon, Jr., who was taxable in Gloucester County in 1769 and 1770 [Tax List 1770-1]. He was taxable on 12-4/5 acres from 1797 to 1820, called "son of Richard" from 1807 to 1820 [Land Tax List 1782-1820]. He was tithable at Dragon Quarter in Gloucester County in 1800 and was called "son of Rich[d]" when he was tithable from 1804 to 1819 [PPTL, 1800-20]. He may have been the Richard Lemon who was head of a Gloucester County household of 4 "other free" and 2 white women in 1810 [VA:408a].

7 iii. James[2], Jr., born say 1766.
   iv. John[4], born say 1776, taxable in Gloucester County in 1797, called "son of Rich[d]" when he was taxable from 1804 to 1820 [PPTL, 1800-20].

3.   Joshua Lemon, born say 1735, was taxable in Gloucester County in 1769 and 1770 but was not listed as a taxable in 1782 or the years following [Tax List 1770-1; PPTL, 1782-99]. Joshua was the father of

   i.   John[3], born say 1770, "son of Joshua," taxable in Gloucester County from 1791 to 1814 [PPTL, 1782-99].
   ii. Richard[4], born say 1780, "son of Joshua," taxable in Gloucester County from 1804 to 1814 [PPTL, 1800-20]

4.   William[1] Lemon, born say 1745, was a "Negro" chosen as the pastor of Petsworth Parish by its predominantly white congregation in the 1780s. Robert B. Semple, a contemporary, said of him,

*though he was not white...he had been washed in the layer of
regeneration, had been purified and made white in a better sense...he was
a lively and affecting (preacher)* [Daniel, "Virginia Baptists and the Negro
in the Early Republic," *VMHB* LXXX (1972): 62].

He was taxable in Gloucester County in 1770 [Tax List 1770-1, 177] and head
of a Petsworth Parish, Gloucester County household of 8 "white" (free)
persons and 2 slaves in 1783 [VA:53]. He was taxable in Petsworth Parish on
his own free tithe, a slave, 2 horses and 6 cattle in 1782, taxable in Ware
Parish from 1783 to 1785, taxable on 2 free male tithes in 1787, on 3 males
in 1796 and taxable until 1807. His widow was probably Mary Lemon who
was taxable on a slave and a horse in 1807 and 1809 and taxable on a horse
in 1810 [PPTL 1782-99; 1800-20]. Molly was head of a Gloucester County
household of 6 "other free" in 1810 [VA:407b]. William was the father of

    i.   William[3], born say 1766, called William Jr. when he taxable in
           Gloucester County in 1789, called "son of Wm." when he was taxable
           in 1792 and 1816 [PPTL 1782-99; 1800-20].
    ii.   John[2], born say 1769, listed himself as a tithable on the same day as
           William Lemon, Jr., in 1790, called "son of Wm" when he was taxable
           from 1804 to 1820 [PPTL, 1782-99; 1800-20].
8   iii. Edward, born say 1770.
    iv. Robert[2], born say 1775, called "son of Wm" when he was taxable in
           Gloucester County in 1796 and 1797 and called "Robert Jr." from 1804
           to 1811 [PPTL, 1782-99].

5. John[1] Lemon, born say 1746, was head of a Petsworth Parish, Gloucester
County household of 8 free persons and 2 slaves in 1783 [VA:53]. He was
taxable in Petsworth Parish on 2 free male tithes, a slave over 16 years of age,
a horse and 7 cattle in 1782, taxable on 3 free tithes from 1801 to 1803, 2 in
1804 and a free tithe in 1809 [PPTL, 1782-99; 1800-20]. He was a "Mul°"
taxable on 125 acres from 1782 to 1812, taxable on another 35 acres from
1797 to 1812 and on another 38 acres in 1811 and 1812. From 1813 to 1820
Mordecai and Robert Lemon were each taxable on 20 acres of his land;
Mildred, Hannah, Mary, and Sally Lemon and his widow Elizabeth Lemon
were each taxable on 17 acres of his land, and his estate was taxable on 38
acres. From 1814 to 1820 Haley Lemon was taxable on 17-1/2 acres with the
notation "transferred to him by John Lemon deed recorded in Gloucester Court
office" [Land Tax List, 1782-1800]. Robert, Richard, and John Lemon were
called sons of John Lemon when they listed their personal property [PPTL,
1800-20]. His "mul°" widow Elizabeth was listed in Gloucester County in
1813 and was taxable on 5 head of cattle in 1815 [PPTL, 1800-20]. She was
head of a Gloucester County household of 4 "other free" in 1810 [VA:408a].
John was the father of

    i.   Richard[3], born say 1776, called "son of John Lemon" in 1810 when he
           was head of a Gloucester County household of 5 "other free"
           [VA:407b].
    ii.   John[5], born say 1780, taxable in Gloucester County from 1797 to 1815,
           called "son of John Lemon" in 1806 [PPTL, 1800-20] and in 1810
           when he was head of a Gloucester County household of 7 "other free"
           and a white woman 26-45 years of age [VA:408a].
   iii. Mildred, taxable on 17 acres from 1813 to 1820.
    iv. Hailey, born say 1776, listed himself as a taxable on the same day as
           John Lemon in 1797 [PPTL, 1782-99]. He was head of a Gloucester
           County household of 6 "other free" in 1810 [VA:662] and was a
           "Mulatto" listed with his unnamed wife in 1813 [PPTL, 1800-20]. He
           received 17-1/2 acres from (his father?) John Lemon by deed recorded
           in Gloucester County [Land Tax List 1782-1820 (1814, p.15)].

    v.   Mordecai, born say 1780, head of a Gloucester County household of 4 "other free" and a white woman 26-45 years of age in 1810 [VA:407b]. He was a "Mulatto" taxable in Gloucester County from 1801 to 1820 [PPTL, 1800-20] and taxable on 20 acres from 1813 to 1820 [Land Tax List 1782-1820].

    vi.   Hannah, a "mul°," called "daughter of John Lemon" when she was listed in Gloucester County in 1813 [PPTL, 1800-20]. She was taxable on 17 acres from 1813 to 1820, called "alias King" in 1818, so she may have married a member of the **King** family [Land Tax List 1782-1800].

    vii.   Robert[3], "mul°" son of John Lemon, taxable in Gloucester County in 1813 and 1814 [PPTL, 1800-20]. He was taxable on 20 acres in Gloucester County from 1813 to 1820 [Land Tax List, 1782-1820].

    viii.   Sarah, a "mul°," called "daughter of John Lemon" when she was listed in Gloucester County in 1813 [PPTL, 1800-20].

    ix.   Mary, a "mul°," called "daughter of John Lemon" when she was listed in Gloucester County in 1813 [PPTL, 1800-20]. She was taxable on 17 acres from 1813 to 1817. She died before 1818 when the tax was charged to her estate [Land Tax List 1782-1820].

6.   Lucy Lemon, born say 1760, was taxable in Gloucester County on a free male tithable in 1804, taxable on a slave and a horse in 1807, and was called "mother of the Wakes" in 1813 when she was listed as a "mul°" over the age of sixteen. She was probably the common-law wife of James **Wakes**, a "free negro" taxable in Gloucester County in 1795 [PPTL, 1782-99; 1800-20]. Lucy was the mother of

    i.   Lewis, born say 1780, "alias Wakes," a "Mulatto" taxable in Gloucester County from 1801 to 1820, listed with his unnamed wife in 1813 [PPTL, 1800-20], head of a household of 8 "other free" in 1810 [VA:407b] and 9 "free colored" in 1820 [VA:191].

    ii.   John[6], born say 1786, "alias Wakes," a "mul°." taxable in Gloucester County from 1809 to 1820, listed with his unnamed wife in 1813 [PPTL, 1800-20], head of a household of 4 "free colored" in 1820 [VA:191].

    iii.   James, born say 1788, "alias Wakes," taxable in Gloucester County from 1809 to 1820 [PPTL, 1800-20], head of a household of 1 "free colored" in 1820 [VA:191].

5.   James[2] Lemon, born say 1766, was called James Lemon, Jr., when he was taxable in Gloucester County in 1787 and in 1789 when he listed his taxables on the same day as (his father) Richard Lemon. He was taxable on 2 free tithables in 1795 and taxable from 1797 to 1804 [PPTL, 1782-99; 1800-20]. He was taxable on 12 acres from 1797 to 1804, and his estate was taxable on the land from 1805 to 1820 [Land Tax List, 1782-1820]. He was the father of

    i.   George W., born say 1796, taxable in Gloucester County from 1817 to 1820, called "son of James" in 1820 [PPTL, 1800-20].

    ii.   ?Francis, born say 1788, taxable in Gloucester County from 1809 to 1815 [PPTL, 1800-20].

8.   Edward Lemon, born say 1770, listed himself as a tithable on the same day as William Lemon, Sr., in 1791, 1792, 1793 and 1795. He was taxable on a slave from 1801 to 1812, was a "mul°" taxable with his unnamed son in 1813 and was called "son of Wm" when he was taxable on 2 tithes in 1814 [PPTL, 1782-99; 1800-20]. He was head of a Gloucester County household of 2 "other free," a white woman over the age of 45 and a slave in 1810 [VA:407b]. He was taxable on 91 acres, called Cowpen Neck, from 1812 to 1816 and taxable on another 50 acres in 1812 [Land Tax List 1782-1820]. He was the father of

i. William[5], born say 1792, called "son of Edward" when he was taxable in Gloucester County in 1816 [PPTL, 1800-20].

LEPHEW FAMILY

1. Stephen Lephew, born say 1750, entered 100 acres on both sides of Little Rockhouse Creek of the Dan River in Gilford County, North Carolina, on 29 January 1779 and entered another 129 acres on Rockhouse Creek on 15 April 1781 [Grant 48:54; 56:255; entry nos. 1146, 1198; SS records NC Archives call nos. S.108.721, location 235-8; S.108.722, location 1051-4]. He was head of a Rockingham County household of 10 white persons in 1790: 2 males over the age of sixteen, 6 under sixteen, and 2 females. Perhaps his sister was Mary Lefew, counted next to him, head of a household of 1 white female and 3 white males under the age of sixteen [NC:167]. She may have been the Polly Lefew who was head of a Rockingham County household of 3 "other free" in 1800 [NC:491]. Stephen died before 1801 when 400 acres of his land was divided among his widow Elizabeth and his nine sons [DB G:158]. Elizabeth was head of a Rockingham County household of 9 "other free" in 1800 [NC:491]. Their children were
    i. Elihu, sold his interest in his father's land jointly with his brother Enoch in 1805 [DB M:57].
    ii. Elijah, died before 1806 when the sheriff sold his share of his father's land [DB M:109].
    iii. Josiah, head of a Rockingham County household of 3 "free colored" in 1820 [NC:604].
    iv. Elias, sold his land in 1809 [DB N:48].
    v. Uriah. The sheriff sold his land in 1806 [M:156].
    vi. Levi. The sheriff sold his land in 1806 [M:156].
    vii. Joseph, born before 1776, head of a Rockingham County household of 6 "other free" in 1800 [NC:491]. He sold his land in 1806 [DB M:107] and was head of a Grainger County, Tennessee household of 4 "free colored" in 1830.
    viii. Enoch, born 1776-1794, sold his interest in his father's land in 1805, purchased his brother Elias' portion in 1809, and then sold this land about a year later [DB M:57, N:48, 50]. He married Jane Craig, 21 May 1814 Rockingham County bond, William Scott bondsman. Enoch was head of a Rockingham County household of 4 "free colored" and a white woman in 1820 [NC:604].
    ix. Elisha, born 1776-1794, head of a Grainger County, Tennessee household of 7 "free colored" in 1830. The sheriff sold his land in 1804 [DB L:13].
    x. ?John, married Miranda **Underwood**, 8 May 1811 Rockingham County bond, William Scott bondsman.

Other members of the family were
    i. Jonas, married Patsey Moore, 16 September 1812 Rockingham County bond, Uriah Lephew bondsman.
    ii. Phoebe, married William Craig, 2 February 1811 Rockingham County bond.

LESTER FAMILY

1. Isam Lester, born say 1765, married Elizabeth Jones **Volentine (Valentine)**, 11 December 1789 Lunenburg County bond, Zachariah **Valentine** surety. He was counted in a list of "free Negroes and Mulattoes" in the lower district of Lunenburg near Hawkins' Ford in 1802 and 1803 with his children: Ermin, Faith, Bolling, Jones, Anna, and Ellick [Lunenburg County, Free Negro & Slave Records, 1802-1803, LVA]. He was head of a Lunenburg County

household of 7 "other free" in 1810 [VA:350] and 3 males and 7 females in a list of "Free Negroes and Mulattos" in the lower district of Lunenburg in 1814, head of a household with Patty **Richardson** and his children: Jones, Betsy, Anna, Elly (Ellick), and Sally Lester [*Magazine of Virginia Genealogy* 33:268]. Isham and Elizabeth's children were

   i.   Ermin, born say 1790.

   ii.   Faith, born say 1791, married John **Key**(s). She was his widow in 1853 when she began receiving a pension for his services in the Revolutionary War [Jackson, *Virginia Negro Soldiers*, 39].

   iii.   Bolling.

   iv.   Betsy, born about 1794, registered in Lunenburg County in 1818: *about 24 years of age, 4 feet 10 inches high, brown complexion.*

   v.   Jones, born about 1795, registered in Lunenburg County on 11 April 1825: *aged about 30 years, dark complexion, about five feet six inches high.* He was married to Suky and had a daughter named Elizabeth by 1814 [*Magazine of Virginia Genealogy* 33:268]

   vi.   Alexander, born about 1796, registered in 1818: *about 22 years, about five feet high, brown complexion.*

   vii.   Anna.

   viii.   Sally, born about 1800, registered in Lunenburg County on 12 November 1821: *about 21 years, dark Complexion, about 4 feet 10 or 11 Inches high, daughter of Isham Lester & Elizabeth Lester his wife* [WB 5, after page 89, nos. 3, 4, 11, 38].

LETT FAMILY

Members of the Lett family were

1   i.   Mary, born say 1706.

   ii.   Savory, born say 1713, married Simon **Thompson** ("negroes") on 10 November 1734 at St. Paul's Parish, Baltimore [Reamy, *Records of St. Paul's Parish*, I:31].

   iii.   Elijah, head of a Frederick County, Maryland household of 6 "other free" in 1790.

   iv.   Aquilla, head of a Frederick County, Maryland household of 5 "other free" in 1790.

   v.   Rosalin, head of a Frederick County, Maryland household of 5 "other free" in 1790 and 3 in Washington County in 1800 [MD:638].

   vi.   Charles, head of a Jefferson County, Virginia household of 11 "other free" in 1810 [VA:78].

   vii.   Daniel, head of a Shenandoah County, Virginia household of 6 "other free" in 1810.

   viii.   Delilah, born about 1771, obtained a certificate of freedom in Frederick County, Maryland on 13 September 1826: *about fifty five years of age...a bright Mulatto Woman...free Born as appears by the affidavit of Nicholas Willson* [Certificates of Freedom 1808-42, 187].

1.   Mary Lett, born say 1706, was convicted by the Baltimore County court in November 1728 and in March 1730/1 for having "Molatto" children by a "Negro" [Barnes, *Baltimore Families*]. She was the mother of

   i.   Sarah, born before August 1728.

   ii.   Zachariah, born about 1731.

LEVINER FAMILY

1.   Jean Lovina, born say 1660, was the "Negro Woman" slave of John Nichols who freed her children John and Sarah Lovina by his 11 November 1696 will, proved 17 May 1697. He gave the children 350 acres of land and called them "my two Molattos" [WB 6, fol.95a-96]. Jean was the mother of

2   i.   John[1], born say 1680.

       ii.   Sarah, born 23 June 1682 and died 2 October 1762 [Bell, *Bass Families of the South*, Chapter on Nansemond Indian Ancestry of Some Bass Families, 15]. She received 200 acres in the southern branch of the Elizabeth River by Nichols' will. On 21 December 1716 there was some uncertainty about the boundaries of her land when the Norfolk County court ordered that it be processioned [Orders 1710-17, 78]. She married William **Bass** and was still living in Norfolk County when she sold part of this land on 15 March 1757 [DB 18:41].

2.   John[1] Lovina, born say 1680, was an apprentice of Nathan Newby when Nichols made his will. He received 150 acres adjoining his sister's land on the Southern Branch of the Elizabeth River and another 160 acres in the Western Branch of Elizabeth River adjoining land of William Davenoll, deceased. John was witness to the 10 February 1703/4 Norfolk County will of James Jordan [McIntosh, *Brief Abstract of Lower Norfolk County Wills*, 186]. He died before 18 May 1716 when (his wife) Anne Lovinah was ordered to give an account of her deceased husband's estate [Orders 1710-17, 153]. On 12 November 1728 his son William sold his father's Norfolk County land to William **Bass**, Jr. [DB G:110]. One of John's children was

3   i.   William[1], born, born say 1707.

3.   William[1] Leviner, born say 1707, sold 150 acres in Norfolk County on 12 November 1728 which was the land his father received from Major John Nichols in 1696 [DB G:110]. He was taxable in John Bowers' household in 1730 and in his own household in Western Branch District of Norfolk County from 1730 to 1734 [Wingo, *Norfolk County Tithables, 1730-150*, 22, 40, 75, 96, 142]. He purchased 183 acres in Bertie County, North Carolina, on the northeast side of Cashie Swamp on 9 February 1745. He and his wife Martha sold this land to Thomas **Wilson** eleven years later on 26 April 1756 [DB H:221, 326]. He was taxable on two tithes in John Hill's Bertie County list for 1757 and was a free male "molatto" taxable on one tithe in the 1764 and 1766 list of Jonathan Stanley [CR 10.702.1, Box 1]. He was probably the father of

4   i.   John[2], born say 1750.

4.   John[2] Leviner, born say 1750, entered 100 acres in Anson County on 13 January 1773 [Entry no. 767; Book 25:191; NC Archives call no. S.108.403, location 1233-7, file no. 3308]. He was head of a Richmond County, North Carolina household of 8 "other free" in 1790 [NC:46] and was taxable on 100 acres and one poll in 1795. He was called John Viner in his Richmond County will, proved December 1802, which named his children [WB 1:87]. They were

       i.   Abraham, born say 1778, indicted for petty larceny with (his brother?) Zadock Leviner in the April 1800 session of the Richmond County court. Zadock was found not guilty, and Abraham was given one lash [Minutes 1793-1804, 508].

       ii.   Zadock, born say 1780, among the freeholders ordered by the June 1803 Richmond County court to work on the road from Cross Roads to Duncan McFarland's [Minutes 1792-1804, 586].

       iii.   Isaac, born say 1781, among the freeholders ordered by the September 1804 Richmond County court to work on the road from Captain Pate's to the east bank of Joe's Creek [Minutes 1792-1804, 621]. He was head of a white Richmond County household in 1810 [NC:213].

       iv.   William[2], born say 1783, among the freeholders ordered by the September 1804 Richmond County court to work on the road from Captain Pate's to the east bank of Joe's Creek [Minutes 1792-1804, 621]. He was head of a white Richmond County household in 1810 [NC:213].

LEWIS FAMILY

1. Mary Lewis, born say 1693, was presented by the Surry County, Virginia court on 19 December 1711 for having a "mulattoe bastard Child" [Orders 1702-13, 385]. Mary was probably related to Morgan Lewis, a taxable in the list for Southwark Parish, Surry County, Virginia, in 1703 [DW 5:290]. She was out of the county by 18 June 1712 when the sheriff reported that she was not in his bailiwick [Orders 1702-13, 396]. She may have been the Mary Lewis who was taxable in Beaufort County in 1755 [SS 837]. She may have been the ancestor of

  i.   John[1], born say 1725, taxable with his son William on two black tithes in Beaufort County in 1764 [SS 837].
2 ii. Morgan[1], born say 1730.
  iii. William, born say 1731, taxable with his wife Betty on one white and one black tithe in the Granville County list of Gideon Macon in 1754 [CR 44.701.19].
  iv.   Judith, born in 1733 of free parents in Goochland County, Virginia, and freed of servitude (her indenture) by William Stamp of Goochland. She petitioned the 7 September 1757 Granville County, North Carolina court complaining that Sherwood Harris was detaining her [Owen, *Granville County Notes*, vol.II].
3 v.   Violet, born about 1740.
4 vi. Jean, born say 1741.

2. Morgan[1] Lewis, born say 1730, purchased 200 acres near Conconary Swamp in Halifax County, North Carolina, in January 1775. He signed an agreement with William Hall to divide land in Halifax County on 12 March 1783 [DB 13:290; 17:431]. He probably received an additional 100 acres through this land division since he left over 300 acres to his children. His 14 August 1780 Halifax County will was proved in February 1789. He left 200 acres and 8 slaves to his wife Lucy, to be divided at her death among his children and his granddaughter Lucy Lewis [WB 3:162]. His wife probably died soon after because her children sold the land they inherited in 1791. He was head of a household of 2 free males, 3 free females, and 7 slaves in the 1786 State Census for Halifax County. His children named in his will were

  i.   John[2], born say 1750, sold land on 21 January 1791 which he had inherited from his father and on the same day purchased 106 acres in the same area [DB 17:277, 427]. He was head of a Halifax County household of 1 male and 4 females for the 1786 state census, 4 "other free" and 1 white woman in 1790 [NC:62], and 6 "other free" in 1800 [NC:324]. He and his wife Cloey sold 54 acres in Halifax on 10 January 1801 [DB 18:930]. He was probably deceased by 1810 when his wife Chloe Lewis was head of a Halifax County household of 4 "other free" [NC:33].
  ii. Morgan[2], born about 1751, seventy years old on 22 August 1821 when he made a declaration in Halifax County court to obtain a pension for his services as a private in the 10th Regiment of the North Carolina Line. His family at that time consisted of his seventy-year-old wife, two daughters, and a two-year-old grandson [M804-1558]. On January 1791 he sold 72 acres in Halifax County which he had received from his father [DB 17:423]. He was head of a Halifax County household of one male and 2 females for the 1786 state census, 4 "other free" in 1790 [NC:62], 3 in 1800 [NC:324], and 4 in 1810 [NC:33].
  iii. Elizabeth.
5 iv. Charles, born say 1765.
  v.   Suky.
  vi. Warner, head of a Halifax County household of 3 "other free" in 1790 [NC:62], 7 in 1800 [NC:324], and 4 in 1810 [NC:32]. On 25 June

1791 he and his brother Charles sold 82 acres they inherited, and on 23 November 1791 he sold a further 82 acres he inherited from his father [DB 17:357, 419].

3. Violet Lewis, born about 1740, was called by her first name only when John Foy asked the July 1760 Craven County court to bind to him her four-year-old daughter Bett [Minutes 1758-61, 66b]. Later in that same court session at the request of Peter Rhem, the Craven County court ordered John Foy to deliver "Bett a negro Child" to her mother Violet so that Rhem could have her indentured to him [Minutes 1758-61, 68b]. Four years later in July 1764 Rhem asked the court to extend Violet's indenture another two years for having two children during her indenture [Minutes 1762-64, 53b]. She was called Violet Lewis a "Free Born Negroe Woman" on 7 January 1767 when she indentured herself to Peter Rhem for eight years [Minutes 1767-75, 5c]. Her children were

    i.   Bett, born about 1756, four years old in July 1760 when John Foy asked the Craven County court to bind her to him [Minutes 1758-61, 66b]. She was called "Bet a free born Negro Woman" on 13 June 1777 when she complained in Craven County court that John Foy was detaining her as a servant. The court ordered her set free [Minutes 1772-84, 49c].

    ii. Hannah, born about March 1763, one year and four months old on 4 July 1764 when Peter Rhem asked the court to bind her to him [Minutes 1762-64, 53b].

    iii. Abigail, born about 1766, called "Abigail a free born Negroe Girl aged Eleven Years" on 11 March 1777 when the Craven County court bound her to Peter Rhem [Minutes 1772-84, 44a]. She was called Abby Lewis in 1790, head of a Craven County household of 4 "other free" in 1790 [NC:131]. She married Gabriel **Moore**, 15 March 1806 Craven County bond, Thomas Lewis bondsman.

4. Jean Lewis, born say 1741, was taxable in Beaufort County in Mary Lewis' household in 1755: Mary Lewis and Jean - 2 black tithes [SS 837]. She indentured her son Stephen to Alexander Gray on 2 May 1777, but the 13 September 1780 Craven County court declared the indenture illegal when Stephen petitioned the court for relief from the indenture. The court bound him instead to William Tisdale [Minutes 1772-84, 21]. On 14 September 1787 the Craven County court bound Stephen and Fred Lewis, "free Negroes," to William Carter [Minutes 1786-87, 64a, 65d]. Her children were

6   i.   ?Thomas[1], born say 1758.

    ii. ?Nanny, head of a Carteret County household of 3 "other free" in 1800.

    iii. Stephen, born say 1772, a "free Negro" bound apprentice to Alexander Gray in 1777 and bound as an apprentice turner to William Carter by the 14 September 1787 Craven County court [Minutes 1786-87, 64a].

    iv. ?Fred, born 25 March 1775, a "free negro" bound as an apprentice turner to William Carter by the 14 September 1787 Craven County court [Minutes 1786-87, 65d].

    v. ?Isaac, born 25 October 1776, a "Mulatto" bound to Abraham Guslin as an apprentice seaman by the Craven County court on 12 March 1787 [Minutes 1786-87, 35d].

5. Charles Lewis, born say 1765, was head of a Halifax County household of 3 males and 2 females in the 1786 state census, 6 "other free" in 1790 [NC:62], and 5 in 1800 [NC:324]. On 25 June 1791 he and his brother Warner sold 82 acres they inherited from their father, and on the same day he sold his half interest in his father's mill [DB 17:419, 421]. He was deceased by 17 November 1801 when the Halifax County court ordered his children bound out

as apprentices [Minutes, 1799-1802, n.p.]. Perhaps his wife was "Red Lewis," head of a Halifax County household of 8 "other free" in 1810 [NC:45]. His children were

    i.   Milisey, born about 1789, twelve-year-old daughter of "Charles Lewis deceased" ordered by the Halifax County court bound apprentice to Elizabeth Branch on 17 November 1801.

    ii.   Letitia, born about 1793, eight-year-old daughter of Charles Lewis ordered bound apprentice to Abner Knight on 17 November 1801.

    iii. Clayton, born about 1797, four-year-old son of Charles Lewis ordered bound to Abner Knight on 17 November 1801.

6.   Thomas¹ Lewis, born say 1758, may have been the "Tom a free Born Negroe" for whom Thomas Silgreaves petitioned the 14 March 1777 Craven County court saying he was unjustly withheld from his liberty by Mr. John Foy. The court ordered him set free [Minutes 1772-84, 45f, 59b]. Thomas Lewis was head of a Craven County household of 7 "other free" in 1790 [NC:134]. He may have been the father of

    i.   Richard, born say 1777, married Keziah **Dove**, 16 March 1798 Craven County bond, Thomas Lewis bondsman. He was head of a Rutherford County household of 8 "free colored" in 1820 [NC:370].

    ii.   Margaret, born say 1783, married Robert **Sawyer**, 10 October 1801 Craven County bond, Samuel Simpson bondsman. Robert **Sawyer** was head of a New Bern, Craven County household of 6 "free colored" in 1820 [NC:78].

    iii. Lucretia, born say 1785, married William **Powers**, 2 April 1803 Craven County bond, Solomon **Bowers** bondsman.

    iv. Thomas², born say 1787, married Rhoda **Robeson**, 13 September 1809 Craven County bond, Isaac **Ransome** bondsman. He may have been the same Thomas Lewis who married Nancy **George**, 19 August 1815 Craven County bond, (his brother?) Willis Lewis bondsman. He was head of a Craven County household of 5 "free colored" and 4 slaves in 1820 [NC:64].

    v.   Joshua², born say 1788, married Betsey **Goddett**, 30 June 1809 Craven County bond, James **Goddett** bondsman.

    vi. Willis, born say 1790, married Betsey **Moore**, 3 May 1811 Craven County bond, Isaac **Ransome** bondsman. He was head of a Craven County household of 9 "free colored" and 3 slaves in 1820 [NC:65].

    vii. Sally, born say 1791, married Isaac **Ransome**, 1 November 1809 Craven County bond, Robert **Sawyer** bondsman. Isaac was head of a Craven County household of 7 "other free" in 1790 [NC:134] and 3 "free colored" in 1820 [NC:78].[132]

    viii. Mary, born say 1794, married Peter **Gaudett (Goddett)** 12 May 1813 Craven County bond, Stephen **Gaudett** bondsman.

    ix. Julia, born say 1796, married George **Goddett**, 29 October 1813 Craven County bond, George **Goddett** bondsman.

    x.   Barbara, born say 1797, married William **Moore**, 25 December 1813 Craven County bond, Asa **Ransome** bondsman.

Stafford County

1.   Benjamin Lewis, born say 1660, was called a "Negroe now manumitted and set free" in May 1691 Stafford County court when he sued his master, William

---

[132]Other members of Isaac **Ransom**'s family were George **Ransom** (head of a Craven County household of 5 "other free" in 1790 [NC:134]), Simon **Ransom** (head of a Robeson County household of 6 "other free" in 1790 [NC:49], 8 in 1800 [NC:414] and 2 in 1810 [NC:126]), Martin **Ransom** (head of a Robeson County household of 4 "other free" in 1810 [NC:126]), and Willis **Ransom** (head of a Robeson County household of 4 "other free in 1810 [NC:126]).

Harris. Lewis claimed that he was free in England and was indentured to serve Christopher Robinson for four years. The court ruled in favor of Lewis, and Harris appealed to the General Court [Sparacio, *Stafford County Order Book 1691-92*, 20-21]. He was in Charles City County in October 1691 when the court ordered him returned to Stafford County because he had no evidence that he was free [Orders 1687-95, 360]. He may have been the ancestor of the Lewis family of Stafford and Spotsylvania counties:

    i.   Charles, born say 1758, a "Mulatto" child living in King George County on 5 April 1771 when the court ordered the churchwardens of Brunswick Parish to bind him and his brother Ambrose to William Buckham [Orders 1766-90, 158].

    ii. Ambrose, born say 1760, a "Mulatto" child bound out in Spotsylvania County with Charles on 5 April 1771. On 4 May 1787 the Spotsylvania County court called him "a soldier who got wounded in General Gates' defeat" when it ordered that he receive a pension. The order was renewed each year through 1795 [Minutes 1786-7, 102, 158; Orders 1787-92, 48, 236; 1792-5, 78, 240]. He served in the Revolution from Spotsylvania County and later moved to Alexandria [Jackson, *Virginia Negro Soldiers*, 39-40].

2   iii. Sall, born say 1761.

    iv. Fanny, head of a Spotsylvania County household of 4 "other free" in 1810 [VA:112a].

    v. William, born about 1776, registered in Petersburg on 5 June 1818: *a free man of Colour, five feet ten inches high, forty two years old, brown Complection, born free & raised in Fredericksburg p. information of Ashton Johnson* [Register of Free Negroes 1794-1819, no. 909]. He was head of a Spotsylvania County household of 7 "other free" in 1810 [VA:111b].

    vi. Matilda, head of a Spotsylvania County household of 4 "other free" and a slave in 1810 [VA:111a].

    vii. Daniel, head of a Stafford County household of 10 "other free" and a slave in 1810 [VA:127].

    viii. Nancy, head of a Spotsylvania County household of 4 "other free" in 1810 [VA:111a].

2.   Sall Lewis, born say 1761, was a "Mulatto" woman living in Spotsylvania County on 15 March 1781 when the court ordered the churchwardens of St. George Parish to bind out her "Mulatto" son Francis [Orders 1774-82, 155]. She was the mother of

    i.   Francis, born say 1775.

Princess Anne/ Norfolk County

1.   George[1] Lewis, born say 1680, was ordered by the Princess Anne County court on 6 September 1721 to give security for a debt he owed John Stireing's estate. He was called a "free negro" when he was convicted by the Princess Anne County court on 3 December 1729 for concealing a tithable (probably his wife). He petitioned the Princess Anne County court on 7 January 1729/30 to be free from paying taxes, but the court ruled that he was "very able to work and labour" [Minutes 1717-28, 119, 129; 1728-37, 44, 49]. He may have been the father or grandfather of

2   i.   Martha, born say 1734.

    ii. Solomon, born say 1734, a "free Negro" taxable in Norfolk Borough from the south side of Tanners Creek to Spratts Bridge in 1753 and 1757 [Wingo, *Norfolk County Virginia Tithables, 1751-65*, 67, 121].

3   iii. Betty, born say 1742.

    iv. Joshua[1], born say 1744, a "free negro" taxable head of a household in the western district of Norfolk Borough in 1765 and 1767 [Wingo, *Norfolk County Tithables, 1751-65*, 213; *1766-80*, 34].

2.   Martha Lewis, born say 1734, was a taxable head of a household in the western district of Norfolk Borough in 1765 and 1767 [Wingo, *Norfolk County Tithables, 1751-65*, 213; *1766-80*, 34]. She may have been the mother of
   i.   Ann, born say 1752, taxable in Mary Meach's household in the borough of Norfolk in 1768 [Wingo, *Norfolk County Tithables 1766-80*, 85].
   ii. Joseph, born about 1773, head of a Sussex County household of 7 "other free" in 1810. He received one of the "Certificates granted to Free negroes & mulattoes from October 1800" in Sussex County on 25 July 1818: *dark complexion, 5'8-1/2", free born, 45 years old* [Register, no. 333].

3.   Betty Lewis, born say 1742, was taxable in the Norfolk County, Virginia household of Ann Canterdine in 1759 in the district from the south side of Tanners Creek to Great Bridge and taxable in the household of (her sister?) Martha Lewis in 1765 and in her own household in 1767 [Wingo, *Norfolk County Tithables 1751-65*, 141, 213; *1766-80*, 34]. She was a "free negro" living in Princess Anne County on 10 August 1780 when her sons George and John Lewis were bound to William Hancock to be planters [Minutes 1782-4, 26]. She was the mother of
   i.   George², "F.B." head of a Princess Anne County household of 2 "other free" and a slave in 1810.
   ii. John, born before 10 August 1780.

Lancaster County
1.   Mary Lewis, born say 1713, the servant of William Stamps, was presented by the Lancaster County, Virginia court on 10 November 1731 for having an illegitimate "mulatto" child in Saint Mary's White Chappel Parish [Orders 1729-43, 8, 45]. She may have been the mother of
   i.   Ned, "a Molota," born say 1746. He and his unnamed brother petitioned the Onslow County court in December 1767 saying that they were free but held by Emmanuel Jones. Their case was put off to the next court which did not record their fate [Minutes III:10b].
   ii. Jesse, born say 1760, and his wife Sarah, "Free Mulattos," had their son John baptized in Bruton Parish, James City County on 7 November 1781 [Bruton Parish Register, 34].

Dinwiddie County
1.   Matthew Lewis, born about 1755, registered in Petersburg on 31 May 1808: *a dark brown Negro man, five feet four and a half inches high, fifty three years old, born free & raised in Dinwiddie County, a shoemaker* [Register of Free Negroes 1794-1819, no. 421]. Perhaps his wife was Margery Lewis (born about 1760) who registered in Petersburg on 9 June 1810: *a brown Mulatto woman, five feet six inches high, fifty years old, born free & raised in Dinwiddie County* [Register of Free Negroes 1794-1819, no. 572]. They may have been the parents of
   i.   Frederick, born about 1778, registered in Petersburg on 11 July 1805: *a light or yellow brown Mulatto man, five feet six inches high, twenty seven years old, born free & raised in the Town of Petersburg* [Register of Free Negroes 1794-1819, no. 327].
   ii. Nancy, born about 1788, registered in Petersburg on 3 April 1809: *a brown Mulatto woman, five feet six inches high, twenty one years old, born free in Dinwiddie County* [Register of Free Negroes 1794-1819, no. 470].

LIGHTY FAMILY

1. Mary Lighty, born say 1690, won a suit against James Dudley in Middlesex County court for the freedom of her "Mulatto" daughters Betty and Lucy on 1 June 1736 [Orders 1732-7, 67-8]. She was the mother of

    i. Betty, born say 1703, freed from the service of James Duley on 1 June 1736.
2   ii. Lucy, born say 1705.

2. Lucy Lighty, born say 1705, was freed from the service of James Dudley on 1 June 1736. That same day the court bound her "Negro" son Maximus to Dudley until the age of twenty-one [Orders 1732-7, 67-8]. She was the mother of

    i. Maximus, born say 1730.

LIGON FAMILY

1. Martha Ligon, born say 1720, was living in Henrico County in February 1745 when the court ordered the churchwardens of Dale Parish to bind out her "mulatto" children Elizabeth and Francis [Orders 1737-46, 363]. Her children were
2   i.   ?Hannah, born say 1740.
3   ii. Elizabeth, born say 1742.
    iii. Francis[1], born say 1744, perhaps identical to Frank Liggan, a "FN" taxable in the upper district of Henrico County from 1804 to 1807 [Land Tax List 1799-1816; PPTL 1782-1814, frame 536].
4   iv. ?Peg, born say 1750.

2. Hannah Liggon, born say 1740, was the mother of Phebe Liggon who married Thomas **Findley**, 10 May 1788 Henrico County bond, Hannah Liggon, Jerry Liggon, and William Logon witnesses. Samuel **Findley**, guardian of Phobe, gave his consent. She was the mother of

    i.   ?Jeremiah, born about 1762, a witness to the marriage of Phebe Liggon and Thomas **Findley**, 10 May 1788 Henrico County bond. He was a "Mulatto" taxable in Chesterfield County from 1788 to 1810 [PPTL, 1786-1811, frames 37, 183, 542, 619, 661, 717, 753, 799]. He obtained a certificate of freedom in Chesterfield County on 26 August 1816: *fifty four years old, brown complexioned, born free* [Register of Free Negroes 1804-53, 261]. He was security for the 13 September 1813 marriage of Manuel **Valentine** and Nancy **Cox** (free persons of colour), 13 September 1813 Chesterfield County bond [Marriage Register, 122].
    ii. Phebe, born say 1770, married Thomas **Findley**, 10 May 1788 Henrico County bond.
    iii. ?Thomas[1], born about 1772, a "Mulatto" taxable in Chesterfield County from 1798 to 1810 [PPTL, 1786-1811, frames 358, 469, 581, 619, 753, 799]. He obtained a certificate of freedom in Chesterfield County on 13 October 1828: *fifty six years old, black complexion, born free* [Register of Free negroes 1804-53, no. 611].
    iv. Peter, born about 1780, a "Mulatto" taxable in Chesterfield County from 1803 to 1810 [PPTL, 1786-1811, frames 542, 619, 661, 717, 799]. He obtained a certificate of freedom in Chesterfield County on 8 September 1806: *twenty five years old, black complexioned, born free* [Register of Free Negroes 1804-53, no. 28].

3. Elizabeth Ligon, born say 1742, was living in Henrico County in April 1765 when the court ordered the churchwardens of Henrico Parish to bind out her

son Chamberlayne Liggon (no race indicated) [Orders 1763-67, 441]. She was
the mother of

5
    i.   Chamberlayne, born say 1763.
    ii. ?William[1], born say 1765.
    iii. ?Samuel, born say 1784, a "free Negro" taxable in Henrico County in
        1801 [PPTL 1782-1814, frame 434].

4. Peg Ligon, born say 1750, was living in Chesterfield County on 1 April 1774
when the court ordered the churchwardens to bind out her children Beverly
and Frank (no race indicated) [Orders 1774-84, 9]. She was the mother of

    i.   Beverly, a "M°" taxable in Powhatan County in 1791 [PPTL, 1787-
        1825, frame 62].
    ii. Francis[2], born say 1775, a "M°" taxable in Powhatan County from
        1790 to 1794, his tax charged to John Forlines in 1790 [PPTL, 1787-
        1825, frames 46, 62, 79, 94, 107], taxable in the lower district of
        Henrico County from 1796 to 1813: his tax charged to William Liggon
        in 1796 and 1797; called a "free Mulatto" from 1803 to 1805, a "free
        Negro" starting in 1806; taxable on a slave in 1809; taxable in the
        lower district of Henrico County on 29 acres adjoining William
        Roberson's land in 1813; taxable on 20 acres near the Stage Road in
        1815 and 1816 [PPTL 1782-1814, frames 345, 407, 434, 463, 490,
        515, 556, 577, 619, 684, 704, 772; Land Tax List 1799-1816], head
        of a Henrico County household of 7 "other free" in 1810 [VA:991].
    iii. ?John, born say 1780, a "Mulatto" taxable in Chesterfield County from
        1801 to 1809 [PPTL, 1786-1811, frames 469, 542, 581, 661, 753].
    iv. ?Winsey, born say 1785, taxable in William Liggon's Henrico County
        household in 1801.
    v. ?Phebe, born say 1788, married Thomas **Bibby**, "F.N.," 30 December
        1806 Chesterfield County bond, John Ligon bondsman.
    vi. ?William[2], born about 1789, obtained a certificate of freedom in
        Chesterfield County on 9 July 1810: *twenty one years old, yellow*
        complexion, born free [Register of Free Negroes 1804-53, no. 133]. He
        registered in Botetourt County: *William Liggin, 30 years old, Yellow*
        Complexion, 6 feet high...born free as appears by the certificate from
        the clerk of Staunton Corporation court, Registered 17th July 1819
        [Free Negroes &c Registered in the Clerks Office of Botetourt County,
        #22]. And he registered in Halifax County, Virginia, on 21 June 1831:
        a bright Mulatto man, five feet 11 inches high and about forty two
        years old, who was born free as appears by a register of the Clerk of
        the Hustings Court of the City of Richmond [Registers of Free Negroes,
        1802-1831, no. 198].
    vii. ?Elizabeth, born about 1789, married Ned **Bibby**, 13 September 1813
        Chesterfield County bond.

5. William[1] Ligon, born say 1765, married Fanny **Mathews**, daughter of Rachel
Mathews who consented, 14 July 1787 Henrico County bond, surety Nathaniel
Couzins who certified that Fanny was over the age of twenty-one. William
was a "melatto" taxable in the northern district of Campbell County in 1789
[PPTL, 1785-1814, frame 117] and taxable in the lower district of Henrico
County from 1792 to 1814: taxable on Francis Liggon's tithe in 1796 and
1797; taxable on his own tithe, (his son?) Winsey Liggon's tithe and a horse
in 1801; called a "free Mulatto" or "free Negro" starting in 1801; taxable on
a slave in 1806; taxable on his two unnamed sons in 1813: taxable on 26 acres
on the Stage Road in 1813; taxable on 81 acres on the Stage Road in 1815 and
1816. His wife was probably the Fanny Ligon who was counted in a "List of
Female Free Negroes & Mulattoes over the age of 16" in Henrico County in
1813 [PPTL 1782-1814, frames 294, 306, 332, 345, 356, 390, 434, 463, 557,
577, 619, 684, 704, 789; Land Tax List 1799-1816]. He was head of a

Henrico County household of 9 "other free" in 1810 [VA:991]. He may have been the father of

i. Thomas[3], born say 1788, a "free Mulatto" or "free Negro" taxable in the lower district of Henrico County from 1805 to 1814: taxable on a slave in 1813; taxable on 40 acres in the lower district near the Stage Road in 1815 and 1816 [PPTL 1782-1814, frames 515, 557, 577, 619, 684, 704, 772, 789; Land Tax List 1799-1816] and head of a Henrico County household of 3 "other free" in 1810 [VA:991].

ii. Betsy, born about 1793, obtained a certificate of freedom in Chesterfield County on 11 June 1827: *thirty four years old, brown complexion, born free* [Register of Free Negroes 1804-53, no. 571].

Other members of the family were

i. Nancy, born say 1782, head of a Richmond City household of 7 "other free" in 1810 [VA:330].

ii. Thomas[2], born say 1780, head of a Prince Edward County household of 6 "other free" in 1810 [VA:576].

iii. Betty, born about 1774, "Persons of Color," head of a Cumberland County, Virginia household of 3 "other free" in 1810 [VA:103]. She registered in Powhatan County on 19 December 1822: *Age: 48; Color: Black; Stature: 5'1-1/2"; Born Free* [Register of Free Negroes, no.50].

iv. Phobe, "F.B.," head of a Powhatan County household of 8 "other free" in 1810 [VA:10].

v. Tilmon Loggins, a "Mulatto" taxable in Patrick County from 1809 to 1817 [PPTL, 1791-1823, frames 519, 539, 598, 666]. He married Prudence **Fendley**, 27 September 1809 Patrick County bond. He, Prudence, Jeremiah, Polly, Edward, Isaiah, Isham and Saundary Loggins obtained certificates of freedom in Patrick County in December 1829 [Orders 1822-31].

vi. Cam Loggins, a "Mulatto" taxable in Patrick County from 1807 to 1817 [PPTL, 1791-1823, frames 492, 520, 540, 616, 666].

LIVELY FAMILY

Members of the Lively family in Virginia were

i. Thomas, born about 1736, taxable in Chesterfield County from 1793 to 1811, a "Mulatto" living with his 2 children on James Scott's land in 1809 and 1811 [PPTL, 1786-1811, frames 162, 198, 268, 301, 374, 563, 689, 738]. He was a "man of Colour," eighty four years of age on 31 May 1820 when he made a declaration in Petersburg to obtain a pension for his services in the Revolution, stating that he enlisted in Chesterfield County in the 5th Virginia Regiment in 1777. On 27 August 1820 his family consisted of his twenty-three-year-old daughter Sally **Freeman**, her twenty-seven-year-old husband Kit **Freeman** and their seven-year-old son James [M804-1573, frame 0042].

ii. William[1], born about 1750, a twenty-three-year-old indented "Mulatto fellow" who ran away from Lewis Boaten of Roberson Fork, Culpeper County, according to the 15 July 1773 issue of the *Virginia Gazette* [Rind edition].

iii. Sally, born about 1792, obtained a certificate of freedom in Chesterfield County on 18 July 1821: *twenty nine years old, bright mulatto complexion, born free* [Register of Free Negroes 1804-53, no. 448].

iv. Becky, born about 1794, obtained a certificate of freedom in Chesterfield County on 13 July 1818: *twenty four years old, yellow complexion, born free* [Register of Free Negroes 1804-53, no. 323].

v. William[2], born about 1794, registered in Petersburg on 24 April 1815: *a light brown Mulatto man, five feet seven and a half inches high,*

> *twenty one years old, rather yellowish eyes, born free and raised in the County of Chesterfield* [Register of Free Negroes 1794-1819, no. 770].

vi.   Charity, born about 1797, obtained a certificate of freedom in Chesterfield County on 18 July 1821: *twenty five years old, bright mulatto complexion, born free* [Register of Free Negroes 1804-53, no. 447].

vii.   John, born about 1814, registered in York County on 18 June 1832: *a mulatto boy about 18 years of age...long bushy hair...Born in Gloster County* [Free Negroes Register 1831-1850, no. 339].

LIVERPOOL/ POOL FAMILY

1.   Sarah Liverpool, born say 1743, was a free "Negro" who was presented by the Northampton County, Virginia court on 8 May 1764 for having an illegitimate child. She confessed to the offense and was ordered to be whipped [Minutes 1761-5, 113, 119]. She was apparently the ancestor of

2   i.   Solomon, born say 1763.

      ii.   Abel, born say 1770, taxable in Northampton County from 1789 to 1796 [PPTL, 1782-1823, frames 102, 131, 214].

     iii.   Henry, born say 1772, taxable in Northampton County from 1789 to 1791 [PPTL, 1782-1823, frames 102, 131]. He married Keziah **Beckett**, 17 March 1799 Northampton County bond, Solomon Liverpool security. They were called Henry and Kesiah Pool when they registered as "free Negroes" in Northampton County on 12 June 1794 [Orders 1789-95, 358].

     iv.   George, born say 1773, taxable in Northampton County from 1790 to 1798 [PPTL, 1782-1823, frames 117, 214, 252], called George Pool when he married Comfort **Weeks**, 10 May 1793 Northampton County bond, Abraham **Lang** security. They were called George Anderson Pool and Comfort Anderson Pool when they registered as "free Negroes" in Northampton County on 10 and 11 June 1794 [Orders 1789-95, 354]. He may have been the George Pool who married Patience **Stephens**, 27 September 1819 Northampton County bond, Daniel Pool security. George Liverpool was head of a Northampton County household of 4 "free colored" in 1820 [VA:217].

     v.   Anderson Pool, a "free Negro" taxable in Northampton County from 1795 to 1813 [PPTL, 1782-1823, frames 197, 214, 252].

     vi.   Daniel, born say 1774, registered as a "free Negro" in Northampton County on 11 June 1794 [Orders 1789-95], married Elishe **Driggers**, 25 June 1799 Northampton County bond, Josias Liverpool security. Daniel may have been identical to Daniel Pool who was security for the 27 September 1819 Northampton County marriage of George Pool. He was a "free Negro" taxable in Northampton County from 1796 to 1813 [PPTL, 1782-1823, frames 214, 252].

     vii.   Josiah, born say 1776, registered as a "free Negro" in Northampton County on 11 June 1794 [Orders 1789-95], probably identical to Sias Pool who was a "free Negro" taxable in Northampton County from 1795 to 1798 [PPTL, 1782-1823, frames 197] and head of a Northampton County household of 11 "free colored" in 1820 [VA:216A].

     viii.   Sarah, born say 1778, registered as a "free Negro" in Northampton County on 11 June   1794 [Orders 1789-95]. She married Solomon **Beckett**, July 1800 Northampton County bond.

     ix.   Adah, born say 1780, married Solomon **Beckett**, 7 July 1801 Northampton County bond, Josiah Liverpool security.

2.   Solomon Liverpool, born say 1763, was presented by the Northampton County court on 11 November 1788 for tending crops on land belonging to the

Gingaskin Indians. He was called Solomon L. Pool when Isaac **Webb** sued him in Northampton County on 13 May 1789 [Orders 1787-9, 269, 270, 272]. He registered as a "free Negro" in Northampton County on 11 June 1794 together with Betty, Catherine, Charles and Nat who were called children of Solomon and Bridget his wife. Bridget was probably the Bridget Liverpool who registered her children Absobeth and William three days later on 14 June 1794 [Orders 1787-9; 1789-95, 367]. Perhaps Bridget was an Indian since she did not register herself. Solomon was taxable in Northampton County from 1783 to 1813: taxable on 2 slaves, 2 horses and 3 cattle in 1783; taxable on a slave over the age of sixteen in 1788; taxable on 2 free males in 1801; 3 free males and 6 horses in 1802; 2 male and 2 female "free Negroes" above the age of 16 in 1813 [PPTL, 1782-1823, frames 18, 32, 87, 131, 195, 250, 311, 331, 540]. He was head of a Northampton County household of 3 "free colored" in 1820 [VA:217]. He and Bridget were the parents of

   i.   Betty, born say 1776.

   ii.   Catherine, born say 1778.

   iii.   Charles, born say 1779, called Charles Pool when he was taxable in Northampton County from 1795 to 1813, called "Charles Liverpool son of Solomon" in 1806 [PPTL, 1782-1823, frames 197, 413, 540]. He married Anne **Driggus**, 1 January 1820 Northampton County bond, Cudjo **Stephens** security, and was head of a Northampton County household of 9 "free colored" in 1820 [VA:217].

   iv.   William, born say 1779, a "free Negro" taxable in Northampton County from 1795 [PPTL, 1782-1823, frames 197].

   v.   Nat, born say 1782.

   vi.   Absobeth, born say 1784, probably identical to Absel Pool who married Esau **Gutrie** of Accomack County, 23 December 1803 Northampton County bond, Moses **Buckner** security. Esaw **Gutridge** and his unnamed wife were listed with 2 males and a female over the age of 16 in their Accomack County household in 1813 [PPTL 1782-1814, frame 856].

Members of the Pool family in Northampton County were

   i.   Anderson Pool, married Catherine **Drighouse**, 23 June 1800 Northampton County bond, Jacob Holland security.

   ii.   Isaac Pool, married Sophia **Morris**, 17 December 1811 Northampton County bond, John Upchurch security. He was a "N." taxable in Northampton County in 1813 [PPTL, 1782-1823, frame 543]. Isaac Liverpool was head of a Northampton County household of 5 "free colored" in 1820 [VA:217].

   iii.   Marshall Pool, married Margaret **Weeks**, 27 December 1817 Northampton County bond, John **Weeks** security.

LOCKLEAR FAMILY

Jacob Lockeleer, born say 1636, was a Frenchman who arrived in Virginia without an indenture and was bound to Edward Diggs, Esquire, for four years. He completed his indenture in York County, Virginia, on 24 April 1660 [DWO 4:86, 89]. He was probably the ancestor of the Locklears who were early mixed-race residents of Lunenburg County, Virginia, and Edgecombe County, North Carolina.

1.   Robert[1] Locklear, born say 1700, was living in Edgecombe County on 10 December 1738 when Benjamin Rawlings mentioned him in his will. Rawlings allowed him to purchase the plantation he was then living on for 10 pounds [SS 1738-52, 63]. This plantation was probably in the part of Edgecombe County which became Halifax County in 1758. Locklear's land was mentioned in a 1 November 1753 Edgecombe County deed which was recorded later in Halifax County. It adjoined the Roanoke River, Quankey Pocosin, and **Chavis'**

Branch [Halifax DB 17:568; Edgecombe DB 2:97]. Robert may have been renting this land or perhaps he was Benjamin Rawling's son-in-law since he was the first person mentioned in Rawling's will [SS 1738-52, 63]. Robert made a deed of gift of all his goods and chattels in Edgecombe County to his son John on 24 May 1749 with the proviso that he maintain him and his wife for the rest of their lives [DB 3:347]. Robert Locklear's children were

2 i. John[1], born say 1721, died about 1787.

  ii. ?Dudley, born say 1722, the defendant in an Edgecombe County court suit, Campbell vs. Dudley Locklear, in August 1746 [Haun, *Edgecombe County Court Minutes*, I:110, 116]. He was a taxable "Molato" in Bladen County in 1776 [Byrd, *Bladen County Tax Lists*, II:64, 84]. He received a patent for 150 acres in Bladen County on the south side of Drowning Creek and Ashpole Swamp below his improvements on 11 November 1779 and sold 100 acres of this land on 10 September 1783 [DB 19:8; 1:36].

3 iii. ?Major, born say 1724.

  iv. ?Susannah Lakier, born say 1725, no race indicated, who was bound an additional year by order of the 8 November 1743 session of the Bertie County court because she had a bastard child during her indenture [Haun, *Bertie County Court Minutes*, II:417].

4 v. ?Randall, born say 1730.

5 vi. ?William[1], born say 1740.

2. John[1] Locklear, born say 1722, entered 100 acres in Bladen County on the south side of Gum Swamp and Drowning Creek between 5 October and 15 November 1752 [Pruitt, *Bladen County Land Entries 1787-1795*, no.665]. He and his wife were "Mulatto" Cumberland County taxables in 1755 [T&C 1], and he and his wife, son, and daughter were taxable in Bladen County in 1763 [Bladen County Tax List (1763)]. He, his wife, son William, and daughters Sarah and Elizabeth were taxable "Mulatoes" in Bladen County in 1768 (his name torn, but apparent from later lists), taxable with his wife and son William in 1770 and 1771 and taxable with his wife and son Robert in 1772 [Byrd, *Bladen County Tax Lists*, I:5, 46, 58, 82, 124; II:101, 119]. He patented 250 acres in Cumberland County on the East side of Drowning Creek on 28 February 1764, and he and his wife Elizabeth sold 50 acres of this land on 1 May 1787 [Hoffman, *Land Patents*, I:504; DB A:56]. On 5 August 1784 he made his Bladen County will, recorded in Robeson County soon after it was formed in 1787 (no probate date). He left his plantation to his wife and then to son Samuel with a shilling to his other unnamed children [WB 1:8]. His children were

  i. ?Jacob, born say 1745, taxable in Bladen County with his wife from 1768 to 1774 ("Mulatoes"), also taxable on Riding **Kersey**'s tax in 1774, and taxable on 100 acres and one poll in McNeill's District in Bladen County in 1784 [Byrd, *Bladen County Tax Lists*, I:7, 46, 82, 124, 135; II:119; Bladen County Tax List (1784)]. He was head of a Robeson County household of 6 "other free" in 1790 [NC:48] and 5 in 1800 [NC:389b]. He purchased 100 acres on Bear Swamp in Robeson County from James **Lowery** on 13 June 1791 [DB B:341].

  ii. Samuel, born say 1748, perhaps the unnamed son who was taxable in John Locklear's Bladen County household in 1763. He was head of a Robeson County household of 1 "other free" in 1790, 5 in 1800 [NC:389b], 12 in 1810 [NC:231] and 7 "free colored" in 1820 [NC:312].

  iii. William[2], born say 1751, taxable in his father's Bladen County household from 1768 to 1771, head of his own household in 1772, and married by 1774 [Byrd, *Bladen County Tax Lists*, I:5, 46, 58, 82, 124, 135; II:101, 119]. He had put his improvements on land in Bladen County on Juniper Branch on 7 December 1778 [Bladen County envelope 4070, Land Grant Office]. He received a grant for this 100 acres on Juniper Branch in Bladen County on 7 November 1784 [DB 1:73] and was taxable in Bladen County on this land in 1784. On 26 May 1788 the sheriff sold this 100 acres on the east side of Drowning Creek and both sides of Juniper Branch for a debt he owed John Moore [DB A:288]. He sold 100 acres on the east side of Drowning Creek to William[3] Locklear in 1810 [DB P:258]. He was head of a Robeson County household of 11 "other free" in 1790 [NC:48], 12 in 1800 [NC:389b], 7 in 1810 [NC:232], and 7 "free colored" in 1820 [NC:295].

    iv.   Sarah, born before 1752, taxable in her father's Bladen County household in 1763 and 1768.

    v.   Elizabeth, born before 1757, taxable in her father's Bladen County household in 1768.

6   vi.   ?Joseph, born say 1758.

    vii.   Robert[3], born say 1759, taxable in his father's Bladen County household in 1772, head of a Fairfield County, South Carolina household of 4 "other free" in 1800 [SC:226].

    viii.   ?John[2], Jr., born say 1767, entered 100 acres on the east side of Juniper Branch adjoining William Locklear in Robeson County on 22 March 1788 [Pruitt, *Land Entries: Robeson County,* I:15]. He was head of a Robeson County household of 4 "other free" in 1790 [NC:48], was living in Richmond County in 1810 [NC:192], and was head of a Richmond County household of 8 "free colored" in 1820 [NC:216].

    ix.   ?Malcolm Buie, born say 1768, entered 50 acres east of Long Swamp in Robeson County on 12 March 1789 including Charles **Valentine**'s improvements and 50 acres bordering his own line east of Juniper Branch on 29 January 1794 [Pruitt, *Land Entries: Robeson County,* I:23, no. 1462]. He purchased adjoining tracts of 100 acres and 177 acres on the east side of Juniper Branch from James **Lowery** on 27 May 1801 and 4 October 1803, and purchased land from Malcolm McMillan by deed proved in Robeson County on 4 October 1803 [DB L:20; N:187-90; Minutes I:264]. He was head of a Robeson County household of 6 "other free" in 1790 [NC:48], 5 in 1800 [NC:389] and 7 in 1810 [NC:232].

3.   Major Locklear, born say 1724, was the defendant in an Edgecombe County court suit, Campbell vs. Major Locklear, in August 1746 [Haun, *Edgecombe County Court Minutes,* I:110, 116]. He was living on the northeast side of Drowning Creek on White Oak Swamp on 27 August 1753 in what was then Bladen County when a land entry was issued to Dennis McLendle and James McCallam for 100 acres which he was living on [Pruitt, *Bladen County Land Entries,* no. 793; NCGSJ VI:174 (Papers of Colonial Governors 1753-4, #CGP 4)]. He was taxed as a "Mulatto" in Cumberland County in 1755 [T&C 1]. He was listed as a white taxable in Bladen County in 1768 and a "Mulato" taxable in 1770 [Byrd, *Bladen County Tax Lists,* I:7, 45, 143]. He was living in Bladen County on 13 October 1773 when he was listed as a harborer of "free Negors and Mullatus living upon the Kings Land" who included Edward and Tiely Locklear [G.A. 1773, Box 7]. Perhaps his widow was Ann Locklear who was head of a Bladen County household of 1 "Black" person aged 12 to 50 and 6 "Black" persons aged over 50 or under 12 in 1786 [Byrd, *Bladen County Tax Lists,* II:169]. He may have been the father of

    i.   Edward, born say 1750, a taxable "Mulato" in Bladen County in 1772 [Byrd, *Bladen County Tax Lists,* II:72, 143].

    ii.   Tiely, born say 1752.

    iii.   Guttridge, born say 1753, a taxable "Mulato" in Bladen County from 1769 to 1776, living in John **Bullard**'s household in 1770 and listed as white in 1774 [Byrd, *Bladen County Tax Lists,* I:14, 33, 78, 111, 129;

II:64, 84]. He received a patent for 200 acres in Bladen near Haleys Mill Swamp on 23 October 1782 [Hoffman, *Land Patents*, vol. II, no.592] and sold this land near what was then called Cade's Mill Swamp on 23 February 1786 [Robeson DB C:27]. He was counted as white in 1790, head of an Orangeburgh District, South Carolina household of 3 males over 16, 4 under 16, and 4 females [SC:96]. He was listed near Charity **Groom**, Isaac **Groom**, Richard **Groom**, William **Groom**, Benjamin **Sweat**, and Gideon **Bunch**, Jr., who were also counted as white. Benjamin **Sweat**, and the **Groom** family were "free Negors and Mullatus" included in the before mentioned 13 October 1773 Bladen County list [G.A. 1773, Box 7].

4. Randolph/ Randall Locklear, born about 1730, was taxable in Lunenburg County, Virginia, in the list of Edmund Taylor for St. James Parish in 1751 [Tax List 1748-52]. He was in the Muster Roll of Captain Smith's Company of the Edgecombe County Militia in the 1750's [Clark, *Colonial Soldiers of the South*, 672]. In 1765 he and wife Sarah were "Black" tithables in Granville County, North Carolina, and in 1766 they were tithable on 3 persons [CR 44.701.20]. He sued Thomas **Evans** in Mecklenburg County, Virginia, on 14 March 1774 for a debt of 2 pounds due by note of hand [Orders 1773-9, 185]. He was taxed on 150 acres and one poll in Bladen County, North Carolina, in 1784. He was granted a patent for 150 acres in Bladen County on the west side of Ashpole Swamp crossing the Boggy Branch on 22 March 1788 [DB 36:493] and made a Robeson County deed of gift of this land to his son Robert on 7 February 1794 [DB F:157]. In 1790 he was head of a Robeson County household of 10 "other free" [NC:48]. His children were

7   i.   ?Thomas, born say 1750.
        ii. Robert[2], born say 1753, brought to court with Nathaniel **Gowen** in Granville County in 1773 on an unspecified charge but released on payment of their prison charges when no one appeared against them [Minutes 1773-83, 1]. "**Chavis** and Robert Locklear" received a patent for 150 acres on the north side of the Little Peedee and west side of the Shoeheel Swamp in Bladen County on 11 November 1779 [DB 19:484, #182]. Robert was taxable on one poll tax in Bladen County in 1784 in McNeill's District and entered 100 acres on Juniper Branch in what was then Robeson County on 4 September 1790 [Pruitt, *Land Entries: Robeson County*, I:38]. On 8 February 1794 he received a deed of gift from his father Randal for 150 acres in Robeson County on the south side of Ashpole Swamp, being the plantation his father was then living on, and sold this land on 25 February 1799 [DB F:157; I:7]. He was head of a Robeson County household of 9 "other free" in 1790 [NC:48], 11 in 1800 [NC:389b], 13 in 1810 [NC:230], and 9 "free colored" in 1820 [NC:301].
        iii. William[3], born say 1765, purchased 100 acres on the east side of Drowning Creek from William[2] Locklear in 1810 [DB P:258]. He was head of a Robeson County household of 7 "other free" in 1810 [NC:220] and 11 "free colored" in 1820, called William Locklear, Jr. [NC:293].

5. William[1] Locklear, born say 1740, was probably living in Halifax County before 1 November 1753 when a Granville grant to Joseph Montfort mentioned land joining **Chavis'** branch and Lockaleer [Halifax DB 17:568]. The family was still in Halifax County on 20 May 1777 when a deed from Alexander McCulloch to John Clayton mentioned land adjoining Lockalear's pocosin [DB 13:455]. William[1] Locklear died before 18 November 1784 when the Halifax County court ordered the sheriff to "sell as much of the estate of William Locklear to satisfy the debts of the decedent." Mary Locklear, head of a

Halifax County household of 8 "other free" in 1800, may have been his widow [NC:324]. Their children may have been

8   i.   Maria, born say 1765.

    ii. Robert⁴, born about 1784, seventeen years old when he, Israel, and Aaron Locklear and Lucy **Cooley** were ordered bound apprentices to Samuel Tunnell by the 18 August 1801 Halifax County court. He was head of a Halifax County household of 2 "other free" in 1810 [NC:33], 8 "free colored" in 1820 [NC:155], and 8 in 1830. He obtained free papers in Halifax County court on 23 February 1850: *Robin Locklear about 65 years old, very dark complexion, 5 feet 10 inches tall. Charlotte Locklear, his wife, 61 years old, bright complexion, 5 feet 3/4 inches tall* [CR 47.301.7, cited by Kent, *Swampers*, 7].

6.   Joseph Locklear, born say 1758, was living in South Carolina on 2 April 1779 when he, Elijah Locklear, Sherwood **Chavis**, and Isaac **Malone**, alias **Rouse**, were jailed in the district gaol of Salisbury on suspicion of robbery.[133] They were released because there was no evidence against them, and they were "willing and desirous of enlisting in the Continental [*Charlotte Gazette*]. Joseph was taxable in 1784 in McNeill's District, Bladen County. He purchased 100 acres in Robeson County from James **Lowry** on 13 June 1791 [DB B:341] and entered 100 acres of land bordering Crickett Lockleir on Bear Swamp on 6 September 1793 [Pruitt, *Land Entries: Robeson County*, I:84]. The sheriff sold 100 acres of his land on the east side of Long Swamp adjoining John Locklear for debt on 5 November 1788 [DB A:211]. He was head of a Robeson County household of 6 "other free" in 1790 [NC:48], 9 in 1800 [NC:389], 7 in 1810 [NC:230], and 8 "free colored" in 1820 [NC:294]. He was probably the father of

    i.   Wiley, married Nancy **Evans**, 25 May 1817 Robeson County bond, Joseph Locklear bondsman.

7.   Thomas Locklear, born say 1750, may have been one of three taxables in the 1766 Granville County household of (his father?) Randall Locklear. He was sued in the October 1770 Granville County court by William **Chavis**:

Take body of Thomas lockery of your sd County Free Negro...answer William Chavers of a plea of Trespas on the case ...at Oxford [CR 44.928.15].

His taxable property in Granville was assessed at 120 pounds in 1780, and in 1782 he was taxable on a horse and 5 cattle in Fishing Creek District. He was head of a Dutch District household of 3 males and 3 females in 1786 for the North Carolina State Census, head of a Wake County household of 13 "other free" in 1790 [NC:103], and head of a Wake County household in 1800 [NC:779]. He was taxable on 180 acres in Captain Ray's district of Wake County in 1793 and 1794 [MFCR 099.701.1, frames 46, 121]. He may have been the father of

    i.   Polly, born say 1786, married David **Mitchell**, 1 January 1804 Granville County bond with John **Tyner** bondsman.

    ii. Rachel, born say 1790, married Peter **Chavis**, 29 April 1807 Wake County bond, Irby Phillips bondsman.

    iii. Elizabeth, born say 1795, married Robert **Chavis**, 29 September 1813 Wake County bond, James Shaw bondsman.

---

[133]Elijah Lockelaire was counted as white in Marlboro County, South Carolina, in 1800 with (sons?): John, Stephen, and Major [SC:54].

     iv. Solomon², born say 1797, married Phillis **Dunston**, 19 January 1818 Wake County bond, John Phillips bondsman.

     v. Catherine, married Edward **Bass**, 28 August 1821 Wake County bond, Samuel **Bass** bondsman.

8. Maria Locklear, born say 1765, was head of a Halifax County household of 4 "other free in 1800 [NC:324]. She may have been the Mary Locklier who was cited by the 28 November 1801 Halifax County court to bring her children to court so they could be bound out [Minutes 1799-1802]. Her 9 May 1832 Halifax County will, proved August 1832, mentioned her granddaughters Eliza and Maria Locklear, and children: Gabriel Locklear and Maria and Polly **Scott** [WB 4:90]. Her children were

     i. Gabriel, born about 1787, a fourteen-year-old "base born child" ordered bound apprentice to Julius Horton by the 18 August 1801 Halifax County court. He was head of a Halifax County household of 8 "free colored" in 1830 and was executor of his mother's 1832 will. On 20 November 1837 the Halifax County court bound to him three children "of color:" Catherine, Jethro, and Mary Locklayer. The 25 February 1842 and 18 August 1845 sessions of the court allowed him to carry his gun, and the 19 August 1845 session ordered him jailed until he paid a fine [Minutes 1832-46].

     ii. Polly **Scott**, probably the wife of Joseph **Scott** who was also mentioned in Maria's will.

     iii. Maria, born about 1795, a six-year-old "base born Child" ordered bound to Edith Clifton by the 18 August 1801 Halifax County court [Minutes 1799-1802]. She married Harwood **Scott**, 25 February 1819 Halifax County bond with Joseph **Scott** bondsman. Her husband Harwood **Scott** was mentioned in her mother's will.

     iv. ?Samuel, head of a Halifax County household of 1 "other free in 1810 [NC:33]. He was in the First Company detached from the Halifax County Regiment in the War of 1812 [N.C. Adjutant General, *Muster Rolls of the War of 1812*, 19].

     v. ?Solomon¹, head of a Rowan County household of 2 "free colored" in 1820 [NC:336]. He was in the First Company detached from the Halifax County Regiment in the War of 1812.

Other members of the family were

     i. Major, taxable in Captain Ward's District of Warren County in 1799 [Tax List 1781-1801, 387].

     ii. Levinia, born before 1776, head of a Warren County household of 1 "free colored" in 1820 [NC:796].

LOCKSAM/ LOCKSON FAMILY

1. Rebecca Locksam, born say 1750, was a "Mullatto" woman claimed as a servant by James Robb, merchant of Fredericksburg, but in the possession of Doctor Archibald Campbell on 24 August 1771 when she petitioned the Orange County, Virginia court for her freedom. The court ruled that she was entitled to her freedom but bound her illegitimate "Mulattoe" son Billey to Alexander Waugh, Jr., on 26 November 1772 [Orders 1769-77, 92, 135, 145, 156, 167, 230]. She was the mother of

     i. William Locksam, born say 1770.

     ii. ?George Lockson, head of a Madison County, Virginia household of 1 "other free" and 4 slaves in 1810 [VA:395].

     iii. ?Rachel Lockson, "F.N." head of a Rockingham County, Virginia household of 1 "other free" in 1810 [VA:27].

LUCAS/ LOCUS(T) FAMILY

The Lucas/ Locus/ Locust family may have originated in Charles City County where Elizabeth Lucie was presented by the churchwardens of Weynoke Parish for having a bastard child by an unknown father. Her son, a "molotto boy the sonne of Elizabeth Lucie dec'd," was bound to Howell Pryse on 4 December 1665. Perhaps his father was Jack (John[1] **Tann**), "a negro servant to Mr. Rice Hoe," who was ordered freed from his service on 8 February 1665/6 by virtue of a note given him by his former master, Rice Hoe, Sr. A former servant of Hoe claimed that "Hoe had never a servt. maid but the sd Jack the Negro lay w'th her or got her w'th child" [Orders 1655-65, 601, 617, 618, 632]. One of Hoe's descendants, Howson Hooe of Prince William County, was the master of Hester Lucas, a "mulatto woman servant" whose son was bound to Hooe in 1763. Perhaps the descendants of Elizabeth Lucie and Jack were

1	i.	Francis Locus, born say 1728.
2	ii.	James Locus, born say 1730.
3	iii.	Joseph[1] Lucas, born 16 July 1735.
	iv.	William Lucas, born 25 August 1737 in St. Peter's Parish, New Kent County, "a mulatto Boy belong. to Mich'l Harfield" [NSCDA, *Parish Register of St. Peter's*, 133].
4	v.	Hester Lucas, born say 1740.
5	vi.	Susannah, born say 1741.
6	vii.	Anthony[1], born say 1742.
7	viii.	Daniel[1] Lucas, born say 1745.
	ix.	Thomas Locus, born about 1748, about five years old on 3 December 1753, called a "base born son of ____ Locus "a free Negro woman," when he was bound an apprentice shoemaker to Sherwood Haywood of Granville County, North Carolina [CR 44.101.2]. He was head of a District 11, Nash County household of 8 "free colored" in 1820 [NC:432].
8	x.	Anthony[2], born say 1750.
9	xi.	Mary, born say 1755.

1. Francis Locus(t), born say 1728, charged Thomas and William Tabers (**Taborn**) with trespass in the 14 September 1749 Southampton County court. The suit was discontinued on the agreement of all parties [Orders 1749-54, 17]. His wife may have been a member of the **Jeffries** family since William **Sweat** and his wife Margaret **Jeffries**, Francis Locust and his wife Hannah, and Margaret **Jeffries**, daughter of the aforesaid, lost their right to 190 acres on the north side of the Meherrin River in Southampton County in a dispute with Arthur Taylor heard at the Council of Virginia on 8 November 1753 [Hall, *Executive Journals of the Council*, V:448]. On 11 April 1754 he was one of fourteen householders sued in Southampton County by William Bynum (informer) for failing to pay the discriminatory tax on free African American and Indian women.[134] He was found not guilty on 15 November 1754, but Bynum was granted a new trial because his witness Joseph Norton had not appeared. Francis was found guilty at the new trial on 13 February 1755 with Joseph Everett as Bynum's witness. Francis was fined 1,000 pounds of tobacco which was the fine for concealing two tithables, so he probably had two women in his household over the age of sixteen. Bynum sued him again on 14 March 1755 on another matter, but Francis was found not guilty [Orders 1749-54, 473, 495, 507, 512; 1754-9, 23, 32, 34, 40, 69]. In June 1759 he was one of the freeholders of Edgecombe County, North Carolina, who were ordered

---

[134]The other householders were John **Porteus**, John **Demery**, Isaac **Young**, Thomas **Wilkins**, James **Brooks**, Jr. and Sr., John **Byrd**, Jr. and Sr., Abraham **Artis**, Lewis **Artis**, William **Brooks**, Ann **Brooks**, and William **Tabor**.

to work on the road from Bryant's Creek to the Granville line [Haun, *Edgecombe County Court Minutes*, I:238]. He received a grant for 525 acres on Turkey Creek in Nash County, North Carolina, on 9 October 1783 and a further 150 acres on the south side of the creek on 1 November 1784 [DB 3:119; 2:146]. He was taxed on 800 acres, 20 cattle, and 6 horses in Nash County in an undated tax list which should perhaps be 1784. He sold 300 acres of this land to Francis **Anderson** on 11 February 1785 [DB 1:174]. He was head of a Nash County household of 8 "other free" in 1790 [NC:70]. He was called Francis Locust of Granville County in an undated power of attorney to Samuel Bailey to recover his lands in Southampton County, Virginia, proved in the February 1803 Granville County court [WB 5:291]. He sold to Jesse **Hammons** 250 acres on the north side of Turkey Creek on 20 November 1792 and 150 acres on the west side of the creek on 13 January 1798 [DB 6:114, 366]. In 1800 he was in Anson County where he was head of a household of 9 "other free" [NC:221]. He may have been the father of

    i.   Billing Lucas, "man of color," enlisted for nine months in the 10th North Carolina Regiment and died September 5, 1779 [Crow, *Black Experience in Revolutionary North Carolina*, 101].

    ii.   Arthur, born say 1760, taxed on 3 cattle in a Nash County tax list circa 1784. He may have been living on land of (his father?) Francis Locus. He was head of a Nash County household of 7 "other free" in 1790 [NC:70], 8 "other free" in Darlington District, South Carolina, in 1800 [SC:116], and 4 "other free" in 1810 [SC:667].

   iii.   Joshua, born about 1782, head of a Darlington District, South Carolina household of 8 "other free" in 1810 [SC:667]. In 1860 he was a seventy-eight-year-old "Mulatto" living in household #1010, Cass County, Michigan, in the household of (his son?) Henry Lucas who was born in South Carolina.

2.   James Locus, born say 1730, was a "Black" taxable living with his wife in the Granville County tax list of Robert Harris in 1754 [CR 44.701.19]. They may have been the parents of

10   i.   Valentine, born say 1750.
11   ii.   James, born say 1755.
       iii.   Barnaby, born say 1755, head of a Nash County household of 8 "other free" in 1790 [NC:70].
      iv.   John, born say 1757, head of a Nash County household of 6 "other free" in 1790 [NC:70], 6 in 1800 [NC:109], and 4 in 1810 [NC:660].
       v.   George, born say 1758, head of a Nash County household of 5 "other free" in 1790 [NC:70].

3.   Joseph[1] Lucas, born 16 July 1735 in St. Peter's Parish, New Kent County, a "Mulatto Boy," was bound to Michael Harfield until the age of thirty-one [NSCDA, *Parish Register of St. Peter's*, 36]. He sold property in Henrico County by deed proved on 7 September 1789 [Orders 1789-91, 77]. He was taxable in the lower district of Henrico County on a horse from 1783 to 1797 and taxable on 18 acres in 1799 and 1800. He was deceased by 1801 when his estate was taxable on the land [PPTL 1782-1814, frames 12, 46, 107, 163, 181, 239, 256, 294, 332, 356; Land Tax List 1799-1816]. He may have been the father of

    i.   Solomon Lucas, a "free Negro" taxable in the lower district of Henrico County from 1797 to 1814: his tax charged to Robinson Lord from 1797 to 1801, called a "free Mulatto" in 1803 and 1804 [PPTL 1782-1814, frames 356, 390, 423, 515, 557, 577, 619, 684, 704, 772, 789; Land Tax List 1799-1816], head of a Henrico County household of 2 "other free" and a white woman in 1810 [VA:993].

    ii.   George Locus(t), born say 1780, a "free Negro" taxable in the upper district of Henrico County from 1806 to 1814 [PPTL 1782-1814,

frames 490, 536, 598, 641, 725, 824], head of a Henrico County
household of 6 "other free" in 1810 [VA:1015].

4. Hester Lucas, born say 1740, a "mulatto woman" servant of Howson Hooe,
was the mother of several illegitimate children born in Prince William County,
Virginia. She may have been the common-law wife of one of Hooe's slaves.
Her children were

 i. Francis (Frances), bastard female born 28 July 1761 to Hester Lucas,
bound to Howson Hooe on 3 May 1763 [Historic Dumfries, *Records
of Dettingen Parish*, 113]. Perhaps she was the Francis Lucas, "F.
Negro," who was head of a Fairfax County household of 1 "other free"
in 1810 [VA:276].

 ii. James, born 24 July 1764 to Hester Lucas, bound to Howson Hooe on
4 June 1765 until the age of thirty-one [Historic Dumfries, *Records of
Dettingen Parish*, 113]. He was taxable in Prince William County in
1787 (listed with Howson Hooe, Esq.), 1801 and 1802 [PPTL, 1782-
1810, frames 87, 478, 491], head of a Prince William County
household of 2 "other free" in 1810 [VA:523].

 iii. Sarah, born about 1764, registered at the court of the District of
Columbia in Alexandria on 10 July 1804: *a Mulatto woman aged about
forty years, was born free...all her female ancestors were born free,
particularly her mother who I well know, Barthw. Dade* [Arlington
County Register of Free Negroes, 1797-1861, no. 8, p.9].

 iv. Betsy, married to Benjamin **Nickens** on 5 August 1805 when they
obtained certificates of freedom in Prince William County [Orders
1804-6, 204].

 v. ?Charles[1], taxable in the upper district of Prince William County from
1787 to 1810: listed with William Mitchell in 1787, called a "black"
man in 1802 [PPTL, 1782-1810, frames 88, 128, 156, 222, 285, 352,
491, 545, 509, 723]. He was head of a Prince William County
household of 15 "other free" in 1810 [VA:523].

 vi. ?Philip[1], taxable near Occoquan in Prince William County from 1791
to 1810, called a "Mul" in 1802 [PPTL, 1782-1810, frames 168, 273,
462, 509, 545, 597, 736], head of a Prince William County household
of 4 "other free" in 1810 [VA:503], listed with his wife Susanna in
Fauquier County in 1813 [Waldrep, *1813 Tax List*].

5. Susannah Lucas, born say 1741, was living in Cumberland County, Virginia,
on 25 May 1761 when the court ordered the churchwardens of Southam Parish
to bind out her "Mulatto" infant son Joseph Lucas until the age of thirty-one
"according to the condition of his mother" [Orders 1758-62, 320]. She was the
mother of

12 i. Joseph[2], born say 1760.

6. Anthony[1] Lucas, born say 1742, was taxable in Prince William County from
1782 to 1796: listed with slaves Harry and Sarah, 4 horses and 13 cattle in
1782, taxed on Benjamin Cunningham's tithe in 1787. He purchased 142 acres
near Blandsford in Prince William County from Thomas Blackburn for 142
pounds in 1794 [DB Z:92-3]. He left a 16 March 1796 Prince William County
will, proved 6 February 1797, by which he divided his land among his sons
Thomas, Samuel, Semer and Anthony Lucas and his grandson Alexander
Lucas after the death of his wife Rebecca. His land included the 142 acres he
had purchased from Blackburn as well as another 57 acres he leased from
Blackburn for three lives. He divided his estate among his children Thomas,
Nancy, Dosha, Samuel, Semer, Tamer, Anthony, Rebecca, and his grandson
Alexander Lucas after his wife's death. He appointed Bernard Hooe, Sr.,
executor. His estate was appraised at $642 [WB H:192-3, 211]. His widow
Rebecca Lucas was taxable from 1797 to 1813, in a list of "FNs and

Mulattoes" above the age of 16 in 1813 [PPTL, 1782-1810, frames 18, 51, 65, 88, 128, 212, 246, 298, 327, 380, 493, 559, 695, 723] and head of a Prince William County household of 5 "other free" in 1810 [VA:524]. His children were

   i.   Nancy, born say 1777, in a list of "FNs and Mulattoes above the age of 16" in Prince William County in 1813, perhaps the mother of Alexander Lucas who was in the same list [PPTL, 1782-1810, frame 723].
   ii. Thomas, born say 1780, taxable in Prince William County in 1798 and 1799 [PPTL, 1782-1810, frames 352, 380].
   iii. Samuel, born say 1783, taxable in Prince William County in 1800 [PPTL, 1782-1810 frames 422], head of a Prince William County household of 7 "other free" in 1810 [VA:518].
   iv. Dosha.
   v.   Semer.
   vi. Tamer.
   vii. Anthony[3], in a list of "FNs and Mulattoes" above the age of 16 in Prince William County in 1813 [PPTL, 1782-1810, frame 723].
   viii. Rebecca.

7. Daniel[1] Lucas, born say 1745, and his wife Sarah were the "mollatto" parents of several children born in St. Peter's Parish, New Kent County [NSCDA, *Parish Register of St. Peter's,* 166]. He was taxable in New Kent County from 1782 to 1786, in 1790, and from 1793 to 1807: called Daniel Lucas, Sr., from 1798 to 1807; listed as a "M"(ulatto) starting in 1801 [PPTL 1782-1800, frames 8, 17, 90, 148, 211; 1791-1828, frames 269, 283, 296, 308, 319, 331, 344, 358, 371, 383, 396, 408, 420, 432]. Their children were
   i.   Thomas, born 7 May 1771, baptized 10 June 1771.
   ii. Joseph[3], born 7 February 1773, baptized 14 March 1773. He was taxable in New Kent County from 1793 to 1795, called Joseph Lucas, Jr. [PPTL 1791-1828, frames 255, 269, 283].
   iii. Daniel[2], born 19 March 1775, taxable in New Kent County from 1798 to 1810: called Daniel Lucas, Jr., from 1797 to 1810; listed as a "M"(ulatto) starting in 1801 [PPTL 1791-1828, frames 308, 319, 331, 344, 358, 371, 383, 396, 420, 432, 443, 455].

8. Anthony[2] Lucas, born say 1750, registered in King George County on 13 May 1800: *a dark Mulatto man aged about ___ years & about five feet ___ Inches, was born in this County of a free woman* [Register of Free Persons 1785-1799, no.13]. He was head of a Loudoun County household of 11 "other free" and a slave in 1810 [VA:258]. He was the father of
   i.   Susannah, born 25 April 1793, daughter of Anthony Lucas, married Elihu **Goins**, and they registered as "free Negroes" in Loudoun County [Certificates of Free Negroes at the Loudoun County courthouse by Townsend Lucas].

9. Mary Lucas, born say 1755, was a "free mulatto hireling" living in Richmond City with her unnamed six-year-old son and infant daughter in 1782 [VA:112]. She was head of a Henrico County household of 8 "other free" in 1810 [VA:993]. She may have been the mother of
   i.   Eliza, head of a Richmond City household of 5 "other free" in 1810 [VA:321],
   ii. Charity Lucis, head of a Richmond City household of 7 "other free" [VA:368].

10. Valentine Locus, born say 1750, married Rachel **Pettiford**, 1780 Granville County bond. Rachel received a pension for his services in the Revolutionary War. He was living in Oxford District, Granville County, in 1790 [NC:91]

and was head of a Wake County household of 8 "other free" in 1790 (abstracted as Valentine Dorus) [NC:106] and 9 "other free" in 1800 [NC:778]. He was taxable in Henry King's list for Wake County on 60 acres from 1793 to 1802 but not charged with poll tax in 1802 [MFCR 099.701.1, frames 54, 227, 253]. He was called an "aged free Negro, who resides on Leek Creek in Wake County" in the 6 October 1801 edition of the *Raleigh Register* which reported that four men entered his home with clubs, beat him and his wife until they were near death, and stole two of their children. Luckily, the children managed to escape later while their captives slept [*Raleigh Register*, October 6, 1801, cited by Franklin, *Free Negro in North Carolina*, 54]. According to Rachel's declaration on 24 May 1838 in Wake County court to obtain a pension, she was an eighty-year-old "free woman of color" whose husband died about a month before Christmas 1812. Bartlett **Pettiford**, "a person of respectability" testified that Rachel was his sister, that he had witnessed their marriage, and that they had eight children: Martin, Phereby, Kinchen, Nancy, Ruthy, Polly, Jordan, and Absalom [M805-533, frame 766]. Their children were

i. Martin, born about 1780, head of a Wake County household of 3 "other free" in 1800 [NC:778]. He married Molley **Mitchell**, 24 January 1800 Orange County bond, Lawrence **Pettiford** bondsman.

ii. Pheraby, also mentioned in Valentine's will. She married Jonathan **George**, 27 January 1802 Orange County bond, Lawrence **Pettiford** bondsman.

iii. Kinchen, head of a Nash County household of 2 "other free" in 1810 [NC:663].

iv. Nancy.

v. Ruthy, probably identical to Ruthy Lucas who married Brittain **Pitman**, 21 February 1815 Wake County bond, William Curtis bondsman. Brittain may have been the brother of Archibald **Pitman**, a "mulatto boy" aged five years the 26 December 1798, ordered bound to Nathan Bradley as an apprentice wheelwright by the Wednesday session of the August 1799 Edgecombe County court [Minutes 1797-1800, n.p.].

vi. Polly.

vii. Jordan.

viii. Absalom.

11. James Locus, born say 1755, was taxable on six head of cattle in Nash County in 1784. He was head of a Nash County household of 6 "other free" in 1790 [NC:70] and 9 in 1800 [NC:108]. He died before 14 August 1809 when his orphans were bound by the Nash County court to Jesse **Booth**, Benjamin **Tann**, and John Locus [Rackley, *Nash County North Carolina Court Minutes* VI:71]. His children may have been

i. Berry, born about 1796, thirteen years old on 14 August 1809 when he was bound by the Nash County court to Jesse **Booth** until the age of twenty-one. He was married to Beady **Taborn**, daughter of Burrell **Taborn**, on 9 January 1842 when her brother Hardimon applied for a pension for their father's service in the Revolution [M804-2335, frame 744].

ii. Elijah, born about 1807, two years old on 14 August 1809 when he was bound to Jesse **Booth**.

iii. Susanna, born about 1798, about eleven years old on 14 August 1809 when she was bound to Benjamin **Tann**.

iv. John, born about 1799, about ten years old on 14 August 1809 when he was bound to Benjamin **Tann**.

v. James, born about 1801, about eight years old on 14 August 1809 when he was bound to John Locus.

vi. Obedience, born about 1805, four years old on 14 August 1809 when she was bound to John Locus.

12. Joseph[2] Lucas, born say 1760, was bound out in Cumberland County, Virginia, on 25 May 1761. He was a "yellow" complexioned man living in Powhatan County when he was listed as a soldier who served as a substitute in the Revolution [NSDAR, *African American Patriots*, 151]. He was a "free B[k]" taxable in Powhatan County in 1790 [PPTL, 1787-1825, frame 48]. He and his wife Lucy Lucas were the parents of William, Nancy, Josiah and Abraham Lucas (no race mentioned) whose births were registered in St. Peter's Parish, New Kent County, from 1786 to 1794 [NSCDA, *Parish Register of St. Peter's*, 166]. He was taxable in New Kent County from 1792 to 1809: called a "F. Negroe" in 1792 and 1794; taxable on 2 tithes in 1805 and 1806 [PPTL 1782-1800, frames 188, 211; 1791-1828, 269, 283, 296, 308, 319, 331, 344, 358, 383, 396, 408, 420, 432, 443]. He was called "Joseph Locust, free Negro" when he was taxable in the upper district of Henrico County in 1811 and 1812, charged with William Locust's tithe in 1812 [PPTL 1782-1814, frames 666, 726]. He registered as a free Negro in Goochland County on 18 July 1809: *five feet nine and an half inches high, about forty five years of age, short curled hair intermingled with Grey...free born* [Register of Free Negroes, p. 32]. He was head of a Henrico County household of 6 "other free" in 1810 [VA:998]. His children were

    i.   William, born 28 January 1786 [NSCDA, *Parish Register of St. Peter's*, 166], a "M"(ulatto) taxable in New Kent County from 1807 to 1810, taxable on a slave aged 12-16 and a horse in 1807 [PPTL 1791-1828, frames 432, 443, 455]. He was a "free Negro" taxable in the upper district of Henrico County from 1811 to 1814: his tax charged to Joseph Locust in 1812; listed with his unnamed wife in 1813 [PPTL 1782-1814, frames 666, 726, 759, 824], head of a Henrico County household of 2 "other free" in 1810 [VA:1015]. He registered in Henrico County on 11 November 1831: *age 44, a mullatto man, 5 feet 9-3/4 inches, Free as appears from his register from the County of New Kent* [Register of Free Negroes and Mulattoes, 1831-1844, p.7, no. 638].

    ii.   Nancy, born 23 February 1788, perhaps the Nancy Lucas who was head of a Richmond City household of 4 "other free" and one slave in 1810 [VA:353].

    iii. Josiah, born 8 December 1792.

    iv. Abraham, born 5 October 1794.

Westmoreland and King George County, Virginia

1.   Elizabeth Lucus, born say 1717, the servant of John Footman, confessed to the Westmoreland County, Virginia court on 30 March 1736 that she had an illegitimate "Mulatto" child. The court ordered that she pay fifteen pounds after completing her indenture or be sold by the churchwardens of Cople Parish for five years [Orders 1731-9, 189a, 192a]. She and her children were listed in the inventory of John Footman's Westmoreland County estate which was taken on 21 March 1739/40:

1 Negro man named Sambo	*26 pounds*
1 Negro Boy named Anthony	*10 pounds*
1 white servant woman that has four years & a half to serve	*9 pounds*
1 Mulatto Boy named Nathaniel Lucas	*15 pounds*
1 Mulatto Boy named John Lucas	*12 pounds*
1 Mulatto Boy named Leonard Lucas	*10 pounds*
1 Mulatto Boy named Abraham Lucas	*5 pounds*

[Estate Settlements, Records, Inventories 1723-46, 221].

On 28 May 1745 she was presented by the court for "entertaining Negroes & Servants & keeping a disorderly house" [Orders 1743-7, 76, 178a]. She was the ancestor of

i. Nathaniel[1], born say 1733, a "Mulatto" boy listed in the account of the estate of John Footman, Gent., on 21 March 1739/40. He was taxable in Westmoreland County from 1782 to 1815: taxable on 3 tithes from 1788 to 1790 [PPTL, 1782-1815, frames 246, 327, 358, 372, 399, 696, 628, 784, 835]. He married Nelly **Lawrence**, 31 May 1791 Westmoreland County bond, John Lucas security. He was a "Molatto" farmer living with his wife Nelly Lucaus and children Meredith, Alcey, and Fanny Locust on William Fitzhugh's land in Westmoreland County in 1801 [*Virginia Genealogist* 31:42].

ii. John, born say 1735, a "Mulatto" boy listed in the account of the estate of John Footman, Gent., on 21 March 1739/40.

iii. Leonard, born say 1737, a "Mulatto" boy listed in the account of the estate of John Footman, Gent., on 21 March 1739/40. He was taxable on 2-3 horses and 6 cattle in King George County in 1782 and 1783 [PPTL, 1782-1830, frames 5, 10]. and taxable in Westmoreland County from 1787 to 1793: taxable on 2 tithes and 2 horses in 1791 [PPTL, 1782-1815, frames 317, 346, 372, 399]. His widow may have been Milly Locus, a "Molatto" farmer living on Thomas Sanford's land in Westmoreland County in 1801 with children Mark, Naney, Dulcey, Harraway, and Betsey Locust [*Virginia Genealogist* 31:41]. She was head of a Westmoreland County household of 6 "other free" in 1810 [VA:777].

iv. Abraham, born say 1739, a "Mulatto" boy listed in the account of the estate of John Footman, Gent., on 21 March 1739/40. He was taxable in King George County from 1786 to 1795 [PPTL, 1782-1830, frames 35, 42, 60, 105, 118, 137].

v. James, born say 1756, a seaman in the Revolution from King George County [Jackson, *Virginia Negro Soldiers*, 40]. He was taxable in King George County from 1786 to 1793, called "free Jim Lucas" [PPTL, 1782-1830, frames 28, 48, 100, 111, 118]. He registered in King George County on 1 May 1800: *a dark Mulatto man aged about ___ years, and about five feet ___ Inches, was bound to Thomas Massey, Senr. of this County to serve till the age of thirty one years* [Register of Free Persons 1785-1799, no.12].

vi. Charles[2], born about 1780, registered in King George County on 9 October 1800: *a dark molatto man, aged about twenty years, & about five feet five inches high, was born in this County of a free malatto woman* [Register of Free Persons 1785-1799, no.14]. He was head of a Spotsylvania County household of 5 "other free" in 1810 [VA:112b].

vii. Harriet, born about 1796, registered in King George County in March 1820: *a dark mulatto woman, about 24 years of age, about 5 feet high, stout made, born in this County of free Parents* [Register of Free Persons, 1785-99, no.57].

viii. Barbary, born say 1780, a "Molatto" farmer living with children Rubin and George Locus on Thomas Sanford's land in Westmoreland County in 1801 [*Virginia Genealogist* 31:41]. She was head of a Westmoreland County household of 5 "other free" in 1810 [VA:777].

ix. Agatha, born say 1770, married Newman **Harrison**, 15 April 1791 Westmoreland County bond. He was called Newman **Hammon** in 1801 when he was counted with his wife Aggy in a List of "Free Mulattoes & Negroes in Westmoreland County" [*Virginia Genealogist* 31:42].

x. John, perhaps the one who served as a seaman in the Revolution from King George County [Jackson, *Virginia Negro Soldiers*, 40]. He was taxable in Westmoreland County from 1794 to 1803 [PPTL, 1782-1815, frames 409, 425, 501, 587] and a "Molatto" farmer living with Margaret Locus and children Penny, Margaret, and Joyce Locus on D. McCarty's land in 1801 [*Virginia Genealogist* 31:41, 42]. Margaret was taxable on a horse in the upper district from 1804 to 1807 [PPTL,

1782-1815, frames 606, 666] and head of a Westmoreland County household of 6 "other free" in 1810 [VA:777].

xi.   Elizabeth, born say 1772, married Allen **Ashton**, 24 December 1793 Westmoreland County bond.

xii. Elizabeth, born say 1773, married Thomas **Sorrell**, 3 December 1794 Westmoreland County bond.

xiii. Spencer, born say 1780, taxable in Westmoreland County from 1801 to 1815 [PPTL, 1782-1815, frames 551, 635, 784, 835], a "Molatto" working as a distiller for Daniel McCarty in 1801 [*Virginia Genealogist* 31:42].

xiv. Philip^2, taxable in King George County from 1794 to 1813, listed as a "Mulatto" in 1813 [PPTL, 1782-1830, frames 127, 169, 178, 203, 218, 230, 240, 279, 305, 330, 341], head of a King George County household of 2 "other free" in 1810 [VA:206].

xv.   David, head of a King George County household of 4 "other free" in 1810 [VA:206].

xvi. Jane, born about 1780, registered in King George County on 7 September 1820: *daughter of ___ Lucas, a dark mulatto about 40 years of age, 5' 1/12 Inch high...born free in this County* [Register of Free Persons 1785-1799, no.63].

xvii. Nat^2 Lucust, listed with wife Jenney in Stafford County in 1813 [Waldrep, *1813 Tax List*], head of a Stafford County household of 4 "other free" in 1810 [VA:128].

xviii. John, listed with wife Mary in Stafford County in 1813 [Waldrep, *1813 Tax List*], head of a Stafford County household of 3 "other free" in 1810 [VA:126].

xix. Hannah, born say 1788, married Samuel **Tate**, 30 December 1809 Westmoreland County bond, Lawrence **Ashton** security.

xx.   William, born about 1792, registered in King George County on 4 December 1817: *a black man aged about Twenty five years, about five feet six and a half Inches high...born of a free black woman* [Register of Free Persons 1785-1799, no.49].

Other members of the Lucas family in Virginia were

i.   Samuel, head of a Loudoun County household of 10 "other free" in 1810 [VA:258].

ii.   Catey, "F. Negroe," head of a Fauquier County household of 5 "other free" in 1810 [VA:379].

iii. Francis, "F. Negro," head of a Fairfax County household of 1 "other free" in 1810 [VA:276].

iv.   William, head of a Prince William County household of 1 "other free" in 1810 [VA:523].

LONGO FAMILY

1.   Anthony Longo, born say 1625, was called Tony Longo "a negro" on 1 February 1647 when the Northampton County, Virginia court ordered him to pay his debt of 384 pounds of tobacco to Francis White. He was taxable on one tithe in Northampton County in 1660 [Orders 1657-64, 102]. Edmund Morgan in *American Slavery - American Freedom* quoted a confrontation that Anthony had with a Northampton County court official as evidence that racism had not yet taken hold on the Eastern Shore in the seventeenth century and how quickly Africans assumed typical English disdain for authority:

> *Anthony Longo: What shall I go to Mr. Walkers for: go about your business you idle rascal: I told him I had a warrant for him: shitt of your warrant have I nothing to do but go to Mr. Walker, go about your business you idle rascal as did likewise his wife, with such noise that I could hardly hear my*

own words, when I had done reading the warrant: stroke at me, and gave me some blows [Orders DW&c 1654-5, 60a].

He was apparently the father of

2   i.   James[1], born say 1652.

2.   James[1] Longo born say 1652, was a tithable head of household in Accomack County from 1676 to 1692 [Orders 1676-78, 32, 58, 1678-82, 17, 101; W&cO 1682-97, 192, 228a, 258a]. He was a delinquent Accomack County militiaman in January 1685. On 20 September 1687 he and Jane Fitzgerald posted bond for Dorothy Bestick, servant of George Nicholas Hack of Pungoteague, who was presented by the court for having an illegitimate child by "George Francis Negro Slave to ye sd Geo Nich Hack." In 1687 Dorothy bound her daughter Sarah to him until the age of eighteen years [W&cO 1682-97, 57, 119a, 142a].[135] On 20 September 1687 James was fined 100 pounds of tobacco for assaulting Richard Shulster. Shulster testified that when he passed by James Longo's house on horseback,

> *James...leaped over his fence furiously...laye hold of ye Deponts. horses bridle...calling the deponent Rogue, Rascall, and severall other scurrilous words over and over againe threatning to beate him and asked me why I did not come to pay him a dayes work...layd his hands on my shoulder in a violent manner...caused great paine.*

The next day he brought suit in court against Shulster. He was sued by William Twyford on 20 November 1689 for failing to perform carpentry work which he had contracted for, and on 16 June 1691 the Accomack County court presented him for working on holy days [W&cO 1682-97, 119, 170a]. He was called James Longo, "the Molatta," on 21 February 1694 when he was presented by the grand jury for turning a road which passed through his land [Orders 1690-7, 32, 123a, 124a]. On 2 April 1706 he petitioned the Accomack County court to permit him to turn this road. The court gave him permission to do so as long as the new road was as near to or nearer to Pungoteague and was well maintained. The court was not satisfied with the new road, and on 9 October 1707 the justices ordered him to reopen the original road. On 5 May 1708 he posted bond for the illegitimate child he had by Isabel Hutton (a white woman) who was presented by the court on 3 June 1707 for having a "Mulatto Bastard Child." On 5 May 1708 she testified in Accomack County court that James Longo, "negro or mullatto," was the father of the child she was pregnant with, and on 5 August the same year she was called "Isabel Hutton who lives at James Longoes" when she was convicted of "having a Bastard Child by a Mulatto." The same court ordered that he be arrested for acting in a contemptuous manner when an officer of the court attempted to serve him with a warrant [Orders 1703-9, 68, 74, 98, 101a, 114, 114a, 122, 125]. He left a 13 August 1729 Accomack will, proved 1 September 1730. He left 70 acres of his land to his son James, 70 acres to his daughter Mary **Huten**, and 70 acres to his daughter Elizabeth, and the remainder of his estate to his wife Isabel. His wife and daughters were executrices of the will [Wills 1729-37, pt.1, 101]. His children were

i.   ?Ann Longo, born say 1683, a "Mallatta Woman" living at William Smith's who was presented by the Prince George's County, Maryland court on 28 March 1703/4 for having an illegitimate child. She was

---

[135]On 19 February 1690 Dorothy Bestick was presented for having another illegitimate child [W&cO 1682-97, 175a, 181a, 187]. Perhaps her descendants were the two John **Bosticks** who were heads of "other free" Kent County, Delaware households in 1810 [DE:185, 188].

called "Ann Congo," servant of William Smith, on 22 August 1704 when he paid her fine [Court Record 1699-1705, 289a, 309a].

ii. James², taxable head of a Matapony Hundred, Somerset County, Maryland household in 1727, and head of a household in Wicomoco Hundred from 1731 to 1740. In March 1740/1 Thomas and William Selby were indicted by the Somerset County court for stealing seven turkeys from him [Judicial Record 1740-2, 92, 96]

iii. Elizabeth.

iv. Mary **Hutton**, born about 1708. Her descendants were John **Hutton**, head o' a Washington, D.C. household of 1 "other free" in 1800 and Sarah **Hutton**, head of a Kent County, Delaware household of 2 "other free" in 1810 [DE:198].

Their Longo descendants were

i. Daniel, "Mulatto" taxable in Little Creek Hundred, Kent County, Delaware, in 1797 and 1798 [Assessments, frames 7, 483].

LOWRY FAMILY

1. James¹ Lowry, born say 1735, received a grant for land in Bladen County on 26 October 1767 [DB 23:216-7], and between 1770 and 1772 he received patents on more than 1000 acres of land in Bladen County [Hoffman, *Land Patents*, II:191, 221, 356, 600]. He was taxable in Bladen County with his wife from 1768 to 1774 ("Mulatoes"), taxable on William **Jones** (a "Mulato") from 1768 to 1771, taxable on a slave named Jack in 1769 and on slaves Jack and Hansom in 1776. In 1779 he was taxable on 2 slaves, 400 acres of improved land. 4 horses, and 100 head of cattle [Byrd, *Bladen County Tax Lists*, I:5, 17, :5, 60, 123, 136; II:63, 84, 101, 115]. He sold more than 300 acres, part on Drowning Creek and part on Raft Swamp, by deeds dated 7 January 1772, May 1772, no month 1772, and 29 January 1773 but was still taxable on 400 acres in 1784. He received a patent for 100 acres on Middle Swamp on 7 November 1784 and sold it on 27 June 1785. He purchased 100 acres on the north side of Drowning Creek in 1786 [DB 1:4, 183; 23:216, 217, 431, 299]. On 1 April 1805 the Robeson County court appointed him overseer of the road from his house to the house where Neil Buie formerly lived, a position usually reserved for whites [Minutes I:321]. He was head of a Robeson County household of 6 "other free" and 3 slaves in 1790 [NC:49] and 6 "other free" and 6 slaves in 1800 [NC:389]. By his 13 March 1810 Robeson County will he left land and nine slaves to his wife, not named, and his children [WB 1:121]. His wife was most likely Celia Lowry who was appointed administratrix of his estate by the Robeson County court on 26 November 1810 [Minutes II:207]. His children were

2   i. William, born say 1754.

ii. Thomas, born say 1760, purchased land in Robeson by deeds proved on 9 O' tober 1800, 7 October 1805, and 5 Oct 1807 [Minutes I:128, 339; II.𝚓2] and purchased 100 acres on the north side of Back Swamp from Ishmael **Chavers** on 17 May 1804 [DB O:163]. He was head of a Robeson County household of 3 "other free" in 1800 [NC:389] and 5 whites and 1 "other free" in 1810 [NC:220]. Nancy **Deas** was living with him on 24 November 1812 when the Robeson County court ordered her to bring two of her illegitimate children by James Lowry to the next court [Minutes 1806-13, 351].

3   iii. James², born before 1776.

iv. Mary.

v. Ceily, head of a Robeson County household of 6 whites and 10 slaves in 1810 [NC:219]. She was called Celia, Junr., in a deed to her from her brother James Lowery, proved in Robeson County in February 1827 [Minutes 1829-39, 142]. She died before August 1829 when her lands were ordered partitioned among her brothers Thomas, William, and James Lowry [Minutes 1829-39, 20].

2. William Lowry, born say 1754, was called the son of James Lowry in an 18 February 1775 deed by which he purchased land in Bladen County from Ann **Perkins**. He sold land in Bladen County shortly afterwards on 2 May 1775 [DB 23:481-2; 36:381] and was head of a Bladen County household of 5 "other free" in 1800 [NC:9] and 9 "free colored" in Robeson County in 1820 [NC:304]. On 23 August 1831 he challenged the right of his brother Thomas to administer the estate of their younger brother James[2], claiming that he as elder brother should have been administrator. However, the court ruled that Thomas was more competent. William's children were

    i.   ?Daniel, married Betsey **Locklear**, 2 July 1805 Robeson County bond.

4   ii.   Allen, born say 1795.

    iii.   ?Alfred, born say 1802, not mentioned in the Lowrie History. William transferred land to him by deed proved in November 1829.

3. James[2] Lowery, born before 1776, sold 50 acres on Ashpole Swamp in Robeson County to Emmanuel **Carter** by a deed proved in 1797 [DB G:142]. He sold two tracts of land to Malcolm **Locklear**, one for 100 acres on the east side of Juniper Branch on 27 May 1801 and one for 177 acres adjoining this land on 4 October 1803 and purchased land by deed proved on 7 October 1807 and 27 August 1811 [DB L:20; N:187-190; Minutes I:340; II:280]. He was head of a household of 3 male and 2 female "free colored" and 9 slaves in 1820 [NC:294]. After his death, Doctor Edmund McLucen was appointed guardian to Catherine, "an infant daughter the only legitimate child of James Lowrie decd" in Tuesday court, February 1833. His wife probably predeceased him since she was not mentioned. In addition, he had at least six illegitimate children by several Robeson County women. Administration on his estate was granted to his brother Thomas Lowery on 22 August 1831 on a bond of 700 pounds. His administrator sold some of his land and one of his slaves, Dick, by deed proved on 28 November 1831 in order to pay the debts of the estate [Minutes 1829-39, 106]. About 1,100 acres of land remained for his daughter Catherine [Minutes 1839-43, 39]. Some of his children were

    i.   a child by Sarah **Hammons**, who the 27 August 1810 Robeson County court ordered him to support [Minutes II:217].

    ii.   a child by Ann **Deas**, who he was ordered to support on 27 August 1811 [Minutes II:217].

    iii.   Parker **Deas**, a child by Nancy **Deas** [Minutes II:328, 351].

    iv.   Sally **Deas**, a child by Nancy **Deas** [Minutes II:328, 351].

    v.   a child by Eliza **Carter**, charged to him by the 24 November 1812 Robeson County court [Minutes II:350].

    vi.   Turner, an illegitimate son by Mary **Sweat** charged to him by the May 1833 Robeson County court.

    vii.   Catherine, his only legitimate child.

4. Allen Lowry, born say 1795, married Catherine **Locklear**, 27 April 1816 Robeson County bond. Allen's father William Lowry transferred land to him by deeds proved in Robeson in Wednesday court 1837 and November court 1838 [Minutes 1829-39]. He and his son William, suspected of supporting the Union cause, were murdered by the white Home Guard near the end of the Civil War in March 1865. His son Henry Berry Lowry led a band of his relatives and friends who killed or drove from the county all those responsible for the murders. According to reporter Alfred Townsend, Allen married Mary **Combes** (Cur?ho?) and was the father of Patrick, Purdie, Andrew, Sinclair, William, Thomas, Stephen, Calvin, Henry Berry, and Mary [Townsend, *The Swamp Outlaws*, 47]. Four of his children were part of the infamous Lowry band:

    i.   William.

    ii.   Steve. ·

    iii. Thomas.

    iv. Henry Berry, born about 1846, described by Robeson County residents to a reporter for the New York Herald as: *of mixed Tuscarora, mulatto, and white blood, twenty-six years of age, five feet nine inches high...straight black hair, like an Indian: a dark goatee, eyes of a grayish hazel..His forehead is good and his face and expression refined--remarkably so, considering his mixed race, want of education and long career of lawlessness...The color of his skin is of a whitish yellow sort, with an admixture of copper...there being no negro blood in it except that of a far remote generation of mulatto, and the Indian still apparent...one of the handsomest mulattoes you ever saw* [Townsend, *Swamp Outlaws*, 12-14].

LUGROVE FAMILY

1.   Bridget Lugrove, alias Churchhouse, born say 1668, the servant of Thomas Chamberlayne, confessed in Henrico County court on 1 October 1687 that she had delivered a bastard child. She petitioned the court for her freedom on 1 December 1691, but her master informed the court that she had delivered a second bastard child for which the court ordered she serve an additional two years. On 16 May 1692 she was presented by the court for having a child by a "Negro" [Orders 1678-93, 248, 396, 406, 419, 421, 435]. She was probably the mother of

    i.   Jane, born say 1691, petitioned the court against her master Thomas Chamberlayne in August 1712. She was discharged from his service in September 1712 [Orders 1710-4, 172, 185].

LYNCH FAMILY

1.   Ann Lynch, born say 1750, was indentured to George Payne in Goochland County in September 1773 when her son Thomas (no race mentioned) was also bound apprentice to Payne [Orders 1771-78, 360]. Thomas was baptized on 22 April 1775, "a mulatto of Co: Paynes." Ann married Bristol **Matthews** on 25 September 1775, "Mulattoes, he in this parish and she in Hanover" [Jones, *The Douglas Register*, 348, 347]. Ann was the mother of

2   i.   ?Polly, born say 1768.

    ii. Thomas, born Whitsunday 1772, baptized 22 April 1775, married Sally **Banks**, daughter of John **Banks**, 29 July 1801 Goochland County bond, Edward **Fuzmore** surety, 29 July marriage [Minister's Returns, 78]. He was taxable in the upper district of Goochland County from 1791 to 1814: his tax charged to Agatha Payne from 1791 to 1797, charged with his own tax in 1798, a "Mulatto" planter on Thomas Thurston's land in 1804, listed with wife Sally in 1813 [PPTL, 1782-1809, frames 286, 302, 346, 470, 484, 672, 692, 744, 785, 828, 870; 1810-3?, frames 11, 77, 102, 165, 198]. He was head of a Goochland County household of 6 "other free" and a slave in 1810 [VA:701]. His wife Sally Lynch registered as a free Negro in Goochland County on 5 September 1829: *yellow complexion, about fifty years of age, about five feet three & an half inches high* [Register of Free Negroes, p.202]. Perhaps they were the parents of Edmund Lynch, head of a Campbell County household of 1 "other free" in 1810 [VA:853].

    iii. ?Robert, born say 1773, head of a Goochland County household of 9 "other free" in 1810 [VA:701].

3   iv. ?Patsy, born say 1774.

2. Polly Lynch, born say 1768, was a "Mulatto" spinner living at Sarah Bowles' in the upper district of Goochland County from 1804 to 1814: taxable on John Lynch's tithe in 1804 and 1805, charged with Billy Lynch's tithe and a slave above the age of sixteen in 1811 and 1812, charged with J. **Brooks'** tithe and a slave in 1814 [PPTL, 1782-1809, frames 692, 744, 828, 870; 1810-32, frames 77, 102, 199]. She was the mother of
   i. ?John, born say 1787, taxable in the upper district of Goochland County from 1804 to 1814, a "Mulatto" blacksmith on John Richards, Jr.'s land in 1806 [PPTL, 1782-1809, frames 785, 827; 1810-32, frames 102, 199].
   ii. ?William, born say 1790, taxable in the upper district of Goochland County from 1807 to 1814: a "free boy" listed with John Glass in 1807, listed with Polly Lynch in 1811, a "Mulatto" blacksmith at N. Perkins' in 1813 and 1814 [PPTL, 1782-1809, frames 824; 1810-32, frames 77, 165, 199].
   iii. Nancy, born say 1794, daughter of Polly Lynch, married Elisha **Banks**, 10 March 1813 Goochland County bond, Robert Lynch surety, 11 March marriage, "both people of color."

3. Patsy Lynch, born say 1774, was head of a Halifax County, North Carolina household of 4 "other free" in 1800 [NC:324]. She charged James **Weaver** with bastardy in Halifax County court on 24 May 1798. Their son was probably Charles Lynch, two months and eleven days old, who was ordered bound apprentice to James **Weaver** on the same day to learn the trade of cooper [Minutes 1796-98]. She was the mother of
   i. ?Stephen, born 1776-1794, head of a Halifax County household of 7 "free colored" in 1820 [NC:155] and 11 in 1830.
   ii. ?Mary, born 1776-1794, head of a Halifax County household of 2 "free colored" in 1820 [NC:155].
   iii. ?Nancy, born 1794-1806, head of a Halifax County household of 6 "free colored" in 1830.
   iv. Charles, born in March 1798, two months and eleven days old on 24 May 1798 when he was bound apprentice to (his father) James **Weaver** by the Halifax County court. He married Lizzy **Coley**, 27 May 1817 Halifax County bond and was head of a Halifax County household of 4 "free colored" in 1830.

LYON(S) FAMILY

1. Elizabeth **Armfield**, born say 1742, was sued for trespass, assault and battery in York County by Anne **Gwinn** and her "next friend" Jane **Savy (Savoy)** on 16 May 1763. She was found guilty and ordered to pay 20 shillings [Judgments & Orders 1763-5, 14, 37]. She was called "a free mulatto" when she registered the birth of her son James in Bruton Parish in 1766. She sued Samuel Timson in York County court for trespass, assault and battery on 18 September 1769 [Judgments & Orders 1768-70, 351, 406]. She was taxable on her property in York County from 1782 to 1803: on 13 cattle in 1782, on from 1-2 slaves from 1792 to 1797, on 2 free tithables in 1802, and was called Betty Lyons in 1790, 1791 and 1793 [PPTL, 1782-41, frames 69, 72, 106, 138, 147, 163, 173, 180, 193, 199, 209, 218, 227, 274, 284]. Elizabeth probably had children by William Lyon, Jr., who was sued by her father Daniel **Armfield** for trespass, assault and battery on 19 December 1763

[Judgments & Orders 1763-5, 126, 171].[136] She was called Betty Armfield when she was head of a York County household of 7 "other free" in 1810 [VA:870]. Her children were

   i. ?Milly **Armfield**, born say 1760, a "Poor orphan" ordered bound out by the churchwardens of Bruton Parish on 19 May 1760 [Judgments & Orders 1759-63, 143].

   ii. James **Armfield**, born 16 March 1766, "Bastard son of Elizabeth Armfield" [Bruton Parish Register, 27], called James Lyons when he was taxable in York County in 1788 [PPTL, 1782-1841, frame 141]. Peter and Robert **Gillett** sued James Lyon and Charles Orrell in York County court for trespass, assault and battery on 22 November 1787 [Orders 1784-7, 520].

   iii. Daniel[2] **Armfield**, born 15 February 1768, baptized 3 April [Bruton Parish Register, 32], called Daniel Lyons when he was taxable in York County from 1788 to 1814, taxable on a slave from 1795 onwards [PPTL, 1782-1841, frames 141, 152, 163, 211, 221, 230, 238, 245, 256, 266, 277, 287, 297, 307, 328, 391, 408]. On 22 November 1796 the York County court awarded Peter **Hailey** 25 pounds in his suit against Daniel Lyons for trespass, assault and battery. Daniel then brought a suit in chancery to stay the execution of the judgment, and this case was continued until 19 November 1798 when Daniel was again found guilty [Orders 1795-1803, 138, 144, 192, 239, 249, 250, 292-3].

   iv. ?Matthew[2] **Armfield**, born about 1779.

   v. ?Warren **Armfield**, born say 1781, taxable in York County in 1803 and 1805 [PPTL, 1782-1841, frames 284, 304].

   vi. John Lyons, born 22 January 1783, baptized 26 March 1783, son of Betty Armfield [Bruton Parish Register, 35].

   vii. ?Martha **Armfield**, taxable in York County on a free tithable in 1803, taxable on a free tithable and a slave in 1805 [PPTL, 1782-1841, frames 284, 304].

   viii. ?William Lyons, born about 1787, registered in York County on 16 December 1822: *a bright Mulatto about 35 years of age...has short hair...born free.* When William renewed his registration nine years later on 28 September 1831, the clerk added the notation: *since the above has become bald, wears whiskers, grey Beard & much the appearance of an Indian* [Free Negro Register, 1798-1831, no. 194].

   ix. ?Nancy Lyons, head of a Richmond City household of 1 "other free" in 1810 [VA:340].

LYTLE FAMILY

1. Frank Lytle, born about 1774, was freed in 1795 after the death of his master, Thomas Lytle of Randolph County, North Carolina. Thomas Lytle came to North Carolina from Pennsylvania about 1760. His family was probably responsible for the freedom of the two "other free" Little families in Pennsylvania in 1790:

   i. George, head of a Bedford County household of 9 "other free."

   ii. James, head of a Westmoreland County household of 1 "other free."

Before his death Thomas Lytle required his heirs and executors to sign a bond on 25 January 1794 to give Frank his freedom and 200 acres. The General

---

[136]The Lyon family probably originated in Rhode Island. Enoch Lyon left a 2 December 1788 Yorktown, York County will by which he left all his estate to his friend William Gossley who was to repay the Synagogue of Newport, Rhode Island, 10 pounds per annum for supporting and burying his deceased mother [W&I 23:621-2].

Assembly passed a bill which legalized his freedom on 24 January 1795 for "meritorious Services" [by Rik Vigeland in *North Carolina African American Historical & Genealogical Society Journal*, V, no.1, p.4]. On 20 March 1795 Thomas' wife Catherine and his executors deeded the 200 acres on Caraway to him:

> *for and in consideration of fidelity of Frank Lytle to his former master and also desire of said master that he should be provided for* [DB 6:72].

And they deeded an additional 132 acres on the waters of the Uwharrie River to him for the same consideration a month later on 20 April 1795 [DB 6:73]. He purchased 175 acres on the Caraway for $500 in 1806 and another 220 acres for $275 in 1831 [DB 12:113; 19:18]. He was counted in the 1860 Randolph County census as a "Mulatto," born in North Carolina, with $6,000 real estate [NC:157]. According to the 1870 mortality schedule for Randolph County he died in September 1869 at the age of ninety-five. His children married whites and light-skinned African Americans, and most of his ancestors were considered white [*NCAAHGS* V, no.1, p.4]. His children were

  i.   Francis Jr, head of a Randolph County household of 5 "free colored" in 1830.
  ii. Elizabeth, married William **Walden**, Sr., 6 February 1819 Randolph County bond.
  iii. Albert, head of a Randolph County household of 6 "free colored" in 1830.
  iv. Catherine Lytle.
  v.   Deborah Robbins, married Emsley **Robbins** on 30 June 1827. He was the son of Ezekiel **Robbins** and Mary Arnold [*NCAAHGS* V, no.1, 7].
  vi. Dorcas Swaney.
  vii. Mary Laughlin.
  viii. Alfred.
  ix. Rebecca Lytle.

MCCARTY FAMILY

1. Margaret McCarty, born say 1712, was a servant woman with two years to serve on 5 April 1734 when she was listed with three-year-old "Mulatto" John McCarty in the inventory of the Stafford County estate of Edward Clement, deceased [WB Liber M, 1729-48, 134-5]. She was the mother of
  i.   John, born about 1731, about three years old on 5 April 1734 when he was listed as a "Mulatto" boy bound to serve until thirty-one in the inventory of Edward Clement's Stafford County estate.
  ii. ?Sarah, "a Molatto" born 3 September and baptized 8 October 1732" in St. Paul's Parish, King George County (no parent named) [St. Paul's Church, King George County, Virginia, 46].
  iii. Catherine, born 19 March and baptized 9 May 1736 in St. Paul's Parish, "Daughter of Margaret McCarty" (no race indicated) [St. Paul's Church, King George County, Virginia, 56].

McCOY/ McKEY FAMILY

1. Samuel[1] Mackie, born say 1720, and his wife Batsheba, "free Malattos," registered their children's births and baptisms in St. Paul's Parish, King George County. Their children were
  i.   John, born 23 November, baptized 24 November 1745.
  ii. Elijah, born 25 August, baptized 19 September 1748.
  iii. Jane, born 2 February, baptized 29 March 1752 [St. Paul's Parish Register, 102, 115, 123].
2 iv. James[1], born say 1750.

3   v.   Bennett, born about 1757.
4   vi.   George McCoy, born say 1759.
        vii. ?Mary Mackey, born say 1760, the servant of Stephen Donaldson,
              Gent., on 11 April 1781 when the Loudoun County court bound her
              "Mulatto" son Anthony (born 17 August 1778) to her master [Orders
              1776-83, 350].
5   viii. ?Verlinda, born say 1763.
        ix.   ?Malinsa M'Guy, head of an Essex County household of 4 "other free"
              in 1810 [VA:208]. She may have been the mother of Mary McGuy
              who registered in Essex County on 14 December 1810: *born free by
              certificate of the clerk of Richmond County, dark Mulattoe, about 27
              years of age, 5 feet 3-3/4 inches* [Register of Free Negroes 1810-43,
              p.17, no.39].
        x.   ?Samuel[2] Magee, head of a Spotsylvania County household of 3 "other
              free" and a white woman over the age of 45 in 1810 [VA:101b].
        xi.   ?Thomas Magee, head of a Spotsylvania County household of 1 "other
              free," a slave and a white woman over the age of 45 in 1810
              [VA:102a].
        xii. ?George[2] Makee, a "yellow" taxable in the lower district of Prince
              William County in 1809 and 1810 [PPTL, 1782-1810, frames 708,
              736], head of a Prince William County household of 3 "other free" in
              1810 [VA:508]. He registered as a free Negro in Washington, D.C.,
              on 25 August 1821: *born free of a free woman in the neighborhood of
              Dumfries, Virginia*. Perhaps his wife was Nancy Makee who registered
              on 25 March 1826 and was also born free in Dumfries. Her sixteen-
              year-old "mulato" daughter Betsy and seventeen-year-old daughter
              Maria registered in October 1827 [Provine, *District of Columbia Free
              Negro Registers*, 7, 60, 74, 100]. George may have been identical to
              ____ McGee, a "yellow" complexioned soldier from King George
              County who enlisted as a substitute in the Revolution [NSDAR, *African
              American Patriots*, 151].

2.   James[1] McCoy, born say 1750, was taxable in the lower district of
     Westmoreland County from 1782 to 1815: taxable on 2 tithes in 1787 and
     1788; 3 from 1789 to 1792; charged with John, George and Garard McKie's
     tithes from 1793 to 1796; called McGuy from 1782 to 1793, McKey from
     1794 to 1815 and McKoy in the 1810 census [PPTL, 1782-1815, frames 247,
     269, 318, 327, 347, 358, 381, 410, 434, 450, 461, 476, 492]. He was listed
     as a "free Molatto" farmer living on his own land in Westmoreland County
     with (his wife?) Polley McKey and child James McKey in 1801 ["A List of
     Free Mulattoes & Negroes in Westmoreland County" *Virginia Genealogist*,
     31:40]. He was head of a Westmoreland County household of 4 "other free"
     in 1810 [VA:778]. He received a pension for his service as a soldier in the
     Revolution [Jackson, *Virginia Negro Soldiers*, 40]. His children were most
     likely
        i.   Catherine, born say 1770, called Catherine McGuy when she married
              Henry **Thompson**, 29 September 1789 Westmoreland County bond,
              Bennett McGuy security. She may have been the Kitty **Thompson** who
              was a "Molatto" living alone in Westmoreland County in 1801, a
              farmer on James Cox's land [*Virginia Genealogist* 31:46].
6   ii.   Rodham, born say 1770.
        iii. George[3], born say 1772, married Nancy McCoy, 4 January 1808
              Westmoreland County bond, William Brown security. He was head of
              a Westmoreland County household of 5 "other free" in 1810 [VA:780].
        iv.   Gerard/ Jerrard, born say 1774, married Winney **Davis**, 17 March
              1801, with the consent of Winney **Davis** dated the same day. He and
              Winney were "Molattoes" farming Mrs. Cox's land in Westmoreland

County in 1801 [*Virginia Genealogist* 31:40], and he was head of a Westmoreland County household of 5 "other free" in 1810 [VA:780].

    v.   John[1], born say 1778, a "Molatto" farmer living with (his wife?) Margaret McKey on Nathaniel Oldham's land in Westmoreland County in 1801 [*Virginia Genealogist* 31:40].

    vi.   James[2], listed in James McKey's household in 1801.

3.   Bennett McCoy, born about 1757, was drafted into the service from Westmoreland County to serve in 1777. He was allowed a pension in 1818 [Jackson, *Virginia Negro Soldiers*, 40]. He was taxable in Westmoreland County from 1789 to 1815: taxable on a slave in 1800 and 1801, in the "list of Free Negroes & Mulattoes" in 1813, called McGuy from 1789 to 1793, McKey from 1794 to 1815 and McKoy in the 1810 census [PPTL, 1782-1815, frames 347, 358, 399, 434, 476, 512, 542, 657, 771, 821]. In 1801 he was listed as a "free Molatto" farmer with Hannah McKey and child Nancy McKey, living on their own land [*Virginia Genealogist* 31:40]. He was head of a Westmoreland County household of 4 "other free" in 1810 [VA:780]. His child was

    i.   Nancy, married George McCoy, 4 January 1808 Westmoreland County bond, William Brown security.

4.   George[1] McCoy, born say 1759, married Elizabeth **Nickens**, twenty-four-year-old daughter of Nathaniel **Nickings**, 10 March 1788 Orange County, Virginia bond, 11 March marriage by Rev. George Eve. He was head of a Rockingham County household of 3 "other free" in 1810 [VA:130b]. According to his Revolutionary pension file, he died in the poorhouse in Rockingham County in 1821 [Jackson, *Virginia Negro Soldiers*, 40]. He was probably the father of

    i.   John[2], born 26 January 1788 of free parents in Augusta County, Virginia, registered as a "free Negro" in Rockingham County on 17 October 1815 and recorded his "free papers" in Ross County, Ohio: *a black man, aged 28 years the 26 January 1816, 6 ft 3/4 in., straight and well made, was born free* [Turpin, *Register of Black, Mulatto, and Poor Persons*, 22; Rockingham County Register of Free Negroes, no.24, p.10].

    ii.   Hannah, born about 1790, registered as a free Negro in Rockingham County on 11 July 1811: *about 5 feet 8 Inches high...about 21 years of age...a Dark Mulatto* [Register, no.8, p.5].

    iii.   George[4], born 1 June 1794, registered in Rockingham County on 20 June 1815: *about 21 years the 1st of this Month...bound an apprentice by order of the County Court of Rockingham to Joshua Peters also a free man of Colour to learn the trade of a Sadler, about 5 feet 7 inches high a dark Mulatto* [Register, no.22, p.10].

5.   Verlinda McKee, born say 1763, was called a "mulatto woman" who had once been indentured to James Gwatkin on 5 August 1805 when her daughter registered as a free Negro in Prince William County [Orders 1804-6, 205]. She was the mother of

    i.   Polly Sanford **Thornton**, born about 1783, daughter of Verlinda McKee a free Mulatto, twenty-two years old when she registered as a free Negro in Prince William County on 2 September 1805 [Orders 1804-6, 239, 243].

    ii.   Sally, born about 1786, nineteen years old when she registered in Prince William County on 5 August 1805 [Orders 1804-6, 205].

6.   Rodham McCoy, born say 1772, married Mary **Askins**, 23 December 1793 Westmoreland County bond, John Kirk security. He and his wife Molly McKey and children were listed as "free Molattoes" farming William Ball's land in Westmoreland County in 1801 [*Virginia Genealogist* 31:40]. He was

head of a Westmoreland County household of 8 "other free" in 1810 [VA:778]. He married, second, Elizabeth **Brinn**, 28 December 1816 Westmoreland County bond, William King security. His children listed with him in 1801 were
   i. Bob.
   ii. Fanny.
   iii. Betsey, married Jarrat **Thompson**, 21 May 1822 Westmoreland County bond. Gerard **Thompson** was living in the household of (his parents?) John and Haney **Thompson** in the list of "free Molattoes" in Westmoreland County in 1801 [*Virginia Genealogist* 31:45].

They may have been the ancestors of
7   i. William Megee, born say 1750.
   ii. Robert Macky, head of a Hyde County, North Carolina household of 2 "other free" and a white woman in 1800 [NC:372].
   iii. Easter Mackey, born 1776-1794, head of a Hyde County household of 4 "free colored" in 1820 [NC:248].
   iv. William McKey, head of a Beaufort County, North Carolina household of 2 "other free" in 1810 [NC:118].

7.   William Megee, born say 1750, was head of a Halifax County, North Carolina household of 9 "other free" in 1790 [NC:66] and 6 in 1810 [NC:38]. His widow was probably Winney McGee, born before 1776, head of a Halifax County household of 6 "free colored" in 1820 [NC:156] and 5 in 1830. Their children were most likely
   i. William J., head of a Halifax County household of 1 "other free" in 1810 [NC:36].
   ii. Henry, head of a Halifax County household of 3 "free colored" in 1820.
   iii. Tamzy, head of a Halifax County household of 2 "free colored" in 1820.

McDANIEL FAMILY

1.   James[1] McDaniel, born say 1725, was a taxable with Kate, "a fr. mulattoe," in the 1751 Bertie County tax list [CCR 190].[137] Kate was Catherine **Hammon**, his common-law wife, as is apparent from the 1759 list of John Brickell and later lists:

James McDaniel, his son James & Catherine Hammon

In 1763 both he and Catherine were taxed as "free molattos" in John Nichols' list. James probably died about 1769 when Kate was taxable in the household of his son James in the list of Edward Rasor [CR 10.702.1]. She was still living in Bertie County in 1810, called Catherine McDaniel, head of a household of 3 "other free" and 1 white male [NC:187]. James' son was
2   i. James[2], probably born circa 1745.

2.   James[2] McDaniel, born about 1745, was probably the third (unnamed) person taxed in his father's household in the 1757 list of Henry Hunter. He was married by 1763 to Sarah, a taxable in his household in John Nichols' list, identified as his wife in the 1769 list of Edward Rasor [CR 10.702.1, box 2].

---

[137]James[1] McDaniel may have been related to Alice McDaniel, born 18 March 1705, a twenty-one-year-old "Mallatto Born of a white Woman" who was living in Charles County, Maryland, on 13 August 1728 when the court ordered that she serve John Howard (the highest bidder) to the age of thirty-one [Court Record 1727-31, 153].

He was head of a Martin County household of 6 "other free" in 1790 [NC:68]. His children were most likely

  i.   Clary, head of a Halifax County household of 2 "other free" in 1800 [NC:358].
  ii. Charles, head of a Halifax County household of 2 "other free" in 1810 [NC:38].

MCINTOSH FAMILY

1. Anne[1] Macentosh, born say 1686, was living in York County on 24 May 1706 she was summoned to court to answer the information of Charles Chiswell for having a "Mullato Bastard Boy." On 24 July the case was deferred for the publication of a new law which had not yet come to the county [DOW 12:406, 424, 433]. She was probably the ancestor of

2   i.   Ann[2], born say 1733.

2. Ann[2] McIntosh, born say 1733, was living in Richmond County, Virginia, in August 1752 when she was ordered to serve her master Arjalon Price an additional thirty-one days for running away and an additional two years for his curing her of "the foul disease" [Orders 1746-52, 416]. He brought her before the Orange County court on 28 October 1756 for having an illegitimate "Mulatto" child. After seeing the child, the court ordered that after the completion of her indenture she serve her master another year and pay the churchwardens of St. Thomas Parish 15 pounds currency or be sold for five years. She was called the servant of John Simpson on 27 April 1758 when the churchwardens of St. Thomas Parish complained that she had delivered a bastard child. She petitioned the court for her freedom from Simpson on 28 September 1758, and on 26 April 1759 she was ordered to serve him additional time for running away for thirteen days [Orders 1754-63, 283, 367, 368, 437, 455]. Her daughter was

3   i.   Mary, born say 1756.

3. Mary McIntosh, born say 1756, was indentured to Arjalon Price of Orange County, Virginia, when he called her his "Mallatto Woman" and left her to his wife by his 29 April 1773 will. She was a "Molatto Girl" valued at 20 pounds in Price's 28 October 1773 inventory [WB 2:470-3, 475]. She was taxable in Orange County on herself, two unnamed daughters and a son in 1813 [Waldrep, *1813 Tax List*]. She was the mother of

  i.   ?William, born say 1785, head of a Culpeper County household of 1 "other free" in 1810 [VA:55].
  ii. ?Joseph, born say 1785, head of a Culpeper County household of 1 "other free" in 1810 [VA:55].
  iii. Mary, born about 1787, obtained a certificate from David Jamison, a justice of the peace from Culpeper County, and produced it in the District of Columbia court in Alexandria on 17 November 1803: *daughter of Molley McIntosh who was born free...about sixteen years old. I have known Mary als. Molly McIntosh from the time she was a girl, lived in the family of Arjalone Price of Orange County...said Molly was the mulatto bastard child of Ann McIntosh a Scotch servant woman. Said Molly was bound till thirty one years old according to Law* [Arlington County Register of Free Negroes, 1797-1861, no. 5, p.5].

MACLIN FAMILY

Members of the Maclin family were

1   i.   Thomas[1], born say 1704
2   ii. Godfrey[1], born say 1720.

1. Thomas[1] Maclin, born say 1704, was taxable in Lunenburg County in 1749 and 1750, taxable on 2 tithes in 1751 and taxable in 1752 on his own tithe, Edward **Peters** and Benjamin **Scott** in the list of Peter Jefferson [Bell, *Sunlight on the Southside*, 110, 140, 169, 192]. He received a patent for 315 acres in Lunenburg County on the branches of Dockery's Creek and Flat Creek on 5 February 1753 [Patents 32:34]. On 10 May 1764 the Lunenburg County court declared him to be levy free [Orders 1764-5, 3]. On 1 July 1769 he sold (signing by mark) 60 acres in Mecklenburg County adjoining Lewis Parham to Lewis Parham for 10 pounds [DB 2:253]. By his 11 August 1761 Mecklenburg County will, recorded 8 March 1773, he left his entire estate to his wife Easter Maclin "to handle as she desires" [WB 1:157]. A few months later on 14 July 1773 she sold (signing by mark) 127 acres in Mecklenburg County adjoining Lewis Parham on the Wheat Stone Branch to Thomas Maclin, Jr., of York County for 20 pounds. On 2 April 1777 she was living in Lunenburg County when she sold 127-1/2 acres in Mecklenburg County on the branches of Dockery's Creek and Flat Creek to Thomas Maclin of Mecklenburg County [DB 4:268; 5:234]. Thomas and Esther may have been the parents of

3   i.   Thomas[2], born say 1746.

2. Godfrey[1] Maclin (Miklin), born say 1720, was presented by the York County court in November 1746 for not listing his wife as a tithable [OW 19:472, 486]. He was the "free mulatta" father of several children who were baptized in Bruton Parish, James City and York counties. His wife was probably named Mary since a "Godfrey and Mary his wife" (no last name or race indicated) had a child named Mildred whose 17 November 1744 birth was registered in Bruton Parish [Bruton Parish Register, 5, 8]. He died before 11 November 1765 when the Mecklenburg County, Virginia court bound his orphan son John to William Terrell Mills [Orders 1765-8, 154]. His children were

   i.   ?Lucretia, born about 1742, wife of David **Bartley**, called "free Mulattas" when they registered the 29 November 1764 birth of their son Godfrey Macklin in Bruton Parish, York County [Bruton Parish Register, 27]. She was called Lucretia Maclin in York County on 17 May 1773 when she sued William **Roberts** for trespass, assault and battery [Judgments & Orders 1772-4, 273]. Lucretia was in Halifax County, Virginia, on 19 November 1778 when she was charged with the murder of Mary Scandling. At her hearing, George **Jones** (who was also from York County) deposed that he had been riding on a horse with Mary Scandling when they met Lucretia who insulted him, tried to strike him with a stick about the size of his arm, and struck Mary Scandling instead. Lucretia was sent to Williamsburg for further trial. Oddly enough, on 20 April 1775 three years prior to her death, Mary had been discharged from her indenture to George **Jones** by the Halifax County because George was a "free Mulatto." Two years later on 20 February 1777 the court bound Mary's daughter Macklin Scandling to George **Jones** [Pleas 1774-79, 109, 193, 379]. Lucretia was listed in the 1782 census for Richmond City, a forty-year-old woman living in Hannah McLin's household, perhaps the mother of Milley McLin, an eighteen-year-old in the same household [VA:111].

   ii.   Mildred, born 17 November 1744, "Daughter of Godfrey and Mary his Wife" (last name and race not indicated). She was probably the Milly Roberts, wife of William **Roberts**, "free Mulattos" who registered the 22 March 1765 birth of their son Macklin in Bruton Parish, James City and York counties [Bruton Parish Register, 5, 29].

4   iii.   Elizabeth[1], born say 1747.

   iv.   John[1], born say 1748, baptized in Bruton Parish on 7 May 1748, described as a "free mulatto" who lived near the lower Mecklenburg County store of Dinwiddie, Crawford, & Company and owed them 3 pounds on 1 September 1775 [*Virginia Genealogist* 15:291]. He may have been identical to John Macklin, "a poor soldier in the service of the United States," whose wife Frances was living in Mecklenburg County on 13 March 1780 when the court ordered Reuben Morgan to supply her with 2 barrels of corn for her support [Orders 1779-84, 19].

5   v.   ?Hannah, born say 1749.

6   vi.   Rebecca, born say 1760.

3.   Thomas[2] Maclin, born say 1746, and his wife Thomason Maclin, "both free mulattoes," registered the birth of their son Godfrey in Bruton Parish, James City and York counties on 23 February 1766 [Bruton Parish Register, 27]. On 21 July 1766 he and Robert **Evans** were securities in York County for a 55 shilling debt William **Roberts** owed Lawson Burfoot [Orders 1765-68, 91]. He was called Thomas Maclin, Jr., of York County on 14 July 1773 when he purchased 127 acres in Mecklenburg County, Virginia, adjoining Lewis Parham from Esther Maclin. He was living in Mecklenburg County on 2 April 1777 when he purchased another 127-1/2 acres from Esther Maclin for 30 pounds. He purchased 65 acres adjoining his land from Reuben Morgan for 150 pounds on 9 January 1779 and sold 10 acres on the Church Road for 10 pounds on 12 August 1782 [DB 4:268; 5:234, 379; 6:191]. On 8 November 1779 the Mecklenburg County court ordered that he be added to the list of tithables, and on 9 April 1782 the court allowed his claim for 325 pounds of beef provided to the Continental Army [Orders 1779-84, 1, 125]. He was head of a Mecklenburg County household of 11 persons in the list of Lewis Parham in 1782 [VA:34]. He was taxable on 16 head of cattle and 4 horses in 1782 and taxable on slaves Cate and Jerry in 1784 [PPTL, 1782-1805, frames 16, 48, 67, 97, 198]. He sued Benjamin Ferrell in Mecklenburg County court for trespass, assault and battery on 14 March 1785. The suit was discontinued on 9 October 1786 on agreement of the parties. He was sued for 8 pounds on 13 June 1785 and was security for Susanna **Chavers** in the suit of James King. On 9 July 1787 the court excused him from paying tax on his infirm son Godfrey [Orders 1784-7, 215, 269, 615]. He was a "Mulatto" taxable on 310 acres in the lower district of Mecklenburg County in 1787 [Land Tax List 1782-1811-A]. He sold land by deed proved in Mecklenburg County court on 8 December 1788 and 9 February 1789 [Orders 1787-92, 324, 329]. By 1790 he was in Wake County, North Carolina, where he was head of a household of 11 "other free" [NC:105]. He died before 25 June 1791 when his estate was administrated. Matthew, Elizabeth, John, and Thomason Maclin, William **Stewart** and Stephen **Haithcock** were buyers at the sale of his estate [Wynne, *Wills, Inventories, Settlement of Estates, Wake County*, 76]. In September 1791 the court appointed guardians for his children Godfrey, James, and Peggy. His children were

    i.   ?Matthew, born say 1764, listed in Mecklenburg County in Thomas Maclin's household in 1785 and listed in his own household on a slave named Liza in 1787 [PPTL, 1782-1805, frames 138, 197]. He married Sally **Jones**, 9 November 1787 Warren County bond, Isaac **Evans** bondsman. Matthew was head of a Wake County household of 6 "other free" in 1790 [NC:105], 7 in 1800 [NC:781], and 7 in Stokes County in 1810 [NC:579]. He purchased half of lot 173 in Raleigh for 18 pounds on 20 March 1797 and sold it for 110 pounds on 24 September 1799. He purchased 100 acres on the north side of Crabtree Creek in Wake County on 3 September 1800 and sold it in 1803 [DB Q:405-6, 444; R:302].

    ii.   Godfrey[2], born 23 February 1766 [Bruton Parish Register, 27], listed in Thomas Maclin's Mecklenburg County household in 1785 and 1787 [PPTL, 1782-1805, frame 97, 198].

iii. Mary[3], born 11 July 1768, baptized 14 August, "daughter of Thomas Macklin & Tomison His Wife Both free mulattoes" [Bruton Parish Register, 33].

iv. ?Jonathan, born say 1769, married Martha **Nickins**, 10 February 1790 Halifax County, Virginia bond. He was taxable in the lower district of Halifax County in 1798 [PPTL, 1782-99, frame 827].

v. ?William, born about 1769, about twenty-four years old on 23 March 1793 when the following article appeared in the *North Carolina Gazette of New Bern*: *committed to the jail of this district a Mulatto fellow, about 24 years of age 5'7" high. He says his name is William Maclin and that he came from Mecklenburg county Va. has a pass which he says he got from Col. Richard Cannon* [Fouts, *NC Gazette of New Bern*, II:15].

vi. ?John[2], born say 1771, taxable in Thomas Maclin's Mecklenburg County household in 1787 [PPTL, 1782-1805, frame 198]. He married Olivia **Williams**, 16 December 1791 Wake County bond, Matthew Maclin bondsman.

vii. ?James, born say 1772, married Mary **Heathcock/ Haithcock**, 5 October 1799 Wake County bond. He was taxable in Wake County on 398 acres in 1794 and taxable on 1 poll in 1802 [MFCR 099.701.1, frames 128, 270].

viii. ?Thomas[3], born say 1773, married Delilah **Evans**, 23 December 1794 Mecklenburg County, Virginia bond, John **Guy** bondsman. He was called "Thomas Maclin (mulatto)" when he was taxable in Mecklenburg County on one "white" tithe and a horse in 1810 [Yantis, *Supplement to the 1810 Census of Virginia*, M-1]. He was head of a Mecklenburg County household of 11 "free colored" in 1820 [VA:154] and was seventy-five years old when he was counted in the 1850 Mecklenburg County census [VA:55b].

ix. ?Fanny, born say 1780, married Earby **Chavous**, 9 March 1797 Mecklenburg County, Virginia bond, Thomas McLin security.

x. Margaret[3], born say 1782, married Barnabus **Scott**, 28 August 1803 Wake County bond. He married second, Peggy **Corn**, 1829 Wake County bond, Gilford **Scott** bondsman.

4. Elizabeth[1] Maclin, born say 1747, was baptized in Bruton Parish on 7 May 1748 [Bruton Parish Register, 8]. She was the "free Mulatto" mother of a bastard child Edy whose birth and baptism were recorded in Bruton Parish in 1765 [Bruton Parish Register, 26]. She may have been the Elizabeth Maclin who was head of a Cumberland County, North Carolina household of 3 "other free" and a slave in 1800. Her children were

i. Edy, born 2 August 1765, baptized 6 October.

ii. Mary[2], born 27 September 1767 [Bruton Parish Register, 32].

5. Hannah Maclin, born say 1749, was called a "free Mulatto" when the 8 March 1765 birth of her bastard child Edmund was recorded in Bruton Parish [Bruton Parish Register, 29]. She was called "Han McLin" in 1782, head of a family of 5 "free mulattoes" including Peggy, Milley, and Lucretia McLin and Edward **Smith**, with one tithable slave and two cattle, living on lots 498 and 479 in Wardship no. 3, Richmond, Virginia, in 1782 [VA:111]. Her children were

i. Edmund, born 8 March 1765, "a Bastard child son of Hannah Macklin a free Mulatto."

ii. Margaret[2], born 9 May 1768, baptized 5 June [Bruton Parish Register, 32], a fourteen-year-old in her mother's Richmond City household in 1782 [VA:111].

6. Rebecca Maclin, born say 1760, was living in Mecklenburg County, Virginia, on 8 June 1789 when the court bound out her illegitimate son Godfrey McLin. On 9 March 1801 the court bound him to John Bugg [Orders 1787-92, 406; 1798-1801, 512]. She was the mother of

    i.   Godfrey³, born about 1785, issued a certificate in Mecklenburg County by John Bugg on 3 January 1814: *Godfrey Maclin was born and raised in the County of Mecklenburg, Virginia, is a free man, is Six feet two inches high, is a mahogany Colour & is about twenty nine years old. The said Godfrey Maclin lived in the family of my father & in my own family from about four years old, until he was twenty two years old, during the whole of which he Conducted himself in an honest & Orderly manner...John Bugg* [Free Person of Color, no.5, p.3].

    ii. ?Betty, bound by the Mecklenburg County court to John and Sally Bugg on 14 December 1801 [Orders 1801-3, 127].

    iii. ?An(?)visa, bound by the Mecklenburg County court to Henry and Martha Finch on 14 December 1801 [Orders 1801-3, 127].

Other members of the family in Virginia were

    i.   Mary¹ Mackland, born say 1734, living in Bruton Parish on 15 July 1754 when the York County court fined her 500 pounds of tobacco for having a bastard child [Judgments & Orders 1752-4, 463].

    ii. James Maclin, alias **Roberts**, born say 1745, added to the list of tithables in Elizabeth City County on 7 November 1764 [Court Records 1760-9, 262].

    iii. Margaret¹, born about 1754. She and Lizza (no last name indicated) ran away from Jonathan Patteson of New Kent County about 20 November 1766. He advertised for their return in the 29 January 1769 issue of the *Virginia Gazette* describing her and (her sister?) as: *two Mulatto girls, named Margaret and Lizzy. The former is about 12 years old, of a dark complexion, and has a thin visage; the other is of a yellow complexion, and has a long woolly head. They are both bound to me as the law directs, viz. to serve until the age of 21 years* [Windley, *Runaway Slave Advertisements* 1:49]. Margaret Maclin complained to the Lunenburg County court on 8 April 1773 that her master John Patteson, Sr., was holding her and Lizza Maclin in servitude. The court discharged her from Patteson's service as an apprentice on 9 September 1773 but dismissed Lizza's complaint [Orders 1769-77, 309, 350, 365].

    iv. Elizabeth²/ Lizza, born say 1756, complained to the Lunenburg County court on 8 April 1773 that her master John Patteson, Sr., was holding her in servitude, but the court dismissed her complaint after hearing both parties on 15 October 1773 [Orders 1769-77, 309, 365].

    v.   Patty, married William **Banks**, 8 September 1787 York County marriage by Rev. John Davenport [*VMHB* XXV:300].

    vi. Winnifred, married Reuben **Gillett**, 11 July 1790 York County bond.

    vii. Jones, born about 1792, issued a certificate in Mecklenburg County on 20 October 1817: *of a bright yellow complexion, Five feet eleven & a half inches high about twenty five years old* [Free Person of Color, no.15, p.8].

    viii. Patty, head of a York County household of 5 "other free" in 1810 [VA:878].

MADDEN FAMILY

1. Mary Madden, born say 1740, was a white servant woman living in St. George Parish, Spotsylvania County, Virginia, on 17 April 1760 when her "mulatto" daughter Sarah was bound apprentice. Mary had at least one other child (unnamed) by 1770 when the vestry of St. George Parish paid Mary

Turnley, wife of Francis Turnley, for helping her deliver it [Madden, *We Were Always Free*, 6, 5]. Mary was the mother of

    i.   Sarah, born 4 August 1758. See the two hundred-year-long history of Sarah Madden's descendants in T.O. Madden's book, *We Were Always Free*.

MAHORNEY FAMILY

Members of the Mahorney family were

    i.   Thomas, born about 1733, living with Sarah Weedon when he was taxable in Prince William County in 1800 [PPTL, 1782-1810, frame 443]. He was about 85 years old on 22 May 1818 when he made a declaration in Prince William County court to obtain a pension for his services in the Revolution. He stated that he enlisted in January 1777 in Westmoreland County. He was called a "free man of colour," aged about ninety-one, on 3 October 1820 when he appeared in court again, declaring that his family residing with him was his wife Mima and son Jack, both slaves [M804-1615, frame 0568].

    ii.   Winny, born about 1759, registered in King George County on 5 August 1801: *a dark mulatto woman about forty two years of age...is a free woman, she having served in the estate of Richard Bernard, decd., the term of thirty one years* [Register of Free Persons, no. 28]. She was called Winny McHorney in Westmoreland County, head of a household of 3 "other free" in 1810 [VA:780].

    iii.   James, born about 1763, registered in King George County in February 1797: *a black man, about thirty four years old...having served his time with William Bernard, Gent., of this County, p. order or certificate of said County of King George* [Register of Free Persons 1785-1799, no. 7].

    iv.   Sukey, born about 1775, registered in King George County on 5 August 1801: *a black woman, aged about twenty six years...is a free woman, she having served William Bernard, Esqr., the term of twenty one years* [Register of Free Persons, no. 30]. She was called Susan McHorney in Westmoreland County, head of a household of 5 "other free" in 1810 [VA:780].

    v.   Rachel, born about 1780, registered in King George County on 5 August 1801: *a black woman, aged about twenty one years...is a free woman, she having served in the estate of Richard Bernard, decd., the term of twenty one years* [Register of Free Persons, no. 29].

    vi.   Caty, born about 1792, registered in King George County on 7 April 1814: *a black woman aged about twenty two years, spare made about five feet four and a quarter Inches high...was born free of a woman emancipated by Richd. Bernard late of King George County decd.* [Register of Free Persons, no.46].

MANLY FAMILY

1.   Gabriel[1] Manly was born before 28 September 1703 when his mother Elizabeth Manly, a servant of John Wilkins, was presented for bastard bearing by the grand jury of Northampton County, Virginia [Orders 1698-1710, 165]. He was called "a Malatto" child on 28 January 1703/4 when John Wilkins, Sr., recorded his indenture in court [OW&c 1698-1710, 183]. He was a taxable in John Wilkins' Northampton County household from 1720 to 1731, called Gabriel Manly in 1720, "Gabriel negro" in 1723, and Gabriel Manly "molato" in 1727 [L.P. 1720-1731]. He married Dinah **Webb**, born in 1704, the daughter of Jane **Webb**, and Left, a slave of Thomas Savage on whose plantation they lived. She was tithable in her mother's household, called Dinah **Webb** in 1728, Dinah Manly in 1729 and 1730, and she was head of her own

household with her mother in 1731, living near Gabriel who was still serving his indenture to John Wilkins. Gabriel and Diana moved to Norfolk County, Virginia, where they were taxable in 1735 [Wingo, *Norfolk County Tithables, 1730-50*, 158 & 167]. By 1742 they were in Bertie County, North Carolina, where he purchased 100 acres of land by deed witnessed by Francis **Brown** and Benjamin Wynn. He purchased 140 acres adjoining his land from Joseph Wynns on 23 February 1746/7, and as Gabriel Manley, cooper, he purchased another 100 acres of adjoining land near the Holley Swamp on 12 November 1750 [DB F:339; G:347, 236]. He, his wife Diana, and 3 children were "Fr mulatoes," taxable in Bertie County in 1751 [CCR 190].

He sold the 200 acres on which he was living on 7 September 1754, and in 1755 his son Abel signed with him when he swapped his remaining 140 acres of land adjacent to Culmer Sessums for 150 acres from James Davis near the "end of a capway running." Soon afterwards on 22 January 1756 he bought another 160 acres near his old property on the Holley Swamp [DB H:212, 319; I:103]. He was taxable in the 1757 list of Henry Hunter [CR 10.702.1], and on 26 July 1758 he signed a promissory note to Blake Baker for 3 pounds [CR 10.908.1]. He was living in the part of Bertie County which became Hertford County in 1759. The records for this period were destroyed by a courthouse fire, so there is no further information on him and his wife. His children were

- 2   i.   Abel, born say 1730.
- 3   ii.   Littleton[1], born say 1732.
-      iii.   Solomon, born say 1733, a taxable in his own household in 1751 [CCR 190], taxable in 1759 in the constable's list of William Witherington for Captain Benjamin Wynn's District, and taxable in Hertford County on two persons in 1768 and 1770 Fouts, *Tax Receipt Book*, 55].
-      iv.   Susannah, born before 1740, taxable in her father's Bertie County household in 1751.
-      v.   Gabriel[2], Jr., born before 1740, taxable in his father's Bertie County household in 1751. He was taxable in Hertford County on one person in 1770 [Fouts, *Tax Receipt Book*, 20] and head of a Hertford County household of 2 "other free" in 1790 [NC:25].
-      vi.   Moses[1], born before 1740, taxable in his father's Bertie County household in 1751. He was taxable in an untitled Bertie list with Francis **Brown**, 2 "black" taxables in 1758, and with Francis **Brown** in the list of John Brickell in 1759. He was taxable in Hertford County on two persons in 1768 and on 50 acres and one horse in District 4 of Hertford County in 1779 [Fouts, *Tax Receipt Book*, 47; GA 30.1]. He was head of a Hertford County household of 11 "other free" in 1790 [NC:26], 10 in 1800, 5 in 1810 [NC:92], and he was a "free colored" man over forty-five years of age living in Hertford County with a "free colored" woman in 1820 [NC:184].
-      vii.   ?Southerland, born say 1747, taxable in Hertford County on one person in 1768, two in 1769 and 1770 [Fouts, *Tax Receipt Book*, 54], and head of a Northampton County household of 9 "other free" in 1800 [NC:461].

2.   Abel Manly, born say 1730, was a taxable head of a Bertie County household with Ann **Archer**, "free Milats.," in 1751 [CCR 190]. She was called his wife Ann in the 1757 tax list of William Wynns. He was taxable in Hertford County on five persons in 1768 and 1769 Fouts, *Tax Receipt Book*, 8]. Possible children:

- 4   i.   Moses[2], born about 1761.
-      ii.   Hardy, head of a Halifax County household of 7 "other free" in 1800 [NC:331], 11 in 1810 [NC:37], and 6 "free colored" in 1820 [NC:157].

iii.   Lud, head of a Halifax County household of 15 "free colored" in 1820 [NC:156].

3.   Littleton[1] Manly was probably born about 1732 since he was head of a household with Sarah in 1751 in the Bertie tax list. He was taxable in Hertford County on two persons in 1768, three in 1769, two in 1770, and taxable on two lots in Winton and a horse in District 3 of Hertford County in 1779 [Fouts, *Tax Receipt Book*, 45; GA 30.1]. He was in the neighboring county of Northampton in 1790 where he was head of a household of 5 "other free" [NC:75]. He may have been the father of

    i.   William, called "William Munley Mulatto" in the state census for Northampton County in 1786, head of a Northampton County household of 4 "other free" in 1790 [NC:75], and a Halifax County household of 7 in 1800 [NC:330], 10 in 1810 [NC:38], and 7 "free colored" in 1820 (Billie Manly) [NC:157].

    ii.   Littleton[2], taxable in Norfolk County from 1798 to 1806: a labourer in Western Branch District in a "List of Free Negroes and Mulattoes" in 1801 [PPTL, 1791-1812, frames 254, 359, 384, 434, 467, 486A, 564, 579]. He was a "free colored" man over forty-five years of age living in Hertford County with a "free colored" woman thirty-six to forty-five years old in 1820.

    iii.   John, head of a Northampton County household of 1 "other free" in 1800 [NC:461], perhaps the John Manley who was head of a Norfolk County household of 4 "other free" in 1810 [VA:814].

4.   Moses[2] Manly, born about 1761, enlisted with Colonel Lytle in the Tenth North Carolina Regiment for nine months in August 1781. He made a declaration in Hertford County court for a pension on 17 August 1819 and a second declaration in Halifax County court on 26 October 1821. He named his wife Chloe and three of his daughters: Sally, Esther, and Candys [M805, reel 549, frame 703]. He was head of a Bertie County household of 3 "other free" in 1790 [NC:14] and a Halifax County household of 5 in 1800 [NC:328], 7 in 1810 [NC:36], and 7 "free colored" in 1820 [NC:157]. On 18 August 1834 his widow Chloe Manley applied to the Halifax County court to receive her husband's Revolutionary War pension and proved to the court's satisfaction that: *said Chloe is the widow of said Moses & that said Moses departed this life on 16 May 1834.* Their children were

    i.   ?Arthur, born before 1776, head of a Halifax County household of 4 "free colored" in 1820 [NC:157]. He was in the First Company detached from the Halifax County Regiment in the War of 1812 [N.C. Adjutant General, *Muster Rolls of the War of 1812 from the Militia of North Carolina,* 19]. He was living in Weldon in May 1844 when he made a declaration in Halifax County court to obtain the pension of Moses Manly, deceased [M805, reel 807, frame 712].

    ii.   Sally, born about 1800.

    iii.   Esther, born about 1804.

    iv.   Candys, born about 1806.

Fairfax County, Virginia

1.   Phillis Manley, born say 1728, was the servant of Moses Linton on 20 June 1749 when the Fairfax County court ordered the churchwardens to bind her "Mullatto" son Isaac to her master. She was the servant of Thomas Fields on 19 April 1754 when she won a suit against him for her freedom. On 18 March 1756 the court ordered the churchwardens of Cameron Parish to bind her daughter Jemima (no race indicated) to Paul Turley [Orders 1749-54, 16, 85; 1754-6, pt. 2, 496]. She was living in Loudoun County on 14 December 1757 when she acknowledged her indenture to serve Thomas Fields for seven years [Orders 1757-62, 57]. She may have been identical to Phillis, one of the

"Negro" tithables in Thomas Field's Loudoun County household in 1762. She was called Phillis Manly in 1765 when she was tithable in Henry Potter's Loudoun County household [Sparacio, *Loudoun County Tithables*, 1758-1769, 22, 41]. She was the mother of

2   i.   ?Sarah, born say 1747.
    ii. Isaac, born say 1749.
3   iii. ?Ann, born say 1750.
    iv. Jemima, born say 1755.

2. Sarah Manley, born say 1747, was living in Fairfax County on 19 March 1771 when the court ordered the churchwardens of Truro Parish to bind out her two-year-old "Molatto" daughter Hannah to Paul Turley. Her suit against John Gibson for trespass abated on 22 August 1786 by her death [Orders 1770-2, 183; 1783-8, 259]. She was the mother of
    i. Hannah, born about 1769.

3. Ann Manley, born say 1750, was living in Fairfax County on 19 March 1771 when the court ordered the churchwardens of Truro Parish to bind out her one-year-old "Molatto" son George to Paul Turley. She petitioned the court for her freedom from Turley on 20 March 1771 and was discharged from his service a month later on 23 May [Orders 1770-2, 183, 185, 227]. She was living in Loudoun County on 10 August 1779 when she complained to the court that Thomas Jacobs was detaining her son Vincent Manly [Orders 1776-83, 183, 201,]. She was the mother of
    i. ?Benjamin Fairfax, born about 1769, an eighteen-year-old (no race indicated) ordered bound by the overseers of the poor of Truro District, Fairfax County, to John Brumback on 19 June 1787 [Orders 1783-8, 420]. He was probably the Benjamin Manly who was bound to John Turley by the Loudoun County court on 14 August 1780 [Orders 1776-83, 256]. The Prince William County court certified his registry (as a free Negro) on 5 August 1805 [Orders 1804-6, 205].
    ii. George, born about 1770.
    iii. Vincent, bound to Thomas Jacobs on 10 August 1779 when his mother Ann complained to the Loudoun County court. The court bound him to William McClelon on 14 December 1779 and ordered the churchwardens of Cameron Parish to bind him to William Beavers on 13 March 1780 [Orders 1776-83, 135, 229].
    iv. ?Dorcas, bound by the churchwardens of Cameron Parish, Loudoun County, to John Turley on 14 August 1780 (no race indicated) [Orders 1776-83, 256]. She and her son Leck were listed as "F.N.s" in the 1813 tax list for Loudoun County [Waldrep, *1813 Tax List*].
    v. ?Henry, bound by the churchwardens of Cameron Parish, Loudoun County, to Peter Harmon on 14 August 1780 [Orders 1776-83, 320].
    vi. ?Rose, head of a Loudoun County household of 3 "other free" in 1810 [VA:246].
    vii. ?Charles, head of a Dinwiddie County household of 2 "other free" in 1810 [VA:154].

MANN FAMILY

1. Sarah[1] Mann, born say 1720, was the servant of John Sutton in August 1765 when she and her children brought suit against him for their freedom in Caroline County court. The court ordered that depositions be taken from several elderly witnesses regarding her freedom and ordered her master to deliver her and her son Glasgow to court in November 1766. She appeared in court on 15 July 1768 when she stated that she had withdrawn her suit because her master had severely beaten her and that others had warned her that her children "would be removed to the Indians where she would never hear from

them." The court found in her favor [Orders 1765-7, 135, 434, 442; 1767-8, 198-9]. She was the mother of

2 i. ?Frank, born say 1739.

   ii. ?Hannah, born say 1740, discharged from John Sutton's service by the Caroline County court on 12 April 1771 [Orders 1770-1, 175].

   iii. ?Remers, born about February 1742, released from servitude by consent of his master John Sutton on 11 February 1773 [Orders 1772-6, 171].

   iv. Glasgow, born say 1744.

   v. ?Caesar, born say 1745, petitioned the Caroline County court for his freedom from John Sutton on 12 April 1771. The court ordered that he serve until 1 November 1776. He was sued by William Bowler in November 1771 [Orders 1770-1, 175, 376].

3 vi. ?Benjamin, born say 1758.

4 vii. ?Rachel, born about 1761.

   viii. ?Patty, brought suit in Caroline County court for her freedom from John Sutton on 11 June 1772. The case was dismissed, probably because she had not yet completed her indenture [Orders 1772-6, 18].

2. Frank/ Frances Mann, born say 1739, was discharged from John Sutton's service by the Caroline County court on 12 April 1771. She was probably living in Louisa County on 11 November 1771 when the court ordered the churchwardens of Trinity Parish to bind out (her daughter?) Judy Mann, a "Melatto Bastard," to John Byarse. She was called Frances Mann "a Free Mulatto" on 10 May 1773 when the Louisa County court ordered the churchwardens of Trinity Parish to bind out her children Charity and Rose Mann to John Smith [Orders 1770-1, 175; 1766-74, 109; 1766-72, 511; 1773, 33]. She was the mother of

   i. ?Judy, born say 1770, a "Melatto" child ordered bound out by the churchwardens of Trinity Parish on 11 November 1771.

5 ii. Charity, born say 1771.

   iii. Rose, born say 1773.

6 iv. James, born say 1778.

3. Benjamin Mann, born say 1758, was in the Continental service on 8 October 1781 when the Louisa County court ordered that needy relief be supplied to his wife Milley Mann and four small children [Orders 1774-82, 335]. Milly complained to the Spotsylvania County court on 6 May 1788 that Abner Yates intended to move to Kentucky and take her sons Daniel and Billy who were bound to him by the Caroline County court. The court bound her ten-year-old son Daniel and eight-year-old son Billy to Thomas Herndon [Minutes 1786-8, 171]. Milly was the mother of

   i. Daniel^2, born about 1778, ten years old on 6 May 1788.

   ii. William, born about 1780, eight years old on 6 May 1788.

4. Rachel^1 Mann, born about 1761, was a "poor orphan" of Essex County on 16 July 1770 when the court ordered the churchwardens of St. Ann's Parish to bind her out [Orders 1767-70, 371]. She was taxable on a free male tithe aged 16-21 in Essex County in 1783 [PPTL, 1782-1819, frames 46]. She was head of an Essex County household of 10 "other free" in 1810 [VA:199] and 3 "free colored" in Spotsylvania County in 1830. She registered in Essex County on 19 August 1811: *born free by info" of Thomas Pitts, colour Black, about 50 years of age, 5 feet 3-3/4 Incs.* [Register of Free Negroes 1810-43, p.20, no.49]. She may have been the mother of

7 i. Clary, born about 1779.

   ii. Betsy, counted in a "List of Free Negroes & Mulattoes in the Parish of St. Ann's" in Essex County in 1813, with a male and female above the age of sixteen in the same list as Rachel Mann [PPTL, 1782-1819, frame 510].

   iii. Rachel[2], born about 1791, registered in Essex County on 22 April 1817: *born free by statement of Thomas Pitts, Esq., light black, about 26 years of age, 5 feet 1 inch* [Register of Free Negroes 1810-43, p.27, no.70].

   iv. Henry, born about 1794, registered in Essex County on 22 April 1817: *born free by statement of Thomas Pitts, Esq., colour black, about 23 years of age, 5 feet 11-3/4 inches* [Register of Free Negroes 1810-43, p.28, no.72]. He was a "free Negro" taxable in Essex County in 1814 [PPTL, 1782-1819, frame 545]. He may have been the Henry Mann who was a "free Negro" taxable in St. Ann's Parish, Albemarle County, from 1809 to 1813 [PPTL, 1800-1813, frames 369, 415, 548].

   v. John, a "free Negro" taxable in Essex County in 1814 [PPTL, 1782-1819, frame 545].

   vi. Jane, born about 1802, registered in Essex County on 22 April 1817: *born free by statement of Thomas Pitts, Esq., colour light black, about 15 years of age, 4 feet 10-1/2 inches* [Register of Free Negroes 1810-43, p.28, no.71].

5. Charity Mann, born say 1771, was living in Louisa County when her children registered as free Negroes. Her children were

   i. Edmund, born about 1794, registered in Louisa County on 19 June 1816: *(son of Charity Mann) a free person of colour, about 22 years of age, dark complexion...formerly bound as an apprentice to William Terry and William Fortune.*

   ii. Stephen, born about 1796, registered in Louisa County on 13 May 1817: *(son of Charity Mann) who was bound to Richard Harris of sd. county as an apprentice, 21 years old, black complexion.*

   iii. Nelson, born about 1797, registered in Louisa County on 8 September 1818: *son of Charity Mann, a person of colour free born, 21-22 years of age, black complexion.*

   iv. Sarah[2], born about 1798, registered in Louisa County on 8 November 1819: *daughter of Charity Mann (the said Charity Mann was born free) and Sarah was formerly bound to John Gunnell of this county, 21 years, dark complexion, thick lips* [Abercrombie, *Free Blacks of Louisa County*, 23, 25, 26, 50]. She registered in Botetourt County on 18 March 1823: *25 years of age; Black; Born free as per Certificate from Clk. Louisa Cty. Court* [Free Negroes &c Registered in the Clerk's Office of Botetourt County, no. 36].

   v. William, born about 1798, registered in Louisa County on 12 October 1835: *son of Charity Mann who was born free, dark complexion, age 37 years* [Abercrombie, *Free Blacks of Louisa County*, 50].

6. James Mann, born say 1774, "Base Born child of Frances Mann," was living in Louisa County on 9 August 1779 when the court ordered the churchwardens of Trinity Parish to bind him out [Orders 1774-82, 259]. He was a "free Negro" aged 16-21 when he was taxable on a horse in Essex County in 1783. He was taxable in Essex County on a slave over the age of sixteen and a horse in 1806 and taxable on a free tithe and a horse in 1809 and 1814 [PPTL, 1782-1819, frames 46, 398, 416, 431, 545]. He was a "free Negro" taxable in Hanover County in 1800 [*Virginia Genealogist* 29:105] and a "free Negro" taxable in St. Ann's Parish, Albemarle County, in 1807, 1810 and 1811 [PPTL, frames; 1800-1813, frames 326, 416, 461]. He was the father of

   i. Sukey, born about 1802, registered in Essex County on 18 June 1821: *emancipated by her father James Mann in Essex County Court by deed of record, colour Tawny, about 19 years of age, 5 feet 2 inches* [Register of Free Negroes 1810-43, p.36, no.91].

7. Clary Mann, born about 1779, registered in Essex County on 22 April 1817: *born free by statement of Thos. Pitts, Dark Mulattoe, about 38 years of age, 5 feet 2-1/4 Ins.* [Register of Free Negroes 1810-43, p.27, no.69]. She was the mother of

    i. Stanton, born about 1796, registered in Essex County on 20 December 1819: *born free appearing by the register of her mother Clary Mann, colour Tawny, about 23 years of age, 5 feet 2 Inches* [Register of Free Negroes 1810-43, p.32, no.83].

    ii. Susan, born about 1803, registered in Essex County on 20 December 1819: *born free appearing by the register of her mother Clary Mann, colour Black, about 16 years of age, 5 feet 1/4 Inches* [Register of Free Negroes 1810-43, p.33, no.84].

Other members of the Mann family were

    i. George, born say 1764, bondsman for the 7 September 1785 Albemarle County marriage of Lucy **Bowles** and Charles **Barnett**. George was a "free Negro" taxable in St. Ann's Parish, Albemarle County, in 1783, 1793, from 1800 to 1807, and taxable in Fredericksville Parish in 1813 [PPTL, 1782-1799, frames 31, 368, 437; 1800-1813, frames 12, 144, 186, 277, 326, 573]. He was head of an Albemarle County household of 3 "other free" in 1810 [VA:166b].

    ii. Nancy, born about 1768, complained to the Henry County court that John Pace was detaining her in slavery. On 29 August 1796 the court liberated her from servitude, "it appearing to the court she has arrived to the full age of eighteen years" [Orders 1792-7, 265].

    iii. Daniel[1], born about 1769, obtained a certificate of freedom in Baltimore County, Maryland, on 4 September 1794 and recorded the certificate in Kershaw County, South Carolina, on 4 October 1797: *Daniel Man a free negro... born in Prince George County, state of Maryland, he's about 38 years of age...5 ft. 5 1/2 inches high without shoes, a yellow negro man, with short curly hair* [Journal of the Court of Common Pleas and Sessions 1791-1799, WPA transcript].

    iv. William, "F. Negroe" head of a Fauquier County household of 4 "other free" and 3 slaves in 1810 [VA:366].

    v. Nanny, born about 1779, registered as a "free Negro" in Lancaster County on 21 April 1806: *Age 27, Color yellow...born free* [Burkett, *Lancaster County Register of Free Negroes*, 2].

    vi. Molly Mans, born about 1779, registered as a "free Negro" in Lancaster County on 19 January 1807: *Age 28 years, Color mulatto...born free* [Burkett, *Lancaster County Register of Free Negroes*, 3].

    vii. John, a "free Negro" taxable in St. Ann's Parish, Albemarle County, in 1805, 1807, and 1810: taxable on a slave over the age of sixteen in 1807 [PPTL, 1800-1813, frames 233, 326, 416].

    viii. John, head of a Frederick County household of 1 "other free" in 1810 [VA:510].

MANNING FAMILY

1. George Manning, born say 1740, was a "Mullatto" taxable in Pasquotank County, North Carolina, in 1769 [N.C. Archives, SS 837]. He may have been the father of

    i. Keziah, born say 1760, married George **Perkins**, 5 April 1780 Bladen County marriage bond, John Cade bondsman.

    ii. Ann, born say 1761, a "Mulatto" taxable in Bertie County, North Carolina, in Abraham Taylor's household in 1775 [C.R. 10.702.1].

    iii. John, born say 1775, head of a Sumter District, South Carolina household of 6 "other free" in 1810 [SC:218a].

Mecklenburg County, Virginia

Mixed-race members of the Manning family living in Mecklenburg County, Virginia, before 1800 were probably related to Samuel Manning. On 18 September 1766 the churchwardens of St. James Parish, Mecklenburg County, bound Nancy **Chavis**, daughter of Findwell **Chavis**, to him. And on 13 September 1768 Samuel's wife testified on behalf of Susannah **Chavis** when the churchwardens sued her for debt [Orders 1765-8, 212; 1768-71, 38, 54]. Members of the family in Mecklenburg County were

    i.   Polley, married John Ginnet **Stewart**, 9 December 1794 Mecklenburg County, Virginia bond, Earbe **Chavous** (**Chavis**) security, with a note from Polly's mother Susanna **Chavous**.

    ii. Benjamin, married Fanny **Guy**, 5 May 1796 Mecklenburg County bond, Earbe (Yarborough) **Chavis** security.

MANUEL/ EMANUEL FAMILY

1.   Nicholas[1] Manuel, born say 1680, and his wife Bungey were freed by the 28 October 1718 will of Edward Myhill of Elizabeth City County, Virginia. Other members of his family did not fare as well:

> *For serving well and faithfully for many years past, two negro slaves Nicholas Manuell and Bungey his wife are to be freed immediately....slaves Hanah Manuell, David, William, George, Nicholas the younger, and Elizabeth Manuell are devised to Elizabeth Myhill for life & then divided among children* [Deeds, Wills 1715-21, 194-5].

    They were probably the parents of

2   i.   Ephraim, born about 1725.

2.   Ephraim Emanuel, born about 1725, was listed in the muster roll of Captain Elisha Williams' Edgecombe County Militia in the 1750's [Clark, *Colonial Soldiers of the South*, 675]. He may have been the husband of Hannah Mannuel who was paid by the estate of James Harris of Halifax County, North Carolina, between 10 August 1774 and December 1776 [Gammon, *Record of Estates* II:26]. He was taxable on 500 acres and one poll in Sampson County in 1784 [L.P. 64.1 by *N.C. Genealogy* XIV:2174]. The Sampson County court recommended that he be exempt from paying tax on 20 September 1785 [Minutes 1784-1800]. He made a deed of gift to his son Jesse of 300 acres on the west side of Coharie Swamp in Sampson County on 15 September 1789 and sold land to Levy Manuel in the same area of Sampson County on 1 April 1795 [DB 8:414; 9:485]. Ephraim was head of a Sampson County household of 3 "other free" in 1790 [NC:51]. His children were

4   i.   ?Christopher, born about 1752.

      ii. ?John[1], born say 1755, purchased 100 acres on the upper side of Edge's Branch on the great swamp in Sampson County on 15 September 1773 [DB 6:199]. He was head of a Sampson County household of 5 "other free" in 1790 [NC:51]. He purchased 230 acres on the west side of the Coharie Swamp on 20 November 1794 and sold this land a few years later on 6 March 1797 [DB 10:52, 375]. He was head of a Sampson County household of 8 "other free" in 1800 [NC:517] and 7 "free colored" in 1820 [NC:310]. In 1810 he was counted as white: over forty-five years old, head of a family of 12 persons [NC:472].

5   iii. ?Nicholas[2], born say 1757.

      iv. Jesse, born about 1760, received his final settlement certificate as a twelve months soldier in the Revolution on 25 December 1787 [*NCGSJ* XIII:93]. His father gave him 300 acres on the west side of Coharie

Swamp in Sampson County by deed of gift on 15 September 1789. He sold this land on 1 May 1792 [DB 8:404; 9:126]. He provided bail for John **Walden**'s appearance in Sampson County court on 15 August 1786 [Minutes 1784-1800, 42]. He was head of a Sampson County household of 6 "other free" in 1790 [NC:51], and he was over forty-five years of age with 6 persons counted as white in 1810 [NC:474]. He was about sixty years old on 6 October 1820 when he made a declaration in Sampson County court to obtain a Revolutionary War pension. He enlisted in Bladen County in April 1782 and served in the 2nd North Carolina Regiment. In 1820 his family consisted of his sixty-two-year-old wife and his nine-year-old granddaughter. He was in Wake County on November 1821 when he made and amendment to his declaration, stating that he had been a resident of Wake for seven years and that he had resided in the city of Raleigh for about three years out of the seven. Henry and Moses **Carter** testified for him. Henry stated that he had been acquainted with him since they were boys, that they were near-neighbors in Duplin County, that they met while both were in the service, and that he could not be mistaken about Jesse because he was such a remarkably tall man [M804-1627].

    v.   ?Levy, born say 1762, taxable on 125 acres in Sampson County in 1784 [L.P. 64.1 by *N.C. Genealogy* XIV:2171]. He purchased 100 acres on the west side of Coharie Swamp from (his father?) Ephraim Manuel on 1 April 1795, purchased a further 205 acres in the same area of Coharie Swamp on 22 February 1796, and purchased 150 acres on the east side of the swamp on 15 October 1798 [DB 9:485; 10:110; 11:38]. He was head of a Sampson County household of 5 "other free" in 1790 [NC:53], counted as white in 1810 [NC:486].

3.   Jesse Manuel, born say 1775, was head of a Cumberland County, North Carolina household of 6 "other free" in 1810 [NC:575]. He may have been the husband of Elizabeth Manual who was discharged by the 6 June 1838 Cumberland County court as an insolvent. He was probably the father of

    i.   Isaac, born say 1800, "a free man of colour," ordered by the 9 December 1841 Cumberland County court to show cause why his children should not be bound out.

    ii.   John[2], born say 1795, head of a Cumberland County household of 4 "free colored" in 1820 [NC:167].

    iii.   Jacob, head of a Cumberland County household of 3 "free colored" in 1820 [NC:178].

4.   Christopher Manuel, born about 1752, was head of a Northampton County, North Carolina household of 6 males 21-60 years old, 1 male less than 20 or more than 60, and 3 females in the 1786 state census, head of a Northampton County household of 8 "other free" in 1790 [NC:75], 11 in Sampson County in 1800 [NC:517] and 6 "free colored" in Sampson County in 1820 [NC:308]. He was about eighty years old on 19 November 1832 when he made a declaration in Sampson County court to obtain a pension for his services in the Revolution. He stated that he was born in Halifax County, North Carolina, and moved to the part of Duplin County which became Sampson County before the war [M804-1627]. He may have been the father of

    i.   Lemuel, born before 1776, head of a Sampson County household of 5 "free colored" in 1820 [NC:290].

    ii.   Michael, born 1776-1794, head of a Sampson County household of 5 "free colored" in 1820 [NC:292].

5.   Nicholas[2] Manuel, born say 1757, was taxable on 150 acres and one poll in Sampson County in 1784 [L.P. 64.1 by *N.C. Genealogy* XIV:2174] and purchased 20 acres on the east side of the Coharie Swamp on 5 March 1792

[DB 9:126]. He was head of a Sampson County household of 5 "other free" in 1790 [NC:51], 9 in 1800, was counted as white in 1810 [NC:472], and was a "sleymaker," head of a Sampson County household of 3 "free colored" in 1820. His widow Milly Manuel was about eighty-eight years old on 11 November 1845 when she made a declaration in Sampson County court to obtain a widow's pension for her husband's services in the Revolution. She stated that they were married by Fleet Cooper, Esq., in Duplin County and that her son Shadrack Manuel was born the day (Corn)Wallis was captured. Her husband died on 27 March 1835. Milly died before 30 March 1855 when Shadrack, heir at law of Nicholas Manuel, appointed attorneys to receive his survivor's pension [M804-1627]. Their son was

    i. Shadrack, born say 1780, head of a Sampson County household of 8 "white" persons in 1810 [NC:476] and 11 "free colored" in 1820 [NC:298].

A member of the Emanuel family in Virginia was

    i. Ritter, a "poor Mulatto Girl" living in Surry County on 22 February 1774 when the court ordered the churchwardens of Southwarke Parish to bind her out [Orders 1764-74, 421].

MARSHALL FAMILY

1. Thomas Marshall, born say 1723, was fined by the Charles City County court on 6 September 1758 for failing to list his wife as a tithable. He may have been identical to Thomas Marshall, a white planter, who married Anne **Perle**, a "Mulatto" woman, in Prince George's County, Maryland, before 23 August 1743 when the court ordered that he be sold for seven years. He was ordered to be released from prison so the case could be tried at the Provincial Court [Court Record 1743-4, 17]. He was living in Halifax County, North Carolina, on 1 December 1762 when his deed of bargain and sale was proved in Charles City County [Orders 1758-62, 57, 496]. He purchased 17-1/2 acres in Halifax County on 11 June 1760, 100 acres on 25 September 1760, was granted 640 acres there on 10 December 1760, and purchased 100 acres on Cain Quarter Creek on 18 January 1764. On 10 February 1769 he gave his daughter Martha **King** 640 acres which had been a Granville grant to him and gave her 100 acres on Cain Quarter Creek, reserving 10 acres for his lifetime. He was married to Winnifred Marshall on 7 May 1774 when he and his wife sold tracts of 17-1/2 acres, 100 acres joining John Marshall, and an 8 acre tract [DB 7:163, 164, 219; 8:369; 10:524; 13:1]. Administration on his Halifax County estate was granted to Willifred Marshall in November 1784. The same November 1784 court called him a "very improper person" when it bound his apprentice Abner Booth, base born child of Sarah Boothe, to someone else [Gammon, *Record of Estates, Halifax County*, 45 (no.571), 50 (no.652)]. His will was recorded in Will Book 2, page 31, but that page is missing from the microfilm copy of the deed book. His daughter was

    i. Martha, married William King. William left a Halifax County will by which he left 100 acres to his son Thomas Marshall King and left 440 acres to his father-in-law Thomas Marshall. They may have been the ancestors of William **King** who was born before 1776 and head of a Halifax County household of 7 "free colored" in 1830.

MARTIN FAMILY

1. Hanna Martyn, born say 1703, was the servant of Martha Rust on 20 August 1721 when she confessed to the Westmoreland County, Virginia court that her child was "begott by a Negro" [Orders 1721-31, 7]. She may have been the ancestor of

2   i. Ann, born say 1734.

  ii. Mary, born say 1740, married Francis **Cousins**, "Mulattoes both of Maniken Town" (Goochland County) on 15 December 1759 [Jones, *The Douglas Register*, 347].

3 iii. Absalom[1], born about 1745.

4 iv. Judith, born say 1750.

5 v. Edmund, born say 1760.

  vi. Jacob[1], a "Mulatto" taxable in the upper district of Goochland County in 1798, a carpenter living on William George's land from 1805 to 1807, living on George Holman's from 1809 to 1812, living with wife Fanny on William Gammon's land in 1813, over the age of forty-five in 1815 when he was charged with William and John Martin's tithes [PPTL, 1782-1809, frames 484, 746, 786, 832, 871; 1810-32, frames 13, 77, 104, 202, 265], head of a Goochland County household of 10 "other free" in 1810 [VA:705].

  vii. William[1], born about 1765, obtained a certificate of freedom in Chesterfield County on 9 September 1805: *forty years old, dark Mulatto, born free* [Register of Free Negroes 1804-53, no. 12]. He was a "M°" taxable in Powhatan County from 1788 to 1796 [PPTL, 1787-1825, frames 23, 35, 94, 108, 120, 134], a "Mulatto" taxable in Chesterfield County from 1799 to 1810 [PPTL, 1786-1811, frames 393, 470, 543, 717, 753, 799] and head of a Chesterfield County household of 3 "other free" in 1810 [VA:70/1062]. He may have been the William Martin, a "yellow" complexioned man, who was born in Cumberland County and was living in Pittsylvania County when he was listed as a soldier who enlisted in the Revolution [NSDAR, *African American Patriots*, 151].

  viii. Samuel[1], born before 1766, a "Mulatto" taxable in Goochland County on a tithe, a horse, and 3 cattle in 1787 and 1788 [PPTL, 1782-1809, frames 154, 180], perhaps the Samuel Martin who was a "Free Negro" taxable in St. Ann's Parish, Albemarle County, from 1803 to 1812 [PPTL, 1800-13, frames 145, 186, 255, 326, 369, 505].

6 ix. Jane, born about 1779.

2. Ann Martin, born say 1734, "a free Molota Woman," complained to the Onslow County, North Carolina court on 13 September 1763 that John Humphrey was illegally keeping her two children. The court ordered the children returned to her because the indentures were obtained by deceit. In March 1764 she bound her son Robert to William Williams, Jr., and her son Daniel to Elizabeth Brack [Minutes 1749-65, 63a, 66a]. Her children were

7 i. Robert[1], born about 1753.

  ii. Daniel, born about 1755, nine years old when he was ordered bound apprentice to Elizabeth Brack by the Onslow County court. He was head of a Wilmington, New Hanover County, household of 8 "free colored" in 1820 [NC:206].

8 iii. ?Jesse, born about 1756.

9 iv. ?John, born say 1757.

3. Absalom[1] Martin, born about 1745, enlisted in the town of Beaufort, North Carolina, for twelve months in Captain William Dennis' Company in the 1st North Carolina Regiment in April 1781. He made a declaration in Carteret County court to obtain a pension on 22 August 1820, declaring that he was married to Rachel, also born about 1745, and had 3 grandchildren living with him: William, born 1807; Jacob, born 1808; and David born 1811. He owned 140 acres of "barren pine land." He died eight years later on 20 September 1828 [M805, reel 0555, frame 20]. He was head of a Carteret County household of 9 "other free" in 1790 [NC:128], 12 in 1800, 16 in 1810 [NC:443], and 7 "free colored" in 1820 [NC:121]. His children were most likely:

      i.   Tamer, head of a Carteret County household of 4 "other free" in 1800.

     ii.   Samuel[2], born before 1776, married Keziah **Black**, Carteret County bond 4 June 1819, head of a Carteret County household of 4 "free colored" in 1820 [NC:121], mentioned in the 16 September 1821 Carteret County will of his father-in-law, Martin **Black** [D:57].

   iii.   Absalom[2], born 1776-1794, head of a Carteret County household of 4 "free colored" in 1820 [NC:115].

4.   Judith Martin, born say 1750, was living in Cumberland County, Virginia, on 22 August 1774 when her "mulattoe" daughter Rhoda Martin was bound to James Cannifax [Orders 1774-8, 276]. She had married a member of the **Fox** family by 22 September 1794 when her daughter Rhoda married in Goochland County. She was as the mother of

      i.   Rhoda, born say 1773, "orphan" of Judith Martin ordered bound to James Canifax by the Cumberland County court on 22 August 1774, a "mulattoe" orphan (no parent named) bound to James Cannifax on 26 March 1777 [Orders 1774-8, 276, 402]. She was called the "of age daughter of Judith Fox" when she married Edward **Fuzmore**, 22 September 1794 Goochland County bond, Thomas T. Bates surety.

     ii.   ?William[2], born say 1789, taxable in the upper district of Goochland County from 1806 to 1814: listed with Edward **Fuzmore** in 1806 and 1807, a "Mulatto Waterman" listed with wife Judith on Thomas Miller's land in 1813 [PPTL, 1782-1809, frames 780, 823; 1810-32, frames 79, 103, 167, 202]. He was called a "Man of color" when he married Judith **Jenkins**, 1 January 1811 Goochland County bond, James **Shelton** surety, 2 January marriage.

5.   Edmund Martin, born say 1760, was taxable in the upper district of Goochland County from 1804 to 1815: a "Mulatto" farmer living near William George's in 1804, living on William Richardson's land in 1809 and 1810 when he was charged with Samuel Martin's tithe, charged with Samuel and Jacob Martin's tithes and 2 horses in 1811 and 1812; listed with his wife Polly, Jacob and Bartlet Martin in 1813, over the age of forty-five in 1815 when he was charged with Jacob and Bartlet Martin's tithes [PPTL, 1782-1809, frames 692, 746, 786, 829, 872; 1810-32, frames 12, 79, 169, 201, 266]. He may have been the father of

      i.   Samuel[3], born about 1786, registered as a free Negro in Goochland County on 16 February 1807: *about five feet five inches and one quarter high, about twenty one years of age, yellow complexion...with straight Black hair* [Register of Free Negroes, p.14, no.32]. He married Nancy **Isaacs**, 7 March 1808 Goochland County bond, Francis **Cousins** surety, 10 March marriage by Rev. Chaudoin [Minister's Returns, 100], and was head of a Goochland County household of 3 "other free" in 1810. He was a "Mulatto" planter on Maria Woodson's land from 1809 to 1814, listed with wife Nancy in 1813 [PPTL, 1782-1809, frame 871; 1810-32, frames 12, 77, 103, 168, 200].

     ii.   Nancy, born say 1788, married William **Banks**, 16 February 1808 Goochland County bond, John Martin surety.

   iii.   Jacob[2], born say 1794, his tax charged to Edmund Martin in 1811.

   iv.   Bartlet, born say 1796, his tax charged to Edmund Martin in 1813.

6.   Jane Martin, born about 1779, was counted in "A List of Free Negroes & Mulattoes in the District of John Holloway, Commissioner, in Botetourt County for the Year 1802" with daughter Betsy and son Jefferson and listed with them again in 1803 [Orders 1800-04, Loose Papers, no. 38, 45-7]. She registered as a free Negro in Botetourt County on 30 September 1829: *50 years of age; Dark Mulatto...Born free as per Certificate of Clerk of Halifax.* Jenny was the mother of

    i.   Betsy, listed with her mother in 1802 and 1803.

    ii.   Jefferson, listed with his mother in 1802 and 1803.

    iii.   Judy, born about 1808, registered in Botetourt County in January 1829: *daughter of Jane; 21 years of age; Mulatto; Born free.*

    iv.   Meshack, born about 1805, registered in Botetourt County in January 1829: *son of Jane; 24 years of age; Mulatto; Born free.*

    v.   Harriet, born about 1810, registered in Botetourt County in January 1829: *daughter of Jane; 19 years of age; Mulatto; Born free.*

    vi.   ?Mary Jane, born about 1811, registered in Botetourt County in September 1828: *17 years of age; Mulatto...Born free* [Free Negroes &c Registered in the Clerk's Office of Botetourt County, nos. 48, 55-8, 96].

7.   Robert[1] Martin, born about 1753, was eleven years old when he was ordered bound apprentice to William Williams, Jr. by the Onslow County court. He was head of a New Hanover County household of 4 "other free" in 1790 [NC:194], 6 "other free" and 2 slaves in Bladen County in 1800, and he may have been the R. Martin who was head of a Brunswick County household of 3 "other free" in 1810 [NC:228]. His children were probably those who were counted as "other free" in Bladen County in 1810:

    i.   Sarah, born before 1776, head of a Bladen County household of 4 "other free" in 1800, 3 in 1810 [NC:218], and 5 "free colored" in 1820 [NC:152].

    ii.   Henry, head of a Bladen County household of 3 "other free" in 1810 [NC:218] and 4 "free colored" in 1820 [NC:152].

    iii.   Ally, head of a Bladen County household of 2 "other free" in 1810 [NC:205].

8.   Jesse Martin, born about 1756, enlisted for nine months in 1780 in Captain Arthur Gatling's regiment of the North Carolina Line commanded by Colonel Armstrong. He was discharged in Stono, South Carolina, in 1781. He was an infirm farmer with no family except his wife Sarah, born about 1765, when he made a declaration to obtain a pension in Gates County court on 15 August 1825 [M805, reel 883, frame 836]. He was head of a Gates County household of 8 "other free" in 1790 [NC:23], 9 in 1800 [NC:273], 7 in 1810 [NC:842], and 7 "free colored" in 1820 [NC:162]. His son may have been

    i.   James, head of a Gates County household of 4 "other free" in 1810 [NC:842] and 8 "free colored" in 1820 [NC:162].

9.   John Martin, born say 1757, was head of a New Hanover County household of 6 "other free" in 1790 [NC:194] and 11 in 1800 [NC:310]. He gave power of attorney to Thomas Nuse to receive his final settlement for service in the Continental Line on 9 September 1791. John Williams, a justice of the peace for New Hanover County, attested that he served in 1782 [*NCGSJ* XIII:94]. He may have been the John Martin who married Mary **Dove**, 28 December 1802 Craven County bond. Perhaps his child was

    i.   Hetty, head of a New Hanover County household of 5 "other free" in 1820 [NC:224].

Other possible descendants of Hanna Martyn were

    i.   Susannah, born about 1764, registered in Petersburg on 23 August 1794: *a light Mulatto woman, five feet two and a half inches high, 30 years old, born free & raised in Chesterfield County* [Register of Free Negroes 1794-1819, no. 82].

    ii.   John, a "Mulatto" taxable in Chesterfield County from 1801 to 1810 [PPTL, 1786-1811, frames 470, 753, 799] and head of a Chesterfield County household of 7 "other free" in 1810 [VA:70/1062].

iii. Molly, a free-born, brown complexioned woman who obtained a certificate of freedom in Chesterfield County on 13 May 1812, no age mentioned [Register of Free Negroes 1804-53, no. 165].

iv. Isham, born about 1783, obtained a certificate of freedom in Chesterfield County on 8 September 1806: *twenty three years old, born free* [Register of Free Negroes 1804-53, no. 32].

v. Zachariah, born about 1785, obtained a certificate of freedom in Chesterfield County on 8 September 1806: *twenty one years old, born free* [Register of Free Negroes 1804-53, no. 33]. He was head of a Petersburg Town household of 7 "other free" in 1810 [VA:332].

vi. Lucky, head of a Petersburg Town household of 8 "other free" in 1810 [VA:126b].

vii. Lucy, born about 1787, registered in Petersburg on 23 December 1808: *a very light colourd Mulatto woman, five feet seven inches high, twenty one years old, born free in the County of Dinwiddie. Jas. Day made oath to her being reputed free* [Register of Free Negroes 1794-1819, no. 431]. She was head of a Petersburg Town household of 3 "other free" in 1810 [VA:123b].

viii. Peggy, head of a Petersburg Town household of 2 "other free" in 1810 [VA:122a].

Another member of the Martin family was:

i. John, "free person of color" who married Sally **Gowens** on 3 October 1819 in St. Philips Parish, South Carolina.

MASON FAMILY

1. Sarah Mason, born say 1723, was living in St. Ann's Parish, Essex County, Virginia, on 21 June 1743 when the court ordered that she be sold for five years as punishment for having a "Mulatto" child [Orders 1742-3, 189]. She may have been the mother of

2   i. Nell, born say 1743.
3   ii. Thomas[1], born say 1750.

2. Nell Mason, born say 1743, no race indicated, was living in Antrim Parish, Halifax County, Virginia, on 16 August 1770 when the court ordered the churchwardens to bind out her six unnamed children [Pleas 1770-2, 7]. She may have been the mother of

i. Patrick, born about 1762, married Patsey **Going**, 3 December 1790 Caswell County bond, Zachariah **Hill** bondsman. He was taxable in St. Lawrence District, Caswell County, in 1790 [NC:83] and was head of a Person County household of 6 "other free" in 1800 [NC:613] and 10 "free colored" in 1820 [NC:498]. He was a "Mulatto" taxable in the southern district of Halifax County, Virginia, from 1805 to 1807 [PPTL, 1800-12, frame 529, 636, 689]. He made a declaration in Person County court on 12 May 1828 to obtain a pension for his services in the Revolution. He stated that he was born about 1762 and enlisted for twelve months on 1 April 1780 [NCGSJ XIV:172].

ii. Ralph, born before 1776, head of a Stokes County household of 2 "free colored" in 1820 [NC:357].

iii. William[1], "F.B." head of a Bedford County household of 9 "other free" in 1810 [VA:472].

iv. Jesse[2], born about 1786, a "FN" taxable in the southern district of Halifax County, Virginia, in 1807 [PPTL, 1800-12, frame 689]. He registered in Halifax County on 25 May 1831: *of Dark complexion, aged 45 years, five feet 6 inches high, was born free* [Registers of Free Negroes, 1802-1831, no. 165].

    v.   Nancy, born about 1795, registered in Halifax County, Virginia, on 25 May 1831: *dark Complexion, about 36 years of age, five feet 2 inches high, was born free* [Registers of Free Negroes, 1802-1831, no. 169].

3.   Thomas[1] Mason, born say 1742, was taxable in St. James District, Caswell County, North Carolina, from 1777 to 1778. He was living in Caswell County on 7 November 1788 when he purchased 133 acres on Cobbs Creek from James Kanedy [DB A:71-2]. He was taxable in St. James District, Caswell County, in 1790 [NC:82]. Person County was formed from this part of Caswell County in 1791 and Thomas sold his land by Person County deed on 4 April 1795 [DB C:472]. He was probably identical to Thomas Mason who was taxable in Louisa County on himself and son Thomas in 1787 [PPTL 1782-1814]. He was the father of

4   i.   Thomas[2], born say 1763.

     ii.   Lawrence, "son of Thomas Mason," married Rosanna Landers, 17 January 1794 Louisa County, Virginia bond, Thomas Mason, Jr., and James Kennedy witnesses. Lawrence was taxable Louisa County in 1801 [PPTL 1782-1814], taxable in Fredericksville Parish, Albemarle County, in 1802 [PPTL 1800-13, frame 121] and head of a Buckingham County household of 3 "other free" in 1810 [VA:796]. His daughter Nancy was named in the 16 March 1828 Amherst County will of Peter **Hartless** [WB 9:124].

   iii.   Sally, born say 1770, "daughter of Thomas Mason," married Zachariah **Hill**, 20 July 1788 Halifax County, Virginia bond, John Jones surety, 31 July marriage by Rev. James Watkins [Minister's Returns, 14].

   iv.   Jean, born say 1774, married Peter **Hartless**, 2 January 1792 Amherst County, Virginia bond with the consent of Thomas and Jane Mason. Peter's 16 March 1828 Amherst County will, proved 17 September 1835, mentioned his wife Jane, Nancy Mason (daughter of Larsons Mason, perhaps identical to Lawrence Mason), and Peter Mason [WB 9:124].

    v.   ?Jesse[1], married Polly Ann **Branham**, 21 March 1796 Louisa County bond, Lawrence Mason, witness. Jesse was taxable in Fredericksville Parish, Albemarle County, from 1800 to 1813: a "Mulatto" listed in 1813 with 3 persons which included females over the age of sixteen [PPTL, 1800-1813, frames 33, 122, 166, 212, 302, 393, 440, 483, 526, 572], head of an Albemarle County household of 9 "other free" in 1810 [VA:203] and 5 "free colored" in 1820.

4.   Thomas[2] Mason, born say 1763, married Elizabeth **Ailstock** in Louisa County in April 1791 according to her application for a survivor's pension for his services in the Revolution. He was listed as a "Mulatto" shoemaker in a "List of free Negroes and Mulattoes" in Louisa County with his wife Elizabeth and children Charles, Susanna, Thomas, Jesse and William (no date but probably about 1801-3) [Abercrombie, *Free Blacks of Louisa County*, 20]. He purchased land in Louisa County on 10 August 1801 and executed a deed of trust on the land on 14 March 1807 (described as 74 acres in 1801 and 24 acres on both sides of Mare Branch when it was sold in 1812) [DB J:222; L:48; M:32]. He was listed as a "Free Negro" in Campbell County in 1813 with a woman over the age of sixteen, taxable on 2 males in 1814 [PPTL, 1785-1814, frames 892, 930]. His widow Elizabeth applied for a pension in Campbell County on 1 May 1854, stating that her husband was a "colored" man who died in October 1832. He was the father of

     i.   Charles.

    ii.   Susanna.

   iii.   Thomas[3], born about 1797, about fifty-seven years old on 1 May 1854 when he made an affidavit to support his mother's application for a survivors pension for his father's Revolutionary War service.

    iv. Jesse³.

    v. William².

Other members of the family in Virginia were

    i. Jack and Will, born say 1680s, two of six Tuscarora Indians accused by five other Tuscarora Indians of murdering Jeremiah Pate of New Kent County on 14 October 1707. The other four accused were Tom Jumper, Charles, Stephen and George. Jack was exonerated when it was shown that he had spent the day of the murder at Colonel Hill's [McIlwaine, *Journals of the Council*, III:158, 167].

    ii. Hatter Wood, born say 1740, a "Molatto" added to the list of tithables in Elizabeth City County on 6 November 1764 [Court Records 1760-9, 258].

    iii. John, a "melatto" taxable in Campbell County in

    iv. Chloe, born say 1778, registered as a free Negro in Northumberland County on 9 January 1809: *bright mulatto about 24, 5 feet 8-3/4 inches high - having 5 children* [Register, no.37]. She was a "free mulatto" head of a Northumberland County household of 7 "other free" in 1810 [VA:989].

    v. James, head of an Essex County household of 4 "other free" in 1810 [VA:202].

    vi. Rane, head of a Buckingham County household of 4 "other free" in 1810 [VA:786].

    vii. Sally, born about 1801, registered in Augusta County on 16 June 1823: *Formerly Sally Mason, wife of Fountain Maxwell, about twenty two years of age, a high mulatto, of slender and rather delicate stature, five feet one and a half inches high, and free born as attested by affidavit of Jno. Dowell* [Augusta County Register of Free Negroes, nos. 26, 62 by http://valley.vcdh.Virginia.edu]. They recorded the certificates in Ross County, Ohio [Turpin, *Register of Black, Mulatto, and Poor Persons*, p.32].

MATTHEWS FAMILY

1. Katherine Matthews, born say 1668, was a white servant woman living in Norfolk County in June 1686 when she was presented by the grand jury for having a "Mulatto" child [Orders 1675-86, 315]. She may have been the ancestor of

    i. Francis, born say 1710, no surname given when he and Gage, two "Mollattoes," were the subject of a dispute between Mr. Maximillian Bush and Mr. Matthew Mathias which was settled by the Norfolk County court on 15 January 1713/4. The court ordered the churchwardens to bind Francis to Maximillian Bush and the younger child Gage to Mr. Mathias [Orders 1710-7, 76]. He was called "Francis Matthews a free Negro" when he successfully petitioned the Norfolk County court for his freedom on 17 August 1732, "being Born of a Free Woman and of Lawful age" [Orders 1723-34, 154].

    ii. Gage, born say 1712, (no surname given) a "free born Negro" formerly belonging to James Ewell, deceased, on 8 January 1735/6 when he petitioned the Princess Anne County court for his freedom. The court ruled that the Act of Assembly which required children to serve until the age of thirty-one did not apply in his case and ordered that he be set free. He was called Gage Matthews and had bound himself as a servant to George Oldner of Princess Anne County by 16 May 1758 when he sued his master for not providing him with sufficient food and clothing. The court ruled in his favor and ordered his master not to punish him without applying to the court for permission [Minutes 1728-37, 298; 1753-62, 318].

       iii. George, born say 1722, a "Mullatto" who was bound by indenture to serve Susannah Hancock, orphan of William Hancock. He sued for his freedom in Princess Anne County on 22 August 1753, and the court ruled that he had served his time required by law and that "he be set at liberty to go where he pleased for employment" [Orders 1753-62, 51].

2   iv. Ruth[1], born say 1728.

3   v. James[1], born say 1730.

      vi. Susannah, born say 1740, married Isaac **Wilson**, 18 August 1785 Halifax County, Virginia bond.

4   vii. Dinah, born say 1746.

2. Ruth[1] Matthews, born say 1728, (no race indicated) was bound to Robert Downing in Bristol Parish on 30 Oct 1732 [Chamberlayne, *Register of Bristol Parish*, 63]. She was called "a free Mulattoe" on 7 March 1756 when her daughter Elizabeth was baptized by the Rev. William Douglas of St. James Northam Parish, Goochland County [Jones, *The Douglas Register*, 348]. She was called an Indian woman on 26 September 1757 when the Cumberland County, Virginia court ordered the churchwardens of Southam Parish to bind her children Betty, Jemmy, Bristol, and Judith to William Fleming [Orders 1752-8, 501]. Her children were

      i. Rachel, born say 1746, consented to the marriage of her daughter Fanny **Mathews** to William **Liggon**, 14 July 1787 Henrico County bond, surety Nathaniel **Couzins** who certified that Fanny was over the age of twenty-one.

5   ii. Elizabeth, born October 1748, baptized 7 March 1756.

     iii. James[2], born say 1750, taxable in Halifax County, Virginia, from 1787 to 1793: called a "Mulatto" in 1792 and 1793 [PPTL, 1782-1799, frames 110, 274, 421, 446]. He married Molly **Cumbo**, daughter of Thomas **Cumbo**, 20 July 1790 Halifax County, Virginia bond, David **Gowing** surety, 29 July marriage. He was a "Free Person of Colour" taxable on Kerr's Creek in Rockbridge County in 1813 [Waldrep, *1813 Tax List*].

     iv. Bristol, born say 1752, married Nanny **Lynch** of Hanover, "Mulattoes," in Goochland County on 25 September 1775 [Jones, *The Douglas Register*, 347].

     v. Judith, born say 1754.

     vi. Joseph, taxable in Halifax County, Virginia, from 1789 to 1792, called a "M°" in 1792 [PPTL, 1782-1799, frames 274, 421]. He married Susanna **Burchfield**, 23 April 1792 Halifax County bond.

    vii. ?Nathaniel, born about 1763, described as "a mulatto, about 12 years old," when Josias Cook of Pittsylvania County, to whom he was bound, advertised in the *Virginia Gazette* that Nathaniel had been stolen from him on 16 March 1775 [*Virginia Gazette*, Purdie edition, p. 4, col. 1].

6   viii. ?_illy, born say 1765.

    ix. Ruth[2], born about 1772, bound apprentice to William Fleming, Esquire, by order of the Chesterfield County court on 7 February 1783 [Orders 1774-84, 393]. She registered in Petersburg on 25 August 1794: *a dark brown Mulatto woman, five feet two inches high, twenty two years old, born free & raised by Wm Fleming in Chesterfield* [Register of Free Negroes 1794-1819, no. 84].

3. James[1] Matthews, born say 1730, was indicted by the court in Henrico County on 6 November 1752 for failing to list his "Mulatto" wife as a tithable [Minutes 1752-5, 19]. He was called a "Negroe" and his wife Susannah Ford a white woman when their son Richardson was baptized on 17 April 1760 by the Rev. William Douglas of Goochland County, Virginia [Jones, *Douglas*

Register, 348]. He was a "Mulattoe" taxable in John Pope's list for Granville County, North Carolina, in 1766. He was taxed with the notation "Mullatoe, has a wife and daughter not listed" [CR 44.701.19]. His children were

    i. a daughter born before 1755, taxable in 1766.

    ii. Richardson, born 17 April 1760, baptized 24 June 1760.

    iii. ?Ford, head of a Franklin County, North Carolina, household of 2 "other free" in 1790 [NC:60].

4.   Dinah Matthews, born say 1746, was taxable on the west side of Church Street in Norfolk Borough in 1767 [Wingo, *Norfolk County Tithables 1766-80*, 34]. She may have been the mother of

    i. Peggy, a "free Negro" bound to John Scott of Elizabeth River Parish by the Norfolk County court on 19 April 1771 [Orders 1768-71, 253].

    ii. Grace, a "free Negro" bound to John Scott of Elizabeth River Parish by the Norfolk County court on 17 August 1771 [Orders 1771-3, 27].

    iii. Phillis, a "free negro" bound to Alexander Guthery of Elizabeth River Parish by the Norfolk County court on 21 August 1772 [Orders 1771-3, 107].

5.   Elizabeth Matthews, born October 1748, was baptized 7 March 1756 by the Rev. William Douglas of St. James Northam Parish, Goochland County [Jones, *The Douglas Register*, 348]. She was living in Halifax County, Virginia, on 20 January 1774 when the court ordered the churchwardens of Anterim Parish to bind her son Peter to William Wyly. She may have been identical to Elizabeth **Haton** whose son David **Haton** was ordered bound to Philip **Gowen** on 20 February 1777. David **Haden** was called the illegitimate son of Elizabeth Matthews when he was ordered bound out by the overseers of the poor on 21 June 1787 [Pleas 1772-4, 335; 1774-9, 193; 1786-9, 172]. She was the mother of

    i. ?Ezekiah/Ezekiel, born say 1772, bound apprentice to William Cole in Halifax County, Virginia, on 15 June 1786 [Pleas 1783-6, 476]. He married Sarah **Cumbo**, 23 April 1793 Halifax County bond, Thomas Maskell surety (Sarah signed her own consent), and 7 May 1793 Caswell County, North Carolina bond with Allen **Going** bondsman. He was head of a Person County household of 5 "other free" in 1800, and 10 in Caswell County in 1810 [NC:489]. He was a "Mulatto" taxable in Halifax County, Virginia, in 1804 and 1805 [PPTL, 1800-12, frames 384, 529].

    ii. Peter, born about 1773, married Lucy **Banger** ("colored people"), 24 October 1791 Halifax County, Virginia bond, surety William P. Martin, 28 October marriage by Rev. William P. Martin. Lucy registered as a "free Negro" in Halifax County, Virginia, on 20 May 1802: *aged about twenty five years, five feet two inches high, between a black and yellow colour, Emancipated by William P. Martin on the 17th day of February 1785 by his Bill of that date* and Peter registered on 31 May 1802: *aged about twenty nine years, five feet seven inches and one quarter high, black colour...born of a free woman* [Halifax County Register, no. 6, 11]. Peter was a "Mulatto" taxable in Halifax County from 1793 to 1812: a planter living with Lucy Matthews who was a spinner in the list of "free Negroes and Mulattoes" in 1801 [PPTL, 1782-1799, frames 446, 607; 1800-12, frames 66, 159, 384, 530, 811, 1036], but not listed there in 1807 when he was a "FN" taxable in the northern district of Campbell County [PPTL, 1785-1814, frame 699].

    iii. ?Elizabeth, ordered bound out by the overseers of the poor in Halifax County, Virginia, on 20 September 1787 and bound to William McDaniel on 18 October 1787 [Pleas 1786-8, 263, 270], married Bartlett **Chavis**, 10 February 1803 Halifax County, Virginia bond.

iv.   David **Haden**, taxable in the upper district of Halifax County in 1801 [PPTL, 1800-12, frame 99] and counted in the list of "Free Negros & Malatters" for Patrick County in 1813 [PPTL, 1791-1823, frame 598].

v.   ?John **Haden**, a "Mul°" taxable in Halifax County from 1795 to 1804 [PPTL, 1782-1799, frame 605; 1800-12, frame 189, 376]. He was probably identical to John **Hatten** who married Susannah **Talbot**, 1 January 1802 Halifax County bond.

vi.   James **Haden**, illegitimate son of Elizabeth Matthews, ordered bound out by the overseers of the poor of Halifax County, Virginia, on 21 June 1787 [Pleas 1786-8, 172].

vii. ?Jordan, a "FN" or "Mulatto" taxable in Halifax County from 1804 to 1806 [PPTL, 1800-12, frames 384, 529, 636].

viii. ?William, a "FN" or "Mulatto" taxable in Halifax County from 1806 to 1809 [PPTL, 1800-12, frames 636, 810].

6.   illy Matthews, born say 1765, was head of a Brunswick County, Virginia household of 5 "other free" in 1810 [VA:724]f, perhaps identical to Nelly Matthews who was a "Mulatto" taxable on a horse in St. Andrew's Parish, Brunswick County, in 1810 and was counted in a list of "Free Negroes & Mulattoes" in Brunswick County in 1813 [PPTL 1782-1850, frames 495, 622]. Her children may have been

i.   Luke, born about 1783, head of a Brunswick County, Virginia household of 3 "other free" in 1810 [VA:724] and 10 "free colored" in 1820 [VA:620]. He registered as a "Free Negro" in Brunswick County on 29 August 1815: *a free black man of a yellow complexion, about five feet nine inches high Thirty two or three years old* [Wynne, *Register of Free Negroes*, 20].

ii.   Thomas, born say 1785, a "Mulatto" taxable in St. Andrew's Parish, Brunswick County, from 1804 to 1810 [PPTL 1782-1850, frames 276, 320, 419, 495, 583], head of a Brunswick County household of one "other free" in 1810 [VA:724].

iii. Edmund, born about 1788, registered in Brunswick County on 24 August 1812, *a free man of a yellow Complexion about twenty two or twenty three years of age about five feet ten or eleven inches high...Who it appears was freeborn.*

iv.   Betsey, born about 1792, registered in Brunswick County on 24 June 1822, *a free woman of colour about thirty years old 5.5 high and yellow complexion...born free in this county as appears from the evidence of Raleigh H. Abernathy* [Wynne, *Register of Free Negroes*, 14, 50].

Members of the Matthews family who registered in Petersburg were

i.   Ned, born about 1760, registered in Petersburg on 9 February 1795: *a dark brown Mulatto man, five feet ten inches high, about thirty five years old, born free and raised in Dinwiddie County* [Register of Free Negroes 1794-1819, no. 98].

ii.   Aldrick, born about 1771, registered in Petersburg on 19 August 1794: *a brown Mulatto man, five feet six inches high, twenty three years old, born free & raised in Dinwiddie County* [Register of Free Negroes 1794-1819, no. 52].

iii. Nancy, born about 1774, registered in Petersburg on 9 August 1799: *a dark brown free Mulatto woman, five feet four inches high, twenty five years old, spare & straight made with bushy hair, born free & raised in the Town of Petersburg* [Register of Free Negroes 1794-1819, no. 147].

iv.   Peggy, born about 1775, registered in Petersburg on 14 August 1800: *a light coloured Mulatto woman, five feet high, small made with blue or grey eyes & strait brown hair, twenty five years old, born free & raised in the Town of Petersburg* [Register of Free Negroes 1794-1819, no. 167].

A member of a Matthews family in Caroline County was
    i. William, born say 1730, an East Indian, produced a warrant in Caroline County court on 13 February 1752 for taking up a runaway servant woman [Orders 1746-54, 296].

Eastern Shore of Virginia
1. Isabel Matthews, born say 1725, a "free Negro," was presented on 15 August 1745 in Northampton County court for bastard bearing. On 8 April 1746 the court ordered that she serve her master John Fathery four months after the completion of her indenture for running away [Orders 1742-8, 245]. She may have been the ancestor of
    i. Okey, head of an Accomack Parish, Accomack County household of 6 in 1800 [*Virginia Genealogist* 1:161].
    ii. Scarborough, head of a St. George Parish, Accomack County household of 7 in 1800 [*Virginia Genealogist* 1:161].
    iii. Betty, head of a St. George Parish, Accomack County household of 5 in 1800 [*Virginia Genealogist* 1:161].
    iv. Moses, a "free Negro child" bound by the churchwardens of St. George's Parish in Accomack County to John Garrison to be a shoemaker on 24 September 1776 [Orders 1774-7, 466].
    v. Candis, head of an Accomack County household of 7 "other free" in 1810 [VA:44].
    vi. Sally, head of an Accomack County household of 4 "other free" in 1810 [VA:39]. She registered in Accomack County: *born about 1782, a black, 5'4" high, born free in Accomack County* [Register of Free Negroes, 1785-1863, no. 714].

A member of the Matthews family in South Carolina was
    i. Peter, head of a Phillip's and Michael's Parish, Charleston, South Carolina household of 4 "other free" and a slave in 1790. He (a "free Negro" butcher), Thomas **Cole**, and Matthew **Webb** petitioned the South Carolina State Legislature on 1 January 1791 to repeal the discriminatory laws against free African Americans [Berlin, *Slaves Without Masters*, 65-6].

MAYO FAMILY

The Mayo family was not free until 1785, but their family history is included here because they had relations with several families who had been free since the colonial period.

Joseph Mayo left a 27 May 1780 Henrico County, proved in November 1791, by which he asked that his executors petition the General Assembly for leave to set free all his slaves. However, if that was not possible, then he bequeathed his "mulattoe women called Maria and Suckey" and his "mulattoe waiting boy Bob" to John Tabb. The administrator procured an act of Assembly for emancipation of the slaves which was carried out by the High Court of Chancery in November 1789 [Catterall, *Judicial Cases* I:98; Hening 12:611]. His slaves over the age of 16 years and from 12-16 years were listed as taxables in his Mecklenburg County estate in 1783:

Slaves aged 16 and over: Fortune, Will, Jack, Bristol, Jeffrey, Sci, Doll, Ciller, Pompey, Sue, Linder. Slaves 12-16 years of age: Jude, Moll, Fanney, Rose, Harry, Ned, Jacob, Mercer, Less? Left?, Cuffie, Patience,

Phillis, Daniel, Joseph, Jupiter, Charles, Cuffey, Tiller, James, Amy, Mingo, Jeaney, Tom, John.

in 1784:
   Slaves aged 16 and over: Fortin, Will, Jack, Bristol, Jeffry, Berry, Cye, Doll, Sinster?, Siller Sue. Slaves 12-16 years of age: Judy, Molly, Fanny, Rose, Henry, Nell, Hutchins, Mar^h, Scipio, Cuffy, Patience, Phillis, Daniel, Will, Amy, Mingo, James, Jenny, Tom, Affey, Tiller, Joseph, Cupit, Charles, Gilbert, Peter, Jacob

and in 1786:
   Slaves aged 16 and over: Fortin, Will, Jack, Brister, Pompey, Jeffrey, Cyfax, Sue, Doll, Siller, Linder, Jude, Ame, Jacob, Tiller. Slaves 12-16 years of age: Moll, Fanny, Rose, Ned, Hany, Fortin, Mingo, James, Jinny, Tom, Affa, Meria, Sipio, Cuffe, Patience, Philis, Daniel, Quominer, Joseph, Jupiter, Charles, Gilbert, Peter [PPTL, 1782-1805, frames 43, 80, 162].

His emancipated slaves Jamey, Jubiter, Charles and Tom were in Mecklenburg County, Virginia, on 14 December 1789 when the court ordered the overseers of the poor to bind them to Benjamin Morton of Halifax County, Virginia, "with the exception that from the peculiar situation of these people that learning them to read, wright and the performance of arithmatick be dispensed with" [Orders 1787-92, 461].

Members of the Mayo family were
1   i.   Fortune^f, born say 1730.
2   ii.   Lenda, born say 1760.
      iii. Susanna, born say 1760, purchased 50 acres in Mecklenburg County near the Warren County line from John **Chavis Walden** for 25 pounds on 25 December 1797 with Moses **Stewart** and Charles **Durham** as witnesses [DB 9:431-2]. She was taxable in Mecklenburg County on 50 acres from 1799 to 1812 [Land Tax List 1782-1811A; 1811B-1824]. She was head of a Mecklenburg County household of 13 "free colored" in 1820 [VA:144a].
      iv.   Pompy, born say 1765, a taxable in Joseph Mayo's estate from 1783 to 1786, married Nancy **Marks**, 17 December 1801 Mecklenburg County bond, Mingo Mayo security. On 10 October 1803 the Mecklenburg County court ordered him, Robert **Brannum**, Thomas **Spence**, William **Stewart**, Humphrey **Wilson**, Joseph **Stewart**, Frederick **Ivey**, Robert **Cole** and Richard **Dunston** to work on the road which Benjamin Edmundson was surveying [Orders 1803-5, 45].
      v.   William, born say 1765, a "Free Negro" taxable in St. Paul's Parish, Hanover County from 1799-1801 [*Hanover County Taxables*, p.88].
      vi.   Judy, born about 1770, 12-16 years old in 1784 and 16 years old in 1786 when she was listed in Joseph Mayo's estate. She was the mother of an illegitimate child named Jeremiah who was bound out by the Mecklenburg County court on 14 September 1795, the same day Fortune Mayo's orphans were bound out [Orders 1792-5, 496]. Jerry was a "free Negro" taxable in Mecklenburg County in 1810 [PPTL, 1806-28, frame 168]. He married Betsy **Pettiford**, 8 December 1813 Warren County bond.
      vii. Thomas, born say 1771, married Abbey **Cousins**, 2 July 1799 Goochland County bond, Joseph Attkisson surety. He may have been the Thomas Mayo who was a "free Negroe" taxable in Charlotte County from 1799 to 1803 [PPTL 1782-1813, frames 452, 489, 554, 591]. He registered in Powhatan County on 16 October 1823: *Age: 50;*

Color: Black: Stature 5'6"; Emancipated by Jos. Mayo [Register of Free Negroes, no. 120].

viii. Hutchings, born say 1772, bondsman (signing) for the 6 July 1803 Warren County marriage of John **Chavis** and Betsy **Carsey**. He married Sally **Stewart**, 10 February 1806 Mecklenburg County, Virginia bond, Daniel Mayo security. Hutchings was head of a Mecklenburg County household of 8 "free colored" in 1820 [VA:160b].

ix. Cuffee, born say 1774, married Celey **Stewart**, 2 April 1802 Mecklenburg County, Virginia bond, Daniel Mayo security. Cuffee was taxable in Haw Tree District of Warren County, North Carolina, in 1808 and 1815 [Tax List CR 100.702.1; Tax List Papers, Vols TC 8, 1795-1815] and head of a Warren County household of 4 "free colored" in 1820 [NC:802].

x. Rhoda, born say 1776, married Elijah **Garnes**, 5 February 1797 Warren County bond. Elijah was head of a Mecklenburg County, Virginia, household of 5 "free colored" in 1820.

xi. Fanny, married Isaac **Garnes**, 17 February 1797 Warren County, North Carolina bond, Elijah Garnes bondsman.

xii. Peter, born about 1780, registered as a "free Negro" in Rockingham County, Virginia, on 1 March 1811: *a black man, about 6 feet high...30 years old the 25 day of December 1810...(by) certificate of the clerk of Cumberland County showing that he was emancipated by the last will of Joseph Mayo, deceased* [Rockingham County Register of Free Negroes, #7, p.4]. He may have been the Peter Mayo who was a "Free Black" head of a Powhatan County household of 9 "other free" in 1810 [VA:9].

xiii. Isaac, born about 1786, registered in Mecklenburg County on 22 May 1827: *a man of dark complexion about Forty one years of age, five feet ten inches high who it appears was emancipated by Joseph Mayo* [Free Person of Color, #35, p.31].

1. Fortune Mayo, born say 1730, sold her property to Samuel Hopkins & Company by bill of sale proved in Mecklenburg County, Virginia, on 13 January 1794: 3 cows, 2 calves, 5 sheep, a mare and colt, 14 hoes, 4 axes, set of cooper's and carpenter's tools, 25 barrels of corn, 400 pounds of seed cotton, frying pan, dishes, and other household items [DB 8:372]. She died before 14 September 1795 when the court ordered the overseers of the poor to bind out Edward, Henry, Fortunatus, and Robert Mayo, orphans of Fortune Mayo deceased, and Jeremiah, a bastard son of Judy Mayo. On 8 February 1795 the court ordered her tithables to work on a road with the tithables of John **C**. **Walden**, Eaton **Walden** and John **Walden** [Orders 1792-5, 496; 1795-8, 11]. Fortune was the mother of

i. Edward, born say 1767, a 12-16 year-old listed in Joseph Mayo's estate from 1783 to 1786.

ii. Henry, born say 1769, a 12-16 year-old listed in Joseph Mayo's estate in 1783, married Margaret **Guarns** (**Garnes**), 17 October 1809 Warren County, North Carolina bond, Richard Russell bondsman. He was head of a Warren County household of 9 "other free" in 1810 [NC:745] and a Mecklenburg County, Virginia household of 9 "free colored" in 1820 [VA:145b].

iii. Fortune[2], born about 1770, 12-16 years of age when she was taxable in Mecklenburg County in 1786, about fifty-five years of age when she registered in Powhatan County on 16 January 1823: *Age: 55 years; Color: Black; Emancipated by Joseph Mayo of Henrico County deceased* [Register of Free Negroes, no. 109].

iv. Robert, born 1776-1794, head of a Mecklenburg County, Virginia household of 5 "free colored" in 1820 [VA:149b].

2. Malinda/ Lenda Mayo, born say 1760, was head of a Mecklenburg County household of 7 "free colored" in 1820 [VA:156b]. The Mecklenburg County court bound her children Jacob and Alpha to John Wilson, blacksmith, on 14 April 1794 [Orders 1792-5, 261]. She was called Melinda Mayo when she was counted as a "free Negro" in Mecklenburg County in 1813 [PPTL, 1806-28, frame 353]. She was the mother of

    i.   Jacob, born about 1780, head of a Mecklenburg County household of 7 "free colored" in 1820 [VA:148b]. He was a seventy-year-old "Black" man counted in the 1850 Mecklenburg County census with (his wife?) sixty-five-year-old Sally Mayo [VA:116b].

    ii. Alpha.

Other members of the family were

    i.   James, head of an Albemarle County household of 6 "other free" in 1810 [VA:166A].

    ii. Dylsy, head of a Cumberland County, Virginia household of 6 "other free" in 1810 [VA:115].

    iii. Cato, head of a Cumberland County, Virginia household of 4 "other free" in 1810 [VA:132].

    iv. Molley, head of a Chesterfield County household of 5 "other free" in 1810 [VA:1062].

    v. Patience, head of a Chesterfield County household of 3 "other free" in 1810 [VA:1062].

    vi. Darkis, head of a Chesterfield County household of 2 "other free" in 1810 [VA:1062].

    vii. Phillis, head of a Chesterfield County household of 3 "other free" in 1810 [VA:1062].

    viii. Anily, head of a Henrico County household of 2 "other free" in 1810 [VA:998].

    ix. Graysey, head of a Henrico County household of 3 "other free" in 1810 [VA:996].

    x. Richard, head of a Fluvanna County household of 4 "other free" in 1810 [VA:441].

    xi. Henry, taxable in Fluvanna County from 1794 to 1813 [PPTL 1782-1826]. He was head of a Fluvanna County household of 2 "other free" in 1810 [VA:441].

    xii. Bob, head of a Henrico County household of 1 "other free" and 1 slave in 1810 [VA:1015]. He was a "free Negro" taxable in Henrico County in 1811 [PPTL 1782-1814, frame 668]. He may have been the "mulattoe waiting boy Bob" mentioned in Joseph Mayo's 1780 will.

    xiii. Elizabeth, born before 1776, head of a Beaufort County, North Carolina household of 2 "free colored" women in 1820 [NC:25].

    xiv. Samuel, born about 1802, registered in Mecklenburg County on 22 May 1827: *a man of dark complexion about twenty five years of age, five feet eleven inches high who it appears was born of a free woman in this County* [Free Person of Color, #34, p.31].

    xv. Lewis, born about 1804, registered in Mecklenburg County on 22 May 1827: *a man of dark complexion about twenty three years of age, five feet seven inches high...who it appears was born free* [Free Person of Color, #36, p.32].

    xvi. Isham, called "Isham (a free boy) on 9 June 1806 when the Mecklenburg County court ordered that he be bound apprentice to Frederick **Ivey** and called Isham Mayo when the order was set aside and he was bound instead to Isham **Garnes** [Orders 1806-8, 215, 221].

    xvii. John, born 1794-1806, head of a Halifax County, North Carolina household of 6 "free colored" in 1830. He and William **Toney** paid Arthur **Toney**'s recognizance to appear in the case of State vs Jack Avant and Arthur Toney on 21 May 1833, and the 17 August 1841

Halifax County court gave him permission to carry his gun in the county.

MAYS FAMILY

1. Mary Mays, born say 1728, was living in Hanover Parish, King George County, Virginia, on 7 November 1746 when the county court presented her for having an illegitimate "Mulatto" child within the previous six months and for attempting to murder the child [Orders 1735-51, pt.2, 503, 504, 507]. She may have been the ancestor of
    i. Jesse, head of a Chesterfield County household of 5 "other free" in 1810 [VA:70/1062].
    ii. Rebecca, head of a Chesterfield County household of 4 "other free" in 1810 [VA:70/1062].
    iii. Lucy, head of a Richmond County household of 3 "other free" in 1810 [VA:346].

MEADE FAMILY

1. Mary[1] Meade, born say 1710, was presented by the churchwardens of Bruton Parish in York County court in August 1741 for having a "Molatto" bastard child and was called Mary Meade alias Bryan when she was presented for the same offense on 19 November 1744. Robert Crichton and John Scrivener sued her in York County in a suit which was dismissed on 15 February 1747/8 by agreement of the parties, and Thomas Hornsby, merchant, sued her for 7 pounds, 12 shillings on 19 March 1749/50. She was paid 1 pound, 13 shillings by the York County estate of Joseph Valentine on 10 March 1773 [W&I 19:52, 72, 79, 314; Judgments & Orders 1746-52, 69, 300; W&I 22:369]. She was probably the ancestor of
    i. Mary[2], born say 1730, called Mary Mead, Jr., on 21 May 1750 when she was presented by the York County court for having a bastard child. She was fined 500 pounds of tobacco. She was called Mary Mead (no Jr.) on 15 July 1751 when the court ordered the churchwardens of Bruton Parish to bind out her children Ann and Frances Mead because she was incapable of supporting them "by reason of her idle, dissolute, and disorderly Course of Life" [Judgments & Orders 1746-52, 307, 326, 435].
    ii. John, head of a York County household of 4 "other free" in 1810 [VA:878]. He was paid 2 pounds, 18 shillings by the estate of Joseph Valentine on 10 March 1773 [W&I 22:369].
    iii. Milley, head of a Richmond City household of 4 "other free" in 1810 [VA:339].
    iv. Milley Meads, head of a Richmond City household of 3 "other free" in 1810 [VA:380].

MEALY FAMILY

1. James[1] Mealy, born say 1720, was a "free Negro" overseer on Philip Lightfoot's Goochland County estate in 1746 [List of Tithables]. He died before 2 October 1778 when his widow Elizabeth married David **Grantum** in Goochland County [Jones, *Douglas Register*, 18]. David left a 17 October 1801 Goochland County will, proved 18 June 1804, by which he lent to his wife Elizabeth land which was to revert to his wife's son James Mealy at her decease. He also mentioned his granddaughter Jenny Mealy [DB 19, part 1: 64]. Elizabeth was a "Mulatto" midwife who was taxable on a horse and lived near Joseph Shelton's in the upper district of Goochland County from 1806 to 1814 [PPTL, 1782-1809, frames 782, 824, 867; 1810-32, frames 8, 73, 99,

193]. She was head of Goochland County household of 2 "other free" in 1810 [VA:693]. James and Elizabeth were the parents of

2   i.   James[2], born about 1764.

      ii. ?Archer, born say 1772, taxable in the upper district of Goochland County from 1789 to 1814: a "free born" tithable living near William Isbell's in 1805, living on Betty **Grantum**'s land from 1806 to 1814 [PPTL, 1782-1809, frames 224, 241, 300, 426, 469, 531, 601, 673, 746, 828, 872; 1810-32, frames 13, 113, 201].

2. James[2] Mealy, born about 1764, was taxable in the upper district of Goochland County from 1787 to 1814: his tax charged to David **Grantum** in 1798, a "Mulatto" planter living near Licking Hole and charged with William Mealy's tithe in 1804 and 1807, living on (his mother) Betty **Grantum**'s land from 1806 to 1814, listed with his wife Frankey in 1813 and 1814 [PPTL, 1782-1809, frames 154, 224, 285, 300, 363, 426, 481, 550, 621, 692, 746, 828, 871; 1810-32, frames 103, 167, 201]. He registered as a frame Negro in Goochland County on 18 December 1822: *about fifty eight years old, about five feet ten inches high...yellowish complexion and was free born.* Perhaps his wife was Frances Mealy who registered on 13 May 1831: *yellow complexion, about fifty three years of age, about five feet two inches high* [Register of Free Negroes, pp.136, 223]. He was a soldier in the Revolution from Goochland County who received a pension in 1831 [Jackson, *Virginia Negro Soldiers*, 41]. He may have been the father of

3   i.   William, born about 1787.

      ii. Jenny, a "Mulatto" who did housework and lived on B. Drumwright's land in the upper district of Goochland County in 1813 [PPTL, 1810-32, frame 169].

     iii. Elizabeth, a "Mulatto" who did housework and lived on B. Drumwright's land in the upper district of Goochland County in 1813 [PPTL, 1810-32, frame 169].

3. William Mealy, born about 1787, registered in Goochland County on 16 February 1808: *a free man of Color, about five feet three inches high, about twenty one years of age, yellow complexion...free born.* He was taxable in the upper district of Goochland County from 1804 to 1814: a "Mulatto" farmer on M.V. Woodson's land from 1809 to 1814 [PPTL, 1782-1809, frames 692, 828, 871; 1810-32, frames 103, 201]. He may have been the father of

    i.   Elizabeth, born about 1808, registered in Goochland County on 18 August 1829: *about twenty one years old, about five feet four inches high of yellow complexion.*

      ii. Margaret, born about 1815, registered in Goochland County on 13 May 1831: *about sixteen years of age of yellowish complexion, about five feet four & a half inches high* [Register of Free Negroes, pp.17, 201, 223].

MEEKINS FAMILY

1. Thomas[1] Meekins, born say 1710, and his wife Mary were "free negroes" who registered the birth and baptism of their children in St. Peter's Parish, New Kent County, Virginia [NSCDA, *Parish Register of St. Peter's*, 98, 119, 141]. He may have been the son of Elizabeth Meekings, born about 1677, who was seventeen years old in 1694 when she petitioned the York County court for her freedom [OW 10:3]. Thomas and Mary Meekins' children were

    i.   Elizabeth, died in St. Peter's Parish in 1734.

      ii. Christmas, born 25 December 1735, baptized 13 February 1736. He may have been the Christmas Meekins who was charged with felony in Halifax County, Virginia court on 1 May 1779 but acquitted after the court examined divers papers that he had in his possession [Pleas 1774-

9, 410]. He was head of a New Kent County household of 5 "Black" persons in 1782 [VA:36]. He was taxable in New Kent County from 1782 to 1814, listed with his unnamed wife in 1813 [PPTL 1782-1800, frames 11, 87, 131, 189, 213; 1791-1828, 297, 320, 397, 455, 491, 503] and head of a New Kent County household of 2 "other free" and a slave in 1810 [VA:761]. He was taxable on 60 acres in 1782 and 1789 [T.L.C. Genealogy, *New Kent County Land Tax Lists*, 30, 57].

iii. Sarah, born 17 August 1739, baptized 23 September 1739 [NSCDA, *Parish Register of St. Peter's*, 141].

iv. Joel, born 29 October 1747, apparently the Joseph Meekins who was head of a "black" New Kent County household of 7 persons in 1782 [VA:36]. He was taxable in New Kent County from 1783 to 1803: taxable on 3 cattle in 1784, taxable on his son Charles in 1785 and 1786, exempt from personal tax starting in 1787; and taxable on a free male tithable and a horse in 1810 [PPTL 1782-1800, frames 21, 44, 64, 99, 117, 131, 149, 169, 189; 1791-1828, frames 359, 371, 384, 455] and head of a New Kent County household of 3 "other free" in 1810 [VA:761]. He was taxable on 60 acres in 1782 and 1789 [T.L.C. Genealogy, *New Kent County Land Tax Lists, 1782-90*, 30, 57].

v. David, born 17 April 1749 [NSCDA, *Parish Register of St. Peter's*, 98], head of a "black" New Kent County household of 4 persons in 1782 [VA:36]. He was taxable in the lower end of St. Peter's Parish on a horse and 3 cattle from 1782 to 1814: listed with his unnamed wife in 1813 [PPTL 1782-1800, frames 11, 44, 100, 149, 189, 213; 1791-1828, frames 359, 384, 409, 432, 455, 491, 503] and head of a New Kent County household of 6 "other free" in 1810 [VA:761].

vi. Isaac[1], born 19 April 1754, "Son of Mary Mekins, a free negroe woman," taxable in New Kent County from 1783 to 1803 and from 1807 to 1814: taxable in 1785 on a slave named Sally who was called his wife Sarah in 1786; taxable on 2 free male tithables in 1807 and 1809, 3 in 1810 and 1811, 2 in 1812, listed with his unnamed wife in 1813. He may have been the father of Richard Meekins, a "FN" tithable in 1812 who was listed with his unnamed wife in 1813 [PPTL 1782-1800, frames 21, 67, 89, 117, 131, 149; 1791-1828, frames 384, 396, 409, 420, 452, 444, 455, 466, 477, 491, 503] and head of a New Kent County household of 9 "other free" in 1810 [VA:762].

Other members of the Meekins family were

i. Peter, taxable in New Kent County from 1793 to 1798 [PPTL 1782-1800, frame 213].

ii. Thomas[2], taxable in New Kent County from 1793 to 1799 [PPTL 1782-1800, frame 213].

iii. Nancy, born about 1779, registered in Henrico County on 11 November 1831: *52 years of age, brown woman, 5 feet 4 inches, born free as appears from her register from the Richmond Hustings Court* [Register of Free Negroes and Mulattoes, 1831-1844, p.10, no.669].

iv. Isaac[2], born about 1785, registered in Henrico County on 14 November 1831: *46 years of age, a man of light complexion, 5 feet 6 inches, Born free as appears from the evidence of George P. Crump* [Register of Free Negroes and Mulattoes, 1831-1844, p.10, no.672].

v. Jane, head of a Richmond City household of 4 "other free" in 1810 [VA:362].

vi. Patteson Meacon, a "free Negro & mulatto over 16" in York County in 1813 [PPTL, 1782-1841, frame 392].

vii. Dandradge, a "free Negro" taxable in York County in 1814 [PPTL, 1782-1841, frame 409].

MEGGS FAMILY

Members of the Meggs family in Virginia were

<blockquote>

i.   Christian, born say 1750, not a Middlesex County tithable herself but taxable on slaves Joan, Francis and Frank (an exempt tithable) in 1783, 3 slaves in 1784, a slave in 1785 and 1790, and taxable on a horse in 1791 [PPTL, 1782-1850, frames 13, 28, 29, 67, 75]. She was head of a Middlesex County household of 5 "Blacks" in 1783 (abstracted as Chatharine Meggs) [VA:56].

ii.   James[1], born say 1760.

iii.   Peter, born say 1766, a "yellow" tithable in the Middlesex County household of James Meggs in 1787, taxable on his own tithe in 1791, a "free negro" tithable in 1803 [PPTL, 1782-1850, frames 45, 75, 116, 124, 188, 272]. He was listed as a "mulatto or Free negro" in Gloucester County in 1819 and 1820 [PPTL, 1800-20].

</blockquote>

1.   James[1] Meggs, born say 1760, was taxable in Middlesex County from 1782 to 1819: taxable on 2 slaves and 2 horses in 1782, a "yellow" tithable in 1787, a "Mulatto" tithable in 1788, taxable on 2 free tithes and a slave over 16 in 1800 and 1801, a "Mulattoe" tithable in 1805, 1806 and 1810, called "James Meggs, Sr., free negro" in 1812 [PPTL, 1782-1850, frames 12, 13, 23, 29, 34, 45, 83, 91, 100, 107, 116, 124, 132, 142, 153, 162, 173, 205, 215, 242, 251, 261, 272, 292, 313, 322]. He was head of a Middlesex County household of 5 "Blacks" in 1783 [VA:56] and a "free negro" head of a Gloucester County household of 1 "other free" and 5 slaves in 1810 [VA:665]. He may have been the father of

<blockquote>

i.   James[2], born about 1782, called "James Meggs, Jr., Mulatoe" when he was tithable in Middlesex County in 1805, 1812 and 1819 [PPTL, 1782-1850, frames 205, 261, 343]. He registered in Middlesex County on 26 June 1805: *born free; 24 years of age; 6'; Tawney complexion* [Register of Free Negroes 1800-60, p.15] and registered in Essex County on 16 March 1818: *born free by affidavit of John B. Burke, Colour: Tawny, 36 years of age, 6 feet 1 inch high* [Register of Free Negroes 1810-43, p.30, no.78].

ii.   Betsy, born about 1782, registered in Middlesex County on 2 December 1832: *born free; 50 years of age; 5'7-1/2"; yellow complexion* [Register of Free Negroes 1827-60, p.6].

iii.   Robert, born about 1784, registered in Middlesex County on 26 June 1805: *born free; 24 years of age; 5'8"; tawney complexion* [Register of Free Negroes 1800-60, p.15]. He was a "negroe" taxable on a slave in Gloucester County in 1809, 1813, and 1814, a "mul°" taxable on 2 slaves from 1815 to 1817 [PPTL, 1800-20]. He was a "free negro" head of a Gloucester County household of 2 "other free" in 1810 [VA:665].

iv.   Parthenia, born about 1793, registered in Middlesex County on 2 December 1833: *born free; 40 years of age; 5'6"; Tawney complexion* [Register of Free Negroes 1827-60, p.6].

v.   Christiana, born about 1798, registered in Middlesex County on 20 June 1825: *born free; 27 years of age; 5'5"; yellow complexion* [Register of Free Negroes 1800-60, p.15].

</blockquote>

MELVIN FAMILY

Members of the Melvin family in Virginia were

<blockquote>

i.   Jane, born 19 November 1764, a "base born Mulatto" child ordered bound to Fielding Turner, Gentleman, in Cameron Parish, Loudoun County, on 9 June 1766 [Orders 1765-7, 83].

</blockquote>

ii. Winney, born April 1769, a "Mullatto" child bound to Fielding Turner on 13 August 1770 [Orders 1770-3, 4].
iii. Rheubin Melvil, a taxable "free Negro" in Fauquier County in 1813 [Waldrep, *1813 Tax List*].

MILES FAMILY

1. Alice Miles, born say 1642, was the servant of John Hill on 10 March 1661/2 when the churchwardens of York Parish presented her in York County court for "fornication with a Negro." The court ordered that she be whipped "till her backe be bloody," but she escaped from the sheriff's custody before he could inflict the punishment. The court ordered her master to produce her in court [DOW 3:151, 159]. She was probably the ancestor of

   i. Richard, born say 1764, taxable in Charles City County on a tithe and a horse from 1788 to 1799 [PPTL, 1788-1814] and taxable in York County in 1804 and 1805 [PPTL, 1782-1841, frames 297, 307].
2   ii. Isaac, born about 1766.
   iii. Jacob, born say 1766, taxable in Charles City County on a horse from 1788 to 1791 [PPTL, 1788-1814].
   iv. James, born say 1767, taxable in Charles City County on a horse from 1788 to 1800 [PPTL, 1788-1814].
3   v. Nat, born say 1780.
   vi. Tabby, head of a Culpeper County household of 6 "other free" in 1810 [VA:56].

2. Isaac Miles, born about 1766, was taxable in Charles City County from 1790 to 1812, a "Mulattoe" taxable in 1813 and 1814 [PPTL, 1788-1814] and head of a Charles City County household of 11 "other free" in 1810 [VA:959]. He obtained a certificate of freedom in Charles City County on 20 October 1831 on testimony of Jesse Ladd: *a bright mulatto man, about 65 years old, born free in this county* [Minutes 1830-9, 79]. He may have been the father of

   i. John, born say 1771, taxable in Charles City County from 1792 to 1799, a "Mulattoe" taxable in 1813 and 1814 [PPTL, 1788-1814].
   ii. Edward, head of a Charles City County household of 4 "other free" in 1810 [VA:959].
   iii. Pleasant, a "Mulattoe" taxable in Charles City County in 1813 and 1814 [PPTL, 1788-1814].
   iv. David, a "Mulattoe" taxable in Charles City County in 1813 and 1814 [PPTL, 1788-1814].

3. Nathaniel Miles, born say 1777, was taxable in Charles City County in 1798, a "Mulattoe" taxable in 1813 and 1814 [PPTL, 1788-1814] and head of a Charles City County household of 11 "free colored" in 1820 [VA:7]. He purchased 75 acres in Charles City County which had belonged to Charles Mackaney, deceased, from James Mackaney for $225 on 15 August 1807 [DB 5:181]. He died before 3 January 1844 when the inventory of his Charles City County estate was taken [WB 4:512]. He was the father of

   i. Harris, born about 1810, registered in Charles City County on 20 October 1831: *son of Nat Miles, a man of yellow complexion, about 21 years old, born free in this county* [Minutes 1830-9, 80].

MILLER FAMILY

1. Ephraim Miller, born say 1710, was taxable in his own household in Norfolk County, Virginia, from 1731 to 1734, and a "free negro" taxable in the household of James Wilson, Sr., in the district from Deep Creek to the Bridge in 1736 [Wingo, *Norfolk County Tithables* 1730-50, 24, 83, 127, 175]. He may have been related to the Miller family of Maryland and Delaware. His

widow may have been Elizabeth Miller, a "free Negro" who was taxable in Currituck County, North Carolina, with her daughter Johanah in 1755. They may have been the ancestors of

- i.   Isaac, born say 1732, a "free Negro" taxable in Currituck County in 1755. He apparently joined the Tuscarora Indian reservation in Bertie County before 12 July 1766 when he signed as one of the chief men in their lease of 8,000 acres of Tuscarora Indian land [DB L:56]. He did not sign the next lease of 1777, so he was probably one of the 155 members of the tribe who went north with them to New York State. (The remainder left in 1802).
- ii. Johannah, born say 1738, taxable in her mother's Currituck County household in 1755.
- iii. Judia, a taxable in Samuel Willoughby's household on the southside of Tanner's Creek in Norfolk County in 1780 [Wingo, *Norfolk County Tithables* 1768-80, 272].
- iv. Hannah, mother of Ezekiel Miller (born about 1789) who registered as a free Negro in Norfolk County on 11 May 1810: *twenty one years of age of a Yellowish complexion...with long hair...Born free* [Register of Free Negros & Mulattos, no.3].
- v.   Jacob L., head of a Stokes County, North Carolina household of 1 "other free" in 1800 [NC:514].
- vi. Polley, head of a Richmond City household of 1 "other free" in 1810 [VA:347].
- vii. Nelly "(free)" head of a Charleston, St. Phillips & Michaels Parish household of 1 "other free" and a slave in 1790.

MILLS FAMILY

1. Frances Mills, born say 1740, was living in Bute/ Warren County, North Carolina, between 10 August 1774 and October 1783 when her "Mulatto" children (called orphans of Francis Mills) were bound to John, William, and Richard Sherry [Bute County Minutes 1767-76, 296; WB 2:95, 96, 97, 98, 243 by Kerr, *Warren County, North Carolina Records*]. She was called Fanny Mills on 7 February 1778 when she sold her cattle and household goods to Stephen Shell in Bute County and called Frances Mills on 11 May 1779 when the Bute County court ordered that John Sherry be paid as a witness for her against Stephen Shell [Minutes 1777-79, 86, 169; WB 2:214]. Warren County was formed from Bute County in 1779, and Fanny's children were bound out there to the Sherry family in February 1782 [Minutes 1780-83, 87]. She was head of a Halifax County, North Carolina household of 10 "other free" in 1800 [NC:327]. Her children were

2   i.   Elizabeth, born about 1758.
3   ii. ?Daniel[1], born about 1761.
4   iii. Sarah, born about 1764.
- iv. James[1], born about 1766, eight-year-old orphan of Francis Mills (no race indicated), bound to Richard Sherry in Bute County on 10 August 1774 [Bute County Minutes 1767-76, 296; Warren County WB 2:243 by Kerr, *Warren County, North Carolina Records*].
- v.   Ann, born about 1769, a five-year-old "mulatto" orphan of Francis Mills, deceased, bound to William Sherry in Bute County on 9 August 1774 [WB 2:96], perhaps the Nancy Mills, born before 1776, who was head of a Halifax County, North Carolina household of 1 "free colored" in 1830 [NC:305].
- vi. John, born say 1771, "mulatto child and orphan of Francis Mills, dec'd," bound to John Sherry in Bute County on 9 August 1774 [WB 2:98], head of a Halifax County household of 2 "other free" in 1810 [NC:34], 6 "free colored" in Nash County in 1820 [NC:416] and 9 in Halifax County in 1830 [NC:306].

vii. ?Polly, born about 1776, a six-year-old, no parent named, bound by the Warren County court to George Webb in February 1782 [Minutes 1780-83, 87].

viii. Isham, born about 1776, seven-year-old, base-born child of Fanney Mills, bound by the Warren County court to George Webb in February 1782, called seven-year-old child of Francis Mills when he was bound to John Sherry in October 1783 [Minutes 1780-83, 87; 1783-7, 15]. He was head of a Warren County household of 4 "free colored" in 1820 [NC:812].

ix. Winnie, born about 1778, six-year-old child of Fanney Mills bound by the Warren County court to George Webb in February 1782, called five-year-old, base-born child of Francis Mills in October 1783 when the court bound her to John Sherry [Minutes 1780-83, 87; 1783-7, 15].

x. Aggey, born about 1778, base-born child of Fanney Mills, bound to George Webb in Warren County in February 1782, called three-year-old child of Francis Mills when she was bound to John Sherry in October 1783 [Minutes 1780-83, 87; 1783-7, 15].

xi. Charlotte, born about 1779, three-year-old child of Fanney mills, bound by the Warren County court to George Webb in February 1782 [Minutes 1780-3, 87].

xii. William Christmas, born in December 1781, two-month-old, base-born child of Fanney Mills, bound by the Warren County court to George Webb in February 1782, called two-year-old child of Francis Mills when he was bound to John Sherry in October 1783 [Minutes 1780-83, 87; 1783-7, 15].

2. Elizabeth Mills, born about 1758, a "young mulatto woman," the sixteen-year-old orphan of Francis Mills, was bound to John Sherry in Bute County on 10 August 1774 [WB 2:97]. She was living in Warren County in February 1782 when the court bound out her son James. She was head of a Halifax County household of 5 "free colored" in 1820 [NC:156] and was a "free colored" woman living alone in Halifax in 1830 [NC:296]. Her children were

i. James[2], born about July 1781, six months old in February 1782 when he was ordered bound to George Webb by the Warren County court [Minutes 1780-83, 87].

ii. ?Isham[2], born about 1790, head of a Halifax County household of 4 "free colored" in 1820 [NC:157] and 9 in 1830 [NC:309]. On 16 February 1836 the Halifax County court bound to him two "free boys of color" Henry Mills (ten years old) and Everett Mills (thirteen years old). The 20 August 1839 Halifax County court bound five children to him: Alfred, Wilson, Franky, Ann, and Penny Mills. He purchased land from Fred Goins (**Gowen**) by a deed proved in Halifax County court on 21 November 1836. He and John Mills were permitted by the 17 August 1841 Halifax County court to carry their guns.

iii. ?Frances, born about 1790, no parent named when the 25 May 1800 Halifax County court ordered her bound as an apprentice to William Pike [Minutes 1799-1802, 105].

3. Daniel[1] Mills, born about 1761, was listed in the Militia Returns of Halifax County, North Carolina, as a twenty-year-old planter born in Halifax County [*The North Carolinian* VI:727]. He appointed Benjamin Hawkins of Warren County his attorney to receive his final settlement pay for service in the North Carolina Continental Line on 23 March 1791 [NCGSJ XIII:98]. His "orphans" were bound out by the Halifax County court. They were

i. Judith, born about 1783, bound out by the Halifax County court on 20 February 1786.

ii. Gilford, born about 1785, sixteen-year-old "orphan of Daniel Mills" ordered bound apprentice by the 18 August 1801 Halifax County court, perhaps the Guilford Mills who married Sally **Goins** 13 January 1834 Halifax County bond with John Jordan bondsman.

iii.   Gideon, born 3 September 1786, "orphan of Daniel Mills," ordered bound to Samuel Tarwell in Halifax County court on 23 May 1799 [Minutes 1799-1802, 37].

4.   Sarah Mills, born about 1764, was the ten-year-old "mulatto" orphan of Frances Mills, deceased, who was ordered bound to Richard Sherry in Bute County on 9 August 1774 [WB 2:95]. She was living in Warren County in February 1794 when the court bound out her son Claiborn. Her children were

i.   Claiborn, born about 1787, seven-year-old, base-born child of Sarah Mills who was bound by the Warren County court to William Ballard on 25 February 1794. He was bound instead to John Moore in February 1799 and called a "boy of colour" in May 1800 when John Moore, Esquire, was ordered to bring him to court and show cause why Claiborn should not be bound to a proper person [Minutes 1793-1800, 45, 152, folio 183]. He was head of a Halifax County household of 3 "other free" in 1810 [NC:34], 9 "free colored" in 1820, and 8 in 1830 [NC:306].

ii.   ?Daniel[2], born about 1797, no parent named when he was bound out by the Halifax County court on 18 August 1801. He was head of a Halifax County household of 8 "other free" in 1830 [NC:305]. On 16 February 1824 the Halifax County court bound to him "Jack Mills, a free boy of color." The same session of the court found Daniel guilty in an issue of traverse with a punishment of twenty lashes on his bare back at the public whipping post. He died before 19 February 1836 when the court ordered the coroner to be paid for summoning jurors to view his body [Minutes 1832-46, n.p.].

iii.   ?Elizabeth, born about December 1799, no parent named when she was bound an apprentice by the 18 August 1801 Halifax County court [Minutes 1799-1802].

Other members of the Mills family were

i.   Jacob, taxable in the Princess Anne County household of "free Negro" Marshall **Anderson** in 1784 [*Virginia Genealogical Society Quarterly* 27:267].

ii.   Taylor, head of a Robeson County household of 3 "other free" in 1800 [NC:423].

MILTON/ MELTON FAMILY

Members of the Milton family were

1   i.   Elisha, born say 1740.
2   ii.   Josiah, born say 1742.
iii.   Hardy, not found by the sheriff in Southampton County on 10 October 1782 when his property was attached for a 3 pound, 12 shilling debt he owed John Wright. The property included a spinning wheel, an iron pot, chairs, a small tub, a pewter dish, spoons, knives, wooden plates and a bedstead [Orders 1778-84, 247].

1.   Elisha Milton, born say 1740, was presented by the Southampton County court on 11 May 1780 for concealing a tithable, on 13 May 1784 for retailing liquor without a license, and on 12 July 1786 for failing to list himself, a slave over the age of 16, 2 horses, and 8 head of cattle as tithables [Orders 1778-84, 111, 389; 1784-9, 189, 271, 286]. He was taxable in Southampton County from 1782 to 1785: taxable on 2 horses and 6 cattle in 1782, taxable on a horse and 9 cattle in 1787, taxable on a slave and a horse in 1788 [PPTL, frames 503, 549, 571, 642, 665]. His 1 December 1788 Southampton County will, proved

21 August 1797, left land to his granddaughter Patsy, daughter of Ann Milton, who was to receive the deed from Ethelred Taylor and named his children Leah and Randolph [WB 5:2]. He was the father of

i. James[1], born say 1762, brother of Ann Melton **Bowzer**, said to have enlisted in the Revolution and died of smallpox at Bunker Hill [Brown, *Genealogical Abstracts, Revolutionary War Veterans Script Act, 1852*, 139; Gwathmey, *Historical Register of Virginians in the Revolution*].

ii. Leah.

iii. Randolph, born say 1768, a witness to the 1 December 1791 St. Luke's Parish, Southampton County will of John Reese [WB 4:649]. He married Amy **Felts**, 13 February 1792 Southampton County bond, Randolph Newsum security. He sued John Wright in Southampton County court on 9 August 1793 for trespass, assault and battery. His witnesses William Jarrell and Lewis Fort failed to appear on 16 August 1794 [Minutes 1793-9, 34, 109]. He was taxable in Southampton County from 1790 to 1811: taxable on 2 free male tithables in 1801 [PPTL 1782-92, frames 765, 821; 1792-1806, frames 58, 86, 166, 197, 274, 323, 385, 419, 522, 698, 813, 847; 1807-21, frames 52, 74, 172, 197]. He was head of a Southampton County household of 8 "other free" in 1810 [VA:71]. He may have been the Randol Milton who was head of an Orange County, North Carolina household of 5 "free colored" in 1820 [NC:336]. His wife Amy was probably related to Jacob **Felts**, head of a Henrico County household of 13 "other free" in 1810 [VA:979].

iv. Ann, born say 1771, married Thomas **Bowser**, 28 December 1792 Southampton County bond, Randolph Milton security. She was called "Ann Milton, alias Ann Bowser," in a codicil to the 20 February 1791 Southampton County will of Ethelred Taylor, recorded 14 July 1791. The will also mentioned Patsey Milton, "so called daughter of Ann Milton, Jr." [WB 4:437]. Ann was called Ann Milton on 9 August 1792 when she sued a member of the Wright family for trespass, assault and battery in Southampton County court [Minutes 1793-99, 33, 153, 155]. She was taxable in Southampton County on a horse from 1790 to 1795, but her name was crossed off the list in 1796 [PPTL 1782-92, frames 764, 821; 1792-1806, frames 58, 86, 166, 197]. She was living in Nansemond County on 8 July 1834 when she made a deposition in court stating that her brother James Melton, a free man of color, enlisted in the Revolution in Southampton County, served under Captain James Gray, and died of smallpox at Bunker Hill. In 1833 her husband Thomas **Bowzer** deposed that his wife lived in Nansemond County for 42 years but her father and family were from Southampton County [Brown, *Genealogical Abstracts, Revolutionary War Veterans Script Act, 1852*, 139; Gwathmey, *Historical Register of Virginians in the Revolution*].

2. Josiah Milton, born say 1742, was taxable on two tithes in Hertford County, North Carolina, in 1770 (called Josiah Meltiah) and one in 1779 [Fouts, *Tax Receipt Book*, 41; GA 30.1]. He was taxable in St. Luke's Parish, Southampton County, from 1782 to 1790: taxable on 2 horses in 1782, and on a tithe and 3 cattle in 1787 [PPTL 1782-92, frames 507, 522, 549, 571, 594, 642, 665, 765]. He was head of a Hertford County household of 10 "other free" in Captain Lewis' District in 1800. Perhaps his children were

i. James[2], born about 1770, head of a Hertford County household of 1 "other free" in 1800, 3 in Southampton County in 1810 [VA:75], and 4 "free colored" in Hertford County in 1820 [NC:188]. He was a eighty-year-old "Mulatto" sailor counted in the 1850 census for Hertford County [NC:653].

ii. Surrell, head of a Hertford County household of 3 "free colored" in 1820, one of whom was a woman over forty-five years of age [NC:186].
iii. John, head of a Hertford County household of 3 "other free" in 1800.
iv. Mourning, born about 1780, head of a Hertford County household of 4 "free colored" in 1820 [NC:186] and 1 in 1830 [NC:404]. She was counted as a seventy-year-old "Black" woman in Hertford County in 1850 [NC:666].
v.   Mills, head of a Hertford County household of 6 "other free" in 1810 (Mills Melton) [NC:107], 12 "free colored" in Orange County in 1820 [NC:336], and a "Negro" head of a Guilford County household of 8 "free colored" in 1830. He married Patsy **Shoecraft** according to the testimony of Jeremiah **Shoecraft**, grandson of William Shoecraft and Bicey **Nickens**, when he applied for Cherokee benefits in 1908 (rejected).
vi. Mary Anna, a sister of Mills Milton, married James **Shoecraft** according to testimony by their grandson Samuel **Shoecraft** when he applied for Cherokee benefits in 1908 (rejected).
vii. Matthias, born about registered in Southampton County on 11 September 1796: *age 21, Mulattoe, 5 feet 4 and 1/2 inches, free born in N. Carolina, Hertford county as p. certificate filed* [Register of Free Negroes 1794-1832, no. 112]. He was head of an Orange County, North Carolina household of 5 "other free" in 1810 (called Matthew Melton) [NC:831]. He was bondsman with Moses **Bass** for the 13 April 1813 Orange County marriage of Polly **Roberts** and Moses **Archer**. He married Betsy **Shoecraft**, 12 June 1821 Orange County bond.
viii. Corde, born 1794-1776, head of a Hertford County household of 3 "free colored" in 1820.
ix. Meede Melton, head of a Hertford County household of 8 "other free" in 1830 [NC:396].
x.   David Melton, among the "Sundry persons of Colour of Hertford County" who petitioned the General Assembly in 1822 to repeal the act which declared slaves to be competent witnesses against free persons of Colour [*NCGSJ* XI:252].

MITCHELL FAMILY

The Mitchell family probably had a very early origin since there were several members of the family born about 1720. The earliest records are for

1   i.   ____, born say 1720, married Mary ____.
2   ii. ____, born say 1722, married Ann **Hawley**.
3   iii. Ann, born say 1730.
4   iv. Jane, born say 1735.
5   v.   Thomas[1], born say 1744.
6   vi. Rachel, born say 1745.
7   vii. Sarah, born say 1747.
    viii. James, born about 1755, about eighteen years old on 20 May 1773 when he complained to the Halifax County, Virginia court against his master Isaac Coles, Gentleman. The court ruled that the indentures were insufficient and bound him instead to Moses Estes. He was called a "Mulatto" the following month on 17 June 1773 when he was bound instead to Leonard Baker [Pleas 1772-3, 117, 146].

1.   ____ Mitchell, born say 1720, was the husband of Mary Mitchell (maiden name unknown) who had eight children before she married Lawrence **Pettiford** according to her great-great-grandchild [28 June 1893 letter from Narcissa

Rattley to her children].[138] By 1752 she was married to Lawrence **Pettiford**, two "Black" taxables in Robert Harris' 1752 Granville County list [CR 44.701.19]. She may have been the mother of the Mitchells who were early taxables in Granville County. They were

8   i.   Archibald, born about 1743.
9   ii.   David[1], born say 1744.
10   iii.   Esther, born say 1747.

2.   ____ Mitchell, born say 1725, married Ann **Hawley**, daughter of Michael **Hawley**. Their son William Mitchell received 60 acres near Cypress Swamp in Northampton County by his grandfather's 1 March 1752 Northampton County will, with the proviso that his mother (unnamed) be allowed to live on the land [SS original]. Ann was not mentioned in the will nor was her husband, but she and William Mitchell sold the 60 acres he received by the will (when he was twenty-one?) on 17 December 1767 [DB 4:133]. Her child was

11   i.   William[1], born say 1746.

3.   Ann Mitchell, born say 1730, was a "free Mulattoe," who petitioned the Bertie County court on 24 October 1758 to apprentice her children to James Boon [Haun, *Bertie County Court Minutes*, II:452].[139] Her children were

     i.   William **Shoecraft**, born about 1749, about nine years old in 1758 when he was indentured to James Boon [*NCGSJ* XVIII:170].
     ii.   Mary Ann Mitchell, born about 1753, ordered bound to James Boon, perhaps the Mary Mitchell who married Burrell **Evans**, 22 July 1779 Granville County bond.
     iii.   ?Nancy Mitchell, born say 1757, married Cato **Copeland**, 11 December 1778 Halifax County bond.

4.   Jane Mitchell, born say 1735, was living in Bertie County in 1755 when Robert **Butler** posted bastardy bonds for two unnamed children he had by her [Camin, *N.C. Bastardy Bonds*, 8]. Her children may have been

     i.   Jeremiah, born say 1751, a free male "Mulatto" in Thomas Pugh's Bertie County household in his list for 1764 [CR 10.702.19].
     ii.   John, born say 1752, a "free molatto" in the household of "free molatto" Robert **Butler** in the 1764 Bertie Summary Tax list [CR 10.702.1]. John's race was not stated when he was bound apprentice in Bertie County to Lemuel Hardy to be a blacksmith on 23 March 1765 [*NCGSJ* XIV:32].
     iii.   Hezekiah, born about 1753, no race stated when he was bound apprentice in Bertie County to Edward Hardy to be a cordwainer on 28 March 1765 [*NCGSJ* XIV:31].

5.   Thomas[1] Mitchell, born say 1744, received a grant for 39 acres in Edgecombe County on 9 November 1784 and sold this land on 20 February 1792 [DB 4:380; 6:535]. He was head of an Edgecombe household of 10 "other free" in 1790 [NC:55], 7 in 1800 (called Free Negro) [NC:221], and 9 in 1810 [NC:741]. Perhaps his widow was Esther Mitchell, born before 1776, head of an Edgecombe County household of 5 "free colored" in 1820 [NC:117]. Thomas may have been the father of

     i.   Stephen, head of an Edgecombe County household of 7 "other free" in 1810 [NC:767].

---

[138]Narcissa Rattley's letter is in the possession of Robert Jackson of Silver Spring, Maryland.

[139]See the Shoecraft family history which assumes that Ann **Shoecraft** was her maiden name.

    ii.   Joel, born before 1776, head of an Edgecombe County household of 9 "free colored" in 1820 [NC:87].

6.   Rachel Mitchell, born say 1745, was head of a Pasquotank County household of one "Mulatto" taxable in 1769 [SS 837], 9 "other free" in 1790 [NC:28] and was still living there in 1810 [NC:915]. Her children may have been
    i.   Tom, head of Pasquotank household of 9 "other free" in 1810 [NC:914].
    ii.   John, head of a Pasquotank household of 8 "other free" in 1810 [NC:914].
    iii.   Robert[1], born before 1776, head of a Pasquotank household of 7 "free colored" in 1820 [NC:271].
    iv.   Ismael, born about 1789, bound as an apprentice wheelwright to James Chamberlain of Pasquotank County in 1806 [*NCGSJ* XI:93].

7.   Sarah Mitchell, born say 1747, was a "Mulatto" head of a Pasquotank County household in 1769 [SS 837]. She may have been the mother of
    i.   Benjamin[1], born say 1767, married Elizabeth **Gregers (Driggers)**, 27 August 1788 Craven County bond, Benjamin **Moore** bondsman. He was head of a Craven County household of 3 "other free" in 1790 [NC:130]. His 7 March 1803 Craven County will, proved December 1817 by George **Godett**, Jr., left 5 pounds to his mother-in-law (stepmother?), Susannah Mitchell, and left all the remainder of his property to his wife Elizabeth Mitchell [WB 1810-21, pt.1, 157].
    ii.   Robert[3], born say 1782, head of a Pasquotank County household of 6 "free colored" and 2 slaves in 1820 [NC:285].

8.   Archibald Mitchell, born about 1743, was taxable with his wife Sealia in Stephen Jett's 1767 Granville County tax list. She was probably the daughter of Benjamin **Bass**, taxed in her father's household in the 1762 list of Samuel Benton [CR 44.701.19]. Archibald was taxed on 2 horses and 5 cattle in Oxford District in 1782. In 1786 he was taxed on 260 acres and one poll, and he was head of an Oxford District household of 10 free males and 3 females in the state census. He was last taxed in Granville in 1793 on 100 acres and no polls, indicating that he was considered to be over fifty years of age [Tax List 1767-1823]. His wife may have been the Cealy Mitchell who was head of a household of 1 "other free" in the 1810 census for Granville County [NC:866]. The Mitchells who were living in Granville and Wake Counties after 1793 may have been some of the nine free males in his 1786 Granville County household:
    i.   Josiah, married Rebecca **Corn**, 23 February 1798 Wake County bond, David **Valentine** bondsman. Josiah was head of Wake County household of 8 "other free" in 1800 [NC:780].
    ii.   Joab, taxable on one poll in Beaverdam District in 1796 [Tax List 1796-1802, 17]. He was head of a Wake County household of 3 "other free" in 1800 and 2 "free colored" in Northampton County in 1820 [NC:244].
    iii.   Joel[1], born before 1776, married Ellis **Pettiford**, 2 January 1801 Wake County household, Martin **Locus** bondsman. He was head of an Orange County household of 12 "free colored" in 1820 [NC:A:404].
    iv.   Zachariah, married Jain **Anderson**, 25 August 1795 Granville County bond, Abel **Anderson** bondsman. He was taxed on one poll in Tabbs Creek District in 1799 [Tax List 1796-1802, 171] and head of a Granville County household of 14 "other free" in 1810 [NC:882]. According to the 2 July 1814 refunding bond on the estate papers of Winny **Anderson**, Zachariah married Joyce **Anderson**.
    v.   William[2], born say 1775, taxable on one poll in Oxford District, and there was another taxable on one poll in Island Creek in 1796 [Tax List

1796-1802, 30, 44]. He was head of a Granville County household of 5 "other free" in 1800 and 9 in 1810 [NC:866]. He was the bondsman for the 31 January 1796 marriage of Rhody **Anderson** and Darling **Bass**. He married Bythea **Hedsbeth**, 11 August 1796 Granville County bond with Darling **Bass** bondsman.

vi. Robert[2], born say 1780, taxable on one poll in 1801 in Napp of Reed District [Tax List 1796-1802, 277]. He was head of a Guilford County household of 12 "other free" in 1810 [NC:991] and 9 "free colored" in 1820 [NC:107]. He married Sopha **Bibba** (**Bibby**), 13 November 1828 Franklin County bond, A.S. Perry bondsman.

vii. Benjamin[2], born say 1782, married Winnie **Anderson**, 19 December 1803 Granville County bond with George **Anderson** bondsman. He was head of a Granville County household of 4 "other free" in 1810 [NC:907].

9. David[1] Mitchell, born say 1744, was taxed in the 1764 Granville County list of Samuel Benton in Jeremiah **Anderson**'s household, and he was taxed with his wife Silvey in Benton's 1765 list. In 1768 he was called "David Mitchell Negro" in Len Henley Bullock's list. Between 1768 and 1770 he married, second, Jane/Jean **Tylor**, a taxable in the 1768 Granville County household of her brother Bartlet **Tyler** [CR 44.701.19]. Olive and William **Bass** called her Jean **Tylor**, alias Mitchell, when they sued her in Granville County court on 7 April 1770 [Minutes 1754-70, 202]. Between 1778 and 1785 as "David Mitchell free Negro" he entered 640 acres in Granville on Beaverdam Creek [Pruitt, *Land Entries Granville County,* 23]. Not long afterwards he made his 18 July 1780 Granville County will which was proved in August court 1781. He mentioned his wife Jean and his children [WB 1:307]. His children: Molley (twelve and one-half years old), Susanna (ten years), Jesse (eight years), and David (four years), "all free negroes," were bound out by the 3 November 1784 Granville County court [Owen, *Granville County Notes,* vol. VI]. His wife Jean/ Jane was taxed on 300 acres, 1 horse, and two cattle as Jane **Tylor** in 1782 and as Jane Mitchell on 365 acres in 1786 and on 200 acres in 1788. She apparently died about August 1799 when her children were indentured by the court, and her son Jesse was taxable on the land. The ages of Mary, Susannah, and Jesse were stated in the indentures and certified by "me Susannah Harris that was present the time they were born" [CR 044.101.2]. David's children were

i. Drury, born say 1765, bound apprentice to Drury **Pettiford** on 6 February 1781 [Owen, *Granville County Notes,* vol. VI]. He received 100 acres by his father's will. He probably sold this land since he was taxed on one poll only in 1786. The February 1799 Granville County court reported that he had deserted his wife Mary **Jones** when it bound out their son Ephraim **Jones** Mitchell (born 1789). He married Mary, widow of John **Harris**, in Wilkes County. He was head of a Wilkes County household of 8 "other free" in 1810 [NC:867]. He was probably related to Daniel Mitchell (born about 1778) and Absolem Mitchell (born about 1780) "free Negro" orphans bound to Maxwell Chambers by the Rowan County court on 8 November 1786 [Minutes 1773-7, 6 (abstract p. 420)].

ii. Martha.

iii. Ann.

iv. Mary, born 24 March 1774, called Molly Mitchell on 24 January 1800 when she married Martin **Locust**, Orange County bond.

v. Susannah, born 28 September 1776.

vi. Jesse, born 29 March 1778. He received the balance of his father's land after his mother's death and was taxable on 263 acres in Beaverdam District in 1800 and 1801 [Tax List 1796-1802, 294].

    vii.   David², born about 1780, four years old on 3 November 1784 [Owen, *Granville County Notes*, vol. VI]. He married Polly **Locklear**(?), 1 January 1804 Granville County bond with John **Tyner** bondsman. He was head of a Caswell County household of 6 "free colored" in 1820 [NC:72].

10.   Esther¹ /Easter Mitchell was probably born about 1747 since her oldest child was born circa 1763. She was taxable in the 1767 Granville County tax list of Stephen Jett in Lewis **Pettiford**'s household [CR 44.701.19]. She was head of a Franklin County household of 2 "other free" in 1810 [NC:825]. Many of her children were identified in Granville County indentures [CR 044.101.2]. Others may have been those counted as "other free" in Franklin County. Her children were

    i.   Isaac Cursi(?) (**Kersey**?) Mitchell, born about 1763, orphan of Hester Mitchel, bound to Malichiah **Reaves** on 21 July 1769.

    ii.   Judah, "base born Mulatto of Esther Mitchel," bound on 1 October 1771.

    iii.   Abigail, born about 1767, "base born Mulatto of Esther," bound to Sarah White on 18 May 1772. She was called "Abby" Mitchell, head of a Franklin County household of 6 "other free" in 1810 [NC:825]. Her six-year-old child James was bound apprentice to Ross Conyers in Franklin County in March 1792 [Minutes 1789-93, 286]. Her 22 November 1817 Franklin County will, no probate date, left 20 shillings each to her sons John and Isaac Mitchell and the rest of her property to her children: Samuel, Polly, Keziah, Henry, and Winney, and her grandson Willis **Dunce** (**Dunston**) [Bradley, *Franklin County Wills*, I:58].

12   iv.   Winnifred, born June 1768.

    v.   Fanny, born say 1770, "base born child of Easter Mitchell," bound to Jeremiah Frazier on 6 November 1777. She may have been the F. Mitchell whose son Chesley, born about 1789, was bound apprentice in Granville County on 7 February 1799.

    vi.   Edward, born say 1771, "base born child of Easter Mitchell," bound to Jeremiah Frazier on 6 November 1777. He married Mariah **Bass**, 5 January 1795 Granville County bond, Thomas **Bass** bondsman.

    vii.   ?Polly, head of a Franklin County household of 6 "other free" in 1810 [NC:826].

    viii.   ?Prissy, head of a Franklin County household of 4 "other free" in 1810 [NC:825].

11.   William¹ Mitchell, born say 1746, received 60 acres on Cypress Swamp in Northampton County by the 1 March 1752 Northampton County will of his grandfather Michael **Hawley** [SS original]. He and (his mother?) Ann Mitchell sold this land (when he was 21?) on 17 December 1767 [DB 4:133]. He may have been the William Mitchel who was a "Mixt Blood" taxable in Bladen County in 1774 [Byrd, *Bladen County Tax Lists*, I:123] and head of a Bladen County household of 4 "other free" in 1790 [NC:188]. Perhaps his descendants were

    i.   Joyce, head of a Northampton County household of 2 "other free" in 1790 [NC:76] and 2 in Halifax County, North Carolina, in 1810 [NC:38].

    ii.   Meney, head of a Gates County household of 2 "other free" in 1790 [NC:24].

    iii.   Thomas², born say 1770, head of a Bladen County household of 7 "other free" in 1800.

    iv.   Elizabeth, head of a Northampton County household of 5 "other free" in 1800 [NC:461].

v.   Olive, born before 1776, head of a Halifax County, North Carolina household of 5 "free colored" in 1820 [NC:157].

vi. Michael, born say 1780, married Lucy **Bass**, 25 April 1805 Granville County bond. He was head of a Granville County household of 7 "other free" in 1810 [NC:877]. Perhaps she was the Lucy Mitchell, born before 1776, who was head of a Northampton County household of 8 "free colored" in 1820 [NC:244].

12. Winnifred Mitchell, born June 1768, "base born of Esther," was bound an apprentice in Granville County on 20 August 1771 [CR 044.101.2]. She was head of Franklin County household of 4 "other free" in 1810 [NC:826]. Her children were bound apprentices in Granville County in May 1793 [Minutes 1792-95, 64-5]. Her children were

i.   Esther², born about 1787.
ii. Lewis, born about 1788.
iii. Jemima, born about 1790.

MICHAM/ MITCHAM FAMILY

Members of the Micham family in North Carolina were

i.   Joseph, head of a Halifax County household of 6 "other free" in 1800 [NC:330].
ii. Jacob, head of a Halifax County household of 6 "other free" in 1800 [NC:330] and 8 in 1810 [NC:38].
iii. Paul, born before 1776, head of a Halifax County household of 5 "other free" in 1810 [NC:38] and 8 "free colored" in 1820 [NC:156].
iv. Mary, head of a Halifax County household of 7 "other free" in 1810 [NC:38].
v.   William, head of a Pasquotank County household of 8 "free colored" in 1820 [NC:275].

Members of the Mitcham family in South Carolina were

i.   Elizabeth, head of a Sumter County household of 8 "other free" in 1800 [SC:953].
ii. Joseph, head of a Sumter County household of 3 "other free" in 1800 [SC:934] and 3 in 1810 [SC:218a].
iii. Jesse, head of a Sumter District household of 5 "other free" in 1810 [SC:218a].
iv. Thomas, head of a Sumter District household of 3 "other free" in 1810 [SC:218a].
v.   Nelly, head of a Sumter District household of 6 "other free" in 1810 [SC:218a].
vi. Gudon(?), head of a Sumter District household of 4 "other free" in 1810 [SC:218a].

MONGOM/MONGON FAMILY

1.   Philip¹ Mongom, born say 1625, was the slave of Captain William Hawley who claimed him as a headright in 1646 in Northampton County court [DW 1645-51, 39 by Deal, *Race and Class*, 383-93]. In 1645 he was whipped in court for entertaining and concealing Sibble Ford, a runaway English maidservant [DW 1645-51, fol.2]. He and Mingo **Mathews** were slaves hired out by Hawley to John Foster who complained that

the Negros which hee had of Capt. William Hawley were very stubborne and would not followe his business.

In 1649 Hawley made an agreement with them that they would be free upon payment of 1700 pounds of tobacco or one white servant [DW 1654-55, fol.25, 54]. However, there is some evidence to suggest that they were freed not by this payment but by warning the local English population of an Indian plot to poison their wells in July 1650 [DW 1645-51, fol.217]. In 1651 he arranged to marry Martha Merris, an English widow, signing a deed of jointure with her to reserve her property for herself and her children [DW 1651-54, 33, fol.33]. In May 1660 he was acquitted of stealing hogs but was fined 100 pounds of tobacco for throwing some hogs' ears on the table where the justices were sitting [Orders 1657-64, 68]. In 1663 he was fined for having an illegitimate child by Margery Tyer, a white woman [Orders 1657-64, fol.173, 175]. In 1666 he recorded his livestock mark in court [DW 1651-54, at end of volume, 6]. Philip was a taxable head of a Northampton County household in 1664 and was taxable with his then wife Mary (a free African American) from 1665 to 1677 [Orders 1657-64, 198; 1674-79, 190]. He and two white men, Edward Parkinson and Peter DuParks, were renting 300 acres on the bay side on Mattawaman Creek from John Savage when he made his 26 August 1678 will, and in 1680 he leased 200 acres near the Pocomoke River by the Maryland-Virginia border [Orders 1674-9, 316; 1678-83, 151; Whitelaw, *Virginia's Eastern Shore*, I:228; II:1216]. On 20 August 1678 Canutus Benne/ Bents confessed in Accomack County court to owing him 555 pounds of tobacco [Orders 1678-82, 7]. On 29 January 1684/5 he submitted to the court that he had notoriously abused and defamed his most loving friends and neighbors John Duparkes and Robert Jarvis. In November 1687 a group of his white neighbors gathered at his house with him, his wife Mary, and his son Philip, Jr. After much "drinkinge and carrousinge," his guests began beating one of the white members of the group, and Philip and his wife and son joined in the melee. The fight broke up when Philip threatened one of them with his gun. They were all fined 500 pounds of tobacco in Northampton County court [OW 1683-89, 118-9, 320-322]. He was last mentioned in the court record of 30 September 1691: "Phillip the Negro planter" [DW&c 1680-92, 306]. He was the father of

2   i.   Philip^2, born say 1659.

2.   Philip^2 Mongom, born say 1659, rented 200 acres in Accomack County near Guilford Creek from John Parker on 18 January 1679/80 (called Philip Mongon) [WD 1676-90, 185-6]. He and his wife Mary died before 15 June 1700 when their estate, consisting of livestock, household goods, and a sword, was sold to pay their creditors [DW&c 1692-1707, 262; OW&c 1698-1710, 44]. Their children were

      i.   Philip^3, born about 1690, the twelve or thirteen year-old "Negro" son of Philip Mongom bound by the Northampton County court to his grandmother Mary Mongom until the age of twenty-one on 1 March 1702/3 [OW&c 1698-1710, 126-7]. He was granted administration on the estate of William **Harmon** on 12 January 1725/6 when William's orphans Edward and Jane **Harmon** chose him as their guardian [Orders 1722-9, 225]. He was taxable in Abraham Bowker's household in 1723, head of his own household in 1726 with Edmund and Jean **Harmon**, and taxable with his wife Dinah Mongon and (her sister?) Jane **Harmon** in 1727 [Bell, *Northampton County Tithables*, 102, 119]. He made a 5 January 1727/8 will, proved a few days later on 9 January, by which he left all his estate and a "Negro girl named Jane Harman" until she arrived at lawful age to his wife Dinah [WD 1725-33, 102, 106]. Dinah was head of a household in 1728 with Jean **Harmon**. Dinah married Richard **Malavery/ Munlavery** about a year later. In one list for 1729 she was called Dinah Mongom when she and Jean **Harmon** were in Richard ___ery's household, and in another list for 1729 she was called Dinah **Malavery** when she and Jane were tithable in Richard **Malavery**'s household. Richard and Dinah were tithables in 1731 but were not taxed again in any of the surviving lists [Bell, *Northampton County Tithables*, 169, 201, 221]. They probably moved to Somerset County, Maryland where Thomas **Malavery** was a taxable in 1743 [List of Taxable Persons].

ii. Mary, born about 1691, daughter of Philip Mongom, twelve years old on 29 December 1702 when she consented to her indenture to George Corbin in Northampton County court on 29 January 1704/5. And she consented to her indenture on 29 January 1704/5 to Thomas Roberts who obliged himself to give her a two-year-old heifer and new clothing when she came of age [OW&c 1698-1710, 122, 215]. She was tithable in Thomas Savage's household in 1724 [Bell, *Northampton County Tithables*, 66] and was presented by the grand jury of Northampton County on 11 May 1725 for having a bastard child. On 12 August 1725 the court excused Captain Thomas Savage from paying her fine because he had given due notice that she was out of the county [Orders 1722-29, 181, 189, 202, 387].

iii. Jane, born about 1693, the nine-year-old "Negro" daughter of Philip Mongom, "free Negro," deceased, bound apprentice to George Corbin at her own request on 29 December 1702 [OW&c 1698-1710, 122].

iv. Esther, born say 1698, chose her guardian in Northampton County court in 1714 [Orders 1711-16, 155]. She was tithable in John and Henry Smaw's households from 1724 to 1727, in the household of Jean **Left** (**Webb**) in 1729, and in Thomas **Drighouse**'s household in 1731. She probably married Henry **Stephens**, Thomas **Drighouse**'s neighbor, the Esther **Stephens** tithable in Henry's household from 1737 to 1744 [Bell, *Northampton County Tithables*, 72, 103, 119, 167, 226, 266].

MONOGGIN FAMILY

Members of the Monoggin family in Gloucester County were

i. Samuel, born say 1758, a soldier in the Revolution from Gloucester County [Jackson, *Virginia Negro Soldiers*, 29]. He was head of a Petsworth Parish, Gloucester County household of 5 free persons in 1783 (called Samuel Menoggin) [VA:53], and was taxable in Ware Parish, Gloucester County, on 4 horses in 1783 and 2 horses in 1785 (called Samuel Menorgan), taxable from 1786 to 1791 (called Samuel Nogin/ Noggin): taxable on 2 slaves in 1786, a slave in 1789, and taxable on a horse in 1790 and 1791. He was called Samuel Morgan negro in 1806 and 1809, Samuel Monoggon mul° in 1814, Samuel Morgan negroe in 1815 and Samuel Monoggin from 1816 to 1820 when he was taxable in the "List of Mulattos and Free negroes" [PPTL, 1782-99; 1800-20]. He was head of a Gloucester County household of 3 "other free" in 1810 (called Sam Manoggin) [VA:409a] and 3 "free colored" in 1820 [VA:192]. From 1807 to 1813 he was called "Samuel Morgan, Negro" or "Samuel Morgan mul°" when he was taxable in Gloucester County on 60 acres of forest land called "Mulattoe Town." In 1814 he was called "Samuel Monoggin negro" when he transferred 15 acres of this land to "George Noggins, mul°, by deed recorded in Gloucester Court office" [Land Tax 1782-1820]. He may have been the ancestor of a slave named Samuel Noggin who was freed by Robert Richeson by deed recorded in York County on 20 October 1794 [Orders 1788-95, 662].

ii. Jesse, born before 1770, a "mulo." taxable in Gloucester County from 1809 to 1820, listed in 1813 with his wife Cate, a "negroe," over the age of 45 in 1815 [PPTL, 1800-20]. He was head of a Gloucester County household of 3 "free colored" in 1820 [VA:192].

    iii.   George, born before 1770, called George Noggins in 1814 when he was taxable on 15 acres in Gloucester County which had been transferred to him by Samuel Monoggin [Land Tax 1782-1820]. He was taxed in the "List of Mulattos and Free negroes" from 1815 to 1820, called George Monoggon (over the age of 45 in 1815) [PPTL, 1800-20]. He was head of a Gloucester County household of 4 "free colored" in 1820 [VA:192].

MONTH FAMILY

1.   Mary[1] Month, born say 1690, was a free Indian whose son Henry was baptized in Christ Church Parish, Middlesex County, on 14 April 1717. She was called Mary Moneth in Middlesex County court on 7 April 1719 when the court ruled for the defendant in her petition against Jacob Rice. Mary alleged that the ruling was contrary to evidence, but the court was divided over whether she should have a new trial [Orders 1710-21, 421, 424, 431, 434, 435, 439]. She was the mother of

2   i.   ?Sarah, born say 1714.
3   ii.   ?Susannah[1], born say 1717.
      iii.   Henry[1], born 24 February 1717/8, baptized 14 April 1718 in Christ Church Parish, died 14 November 1718 and was buried the same day [NSCDA, *Parish Register of Christ Church*, 99, 175].

2.   Sarah Month, born say 1714, was a "free Indian" living in Spotsylvania County on 7 April 1742 when the court ordered the churchwardens of St. George Parish to bind out her children Robin, Nat and Harry because she was neglecting to bring them up [Orders 1740-2, 165]. She was the mother of

      i.   Robin, born say 1734, called Robert Month in June 1765 when John Downer sued him for debt in Caroline County court. The sheriff attached some of his effects to pay the debt. In August 1771 his estate was attached to pay a debt to Thomas Pennington. On 1 July 1774 he was tried for breaking into the house of Nathaniel Holloway and stealing cloth, but the court ruled that the evidence was not sufficient to subject him to further trial [Orders 1765-7, 81, 186, 344; 1767-70, 7; 1770-2, 280; 1772-6, 14, 210, 265, 414, 516, 564].
      ii.   Nat, born say 1736.
      iii.   Harry[2], born say 1738.

3.   Susannah[1] Month, born say 1717, (no race indicated) petitioned the Spotsylvania County court for her freedom from Larkin Chew on 2 May 1738. On 1 August 1738 the court ruled that she was free and ordered Chew to pay her five shillings for one month's pay. On 7 October 1740 the court called her "Indian Sue" when she was added to the list of Larken Chew's tithables. She was a "free Indian" living in Spotsylvania County on 6 May 1760 when the court ordered her "free Mulatto" children Ambrose and Mary bound out as apprentices to Larken Chew, Gent. [Orders 1738-40, 6, 15, 17; 1740-2, 104; 1755-65, 158; 17]. She was the mother of

4   i.   Ambrose, born say 1750.
5   ii.   Mary[2], born say 1752.
      iii.   ?Susannah[2], born say 1754, called "Susannah Month alias **Mann**" on 5 September 1789 when she testified in Spotsylvania County court that a slave belonging to Spilsbe Coleman named Gimboes Sam broke into the house of James and William Month and raped her on the night of 27 August 1789. The court found the slave innocent after hearing Susannah's testimony and the testimony of John Lahone [Minutes 1787-92, 312].
      iv.   ?James, born say 1760, living in Spotsylvania County in August 1789, a "Mul°" taxable in Halifax County, Virginia, from 1794 to 1812

(sometimes called James Munt) [PPTL, 1782-1799, frame 542; 1800-12, frames 199, 328, 529, 810, 1036].

4. Ambrose Month, born say 1750, indentured his children Charity **Grymes Penn**, David **Penn**, and Averilla **Penn** (**Pinn**) to Micajah Poole in Spotsylvania County on 13 February 1779 [DB J:431]. They were called David **Pinn** Month, Charity **Grimes** Pinn **Month** and Averilla **Pinn** Month on 21 December 1780 when the court ordered the churchwardens of Berkeley Parish to bind them out [Orders 1774-82, 151]. The mother of his children was apparently Patsey **Maclin** whose son David **Pinn** received land by the Halifax County, Virginia will of David **Pinn**, Sr. [WB 3:359]. Ambrose received a pension for his services in the Revolution based on his application from Knox County, Tennessee, in 1834. He stated that he was born in Spotsylvania County and was a free man who was part Shawnee and part Negro [National Archives pension file cited by NSDAR, *African American and American Indian Patriots of the Revolutionary War*, 138]. He was the father of
    i.   Charity **Grimes Pinn**, born say 1772.
    ii. David **Pinn**, born say 1774.
    iii. Averilla[1] **Pinn**, born about 1776, an eleven-year-old "bastard" child bound to Micajah Poole in Spotsylvania County on 7 August 1787 [DB L:364].

5. Mary[2] Month, born say 1752, may have been the mother of two "Mulatto" children bound out by the Spotsylvania County court on 21 May 1778. Her children were
    i.   ?Sally, born before 1776, head of a Spotsylvania County household of 5 "free colored" in 1820 [VA:65].
    ii. Jane, born say 1775, a "Mulatto" child ordered bound out by the churchwardens of St. George Parish, Spotsylvania County, on 21 May 1778.
    iii. William, born say 1777, a "Mulatto" child bound out by the churchwardens of St. George Parish, Spotsylvania County, on 21 May 1778 [Orders 1774-82, 90].
6   iv. ?Nancy, born say 1795.

6. Nancy Month, born say 1795, was living in Louisa County on 11 December 1849 when her daughter Avey registered as a "free Negro." Her daughter was
    i.   Avey/ Averilla[2], born about 1817, registered on 11 December 1849: *daughter of Nancy Month both born free, woman of dark complexion, about 5'4-3/4" high, between 31-32 years old, thick lips* [Abercrombie, *Free Blacks of Louisa County*, 77].

MOORE FAMILY

1. Abraham[1] Moore, born say 1665, was one of the "Negroes" taxable in Robert Caufield's Lawnes Creek Parish, Surry County, Virginia household from 1683 to 1685. He was called "Abraham a free Negro" in 1686 when he was taxable in Thomas Patridge's household in Lawnes Creek Parish, Surry County, Virginia, with an unnamed "Negro" woman. She was probably "Joy a Negro Woman" who was taxable in Patridge's household in 1685 [*Magazine of Virginia Genealogy*, vol.23, no.1, 38, 43, 50; no. 2, p.58]. Thomas Patridge was the agent for Robert Caufield and Major Allen who purchased goods and a slave on the Island of Barbados in February 1685/6 [Haun, *Surry County Court Records*, IV:623-5]. Abraham was called Abraham Moore in 1687 when he was a "Negro" tithable with Joy in Patridge's household, called "Abraham ye Negro at Mr. Allens quarter" in 1689, tithable at Major Allen's quarter in 1691: "Abraham Moor, Joy a Negroe - 2," and head of his own household

with "Negro Joy" adjacent to Major Allen's tithables from 1693 to 1695. In 1694 Joy was identified as his wife [*Magazine of Virginia Genealogy*, vol. 23, no. 2, p. 65; no. 3, 58, 66; no. 4, 65, 72; vol. 24, no.1, p.70]. On 5 July 1692 the Surry County court ruled that he owed a debt of seven barrels of corn to William Edwards, assignee of William Miles. On 3 January 1692/3 James Dykes sued him for slander, but the court ruled in Abraham's favor. And in November court 1694 he was listed among four residents of Surry County who were paid 200 pounds of tobacco for a wolf's head [Haun, *Surry County Court Records,* V:40, 44, 59, 119]. He may have been the Abraham Moore who sold 100 acres in Beaufort County, North Carolina, on the head of the west branch of Town Creek on 16 February 1716/7. This was part of 320 acres he had purchased from Samuel Oxdale [DB 1:241]. He may have been the father of

2   i.   Keziah, born say 1710.

2.   Keziah Moore, born say 1710, was a "free Negro" taxable, head of a household of herself and two unnamed daughters in the 1755 Beaufort County tax list [SS 837]. In March 1756 she was sued for debt by Robert Peyton in Beaufort County court, but the jury found in her favor in March court 1757 [Minutes 1756-61, 1:2d (March 1756 Appearance Docket no.19); 1:24b (March 1757 Appearance Docket no.5)]. She purchased 30 acres in Beaufort County at a Cypress Landing near John Lesley's on 8 February 1757 [DB 3:299]. The June 1758 Session of the Beaufort County court ordered that:

> a free Negroe Woman named Rachel Blango, another named Sarah Blango the younger, another named Dinah Blango and a Man named Gabe and another Negroe Woman named Bett Moore, another Mary Moore, and Keziah Moore be Summoned to appear at next court to produce a Master for their Children in order they may be bound out as the law directs [Minutes 1756-61, 1:46d].

She was a Beaufort County taxable in 1764, head of a household with John, James, and Penelopy Moore [SS 837]. She sold her Beaufort County land on 28 September 1768 [DB 4:239] and was a Craven County taxable in 1769, head of a household of 2 "Black" females. Administration on her estate was granted to Robert **Mitchell** on 200 pounds security on 13 June 1775 in Craven County court [Minutes 1772-84, 63].[140] Her children may have been

        i.   Abraham[2], born say 1730, a "free negro" taxed by himself in 1755 in Beaufort County. He and (his brother?) Simon were called "free Negroes" when they purchased 300 acres on the south side of Terts Swamp and Durham's Creek in Beaufort County on 28 March 1758 [DB 3:383]. He was taxable in Craven County in 1769, head of a household of 1 "Black" male and 1 "Black" female and head of a Craven County household of 1 "other free" in 1790 [NC:134]. He may have been the Abraham Moore who married Betsy **Carter** 21 November 1799 Craven County bond, John C. **Stanly** bondsman.[141]

3   ii.   Simon[1], born say 1733, died 1819.
4   iii.   James[1], born say 1735.
5   iv.   Mary, born say 1737.
       v.   William, born say 1738, nearly twenty-one years old in 1758. He was called "a free Negroe" in June 1758 Beaufort County court when he moved by his attorney, Malloy Chauncy, that he could prove that he was twenty-one years old and should be free from his indenture to

---

[140]The same court called him "Robert Mitchell Free Negro" when it ordered that he be exempt from working on roads since he was "upwards of sixty years of age" [Minutes 1772-84, 63, 33c].

[141]See Franklin's *The Free Negro in North Carolina* for details of the life of John C. **Stanly**.

Thomas Crimpen. The court denied his request after checking the record [Minutes 1758-61, 1:46c].

  vi. Susan, born say 1739, a "free Negro" taxable with Mary Moore in Beaufort County in 1755. She was head of a Craven County household of 3 "other free" in 1790 [NC:134].
6 vii. Rachel, born say 1740.
7 viii. John[1], born say 1742.
  ix. Kuffie (free Negro), born say 1750, a "Black" taxable in his own household in 1769.
  x. Penelopy[1], born before 1753, taxable in 1764 in Keziah's Beaufort County household.

3. Simon[1]/ Simeon Moore, born say 1733, was living in Beaufort County when he and (his brother?) Abram, called "free Negroes," purchased 300 acres on the south side of Terts Swamp and Durham's Creek on 28 March 1758 [DB 3:383]. He was called "Simon Moore, a free Neg.," in March 1759 court, when Michael Coutanche had a case against him and Will Peyton for which Coutanche failed to appear [Minutes 1756-61, 2:12c (March 1759 Reference Docket no.31)]. Simon was head of a Craven County household of 1 "Black" male and 2 "Black" females in 1769 and head of a Craven County household of 11 "other free" in 1790 [NC:134]. His 10 October 1819 Craven County will, proved in December 1819, mentioned his wife (unnamed) and children [WB C:189]. His children mentioned in the will were
  i. Simon[2]/ Simeon, born say 1762. On 13 September 1782 he and Benajah Bogey were charged in Craven County court with having joined the British. They were released when they consented to join the Continental Army [Minutes 1779-84, 47b]. He married Mary **Davis** ("widow"), 27 January 1790 Craven County bond, John Moore bondsman. Simon was head of a Jones County household of 5 "other free" in 1810 [NC:270].
  ii. Hardy, born 1776-1794, head of a Lenoir County household of 4 "free colored" in 1820 [NC:295] and 10 in Jones County in 1830 [NC:132].
  iii. Selah, perhaps the Sealy Moore whose fourteen-year-old daughter, Susanna Moore, was bound apprentice to Alexander Reddit by the June 1814 Beaufort County court [Minutes 1809-14, n.p.].
  iv. Abner.
  v. Polly.

4. James[1] Moore, born say 1735, was called "James Moor free negroe" when he was sued by John Barker and Ed Satter in Beaufort County court in March 1756. He lost the case by default when he "made his escape." He was probably the James Moor who was sued by Coleman Roe in the same court. The September 1757 court ruled that a deposition be taken from him in a case against Thomas **Blango**, Jr., and Sarah **Blango** [Minutes 1756-61, 1:3a (Reference Docket no.28), 1:13b (Appearance docket no.22), docket no.47; 1:34c (Dockets no.8 & 9)]. He was taxable in 1764 in Keziah Moore's Beaufort County household, and was a taxable head of his own Craven County household of one "Black" male in 1769 [SS 837]. His 21 May 1793 Bladen County will named Abraham **Freeman** and Abigail **Chavis** as executors [Campbell, *Abstracts of Wills, Bladen County*, 54]. He named his daughters
  i. Eardice.
  ii. Lydia, born before 1776, head of Columbus County household of two "free colored" in 1820 [NC:50].[142]
  iii. Hannah.

---

[142]Columbus County was formed from Bladen and Brunswick Counties in 1808.

5. Mary Moore, born say 1737, was a "free Negro" taxable with Susan Moore in Beaufort County in 1755. The June 1758 Session of the Beaufort County court ordered that she be summoned to appear in the next court with a master for her children to be bound to. She may have been the Mary Moore who was a plaintiff in a Craven court case in August 1759 and January 1761 [Minutes 1756-61, 1:46c, 37b; 1761-2, 92b]. Her children may have been

    i. Lemuel, born 1757, a fourteen-year-old "Free Negroe Boy" ordered bound apprentice to John Davis to be a house carpenter by the Craven County court on 14 December 1771 [Minutes 1767-75, 189b], perhaps the Lamuel Moore who was in Pitt County on 27 July 1791 when he gave John Moye, Esq., his power of attorney to receive his pay for twelve months service in the Continental Line under Captain Anthony Sharpe [*NCGSJ* XIII:237].

    ii. Joseph, born about 1758, "a free born Negroe Boy Aged Sixteen Years," bound an apprentice house carpenter to Nathaniel Scarbrough by the 17 June 1774 Craven County court [Minutes 1772-84, 18d].

    iii. James[2], born say 1764, was probably twenty-one years old on 17 March 1785 when he and James **York** successfully petitioned the Craven County court to release them from their service to James Ellis.[143] The following day General Caswell made an appeal on Ellis' behalf, but the court refused to grant it [Minutes 1784-86, 11c, 12c].

6. Rachel Moore, born say 1740, was probably the Rachel who was taxed in Beaufort County in 1764: "John and Rachel F.N., 2 black tithes" [SS 837]. She apparently married a former slave named Punch (John Punch?) as this would explain the June 1786 Beaufort County court Docket no.41 which records the case of Richard Cogdell against "Old Punch and Rachel Moor."[144] He may have been the Williams Punch (Williams' Punch, the former slave of the Williams family?) who was taxable on an assessment of 230 pounds in Beaufort County in 1779 [*NCGSJ* XV:143 (LP.30.1)]. This may have been an assessment on the 213 acres on Blounts Creek which was patented by Rachel Moore according to a Moore family Beaufort County deed of 7 January 1811 [DB 9:14]. Rachel Moore was head of a Beaufort County household of 2 "other free" in 1800 [NC:15]. Rachel and Punch may have been the parents of

8   i. Lucy, born say 1758.
9   ii. John Punch Moore, born say 1760.
    iii. Giles[1], born before 1776, head of a Beaufort County household of 6 "other free" as Giles **Punch** in 1800 [NC:15], 6 in 1810 (as Giles Moore) [NC:118], and head of a Beaufort County household of 5 "free colored" as Giles Moore in 1820 [NC:27].

7. John[1] Moore, born say 1742, was called "John Moor a free negroe boy" when he was bound apprentice to Robert Palmer, Esq., in Beaufort County court on

---

[143]James **York** was head of a Craven County household of 1 "other free" in 1790 [NC:131].

[144]The case against "Old Punch" and Rachel Moore was decided for the plaintiff for one penny in September 1786 Court [Minutes 1785-86, June Reference Docket no.41; September Reference Docket no.20]. The 1744-45, 1756-61 and 1785-86 records are among the few surviving eighteenth century court minutes and dockets for Beaufort County. The name Punch suggests some connection between the free Moore family of Beaufort and the James family of Bertie County. David **James** of Bertie County was a defendant in a December 1757 Beaufort County Court case (called "David James, free negro") which was settled in March 1758 [Minutes 1756-61, 1:39d, 43b (docket no.26)]. Andrew and Ann **James** of Bertie County had a son named Punch born about 1758 [Haun, *Bertie County Court Minutes*, IV:157].

December 1757 on the motion of Coleman Roe [Minutes 1756-61, 1:37b].[145]
He was taxable in 1764 in Keziah Moore's Beaufort County household [SS
837]. He was called "John Moore free Negro" when he was acquitted of an
unspecified charge in the January 1762 Craven County court [Minutes 1761-2,
64a]. And he was called "John Moore A free Negroe" when he purchased 100
acres in Craven County by deed proved in April 1763 [Minutes 1762-66, 13d].
He was called a cooper in this deed which was for 100 acres on Batchelor's
Creek [DB 11:59]. He was a taxable head of a Craven County household of
a "Black" male and a "Black" female in 1769 and head of a Craven County
household of 12 "other free" in 1790 [NC:134]. On 22 November 1792 he
petitioned the General Assembly for permission to liberate his children who
were "illegitimate being born of a negro woman slave belonging to himself"
because he had worked for fifty years to acquire a small amount of property
and wished to pass it on to his children [Schweninger, *Race, Slavery and Free
Black Petitions*, no. 11279207]. He named his children in his 1816 Craven
County will and left his grandsons, children of his son John Moore, 150 acres
with their father having a life right in their part [WB C:120]. His children
named in the will were

- 10   i.   John[3], born say 1769.
-       ii.   Edward.
-      iii.   Sarah, born say 1775, wife of James **Morgan**, head of a Craven County household of 1 "other free" in 1790 [NC:134] and 8 "free colored" in 1820 [NC:59].
-      iv.   June, born say 1778, wife of William **Dove**, head of a Craven County household of 8 "free colored" in 1820 [NC:65].
-       v.   Simon[3].

8.   Lucy Moore, born say 1758, alias Lucy **Punch**, was head of a Beaufort
County household of 5 "other free" (as Lucy **Punch**) in 1800 [NC:15], 3 in
1810 (as Lucy Moore) [NC:113], and one "free colored" in 1820 (as Lucy
Moore) [NC:28]. Her children were identified in the 23 August 1823 will of
her son Willowby who named his mother "Lewsea" and siblings: William,
John, Giles, and Peggy [Beaufort County Genealogical Society, *Will Abstracts*,
225]. Lucy's children were

-       i.   William, born before 1776, head of a Beaufort County household of 5 "other free" in 1800 [NC:13], 5 in 1810 [NC:113], and 8 "free colored" in 1820 [NC:27]. His land on the south side of Round Pole Branch was mentioned in the 17 May 1803 Beaufort County will of Catherine **Healy/ Ealey**.
-      ii.   Sarah, head of a Beaufort County household of 7 "other free" in 1810 (called Sally Moore) [NC:118].
-      iii.   John[4], born 1776-94, head of a Beaufort County household of 5 "other free" in 1810 [NC:114] and 9 "free colored" in 1820 [NC:27]. He was probably the John Moore who was married to Elsey **Carter** on 4 November 1821 when they sold Craven County land she inherited from her father George **Carter** [DB 43:82].
-      iv.   Giles[2], born 1776-94, head of a Beaufort County household of 4 "free colored" in 1820 [NC:27].
- 11   v.   Willowby, born 1776-94.
- 12   vi.   Margaret/Peggy, born 1776-94.

9.   John Punch Moore, born say 1760, was head of a Beaufort County household
of 5 "other free" in 1790 (called John P. Moore) [NC:126] and 9 in 1800
(called John Moore) [NC:9]. He may have been the John Moore who gave

[145]Coleman Roe was a witness to the 8 February 1757 Beaufort County deed to Keziah Moore for 30 acres [DB 3:299].

Thomas Armstrong his power of attorney to collect his pay due for nine months service as a soldier in the Continental Line in Beaufort County on 5 June 1792 [*NCGSJ* XIII:236]. Property called "the John P. Moore Land and Plantation" was mentioned in Alexander Redditt's will proved in June Term 1814 Beaufort County court [Camin, *Beaufort Orphans Book A*, 81]. John's widow was most likely Mary Punch Moore who was granted administration on his Beaufort County estate in the September 1809 session of Beaufort County court on a bond of 150 pounds. She exhibited the account of sales in the March 1811 Session [Minutes 1809-14, first page of September 1809 Minutes; March 1811 Session, no page number]. She was called Mary Moore, head of a Beaufort County household of 10 "other free" in 1810 [NC:113]. One of their children may have been

    i.   Anthony, head of a Beaufort County household of 6 "other free" and 3 slaves in 1810 [NC:114] and 8 "free colored" in 1820 [NC:27].

10. John³ Moore, born say 1769, was head of Craven County household of 2 "other free" in 1790 [NC:134]. His children mentioned in his father's 1816 Craven County will [WB C:120] were

    i.   Amos.
    ii. Abraham³.
    iii. Nathan.

11. Willowby Moore, born 1776-94, purchased 183 acres on Nevil's Creek in Beaufort County from John Gray Blount of the town of Washington on 1 July 1801 and purchased 71 acres from Sarah and Giles Moore on 7 January 1811 (their 2/6 share of 213 acres) [DB 2-3:127; 9:14]. He was head of a Beaufort County household of 3 "other free" and 1 slave in 1810 [NC:114] and 6 "free colored" in 1820 [NC:27]. His 23 August 1823 Beaufort County will was proved in February 1824 by Lodowick Redditt, a witness to the will. Willowby mentioned his sister Peggy Moore; brothers John, William and Giles Moore; mother Lucy Moore; gave his wife Amy Moore 50 acres; and left the remainder of his land to his daughter Mary Ann **Keis** [Beaufort County Genealogical Society, *Will Abstracts*, 225]. His daughter was

    i.   Mary Ann **Keis**, head of a Beaufort County household of 4 "other free" in 1820 [NC:23].[146]

12. Margaret/Peggy Moore, born 1776-94, was head of a Beaufort County household of 10 "other free" in 1810 [NC:113] and 8 "free colored" in 1820 [NC:27]. Her children were

    i.   Patience, born about 1806, the eight-year-old daughter of Margaret Moore bound apprentice to Alexander Reddit by the June 1814 Beaufort County court [Minutes 1809-14, n.p.].

Wives and Children of Unnamed Members of the Moore Family
13. Betty **Sutton**, born say 1720, was a "free negro" tithable in 1755 and head of her own Beaufort County household [SS 837]. She may have been the Bett Moore who was ordered by the June 1758 Beaufort County court to produce a master for her children [Minutes 1756-61, 1:46d]. She may have had a child by a member of the Moore family since a young woman called "Betty Moore Alˢ Sutton" appeared in Craven County court on 10 April 1762 [Minutes 1761-62, 80b]. Her daughter was most likely

14   i. Betty Moore, born about 1738.

---

[146]Other members of the family were Amey **Keaes** (head of a Beaufort County household of 2 "other free" in 1810 [NC:114]), Clary **Keaes** (head of a Beaufort County household of 5 "other free" in 1810 [NC:114]), and Silvy **Keais** (head of a Beaufort County household of 4 "other free" [NC:127]).

14. Betty Moore, alias **Sutton**, born about 1738, was called "Betty a Negro Servant to Peter Conway" when she was ordered by the 10 October 1761 Craven County court to serve Conway another year because she had a child during her indenture. And she was called "Betty Moore Al^s Sutton" when her son Jack was bound out on 10 April 1762, and called "Betty Moore, a Negro Wench" on 9 April 1763 when she was ordered to serve an additional year of her indenture to Peter Conway because she had a child Molly during her indenture [Minutes 1761-62, 53a, 80b; 1762-66, 14d]. Betty's children were

    i. John^2/ Jack Moore, born about July 1761, nine-month-old "Base free Born Negro Son to Betty Moore Al^s Sutton," ordered bound to Peter Conway on 10 April 1762 by the Craven County court [Minutes 1761-62, 80b]. He was called John Moore in Craven County court on 14 September 1777, a thirteen-year-old (no race indicated) bound as an apprentice blacksmith to James Saunders [Minutes 1772-78, 24a]. He was head of a Craven County household of 2 "other free" in 1790 [NC:134].

    ii. Molly Moore, born about February 1763, two months old on 9 April 1763 [Minutes 1762-66, 14d]. She was head of a Beaufort County household of 7 "other free" in 1810 [NC:113].

    iii. ?Peter **Sutton**, head of a Beaufort County household of one "other free" in 1790 [NC:127].

    iv. ?Fab **Sutton**, head of a Carteret County household of 7 "other free" in 1800.

    v. ?Peggy **Sutton**, head of a Beaufort County household of 6 "other free" in 1810 [NC:115].

15. Sarah **Blango** Moore, born about 1740, was taxable as Sarah Blango Jr., "free Negro," in Rachel **Blango**'s 1755 Beaufort County household [SS 837]. The 9 October 1778 issue of the North Carolina Gazette of New Bern carried an order to the sheriff to search for her stolen children:

> she was last night robbed of her own children, by three men in disguise, one a boy about six years old named Ambrose, the other a girl named Rose, of the same age, they being twins... [Fouts, NC Gazette of New Bern, I:80-1].

Her children were

    i. Ambrose Moore, born about 1772, married Hannah **Howard**, 24 December 1803 Carteret County bond with Jacob **Moore** bondsman and second, Polly **Carter**, 29 December 1804 Craven County bond with Jacob **Moore** bondsman. He was head of a Craven County household of 2 "free colored" in 1820 [NC:67]. On 4 November 1821 he and his wife Polly sold land in Craven County which she inherited from her father George **Carter** [DB 43:82].

    ii. Rose, born about 1772, perhaps the Rose **Carter**, born 1776-94, who was head of a Carteret County household of 3 "free colored" in 1820 [NC:123].

    iii. ?Abel, born before 1776, head of Craven County household of Craven County household of 6 "free colored" in 1820 [NC:67]. On 4 November 1821 he and his wife Elizabeth **Carter** sold land in Craven County which she inherited from her father George **Carter** [DB 43:82].

16. Catherine **Ealey**, born say 1755, was head of a Beaufort County household of 3 "other free" in 1790 (called Catherine Healy) [NC:125], 3 in 1800 (called Katy Ely) [NC:7], and 3 in 1810 (called Cate Ele) [NC:113]. She (or her husband) was probably a descendant of John **Eley** who was presented by the 21 November 1758 Surry County, Virginia court for not listing his tithable "Mulatto" wife [Orders 1757-64, 135]. Her 17 May 1803 Beaufort County will

(called Cathron Ealey) left 100 acres on the south side of Round Pole Branch adjoining William Moore to her daughter Philpiny (Penelopy) Moore, 100 acres to her daughter Betsy Moore, and named her grandchild Hardy Moore.[147]   Penelopy and Betsy were named as her executors [Camin, *Beaufort Orphans Book A,* 67]. Her children named in the will were

    i.   Mary, "eldest daughter."

    ii. Penelopy[2].

    iii. Betsy, "youngest daughter," born before 1776, head of a Beaufort County household of 5 "free colored" in 1820 [NC:28].

MORDICK FAMILY

1. Benjamin[1] Mordick, born say 1705, was a "Mullatto Boy" freed by the 26 January 1726 Hyde County will of Sarah White. She gave him her livestock and her plantation on the Machepunga River "till the leas is out if he think fitt" [SS Wills]. He may have been married to a white woman since the June 1755 Hyde County court ruled that only his male dependents were tithable, but the September 1755 court reversed this ruling and required him to pay tax on his female dependents as well. He purchased two brass skimmers and a pewter dish at the sale of the estate of James Batchelor on 13 and 14 March 1761 [Haun, *Hyde County Court Minutes,* I:207, 213; II:218]. The Hyde County court recommended to the State Legislature that he and Michael Mordick (both Mullatos) be exempt from payment of tax on 25 October 1769 [Saunders, *Colonial Records of North Carolina,* VIII:109]. He named his children in his 14 August 1776 will [RW 1/481]. He left his land to be divided amongst his sons Benjamin and John, gave a church bible to his daughter Lydia, and named daughters: Mariam, Ruth, Rachel, Bridget, and Michael. His children were

    i.   Levy, born say 1729, recorded his livestock mark in the June 1754 session of the Hyde County court. He purchased 200 acres from John Harvey by deed proved in March 1757 court, purchased a cow and calf at the sale of John Harvey's estate, and purchased 300 acres from Richard Harvey by deed proved in September 1760 Hyde County court [Haun, *Hyde County Court Minutes,* I:186; II:2, 41, 206]. He was not mentioned in his father's will because he predeceased him. His 21 April 1771 Hyde County will (which he wrote himself) was proved December Term the same year. He left 200 acres called "Strides(?) nack" and 100 acres on North Harbor to his brother Benjamin, a long list of items to his sister Bridget, and mentioned sisters Michel and Letitia, and John Mordick. His land on "Torkil nake" was to be sold to pay his debts and pay for schooling for his sister Bridget's children. His father and brother Benjamin were executors [RW 1/25].

    ii. Lydia, born say 1731, recorded her livestock mark in the September 1754 Hyde County court [Haun, *Hyde County court Minutes,* I:187].

    iii. Bridget, born say 1732, recorded her livestock mark in the September 1754 Hyde County court. She received a long list of items by the 1771 will of her brother Levi. He also provided schooling for her unnamed children.

    iv. Shadrack, born say 1734, recorded his livestock mark in the March 1755 Hyde County court [Haun, *Hyde County Court Minutes,* I:203]. He was not mentioned in Benjamin's will, so he probably predeceased him.

    v. Benjamin[2], received three hundred acres by the 1771 will of his brother Levy. His Hyde County estate was administered in 1778 [SS 945].

    vi. Michel, a daughter.

---

[147]Harden Moore was head of a Lenoir County household of 4 "free colored" in 1820 [NC:295].

vii. Letitia.

viii. Mariam.

ix. Ruth.

x. Rachel, perhaps the Rachel Morrick who was head of a Craven County household of 4 "free colored" in 1820 [NC:69]. There was also a Vensiter Morrick, born before 1776, head of a Craven County household of one "free colored" woman in 1820 [NC:76].

xi. John.

MORGAN FAMILY

1. Elizabeth Morgan, born say 1685, was a white servant of Henry Ashton, Gent., on 25 July 1705 when the Westmoreland County, Virginia court convicted her of having a "mulatto" child [Orders 1698-1705, 268]. She was probably the ancestor of

    i. Anthony, born say 1705, living in Richmond County, Virginia, in May 1736 when his white servant, James Talent, complained that he was being misused by his master and that his master was a "Mulatto." The court ruled that Sallent be immediately discharged from his service [Orders 10:394].

    ii. Thomas[1], born about 1731, a soldier from Suffolk, Virginia, in the French and Indian War who deserted from the Virginia Regiment in September 1757 and was described as: *age 26, 5'7", mulatto* [*Magazine of Virginia Genealogy* 31:96].

Several members of the Morgan family, all born about 1740, perhaps brothers and sisters or cousins of Anthony or Thomas Morgan, were living in North Carolina between 1760 and 1770. They were

2   i. Cerra (Sarah?), born say 1737, mother of a "Mulatto" bound in Edgecombe County in 1763.

3   ii. John[1], born say 1740, purchased land in Northampton County in April 1762.

4   iii. William[1], born say 1741, purchased land in Edgecombe County in September 1762.

5   iv. Lucy, born say 1743, a "Mulatto" bound apprentice in Edgecombe County in 1758.

6   v. George, born circa 1745, a Craven County taxable in 1769.

2. "Cerra" (Sarah?) Morgan, born say 1737, was living in Edgecombe County on 25 January 1763 when her daughter Mary, "a Mulatto girl," was bound out [Minutes 1759-64, 51]. Cerra was the mother of

    i. Mary, a "Mulatto girl" ordered bound to John Fort by the 25 January 1763 session of the Edgecombe County court. She may have been the same Mary Morgan, born about 1753, sixteen-year-old "Mulatto," who was ordered bound to Samuel Henderson, Jr., in Granville County on 16 July 1769 [Owen, *Granville County Notes*].

7   ii. ?Elizabeth, born say 1755.

    iii. ?Patience, born before 1776, head of a Franklin County household of 8 "other free" in 1810 [NC:826], 11 "free colored" in Halifax County in 1820 [NC:156], and 3 "free colored" in Halifax in 1830.

3. John[1] Morgan, born say 1740, purchased 200 acres in Northampton County, North Carolina, on 6 April 1762. He and his wife Barbary sold 45 acres of this land near the county line (Greensville County, Virginia) to (their son?)

John Morgan, Jr., in March 1785, proved by the oath of Mark Morgan.[148]
He and Barbary sold a further 66 acres adjoining this land on 3 August 1786.
James **Haithcock** was witness to this deed [DB 3:245; 9:264; 10:297]. John
Morgan, Sr., was head of a Northampton County household of one free male
and 4 free females in Captain Williams' District for the state census of 1786,
4 "other free" in 1790 [NC:72], and 6 "other free" and 4 slaves in 1810
[NC:736]. His 11 October 1820 Northampton County will, proved June 1821,
left all his estate to his unnamed wife, to be divided equally between his
children. William Fox was executor [WB 3:250]. His children mentioned in
his will were

    i.   Joseph, born say 1760.
8   ii. John³, Jr., born say 1762.
   iii. William², born say 1764, cosigner of a Northampton County deed with
       John Morgan on 3 March 1792. He was head of a Northampton County
       household of 3 "other free" in 1790 [NC:72] and 6 in 1810 [NC:736].
   iv. ?Mark, not mentioned in the will, head of a Halifax County household
       of 1 free male in district 2 in 1786 for the state census and 7 "other
       free" in Northampton County in 1790 [NC:72]. He received a deed of
       gift for 59 acres near the county line from John Morgan, Senior, on 3
       March 1792. He may have been the Mark Morgan who married
       Elizabeth Good, 5 March 1793 Warren County bond, Daniel **Mills**
       bondsman. He and his wife Elizabeth sold their Northampton County
       land to William Fox, Junr., on 2 December 1796 [DB 9:263; 10:282].
    v. Joshua.
9   vi. Matthew, born say 1770.
   vii. Benjamin.
  viii. Daniel.
   ix. Archibles.

4.   William¹ Morgan, born say 1741, purchased 100 acres on the south bank of
White Oak Swamp at the mouth of Cabin Branch in Edgecombe County on 4
September 1762 and sold this land without a dower release on 19 April 1774.
He purchased 107 acres adjoining this land on the south side of Fishing Creek
on 3 May 1773, purchased another 240 acres on Long Branch on 23
November 1773, and purchased 140 acres in this same area from William
Jackson on 12 October 1774. He and his wife Sarah sold 300 acres of their
land to Jonas Shivers (**Chavis**?) on 22 November 1779 and 50 acres on 13
August 1783 [DB 1:602; 2, 72, 73, 87; 3:362, 501; 4:27]. His 10 November
1794 Edgecombe County will, proved February 1795, left all his land to his
son William, and named his grandson David Morgan, and daughters Martha
Price and Keddy **Jenkins**. William, David, and Isaac Morgan were buyers at
the estate sale proved in August court 1796. His children were

    i. William³, born say 1775, a "Mulatto" head of an Edgecombe County
      household of 5 "other free" in 1800 [NC:223] and 2 "free colored"
      males in 1820 [NC:126].
    ii. Martha **Price**.
   iii. Keddy (Kitty) **Jenkins**.

5.   Lucy Morgan, "a Mulatto girl" born say 1743, was ordered bound to William
Lane by the 23 February 1758 session of the Edgecombe County court
[Minutes 1757-59, 15]. Four years later the court ordered her and her son Jack
bound to Robert Young [Minutes 1759-64, 27]. Her children were

    i. John²/ Jack, born say 1760, ordered bound with his mother to Robert
      Young by the Edgecombe County court in September 1762. He may

---

[148]This land was located in the northeast corner of Northampton County where it borders Halifax
County and the Virginia counties of Brunswick and Greensville.

have been the John (Moore) Morgan who was head of an Orange County household of 4 "other free" and one white woman in 1800 [NC:589].

ii. ?Isaac, born about 1766, sixteen years old in 1782 when he was a "Mulatto" listed among the Drafts & Substitutes from Edgecombe County in the Revolutionary War [*The North Carolinian* VI:752]. He was a buyer at the sale of William[1] Morgan's estate proved in August 1796 Edgecombe County court. He was counted as white in 1790, head of an Edgecombe County household of 3 males and 2 females [NC:57] and was a "Mulatto" head of an Edgecombe County household of 6 "other free" and one white woman in 1800 [NC:223].

6. George[1] Morgan, born circa 1745, was head of a Craven County household of 2 Black males and 2 Black females in 1769 [SS 837]. His children were probably those counted as "other free" in Craven County and the adjoining counties. They were

    i. Elisha, head of a Jones County household of 4 "other free" in 1790 [NC:144]. Perhaps Rebecca Morgan was his widow. She was head of a Lenoir County household of 5 "other free" in 1800 [NC:17] and 5 "other free" in Jones County in 1810 [NC:270].

    ii. James, head of a Craven County household of 1 "other free" in 1790 [NC:134] and 8 "free colored" in 1820 [NC:59]. His wife Sarah **Moore** was mentioned in the 1816 Craven County will of her father John **Moore** [WB C:120].

    iii. Isham, head of a Lenoir County household of 7 "other free" in 1810 [NC:292].

    iv. Jesse, head of a Lenoir County household of 6 "other free" in 1810 [NC:292] and 8 "free colored" in Craven County in 1820 [NC:62].

7. Elizabeth Morgan, born say 1755, was living in Edgecombe County in 1774 when the October session of the county court ordered her "base born child" Selah bound out [Minutes 1772-84, first page of October 1774 Minutes]. She may have been the Betsy Morgan who was head of an Orange County household of 8 "free colored" in 1820 [NC:A:400]. Her children were

    i. Selah, born about 1771, bound to James Brown to learn carding and spinning (no race stated).

10   ii. ?Thomas[2], born say 1773.

8. John[3] Morgan, Jr., born say 1762, was head of a Northampton County household of 1 male 21-60, 2 males less than 20 or 60 plus, and 1 female in Captain William's District for the 1786 state census. He was head of a Halifax County household of 16 "other free" in 1790 [NC:64] and 3 in 1800 [NC:328]. He was the father of

    i. ?Fanny, born before 1776, head of a Halifax County household of 6 "free colored" in 1820 [NC:157].

    ii. ?Gardner, born before 1776, head of a Halifax County household of 9 "free colored" in 1820 [NC:158].

    iii. ?Randall, born before 1776, head of a Halifax County household of 10 "free colored" in 1820 [NC:157].

    iv. Lucy, born about 1813 in Halifax County, married (William) Riley **Jones**, 26 February 1838 Robeson County bond, and registered as a forty-year-old "free Negro," in Bartholomew County, Indiana, on 22 August 1853. According to her death certificate in Washtenaw County, Michigan, she was the daughter of John Morgan, born 16 March 1807, died 19 February 1907 [Vol.3, p.171, #429].

9. Matthew[1] Morgan, born say 1770, was head of a Halifax County household of 13 "other free" in 1810 [NC:36], 11 "free colored" in Robeson County in

1820 [NC:323], and 10 in Robeson County in 1840 [NC:201]. He sold 100 acres in Robeson County on the east side of First Swamp to (his son?) George Morgan on 28 November 1835 [DB W:290]. His children were most likely

    i.   Matthew², born say 1805, married Nancy **Bass**, 12 February 1828 Robeson County bond, Henry Parker bondsman. He was head of a Robeson County household of 5 "free colored" in 1830. He purchased 200 acres on both sides of the first branch of Wilkinson's Swamp from George Morgan on 29 October 1839 [DB BB:814].

    ii. Lewis, born say 1808, head of a Cumberland County household of 4 "free colored" in 1820 [NC:208]. He married (second?) Kitty **Goins**, 29 January 1829 Robeson County bond, Findl **Ivy** bondsman.

    iii. George², born about 1810, married Delila **Bass**, 6 June 1836 Robeson County bond, Lewis Morgan bondsman. They moved to Canada about 1853, to Haiti in 1861, and returned to the United States (Maryland) in 1868.[149] In 1880 they were in Pilson Township, Charlevoix County, Michigan [Census 55/3/49].

10. Thomas² Morgan, born say 1773, was head of an Orange County household of 5 "other free" and one white woman in 1800 [NC:589]. Perhaps those counted as "other free" in Orange County were his children. They were

    i.   Thomas³, Jr., head of an Orange County household of 4 "other free" and one white woman in 1800 [NC:587] and 9 "free colored" in 1820 [NC:318].

    ii. Paul, head of an Orange County household of 2 "other free" in 1800 [NC:587].

MORRIS FAMILY

Norfolk County
1. Ann Morris, born say 1673, the (white) servant of Isabella Spratt, was living in Norfolk County on 16 March 1690/1 when the court ordered that she serve her mistress an additional two years because she "was delivered of a Bastard Child begotten by a negro" [DB 5, pt. 2, 214]. She may have been the ancestor of

    i.   Mary, born say 1750, taxable in the Norfolk County household of John Willoughby, Sr., on the north side of Tanners Creek in 1768 [Wingo, *Norfolk County Tithables, 1766-80*, 74].

Middlesex, Gloucester, Chesterfield, York and Charles City counties
1. Elizabeth¹ Morris, born say 1688, the servant of Francis Weekes, was presented by the grand jury of Middlesex County, Virginia, on 8 January 1705/6 for having a "mulatto bastard child." The court ordered the sheriff to give her twenty-five lashes and ordered the churchwardens of the parish to sell her after she completed her indenture to Weekes. She was presented for the same offense on 7 June 1708 [Orders 1705-10, 19, 28, 177, 182, 185, 188, 196, 203, 212]. She was a "Mulatto Woman" whose son James Morris was baptized in Christ Church Parish, Middlesex County, on 15 March 1705/6 [NSCDA, *Parish Register of Christ Church*, 75, 195, 245]. She was the mother of

2   i.   James¹, born say December 1705.
3   ii. ?Winnifred, born 9 May 1707.

---

[149]The original agreement between the Republic of Haiti and George Morgan's son-in-law is in the possession of Mrs. Maxine (Bass) Collins of Ann Arbor Michigan. William E. Calbert of Washington, D.C., provided the information on George Morgan and Lucy Morgan Jones.

2. James[1] Morris, born say December 1705, was baptized 15 March 1705/6 in Christ Church Parish, Middlesex County [NSCDA, *Parish Register of Christ Church,* 58]. He may have been the father of

4   i.   Thomas[1], born say 1743.
5   ii.   William[1], born say 1745.

3. Winnifred Morris, born 9 May 1707, "a Molatto belonging to Francis Weekes, Jun[r]," was baptized in Christ Church Parish, Middlesex County, on 25 January 1707/8. And she was called a "Mulatto" on 19 December 1740 when she registered the birth of her son George in the same parish. She died on 18 April 1745 [NSCDA, *Parish Register of Christ Church,* 75, 195, 245]. On 3 September 1745 the Middlesex County court ordered the churchwardens of Christ Church Parish to bind out her "two Mulatto children" George and James Morris [Orders 1745-52, 26]. She was the mother of

6   i.   ?Biddy, born say 1722.
       ii.   ?Francis, born say 1731, a "malatto" taxable in Chesterfield County in 1756. He was probably identical to "Frank Malatto" who was taxable in his own household in 1752 [Tax List 1747-1821, frames 11, 26]. He brought a suit against Anthony **Jasper** which was dismissed by the Chesterfield County court in September 1760. He was called a "Mulatto" on 4 December 1767 when he was charged with being a vagrant in Chesterfield County. Edward Cox posted bond for his good behavior [Orders 1759-67, 85; 1767-71, 155]. He was a "yellow" complexioned man born in Henrico County who was living in Petersburg when he was listed in the size roll of troops who enlisted at Chesterfield Courthouse [The Chesterfield Supplement cited by NSDAR, *African American Patriots,* 151]. He may have been the Francis Morris who was taxable in Gloucester County from 1793 to 1800 [PPTL, 1782-99; 1800-20].
7   iii.   George[1], born 19 December 1740.
8   iv.   James[2], born say 1742.

4. Thomas[1] Morris, born say 1743, was head of a Petsworth, Gloucester County household of 7 free persons in 1784 [VA:69]. He was taxable in Gloucester County from 1782 to 1800: listed the same day as Seth, William, Jr., and James Morris in 1789, taxable on 2 tithes in 1796, taxable on a slave in 1798 and 1799, taxable on 3 tithes in 1804 [PPTL 1782-1799; 1800-20], and head of a Gloucester County household of 5 "other free" in 1810 [VA:664]. Betsy **Gladman** was living with him "as a wife" in 1813 [PPTL, 1800-20]. He was the father of

       i.   Thomas[2], born say 1783, "mulatto son of Tho[s]," taxable in Gloucester County in 1804, called "Thomas, Jr., miller," in 1806 and 1807 [PPTL, 1800-20].
       ii.   William[6], born say 1787, "mul[o], son of Tho[s]," taxable in Gloucester County in 1813 [PPTL, 1800-20].
       iii.   Frances, "mul[o], daughter of Tho[s]," taxable in Gloucester County in 1813 [PPTL, 1800-20].
       iv.   Cary, "mul[o], son of Tho[s]," taxable in Gloucester County in 1813 [PPTL, 1800-20].

5. William[1] Morris, born say 1745, was taxable in Gloucester County from 1782 to 1805, listed with 2 "mulatto" tithes in 1802 and 1803 [PPTL 1782-99; 1800-20], taxable on 40 acres in Gloucester County in 1800 [1800 Land Tax List, p.13], and head of a household of 6 "other free" in 1810 [VA:664]. He was called William Morriss, Sen., "mul[o]," in Gloucester County in 1813 when Sarah, a "negroe" was living with him as his wife [PPTL, 1800-20]. He was the father of

    i.   ?William[4], born say 1768, called "William Jr." when he was taxable in Gloucester County from 1789 to 1813, listed with his unnamed wife in 1813 [PPTL, 1800-20].

    ii.   Polly, head of a Gloucester County household of 5 "other free" in 1810 [VA:664]. She was called the "mul° daughter of W[m] Morris Sen[r] when she was listed in 1813 [PPTL, 1800-20].

    iii. ?Grymes, born say 1780, a "mulatto" taxable in Gloucester County from 1801 to 1820 [PPTL, 1800-20].

    iv. ?George[5], born say 1783, a "mulatto" taxable in Gloucester County from 1804 to 1817, listed with his unnamed wife in 1813 [PPTL, 1800-20], head of a Gloucester County household of 6 "other free" in 1810 [VA:664].

    v.   ?Philip, born say 1785, a "mulatto" taxable in Gloucester County from 1806 to 1820, listed with his unnamed wife in 1813 [PPTL, 1800-20].

    vi. ?James[4], born say 1792, called "James Morriss, Jr., mul°," when he was taxable in Gloucester County in 1813 [PPTL, 1800-20].

6.   Biddy Morris, born say 1722, may have been identical to Bidde (no family name), a "Mullatto" child living in Bristol Parish on 24 July 1727 when the court ordered the churchwardens to bind her to Godfrey Ragsdail [Chamberlayn, *Register of Bristol Parish*, 36]. Biddy Morris was living in Chesterfield County on 7 September 1750 when her son Jack (no race indicated) was bound apprentice [Orders 1749-54, 77]. She was the mother of

    i.   Abraham, born say 1745, taxable in Chesterfield County on a horse from 1786 to 1796 and on 2 tithes from 1797 to 1804, taxable on a horse in 1805 [PPTL, 1786-1811, frames 16, 88, 162, 235, 339, 375, 450, 488, 526].

9   ii.   Jack[1], born say 1746.

    iii. ?Matt, born about 1748, registered in Petersburg on 18 August 1794: *a black Man, five feet five and a half inches high, about forty six years old, born free & raised in the county of Chesterfield* [Register of Free Negroes 1794-1819, no. 43].

10   iv. ?Elizabeth[2], born about 1754.

7.   George[1] Morris, born 19 December 1740, was called the son of Winefred Morris, a "free Mullatto," when his birth was registered in Christ Church Parish, Middlesex County. He was taxable on 2 tithes in Gloucester County in 1770 and 1771 [Tax List 1770-1, 99], taxable in Petsworth Parish, Gloucester County, on 2 free tithes and 8 cattle in 1782 and 1784, taxable in Ware Parish in 1785 and 1786, taxable on 3 tithes in 1787, and taxable on himself and (his son?) James Morris in 1788 [PPTL, 1782-99]. He may have been the father of

    i.   Seth, born say 1765, taxable on a horse in Gloucester County from 1789 to 1792 and taxable there from 1793 to 1799 [PPTL 1782-99], jointly taxed with James Morris on a 40 acre plot in Gloucester County from 1797 to 1820 [Land Tax List, 1782-1820], head of a Gloucester County household of 1 "other free" and 2 slaves in 1810 [VA:664], a "mul°" taxable in Gloucester County from 1801 to 1820 [PPTL, 1800-20].

    ii.   James[3], born say 1767, taxable in Gloucester County from 1789 to 1799 [PPTL 1782-99], jointly taxed with Seth Morris on a 40 acre plot in Gloucester County from 1797 to 1820 [Land Tax List, 1782-1820], head of a Gloucester County household of 1 "other free" and 3 slaves in 1810 [VA:664], a "mulatto" taxable from 1804 to 1819, called "James Sr." after 1812, over forty five years of age in 1815 when he was taxable on a slave [PPTL, 1800-20].

    iii. Elizabeth[2], born say 1769, head of a Gloucester County household of 8 "other free" in 1810 [VA:663]. She was called Elizabeth Morriss,

Sen., "mul°," in 1813 when she was head of a Gloucester County household with (her daughter?) Dianna who was over the age of sixteen [PPTL 1800-20].

8. James[2] Morris, born say 1742, was ordered bound apprentice by the churchwardens of Christ Church Parish, Middlesex County, on 3 September 1745 [Orders 1745-52, 26]. He was called "James Morris a free born Negro" by the Richmond County court on 4 February 1754 when it ordered the churchwardens of Lunenburg Parish to bind him to Stuart Redman [Orders 1752-5, 117]. He may have been the James Morris who was head of a Charles City County household of 7 "other free" in 1810 [VA:957]. He was the father of

11   i.   ?George[2], born say 1762.
      ii. ?Charles, born about 1766, a man of color from Charles City County listed in the size roll of troops who enlisted at Chesterfield Courthouse [The Chesterfield Supplement cited by NSDAR, *African American Patriots*, 151]. He was a "Mulatto" taxable in Chesterfield County from 1798 to 1810 [PPTL, 1786-1811, frames 358, 543, 620, 662, 717, 753, 799] and head of a Chesterfield County household of 2 "other free" in 1810 [VA:70/1062]. He obtained a certificate of freedom in Chesterfield County on 8 August 1814: *about forty eight years old, brown complexioned, born free* [Register of Free Negroes 1804-53, no. 224].
      iii. Elvy, "daughter of James Morris," married Philip **Wallace**, 24 March 1815 Charles City County bond [*Wm & Mary Quarterly Historical Papers* Vol. 8, No.3, p.195].

9. Jack Morris, born say 1746, an orphan, no race indicated, was bound apprentice in Chesterfield County on 7 September 1750 [Orders 1749-54, 77]. He was a soldier in the Continental Line on 7 February 1778 when the Chesterfield County court ordered that his wife Mary receive 6 pounds public money [Orders 1774-8, 158]. He may have been the John Morris who was head of a Chesterfield County household of 4 free persons in 1783 [VA:50] and a John Morris was head of a Charles City County household of 5 "other free" in 1810 [VA:942]. His wife may have been the Mary Morris (born about 1746) who registered in Petersburg on 19 August 1794: *a brown Mulatto woman, five feet one inches high, forty eight years old, born free & raised in Chesterfield County* [Register of Free Negroes 1794-1819, no. 57]. They may have been the parents of
      i.   Peter, a "free negro" taxable in Henrico County in 1790 [PPTL B, p.2].
      ii. Patsy, born about 1776, registered in Petersburg on 25 August 1794: *a dark brown Mulatto woman, five feet three and a half inches high, eighteen years old, born free & raised in Chesterfield County* and registered again on 14 August 1800 [Register of Free Negroes 1794-1819, nos. 85, 166].
      iii. Arthur, born say 1777, a "Mulatto" laborer who was taxable in Chesterfield County from 1798 to 1810 [PPTL, 1786-1811, frames 358, 470, 753, 799, 824].
      iv. Obedience, born about 1778, registered in Petersburg on 18 August 1800: *a dark brown, spare made Mulatto woman, five feet six inches high, twenty two, short bushy hair, born free and raised in the County of Chesterfield* [Register of Free Negroes 1794-1819, no. 190].

10. Elizabeth[2] Morris, born about 1754, was "a poor child" who was bound out in Chesterfield County in March 1769 [Orders 1767-71, 266]. On 2 April 1779 the court ordered the churchwardens to bind out her daughter Nancy to Daniel McCallum, and on 6 June 1782 the court ordered the churchwardens to bind

out her children William, John and Elizabeth Morris [Orders 1767-71, 266; 1774-84, 210, 358]. She was called a "free Mulatto woman" when she appeared before Mayor John Beckley of Richmond City and made oath that William **Bowman** was the only surviving brother and heir at law of James **Bowman**, deceased, a soldier in the Virginia Line. The affidavit was certified by the Henrico County court on 6 October 1783 [Orders 1781-4, 439]. She registered in Petersburg on 18 August 1794: *a light brown Mulatto woman, five feet five inches high, about forty years old, born free in Chesterfield County* [Register of Free Negroes 1794-1819, no. 25]. She was the mother of

    i.   William², born say 1769, taxable in Chesterfield County from 1791 to 1811, a blacksmith living on Colonel Walthal's land in 1809 [PPTL, 1786-1811, frames 88, 235, 339, 450, 488, 602, 689, 738].

    ii. ?David, born say 1770, a "poor" child bound apprentice in Chesterfield County on 4 February 1774 [Orders 1771-4, 398], a "Mulatto" carpenter taxable in Chesterfield County from 1791 to 1811, living on P.T. Edward's land in 1809 [PPTL, 1786-1811, frames 88, 203, 269, 339, 526, 641, 738, 782, 824].

12   iii. Elizabeth⁴, born about 1772.

    iv. John born about 1773, registered in Petersburg on 29 June 1795: *a brown Mulatto man with Bushy Black hair, five feet seven inches high, twenty two years old, born free in Chesterfield County & raised in the Town of Petersburg* and registered again on 11 July 1797 [Register of Free Negroes 1794-1819, nos. 102, 121].

    v. Wilson, born say 1775, son of Elizabeth Morris bound out in Chesterfield County on 7 September 1781 [Orders 1774-84, 324]. He was a "Mulatto" taxable in Chesterfield County from 1796 to 1799 [PPTL, 1786-1811, frames 269, 340, 375].

11. George² Morris, born say 1762, was taxable in York County from 1784 to 1814: taxable on 3 horses and 9 cattle in 1784, taxable on a slave in 1788 and 1789, called George Morris, Sr., when he was taxable on 2 tithes in 1794 and 1799, listed as a "free Negro" in 1814 [PPTL, 1782-1841, frames 87, 142, 163, 203, 212, 288, 318, 341, 355, 409]. On 20 March 1790 he and Elizabeth **Armfield** were sued in York County court for a 10 pound debt, and on 19 December 1791 his suit against Elizabeth for debt was dismissed by the court. Elizabeth **Lyons** was a witness for Elizabeth **Armfield**, and Richard **Roberts** of James City County was a witness for George. He sold property by bill of sale proved in court on 15 September 1794. On 19 May 1800 the court ordered Godfrey **Roberts** to stand trial in Williamsburg for stealing his horse [Orders 1788-95, 233, 409, 525, 651; 1795-1803, 233, 398, 409, 525]. He may have been the father of

    i.   George⁴, born about 1782, registered in York County on 20 March 1809 and again on 14 March 1817: *a light Mulatto about 35 years of age, 5 feet 3-1/2 Inches high, short stout fellow, large flat nose, thick lips, long bushy hair, & when in conversation has a simple smile which appears to be more natural than forced...he has high cheek bones, born of free parents* [Register of Free Negroes 1798-1831, nos. 36, 95]. He was called George Morris, Jr., when he was taxable in York County from 1803 to 1814: taxable on a slave in 1809 and 1810 and head of a household of 1 "free Negro & mulatto over 16" and 2 slaves in 1813 [PPTL, 1782-1841, frames 288, 318, 341, 355, 377, 392, 489]. He was head of a York County household of 4 "other free," a slave, and a white woman 26-45 years of age in 1810 [VA:878].

    ii. Anthony, head of a York County household of 5 "other free" and a slave in 1810 [VA:878] and 3 "free Negroes & mulattoes over 16" in 1813 [PPTL, 1782-1841, frame 392]. He registered in York County on 18 August 1812: *(blank) years of age, 5 feet 5-1/2 Inches high...dark complexion...large round fierce Eyes & when conversing has a smile on his countenance. Born of free parents* [Register of Free Negroes 1798-1831, no. 66].

12. Elizabeth[4] Morris, born about 1772, registered in Petersburg on 1 March 1798: *a light brown Mulatto woman, five feet one and a half inches high, twenty seven years old, born free and raised in the County of Chesterfield* [Register of Free Negroes 1794-1819, no. 137]. She may have been the Betty Morris who was head of a Petersburg Town household of 6 "other free" and 2 slaves in 1810 [VA:120a]. She was the mother of

    i.   William[5], born about 1785, registered in Petersburg on 24 April 1804: *a dark brown Mulatto man (son of Betty Morris, a free mulatto woman) five feet six inches high, nineteen years old, born free & raised in the Town of Petersburg* [Register of Free Negroes 1794-1819, no. 269].

    ii. ?Abraham, born about 1786, registered in Petersburg on 5 June 1809: *a dark brown Negro man, five feet seven inches high, twenty two years old, a waterman, born free & raised in the Town of Petersburg* [Register of Free Negroes 1794-1819, no. 47?].

Other members of the Morris family in York County were

    i.   George[3], born say 1771, married Nancy **Carter**, 1 April 1792 York County bond, David **Poe** surety [*WMQ* 1:58]. He was taxable in York County in 1795 and 1798, called George Morris, Jr. [PPTL, 1782-1841, frames 212, 239].

    ii. Peggy, born about 1779, registered in York County on 16 December 1822: *about 5 feet 3-3/4 inches & about 43 years of age, has thick pouting lips* [Register of Free Negroes 1798-1831, no.178]. She was taxable in York County on a free male tithable in 1811 [PPTL, 1782-1841, frame 366].

Other members of the Morris family in the town of Petersburg or in Chesterfield County were

13   i.   Mary, born about 1764.

    ii. Nancy, born about 1767, registered in Petersburg on 24 March 1817: *a free woman of colour, five feet eight inches high, fifty years old, light brown complection, short bushy hair, born free in Jas. City County* [Register of Free Negroes 1794-1819, no. 840].

    iii. Rebecca, born about 1769, registered in Petersburg on 30 October 1809: *Rebecca Brown formerly Morris, a dark brown free negro woman five feet and a half inches high, forty years old, born free & raised in the State of Maryland & migrated to this state prior to January 1794 as appears by the affidavit of Jas Minton of Maryland & Wm Burton of this town* [Register of Free Negroes 1794-1819, no. 498].

    iv. Sally, born about 1770, obtained a certificate of freedom in Chesterfield County on 8 September 1806: *thirty-six years old, brown complexioned, born free* [Register of Free Negroes 1804-53, nos. 30, 147, 235, 314, 315]. She was counted in a list of "free Negroes and mulattoes" with her 6 children living on Elizabeth Walthall's land in Chesterfield County in 1811 [PPTL, 1786-1811, frame 824].

    v. Sukey, a "poor" child bound apprentice in Chesterfield County on 4 February 1774 [Orders 1771-4, 398].

    vi. Peg, a "poor" child bound apprentice in Chesterfield County on 4 February 1774 [Orders 1771-4, 398].

    vii. Nancy, born about 1773, counted in a list of "free Negroes and mulattoes" with her 3 children living on Elizabeth Walthall's land in Chesterfield County in 1811 [PPTL, 1786-1811, frame 824]. She obtained a certificate of freedom in Chesterfield County on 26 August

1816: *forty-three years old, yellow complexioned, born free* [Register of Free Negroes 1804-53, no. 262].

viii. John, born say 1779, a "Mulatto" blacksmith who was taxable in Chesterfield County from 1791 to 1811 [PPTL, 1786-1811, frames 88, 163, 203, 302, 340, 782, 824].

ix. William[3], born about 1775, registered in Petersburg on 17 July 1806: *a dark brown free Negro man, five feet six and a half inches high, twenty one years old April last, born free & raised in the Town of Petersburg* [Register of Free Negroes 1794-1819, no. 387].

x. Gabriel, born about 1780, registered in Petersburg on 10 July 1805: *a dark brown stout made Negro man, five feet six inches high, large red eyes, twenty five years old, born free and raised in the County of Chesterfield* [Register of Free Negroes 1794-1819, no. 320]. He obtained a certificate of freedom in Chesterfield County on 26 August 1816: *thirty-eight years old, dark brown complexioned, born free* [Register of Free Negroes 1804-53, nos. 230, 266].

xi. Elijah, born about 1781, obtained a certificate of freedom in Chesterfield County on 9 January 1809: *twenty-eight years old, brown complexioned, born free* [Register of Free Negroes 1804-53, no. 88]. He was a "Mulatto" taxable in Chesterfield County from 1805 to 1811, a blacksmith living on Edward Archer's land [PPTL, 1786-1811, frames 602, 641, 689, 738, 782, 824].

xii. Lucy, born about 1782, obtained a certificate of freedom in Chesterfield County on 13 July 1807: *twenty-five years old, yellow complexioned, born free* [Register of Free Negroes 1804-53, no. 42].

xiii. Polly, born about 1785, obtained a certificate of freedom in Chesterfield County on 13 July 1807: *twenty-four years old, brown complexioned, born free* [Register of Free Negroes 1804-53, nos. 120, 232]. She may have been identical to Polly Morris, born about 1783, who obtained a certificate of freedom in Chesterfield County on 25 March 1816: *thirty three years old, dark brown complexioned, born free* [Register of Free Negroes 1804-53, no. 272]. She was counted in a list of "free Negroes and mulattoes" with her 3 children living on Jesse Cogbill's in Chesterfield County in 1811 [PPTL, 1786-1811, frame 824].

xiv. Jack, born about 1792, obtained a certificate of freedom in Chesterfield County on 13 July 1812: *twenty-four years old, bright yellow complexioned, born free* [Register of Free Negroes 1804-53, no. 169].

13. Mary Morris, born about 1764, was forty-two years old on 8 September 1806 when she obtained a certificate of freedom in Chesterfield County: *yellow complexioned, born free* [Register of Free Negroes 1804-53, nos. 29, 145, 231, 310]. She may have been the mother of

i. Archer, born about 1785, a twenty-one-year-old, free-born, dark brown complexioned man who obtained a certificate of freedom in Chesterfield County on 12 March 1806 [Register of Free Negroes 1804-1853, nos. 23, 109, 234].

ii. Nancy, born about 1786, a twenty-year-old, free-born, yellow complexioned woman who obtained a certificate of freedom in Chesterfield County on 8 September 1806 [Register of Free Negroes 1804-1853, nos. 31, 146, 311].

iii. Franky, born about 1794, a twenty-year-old, free-born, brown complexioned woman who registered in Chesterfield County on 10 October 1814 [Register of Free Negroes 1804-1853, nos. 233, 312].

Other members of the Morris family in nearby Virginia counties were

i. Rosanna, a "M°" taxable in Powhatan County on 2 slaves and 4 horses from 1811 to 1815 [PPTL, 1787-1825, frames 403, 424, 442, 462,

487], "F.B." head of a Powhatan County household of 5 "other free" and 4 slaves in 1810 [VA:5].

ii. Edward, born say 1785, a "melatto" taxable in the northern district of Campbell County in 1792 [PPTL, 1785-1814, frame 237], a "M°" taxable in Powhatan County from 1801 to 1806 [PPTL, 1787-1825, frames 227, 242, 260, 322], and head of a Goochland County household of 5 "other free" in 1810 [VA:705]. He married Susanna **Johns**, 24 May 1806 Goochland County bond.

iii. John, head of a New Kent County household of 2 "other free" in 1810 [VA:762].

<u>Accomack and Northampton counties</u>

1. William[1] Morris, born say 1689, was living in Accomack County on 6 December 1704 when John Willis accused him of assault. He was called "William Morris Mallatto" when several persons reported that he was threatening people with a gun [Orders 1703-9, 38, 42a]. And he was living in Accomack County on 16 December 1717 when he bound his children Sarah and Jacob Morris to Arthur Robins by Northampton County indenture [W&D 1711-18, 130]. He may have been a descendant of Martha Merris, an English widow, who made a deed of jointure to marry Philip **Mongon** in Northampton County in 1651 [DW 1651-54, 33, fol.33]. Perhaps William's wife was Sarah Morris, a "mulatto" taxable in the Northampton County household of Arthur Robins from 1724 to 1728 [Bell, *Northampton County Tithables*, 63, 113, 142]. She bound her sons Abraham and John to Arthur Robins of Northampton County on 1 September 1726. She was probably an elderly woman on 9 July 1745 when the court ordered that she be tax-free [Orders 1722-9, 252; 1742-8, 224]. William and Sarah's children were

  2   i. Sarah, born about 1710.
  3   ii. ?Tabitha, born say 1712.
  4   iii. Jacob[1], born about 1714.
       iv. Abraham[1], born in January 1718, eight-year-old son of Sarah Morris, bound apprentice to Arthur Robins in Northampton County on 1 September 1726 [Orders 1722-29, 252].
       v. John/ Jack, born Christmas 1720, four-year-old "son of Sarah Morris," bound apprentice in Northampton County to Arthur Robins on 1 September 1726 [Orders 1722-29, 252]. He was a "negro" taxable in Jonas Jackson's household in 1743, and he was taxable in Jacob Henderson's household in 1744. He was a "Negro" sued for debt in Northampton County by Benjamin Dingly Gray on 10 September 1751 [Orders 1751-3, 12]. He was head of his own household with (his wife?) Esther Morris in 1765 [Bell, *Northampton County Tithables*, 347, 365]. Perhaps Esther was Esther **Driggers**, daughter of Thomas **Drighouse** and Jean **Beckett**, a taxable in Thomas **Drighouse**'s household in 1744.

  5   vi. ?Sabra, born say 1724.
  6   vii. ?Rachel[1], born say 1726.

2. Sarah Morris, born about 1710, daughter of William Morris of Accomack County, was about seven years old on 16 December 1717 when her father bound her to Arthur Robins until the age of twenty-one by Northampton County indenture [W&D 1711-18, 130]. She was taxable in Joachim Michael's household from 1727 to 1729 [Bell, *Northampton County Tithables*, 122, 141, 188]. On 10 February 1731 she consented to serve Arthur Robins for three years after she attained the age of twenty-one in exchange for his paying her fine for a bastard child [Orders 1729-32, 68]. On 14 June 1732 Robins agreed to pay her fine and indemnify the parish from a child she had by William **Allen** [Orders 1732-42, 8, 28, 36, 42]. She was again taxable in Joachim

Michael's household from 1737 to 1744 [Bell, *Northampton County Tithables*, 262, 274, 289, 308, 326, 353, 362]. She may have been the mother of

    i.   Abraham[2], born 1 March 1743, an eleven-year-old bound to Thomas Dolby on 14 January 1755 perhaps identical to the Abraham Morris who was about eight years old on 10 September 1754 when the court ordered him bound to William Galt [Orders 1753-8, 129, 180]. He was a "Mulatto" taxable in Northampton County from 1787 to 1794, levy free in 1793 and 1794 [PPTL, 1782-1823, frames 74, 155, 182].

    ii.   Rachel[2], daughter of Sarah Morris, bound apprentice to Arthur Robins on 10 June 1747 [Orders 1742-8, 425].

    iii. Adah, daughter of Sarah Morris, bound apprentice to Arthur Robins on 10 June 1747 [Orders 1742-8, 425].

3.   Tabitha Morris, born say 1712, was a "Mulattoe" whose base-born child was bound to John Foscew by the Accomack County court on 6 August 1728. She was presented by the court for having a another bastard child on 6 May 1729 [Orders 1724-31, 115a, 152]. She was living in Northampton County on 12 February 1733/4 when she consented to the indenture of her "poor Mulatto" children Isaac and Elishe to Thomas Marshall, Gentleman [Orders 1732-42, 91]. Her children were

7   i.   Elishe, born in September 1730.

    ii.   Isaac[1], born in July 1732, two-year-old "Mulatto" son of Tabitha Morris, bound apprentice on 12 February 1733/4 [Orders 1732-42, 91].

4.   Jacob[1] Morris, born about 1714, the three-year-old son of William Morris of Accomack County, was bound by his father to Arthur Robins on 16 December 1717 by Northampton County indenture [W&D 1711-18, 130]. He was taxable in Jacob Andrew's Northampton County household in 1740 and in Abel Upshur's household with his wife Comfort Morris and (sister?) Rachel Morris in 1743. His wife was most likely Comfort **Beckett**, a tithable in the household of his neighbor, Thomas **Drighouse**, in 1739 and 1740. Jacob was head of his own household in 1744 [Bell, *Northampton County Tithables*, 289, 313, 331, 353, 362]. He was sued by Samuel Grafton in a suit for trespass which was agreed on 10 May 1750 [Orders 1748-51, 218]. He was called Jacob Morris Negro, deced., on 11 June 1751 when "Comfort Morris Negro" recorded the inventory of his estate, valued at 35 pounds, in Northampton County court [Wills, Inventories, Deeds, 1750-54, 87-88; Orders 1751-3, 37, 57, 90]. Comfort sued Daniel **Stephens** for a 3 pounds, 1 shilling debt on 15 April 1752, and Daniel **Stephens** was paid 30 shillings for maintaining Jacob's orphans Isaac, Jacob and Esther Morris on 10 September 1754 and was paid 30 shillings for maintaining Jacob Morris on 13 August 1755 [Orders 1753-8, 129, 243]. Comfort probably married Daniel **Stephens** since a Comfort **Stephens** was taxable in his household in 1769 [Bell, *Northampton County Tithables*, 401]. Jacob's children were

    i.   Isaac[2], born say 1740, called Aise Morris when he registered as a "free Negro" in Northampton County on 12 June 1794 [Orders 1789-95, 358].

    ii.   Jacob[2], born say 1745, a tithable in the Northampton County household of Solathiel Harrison in 1769 [Bell, *Northampton County Tithables*, 398]. He was taxable in Northampton County in 1798, called "Jacob Morris Senr." [PPTL, 1782-1823, frames 251], head of a St. George Parish, Accomack County household of 5 "other free" in 1800 [*Virginia Genealogist* 2:158] and 6 in 1810 [VA:42].

    iii. Esther, registered as a "free Negro" in Northampton County on 13 June 1794 [Orders 1789-95, 364].

5.   Sabra Morris, born say 1724, was the mother of

    i.   Lazarus, born in February 1743/4, three-year-old son of Sabra Morris, bound apprentice in Northampton County on 9 December 1746 [Orders 1742-48, 373]. He was a "Mulatto" taxable in Northampton County from 1787 to 1796 [PPTL, 1782-1823, frames 74, 125, 196].

6.   Rachel[1] Morris, born say 1726, was taxable in the Northampton County household of Jacob Morris in 1743. The churchwardens sued her for debt on 14 December 1743, and they presented her on 8 July 1746 for having a bastard child [Orders 1742-48, 136, 344]. She was the mother of
    i.   Isaac[3], born 23 September 1743, son of Rachel Morris, bound apprentice to George Fosque on 11 February 1745/6, eighteen-year-old son of Rachel Morris bound apprentice on 3 October 1761 [Orders 1742-8, 300; Minutes 1754-61, 275].
8   ii. ?Sarah, born say 1746.

7.   Elishe Morris, born in September 1730, the four-year-old "Mulatto" daughter of Tabitha Morris, was bound apprentice in Northampton County on 12 February 1733/4. She was presented for having an illegitimate child born on 9 November 1751 [Orders 1732-42, 91; 1751-3, 56, 70]. She was the mother of
    i.   Isaac[4], born 3 October 1743, "Mulatto" son of Elishe Morris, bound to Elijah Mears on 10 November 1761, apparently because of his complaint to the court against Elishe Dowty on 13 October 1761 [Minutes 1754-61, 274-5].
    ii. Abraham[3], born in December 1750, ten-year-old son of Elishe Morris bound apprentice to Henry Gascoigne on 12 August 1760 [Minutes 1754-61, 19, 230], perhaps the Abraham Morris who was taxable in Northampton County from 1795 to 1813, called "Abraham Morris Senr." [PPTL, 1782-1823, frames 196, 541].
9   iii. Rebecca, born say 1758.

8.   Sarah Morris, born say 1746, registered as a "free Negro" in Northampton County on 12 June 1794 [Orders 1789-95, 358]. She was the mother of
    i.   Levin, born 29 September 1763, three-year-old "negro" son of Sarah Morris, bound apprentice to Caleb Scott on 14 April 1767 and bound to David Stott on 11 October 1768 [Minutes 1765-71, 107, 243]. He was a "Mulatto" taxable in Northampton County from 1787 to 1796 [PPTL, 1782-1823, frames 74, 81, 125, 182, 196]. He was head of a Northampton County household of 5 "free colored" in 1820 [VA:216A].

9.   Rebecca Morris, born say 1758, was the mother of
    i.   Jacob[3], born about January 1779, son of Beck Morris, bound apprentice by the Northampton County court to Henry Abdeel on 14 June 1785 [Orders 1783-87, 293], married Phillis **Only**, 23 August 1802 Northampton County bond, York **Stepney** security.

Other members of the family on the Eastern Shore of Virginia were
    i.   George, born 28 April 1755, bound apprentice to John Upshur in Northampton County on 12 June 1770 [Minutes 1765-71, 372]. He married Mary **Stevens**, 19 October 1785 Northampton County bond, David Jones security. He was taxable in Northampton County from 1784 to 1787: called a "Mulatto" in 1787 and 1788 [PPTL, 1782-1823, frames 29, 74, 81].
    ii. John, born about 1759, registered in Petersburg on 11 May 1804: *a dark brown Mulatto man, five feet seven and a half inches high, forty five years old with short napt hair, born free & raised in the County of Northampton* [Register of Free Negroes 1794-1819, no. 272].

    iii.   Isaac[5], a "free Negro orphan" ordered bound by the churchwardens of St. George Parish in Accomack County to Archibald Garrison to learn shoemaking on 28 March 1775 [Orders 1774-7, 327].

    iv.   Sukey, born say 1774, married Jacob **Thomson**, 26 May 1795 Northampton County bond, Thomas Lewis security.

    v.   Revel, married Dilly **Drighouse**, 7 September 1801 Northampton County bond, James Smith security. He was taxable in Northampton County from 1795 to 1796 [PPTL, 1782-1823, frames 196].

    vi.   Mary, married Hezekiah **Beavans**, 31 July 1798 Northampton County bond, Revel Morris security.

    vii.   Nancy, married Daniel **Weeks**, 6 July 1803 Northampton County bond, Abraham Lang security.

    viii.   Dennard, married Rebecca **Costin**, 1808 Northampton County bond.

    ix.   Sophia, married Isaac **Pool**, 27 December 1811 Northampton County bond, John Upchurch security.

    x.   John, head of an Accomack County household of 9 "other free" in 1810 [VA:115].

    xi.   York, head of an Accomack County household of 3 "other free" and one slave in 1810 [VA:44].

    xii.   William, head of an Accomack County household of one "other free" and 4 slaves in 1810 [VA:182].

    xiii.   Daniel, born in 1786, registered in Accomack County on 29 September 1807: *Dark Mulatto, 5 feet 8 Inches...Born free* [Free Negro Register, 1785-1863, no. 23].

MOSELY FAMILY

1.   Thomas Moseley, born say 1725, was living in Henrico County on 6 November 1752 when he was indicted by the court for failing to list his "Mulatto" wife as a tithable. The case against him was dismissed at the next session of the court [Minutes 1752-5, 19, 27]. On 6 March 1769 the court ordered the churchwardens of Henrico Parish to bind out his children Leonard, Anne and Mary Moseley [Orders 1767-9, 397]. He was the ancestor of

    i.   Leonard, bound apprentice in 1769.

    ii.   Anne, bound apprentice in 1769.

    iii.   Mary, bound apprentice in 1769.

Other members of the Mosely family were

    i.   Beersheba, petitioned the Frederick County, Virginia court on 7 November 1770 for her freedom from Godwin Swift who was illegally detaining her as a slave. She was released on the testimony of witnesses that she was the daughter of a free Indian commonly called the "Indian Doctor" who lived in Queen Anne's County, Maryland. She paid Thomas Lewis for attending as a witness for her for two days [Orders 1770-2, 39, 126].

    ii.   Caty, head of a Craven County, North Carolina household of 3 "other free" in 1790 [NC:134].

    iii.   David, head of a 96 District, Spartanburgh County, South Carolina household of 8 "other free" in 1800 and 7 "other free" in 1810 [SC:181].

    iv.   Nancy, born before 1776, head of a New Hanover County, North Carolina household of 5 "free colored" in 1820 [NC:230].

    v.   Jinny, head of a Petersburg Town household of 1 "other free" in 1810 [VA:117a].

MOSES FAMILY

1.   Ezekiel[1] Moses, born say 1710, was the "Negro fellow" (slave) of Elizabeth
Harmonson in January 1739/40 when Elizabeth **Webb**, "a malatto," appeared
in Northampton County, Virginia court and offered to serve Ezekiel's mistress
for sixteen years on condition that she allow her to marry Ezekiel. She was
called Betty Moses on 10 September 1745 when the court bound her sons Left
and Luke to George Kendall [Orders 1732-42, 382; 1711-6, 255; 1742-8,
255]. Ezekiel and Elizabeth were the ancestors of
   i.   Left, born say 1741, bound to George Kendall on 10 September 1745.
   ii.   Luke, born say 1743, bound to George Kendall on 10 September 1745.
         He may have been the member of the Moses family, first name not
         indicated, who sued a member of the **Jeffery** family for 10 shillings in
         Northampton County in June 1762 and sued John Daniel (an Indian) in
         September 1762 [Minutes 1761-5, 30, 41, 42, 51, 56]. He was taxable
         in Northampton County from 1800 to 1813 [PPTL, 1782-1823, frames
         290, 304, 433, 541].
   iii. Ezekiel[2], born say 1762, married Diana **Beckett**, "ward of Mark
         Becket," 22 August 1791 Northampton County bond, William Stith
         security. He was a "Mulatto" delinquent taxable in Northampton
         County in 1786 [*Virginia Genealogist* 20:269] and taxable in
         Northampton County from 1792 to 1796 [PPTL, 1782-1823, frames
         140, 182]. He was a "yellow" complexioned seaman who enlisted as
         a substitute from Northampton County. He was later listed as a
         silversmith from Northumberland County [NSDAR, *African American
         Patriots*, 151; Jackson, *Virginia Negro Soldiers*, 41]. He was taxable
         in York County from 1803 to 1814 [Personal Property Tax List, 1782-
         1841, frames 288, 297, 307, 341, 392, 409].
   iv.   Mark, born say 1764, married Mary **Beckett**, 13 December 1785
         Northampton County bond, Isaac **Beckett** security. Mark was a
         "Mulatto" delinquent taxable in Northampton County in 1786 [*Virginia
         Genealogist* 20:269], a "Mulatto" taxable in Northampton County from
         1787 to 1794 [PPTL, 1782-1823, frames 74, 125, 182], head of an
         Accomack County household of 9 "other free" in 1800 [*Virginia
         Genealogist* 1:160], and 6 in 1810 [VA:111].
   v.   Betty, probably born about 1766, a "Negro" orphan bound to Savage
         Cowdry by the Northampton County court on 9 April 1766. She was
         said to have been about ten years old on 8 July 1777 when the court
         bound her to Esther Davis [Minutes 1765-71, 35; 1777-83, 2].
   vi.   Daniel, born say 1780, married Rachel **Teague**, 25 September 1802
         Northampton County bond, Levin **Morris** security.

MOSS FAMILY

Members of the Moss family were
1   i.   Dorothy[1], born say 1700.
2   ii.   Thomas[1], born about 1728.
3   iii. Richard[1], born say 1730.
4   iv.   William[2], born say 1734.

1.   Dorothy[1] Moss, born say 1700, left a 2 April 1764 Cumberland County,
Virginia will, proved 25 June 1764, by which she divided her household goods
and a mare among her children William Moss, Joseph Moss, Elizabeth
Morris, John Moss, and granddaughter Elizabeth, daughter of Joseph Moss.
Nathaniel **Morris** was a witness. She appointed her sons Joseph and John her
executors [WB 1:294]. She was the mother of
5   i.   Joseph[1], born say 1725.

       ii.   William[1], born say 1728, a "free Negro" taxable in Campbell County from 1785 to 1794: taxed on his unnamed nephew in 1785 [PPTL, 1785-1814, frames 6, 43, 136, 216, 305].

      iii. Elizabeth[1], probably wife of Nathaniel **Morris**.

      iv. John, born say 1735.

2.   Thomas[1] Moss, born about 1728, was a carpenter indentured to Lawrence Egmond and employed by William Lightfoot of Charles City County. He ran away, and Lightfoot placed an advertisement in the *Virginia Gazette* on 11 July 1754 offering a reward for his return, describing him as: *a Negroe Man…a slim made Fellow, about 5 Feet 8 Inches high and about 25 or 26 Years of Age, had on when he went away, a blue Cloth Coat, wide Trousers, and hath Oznabrigs and checked Shirts…subject to Drink and very talkative when drunk.* The ad went on to say he was probably headed towards Newcastle where his wife lived [*Virginia Gazette*, p. 3, col. 2]. He appeared in Charles City County court on 2 July 1760 and again on 3 February 1762 and agreed to serve his master William Lightfoot, Esq., an additional year after the completion of his service [Orders 1758-62, 197, 352]. Perhaps he and his wife were the parents of

6   i.   Judith, born say 1751.

7   ii. Sarah, born say 1753.

8   iii. Temp, born say 1754.

3.   Richard[1] Moss, born say 1730, may have identical to Richard, a "Muletto" (no last name) who was bound out by the Henrico County court in April 1741 [Orders 1737-1746, 138]. Richard Moss died before 4 April 1778 when the Chesterfield County court ordered the churchwardens of Manchester Parish to bind his orphan William Moss to William Gibson [Orders 1774-84, 162]. He was the father of

9   i.   ?Richard[2], born about 1752.

      ii. ?Henry[1], born about 1754, head of a Powhatan County household of 3 persons in 1783 [VA:58]. He was taxable in Powhatan County from 1789 to 1791 and from 1803 to 1817: called a "Mull°" in 1790, charged with William Pollock's tithe in 1791, called a "F.B." from 1813 to 1815 [PPTL, 1787-1825, frames 36, 48, 63, 262, 280, 321, 366, 443, 463, 488, 538]. He was about forty two years old on 1 July 1796 when he was described by the 1 July 1796 issue of a Virginia newspaper as: *born a free Negro in one of the lower Counties of this state…his father was a black and his mother a mulatto, but he has turned white; he was in the Virginia Line in the last war* [Headley, *18th Century Newspapers*].

10   iii. ?John, born say 1760.

      iv. Benjamin[1], born say 1762, made choice of his guardian Jesse Cogbill in Chesterfield County court on 4 December 1778 [Orders 1774-84, 201]. He was head of a Powhatan County household of 2 persons in 1783 [VA:58] and a "Mull°" taxable in Powhatan County from 1787 to 1797 [PPTL, 1787-1825, frames 8, 22, 48, 63, 81, 95, 134], perhaps the Benjamin Moss who was a "Mulatto" taxable in Buckingham County from 1800 to 1807 [PPTL, 1782-1809].

      v.   ?Dorothy[2]/ Dolly married Shadrack **Battles** in Louisa County on 25 July 1780 [Jones, *The Douglas Register*].

      vi. William[3], born say 1764, bound apprentice to William Gibson In Chesterfield County on 4 April 1778. He was a "M°" taxable in Powhatan County from 1792 to 1805 [PPTL, 1787-1825, frames 81, 95, 107, 121, 148, 165, 188, 209, 227, 242, 261, 281, 299].

      vii. ?Nancy, born say 1765, married David **Howell**, 24 April 1786 Powhatan County bond.

    viii. ?Patty, head of a Chesterfield County household of 10 "other free" in 1810 [VA:70/1062].

    ix. ?Elisha, a "M°" taxable in Powhatan County in 1792, 1793, 1798, and 1801 [PPTL, 1787-1825, frames 80, 95, 166, 227].

3. William² Moss, born say 1734, may have been identical to William, a "Mulleto" (no last name), who was bound out by the Henrico County court in April 1741 [Orders 1737-1746, 138]. William Moss was taxable in the upper district of Henrico County from 1799 to 1807: taxable on a horse and 3 cattle in 1785; called William Moss, Sr., a "free Negro," from 1799 [PPTL 1782-1814, frames 376, 408, 449, 491, 537]. And he was taxable in the upper district of Henrico County on 6 acres from 1799 to 1816, called a "fn" in 1804, 1812, 1815 and 1816 [Land Tax List 1799-1816]. He may have been the father of

    i. William⁴, born say 1770, a "Mulatto" taxable in Chesterfield County on a tithe and a horse from 1788 to 1794 [PPTL, 1786-1811, frames 107, 144, 185, 218]. He married Nancy **Auter (Otter)**, "daughter of Sarah Auter," 5 January 1793 Henrico County bond, Nathaniel **Cousins** surety. He may have been the William Moss, Jr., who was a "free Negroe" taxable in Henrico County from 1799 to 1814, listed with his unnamed wife in 1813 [PPTL 1782-1814, frames 376, 449, 491, 537, 726, 758, 824]. He was head of a Henrico County household of 5 "other free" in 1810 [VA:985].

    ii. Archer, born about 1782, obtained a certificate of freedom in Chesterfield County on 14 March 1814: *thirty two years old, dark brown complexion, born free* [Register of Free Negroes 1804-53, no. 218]. He was a "free Negro" taxable in the upper district of Henrico County in 1814 [PPTL 1782-1814, frame 824].

5. Joseph¹ Moss, born say 1725, was named in his mother's 2 April 1764 Cumberland County will. He was living in Cumberland County on 22 May 1775 when the court bound Elizabeth Moss's "mulattoe" son Joseph to him [Orders 1774-8, 331]. He was the father of

11   i. Elizabeth², born say 1750.

12   ii. ?Anna, born say 1753.

6. Judith Moss, born say 1751, was living in Prince Edward County on 19 October 1772 when the court ordered the churchwardens of St. Patrick's Parish to bind out her son Burwell (no race indicated). She was the mother of

    i. Burwell, born say 1770, son of Judith Moss, bound apprentice on 19 October 1772 [Orders 1771-81, part 1, 177]. He was a "free Negro" head of a Charlotte County household of 4 "other free" in 1810 [VA:68].

    ii. Jesse, born say 1772, orphan of Judith Moss, bound apprentice in Prince Edward County on 15 August 1774 [Orders 1771-81, part 2, 458]. He may have been the Jesse Moss who was a "free Negro" taxable in the upper district of Henrico County from 1799 to 1814: listed with his unnamed wife in 1813 [PPTL 1782-1814, frames 147, 376, 449, 491, 537, 759]. He was head of a Henrico County household of 3 "other free" in 1810 [VA:985].

    iii. Siller, born say 1775, daughter of Judith Moss, bound to Charles Smith in Prince Edward County on 18 March 1781 [Orders 1771-81, part 2, 94].

7. Sarah Moss, born say 1753, had a "free Negro" son Julius Moss whose 25 March 1782 birth was registered in St. Peter's Parish, New Kent County, Virginia [NSCDA, *St. Peter's Parish Register*, 169]. She was the mother of

    i.   Richard³, born about 1772, a "Negro," married Sarah **Johns**, "mulatto" daughter of Mallory **Johns**, Jr., who consented, 14 May 1791 Campbell County bond, Henry Moss witness. He was taxable in Campbell County from 1787 to 1790 [PPTL, 1785-1814, frames 43, 73, 102, 136], a "Mulatto" taxable in Chesterfield County on a tithe and a horse from 1792 to 1810 [PPTL, 1786-1811, frames 144, 184, 470, 543, 799] and head of a Chesterfield County household of 5 "other free" in 1810 [VA:70/1062]. He obtained a certificate of freedom in Chesterfield County on 10 May 1813: *forty one years old, dark brown complexion, born free* [Register of Free Negroes 1804-53, no. 188]. The administrator of the Chesterfield County estate of Andrew **Scott** obtained a judgment against Richard before 1831 when Richard claimed that **Scott** was indebted to his brother Julius Moss [LVA chancery case 1831-030].

    ii.   Julius, born 25 March 1782, a "FN" taxable in New Kent County from 1811 to 1815 [PPTL, 1791-1828, frames 466, 491, 515], head of a New Kent County household of 1 "other free" in 1810 [VA:762].

   iii. ?Elizabeth, counted with 3 females over the age of sixteen in a list of "free Negroes" in Chesterfield County in 1813 [Waldrep, *1813 Tax List*].

    iv. ?George, a "FN" taxable in New Kent County from 1801 to 1815 [PPTL, 1791-1828, frames 359, 408, 420, 444, 455, 477, 491, 515], head of a New Kent County household of 3 "other free" in 1810 [VA:761].

8.   Temp Moss, born say 1754, was living in Prince Edward County on 20 January 1777 when the court ordered the churchwardens of St. Patrick's Parish to bind her son Robert Moss (no race indicated) to Charles Smith to learn the trade of cooper [Orders 1771-81, part 2, 507]. She was the mother of a "Mulattoe" child named Joe Moss who was bound to Baker Ewing in Bedford County on 25 January 1779 [Orders 1774-82, 220]. She was the mother of

    i.   ?Edward², born say 1772, married Rachel **Hill**, 20 July 1793 Bedford County bond, Robert **Hill** bondsman. He was a "free Black" head of a Bedford County household of 5 "other free" in 1810 [VA:473] and a "free N." taxable in Bedford County on two persons in 1813 [Waldrep, *1813 Tax List*]. Perhaps his wife was Sall Morse, Senr., who registered in Bedford County on 24 October 1831: *5 feet 3/4 inch high, bright mulatto, straight hair, 56 or 57 years old, Born free* [Register of Free Negroes 1820-60, p.15].

    ii.   Joseph⁴, bound to Baker Ewing in Bedford County on 25 January 1779.

   iii. Robert, bound apprentice to Charles Smith in Prince Edward County on 20 January 1777, called Bob Moss when he was bound to Robert Ewing, Jr., in Bedford County on 25 September 1780 [Orders 1774-82, 297].

9.   Richard² Moss, born about 1752, was head of a Powhatan County household of 8 persons in 1783 [VA:58] and a "Mull°" taxable in Powhatan County from 1787 to 1791 [PPTL, 1787-1825, frames 8, 21, 36, 48, 63]. He married Dorothy Moss, 30 December 1786 Powhatan County marriage bond. He was taxable in Goochland County from 1797 to 1813: taxable on a free male tithable aged 16-21 in 1799; 2 tithes aged 16-21 in 1800; 2 in 1801 when he was called a "free negroe planter," called a "Mulatto" from 1802 to 1813 [PPTL, 1782-1809, frames 453, 499, 512, 568, 583, 639, 654; 1810-32, frames 144]. He was head of a Chesterfield County household of 8 "other free" in 1810 [VA:70/1062]. He obtained a certificate of freedom in Chesterfield County on 13 May 1812: *sixty years old, dark brown complexion, born free* [Register of Free Negroes 1804-53, no. 163]. He was the father of

i. ?Henry[2], born say 1770, taxable in Campbell County from 1787 to 1790 and a "F.N." taxable there from 1809 to 1811 [PPTL, 1785-1814, frames 43, 73, 102, 136, 734, 771, 807]. He married Winney **Valentine**, "free negroes," 15 June 1806 Campbell County bond, Benjamin **Armstrong** and Harry Moss bondsmen.

ii. Celia, born say 1771, "daughter of Richard Moss," married Aaron **Goen (Gowen)**, 29 December 1792 Powhatan County bond.

iii. Benjamin[2], a "Mul°" taxable in Powhatan County on a horse in 1787, called Ben Moss, Jr. [PPTL, 1787-1825, frames 8]. He was a "Mulatto" taxable in Goochland County in 1811 [PPTL, 1810-32, frame 56].

iv. ?Edward[3]/ Ned, born about 1778, obtained a certificate of freedom in Chesterfield County on 14 June 1813: *thirty five years old, black complexion, born free* [Register of Free Negroes 1804-53, no. 187].

v. ?Sally, married Jeremiah **Mayo**, "free man of color," 12 October 1807 Chesterfield County bond, Richard Moss security and witness.

vi. John, a "Mulatto" taxable in Goochland County from 1803 to 1814: a ditcher at George Payne's" in 1809, a waterman at Colonel Payne's in 1810, a ditcher on Robert Pleasants' land in 1811 who was taxable on a slave over the age of 16 from 1811 to 1814, also taxable on a slave aged 12-16 in 1814. John was over the age of forty-five in 1815 [PPTL, 1782-1809, frames 654, 764, 808, 871; 1810-32, frame 12, 79, 104, 169, 200, 265].

vii. Daniel, a "Mulatto" taxable in Goochland County from 1809 to 1811 [PPTL, 1782-1809, frames 849; 1810-32, frame 56].

10. John Moss, born say 1760, was head of a Powhatan County household of 4 persons in 1783 [VA:58] and a "Mull°" taxable in Buckingham County in 1788 [PPTL A, p.10]. He was a "M°" taxable in Powhatan County from 1794 to 1804 [PPTL, 1787-1825, frames 108, 120, 147, 166, 188, 209, 241, 261, 280], a "FN" taxable in the northern district of Campbell County from 1807 to 1810 [PPTL, 1785-1814, frame 699, 734, 771] and head of a Campbell County household of 7 "other free" in 1810 [VA:848]. He may have been the father of

i. Lucy, registered as a "Free Negro" in Campbell County on 15 October 1836: *Age: 56; 5 feet 6-1/2 Inches; Born free in said County* [Register of Free Negroes, 1801-50, p.14].

ii. Elizabeth[2], born about 1791, registered in Campbell County on 15 October 1836: *Age: 45; 5 feet 4-1/2 Inches; Born free in said County of Campbell* [Register of Free Negroes, 1801-50, p.14].

iii. Littleberry[2], born about 1794, registered in Campbell County on 3 October 1834: *Age: 40; 6 feet; Bright Malattoe; left Eye smaller than the right, born free* [Register of Free Negroes, 1801-50, p.14]. He was a "FN" taxable in Campbell County in 1814 [PPTL, 1785-1814, frames 931].

iv. Keziah, born about 1802, registered in Campbell County in September 1837: *Age 33; 5 ft 2 in. Bright complexion* [Register of Free Negroes, 1801-50, p.15].

11. Elizabeth[2] Moss, born say 1750, was living in Cumberland County, Virginia, on 23 April 1770 when the court ordered the churchwardens of Southam Parish to bind out her "mulattoe" son Joseph Moss to Thomas Epperson [Orders 1767-70, 503]. She married Zachariah **Goff** in June 1796 in Campbell County according to her application for a pension for his services in the Revolution [M805-362, frames 285-96]. She was the mother of

i. Joseph[3], ordered bound by the Cumberland County court to Thomas Epperson on 23 April 1770 and bound to (his grandfather?) Joseph Moss on 22 May 1775 [Orders 1774-8, 331]. He was a "Melatto" or

"F.N." taxable in the southern district of Campbell County from 1787 to 1794 [PPTL, 1785-1814, frames 43, 73, 136, 256, 293]. He married Phebe **Martin**, 25 December 1786 Powhatan County bond, surety Dick **Moss**.

12. Anna Moss, born say 1753, was a "Mull°" taxable in Buckingham County on a horse in 1788, taxable on her 3 unnamed sons and 5 horses in 1798, taxable on James, Drury and Thomas Moss in 1799, taxable on Thomas Moss in 1801 [PPTL, 1782-1809], a "Mulatto" taxable on her unnamed son in St. Ann's Parish, Albemarle County, in 1811, taxable on a horse in 1813 [PPTL, 1800-13, frame 461, 548]. She was the mother of

    i.   Thomas[2], born say 1774, a "Mulatto" taxable on 3 free males and 3 horses in Buckingham County in 1795, taxable on John Moss's tithe in 1796, John and James Moss's tithe in 1797, listed with Ann Moss in 1799 and 1801 [PPTL, 1782-1809], a "free Negro" taxable in St. Ann's Parish, Albemarle County, in 1802 and 1803 [PPTL, 1800-13, frames 100, 144]. He was a "FN" taxable in Campbell County from 1809 to 1814: listed with a woman over the age of sixteen in 1813 [PPTL, 1785-1814, frames 734, 771, 806, 892, 931].

    ii. John, born say 1778, taxable in the Buckingham County household of Thomas Moss in 1796 and 1797, taxable on a horse in 1799 (called Jonathan Moss) [PPTL, 1782-1809], a "Mulatto" taxable in St. Ann's Parish, Albemarle County, from 1800 to 1812: taxable on an unnamed apprentice in 1802, taxable on a slave in 1803, taxable on apprentices P. **Cuzins** and Alexander Moss in 1804, taxable on his unnamed brother in 1805, taxable on a slave in 1806, taxable on his brother Richard in 1811, called Jonathan Moss in 1809, 1812 and 1813 [PPTL, 1800-13, frames 12, 145, 186, 232, 232, 277, 548], head of a Prince Edward County household of 4 "other free" in 1810 [VA:577].

    iii. James, born say 1780, listed as a taxable with Ann Moss in Buckingham County in 1799.

    iv. Drury, born say 1782, listed with Ann Moss in Buckingham County in 1799 [PPTL, 1782-1809], a "Mulatto" taxable in Albemarle County from 1804 to 1809 and in 1812 [PPTL, 1800-13, frames 186, 233, 277, 326, 369, 505], head of a Nelson County household of 5 "other free" in 1810 [VA:712].

    v. Alexander, a "Mulatto" taxable in Albemarle County from 1806 to 1813 [PPTL, 1800-13, frames 278, 327, 506, 553], head of a Nelson County household of 1 "other free" in 1810 [VA:712], a "FN" taxable in Campbell County in 1814 [PPTL, 1785-1814, frame 931].

    vi. ?Littleberry[2], a "Mulatto" taxable in Albemarle County from 1809 to 1813 [PPTL, 1800-13, frames 369, 506], 548].

    vii. ?Lucy, listed as a "free Negro" in Albemarle County in 1813 [PPTL, 1800-13, frame 553].

    viii. Richard, born say 1795, taxable in Albemarle County in 1811.

Other members of the family were

    i.   Peter, born say 1770, a "FN" taxable in Campbell County in 1810 [PPTL, 1785-1814, frame 771], head of a Campbell County household of 5 "other free" in 1810 [VA:853]. He married Fanny **Armstrong**, daughter of Benjamin **Armstrong**, 27 December 1809 Campbell County bond, Peter Moss and Benjamin **Armstrong** bondsmen.

    ii. Aggy, head of a Henrico County household of 4 "other free" in 1810 [VA:985].

    iii. Matilda, head of a Richmond City household of 5 "other free" and 2 slaves in 1810 [VA:326].

    iv. Polly, head of a Richmond City household of 4 "other free" in 1810 [VA:374].

v. Ridley, obtained a certificate of freedom in Chesterfield County on 13 May 1812: ___ *years old, yellow complexion, born free* [Register of Free Negroes 1804-53, no. 162].

MOZINGO FAMILY

1. Edward[1] Mozingo, born say 1641, was a "Negro man" whose apprenticeship to Colonel John Walker was completed on 5 October 1672 [McIlwaine, *Minutes of the Council*, 316]. He was a tenant on Andrew Boyer's land in Old Rappahannock County in March 1680/1. In 1683 the Old Rappahannock County court granted him judgment against Rees Evans for three barrels of Indian corn and ordered him and his wife Margaret to post security for their good behavior towards Colonel John Stone [D&W 6:134-5; Orders 1683-6, 30, 166-7]. Edward's 30 July 1711 Richmond County will was proved 7 May 1712. He left two guns to his son Edward and divided his land and property among his wife Margaret and sons Edward and John who he also named as executors. Edward Barrow was a witness to the will and returned an inventory of the estate [Wills & Inventories 1709-17, 75-6, 87]. He was the father of

2   i.   Edward[2], born say 1664.
    ii. John[1], born say 1668, petitioned the Richmond County court on 28 October 1709 for his "nearest Friend" Edward Mazingoe. On 2 April 1712 the Richmond County court reported that he had refused to procession his land in North Farnham Parish where he was living because he did not know the bounds between the land he held under Colonel Pierce's patent and the land of Samuel Bayley [Orders 1711-6, 13]. On 31 May 1733 John Minor brought a suit against him in Westmoreland County court which was agreed to by both parties [Orders 1731-9, 86a].

2. Edward[2] Mozingo, born say 1664, brought suit against Edward Barrow in Richmond County, Virginia court on 5 April 1705 [Orders 1702-4, 327]. His mother-in-law Elizabeth Booth mentioned him and his children Sarah and John in her 27 October 1708 Cople Parish, Westmoreland County will, proved 26 January 1708/9. She left Edward 500 pounds of tobacco and five head of cattle, and left his daughter Sarah furniture and pewter dishes. Elizabeth also named her daughter Ann **Grimstead**, grandchildren William and Thomas **Grimstead**, and named son-in-law Thomas **Grimstead** executor [WB 4:169-70]. On 28 October 1709 Edward appeared in Westmoreland County, Virginia court as the "nearest Friend" of Sara Mazingoe in her suit against Thomas **Grinstead**, executor of the estate of Elizabeth Booth. **Grinstead** was ordered to deliver to Sarah a bed, furniture, and pewter dishes which were willed to her by Elizabeth Booth. And in the same court Edward and his wife Elizabeth brought a successful suit against **Grinstead** to deliver to Edward five head of cattle and 500 pounds of tobacco which was his legacy from Elizabeth Booth [Orders 1705-21, 133a]. The **Grinstead/ Grimstead** family descended from Elizabeth **Key**, a mixed-race slave who sued for her freedom in Northumberland County in 1656 and later married her white attorney William Grimstead [Northumberland County Record Book 1652-58, 66, 67, 85a, 85b; 1658-66, 27, 43, 44]. Edward Mozingo appeared in Richmond County court numerous times between 1721 and 1752 [Orders 9:61, 97, 284, 343, 358, 370; 10:403; 11:29, 294, 379, 395, 403, 442, 457, 542; 12:48, 69, 79, 340]. On 27 March 1734 he and Ephraim McCarty were acquitted in a trial held in Westmoreland County court in which they were charged with breaking open a tobacco house and stealing tobacco which belonged to Nicholas Minor [Orders 1731-9]. His 10 November 1753 Richmond County will was proved by his son Edward on 1 April 1754. He left his land, tobacco house, and property to his sons Edward, George and John, and pewter dishes to his daughter Margaret. He allowed (his son-in-law) George Henson and (daughter)

Margaret Henson to lease the land they were then living on for seven years. He also named his daughter-in-law Hannah and his daughter Sarah **Chandler** [Wills 1753-67]. Edward[2] and Elizabeth were the parents of

    i.   Edward[3].
    ii.   George.
    iii. John[2].
    iv. Margaret, married Francis **Chandler** in North Farnham Parish, Richmond County on 18 July 1731 [King, *Registers of North Farnham Parish*, 135]. She was called the wife of Francis **Chandler** on 26 May 1741 when the Westmoreland County court presented George Hinson of Washington Parish for living in adultery with her and presented Francis **Chandler** and Rebecca **Payn** for cohabiting together. The case against George Hinson was dismissed on 27 February 1741/2 when it was suggested to the court that he had run away [Orders 1739-43, 100, 115a, 134].
    v.   Sarah, married John **Chanler** in North Farnham Parish on 25 August 1729 [King, *Registers of North Farnham Parish*, 135]. He was called John **Chandler**, a "Mulatto," when he was sued in Westmoreland County, Virginia court for a two pound debt on 30 September 1755 [Orders 1755-8, 7a].

Most of their descendants were considered white by 1790. However, three descendants were counted in "A List of Free Mulattoes & Negroes in Westmoreland County" in 1801 [*Virginia Genealogist* 31:42]:

    i.   Thomas, taxable in the upper district of Westmoreland County from 1787 to 1810 when his name was crossed off the list [PPTL, 1782-1815, frames 310, 333, 443, 521, 587, 707], married Mary Cannady, 24 September 1793 Westmoreland County bond.
    ii.   Richard, taxable in the upper district of Westmoreland County from 1789 to 1801 [PPTL, 1782-1815, frames 341, 426, 484, 501, 532], married Nancy Yardly, 10 May 1796 Westmoreland County bond.
    iii. William, taxable in the upper district of Westmoreland County from 1790 to 1809 [PPTL, 1782-1815, frames 353, 388, 426, 532, 686].

MUCKELROY FAMILY

1.   James[1] Muckelroy, born say 1720, was a witness to the 10 October 1739 Beaufort County deed from William Carruthers to William Phipps. He purchased 330 acres from Moses Prescott on the north side of Bay River on 2 December 1751. This was land on Chapel Creek adjoining Abraham **Johnston** [Hoffman, *Land Patents*, II:667]. He was a "black" taxable with his unnamed wife and William **Tyre** in Beaufort County in 1755 and with his son in 1764 [SS 837]. The December 1757 Session of the Beaufort County court recorded that he married Eliza Humes, daughter of James Humes, decd., and was appointed guardian to her sister Abigail Humes. He complained to the court that: *there is a negro man, Hercules, that falls among the sd. two daughters and another daughter of the sd. decd...* [Minutes 1757-61, I:37c]. He purchased 200 acres in the fork of Trent Creek on the south side of Bay River near the Cedar Landing adjoining his own land on 13 June 1770, John **Curtis** and John Mackelroy witnesses [DB 18:125]. His 23 April 1773 Beaufort County will was proved 20 October the same year. He appointed his wife Elizabeth as executrix and gave land to his children:

    i.   David, "my plantation."
    ii.   Adam[2], land on the south prong of Trents Creek.
    iii. James[2], land in the fork of Trent Creek.
    iv.   Sarah, land on Neale's Creek.
    v.   Elizabeth, land on Neale's Creek.

vi. Mary **Cirtis**, land on Raccoon Creek. Perhaps she was the wife of Richard **Curtis**, a "free negro" taxable with his wife in Beaufort County in 1755 [SS 837].

2. Adam[1] Muckelroy, born say 1715, was witness to the 10 October 1739 Beaufort County deed of William Carruthers to William Phipps. He was probably the Adam McCoy who purchased 100 acres on the northwest prong of Bay River on 5 May 1745 with James Mackelroy as witness. He and his wife were taxables with their son Thomas and his wife, and (son?) William in Beaufort County in 1755, and he was taxable on only himself in 1764 [SS 837]. He was taxable on an assessment of 3,384 pounds in 1779 [GA 30.1 by *NCGSJ* XV:145]. His children were

   i. Thomas, born say 1735, taxable with his wife in 1755 in his father's household and in his own household in Beaufort County in 1764 on two "black" tithes. He was head of a Craven County household of 3 "other free" in 1790 [NC:131].

   ii. ?William, born say 1740, taxable in 1755.

MUMFORD/ MUNFORD FAMILY

The Mumford family was probably related to Munford **Blanks**, head of a New Hanover County, North Carolina household of 4 "free colored" in 1820 [NC:221]. Members of the Munford/ Mumford family in North Carolina and South Carolina were

   i. Lydia, head of a Chesterfield County, South Carolina household of 6 "other free" in 1800 [SC:105a], perhaps identical to the Lydia Mumford who was head of an Anson County, North Carolina household of 4 "other free" in 1800 [NC:233] and 4 in 1810 [NC:28].

   ii. Eliza, head of a Chesterfield County, South Carolina household of 5 "other free" in 1800 [NC:105a].

   iii. Samuel, head of a Marion District, South Carolina household of 3 "other free" and a white woman in 1810 [SC:79a].

   iv. Henry, head of a Marion District, South Carolina household of 2 "other free" in 1810 [SC:79a].

MUNDAY FAMILY

1. Cretia Munday, born about 1747, registered in Southampton County on 30 July 1810: *age 63, Dark Mulatto, 5 feet 1/2 inch, free born* [Register of Free Negroes 1794-1832, no. 742]. She was probably the mother of

   i. Pherebe, born about 1776, registered in Southampton County on 30 July 1810: *age 34, Dark Mulatto, 5 feet 2 inches, free born* [Register of Free Negroes 1794-1832, no. 743].

   ii. Etheldred, born about 1783, registered in Southampton County in December 1804: *age 21, Blk., 5 feet 6 inches, free born*. He registered again on 30 July 1810: *age 27, Dark Mulatto Man, 5 feet 9 inches, free born* [Register of Free Negroes 1794-1832, nos. 316, 740]. He was listed in Southampton County as a "fn" with his wife Abby in 1813 and 1814 [PPTL 1807-21, frames 321, 421].

   iii. Jacob, born about 1787, registered in Southampton County on 30 July 1810: *age 23, Dark Mulatto Man, 5 feet 8-1/2 inches, free born*. He registered again on 12 June 1816 [Register of Free Negroes 1794-1832, nos. 741, 1013].

   iv. Isaac, listed in Southampton County as a "fn" with his wife Kesiah in 1813 and 1814 [PPTL 1807-21, frames 321, 421].

   v. Isham, listed in Southampton County as a "fn" with his wife Judah in 1813 and 1814 [PPTL 1807-21, frames 321, 421].

vi.   Thomas, born about 1792, registered in Southampton County on 26 August 1816: *age 24, Mulatto, 5 feet 6-1/4 inches, free born* [Register of Free Negroes 1794-1832, no. 1024].

MUNS FAMILY

1.   Elizabeth Munds, born say 1748, was a "Molatto" woman living in Sussex County, Virginia, on 19 June 1777 when the court ordered the churchwardens to bind out her children Stephen and Anne Munds [Orders 1777-82, 17]. Elizabeth was taxable in Sussex County from 1789 to 1812: taxable on a horse in 1789; taxable on a slave and 2 horses in 1803; taxable on 2 horses from 1810 to 1812 [PPTL 1782-1812, frames 96, 106, 204, 233, 265, 553, 600, 614, 651, 706, 787, 820, 841]. She was the mother of

    i.   Anne, perhaps identical to Nancy **Brown**, born 9 December 1770, who registered in Petersburg on 26 January 1798: *Nancy Brown, a light brown Mulatto woman, short bushy hair, five feet high, twenty seven years old the 9 Dec. 1797, daughter of Elizabeth Muns of this town a free woman & now wife of Jack Brown a free man* [Register of Free Negroes 1794-1819, no. 128].

    ii.   Stephen, born in January 1774, registered in Petersburg on 9 July 1798: *a light brown, straight well made Mulatto man, five feet seven inches high, short bushy hair, twenty five Jan. next, born free & raised in the County of Sussex* [Register of Free Negroes 1794-1819, no. 140].

MURRAY FAMILY

1.   Mary Murray, born say 1700, was the servant of Nicholas Minor on 25 March 1719 when the Westmoreland County court presented her for having an illegitimate "Mulatto" child. The court ordered that she be sold by the churchwardens after she completed her indenture to Minor [Orders 1705-21, 367]. She was probably the mother of

2   i.   Ann, born about 1719.

2.   Ann Murray, born about 1719, was a "Mulatto woman" living in Yorktown, York County, on 18 June 1753 when she bound her son Gabriel as an apprentice to John Richardson, carpenter and joiner [Deeds & Bonds 5:550]. She was indicted in York County for selling liquor without a license on 19 November 1759 and fined 10 pounds currency. On 21 November 1763 the court presented her for not listing herself as a tithable, and on 16 July 1764 Mary Brown paid her as a witness in the York County suit of James Reade. On 17 November 1766 the court again presented her for not listing herself as a tithable [Judgment & Orders 1759-63, 90, 126; 1763-5, 90, 126, 248; Orders 1765-8, 161, 206]. Her children were

3   i.   ?Lucy[1], born say 1738.

    ii.   Gabriel, born about 1746, seven years old when he was bound apprentice to John Richardson of Yorktown on 18 June 1753 [Deeds & Bonds 5:550]. He may have been the Gabriel Murray who sued Robert Goode for trespass, assault and battery in Henrico County on 6 September 1768. The court awarded him 5 pounds currency [Orders 1767-9, 352, 449].

    iii.   ?Margaret, born say 1748, living in Henrico County on 4 April 1768 when the court ordered the churchwardens of Henrico Parish to bind out her "mulatto" daughter Milley [Orders 1767-69, 211]. Perhaps one of Milly's children was Charlotte Murray who registered in Chesterfield County on 14 June 1830: *thirty two years old, dark brown complexioned, born free* [Register of Free Negroes 1804-53, no. 721].

3. Lucy[1] Murray, Sr., born say 1738, may have been identical to the Lucy Murray, no race indicated, who was living in Chesterfield County on 5 October 1759 when the court dismissed the suit of the churchwardens against her for debt (for having a bastard child?) [Orders 1759-63, 28]. She left a 15 November 1815 Halifax County, North Carolina will, proved in August 1816. She devised 100 acres near Zachariah **Archer** to her son Mark Murray and 50 acres to David **Winborn**, no relationship stated; a dollar to each of her daughters Polly **Brown** and Patty **Jones**; a heifer to Patty **Jones**'s son William **Jones**; and a dollar to the heirs of her daughter Fanny **Curtis** [WB 3:587]. Her children were

    4 i. Mark, born about 1760.
       ii. ?Lucy[2], born say 1761, not named in the will. She married Benjamin **James**, 8 March 1779 Bertie County bond.
       iii. Fanny **Curtis**, deceased when her mother's will was written. She was called Frances Murray in 1790 when she was head of a Halifax County household of 6 "other free" [NC:64].
       iv. Polly **Brown**.
       v. Patty **Jones**, mother of William **Jones**.

4. Mark Murray, born in Virginia about 1760, was head of a household of 1 male and 7 females in District 12 of Halifax County, North Carolina, in the 1786 state census. He was head of a Halifax County household of 9 "other free" in 1790 [NC:64], and he was also counted with 9 in his household in Martin County in 1790 [NC:69]. He sold his land in Halifax County to Thomas **Winborn**, Senior [WB 4:52]. On 23 October 1832 he testified in Halifax County court to obtain a pension for his services in the Revolution. He stated that he was about seventy-two years old, born and raised in Caroline County, Virginia, moved from there to Hanover County and from there to Halifax County, North Carolina, about 1792. He gave his age as eighty-nine years on 5 May 1845 when he applied for a pension while living in Wilson County, Tennessee. He stated that he enlisted in 1780, but had no record of his service because he left his discharge papers with his father who died shortly after the Revolution. On 18 September 1851 he gave his age as ninety-six years when he again appeared in Wilson County court and testified that:

    > his Great Grandmother came from Ireland, had to be sold for her passage, and his parents always told him that a gentleman by the name of Col. Walk brought her. She was free and fair skinned and after serving out her passage Murrey had children by a Negro which accounts for his being mixed blooded.

    Elizabeth Pope (a white woman) deposed in Smith County Tennessee on 15 October 1851 that:

    > Mark and his wife use to come across (Deep Creek) to go to meetings on Fishing Creek. They were verry Respectable for coulored people. The old Sady, Marks Mother, was a great midwife was sent for a great deal among the most Respectable people.

    Thomas Hale deposed in Smith County that:

    > (Mark) was a man of first rate character although a Mixed Couloured Man...a light Mulatto, was highly respected...Mark's Mother was called a Portague.

    Jesse Grimes testified that as a boy in Halifax County he had often seen Mark joking at log-rollings and house-raisings with other former (white) soldiers about their service in the Revolution [M840-1796, frames 1-57]. In 1850 he was ninety-four years old, living in Wilson County, Tennessee, with (wife?) Lucy, sixty-one years old [TN:221]. Their probable children were

    i.   John, born about 1784 in North Carolina, a "male Mulatto" living near Mark Murray in the 1850 census for Wilson County, Tennessee [TN:223].

    ii. Polly, born about 1805 in North Carolina, living near Mark Murray in 1850 [TN:224].

    iii. Martha **Richardson**, born about 1805, living nearby Mark Murray's household in 1850 [TN:222].

MURROW FAMILY

1.   Margaret Murrow, born say 1668, was the servant of Charles Lee on 17 April 1689 when the Northumberland County court ordered that she serve her master additional time for having a child by a "negro" [Orders 1678-98, 448, 460]. She was probably the ancestor of

    i.   John, a white tithable in the Bertie County, North Carolina list of David Standley from 1769 to 1772 and a "Mulatto" tithable in 1774 [C.R. 10.702.1, box 13].

NASH FAMILY

Members of the Nash family were

1   i.   John[1], born say 1752.

    ii. James, born say 1754, a "Mulata" boy bound apprentice by the 1 September 1761 New Hanover County, North Carolina court: _ah Hand brought into Court a Mulata boy born of ___ oman, Named James Nash praying he may be bound __ him...[Minutes 1738-69, 203].

2   iii. Thomas, born say 1762.

1.   John Nash, born say 1752, was taxable in Chesterfield County on a tithe and a horse in 1792 and 1793 and 2 tithes and 2 horses in 1794 [PPTL, 1786-1811, frames 145, 183, 219]. He may have been the father of

    i.   Moses, born say 1773, a "Mulatto" taxable in Chesterfield County in 1805, 1806 and 1807, called Moses **Ash** in 1811 when he was laborer living with his wife and three children on Samuel Davis's land [PPTL, 1786-1811, frames 603, 641, 689, 824]. He was called Moses Nash in 1813 when he was a "free Negrow" tithable living on Samuel Davis's land [Waldrep, *1813 Tax List*]. He and Nathaniel **Stewart** were security for the 4 March 1812 Chesterfield County marriage bond of Mima **Norton** and Isham D. **Valentine**.

2.   Thomas Nash, born say 1762, (called Thomas **Ash**) was head of a Opelousas, Louisiana household of 7 "other free" in 1810 [LA:316]. He was counted as white in Natchitoches in 1820 [LA:92] and 1830: born 1760-70, head of a household of 5 persons [LA:58]. He was the father of

    i.   Mary, born 6 June 1781, daughter of Thomas Nash, married James **Groves** [Wise, *Sweat Families of the South*, 120]. James was head of a Natchitoches, Louisiana household of 3 "other free" in 1810 [LA:325].

Mecklenburg County, Virginia

1.   Elizabeth Naish/ Nash, born say 1778, was head of a Mecklenburg County household of a white woman 26-45 years of age in 1820 [VA:141a]. She was taxable on her son Irbey and 2 horses in 1812 [PPTL, 1806-28, frame 293]. She rented land in Mecklenburg County from Jacob **Chavis** from about 1800 to 1819 [LVA chancery file 1819-006]. She was the mother of

i. ?John, born about 1794, registered in Mecklenburg County, Virginia, on 28 October 1826: *a free mulatto about thirty two years old, five feet six and three eighths Inches high...born of a free Woman in this County* [Register of Free Negroes 1809-41, no.16, p.20]. He married Olive **Ivey**, 1823 Mecklenburg County bond.

ii. Irbey, born about 1795, head of a Mecklenburg County household of 3 "free colored" in 1820 [VA:141a]. He married Ann **Dunston**, 1830 Mecklenburg County bond. He and Ann were counted as "Mulatto" in the 1850 Mecklenburg County census [VA:138b].

iii. ?Willie, bound by the Mecklenburg County court to Jacob **Chavous**, wheelwright, on 12 October 1807 [Orders [Orders 1807-9, 239].

iv. ?Archibald, bound by the Mecklenburg County court to Jacob **Chavous**, wheelwright, on 12 September 1808 [Orders [Orders 1807-9, 467].

v. ?Banister, married Temperance **Dunston**, 1835 Mecklenburg County bond.

vi. ?Luvenia, born say 1808, married John **Chavous**, 24 February 1829 Mecklenburg County bond.

Another member of the Nash family in Mecklenburg County was

i. Mary, born about 1787, a sixty-three-year-old "Mulatto" counted in the 1850 Mecklenburg County census [VA:139b].

NEAL FAMILY

Members of the Neal family were

i. John, born say 1738, a "Mulatto boy" valued at 10 pounds in the 1 April 1748 inventory of the King George County, Virginia estate of Robert Rankins. He was called a "Mulatto Boy named Jno. Neal under indentures for 31 years from his birth" in the 2 June 1749 inventory of the King George County estate of George Harrison [Inventories 1745-65, 28, 45].

1   ii. William, born say 1740.

1. William Neal, born say 1740, was a "mulatto" taxable in New Hanover County, North Carolina, in 1763 [SS 837] and in Brunswick County, North Carolina, in 1769 [*NCGSJ* V:242]. He may have been the father of

i. Arthur, head of a Richland District, South Carolina household of 5 "other free" in 1800 [SC:60].

ii. S., head of a Brunswick County, North Carolina household of 2 "other free" in 1810 [NC:226].

iii. Nancy, head of a Darlington District, South Carolina household of 6 "other free" in 1810 [SC:669].

iv. James, head of a Darlington District, South Carolina household of 4 "other free" in 1810 [SC:669].

v. Benjamin, head of a Marlboro District, South Carolina household of 5 "other free" in 1800 [SC:60], 4 in Richland District in 1810 [SC:177], perhaps the Benjamin Neale who was head of a Craven County, North Carolina household of 3 "free colored" in 1820 [NC:65].

NEWSOM FAMILY

1. Moses[1] Newsom, born about 1710, was the (white) son of Thomas Newsom (William, William) of Isle of Wight County, Virginia, and his wife Elizabeth

Crawford [*Genealogy of Virginia Families* IV:499-500].[150] He was mentioned in the 18 September 1752 Southampton County will of his mother Elizabeth Newsom [WB 1:175]. He purchased 150 acres on the south side of the Nottoway River in Isle of Wight County from his father for 5 shillings on 21 February 1736 and sold this land "conveyed to sd Moses Newsom by Thomas Newsom, father of the sd Moses" on 22 July 1745 [DB 5:94; 7:143]. This part of Isle of Wight County became Southampton County when it was formed in 1749. On 20 August 1744 he purchased 150 acres near this land, just across the county line in Northampton County, North Carolina, on the south side of Meherrin River near Kirby's Creek. He sold half this land on 25 February 1757 and purchased another acre on Ivey Branch from Over Jordan for 2-1/2 shillings for use as a water grist mill on 3 November 1760 [DB 1:135; 2:365; 3:87]. He died before May 1764 when his wife Judah was granted administration of his estate on 150 pounds bond in the Northampton County court [*NCGSJ* XIV:157]. The court sold the grist mill and the other 75 acres of her land on 20 October 1766 to pay her deceased husband's debts [DB 4:7]. Judah was apparently African American since their children were counted as African American. They were most likely

2	i.	John, born say 1731.
3	ii.	Moses[2], born say 1735, died 1805.
	iii.	James[1], born say 1740, purchased 103 acres on 3 December 1761 near Nathan Stancell's corner, which was near the land of (his brother?) Moses[2] Newsom and sold this land on 9 October 1769 [DB 3:158; 5:21]. He was a "Black" member of the undated Colonial Muster of Captain James Fason's Northampton County militia [Mil. T.R. 1-3]. He was a Northampton County taxable in 1780 on an assessment of 370 pounds [G.A. 46.1]. He was head of a Northampton County household of 5 "Black" persons 12-50 years old and 5 "Black" persons less than 12 or over 50 years old in Dupree's District for the 1786 state census, 11 "other free" in 1790 [NC:74] and 10 in 1800 [NC:463].
4	iv.	Booth, born before 1760.

2.   John Newsom, born say 1731, was a resident of Southampton County, Virginia, on 7 January 1752 when he purchased 150 acres near Kirby's Creek in Northampton County. He sold 15 acres of this land on 2 August 1769 [DB 2:84; 4:266]. He was a "Black" member of Captain Fason's Northampton County militia [Mil. T.R. 1-3]. In September 1774 he bought 100 acres in Northampton County adjacent to William Crumpler [DB 6:45]. He was a Northampton County taxable in 1780 on an assessment of 562 pounds [GA 46.1]. He, called John Sr., and his wife Martha made a deed of gift of their 150 acres on Kirby Creek to (their son?) Amos Newsom of Southampton County on 2 October 1782 [DB 7:121]. John and Martha may have been the parents of

   i.   Amos, born say 1756, a resident of Southampton County, Virginia, when (his parents?) John and Martha Newsom made a deed of gift to him of 150 acres of their land near Angelico Branch of Kirby Creek on 2 October 1782. He was head of a Northampton County household of 4 "Black" persons 12-50 years old and 4 "Black" persons less than 12 or over 50 years old in Dupree's District for the 1786 state census, 6

---

[150]According to the Newsom genealogy, Moses Newsom "perhaps moved to North Carolina."

"other free" in 1790 [NC:74], 7 in 1800 [NC:463], 11 in 1810
[NC:737], and 6 "free colored" in 1820 [NC:248].[151]

5   ii.   Ethelred, born say 1760.

3.   Moses[2] Newsom, born say 1735, received a grant for 480 acres in
Northampton County on 4 March 1761 and sold this land on 3 February 1768
[DB 4:147]. He was listed among the "Black" members of the undated
Colonial Muster Roll of Captain Fason's Northampton County Militia [Mil.
T.R. 1-3]. On 10 August 1778 he repurchased 462 acres adjoining John
Newsom's line which was part of the land he sold in 1768. He sold 22 acres
of this land on 12 February 1780 and sold a further 314 acres adjoining James
Newsom's line on 6 April 1785 [DB 6:256: 7:47, 236]. He was taxed in
Northampton County on an assessment of 2,430 pounds in 1780 [GA 46.1].
He was head of a Northampton County household of 9 "Black" persons 12-50
years old and 7 "Black" persons less than 12 or over 50 years old in Dupree's
District of Northampton County in 1786 for the state census, 14 "other free"
in 1790 [NC:74], and 10 in 1800 [NC:463]. He may have been the Moses
Newsom who entered tracts of 100 acres and 125 acres on Potts Branch near
Thomas **Ivey** in Robeson County on 19 April 1791 [Pruitt, *Land Entries:
Robeson County,* I:45, 53]. This was near the land of (his nephew?) Ethelred
Newsom. Between 1796 and 1802 he married Winnifred **Walden**, widow of
John **Walden**. Winnifred was granted administration on John **Walden**'s estate
in 1796, but Moses Newsom was the estate representative mentioned in the 6
February 1802 account of sales [CR 71.801.20]. Moses Newsom's 17
September 1805 Northampton County will was proved in December of that
year. He left 50 acres on Little Swamp near the Roanoke River to his wife
Winnie, one silver dollar to George **Artist**, named some of his children:
Tabitha **Cumbo**, Henry Newsam, and James Newsam; divided the residue
among other unnamed children; and named his son Nathaniel Newsom
executor [WB 2:297]. Winnie Newsom by her 4 November 1807 will, proved
December the same year, gave land to Harwood **Dukes** in return for his
lending money to her son by her previous marriage, Harrod/ Harwood
Walden. She also divided four head of cattle among the unnamed children of
Joel Newsom and Howell **Wade** and made small bequests to her daughter
Penny Newsom and granddaughters Winnie **Walden** and Lucy Newsom.[152]
Drury **Walden** was her executor [WB 2:353]. Moses Newsom's children were
identified in a chancery suit in Champaign County, Ohio, brought by Henry
Newsom on 30 July 1832 against the heirs of (his brother) James Newsom.
They were Nathaniel Newsom of North Carolina, Moses Newsom of North
Carolina, Nathan Newsom of Pennsylvania, Naomi **Banks** (wife of Cyrus
Banks) of North Carolina, Cloe **Rand** (wife of Micajah **Rand**) of North
Carolina, the heirs of Joel Newsom, the heirs of Tabitha **Cumbo** (late Tabitha
Newsom), the heirs of Martha **Artist** (late Martha Newsom), and Turner **Byrd**
of Logan County in right of his mother Judith **Byrd**, deceased (late Judith
Newsom) [Court of Common Pleas, Champaign County reel 14-344]. Moses
Newsom's children were

6   i.   Nathaniel[1], born say 1765-70.

---

[151]In May 1763 another Amos Newsom signed a petition to the North Carolina Assembly to repeal
the law which placed additional tax on free Negroes [Saunders, *Colonial Records of North Carolina,*
VI:982-3]. He was probably the (white) brother of Moses[1] Newsom [*Genealogy of Virginia Families*
IV:499].

[152]Harwood **Dukes** was head of a Northampton County household of 5 "other free" in 1800
[NC:435]. Howell **Wade** was head of a Northampton County household of 7 in 1800 [NC:485], 7 in
1810 [NC:751], and 8 "free colored" in Halifax County in 1820.

    ii. a daughter, married George **Artis**. She apparently died before 1807 when George married Hannah **Archer**, widow of Luke **Archer**.

    iii. Moses³, Jr., born say 1776, head of a Northampton County household of 1 "other free" in 1800 [NC:463], 3 "other free in 1810 [NC:737], and 1 "free colored" in 1820 [NC:248]. He made deeds of trust for the 24 acres on which he was living on 5 September 1830 and 28 August 1835 [DB 28:176, 308]. He was called "Moses Newsoms son" in the 28 August 1835 deed. His 25 May 1840 Northampton County will was proved in June 1846. He named only his nephew Everett **Banks** [WB 5:48].

    iv. Nathan, living in the state of Pennsylvania when the suit for partition was filed in Champaign County.

    v. Naomi **Banks**, born about 1765, wife of Cyrus **Banks** of North Carolina who was apparently identical to Silas **Banks** of Northampton County, North Carolina. Ona **Banks** was about eighty-five years of age in 1850 when she was counted with (her son) Everett **Banks** in the Northampton County household of (her son-in-law) Thomas **Smith** [household no. 1041].

    vi. Tabitha **Cumbo**, who was deceased when Moses² Newsom made his will. Her children mentioned in the will were Jinny, Henry, and John. Henry, John and Jensy **Cumbo** were named in the Champaign County suit for partition. By 1832 when the suit was filed, Henry and John were living in North Carolina; Jensy had married John Newsom and was living in Logan County.

7   vii. Henry¹, born say 1780.

    viii. James², died intestate in Logan County, Ohio, before 6 August 1832 when (his brother) Henry Newsom was granted administration on his estate on $1,600 security [Administrative Docket Book B:3, 22]. Pm 30 July 1832 Henry brought suit against James's heirs for partition of his land. The land included 200 acres which James had purchased by deed of 29 January 1817 and four lots in the town of Milford which he had purchased by deed of 4 February 1818 [Court of Common Pleas, July Term 1836, Champaign County reel 14-344, pp. 344-52].

    ix. Chloe **Rann**, sister of James Newsom, and wife of Michael **Rann** who stated in his 10 November 1847 Halifax County, North Carolina will that he had a claim on part of James Newsom's Ohio estate [WB 4:295].

    x. Joel, born 1776-94, head of a Northampton County household of 7 "other free" in 1810 [NC:737] and 9 "free colored" in 1820 [NC:248]. His heirs listed in the Champaign County suit for partition were Angelina **Artist** (wife of James **Artist** of Logan County), Henry Newsom of North Carolina, Moses Newsom of North Carolina, Lucy **Hunt**, wife of James **Hunt** of North Carolina, and four others whose names were unknown to Henry Newsom at the time of the Champaign County suit.

    xi. Martha **Artist**, wife of George **Artist**. Her heirs (sons) Kinchen **Artist** of Logan County and Newsom **Artist** of North Carolina were named in the Champaign County suit for partition as well as in George **Artis**'s 30 December 1819 Northampton County will [WB 3:296].

    xii. Penny, received a hat by the 4 November 1807 Northampton County will of her mother Winna Newsom.

    xiii. Judith **Byrd**, whose only heir was Turner **Byrd** of Logan County when the Champaign County suit was filed.

4. Booth Newsom was born before 1760 since he was listed in the Colonial Muster Roll of Captain James Fason's Northampton County Militia [Mil. T.R. 1-3]. He was taxable in Northampton County on an assessment of 215 pounds in 1780 [GA 46.1] and was head of a Northampton County household of 1

"Black" person 12-50 years old and 2 "Black" persons less than 12 or over 50 years old in Elisha Webb's District in 1786 for the state census. He was head of a Northampton County household of 3 "other free" in 1790 [NC:74] and 8 in 1800 [NC:463]. He may have been the Boothe Newsom who was declared an insolvent debtor by the Halifax County court on 28 November 1844. Perhaps his children were the Newsoms counted in the census for Halifax County, North Carolina, in 1820:

i.   Patience, born before 1776, head of a household of 9 "free colored" in 1820 [NC:159].

ii. Seymour, head of a household of Northampton County household of 1 "other free" in 1810 [NC:737], 7 "free colored" in Halifax County in 1820 [NC:159] and 9 in 1830. He was permitted to carry a gun by order of the 17 August 1840 session of the Halifax County court [Minutes 1732-46, vol.2].

iii. Arthur, born about 1790, an eight-year-old "base born child" bound out by the Halifax County court on 21 August 1798. He married Tempy **Ash**, 13 April 1820 Halifax County bond, and was head of a Halifax County household of 8 "free colored" in 1820 [NC:159].

5. Ethelred[1] Newsom, born say 1760, may have been named for Ethelred Taylor who sold John Newsom his land on 7 January 1752 and witnessed the will of Jacob Newsom in Southampton County, Virginia, on 2 October 1771 [WB 3:240]. He was a soldier in the Tenth Regiment of the North Carolina Continental Line [Clark, *State Records of North Carolina*, XVI:1126], called "Netheneldred Newsom of Robeson County" on 18 April 1792 when he appointed Jacob Rhodes his attorney to receive his final settlement for serving in the war [*NCGSJ* XIV:111]. He entered 100 acres on the east side of Five Mile Branch near Thomas **Ivey** in Robeson County on 24 December 1787 and another 200 acres on 12 September 1788 [Pruitt, *Land Entries: Robeson County*, I:12, 18]. He purchased land by deed proved in Robeson County on 2 July 1801 [Minutes I:331]. He was head of a Robeson County household of 3 "other free" in 1790 [NC:50], 3 in 1800 [NC:408], and 4 in 1810 [NC:241]. He may have been in Northampton County in 1800 when he was counted in the census for that county with 6 "other free" in his household. He sold 320 acres in Chatham County on the west side of the Haw River on 18 November 1817 [DB V:89]. His 20 December 1820 Robeson County will, no probate date, mentioned his wife Lucy and left land to his grandsons [WB 1:325]. Lucy transferred land to Nelson **Roberts** by deed proved in May 1838 Robeson County court [Minutes 1829-39]. Ethelred's children were

i.   a daughter, married _____ **Terry**, mother of Newsom **Terry**. Her husband was probably Philip **Terry**, head of a Cumberland County household of 4 "free colored" in 1820 [NC:191] who may have been a son of David **Terry**, head of a Sampson County household of 4 "other free" in 1790 [NC:51].

ii. Mary **Roberts**, mother of Ishmael **Roberts**. Ishmael was also mentioned in the Chatham County will of his grandfather Ishmael **Roberts** [CR 22.801.16].

iii. Sarah **Roberts**, mother of Ethelred **Roberts**, and wife of Aaron **Roberts** according to Aaron's free papers recorded in Owen County, Indiana [DB 3:280].

8   iv. ?Henry[3], born about 1800.

6. Nathaniel[1] Newsom, born 1765-70, was head of a Northampton household of 3 "other free" in 1790 [NC:74], 6 in 1800 [NC:463], 11 in 1810 [NC:737], and 7 "free colored" in 1820. His wife was Edy **Hawley** whose father Benjamin **Hawley** mentioned her and her daughter Charlotte Newsom in his 9 July 179_ Northampton County will, proved March 1805 [WB 2:276]. Nathaniel's 31 July 1835 Northampton County will was proved in September

the same year [WB 4:37]. He left land in Northampton County and land in Logan County, Ohio, to his children:

    i.   Nathaniel[2], who received 157 acres where his father lived. In 1860 he was head of a Jefferson Township, Logan County, Ohio household with $3,650 real estate [OH:43].

    ii.   Willis, who received the land he was living on.

    iii.   Dorothy **Archer**, who received land in Logan County, Ohio.

    iv.   Sally **Byrd**.[153]

    v.   Charlotte, married Sterling **Haithcock**, 24 November 1813 Northampton County bond.

    vi.   Edith **Roberts**.

    vii.   Elizabeth Newsom.

    viii.   Tilitha **Hawley**.

7.   Henry[1] Newsom, born say 1780, was head of a Northampton County household of 2 "other free" in 1810 [NC:737]. He was taxable on 100 acres in Champaign County, Ohio, in 1816 based on military title [*Champaign County Genealogical Society Newsletter July/Aug/Sep 1999*: 90]. He left a 4 September 1841 Logan County will, proved 28 October 1841. He devised to his wife Dorothy 70 acres of his land on the north side of the road leading from Zanesfield to Middleburgh. The profits from the remainder of his farm land was to be used to pay for the education to his youngest sons John and Henry. When John reached the age of twenty-one and at the death of his wife, all the land was to be divided between John and Henry who were also to receive forty acres of land in Mercer County adjoining land he had deeded to Judith and Nancy Newsom. He left $1 each to his children Priscilla **Dick**, Nathan Newsom, Levina **Witsell**, Martha **Byrd**, Eliza **Allen** and divided the remainder of his estate equally between his children Lydia, Ann, Judith, Nancy, Alice, John and Henry. Buyers at the sale of his estate included Sterling **Heathcock** (**Haithcock**), Owen **Byrd**, Green **Allen**, Kinchen **Artis**, Peter **Byrd**, Joshua **Hunt**, David **Hunt**, Joseph **Allen**, Martha Newsom, William **Dempsey**, Matthew Newsom, Leonard **Whitfield**, Benjamin **Hawley**, Hardy **Wade** and Jonathan **Bowser** [Administrative Docket Book B:146, 263-270]. He was the father of

    i.   Lydia.

    ii.   Ann.

    iii.   Judith.

    iv.   Nancy.

    v.   Alice.

    vi.   Priscilla **Dick**.

    vii.   Nathan.

    viii.   Levina **Witsell**, probably wife of Felix **Whitsel** who was a buyer at the sale of Henry Newsom's estate [WB, 270].

    ix.   Martha **Byrd**.

    x.   Eliza **Allen**.

    xi.   John.

    xii.   Henry[4].

8.   Henry[3] Newsom, born about 1800, received twenty lashes by order of the 7 December 1829 Cumberland County court, and on 11 June 1830 he took the oath of an insolvent debtor. He obtained "free papers" in Cumberland County on 15 and 17 March 1834 and recorded them in Owen County, Indiana, on 10 November 1845: *he is the son of Lifsy (Lucy?) Newsom, a free born woman*

---

[153]There was also a Jinny **Byrd** who received her Northampton County, North Carolina, "free papers" on 14 March 1835 and registered in Logan County, Ohio: *Jinny Newson, wife of Everett Byrd, bright complexion, 37 years old, was free...* [Turpin, *Register of Black, Mulatto, and Poor Persons*, 11].

of colour...is married to one Polly George, a free born woman of color and has seven children namely: Isham (about fifteen years old), Dred (about thirteen years old), Lifsy (about eleven years old), Sarah (about eight years old), Henry (about five years old), Martha (about four years old), and Elijah (about fifteen months old)...he is of dark complexion...about thirty four years old about five feet five inches high...for many years a resident in this Town. His wife Polly also obtained free papers in Cumberland County (on 19 March 1834) and recorded them in Owen County on 10 November 1845: *wife of Henry Newsom, daughter of Elizabeth George, a Freeborn woman of colour, about thirty two years old, of a tolerably light complexion...said Polly & her mother are coloured persons of free parentage* [DB 8:433]. Henry was head of a Franklin Township, Owen County, Indiana, household of 7 "free colored" in 1840 [IN:25]. He called himself Henry A. Newsom on 12 December 1835 when he speculated in corn futures, contracting with the inhabitants of Township Nine of Owen County to deliver 350-3/4 bushels of corn three years from that date [DB 8:433]. He probably profited from this trade since he offset this obligation by contracting with other parties to supply this corn in January 1838 after the price of corn fell 30-40% in Cincinnati as a result of the Panic of 1837 [Circuit Order Book 13:148-149; Buley, R.C., *The Old Northwest Pioneer Period, 1815-40*, 2 vol. Indianapolis: n.p. (1850):273]. In 1845 he and his son Dred O. Newsom were sued in Owen County for $36 in corn and pork which they failed to deliver on 29 May 1843 [Orders 4:120].

Other members of the Newsom family were

      i. Stephen, born say 1758, a "Negro" taxable in Southampton County from 1787 to 1790 [PPTL 1782-92, frames 643, 765].

10   i. Hannah, born say 1768.

      ii. Aaron, born about 1772, taxable in Greensville County from 1799 to 1804 [PPTL 1782-1807, frames 247, 266, 276, 289, 305, 323], a "Free Negro" taxable in Meherrin Parish, Brunswick County, Virginia, from 1810 to 1815 [PPTL 1799-1815, frames 477, 520, 559, 637, 675, 730]. Thomas **Stewart** left him 10 pounds by his 14 October 1790 Greensville County will [WB 1:181-3]. Molly **Stewart** charged him with breach of the peace, but the case was dismissed by the Greensville County court on 10 May 1802 [Orders 1799-1806, 217]. He and his wife Christian of Brunswick County, Virginia, sold his part of the Greensville County estate of Jesse Jones to Henry **Stewart** on 13 October 1806 [Greensville County DB 3:507]. He registered in Petersburg on 30 August 1794: *a dark brown man, five feet ten inches high, twenty two years old, appears to have been born free & raised in Greensville County* [Register of Free Negroes 1794-1819, no. 89] and recorded the certificate in Brunswick County, Virginia court in January 1826. He was married to Susan Newsom by January 1826 when she registered in Brunswick County: *Wife of Aaron Neusum, a free bright mulatto woman, about 27 years old, 5 feet 4 inches high with long bushy hair* [Wynne, *Register of Free Negroes*, 81-2]. He was head of a Freetown, Brunswick County, Virginia household of 4 "other free" in 1810 [VA:769] and 7 "free colored" in 1820 [VA:664].

11   iii. Sarah, born before 1776.

     iv. James[3], born before 1776, head of a Botetourt County household of 9 "free colored" in 1820.

     v. Nathan[3], born about 1776, registered in Southampton County on 25 June 1802: *age 26, Mulatto, 6 feet high, free born* [Register of Free Negroes 1794-1832, no. 229]. He recorded his free papers in Norfolk County, Virginia [Freed Negro Papers, Chesapeake County courthouse loose papers].

    vi.   Nelson, head of a Northampton household 1 white male over the age of 16 in 1790 [NC:75] and 3 "other free" in Sampson County, North Carolina, in 1800 [NC:521].

   vii. Henry[2], born about 1787, head of an Owen County, Indiana household of 2 "free colored" in 1840 (a man and woman over fifty-five years of age) [IN:24] and a sixty-three-year-old man living in Harrison Township, Vigo County, Indiana, in 1850 [IN:542].

  viii. Elias, born about 1791, registered in Southampton County on 25 August 1818: *age 27, Mulatto, 5 feet 5-1/2 inches, free born.* His wife Winny registered on 26 April 1819: *age 32, wife of Elias Newsom, 5 feet 3-1/2 inches high, rather of a bright complexion, free born* [Register of Free Negroes 1794-1832, no. 1157, 1177].

    ix. Etheldred[2], born about 1793, registered in Southampton County on 13 August 1816: *age dark complection, 5 feet 6 1/2 inches high, free born* [Register of Free Negroes 1794-1832, no. 1023].

    x. Carter, born about 1794, registered in Southampton County on 13 January 1817: *age 23, Black, 5 feet 6 inches high, free born* [Register of Free Negroes 1794-1832, no. 1044].

10. Hannah Newsom, born about 1768, was living in the lower district of St. Luke's Parish on 22 May 1798 when the Southampton County court ordered the overseers of the poor to bind out her illegitimate son Anthony Newsum [Minutes 1793-99, 347]. She registered in Southampton County on 19 November 1831: *bright (Colour), 5 feet 1/4 inch high, free born* [Register of Free Negroes 1794-1832, no. 1931]. Hannah was the mother of

    i. Anthony, born about 1785, taxable in James Wilinson's household in St. Luke's Parish, Southampton County, in 1805, listed in his own Southampton County household in 1807 and 1811 [PPTL 1792-1806, frame 823; 1807-21, 54, 173, 198] and head of a Southampton County household of 6 "other free" in 1810 [VA:88]. He registered in Southampton County on 2 August 1810: *age 25, yellow, 5 feet 9 inches, free born* [Register of Free Negroes 1794-1832, no. 813].

11. Sarah Newsom, born before 1776, was head of a Northampton County household of 3 "other free" in 1800 [NC:463] and 4 "free colored" in 1820 [NC:248]. She may have been the mother of

    i. Felson, born about 1806, bound an apprentice farmer to Samuel Stancell by the 8 September 1813 Northampton County court [Minutes 1813-21]. He was listed as a forty-four-year-old blacksmith in the 1850 Northampton County census in household number 484.

NEWTON FAMILY

1. Abraham Newton, born say 1700, was a "Mulatto" slave who was purchased by his wife Elizabeth **Young**, "a free Mulatto" woman of Norfolk County. She died in November 1743 and left a will (not recorded) which gave him his freedom. The Legislative Council ordered him set free [Hall, *Executive Journals of the Council,* V:196, 215]. Their children were probably

    i. Henry, born say 1723, taxable head of a Norfolk County household with Benjamin and William Newton in Western Branch District in 1759 [Wingo, *Norfolk County Tithables, 1751-65,* 133].

2   ii. Benjamin, born say 1725.

   iii. William[1], born say 1730, a tithable in Henry Newton's household in 1759, in Benjamin Newton's household in 1761 and tithable in Richard Carney's household in Norfolk County on the north side of Western Branch in 1770 (called William Neowton) [Wingo, *Norfolk County Tithables, 1751-65,* 133, 167; *1766-80,* 107].

2. Benjamin Newton, born say 1725, was taxable in the household of (his brother?) Henry Newton in 1759 and was head of a Norfolk County household in 1761: taxable with (his wife?) Elizabeth Newton and (brother?) William Newton. He was taxable with Elizabeth in 1765 and 1767 and taxable by himself until 1774 [Wingo, *Norfolk County Tithables, 1751-65*, 133, 167, 190; *1766-80*, 15, 72, 88, 106, 150, 213, 228]. Benjamin and Elizabeth may have been the parents of

    i.   Sarah, born say 1752, a tithable in Richard Carney's household in Norfolk County on the north side of Western Branch in 1770 (called Sary Neowton) [Wingo, *Norfolk County Tithables, 1766-80*, 107].

    ii. James, born about 1754, a "Mulatto" apprenticed to Josiah Deans of Norfolk County to be a carpenter on 10 December 1769 [DB 25:52]. He was one of eight tithables in William Deans' Norfolk County household in 1770: *William Deans, Sr., Josiah Deans & negroes James, Neowton, Dempo, Will, Sam & Lead - 8* [Wingo, *Norfolk County Tithables, 1766-80*, 107]. He was taxable in Norfolk County from 1795 to 1812: called a "M"(ullato) starting in 1798; a labourer living on Western Branch in a "List of Free Negroes and Mulattoes" in 1801 [PPTL, 1791-1812, frames 144, 255, 359, 384, 467, 650, 728, 778].

3   iii. Thomas, born say 1770.

    iv. William[2], a "M"(ulatto) taxable in Norfolk County from 1802 to 1817, a "B.M." (Black Man) living on Western Branch and taxable on a "free Negro" tithe in 1816 [PPTL, 1791-1812, frames 434, 486A, 581, 694, 746; 1813-24, frames 105, 145, 263]. He married Margaret **Nickens**, 30 March 1805 Norfolk County marriage [Ministers' Returns].

    v.   Wilson, a "free Mulatto" bound by the Princess Anne County court as an apprentice to John Williams on 10 August 1772 to learn the trade of blacksmith [Minutes 1770-3, 298].

3. Thomas Newton, born say 1770, was taxable in Portsmouth and Elizabeth River Parishes in Norfolk County from 1789 to 1817: called a "M"(ulatto) starting in 1798; a labourer living on Western Branch in a "List of Free Negroes and Mulattoes" in 1801; a "B.M." (Black Man) taxable on a horse and 4 cattle in 1815 [PPTL, 1782-1791, frames 647; 1791-1812, frames 87, 231, 255, 359, 384, 434, 564, 694; 1813-24, frames 105, 263]. He was head of a Norfolk County household of 9 "other free" in 1810 [VA:820]. He may have been the father of

    i.   Mary, married Richard **Anderson** (free blacks), 4 December 1824 Norfolk County bond, Isaac **Fuller** security.

Other members of a Newton family in Virginia were

    i.   Isaac, born say 1752, head of a Richmond County, Virginia household of 3 "other free" and 2 slaves in 1810 [VA:411], a levy free "free black" in 1813 with (his wife?) Judith Newton who was above the age of sixteen [Waldrep, *1813 Tax List*].

    ii. John, born about 1756, the runaway servant of William Brown on 13 July 1776 when Brown advertised for his return in the Virginia Gazette: *about 20 Years of Age, 5 feet 5 or 6 Inches high, slender made, is an Asiatic Indian by Birth, has been twelve Months in Virginia, but lived ten years (as he says) in England, in the service of Sir Charles Whitworth. He wears long black Hair, which inclines to curl, tied behind, and pinned up at the Sides; has a very sour Look, and his Lips project remarkably forward...He has been at Richmond, Williamsburg, and in other Parts of the Country, in the Service of Mr. George Rootes of Frederick, and Col. Blackburn of Prince William, of whom I had him; and as he is a good Barber and Hair-Dresser, it is probably he may endeavor to follow those Occupations as a free Man.*

> *Whoever takes up said Servant...shall have eight dollars reward; and if delivered to me at Westwood, in Prince William, further reasonable Charges* [*Virginia Gazette* (Dixon & Hunter edition)].

NICHOLS/ NICHOLAS FAMILY

1. Margaret Nicholas, born say 1690, was presented by the Princess Anne County court on 2 February 1708/9 for having a "Mullatto" child. On 7 February 1710/11 the court ordered that she pay a fine of fifteen pounds or be sold by the churchwardens for five years. On 6 March 1710/11 the court ordered the sheriff to search for her because she had escaped from the churchwardens when they were endeavoring to sell her. On 9 May 1712 her master Tully Smyth sued Lewis Purvine for keeping his servant for twenty-one days, but the jury accepted Purvine's excuse that she was his servant at the time. On 2 April 1714 she was convicted by the court for having another "Molatto" child. The court ordered that she serve her master Tully Smyth three months for absenting herself from his service and also for having a child in his house and ordered that she be sold for five years for the benefit of Lynhaven Parish after her service was completed. The sheriff sold Margaret before 1 November 1721 when the sale was recorded in court [Minutes 1691-1709, 491; 1709-17, 48, 53, 92, 151; 1717-28, 115, 121, 124]. She was apparently the mother of

    i.   Samuel, born say 1714, a "free mullatto" who sued Henry Chapman for trespass in Princess Anne County court on 2 June 1742. He was called a "free Negro" when he recorded his livestock mark in Princess Anne County on 30 April 1746. He was called Sam Nichols when he won a judgment for twenty-three shillings against Lewis Thelaball in Princess Anne County court on 18 July 1750. On 22 November 1752 the court ordered John Chapman to post fifty pounds security for his good behavior towards Sam, and on 19 June 1753 the court ordered Sam to post fifty pounds bond for his good behavior towards John Chapman. On 16 October 1759 the court bound "free Mullatto" Nanny **Duncan** to him as an apprentice [Minutes 1737-44, 174; 1691-1709, 17; 1744-53, 214, 341; 1753-62, 25, 365]. He was probably the ancestor of Sam Nichols, head of a Norfolk County household of 1 "other free" and 3 slaves in 1810 [VA:913].

NICKENS FAMILY

1. Richard[1] Nickens, born say 1660, was called Black Dick when he and his wife Chriss were freed "after the finishing of the Crop that is now on the Grounde" by the 4 June 1690 Lancaster County will of John Carter, proved 11 December the same year. Each was given a cow, three barrels of corn and peas, and allowed the use of some land for farming. Chris' unnamed daughter was also freed as were slaves, Diana and "little Chriss," when they reached the age of eighteen years [WB 8:5].[154] They were all apparently free by July 1691 since they were not included in the inventory of Carter's estate [WB 8:24, 24a, 33]. Dick was taxable on a tithe in Lancaster County in 1699 (Black Dick), 2 in 1700 (Black Dick), 3 in 1701 and 1702 (Free Dick), 4 in 1703 (Free Richard), 2 in 1704 (Richard Yoconohawcon), and 4 in 1706 (Free Dick). Chris may have been identical to "Criss a free negroe woman" who was owed 200 pounds of tobacco by the estate of William Flinston, deceased, for funeral

---

[154]Edward Nickens may have been identical to "new Ned" who was listed in the account of Carter's estate [WB 8:24]. Perhaps Little Chriss was the mother of *Betty a negro child the Daughter of Criss, a free negro woman* (no surname mentioned) who was five years old on 19 September 1716 when she was bound apprentice to Charles Craven in adjoining Northumberland County [Orders 1713-19, 180].

charges on 10 March 1708 [Orders 1696-1702, 93, 128, 153; 1702-13, 12, 55, 108, 162, 185]. Their children (who shortened the name to Nickens) were most likely

2   i.   Edward[1], born say 1680.

3   ii.   Elizabeth[1], born say 1685.

2.   Edward[1] Nickens (Richard[1]), born say 1680, was called Edward Yockohoc when he was taxable on 2 tithes in Lancaster County in 1707 and called Edward Yockonhawken in 1709 when he was a Christ Church Parish taxable on 1 tithe. He was called Edward Nicken on 12 December 1712 when he was sued in Lancaster County court by David Williams, and he was called Edward Nicken from 1715 to 1719: "a negro" in 1716 and 1717 when he was taxable on 1 tithe, and called Edward Nicken in 1720 when he was taxable on 2 tithes [Orders 1702-13, 179, 231, 298; 1713-21, 118, 168, 223, 258, 302, 335]. He purchased 50 acres in Christ Church Parish, Lancaster County for 4,000 pounds of tobacco on 6 March 1713/4 and sold this land on 20 March 1722. On 2 November 1722 he purchased 40 acres on the west side of Corrotoman River and another 50 acres adjoining this land and land of Colonel Robert Carter on 13 September 1726. He sold this land on 5 March 1730, with Simon **Showcraft** as a witness [DB 9:478-9; 11:212-3, 222-3; 305-6; 12:147-9]. On 18 July 1723 Abraham **Shoecraft** acknowledged in Northumberland County court that he was indebted to him for 1,500 pounds of tobacco, and on 14 August 1728 he was sued by Robert Biscoe in Lancaster County court [Orders 1719-29, 109; 1721-29, 287]. His 21 September 1735 Lancaster County will was proved 12 November the same year, Richard and Elizabeth **Weaver** and Simon **Shewcraft** witnesses. The will (which he signed) named his wife Mary and children: Tun, Sarah, John, Robert, Aner, Edward, Richard, and James [WB 12:355]. Mary may have been the Mary Nickens who was presented by the Lancaster County court on 12 November 1742 [Orders 1729-43, 364]. Their children were

     i.   Tun.

    ii.   Sarah.

4   iii.   John[1], born say 1720.

5   iv.   Robert[1], born say 1721.

     v.   Aner, born say 1723.

6   vi.   Edward[2], born say 1725.

7   vii. Richard[3], born say 1727.

8 viii. James[1], born say 1729.

3.   Elizabeth[1] Nickens (Richard[1]), born say 1685, may have been the unnamed daughter of Chris (Nickens) who was freed by the 4 June 1690 Lancaster will of John Carter. She may have been identical to Elizabeth Nigings of Lancaster County who "of her own free & Voluntary will" bound her son Richard Niggins as an apprentice carpenter to Henry and Ann Tapscott in Northumberland County on 16 May 1711 [Record Book 1710-13, 21]. A case against her for having a bastard child was dismissed by the Lancaster County court in 1715 [Orders 1713-21, 137]. She may have been the same Elizabeth Nickens who was presented by the Lancaster County court on 19 November 1764 for concealing three tithables. The case was dismissed on 17 December 1764 [Orders 1764-67, 76].[155] Elizabeth was the mother of

9   i.   Richard[2], born in August 1705.

---

[155]Perhaps Elizabeth Nickens failed to list the female members of her household as tithables. No free women were listed as tithables in Lancaster County in the surviving colonial tax lists of 1745 and 1746 [Tithables 1745-1795], so this may have been the first time the court was enforcing the 1723 amendment which made female members of African American and Indian households tithable.

ii.   ?Murrough, born say 1708, sued Robert Scofield for trespass, assault and battery in Lancaster County court on 9 June 1731. The jury awarded her six pence and costs [Orders 1729-43, 40, 44, 90].

10   iii.   ?Catherine /Kate, born say 1710.

11   iv.   ?Christian, born say 1711.

v.   ?Thomas, born say 1720, living in Northumberland County when he made his 22 April 1778 will, proved 14 September the same year. He left a cow and a colt to his wife's grandchild Ann **Weaver Kelly** and the remainder of his estate to his wife Ann [RB 10:375]. His estate was valued at 159 pounds [Orders 1776-80, 494]. His wife was Ann **Weaver**, mentioned in the 30 November 1777 Lancaster County will of her brother Isaac **Weaver** [WB 20:120]. She was taxable on 5 cattle and a horse in Northumberland County in 1782 [PPTL, 1782-1812, frame 232].

12   vi.   ?William[1], born say 1725.

4.   John[1] Nickens (Edward[1], Richard[1]), born say 1720, was a taxable head of household in Lancaster County in 1775 and 1776 with James Nickens and taxable with (his son?) John Nickens, Jr., from 1777 to 1781 [Tithables 1745-95, 14, 18, 20, 35, 42, 51]. He was head of a Lancaster County household of 7 "white" (free) persons in 1783 [VA:55]. He was taxable in Northumberland County on 9 cattle and a horse in 1782 [PPTL 1782-1812, frame 232] and taxable in Lancaster County from 1783 to 1801: taxable on 2 free males in 1790, 3 in 1791, taxed on Benjamin and Bartley Nickens' tithes in 1794 and 1796 [PPTL, 1782-1839, frames 16, 74, 86, 121, 144, 216]. He was the father of

i.   ?Richard[4], born about 1751, served in the Revolution aboard the galley *Hero* and received 1,000 acres on 2 August 1783 for serving three years. He was listed as William Brent's Lancaster County tithe in 1775, and listed as John Clayton's tithe in 1776 [Tithables 1745-95, 14, 18]. He was in the personal property tax lists in Lancaster County from 1784 to 1794: taxable on 3 slaves in 1787, taxable on taxable on Philip **Boyd**'s tithe in 1792 and 1793 [PPTL, 1782-1839, frames 23, 45, 62, 97 109, 121, 157; Tithables 1745-95, 51]. He registered in Lancaster County on 17 October 1803: *Age 52, Color mulatto...born free* [Burkett, *Lancaster County Register of Free Negroes*, 1]. He married Elizabeth **Hamilton**, 20 August 1806 Lancaster County bond and was head of a Lancaster County household of 4 "other free" in 1810 [VA:355]. He was said to be eighty-two years old when he applied for a pension in Lancaster County court on 17 December 1832 [M805, reel 0615, frame 0187], and his age was estimated at eighty years on 7 January 1834 when he testified for John Jackson's pension application [Hopkins, *Virginia Revolutionary War Land Grant Claims*, 119]. His 17 January 1835 Lancaster County will, proved 16 March 1835, mentioned his niece Zelia Nicken and her children Assenath and Nancy Nicken [WB 28:329].

ii.   John[2], Jr., born say 1756, taxable in the Lancaster County household of (his father?) John Nickens, Sr., from 1777 to 1781 [Tithables 1745-95, 51, 57]. He was head of a Lancaster County household of 1 "white" (free) person in 1783, listed next to John, Sr. [VA:55] and taxable in Lancaster County from 1783 to 1813, in the list of "free Negroes & Mulattoes" in 1813 [PPTL, 1782-1839, frames 16, 276, 230, 319, 350, 385]. He was a "free mulatto" head of a Northumberland County household of 10 "other free" in 1810 [VA:990]. He was called John Nickens, Jr., when he married Ann **Mills**, 17 September 1791 Lancaster bond.

iii.   ?Robert[2], born say 1762, served as a soldier in the Revolution from Lancaster County [Jackson, *Virginia Negro Soldiers*, 41]. He was taxable in Lancaster County in John McTire's household in 1779, in John Davis' household in 1787, and taxable in his own household in 1794 and 1795, called Robert Nickens, Junr. [Tithables 1745-95, 33, 51, 57] and taxable from 1796 to 1804 [PPTL, 1782-1839, frames 144, 189, 216, 256]. He posted bond to marry Elizabeth **Gray**, 12 August 1786 Lancaster bond but married Nancy **Howe** (spinster over 21), 5 March 1793 Lancaster bond. Nancy registered in Lancaster County on 19 September 1803: *Age 31, Color mulatto...born free*. Elizabeth **Gray** registered on 21 January 1811: *Age abt. 42, Color mulatto...born free* [Burkett, *Lancaster County Register of Free Negroes*, 1, 5].

    iv. ?Bridger, taxable in Lancaster County from 1786 to 1788, in 1805, and from 1813 to 1816, in a list of "free Negroes & Mulattoes in 1813 [PPTL, 1782-1839, frames 36, 53, 274, 385, 421].

    v. Benjamin², born about 1772, taxable in Lancaster County in 1794, adjoining John and Bartley Nickens [Tithables 1745-95, 51]. He married Mary Nickens, daughter of Amos¹ Nickens, 11 April 1796 Northumberland County bond. Benjamin was taxable in Northumberland County in the same district as his father-in-law Amos Nickens, Sr., in 1797 and 1802 [PPTL, 1782-1812, frames 464, 531]. He registered in Lancaster County on 20 June 1803: *s/o Jno., Age 31, mulatto, rather dark* [Burkett, *Lancaster County Register of Free Negroes*, 1].

    vi. Bartley, born say 1774, taxable in Lancaster County from 1792 to 1803 [PPTL 1782-1839, frames 98, 203, 242]. His 20 December 1804 Lancaster County will, proved 16 April 1805, gave Uriea? Nicken, son of Robert Nicken, his house "where my father now lives" and named Elizabeth Nicken, daughter of John Nicken. Richard Nicken was one of the executors [WB 28:89].

5. Robert¹ Nickens (Edward¹, Richard¹), born say 1721, purchased 3 acres on the east side of the Eastern Branch of the Corrotoman River in Lancaster County on 21 October 1763 [DW 17:24]. He was sued in Lancaster County court by Thomas Pollard on 16 March 1769 and by Mungo Harvey on 16 December 1773 [Orders 1768-70, 8; 1770-78, 371]. He was head of a Lancaster County household of 3 "Blacks" in 1783 [VA:55] and taxable in Lancaster County from 1782 to 1800 [PPTL, 1782-1839, frames 5, 29, 74, 98, 174, 189, 203]. He may have been the father of

13   i. Nathaniel, born say 1745.
14   ii. James³, born say 1748.
15   iii. Amos¹, born say 1754.
    iv. Benjamin¹, born say 1760, taxable in Prince William County from 1782 to 1813, called a "yellow" man in 1809 and 1813 [PPTL, 1782-1810, frames 27, 52, 77, 142, 236, 274, 315, 368, 444, 510, 598, 709]. He and his wife Betsy, "formerly Betsy **Lucas**" obtained certificates of freedom in Prince William County on 5 August 1805 [Orders 1804-6, 204]. He was head of a Prince William County household of 1 "other free" in 1810 [VA:506].
    v. Daniel, born say 1780, taxable in Prince William County from 1796 to 1813, called a "yellow" man in 1809 and 1813 [PPTL, 1782-1810, frames 315, 441, 444, 578, 667, 709]. He was head of a Prince William County household of 3 "other free" [VA:506].

6. Edward² Nicken (Edward¹, Richard¹), born say 1725, and his wife Susannah sued George Miller for trespass, assault, and battery in Lancaster County court on 17 April 1756 [Orders 1752-56, 435]. He was deceased by 18 February 1757 when his son Edward Jones Nicken was bound apprentice in Lancaster County with the consent of his mother. And on 17 February 1758 she bound

their daughter Lucy to Henry Tapscott [Orders 1756-64, 40, 118]. Two of their children were

16   i.   Edward Jones Nicken, born say 1748.
     ii.   Lucy, born say 1752.

7. Richard³ Nickens (Edward¹, Richard¹), born say 1727, was head of a Northumberland County household of 4 "black" persons in 1782 [VA:37] and taxable on himself and 4 cattle in Northumberland County in 1782 [PPTL, 1782-1812, frame 232]. He was taxable in Lancaster County from 1784 to 1786 [PPTL 1782-1839, frames 23, 30]. He may have been the father of

     i.   Limas, born say 1752, head of a Northumberland County household of 5 "black" persons in 1782 [VA:37]. He was taxable on himself and a horse in Northumberland County in 1782 [PPTL, 1782-1812, frame 232]. Elimas/ Elimaleck was taxable in Lancaster County in 1785 and 1786 [PPTL, 1782-1839, frames 30, 36]. Amelick was taxable on 2 tithes in Augusta County in 1800 in the same list as Abraham, Edward and Jacob Nickens [1800 PPTL, p.22]. On 23 November 1801 the Orange County, Virginia court certified that he and Moses Nickens were free and allowed them to hire themselves out [Orders 1801-3, 179]. Amlick and his wife Sarah and their children: James, Agnes, Lot, Easter, Amlick, and Moses resided in Ross County, Ohio, on the farm of Benjamin Kerns in 1804 according to a certificate of residency he obtained from Kerns on 18 August 1812 and recorded at the Ross County courthouse [Turpin, *Register of Black, Mulatto, and Poor Persons*, 17].
     ii. Moses, taxable in Lancaster County in 1786 [PPTL, 1782-1839, frame 36].
    iii. Edward, taxable in Lancaster County in 1786 [PPTL, 1782-1839, frame 36]. He was "a coloured man," who brought David Nickins, a Baptist Minister, to Ross County, Ohio, in 1804 or 1805 to the farm of Benjamin M. Kerrin (Kern) [Turpin, *Register of Black, Mulatto, and Poor Persons*, 25, 27]. David Nickens was head of a Washington Township, Pickaway County, Ohio household of 6 "free colored" in 1820.
    iv. Abraham, born say 1760, taxable on a tithe and two horses in Augusta County in 1800 [1800 PPTL, p.22]. He moved to Ross County, Ohio, where he resided on the farm of Benjamin Kerns in the Fall of 1805 with his wife Polly and children: Rachel, Kissy, Betsey, Nathaniel, Bill, James, Sam, and Palt [Turpin, *Register of Black, Mulatto, and Poor Persons*, 16].[156]

8. James¹ Nickens (Edward¹, Richard¹), born say 1729, "orphan of Edward Nicken," was bound as an apprentice shoemaker to John Hubbard in Lancaster County until the age of twenty-one on 11 February 1736 [Orders 1729-43, 161]. He and his wife Margaret received 200 acres on the east side of Potecasi Creek in Society Parish, Bertie County, North Carolina, by deed of gift from her parents Edward and Margaret **Carter** on 10 May 1750 [DB G:354]. James and Margaret were taxed as "fr. Muls." in the 1750 Bertie County summary filed with the central government [CCR 190], and in the 1757 list of John Brickell [CR 10.702.1 Box 1]. This part of Bertie County became Hertford County in 1759, and James was taxed there on 2 persons in 1768, 3 in 1769, 2 in 1770, and on 200 acres, 3 horses, and 3 cattle in District 3 in 1779 [Fouts, *Tax Receipt Book*, 35; GA 30.1]. He was head of a Hertford County household of 3 "other free" in 1790 [NC:27]. Perhaps his children were

---

[156]Benjamin Kerns was probably related to Henry Kern, head of a white Lancaster County household in 1783 [VA:55].

i. Carter, born say 1748, taxable in Hertford County on 1 person in 1768 and 1769, on 2 persons in 1770, and taxable on 2 horses and 2 cattle in the 1779 [Fouts, *Tax Receipt Book*, 13; GA 30.1]. He was paid for services to the Revolution [Haun, *Revolutionary Army Accounts*, vol. I, Book 4:232].

ii. William[2], born say 1750, died in Wilson County, Tennessee, in 1820 leaving ten children [Wilson County Quarterly Court Minutes 1830, 34]. In 1833 his sons Marcus, Andrew and Calvin presented a petition to the General Assembly of Tennessee stating that their parents were from Portugal, had settled in the United States many years since and that "their colour is rather of the mixed blood by appearance." They asked to have the same rights as other citizens of the state. One supporting statement said that their grandfather was from Portugal and another that their father bore the name "of a desent of the Portagee" [Tennessee Legislative Petition 77-1831]. In the 1880 census two of their siblings listed North Carolina as the place of birth of their parents.

iii. Richard[6], born say 1763, taxable on 1 poll in Captain Joseph Bridgers' Hertford County Company in 1784 adjacent to James Nickens [L.P. 64.1]. His field adjoining Thomas Cotten was mentioned in Cotten's 18 April 1787 Hertford County will [P.C. # 122.2 by *NCGSJ* XI:251]. He was head of a Hertford County household of 8 "other free" in 1800.

iv. Malachi, born about 1765, living in Hertford County in 1781 when he enlisted as a private in Colonel Armstrong's North Carolina Regiment. He was about fifty-six years old on 13 November 1821 when he testified in Hertford County court that he was a common laborer living with his wife Margaret and a seventeen-month-old child (his grandson?) Manuel **Murfee**. James **Smith** testified on his behalf [M805, frame 0198]. Malachi was head of a Hertford County household of 5 "other free" in 1790 [NC:26], 3 in 1800, and 3 "free colored" in 1820 [NC:190]. He was one of the "Sundry persons of Colour of Hertford County" who petitioned the General Assembly in November- December 1822 to repeal the act which declared slaves to be competent witnesses against free African Americans [*NCGSJ* XI:252].

v. Jonathan, born say 1780, married Kesiah **Blizzard**, 18 January 1803 Duplin County bond, Solomon **Carter** bondsman. He purchased 146 acres in Duplin County on the east side of the Northeast Cape Fear River and the north side of Matthews and Juniper Branches from Alexander **Carter** on 10 November 1811 [DB 4A:392]. He was head of a Duplin County household in 1810 (counted as white) [NC:690] and 8 "free colored" in 1820 [NC:189]. He sold land by deed registered in Dobbs County between 1810 and 1819 [DB 24:98; 26:370].

9. Richard[2] Nickens (Elizabeth[1], Richard[1]), born in August 1705, was "6 years old next August" on 16 May 1711 when he was apprenticed by his mother Elizabeth Nigings of Lancaster County to Henry and Ann Tapscott in Northumberland County to be a joiner carpenter [Orders 1710-13, 21]. He was probably the Richard Nickens who was number 37 in the Muster Roll of Major William Shergold's Regiment of Currituck County, North Carolina Militia in the 1750's, in the same list as Simon **Shewcraft**, a witness to Edward[1] Nicken's 1735 Lancaster County will [Clark, *Colonial Soldiers of the South*, 657-8]. He was called "Richard Nickins of Currituck County Tailor" on 26 March 1751 when he purchased 70 acres in Pasquotank County on the south side of Great Swamp near the Great Swamp Bridge on 26 March 1751 [DB B:144]. This land is located in present-day Camden County. He purchased 50 acres adjoining this land near the Great Swamp in adjoining Currituck County on 19 April 1768, another 50 acres adjoining this land a year later on 1

September 1769, and another 120 acres on 1 June 1771 [DB 2:44, 135, 318]. His 2 February 1774 Currituck County will was proved 20 June the same year. His wife Rachel and son Edward were his executors. His estate consisted of several hundred acres of land, a slave woman named "Sooke," and four guns. He left land "near the great swamp" in Pasquotank County to his daughters and his shoemaking tools to Edward. The will mentioned his children and grandchildren: Philip, Edward, Roland, and Proskate Nickens [WB 1:92-94]. His children were

17   i.   Edward[3], born say 1730.

     ii.   Leah Rael.[157]

     iii.   Margaret Nickens, head of a Currituck County household of 3 "other free" in 1790 (called Margaret Mekins) [NC:22].

     iv.   Rachel **Hall**, who received the use of her father's land in Pasquotank County near the Great Swamp Bridge. She was probably related by marriage to Lemuel **Hall**, head of a Pasquotank County household of 9 other free in 1810 [NC:902].[158]

10.   Catherine /Kate Nicken (Elizabeth[1], Richard[1]), born say 1710, "a negro woman named Kate Nicken," was living in Christ Church Parish, Lancaster County on 8 May 1728 when the court presented her for having a bastard child. Valentine Bell was security for the payment of her fine [Orders 1721-29, 270, 275, 278].[159] Her children may have been

     i.   Stephen, born say 1732, obtained an attachment against the estate of Thomas Loney for about 2 pounds on 10 July 1753 in Northumberland County court [Orders 1753-56, 21]. He was taxable on himself and a horse in Northumberland County in 1787, taxable in 1791 and 1792, and exempt in 1794 [PPTL, 1782-1812, frames 380, 394, 424].

11.   Christian Nickens (Elizabeth[1], Richard[1]), born say 1711, was living in Lancaster County on 9 August 1729 when the court ordered that she receive twenty-five lashes for failing to pay her fine of 50 shillings for having a bastard child [Orders 1721-29, 252]. Her children may have been

     i.   Martha[1], born say 1735, mother of Rhoda Nickens, who was bound apprentice to (her great-grandmother?) Betty Nickens on 21 October 1765 in Lancaster County [Orders 1764-67, 168].

18   ii.   James[2], born say 1737.

12.   William[1] Nicken (Elizabeth[1], Richard[1]), born say 1725, was sued by David Galloway in Lancaster County for a 6 pound debt on 15 July 1765 and was sued by Thomas Pollard for a 3 pound debt in Lancaster County on 16 March 1769 [Orders 1764-67, 145, 199, 213; 1768-70, 8]. He was charged with breaking and entering the house of John Mason on 29 June 1772 [Orders 1770-78, 4], but was acquitted by the Grand Jury at Williamsburg according to a notice in the 22 April 1773 issue of the *Virginia Gazette* [Purdie & Dixon edition, p.3, col. 1]. His children James, Mary Ann, Richard, and William were named by the Lancaster County court when it ordered them bound apprentices while he awaited trial. The apprenticeships were reversed on 18

---

[157]Perhaps Leah **Rail/ Rael** was the wife of Jesse **Rowals**, head of a Hertford County household of 11 "other free" in 1790 [NC:25].

[158]The **Hall** family also originated in Lancaster County.

[159]Valentine Bell was charged with felony in Lancaster County Court on 19 December 1728. He testified that, in company with Robert Scofield and "free Robin a Mulatto," he killed a heifer that wandered into his cornfield. Bell was sent to the General Court in Williamsburg for trial [Orders 1721-9, 310-1].

February 1773 after his acquittal [Orders 1770-78, 292, 299]. He was taxable in Lancaster County in 1775 [Tithables 1745-95, 15]. He may have been the William Nicken who enlisted early in the Revolutionary War as a drummer, was in a short time made drum major, and returned to Northumberland County at the close of the war [Hopkins, *Virginia Revolutionary War Land Grant Claims,* 39]. His children were

    i.   James[4], born about 1759, taxable in Prince William County from 1796 to 1798 and from 1806 to 1813: called a "Dark" man in 1805 and 1806, a "yellow" man in 1809 and 1813 [PPTL, 1782-1810, frames 315, 341, 368, 598, 645, 709]. He was head of a Prince William County household of 5 "other free" in 1810 [VA:506]. He was about fifty-nine years old and living in Falmouth when he applied for a pension on 27 April 1818. He was a sixty-two-year-old "Free Man of Color" living alone in Stafford County on 16 August 1820 when he applied for a pension. He testified that he enlisted in Lancaster County where he served aboard the ships *Tempest, Revenge,* and *Hero,* and then served in the army for two or three years [M805, reel 615, frame 0192].

    ii.   Mary Ann, born say 1760, bound to Bridger Haynie in Lancaster County on 18 February 1773 [Orders 1770-78, 299].

    iii.   Richard[5], born say 1761.

    iv.   William[3], born say 1765, "a black man," and his wife Rose and four or five unnamed children living in Ross County, Ohio, about 1807 according to a certificate of residency signed by William Lewis and recorded at the Ross County courthouse [Turpin, *Register of Black, Mulatto, and Poor Persons,* 17].

13. Nathaniel Nickens, born say 1745, was a Lancaster County seaman who served in the Revolution [Jackson, *Virginia Negro Soldiers,* 41] and head of a Lancaster County household of 3 "Blacks" in 1783, listed next to Robert Nickens [VA:55]. He was taxable in Lancaster County from 1782 to 1786: listed with 2 tithables in 1784, charged with Moses **Cook**'s tithe in 1786 [PPTL, 1782-1839, frames 7, 23, 38]. He was the father of

    i.   Elizabeth[3], born about 1764 according to the affidavit of her father Nathaniel Nickings when she married George **McCoy**, 10 March 1788 Orange County, Virginia bond, 11 March marriage by Rev. George Eve.

14. James[3] Nickens (Robert[1], Edward[1], Richard[1]), born say 1748, was the father of Jemima **Bass**, widow of Willis **Bass**. She was sixty-six years old on 10 April 1835 when she deposed that she was the only child of James Nickens who served as a seaman in the Revolution [Hopkins, *Virginia Revolutionary War Land Grant Claims,* 166; M805-0615, frame 0192]. Willis was deceased on 19 May 1834 when the Norfolk County court certified that she was his widow and only heir of her father James Nickens and his brother Nathaniel Nickens. James served aboard the *Caswell* [Minutes 24:139]. He was the father of

    i.   Jemima, born about 1769, married Willis **Bass**.

    ii.   ?Margaret, married William **Newton**, 30 March 1805 Norfolk County marriage [Ministers' Returns].

15. Amos[1] Nickens (Richard[3], Edward[1], Richard[1]), born say 1754, was a "free head of a Northumberland County household of 4 "Black" persons in 1782 [VA:37]. He was taxable in Northumberland County on himself, 3 cattle, and 2 horses in 1787 and taxable there from 1789 to 1802 [PPTL, 1782-1812, frames 335, 374, 401, 464, 531]. He purchased 25 acres in Northumberland County in the Parish of Great Wicomico adjoining the Church yard and 10 acres adjoining this land on 7 December 1793 [RB 9:3; 14:723]. His 6 April

1807 Northumberland County will, proved 8 June the same year, mentioned his wife Sally and grandson Darius and left his land and personal estate to his son and executor Amos [RB 17:529]. Sally was probably the sister of John **Pinn** who mentioned her in his 9 July 1785 Northumberland County will [*Northumberland County Wills and Administrations*, 80]. Amos was the father of

    i.   Amos[2], born about 1775, registered in Northumberland County on 12 June 1809: *blackman, about 34 years old, 5 feet 8-1/2 Inches high* [Register of Free Negroes and Mulattos, #43, Northumberland County courthouse]. He was probably first taxable in Northumberland County in 1797 when he was one of two unnamed taxables in the household of his father Amos[1] Nickens. He was taxable in his own household, called Amos Nickens, Jr., adjoining Amos Nickens, Sr., in 1802 [PPTL, 1782-1812, frames 464, 531]. He was called A. Nickens when he married Elizabeth **Causey**, "daughter of William **Causey**," 5 July 1800 Northumberland County bond, Joseph Mott security; and called Amos Nickens when he married, second, Caty **Griffin**, 6 March 1810 Northumberland County bond, Joseph **Weaver** security. He was head of a Northumberland County household of 7 "other free" in 1810 [VA:990]. He was a "Black" taxable in Northumberland County in 1812 and was listed with a female in his household in "A list of Free Negroes and Mulattoes over the age of 16 years" in the year 1813 [PPTL, 1782-1812, frame 640; 1813-49, p. 22]. He and his wife Catherine sold 40 acres "being the land his father left near Wiccomoco Church" on 25 June 1813 and another 10 acres on 16 December 1815 [DB 19:275; 20:113]. He purchased 27 acres in Lancaster County on 13 May 1819 [DB 14:723]. On 22 May 1843 he testified for Fortunatus Pittman's Northumberland County application for a Revolutionary War pension [Hopkins, *Virginia Revolutionary War Land Grant Claims*, 175]. His Northumberland County will was written on 15 October 1850 [WB A:25].

    ii.   Mary, born say 1778, "daughter of Amos Nicken," married Benjamin Nicken, 11 April 1796 Northumberland County bond, Asa Swanson security.

16. Edward Jones Nicken (Edward[2], Edward[1], Richard[1]), born say 1748, was called "son of Edward Nicken, deceased" when he was bound an apprentice shoemaker to John Nicholds in Lancaster County on 18 February 1757 [Orders 1756-64, 40]. His children may have been

    i.   Polly **Armstead** Nickens, born about 1767, married Charles **Lewin**, 1 January 1805 Lancaster County bond. Charles, born about 1768, registered in Lancaster County on 23 May 1804: *Age 36, Color mulatto...born free*. Polly may have been identical to Mary **Lewin** who registered on 18 August 1815: *Age 48, Color tawny...born free* [Burkett, *Lancaster County Register of Free Negroes*, 2, 6]. Charles was head of a Lancaster County household of 9 "other free" in 1810 [VA:352]. Charles may have been the brother of Molly **Lewin** who was head of a Lancaster County household of 4 "other free" in 1810 [VA:352].

    ii.   Armstead, born about 1781, registered in Lancaster County on 16 September 1805: *Age 24, Color mulatto* [Burkett, *Lancaster County Register of Free Negroes*, 2]. He married Polly **Weaver**, 21 January 1819 Lancaster County bond.

17. Edward[3] Nickens (Richard[2], Elizabeth[1], Richard[1]), born say 1730, was probably a shoemaker like his father since he was required by his father's will to make his mother's shoes. He was a soldier in the Revolutionary War who was deceased by 5 December 1792 when a petition by his son and heir Richard

Nickens was placed before the North Carolina General Assembly [LP 117 by *NCGSJ* IV:174]. His oldest children: Philip, Edward, Roland, and Proskate were mentioned in his father's Currituck County will [WB 1:92-94]. His children were

    i.   Philip, born say 1762.

    ii. Edward[5], born say 1765, perhaps the Edward Nickins who was head of a Hertford County household in 1810 [NC:96].

    iii. Roland, born say 1767.

    iv. "Proskate"/ Prescott, born say 1768. On 27 June 1791 he purchased from John and Dolly Northern for 5 pounds 25 acres near the Great Swamp Bridge which had been devised to his sister Leah **Rail**, and on 5 January 1793 he sold for 200 pounds the 25 acres he purchased from the Northerns as well as 25 acres he was devised in his grandfather's will near Moyock Mill [DB 6:155, 260]. He was head of an "other free" household in Captain Lewis' District of Hertford County in 1800.

    v.   Richard[7], born say 1770, not mentioned in the will of his grandfather Richard Nickens, but named as the son of Edward Nicken in his own petition to the General Assembly. On 27 June 1791 he purchased from John and Dolly Northern 100 acres of land in Currituck County "which Rich[d] Nickin Deces[d] Give to his Son Edward Nickin by his will." On 13 February 1793 he and his wife Elizabeth sold 10 acres of their land and another 160 acres near the Great Swamp about a year later. And in 1794 he sold land near the Great Swamp Bridge which his grandfather Richard Nickens had devised to his father Edward Nickens [DB 6:167; 7:18, 46-48]. He was head of a Currituck County household of 3 "other free" in 1790 (called Richard Mekins) [NC:22] and 8 "other free" in Captain Lewis' District of Hertford County in 1800. Perhaps his wife Elizabeth was identical to the Betsy Nickens who was head of a Pasquotank County household of 2 "other free" in 1810 [NC:916].

18. James[2] Nickens (Christian, Elizabeth[1], Richard[1]), born say 1737, sued Edward Ingram for his freedom from his indenture on 11 September 1764 in Northumberland County court. He was called James Nicken alias Bateman when the court ordered him to serve Ingram for four more years [Orders 1762-66, 411, 435]. He was taxable in Lancaster County in John Nickens' household in 1775 and 1776 and his own household in 1781 [Tithables 1745-95, 14, 18, 37] and was taxable there from 1782 to 1786 [PPTL 1782-1839, frames 5, 16, 23, 38]. He was head of a Lancaster County household of 9 "Blacks" in 1783 [VA:55] and a "F. Negroe" head of a Fauquier County household of 8 "other free" in 1810 (called James Nickens, Sr.) [VA:368]. On 3 September 1834 James Nickens, Elizabeth Nickens, and Judy **Watkins** appeared in Frederick County court to apply for the survivors' pension of their father James Nickens and their brother Hezekiah Nickens, a seaman in the Virginia State Navy who died during the war. They testified that their father died about 1825 and their mother Sally was also deceased, and they were their only heirs [Minutes 1834-38, 61]. His children named in his pension file were

    i.   Hezekiah, born say 1758, served as a seaman in the Revolution from Lancaster County.

    ii. Elizabeth[2], born say 1762.

    iii. James[5], Jr., born say 1764, head of a Fauquier County household of 11 "other free" in 1810 [VA:368]. He married Mary Peggy **Berden**, 17 July 1793 Culpeper County bond.

    iv. Judy **Watkins**, born say 1766.

Other members of the Nickens family were

i. William, confessed in York County court on 17 May 1773 that he owed 10 pounds to Thomas Mason, Esquire [Judgments & Orders 1772-4, 266].

ii. Edward[4], born say 1760, served as a seaman aboard the *Gloucester* in the State Navy for which he received bounty land on 9 February 1784. He moved to New Kent County where he lived near James **Lafayette** [Jackson, *Virginia Negro Soldiers*, 41]. He was taxable in the lower end of New Kent County on the south side of Warrenny Road from 1782 to 1815: taxable on a slave named Roger in 1785; taxable on a slave in 1792; removed to Richmond in 1794; taxable on a slave in 1796 and 1804; called a "FN" in 1806; taxable on 2 free males in 1809; listed as a "Person of Colour" with his unnamed wife in 1813. His children may have been Edward Neekins, Jr., and Bartholomew Neekins who were taxable in New Kent County in 1820 [PPTL 1782-1800, frames 36, 100, 190, 213; 1791-1828, frames 372, 409, 432, 455, 476, 491, 503, 516, 574].

iii. Julius Nickern, born say 1761, married Susanna **Prewit**, 20 June 1782 Pittsylvania County bond. She was probably related to Samuel **Prewet**, head of a Campbell County household of 2 "other free" in 1810 [VA:882]. Perhaps Susanna was the Suckey Nickings who was head of a Richmond County household of 10 "other free" in 1810 [VA:408].

iv. Isaac, born about 1772, registered in Orange County, Virginia, on 27 August 1799: *Isaac Nickins, a negro, 27, black complexion, 5'5", born free in Northumberland County*. On 5 November 1816 he purchased "three negroes, a woman, Jean, a boy, Owins, and a girl, Dicy" (his wife and children?) in Jackson County, Tennessee, and recorded the purchase in Ross County Ohio [Turpin, *Register of Black, Mulatto, and Poor Persons*, 21].

v. James, taxable in Essex County in 1795 [PPTL, 1782-1819, frame 266].

vi. William, taxable on a horse in Essex County from 1802 to 1813 when he was counted in a list of "Free Negroes & Mulattoes" over the age of sixteen in St. Ann's Parish [PPTL, 1782-1819, frames 348, 483, 510].

vii. Walker, listed as a "Free Negro & Mulatto" in Essex County in 1814 [PPTL, 1782-1819, frame 547].

viii. Martha[2], born say 1774, married Nathan **Mackling (Maclin)**, 10 February 1790 Halifax County, Virginia bond, Robert Hill surety, 11 February marriage.

ix. Frances Nicklens, born say 1776, mother of Polly Nicklens, who consented to Polly's marriage to William **Balfour**, "free persons of colour," 26 December 1812 Fredericksburg bond. Frances may also have been the mother of Sarah Nickens who married William **Skinker**, "both free persons of colour," 19 October 1820 Fredericksburg bond. Frances was head of a Stafford County household of 2 "free colored" in 1830, and William **Skinker** was head of a Stafford County household of 5 "free colored" in 1830.

x. Bridget, head of a Lancaster County household of 4 "other free" in 1810 [VA:355].

xi. Elizabeth[4]/Betsy, married Thomas **Spriddle**, 11 August 1817 Northumberland County bond, Joseph **Weaver** security.

xii. Catherine Nigenes, head of a Washington, D.C. household of 1 "other free" in 1800.

NORMAN FAMILY

1. Elizabeth Norman, born say 1695, was the servant of Benjamin Belt on 23 August 1715 when the Prince George's County, Maryland court ordered him to keep her and her "Mallatoe" child until the November court. The court sold her and her child to Richard Keene, the constable for Patuxent Hundred, for 3,600 pounds of tobacco later that year on 22 November. Five years later on 22 November 1720 she confessed to the court that she had an illegitimate child by a "Mullato man of William Digge's." The court sold her to her master for seven years and sold the child to William Maccoy until the age of thirty-one. On 28 August 1722 she confessed to having another "Malatto" child, and the court ordered her sold to Richard Keene for seven years and gave her child to William Harris until the age of thirty-one. In March 1749/50 the court allowed her 200 pounds of tobacco a year for her support [Court Record 1710-5, 693, 721, 790; 1715-20, 4; 1720-2, 20-1, 84, 622-3; 1748-9, 133]. She was the mother of

    2   i.   Jane, born say 1715.

2. Jane Norman, born say 1715, was called "a Mallatto woman named Jane (no last name) Living at Mr. Richard Keen's" on 23 August 1737 when she confessed to the Prince George's County, Maryland court that she had an illegitimate child by a "free Mallatto." The court ordered that she receive twenty lashes and serve her master an additional year and one-half and sold her two-month-old son James to Edward Swann until the age of twenty-one. She had another child by a free person before 28 November 1738 when the court ordered that she receive fifteen lashes and serve her master twelve months for the trouble of his house, bound her male child to Keene until the age of twenty-one years, and ordered Keene to give the boy a year of schooling and a decent suit of clothes at the end of his indenture. She was called "Jan Molato Norman" on 26 November 1745 when the court bound her son Joseph to her master until the age of twenty-one. On 28 June 1748 and 28 March 1748/9 she was convicted of having illegitimate children by a free person. On 27 November 1750 she confessed to having another child named Basil who was bound to her master until the age of twenty-one [Court Record 1736-8, 497, 505; 1738-40, 192, 200; 1744-6, 248, 279; 1747-8, 168; 174; 1748-9, 181; 1749-50, 244]. She was the mother of

    i.   James, born in June 1737, head of a Hampshire County, Virginia household of 2 "other free" in 1810 [VA:770].
    ii. ?Catherine, head of a Montgomery County, Maryland household of 6 "other free" in 1790.
    iii. ?George, head of a Washington County, Maryland household of 1 "other free" in 1790.
    iv. ?Delpha, "Mulo." head of a King and Queen County, Virginia household of 7 "other free" in 1810 [VA:172].
    v. Bazil, born in 1750, head of a Frederick County, Virginia household of 7 "other free" in 1810 [VA:569].
    vi. ?Betty, head of a Frederick County, Virginia household of 3 "other free" in 1810 [VA:575].

Other members of the Norman family were

    i.   John, born say 1765, bound his "Negro" son John to Robert Mitchell in Richmond City, Virginia, on 20 June 1793 [Hustings Court Deeds 1792-9, 69 by Gill, *Apprentices of Virginia*, 186-7].
    ii. Lilly, born say 1773, a "Mulatto" living in Hamilton Parish on 22 August 1774 when the Fauquier County court ordered her bound to Judith Neale Grant [Orders 1773-80, 203].
    iii. Reuben, head of a Warren County, North Carolina household of 5 "other free" in 1800 [NC:822].

   iv. Samuel, head of a Warren County, North Carolina household of 2 "other free" in 1790 [NC:].

   v. Polly, head of a Chowan County, North Carolina household of 3 "free colored" in 1820 [NC:129].

NORRIS FAMILY

1. Ann Norris, born say 1740, confessed to the Fairfax County court on 17 June 1760 that she had a "base born Mulatto child." On 15 July the court ordered her sold for five years and bound (her son) Samuel Norris to her mistress Ann Jenkins [Orders 1756-63, 474, 489]. She was the mother of

   i. Samuel, born in January 1760, a "base born Mulatto child" bound out by the churchwardens of Trinity Parish, Fairfax County. On 19 June 1764 the court ordered the churchwardens of Truro Parish to bind him to Ann Jenkins [Minutes 1763-5, n.p.].

NORTON FAMILY

1. Elizabeth Norton, born about 1734, registered in Petersburg on 20 August 1794: *a brown Mulatto woman, five feet one inches high, sixty years old or upwards, born free and raised in Chesterfield County near Petersburg* [Register of Free Negroes 1794-1819, no. 72]. She may have been the ancestor of

   i. Jacob, born say 1760, a "man of colour" who died in Revolutionary War service and left no heirs according to a deposition by Charles **Hood** in Orange County, North Carolina, in 1820 [*The North Carolinian*, p. 2578].

   ii. Thomas, a "free" taxable head of a household with David Norton and Nick **Harris** in the Dinwiddie County list of Braddock Goodwyn from 1793 to 1796 [PPTL, 1791-99 (1793 A p.10), (1794 B, p.10) (1796 A, p.10].

   iii. Sealer, born about 1768, registered in Petersburg on August 19, 1794: *a dark brown Mulatto woman, five feet eight inches high, twenty six years old, born free & raised in Chesterfield County* [Register of Free Negroes 1794-1819, no. 54].

   iv. Sarah, head of a Randolph County, North Carolina household of 3 "other free" in 1790 [NC:99].

   v. William[1]/ Willie, head of a Halifax County, North Carolina household of 3 "other free" in 1800 [NC:330] and 4 in 1810 [NC:39].

   vi. William[2], a cooper, counted with his wife Elizabeth in a list of "free Mulattoes" living on Bears Element Creek in Lunenburg County with Eppes **Allen** and Betsy **Hobson** in his household in 1802 and 1803 [Lunenburg County Free Negro & Slave Records, 1802-3, LVA], perhaps identical to Billey Norton who was head of a Petersburg household of 4 "other free" in 1810 [VA:118a].

   vii. Aaron, counted in a list of "free Mulattoes" in James and Ritter **Stewart**'s household on Beaver Pond in Lunenburg County in 1802 [Lunenburg County Free Negro & Slave Records, 1802-3, LVA].

   viii. Polly, mother of Mima Norton who married Isham D. **Valentine**, "free persons of color," 4 March 1812 Chesterfield County bond, Nathaniel **Stewart** and Moses **Nash** securities. Isham, Nathaniel, and Moses were counted in the Chesterfield County list of "Free Negrows of Colour" in 1813 [Waldrep, *1813 Tax List*].

   ix. Peter, taxable in Dinwiddie County in 1790 [PPTL, 1791-9 (1790 A, p.9)], a "Molatto" taxable in Chesterfield County in 1805 [PPTL, 1786-1811, frame 620].

x. David, a "free" taxable in Dinwiddie County from 1793 to 1798 [PPTL, 1791-9 (1798 B, p.11)].

NORWOOD FAMILY

1. Theophilus[1] Norwood, born say 1700, was the Carteret County Deputy Marshall and kept the ferry at the head of North River in 1728 [Minutes 1723-47, 8a, 10b]. He married Elizabeth **Johnson**, a daughter of William[1] **Johnson**, and was named in her father's 5 November 1726 Carteret County will [SS Wills 1722-35, 140]. He and Elizabeth's brother, Jacob **Johnson**, purchased 130 acres in Carteret County on Core Sound on the east side of North River from (Jacob's uncle?) Richard[2] **Johnson** on 2 October 1724. He sold his half of this land to Jacob on 6 June 1727. He purchased 160 acres on the west side of the head of North River on 3 June 1727 from William Russell, and he and his wife Elizabeth signed over their right to this land to Richard Russell on 3 September 1729 [DB C:113, 171; D:20-23]. He was listed in the muster roll of Colonel Gabriel Powell's Battalion of South Carolina Militia in the 1759 Cherokee Expedition, Captain John Hitchcock's Company [Clark, *Colonial Soldiers of the South*, 896, 917, 930]. Theophilus and Elizabeth's children were

    i.   William, born before 5 November 1726 when he was mentioned in the will of his grandfather William **Johnson**.
2   ii. ?Ann Norwood, born say 1730.

2. Ann[1] Norwood, born say 1730, a "Woman of Mixt blood," appeared in Carteret County on 5 March 1750 requesting that her children Ann and Sampson be bound to James Shackleford. Her children were

    i.   Sampson, born about 1748, bound to James Shackleford on 5 March 1750 with the consent of his mother [Minutes 1747-64, 181].
    ii.   Ann[2], born about 1749, ordered bound to James Shackleford on 5 March 1750 with the consent of her mother. She was head of a Carteret County household of 2 "other free" in 1790 [NC:129].
    iii. Esther, born about 1752, eighteen years old in June 1770 when the court ordered her bound to James Shackleford [Minutes 1764-77, 388].
    iv.   Theophilus[2]/Foy, born about 1753, a six-year-old "Molato" boy of Nan Norwood, a "Molato" woman, ordered bound to Keziah Shackleford on 6 September 1759 [Minutes 1747-64, 251]. His age was estimated at fifteen years in June 1770 when he consented to his indenture to William Fulford [Minutes 1764-77, 388]. He was twenty-seven years old in 1778 when he was listed in the Carteret County Militia Returns [*The North Carolinian* VI:728].
    v.   Sophia/Phias, born about 1755, a "Molato" girl of Nan Norwood, ordered bound to Keziah Shackleford on 6 September 1759 [Minutes 1747-64, 259]. She was fifteen years old in June 1770, called Sophia Norwood, when she was ordered bound to William Fulford [Minutes 1764-77, 388].
    vi.   Obed, born about March 1758, a "Molato" boy of Nan Norwood, ordered bound to Keziah Shackleford on 6 September 1759 [Minutes 1747-64, 259]. His age was estimated at thirteen years in June 1770 when James Shackleford asked that he be bound to him as a cooper [Minutes 1764-77, 388]. He was called Obid Norward on the 1778 Carteret County Militia Returns [*The North Carolinian* VI:728]. He married Nelly **Neale**, 3 August 1810 Craven County bond.
    vii. Betty, born about 1760, ordered bound to Keziah Shackleford on 5 March 1761 [Minutes 1747-64, 259].
    viii. ?Tabitha, born about 1765, five years old in June 1770 when the court ordered her bound to James Shackleford (no parent named) [Minutes 1764-77, 388]. She was head of a Portsmouth, Carteret County

household of 7 "other free" in 1810 (called Tabitha Nored) [NC:440] and 4 "free colored" in 1820 [NC:128].

ix.   ?Alice, born about 1768, one year and nine months old in June 1770 when the court ordered her bound to James Shackleford (no parent named) [Minutes 1764-77, 388]. She was head of a Carteret County household of 3 "other free" in 1810 (called Alice Nored) [NC:435].

NUTTS FAMILY

Members of the Nutts family were
  i.   William, born say 1750, an Indian living in Accomack County on 25 October 1774 when he and Nathan Addison's slave Jacob were charged with felony [Orders 1774-7, 270, 277].
  ii.   Daniel, born December 1760, a four-year-old "Mulattoe" bound to Major Joyne by the Northampton County, Virginia court on 11 September 1765 [Minutes 1765-71, 11]. He was head of an Accomack County household of 4 "other free" in 1810 [VA:45].
  iii. Edmund, born Christmas 1774, bound by the Northampton County court to Margaret Addison on 12 February 1782 [Minutes 1777-83, 336]. He was a "free Negro" taxable in Northampton County from 1798 to 1803 [PPTL, 1782-1823, frames 251, 270, 312, 353]. He married Mary **Bibbins**, 18 June 1800 Northampton County bond, Southy **Collins** security, consent of Nanny **Bibbins**. He was head of an Accomack County household of 8 "other free" in 1810 [VA:45]. He was called an Indian when his wife Mary was counted as a "free negro" in Accomack County in 1813 [PPTL 1782-1814, frame 833].
  iv.   Thomas, head of an Accomack County household of 5 "other free" in 1800 [*Virginia Genealogist* 2:158].
  v.   Bridget, married Toby **Stephens**, 7 September 1804 Northampton County bond, Ben Dunton security.
  vi.   Sabra, married Isaac **Stephens**, 16 August 1809 Northampton County bond, Isaac Stevens, Sr., security.
  vii. Ariena, born say 1779, married Peter **Beckett**, 10 January 1800 Accomack County bond, Babel **Major**, surety. Babel **Major** was head of an Accomack County household of 6 "other free" in 1810 [VA:43]. Ariena may have been the Arena **Becket** who married Thomas **Bibbins**, 2 August 1800 Accomack County bond, Peter **Bibbins** surety.

OATS FAMILY

Members of the Oats family were
  i.   Charles, born say 1752, called Charles Oats alias Jackson when he was presented by the York County court on 15 November 1773 for failing to list himself as a tithable in Bruton Parish [Judgments & Orders 1772-4, 436, 442]. He was a "free negro" who was accused of breaking into a cellar in Williamsburg which belonged to James Smith. On 9 August 1776 Smith placed an ad in the *Virginia Gazette* offering a reward for his capture, stating that Charles had a wife in Back River [*Virginia Gazette*. 16 August 1776. Supplement (Purdie edition)].
  ii.   William, a seaman in the Revolution from Northumberland County [Jackson, *Virginia Negro Soldiers*, 41]. He was a "free mulatto" head of a Northumberland County household of 4 "other free" in 1810 [VA:991].
  iii. John, head of a Dauphin County, Pennsylvania household of 1 "other free" in 1790.

OKEY FAMILY

The Okey family probably descends from Mary Vincent, wife of John Okey, an early resident of Sussex County, Delaware. Before marrying John Okey (a white man), Mary had a son named Aminadab **Hanser** by a slave in Accomack County, Virginia, about 1664. (See the Okey and **Hanser** family histories in *Free African Americans of Maryland and Delaware*). A mixed-race man named Aminadab Okey appeared in the Sussex County, Delaware, records in 1713. Perhaps he was another mixed-race child of Mary Okey.

1. Aminadab Okey, born say 1680, may have been the "strang Child...which is not Certainly known Whose it is" who was living at John Okey's house in March 1682 when the Sussex County court bound him to Henry Bowman. Aminadab Okey was sued by Aminadab **Hanser** in Sussex County court on 3 May 1704 [Horle, *Records of Sussex County*, 155, 1191]. He and Aminadab **Hanser** were apparently neighbors because on 9 April 1713 he was required to give 100 pounds security to Aminadab **Handsor** in Sussex County court to guarantee that he would abide by the arbitrators' decision regarding the removal of a fence. And Aminadab **Hanser**'s wife Rose mentioned Aminadab Okey's land adjoining hers in her 8 December 1725 deed of sale [DB D-4:225-6; F-6:220-2]. Aminadab Okey died before 1734 when the account of his estate was recorded in Sussex County court. The account totalled 44 pounds and included 22 pounds for the sale of land [Orphans Court 1728-44, 65]. He was most likely the ancestor of

    i. Robert[1], born say 1698, living on land adjoining Samuel and Ann **Hanser** on 20 May 1733 when they sold 124 acres near Rehoboth Bay, Sussex County. He was mentioned in the 11 June 1742 Sussex County, Delaware, deed of his son Samuel who sold land which had formerly belonged to Aminadab Okey and Robert Okey [DB G-7:34-5; H-8:14]. He died before 3 September 1745 when his daughter Sabria and her husband John **Parsons** petitioned the Sussex County court to divide his land among his heirs [Orphans Court 1744-51, 17].

2   ii. Joseph, born say 1725.

    iii. Saunders, born say 1750, and his wife Mary, "melattoes," registered the 20 October 1771 birth of their daughter Rhoda at St. George's Protestant Episcopal Church, Indian River [Wright, *Vital Records of Kent and Sussex Counties*, 101]. He was taxable in Lewes and Rehoboth, Sussex County in 1774 and a delinquent taxable in 1787. He married, second, Johannah **Hansor**, widow of Nehemiah **Hansor** about 1786.

    iv. Robert[2], born say 1752, taxable in Lewes and Rehoboth Hundred, Sussex County, in 1774. He was called a tanner on 2 February 1789 when he and Jennett Okey, spinster, purchased as tenants-in-common four acres in Lewes and Rehoboth Hundred on the edge of the Rehoboth Road [DB O-14:161]. He was head of a Sussex County household of 9 "other free" in 1800 [DE:438] and 11 in 1810 [DE:462].

    v. Thomas, Jr., born say 1757, taxable in Lewes and Rehoboth Hundred in 1774.

    vi. Jonathan[1], born say 1757, perhaps the John Okey, Jr., who was taxable in Lewes and Rehoboth Hundred in 1774. Jonathan was head of a Little Creek Hundred, Kent County household of 4 "other free" in 1800 [DE:41].

    vii. William[1], born say 1763, and his wife Sarah registered the 5 April 1785 birth of their daughter Polley at St. George's Protestant Episcopal Church, Indian River Hundred, Sussex County, Delaware [Wright, *Vital Records of Kent and Sussex Counties*, 106]. He was taxable in Indian River Hundred, Sussex County in from 1784 to 1790.

    viii.   Jonathan², head of a Saint Jones Hundred, Kent County household of 2 "other free" in 1800 [DE:45] and 3 in Sussex County in 1810 [DE:416].

    ix.   Robert³, head of a Little Creek Hundred, Kent County household of 3 "other free" in 1800 [DE:40] and 9 in Sussex County in 1810 [DE:468].

    x.   Robert⁴, born 1776-1794, head of a Sussex County household of 7 "other free" in 1810 [DE:415] and 8 "free colored" in Lewes and Rehoboth Hundred in 1820 [DE:306].

    xi.   William², born 1776-1794, head of a Lewes and Rehoboth Hundred, Sussex County household of 6 "free colored" in 1820 [DE:306].

    xii.   Levin, taxable in Broadkiln Hundred, Sussex County, in 1784.

    xiii.   Betty, head of an Accomack County household of 4 "other free" and a slave in 1810 [VA:117].

2.   Joseph¹ Okey, born say 1725, purchased 212 acres in Broadkill Hundred, Sussex County, Delaware, from the sheriff on 5 August 1762 [DB I-9:390]. He was a "Molatto" taxable in William Burford's District, Granville County, North Carolina, in 1765. He was taxable on two tithes in 1769 and 1771 and was taxed on an assessment of 329 pounds in Nap of Reeds District, Granville County, in 1780. In 1786 he was called Joseph Oakey, Sr., in Nap of Reeds District of Granville County when he was head of a household of 2 "white" men over sixty or under twenty-one years and 4 "white" women in the state census. He was taxable on 250 acres from 1786 to 1804 and taxable on one poll in 1786 but not free from poll tax by 1790. He was called Joseph Oakley in 1800 when he was head of a Granville County household of 8 "other free." Perhaps his widow was Sarah Oakey who was taxable on 50 acres in Ledge of Rock District, Granville County, from 1805 to 1808 [Tax List 1803-1811, 142, 199, 212, 268]. Joseph may have been the father of

3   i.   Joseph², Jr., born say 1750.

    ii.   Micajah, head of a household of 1 "white" male under twenty-one years of age and 2 "white" females in Nap of Reeds District in the state census for Granville County in 1786. Administration of his Granville County estate was granted to Joseph Okey in February 1791 on 200 pounds security [Minutes 1789-91, n.p.].

3.   Joseph² Okey, born say 1750, was taxable on an assessment of 1,810 pounds in Granville County in 1780. He was called Joseph Oakey, Jr. in 1790 when he was taxable in Dutch District, Granville County, North Carolina, and called "Joseph Oakley, Jr." in 1800 when he was head of a Granville County household of 8 "other free." He was taxable on 447 acres Dutch District, Granville County from 1786 to 1796 and taxable on 250 acres from 1802 to 1804. His 8 August 1804 Granville County will was proved by his wife Elizabeth in August 1805. He (signing) left 100 acres to his son Aaron, 150 acres to his son Willie and daughter Selah, and named his other children: Joseph, Susanna, Elizabeth, and Deborah [Original at N.C. Archives, CR.044.801.29]. His widow Elizabeth Okey was taxable on 250 acres in Ledge of Rock District in 1805 [Tax List 1796-1802, p.283; 1803-1811, 89, 142, 199, 212], and head of a Ledge Neck, Granville County household of 3 "free colored" women in 1820 [NC:18]. They were the parents of

    i.   Aaron.

    ii.   Selah.

    iii.   William⁴/ Willie.

    iv.   Joseph³.

    v.   Susanna.

    vi.   Elizabeth.

    vii.   Deborah.

OLIVER FAMILY

1. Mary Oliver, born say 1692, was living in St. Stephen's Parish, Northumberland County, on 18 December 1712 when the grand jury indicted her for having a "Mulatto" child the previous May. She did not appear in court until 18 November 1713 when she was ordered to pay a fine of 500 pounds of tobacco [Orders 1699-1713, 812; 1713-19, 6]. She may have been the ancestor of

   i. William[1], head of a Westmoreland County household of 12 "other free" in 1810 [VA:781].
   ii. William[2], head of a Lancaster County household of 5 "other free" in 1810 [VA:355].
   iii. James, "free negro" head of a Gloucester County household of 1 "other free" in 1810 [VA:665].
   iv. Benjamin, "free Negro" taxable in Hanover County in 1800 [*Virginia Genealogist* 29:105].

OTTER/ AUTER FAMILY

1. Sarah Otter, born say 1750, was called Sarah Otway and was living in Cumberland County, Virginia, on 28 August 1775 when the court ordered the churchwardens of Littleton Parish to bind out her "mulattoe" children Kitty and Billy to Benejah Thompson. She was called Sarah Otry on 25 March 1776 when the court bound her "mulattoe" children Kitty, Billy, and Nancy to Bartlet Thompson. And she was called Sarah Otrey on 28 July 1777 when the court bound her "mulattoe" son James to Bartlet Thompson [Orders 1774-8, 339, 364]. She was called Sarah Otter in Chesterfield County on 7 May 1779 when the court ordered her children James and John Otter bound out [Orders 1774-84, 224]. She was called Sally Auter in Henrico County on 5 January 1793 when she consented to the marriage of her daughter Nancy Auter to William Moss. She purchased a lot of about 1-3/8 acres in Swansboro, Chesterfield County, in 1799 and was called Sally Allen alias Otter when she was taxable on the land until 1820 when it was divided among Royal (1/2 lot), Milley (1/2 lot), and Kittey Auter (32/40 lot) [Land Tax List 1791-1822, B lists]. She was counted in a list of "Free Negroes" in Chesterfield County in 1813 with two women in her household over the age of sixteen [Waldrep, *1813 Tax List*]. She was the mother of

2 i. Kitty, born about 1772.
   ii. Billy, born say 1774, bound apprentice in Cumberland County on 28 August 1775.
   iii. Nancy, born say 1775, bound to Bartlet Thompson on 25 March 1776, called Nancy Otter, a "poor orphan" when the Cumberland County court ordered the churchwardens of Littleton Parish to bind her to Benjamin Martin on 25 November 1782 [Orders 1779-84, 289]. She married William Moss, 5 January 1793 Henrico County bond.
   iv. James, bound to Bartlet Thompson on 28 July 1777.
   v. ?Henry, born say 1778, a "F. Negroe" taxable on a tithe and 2 horses in Chesterfield County from 1801 to 1804, a "Mulatto" taxable in 1805 to 1807, died before 1809 when his estate was taxable on a horse [PPTL, 1786-1811, frames 470, 506, 583, 620, 717, 753].
   vi. John Auter, born 13 December 1779, registered in Petersburg on 26 July 1805: *a brown Mulatto man, born 13 December 1779, five feet four and a half inches high, born free and raised in the County of Chesterfield* [Register of Free Negroes 1794-1819, no. 345]. He was called Jack Otter when he was taxable in Chesterfield County from 1802 to 1804 [PPTL, 1786-1811, frames 506, 583].

vii.   ?Patty, born about 1783, obtained a certificate of freedom in Chesterfield County on 26 August 1818: *thirty five years old, yellow complexion, born free* [Register of Free Negroes 1804-53, no. 263].

2.   Kitty Otter/ Auter, born about 1772, obtained a certificate of freedom in Chesterfield County on 16 March 1814 (and on 12 July 1819 and 11 June 1827): *forty two years old, brown complexion, born free* [Register of Free Negroes 1804-53, nos. 216, 340, 580]. She may have been the mother of
  i.   Royall Otter, born about 1793, obtained a certificate of freedom in Chesterfield County on 16 March 1814: *twenty one years old, yellow complexion, born free* [Register of Free Negroes 1804-53, no. 211].
  ii.   Betsey Otter, born about 1795, obtained a certificate of freedom in Chesterfield County on 16 March 1814: *nineteen years old, yellow complexion, born free* [Register of Free Negroes 1804-53, no. 214]. She married Ned **Bowman**, 7 March 1815 Chesterfield County bond, Martin **Bowman** security.
  iii.   Milly, married Watt **Logan**, "free persons of color," 27 May Chesterfield County bond, Royal Otter security.

OVERTON FAMILY

1.   Sarah Overton, born say 1713, a "Mallatto Woman," was freed from her indenture to Edmund Chancey after being allowed by the October 1745 Pasquotank County court to "go up the river to see for her age in a Bible there." She was the mother of three "Mallatto Children" Bob, Jack Spaniard, and Spanial **Bow** who were bound to Edmund Chancey until the age of twenty-one by the Pasquotank County court on 12 July 1738 [Haun, *Pasquotank County Court Minutes 1737-46*, 32, 179, 186]. Chancey left a Pasquotank County will on 15 March 1753 by which he bequeathed the remainder of the service of "Jack Spanyerd boe and Spanyoll Boe" to his son Daniel Chancey and left the remainder of the service of Bob Boe, Rachel Boe, and Frank Boe, and her two children to his daughter-in-law Rachel Chancey [Grimes, *Abstract of North Carolina Wills*, 114-7]. Her children were
  i.   Robert **Bow**, born 10 December 1729(?), a "Mulatto" head of a Pasquotank County household in 1769 [SS 837]. See further the **Bow** history.
  ii.   Frank **Bow**, born say 1731.
  iii.   Rachel **Bow**, born say 1733.
  iv.   Jack Spaniard **Bow**, born November 1734.
  v.   Spanial **Bow**, born May 1738.
  2   vi.   ?Parthenia[1] Overton, born say 1740.
  3   vii.   ?Titus Overton, born say 1742.
  4   viii.   ?Samuel Overton, born say 1744.

2.   Parthenia[1] Overton, born say 1740, was head of a Perquimans County household of 10 "other free" in 1790 [NC:31], 12 in 1800 [NC:657], and 2 in 1810 [NC:917]. She may have been the mother of
  5   i.   Jonathan, born about 1754.
  6   ii.   Rachel, born about 1760.
  7   iii.   Lemuel[1], say 1762.

3.   Titus Overton, born say 1742, was taxable with his wife in Bladen County in 1763, was taxable on 2 "Mulatto" tithes in Cumberland County in 1767, was taxable with his wife ("Mulatoes") in Bladen County from 1770 to 1776 and was taxable in Bladen County on 500 acres, 3 horses, and 3 head of cattle in 1779 [SS 837; *N.C. Genealogy* XXI:3136; Byrd, *Bladen County Tax Lists*, I:32, 89, 123; II:90, 146]. He lived on the east side of the Northwest River according to a 3 February 1770 Bladen County deed from John **Johnston** to

Silvanus Wilson for sale of 100 acres in Cumberland County where Titus Overton formerly lived [DB 23:227-8]. He received 2 pounds, 2 shillings for twenty-one days service in the Bladen County Militia between 1775 and 1776 under Captain James Council [Haun, *Revolutionary Army Accounts, Journal "A"*, 22]. He was called Titus Overton, cooper of Bladen County, on 12 April 1783 when he purchased 100 acres in Cumberland County on the Northwest Branch of Cape Fear River on Locks Creek which Peter Shaver patented on 2 March 1754. The size of this plot was corrected to 125 acres by deed of 13 August 1804. On 28 February 1786 he sold 150 acres in this same area of Cumberland County on Harrison's Creek which had been conveyed to him by William Anderson by an unrecorded deed. He was called Titus Overton, planter, on 19 September 1792 when he sold 100 acres on the northeast side of the Northwest River near Beaverdam Pond which had been conveyed to John **Johnston** and his wife on 27 April 1767 and on which they were buried, and he sold 111 acres of his land on Locks Creek on 25 August 1804 [Cumberland County DB 11:66; 12:326; 20:245, 252; 28:151]. On 16 July 1791 he was appointed administrator of the Cumberland County estate of John Overton, a soldier in the North Carolina Line [*NCGSJ* XIV:115-6]. He was head of a Cumberland County household of 11 "other free" in 1790 [NC:31], 7 in 1800, and 1 in 1810 [NC:600]. Titus' children were most likely

    i.   John[1], died before 16 July 1791 when Titus Overton was granted administration on his Cumberland County estate on security of 60 pounds [Minutes 1791-97, Saturday, 16 July 1791].

    ii.   Dyer, born before 1776, head of a Cumberland County household of 5 "other free" in 1810 [NC:570], and 7 "free colored" in 1820 [NC:181]. On 28 December 1811 he purchased 40 acres in Cumberland County on the northwest side of Cape Fear River [DB 26:540].

    iii.   Isom, who purchased 133 acres adjoining Titus Overton on 26 July 1804 [DB 20:253]. His 20 November 1807 Cumberland County will, proved 18 December the same year, mentioned his wife Charity, her unnamed child she was then pregnant with, and his sister Betsy Howard [WB A:109].

    iv.   Elizabeth, married William Howard according to the will of her brother Isom. William was head of a white Cumberland County household in 1810 [NC:602].

4.   Samuel Overton, born say 1744, was a "Molatto" Perquimans County taxable in 1771 [CR 77.701.1]. His freedom papers issued in Edenton in 1783 stated that he was a

    Mulatto, Free man and is entitled to all the rights, privileges Immunities of a Citizen of the State of North Carolina [Crow, *Black Experience in Revolutionary North Carolina*, 33].

He was head of a Pasquotank County household of 3 "other free" in 1790 [NC:31], 4 in 1800 [NC:634], and 13 "free colored" in 1820 [NC:277]. He was called a "free man of Colour" on 8 March 1825 when he made a declaration in Pasquotank County court to obtain a Revolutionary War pension. He claimed that he was ninety-six years old, the father (grandfather?) of a five-year-old boy, David, and that he had lost all his property by a fire in July 1824 [M804-1854, frame 0826]. He may have been the father of

    i.   Susannah, head of a Pasquotank County household of 2 "other free" in 1790 (Susanna Everton) [NC:28] and 5 in 1810 [NC:917].

5.   Jonathan Overton, born about 1754 in Perquimans County, was the apprentice of John Bateman of Chowan County when he entered the service as a substitute for him under Colonel Lytle. He was at sea for a while and then returned to Edenton. He was about 79 years old on 19 December 1832 when

he made a declaration in Chowan County court to obtain a pension for three years service [M804-1854, frame 0788]. He was head of a Chowan County household of 9 "other free" in 1810 [NC:535] and 7 "free colored" in 1820 [NC:129]. He was described in a 1849 newspaper account as: *a colored man, a soldier in the Revolution...at the advanced age of 101 years* [Crow, *Black Experience in Revolutionary North Carolina*, 101]. He may have been the father of

    i.   Benjamin, born say 1774, head of a Perquimans County household of 10 "other free" in 1810 [NC:961].

    ii. James, born say 1775, head of a Pasquotank County household of 4 "other free" in 1810 [NC:918] and 7 "free colored" in 1820 [NC:285]. He married Nancy **Bowe**, 19 January 1809 Pasquotank County bond. He was called "James Overton Freeman of color" when he purchased 3 acres in Pasquotank County about a half mile below Nixenton on 11 February 1839 [DB DD:89].

    iii. David, born say 1778, head of a Chowan County household of 1 "other free" in 1800 NC:118], 1 "other free" and a slave in 1810 [NC:118] and 1 "free colored" in 1820 [NC:114].

    iv. Jesse, born about 1780, a "Mulato" house carpenter apprenticed to Isacha Branch in Perquimans County on 14 February 1792 [CR 77.101.6] and head of a Pasquotank County household of 5 "other free" in 1810 [NC:918].

    v.   Betsy, head of a Chowan County household of 3 "other free" in 1810 [NC:535].

6.   Rachel Overton, born about 1760, was a twelve-year-old "Mullatto" girl bound to James Shannonhouse by the Pasquotank County court in September 1772, no parent named [Minutes 1768-75, Wednesday, September court, n.p.]. She was head of a Perquimans County household of 7 "other free" in 1790 [NC:31] and 6 in Pasquotank County in 1810 [NC:917]. Her children were bound out in Perquimans County in 1819 and 1821 [CR 077.101.6]. They were

    i.   John[3]/ Jack, bound to James Leigh on 10 February 1819. He registered in Pasquotank County about 1831: *about Twenty Years of Age...black Complexion...Son of Rachel Overton, a free Person of Colour* [Byrd, *In Full Force and Virtue*, 193].

    ii. Livinia, "of color," bound to Sophia Barker on 10 February 1819.

    iii. William, bound to James Leigh on 10 February 1819.

    iv. Alexander, "colored son of Rachel," bound to Myles Elliot on 14 August 1821.

    v.   Miley, bound to Edward Wood on 14 August 1821.

    vi. Parthenia[2], bound to Jesse Murden on 14 August 1821.

7.   Lemuel[1] Overton, born say 1762, was head of Perquimans County household of 2 "other free" in 1790 [NC:31]. He was the husband of a slave named Rose and children John and Burdock who were emancipated by order of the North Carolina General Assembly. They were probably his slaves since the owner's name was not stated [Byrd, *In Full Force and Virtue*, 298]. He was living in Pasquotank County on 10 July 1820 when he appointed James Freeman his attorney to obtain a land warrant for his services as a soldier in the 10th Regiment of the North Carolina Line [*NCGSJ* VII:93]. He was deceased on 12 February 1822 when his son Lemuel was bound apprentice in Perquimans County [CR 77.101.6]. His children were

    i.   John[2], son of Lemuel and his wife Rose, registered as a "free man of Colour" in Pasquotank County on 26 October 1830. His wife Abby (daughter of Tully and Betty **Bowe**) registered the same day [*In Full Force and Virtue*, 191-2].

ii. Braddock, son of Rose and Lemuel, registered as a "free born" person in Pasquotank County on 1 November 1830. His wife Molly, daughter of Lemuel and Jenny **Hall**, registered the same day [Byrd, *In Full Force and Virtue*, 191, 193].

iii. William, "son of Lemuel" bound to Benjamin Jones in Perquimans County on 10 May 1819 [CR 77.101.6].

iv. Lemuel², bound to Jesse Murden on 12 February 1822.

OWENS FAMILY

1. Mary Owen, born say 1702, was presented by the grandjury of Prince George County, Virginia, on 10 May 1720 for having a "Mallatto" child [Orders 1714-20, 320]. She was probably the mother of

2   i. Sarah, born say 1744.

2. Sarah Owen, born say 1744, gave consent to the Petersburg marriage of her daughter Anne Owens to James **Valentine**, 10 December Petersburg Hustings Court bond, William **Cypress** surety, 11 December 1785 marriage. She was the mother of

i. Anne, born say 1764.

ii. ?Dilcey, born about 1768, registered in Petersburg on August 19, 1794: *a brown Mulatto woman, five feet one and a half inches high, twenty six years old, born free & raised in the County of Prince George* [Register of Free Negroes 1794-1819, no. 64].

iii. ?James, born about 1775, registered in Petersburg on 19 July 1817: *a free man of colour, five feet four and a half inches high, forty two years old, dark brown complection, born free in Dinwiddie County, a carpenter* [Register of Free Negroes 1794-1819, no. 853].

iv. ?Polly, born about 1784, registered in Petersburg on 9 June 1810: *a dark brown Mulatto woman, five feet three & a half inches high, twenty six years old, born free in Dinwiddie County* [Register of Free Negroes 1794-1819, no. 580].

Other members of the family were

i. William, born about 1782, registered in Petersburg on 13 June 1807: *a Brown Mulatto man, five feet two inches high, twenty five years old, raised in Sussex County with Mason Harwell, by trade a shoe maker, born free.* He registered again on 29 May 1812 [Register of Free Negroes 1794-1819, nos. 408, 706].

ii. James Owens, head of a Burke County, North Carolina household of 5 "other free" in 1810 [NC:349].

iii. Polly, born about 1776, registered in Brunswick County, Virginia, on 23 June 1823: *about forty seven Years old, five feet five & a half Inches high...born free from the evidence of David B. Stith* [Wynne, *Register of Free Negroes*, 55].

iv. Nathaniel, "m" head of a Brunswick County, Virginia household of 1 "other free" in 1810 [VA:726].

OXENDINE FAMILY

1. John¹ Oxendine, born say 1694, was called "John Figrow (Mallatto)" on 18 November 1719 when Judith Bowling, servant of Ann Hould, came into Northumberland County, Virginia court and swore that he was the father of "the child she was lately brought to bed with."[160] He was called "John Oxendine alias Figro" on 20 January 1724/5 when he brought a successful suit

---

[160]Judith may have been the ancestor of the "Melungeon" **Bowling** family of Tennessee.

against Ann Hould and William Wildey and his wife Elizabeth in Northumberland County, Virginia, for his freedom from any service due to them [Orders 1713-19, 347; 1719-29, 167]. He was living in Northumberland County in the 1730's when the birth dates were recorded for his children Benjamin, Jenne, Clark, and John [Fleet, *Northumberland County Births*, 112]. He was living in Bladen County, North Carolina, on 27 August 1753 when John **Johnson**, Jr., entered 100 acres whereon John Oxendine was living. He was called John Oxendine, Senr., when his improvements on the east side of Drowning Creek were mentioned in the 5 March 1759 Bladen County land entry of his son John Oxendine [Philbeck, *Bladen County Land Entries*, nos. 805, 1126]. On 28 November 1758 the Bladen County court recommended him to the General Assembly as a person to be excused from paying his taxes [Saunders, *Colonial Records of North Carolina*, V:1045]. His wife may have been Sarah Oxendine who was a white head of household in Bladen County in 1770, taxable on William Taner, a white man [Byrd, *Bladen County Tax Lists*, I:35]. John's children were

    i.   Benjamin[1], born 12 April 1733, sued in Cumberland County, North Carolina court by William Hodges on 18 April 1758 [Minutes 1755-59, 34].

    ii. Jenne, born 14 February 1735.

    iii. Clark, born 28 November 1736.

    iv. John[2], born 10 June 1739, entered 100 acres on the east side of Drowning Creek on 5 March 1759 which included the improvements of John Oxendine, Senr. He was living in South Carolina on 25 February 1773 when he was presented by the Court of General Sessions for retailing liquor without a license [Journal of the S.C. Court, p.229]. He was taxable in Christ Church Parish, South Carolina, from 1786 to 1795, on two slaves in 1786 and on six slaves in 1794 [Tax Returns 1783-7, frames 112, 189; 1787-1800, frames 39, 153, 172, 194].

2   v. ?Charles[1], born say 1741.

    vi. ?Cudworth, a taxable "Mulato" in Bladen County in 1768 and 1769 [Byrd, *Bladen County Tax Lists*, I:5, 14], head of a Liberty County, South Carolina household of 8 "other free" in 1800 [SC:806] and a Marion District household of 6 "other free" in 1810 [SC:83].

2. Charles[1] Oxendine, born say 1741, received a patent for 150 acres northeast of Drowning Creek in Bladen County on 23 October 1767 [Hoffman, *Land Patents*, II:450].[161] He was a "mixt Blood" taxable in Bladen County from 1766 to 1768 and a "Molato" taxable in 1770 and 1771 [Byrd, *Bladen County Tax Lists*, I:7, 35, 59]. He entered a further 200 acres in Robeson County bordering his land by two land entries of 100 acres each on 22 January and 23 September 1793 [Pruitt, *Land Entries: Robeson County*, I:70, 85]. On 23 November 1797 he made an unsuccessful claim for payment for three steers he provided the army commanded by General Rutherford [*NCGSJ* II:151]. He was head of a Robeson County household of 11 "other free" in 1790 [NC:49] and 10 in 1800 [NC:409]. By his 7 September 1808 Robeson County will he left 150 acres to his son David and 200 acres and a grist mill to his daughters [WB 1:206]. His children were

    i.   Benjamin[2], executor of his father's will, head of a Robeson County household of 1 "other free" in 1790 [NC:50], 1 "other free" and 1 white woman in 1800 [NC:409], 2 "other free" in 1810 [NC:228], and 1 "free colored" in 1820 [NC:313]. The county sold 150 acres of his land for debt on 4 January 1809 [Minutes II:128].

---

[161]Robeson County was formed from this part of Bladen County in 1787.

ii. John[3], head of a Robeson County household of 1 "other free" in 1790 [NC:48]. He entered 100 acres on the north side of Drowning Creek on 18 June 1794 [Pruitt, *Land Entries: Robeson County,* I:96] and sold land by deed proved in Robeson County on 1 January 1810 [Minutes II:174]. He was head of a Cumberland County household of 6 "other free" in 1800 and 9 in 1810 [NC:620]. He married Margaret **Mainor**, 30 October 1810 Cumberland County bond.[162]

iii. Charles[2], head of a Robeson County household of 1 "other free" in 1790 [NC:48], 3 in 1800 [NC:409], 4 in 1810 [NC:232], and 5 "free colored" in 1820 [NC:301]. He was probably the Charles Oxendine who was indicted for assault and battery and fined fifteen dollars by the Robeson court in 1837. Since he was unable to pay his fine, as a "free negro" he was liable to be hired out by the sheriff. He successfully fought this judgment in the Supreme Court of North Carolina with the help of two eminent Fayetteville lawyers, Robert Strange, a U.S. senator, and George E. Badger, later Secretary of the Navy and a Whig senator [Franklin, *Free Negro in North Carolina,* 86].

iv. Jesse, entered 100 acres east of Drowning Creek and north of Mill Branch in Robeson County on 22 January 1793 [Pruitt, *Land Entries: Robeson County,* I:70]. He was head of a Robeson County household of 4 "other free" in 1800 [NC:409] and 8 in 1810 [NC:232]. He purchased land by deed proved in Robeson County on 7 July 1801 [Minutes I:158].

3 v. Moses.

vi. Aaron, head of a Sumter District, South Carolina household of 5 "other free" in 1810 [SC:224a].

vii. David, head of a Robeson County household of 1 "other free" in 1800 [NC:409], 6 in 1810 [NC:230], and 2 "free colored" in 1820 [NC:305].

viii. Nancy, born about 1765, living in South Carolina in 1795 when the 25 July issue of the *North Carolina Central and Fayetteville Gazette* offered a: *$10 reward to deliver to the subscriber in Georgetown, a mustie servant woman named Nancy Oxendine, she is a stout wench, of a light complexion about 30 years old. It is supposed she has been ??elks away by her brother and sister, the latter lives in Fayetteville* [Fouts, *Newspapers of Edenton, Fayetteville, & Hillsborough,* 81]. Her brother John[3] and sister Betsy lived in Cumberland County.

4 ix. Betsy, born say 1766.

x. Mary, perhaps the Polly Oxendine who was a 36-45 year old head of a Cumberland County household of 3 "free colored" in 1820.

xi. Catherine.

xii. Sarah.

3. Moses Oxendine was head of a Robeson County household of 3 "other free" in 1810 [NC:232] and 7 "free colored" in 1820 [NC:311]. His 20 September 1856 Robeson County will was proved in August 1857. He left 31 acres to his daughter Sylvanah and mentioned her son Archibald [WB 2:122]. His daughter was

i. Sylvanah, mother of Archibald Oxendine.

---

[162]Margaret **Mainor** was probably the daughter of John **Manor**, head of a Sampson County household of 1 "other free" in 1790 [NC:53], and 4 in Cumberland County in 1810 [NC:603]. Jesse **Maner** (born about 1786), Isaac **Maner** (born about 1791), and Stephen **Manor** (born 19 October 1812) were "Mulatto" or "coloured" children bound apprentices in Cumberland County [Minutes 1801-4, 17 April 1801; Minutes 1823-7, 12 June 1824].

4.   Betsy Oxendine, born about 1766, was living in Cumberland County in
      October 1786 when the court ordered that her child Nance Oxendine be bound
      out. She was the mother of
      i.   ?John[4], born about 1782, "a Mullattoe Base Born Child," no parent
            named when he was ordered bound to Neil McRainy by the 28 October
            1786 Cumberland County court [Minutes 1784-7, n.p.].
      ii. Nance, born about 1787, a "mulato" girl about eighteen months old
            who was ordered bound to James Dyer, Esq., by the 28 October 1788
            Cumberland County court [Minutes 1787-91, n.p.].

5.   Henry Oxendine, born say 1765, was head of a Richmond County household
      of 5 "other free" in 1790 [NC:46]. On 22 June 1790 he entered 100 acres in
      Richmond County on Powells Branch of Rockey Fork of Hitchcock Creek
      [Pruitt, *Land Entries: Richmond County,* no. 544]. The April 1792 Richmond
      County court called him Henry Auxendine when it ordered the sheriff to sell
      his land to satisfy a judgment against him by Thomas Dockery, Esquire
      [Minutes 1779-92, 226]. And he was called Henry Auxendine when he married
      Sarah **Collins** in Richmond County between 1 December 1788 and 31
      December 1789 [*NCGSJ* XII:168 (T&C Co. Sett., Box 75)]. He was head of
      a Robeson County household of 5 "free colored" in 1820 [NC:308]. He may
      have been the father of
      i.   Charles[3], head of a Marion District, South Carolina household of 5
            "other free" in 1810 [SC:83].

6.   Hector Oxendine was killed by the White Home Guard in Robeson County
      near the end of the Civil War in May 1865. He was suspected of helping
      General Sherman when his army marched through Robeson County [Blu, *The
      Lumbee Problem,* 52-53].

PAGE FAMILY

Several members of the Page family, perhaps siblings, were taxables in Norfolk
County in the 1750s. They were
      i.   Sam, born say 1728, taxable in Norfolk County near Tanner's Bridge
            in 1752 [Wingo, *Norfolk County Tithables, 1751-65,* 31].
1   ii. Ann, born say 1730.
      iii. Abraham, a "Free Negro" who was indentured to William Denby when
            Denby made his 2 September 1749 Norfolk County will [McIntosh,
            Brief Abstracts of Norfolk County Wills, 300].
      iv. Rachel, born say 1734, a taxable "free negro" head of her own Norfolk
            County household in the District of the Borough of Norfolk on the
            South Side of Tanner's Creek to Spratt's Bridge between 1757 and
            1765 [Wingo, *Norfolk County Tithables, 1751-65,* 122, 145, 217].
      v.   Margaret, born say 1736, a taxable "free negro" head of her own
            Norfolk County household in the District of the Borough of Norfolk on
            the South Side of Tanner Creek to Great Bridge in 1759 [Wingo,
            Norfolk County Tithables, 1751-65, 145].
      vi. Sarah, born say 1745, a taxable in the east side of the borough of
            Norfolk in 1765 [Wingo, *Norfolk County Tithables, 1751-65,* 217].

1.   Ann Page, born say 1730, was taxable in Ann **James'** household in 1754 in
      Norfolk County near Tanner's Creek and head of her own household from
      1754 to 1765, called "free negro" in some years and "Mollata" in others
      [Wingo, *Norfolk County Tithables, 1751-65,* 92, 122, 145, 182, 217]. She may
      have been the mother of
      i.   Thomas, born say 1759, a "free Negro" ordered bound apprentice by
            the churchwardens of Elizabeth River Parish in Norfolk County court
            on 16 May 1760 (no parent named) [Orders 1759-63, 36].

ii. James, born say 1765, head of a Bertie County, North Carolina household of 2 "other free" in 1790 [NC:14].

Their descendants were most likely

i. Maria, head of a Richmond City household of 2 "other free" and 2 slaves in 1810 [VA:345].

ii. Nathaniel, head of a Richmond City household of 2 "other free" in 1810 [VA:345].

iii. John, head of a Henrico County household of 2 "other free" in 1810 [VA:996].

PAGEE FAMILY

1. Nanny Pagee, born say 1770, won freedom for herself and her children from a family named Hook by a judgment confirmed in the Virginia Court of Appeals in 1814. The jury in the case found that she was brought to Virginia from North Carolina by Thomas Jones illegally if she was a slave and that, from inspection, she was a white woman [Catterall, *Judicial Cases*, I:121]. She was probably identical to Nancy Pegee, a spinster counted in "A List of Free Negroes & Mulatters" in Botetourt County in 1804 [Orders 1800-4, Loose Papers, no. 48]. She was apparently the mother of

    i. Polly, born about 1795, registered in Botetourt County on 7 August 1823: *age 28, Bright Mulatto, 5 feet 5 inches high, Free as per certificate from Court of Bedford* [Free Negroes &c Registered, no. 39].

    ii. Daniel, born about 1798, registered in Bedford County on 7 August 1823: *age 25, dark Mulatto, 5 feet 8 inches high, free as per copy Judgt. of Court of appeals* and registered again on 9 June 1834: *age 39, Dark Mulatto, five feet eight Inches high a Barber by trade, free as per Copy of Judgment of Court of appeals, by a Certificate from Charlotte County* [Free Negroes &c Registered, nos. 40, 91].

    iii. Celia, registered on 9 September 1828, *age --, Mulatto, 5 feet 6 inches high, free by a decree of the Court of Appls Dated 22 June 1811* [Free Negroes &c Registered, no. 46].

    iv. Judy, born about 1808, registered in Botetourt County on 9 June 1836: *age 28, bright Mulatto, five feet 2 or 3 inches high, Born free* [Free Negroes &c Registered, no.92].

PALMER FAMILY

1. Ann Palmer, born say 1706, was the servant of Michael Gilbert of Cople Parish, Westmoreland County, Virginia, on 24 July 1724 when she acknowledged having a "Mulatto" child "begott of her body by a negro Man" [Orders 1721-31, 70a]. She may have been the ancestor of

    i. John, head of a Loudoun County household of 5 "other free" in 1810 [VA:313].

    ii. Betty, head of a Queen Anns County, Maryland household of 2 "other free" in 1790.

    iii. Samuel, head of a Kent County, Maryland household of 3 "other free" in 1800 [MD:165].

Members of the family in North Carolina were:

i. William, head of a Pasquotank County household of 7 "other free" in 1800 [NC:635] and 6 in 1810 [NC:919].

ii. David, head of a Pasquotank County household of 6 "other free" in 1800 [NC:635].

iii. Jerry, head of a Pasquotank County household of 5 "other free" in 1810 [NC:919].

   iv.   Henry, head of a Pasquotank County household of 3 "other free" in
         1810 [NC:919].

Another Palmer family:
Priscilla Palmer, born say 1702, a single white woman of Christ Church Parish,
Lancaster County, Virginia, had a male child by Robert Carter's slave named
"Mullatto Billy" on 26 March 1723 [Orders 1721-9, 98-100].

PARKER FAMILY

Members of the Parker family were
1   i.   Elisha, born about 1752-1759.
     ii.   Samuel, born before 1776, head of a Nansemond County household of
           2 "free colored" in 1820 [VA:71].
    iii.   Milley, born before 1776, head of a Nansemond County household of
           7 "free colored" in 1820 [VA:74A].

1.   Elisha Parker, born about 1752-1759, a "man of color," was about eighty
     years old on 20 November 1832 when he made a declaration in Gates County,
     North Carolina, to obtain a pension for his services in the Revolution. He
     stated that he was born in Nansemond County, Virginia, near the North
     Carolina line about 1752. He was said to have been about seventy-five years
     old on 10 February 1834 when he made a similar declaration in Nansemond
     County court, stating that he entered the service in Gates County about 1779
     as a substitute for Francis Speight and had been a resident of Nansemond
     County for the previous forty-five years [M804-1871, frame 0787]. He was
     head of a Gates County household of 4 "other free" in 1790 [NC:23] and 3
     "free colored" in Nansemond County in 1820 [VA:79]. He may have been
     related to
      i.   Thomas, head of a Cumberland County, North Carolina household of
           8 "other free" in 1810 [NC:605].

PARR FAMILY

1.   Anne Parr, born say 1732, was the servant of Archibald Stewart on 30 April
     when the Augusta County court adjudged that her bastard child was a
     "Mulato" and bound the child to her master [Orders 1753-5, 192]. She was
     probably the mother or grandmother of
      i.   Will, head of an Augusta County household of 8 "other free" in 1810
           [VA:373].

PARROT FAMILY

Members of the Parrot family were
      i.   William, born say 1725, presented by the York County court on 20
           November 1749 for failing to list himself as a tithable [Judgments &
           Orders 1746-52, 256, 277, 284].
     ii.   Sarah, born say 1727, presented by the York County court on 20
           November 1749 for failing to list herself as a tithable [Judgments &
           Orders 1746-52, 256, 277, 284].
    iii.   Susan **Jarvis**, born say 1727, a "Poor Mulatto" woman living in York
           County on 17 December 1759 when the court ordered the
           churchwardens of Yorkhampton Parish to bind out her children because
           she was unable to provide for them [Judgments & Orders 1759-63,
           103]. She was head of a York County household of 2 "other free" in
           1810 [VA:876]. She was called Susanna Parrott alias Susanna Jarvis
           when she was sued by Thomas Fauntleroy in a case heard in York
           County court between May 1801 and May 1802. James Trice, Thomas

Trice (of King and Queen County) and John Bowden (of James City County), and Thomas Drewry were witnesses. The case was discontinued with each party paying their own costs [Orders 1795-1803, 457, 482, 483, 498, 516-8, 522].

PATRICK FAMILY

1. Ezekiel Patrick, born say 1730, was head of a Georgetown District, Prince George's Parish, South Carolina household of 5 "other free" in 1790 and 7 in Liberty County in 1800 [SC:785]. He may have been the father of
    i.   David, head of a Bladen County, North Carolina household of 7 "other free" in 1800.
    ii.   "Luke & John," heads of a Colleton District household of 10 "other free" and a slave in 1810 [SC:617].
    iii. Sam, head of a Colleton District household of 4 "other free" in 1810 [SC:591].
    iv.   Right, head of a Colleton District household of 3 "other free" in 1810 [SC:591].
    v.   Jeremiah, head of a Colleton District household of 1 "other free" in 1810 [SC:617].

PATTERSON FAMILY

1. Anne Patterson, born about 1732, was described as a "free mulatto woman" on 29 July 1750 when she registered the birth of her daughter Elizabeth in St. Peter's Parish, New Kent County, Virginia [NSCDA, *Register of St. Peter's Parish*, 100]. On 7 October 1765 the Henrico County court ordered the churchwardens of Henrico Parish to bind out her "Mulatto" children John, Sall, and Iris [Orders 1763-7, 525]. She was a fifty-year-old "mulatto" living in Ward 3 of Richmond, Virginia, in 1782 [VA:114]. Her children were
    i.   Elizabeth[1], born 29 July 1750.
    ii.   John, bound apprentice in Henrico County on 7 October 1765. He may have been the John Patterson who was a "F.B." head of a Bedford County, Virginia household of 4 "other free" in 1810 [VA:469].
    iii. Sall, bound apprentice in Henrico County on 7 October 1765.
    iv.   Rice (Iris?), born about 1762, a twenty-year-old "Free mulatto" listed in Anne Patterson's Richmond City household in 1782 [VA:114].

2. Susannah Patterson, born say 1740, perhaps a sister of Anne Patterson, was living in New Kent County, Virginia, in 1758 when the birth and baptism of her daughter were recorded [NSCDA, *Register of St. Peter's Parish*, 98, 171]. She was head of a household with no whites, one dwelling, and one other building in the Upper Precinct of New Kent County in 1785 [VA:92]. She was taxable in New Kent County from 1783 to 1810: taxable on a slave named Sam, 2 horses and 7 cattle in 1783; taxable on her son Jesse in 1784 and 1785; taxable on a horse from 1797 to 1800; taxable on a free male tithable, 2 slaves aged 12-16 and a horse in 1804; taxable on a free male tithable from 1805 to 1809; taxable on a slave aged 12-16 in 1810 [PPTL 1782-1800, 19, 55, 73, 75, 101]. Her children were
    i.   Mary, born 12 February 1758 and baptized 4 September the same year, "daughter of Susannah Patterson" (no race stated). She was living in New Kent County on 31 December 1776 when she registered the birth of her daughter Elizabeth[2] (Betsey) Patterson (no race stated) [NSCDA, *Register of St. Peter's Parish*, 171, 174].
    ii.   Jesse, born say 1763, taxable in New Kent County from 1790 to 1820: called son of Susannah Patterson in 1784; a "Mulatto" taxable from 1790 to 1792 [PPTL 1782-1800, 55, 73, 150, 170, 191, 314; 1791-

He was head of a New Kent County, Virginia household of 1 "other free" in 1810 [VA:765].

iii. ?Moses, born say 1762, listed as a taxable in New Kent County adjacent to Susannah Patterson in 1783 and taxable from 1786 to 1794 [PPTL 1782-1800, 19, 89, 101, 149, 170, 191, 215].

iv. ?Dandridge, a "M"(ulatto) taxable in New Kent County from 1805 to 1820 [PPTL 1791-1828, frames 409, 421, 433, 444, 456, 491, 503, 516, 579].

v. ?Randolph, a "M"(ulatto) taxable in New Kent County in 1811 [PPTL 1791-1828, frame 466].

Their descendants may have been:

i. Elizabeth[2], a "free born Mulatto" apprenticed to Willoughby Old by the Princess Anne County court on 5 July 1770 [Minutes 1770-3, 12].

ii. Nancy, head of a Henrico County, Virginia household of 4 "other free" in 1810 [VA:1015].

iii. Joseph, born before 1776, head of a Granville County, North Carolina household of 6 "other free" in 1810 and 11 "free colored" in Guilford County in 1820 [NC:113].

iv. Jacob, head of a Currituck County household of 3 "other free" in 1810 [NC:88].

v. Lucy, born before 1776, head of a Surry County, North Carolina household of 11 "free colored" in 1820 [NC:722].

vi. George, head of a Buckingham County household of 3 "other free" in 1810 [VA:815].

vii. Squire, head of a Buckingham County household of 2 "other free" in 1810 [VA:815].

PAVEY/ PEAVEY FAMILY

1. Joshua[1] Pavey, born say 1725, was called Joshiah Pavee on 20 June 1745 when he made a successful appeal to the Craven County, North Carolina court [Haun, *Craven County Court Minutes*, III:463]. He was listed in the 27 November 1752 muster of the Wilmington Company commanded by Captain George Merrick [Clark, *Colonial Soldiers of the South*, 683]. He was called "Pavey" in the 1755 New Hanover List of Taxables in which he was taxable on 4 "Negro Males" [N.C. Archives File T.O. 105]. He purchased 200 acres on the east side of the mouth of Nichols Creek and the sound in New Hanover County on 28 April 1764, and sold half this land to Daniel **Webb** on 1 October 1764 [DB E:272, 274]. He was called a "Mulatto" and Daniel **Webb** was called a "free Negro" when the deed was proved in New Hanover County on 2 September 1766 [Minutes 1738-69, 274]. He was taxable in Bladen County (in the list next to John **Webb**) on 4 "Mixt Blood" males and a female in 1774 and taxable on 4 "Black" taxables (his wife and two sons) in 1775 and 1776 [Byrd, *Bladen County Tax Lists*, I:124; II:36, 47, 90]. He was head of a household of 1 male "Molatto" 21-60 years of age in the state census for New Hanover County in 1787. He was probably the ancestor of

i. Charles Peavy, taxable in Bladen County on a male and a female "Mixt Blood" in 1774 [Byrd, *Bladen County Tax Lists*, I:124], head of an Onslow County household of 11 "other free" in 1790 (abstracted as Charles Perry) [NC:197] and 14 "other free" in Brunswick County in 1800 [NC:13A].

ii. James Pevee, head of a Fayetteville, Cumberland County household of 1 "other free" in 1790 [NC:42].

iii. Caleb/ Calop Peavy, entered 200 acres on the west side of Slap Arse Swamp in Bladen County on 11 November 1771 [NC Archives, SS call no. S.108.494, location 863-9, file no. 774]. He was head of an Onslow County household of 4 "other free" in 1790 (abstracted as

Colop Perry) [NC:197], 3 "other free" in Brunswick County in 1800 [NC:13], and probably the C. Peavy who was head of a Brunswick County household of 7 "other free" in 1810 [NC:236]. Administration of his Marlboro County, South Carolina estate was granted to Ephraim **Sweat** on 3 April 1818 on $500 bond [Minutes of the Court of Ordinary, 125].

iv.   Thomas Peavey, head of a New Hanover County household of 1 "Molatto" 21-60 years old with 3 "Molatto" females for the state census in 1787, probably the T. Peavy who was head of a Brunswick County household of 4 "other free" in 1810 [NC:234].

v.   J. Peavy, head of a Brunswick County household of 3 "other free" in 1810 [NC:234]. This was probably Reverend Joshua[2] Peavy, born 3 July 1784 in Brunswick County, North Carolina. Although he was scarcely able to read, he started preaching in South Carolina and was ordained by Bishop Enoch George in 1821 in Alabama. He was described as being of "very dark complexion" (for a white man) [West, Rev. Anson, *History of Methodism in Alabama*, Nashville (1893): 206-9]. He married Martha **Smith** [Owen, Thomas McAdory, *History of Alabama and Dictionary of Alabama Biography*, Chicago (1921): IV:1334], probably a daughter of H. **Smith**, head of a Brunswick County, North Carolina household of 8 "other free" in 1810 [NC:234].

vi.   N. Peavy, head of a Brunswick County household of 2 "other free" in 1810 [NC:236].

In June 1856 a member of the Peavey family in North Carolina accused an election inspector of refusing to receive his vote. He claimed that his mother and grandmother were white women and that: *his father was a dark colored man with straight hair, his grandfather a dark red-faced mulatto, with dark straight hair.* He lost his case [Catterall, *Judicial Cases Concerning American Slavery* II:198].

PAYNE FAMILY

1.   Francis[1] Payne, born say 1620, was a slave called "Francisco a Negroe" when Philip Taylor claimed him as a headright in 1637 [Nugent, *Cavaliers and Pioneers* I:74]. The relationship between some masters and their slaves before slavery became institutionalized is illustrated by an agreement between Taylor and one of his slaves who stated in Northampton County court that

> *Now Mr. Taylor and I have divided our corne and I am very glad of it now I know myne...owne ground I will work when I please and play when I please* [Orders 1640-45, 457].

Thomas Yeoman, a poor white Northampton County planter, called him "Frank Capt. Taylor's Negro" in 1646 when he bequeathed him his estate consisting of 400 pounds of tobacco, 3 barrels of corn, and a shirt in gratitude for Francis looking after him while he was sick [DW 1645-51, 20].

Taylor died the same year and left Francis to his widow Jane who remarried and moved to Maryland with her husband William Eltonhead [DW 1645-51, 14 by Deal, *Race and Class*, 310-321]. On 13 May 1649 Jane called him "Francis Payne my Negro servant" when she gave him the right to a crop he was raising and the "power from tyme to tyme to make use of the ground and plantation" in return for 1,500 pounds of tobacco and six barrels of corn after the harvest [DW 1651-4, fol. 118]. This land was in Northampton County on Old Town Neck [Whitelaw, *Virginia's Eastern Shore*, 281-2]. A few months afterwards she agreed to sell him his freedom in exchange for three male servants with six to seven years to serve [DW 1651-54, fol. 118]. Still later that year Jane's husband wrote a letter to him about his progress in helping him acquire these three servants:

> *After my love to thee etc. I cannot heare of any servants in Yorke...But if you doe get your tobacco in caske, I question not but to gett them, when I come downe againe...I will bringe downe some caske with mee...your lovinge mayster* [DW 1651-54, fol. 174].

A few months later Eltonhead received a bill for two servants "which is for the use of Francis Payne Negro towards his freedom," and within a year Payne completed the payments. He was free by 1651 when he successfully sued Joseph Edlowe of Maryland for a debt of 300 pounds of tobacco for a heifer Edlowe purchased from him, and he had to pay Randall Revell a 400 pound debt later that same year [DW 1651-54, 119, p.38, fol.50, p.69]. He purchased a mare in June 1655 and sold its colt to Anthony **Johnson** on 31 January 1660 [DW 1655-68, fol. 19; 1657-66, fol. 74]. His former mistress confirmed his freedom in the July 1656 Northampton County court

> *I Mrs Jane Eltonhead...have hereunto sett my hand that ye aforesd Payne (a negro) shall bee discharged from all hinderances of servitude (his child) or any that doth belong to ye sd Payne* [DW 1654-55 fol.100].

By September 1656 he had married Amy, a white woman, who he gave a mare by deed of jointure. Later that year he sued John **Gussall** for failure to pay him rent [Orders 1665-56, 15; DW 1654-55, fol. 138; DW 1655-68, fol. 19, 21]. In 1665 he and Emmanuel **Driggus** were security for Hannah **Carter** when she was manumitted by her master, Francis Pigot [DW 1665-68, pt.2, 15]. He was called "Francis Pane Negro" in the Northampton County tithe lists on which he was taxable on two tithes in 1663 and only one tithe from 1664 to 1668. He left a 9 May 1673 Northampton County will, proved 29 September 1763 leaving all his estate to Agnes Pane, stating that Devrox **Dregushe (Driggers)** was to have nothing [Orders 1657-64, 176, 198; 1664-74, fol.14, p.42, fol.54, 217, 220-1]. The only evidence that Francis Payne ever had any children was the mention of a child in Jane Eltonhead's 1656 confirmation of his freedom. However, the following may have been his descendants:

2   i.   Rebecca, born say 1720.

       ii.   William, born say 1750, a "Mulatto" boy bound to William Hancock, then to Robert Wooding, Gent., who then sold the indenture to Joseph Gill in May 1764. The Halifax County, Virginia court ordered him returned to Wooding [Pleas 4:266, 279].

      iii.   Francis[2], head of a Gloucester County household of 5 "other free" in 1810 [VA:666]. He and his unnamed wife were "Mulattoes" living in Gloucester County in 1813. He was over the age of forty-five in 1815 [PPTL 1800-20].

      iv.   Evan, born say 1757, a "mulatto" listed among fourteen deserters from Lieutenant John Tankersley's troops. Tankersley offered a reward for their delivery to King George courthouse in the 3 October 1777 issue of the *Virginia Gazette* [Purdie edition, p. 3, col. 1].

      v.   Benjamin, born say 1760, a "yellow" complexioned soldier from Buckingham County listed in the size roll of troops who enlisted at Chesterham Courthouse [The Chesterfield Supplement cited by NSDAR, *African American Patriots*, 152]. He enlisted in Goochland County [Jackson, *Virginia Negro Soldiers*, 41].

      vi.   Joshua, born say 1760, a man of color born in Westmoreland County who was living in King George County when he was listed in a register of soldiers who served in the Revolution [NSDAR, *African American*

Patriots, 152]. He was head of a Rockingham County, North Carolina household of 5 "other free" in 1800 [NC:491].

vii. Sarah, head of a Accomack Parish, Accomack County household of 2 "other free" and 3 slaves in 1800 [*Virginia Genealogist* 2:13].

viii. Thomas, head of a Prince William County household of 6 "other free" in 1810 [VA:510].

ix. Joanna, "Free Negroe" head of a Fauquier County household of 2 "other free" in 1810 [VA:375].

x. Molly, head of a Queen Ann's County, Maryland household of one "other free" in 1790.

xi. Ben, a "Mulatto" head of a 96 District, Abbeville County, South Carolina household of one "other free" in 1790 [SC:57].

2. Rebecca Paine, born say 1720, was living in Westmoreland County, Virginia, on 1 April 1741 when the court presented Francis **Chandler** for cohabiting with her. He was the husband of Margaret **Chandler**, a "Mulatto" woman. Rebecca was called a "Molatto" on 12 May 1746 when she agreed to serve William Bayley for four years to pay a ten pound debt she owed him [Orders 1739-43, 100; 1743-7, 137]. She may have been the mother of

3   i. Virgin, born say 1745.
4   ii. Lawrence, born 4 October 1748.

3. Virgin Payne, born say 1745, was the mother of Rice and John Payne whose births were recorded in St. Paul's Parish, King George County (no race indicated) [St. Paul's Parish Register]. She was the mother of

i. ?Charles, born about 1766, registered in King George County on 10 November 1801: *a dark mulatto man aged about thirty five years, about five feet six inches high, rather spare...born in this County of free parents* [Register of Free Persons, no.36].

ii. Rice, born 28 August 1766, registered in King George County on 25 November 1800: *a dark mulatto man, aged about thirty two years, five feet seven inches high...Slender make...born in this County of a free Woman* [Register of Free Persons, no.18]. He was head of a Prince William County household of 4 "other free" in 1810 [VA:515].

iii. Jack, born 13 October 1772, registered in King George County on 5 February 1804: *a dark mulatto man, aged about twenty eight years, short and curled hair, five feet ten Inches high, well set, though not corpulaent, born of a free mother of this County* [Register of Free Persons, no.38].

iv. ?Polly, born about 1793, registered in King George County on 3 September 1818: *a Black woman about 25 years of age, about 5 feet, stout made, born free* [Register of Free Persons, no.52].

4. Lawrence Payne, born 4 October 1748, registered in King George County in November 1794: *a mulatto man born October the 4th 1748 about five feet nine inches high, was bound by indenture to Langhern Dade to serve the term of thirty one years.* His wife Susannah, born about 1742, registered the same month: *the wife of Laurence above, is about fifty two years old, about four feet six inches high, of a dark yellow colour, served to the age of thirty one years & is now free* [Register of Free Persons 1785-1799, no.1, 5]. He was taxable in King George County from 1782 to 1814 [PPTL 1782-1830, frames 10, 54, 118, 138, 204, 306, 342, 354] and head of a Rockingham County household of 4 "other free" in 1810 [VA:36]. Lawrence and Susannah may have been the parents of

i. Alice, born about 1768, registered in November 1794: *a mulatto woman, twenty six years old, about four feet six inches high, was bound by indenture to Townshend Dade, Gent., of this County to serve till eighteen years old & is now a free woman* [Register, no.3].

    ii.   Elizabeth, born about 1770, registered in November 1794: *a mulatto woman, twenty four years old & about five feet high, was bound to William Lord & his wife of this County to serve till the age of eighteen years, & is now a free woman* [Register, no.2].

    iii. Lett, born about 1773, registered in November 1794: *of a dark yellow colour, twenty one years old 7 about five feet high, was born free & of course is a free woman* [Register, no.4].

    iv. Lawrence, Jr., a "Mulatto" taxable in King George County from 1806 to 1815 [PPTL, 1782-1830, frames 265, 354, 375], head of a King George County household of 1 "other free" in 1810 [VA:212].

PEACOCK/ POE FAMILY

1.   Mary Peacock, born say 1693, was a white servant with three years and three months to serve when she was listed in the 20 July 1712 inventory of the Richmond County, Virginia estate of Colonel Samuel Peachey [Wills & Inventories 1709-17, 170-2]. She was called the servant of Samuel Peachey on 5 August 1713 when the Richmond County court ordered her to serve him or his assigns an additional year for having an illegitimate "Mulatto" child. The court also ordered that upon completion of her service, she pay ten pounds to the churchwardens of North Farnham Parish or be sold by them for five years [Orders 1711-6, 123]. She may have been the ancestor of

2   i.   Jane, born say 1710.

    ii. William Peacock, head of a Kent County, Maryland household of 5 "other free" in 1800 [MD:164, 165].

2.   Jane Peacock/ Poe, born say 1710, was a "Molatto" presented by the York County court for not listing herself as a tithable on 20 November 1727 (called Jane Peacock) and on 17 November 1735 (called Jane Poe). She was called "Jane Po alias Peacock" on 20 August 1744 when Landon Carter, Esq., sued her in York County for a cow and a calf of the value of 40 shillings. The court ruled that they were her property and dismissed the suit [OW 16:489; W&I 18:237, 245; 19:302, 317]. She was the ancestor of

    i.   William Poe, head of a York County household of 4 "other free" in 1810.

PENDARVIS FAMILY

1.   Joseph[1] Pendarvis, born say 1675, was a white planter of Colleton County, South Carolina, who wrote a will on 11 February 1735, proved 17 March the same year, leaving 1,009 acres near Green Savanna and a plantation on Charleston Neck to the "children of a Negro woman named Parthena deceased that lived with me." Their children, underage when Pendarvis wrote his will, were James, Brand, William, John, Thomas, Mary, and Elizabeth [Moore, *Wills of the State of S.C. 1670-1740*, I:300]. Their daughters Mary and Elizabeth married white planters, and their descendants were considered white [Koger, *Black Slaveowners*, 13]. Joseph and Parthena were the parents of

2   i.   James, born say 1718.

    ii. Brand, born say 1720, married Ursetta Jennings in Orangeburgh in 1748.

    iii. William[1], head of a South Orangeburgh District, South Carolina household of 5 "other free" and a slave in 1790 [SC:102].

    iv. John, head of a South Orangeburgh District, South Carolina household of 4 "other free" and a slave in 1790 [SC:102].

    v.   Thomas.

    vi. Mary.

    vii. Elizabeth.

2. James Pendarvis, born say 1718, married Catherina Rumph (a white woman) on 3 September 1741 in Orangeburgh. He was taxable on 3,250 acres and 113 slaves in St. Paul's Parish, Charleston District, Colleton County, from 1785 to 1787 and taxable on 4,710 acres and 123 slaves in 1792. He died about 1797 when his estate was taxed on 4,709 acres and 151 slaves [South Carolina Tax Returns, microfilm AD 941, frames 100, 179; AD 942, frames 19, 67, 82, 146, 218, 231, 288]. He was the father of
   i. William², a minor whose estate was taxable on 39 slaves in St. Paul's Parish in 1785 and 59 slaves in 1799.

Other members of the family were
   i. Joseph², taxable in Winton County on 100 acres and 44 slaves in 1788 [South Carolina Tax Returns, microfilm AD 942, frame 33] and head of a household of 6 "other free" and 41 slaves in 1790 in the south part of Orangeburgh District [SC:102].
   ii. Joseph³, Jr., head of a Colleton District household of 5 "other free" in 1810 [SC:618].

PENDERGRASS FAMILY

1. Richard¹ Pendergrass, born say 1755, was called "Negro Richd Pendegrass" on 17 March 1781 when he was listed as one of General Cornwallis' prisoners at his Guilford Courthouse headquarters [*NCGSJ* V:81]. He was taxable in St. Lawrence District of Caswell County in 1790 [NC:83]. He died before 25 December 1817, leaving a Caswell County nuncupative will which made bequests to his daughters Sally **Roe** of Person County and Nancy **Curtis** of Caswell County and stated that he had already provided for his other children [WB H:132]. He was the father of
   i. ?Richard², married Elizabeth **Curtis**, 6 December 1798 Person County bond, Richard **Pendergrass** (Sr.?) bondsman. He was head of a Person County household of 3 "other free" in 1800 (called Richard, Jr.) [NC:601]. He married, second, Mary **Roberts**, 26 November 1800 Person County bond, Julius Justice bondsman.
   ii. Nancy ("colored"), married James **Curtis**, 19 February 1800 Person County bond with Byrd Rogers bondsman.
   iii. Sarah, married John **Roe**, 2 March 1802 Person County bond.

PERKINS FAMILY

1. Esther¹ Perkins, born say 1710, was in Accomack County on 8 December 1730 when Thomas Blair, Gentleman (her master?), paid her fine for having a bastard child [Orders 1724-31, 201, 115a].[163] Esther died before 1 June 1748 when her son Jacob was bound apprentice in Accomack County: "Mulatto Boy Son of Esther Perkins, deced" [Orders 1744-53, 273]. Esther's children were
2   i. ?Ann, born say 1726.
3   ii. ?Darky, born about 1728.
4   iii. ?Joshua¹, born about 1732.
5   iv. ?George¹, born say 1735.

[163]Esther Perkins may been the sister of Isaac and Joshua Perkins who owned land in Craven County, North Carolina, in 1738 and 1750 respectively [Craven DB 1:406; 7:88, 90, 98 100; Haun, *Craven County Court Minutes*, IV:93, 113]. Isaac recorded a memorial for 100 acres on Reedy Creek in Craven County, South Carolina, on 9 May 1761 based on a plat of 10 May 1756 [S.C. Archives Memorials 14:82; Colonial Plats 6:162]. He was probably the Isaac Perkins who was head of a Cheraw District, South Carolina household of one white male over 16, two under 16, one white female, and 2 "other free" in 1790 [SC:46].

    v. Jacob[1], born December 1745, a "Mulatto Boy Son of Esther Perkins, deced," aged two years last Christmas, bound as an apprentice shoemaker to George Bundick, Jr., on 1 June 1748 and then bound instead to James Gibson [Orders 1744-53, 273, 280].

    vi. ?Arcadia, born about 1746, a six-year-old "Mulatto" bound to George Hoyetil on 29 January 1752 [Orders 1744-53, 570].

2. Ann Perkins, born say 1726, was granted a patent for land in Bladen County, North Carolina, on 25 April 1767. She sold 50 acres on a branch of Raft Swamp on 12 December 1768 and sold another 100 acres on Beaver Dam Branch of Raft Swamp to William **Lowry**, son of James **Lowry**, on 18 February 1775 [DB 23:71, 481]. She was taxable in Bladen County on two "Mulatoes" in 1771: her son Jordan Perkins and Thomas **Sweat** [Byrd, *Bladen County Tax Lists*, I:60]. She was the mother of

    i. Jordan[1], born say 1758.

    ii. ?Olive, born say 1762, married Ephraim **Sweat** according to the 18 April 1811 Opelousas, Louisiana marriage bond of their son Gideon **Sweat** [Opelousas license no.6].

    iii. ?Nancy, born before 1776, head of a St. Landry Parish household of 6 "free colored" in 1820 [LA:108].

3. Darky (Dorcas) Perkins (Esther[1]), born about 1728, was six years old in September 1734 when she was bound apprentice to James Gibson in Accomack County court [Orders 1731-36, 133]. Dorcas or another daughter of Esther may have been the mother of the members of the Perkins family who remained in Accomack County.[164] They were

    i. Jemmy (James), born about 1748, a four-year-old "Mulatto" bound as an apprentice shoemaker to George Hoyetil in Accomack County in 1752 [Orders 1744-53, 571].

    ii. Joshua[2], born about 1752, a member of Captain Windsor Brown's Virginia Company of troops when Brown advertised in the 6 June 1777 issue of the *Virginia Gazette* that he had deserted. Brown described him as: *a mulatto, about 5 feet 6 or 7 inches high, 24 or 25 years old, and is a straight made fellow; had on a short striped jacket, a felt hat bound round with French lace* [*Virginia Gazette*, Purdie edition, p. 3, col. 3]. His only heir Sally Perkins applied for his pension in Accomack County on 29 March 1834 for Revolutionary War service as a seaman [Orders 1832-36, 21, 313].

    iii. Nimrod, born say 1755, bound an apprentice shoemaker to William Sacker James in Accomack County on 28 August 1765 [Orders 1764-65, 489]. He was taxable in Accomack County in 1785 and 1790 [PPTL, 1782-1814, frames 154, 347], a "Mulatto" taxable in Northampton County in 1787 and 1788 [PPTL, 1782-1823, frames 74, 81], and head of an Accomack County household of 2 "other free" and a white woman in 1800 [*Virginia Genealogist* 2:13]. He was about seventy-two years old on 31 July 1832 when he testified in Accomack County court that he enlisted as a drummer on board the galley *Diligence* from 1777 until 1781 and that he had received a Virginia Military Land Warrant for 100 acres [Orders 1828-32, 537].

6   iv. Cady, born say 1758.

    v. Abraham, born say 1760, a "free Negro" taxable in Accomack County from 1798 to 1812 [PPTL, 1782-1814, frames 363, 499, 698, 732,

---

[164]Dorcas Perkins apparently had at least one child. The 27 January 1746 session of the Accomack County Court recorded that the charges against her by the churchwardens were abated due to her death which would have been about the same year as her mother died [Orders 1744-53, 181]. Perhaps the court confused Dorcas with Esther Perkins.

796], head of St. George's Parish, Accomack County household of 7 "other free" in 1800 [*Virginia Genealogist* 2:159] and 8 in 1810 [VA:48].

7   vi.   Adam, born say 1765.

     vii.   Esther², born about 1773, ordered bound out by the churchwardens of Accomack Parish in Accomack County to Leah James on 30 May 1775 [Orders 1774-7, 352], head of an St. George's Parish, Accomack County household of 3 "other free" in 1800 [*Virginia Genealogist* 2:159]. She registered in Accomack County about 1832: *born about 1773, yellow complexion, 5'5-3/4" high, born free in Accomack County* [Register of Free Negroes, 1785-1863, no. 593].

     viii.   Oliver, a "free Mulatto" ordered bound out by the churchwardens of Accomack Parish to Shadrack Bayly on 30 May 1775 [Orders 1774-7, 354].

     ix.   Comfort, head of a St. George's Parish, Accomack County household of 5 "other free" in 1800 [*Virginia Genealogist* 2:160].

4.   Joshua¹ Perkins (Esther¹), born about 1732, was two years old (no parent or race indicated) on September 1734 when he was bound to James Gibson in Accomack County court [Orders 1731-36, 133]. He was probably one of the mixed-race sons of Esther Perkins since her son Jacob was also bound to James Gibson. Joshua owned land in Bladen County, North Carolina, on the province line adjoining land entered by Benjamin Davis before 20 October 1761 [Philbeck, *Bladen County Land Entries,* no. 1210 (called Joshua Parkins)]. He purchased 125 acres in Bladen County on Wilkerson Swamp, a branch of the Little Pee Dee River, on 1 November 1768 and sold this land on 26 April 1770. This was part of a tract of 250 acres, the other half owned by Robert **Sweat** in 1754 and sold by Philip **Chavis** in 1768. And he was granted 100 acres on Wilkerson Swamp on 22 Dec 1769 [Bladen DB 23:80, 121, 104-5, 424-5, 147-8]. These lands are on the present-day border of Robeson County near the county line of Dillon and Marlboro Counties, South Carolina. He was a "Mulato" taxable in Bladen County with his wife and sons George and Isaac in 1768 and 1769 [Byrd, *Bladen County Tax Lists,* I:7, 17]. He was taxable in Washington County, Tennessee, in 1787 (called Joshua Perkins, Sr.) but not in 1788, perhaps because he was over age [Creekmore, "Early East Tennessee Taxpayers," *East Tennessee Historical Society's Publications,* (1963):108; *Tennessee Ancestors,* 5:37].

Joshua and his children's race and color were described in detail in an 1858 Johnson County, Tennessee trial in which his great-grandson, Jacob F. Perkins, sued John R. White for slander because he called him a "free Negro." The race of Joshua's great-grandchildren was not self evident since Joshua and his descendants had married white or light-skinned women. Eighteen elderly deponents, many who had known the family when they lived near the Pee Dee River in South Carolina (where Joshua had apparently moved after selling his Bladen County land), deposed that they had known Joshua/ Jock and his children: George, Jacob, Joshua, Isaac, Lewis, and Polly. He kept race horses and a ferry by Roan's Creek and associated with "decent, respectable" white people like Landon Carter.¹⁶⁵ He married Mary/ Polly Black in 1753. She was fair skinned, called a Scotch woman. He moved back to North Carolina in 1785 (Washington County?) and died on 10 April 1801 [The Perkins File in the T.A.R. Nelson Papers in the Calvin M. McClung Collection at the East Tennessee Historical Center, depositions of Anna Graves and John J. Wilson].

---

¹⁶⁵Landon Carter was taxable on 3,716 acres in Washington County, Tennessee, in 1795 [McCown, *Washington County, Tennessee Records, Vol. I,* Privately Printed, Tennessee (1964):135].

The Johnson County court decided that Jacob F. Perkins was indeed a "free Negro" [Johnson County, Tennessee, Circuit court Minutes 1855-58, July 17, 1858, 427], but it considered depositions from fifty-nine persons before making this decision. The depositions provide the physical descriptions of many members of the family as well as a description of their life in the white community. Sixteen of twenty-two elderly deponents who had actually seen old Joshua Perkins said he was of African descent:

> *Can't say whether...full blooded. The nose African. Believe they were Africans...always claimed to be Portuguese. All married white women* [The Perkins File, deposition of John E. Cossen].

> *as black as any common mulatto. Hair short and curled and kinky...*[The Perkins File, deposition of Larkin L. White].

> *He was a very black and reverend negro...*[The Perkins File, deposition of Reuben Brooks].

> *black man, hair nappy...Some called Jacob (his son) a Portuguese and some a negro...I helped Jock shell corn. He was said to be a hatter* [The Perkins File, deposition of John Nave, 88 years old].

> *Knew old Jock (Joshua) in North Carolina on Peedee...right black or nearly so. Hair kinky...like a common negro* [The Perkins File, deposition of Abner Duncan, 86 years old].

However, six persons who had seen old Joshua Perkins said he was dark-skinned but not African. They seem to have argued in their depositions that the Perkins family must have been something other than African - Portuguese or Indian - since they were relatively affluent and had good relations with their white neighbors:

> *dark skinned man...resembled an Indian more than a negro. He was generally called a Portuguese. Living well...Kept company with everybody. Kept race horses and John Watson rode them* [Ibid., deposition of Thomas Cook, 75 years old].

> *mixed blooded and not white. His wife fair skinned...They had the same privileges* [Ibid., deposition of Catherine Roller, 80 years old].

> *Hair bushy & long - not kinky. Associated with white people...Associated with...the most respectable persons. Some would call them negroes and some Portuguese* [Ibid., deposition of John J. Wilson, about 70 years old].

> *He was known of the Portuguese race...Four of his sons served in the Revolution...Jacob and George drafted against Indians...they came from and kept a ferry in South Carolina* [Ibid., deposition of Anna Graves, 77 years old].

> *They kept company with decent white people and had many visitors* [Ibid., deposition of Elizabeth Cook, about 71].

> *I taught school at Perkins school house...they were Portuguese...associated white peoples, clerked at elections and voted and had all privileges* [Ibid., deposition of David R. Kinnick, aged 77].

Some who testified in favor of the Perkins family had never seen Joshua
Perkins and seem to have been genuinely confused about the family's ancestry:

> *I was well acquainted with Jacob Perkins* (one of Joshua's sons). *A
> yellow man - said to be Portuguese. They do not look like negroes.
> I have been about his house a great deal and nursed for his wife.
> She was a little yellow and called the same race. Had blue eyes and
> black hair. Was visited by white folks* [Ibid., deposition of Mary
> Wilson].

One of the deponents, seventy-seven-year-old Daniel Stout, explained very
simply how people of African descent could have been treated well by their
white neighbors:

> *Never heard him called a negro. People in those days said nothing
> about such things* [Ibid., deposition of Daniel Stout].

According to the depositions, Joshua and Polly's children were

8   i.   George², born 22 March 1754 in Liberty County, South Carolina.
9   ii. Jacob², born say 1756.
10   iii. Isaac³, born say 1758.
11   iv. Joshua³, born in November 1759.
       v.   Lewis¹, born say 1762, perhaps the Lewis Perkins who was taxable in
Carter County, Tennessee in 1805 [1805 Carter County Tax List]. He
was said to be a dark-skinned man with red complexion [The Perkins
File, deposition of John J. Wilson]. A sixty-five-year-old woman
deposed in 1858 that she had known Lewis, and that Lewis [had] *kinky
hair* [Ibid., deposition of Sarah Oaks], and a sixty-nine-year-old man
deposed that *Lewis* [was] *dark and bushy headed* [Ibid., deposition of
Goulder Hicks].
     vi. Polly, perhaps identical to Mary Perkins, born before 1776, head of a
St. Landry Parish, Louisiana household of 2 "free colored" in 1820
[LA:105], mother of Eady Perkins according to the 10 October 1825
Opelousas license for her daughter's marriage to James F. **Carr**
[Opelousas license no.42]. She was called Polly Perkins when her
daughter Edith Perkins married Stephen **Goin** of South Carolina on 17
November 1826 in Opelousas [License no.78]. James **Carr**, born 1776-
94, was head of a St. Landry Parish household of 2 "free colored" in
1820 [LA:101].

5.   George¹ Perkins (Esther¹), born say 1735, was a "Mulatto" servant charged in
Accomack County court with absenting himself from the service of Andrew
Gilchrist, administrator of James Gibson, on 28 August 1751 [Orders 1744-53,
522, 554]. He may have been the George Perkis who was in the Berkeley
County, South Carolina Detachment of Captain Benjamin Elliot, drafted
November 1759 and discharged January 8, 1760, in the same list with "Carter,
a free Negro," Gideon **Bunch**, Ephraim **Bunch**, James **Bunch**, and Jacob
Bunch [Clark, *Colonial Soldiers of the South*, 939]. He was living in Craven
County, North Carolina, when he was acquitted of an unspecified crime by the
October 1761 Craven County court. He was ordered to pay a little over 12
pounds damages to Edmond Morgan on 13 June 1769 [Minutes 1761-62, 45a;
1766-75, 115b]. He was called a husbandman on 27 February 1771 when he
purchased 200 acres in Craven County on the west side of Cahoogue Creek for
sixty barrels of tar. He sold half of this land on 3 October 1774 and was called
a "free Negro" when he sold the remainder by deed proved in September 1785
Craven County court [DB 19:202; 26:124-5, 130]. He was a taxable head of
his own "Black" Craven County household in 1769 [SS 837] and head of a
Craven County household of 4 "other free" in 1790 [NC:131]. He was

bondsman for the 3 February 1786 Craven County marriage of Sarah Perkins to Isaac **Carter**. He may have been the father of

  i.   Isaac[2], born about 1756, head of a Craven County household of 2 "other free" in 1790 [NC:131] and 2 "free colored" in Craven County in 1820 [NC:67]. He married Deborah **Godett**, 24 March 1784 Craven County bond. She was named in the 1803 Craven County will of her father George **Godett** [CR 28.801.20]. Isaac entered land on the south side of the Neuse River and west side of Macock's Branch on 9 December 1813 [Grants 4:177]. He was living with his wife Deborah, born 1763, when he made a declaration in Craven County court to obtain a Revolutionary War pension on 13 May 1829. He testified that he enlisted for three years in May 1778 and was granted pension certificate no. 4666 on 30 November 1818. He still had 100 acres of land in his possession, and included with his pension application was a copy of his deed of 30 January 1827 by which he sold 150 acres on the south side of the Neuse River and head of Handcocks Creek near the head of Macocks Branch to Isaac **Carter**. Joseph Physioc testified that: *from a long and intimate acquaintance with the General Conduct and Character of the Said Isaac Perkins, we do not hesitate to declare that (though a man of Colour) we do believe him to be too honest in principal to practice anything like a fraud.* His lawyer, Samuel Gerock, called him a "Negroe Man, and Old Soldier of the Revolutionary Army" when he appealed for the restoration of his pension [National Archives Inv. File 41.953]. His will, proved in Craven County in August 1830, mentioned his wife Deborah and sister Sarah **Carter** and her children [WB C:326].

  ii. Sarah, married Isaac **Carter**.

6. Cady Perkins (Dorcas[1], Esther[1]), born say 1758, was the mother of George Perkins who was ordered bound by the overseers of the poor to Sarah Bradford by the Accomack County court to be a farmer on 31 January 1792. She may also have been the mother of Stephen and Lott Perkins who were ordered bound to Caleb Harrison to be farmers on 1 March 1792. On 27 March Sarah Bradford brought a case against John Mears, George's former master, for detaining George in his service. After a hearing, the court ordered the overseers of the poor to bind George to Elizabeth Bradford [Orders 1790-6, 305, 324, 326, 343]. Cady was the mother of

  i.   George[3], Sr., registered in Accomack County about 1832: *born about 1780, a dark yellow, 5'8-3/4", born free in Accomack County* [Register of Free Negroes, 1785-1863, no. 602].

  ii. ?Stephen[1], registered in Accomack County on 29 September 1807: *born 1 February 1780, a Dark Mulatto colour or Brown, 5 feet 5 Inches, Dark hair, Dark Eyes* [Register of Free Negroes, 1785-1863, no.12].

  iii. ?Lot, born 22 April 1785, registered in Accomack County on 29 September 1807: *a light Black Dark Mulatto, 5 feet 6-1/2 Inches...Born Free* [Register of Free Negroes, 1785-1863, no.8].

7. Adam Perkins, born say 1765, was taxable in Norfolk County from 1791 to 1812: called a "N"(egro) in 1797; a labourer on Western Branch in a "List of Free Negroes and Mulattoes" in 1801, head of a household with males Nathan and Wright Perkins and females Annas, Betsey and Lucretia Perkins; called a "M"(ulatto) in 1802; taxable on a slave aged 12-16 in 1803 [PPTL, 1791-1812, frames 29, 88, 145, 231, 304, 384, 434, 468, 487, 582, 695, 747]. He was head of a Norfolk County household of 6 "other free" in 1810 [VA:820]. He purchased 5 acres in Norfolk County at the head of the Western Branch of the Elizabeth River for 7 pounds, 10 shillings on 4 September 1790 and purchased another 7 acres adjoining Thomas **Archer** and John **Weaver** for 14 pounds on 1 November 1797 [DB 32:87; 37:143]. Annias was a "B." (Black)

taxable on 2 horses in Western Branch in Norfolk County from 1815 to 1817 [PPTL, 1813-24, frames 110, 148, 265]. Adam and Annias may have been the parents of

  i. Betsey, born say 1792, married William **Bass**, 2 November 1812 Norfolk County bond, Adam Perkins surety.
  ii. Nathan, born say 1794, a "B.M." (Black Male) taxable in Western Branch in Norfolk County from 1815 to 1817 [PPTL, 1813-24, frames 110, 266].
  iii. Wright.
  iv. Lucretia.

8. George[2] Perkins (Joshua[1], Esther[1]), was born on 22 March 1754 in Liberty County (present-day Marion County), South Carolina, according to his pension application [National Archives Pension File RF-8113]. He applied for a pension while living in Lawrence County, Kentucky, on 15 March 1834. He was living in South Carolina when he entered the service in Charleston. He served four tours of ten days each in the militia under Lieutenant Richard Whittington in 1780. He lived for about twenty-six years (1787-1813) on the Watauga River in the part of North Carolina which later became Washington County, Tennessee, and lived in Lawrence County, Kentucky, for another twenty-one years (1813-34). A copy of his 5 April 1780 Bladen County marriage bond to Keziah **Manning**, with John Cade (one of the captains he served under) as bondsman, was included in Keziah's application for a widow's pension [RF-8113]. He was taxable in Washington County in 1788 and received a grant for 100 acres in Washington County on Little Doe Creek near Roans Creek from the State of North Carolina on 17 November 1790 and another 100 acres on the Watauga River on 16 October 1797 [Creekmore, *Tennessee Ancestors,* 5:37; Carter County, Tennessee DB A:141, 149 (This part of Washington County became Carter County, Tennessee)]. He purchased 200 acres in Washington County, Tennessee, on Little Doe Creek of the Watauga River on 24 May 1793 [Washington County DB 2:273-275]. He sold 200 acres of this land on 21 October 1795, another 100 acres on 28 December 1797 [Carter County DB A:104, 136], sold 100 acres on the Watauga River on 10 February 1804, 100 acres on Roans Creek on 26 November 1804, 50 acres on Little Doe Creek on 26 August 1805, and another 50 acres in this area on 10 April 1807 [Carter DB A:468-9, 532-3; B:16, 108-9]. George died in Lee County, Iowa, on 16 November 1840 and Keziah died on 12 August 1849 according to their only surviving child Ann **Graves** [National Archives Pension File RF-8113]. Their children were

  i. Stephen[2], born 6 September 1783, purchased 190 acres on Doe River on 12 September 1806 and sold this land on 10 August the same year [Carter County DB A:111-3]. He married Catherine Summa and had eleven children.
  ii. Anna **Graves**, born about 1780 since she was seventy-seven years old in 1858 when she made a deposition in Missouri for the Johnson County, Tennessee trial of Jacob F. Perkins [The Perkins File, deposition of Anna Graves].

9. Jacob[2] Perkins (Joshua[1], Esther[1]), born say 1756, was taxable on 200 acres in Washington County, Tennessee, in 1787, 1788, and 1789 [*East Tennessee Historical Society's Publications,* (1963):108; *Tennessee Ancestors,* vol. 5, No.1 (April 1989):37, 82]. He purchased 200 acres on Little Doe Creek of the Watauga River in Washington County, Tennessee, on 11 May 1791 [DB 2:272-3]. He was a school teacher who married Nancy **Graves**, daughter of John **Graves**, a constable, and his wife Susan, a white woman [The Perkins File, deposition of James Bradley]. Johnson Hampton testified for the pension application of his son Jacob[3] Perkins that Jacob[2] Perkins came to Carter County, Tennessee, about 1802 and that Jacob[2] told him he had lived in South

Carolina near the Little Pee Dee River during the time of the Revolution. Jacob served in the Revolution under General Marion and: *was [a] respectfully up right honest man and was considered by his neighbors.* John J. Wilson, who helped to bury him, testified that [Jacob]: *and wife were both members of the Babstez Church he was a respectable man and a good citizen and was regarded by his neighbors.* His son Jacob[3] Perkins testified that Jacob[2] Perkins also served several tours against the Indians after coming to Carter County (then Washington County, North Carolina). And he was married to Ann **Graves** by Jonathan Mulkey, a Washington County preacher while the county was still a territory of North Carolina (1790-96). He further testified that his father died on 4 April 1819, and his mother lived with him until her death on 8 November 1842 [National Archives Pension File R-8105]. James Bradley deposed that he knew Jacob's children: Joseph, Sally, Esther, Joshua, Amos, John, Susan, and Keziah [The Perkins File]. In his 22 March 1819 Carter County, Tennessee will, he mentioned his wife Nancy and their children: Joseph, Joshua, Amos, Jacob, John, Sarah, Esther, Keziah, Lydia, and Susanna, and he asked that land he owned in Burke County, North Carolina, be sold and divided between William and Benjamin (no last name mentioned), the two children of his daughter Sarah [WB 1:387-8]. His children were

   i.   Joseph. He and his brothers, Joshua, Amos, Jacob, and John Perkins entered land on Cranberry Creek in 1827 [Burke, *The History of the North Carolina Country, 1777-1920*, 212]. They were the original owners of the Cranberry Iron Forge in Watauga County [Arthur, *History of Watauga County*, 264].

   ii.   Sarah, mother of William and Benjamin **Graves**.

   iii.   Esther[3].

   iv.   Joshua[5], born in 1796, married Elizabeth Kite. They were the parents of Jacob F. Perkins, plaintiff in the 1858 Johnson County suit [The Perkins File, Plaintiff's Attorney's Notes/ Outlines of Argument]. Jacob F. Perkins was a school teacher. He clerked at elections, voted, and associated with whites.

   v.   Amos.

   vi.   Jacob[3], born about 1799, since he was about fifty-three years old on 16 October 1852 when he testified for a survivor's pension [National Archives File R-8105]. He was a school teacher [The Perkins File, deposition of Dr. John E. Cossen].

   vii.   John.

   viii.   Susan.

   ix.   Keziah.

   x.   Lydia.

10. Isaac[3] Perkins (Joshua[1], Esther[1]), born say 1758, received a grant for 100 acres in Washington County on Campbell's Creek from the State of North Carolina on 17 November 1790 and was living in Granville County (Greenville?), South Carolina, on 19 January 1796 when he sold this land to Jacob Perkins [Carter County DB A:110, 147]. He purchased 100 acres in Greenville District, South Carolina, in 1796 and sold 200 acres there in 1797. He purchased 100 acres in Greenville District on 8 September 1796. On 29 March 1798 he sold by two deeds (signing) a total of 500 acres of land in Greenville County on the waters of "Guilden Creek of Enoree Reiver" which was land he had been granted on 1 December 1794 [DB D:320, 509, 511]. He was head of a Buncombe County, North Carolina household of 12 "other free" in 1800 [NC:183], 11 "other free" in Opelousas, Louisiana in 1810 (living near Gilbert **Sweat**) [LA:325], and one "free colored" over forty-five years of age in 1820 [LA:108]. He married Hannah **Sweat** according to the 16 January 1819 Opelousas Courthouse marriage license of their son Stephen Perkins of South Carolina [Opelousas license no.3]. Isaac and Hannah's children were

    i.   George[4], born say 1785, married Polly **Ashworth**, daughter of James **Ashworth** and Keziah **Dial** of South Carolina, 4 December 1810. George was head of a St. Landry Parish household of 5 "free colored" in 1820 and 10 in 1830 [LA:107, 27].

    ii.   Isaac[4], born say 1787, married Sarah **Singleton**, 24 May 1810 St. Landry Parish bond; and second, Mary **Sweat**, 23 September 1811 Opelousas marriage [Opelousas marriage license no.3]. He was head of a St. Landry Parish household of 3 "free colored" in 1820 [Census p.108].

    iii.   Stephen[3], born say 1790 (in Craven County, South Carolina), son of Isaac Perkins and Hannah Sweat, married Nancy **Johnson**, daughter of Isaac **Johnson** and Mary **Willis**, on 16 January 1819 in Opelousas [Opelousas marriage license no.3].[166]

    iv.   ?Lewis[2], born say 1792, head of a St. Landry Parish household of 4 "free colored" in 1820 [LA:107].

11. Joshua[4] Perkins (Joshua[1], Esther[1]), born in November 1759 in present-day Marion County, South Carolina, was taxable on one poll in Washington County, North Carolina, in 1788 (called Joshua Perkins, Jr.) in the same list as George Perkins and Gilbert **Sweat**, and he was taxable on 100 acres in 1791 [Creekmore, *Tennessee Ancestors*, 5:37, 72, 81]. He was head of a Buncombe County, North Carolina household of 7 "other free" in 1800 [NC:183]. He married Mary Mixon according to the 2 October 1810 Opelousas Marriage of his daughter Sarah Perkins [Opelousas Parish Courthouse, marriage license no.14].[167] He was head of an Opelousas, St. Landry Parish, Louisiana household of 6 "other free" in 1810, one "free colored" over forty-five years of age in 1820, and one over fifty-five years of age in 1830 [LA:26]. On 25 May 1830 he was called a "f.m.c." (free man of color) when he made a deposition for Gilbert **Sweat**, "f.m.c.," in a case held in St. Landry Parish in which he testified that he would be seventy-one years old in November 1830, was born on the Little Peedee River in what was then called Marion County, South Carolina, in the same area as Gilbert **Sweat**. About the year 1777 he helped **Sweat** run off with Frances Smith, wife of John Barney Taylor. They travelled the same route from South Carolina: to North Carolina to Tennessee to Big Black River, Mississippi, and finally to Louisiana about 1804. However, they sometimes did not see each other for several years at a time [Parish of St. Landry, case no.1533]. On 15 June 1837 when he was about seventy-eight years old, his three daughters filed suit in the Court of Probate of St. Landry Parish to have a curator appointed to administer his estate because he was blind and supposedly feeble. They were Mary Perkins (wife of James **Ashworth**), Sarah Perkins (wife of Jesse **Ashworth**), and Elizabeth

---

[166]He was probably the same Isaac **Johnston** who was head of a Robeson County household of one "other free" in 1790 [NC:48], perhaps a descendant of the **Johnson** Family of Northampton County, Virginia. Joseph Willis was the slave of Agerton Willis of Bladen County who manumitted him and gave him "considerable property." The manumission was approved by the North Carolina General Assembly in 1787 [Byrd, *In Full Force and Virtue*, 292]. Joseph was a "Molatto" taxable on 320 acres, 1 "white" (free) poll and 2 black (slave) polls in Captain Burn's Bladen County District in 1784, counted as white in 1790, head of a Cheraw District household of 1 male over 16 and 2 females [SC:46], head of a St. Landry Parish household of 13 "other free" and 7 slaves in 1810 [LA:325] and 11 "free colored" and 4 slaves in 1820 [LA:108]. He was buried in Ten Mile Cemetery at Occupy Church in Lower Rapides Parish: Rev. Joseph Willis, 1764-1854, First Baptist preacher of the word in Louisiana west of the Mississippi River [Wise, *Sweat Families of the South*, 100].

[167]Members of the Mixon family were in Craven County, North Carolina, between 1737 and 1756 [Haun, *Craven County Court Minutes*, II:107, IV:362] and were in Cheraw District, South Carolina, in 1790 [SC:46].

Perkins (wife of James **Goings**). He was living with his son Jordan Perkins at the time. The estate was said to contain considerable property, mainly cattle. The case was dismissed on 3 April 1840, apparently due to the death of Joshua. His children were

    i.   Elizabeth, born say 1787, married James **Goings**. He was born before 1776, head of an Opelousas Parish household of 3 "other free" in 1810 [LA:305] and 7 "free colored" in 1820 [LA:101].

    ii.   Jordan, born say 1789, married Jinny **Goen** on 12 March 1814 in Opelousas [Opelousas license no.9]. He was head of a St. Landry Parish household of 6 "free colored" in 1820 [LA:101].

    iii. Sarah, born about 1791, daughter of Joshua Perkins and Mary Mixon, married Jesse **Ashworth**, "of South Carolina," son of James **Ashworth**, Sr., and Keziah **Dial**, on 2 October 1810 [Opelousas license nos.14, 17]. James **Ashworth**, Sr., was head of an Opelousas household of 11 "other free" in 1810 [LA:306]. Sarah **Ashworth** was a fifty-nine-year-old "Mulatto" in the 1850 Calcaisieu Parish, Louisiana census.

    iv. Mary, born about 1796, daughter of Joshua and Mary Perkins, married James **Ashworth**, Jr., son of James and Keziah **Ashworth**, on 23 September 1811 in St. Landry's Parish, Louisiana [Opelousas license no.13].

PETERS FAMILY

1.   Mary Peters, born say 1688, was the "Mullatto Woman Servant" of Edward Couch on 5 July 1708 when she confessed to the Middlesex County court that she had an illegitimate "Mullatto" child. Couch paid her fine of 500 pounds of tobacco [Orders 1705-10, 178, 182]. Her descendants may have been

2   i.   Edward, born say 1720
3   ii.   Catherine, born say 1723.

2.   Edward Peters, born say 1720, was sued for a 5 pound, 10 shillings debt in Sussex County, Virginia, in October 1755 [Orders 1754-56, 252, 288]. He was married before 21 November 1758 when the Surry County, Virginia court issued a presentment:

    Against...Edward Peters, for each and every of them not listing their wife's according to law supposing the said persons to be Mulattoes...[Orders 1757-64, 135].

He may have been the father of

4   i.   Aaron[1], born say 1737.
5   ii.   Armstead, born about 1739.
6   iii. Anthony[1], born say 1741.
7   iv. Lucy[1], born say 1743.
8   v.   Jasper, born say 1744.

3.   Catherine Peters, born say 1723, was a "free negro" who was tried in Williamsburg, Virginia, in October 1744 for murdering a bastard child, born 19 July 1744 [Orders 1744-1822, 1]. In December 1744 the Surry County, Virginia court clerk was paid for attending the trial [Orders 1744-48, 14]. She may have been the mother of

9   i.   Rebecca, born say 1738.
         ii.   Samuel, born say 1740, brother of Rebecca Peters, bound apprentice by the churchwardens of Henrico Parish in August 1754 Henrico County court (no parent or race mentioned) [Orders 1752-55, 218].
10   iii. William, born say 1745.

4. Aaron[1] Peters, born say 1737, was godparent for the christening of Samuel and Sarah Blizzard's daughter Lucy in Albemarle Parish, Sussex and Surry counties, on 16 May 1762 [Richards, *Register of Albemarle Parish*, 214]. He lost a suit brought by Daniel Ellis in Sussex County court in December 1764 for 10 pounds due on a judgment obtained in Surry County court [Orders 1764-66, 168]. He may have been the father of

11 i. Gilliam, born say 1765.
    ii. Aaron[2], born say 1771, head of a Halifax County, North Carolina household of 11 "free colored" in 1820 [NC:161] and 14 in 1830 [NC:322]. On 19 February 1836 there were five suits against him in Halifax County court for debts.
12 iii. Isham, born say 1773.
    iv. Cullen, born say 1775, head of a Halifax County, North Carolina household of 4 "other free" in 1800 [NC:336] and 7 in 1810 [NC:41].

5. Armstead Peters, born about 1739, appeared in Surry County, Virginia court on 15 May 1764 when he and William **Walden** were sued by the administrator of John Peters' estate for the price of articles which they purchased at the sale of the estate in 1762 but had not yet paid for [Orders 1764-74, 25, 33]. He was head of a Surry County household of 15 "whites" (free persons) in 1782 [VA:43]. He was taxable in Cabin Point district of Surry County from 1782 to 1812: taxable on Jesse Peters' tithe in 1782; charged with Drury **Walden's** tithe in 1788; charged with Aaron **Taylor's** tithe in 1791; taxable on a slave named Phil over the age of sixteen in 1793; taxable on slave Harry and 2 others from 1794 to 1804; taxable on James **Taylor's** tithe in 1801 and 1802 [PPTL, 1782-90, frames 350, 379, 458, 479; 603, 1791-1816, 15, 115, 166, 269, 302, 341, 421, 459, 598, 615, 674, 713].[168] He purchased 100 acres in Surry on 26 September 1786, and he and his wife Jenny sold this land two years later on 2 June 1788. He purchased another tract of 100 acres on 28 December 1790 from John **Debereaux** [DB 12:218; 13:236, 295]. He married, second, Elizabeth **Blizzard**, 26 April 1792 Surry County bond. She may have been the Betsy Peters whose son Charles **Pickett**, born about 1788, registered as a "free Negro" in Surry County on 25 March 1807 [Hudgins, *Surry County Register of Free Negroes*, 32]. Armstead was taxed on 100 acres until 1803 when the Surry Tax Alterations recorded the transfer of this land [Land Tax Lists]. He registered as a "free Negro" in 1795: *a mulatto man...aged about 56 years, born free, of a yellowish complexion, about 5'10 or 11" high and pretty stout made* [Back of Guardian Accounts Book 1783-1804, no.1]. He was head of a Surry County household of 5 "other free" in 1810 [VA:614]. Betsy was listed in Surry County in 1813 with 2 free "Negroes & Mulattoes over 16 years old" [PPTL, 1791-1816, frame 752]. His children may have been
    i. Lucy[2], born about 1770, registered as a "free Negro" in Surry County on 16 September 1800: *a mulatto woman of yellowish complexion, aged about 30 years, 5'5" high, born of free Parents, residents of this county* [Back of Guardian Accounts Book 1783-1804, no.63]. She registered in Petersburg on 9 July 1805: *a Mulatto woman of yellowish brown complexion, five feet four and a half inches high, thirty five years old, has holes in her ears, raised in the County of Surry as appears by a certificate of her registry from the Clerk of that County* [Register of Free Negroes 1794-1819, no. 299] and was head of a Petersburg Town household of 5 "other free" and one slave in 1810 [VA:125a].
    ii. Patsy, born say 1773, mother of William **Collins** Peters who registered as a "free Negro" in Surry County on 27 August 1816: *William*

---

[168]Aaron **Taylor** was probably identical to Aaron Peters who was taxable in Cabin Point district of Surry County in 1789 and 1790, the years Aaron **Taylor** was omitted from the list [Personal Property Tax List, 1782-90, frames 557, 603].

Collins, alias William Collins Peters, a mulatto, son of Patsy Peters, and is free born, age ca 25...of bright complexion, long hair and 5'9" tall [Surry County Registry of Free Negroes, p.85, no.205].

6. Anthony[1] Peters, born say 1741, sued William **Wilson** in York County court on 15 March 1765 for a 31 shillings debt due by account. And he and Jasper Peters were found guilty by the same court for trespass, assault and battery against John **Poe** [Judgments & Orders 1763-5, 357, 361]. He may have been the father of

    i. Anthony[2], born say 1763, married Anne **Carter**, 10 June 1786 York County bond, James **Ashby** security. He was taxable in Simon **Gillett**'s York County household in 1784 and 1786 (perhaps identical to Anthony **Jasper**, a 16-21 year-old in Simon's household in 1785), taxable in his own household in 1788, 1789, 1793, 1794, 1798, 1799, 1800, 1803 (taxable on a slave), 1809, 1810, 1811, 1812, and head of a household of 2 "free Negroes & mulattoes over 16" in 1813 [PPTL, 1782-1841, frames 91, 107, 130, 394, 410]. He married, second, Druscilla Daily, 16 January 1790 Henrico County bond, Lewis **Fortune** bondsman. He testified in Henrico County on 20 April 1791 at the trial of Hugh **Shavers (Chavis)** who was accused of stealing from the home of Mary Williamson a bed, blanket and mirror which were later found in the possession of Toby **Jackson** of Richmond City. Anthony testified that at the end of February 1791 **Chavers** came into his shop to have his shoes mended and complained that Toby **Jackson** had purchased a bed and mirror from him but failed to pay the balance. (Toby **Jackson** was emancipated by deed proved on 3 July 1786 by his wife Rebecca **Jackson**, a "Mulatto woman" emancipated by Thomas Johnson by deed proved on 4 November 1782 [Orders 1781-4, 114; 1784-7, 509; 1789-91, 493]). Anthony was head of a York County household of an "other free" man, 7 slaves and a white woman aged 26-45 in 1810 [VA:304].

    ii. Sally, head of a York County household of 4 "other free" in 1810 [VA:880].

7. Lucy[1] Peters, born say 1743, was a resident of Surry County, Virginia, on 9 January 1796 when her son Jesse registered as a "free Negro" [Back of Guardian Accounts Book, 1783-1804, no. 17]. She was the mother of

13   i. Jesse, born about 1764.

8. Jasper Peters, born say 1744, and Anthony Peters were sued in York County court by John **Poe** for trespass, assault and battery on 18 March 1765. They were found guilty and ordered to pay **Poe** 20 shillings. Jasper was sued for debt on 21 May 1770 [Judgments & Orders 1763-5, 357; Orders 1768-70, 471]. He and his wife Molly, "free mulattoes," baptized their daughter Ann Peters in Bruton Parish. Their daughter was

    i. Ann, born 18 March 1768, baptized 5 June 1768 [Bruton Parish Register, 32].

9. Rebecca Peters, born say 1738, and her brother Samuel Peters were ordered bound out by the churchwardens of Henrico Parish, Henrico County, on 5 August 1754 (no parent or race mentioned). She was called a "Free Mulatto" on 3 November 1760 when the court bound out her children Anne and Elisha. Her "Mulatto" children Frank and Milley were bound out by the court on 1 February 1768, and on 7 August 1769 the court ordered her children Frank and Milley bound to Ann Vanderwall and ordered her daughter Rachel bound out [Minutes 1752-55, 218; Orders 1755-62, 479; 1767-69, 207, 491, 510]. She may have been the Rebecca Peters who was head of a Richmond City

household of 4 "other free" and one slave in 1810 [VA:328]. Her children were

    i.   Anne, born say 1757.

    ii. Elisha, born say 1759.

   iii. Frank, born say 1765.

   iv. Milley, born say 1767.

    v. Rachel, born say 1769.

   vi. ?Betty, head of a Hanover County household of 3 "other free" in 1810 [VA:857].

10. William Peters, born say 1745, was surety for the 19 March 1785 Stafford County marriage bond of Hannah Peters and William **Clark**. Hannah's mother was living at Charles Carter's place in Frederick County on 7 December 1817 when her husband William Clark obtained free papers in Culpeper County: *William Clerke, a Mulatto man, 50 or 60, 5'7", served in the Revolutionary War in 1780 and 1781...is a free man, who has a wife and several children, and wishes to visit his mother in law in Frederick Co., at Charles Carter's place*. [Madden, *We Were Always Free*, 195]. He may have been the father of

    i.   Joshua, head of a Rockingham County household of 4 "other free" in 1810 [VA:3]. George **McCoy** was apprenticed to Joshua as a saddler when George registered as a "Free Negro" in Rockingham County on 20 June 1815 [Rockingham County Register of Free Negroes, no.22, p.10]. Perhaps his wife was Sally Peters, a free woman of color who testified in Rockingham County on 12 December 1816 that Coleman and Nicholas **Clerke** were sons of William and Hannah **Clerke** (**Clark**) [Turpin, *Register of Black, Mulatto and Poor Persons*, 21].

    ii. Hannah, born say 1764, married William **Clark**, 19 March 1785 Stafford County bond [Madden, *We Were Always Free*, 195].

   iii. Reuben, born about 1776, a "free Negroe" taxable in Amherst County in 1805, 1806 and 1812, and from 1816 to 1821 [PPTL 1804-23, frames 71, 111, 239, 403, 503, 554, 541, 604]. He was called "free Negro" when he married Susanna **Hartless**, "a free mulatto," in Amherst County on 8 January 1812 [Marriage Register, 229]. He was a "free Negro" taxable on Irish Creek in Rockbridge County in 1813 [Waldrep, *1813 Tax List*]. He registered as a "free Negro" in Amherst County on 17 September 1822: *a free man of Colour aged about 46 years five feet seven inches high* [Register of Free Negroes, no.13]. He purchased 141 acres on Pedlar River in Amherst County from John and Mary **Clark** on 8 April 1823 [DB R:39].

   iv. Molly, head of a Northumberland County household of 3 "other free" in 1810 [VA:991]. She registered as a "free Negro" in Northumberland County on 30 July 1814: *light Mulatto, about 46 years, Born of free parents in Lancaster County* [Register of Free Negroes, no.71].

    v. Thornton, born say 1785, a "blackman" taxable in Amherst County in 1806 [PPTL 1804-23, frame 111].

   vi. Lucy[3], born say 1789, head of a Spotsylvania County household of 4 "other free" in 1810 [VA:111b]. She married William **Jones** ("free persons of color"), 29 September 1810 Fredericksburg bond, James **Ferguson** surety. James **Ferguson** was head of a Spotsylvania County household of 4 "other free" in 1810 [VA:103b].

11. Gilliam Peters, born say 1765, was head of a Northampton County, North Carolina household of a white male and 2 white females in 1790 [NC:72], 5 "other free" in 1800 [NC:471], and 5 in 1810 [NC:741]. His Northampton County estate was administered on 4 March 1816. Purchasers at the sale of the estate, recorded in June 1816, included Mrs. Peters, Tabitha Peters, and Washington Peters. His children were probably

     i.   Tabitha, married William **Coley**, 25 April 1818 Halifax County bond. She may have been the same Tobby **Cooley** who married Henry Peters, 8 November 1826 Halifax County bond.

    ii. Washington, born 1776-94, head of a Northampton County household of 4 "free colored" in 1830.

12. Isham Peters, born say 1773, was head of a Halifax County, North Carolina household of 10 "free colored" in 1820 [NC:161] and 5 in 1830 [NC:353]. His children may have been

     i.   David, born 1776-94, head of a Halifax County household of 6 "free colored" in 1830 [NC:353].

    ii. Henry, born 1776-94, married Tobby **Cooley**, 8 November 1826 Halifax County bond, head of a Halifax County household of 4 "free colored" in 1830 [NC:353].

   iii. Susan, born 1794-1806, married John **Scott**, Jr., 22 January 1822 Halifax County bond.

   iv. Bur., born 1806-20, married 26 February 1824 Halifax County bond, Micajah **Mitchum**, perhaps the son of Mary **Michum**, head of a Halifax County household of 7 "other free" in 1810 [NC:38].

    v. Thomas, born about 1810, a "Mulatto" counted in Halifax County in 1850, with his wife Catherine and children: Eliza, Isham, and Joshua.

13. Jesse Peters, born about 1764, was taxable in Surry County, Virginia, in 1782, his tax charged to Armstead Peters [PPTL, 1782-90, frame 350]. He was a "Mulatto" taxable on himself and a slave over the age of sixteen in Warwick County in 1789 [PPTL, p. 3]. He married Sally **Debreaux**, 9 January 1796 Surry marriage bond, Armstead Peters surety, 15 January 1796 marriage. He registered as a "free Negro" in Surry County on 9 January 1796: *son of Lucy Peters a free mulattoe, a resident of the county, a dark mulattoe man aged about 32 years, pretty well made short hair, 5'11" high* [Back of Guardian Accounts Book 1783-1804, no.17]. He was taxable in Surry County from 1802 to 1816: listed with 3 "free Negroes & Mulattoes" in 1813 [PPTL, 1782-90, frames 350; 1791-1816, frames 498, 540, 598, 636, 674, 713, 752, 863]. His wife Sally registered in Surry County on 20 August 1804: *wife of Jesse Peters was born of free parents of this county to wit, John Debrix and Lucy his wife, the said Sally is of a bright complexion, aged about 30 years, her hair pretty long, she is 5'3/4" high.* She registered again on 24 March 1838 at the age of sixty-four [Surry County Registry of Free Negroes, p.5, no.15]. Jesse was called a "Free man of Color" in his application for a pension in May 1835 in which he stated that he was seventy-one years old and fought at the Battle of Guilford Courthouse under Captain John Lucas [National Archives File, R 8146]. His children were

     i.   Anna, born say 1800, married Richard **Debrix**, 21 January 1817 Surry County bond, with the consent of her father Jesse.

PETTIFORD FAMILY

Three members of the Pettiford family were "Black" taxables in the Granville County tax lists in the 1750s. They were probably brothers, born in the 1730s and married before 1755. They were

1   i.   Lawrence[1], born say 1732.
2   ii. Lewis[1], born say 1734.
3   iii. George[1], born say 1736.

1. Lawrence[1] Pettiford, born say 1732, was taxable in the earliest Granville Tax List, dated 1746 or 1748, and was taxable with his wife Mary in Robert Harris' Granville County list for 1752: two "Black" taxables [CR 44.701.19]. According to Mary's great-great-granddaughter she was married to a **Mitchell**

and had eight children before she married Lawrence Pettiford with whom she also had eight children [28 June 1893 letter from Narcissa Rattley to her children].[169] Lawrence was in the 8 October 1754 Granville County muster of Colonel Eaton [Clark, *Colonial Soldiers of the South*, 728]. On 14 September 1757 he purchased 70 acres in Granville County on the south side of Fishing Creek and another 15 acres adjoining this land on 17 March 1762 [DB C:451; E:360]. He sold 50 acres of this land to Reuben **Bass** on 20 October 1768 [DB H:473]. On 30 September 1767 he purchased 300 acres on Beaverdam Creek and sold this land on 16 December 1776 [DB H:406; L:146]. He was taxable on five persons in the Summary Tax List of 1769, taxable in Fishing Creek District on 150 acres, 2 horses, and 10 cattle in 1782; and he was taxable on 170 acres in 1787 but not subject to poll tax because he was "aged" [Tax List 1786-91]. He sold this 170 acres on 9 October 1787 to Nathan **Bass** [DB O:537] and moved to Wake County where he was head of a household of 8 "other free" in 1790 [NC:104]. His children were

i.   Isham, born about 1753, first taxable in his father's household in the 1765 tax list of Samuel Benton.

4 ii. Philemon/ Philip, born about 1754.

iii. ?Bartlet, born say 1758, purchased 50 acres adjacent to Lawrence Pettiford's 50 acres in Wake County on 12 February 1795. They sold their land as one parcel of 100 acres on 26 March 1800 [DB Q:57, 444]. He was probably the Bartley Petiford who was head of a Marion District, South Carolina household of 4 "other free" in 1810 [SC:83]. By 1820 he was back in North Carolina where he was called "Bartely Bettingford" in the census for Robeson County, over forty-five years old and head of a household of 2 "free colored" [NC:306]. In 1831 he was in Wake County where he married Sallie **Woodward**, 30 March 1831 bond. He testified for the pension application of his sister Rachel **Locus** in 1838. In 1840 he married Zilpha **Williams**, Franklin County bond, and was counted as a ninety-year-old pauper in the 1850 Franklin County census [NC:306].

5 iv. William[1], born about 1761.

v.   ?George[2], born say 1762, received a bed by the 1771 will of George **Anderson** [Original in County, not recorded]. He was taxable on 1 poll in Granville County in 1785, head of a Ragland's District household of 1 male and 1 female in 1786 for the state census, and head of a Granville County household of 7 "other free" in 1800. He was one of the freeholders ordered to work on the road from Fishing Creek at Taylor's Mill to the courthouse in November 1794 [Minutes 1792-5, 178]. He married Taby **Johnson**, 1 May 1837 Granville County bond, Edmond Pettiford bondsman. He was about sixty-three years old on 10 February 1821 when he made a declaration in Granville County court in order to obtain a Revolutionary War pension. His wife Tabitha applied for a widow's benefit in 1853 [M805-648; *NCGSJ* XV:162].

vi. ?Rachel, born say 1764, married Valentine **Locus**, 12 August 1780 Granville County bond. On 24 May 1838 she applied for a survivor's pension for her husband's service in the Revolution, testifying that she was eighty years old at the time. Her brother Bartlet Pettiford, a "person of respectability," testified that he had witnessed her marriage [M805-533, frame 768].

vii. ?Lawrence[2], born say 1766, not identified as Lawrence[1]'s son, but testified with Martha Pettiford for the 1838 pension application of Rachel **Locus** that he remembered that she was married at a place "about one mile from their father's." He was probably referring to Lawrence[1] Pettiford's home since George[1] and Lewis[1] Pettiford had left

---

[169]Narcissa Rattley's letter is in the possession of Robert Jackson of Silver Spring, Maryland.

the county by then (the early 1780s). He may have been the Lawrence Pettiford who purchased 50 acres in Wake County on the west side of Crabtree Creek on 11 February 1795 and sold this land together with the adjoining 50 acres belonging to Bartlet Pettiford (his brother?) as one parcel to Matthew **Maclin** on 25 March 1800 [DB Q:58, 444]. He was taxable on 100 acres in Wake County in 1793, and he and Lewis Pettiford were taxable on 1 poll in 1802 [MFCR 099.701.1, frames 61, 253]. His estate papers were filed in Guilford County on 4 July 1838 [CR 046.508.194].

viii. ?Martha, born say 1768, perhaps the Martha Pedford who was an eighty-four-year-old "Black" head of household, born in North Carolina, living in Jefferson Township, Logan County, Ohio, in 1850 [OH:312].

2. Lewis[1] Pettiford, born say 1734, was a "Black" taxable in the 1758 Granville County Tax List of Nathaniel Harris, taxable in 1764 with his wife Catherine and daughter in Samuel Benton's list. He was probably married before 1753 since he had two daughters over twelve years old in the 1766 list of Stephen Jett. Easter **Mitchell**, also taxable in his 1766 household, may have been his wife's daughter by a previous marriage [CR 44.701.19]. He purchased 50 acres on the north side of Harrell's Creek near the mouth of the Mirey Branch in Granville County on 6 April 1765 and sold this land including the house in which he had lately dwelt on 8 November 1768 [DB H:47, 515]. On 11 May 1772 John Gordon & Company sued him in Mecklenburg County, Virginia, for a debt of 16 pounds, and the Mecklenburg County court ordered his son Edward bound to Richard Epperson on 9 March 1778 [Orders 1771-73, 198, 243, 308, 457; 1773-9, 395]. He was a "Mul°" taxable in the southern district of Halifax County, Virginia, in 1794 [PPTL, 1782-1799, frame 544]. Lewis' children can be identified from the Granville County tax lists:

i. Cortney, born about 1752, taxable in her father's household in Samuel Benton's list in 1764. She married I. **Burrell** of Petersburg, Virginia [Hustings Court Records]. He registered in Mecklenburg County, Virginia, on 30 December 1810 by testimony of J. Nelson and R. Boyd of Mecklenburg County: *Free John (commonly called John Burwell) was emancipated by his master Edwin Burwell, who gave him a tract of land adjoining mine, on which he has lived many years, within half a mile of my house, and Conducted himself in an Orderly & peaceable manner, his wife Courtney Pettifort, was born free and has always supported an excellent Character* [Free Person of Color, no.2, p.1]. They were probably the parents of Clarissa **Burwell**, head of a Petersburg Town household of 3 "other free" in 1810 [VA:121b], and Peachey **Barrell** who registered in Rockingham County in 1812: *a woman of a Dark Complexion aged 23 years five feet four inches* [Register of Free Negroes, #11]. A deed from free John Burwell and Anderson Pettiford was proved in Mecklenburg County on 13 November 1809, and an indenture of bargain and sale from free John Burwell, Anderson Pettiford and Caty Pettiford was proved on 18 February 1811 [Orders 1809-11, 76, 369].

6 ii. Molly[1], born about 1754.
7 iii. ?Drury[1], born say 1755.
8 iv. Catherine[2]/Caty, born about 1757.
   v.   ?Elias, born say 1759, taxable in Granville County on 200 acres and 1 poll in 1785 and head of a Tar River District household of 1 male and 2 females in the 1786 state census.
9 vi. ?Easter, born say 1761.
   vii. Edward, ordered bound apprentice in Mecklenburg County, Virginia, on 9 March 1778 [Orders 1773-9, 395].

viii. ?Lewis[2], born say 1769, married Elizabeth **Sweat**, 2 January 1788 Granville County bond with Elias Pettiford bondsman. He was taxable one poll in Granville County in 1790 and was bondsman for the 31 October 1799 marriage of Mordecai **Bass** and Nancy Askew. On 15 April 1815 he was described as a "free man of color" in a Wake County indenture by which his wife at that time, Lydia, petitioned the court to bind out her two boys to her father Reuben **Bass**. The indenture explained that the boys, Ned and Thomas, eighteen and nineteen years old, were illegitimate children born before her marriage to Lewis, and Lewis was hiring them out without her consent [CR 99.101.1].

ix. ?William[2], born say 1780, head of a Petersburg, Virginia household of 4 "other free" in 1810 [VA:127a].

3. George[1] Pettiford, born say 1736, was a "Black" taxable in the 1754 Granville County tax list of Robert Harris, and he was listed in the Muster Roll of Colonel William Eaton's Granville County Militia [Clark, *Colonial Soldiers of the South*, 723]. He and his wife Lucy were "Black" taxables in the 1755 summary list for Granville and the 1757 list of Richard Harris. In the 1762 list of Samuel Benton for Oxford and Fishing Creek Districts he was taxable on his wife and (his wife's sister?) Rachel **Butler** and taxable on only two tithes in 1763. He had 4 "Black" taxables in the 1769 summary list for Granville County, but the taxables were not named. In August 1768 he tarred the courthouse and jail of Granville County [Minutes 1765-72, 126-7]. In 1777 he was a taxable in the Nash District of Caswell County, and in 1780 he was taxable there on 200 acres, one horse, and six cattle [SS 837]. he may have been the father of

10   i. Mary, born say 1765.

4. Philip Pettiford, born about 1754, was taxable in his father's household in the 1768 list of John Pope (called Phelimon Petteford). He married Patience **Bass** [28 June 1893 letter from his great-granddaughter, Narcissa Rattley, to her children]. Philip was taxable in Granville County on 2 horses and 5 cattle in 1782 (as Philemon), taxable on one poll in 1785 (as Philip), and was head of an Oxford District household of 5 male and 3 female "Blacks" and one white male in 1786 for the state census. He and George Pettiford were found guilty of forgery in Granville County court on 8 February 1787, but the judgment was arrested [Minutes 1786-7, n.p.]. In 1789 he was taxed in Captain Wyatt's Wake County List, but he had moved to Cumberland County by 1790 where he was head of a household of 9 "other free" [NC:40]. On 5 September 1820 in Granville County court he applied for a Revolutionary War pension and swore that he was sixty-six years old and living with his eighty-four-year-old wife [*NCGSJ* XV:162]. His final pension payment papers recorded his death on 13 April 1825 [National Archives]. Administration on his Cumberland County estate was granted on 5 September 1825 to John Pettiford with Bartly Pettiford and Frederick Moore providing security of 100 dollars [Minutes 1823-35].[170] This confirms the statement in the 28 June 1893 letter of Narcissa Rattley that Philip died in Fayetteville where he went to draw his pension. His children were most likely Sarah, Maria, Nance, and Gillica, "mulattos" (no surname given) who were bound apprentices to Duncan McNeill and his family in Cumberland County court on 29 October 1790 [Minutes 1787-91]. Philip's children named in Narcissa Rattley's letter were

---

[170]John Pettiford was an insolvent Fayetteville District taxpayer in 1825 according to the minutes of the 9 September 1826 Cumberland County Court, perhaps the J(?). Pettiford who was head of a Cumberland County household of 3 "other free" in 1810 [NC:622].

Milley, Sally, Nanny, Gillie, Betsy, Jefferson, and William. Philip's children were

   i.   Milley², born say 1775.

   ii.   Sally, born about 1779, an eleven-year-old "mulatto" bound to Duncan McNeill in Cumberland County court on 29 October 1790.

   iii. Maria, born about 1784, six years old in 1790. Perhaps she died young since she was not mentioned by Mrs. Rattley.

   iv. Nanny/ Nance, born about 1787, three years old in October 1790.

   v.   Gillie/ Gillica, born about May 1790, five months old in October 1790.

   vi. Betsy.

   vii. Jefferson.

   viii. William³, born say 1796.

5.   William¹ Pettiford, born about 1761, was called the son of Lawrence Pettiford in George **Anderson**'s 1771 Granville County will [Original Granville County will, not recorded]. In the 1778 Militia Returns for Granville County he was listed in Captain William Gill's Company as a seventeen-year-old "black man" [*The North Carolinian* VI:726 (Mil. TR 4-40)]. William was head of a Granville County household of 1 male and 3 females in Fishing Creek District in the 1786 state census and head of an Orange County household of 14 "other free" in 1810 [NC:863] and 8 "free colored" in 1820 [NC:312]. He was about fifty-eight years old on 19 February 1819 when he made a deposition before one of the justices of Orange County to obtain a pension for his services in the Revolution. He made a second deposition on 1 September 1820 when he testified that his wife was fifty-two years old and very infirm. He had a fifteen-year-old son named Reuben living with him as well as five daughters: aged nineteen, seventeen, twelve, ten and three. He was described as Philip Pettiford's brother in Philip's pension application and in his own application [National Archives Pension files]. He left a 3 July 1836 Wake County will which named William **Croker**, Sr., William **Day**, Sr., Jesse **Day**, Jr., Nelson Pettiford, Sr., Lavina **Roberts** and James E. **Franklin** but did not state his relationship to them [WB 24:28]. William was the father of

   i.   ?Viney, married Dempsy **Roberts**, 9 April 1812 Orange County bond.

   ii.   ?Levice, married Francis **Croker**, 5 September 1812 Orange County bond, William **Croker** bondsman.

   iii. ?Lucy, married William **Croker**, 27 November 1813 Orange County bond.

   iv. ?Love, born about 1798, married Jesse **Day**, 27 January 1819 Orange County bond, William **Day** bondsman. They were counted in the census for Lawrence County, Illinois, in 1850.

   v.   ?Jinsey, born about 1799, married William **Day**, 6 October 1818 Orange County bond. They were counted in the census for Lawrence County, Illinois, in 1850.

   vi. ?Nelson, born about 1800, married Clara **Collins**, 19 August 1823 Orange County bond. They were counted in the census for Lawrence County, Illinois, in 1850.

   vii. Reuben, born about 1805, married Agnis **Griffin**, 12 June 1826 Orange County bond.

6.   Molly¹ Pettiford, born about 1754, was taxable in her father's household in the list of Stephen Jett in 1767 but not listed in his household in 1768. Her "base born child" Lucy Pettiford was bound as an apprentice in Granville County on 4 February 1777. She may have been the mother of Thornton Pettiford who was bound to Nathan **Bass** on 1 February 1779 [CR 044.101.2-7]. And she may have been the Milly Pettiford who married Benjamin **Bass**, 2 January 1781 Granville County bond. Her children born before her marriage were

   i.   Lucy, "base born child of Molly Pettiford," bound apprentice to Jesse Barnet on 4 February 1777. She may have been the same Lucy

Pettiford (born about 1780) who was bound apprentice in Caswell County on 17 July 1786 [CR 20.101.1].

ii. Thornton, born about 1772, no parent named, a seven-year-old bound apprentice to Nathan **Bass** in Granville County on 1 February 1779 [CR 44.101.2], perhaps identical to Thomas Pettiford, son of Milley Pettiford, who was bound to Nathan **Bass** on 1 February 1779 according to Thomas McAdory Owen's notes [Owen, *Granville County Notes*, vol. II]. In October 1792 Thornton was bondsman for Mary Pettiford who was charged with having a bastard child [Camin, *N.C. Bastardy Bonds*, 87]. He married Alice **Goff**, 31 March 1804 Petersburg Town, Virginia bond [Hustings Court Records] and was head of a Petersburg, Virginia household of 2 "other free" and 2 slaves in 1810 [VA:128a].

7. Drury[1] Pettiford, born say 1755, married Tycey **Bass**, 12 November 1781 Granville County bond with (his brother?) Elias Pettiford bondsman. He was taxable on one poll in Granville County in 1785, head of a household of 2 males and 2 females in Granville in the 1786 state census, and taxable in Granville County on 2 polls and 90 acres in 1788. He moved to Stokes County where he was head of a household of 11 "other free" in 1810 [NC:607]. In his application for a pension on 25 August 1820 he stated that he enlisted in Virginia, that his age was sixty-nine years, and the age of his wife Dicy was sixty-six. He listed the ages of his children who were more likely his grandchildren [CR 099.928.11 by *NCGSJ* XV:162]. His wife was probably Dicey **Bass**, "the base born child of Lovey Bass," who was born about 1766 [CR 44-101.2-7]. His (grand) children were

    i. Jesse, born about 1802.
    ii. Nicholas, born about 1804, married Jane **Evans**, 12 October 1821 Wake County bond.
    iii. Jincy, born about 1808.
    iv. Drury[3], born about 1811.
    v. Sally, born about 1813.
    vi. Franky, born about 1814.
    vii. Thomas[2], born about 1818.

8. Catherine[2] Pettiford, born about 1757, was living in Mecklenburg County, Virginia, on 14 June 1784 when the court ordered the churchwardens to bind out her sons Byrd and Anderson Pettiford. On 12 June 1786 the court bound out her seven children, called "Bastards of Caty Peteford," as apprentices to Caleb Johnson. They complained to the court on 13 July 1795 that Johnson was mistreating them, but the case was discontinued for want of prosecution on 11 April 1796 [Orders 1784-87, 51, 524; 1792-5, 474; 1795-8, 57]. She registered in Petersburg on 23 May 1812: *a light brown Mulatto woman, five feet eleven and a half inches high, fifty five years old, born free & raised in Mecklenburg County* [Register of Free Negroes 1794-1819, no. 704]. Her children were

    i. Anderson, born say 1771, ordered bound apprentice on 14 June 1784 [Orders 1784-7, 51]. He purchased 6 acres on Field's Mill Road in the upper district of Mecklenburg County by indenture of bargain and sale acknowledged in court on 14 July 1806 and was taxable on the land from 1807 to 1812. He sued William Fisher in court for trespass, assault and battery and was awarded $183 by the jury on 13 May 1807 [Orders 1805-6, 226, 369; 1807-9, 67, 129; Land Tax List 1782-1811A; 1811B-1824A, A lists]. He married Annis **Anderson**, 4 December 1817 Granville County bond and was head of a Granville County household of 3 "free colored" in 1820 [NC:34].
    ii. Catherine[3]/Cate, born say 1773.

iii.   Boling, born say 1775, bound apprentice to Caleb Johnson in Mecklenburg County on 12 June 1786. He ran away from Johnson in 1797 and, with the help of his uncle Benjamin **Bass**, found work driving a wagon for William Hester of Granville County for $5 a month. In September 1801 Johnson sued for his return, and Hester offered to pay for the remainder of his apprenticeship [LVA, Mecklenburg County chancery case 1804-001].

iv.   Martin, born say 1777.

v.   Hannah, born say 1779, married Jacob **Garrett**, 4 November 1802 Mecklenburg County, Virginia bond, 6 November marriage, (her brother) Drury Pettiford surety. Jacob **Garatt** was freed by deed of emancipation from John Finney according to a certificate of the Amelia County court recorded in Mecklenburg County on 13 August 1804 [Orders 1803-5, 206]. He was living near Petersburg in 1813 when he was counted in a list of "Free Negroes and Mulattoes" in Dinwiddie County [PPTL, 1810-14].

vi.   Drury², born say 1781.

vii.   Bird, born say 1784, bound apprentice in Mecklenburg County on 14 June 1784 and bound to Harrison Wynne on 8 December 1794. On 9 September 1805 he complained of mistreatment by Wynne, and on 10 February 1806 Wynne moved that he be bound instead to (his brother) Anderson Pettiford [Orders 1784-7, 51; 1792-5, 380; 1803-5, 462].

viii.   ?Winny, born say 1788, registered in Petersburg on 9 May 1809: *a dark brown ~~Negro~~ woman of Colour, five feet one and a half inches high, twenty one years old, born free & raised in the Town of Petersburg* [Register of Free Negroes 1794-1819, no. 465].

9.   Easter Pettiford, born say 1761, was living in Granville County in August 1777 when her six-week-old son Collin was bound apprentice. She was head of a Granville County household of 5 "free colored" in 1820 [NC:27]. Her children were

i.   Collin, born about June 1777, "orphan of Easter Pettiford," bound an apprentice to Thomas Satterwhite on ___ August 1777 [CR 044.101.2-7]. He married Polly **Chavis**, 16 June 1802 Granville County bond. He was taxable on one poll in Island Creek District in 1804 and 1805, one poll in Abrams Plains District in 1806-09, and taxable on 81 acres on Grassy Creek in Country Line District in 1820 and 1823 [Tax List 1767-1823, 63, 124, 188, 204, 255, 311]. He was head of a Granville County household of 7 "other free" in 1810 [NC:860] and 7 "free colored" in 1820 [NC:36].

ii.   ?Augustine, born about 1779, a two-year-old boy bound apprentice to Thomas Satterwhite in Granville County on 6 November 1781, no parent named [Minutes 1766-95].

10.   Mary Pettiford, born say 1765, was the mother of Charity Pettiford who was bound to Mary Badgett by the Granville County court in May 1793. In August that year she petitioned the court to have her daughter removed from Badgett and bound to some other person [Minutes 1792-5, 91]. She was the mother of

i.   Charity, born about 1786, seven-year-old daughter of Mary Pettiford bound to Mary Badgett in Granville County in May 1793 [Minutes 1792-5, 64].

ii.   Elizabeth, born about 1789, four years old in August 1793 when she was bound to William Pinn [Minutes 1792-5, 92]. She married William **Anderson**, 12 November 1808 Granville County bond, and a Betsy Anderson married Moses **Bass**, 28 August 1809 Granville County bond.

iii.   Merriman, born about 1792, one and a half years old in August 1793 when he was bound to William Pinn [Minutes 1792-5, 92], perhaps the

Meredith Pettiford who married Ann **Tyler**, 6 August 1818 Granville County bond.

Other members of the Pettiford family were

    i.   Moses, born say 1775, bound as an apprentice farmer to William Creath by the Granville County court on 2 November 1790 [Minutes 17]. He was head of a Guilford County household of 5 "free colored" in 1820 [NC:111].

    ii. Archilus, born about 1781, a five-year-old bound to Nicholas Talley by the Granville County court on 9 November 1786 to be a cordwainer [Minutes 1786-7]. He was called Cillis Pettiford in November 1795 when the Granville County court reported that Talley had moved to Guilford with the boy several years previous, but had since died and left him with someone who was not treating him well [Minutes 1792-5, 287]. He may have been identical to Archibald Pettiford who was head of a Stokes County household of 6 "other free" in 1810 [NC:606] and 11 "free colored" in 1820 [NC:364].

    iii. Polly, born about 1783, bound apprentice in Caswell County on 17 July 1786 (no parent named) [CR 20.101.1].

    iv. Stephen, born about 1785, bound apprentice in Caswell County on 17 July 1786 (no parent named) [CR 20.101.1].

    v. Thomas[1], born say 1786, married Patsey **Tyner**, 1 September 1807 Granville County bond, Jonathan **Tyner** bondsman. He was head of a Stokes County household of 5 "other free" in 1810 [NC:610] and 5 "free colored" in 1820 [NC:364].

PHILLIPS FAMILY

1. Mary Phillips, born say 1670, was the servant of Mr. Thomas Banks on 16 July 1690 when she confessed in Northumberland County court that she had a child by her master's "negro" named William Smyth. On 15 August 1694 she bound her "mulatto" son Thomas as an apprentice to Thomas Downing until the age of thirty years by indenture recorded in Northumberland County [Orders 1678-98, pt. 2, 668; 1699-1713, pt. 2, 511, 684]. She was probably the mother of William Phillips, a "Mulatto," who was bound apprentice in Northumberland County in 1710. She was the mother of

    i.   William[1], born 16 March 1690, a twenty-year-old "Mulatto" belonging to Mrs. Elizabeth Banks on 19 July 1710 when he was bound to serve her as an apprentice until the age of twenty-four

    ii. Thomas, born 16 January 1693/4 [Orders 1678-98, pt. 2, 668].

They may have been the ancestors of

    i.   John, born say 1750, a taxable "Molato" in Benjamin **Ivey**'s Bladen County, North Carolina household in 1770 [Byrd, *Bladen County Tax Lists*, I:34].

    ii. Sylvia, head of a Buckingham County household of 18 "other free" in 1810 [VA:799].

    iii. William[2], "F.N." head of a Culpeper County household of 4 "other free" and a white woman in 1810 [VA:66].

    iv. James, head of a Richmond City household of 4 "other free" in 1810 [VA:369]. He was probably the James Phillips who married Jenny, "a dark mulatto" who was emancipated by verdict of the Richmond District Court, by 29 May 1807 Henrico County bond.

    v. B., head of a Brunswick County, North Carolina household of 3 "other free" in 1810 [NC:234].

PICKETT FAMILY

1. Mary Pickett, born say 1664, was living in Elizabeth City County on 20 May 1724 when the court granted her petition to be levy free [Orders 1724-30, 15]. She may have been the ancestor of

2   i.   Susannah, born say 1718.
     ii. Samuel, born about 1723, a "Mulatto" ordered to be released from the Surry County estate of John Simmons, deceased, in December 1744 because he was over twenty-one [Orders 1744-48, 108, 12].
     iii. Sarah **Pickart**, born say 1735, whose "Molatto" son Stafford was born in Overwharton Parish, Stafford County, on 22 October 1757 [Overwharton Parish, Stafford County, Registry 1724-76, 192].
3   iv. Elizabeth, born say 1742.

2. Susannah Pickett, born say 1718, was called Susannah Pickett alias **Taylor** when her children: Sarah, Edward, Lydia, and James were bound out by the Surry County, Virginia court in January 1745/6. She was the mother of
     i.   Sarah, born say 1739.
     ii. Edward, born say 1741, complained to the Surry County court on 16 January 1754 against his master Joseph Eelbeck. The court noted that Eelbeck had moved to North Carolina and ordered the churchwardens of Southwarke Parish to take him under their care [Orders 1753-7, 43]. He may have been the Edward **Taylor** whose son Aaron **Taylor** registered as a "free Negro" in Surry County in 1796.
     iii. Lydia, born say 1743, called Lydia **Taylor**, a "Mulatto," when she was bound out in Surry County on 19 June 1753 [Orders 1751-3, 443].
     iv. James, born say 1745.

3. Elizabeth Pickett, born say 1742, (no race indicated) was living in Charles Parish on 17 May 1762 when the York County court presented her for having a bastard child [Judgments & Orders 1759-63, 358]. She was living in Warwick County in 1765 when she baptized her son William Picket, "bastard son of Eliza Picket," in Charles Parish [Bell, *Charles Parish Registers*, 152]. Her children were
4   i.   ?John, born say 1761.
     ii. William[1], baptized 24 November 1765, head of a Montgomery County, Pennsylvania household of 5 "other free" in 1790, perhaps the William Pickett who was head of a Philadelphia County household of 5 "other free" in 1790.
     iii. Robert, born 23 October 1768, baptized 12 February 1769, son of Eliza by William **Sandefer** [Bell, *Charles Parish Registers*, 152].

4. John Pickett, born say 1761, and his wife Elizabeth, were living in Warwick County on 18 March 1785 when they registered the birth and baptism of their "mulatto" son William, in Charles Parish, York County [Bell, *Charles Parish Registers*, 152]. He was a "Mulatto" taxable in Warwick County in 1789 and a taxable there in 1798 [1789 PPTL, p.3; 1798, p.5]. Their children were
     i.   Patsey, born 18 September, baptized 3 November 1782, daughter of John and Eliza Pickett."
     ii. William[2], born 7 August 1784, baptized 18 March 1785, "mulatto son of John and Elizabeth."

PIERCE FAMILY

1. Deborah Pierce, born say 1708, was the servant of James Halloway on 19 June 1729 when she was a witness for Christopher Needham in Elizabeth City County court. On 15 December 1731 she was presented for having a bastard

child. And on 7 June 1748 she was presented for having a "Mulatto Bastard" [Orders 1723-9, 332; 1731-47, 15; 1747-55, 42, 149]. She was the mother of

2   i.   ?Thomas, born say 1722.

       ii. Elizabeth, a "Mulatto Bastard," bound to John Selden on 15 February 1749/50 [Orders 1747-55, 149]. She may have been the mother of Sarah Pierce (no race indicated) who was fined 500 pounds of tobacco by the Elizabeth City County court on 7 January 1767, probably for having an illegitimate child [Court Records 1760-9, 419].

2.   Thomas Pierce, born say 1722, received a warrant for 57 acres in Tyrrell County, North Carolina, on 21 March 1743 [Saunders, *Colonial Records of North Carolina* IV:628] and was taxable on 265 acres, 4 horses, and 10 cattle in Tyrrell County in 1782 [*NCGSJ* X:244]. He was a "free colored" head of a Tyrrell County household of 4 free males and 4 free females in 1790 [NC:34]. On 13 June 1795 he was called "Thomas Pierce of Tyrrell County, administrator of William Pierce," when he gave power of attorney to Samuel Warren, an attorney, to receive the final settlement due to (his son?) William Pierce for his service in the North Carolina Continental Line [*NCGSJ* XIV:230]. Thomas' widow Mary Pierce appeared in Tyrrell County court in January 1797 to claim her dower rights to two tracts of land, one for 50 acres on the sound and one for 140 acres joining Samuel Chessons. She was head of a Washington County household of 2 "other free" in 1800 [NC:708]. Their children were most likely

        i.   William, born say 1750, died before 13 June 1795.

3   ii. Israel, born say 1755.

4   iii. Sarah, born say 1770.

      iv. Stevens, born say 1785, head of a Tyrrell County household of one "other free" and one slave in 1810 [NC:785].

3.   Israel Pierce, born say 1755, was a "free colored" head of a Tyrrell County household of 3 free males and 3 free females in 1790 [NC:34], 7 "other free" in Hyde County in 1800 [NC:374], 11 in Hyde County in 1810 [NC:119] and 8 "free colored" in Beaufort County in 1820 [NC:32]. He was in Tyrrell County on 21 June 1791 when he gave power of attorney to Samuel Warren, an attorney, to receive his final settlement due him as a soldier in the North Carolina Continental Line [*NCGSJ* XIV:230]. He may have been the father of Simon Pierce, born 28 December 1798, and Lewis Pierce, born September 1801, "free Mullattos" bound as apprentices to William and Mercer Cherry in Beaufort County by the September court [Minutes 1809-14, 10th page of September Minutes].

4.   Sarah Pierce, born say 1770, was living in Tyrrell County on 8 April 1796 when her nine-year-old son James **Simpson** was bound to Isaac Bateman [CR 96.102.1, Box 1]. She was head of a Washington County household of 3 "other free" in 1800 [NC:708] and 5 in 1810 [NC:787]. Her son was

        i.   James **Simpson**, born about 1787, perhaps the James **Swinson** who was head of a Beaufort County household of 2 "free colored" in 1820 [NC:34].

Other members of the Pierce family were

        i.   William Pierse, head of a Beaufort County, South Carolina household of 10 "other free" in 1800 [SC:116].

       ii. Joseph, a "Mulatto" soldier born in Nansemond County who was living in New Kent County when he was listed in the size roll of troops who enlisted at Chesterfield Courthouse [The Chesterfield Supplement cited by NSDAR, *African American Patriots*, 153].

     iii. Francis, a man of color born in Caroline County who enlisted as a soldier in the Revolution NSDAR, *African American Patriots*, 153].

iv.   William, head of a Loudoun County household of 6 "other free" in 1810 [VA:268].
v.   Henry, born about 1779, registered in Amelia County on 24 October 1805: *a brown Mulatto man about 5 feet 5 inches high about 26 years of age, born free as appears by the certificate of George Gorden and a register from the County of Fouqerire* [Register of Free Negroes 1804-35, no. 20].
vi.   Benjamin, "F. Negroe" head of a Fauquier County household of 1 "other free" in 1810 [VA:412].

PINN FAMILY

Members of the Pinn family were probably descendants of Thomas Pin who was taxable in Lancaster County in 1695 but was declared levy-free in June 1697 because he was "very aged" [Orders 1686-96, 332; 1696-1702, 20]. He was most likely the ancestor of

1   i.   Robert[1], born say 1710.
2   ii.   David[1], born say 1725.
3   iii. Patsey **Maclin**, born say 1750.

1. Robert[1] Pinn, born say 1710, was presented by the churchwardens of Wicomico Parish, Northumberland County, on 16 August 1733 for absenting himself from church [Orders 1729-37, 109]. He was in Lancaster County on 13 January 1744 when his son Robert, no age or race mentioned, was bound to Thomas Dogget as an apprentice cooper. He was probably married to Margaret Pinn who bound her son Robert to William Downman as an apprentice shoemaker in Lancaster County on 11 May 1751 [Orders 1743-52, 9, 251]. Margaret may have been the ancestor of a "free Negro boy" named Thomas Pinn bound out by the court in Richmond County, Virginia, on 7 May 1764 to William Downman, the same man Robert Pinn was bound to in Lancaster County [Orders 1762-5, 227]. Robert and Margaret's were the ancestors of

4   i.   Robert[2], born say 1740.
5   ii.   ?Rawley, born say 1750.
        iii. ?John[1], born say 1752, a "Free" head of a Northumberland County household of 3 "Blacks" in 1782 [VA:37]. His 9 July 1785 Northumberland County will, proved 9 July 1792 but not recorded, mentioned (his wife?) Ann **Kesterson**, who was to receive all his estate as long as she remained single or married a free person. However, if she married a slave, then the entire estate was to go to his sister Sally **Nickens** [*Northumberland County Wills and Administrations*, 80]. Ann **Kesterson** was probably the sister of Judith **Kesterson** who married Edward **Sorrell**, 13 April 1789 Northumberland County bond.
        iv.   ?Sally **Nickens**, called the sister of John Pinn in his 9 July 1785 Northumberland County will, probably the wife of Amos **Nickens**.
        v.   ?Thomas, born say 1758, a "free Negro boy" living in Richmond County, Virginia, on 7 May 1764 when the court ordered the churchwardens of North Farnham Parish to bind him out to William Downman, the same man Robert Pinn was bound to in Lancaster County on 11 May 1751 [Orders 1762-5, 227].

2. David[1] Pinn, born say 1725, an "Indian," was taxable in Benjamin George's Christ Church Parish, Lancaster County household in William Tayloe's list for 1745 and called David Pinn, "an Indian," in Benjamin George's Christ Church Parish household in the 1746 list of Dale Carter [Tithables 1745-95, 1, 6]. He was a shoemaker on 11 February 1764 when he and his wife Averilla (**Grimes**) leased 50 acres in Spotsylvania County from John Waller. They conveyed a life interest in this land to Oliver Towles on 31 November 1774

[DB F:362; J:41]. He purchased land by deed proved in Halifax County, Virginia, on 17 November 1774, 17 May 1781 and 20 December 1787 [Pleas 1774-9, 88; 1779-83, 191; 1786-8, 298]. He was taxable in Halifax County from 1782 to 1796: listed with 2 tithes and 3 horses in 1782, called a "Mul°" in 1791 and 1796 [PPTL, 1782-1799, frames 4, 27, 47, 142, 422, 681] and head of a household of 4 whites (free persons) in 1785 [VA:90]. He left a 30 September 1796 Halifax County will, proved 25 September 1797, by which he left all his estate to his wife Avery except for 50 acres which he left to Patsey **Macling (Maclin)**. After Patsey's death the land was to go to her son David Pinn who was to care for David Pinn, Sr.'s wife for the rest of her life. After Avery's death, her portion was to be divided between David Pinn and Nancy Pinn [WB 3:359]. Averilla was taxable on 1-2 horses in Halifax County from 1797 to 1809, called a "Mulatto" starting in 1805 [PPTL, 1782-1799, frames 707, 831, 924; 1800-12, frame 69, 146, 389, 533, 640, 814]. David may have been the father of

    i.   John[3], a "Mul°" taxable in the southern district of Halifax County in 1796 [PPTL, 1782-1799, frame 681].

3.   Patsey **Maclin**, born say 1750, may have been the partner of Ambrose **Month** who bound his children Charity **Grymes** Penn, David Penn, and Averilla Penn (Pinn) to Micajah Poole in Spotsylvania County on 13 February 1779 [DB J:431]. She received 50 acres where she was then living by the 30 July 1796 Halifax County, Virginia will of David Pinn. After her death, the land was to pass to her son David Pinn. She was the mother of

6   i.   Charity **Grimes**, born say 1772.

    ii.   David[2] Pinn **Month**, born say 1774, bound out by the churchwardens of Berkeley Parish in Spotsylvania County on 21 September 1780 [Orders 1774-82, 151]. He was taxable in Dinwiddie County in 1790, his tax charged to Thomas Woodward [PPTL, 1800-19, list B, p.20] and taxable in Halifax County, Virginia, in 1809 [PPTL, 1800-12, frame 814]. He married (his cousin?) Nancy Pinns who was to receive half the property left to Averilla Pinn by her husband David Pinn, Sr.'s Halifax County will. She was called Nancy **Grimes** in the 4 January 1812 Caswell County deed by which she and her husband David sold the land which had been willed to her by "her uncle" David Penn. This deed was not legal since it was recorded in Caswell County [DB R:433]. David and Nancy were living in Grainger County, Tennessee, on 20 November 1817 when they sold the land by deed proved in Halifax County, Virginia [DB 26:639]. David was head of a Knoxville County, Tennessee household of 2 "free colored" in 1830 (born before 1776). David was called David Penn "sometimes known and called by name David Month" when he sold his land on Winn Creek in Halifax County by deed proved in Caswell County, North Carolina [Caswell DB R:433].

    iii.   Averilla, born say 1776.

4.   Robert[2] Pinn, born say 1740, was taxable on 2 free tithes in Lancaster County from 1787 to 1790, called Robert Pinn, Sr. [PPTL, 1782-1839, frames 45, 53, 62, 74, 86]. He and his wife Ann were identified as the parents of Benjamin Pinn when he married Betty **Bell**, 25 April 1789 Lancaster County bond. Ann Pinn, born about 1748, registered as a "free Negro" in Lancaster County on 19 September 1803: *Age 55, Color black, Height 5'3"...born free* [Burkett, *Lancaster County Register of Free Negroes*, 1]. She was probably the Nanny Pin who was head of a Lancaster County household of 3 "other free" in 1810 [VA:357]. Robert was the father of

    i.   William[1], born say 1758, mentioned in the Revolutionary War pension application of his brother John Pin, perhaps the William Penn who was head of a Maryland household of one "other free" in 1790 [MD:52].

    ii. John[2], born about 1760, married Anne **Cassady**, 12 September 1785 Northumberland County bond. He was living in Boston, Massachusetts on 28 October 1842 when he applied for a pension for his services in the Revolution. He stated that his father Robert Pin was a Mustee and his mother a Cherokee who were inhabitants of Lancaster County, Virginia, at a place called Indian Town near Carter's Creek. He and his father served in Captain William Yerby's Company of Artillery, he as a powder boy. He had moved to Boston about 1792 and married Nancy **Coffin** about ten years later. She died about 1820. He had owned a small house and lot, but the house had been lost in an accidental fire. He testified that his brothers Jim and William also served and that Jim died in the service. He was described as "a coloured man - apparently of Indian Origin and is a person of good report amongst our mercantile community both here and at Salem" [M804-1938, frames 0637-51].

    iii. James[1], born say 1762, mentioned in the Revolutionary War pension application of his brother John Pin, said to have died in the service.

    iv. Benjamin, born about 1768, a twenty-one-year-old carpenter, "son of Robert and Ann Pin," married Betty **Bell**, "daughter of Elias Bell, deceased," 25 April 1789 Lancaster County bond. He was taxable in Lancaster County from 1791 to 1798 [PPTL, 1782-1839, frames 86, 110, 122, 144, 175] and head of a Norfolk County household of 6 "other free" in 1810 [VA:915].

    v. ?Robert[3], born about 1768, registered as a "free Negro" in Lancaster County on 22 April 1806: *Age 38, Color dark, Height 5'10-1/4", Born free; a little grey* [Burkett, *Lancaster County Register of Free Negroes*, 2]. He was taxable in Lancaster County from 1792 to 1817, in the list of "free Negroes & Mulattoes" in 1813 and 1814 [PPTL, 1782-1839, frames 98, 133, 175, 304, 385, 399, 431] and head of a Lancaster County household of 7 "other free" in 1810 [VA:357].

    vi. ?Aaron, born about 1772, taxable in Lancaster County from 1792 to 1807 [PPTL, 1782-1839, frames 98, 122, 157, 216, 242, 304]. He married Mary **Kelly Weaver**, 3 March 1794 Lancaster bond. He purchased 57 acres in Christ Church Parish, Lancaster County, on 3 November 1800 [DB 23:298]. He registered as a "free Negro" in Lancaster County on 20 June 1803: *Age 31, Color black, 5'8-1/2" Height...born free*, and (his wife?) Mary Pinn, born about 1775, registered on 19 September 1808: *age 33, Color yellow, Height 5'4"...born free* [Burkett, *Lancaster County Register of Free Negroes*, 1, 4]. Perhaps his widow was the Mary Pin, Senr., who was head of a Lancaster County household of 7 "other free" in 1810 [VA:356]. She may have been the Mary Pinn who was named as one of the heirs of Elijah **Weaver** on 15 September 1834 in Lancaster County court [Orders 1834-41, 37].

    vii. ?Molly, head of a Lancaster County household of 4 "other free" in 1810 [VA:357].

5. Rawley[1] Pinn, born say 1750, was a "Mulatto" taxable in Buckingham County in 1774 [Woodson, *Virginia Tithables From Burned Counties*], head of an Amherst County household of 7 persons in 1783 [VA:47], and 8 "Mulattos" in 1785 [VA:84]. He was a free man of color who served in the Revolution from Amherst County [NSDAR, *African American Patriots*, 152]. Edmund Wilcox sued him in Amherst County court for 550 pounds of crop tobacco in May 1784 [Orders 1782-4, 249]. He was taxable in Amherst County from 1782 to 1794 and from 1799 to 1804, taxable on 2 tithes in 1800 [PPTL 1782-1803, frames 4, 17, 38, 69, 106, 138, 169, 229, 261, 329, 455, 485, 522, 556, 593; 1804-23, frames 29]. He was surety for the 29 November 1792 Amherst County marriage bond of Francis **Beverly** and Mary **Williams**. He

purchased land by deed proved in Amherst County court on 1 December 1788 [Orders 1787-1790, 408], and he and his wife Sarah (signing) sold land in Amherst County on Mill and Porridge Creeks to George and William **Clark** for 100 pounds on 18 March 1800 [DB I:161]. They were the parents of

7   i.   ?James², born say 1775.

      ii.   Ann, born say 1778, daughter of Rolly Pinn (farmer) and Sarah Pinn, married Thomas **Evans**, 2 November 1795 Amherst County bond, John Lonogan security.

8   iii.   ?Turner, born about 1782.

     iv.   ?Edy, married William **Beverly** in November 1800 in Amherst County by the Rev. James Boyd.

6.   Charity **Grimes** Pinn **Month**, born say 1772, was ordered bound out by the churchwardens of Berkeley Parish in Spotsylvania County on 21 September 1780 [Orders 1774-82, 151]. She may have been identical to Charity Pinn, the mother of Alexander Pinn who was born in Dinwiddie County about 1800. Her children were

       i.   ?Avey, born about 1790, registered in Petersburg on 30 June 1817: *a dark brown free woman of colour, five feet two inches high, twenty seven years old, born free in Dinwiddie County, a Spinner* [Register of Free Negroes 1794-1819, no. 851].

      ii.   ?Henry, born about 1795, registered in Lunenburg County on 12 August 1822: *aged about 27 years...dark complexion, born free* [WB 5, after page 89, no. 16 (not in order, between nos. 27 & 28)]

     iii.   Alexander, born about 1800, registered in Lunenburg County on 13 August 1821: *aged about twenty one years, black complexion, son of Charity Pinn, born free in Dinwiddie County*, perhaps identical to Sandy Pinn who registered at about the age of fifty, no date: *of dark complexion* [WB 5, after page 89, nos. 27, 76].

7.   James² Pinn, born say 1777, married Nancy **Redcross**, daughter of John **Redcross**, 27 August 1799 Amherst County bond, Rawleigh Penn surety; and married second, Jane **Cooper**, 6 October 1812 Amherst County bond, John **Cooper** security. He was taxable in Amherst County from 1800 to 1820: taxable on 2 tithes in 1809, 2 slaves in 1811, called a "man of color" in 1811, 1812, 1815 and 1820, a "Mulatto" in 1813, in a list of "Free Mulattoes & Negroes" in 1814, 1817, and 1818 [PPTL 1782-1803, frames 485, 522, 593; 1804-23, frames 29, 71, 151, 172, 216, 239, 259, 284, 418, 489]. He was head of an Amherst County household of 6 "other free" and a slave in 1810 [VA:302]. On 21 July 1817 James and his wife Jinsey sold 108 acres in Amherst County on Porridge Creek to Turner Pinn, sold 112 acres on Porridge Creek where James was then living, and purchased 130 acres on Porridge Creek for $1,000 [DB N:349, 354]. He purchased another 19 acres on Porridge Creek for $360 on 19 January 1818 and 145 acres on the east side of Glade Road for $1,700 on 19 May 1820 [DB N:463; O:698]. He sold 150 acres on Porridge Creek to John **Cooper** on 27 September 1821, and his wife Jincy and John **Cooper** sold 45 acres on Porridge Creek on 3 August 1822 [DB P:217]. James and Jane/ Jincy were the parents of

       i.   Robert⁵, born about 1813, registered in Amherst County on 5 January 1836: *light complexion for a Negro 5 feet Eight and a half inches high son of James & Jincey Pinn...twenty three years of age.*

      ii.   Christina, born about 1815, registered on 11 August 1834: *daughter of James Pinn and Jincey his wife free born about 19 years light complexion for a Negro five feet one inch high.*

     iii.   George Washington Lafayette, born about 1821, registered on 13 March 1841: *About 20 years of age - Bright Mulatto - 5 feet 11 inches high...Son of Jincy Pinn* [McLeRoy, *Strangers in Their Midst*, 60, 61 63].

8. Turner Pinn, born about 1782, was taxable in Amherst County from 1800 to 1820: taxable on a slave in 1811, called a "man of color" in 1811, 1812, 1815 and 1820, a "Mulatto" in 1813, in a list of "Free Mulattoes & Negroes" in 1814, 1817 and 1819 [PPTL 1782-1803, frames 485, 551, 593; 1804-23, frames 29, 151, 195, 216, 239, 259, 284, 308, 418, 528, 578]. He married Joyce **Humbles**, 13 August 1807 Amherst County bond, William Solle security. He was head of an Amherst County, Virginia household of 8 "other free" in 1810 [VA:302]. He purchased 108 acres in Amherst County where he was living on 21 July 1817 from (his brother?) James Pinn, and on the same day he and his wife Joyce and James Pinn and his wife Jincy Pinn sold 112 acres on Porridge Creek where James was then living [DB N:349, 350]. Turner registered as a "free Negro" in Amherst County on 26 September 1828: *of dark brown complexion, about five feet ten inches high aged 46 years born free.* His wife Joyce Pinn registered on 20 October the same year: *wife of Turner Pinn a free woman of color rather light complexion about five feet in hight stout built about forty five was born free* [McLeRoy, *Strangers in Their Midst*, 55, 56]. Their children were

    i.   Maria, born about 1802, daughter of Turner Pinn, married Bartlet **Sparrow**, 26 December 1827 Amherst County bond, Jonathan **Beverly** security. She registered in Amherst County on 11 October 1831: *wife of Bartlet Sparrow formerly Maria Pinn a free Negro of light complexion daughter of Turner Pinn 29 years of age 5 feet 8-1/2 inches high.*

    ii. ?William[2], born about 1805, registered on 27 October 1828: *dark complexion about six feet & half an inch in hight of spare stature aged 23 years.*

    iii. Polly, born about 1805, registered in Amherst County on 27 October 1828: *a free woman of colour aged twenty three years rather dark mulatto complexion about five feet nine inches in height.* She was called the daughter of Turner Pinn when she married Richard **Tuppence**, 14 August 1829 Amherst County bond. Richard **Tuppence** registered on 14 August 1829: *a free man of light complexion (nearly white) light hair slightly curled five feet six inches and a half high...aged Twenty five years* [McLeRoy, *Strangers in Their Midst*, 55, 56, 57-8]. He was probably related to David **Topence**, head of a Richmond City household of 4 "other free" and a slave in 1810 [VA:325], S. **Twopence**, "Free Negro" head of a King & Queen County household of 4 "other free" in 1810 [VA:179], Huley **Twopence**, head of a Campbell County household of 4 "other free" in 1810 [VA:853], and Nancy **Twopence**, head of a Middlesex County household of 4 "other free" in 1810 [VA:470].

    iv. ?Saunders, born about 1806, registered on 20 October 1828: *dark complexion about six feet in hight aged 22 years.*

    v.   Segis, born about 1806, registered on 11 October 1831: *daughter of Turner Pinn a dark Mulatto 5 feet 4-3/4 inches high 25 years of age.* She married Daniel **Jackson** in 1840.

    vi. ?Raleigh[2], born about 1808, registered on 27 October 1828: *dark complexion about five feet ten inches high aged 20 years.* He married Susanna **Scott**, eighteen-year-old daughter of Samuel **Scott**, 18 June 1827 Amherst County bond, Thomas Jewell security.

    vii. Betsy, born about 1813, registered on 11 October 1831: *daughter of Turner Pinn a verry dark Mulatto 5 feet 8-3/4 inches high 18 years of age.*

    viii. Lavinia, born about 1815, registered on 11 October 1831: *daughter of Turner Pinn verry light complexion for a Negro, or perhaps more properly a very dark Mulatto 5 feet 8 3/4 inches high about 16 years of age* [McLeRoy, *Strangers in Their Midst*, 55, 56, 58].

Other members of the Pinn family were

    i. ?Minor, head of a Fauquier County household of 5 "other free" in 1810 [VA:380], perhaps the father of Samuel Pinn, born about 1795, who registered in Fauquier County on 24 August 1819: *21 years of age in June last, 5 feet 7 inches high, a Bright Mulatto, Bushy hair...flat nose prominent* [Register of Free Negroes, no.13].

    ii. ?Peggy, "F. Negroe," head of a Fauquier County household of 4 "other free" in 1810 [VA:418].

    iii. Robert[4], born about 1786, a turner, counted in the "List of Free Negroes and Mulattoes in the Lower District of Lunenburg for the Year 1814" [*Magazine of Virginia Genealogy* 33:266]. He registered in Lunenburg County on 10 April 1820: *about 34 years of age, yellowish Complexion, five feet four and one half inches high, born in Dinwiddie County.* Lucretia was probably his wife. She registered in Lunenburg County on 5 December 1818: *Lucretia Pinn formerly Mills, born free, about 28 years, five feet six inches high, yellow Complexion* [WB 5, after page 89, nos. 6 & 9]. Cretia, Eliza, Franky and Ned Mills were counted near Robin Pen in the "List of Free Negroes and Mulattoes" in Lunenburg in 1814 [*Magazine of Virginia Genealogy* 33:266].

    iv. David[3], born 1775-1794, head of a New Hanover County, North Carolina household of 1 "free colored" in 1820 [NC:235].

PITTMAN FAMILY

1. Ann Pittman, born say 1700, was the servant of Nathan Hutchings of Princess Anne County on 5 September 1722 when she was convicted of having a "mullatto" child. The court ordered the churchwardens to sell her after the completion of her indenture [Princess Ann County Orders 1717-28, 151]. She may have been the ancestor of

    i. Reuben, born about 1790, no race indicated when he was bound to Richard Bradley in Edgecombe County, North Carolina, on 24 November 1799.

    ii. Archibald, born 26 December 1793, a five-year-old "mulatto" boy bound to Nathan Bradley in Edgecombe County as an apprentice wheelwright on the fourth Monday in August 1799 [Minutes 1797-1800, n.p.].

PITTS FAMILY

1. Ann Pitts, born say 1670, was the servant of Joseph Hoult of Northumberland County on 20 1688/9 when she was convicted of having a child by a "negro" [Orders 1678-98, part 2, 430]. She may have been the ancestor of

    i. Nancy, head of a Stokes County, North Carolina household of 4 "free colored" in 1820 [NC:362].

PLUMLY FAMILY

1. Obediah Plumly, born say 1760, was a yellow complexioned soldier from New Kent County, Virginia, who served as a substitute in the Revolution [Register & description of Noncommissioned Officers & Privates at Chesterfield Court House, cited by NSDAR, *African American Patriots*, 153]. He was head of a "white" household of a male aged 21-60 with three males younger than 21 or over 60 in the 1786 census for Northampton County, North Carolina, head of a Northampton County household of 7 "other free" in 1790 [NC:76], 11 in 1800 [NC:469] and 3 in 1810 [NC:739]. He was probably the father of

    i. Josiah, head of a Northampton County household of 7 "other free" in 1810 [NC:739] and 4 "free colored" in 1820 [NC:250].

ii.   Keziah, married Eli **Kemore** (**Keemer**), 6 July 1815 Northampton
County bond, Jesse **Ash** bondsman.

POE FAMILY

1.   Jane Peacock/ Poe, born say 1700, was a "Molatto" presented by the York
County court for not listing herself as a tithable on 20 November 1727 (called
Jane Peacock) and on 17 November 1735 (called Jane Poe). She was called
"Jane Po alias Peacock" on 20 August 1744 when Landon Carter, Esq., sued
her in York County for a cow and a calf of the value of 40 shillings. The court
ruled that they were her property and dismissed the suit [OW 16:489; W&I
18:237, 245; 19:302, 317]. The court presented her on 19 November 1750 for
not listing herself as a tithable, but the sheriff reported that she was not to be
found in the county [Judgments & Orders 1746-52, 364, 393]. She may have
been the mother of

    i.   Ann, born say 1724, presented by the York County court on 20
November 1749 for failing to list herself as a tithable in Bruton Parish.
The court fined her 1,000 pounds of tobacco for the offense. The court
presented her for the same offense the following year on 19 November
1750, but the sheriff reported that she was not to be found in the
county [Judgments & Orders 1746-52, 256, 277, 364, 393].

2   ii.   John, born say 1726.

3   iii.   Thomas[1], born say 1728.

    iv.   Elizabeth, born say 1730, presented by the York County court on 20
November 1749 for failing to list herself as a tithable [Judgments &
Orders 1746-52, 256, 277].

2.   John Poe, born say 1726, was sued in York County court on 17 July 1749 by
Elizabeth **Savey** (**Savoy**). The case was dismissed later that year on 21 August
1749 when she failed to prosecute. On 20 November 1749 the court presented
him for failing to list himself as a tithable, on 16 November 1761 for
concealing two tithables and on 17 December 1764 for failing to list his wife
as a tithable. On 15 August 1763 he sued John **Bird** for debt, but the suit was
dismissed on agreement between the parties. He was a witness for George
Jones in his suit against Peter **Gillett** on 19 September 1763. On 18 March
1765 he sued Anthony and Jasper **Peters** for trespass, assault and battery and
was awarded 20 shillings. Sarah **Gillett**, Patience **Alvis**, and William **Wilson**
were his witnesses [Judgments & Orders 1746-52, 225, 238, 256, 277, 284;
1759-63, 298, 312; 1763-5, 63, 79, 320, 357, 358]. He was taxable on 2
horses and 6 cattle in James City County in 1782. His widow may have been
Mary Poe who was taxable in James City County on a horse and 2 cattle in
1783 and 1786 [PPTL, 1782-99]. They may have been the parents of

    i.   William, born say 1765, taxable in Bruton Parish, York County, in
1786, taxable in James City County in 1787 [PPTL, 1782-99], and
taxable in York County from 1788 to 1813 when he was head of a
household of 2 "free Negroes & mulattoes over 16" [PPTL, 1782-
1841, frames 128, 143, 153, 246, 267, 367, 393]. He was head of a
York County household of 4 "other free" in 1810 [VA:880].

3.   Thomas[1] Poe, born say 1728, sued Peter **Gillett** in York County on 16
September 1751 for a debt due by account. The case was dismissed. The York
County court presented him on 16 November 1761 for concealing two
tithables, on 17 December 1764 for failing to list his wife as a tithable, and on
15 November 1773 for failing to list himself and his unnamed son. On 18 June
1787 the court discharged him from paying taxes, probably due to old age
[Judgments & Orders 1746-52, 473; 1759-63, 298, 312; 1763-5, 320; 1772-4,
437; 1784-7, 468]. He and his wife Sarah Pow, "free Mulattas," registered the
____ 1766 birth of their son Thomas in Bruton Parish [Bruton Parish Register,

30]. He was taxable in York County on 2 tithables, 3 horses and 9 cattle in 1782, 2 horses and 6 cattle in 1785, 2 tithables in 1786, and exempt from personal tax from 1788 to 1792 when he was taxable on 2 horses [PPTL, 1782-1841, frames 69, 92, 109, 131, 143, 164, 184]. On 29 September 1789 he was charged in Brunswick County, Virginia court with horse stealing. Joseph Hill claimed that his black mare was stolen or strayed from the house of a certain William Gray of Greensville on the fourth Thursday in August and that he found her the 28th September and that Fortunatus Sidnor swore in his presence before an alderman of the city of Richmond that he took the mare from Thomas Poe. John Smith deposed that Poe came up to his gate and tied his horse up to his door on 24 August. He asked Poe who he belonged to, where he was from, and where he was going to which Poe replied that he belonged to himself, was from York and was going to Eaton's Ferry on the Roanoke River. The court ordered that he be sent for trial at the district court of Brunswick [Orders 1788-92, 227]. He purchased property by indenture of bargain and sale from John Ferguson acknowledged in York County court on 17 May 1790, and he mortgaged property to Ferguson on 1 June 1790 [Orders 1788-95, 282-3]. Thomas and Sarah were the parents of

    i.   ?David, born say 1755, taxable in York County from 1782 to 1796: taxable on 3 horses and 3 cattle in 1782 and taxable on a slave in 1795 [PPTL, 1782-1841, frames 69, 72, 109, 127, 143, 164, 203, 212].

    ii.   Thomas², born in 1766 [Bruton Parish Register, 30], sent by the York County court to the General Court in Richmond on 15 February 1786 on a charge of breaking and entering the dwelling house of John Peal and stealing property worth 25 shillings [Orders 1784-7, 271]. He was taxable in York County from 1794 to 1800 [PPTL, 1782-1841, frames 203, 231, 257].

    iii.   ?Charles, born say 1767, a 16-21 year old taxable in Thomas Poe's household in 1785 and taxable in his own household in 1788, 1789, 1794 and 1795 [PPTL, 1782-1841, frames 109, 143, 153, 203, 212].

POMPEY FAMILY

1.   John Pompey, born say 1710, was living in Brunswick County, Virginia, on 5 October 1733 when a case brought against him by Miles Thweet was dismissed. He and his wife Anne sued George Smith in court in September 1739, and they were sued for debt by Anthony Haynes and Clement Reed in September 1740. Charles **Valentine** sued him for debt in April 1741. A suit brought against him by Andrew King was dismissed at King's costs in June 1749 [Orders 1732-41, 40, 266, 357, 382, 412, 440, 441, 443; 1741-2, 45; 1745-9, 415, 505]. John and Anne were probably the parents of

    i.   James, born about 1735, a "Negro planter" from Sussex County, Virginia, listed in the Size Roll of Captain Thomas Waggener's Company at Fort Holland in August 1757: *22 years old, 5 feet 4 inches tall* [Clark, *Colonial Soldiers of the South*, 463].

2   ii.   Littleberry, born say 1740.

2.   Littleberry¹ Pompey, born say 1740, was apprenticed to John Quarles on 25 January 1753 when he complained to the Brunswick County, Virginia court against his master for ill treatment and neglecting to teach him a trade. They reached agreement by 26 September 1753 when the case came to trial [Orders 1751-3, 409; 1753-6, 66]. He was living in Sussex County on 11 January 1774 when he and James **Stewart** purchased 270 acres in Meherrin Parish, Brunswick County, to be equally divided between them as if two separate deeds had been made. He purchased 50 acres on the north side of the Meherrin River in Brunswick County adjoining Richard Branscomb and Thomas Evans on 23 November 1778. He purchased 50 acres in Brunswick County on Tomlins Run on 26 January 1778. On the same day he and his wife

Nanny and James **Stewart** sold 135 acres in Brunswick County in Meherrin Parish on **Steward**'s Branch. They were living on land in Brunswick County on the south side of the Meherrin River adjoining Drury **Going** and Rebecca **Stewart** on 10 October 1787 when **Going** sold his land [DB 11:251-3; 13:44-5; 14:366]. Nanny may have been James **Stewart**'s sister and the daughter of Rebecca **Stewart**. Nanny was called a widow when she was taxable in Meherrin Parish, Brunswick County, on a horse from 1787 to 1794 and on a free male tithe and a horse from 1796 to 1800, taxable on a horse in 1801 [PPTL 1782-98, frames 205, 237, 270, 307, 324, 362, 399, 436, 543, 592, 640; 1799-1815, frames 41, 91, 139]. They were probably the parents of

   i.   Mary, head of a Free Town, Brunswick County household of 3 "other free" in 1810 [VA:770].

   ii.   Littleberry[2], born say 1780, taxable in Meherrin Parish, Brunswick County, in 1802 and 1803 [PPTL 1799-1815, frames 196, 258].

   iii. William[2], born say 1790, taxable in Meherrin Parish, Brunswick County, from 1806 to 1810, listed as a "free person of colour" in 1810 and 1811 [PPTL 1799-1815, frames 393, 437, 477, 519, 559, 637, 675], head of a Free Town, Brunswick County household of 1 "other free" in 1810 [VA:770].

3   iv.   Betty, born about 1771.

   v.   Rebecca, born 1776-1794, head of a Free Town, Brunswick County household of 3 "other free" in 1810 [VA:770] and head of Northampton County, North Carolina household of 1 "free colored" in 1820 [NC:250].

   vi.   Maria, married William **Banks**, 9 August 1825 Northampton County, North Carolina bond, Silas **Banks** bondsman.

3.   Betty Pompey, born about 1771, was head of a Brunswick County household of 7 "free colored" in 1820 [VA:666]. She registered as a free Negro in Brunswick County on 26 September 1831: *a free woman of dark complexion about sixty years old five feet four inches high...born free as appears by the evidence of Phebe Harrison* [Wynne, *Register of Free Negroes*, 113]. She may have been the mother of

   i.   Claiborne, born about 1788, listed in Thomas Branscomb's Greensville County, Virginia household from 1810 to 1812, a "Mulatto" taxable in Meherrin Parish, Greensville County, in 1813 [PPTL 1782-1850, frame 445], in a list of "Free Negroes and Mulattoes" in Meherrin Parish, Brunswick County, in 1814 and 1815 [PPTL 1799-1850, frames 675, 732], registered there on 25 August 1823: *a free man of black Complexion five feet 8 Inches high about thirty five Years old...born free as appears from the evidence of Phil Claiborn and by Occupation a farmer*.

   ii.   Peggy, born about 1789, in a list of "free Negroes and Mulattoes" in Meherrin Parish, Brunswick County, in 1813 [PPTL 1799-1815, frame 637], head of a Brunswick County household of 7 "free colored" in 1820 [NC:666]. She registered in Brunswick County on 24 May 1824: *a free woman of a Yellow complection about thirty five years of Age five feet five Inches high...born free in this County as appears from the Evidence of Phil Claiborne*.

   iii. Cresy, born about 1795, head of a Brunswick County household of 4 "free colored" in 1830 [VA:267], registered in Brunswick County on 26 September 1831: *a free woman of dark complexion about thirty six years old five feet two inches high...as appears from evidence of Phebe Harrison*.

   iv.   Caleb, a "Mulatto" taxable in Meherrin Parish, Greensville County, in 1814 [PPTL 1782-1850, frame 464], a "Free Negro" taxable in Meherrin Parish, Brunswick County, in 1815 [PPTL 1799-1815, frame 732].

    v.   Thomas, born 1794-1806, head of a Greensville County, Virginia household of 3 "free colored" in 1820 [VA:264].

    vi. Turner, born about 1800, registered in Greensville County on 10 March 1825: *a free Colored man of a light yellow Complexion about 25 years old, 5'10-5/8 inches high in shoes...by occupation a planter* [Register of Free Negroes, no.137]. He was head of a Brunswick County household of 4 "free colored" in 1830, one of whom was a woman over fifty-five years of age [VA:247].

    vii. Dostin, born about 1802, registered as a free Negro in Brunswick County on 28 July 1823: *a free man of Yellow complexion, about twenty one years of Age Six feet high...born free as appears from the evidence of Phil Claiborne and by Occupation a Carpenter.*

    viii. Rowana, born about 1811, registered on 26 September 1831: *a free woman of dark complexion about twenty years old, five feet two inches high...born free as appears by the evidence of John Wyche.*

    ix. Lucinda, born about 1811, registered on 28 November 1831: *a free woman of dark complexion about twenty years of age, five feet and a half inch high has two small scars on the back of the right hand, and no others perceivable, was born free as appears by the evidence of John Wyche* [Wynne, *Register of Free Negroes*, 67, 112, 119, 120, 195].

Another member of the Pompey family was

    i.   William[1], taxable in St. Luke's Parish, Southampton County from 1805 to 1814: a "f.n." on Ben Jordan's land in 1812, listed with wife Abby in 1813 and 1814 [PPTL 1792-1806, frames 817, 850; 1807-21, frames 77, 175, 200, 323, 423].

PORTIONS FAMILY

Members of the Portions family were

    i.   John Portions, born say 1717, the "Molatto Man" servant of William Moore of Warwick County taken up as a runaway by William Carter who received a certificate for it in York County on 12 October 1738 [W&I 18:457].

    ii. William Pattins, presented by the York County Court on 20 November 1727 for not listing himself as a tithable [DOW 16:489].

PORTIS FAMILY

1.   John Portis, born say 1718, purchased 97 acres in Isle of Wight County on the south side of Lightwood Swamp from John and Bridget **Demmira (Demery)** on 28 October 1745 [DB 7:205]. On 13 June 1754 he (called John Porteus) and John **Demery** were among fourteen heads of household who were sued in Southampton County court by William Bynum (informer) for failing to pay the discriminatory tax on free African American and Indian women.[171] He was fined 1,000 pounds of tobacco, the fine for concealing two tithables, so he probably had two women in his household over the age of sixteen [Orders 1749-54, 500, 512; 1754-9, 5, 22-3, 42-3]. He may have been related to John Portee, Sr., who was taxable on the female members of his household in Granville County, North Carolina in the list of Phil. Pryor in 1762:

    John Portee, Senr., John Portee, Junr., Uriah Portee, Rachael Portee, Milly Portee, Sarah Ason, Lucy Wilson, Basel Wilson [CR 44.701.19].

---

[171]The other householders were Isaac **Young**, Thomas **Wilkins**, Francis **Locust**, James **Brooks**, Jr. and Sr., John **Byrd**, Jr. and Sr., Abraham **Artis**, Lewis **Artis**, William **Brooks**, Ann **Brooks**, and William **Tabor**.

Rachel Portie, Sarah Portie and members of the **Wilson** family were residents of Richland District in 1806 when they petitioned the South Carolina legislature to be exempted from the tax on free Negro women [S.C. Archives series S.165015, item 01885]. John may have been the father of

2   i.   Robert, born say 1740.

2.   Robert Portiss, born say 1740, was one of the freeholders in Edgecombe County, North Carolina, in June 1761 who were ordered to work on the road from Fishing Creek to the road that led to Tarborough [Minutes 1744-62, 24]. He purchased 240 acres on Fishing Creek in Halifax County, North Carolina, on 6 April 1767 [DB 9:490]. Land adjoining his was mentioned in the record of an Edgecombe County estate on 25 February 1793 [Gammon, *Record of Estates, Edgecombe County I:*71]. He was head of an Edgecombe County, North Carolina household of 1 "other free" in 1790 [NC:58], 7 in 1800 (a "Mulatto") [NC:232] and 2 in 1810 [NC:759]. He may have been the father of

    i.   Elizabeth, born say 1759, called a "young Woman of mixed Blood named Bet...of free Parents" in her suit, Portess vs. Hodges, when the Edgecombe County court summoned Thomas Hodges to the November 1780 session to show cause why he held her in slavery [Byrd, *In Full Force and Virtue*, 140]. She was head of an Edgecombe County household of 6 "other free" in 1810 [NC:760].

    ii.   Martin, head of an Edgecombe County household of 2 "other free" in 1810 [NC:759].

    iii. Samuel, head of an Edgecombe County household of 1 "other free" in 1810 [NC:759].

POWELL FAMILY

1.   Margaret Powell, born say 1660, was a servant (no race mentioned) who several times ran away from her master, Captain Barham, and was ordered by the 4 March 1678 Surry County, Virginia court to serve William Gray for six months, apparently because he was the only one she was willing to serve

> *haveing dureing the time shee served Capt. Barham Runaway severall times & now appeareing in Cort and being Willing to serve six months, It is Ordered that shee doe serve ye. said six months.*

On 4 January 1680 she was ordered to serve additional time for having a bastard child while in Gray's service. On 5 September 1682 the court ruled that she was tithable, so she was probably an African American [Haun, *Surry County Court Records*, III:246, 332, 385]. She was taxable in Augustine Hunicutt's household in Chipoaks Precinct of Lawnes Creek Parish in 1681 and in Hansell Bayly's household in 1682 [*Magazine of Virginia Genealogy*, vol.22, no.4, 53, 58]. She may have been the mother of

2   i.   Mary, born say 1695.
3   ii. Stephen[1], born say 1700.

2.   Mary Powell, born say 1695, was called "Mary Powell a mullatto" on 12 June 1755 when the Southampton County court ordered that she be exempt from paying levies [Orders 1754-9, 92]. She may have been the ancestor of

    i.   Elijah, born say 1755, mentioned in the May 1786 Johnston County court which ordered the sheriff to deliver an "orphan" child of his to be bound out [Haun, *Johnston County Court Minutes*, IV:325]. He was head of a Johnston County household of 1 "other free" in 1800, 6 in Chatham County in 1810 [NC:200], and 10 "free colored" in Chatham in 1820 [NC:211]. He was one of the freeholders of Chatham County who were ordered by the court to work on the road from New Hope

Bridge to William Goodwin's in February 1814 [Minutes 1811-18, 147]. His will was proved in Chatham County court on Monday, 13 August 1832.

ii. Nancy, born say 1760, mentioned in the May 1786 session of the Johnston County court which ordered the sheriff to deliver two of her "base born" children to court to be bound out. In September 1789 Stephen **Haithcock** entered into bond for having an illegitimate child by her [Haun, *Johnston County Court Minutes*, III:325; IV:84]. She was head of a Johnston County household of 2 "free colored" in 1820 [NC:259].

iii. Artis, removed from his master Jacob Newsum and bound instead to James Williams by the Southampton County court on 14 July 1785 [Orders 1784-9, 102]. He married Levinia (Viney) **Artis**, with Absolem **Artist**'s consent, 23 July 1800 Southampton County bond, Hanson Pope security, 18 August marriage.

iv. Mason, married Charles **Artis**, 30 December 1801 Southampton County bond, Evans Pope, surety.

v. Blytha, married John **Artis**, 15 February 1802 Southampton County bond, John Pope surety, Evans Pope witness.

vi. Phillis, born say 1785, head of a Southampton County household of 5 "other free" in 1810 [VA:57].

vii. James, head of a Halifax County, North Carolina household of 2 "other free" in 1800 [NC:336] and 8 "free colored" in Northampton County in 1820 [NC:250].

viii. Miles, head of a Northampton County, North Carolina household of 4 "other free" in 1810 [NC:739] and 8 "free colored" in 1820 [NC:250].

ix. Natt, "Free Negro" taxable on one head of cattle in Nansemond County in 1815 [Yantis, *Supplement to the 1810 Census of Virginia*, S-14].

x. Ruth, head of a Johnston County household of 7 "other free" in 1810 [NC:246].

xi. Jacob, born 1776-94, head of a Johnston County household of 1 "other free" in 1800 and 5 "free colored" in 1820 [NC:259]. He married Sally **Dempsey**, 13 December 1819 Halifax County bond, James **Dempsey** bondsman.

3. Stephen[1] Powell, born say 1700, was married to Mary Powell, the daughter of John[1] **Jeffries**, when she was named in her father's 3 November 1746 Albemarle Parish, Surry County will [D&W 1738-54, 798]. He was granted a patent for 195 acres on the north side of the Meherrin River by the side of Horse Meadow Branch in Isle of Wight County on 30 March 1743 [Patents 21:432]. Mary was called "the wife of Stephen Powell" on 14 June 1759 when the Southampton County court ordered that she be exempt from paying levies [Orders 1754-9, 509]. He and his wife Mary sold their land to John Powell by Southampton County deed of 5 July 1765 [DB 3:350-2]. Stephen was head of a Cumberland County, North Carolina household of 3 "Mulatto" tithables in 1767 [*N.C. Genealogy* XXI:3136]. By his 20 December 1780 Johnston County will he left his personal estate to his wife Mary, left his son Stephen his clothes, and left $1 each to his son William and daughters Sarah **Haithcock** and Mary **Reed** [Original at NC Archives]. He was the father of

4 i. Stephen[2], born say 1740.

ii. Sarah **Haithcock**.

iii. Mary **Reed**, perhaps the wife of David **Reid**, head of a Chatham County household of 11 "other free" in 1810 [NC:193].

iv. William[1], born about 1761, head of a Southampton County household of 8 "other free" in 1810 [VA:75]. He married Beedy **Husk**, 23 July 1797 marriage in Southampton County by Rev. Benjamin Barnes, Methodist [Minister's Returns, 648]. He was listed in Southampton County as a "free Negro" with his wife Bedy on Drew Bryant's land in 1813. His wife was called Judah in 1814 [PPTL 1807-21, frames 323, 423]. He registered in Southampton County on 9 June 1818: *age 57, Mulatto, 5 feet 9-1/2 inches, free born* [Register of Free Negroes 1794-1832, no. 1143]. In 1820 he was head of a Northampton County, North Carolina household of one "free colored" born before 1776 [NC:250]. His wife Beedy was probably related to Lewis **Husk**, head of a Northampton County, North Carolina household of 3 "other free" in 1800 [NC:449], and Edward **Husk**, head of an Orange County, North Carolina household of 2 "other free" in 1800 [NC:571].

4. Stephen[2] Powell, born say 1740, entered land on the north side of Black Creek in Johnston County on 1 September 1778 and entered another 150 acres adjoining this land on the north side of White Oak Swamp in August 1780 [Haun, *Johnston County Land Entries*, 23, 142]. In November 1782 he was granted administration on the Johnston County estate of Archibald **Artis** on a bond of 200 pounds [Haun, *Johnston County Court Minutes*, III:232] and was taxable on 150 acres and one poll in Johnston County in 1784 [GA 64.1]. He was about fifty-two years old on 29 February 1792 when he made a deposition in Johnston County court that his son Stephen, aged about eighteen or nineteen years old, enlisted for eighteen months and died in the service in 1783 [*NCGSJ* XIV:234]. He was granted administration on his son's Johnston County estate in November 1792 [Haun, *Johnston County Court Minutes*, IV:234]. He entered 150 acres adjoining his own line on the north side of Whiteoak Swamp in Johnston County on 17 January 1793 [Haun, *Johnston County Land Entries*, no.323]. He was head of a Johnston County household of 11 "other free" in 1790 [NC:142], 11 in 1800, and 4 in Chatham County in 1810 [NC:197]. His children were
    i.   Stephen[3], Jr., born about 1764, died in 1783.
    ii. William[2], head of a Johnston County household of 1 "other free" and 2 slaves in 1810 [NC:246].

A member of the Powell family in Chesterfield County, Virginia, was
    i.   Elizabeth, born say 1745, a "Mulato" bound by the churchwardens to William Bradley until the age of thirty-one. He assigned her to John Almond, but on 1 August 1766 the court ruled that the indenture was not assignable [Orders 1759-67, 748]. She ran away from Almand in December 1768 and he placed an ad in the 11 May 1769 edition of the *Virginia Gazette*: *Run away from the subscriber, some time in December last, a Mulatto woman, named Elizabeth Powell; she is a large woman though not tall. Any person that will take her up, and send the said woman to me, at Goochland Court-house, shall receive three pounds reward, besides what the law allows* [*Virginia Gazette*, Rind edition]. She may have been the mother of several children bound out in Chesterfield County, no parent or race indicated: James Powell, a poor child, who was ordered bound out on 5 July 1771, William Powell who was ordered bound out by the churchwardens of Manchester Parish in June 1784 and Betsy Powell who was ordered bound out by the churchwardens of Manchester Parish in June 1784 but allowed to stay with her unnamed mother [Orders 1771-4, 9; 1774-84, 541, 546].

POWERS FAMILY

1. Betty[1] Powers, born say 1738, appeared in Beaufort County court in September 1756 in her suit against Joseph Adams and his wife. The court ordered that depositions be taken from several persons in Northampton and Bertie counties and that she return to the Adams' service until the case was settled. However, the court dismissed the case in September 1757 because her

proof was insufficient [Minutes 1756-61, 1:14a (Docket #59), 34d (Docket #11)]. She was called "a free Molatto Woman named Bett" in the June 1758 Beaufort County court when the court ordered her to serve two additional years for having two bastard children during her indenture. The same court bound her four-year-old son Simon to Thomas Jasper, and her one-year-old daughter Betty to Mrs. Celia Payton [Minutes 1756-61, 1:46c; 2:46d (June court 1758)]. She was called "Betty Power a free Melatto woman" and was apparently free of her indenture by June court 1761 when she moved by her attorney, William Herritage, that "a negro Boy Named Simon, being formerly Bound to Thos Jasper & he going out of the Country, ..." be Bound to James Calef [Minutes 1756-61, 2:43c]. Her children were

    i.   Simon, born March 1754, according to the June 1758 court minutes.

    ii.   Betty[2], born about December 1756, one year and six months old in June 1758, perhaps the Elizabeth Powers who was head of a Hyde County household of 3 "other free" in 1790 [NC:139]. She may have been the mother of George[2] **Godett**'s daughter Betsy Powers.

2   iii. ?Jeremiah, born say 1759.

2.   Jeremiah Powers, born say 1759, was called a "Free Negroe" by the 13 March 1777 Craven County court when he was charged with entertaining slaves [Minutes 1772-78, 45f]. He was head of a Craven County household of 5 "other free" in 1790 [NC:131] and 6 "free colored" in 1820 [NC:77]. He may have been the father of

    i.   William, born say 1780, married Lucretia **Lewis**, 2 April 1803 Craven County bond, Solomon **Bowers** bondsman.

POYTHRESS FAMILY

1.   Odam Poythress, born about 1755, purchased 50 acres adjoining Peter Nowles and James Sexton in Northampton County, North Carolina, on 3 December 1777, and he and his wife Sele sold this land two years later on 23 August 1779 [6:237, 351]. He was head of a Northampton County household of 4 free males and 4 free females in Captain Williams' District in 1786 for the state census, 9 "other free" in 1790 [NC:72], 12 in 1800 [NC:469], and 10 in 1810 [NC:742]. He purchased 100 acres on Jack Swamp on 9 February 1785 [DB 10:51]. Administration of his estate was granted John Sandifer on 3 December 1817 on a bond of 1,000 pounds [Minutes 1813-21, 68]. His children were probably

    i.   Thomas, who paid money to the Northampton County estate of Robert Crow between January and March 1801 [Gammon, *Record of Estates, Northampton County*, I:120].

    ii.   Littleberry, tithable in Meherrin Parish, Greensville County, Virginia, in 1805, his tax charged to William Dancy [PPTL 1782-1850, frame 336]. He sold land in Northampton County in 1819, two years after Odam's death.

    iii. Francis, who gave Littleberry his power of attorney in Northampton County court on 9 June 1819 [Minutes 1813-21, 177].

2.   Hardimon Poythress, born about 1757, was head of a Northampton County household of 3 free males and 2 free females in Captain Williams' District of the state census and 5 "other free" in 1790 [NC:72]. He died before 7 March 1796 when Jesse Mitchell was granted administration on his estate by the Northampton County court on only 50 pounds bond [Minutes 1792-96, 219]. Temperance Poythress, head of a Northampton County household of 6 "other free" in 1800 [NC:471], was most likely his wife. Their children were probably

    i.   Odam, Jr., who died before 4 March 1817 when his next of kin, John Poythress, was required to show cause why administration on his estate should not be granted to the greatest creditor [Minutes 1792-96, 7].

    ii.   John, whose estate administration was granted Hardimon Poythress in Northampton County court on a bond of 50 pounds [Minutes 1792-6, 18].

Other descendants were

    i.   "Sterling and Lucy Poltress, children of color," bound apprentices to Ransom Sherrin in Halifax County on 15 February 1824.

    ii.   Sebastian and Frances Portres, (paupers) bound out on 4 March 1824 by the Northampton County court [Minutes 1821-25, 373].

PRISS/ PRESS FAMILY

1.   Priscilla, born say 1688, was called "Priss alias Priscilla a Malatta or Mustee bigg with a bastard Child got in Somerset County in Maryland" in Accomack County court on 7 August 1706 when Edward Bagwell "Indian" appeared in court and agreed to have her child bound to him [Orders 1703-9, 75]. Her child was

2   i.   William, born in 1706.

2.   William Priss/ Press, born in 1706, was called "an Indian who was born in Accomack (County) of the body of a free Negro called Priscilla" in March 1730/1 when he was fined 1,000 pounds of tobacco for failing to list himself as a tithable in Northampton County, Virginia. Thomas Fisherman, who was also an Indian, was paid 1,000 pounds of tobacco for informing on him. His mother-in-law, an Indian woman named Ibby, called William a "Mulatto" on 10 October 1732 when she complained to the court that he had beaten and abused her. The court ordered him to post five pounds security for his good behavior towards her [Orders 1732-42, 26, 35; Mihalyka, *Loose Papers* I:239; II:11]. William was apparently the ancestor of the following members of the Press family:

    i.   Littleton, married Molly **Fisherman** 14 December 179_ Northampton County bond, Reubin **Reed** security.

    ii.   Elsey, head of an Accomack County household of 3 "other free" in 1800 [*Virginia Genealogist* 2:160].

    iii. Tabby, married Thomas **Francis**, 26 December 1796 Northampton County bond, Edmund Press security.

    iv. Molly, married Sam **Beavans**, 19 August 1797 Northampton County bond, Abraham **Lang** security.

    v.   Edmund, married to Rachel on 10 April 1793 when they were charged in Northampton County court with breach of the peace by William **Roberts**, Sr. [Minutes 1789-95, 284-5]. He was security for the 24 September 1796 Northampton County marriage of Solomon **Beavans** and Esther **Casey** and head of a Northampton County, Virginia household of 4 "free colored" in 1820 [VA:216A]. He was an "Indian" taxable on a horse in Northampton County in 1812 [PPTL 1782-1823, frame 515].

    vi. ?John, born 15 March 1779, bound by the Northampton County court to William Roberts on 12 December 1792 [Minutes 1789-95, 265], head of a Sussex County, Delaware family of 8 "other free" in 1810 [DE:375].

PRICE FAMILY

1. Elizabeth[1] Price, born say 1675, left a 26 December 1735 Norfolk County will, proved 19 January 1735/6, leaving a bed to her granddaughter Elizabeth, Price, a heifer to her granddaughter Mary Price, a shilling each to her children Susan, William, Edward, Elizabeth, Eleanor and Ann Price, and the remainder to her son Richard Price who was to be her executor [McIntosh, *Brief Abstracts of Norfolk County Wills*, 134]. Her children were

    2   i.   Elizabeth[2], born say 1700.
         ii. Susan.
    3   iii. Richard[1], born say 1705.
    4   iv. William[1], born say 1710.
         v.   Edward.
         vi. Eleanor.
         vii. Ann.

2. Elizabeth[2] Price, born say 1700, was called "Eliza Price Junr." on 20 June 1718 when she was presented by the Norfolk County Grand Jury for bearing a base born child (no race indicated) [DB 10:11, 34, 38]. She was taxable in the household of (her brother) Richard Price in Norfolk County in 1736 [Wingo, *Norfolk County Tithables, 1730-50*, 185]. She may have been the mother of

    5   i.   Elizabeth[3], born say 1718.

3. Richard[1] Price, born say 1705, was a taxable head of a Norfolk County household in the Western Branch District with his brother William Price living near William **Bass** from 1730 to 1732. He was taxable in 1734 and taxable with (his sister) Eliza Price in 1736 [Wingo, *Norfolk County Tithables, 1730-50*, 20, 39, 71, 138, 185]. He was the father of

    6   i.   John[1], born say 1735.

4. William[1] Price, born say 1710, was taxable in the Norfolk County household of his brother Richard Price in Western Branch District from 1730 to 1732, taxable in his own household in 1734, and taxable with his unnamed wife in 1736 [Wingo, *Norfolk County Tithables, 1730-50*, 20, 39, 71, 138, 183]. They may have been the parents of

         i.   Richard[2], head of a Halifax County, North Carolina household of 8 "other free" in 1810 [NC:40].

5. Elizabeth[3] Price, born say 1718, was a "Mullatto" bound to Martha Reding in April 1743 when the Pasquotank County, North Carolina court ordered that she serve her mistress an additional year for having a child born four to six months previous. The court also bound her unnamed child to Reding until the age of thirty-one [Haun, *Pasquotank County Court Minutes 1737-46*, 108]. Martha Reding was the widow of Joseph Reding who was probably related to the Redding family of Norfolk County [Pasquotank County court Minutes 1737-55, April court 1744; Wingo, *Norfolk County Tithables, 1730-50*, 130]. Elizabeth was probably the mother of a "Malatto" girl named Kesiah Price who was bound by the Pasquotank County court to Jonathan Reding until the age of thirty-one in July 1751. In December 1755 the court bound Elizabeth's daughter Rachel (no race indicated) to Jonathan Reding [Minutes 1751-2, July court, n.p.; 1755-77, last page of December court]. Her children were

         i.   ?Kesiah, a "Malatto" bound to Jonathan Reding in July 1751.
    7   ii. Rachel, born say 1755.

6. John[1] Price, born say 1735, sold two tracts of swamp land of 50 acres each near the head of the Western Branch in Norfolk County for a total of 8 pounds, 5 shillings on 15 January 1759. He made his mark and his wife Mary

signed. And he sold another 1-1/2 acres of land in the same area for thirty shillings on 24 October 1759, explaining in the deed that it was land which formerly belonged to his father Richard Price and that he had purchased it from William Price who was Richard's brother [DB 18:175; 19:37a&b]. He was taxable in the Norfolk County household of John **Bass** in 1756 and 1757, in his own Western Branch District household in 1759, with his wife Mary in 1761, taxable on 50 acres in 1765, taxable on himself and his wife in 1767, and by himself in 1769 and 1770. He probably died before 1771 when Mary was taxable on 50 acres [Wingo, *Norfolk County Tithables, 1730-50*, 100, 115, 135, 171, 190; 1766-80, 15, 88, 106, 150]. They may have been the parents of

    i.   John², taxable on a horse in Portsmouth and Elizabeth River Parishes, Norfolk County, from 1790 to 1817: listed as a "M"(ulatto) from 1800 to 1804; taxable on 2 free males when he was a shoemaker living in Portsmouth in a list of "free Negroes and Mulattoes" in 1801; taxable on 2 free males in 1804; taxable on a slave in 1811; 2 free males, a slave, and a two-wheel carriage in 1812; in a list of "free Negroes and Mulattoes" in 1813; a "B.M." (Black Man) living in Portsmouth in 1815 when he was taxable a slave over 16 and a two-wheel riding carriage [PPTL, 1782-1791, frame 688; 1791-1812, frames 26, 145, 379, 383, 434, 468, 779; 1813-24, frames 109, 264].

    ii.   William², taxable on a horse in Portsmouth and Elizabeth River Parishes from 1791, to 1812: called a "M"(ulatto) from 1800 to 1804; a labourer living on Western Branch when he was in a list of "free Negroes and Mulattoes" in 1801; taxable on 2 free tithes and a horse in 1803 and 1804; taxable on a slave in 1805 and 1812 [PPTL, 1791-1812, frames 26, 360, 379, 383, 434, 468, 487, 565, 778].

    iii.   James, a "Molato" taxable in the household of (his brother-in-law and sister?) Edward and Sarah **Wiggins** in the 1774 Bertie County, North Carolina tax list of Samuel Granberry [CR 10.702.1, box 3]. He was taxable in Portsmouth and Elizabeth River Parishes in Norfolk County from 1790 to 1817: a labourer living on Western Branch in a list of "free Negroes and Mulattoes" in 1801; called a "M"(ulatto) in 1802; called a "B.M." (Black Man) in 1815 [PPTL, 1791-1812, frames 26, 383, 434; 1813-24, frames 110, 266].

    iv.   Stephen, taxable in Portsmouth and Elizabeth River Parishes from 1790 to 1817: listed as a "N"(egro) in 1797, a "M"(ulatto) in 1800, a labourer living on Western Branch when he was in a list of "free Negroes and Mulattoes" in 1801 [PPTL, 1791-1812, frames 26, 231, 383, 434; 1813-24, frames 265].

    v.   Nancy, married Nelson **Bass** 9 December 1817 Norfolk County bond, James Price surety.

    vi.   Sally, a "free woman of colour," married John Gibbs **Bass**, a "free man of colour," 12 August 1812 Norfolk County bond, William **Bass** surety.

7.   Rachel Price, born say 1755, was living in Gates County in August 1798 when the court bound out her sons Benjamin and Robert [Fouts, *Minutes, Gates County*, I:202]. She was head of a Chowan County household of 2 "other free" in 1810 [NC:534] and 3 "free colored" in Edenton in 1820 [NC:320]. She was the mother of

    i.   ?Demsey, born say 1774, head of a Camden County household of 3 "other free" and one white woman in 1800 [NC:97].

    ii.   ?Samuel, born say 1776, head of an Onslow County household of 1 "other free" and 3 slaves in 1800 [NC:163].

    iii.   ?Aaron, head of a Pasquotank County household of 3 "other free" in 1810 [NC:921].

iv. Benjamin, born about 1787, bound as an apprentice farmer to Willis Brown in Gates County by the August 1798 court.

v. Robert, born about 1789, bound as an apprentice farmer to Willis Brown in Gates County.

vi. John[3]/ Jack, born about 1797, illegitimate son of Rachel Price who was bound to George Williams by the Gates County court in August 1799 [Fouts, *Minutes, Gates County,* I:247].

PRICHARD FAMILY

1. Herbert[1] Prichard, born say 1690, was living in Bertie County on 14 May 1738 when the Bertie County court ordered him, Henry **Bunch**, and other freeholders to lay out a road from Connaritsa Swamp to the road leading to Wills Quarter Swamp [Haun, *Bertie County Court Minutes,* I:118]. His 23 September 1738 Bertie County will, proved in February 1738/9, appointed Jonathan Standley, Jr., his executor and gave his land and plantation to his sons John and William. The will was witnessed by Ann Williams [SS 1724-43, no. 95]. His children were

     i. John, born say 1720, a taxable "Free Mulatto Male" in the 1763 list of Jonathan Standley in Edward Callum's household and a "free male molattor" head of his own household in Standley's 1764 list [CR 10.702.1]. He purchased land from Jonathan Standley by deed proved in Bertie court in 1772 and sold land to his brother William by deed proved later that year [DB L:329; M:10]. He was taxed on an assessment of 121 pounds in the 1778 county summary and on 173 acres in Wynn's and King's District in 1779.

2   ii. William, born say 1725.

3   iii. James[1], born say 1730.

4   iv. ?Herbert[2], born say 1738.

2. William Prichard, born say 1725, purchased land by deed proved in Bertie County in 1762 and 1766, and purchased land from his brother John in 1772 [DB K:228; L:90; M:10]. He was a taxable "Free Mulatto Male" in the 1763 list of Jonathan Standley in William Holland's household and a "free male molattor" head of his own household in Standley's 1764, 1769, and 1771 list. He and his brothers probably married white women since their wives were never taxed in Bertie County [CR 10.702.1].[172] His Bertie County will was proved in February 1775 and named his wife Christian and children [Dunstan, *The Bertie Index,* 1927]. Christian was taxed on an assessment of 157 pounds in the 1778 summary list and 300 acres in the 1779 list for Wynn's and King's District. His children were

     i. ?Richard, born say 1749, a "White Servant" taxable in William's household in the 1765 list of Jonathan Standley.

    ii. Jonathan, head of a white Bertie County household of 2 males and 4 females in 1790 [NC:14]. He married Patsy **Butler**, 2 February 1797 Bertie County bond.

   iii. Christopher, head of a white Bertie County household of 2 males in 1790 [NC:14].

   iv. Mary.

    v. Ruth.

   vi. Keziah, married John **Butler**, 27 December 1797 Bertie County bond, her brother Christopher Prichard bondsman.

---

[172]The white wives of free African Americans were taxable, but the courts of many counties seemed to be unsure of this.

3.   James[1] Prichard, born say 1730, was a taxable "Free Mulatto Male" in the
      1763 list of Jonathan Standley in John Higges' household. He purchased land
      by deed proved in Bertie County in 1763 [DB K:236]. On 29 March 1770
      Nathan **Cobb**, sixteen-year-old orphan of John **Cobb**, was bound to him to be
      a cooper [CR 010.101.7 by *NCGSJ* XIV:34] and Nathan was listed as a "Free
      Malletor" in his household in the 1770 list of Jonathan Standley. He was taxed
      on an assessment of 191 pounds in the 1778 summary list and on 150 acres in
      an untitled 1779 list. James' will, proved in May 1786 Bertie County court,
      named his wife Dorcas and children [Dunstan, *The Bertie Index*, 1927]:
      i.   Reuben/ Rigdon, born say 1765. He married Ann **Bunch**, 29 February
            1792 Bertie County bond with James Prichard bondsman. He sold 50
            acres on Connaritsa Swamp (which he received by his father's will?)
            on 29 January 1797 to his brother James [DB R:361].
      ii.   James[2], head of a white Bertie County household of 2 males and one
            female in 1790 [NC:14]. His Bertie will was proved in November 1807
            and named his children: Absilla, Solomon, James[3], and David
            [Dunstan, *The Bertie Index*, 1927].

4.   Herbert[2] Prichard, born say 1738, may have been a son of Herbert[1] Prichard,
      but he was not named in his will. He was a taxable "Free Mulatto Male" in
      the 1763 list of Jonathan Standley in Jonathan Robson's household. He
      purchased 105 acres adjoining his own line, Thomas **Wilson**'s, and William
      Leviner's by a deed proved in December 1763 by Jeremiah **Bunch**. He
      purchased 100 acres on Pellmell Pocosin in December 1766 [DB K:245;
      L:44]. In 1767 he was taxed in Standley's list as a free white head of
      household and a "Free Mallator" head of household in Standley's 1769 list. In
      1775 he was a "free mulatto" in Peter Clifton's list. He purchased 250 acres
      at the mouth of Poplar Branch on 30 May 1774 and 200 acres on the north
      side of White Oak Swamp on 11 May 1778 [DB M:161, 350]. He was taxable
      on an assessment of 165 pounds in the 1778 Bertie summary list and was taxed
      in two districts in 1779, 200 acres in Wynn's and King's District and 100
      acres in Thomas Ward's list for Captain Walton's District. He was witness to
      numerous deeds which he proved in Bertie court and was several times called
      upon to settle the estates of Bertie residents [Haun, *Bertie County Court
      Minutes*, V:477; VI: 707, 732, 746, 755, 757, 758, 806, 807, 843, 878, 917].
      He purchased a further 300 acres near the Chowan River on 22 March 1782
      and 217 acres for 235 pounds on 17 December 1797 [DB M:541; R:404]. The
      February 1789 Bertie County court ordered a "Mollatto child" Polly **Carter**
      bound to him because her master, Robert Rawlings, was treating her badly
      [Haun, *Bertie County Court Minutes*, VI:734]. His Bertie County will, proved
      in May 1797, named his wife Elizabeth, executor, and his children [Dunstan,
      The Bertie Index, 1926]. His heirs purchased a half-acre lot, no. 91, in the
      town of Colerain on 10 August 1799 [DB S:102]. His children were
      i.   Absolem, born say 1770, purchased land by deeds proved in Bertie in
            1789 and sold land by deeds proved in 1798 [DB S:10, 46, 47]. He
            married Sarah Brown, 25 January 1800 Bertie County bond.
      ii.   Zadock.
      iii. Hugh.
      iv.   Martha.

PROCTOR FAMILY

The Proctor family of North Carolina may have originated in Charles County,
Maryland, where Elizabeth Proctor had a "Mollatto" child named Charles about
1705. There was also a Mary Procter who was indicted by the Loudoun County,
Virginia court for cohabiting with a "Negro" named Peter, the slave of Thomas
Kelly, and having a "Mulatto" child [Orders 1757-62, 233]. Members of the family
in North Carolina were

1   i. Joseph, born before 1776.
      ii. Edward, born before 1776, head of a Craven County household of 2 "free colored" in 1820 [NC:65].

1. Joseph Proctor, born before 1776, was head of a Granville County household of 2 "free colored" men and 6 slaves in 1820 [NC:24]. He may have been the father of
    i. Lucy, born say 1795, married Jones **Thomasson**, 25 December Granville County bond, Bannester Royster surety.
    ii. Charles, born 1794-1776, head of a Granville County household of 1 "free colored" in 1820 [NC:24]. He was called Charles M. Proctor when he married Tabitha Simmons, 18 May 1821 Granville County bond, Benjamin Davis bondsman.

PRYOR FAMILY

1. Alice Pryor, born say 1745, was the mother of Leviny Pryor who registered as a free person in King George County on 7 September 1820. She was the mother of
2   i. Leviny, born about 1764.
    ii. ?George, born about 1764, registered in Augusta County on 23 February 1824: *of a light black colour, aged 60 years, 5 feet 8 inches high* [Register, no. 80].
    iii. ?Syllah, born say 1772, mother of Winny Pryor who registered in King George County on 23 August 1820: *daughter of Syllah Pryor, a bright mulatto woman, about 28 years of age, about 5 feet 4 inches high...born free in the County of King George* [Register of Free Persons, no.60].
3 iv. ?Joseph, born before 1776.
    v. ?Andrew, born about 1775, registered in King George County on 12 January 1775: *a black man, about twenty two years old and about five feet six inches high, was born of a free woman and served to the age of twenty one years with Richard Potes of this County* [Register, no.6].

2. Leviny Pryor, born about 1764, registered in King George County on 7 September 1820: *daughter of Alice Prior, a very dark mulatto about 56 years of age...born free in the county of King George* [Register of Free Persons, no.61]. She was the mother of
    i. Milly, born about 1783, registered in King George County on 7 September 1820: *Daughter of the above named Leviny, about 37 years of age, 4 11/12 feet high - was born free in this County* [Register no.62].
    ii. ?Tabathy, head of a Hanover County household of 3 "other free" in 1810 [VA:852].

3. Joseph Pryor, born before 1776, was head of a Halifax County, North Carolina household of 8 "other free" in 1810 [NC:39] and 5 "free colored" in 1820 [NC:162]. He was probably the father of
    i. Peter, head of a Halifax County, North Carolina household of 1 "other free" in 1810 [NC:39].

PUGH FAMILY

1. Sarah[1] Pugh, born say, 1730, was a "free molatto" Bertie County taxable in 1763 [CR 010.702.1, box 1]. Her children were
    i. Pen, born about 1748, the nine-year-old daughter of Sarah Pugh, a "Free Mullattoe," bound to Margaret Dukinfield on 27 January 1756 [CR 010.101.7 by *NCGSJ* XIII:169]. She was called "a mulatoe girl

aged 17 years" when she was bound to John Pearson in Bertie County on 27 June 1766 [*NCGSJ* (1988):32]. She may have been the Penelope Pugh who married Thomas Whitmell, Jr., (a white man), 20 October 1768 Bertie County bond.

2   ii.   Isaac, born about 1750.

      iii.   Mary, born about 1755, the four-year-old minor of Sarah Pugh, bound to James Jones on 26 July 1759 [*NCGSJ* XIII:171], taxable in her own household in George Lockhart's list for Bertie County in 1774.

      iv.   ?Jesse, born about 1755, a "free Mulatto" taxable in John Pearson's Bertie County household in 1767.

      v.   David, born about 1757, the two-year-old minor of Sarah Pugh, bound to James Jones on 26 July 1759 to be a cooper [*NCGSJ* XIII:169]. He was head of a Hertford County household of 6 "other free" in 1800 and was listed in the roster of soldiers from North Carolina in the American Revolution.

      vi.   Arthur, born about 1761, described as a Mulatto bastard of Sarah when he was bound as an apprentice cooper to James Holley on 30 March 1767 [Haun, *Bertie County Court Minutes*, III:765]. He was listed in the roster of soldiers from North Carolina in the American Revolution.

      vii.   ?Sarah[2], born about 1762, ordered bound to Mrs. Pearson in August 1777, parent and race not identified.

      viii.   ?Darbe, born about 1768, ordered bound to Mrs. Pearson in August 1777, parent and race not identified [Haun, *Bertie County Court Minutes*, IV:241].

2.   Isaac Pugh, born about 1750, the six-year-old son of Sarah Pugh, was bound to Margaret Dukinfield in Bertie County on 27 January 1756. He was head of a "Mulatto" household in Buxton's list for Nansemond County, Virginia, in 1784 (number of persons in household not recorded) [VA:74] and a "Free Negro" taxable on one head of cattle and 6 horses in Nansemond County in 1815 [Yantis, *Supplement to the 1810 Census of Virginia*, S-14]. He was probably the ancestor of

      i.   Jasper, head of a Norfolk County household of 6 "other free" in 1810 [VA:841].

      ii.   Toney, a "Free Negro" taxable on 3 slaves, one head of cattle, and 11 horses at "B. Church" in Nansemond County in 1815 [Yantis, *Supplement to the 1810 Census of Virginia*, S-14].

      iii.   Sarah[3], born about 1780, registered in Norfolk County on 16 December 1811: *5 feet 6 1/2 In. 31 years of age of a Yellowish Complexion with a scar on her forehead, Born free* [Register of Free Negros & Mulattos, #67].

PURSLEY FAMILY

1.   Ann Pursley, born say 1715, was living in Cople Parish on 30 June 1736 when the Westmoreland County, Virginia court convicted her of having a "Mulato" child [Orders 1731-9, 252a]. She was the ancestor of

      i.   Jeremiah, an overseer for William Weatherspoon, counted in "A List of Free Mulattoes & Negroes" in Westmoreland County in 1800.

      ii.   Baker Purse, a gardener for Taker Carter, counted in "A List of Free Mulattoes & Negroes" in Westmoreland County in 1801 [*Virginia Genealogist* 31(1987):42], head of a Westmoreland County household of 1 "other free" in 1810.

      iii.   ?James Percey, a taxable in Bladen County with Gilbert **Cox** in 1770 [Byrd, *Bladen County Tax Lists*, I:34].

RAINS FAMILY

Members of the Rains/ Reins family were

    i.   Robert Reins, head of a Norfolk County household of 9 "other free" in 1810 [VA:839], probably identical to Robert Rains, a "free negro" farmer listed with his unnamed wife, "a free negro woman," in Hardy County in 1813 [Waldrep, *1813 Tax List*].

1   ii.   Bethena, born about 1779.

    iii.   Hannah Rains, head of a Spotsylvania County household of 2 "other free" in 1810. She was counted in a list of "Free Negroes & Mulattoes" in Fredericksburg in 1813 [Waldrep, *1813 Tax List*].

1.   Bethena Reines, born about 1779, registered in Essex County on 10 August 1829: *born free by cert. of Richard Rowzee, dark Mulattoe, 50 years of age, 5 feet 2 inches* [Register of Free Negroes 1810-43, p.72, no.163]. She was the mother of

    i.   Polly, born about 1802, registered in Essex County on 10 August 1829: *born free by cert. of Richard Rowzee, bright Mulattoe, 27 years of age, 5 feet 5-1/8 inches.*

    ii.   Catherine, born about 1804, registered in Essex County on 10 August 1829: *born free by cert. of Richard Rowzee, bright Mulattoe, 25 years of age, 5 feet 5-7/8 inches* [Register of Free Negroes 1810-43, p.73, nos.165-6].

RALLS FAMILY

1.   Rebecca Ralls, born say 1720, complained to the Caroline County court on 13 October 1768 that Mary Stevens was detaining her children, but in April 1769 the court ordered that her children Hampton, Harry, and Cloe serve her mistress until the age of thirty-one. She was called "Beck, a Mulatto" in the suit brought by her son Harry for freedom from Mary Stevens in July 1771 [Orders 1768-70, 262, 292, 315; 1771-2, 244]. Rebecca was the mother of

    i.   Harry, born about 1739 according to Muriah Mullin who testified for him in his suit for freedom from Mary Stevens in Caroline County court on 14 June 1771. She stated further that he was "the whitest child she ever saw to have so dark a Mother and that she was sure it was a white man's child" [Orders 1771-2, 221, 244-5, 301, 371].

    ii.   ?John Ralls/ Rolls, born about 1739 in Caroline County, a "free man of colour" living in Culpeper County in 1779 when he enlisted in the Revolution. He was about eighty-two years old and had been living alone in Shenandoah County for "some years" before 9 January 1821 when he made a declaration to obtain a pension. David Jamison, a justice of the peace in Culpeper County, testified for him, noting that John had been one of four brothers and a sister in the county, and that he had had a wife and children living there while he was in the service [M804-2079, frame 0520; Revolutionary Army, vol. 1, Register 1777-1783, LVA accession number 24296, cited by NSDAR, *African American Patriots*, 153].

    iii.   Hampton, perhaps identical to "Hampton, a Negro boy belonging to John & Mary Stevens born January the 20th 1746." The birth date was recorded in Harry Rall's petition for his freedom in 1771. Hampton petitioned for his freedom from Edward Stevens in October 1772 (no race indicated), but the court ruled that he was not entitled to his freedom until 20 January 1777 [Orders 1772-6, 143, 160, 164, 225].

    iv.   Cloe, born say 1750.

Their descendants were probably:

    i.   Samuel Rawls, "free black" taxable in Orange County, Virginia, in 1813 [Waldrep, *1813 Tax List*].

    ii.   Agatha Rolls, a "Mulatto" taxable in Culpeper County in 1813 [Waldrep, *1813 Tax List*].

RANDALL FAMILY

Members of the Randall family of Virginia were

    i.   George, head of a Prince William County household of 12 "other free" in 1810 [VA:508].

    ii.   Robert, head of a Norfolk County household of 8 "other free" in 1810 [VA:917].

    iii.   Thomas, head of a Norfolk County household of 2 "other free" and a slave in 1810 [VA:802].

    iv.   Mason, head of a Frederick County household of 2 "other free" in 1810 [VA:513].

    v.   Lucy, born about 1795, registered as a free Negro in Botetourt County on 10 June 1836: *41 years of age; Mulatto...Born free as per Order of Botetourt Court April Term 1814* [Free Negroes &c Registered in the Clerk's Office of Botetourt County, no. 93].

RANGER FAMILY

1.   Mary Range, born say 1722, was the servant of Winder Kenner on 11 August 1740 when she was convicted in Northumberland County court of having an illegitimate "mulatto" child. On 14 December 1741 the court ordered her sold for five years. She was the ancestor of

    i.   Nicholas Ringe, born 13 November 1741, "Mulato son to Mary" [Fleet, *Northumberland County Record of Births*, 76]. Nicholas Ranger was taxable in Prince William County from 1793 to 1802 [PPTL, 1782-1810, frames 236, 261, 316, 446, 464, 511].

    ii.   Hannah Range, born 9 March 1744, "Daugr. to Mary Born a Mullatto" [Fleet, *Northumberland County Record of Births*, 76].

    iii.   ?Solomon Ranger, taxable in Prince William County from 1793 to 1809, called a "Free Black" in 1799 [PPTL, 1782-1810, frames 237, 342, 407, 445, 511, 668], head of a Prince William County household of 4 "other free" in 1810 [VA:508].

    iv.   ?Joseph Rantger, an African American seaman in the Revolution from Northumberland County who moved to Elizabeth City County [NSDAR, *African American Patriots*, 153; Jackson, *Virginia Negro Soldiers*, 42]. Joseph Ranger was in a list of "free negroes & mulattoes" in Elizabeth City County in 1813 [Waldrep, *1813 Tax List*].

RANN FAMILY

1.   Matthew[1] Rann, born say 1740, was mentioned in a 3 September 1767 letter from Anthony Armistead of Northampton County, North Carolina, to Col. Samuel Benton, clerk of Granville County. Armistead wrote: *Mathew Ran, while he Lived with me got in my debt...he's now Run away and is got with old William Chavers, or one Asa Tiner that Married his daughter... old Chavers Lives in Granville or Bute County...(Mathew Ran is a Lusty Man... a Carpenter by Trade and Squints)* [CR 44.928.8 by *NCGSJ* XI:35]. He may have been the father of

2   i.   Mary, born say 1768.

3   ii.   Michael, born say 1770.

2.   Mary Rann, born say 1768, was living in Southampton County on 15 July 1799 and 22 July 1800 when the court ordered the overseers of the poor in the

lower district of Nottoway Parish to bind out her children Matthew, Archer, Patty, Isaac, and Betty [Minutes 1799-1803, 25, 103, 108]. She was head of a Southampton County household of 8 "other free" in 1810 [VA:60]. She was listed in St. Luke's Parish, Southampton County, in 1813 with her daughters Disey and Nanny on Henry Blow's land [PPTL 1807-21, frames 324]. She was the mother of

    i.   Matthew², born about 1785, a "poor child of Mary Ran," ordered by the Southampton County court bound to John P. Pettway on 15 July 1799. He registered in Southampton County on 5 September 1809: *age 27, light complexion, 5 feet 6 inches, free born.* He registered again on 31 July 1810: *age 28, Dark Mulatto, 5 feet 6 inches, free born.* And he registered again on 14 November 1816: *age 31, Dark Mulatto, 5 feet 7 inches, free born* [Register of Free Negroes 1794-1832, no. 435, 449, 765, 1036].

    ii.   Disey, born about 1786, registered in Southampton County on 6 July 1810: *age 24, yellow (Colour), 5 feet 4 inches, free born.* She registered again on 24 December 1823: *age 36, dark complection, 5 feet 4-1/2 inches, free born* [Register of Free Negroes 1794-1832, nos. 561, 1430].

    iii.   Sam, born about 1786, son of Mary Rand who complained to the Southampton County court on 20 February 1804 about the treatment he was receiving from his master Sam Calvert. The court ordered Benjamin Lewis to take the boy into his care until the case was heard, and on 18 September 1804 the court ordered the overseers of the poor to take him into their care [Minutes 1803-4, unpaged]. Sam registered in Southampton County on 31 July 1810: *age 24, Dark Mulatto, 5 feet 9-1/2 inches, free born.* He registered again on 7 July 1813 and 11 June 1816 [Register of Free Negroes 1794-1832, no. 770, 818, 1012].

    iv.   Patty, born say 1790, ordered bound out to Samuel Kello on 22 July 1800.

    v.   Archer, born about 1791, ordered bound out to Samuel Kello on 22 July 1800. He registered in Southampton County on 22 April 1813: *age 22, yellow (Colour), 5 feet 6-1/4 inches, born of free parents* [Register of Free Negroes 1794-1832, no. 815].

    vi.   Betty, born about 1792, ordered bound out to William Blow on 22 July 1800. She registered in Southampton County on 1 April 1822: *Betsey Williams formerly Rann, age 30, 5 feet 2 inches, free born* [Register of Free Negroes 1794-1832, no. 1312].

    vii.   Isaac, born about 1793, ordered bound out to Isaac Hill on 22 July 1800. He was a "Mullatto boy" accused in Southampton County court on 20 January 1806 of stealing $5 from a boy slave named Burwell belonging to James Crichlow. Mason **Chavis** was a witness against him. He was sent to the district court in Suffolk for trial [Minutes 1799-1803, 85]. He registered in Southampton County on 26 July 1815: *age 22, yellow complexion, 5 feet 10-1/4 inches, free born* [Register of Free Negroes 1794-1832, no. 964]. He was a "f.n." taxable in Nottoway Parish, Southampton County, in 1818 [PPTL 1807-31, frame 650].

    viii.   Nancy, poor child of Mary Rand, ordered bound apprentice in Southampton County on 23 November 1803 [Minutes 1803-4, unpaged]. She was over the age of sixteen when she was listed in her mother's household in 1813.

3.   Michael Rann, born say 1770, was taxable in St. Luke's Parish, Southampton County, in Lazarus Cook's household from 1794 to 1796 [PPTL 1792-1806, frame 76, 185]. He was head of Northampton County, North Carolina household of 6 "other free" in 1800 [NC:473], 7 in Halifax County in 1810 [NC:44], and 8 "free colored" in Halifax in 1820 [NC:163]. He was in the

First Company detached from the Halifax County Regiment in the War of 1812 [N.C. Adjutant General, *Muster Rolls of the War of 1812*, 19]. On 18 May 1841 the Halifax County court ordered William and Joseph Rand bound as apprentices to him. His 10 November 1847 Halifax County will was proved in November 1850. He left his children Mary and Willis Ran his property as well as his portion of the estate of his deceased wife Cloe Ran, formerly Cloe **Newsom**. He claimed a share of the estate of her brother James **Newsom** who died intestate in Ohio about 1835-1837. Fred A. McWilliams of Halifax County was his executor as well as his agent to recover his claim on James **Newsom**'s Ohio estate [WB 4:295]. His children were

   i.   Maria, born 1806-20, head of a Halifax County household of 3 "free colored" in 1830.
   ii. ?James, born 1806-20, head of Halifax County household of one "free colored" in 1830.
   iii. Willis, born 1806-20, head of Halifax County household of one "free colored" in 1830.

RAPER FAMILY

1. Hannah Raper, born say 1710, was living with her son William Raper when he made his 6 June 1787 Charleston, South Carolina will. She was the mother of

   i.   William, Born say 1730.
   ii. Ruth, born say 1735, married Thomas **Cole**.

1. William Raper, born say 1730, married Susanna **Cole**, "Mulattoes," in St. Philip's Parish, Charleston. He was executor of the 21 October 1771 Charleston will of his brother-in-law Thomas **Cole**. He called himself a bricklayer in his own 6 June 1787 Charleston will which was proved 27 October 1787. He allowed his mother Hannah the use of a room in his house on the east side of Meeting Street, left his wife Susanna a slave named Ichabod and the use of three other slaves who were to go to his granddaughter Elizabeth Susanna **Gardner** after his wife's death. He left his house on Meeting Street to his daughter Ruth **Gardener**. He also provided for the emancipation of one of his slaves, a "Mulatto Boy named John," the son of Tamer, when he reached the age of twenty-five years. He named his wife, son-in-law George **Gardener**, and John Webb executors [WB 14:109-10; 22:194-6]. The account of his estate returned by his wife in 1788 included nine slaves [Inventories B:15-16]. William and Susanna were the parents of

   i.   Ruth, married George **Gardner**.

RATCLIFF FAMILY

1. Mary Ratcliff, born say 1733, was living in Truro Parish, Fairfax County, on 20 March 1753 when the court ordered the churchwardens to bind her "Mulatto" son Ned to Thomas Sorrell [Orders 1749-54]. She was the ancestor of

   i.   Ned, born say 1753.
   ii. ?Sarah Ratliff, born 1776-1794, head of a Guilford County, North Carolina household of 8 "free colored" in 1820 [NC:115].

RAWLINSON FAMILY

1. Elizabeth[1] Rawlinson, born say 1663, was the servant of Ralph Flowers in November 1684 when she confessed to the York County court that she had an illegitimate child by John Hall [DWO 6:606]. She may have been the mother of

2   i.   Elizabeth[2], born say 1684.

2. Elizabeth² Rawlinson, born say 1684, was presented by the Grand Jury of York County, Virginia, on 20 November 1727 for not listing herself as a tithable. She owed William Timson 3 pounds, 10 shillings according to the settlement of his York County estate recorded on 21 February 1725/6. Perhaps she was the mother of a "Mollatto Servt. boy to be free" who was listed in the inventory of the York County estate of Captain William Timson (of Queen's Creek) on 11 November 1719. Elizabeth's 4 October 1748 Bruton Parish, York County will was proved on 17 December 1750. She left her estate to her son John Rollinson and a shilling each to her son George Rollinson and daughter Joanna Inscho [OW 13:19, 51; 15, pt. 2, 354, 374, 491-2, 515; 16, pt. 2, 373, 489; Wills & Inventories 1746-1759, 197-8]. She was the mother of

    i.   George, born say 1705, apparently married Tabitha **Gibson**, who received a girl slave named Nanny by the 7 September 1726 Charles City County will of (her father?) Gibby **Gibson**. He was called George Rollison when he received a girl slave named Nanny by the 6 May 1727 distribution of the estate [DW 1724-31, 161-2, 167].

    3   ii. ?Elizabeth³, born say 1708.

    iii. Joanna **Insco**, born say 1710, presented by the York County court on 20 November 1727 for not listing herself as a tithable, called Joanna Inscow alias Rollinson on 16 July 1733 when she was presented by the churchwardens of Bruton Parish. On 21 June 1736 she was presented for having a bastard child. On 15 December 1735 Isaac Bee was presented for not listing her as a tithable, and on 15 May 1738 she was presented for not listing herself. On 21 August 1738 she proved to the court that she was "not a Molatto," but she was again presented for not listing herself as a tithable on 19 January 1746/7 [OW 18:60, 67, 293, 414, 440, 489, 499; 19:486]. She may have been identical to Hannah Insco who sued Thomas Dickson, administrator of Isaac Bee's estate [OW 19:249]. On 17 December 1753 a deed to her from her son John **Insco** was proved in York County [Judgments & Orders 1752-4, 363].

    iv. John, born in 1725, chosen by his nephew John **Insco** as his guardian in York County court on 17 November 1746 [OW 19:474]. He was called a "Mulatto" by the York County court on 1 November 1748 when he was presented for not listing his wife and mother as taxables. He sued John Glass for debt in York County court on 15 May 1749 and was security for George Kerby's appearance at court on 18 November 1751. Humphrey **Jones** brought a suit in chancery against him on 17 August 1752 in which the parties by their counsel agreed that the plaintiff and a witness named Thomas **Carter** were "Mulattos." The court ruled that the lease involved in the suit was obtained fraudulently and was, therefore, cancelled. John appealed to the General Court. Humphrey **Jones** sued him for a 93 pound, 16 shilling debt on 19 November 1753 [Judgments & Orders 1746-52, 101, 112, 141, 153, 156, 163, 182, 491; 1752-4, 119, 153, 166, 168, 170-1, 178, 196, 285, 343-4, 353, 495]. His 6 February 1780 Bruton Parish, York County will was proved on 16 October 1780. He left 500 pounds to Elizabeth Garrett for her services, 500 pounds to Samuel Garrett when he came of age, 100 pounds to Judith and Sarah Garrett when they arrived at eighteen years, and the remainder of his estate to his son Hulett Rollinson and his daughter Elizabeth, wife of William Cole. His inventory included eight houses in Williamsburg, a saddle, and "an old negro fellow." He was a shoemaker [WI 22:500-1; OWI 23:67, 68].

3. Elizabeth² Rawlinson, born say 1708, was called "Elizabeth Rawlinson the younger" when she was presented for not listing herself as a tithable in York County on 20 November 1727, perhaps the same Elizabeth Rawlinson who

968   *Rawlinson Family*

was presented again in York County on 15 May 1738 [OW 16:489; 18:414]. She was probably the mother of

4   i.   William[1] Rollison, born say 1727.

4.   William[1] Rollison, born say 1727, was a "mollatoe" taxable with his unnamed wife in William Person's Granville County, North Carolina Tax List in 1750 [CR 44.701.23]. On 1 August 1764 he recorded a plat for 400 acres adjoining his land in South Carolina on the north side of the Santee River near present-day Richland County [South Carolina Archives, Plats 8:62]. He was head of a Camden District, Richland District household of 3 "white" males and 3 "white" females in 1790, living near Henry **Bunch** and Benjamin and Isaac **Jacobs** who were also counted as white [SC:26]. He was probably the father or grandfather of

    i.   Benjamin[1], granted a memorial for 200 acres in Craven County, South Carolina, in the fork of the Wateree and Congaree Rivers in present-day Richland County on 15 February 1769 and granted a memorial for 300 acres in the same area adjoining William Rollinson on 6 February 1770 [South Carolina Archives, Memorials 8:420; 10:57]. He was head of a Richland District household of 7 "other free" in 1810 [SC:176a].

   ii.   Abigail, recorded a plat for 250 acres in Craven County, South Carolina, in the fork of the Wateree and Congaree Rivers adjoining William Rollinson on 22 May 1771 and sold this land on 14 September 1773 [South Carolina Archives, Memorials 20:180; Charleston Deeds H-4:222-6].

  iii.   Sam, head of a Richland District household of 6 "other free" and 2 slaves in 1810 [SC:178].

  iv.   William[2], head of a Richland District household of 7 "other free" in 1810 [SC:171].

   v.   Nathaniel, head of a Richland District household of 6 "other free" in 1810 [SC:171].

  vi.   John[2], recorded a memorial for 100 acres in Craven County, South Carolina, in the fork of the Wateree and Congaree Rivers on 23 May 1771 [South Carolina Archives, Memorials 10:446]. He was head of a Richland District household of 6 "other free" in 1810 [SC:179].

  vii.   Benjamin[2], head of a Richland District household of 6 "other free" in 1810 [SC:179].

viii.   Catherine, head of a Richland District household of 6 "other free" in 1810 [SC:175a], a resident of Richland District in 1806 when she petitioned the South Carolina legislature to be exempted from the tax on free Negro women [S.C. Archives series S.165015, item 01885].

  ix.   William[3], head of a Richland District household of 2 "other free" in 1810 [SC:177a].

   x.   John[3], head of a Richland District household of 3 "other free" in 1810 [SC:177a].

  xi.   James, head of a Richland District household of 2 "other free" in 1810 [SC:178].

REDCROSS FAMILY

Mixed-race members of the Redcross family mentioned in early Virginia records were

1   i.   John[1], born say 1730.
2   ii.   _____, born say 1733.

1.   John[1] Redcross, born say 1730, was living in the town of Richmond on 7 March 1774 when he sold a wagon, four horses and other goods to Samuel Williamson of Richmond for 180 pounds by Henrico County deed. The other goods included: a mare, a horse colt, a bed and furniture, four rush-bottomed

chairs, a large seal-skinned trunk, a large chest, three iron pots, an iron skillet, a dozen pewter plates, a pewter basin, a pewter dish, half a dozen knives and forks, half a dozen Queen china cups and saucers, half a dozen Queen china plates, a frying pan, a Queen china tea set and a Queen china dish [Deeds 1767-74, 522]. He was sued in Amherst County court for a debt of 25 pounds in November 1779. In October 1782 he sued William **Ampey** for slander, and **Ampey** sued him for trespass. Both cases were dismissed because they failed to appear [Orders 1773-82, 387; 1782-4, 49-50]. He was head of an Amherst County household of 11 whites (free persons) in 1783 [VA:48] and 1785 [VA:85]. He was taxable in Amherst County from 1782 to 1799 [PPTL 1782-1803, frames 9, 43, 70, 139, 197, 262, 329, 374, 455]. He and William **Ampey** were sued for a debt of 40 pounds on 3 May 1786. On 6 October 1788 the court reversed the indenture of Ann Shacklin's son John Shacklin (who had been bound to Henry Cam(p)den the previous month) and Henry Shacklin (who had been bound to Leroy Pope) on John Redcross's motion that their proper names were Williams and that they were properly brought up. He sued William Camden for slander on 1 March 1790 and Camden had a suit against him on 7 November 1791. His suit against James Warren for slander was dismissed for want of prosecution on 20 May 1793 [Orders 1783-7, 510; 1787-90, 353, 355, 606; 1790-4, 51, 123, 323, 373, 504, 527, 570, 584]. The inventory of his Amherst County estate was recorded 20 July 1801 and administration on his estate was granted to William Bryant in May 1802 [WB 4:13]. His children were

3   i.   ?John², born say 1755.
     ii.   Nancy, born say 1780, daughter of John Redcross, married James **Pinn**, 27 August 1799 Amherst County bond.
    iii. ?Henry, born about 1789 registered as a free Negro in Augusta County on 29 November 1814: *a freeman of colour aged about 25 years of age, five feet 9 inches high of yellow complexion, black eyes black hair and rather finer than common...born free and served his apprenticeship with David L. Garland of New Glasgow as a hostler* [Register of Free Negroes, no.10]. He was taxable in Amherst County in 1803 and a "Mulatto" taxable there in 1813 [PPTL 1782-1803, frame 594; 1804-23, frame 260].

2.   _____ Redcross, born say 1733, probably married a member of the **Evans** family. Her son Daniel Redcross was bound to John **Evans/ Epps** by the churchwardens of Cumberland Parish, Lunenburg County, on 10 December 1767 [Orders 1766-69, fol.122]. He was taxable in John **Evans'** Lunenburg County household in 1772 and 1773 and called Daniel **Evans** in John's household in 1775 [Bell, *Sunlight on the Southside*, 304, 324, 354]. Daniel left a 12 September 1777 Lunenburg County will, proved 10 June 1779, leaving half his estate to his brother Charles **Evans** and the remainder to John **Epps** [WB 3:26]. She was the mother of

4   i.   ?Lucy, born say 1750.
     ii.   Daniel, born say 1752, died before 10 June 1779.
    iii. ?William, born say 1768, taxable in Charles City County from 1789 to 1791, called "William **Evans**, alias Redcross" in 1790 [PPTL, 1788-1814].

3.   John² Redcross, born say 1755, was a soldier in the Revolutionary War from York County [Jackson, *Virginia Negro Soldiers*, 42]. He and his wife Mary were the parents of Fanny Redcross whose birth and baptism were recorded in Bruton Parish, James City County, in 1781 [Bruton Parish Register, 34]. Mary may have been the daughter of Mary **Meade** since a Meade Redcross (their son?) registered as a "free Negro" in York County. He was sued in Henrico County court on 3 December 1783 for a 3 pound, 5 shilling debt due by note of hand [Orders 1781-4, 149]. He was taxable in York County from

1784 to 1814: taxable on 2 horses in 1784, 3 tithes in 1802, 3 from 1809 to 1811, 2 in 1812, and 2 "free Negroes & mulattoes over 16" in 1813. His wife Molly/ Mary was taxable on a free male tithable in 1819 and taxable on a slave and a horse in 1820 [PPTL, 1782-1841, frames 92, 143, 164, 194, 224, 247, 308, 356, 378, 395, 426, 472, 484]. He was head of a York County household of 10 "other free" in 1810 [VA:882]. He was the father of

    i. ?Molly, born about 1776, registered in York County on 22 June 1803: *dark mulatto about 27 years of age, 5 feet high, with woolly Hair and small regular features, born of a free Woman in Bruton Parish* [Free Negro Register 1798-1831, no.23].

    ii. Fanny, born 10 March 1781, baptized 7 October.

    iii. ?John⁵, Jr., born about 1784, registered in York County on 16 October 1804: *a small black fellow about 20 years of age, 5 feet 4-1/4 Inches high...fierce black Eyes, fine Woolly hair...born of free parents on Queens Creek in the parish of Bruton* [Register 1798-1831, no.26]. He was taxable in York County from 1810 to 1814, called John Redcross, Jr. [PPTL, 1782-1841, frames 356, 395, 411].

    iv. ?Thomas, born say 1788, taxable in York County in 1809 and a "free Negro & mulatto" taxable in 1813 [PPTL, 1782-1841, frame 342, 395].

5   v. ?Meade, born about 1791.

    vi. ?George, born about 1802, registered in York County on 17 October 1831: *of light complexion Twenty nine years of age 5 feet 9 1/2 Inches high...large eyes and broad nose* [Free Negroes Register 1831-50, no.307].

4. Lucy Redcross, born say 1750, registered the 26 September 1768 birth of her son John Redcross in St. Peter's Parish, New Kent County. Her son was

6   i. John⁴, born 26 September 1768.

5. Meade Redcross, born about 1791, registered in York County on 21 February 1814: *of light complexion abt. 23 years of age 5 feet 5-1/2 Inches high, has short wooly hair...born of free parents on Queens Creek* [Free Negro Register 1798-31, no.73]. He was the father of

    i. ?Maria, born about 1809, registered in York County on 19 September 1831: *a dark girl about 22 years of age 5 feet 2 1/4 inch high* [Register 1831-50, no.290].

    ii. John⁶ Jr., born about 1811, registered on 18 June 1832: *(son of Meade) a person of tawny complexion about 21 years of age 5 feet 6 inches high* [Register 1831-50, no.341]. He was head of a York County household of 4 "other free" in 1810 [VA:882].

    iii. ?Julia, born about 1815, registered on 18 November 1833: *a person of yellowish complexion about 18 years of age five feet one Inch high* [Register 1831-50, no.357].

6. John⁴ Redcross, born 26 September 1768 in New Kent County [NSCDA, *Register of St. Peter's Parish,* 598], was a "Mulatto" taxable on a horse in St. Martin's Parish, Hanover County, in 1785 and 1786 [PPTL, 1782-1803, pp. 123, 157]. He may have been the John Redcross who married Susanna **Thomas** alias **Humbles** in Amherst County, 13 February 1807 bond, William Bryant security. He was a "Mulatto" taxable in Amherst County in 1813 and 1814 [PPTL 1804-23, frames 260, 284]. He was head of an Amherst County household of 6 "other free" in 1810 [VA:260] and was a seventy-five-year-old "Mulatto" man listed with his wife Susan in the 1850 census for Amherst County. He was the father of

    i. ?William, born about 1805, a forty-five-year-old "Mulatto" listed in the 1850 census for Amherst County with (his wife?) Jane Redcross and children.

ii. Patrick Henry, born about 1810, registered as a "Free Negro" in Amherst County on 30 December 1831: *brown complexion 5 feet 4 3/4 inches high* [Register no.52]. He was called the son of John Redcross when he registered on 17 March 1851 [Register no. 216].

REDMAN FAMILY

1. Ann Redman, born say 1675, a "molatto woman," was the daughter of an English woman named Jane Redman. Ann was freed from the service of Colonel William Lloyd, deceased, and his son Thomas Lloyd by the Richmond County, Virginia court on 7 October 1697 [Orders 1697-99, 249]. Her descendants were most likely

   i. William, born about 1751, head of a Lincoln County, North Carolina household of 11 "other free" in 1800 [NC:900] and 4 "other free" and a white woman in Rutherford County in 1810 [NC:431]. He made a declaration in Buncombe County court on 7 April 1820 to obtain a Revolutionary War pension. He stated that he was about sixty-nine years old and enlisted in 1775. He was the keeper of Samuel Bell's mill and had no family living with him other than his wife who was about sixty years old [M805-679, frame 0652].

   ii. William, Jr., head of a Rutherford County household of 4 "other free" in 1810 [NC:431] and 2 "free colored" over forty-five years old in 1820 [NC:77].

   iii. Lettice, born say 1760, mother of "orphans" Beck, Amy and Godfrey who were bound as apprentices to Benjamin Cleveland in Wilkes County, North Carolina in October 1783. Lettice bound herself "of her own free will" as a slave to Cleveland for three years in July 1784 [WB 1:135].

   iv. Betsy, born about 1778, registered as a "free Negro" in Pittsylvania County and presented her papers to the Botetourt County court on 14 May 1834: *56 years of age; Mulatto...Born free as per certificate from Clerk of Pittsylvania.*

   v. Richard[2], born about 1787, registered in Halifax County, Virginia, on 21 November 1825: *aged about thirty eight years, five feet ten inches high, of a yellow complexion...born of a white woman...registered as a free negro* [Registers of Free Negroes, 1802-1831, no. 82]. He registered in Pittsylvania County and presented his papers to the Botetourt County court on 14 May 1834: *47 years of age; Mulatto...Born free as per certificate from Clerk of Pittsylvania* [Free Negroes &c Registered in the Clerk's Office of Botetourt County, nos. 80, 81].

   vi. Betsy, born about 1788, registered in Halifax County, Virginia, on 26 May 1831: *a bright Mulatto woman, aged 43 years, five feet five inches high, was born free* [Registers of Free Negroes, 1802-1831, no. 176].

   vii. Mary, born about 1790, registered as a free Negro at the Hustings Court of the Corporation of Staunton, Virginia: *a mulatto woman, about forty years old, four feet eleven inches...born free as appears from a certificate of registry signed by P. William, Clerk of Shenandoah County* [Staunton Free Negro Register, no.117].

Other members of the family were taxed as "Free Negroes" in Hardy County in 1810 [Yantis, *A Supplement to the 1810 Census of Virginia*, H-7]:

   i. John, born about 1760, taxable on 3 persons and 2 horses. At the age of sixty years on 11 June 1820, he made a declaration in Hardy County court on 11 June 1820 to obtain a pension for his services in the Revolution. He stated that he enlisted in Winchester, Virginia. His widow Sarah applied for a survivor's pension on 9 August 1838 stating that they had been married about fifty years previous and that her husband died on 8 October 1836. Their son Nimrod was fifty-one years old on 26 May 1849 when he appeared in Hardy County court stating that he was the son of John and Sarah who died 4 November 1848 [M805-679, frame 0611].

ii.   Moses, taxable on one person and 2 horses.

iii. Reuben, taxable on one person and 2 horses.

iv.   Richard[1], taxable on one person and a horse. He testified for the pension application of Sarah Redman, stating that he had been present at the marriage of John and Sarah. He applied for a pension while living in Hardy County on 10 February 1829. He enlisted about 1780 at Fauquier courthouse. His unnamed wife was sixty-five years old in 1829 [M805-679, frame 0630]. He was listed as a "yellow" complexioned soldier in the size roll of troops who enlisted in the Revolution [The Chesterfield Supplement cited by NSDAR, *African American Patriots*, 153].

v.   Aaron, taxable on one person and a horse.

REED FAMILY

1.   William[1] Reed, born about 1673, was a mixed-race child born to a white servant woman in the Charles City County, Virginia household of Robert Jones. Jones bequeathed him a cow and a gun and his freedom from his indenture at the age of twenty-one years. Jones' executors refused to comply with his wishes, so William sued them in Charles City County court. On 3 September 1694 the court ruled in William's favor [Orders 1687-95, 522]. He was a taxable in James Ellis' household in the lower precinct of Southwarke Parish in Surry County from 1699 to 1703: called "Wm Read a Malatta" in 1699 [*Magazine of Virginia Genealogy*, vol.24, 2:77, 84; 3:68, 73; DW 5:289]. In May 1708 he began a suit against William Edwards in Surry County court for which he was awarded 1,285 pounds of tobacco on 21 September 1715 [Haun, *Surry Court Records*, VI:102; VII:89]. He may have been identical to the William Read who was living with his wife Mary Read in Brunswick County in 1729 when they sold 100 acres on the north side of the Nottoway River and both sides of Sappony Creek [Surry DW&c 8:22]. They may have been the parents of

2   i.   Elizabeth, born say 1713.
3   ii.   Ann, born say 1724.
4   iii. John, born say 1738.
5   iv.   Jane, born say 1740

2.   Elizabeth Reed, born say 1713, was fined 6 pounds on 3 May 1735 by the vestry of Chowan County, North Carolina, for having two "Molatto bastards" [Fouts, *Vestry Minutes of St. Paul's Parish*, 51]. Perhaps her descendants were

6   i.   Rachel, born say 1735.
7   ii.   Jemima, born say 1745.
     iii. Shadrack[1], born say 1750, head of a South Orangeburg District, South Carolina household of 7 "other free" and 3 slaves in 1790 [SC:99]. He received a little over 7 pounds on 9 January 1785 for supplying beef to the state commissary [South Carolina Archives, Accounts Audited for Revolutionary War Service, AA 6307].
     iv.   Willis, born say 1755, head of a South Orangeburg District household of one "other free" in 1790 [SC:99], paid a little over 35 pounds for militia duty as a horseman from 15 April 1781 to 15 February 1782 [South Carolina Archives, Accounts Audited for Revolutionary War Service, AA 6309].
     v.   Sarah, born say 1757, married Peter **Gordon** on 14 January 1778 in St. Philip's Parish, South Carolina.

- vi. Hardy[1], head of a South Orangeburg District, South Carolina household of 7 "other free" in 1790 [SC:99].
- vii. Charity, head of a South Orangeburg District, South Carolina household of 2 "other free" in 1790 [SC:99] and 3 in 1800 [SC:53].
- viii. Cloe, head of a South Orangeburg District, South Carolina household of 3 "other free" in 1790 and 3 in 1800 [SC:53].
- ix. Sarah, head of a Barnwell District, South Carolina household of 2 "other free" in 1800 [SC:58].
- x. William[2], head of a Chesterfield County, South Carolina household of 9 "other free" in 1800 [SC:106].

3. Ann Reed, born say 1724, was the servant of James Ridley in Southampton County, Virginia, on 10 January 1752 when the court ordered the churchwardens to bind out her unnamed "Mulatto" child to her master. On 9 April 1752 the churchwardens sued her for debt, and on 18 November that year the court ordered the churchwardens to bind out her "Mulatto" son Isaac and her daughter Winney, "a poor child" [Orders 1749-54, 195, 201, 219; 1754-9, 27]. Her children were

  8   i. Isaac, born about 1740.
  9   ii. Ann[2], born say 1745.
        iii. Winney, born say 1750.
        iv. ?Dempsey, born say 1758, listed in the Revolutionary War accounts, hired as a substitute by Nathaniel Harris in Mecklenburg County, North Carolina [Crow, *Black Experience in Revolutionary North Carolina*, 101]. On 3 June 1779 he purchased 200 acres in Warren County on Buffalo Branch for 200 pounds and sold 75 acres of this land to his neighbor, Joshua Capps, on 25 __ 1784 [DB 7:406; 8:203]. The October 1784 session of the Warren County court allowed him 30 pounds for building the bridge across Fishing Creek, and the April 1786 court ordered Warren **Williams**, base born child of Sarah **Williams**, bound to him as an apprentice cooper [Minutes 1783-87, 62, 67, 127]. He was taxable in Warren County from 1782 to 1791, taxable on 2 polls and 80 acres in 1787 [Tax List 1781-1801, 32, 57, 85, 95, 126, 150, 171, 211], head of a Warren County household of 8 "other free" in 1790 [NC:78], 13 in Mecklenburg County, North Carolina, in 1800 [NC:534], and 12 "free colored" in Cabarrus County in 1820 [NC:160].
        v. ?Frederick, born say 1765, head of a Franklin County, North Carolina household of 4 "other free" in 1790 [NC:60]. He married Toppin Johnson, 25 December 1815 Franklin County bond, James Ferrell bondsman.

4. John Read, born say 1738, was living in Southampton County on 9 September 1762 when he and John **Brooks** were sued for a debt of 9 pounds, 17 shillings [Orders 1759-63, 239]. He was taxable on a horse and 4 cattle in St. Luke's Parish, Southampton County, from 1782 to 1789 and taxable on 4 horses in 1790 [PPTL 1782-92, frames 508, 524, 597, 645, 668, 717, 767]. His 23 August 1790 Southampton County will was proved 10 December the same year. He left a cow to his daughter Patience **Sweat** and left 120 acres of land and the remainder of his estate to his wife Sarah. After her death the land was to go to his son Cordall and the estate was to be divided among his children Tabitha **Byrd**, Priscilla **Byrd**, Patience **Sweat**, Mason Read, Salley Read and Cordall Read. Cordall Francis and Hardy **Hunt** were witnesses [WB 4:395]. Sarah was the daughter of James **Brooks** who mentioned his daughter Sarah Read in his 21 May 1798 Southampton County will, recorded 21 May 1798, James **Sweat** executor [WB 5:58]. Sarah Read was taxable on 4 horses in Southampton County in 1791, 2 in 1792, taxable on John **Brooks'** tithe in 1793, on Cordall Read's tithe in 1795, on 2 horses from 1794 to 1804, called

a "Mulatto" from 1802 to 1806, taxable on a free male tithable and 3 horses in 1806 [PPTL 1782-92, frames 823, 882; 1792-1806, frames 61, 88, 169, 277, 327, 389, 423, 527, 565, 634, 702, 851]. She was head of a Southampton County household of 5 "other free" in 1810 [VA:88]. Their children were

    i.   Patience, born say 1768, "daughter of John and Sarah," married James **Sweat**, 3 March 1790 Southampton County bond, David Reed surety.

    ii.   Cordall, born before 1776, married Delilah **Kersey**, 19 November 1798 Southampton County bond, James **Sweat** surety. He was taxable in St. Luke's Parish, Southampton County, in Sarah Read's household in 1795, charged with his own tax from 1799 to 1813, called a "Mulatto" in 1802 and thereafter, listed with wife Delila in 1812 and 1813 [PPTL 1792-1806, frames 390, 416, 565, 634, 702, 818, 851; 1807-21, frames 56, 77, 175, 200, 298, 324]. He was head of a Southampton County household of 7 "other free" in 1810 [VA:88] and a Northampton County, North Carolina household of 9 "free colored" in 1820 [NC:258].

    iii.   Tabitha **Byrd**, born say 1772, married Godfrey **Scott**, 16 November 1795 Southampton County bond, Cordall Reed surety, 22 November marriage.[173]   Godfrey was a witness to the 9 January 1800 Northampton County will of Philip **Byrd** [WB 2:363].

    iv.   Priscilla **Byrd**, perhaps identical to Priscilla Reed whose children Edward, Vine, and James were ordered bound by the churchwardens of Sussex County to Henry Brown on 15 January 1778 [Orders 1777-82, 32].

    v.   Mason, born say 1775, "daughter of Sary Read," married Claxton **Roberts**, 29 January 1793 Southampton County bond, James **Sweat** surety.

    vi.   Sally.

5.   Jane Reed, born say 1740, was living in Southampton County, Virginia, on 13 December 1759 when the court ordered the churchwardens to bind out her "mullatoe" child Clement [Orders 1759-63, 11]. She was the mother of

    i.   ?Raymond, born say 1758, a "mullatto" child (no parent named) bound out by the Southampton County court for twenty-one years on 11 May 1758 [Orders 1754-9, 434].

    ii.   Clement, born say 1759, married Amy **Malone**, 17 November 1796 Brunswick County, Virginia bond. The **Malone** family were counted as "Free Negroes" in Brunswick County [Wynne, *Register of Free Negroes*].

6.   Rachel Reed, born say 1735, may have been one of the illegitimate children born to Elizabeth Reed in Chowan County before 3 May 1735 when she was presented by the churchwardens of St. Paul's Parish. Rachel was living in Chowan County on 5 January 1758 when she was presented by the churchwardens of St. Paul's Parish for having several base born children. In April 1763 the Chowan County court bound her "Mulatto" children Jacob and Reuben to James Bond, but on motion of her attorney Samuel Johnston on 23 June 1769 the court ordered Bond to show cause why the children should not be moved from their apprenticeship [Minutes 1761-3, 131; 1766-72, 472-3]. Rachel was a "mixt Blood" taxable in Hertford County on one person in 1768 and 1769 and on two persons in 1770 [Fouts, *Tax Receipt Book*, 50]. She was head of a Gates County household of 2 "other free" in 1790 (abstracted as Rude but appears to be Reede in the microfilm copy of the original) [NC:24;

---

[173]Godfrey **Scott** first married Betsey **Francis**, 11 May 1785 Southampton County marriage [Minister's Returns, p.638].

National Archives film M7, p. 329] and 5 "free colored" in Edenton, Chowan County, in 1820 [NC:130]. Her children were

    i. Jacob[1], born about 1755, eight years old in April 1763 when the Chowan County court bound him to James Bond until the age of twenty-one. He served in the Revolutionary War and died before 23 May 1792 when the Gates County court appointed (his mother) Rachel Reid, administratrix of his estate. On 4 August 1792 in Gates County she gave her son Benjamin power of attorney to settle the balance of his army wages from 20 November 1778 to June 1779 [*NCGSJ* XV:103].

    ii. ?Benjamin, born about 1758, enlisted with Colonel Murfree for the term of the war. He made a declaration in Gates County court to obtain a pension on 19 November 1821, saying he had a stiff arm from a wound, and he had a sixty-two-year-old wife named Treasey [M805, reel 680, frame 89]. He was head of a Gates County household of 3 "other free" in 1790 (abstracted as Rude but appears to be Reede in the microfilm copy of the original) [NC:22; National Archives film M7, p. 323], 3 in 1810 [NC:842], and 3 "free colored" in 1820 [NC:154].

    iii. Reuben, born about 1760, three years old in April 1763 when he was bound by the Chowan County court to James Bond until the age of twenty-one to be a cordwainer [Minutes 1761-3, 131].

7. Jemima Reed, born say 1745, a "free Mullatoe," was taxable in Hertford County, North Carolina, from 1768 to 1770 [Fouts, *Tax Receipt Book*, 25]. She was living in adjoining Gates County in November 1785 when the court bound her eighteen-year-old, illegitimate son Abraham as an apprentice cooper to John Duke, Jr. [Fouts, *Minutes of County Court of Pleas and Quarter Sessions 1779-86*, 97]. Her son was

    i. Abraham, born about 1767, head of a Gates County household of one "other free" in 1790 (abstracted as Rude) [NC:22]. He married Charlotte **Bird/ Byrd**, 27 February 1786 Southampton County bond.

8. Isaac Reed, born about 1740, the son of Ann Reed, a "Mulatto," was ordered bound out by the Southampton County court on 14 December 1752 [Orders 1749-54, 285]. He was taxable in Chowan County in John Lewis' list in 1756. He was taxed as a "Negro man" with a "Negro" woman in an untitled 1766 Chowan tax list, and in 1768 and 1769 he and his wife Margaret were taxables in Timothy Walton's list for Chowan County [CR 24.701.2]. His land on the east side of Bennett's Creek was mentioned in an 8 June 1799 Gates County deed [DB 4:345 by Taylor, *Abstracts of Deed Books A-5*, 188]. The Gates County court appointed him administrator of the estate of Jacob Reid on 22 May 1792 [Fouts, *Minutes of County Court of Pleas and Quarter Sessions 1787-93*, 110].[174] As administrator of the estate he appointed Samuel Smith attorney to settle the Continental Army Accounts of (his son?) Jacob Reid, Jr., from 10 December 1778 to 10 April 1779. On 5 June 1792 Captain Arthur Gatling testified in Northampton County, North Carolina court that Jacob was a soldier in a company of new levies on the Continental Establishment which he marched from Hertford to South Carolina from November 1778 to March 1779, and Jacob died in the service in South Carolina [*NCGSJ* XV:102]. Isaac was head of a Gates County household of 4 "other free," one white woman, and one white male over sixteen years of age in 1790 (abstracted as Rude by appears to be Reede in the microfilm copy of the original) [NC:23; National Archives film M7, p.334]. His children may have been

    i. Jacob[2], Jr., born about 1760, died in Revolutionary War service.

---

[174]Gates County was formed from Chowan, Hertford, and Perquimans counties in 1779.

    ii.   Hardy[2], born say 1762, married Tabitha Reed, 20 January 1784 Gates County bond, William Gwinn bondsman. He was head of a Gates County household of 8 "other free" in 1790 (abstracted as Rude but appears to be Reede in the microfilm copy of the original) [NC:23; National Archives film M7, p. 329]. On 22 May 1792 the Gates County court granted him administration on the estate of (his brother?) James Reid, deceased.

    iii. James, born say 1763, died before 22 May 1792 when (his brother?) Hardy Reid was granted administration on his Gates County estate [Fouts, *Minutes of County Court of Pleas and Quarter Sessions 1787-93*, 110].

10   iv. Micajah, born say 1765.

    v. Henderson, born before 1776, head of a Gates County household of one "free colored" in 1820 [NC:155].

    vi. Lettis, head of a Gates County household of 7 "free colored" in 1820 [NC:155].

    vii. Sarah, married Dempsey **Turner** of Pasquotank County, 19 May 1801 Gates County bond. He was head of a Pasquotank County household of 4 "other free" in 1790 [NC:29].

9.   Ann[2] Reed, born say 1745, was living in Southampton County on 14 February 1782 when the court ordered the churchwardens to bind out her "poor children" David and Jeremiah Reed. Jeremiah was ordered bound out again by the overseers of the poor on 11 September 1789 [Orders 1778-84, 183; Minutes 1786-90]. She was taxable in St. Luke's Parish, Southampton County, in 1787, taxable on David Reed's tithe and a horse in 1789 [PPTL 1782-92, frames 645, 718]. She may have been the "Anne Read a free Mulato" who was required by the Halifax County, North Carolina court on 28 August 1799 to post bond of 200 pounds during her stay in North Carolina [Minutes 1799-1802, 54]. She was the mother of

    i.   ?Shadrack[2], born say 1763, head of a Hertford County household of 6 "other free" in 1790 [NC:26], 3 in 1810 [NC:98], and 3 "free colored" in 1820 [NC:192]. He and his brother Jeremiah were two of the "Sundry persons of Colour of Hertford County" who petitioned the General Assembly in 1822 to repeal the act which declared slaves to be competent witnesses against free African Americans [*NCGSJ* XI:252].

    ii. David, born say 1767, taxable on a horse in St. Luke's Parish, Southampton County in 1788 and 1790, taxable in John Robertson's household in 1793 [PPTL 1782-92, frames 669, 718, 768; 1792-1806, frame 61]. He was head of a Chatham County, North Carolina household of 11 "other free" in 1810 [NC:193].

    iii. ?Jeremiah, born about 1773, registered in Southampton County on 12 January 1795: *age 22, no. 98, 22 Jeremiah Read light complexion, 5 feet 10-1/4 high, Free born* [Register of Free Negroes 1794-1832, no. 98]. He was taxable in St. Luke's Parish, Southampton County, from 1793 to 1799 [PPTL 1792-1806, frames 61, 89, 169, 278, 328, 390] and head of a Hertford County household of 7 "other free" in 1800 (called Jeremiah Scotch Reed) and 9 "free colored" in 1820 [NC:186].

    iv. ?Balaam, born about 1781, a poor child living in Sussex County on 15 June 1786 when the court ordered the overseers of the poor on the southside of the Nottoway River in district 3 to bind him to William Brown [Orders 1786-91, 31]. He registered in Sussex County on 10 June 1806: *black complexion, 5 feet 5-1/2 inches high, age 25, free born* [Register of Free Negroes, 1800-50, no. 50]

    v. ?Artis, taxable in St. Luke's Parish, Southampton County, in Isham Newsum's household in 1795 [PPTL 1792-1806, frame 167].

vi. ?Jacob, a "free Negro" listed in Southampton County with his wife Charity on Sophia Powell's land in 1813 and 1814 [PPTL 1807-21, frames 324, 424].

vii. ?Stephen, taxable in St. Luke's Parish, Southampton County in Simon Pope's household in 1794, charged with his own tax in 1802, a "Mulatto" in 1804 [PPTL 1792-1806, frames 87, 565, 703].

10. Micajah Reed, born say 1765, purchased 25 acres in Gates County on Collage Branch on 17 November 1796 and sold this land on 15 August 1807 [DB 4:127; 7:50]. He was head of a Gates County household of 4 "other free" in 1790 [NC:24], 8 in 1800 [NC:277], 10 in 1810 [NC:853], and 11 "free colored" in 1820 [NC:155]. In August 1817 he proved to the Gates County court that he was the lawful heir of Nathaniel **Hall**, who died in Revolutionary War service. Nathaniel may have been the father of Nathaniel **Hall**, a "Molatto Boy," born about 1786, bound an apprentice cooper in Gates County in May 1806 [Fouts, *Minutes of Gates County*, IV:1001; III:499]. One of Micajah's children may have been

    i. James, born say 1787, married Sealy **Robbins**, 25 October 1808 Gates County bond, James Lassiter bondsman. He was head of a Gates County household of 3 "other free" in 1810 [NC:837].

Nansemond County
Members of the Read family in Nansemond County were

    i. Elisha[1], Sr., born say 1760, a "Free Negro" taxable in Nansemond County in 1815 [Yantis, *Supplement to the 1810 Census of Virginia*, S-14].

    ii. Amos, born about 1758, a seventy-five-year-old "free man of Colour by birth" who applied for a pension in Nansemond County on 13 May 1833 for his service in the Revolution [M805-678, frame 0166].

    iii. Ameriah, born about 1762, about seventy-two years old on 13 January 1834 when he applied for a pension for his service in the Revolution. He stated that he enlisted in 1778 and had always lived in Nansemond County [M805-678, frame 0154].

    iv. Abram, born about 1764, a "free man of Colour by birth" who had always lived in Nansemond County and was about seventy-nine years old on 13 May 1833 when he applied for a pension for his service in the militia digging embankments at Portsmouth during the Revolution [M805-678, frame 0148].[175]

    v. Harrison, a "Free Negro" taxable on one head of cattle in Nansemond County in 1815.

    vi. Jonathan, a "Free Negro" taxable in Nansemond County in 1815.

    vii. Elisha[2], Jr., a "Free Negro" taxable in Nansemond County in 1815.

    viii. Jacob[3], a "Free Negro" taxable in Nansemond County in 1815 [Yantis, *Supplement to the 1810 Census of Virginia*, S-14], perhaps the Jacob Reed (born about 1780) who was counted in the 1850 census for Hertford County, North Carolina, with Margaret Reed (born about 1785), both listed as "Black" [NC:666].

Eastern Shore of Virginia
1. Rebecca Read, born say 1745, was taxable in the Northampton County household of Nathan **Drighouse** (**Driggers**) in the List of John Marshall in 1765 [L.P. 1765]. She may have been the ancestor of

---

[175]He was called "Abram of Read," indicating that he was the emancipated slave of a member of the Read family, despite the fact that he was called "a free man of Colour by birth" in the same sentence. The early nineteenth-century Nansemond County tax and census records listed all free persons of color this way regardless of their origins.

    i.   Isaac, born about 1760, a "Mulatto" taxable in Northampton County from 1791 to 1794 [PPTL 1782-1823, frames 126, 183]. He registered as a free Negro in Northampton County on 11 June 1794. Tamer **Stevens** sued him for slander in a case that was agreed to at his costs in Northampton County court on 13 June 1794 [Orders 1789-95, 354, 363]. He registered in Accomack County: *Isaac alias Isaac Read, a light Black inclining to yellow...Born Free* [Register of Free Negroes, no. 115].

    ii.   Reubin, sued in Northampton County by Peter **Toyer** on 9 July 1788, called a "free Negro" on 11 May 1792 when he was charged with plotting and conspiring to rebel and murder the white inhabitants of the county. The court sent him for trial at the next district court held in Accomack County [Minutes 1789-95, 157, 212]. He was security for the 3 January 1793 Northampton County marriage bond of Zerobabel **Weeks** and Nancy **Beavans** and the 23 January 1794 Northampton County marriage bond of Nathan **Driggers** and Elizabeth **Bingham**. He was taxable in Northampton County from 1786 to 1792: taxable on a slave in 1789 [PPTL, 1782-1823, frames 54, 103, 147].

    iii. Rachel, head of an Accomack County household of 4 "other free" and 5 slaves in 1810 [VA:53].

    iv. Betty, born before 1776, head of a Northampton County household of 10 "free colored" in 1820 [VA:216A].

REEVES FAMILY

1.   Malachi Reeves, born say 1720, received a patent for 400 acres on both sides of Tabbs Creek in Granville County on 25 March 1749 [DB C-1:1]. He was a "Black" taxable in the 1752 Granville County tax list of Jonathan White [CR 044.701.19]. On 9 May 1753 he purchased 522 acres on the north side of Fishing Creek from William Reeves for 60 pounds and sold this land to James Reeves for 60 pounds about a year later on 29 August 1754 [DB B:243, 402]. He was a white tithable with his sons William and Jonathan, John Allin, and one slave in Samuel Benton's list for Fishing Creek in 1762 [*NCGSJ* XIII:25]. On 21 July 1769 Isaac Cursi (**Kersey**) **Mitchell** was bound apprentice to him in Granville [CR 044.101.2-7]. His children were

    i.   William, born say 1744, a white tithable in 1762.
    ii.   Jonathan, born say 1746, a white tithable in 1762.

2.   James[1] Reeves, born say 1725, was a "black" taxable with his son James Reeves and "negro" Mary **Anderson** in the 1758 Granville County list of Nathaniel Harris. He purchased 522 acres on the north side of Fishing Creek from (his brother?) Malachi Reeves on 29 August 1754. He and Malachi were witnesses to the 30 March 1758 Granville County deed from Jacob Perry to Joseph **Bass** [DB B:402; E:50]. His children were

    i.   James[2], born say 1746, a black taxable in 1758. He may have been the James Revus who was head of a Wayne County household of 4 "other free" in 1810 [NC:836].
    ii.   ?John, head of a Greene County household of 1 "free colored" and 5 slaves in 1820 [NC:256].

3.   Margaret Reeves, born say 1735, was living "at George **Anderson**s" in Granville County on 7 June 1754 when Eliza Reeves, "supposed to be the child of Margaret Reeves," was bound to William Howlet until she was eighteen years of age [Owen, *Granville County Notes*, vol. I]. Her child was

4   i.   Elizabeth, born say 1752.

4.   Elizabeth Reeves, born say 1752, was living in Granville County on 16 January 1771 when her child Patience was bound apprentice to Valentine

White [CR 44.101.2; Owen, *Granville County Notes*, vol. IV]. Her children
were

    i.   Patience, born about 1765, a base born "Mulatto" bound to Valentine
White in Granville County on 16 January 1771, no parent named on
indenture [CR 44.101.2-7]. She married Augustine **Anderson**, 19
December 1796 Granville County bond.

   ii.   ?Suryeth(?), head of a Cumberland County household of 3 "free
colored" in 1820 [NC:153].

Other Reeves family members were

    i.   Chloe, born March 1764, a "Mullatto" child living in Loudoun County
on 13 June 1768 when the court ordered the churchwardens of
Cameron Parish to bind her to Nathaniel Grigsby [Orders 1767-70, 78].

   ii.   Nancy Reves, a "Mulatto" ordered bound out by the churchwardens of
St. Ann's Parish, Essex County, Virginia, on 18 August 1783 [Orders
1782-3, 401].

  iii.   Page, "F. Negro" head of a Fauquier County, Virginia household of 8
"other free" in 1810 [VA:340].

REVELL FAMILY

The Revell family may have originated in Surry County, Virginia, where
Edward Revell and (his son?) Edward Revell, Jr., were taxables in the same
household in Thomas Holt's list for 1703 [DW 5:291].

1.   Edmund Revell, born say 1725, was among the freeholders who were ordered
by the Edgecombe County, North Carolina court to work on the road near
Plumbtree Bottom in March 1762 [Minutes 1759-64, 38].[176] On 1 April 1763
he received a patent for 700 acres in the part of Edgecombe County which
became Nash County in 1777 [Hoffman, *Granville District Land Grants*, 114].
He sold 350 acres of this land to (his son?) Elijah Revell for 5 shillings on 7
October 1765; he sold 100 acres of this land to (his son?) Micajah Revell for
8 pounds on 25 September 1766; and he sold the remaining 250 acres for 50
pounds on 15 April 1767 [DB C:403; O:224]. Less than two weeks later on
27 April 1767 he received a patent for 500 acres in Dobbs County on the north
side of Bear Creek [Hoffman, *Land Patents*, II:435]. He was taxable on one
tithe in Dobbs County in 1769 [*NCGSJ* XV:80]. He sold land by deed proved
in Dobbs County between April 1773 and April 1775 [DB 10:455]. On 29
April 1768 he patented 150 acres northeast of Drowning Creek in the part of
Bladen County which later became Robeson County [Hoffman, *Land Patents*,
vol. II, no. 6913]. He and his wife were "Mulato" taxables in Bladen County
in 1772 [Byrd, *Bladen County Tax Lists*, I:82]. On 7 November 1784 he was
granted two patents in Bladen: one for 150 acres on both sides of Bear Swamp
and the other east of Long Swamp on [DB 1:26-7], and he was taxable in
Bladen County on 300 acres and one poll in 1784. He was head of a Robeson
County household of 9 "other free" in 1790 [NC:50]. He sold land in Robeson
County by deed proved on 8 April 1800 [Minutes 1797-1806, 104]. His
children may have been

2   i.   Sabra, born say 1742.

3   ii.   Elijah[1], born say 1745.

---

[176]One of the freeholders listed next to Edmund Revell in 1762 was Francis **Jenkins**, who was
called a "mustee" in Edgecombe County Court in October 1765 [Minutes 1764-72, 42]. Edmund was
probably related to Humphrey Revell who received a patent for 318 acres in Northampton County on
30 October 1754 [Hoffman, *Granville District Land Grants*, 234]. He was counted as white in the 1790
Northampton County census [NC:75], but he made a deed of gift on 19 February 1754 to (his son-in-
law?) Peter **Stewart** who was African American [DB 2:161].

4   iii.   Micajah[1], born say 1747.
       iv.   Burwell, born before 1776, head of a Robeson County household of
              one "other free" in 1790 [NC:49] and 4 "free colored" in 1820
              [NC:306]. He purchased land in Robeson County by deeds proved on
              6 April 1801 and 4 April 1803 [Minutes 1797-1806, 142, 239].
       v.   Nathaniel[2], born before 1776, head of a Robeson County household of
              3 "other free" in 1800 [NC:415], 6 in 1810 [NC:240], and 2 "free
              colored" in 1820 [NC:305]. He purchased 50 acres in Robeson County
              on the east side of Saddletree Swamp from Samuel **Hammond** on 4
              May 1801. He sold five head of cattle, five sows, 20 pigs, and
              household goods to Rachel Jones of Robeson County on 30 January
              1829 [DB M:355; V:466].

2.   Sabra Revell, born say 1742, was living in Edgecombe County on 26 April
       1764 when her "base born child" Sal was bound to Joseph Howell [Minutes
       1759-64, 11]. By 20 August 1771 she had moved to Granville County where
       her children were bound out by the court [CR 44.101.2-7]. Her children were
5   i.   ?Peggy, born say 1760, not apprenticed in Granville.
6   ii.   Nathaniel[1], born say 1762.
       iii.   Sal, born about 1764, seven years old when she was bound out in
              Granville County on 21 August 1771.
       iv.   Mackly, born in 1766, "base born female child of Sabra Revell aged
              about six months," ordered bound to Joseph Howell by the 14 October
              1766 Edgecombe County court [Minutes 1764-72, 48], six years old
              when she was bound out in Granville County on 21 August 1771.
       v.   Barbara, born about 1768, three years old when she was bound out in
              Granville County on 21 August 1771.
       vi.   Elijah[2], born 1770, one-year-old child of "Savory Revell" bound to
              Thomas Harris by the Granville County court. He may have been the
              Elijah Revell who was head of a Sampson County household of 6
              "other free" in 1800 [NC:525].

3.   Elijah[1] Revell, born about 1745, petitioned the Edgecombe County court of
       Pleas and Quarter Sessions on 28 March 1759 against Thomas Lane who was
       "holding him in bondage without right." His petition was rejected as it was
       entered in the wrong county [Minutes 1757-59, 35]. On 7 August 1765 he
       bought for 5 shillings, 350 acres of Edmond Revell's land [DB C:403]. On In
       May 1772 the Edgecombe County court ordered him and (his brother?)
       Micajah to work on the road near the Sapony Road [Minutes 1772-84, n.p].
       On 3 June 1773 he bought an additional 340 acres on the north side of Stony
       Creek in the part of Edgecombe which later became Nash County [DB 2:101],
       and in 1782 he was taxable in Nash County on 970 acres, 4 horses, and 22
       cattle. On 25 August 1785 he sold Micajah 100 acres of his land in Nash
       County for 25 pounds. He sold 250 acres of his land on the south side of
       Stony Creek for $250 on 11 February 1794, and bought 181 acres on the north
       side of the creek for $301 on 9 September 1795 [DB 4:129; 6:25, 111]. He
       was head of a Nash County household of 12 "other free" in 1790 [NC:71] and
       8 "other free," six slaves, and one white male 26-45 years of age (his son-in-
       law?) in 1800 [NC:117]. His 22 November 1806 Nash County will named his
       wife Dolly and divided his eight slaves among his children [WB 1:173]. Dolly
       was head of a Nash County household of 5 "other free" in 1810 [NC:639].
       Their children were
       i.   Elias, born say 1765, purchased 75 acres on the north side of Kirby's
              Creek in Nash County on 5 June 1786 [DB 4:129]. While a resident of
              Northampton County on 30 March 1792, he sold this land to (his
              cousin?) Henry Revell [DB 6:130]. He was deceased by 22 November
              1806 when his father wrote his Nash County will. His heirs received
              $10 from their grandfather. They were probably Rabourn Revel and his

sister Bedah and brother Ezekiel, who sold 75 acres on the north side of Kirby's Creek jointly with Elias's brothers and sisters on 16 February 1809 [DB 3:290].

7   ii.   Jonathan[2], born before 1776.
    iii. Paul, born say 1770.
    iv.   Edith Revell, born say 1772.
    v.   Celah Malone, born say 1775. Her husband was probably John Malone who signed a joint deed of sale of Elias' 75 acres in Nash County on 16 February 1809 [DB 3:290].
    vi.   Faithful Malone, probably the wife of Charles Malone who signed a joint deed of sale of Elias' 75 acres in Nash County on 16 February 1809 [DB 3:290].
    vii. Barnabas, head of a Nash County household of 2 "other free" in 1810 [NC:639]. He sold one third of a 100 acre tract adjacent to his brother Matthew and Faithy Malone on 8 March 1811 [DB 5:286].
    viii. Matthew, born before 1776, head of a Nash County household of one "other free" in 1810 [NC:639] and 4 free colored and one slave in 1820 [NC:425].
8   ix.   Humphrey, born 1776-94.

4. Micajah[1] Revell, born say 1747, purchased 100 acres in Edgecombe from (his father?) Edmond Revell on 25 September 1766 [DB C:403]. On 10 February 1770 he bought a 100 acre plantation on the north side of Stony Creek for 12 pounds, and on 4 August 1774 he bought 50 acres of the land that Edmund Revell formerly held on the north side of the Tar River. On 31 December 1774 he bought a 50 acre plantation on the south side of Stony Creek [DB 2:149, 290; 3:70]. He sold 2 acres of this land on 1 August 1777 in what was then Nash County [DB 1:81]. He was head of a Nash County household of 12 "other free" in 1790 [NC:71]. On 13 July 1807 he had an account with William White's store on present-day Tarboro Street in Wilson [*NCGSJ* XVI:215]. He may have been the M. Revell who was head of a Cumberland County household of 6 "other free" and one slave in 1810 [NC:624]. His children may have been
    i.   Henry, born say 1774, head of a Nash County household of two "other free" in 1800 [NC:117]. He purchased 75 acres from Elias Revell of Northampton County on 30 March 1792 [DB 6:130].
9   ii.   Elijah[3], born before 1776.
    iii. Larey, born say 1790, head of a Cumberland County household of 2 "other free" in 1810 [NC:564].
10 iv.   James, born say 1795, died in 1842.

5. Peggy Revell, born say 1760, was head of an Orange County household of 3 "other free" in 1800 [NC:618]. She may have been the mother of
    i.   Hezekiah, born about 1776, a "Mulatto" child bound by the 23 November 1790 Orange County court to Robert Neil. As Kiah Revill he married Susannah **Freeman**, 15 September 1805 Orange County bond. He was head of an Orange County household of 7 "other free" in 1810 [NC:942].
    ii.   Chia, born about 1778, a "Mulatto" child bound by the 23 November 1790 Orange County court to Robert Neil. He may have been the Coy Revell who was head of an Orange County household of 12 "free colored" in 1820 [NC:332].

6. Nathaniel[1] Revell, born say 1762, was bound to Mary Fort to be a farmer by the July 1764 Edgecombe County court [Minutes 1759-64, 26]. He may have been the Nathaniel Revell who was taxable on one poll in Sampson County in 1784 [L.P. 64.1 by *N.C. Genealogy* XIV:2174]. He was one of the freeholders of Sampson County who was ordered to clear South River from the New

Hanover County line as far as the Tarr Landing on 22 June 1784 [Minutes 1784-1800, 3]. He was head of a Sampson County household of 13 "other free" in 1790 [NC:52] and 10 in 1800 [NC:526]. Along with several other free African Americans he was counted as white in 1810, head of a Sampson County household of 4 males and 4 females [NC:486]. He purchased 100 acres of land he was living on in Sampson County between the Little Coharie and the great swamp on the south prong of the running branch on 9 April 1801 [DB 12:143]. His children may have been

   i.   Stephen, born say 1778, purchased 200 acres in Sampson County on 21 April 1798 on John Odam's line [DB 11:76]. He was head of a Sampson County household of 2 "other free" in 1800 [NC:501], counted as white in 1810 with 4 males and 2 females [NC:486].

   ii.   Micajah², born 1765-84, counted as white in Sampson County in 1810, head of a household of 2 males and 3 females [NC:476].

7.   Jonathan² Revell, born before 1776, was head of a Nash County household of 4 "other free," 7 slaves, and one white woman aged 26-45 in 1800 [NC:117] and head of a Cumberland County household of 6 "free colored" in 1820 [NC:157]. He purchased land on the east side of the Raleigh Road, about two and one-half miles above Fayetteville, by a deed recorded in 1819, sold a half acre lot on the east side of the Raleigh Road about two and one-half miles above Fayetteville with a frame house and brick chimney on 21 December 1819 [DB 31:493, 521; 34:493], and sold another lot in Fayetteville by deed proved in 1823. He may have been the father of

   i.   Elijah⁴, head of a Cumberland County household of 9 "free colored" in 1820 [NC:170].

   ii.   Nancy, head of a Cumberland County household of 4 "free colored" in 1820 [NC:170].

8.   Humphrey Revell, born 1776-94, married Dilly **Hammonds**, 28 December 1811 Edgecombe County bond with his brother Barnabas Revell bondsman. He was head of a Nash County household of 4 "free colored" and 4 slaves in 1820 [NC:425]. His 8 November 1831 Nash County will was proved in February 1832 [WB 1:379]. He left land and three slaves to his wife Delilah and divided his other slaves and land between his two sons,

   i.   William N., born after 1810 since he was not yet 21 when his father made his will.

   ii.   Elijah H., born after 1810 since he was not yet 21 when his father made his will.

9.   Elijah³ Revell, born before 1776, was head of Robeson County household of 6 "other free" in 1810 [NC:241] and a Cumberland County household of 7 "free colored" in 1820 [NC:152]. He may have been the Elijah Revell to whom Horatio Revell was ordered bound by the Robeson County court on 5 October 1801 [Minutes I:166]. Horatio was removed from his care by order of the 3 January 1803 Robeson court because he was "illy treated by his master" [Minutes I:225]. Horatio, born about 1789, was head of a Cumberland County household of 4 "free colored" in 1820 [NC:177]. Elijah's wife may have been Peggy Revels, "the Barber's wife," who was mentioned in the 3 March 1824 session of the Cumberland County court [Minutes 1823-35, n.p.]. Elijah sold land by deed proved in Robeson County in February 1827 [Minutes III:144]. He may have been the Elias Revell of Cabarrus County who was ordered by the March 1838 Cumberland County court to produce William Lee Revels, "a Free boy of Colour," to the next court [Minutes 1838-40, Saturday March 1838 court]. Perhaps his children were

   i.   Eli B., born about 1809, died in Lincolnton, North Carolina, on 18 June 1841 at the age of thirty-two according to the 23 June 1841 issue of the Lincolnton Republican [*NCGSJ* II:144].

10. James Revell, born say 1795, purchased 514 acres in Cumberland County on Juniper Creek by a deed recorded in 1837 [DB 42:18]. He married his slave named Janet. By his 26 December 1841 Cumberland will, proved September 1842, he entrusted his friend, Malcolm Munroe, with applying to the legislature for his wife's emancipation. He gave her all his lands and stock [WB C:21]. On 6 December 1842 "M. Revell and others" sued the administrator of the will, Daniel Baker, for distribution of the estate [Minutes, 1835-44, n.p.]. Perhaps James Revell was the father of Catherine, Willis, and Mary Jane Revell who were bound out in Cumberland County after his death [Minutes 1835-44, n.p.]. He may have been the father of

> 11   i.   Hiram Rhoades Revell, born 1 September 1822.
>   ii.   Catherine, born about 1830, a thirteen-year-old "free girl of color" bound to Jonathan Jessup on 5 June 1843.
>   iii.   Willis, born about 1833, a nine-year-old "free boy of color" bound to Charles M. Beebe on 6 September 1842.
>   iv.   Mary Jane, born about 1834, an eight-year-old bound to Charles M. Beebe on 6 September 1842.

11. Hiram Rhoades Revell, born in Fayetteville on 1 September 1822, was the first African American elected to the U.S. Senate. He moved from Fayetteville to Lincoln County, North Carolina, before 20 February 1845 when he was bondsman for the marriage of Mrs. Mary Revels and William L. **Mitchell**. Local Lincoln County historians claimed that he was a barber and sold cakes and confections in Lincolnton in a small building on the present site of the North State Hotel lot, between the hotel and Water Street, facing the court square. He moved to Indiana where he was counted in the 1850 census in Cambridge City, Wayne County: twenty-five years old, with (his brother and sister?) John E. Revels (eight years old) and Pheba Revels (seventeen years old) living in the household of William **Mitchell**, a wagon maker from North Carolina [household # 181]. He moved to Illinois where he was educated and ordained a minister in the African Methodist Episcopal Church. He settled in Baltimore where he served as a church pastor and principal of a school. In 1861 he helped organize two volunteer African American regiments for service in the Union Army. As a member of the Mississippi state senate he voted to restore the power to vote and hold office to disenfranchised members of the former Confederacy. In January 1870 he was elected to the U.S. Senate to fill the unexpired term of Jefferson Davis. In 1875 he helped overturn the Republican (Carpetbag) government of Mississippi asserting that too many of their politicians were corrupt. The Democratic administration rewarded him by appointing him president of Alcorn Agricultural and Mechanical College near Lorman, Mississippi [*Encyclopedia Britannica, Micropedia*, VIII:537-8].

REYNOLDS / RUNNELS FAMILY

1. Margaret Reynolds, born say 1710, was living in Bertie County on 16 November 1732 when the court ordered her five-year-old "bastard Mulatto child," James Reynolds, who had been bound to her father Thomas **Kersey**, deceased, bound instead to John Boude [Haun, *Bertie County Court Minutes*, I:79]. She was the mother of

>   i.   James[1], born about 1727.
> 2   ii.   ?Jesse, born say 1745.
> 3   iii.   ?Patience[1], born say 1752.

2. Jesse Runnels, born say 1745, was taxable on two persons in Hertford County in 1770 and on one poll in 1784 in the Hertford County list of William Outland's Company [Fouts, *Tax Receipt Book*, 44; L.P. 64.1]. He was head of a Hertford County household of 11 "other free" in 1790 (abstracted as Jessee Rowals but appears as Jessee Ronals in the microfilm of the original)

[NC:25; National Archives film M7, p.182], 8 in 1800, 6 in 1810 [NC:92], and 7 "free colored" in 1820 [NC:180]. Perhaps his children were those counted as "other free" in Hertford County:

    i.   David, head of a Hertford County household of 4 "other free" in 1800 and 9 in 1810 [NC:106].

    ii.   Benjamin, head of a Hertford County household of 1 "other free" in 1800 and 5 in Edgecombe County in 1810 [NC:727].

    iii.   James[2], born before 1776, head of a Hertford County household of 13 "other free" in 1810 [NC:92] and 9 "free colored" in 1820 [NC:188]. He was one of the "Sundry persons of Colour of Hertford County" who petitioned the General Assembly in November- December 1822 to repeal the act which declared slaves to be competent witnesses against free African Americans [*NCGSJ* XI:252].

3.   Patience[1] Runnels, born say 1752, was head of a Hertford County household of 6 "other free" in 1790 [NC:27], 9 in 1800, and 6 in 1810 [NC:92]. Perhaps her children were

    i.   Hannah, head of a Hertford County household of 6 "other free" in 1800.

    ii.   Patience[2], head of an Edgecombe County household of 2 "other free" in 1810 [NC:720].

    iii.   Parhania, head of a household of 2 "free colored" in Nash County in 1820 [NC:439].

Another Reynolds family:

1.   Mary Reynolds, born say 1713, was living in King George County, Virginia, on 5 November 1731 when she was presented for having a bastard child and on 2 July 1736 when she was taken up as the runaway servant of Israel Illingsworth. On 2 May 1746 she was living in Brunswick Parish, King George County, when the court presented her for "living in fornication and Continually Cohabiting with Joseph a Mulatto Man Slave belonging to John Owens." The presentment abated on 4 July 1747 by her death [Orders 1735-51, pt.1, 485, 515, 526]. She was probably the ancestor of

    i.   George, born about 1778, head of a York County household of 3 "other free" in 1810 [VA:882]. He obtained certificate #94 when he registered as a "free Negro" in King and Queen County on 13 January 1823: *a mulatto born free in the County of King and Queen aged about forty five years, five feet six and a half inches high.* And he registered this certificate in York County on 15 August 1831 [Free Negroes Register 1831-50, no. 283].

    ii.   Dinah, head of a Henrico County household of 1 "other free" and 4 slaves in 1810 [VA:1005].

    iii.   Mary, born before 1776, head of a Pittsylvania County household of 6 "free colored" in 1820 [VA:832].

    iv.   Julian, born 1776-94, head of a Pittsylvania County household of 2 "free colored" in 1820 [VA:832].

    v.   James, taxable on one head of cattle in Nansemond County in 1815 [Yantis, *Supplement to the 1810 Census of Virginia*, S-14].

RICH FAMILY

1.   Christian[1] Rich, born say 1665, was the servant of Anthony Lynton on 21 July 1686 when the Northumberland County court ordered that she serve her master additional time and ordered the sheriff to give her twenty lashes for having a child by a "negroe." She escaped before the sheriff could carry out the order, so the court ordered the constable for Mattapony Precinct to take her into custody. She had another child by a "negro" before 18 September 1689 and

a child by a white man named John Elson before 16 May 1694 [Orders 1678-98, 348, 478, 652]. She was apparently the mother of

2   i. Mary¹, born say 1686.

2. Mary¹ Rich, born say 1686, was a "Mulatto" woman who petitioned the Northumberland County, Virginia court on 17 November 1708 setting forth that she was illegally detained as a servant. The court assigned George Estridge as her attorney to sue for her freedom [Orders 1699-1713, pt. 2, 560]. She was probably the mother of

3   i. Mary², born say 1717.

3. Mary² Rich, born say 1717, a "free mulatto," was living in North Farnham Parish, Richmond County, Virginia, on 2 January 1735 and 30 March 1742 when she registered the birth of her children David and Wilmoth [King, *Register of North Farnham Parish*, 157]. In November 1745 she had a case in Richmond County court against Jonathan Lyell who was ordered to pay her 500 pounds of tobacco which he owed her [Orders 1739-46, 503, 512]. She may have been the wife of "Mulatto William" whose orphan Sarah Rich was bound out by the Lancaster County court with the consent of her unnamed mother on 8 March 1750 [Orders 1743-52, 242].[177] Mary's children were

4   i. David¹, born 2 January 1735.
5   ii. Wilmoth, born 30 March 1742.
6   iii. ?Sarah, born say 1745.

4. David¹ Rich, born 2 January 1735, was ordered bound by the churchwardens of North Farnham Parish, Richmond County, in April 1749 [King, *Register of North Farnham Parish*, 157; Orders 1746-52, 161]. He was head of a Northumberland County household of one "white" (free) person in 1782 [VA:38], and a "free negro" head of a Northumberland County household of 5 "other free" in 1810 [VA:994]. On 2 June 1783 he, Wilmoth Rich and Andrew the slave of William Palmer were tried for hog stealing. Wilmoth and Andrew were found not guilty, but David was found guilty and received twenty-five lashes [Orders 1776-84, 291]. He may have been the father of

7   i. Mahala, born say 1772.
8   ii. Winney, born say 1775.

5. Wilmoth Rich, born 30 March 1742, was ordered bound by the churchwardens of North Farnham Parish, Richmond County, in May 1749 [King, *Register of North Farnham Parish*, 157; Orders 1746-52, 161]. On 4 June 1770 the court ordered the churchwardens of North Farnham Parish to bind his children David, Mary, Ann, and Betty Rich to Ann Palmer--the boy until the age of twenty-one and the girls until eighteen [Orders 1769-73, 117]. He was probably identical to William Rich who was a soldier in the Revolution from Lancaster County [Jackson, *Virginia Negro Soldiers*, 42] and head of a Lancaster County household of 5 "Blacks" in 1783 [VA:55]. He died before 2 May 1785 when the Richmond County court ordered the churchwardens of North Farnham Parish to bind out his son George Ritch [Orders 1784-6, 253]. He was head of a Richmond County household of 2 "other free" in 1810 [VA:408]. He was the father of

9   i. David², born say 1763.
10   ii. Mary³, born say 1765.
    iii. Ann, born say 1767.
11   i. Elizabeth¹/ Betty, born say 1769.

---

[177]Perhaps William was identical to "William a Molatto begotten by a Negro man on a white woman" who was seven years old on 16 March 1709/10 when he was bound by the Northumberland County Court to Mary Price [Orders 1699-1713, pt. 2, 654].

12   ii.   Criss², born say 1772.
      iii. George¹, born say 1775, orphan of Wilmoth Rich, ordered bound as an
            apprentice on 2 May 1785 [Orders 1784-6, 253]. He was head of a
            Richmond County household of 6 "other free" in 1810 [VA:413]. He
            and Betty **Venie** were counted as "free Negroes & mulattoes over 16
            years" in Richmond County in 1813 [Waldrep, *1813 Tax List*]. He
            married Elizabeth Rich, daughter of David Rich, 27 December 1814
            Richmond County bond.

6.   Sarah Rich, born say 1745, "Orphan of Mulatto William," was bound out by
      the Lancaster County court with the consent of her unnamed mother on 8
      March 1750 [Orders 1743-52, 242]. She may have been the mother of
      i.   Robert¹, born about 1766, counted with (his wife?) Sally Rich as "free
            Negroes & mulattoes over 16 years" in Richmond County in 1813
            [Waldrep, *1813 Tax List*]. He registered in Lancaster County on 19
            March 1828: *Age 62, Color bright...born free*.
      ii.   Hannah¹, born about 1771, head of a household of a male and 2 female
            "free Negroes & mulattoes over 16 years" in Richmond County in 1813
            [Waldrep, *1813 Tax List*]. She registered in Lancaster County on 17
            August 1807: *Age 36, Color dark...born free* [Burkett, *Lancaster
            County Register of Free Negroes*, 4, 8].

7.   Mahala Rich, born say 1772, was counted in Richmond County in 1813 with
      (her son?) John Rich in a list of "male & female free Negroes & mulattoes
      over 16 years" with 2 males and 2 females [Waldrep, *1813 Tax List*]. She was
      probably the mother of
      i.   John, born before 1798, over sixteen years of age in 1813.

8.   Winney Rich, born say 1775, was head of a Richmond County household of
      1 "other free" in 1810 [VA:407]. She was counted in Richmond County with
      (her son?) Billy Rich in a list of "free Negroes & mulattoes over 16 years."
      She was the mother of
      i.   ?William/ Billy, born before 1798, over sixteen years of age in 1813.
      ii.   Hannah², born 15 July 1793, daughter of Winney Rich [King, *Register
            of North Farnham Parish,* 157].

9.   David² Rich, born say 1763, was a taxable "free Black" in Richmond County
      in 1789 [PPTL B, p.5] and head of a Richmond County household of 8 "other
      free" in 1810 [VA:407]. He and (his wife?) Susannah were counted as "male
      & female free Negroes & mulattoes over 16 years" in Richmond County in
      1813 [Waldrep, *1813 Tax List*]. He was the father of
      i.   Elizabeth², born say 1796, daughter of David Rich, married George
            Rich, 27 December 1814 Richmond County bond.

10.   Mary³ Rich, born say 1763, was bound apprentice to Ann Palmer in Richmond
      County on 4 June 1770 [Orders 1769-73, 117]. She was the mother of Richard
      Rich, a "free Negro," born in North Farnham Parish on 6 October 1782
      [King, *Register of North Farnham Parish,* 157]. She was head of a Richmond
      County household of 9 "other free" in 1810 [VA:407]. She was the mother of
      i.   Robert², born 22 April 1781, "son of Mary Rich." He was taxable in
            Essex County from 1796 to 1814: counted with a male and female
            "free Negro & Mulatto" in 1813 [PPTL, 1782-1819, frames 279, 292,
            302, 313, 249, 432, 510, 548]. He married Polly **Wood**, November
            1813 Lancaster County bond. He was head of a Richmond County
            household of 7 "other free" in 1810 [VA:407].
      ii.   Richard, born 6 October 1782, "free Negro son of Mary Rich."

11. Elizabeth[1]/ Betty Rich, born say 1769, was living in Northumberland County in 1787 when her daughter Fanny was born: *Fanney Rich Daughter to Bettey Rich a Molatto was born March 25 1787* [Fleet, *Northumberland County Record of Births*, 82]. She was probably the Betty Rich who was head of a Richmond County household of 5 "other free" and one slave in 1810 [VA:407]. Her children were

    i. Fanny, born 25 March 1787.

12. Criss[2] Rich, born say 1772, orphan of Wilmoth Rich, deceased, was ordered bound as an apprentice in Richmond County on 6 June 1785 [Orders 1784-6, 261]. She was head of a Richmond County household of 6 "other free" in 1810 [VA:407] and was counted in Richmond County with (her son) George Rich in a list of "free Negroes & mulattoes over 16 years" in 1813 [Waldrep, *1813 Tax List*]. She was the mother of several children born in North Farnham Parish, Richmond County [King, *Register of North Farnham Parish*, 157]. Her children were

    i. George[2], born 1 August 1793, "son of Criss Rich."
    ii. Kendal, born 12 October 1795, "son of Criss Rich"
    iii. Nancy, born 25 October 1798, "daughter of Criss Rich."
    iv. Robert[3], born 15 January 1799.
    v. Daniel, born 8 May 1802.
    vi. Thaddeus, born 30 August 1804.
    vii. J., born 5 February 1807.

RICHARDSON FAMILY

1. Elizabeth Richardson, born about 1707, "a free Mulatto," was living in Elizabeth City County between 18 August 1731 and 22 September 1737 when the court bound her children Samuel, Matthew, Miles, and James as apprentices to Joseph Banister. She was probably related to John Richardson and his wife Mary who were sued for debt by Joseph Banister on 15 June 1743 and who sued Banister on 5 April 1748. On 15 March 1737/8 the court ruled that Elizabeth was free from her own indenture [Orders 1731-47, 10, 66, 98, 151, 169, 338; 1747-55, 28, 40, 52, 59]. She was the mother of

    i. Samuel, born say 1725, "son of Eliza. Richardson a Mulato," bound to Joseph Banister on 18 August 1731. He may have been related to the Samuel Richardson who was head of a Charlotte County household of 9 "other free" in 1810 [VA:63].
    ii. Matthew[1], born say 1727, "son of Eliza. Richardson a Mulato," bound to Joseph Banister on 18 August 1731. On 6 December 1748 he had a complaint against Banister which was settled between them and acknowledged in Elizabeth City County court on 1 August 1749. And Samuel Walker had a case against Matthew which was dismissed on 6 December 1749 [Orders 1747-55, 64, 105, 131, 137].

2   iii. ?Fanny[1], born say 1730.
    iv. ?Elizabeth, born say 1730, may have been the unnamed "Mulato" child of Elizabeth bound out in Elizabeth City County on 19 September 1733. On 5 September 1759 the court ordered the churchwardens to bind out "all the children of Elizabeth Richerson a Molatto" [Minutes 1756-60, 249].
3   v. Miles, born say 1735.
    vi. James, born say 1737, bound to Joseph Banister on 22 September 1737.

3. Miles Richardson, born say 1735, was a "Mulato Child" bound to Joseph Banister in Elizabeth City County on 17 September 1735. On 7 April 1761 the court bound out his daughter Elizabeth Richardson to Daniel Richardson with the consent of her mother Mary Richardson, "she being unable to maintain him

as appears to this Court" [Court Records 1760-9, 11]. They were the parents of

    i.   Elizabeth, born say 1757.

AMELIA COUNTY

1. Fanny[1] Richardson, born say 1730, was living in Raleigh Parish, Amelia County on 29 February 1755 when the court ordered the churchwardens of Raleigh Parish to bind her "Mallatto" daughter Winney to Thomas Dobson [Orders 1751-5, 217; 1754-8, n.p.]. She was the mother of

2   i.   ?Daphne, born say 1748.
       ii. Winney, born say 1753.

2. Daphney Richardson, born say 1748, a "Free Negro" (no last name), was living in Amelia County on 26 June 1766 when the court ordered the churchwardens of Raleigh Parish to bind her to William Pride. She was probably identical to Daphne Richardson whose "mulatto" daughter Lucy was ordered bound out to Thomas Dobson and his wife by the churchwardens of Nottoway Parish, Amelia County on 25 May 1769. Daphne Richardson was called a "free Mulatto" on 27 December 1770 when the churchwardens of Nottoway Parish were ordered to bind out her daughters Lucy and Fanny to some other person than Thomas Dobson, "it appearing that the sd. Dobson is an improper person" [Orders 1765-7, 95; 1768-9, 131]. She was the mother of

3   i.   Lucy, born say 1766.
      ii. Fanny[2], born say 1768. She may have been the Fanny Richardson, a "Mulatto" who was committed to jail in Culpeper County for want of a certificate of freedom. She was released on 20 May 1799 when Job Strode testified that she had been his servant and that he had known her mother who was a free woman [Minutes 1798-1802, 82].
     iii. ?Lewis, head of a Granville County, North Carolina household of 7 "other free" in 1810 [NC:878].
     iv. ?John, born about 1783, registered in Amelia County in September 1815: *a black man about 32 years of age about 5 feet 7 inches high...born free as appears from a certificate from Pascal McGlassons with whom he served his time* [Register of Free Negroes 1804-1835, no. 85].

3. Lucy Richardson, born say 1766, was a "mulatto" bound to Thomas Dobson in Amelia County on 25 May 1769 and bound to someone else on 27 December 1770. She was in Mecklenburg County, Virginia, on 10 January 1789 when the court ordered the overseers of the poor to bind out her illegitimate children Crecy, Lucy and Kitt (no race indicated) [Orders 1787-92, 337]. She was called "Lucy Richerson, a free woman of color," in August 1812 when the Granville County, North Carolina court complained that she had four bastard children with no visible means of support [CR 044.928.25]. She was apparently the mother of

     i.   Lucreasy, born about 1781, a fourteen-year-old child (no race or parent indicated) bound to Jonathan Knight, Jr., by the Granville County court in May 1795 [Minutes 1792-5, 242].
      ii. Lucy, born about 1782, a thirteen-year-old child bound to Jonathan Knight, Jr., by the Granville County court in May 1795 [Minutes 1792-5, 243].
     iii. Christopher, born about 1784, an eleven-year-old child bound to Jonathan Knight, Jr., by the Granville County court in May 1795 [Minutes 1792-5, 243].
     iv. Nancy, born 20 June 1789, a five-year-old child bound to Jonathan Knight, Jr., by the Granville County court in May 1795 [Minutes 1792-5, 243].

v. Samuel, born 30 July 1793, bound to Jonathan Knight, Jr., by the Granville County court in May 1795 [Minutes 1792-5, 243].

They were probably related to William, Benjamin, and John Richardson, perhaps brothers, who owned land in Halifax County, North Carolina, near the Warren County line and were counted as "other free" in Halifax County.

5. William[1] Richardson, born say 1745, received a grant in Halifax County for 300 acres joining Deans former line and the county line on 1 March 1782 [DB 14:487]. This was land near Little Fishing Creek, Bear Swamp, and the Warren County line. The **Wilkins** and **Hawkins** families were his neighbors. He was head of a Halifax County household of 7 "other free" in 1790 [NC:63]. His undated Halifax County will was proved in August term 1798 [WB 3:309]. He divided his land among his children:

   i. Henry, head of a Halifax County household of 6 "other free" in 1800 [NC:338].
   ii. William[2], head of a Halifax County household of 6 "other free" in 1790 [NC:64] and 8 in 1810 [NC:46].
   iii. Elijah, head of a Halifax County household of 5 "other free" in 1800 [NC:338].
   iv. Matthew[2].
   v. Mourning **Bass**.
   vi. Harty/ Hardy[1].
   vii. Olive, married John **Bass**, 8 December 1798 Granville County bond, Absolem **Bass** bondsman.
   viii. Winney.
   ix. Christian.

6. Benjamin[1] Richardson, born say 1750, received a grant for 120 acres in Halifax County near William Richardson and the county line on 16 May 1780 [DB 17:1]. He married Mary **Bass**, widow of Elijah **Bass**, 13 February 1783 Granville County bond with Philip **Pettiford** as bondsman. She was also called Mary **Bass** on her 13 February 1777 Bute County marriage bond to Elijah **Bass** [M804-2038, frame 0533]. Benjamin and Mary were married on 14 February, the day after the bond was posted, according to her 11 October 1841 application for his Revolutionary War pension. He "went out of Halifax and Warren Counties" and enlisted in the militia in September 1780 [M804-2038, frame 0520]. He was counted in District 11 of Halifax County for the 1786 State Census with 6 free males and 6 free females in his household and was head of a Halifax County household of 10 "other free" in 1800 [NC:338]. His 10 July 1809 Halifax County will, proved November the same year, divided his land between three of his children Benjamin, Jesse, and Absolem [WB 3:506]. He died on 14 July 1809 according to his wife's pension application. She died 20 November 1844 according to an affidavit by Willis Qualls, the brother of the man who made her coffin. John King of Franklin County, born about 1737, and David King of Warren County, born about 1764, testified on her behalf that they also served in the Revolution and were acquainted with both her husbands. The Richardson family claims to be "Haliwa-Saponi Indians," but J.R.J. Daniel of Halifax County called them:

   free persons of color & generally...industrious & well behaved people

   on 24 May 1855 when he wrote an affidavit for the pension application of Benjamin and Mary's children [M804-2038, frames 525-7, 0537]. Their children were
   i. Benjamin[2], born before 1776, head of a Halifax County household of 1 "other free" in 1810 [NC:45] and 7 "free colored" in 1820 [NC:162].
7 ii. Jesse, born before 1776.

    iii.   Lucy **Evans**, named in her mother's pension application.

    iv.   Absolem, head of a Halifax County household of 1 "other free" in 1810 [NC:45], 7 "free colored" in 1820 [NC:163], and 11 "free colored" in 1830. He was residing in Warren County when he applied for a survivor's pension in May 1855.

    v.   ?Moses, born before 1776, head of a Halifax County household of 7 "other free" in 1810 [NC:45] and 7 "free colored" in 1820 [NC:162].

8   vi.   Hardy, born say 1790.

7.   Jesse Richardson, born before 1776, was head of a Halifax County household of 4 "other free" in 1810 [NC:45] and 4 "free colored" in 1830. When he was granted permission to carry his gun in the county on 17 May 1841, the Halifax County court also granted permission to Gideon and Asa Richardson, identifying them as his sons. Two of his children were

    i.   Gideon, born 1776-94, head of a Halifax County household of 8 "free colored" in 1830.

    ii.   Asa.

8.   Hardy[2] Richardson, born say 1790, was head of a Halifax County household of 4 "other free" in 1810 [NC:45], 9 "free colored" in 1820 [NC:163], and 11 in 1830. On 1 March 1822 he sold 35 acres adjoining Lewis Richardson and Falling Creek in Halifax County to Lewis **Boon**, explaining in the deed that it was part of 70 acres he had purchased from William Willy [DB 25:590]. He was not mentioned in his father's will, but he signed a 12 March 1853 letter to the pension office with Lucy, Absolem, and Jesse Richardson, claiming to be the only surviving children and heirs of Mary Richardson. Also, J.R.J. Daniel of Halifax County wrote an affidavit for their survivor's pension application that Hardy was the son of Benjamin and Mary Richardson and that Mary lived and died in Hardy's home. He also wrote that Hardy died "a short time" before 24 May 1855 [M804-2038, frames 535, 537]. Hardy's 20 December 1854 Halifax County will, proved May 1855, lent his wife Dorcas his land which was to be divided at her death among his children. It mentioned the "Dean" tract and land on Falling Creek which was probably land owned by his father as well as land he had purchased himself [WB 5:7]. In 1860 Dorcas was a sixty-seven-year-old "Mulatto" living in household no. 1377: $360 real estate, $427 personal estate, with Martha (seventy-one years old), Edward (twenty-six years old), Frances (fifteen years old), Faulcon (fifteen years old), and Missouri (ten years old). Hardy's children mentioned in his will were

    i.   Elizabeth, born about 1815, received $5 by her father's will. She was living in household no.1382 with five children and $520 real estate in 1860.

    ii.   Alfred, born about 1815, received 100 acres he was then living on. He was living in household no. 1380, $300 real estate, with Eliza, forty-seven years old, and eight children in 1860.

    iii.   Mason, born about 1817, received 50 acres. He was living in household no. 1379, $150 real estate, with Mary, forty years old and Dorcas, twenty years old, in 1860.

    iv.   Emily, received $5 by her father's will. Her daughter Rebecca received 10 acres by her grandfather's will.

    v.   Edward, born about 1834, received the "Evans" tract, the Stephen Marshall tract, and the Dean tract, and was living in his mother's household in 1860.

    vi.   Jane, received $25 by her father's will.

    vii.   Abner, received 60 acres on Falling Creek adjoining his own land.

    viii.   Dorcas, was to receive 25 acres of the land of her brother Mason at his death.

ix. Harriet, was to receive 25 acres of the land of her brother Mason at his death.
x. Louisa, received the tract of land where she was living.
xi. Mary, received 73 acres.
xii. Frances, born about 1845. She received $50 by her father's will, and was living in her mother's household in 1860.

9. John Richardson, born say 1760, received a grant for 119 acres in Halifax County on both sides of Little Fishing Creek near the lands of (his brothers?) Benjamin and William Richardson on 27 November 1792 and sold this land on Falling Creek to Benjamin **Bass** on 22 April 1799. He sold 100 acres on the north side of Little Fishing Creek on 7 February 1795 and purchased 22 acres on Falling Creek joining lands of Benjamin **Bass** on 9 December 1800. Joel **Evans** and Joseph **Lantern** were witnesses to the deed [DB 17:747, 838; 18:460, 916]. He married Sarah **Bass**, (daughter of Benjamin **Bass**), 22 March 1802 Granville County bond with (her brother) Absolem **Bass** bondsman. He was head of a Halifax County household of 6 "other free" in 1800 [NC:338] and 5 in 1810 [NC:45]. He may have been the father of
   i. John Jr., head of a Halifax County household of 2 "other free" in 1800 [NC:338], 1 in 1810 [NC:46], and 7 "free colored" in 1820 [NC:163]. He purchased 17 acres in Halifax County from Cary (Sarah) **Bass** on 24 November 1801. This was land which had belonged to her father Benjamin **Bass** [DB 18:912].

King George County, Virginia
1. Mary Richardson (Richerson), born say 1735, was a "free Negro" woman living in Fredericksburg on 4 October 1757 when she bound herself to Ann Manning for ten years [WB B:398]. She was living in King George County on 4 March 1762 when the churchwardens of Brunswick Parish were ordered to bind out her "natural daughter" Frank to Ann Mannan [Orders 1751-65, pt.4, 973]. She was the mother of
   i. Frank, born say 1761.
   ii. ?Jesse, head of a Westmoreland County household of 10 "other free" in 1810.
   iii. ?Nancy, head of a Lancaster County household of 7 "other free" in 1810 [VA:358].
   iv. ?Clary, head of an Essex County household of 3 "other free" in 1810 [VA:202].

RICKMAN FAMILY

1. John[1] Rickman, born say 1719, was exempted by the Henry County court on 30 July 1779 from paying public levies in the future [Orders 1778-82, 50]. He was the father of
2   i. Peter[1], born say 1740.
     ii. ?William[1], born say 1742, won a suit in Halifax County, Virginia court against Benjamin Echols for a debt of 40 pounds on 22 July 1769 [Pleas 1767-70, 417]. He was a defendant in two suits in Pittsylvania County for debt in March 1774. One was dismissed because he was not an inhabitant of the county [Court Records 1772-5, 336, 347].
3   iii. ?John[2], born say 1750.
     iv. James, born say 1768, orphan of John Rickmond, bound out by the overseers of the poor in Henry County on 27 May 1784 [Orders 1782-5, 150].
     v. Fanny, born say 1770, orphan of John Rickmond, bound out by the overseers of the poor in Henry County on 27 May 1784 [Orders 1782-5, 150].

2. Peter[1] Rickman, born say 1740, was living in Halifax County, Virginia, on 17 May 1759 when a case against him was dismissed on agreement of the parties. On 16 May 1765 the court presented him, Shadrack **Gowin**, and Philip **Dennum** for concealing a tithable on information of John Bates, Gentleman. The tithables were probably their wives. Their cases were dismissed in August 1766, perhaps on payment of the tax. He was sued for a 2 pound debt in May 1763 and in December 1763 his male laboring tithables were ordered to work on a road with Shadrack **Going** and William Rickman [Pleas 1752-5, 384; 1763-4, 46, 228; 1764-7, 46, 358]. David **Gowing** sued him for a debt of 3 pounds in Pittsylvania County on 25 June 1773 [Court Records 1772-5, 211-2]. He was taxable in Henry County from 1782 to 1790: charged with Thomas Rickman's tithe in 1787, listed with 2 tithables from 1788 to 1790 [Personal Property Tax Lists, 1782-1830, frames 15, 232, 356]. A Henry County jury awarded him 150 pounds currency as damages in his suit against Joseph Jones on 29 May 1784. He sold, signing, all his personal property consisting of two horses, a colt, two cows and yearlings, two spinning wheels and other household goods to Henry Lyne by Henry County bill of sale on 22 February 1788 [DB 1:446]. He was called Peter "Sr." when he was taxable in Patrick County from 1791 to 1799: listed with 3 tithables in 1791 and 1792, 2 in 1793 and 1795, 3 in 1797, 2 in 1799 [Personal Property Tax List 1791-1823, frames 155, 182, 211, 240, 273]. He was the father of

4   i.   ?Thomas[1], born say 1762.
    ii. ?William[4], born about 1769, one of two William's taxable in Patrick County from 1809 to 1813 (one called "SC" and the other "HC", in a list of "free Negroes and Mulattoes" in 1813 [Personal Property Tax Lists, 1791-1823, frames 155], head of a White County, Tennessee household of 11 "free colored" in 1820, 7 in 1830 and listed with wife Jane in the Martin County, Indiana household of Dennis C. **Robbins** in 1850.
    iii. ?Isaac, born say 1775, taxable in Patrick County from 1798 to 1801 [Personal Property Tax Lists, 1791-1823, frames 256, 297, 324].
    iv. Peter[2], Jr., born say 1774, taxable in Patrick County from 1791 to 1814, called "son of Peter" in 1800, called Peter Sr. starting in 1804, in the list of "free Negroes and Mulattoes" in 1813 and 1814 [Personal Property Tax Lists, 1791-1823, frames 155, 211, 297, 353, 407, 467, 598, 616].
    v.   ?John[3], born say 1780, married Elizabeth Rickman, 30 April 1801 Stokes County bond, James **Harris** bondsman.
    vi. ?Abner, born say 1780, taxable in Patrick County from 1800 to 1816, called a "Mulatto" from 1812 [Personal Property Tax Lists, 1791-1823, frames 297, 524, 593, 654]. He married Delilah Clark, 1808 Patrick County bond, Peter Rickman surety and was head of a White County, Tennessee household of 8 "free colored" in 1820.
    vii. ?Susannah, born about 1784, married William **Findley**, 1802 Patrick County bond, John **Going** surety. Suckey registered in Patrick County in June 1832: *aged about 45 or 50 years, of dark complexion...with black eyes and somewhat a round face and 5 feet 3 inches and 3 quarters high...Free born in the County of Patrick* [Wilson, Cynthia A., http://ftp.rootsweb.com/pub/usgenweb/va/patrick/courts/colreg.txt].

3. John[2] Rickman, born say 1750, was taxable on 100 acres in St. Martin's Parish, Hanover County, Virginia, from 1782 to 1794 and sold the land to Samuel Luck before 1795. He was taxable there on his own tithe and a horse in 1789, called a "free Mulatto" in 1793, not listed in 1794 [Personal Property Tax List 1782-91, p. 234; 1792-1803, p.38; Land Tax List 1782-1801]. He may have been the John Rickman who married Agnes Rickman, 13 November 1794 Caswell County, North Carolina bond, Patrick **Mason** bondsman. He was taxable in Patrick County, Virginia, from 1798 to [Personal Property Tax

Lists, 1791-1823, frames 256, 297, 324, 353, 379]. He was head of a Stokes County household of 3 "other free" and 3 white women in 1800 [NC:493]. He was the father of

    i.   ?William[3], born say 1774, taxable in Patrick County from 1791 to 1801 [Personal Property Tax Lists, 1791-1823, frames 155, 182, 240, 273, 324]. He married Abigail Gibson, 25 October 1795 Patrick County bond, John Rickman surety. He bought land in Patrick County in 1805, 1806, and 1814 and sold it in 1820 [DB 2:535, 575; 4:6, 163; 5:531]. An inquisition on his death was returned to Patrick County court on 15 June 1820 [Orders 1810-21, n.p.]. Abigail was counted as white in the 1820 Patrick County census.

    ii.   Nicholas, born say 1778, married Sarah **Fendley**, 28 March 1799 Stokes County, North Carolina bond, Charles **Barnette** and John Rickman bondsmen. He registered in Patrick County in November 1823. He was head of a Stokes County household of 2 "other free" and 2 white women in 1800 [NC:494], 2 "free colored" in Wythe County in 1820, 8 in Surry County, North Carolina, in 1830, and 8 in Grayson County, Virginia, in 1840, listed as a "Mulatto" in Shelby Township, Ripley County, Indiana in 1850.

    iii.   Peter[3], born about 1781, married Nancy Rickman, 20 June 1800 Stokes County bond, Nicholas and John Rickman bondsmen. He was called "little" Peter Rickman when he was taxable in Patrick County 1799, called "Peter Jr." from 1804 to 1806, "little Peter" in 1807, 1809 and 1810; "Peter, Jr., Mollatto" in 1812; counted in the "list of "Free Negros & Malatters" in 1813 [Personal Property Tax List 1791-1823, 273, 406, 437, 468, 524, 542, 575, 594, 616]. He was head of a White County, Tennessee household of 3 "free colored" in 1820, 3 "free colored" in Gallia County, Ohio, in 1830, and a "Mulatto" living in Liberty Township, Highland County, Ohio, in 1850 with Thornton **Goen** in his household.

4.   Thomas[1] Rickman, born say 1762, was taxable in Henry County from 1786 to 1790 [Personal Property Tax Lists, 1782-1830, frames 232, 257, 306, 319, 357]. He was paid as a witness for the plaintiff in the Henry County suit of Rickman vs. Going in April 1790 [Orders 1788-91, 108]. He was taxable in Patrick County from 1791 to 1800, called "Sr." in 1795 and 1796 [Personal Property Tax Lists, 1791-1823, frames 155, 182, 211, 224, 256, 297]. He married Nancy Stephens, 25 October 1795 Patrick County bond, John Rickman surety. On 12 August 1824 the Patrick County court ordered that the "whole of" his children under age be bound out, and on 13 June 1828 the court ordered that he and his sons Anderson, Allen, and Daniel "nussenses" and all his lawful hands residing in the precinct be added to Horatio Penn's road gang [Orders 1823-31]. He was the father of

    i.   John[4], born say 1781, taxable in Patrick County from 1798, called a "mollatto" in 1812, in the list of "free Negroes and Mulattoes" in 1813 and 1814. There were two Johns listed in Patrick County between 1798 and 1802, one called "Jr." [Personal Property Tax Lists, 1791-1823, frames 256, 273, 297, 379, 437, 598, 616]. He married Tabitha **Harris**, 1805 Patrick County bond. He obtained a license in Henry County to retail pewter and recorded it in Patrick County on 13 April 1820. He registered in Patrick County in November 1829 as son of Thomas Rickman [Orders 1810-21, n.p.]. A John Rickman was head of a Gallia County, Ohio household of 10 "free colored" in 1830.

    ii.   Thomas[2], born about 1783, married Patsy **Findley**, 23 December 1806 Patrick County bond, Peter **Fendley** surety. He registered in Patrick County in December 1829: *aged 46, five feet nine inches and 3 quarter high, a bright mulatto with black and gray beard with hazle eyes and slender stature. Free born.* Patsy registered the same day: *a free*

woman of color aged 50 years a dark mulatto and of low stature and black eyes [Pilson and Baughan, *Alphabetical List of Lands Taxed in Patrick County*, 7-8]. The court called him "son of old Thom" when it certified his papers [Orders 1823-31].
- iii. Anderson.
- iv. Allen.
- v. Daniel.

RIDLEY FAMILY

1. Margaret Redley, born say 1692, was presented by the churchwardens of Washington Parish, Westmoreland County, Virginia, on 28 June 1710 for having a bastard child. She may have been identical to "Margrett a Servt. to Calleb Butler" who was presented by the churchwardens of Washington Parish on 28 May 1707 and 22 February 1710 for "fornication & haveing a Mulatto bastard." On 24 June 1713 she and Edward **Buss** "a Mulatto" were presented by the grand jury for fornication and cohabiting together [Orders 1705-21, 58, 66, 136a, 140a, 143a, 145a, 155a, 217]. She was probably the mother of
   - i. Moses, born say 1710, owned land in Orange County, North Carolina, adjoining George **Gibson** and Thomas **Collins** [*Orange County Loose Papers*, vol. V, no. 131; vol.VI, no. 579]. He and his wife Mary were "Mulatto" Orange County taxables in 1755 [N.C. Archives T&C 1, p.8]. He was called a poor debtor in February 1761 when William **Chavis** sued him in Orange County court [Haun, *Orange County Court Minutes*, I:459]. He was probably related to Moses Ridle, an "Indian" tithable in John Wilson's Pittsylvania County tax list for 1767.

ROBERTS FAMILY

Members of the Roberts family in Virginia were
1
- i. Mary[1], born say 1664.
- ii. Thomas[1], born say 1668, a "mollotta" servant bound by indenture to William Wise of York County, Virginia. He had twenty-seven months more to serve on 26 January 1690/1, but the York County court added another twenty-two months to his time for running away with Wise's Portuguese servant John Sherly between 18 August 1690 and 1 January 1690/1. Wise's account of the charges he had incurred while taking them up included expenses at New Castle and passage to and from Philadelphia. Thomas was the servant of Ralph Walker on 24 November 1693 when his suit against William Wise was dismissed by the court [DOW 8:527-8, 536; 9:269].

1. Mary[1] Roberts, born say 1664, was living in Elizabeth City County on 17 June 1724 when the court granted her petition to be levy free [Orders 1724-30, 34]. She may have been the ancestor of
2
- i. Mary[2], born say 1685.
3
- ii. John[1], born say 1710.
- iii. Judith, born say 1718, a "Moletto" who Thomas Crips failed to list as one of his tithables in York County in December 1735 [OW 18:245].
4
- iv. Margaret, born say 1725.
- v. Daniel, born say 1725, a "Mulatto" son of "a Free Woman," who brought a case against Charles Hansford, Jr., in York County court in March 1746 for holding him in servitude, apparently after he had already completed his indenture. The court declared him a free man [WI 19:424].
5
- vi. Joseph[1], born say 1740.

	vii.	Esther, born say 1752, a free Negro woman, the wife of Stepney **Blue** who ran away from his owner, Nathan Yancy of York County, in 1774 [*Virginia Gazette* of 29 September and 2 November 1774].
6	viii.	James³, born say 1753.
	ix.	Joseph², a "free Negro" taxable in Isle of Wight County from 1783 to 1803: taxable on his own tithe, a horse and 2 cattle in 1783; taxable on 2 tithes from 1802 to 1804; called Joseph Rober(t)son in 1791, 1795, 1796 and 1798 [PPTL 1782-1810, frames 36, 52, 93, 140, 153, 188, 235, 251, 340, 354, 399, 422, 437, 481, 500, 586, 606, 664].
	x.	Hester, born about 1765, registered in York County on 17 September 1810: *a dark woman abt. 45 years of age 5 feet 3-1/2 Inches high* [Register of Free Negroes 1798-1831, no.56].
	xi.	Nancy, born about 1765, registered in York County on 16 December 1822: *a bright Mulatto woman aged about 57 or 58 years, five feet four Inches and one Quarter high, with woolly hair* [Register of Free Negroes 1798-1831, no.176]. She was taxable on a horse in York County in 1795 [PPTL, 1782-1841, frame 212] and head of a York County household of 7 "other free" and two slaves in 1810 [VA:882].
	xii.	Patsy², born about 1772, registered in York County on 16 December 1822: *about 50 years of age 5 feet 1-1/2 inch high* [Register of Free Negroes 1798-1831, no.177].

2. Mary² Roberts, born say 1685, was a "Molatto" presented by the York County court on 15 November 1735 for not listing herself as a tithable [OW 18:237, 245]. Her 19 September 1749 York County will was proved on 20 November 1749. She left seven head of cattle, a bed and furniture to her son Matthew, left the same to her daughter Ann Robbards, and divided the remainder of her estate between her children Matthew Robbards, Ann Robbards, Anthony Robbards, Mary **Clark**, Elizabeth **Cannady**, Margaret **Wilson** and Sarah **Banks**. Her son Anthony Robbards was her executor [W&I 20:163-4]. Her children were

	i.	Ann, born say 1709.
7		
	ii.	Mary³, born say 1711, presented by the York County court on 17 November 1729 for having an illegitimate child. On 17 May 1731 the court dismissed her petition against John Mundell that he was the father of her bastard children. On 20 December 1731 she was presented for having a bastard child on the information of the churchwardens of Yorkhampton Parish. On 21 August 1732 her mother Mary Roberts was her security for payment of the fine. She was called Mary Roberts, "a Molatto living at Chiscake," on 15 November 1735 when she was presented by the York County court for not listing herself as a tithable [OW 17:5, 13, 27, 161, 248, 273, 295, 308; W&I 18:237, 245]. She had married a member of the **Clark** family before 19 September 1749 when her mother made her will.
	iii.	Matthew, born say 1715, living in Yorkhampton Parish when he was presented by the York County court on 19 November 1770 for failing to list himself as a tithable and on 15 November 1773 for absenting himself from his parish church [Judgments & Orders 1770-2, 105, 337; 1772-4, 438, 443].
	iv.	Sarah **Banks**, born say 1717, perhaps the wife of John **Banks** who was presented by the York County court on 17 November 1735 for not listing his "Molatto" wife as a tithable [W&I 18:237, 245].
	v.	Elizabeth **Cannady**, probably the wife of Joseph **Cannady** who was presented by the York County court on 15 December 1735 for not listing his wife Betty as a tithable [OW 18:245].
	vi.	Margaret **Wilson**, born say 1720.
8	vii.	Anthony, born say 1723.

3. John[1] Roberts, born say 1710, made his mark as witness to the 14 February
    ___ Northampton County, North Carolina deed of Philemon and Ann
    Maurice to Sebastian Squire which was proved in May 1745 [DB 1:189]. He
    was living in Southampton County on 14 May 1752 when he was sued by the
    executors of John Person and on 12 September the same year when he was
    sued by Thomas **Tabor**. Both suits were dismissed. On 13 June 1754 he was
    one of fourteen heads of household who were sued in Southampton County
    court by William Bynum (informer) for failing to pay the discriminatory tax
    on free African American and Indian women. James Kindred testified against
    him. He was fined 500 pounds of tobacco [Orders 1749-54, 224, 266, 319,
    496, 510-11; 1754-9, 24].[178] He was in Northampton County in January
    1762 when he voted in the election.[179] Administration on his Northampton
    County estate was granted to William Arington in May 1764 on 100 pounds
    bond with John Dancy and Arthur Hart securities [*NCGSJ* XII:170, 171;
    XIV:157]. (Arthur Hart lived on land adjoining Cypress Swamp in part of
    Northampton County which is near present-day Greensville County. He may
    have been the father of

9   i.   James[1], born say 1734.
    ii.   Thomas[2], born say 1740, taxable in the Lunenburg County list of
          Edmund Taylor for St. James Parish in 1764 [Bell, *Sunlight on the
          Southside*, 257]. This part of Lunenburg County became Mecklenburg
          County in 1765 and Thomas was counted there in 1782 as a "Mulatto"
          head of a household of 5 persons [VA:34].

4. Margaret Roberts, born say 1725, left a 6 June 1789 Northampton County,
    North Carolina will which was proved in September 1794. She gave two
    shillings to each of her children Ishmael, James, and John Roberts, Mary
    Roberts, Faitha **Scott**, Christian **Stewart**, Phebe Roberts, Hannah Roberts,
    Milla **Anderson**, and Elizabeth Roberts and gave the remainder of her estate
    to her daughter Delpha Roberts. She named her daughter Delpha and (her son-
    in-law) Jeremiah **Anderson** executors [WB 2:54]. Her children were

10 i.   Ishmael[1], born say 1750.
    ii.   James[5], born say 1756.
11 iii. John[2], born say 1759.
    iv.   Mary[5].
    v.   Faitha **Scott**.
    vi.   Christian **Stewart**.
    vii. Phebe Roberts.
    viii. Hannah Roberts.
    ix.   Milla **Stewart**.
    x.   Elizabeth Roberts.
    xi.   Delpha Roberts.

5. Joseph[1] Roberts, born say 1740, was mentioned in the 1772 Surry County,
    Virginia account of the estate of William Seward [WB 12:95]. He was head
    of a Surry County household of 8 free persons in 1782 [VA:43] and no
    "whites" in 1784 [VA:79]. His wife Hannah **Banks** was the heir of Matthew
    Banks from whom she received part of 75 acres. She and her husband and the
    other heirs sold this land in Surry County on 22 February 1796 [DB 1792-99,

---

[178]The other householders prosecuted for not listing their wives as tithables were John **Porteus**,
Isaac **Young**, Thomas **Wilkins**, Francis **Locust**, James **Brooks**, Jr. and Sr., John **Byrd**, Jr. and Sr.,
Abraham **Artis**, Lewis **Artis**, William **Brooks**, John **Demery**, Ann **Brooks**, and William **Tabor**. The
Brooks and **Byrd** families were also from York County.

[179]Other free African Americans who voted in this election were Benjamin **Hawley**, John **Demery**,
Peter **Stewart**, Charles **Byrd**, and James **Scott** [*NCGSJ* XII:170, 171].

344]. He was security for the 31 May 1786 Surry County bond, 1 June 1786 Isle of Wight County marriage, of Faithy **Banks** and James **Wilson**. He was taxable in Surry County from 1784 to 1813: taxable on Edwin Roberts' tithe from 1788 to 1791; taxable on Joseph Roberts, Jr.'s tithe in 1793; James Roberts' tithe in 1794, 1797, and 1798; John Roberts' tithe in 1799; listed with 2 "free Negroes & Mulattoes above the age of 16" in 1813 [PPTL, 1782-90, frames 384, 393, 430, 505, 582; 1791-1816, 44, 143, 193, 221, 304, 344, 384, 573, 616, 656, 695, 753]. Joseph and Hannah were the parents of

i. ?Edwin, born say 1771, taxable in Surry County from 1788 to 1794: his tax charged to Joseph Roberts from 1788 to 1791 [PPTL, 1782-90, frames 505, 582; 1791-1816, 44, 193]. He married Polly **Jones**, 7 January 1796 Isle of Wight County bond, Thomas **Jones** surety. He was a "F.N." Isle of Wight County taxable from 1795 to 1807 [PPTL 1782-1810, frames 368, 382, 411, 513, 565, 624, 641, 702, 741, 760]. He was head of a Norfolk County household of 6 "other free" in 1810 [VA:38].

ii. ?Joseph[3], born in November 1772, registered as a "free Negro" in Surry County on 17 August 1797: *a mulatto man aged 25 years old next Novemr. pretty bright complection, about 5'5" high pretty stout and well made, short hair* [Back of Guardian Accounts Book, 1783-1804, no.26]. He was taxable in Surry County in 1791, 1793 and 1798: his tax charged to Richard Scammell in 1791 and 1798, listed with Joseph Roberts in 1793 [PPTL, 1791-1816, frames 44, 143, 347]. He married Elizabeth **Charity**, 17 May 1802 Surry County bond, David **Charity**, father of Elizabeth, surety. He was head of a Campbell County household of 6 "other free" in 1810 [VA:880].

iii. ?Benjamin, born before 1776, head of a Sussex County household of 3 "free colored" in 1830.

iv. James[7], born about November 1777, registered in Surry County on 28 April 1801: *bright complexion, 5'7-1/2" high, pretty straight & square made, aged about 23-1/2 years, he is son of Joseph & Hannah Roberts free persons of this county* [Back of Guardian Accounts Book, 1783-1804, no.129]. He was taxable in his father's Surry County household in 1794, 1797 and 1798 [PPTL, 1791-1816, 193, 304, 344] and was a "F.N." taxable in Isle of Wight County from 1803 to 1805 [PPTL 1782-1810, frames 624, 641, 702]. He may have been the James Roberts who married Amelia (**Jenkins**?). They were the parents of Joseph **Jenkins** Roberts who was born of free parents in Norfolk County on 15 March 1809. James died in 1823. His son emigrated to Liberia with his widowed mother, two younger brothers, and two younger sisters in 1829. He established one of the most prosperous trading firms in Liberia. He was Liberia's first African American governor in 1841 and its first president in 1847 [Huberich, *Political and Legislative History of Liberia*, 1:770-71, by Wiley, *Slaves No More*].

v. John[4], born in October 1780, registered as a "free Negro" in Surry County on 30 April 1802: *(son of Joseph Roberts) a mulatto man, who is 5'5-1/2" high, aged about 21 years last October...bright complexion, rather bushy hair, straight and well made and by trade a planter* [Back of Guardian Accounts Book 1783-1804, no.137]. He was taxable in his father's Surry County household in 1799 [PPTL, 1791-1816, frame 384] and was a "F.N." taxable in Isle of Wight County from 1802 to 1807 [PPTL 1782-1810, frames 565, 624, 641, 702, 741, 760].

vi. William[3], born 5 April 1789, registered in Surry County on 23 February 1808: *a son of Joseph and Hannah Roberts late of this county a Mulattoe Man who is of a lite complexion, aged about 19 years the 5 April next, 5'6-1/4" high, stout & well made has long hair* [Hudgins, *Surry County Register of Free Negroes*, 36].

    vii.   ?Henry, head of a Campbell County household of 5 "other free" in 1810 [VA:880].

   viii. ?Samuel, head of a Sussex County household of 4 "other free" in 1810 [VA:661].

    ix. ?Nat, head of a Southampton County household of 4 "other free" in 1810 [VA:74].

6.   James[3] Roberts, born about 1753, and his wife Jane, "Mulattoes," were living in Charles Parish, York County, on 20 June 1773 when the birth of their son James was recorded [Bell, *Charles Parish Registers*, 163]. He was taxable in York County from 1784 to 1814: taxable on a slave in 1795 and 1805, taxable on 3 "free Negroes & mulattoes over 16" in 1813, and taxable on 2 free male tithables over 21 in 1814 [PPTL, 1782-1841, frames 92, 394, 411] and head of a York County household of 8 "other free" in 1810 [VA:881] and 5 "free colored" in 1820 [VA:159]. He registered in York County on 16 December 1822: *a dark Mulatto about sixty-nine years old, 5 feet 2-1/2 inches high* [Register of Free Negroes 1798-31, no.151]. His son was

     i. James[6], born 20 June 1773, baptized 1 August in Charles Parish.

7.   Ann Roberts, born say 1709, confessed to the York County court on 18 May 1741 that she had an illegitimate child [W&I 19:12-3]. She may have been the mother of "poor orphans" named James and Mary Roberts who were ordered bound out by the churchwardens of Bruton Parish on 16 May 1748. And she may have been identical to _____ Roberts (damaged order book page), a "free Mulatto" who was living in Bruton Parish on 19 August 1751 when the court ordered the churchwardens to bind her daughter Patt to John Peale [Judgments & Orders 1746-52, 83, 451]. She may have been the mother of

     i. Pat[1], born say 1743, ordered bound apprentice to John Peale in Bruton Parish on 19 August 1751.

    ii. James[2], born say 1745, a "poor orphan" living in York County on 16 May 1748 and 17 December 1750 when the court ordered the churchwardens of Bruton Parish to bind him out [Judgments & Orders 1746-52, 83, 380]. He may have been identical to James **Maclin**, alias Roberts, born say 1745, who was added to the list of tithables in Elizabeth City County on 7 November 1764 [Court Records 1760-9, 262].

   iii. Mary[4], born say 1747, ordered bound out by the churchwardens of Bruton Parish on 16 May 1748.

8.   Anthony Roberts, born say 1723, was executor of the 19 September 1749 York County will of his mother Mary Roberts and was granted administration on the 18 November 1751 York County estate of Margaret **Jasper**, deceased [W&I 20:163-4; Judgments & Orders 1749-53, 483]. He was called "Anthony Roberds Mulatto" when his payment of 5 shillings was entered in the account of the York County estate of John Peters which was recorded in court on 15 September 1760 [W&I 21:20]. The York County court presented him on 20 May 1765 and 17 June 1771 for not attending Yorkhampton Parish Church and on 17 November 1766 for not listing his son as a tithable. He and Francis Peters were sued for debt on 18 April 1768, and he was sued for a debt of 30 shillings on 16 July 1770. He was presented on 19 November 1770, 15 November 1773, and 21 November 1774 for failing to list himself as a tithable [Judgments & Orders 1763-5, 374, 448; Orders 1765-8, 161, 206, 207, 499; 1770-2, 14, 105, 211, 337; 1772-4, 436, 442, 443; 1774-84, 66, 73]. He was taxable on a slave and 2 horses in 1783, presented by the York County court in 1785 for failing to list his tithables, taxable on one tithe, a slave and a horse in 1788, tithable on a horse but exempt from personal tax in 1789, taxable on a free tithable and a horse in 1790, tithable on a slave in 1793, tithable on a horse in 1801 and 1802, and tithable on one free tithe and 2 horses in 1803

[PPTL, 1782-1841, frames 72, 111, 144, 154, 164, 258, 267, 279, 289]. (His son?) William Roberts and he were sued for debt in York County on 19 July 1784. He was awarded 30 pounds in his suit for trespass, assault and battery against Daniel **Lyons** on 22 November 1796. James Roberts, David **Poe** and James **Ashby** were witnesses [Orders 1784-7, 20; 1795-1803, 136-7]. He left a 6 October 1803 York County will, proved 15 July 1805, by which he appointed his son John Robbards his executor, gave his grandson William Robbards all his estate, and by a 6 June 1805 codicil gave a heifer to his grandson Thomas **Hunley** and a calf to Margaret Robbards [W&I 23:677-8]. He was the father of

    i.   ?Hannah, born say 1747, presented by the York County court on 19 November 1770 for selling rum without a license and presented on 15 November 1779 for failing to list her tithables. She was sued by John Cary in 1780 [Judgments & Orders 1770-2, 105; 1774-84, 242, 256].

12   ii. William[1], born say 1744.

   iii. John[3], born say 1763, taxable in York County from 1784 to 1810 [PPTL, 1782-1841, frames 92, 144, 164, 195, 212, 231, 247, 267, 289, 308, 329, 356] and head of a York County household of 8 "other free" in 1810 [VA:881].

   iv. ___, born say 1765, mother of Thomas **Hunley** (born about 1786) who registered in York County on 16 December 1822: *a light complected Mulatto about 36 years old...blue eyes has tolerable short hair...Born free* [Register of Free Negroes 1798-1831, no. 186]. He may have been related to David Hunley who was presented by the York County court on 15 May 1786 for failing to list himself as a tithable [Orders 1784-7, 322].

9. James[1] Roberts, born say 1734, was "a Mulatto" taxable in Lunenburg County in the St. James Parish list of Edmund Taylor in 1764 [Bell, *Sunlight on the Southside*, 256]. He purchased 100 acres in Northampton County, North Carolina, on the south side of Mockerson Branch adjoining George Jordan's land on 12 August 1765 and purchased 220 acres on Licking Branch adjoining George Jordan on 7 December 1785. He made his mark on a deed by which he sold 35 acres of his land adjoining Burwell Jordan to Burwell Jordan of Greensville County on 1 March 1790 [DB 3:408; 10:407; 8:227]. He was taxable in Northampton County on an assessment of 1,810 pounds in 1780 [GA 46.1] and head of a household of 4 "other free" and 2 slaves in 1790 [NC:73] and 3 "other free" in 1800 [NC:472]. He left a 3 March 1803 Northampton County will (making his mark), proved in March 1809, by which he left a cow, calf, and bed to Willis **Scott**; left Jonathan Roberts, William Roberts and Mary **Scott** (no relationship stated) ten shillings; and left the remainder of his personal estate to Claxton Roberts. He divided his 325 acre plantation between his sons Lyas (Elias) and Claxton who were to provide for their mother Ann Roberts. Jonathan and Claxton were named as executors. Jonathan qualified in March court 1809 [WB 3:14]. Mary was head of a Northampton County household of 4 "free colored" in 1820 [NC:256]. Their children were

13   i. James[4], born say 1755.
14   ii. Jonathan[1], born say 1759.
   iii. William[2], born say 1760, head of a Northampton County household of one "other free" in 1790 [NC:73], 7 in 1800 [NC:473], and 9 in 1810 [NC:743]. Administration on his estate was granted to Silas Long on bond of 500 pounds by the 2 December 1817 Northampton County court [Minutes 1817-21, 60].
   iv. Mary[4] **Scott**.
   v. Elias[1], head of a Northampton County household of 4 "other free" in 1790 [NC:73], 11 in 1800 [NC:473], and 15 "other free" and 2 slaves in 1810 [NC:743]. He and Stephen **Walden** were sureties for a 250

pound bond for Elisha **Byrd** to administer the estate of James **Byrd** in the 3 June 1816 Northampton County court [Minutes 1813-16, n.p.].

vi.   Claxton, head of a Northampton County household of 4 "other free" in 1800 [NC:473] and 9 "other free" and a slave in 1810 [NC:743]. He married Mason **Reed**, 29 January 1793 Southampton County, Virginia bond.

10.   Ishmael[1] Roberts, born say 1755, was head of a Robeson County household of 10 "other free" in 1790 [NC:50], 15 in 1800 [NC:415], and 14 in Chatham County in 1810 [NC:195]. He received pay for Revolutionary War service from 3 June 1777 to 3 June 1778 as a private in Colonel Abraham Shepherd's Company. Colonel Shepherd gave him a certificate which stated that he was furloughed *at Head Quarters Valley Forge to come home with me who was Inlisted in my Regement for the Term of three years - and Returned Home with me* [NCGSJ XV:105]. He entered 100 acres in Robeson County on the north side of Saddle Tree Swamp on 5 September 1787, 100 acres on the north side of Five Mile Branch and 100 acres on the east side of Raft Swamp on 14 February 1788, and 100 acres on the west side of Five Mile Branch on 22 January 1793 [Pruitt, *Land Entries: Robeson County,* I:7, 13, 70]. He sold land by deed proved in Robeson County on 5 January 1801 and purchased land by deed proved in Robeson County on 6 July 1803 [Minutes I:130, 256]. On 18 February 1804 he purchased two tracts of land in Chatham County, one of 250 acres on Bear and Bush Creeks for $450, a second of 100 acres on the waters of the Cape Fear River for $150, and he purchased a further 57 acres on Bush Creek for 75 pounds on 9 January 1805 [DB N:456, 437; M:641]. The sheriff sold 260 acres of this land on 12 February 1808 for a debt of about 16 pounds [DB P:118]. However, Ishmael repurchased this same 260 acre tract for about 17 pounds on 14 August 1811. And he purchased 102 acres on Little Lick Creek on 10 April 1818 [DB S:26; V:131]. On 8 and 12 February 1825 he sold (signing) most of his land to his sons: Richard, James, and Aaron [DB AB:166, 221; AA:275]. By his 12 July 1826 Chatham County will, he left his land on the west side of Bush Creek to his wife Silvey and then to his grandson Ishmael, oldest son of Zachariah. He also left one dollar to a list of persons, no relationship stated (who were identified as his children in his May 1829 Estate Papers), and he willed that his land where John **Archie (Archer,** his son-in-law) was living was to be sold and divided among his wife and a second list of persons (which included members of the first list), no relationship stated, and left $20 for the schooling of his grandson Thomas Roberts [CR 022.801.16]. When the will was offered for probate in the Tuesday, May 1827 session of the Chatham County court, the jury ruled that it was his will as regards his personal property but not as regards his real estate [Minutes 1822-27, n.p.]. A committee was appointed to settle the problem, and their report was recorded in the Monday, May 1828 session [Minutes 1828-33]. His estate papers listed seventeen persons and called them his children, but at least two of them, Ishmael and Elias, were probably his grandchildren [N.C. Archives Estate Papers, Chatham County]. The fifteen other persons named in his will and estate papers were

15   i.   Ethelred, born say 1780.

ii.   Zachariah, born say 1782, father of Ishmael[2] Roberts who was not yet twenty-one years old when his grandfather wrote his July 1816 will. Zachariah's wife Mary Roberts, and their son Ishmael were mentioned in the 20 December 1820 Robeson County will of her father Ethelred **Newsom** [WB 1:325].

iii.   Kinchen[2], born say 1784, head of a Chatham County household of 6 "other free" in 1810 [NC:195]. On 15 August 1821 he purchased 154 acres in Chatham County on the south side of Cape Fear River near the Ferry Road and Drake's land for $430 and sold this land seven years later on 25 December 1828 for $200. On 3 April 1829 he sold the 150 acres on Bush Creek which he received as one of the heirs of (his father?) Ishmael Roberts [DB X:320; AB:134, 186]. He was head of a Lost Creek Township, Vigo County, Indiana, household in 1850. He was a sixty-five-year-old, born in Virginia, with $3,000 estate, living with Nancy, fifty-eight years old, born in North Carolina [Household no. 202].

iv. Jonathan[2], born say 1784, head of a Robeson County household of 5 "other free" in 1810 [NC:241]. He entered 100 acres in Robeson County on 1 January 1810 [Pruitt, *Land Entries: Robeson County*, vol. II, no.162] and was living in Cumberland County when his father's estate papers were proved in May 1829 Chatham County court.

v. Elizabeth, born say 1788, married John **Archie**. She may have been the Betsey Roberts who had an illegitimate child by Barna **Stewart**. The August 1805 session of the Chatham County court ordered Barna to pay for the child's support [Minutes 1805-10, 41].

vi. Benjamin, born say 1792, married Sally **Archer**, 30 June 1817 Orange County, North Carolina bond, Jesse **Archer** bondsman. He was one of the freeholders (or son of one) who was ordered to work on the road from Deep River to Little Lick Creek in Chatham County in May 1817 [Minutes 1811-18, 60]. Benjamin was head of a Chatham County household of 6 "free colored" in 1820 [NC:192] and 6 in Orange County, Indiana, in 1840. He and his wife Sally obtained free papers in Chatham County on 6 November 1824 and recorded them in Orange County, Indiana on 11 February 1833 [Orange County Recorder Office Deeds D:433-4].

vii. Elias[2], born say 1793, obtained free papers in Chatham County on 10 February 1823 which stated that he was married to Nancy **Archie**, the daughter of Thomas **Archie**, and that they had been living in Chatham County for twenty-three years. Elias recorded his free papers in Orange County, Indiana on 20 February 1833 [DB D:432].

viii. Aaron, born say 1795, married Jary **Teary** (**Terry**) 10 October 1816 Robeson County bond, William **Carter** bondsman. He purchased 100 acres in Chatham County from his father for $150 on 12 February 1825 [DB AA:275]. On 13 April 1830 he obtained Chatham County "free papers" in which the clerk stated that he was a "free man of color," the son of Ishmael Roberts, an old Revolutionary soldier who served under Colonel Shepherd. Aaron had a wife named Sarah, the daughter of Edward (Etheldred) **Newsom**, another "free man of color" who served in the Revolution, and a daughter named Candassa [Owen County DB 3:280]. Sarah was mentioned in her father's 20 December 1820 Robeson County, North Carolina will [WB 1:325]. Their daughter Candace married John Harper on 15 December 1842 in Owen County [DB B:179]. Aaron was head of a Washington Township, Owen County, Indiana household of 3 "free colored" in 1830 [IN:19] and 5 in 1840 [IN:33].

ix. Margaret **Leucus** (**Locus**), born say 1799. She married Isham **Lucas**, 26 August 1820 Robeson County bond, Ethelred **Newsom** bondsman, and was living in Robeson County when her father's estate was settled in May 1829 in Chatham County.

x. James[10], born say 1800, married Polly **Stewart**, 12 February 1822 Chatham County bond, Thomas Cottrell bondsman. He purchased 62-1/2 acres in Chatham County on the south side of the Cape Fear River on Bush Creek from his father for $150 on 8 February 1825 [DB AB:166] and sold land by deed proved in Chatham County on Wednesday, May 1837 session [Minutes 1833-41].

xi. Richard[3], born say 1802, purchased 100 acres in Chatham County on Bush Creek from his father for $400 on 8 February 1825 [DB

AB:221]. The Thursday session of the August 1821 Chatham County court ordered him to support his child by Elleky **Evans** [Minutes 1805-10]. He married ___ **Bird**, 14 December 1827 Chatham County bond, John **Archy** bondsman. His wife was probably the daughter of Josiah **Bird**, head of a Chatham County household of 8 "free colored" in 1820 [NC:211]. He sold land by deed proved in Chatham County on Wednesday, May term, 1837 [Minutes 1833-41]. Richard may have been the Richard Roberts who was head of a Ripley Township, Rush County, Indiana household of 5 "free colored" in 1840.

xii. Mary[6].
xiii. Delphy, born say 1810. She was married to Henry Trevan before February 1830 when the deed for land they inherited from Ishmael Roberts was proved in Chatham County [Minutes 1828-33].
xiv. Rebecca.
xv.   Lewis.
xvi. "Pardon Boin." He was one of the earliest settlers of the town of Spencer, Owen County, Indiana, where he purchased Lot numbers 251, 261, 119, 105, 228, 126, 5, 52, and 53 between August 1825 and June 1831, and he received a patent for 40 acres in Lafayette Township in 1836. He was called Bowen Roberts when he purchased land from the other heirs of Ishmael Roberts by deed proved in Chatham County court in the Monday, February 1830 session [Minutes 1828-33]. Before travelling back to Owen County, he obtained "free papers" in Chatham County on 1 March 1830 and recorded them in Owen County on 31 October 1831. They mentioned his wife Elizabeth and daughter Patsy and stated that he was the son of Ishmael Roberts, Sr., an "old revolutionary" who had been living in Chatham County upwards of twenty years. They also mentioned Ishmael's widow Silvia and her daughter Rebecca [DB 3:279]. Pardon was head of an Owen County household of 5 "free colored" in 1830 [IN:19].

11. John[2] Roberts, born say 1759, purchased 100 acres in Northampton County, North Carolina, adjoining James Roberts and George Jordan on 10 September 1779 [DB 7:15]. He was a single man in 1780 when he was taxable on an assessment of 350 pounds in Northampton County [GA 46.1] and was head of a Northampton County household of 8 "other free" in 1790 [NC:73]. He purchased 6 acres on the east side of Cypress Swamp in Northampton County on 9 September 1791 [DB 10:66]. On 20 January 1798 he purchased 400 acres in Chatham County on the south prong of Lick Creek for 140 pounds and sold 222-1/2 acres of this land on 17 January 1819 [DB J:285; X:230]. This was land which bordered the part of Orange County which became Durham County in 1881. He was head of a Chatham County household of 14 in 1800 and 10 in 1810 [NC:214]. Perhaps his widow was Molley Roberts, born before 1776, head of a Person County household of 7 "free colored" in 1820 [NC:498]. His children may have been
i.   Polley, married Moses **Archer**, 23 April 1813 Orange County bond, Mathias **Milton** and Moses **Bass** bondsmen. Moses **Archie** was head of a Chatham County household of 4 "other free" in 1820 [NC:192].
ii. Joseph[4], born 1776-94, head of a Person County household of 4 "free colored" in 1820 [NC:498].

12. William[1] Roberts, born say 1744, husband of Milly (**Maclin**?) Roberts, "free Mulattos," registered the 22 March 1765 birth of their son Macklin in Bruton Parish, James City County [Bruton Parish Register, 29]. The York County court presented him on 6 May 1765 for not listing his wife as a tithable. The case was dismissed after he paid her levy and the court costs. On 21 July 1766 he was sued by the executor of Lawson Burfoot for a 55 shilling debt. Robert **Evans** and Thomas **Maclin** were his securities [Judgments & Orders 1763-5,

370; Orders 1765-68, 91]. He was presented by the York County court on 19 November 1770 for failing to list himself as a tithable and for selling rum without a license, and presented on 15 July 1771 for not listing himself as a tithable. Lucretia **Maclin** sued him on 17 May 1773 for trespass, assault and battery [Judgments & Orders 1770-2, 105, 337; 1772-4, 273]. His widow Mildred was taxable in York County on a free tithable in 1782; a free tithable, a slave, 2 horses and 7 cattle in 1783; taxable on a slave named Lewis in 1784; and taxable on (her son?) Richard Roberts and Lewis Wilson in 1785 [PPTL, 1813-24, frames 69, 72, 92, 102]. William and Milly were the parents of

    i.   Macklin, born 22 March 1765 [Bruton Parish Register, 29], perhaps identical to Godfrey Roberts (named for his grandfather Godfrey **Maclin**?) who was presented on 15 May 1786 for failing to list himself as a tithable. On 19 May 1800 the York County court ordered him to stand trial in Williamsburg for stealing a horse belonging to George **Morris** [Orders 1784-7, 322; 1795-1803, 398]. He was taxable in York County from 1788 to 1814 [PPTL, 1782-1841, frames 144, 164, 195, 212, 247, 267, 288, 318, 342, 367, 394, 411] and head of a York County household of 9 "other free" in 1810 [VA:881].

    ii.   ?Richard[1], born about 1766, taxable in the York County household of Mildred Roberts in 1785, taxable on a horse from 1788 to 1814, taxable on a slave in 1798 [PPTL, 1782-1841, frames 102, 144, 164, 239, 258, 279, 299, 318, 342, 367, 394, 411], head of a York County household of 8 "other free" in 1810 [VA:881] and 9 "free colored" in 1820 [VA:159]. He registered in York County on 20 January 1823: *light complexion about 56 years of age 5 feet 6-1/4 Inches high...bony face, fine short hair* [Register of Free Negroes 1798-31, no.202].

13.   James[4] Roberts, born say 1755, was called the son of James Roberts in a promissory note made on 24 July 1778 by which Jonathan Bowing agreed to pay him 80 pounds currency for value received. The promissory note was in a small leather-bound notebook which the Roberts family took with them when they moved to Indiana [Roberts Settlement Papers, Library of Congress Manuscript Division]. He was taxable in 1780 in Northampton County on an assessment of 482 pounds, including 12 pounds, 8 shillings cash in hand [GA 46.1]. He purchased 100 acres adjoining James Saul in Northampton County on 20 May 1774 and another 250 acres on the east side of Cates Hole Mill Swamp adjoining George Jordan in 1779. He sold (signing) 215 acres on Cates Hole Swamp adjoining George Jordan to (his brother) Jonathan Roberts on 9 February 1796. He bought another 96-1/2 acres adjoining his own land in 1797 and sold (signing) 125 acres on Cates Hole Swamp on 24 November 1797 [DB 5:321; 6:331; 10:233, 327, 340]. He was head of a Northampton County household of 7 "other free" in 1790 [NC:73], 10 in 1800 [NC:473], 7 "other free" and a slave in 1810 [NC:743], and 8 "free colored" in 1820 [NC:256]. Perhaps his children were

    i.   Richard[2], born before 1776, head of a Northampton County, North Carolina household of 2 "other free" in 1810 [NC:743] and 9 "free colored" in 1820 [NC:256].

    ii.   Kinchen[1], born say 1780, head of a Northampton County household of 5 "other free" in 1810 [NC:743]. He was among the freeholders of Northampton County who were required to furnish hands for the road from Frederick Stanton's to Nathaniel Stevenson's on 4 March 1816. He was deceased by 3 December 1816 when his wife Lucy was granted administration on his estate with Peter **Stewart** and Stephen **Walden** as sureties. On 3 March 1817 the court bound Kinchen's orphans James, Turner, and Harris to (their grandfather?) James Roberts.

    iii.   Katy, married Herbert **Scott**, 5 January 1816 Northampton County bond, William **Sweat** bondsman.

    iv. Elijah, born 1776-1794, head of a Northampton County household of 3 "free colored" and a female slave under the age of 14 in 1820 [NC:256]. He was one of the freeholders ordered by the Northampton County court to work on a road Frederick Stantons to Nathaniel Stevenson's on 4 March 1816 [Minutes 1813-21].

    v. Anthony[3], born 1795-1806, ordered by the Northampton County court on 7 December 1814 to pay support for a child he had by Elizabeth **Walden**. He was one of the freeholders ordered by the Northampton County court to work on a road Frederick Stantons to Nathaniel Stevenson's on 4 March 1816 [Minutes 1813-21]. He married Betsey **Davenport**, 26 March 1816 Northampton County bond, Tom Hughes bondsman. He was head of a Northampton County household of 4 "free colored" in 1820 [NC:256] and 9 "free colored" in Ripley Township, Rush County, Indiana in 1840.

14. Jonathan[1] Roberts, born say 1759, received 18 shillings, 8 pence pay for 7 days service in the Northampton County, North Carolina Militia under Colonel Allen Jones in 1775-1776 [Haun, *Revolutionary Army Accounts, Journal "A"*, 20]. He was single in 1780 when he was taxable on a 286 pound assessment in Northampton County [GA 46.1]. He kept a leather-bound notebook which recorded the birth on 3 June 1782 of Willis **Scott**, son of Mary **Scott**, and recorded his payment of 2 pounds, 9 shillings for schooling for the year 1803 [Roberts Settlement Papers, Library of Congress Manuscript Division]. He may have married Mary **Scott** because he made a deed of gift to his son Willis Roberts which was proved in Northampton County court on 6 June 1814. However, Jonathan's father James Roberts still referred to Willis as Willis **Scott** when he left him furniture by his 3 March 1803 Northampton County will [WB 3:14]. Jonathan was head of a Northampton County household of 5 "other free" in 1790 [NC:73], 10 in 1800 [NC:473], and 8 "other free" and a slave in 1810 [NC:743]. He purchased 215 acres on the east side of Cypress Swamp from his brother James on 9 February 1796, sold (signing) 106 acres of this land on 26 December 1797. He transferred land to his son Willis Roberts by deed filed on 20 July 1814 and to his son Hansel by deed filed on 9 February 1819 [DB 10:233, 362; 17:45; 20:51]. By his 15 July 1820 Northampton County will, proved 4 December 1820, he left his plantation to his wife Mary and then to his son James, and left five shillings each to son Willis Roberts, daughter Delila **Bass**, daughter Delina **Demcy**, son Ransom Roberts, son Hansel Roberts, and daughter Viny Roberts. He left furniture to his granddaughter Beca Roberts and named son Willis executor [WB 3:241]. His children were

    i. James[9], born 1775-96, head of a Northampton County household of 4 "free colored" in 1820 [NC:256]. He married Martha Roberts, 21 November 1824 Northampton County bond, Ransom Roberts bondsman. He died before March court 1826 when Martha received 41 acres adjoining Willis Roberts' land as her widow's dower. (His brother) Ransom was executor of his estate [C.R. 071.508.178 (estates papers at N.C. Archives)].

    ii. Willis, born 3 June 1782, head of a Northampton County household of 6 "other free" in 1810 [NC:743] and 11 "free colored" in 1820 [NC:256]. His father transferred land to him by deed filed in Northampton County on 20 July 1814, and he transferred land to his brother Hansel by deed filed on 14 December 1833 [DB 17:45; 26:195]. He was head of a Ripley Township, Rush County, Indiana household of 8 "free colored" in 1840.

    iii. Delila **Bass**, perhaps the Delila **Bass**, born about 1800, who married (second) Benjamin **Bass** on 7 January 1830 in Owen County, Indiana [DB A:34]. Benjamin was head of an Owen County household of 6 "free colored" in 1830 [IN:22] and 9 in 1840 [IN:42] and was living with Delilah in household no. 167 of Marion Township, Owen County, in 1850.

   iv. Delina **Dempsey**.

    v. Ransom, born 1775-94, head of a Northampton County household of 4 "free colored" in 1820 [NC:256].

   vi. Hansel, married Priscilla Roberts, 25 December 1813 Northampton County bond, Willis Roberts bondsman. His father transferred land to him by deed filed in Northampton County on 9 February 1819, and his brother Willis transferred land to him by deed filed on 14 December 1833 [DB 20:51; 26:195]. He was head of household no. 261 in Jackson Township, Hamilton County, Indiana, in 1850.

  vii. Viny.

15. Ethelred Roberts, born say 1780, entered land in Robeson County on 5 March 1801 [Pruitt, *Land Entries: Robeson County*, vol. II, no.161] and purchased land by deed proved in Robeson County on 8 January 1805 [Minutes I:314]. He was head of a Robeson County household of 4 "other free" in 1810 [NC:241], 9 "free colored" in 1820 [NC:321], and was living in Robeson County in May 1829 when his father's Chatham County estate was settled. He was probably named for Ethelred **Newsom**. He and his wife Dicey were mentioned in the free papers of their son Elias. They were the parents of

    i. Elias[3], born about 1815, a few months more than fifteen years of age in March 1830 according to free papers which were written for him in Robeson County on 8 June 1834 while he was a resident of Owen County, Indiana. He left Robeson County to go to Indiana with his uncles Aaron Roberts and Pardon Bowen Roberts, the latter of whom resided in Chatham County in 1830. The papers further stated that: *the undersigned ware well acquainted with the said Elias from his infancy and also with his father Etheldred Roberts...and his wife Dicey...persons of Colour are free born and that they have always sustained the reputation of Honest, industrious persons...he was never indentured or otherwise to either of his uncles* [Owen County DB 4:295].

Northampton County, Virginia

1. Elizabeth Roberts, born say 1690, was "a negro" living in Northampton County, Virginia, on 20 December 1715 when she came into court to bind her children John and William Roberts to Thomas Preeson [Orders 1710-16, 235]. Her children were

    i. John[1], born say 1708.

   ii. William[2], born say 1710, a "negro" tithable in the Northampton County, Virginia household of Jonathan Stephens in 1731 and a tithable in John Kendall's household in 1738 [Bell, *Northampton County Tithables*, 224, 281]. On 8 October 1734 John Kendall paid a fine for an illegitimate child William had by Elizabeth **Carter**, "Negroe" [Orders 1732-42, 136]. Perhaps Elizabeth was identical to (his wife?) Elizabeth Roberts who was tithable in his household from 1739 to 1742 [Bell, *Northampton County Tithables*, 286, 308, 316, 331]. He won a suit for trespass, assault and battery against Howson Mapp for 5 shillings on 12 November 1740 [Orders 1732-42, 423].

2   iii. ?Mary, born about 1714.

3   iv. ?Sabra, born say 1718.

2. Mary Roberts, born about 1714, a "free Negro," made choice of Jacob Waterfield as her guardian in Northampton County, Virginia court on 15 May 1728 [Orders 1722-9, 326]. She consented to the indenture of her son Hezekiah to Abel Upshur on 13 November 1739. She was tithable at Mol

Upshur's plantation in 1740 [Bell, *Northampton County Tithables*, 308]. She was the mother of

i. Hezekiah, born in February 1734/5, bound apprentice to Abel Upshur on 13 November 1739 [Orders 1732-42, 373]. The Accomack County court presented him on 30 May 1775 for failing to list himself as a tithable in 1774. The case was dismissed at the next court [Orders 1774-7, 349, 365]. He was head of a St. George Parish, Accomack County household of 3 "other free" in 1800 (called Kiah) [*Virginia Genealogist* 2:160]. He was a soldier who served in the Revolution from Accomack County [Jackson, *Virginia Negro Soldiers*, 42].

ii. Rachel², born 28 June 1733, a ten-year-old "Negroe" bound apprentice to John and Mary Luker in Northampton County on 12 April 1743 [Orders 1742-48, 78]. She may have been the Rachel Roberts who was presented on 13 May 1777 for bastard bearing [Minutes 1771-7, 370].

3. Sabra Roberts, born say 1718, a "Negroe," was presented in Northampton County, Virginia, on 9 November 1736 for bastard bearing and was called "Sabra a Negroe Servant woman to William Smith" on 11 April 1738 when the court bound her daughter Dorothy to her master. On 12 August 1740 the court ordered her released from her indenture to William Smith but deliberated until 15 October before deciding that she was entitled to her freedom dues [Orders 1722-9, 246, 259; 1732-42, 309, 408, 415]. She was taxable in William Smith's household from 1737 to 1740 and taxable in her own household adjoining William and Betty Roberts in 1741 [Bell, *Northampton County Tithables*, 267, 285, 308, 317]. She was the mother of

4   i.   Dorothy¹, born 10 November 1735.

4. Dorothy¹ Roberts, born 10 November 1735, daughter of Sabra, was bound apprentice to William Smith in Northampton County on 11 April 1738 [Orders 1732-42, 309]. She may have been the mother of

5   i.   Dorothy²/ Dolly, born say 1765.

5. Dolly Roberts, born say 1765, was head of an Accomack County household of 6 "other free" in 1800 [*Virginia Genealogist* 2:160] and 5 in 1810 [VA:53]. She was the mother of

i. Robin, born about 1778, registered in Accomack County on 29 September 1807: *Black, 9 feet 1/4 Inches* [Register of Free Negroes, no. 36]. He was called son of Dol Roberts in the list of tithables for Accomack County in 1799 and was married to Mary Roberts by 1813 when they were in the list of "free Negroes" [PPTL 1782-1814, frames 403, 834]

ii. ?Southy, born 14 September 1779, registered in Accomack County on 29 September 1807: *Black, 5 feet 3-5/8 Inches...Born free* [Register of Free Negroes, no. 11].

iii. ?Levin, born in November 1786, registered in Accomack County on 29 September 1807: *Black (rather light), 5 feet 4-1/2 Inches, Born free* [Register of Free Negroes, no. 13].

Other descendants on the Eastern Shore of Virginia were

i. Rachel¹, born about 1723, a twelve-year-old "Negroe" bound apprentice in Northampton County to Lydia Luke on 8 July 1735. On 8 April 1740 the court ordered Jonathan Smith to release her from servitude [Orders 1732-42, 167, 395].

ii. Esther, born about 1725, ten-year-old "Negroe" bound apprentice in Northampton County to Lydia Luke on 8 July 1735 [Orders 1732-42, 167]. On 8 April 1740 the court ordered Jonathan Smith to release her from servitude [Orders 1732-42, 395].

    iii.   Susanna, born say 1727, tithable in the Northampton County household of Joseph Delpeach in 1743 and 1744 [Bell, *Northampton County Tithables*, 351, 367]. On 14 December 1743 James Delpeech paid her court costs when she was whipped for bastard bearing. Solomon Wilson sued her for debt, but the case was dismissed at his costs on 14 May 1746 [Orders 1742-8, 136, 327].

    iv.   Robert, born about 1765, seven years old in July 1772 when he was bound apprentice in Northampton County [Minutes 1771-77, 120]. He was head of an Accomack County household of 7 "other free" in 1800 [*Virginia Genealogist* 2:14].

    v.   Littleton, a "Mulatto" taxable in Northampton County from 1790 to 1792 [PPTL, 1782-1823, frames 112, 141].

    vi.   Oney, head of an Accomack Parish, Accomack County household of 4 "other free" and a slave in 1800 [*Virginia Genealogist* 2:14].

    vii.   Isaac, head of an Accomack County household of 3 "other free" in 1800 [*Virginia Genealogist* 2:161] and 4 "other free" and a slave in 1810 [VA:52].

<u>Augusta, Frederick and Spotsylvania counties</u>
1.   Rebecca Roberts, born say 1730, a "Mulatto" servant, brought a successful suit for her freedom from her master John David Wilpart in Augusta County on 20 May 1761 [Orders 1761-3, 9]. She may have been the mother of

    i.   Anthony, born about 1753, registered in Petersburg on September 3, 1794: *a brown Mulatto man, five feet seven inches high, forty one or forty two years old, born free & raised in Spotsylvania County* [Register of Free Negroes 1794-1819, no. 91].

    ii.   Edward, born 10 April 1755, a "Mulatto Bastard Child" bound to William Cockran by the Frederick County, Virginia court in August 1755. On 8 April 1767 the court ordered him bound instead to William Baldwin until the age of thirty-one [Orders 1753-5, 370; 1765-7, 349].

ROBINS FAMILY

1.   John[1] Robbins, born say 1700, was one of the Chowan County Indians who sold their land on Bennett's Creek in 1734 in the part of Chowan County which later became Gates County:

> *James Bennett, Thos Hoyter, Charles Beasley, Jeremiah Pushin, John Robins, John Reading & Nuce Will Cheif men of the Chowan Indians...*[Chowan DB W-1, 250].[180]

On 12 April 1790 James Robins, Benjamin Robins, George **Bennett** and Joseph **Bennett** sold to Samuel Lewis and Samuel Harrell for $100 the last remaining 400 acres of the original tract of 11,360 acres near Bennetts Creek and Chowan Creek granted to the Chowan Indians in 1724. On 23 October 1790 Lewis and Harrell petitioned the General Assembly for authorization to purchase the land, stating that the Indian men had died,

> *leaving a parcel of Indian women, which has mixed with Negroes, and now there is several freemen and women of Mixed blood as aforesaid which has descended from the sd Indians...the said freemen...did in the*

---

[180]Mary Beasley was probably one of Charles Beasley's descendants. She paid 5 pounds for a five-year lease on a small house and one acre of land in Gates County from David Watson on 2 November 1795 [DB 3:261]. Perhaps she was the Polly **Beasley** ("&d Major") who was head of a Washington County household of 5 "other free" in 1810 [NC:795]. See further the Bennett and Hiter histories.

late Contest with Great Brittain behave themselves as good and faithful soldiers.

Their petition was rejected at first but approved on 28 and 30 December 1791 on petition of James Robins, noting that the money had been paid and the deed signed by all except six Indian women, descendants of the tribe, who were living on land unaffected by the sale [General Assembly Session Records, Nov-Dec 1790, Box 2; Gates County DB 2:272-274].[181] John Robins' likely descendants were

- 2   i.   Nan, born say 1743.
- 3   ii.   Lucy, born say 1750.

2.   Nan/ Nancy/ Ann Robins, born say 1743, was among eight Indians who purchased for 5 pounds thirty acres near the old Indian patent on 1 August 1782 in Gates County: James, Benjamin, Patience, Sarah, Nancy, Elizabeth, Dorcas, and Christian Robbins. The following year she was identified as their mother in a deed for land adjoining theirs [DB A-2:33, 46]. On 20 August 1821 their land was divided among Sarah, Nancy, Elizabeth, Thaney, Lewis, Treasy, and Judith Robbins [DB 11:40]. Ann Robins was head of a Gates County household of 4 "other free" in 1800 [NC:276], 5 in 1810 (called Nancy) [NC:842], and 7 "free colored" in 1820 [NC:155]. Possible children of Ann mentioned in the 1 August 1782 purchase of 30 acres were

- 4   i.   James[1], born say 1760.
-      ii.   Benjamin, born about 1765, a fourteen-year-old Indian ordered bound by the Gates County court as an apprentice planter to James Garritt, Sr., in November 1779. He was about seventeen years old in May 1781 when he was bound to Jethro Miltear [Fouts, *Gates County court Minutes* 1779-86, 10, 32].
- 5   iii. Patience, born say 1763.
- 6   iv.   Sarah, born say 1766.
-      v.   Elizabeth.
- 7   vi.   Thaney, born say 1770.
-      vii. Dorcas, head of a Gates County household of 6 "other free" in 1800 [NC:276] and 4 in 1810 [NC:842].
-      viii. Christian, living in Perquimans County on 23 February 1819 when he sold his rights to 5 acres in Gates County at Indian Town joining lands of Nancy, Elizabeth, and Sarah Robbins [DB 10:366].

3.   Lucy Robbins, born say 1750, was the mother of Samuel Robbins, a fifteen-year-old illegitimate boy, no race indicated, who was bound as an apprentice cooper to Jethro Miltear by the Gates County court in February 1787. She may also have been the mother of Elisha Robbins, an "Indian" boy who was bound to Jethro Miltear six years earlier in May 1781. Lucy was the mother of

- 8   i.   ?Mary, born say 1768.
-      ii.   ?Elisha, born about 1770, an eleven-year-old Indian boy ordered bound apprentice to Jethro Miltear in May 1781. He was an insolvent taxpayer in Gates County in 1794 [Fouts, *Minutes of County Court, Gates County, 1779-86*, 32; *1787-93*, 3, 86; *1794-99*, 80].
-      iii. ?Hardy, born say 1770, head of a Gates County household of one "other free" in 1790 [NC:23], an insolvent taxpayer in 1791 and 1794.
-      iv.   Samuel, born about 1772, son of Lucy Robbins bound as an apprentice cooper in February 1787, an insolvent taxpayer in Gates County in

---

[181]Several members of the Robins family of Virginia, descendants of Indian women brought to Virginia by traders between 1682 and 1748, brought suit in April 1772 against persons who held them in slavery [Catterall, *Judicial Cases Concerning American Slavery*, I:91].

1794 [Fouts, *Minutes of County Court, Gates County, 1787-93*, 3; *1794-99*, 40].

   v. ?James², born about 1780, an eleven-year-old "Indian Boy," no parent named, bound as an apprentice turner to William Gordon by the Gates County court in February 1791 [Fouts, *Minutes of County Court, Gates County, 1787-93*, 81].

4. James¹ Robins, born say 1760, was among eight members of the family named as buyers of 30 acres near the old Indian patent line in Gates County on 1 August 1782 [DB A-2:33]. In 1783 this land was called the "line of children of Nan Robbins," but by 1793 it was called James Robins' land [DB 3:167]. On 12 April 1790, he, (his brother?) Benjamin Robins, and George and Joseph Bennett were called "chief men and representatives of Chowan Indian Nation" when they sold for $100 the last 400 acres of the original 11,360 acres which the tribe held by patent of 24 April 1724 [DB 2:153]. He sued John Odom and William Watson in Gates County court for four pounds damages in May 1795 [Fouts, *Minutes of County Court, Gates County, 1794-99*, 35]. He was head of a Gates County household of 15 "other free" and a white woman in 1790 [NC:23], 3 "other free" and a white woman in 1800 [NC:276], and 2 "other free" in 1810 [NC:842]. Perhaps his children were

   i. Jacob, born 1776-94, head of a Gates County household of 5 "other free" in 1810 [NC:842] and 8+ "free colored" in 1820 [NC:155]. He purchased land by deed proved in Gates County in May 1811 [Minutes 1806-11, 697] and February 1814 [Minutes 1812-17, 827] and was living in Perquimans County on 6 February 1816 when he sold 30 acres in Gates County [DB 10:125].

   ii. Josiah, born 1776-94, head of an Orange County household of 5 "free colored" in 1820 [NC:336]. He married Tabitha **Shoecraft**. They moved with the **Shoecraft** family from Hertford to Orange and then to Guilford County. Josiah's widow Tabitha Robbins, born 1794-1806, was head of a Guilford County household of 7 "free colored" in 1830.

   iii. Lewis, head of a Gates County household of 2 "other free" in 1810 [NC:842].

   iv. Kinston, one of the "sundry persons of Colour of Hertford County" who petitioned the General Assembly in 1822 to repeal the act which declared slaves to be competent witnesses against free African Americans [*NCGSJ* XI:252].

   v. Thomas, born 1776-94, head of a Hertford County household of 4 "free colored" in 1820 [NC:186] and 5 in 1830 [NC:404].

   vi. ?Nancy, born say 1788, married Jethro **Martin**, 8 October 1806 Gates County bond, (her brother?) Jacob Robbins bondsman.

5. Patience Robbins, born say 1763, was among eight members of the family named as buyers of 30 acres near the old Indian patent line on 1 August 1782 [DB A-2:33]. She was the mother of

   i. Judith, who was living in Chowan County on 15 May 1820 when she sold land in Gates County known by the name of Indian Town which was descended to her from her mother [DB 10:523].

6. Sarah Robins, born say 1766, was head of a Gates County household of 2 "other free" in 1800 [NC:276], 4 in 1810 [NC:342], and 10 "free colored" in 1820 [NC:155]. She was the mother of

   i. ?John², born 10 August 1782, bound an apprentice house carpenter and joiner to William Lewis in February 1794 by the Gates County court. He and James Robbins were called "Indian or Molatto Boys" when they were bound to Henry Lee in February 1796 after William Lewis' death [Fouts, *Minutes of County Court, Gates County*, vol. I:6, 53]. He may have been the John Robins who married Mrs. Mary Ann **Weaver**, "free persons of colour," 1816 Norfolk County bond, Robert Barrett surety. He was head of a Gates County household of 7 "free colored" in 1820 [NC:155].

ii.   James[3], born in August 1784, ten-year-old son of Sarah Robbins bound as an apprentice house carpenter and joiner to William Lewis in Gates County in February 1794.

iii. ?Sealy, married James **Reed**, 25 October 1808 Gates County bond, James Lassiter bondsman.

7. Thaney Robins, born say 1770, was living in Gates County in February 1794 when the court bound her son Charles as an apprentice cooper to William Hinton of Indian Neck [Fouts, *Minutes of County Court, Gates County*, I:6]. She received her part of the division of 30 acres in Gates County, formerly called Indian Town, on 20 August 1821 [DB 11:40]. Her children were

i.   Charles, born about 1787.

8. Mary Robins, born say 1768, was living in Gates County in May 1798 when the court bound her twelve-year-old son Jethro to Richard Rawls to learn house carpentry [Fouts, *Minutes of County Court, Gates County*, I:97]. Her son was

i.   Jethro, born about 1786.

ROBINSON FAMILY

1. Mary Robinson, born say 1730, was living in Truro Parish, Fairfax County, on 22 June 1749 when the court ordered the churchwardens of Truro Parish to bind her "Mullatto" child to Hugh West to serve until the age of thirty-one and bound her to her master for an additional year [Orders 1749-54, 20]. And on 22 May 1754 the churchwardens bound her four-year-old "Mulatto" son William Robinson to West. Her children were released from their indentures in Loudoun County about twenty-five years later by (Hugh's son?) George West [Emancipation Papers, Loudoun County Courthouse, by Townsend Lucas in *JAAHGS*, 11:122]. Her children were

2   i.   ?Jane, born about 1747.

ii. William, born about 1750, thirty-one years old when he was discharged from his service by George West on 4 August 1781.

2. Jane Robinson, born about 1747, was thirty-one years old by 17 April 1778 when she completed her apprenticeship to George West in Loudoun County. Her children listed with her in the record of her emancipation were

i.   John, born October 1769 at Cameron.

ii.   Margaret, born about the middle of January 1771.

iii. James, born 14 February, died 1774.

iv.   Mary, born 1 August 1774, discharged from her apprenticeship by Heathy Dade on 1 August 1792.

v.   Amos, born 25 December 1777.

vi.   William, born 29 May 1780.

vii. Henry, born 1 June 1782.

viii. Lewis, born in June, no year stated.

Others in Virginia were

i.   Betty, born say 1730, called a "Christian White servant belonging to William Andrews" when she was charged by the churchwardens of Accomack Parish in Accomack County court on 2 June 1748 with having a bastard child by "Jemmy a Mulatto man Slave belonging to James Pettinger." The court ordered that her fine be paid by selling her for another five years when her servitude was completed [Orders 1744-53, 274].

ii.   Hannah, a "free Negro" living in York County on 17 September 1750 when the court ordered the churchwardens of Charles Parish to bind her to William Sclater [Judgments & Orders 1746-52, 352].

iii. Sampson, "Mulatto" head of a Nansemond County household in Buxton's list for 1784 [VA:74] and a Frederick County household of 5 "other free" in 1810 [VA:597].

iv.   George, a "Free Negro" taxable at G. Church in Nansemond County in 1815.

v.   Nancy, a "Free Negro" taxable on 2 cattle in Nansemond County in 1815 [Yantis, *Supplement to the 1810 Census of Virginia*, S-14].

vi.   Aaron, a "Free Negro" taxable in Nansemond County in 1815.

vii. Abby, head of a Norfolk County household of 4 "other free" and one slave in 1810 [VA:918].

viii. Charles(?), head of a Norfolk County household of 5 "other free" in 1810 [VA:918].

ix.   Olley, head of a Frederick County household of 7 "other free" in 1810 [VA:590].

x.   James, head of a Frederick County household of 6 "other free" in 1810 [VA:596].

xi.   Thomas, head of a Frederick County household of 4 "other free" in 1810 [VA:594].

xii. Susan, head of a Richmond City household of 5 "other free" in 1810 [VA:368].

xiii. Peter, head of a Richmond City household of 2 "other free" and one slave in 1810 [VA:346], perhaps the Peter Robertson, "Free mulatto, who was living in ward 2 of Richmond City in the household of Isaac Armistead, a ship carpenter, in 1782 [VA:112].

xiv. Barnett B., head of a Richmond City household of one "other free" and 2 slaves [VA:328].

North Carolina

1. Mary Robinson, born say 1735, was a "free Molato" woman who petitioned the Onslow County, North Carolina court on 5 January 1756 to order Richard Whitehurst, Sr., to release her unnamed child to her. The court ordered the sheriff to find the child and deliver it to her [Minutes 1749-65, 31c, 37a]. Her children may have been

2   i.   David, born say 1753.

3   ii.   Zachariah, born say 1760.

    iii. Manuel, head of a Richland District, South Carolina household of 6 "other free" in 1810 [SC:173a].

    iv.   Thomas Robison, head of a "Molatto" New Hanover County household of 2 polls aged 21-60 years, 3 under 21 or over 60, and 5 females in 1786 in John Erwin's list for the North Carolina state census; called Thomas Roberson in 1800, head of a New Hanover County household of 7 "other free" [NC:311]. Perhaps the man in his household in 1786 was Joseph Roberson, head of a New Hanover County household of 5 "other free" in 1800 [NC:311], and one "free colored" man over forty-five years old in 1820 [NC:209].

    v.   Edward Robeson, head of a "Molatto" New Hanover County household of one poll aged 21-60 years, one under 21 or over 60, and one female in 1786 in John Erwin's list for the North Carolina state census. He may have been the Edward Robinson of Cumberland County who was ordered by the 21 May 1763 Cumberland County court to appear and show cause why "three Mulatto Children that live with him should not be Bound apprentice as the law directs." They were Rachel, Benjamin, and Juda **Allen** [Minutes 1759-65, 90, 102, 108].

2. David Robinson, born say 1753, was head of a Jones County household of 3 "other free" in 1790 [NC:143]. He may have been the father of
     i. Benjamin, head of a Lenoir County household of 4 "other free," one white woman, and one white boy in 1800 [NC:15].
    ii. Charles Robinson, born 1794-76, head of a Lenoir County household of 3 "free colored" in 1820 [NC:291].
   iii. John Roberson, head of a Lenoir County household of one "other free" and a slave in 1810 [NC:287].
    iv. Lewis Roberson, head of a Lenoir County household of 2 "other free" in 1810 [NC:287] and 2 whites in 1820 [NC:291].

3. Zachariah Robinson, born say 1760, was head of an Anson County household of 10 "other free" in 1810 [NC:56] and 15 "free colored" in 1820 [NC:12]. He may have been the father of
     i. Sarah, born say 1783, married John **Demery** in Anson County in 1801 according to his recollection [*History of Randolph County, Indiana*, 137].
    ii. Moses, head of a Cumberland County household of 8 "free colored" in 1820 [NC:189].
   iii. Thomas, born 1776-94, head of an Anson County household of 6 "free colored" in 1820 [NC:12].
    iv. Martin, head of an Anson County household of 4 "free colored" in 1820 [NC:12].

4. George Robison, born say 1710, and his wife Tiba were taxables in Granville County, North Carolina, in 1750 with their sons George (born say 1733) and Frank Robison (born say 1735) [CR 44.701.23].

ROGERS FAMILY

Sarah Rogers, William Rogers, and Thomas **Swet** (**Sweat**) were the "Negro Children" slaves of Alexander Young who made a 25 December 1726 Isle of Wight County will which was proved 27 January 1728/9. He gave them to his friend John Exum to serve until the age of twenty-one and then to be free on the condition they pay him thirty pounds of tobacco yearly. He also gave Exum a "Negro woman" slave named Fortune who was to serve until her son Thomas **Swet** reached the age of twenty-one and then she was also to be free. The inventory of Young's estate, taken on 25 March 1729, included "1 Negro woman, 1 Negro girle, 2 Negro Boys" [Inventories & Accounts, 1726-34, 143-4, 181-2]. John Exum owned land in the part of Isle of Wight County which later became Southampton County and adjoined the Nottoway Indian reservation [DB 7:244, 246]. Other members of the Rogers family were
     i. Francis **Jenkins** alias Rogers, born say 1740. See the **Jenkins** family history.
    ii. Mary, born say 1748, a "free molatto" taxable in the Bertie County summary list for 1764.
   iii. John, born say 1750, one of the Tuscarora Indians who sold land by 10 February 1777 Bertie County deed [DB M:314-5].
    iv. Jeffry, born about 1761, a "free Mulato" boy aged four years on 5 October 1765 when the Craven County, North Carolina court ordered him bound to Elizabeth Mason to be a shoemaker. His master Thomas Mason died before 11 September 1770 when the court bound him to Thomas Nelson [Minutes 1758-66, 34c; 1767-75, 154b].
     v. Abraham, born 1776-1794, head of a Beaufort County, North Carolina household of 2 "free colored" in 1820 [NC:33].
    vi. Celia, born say 1760, one of the Nansemond Indians who sold 238 acres of the Nottoway reservation in Southampton County on 12 July 1792 [DB 7:714]. She died in September 1805.

vii. Alexander, born about 1797, an eleven-year-old orphan Indian boy listed in the special census of the Nottoway Indians which was taken in Southampton County in 1808. He was the half-brother of Fanny and Solomon **Bartlett** on their mother's side. The three children lived with their relative Celia Rogers until her death in September 1805 when they were taken in by white neighbors [LVA, Box 154a, Executive Papers June 21 - July 22, 1808, 4-7].

Cumberland County, Virginia

1. Prudence Rogers, born say 1735, was the mother of Sarah, Ann and Jane Rodgers who were bound by the churchwardens of Southam Parish, Cumberland County, to Job Thomas on 27 April 1761. On 23 September 1765 she complained to the court about his treatment of her children. On 27 March 1775 the court ordered the churchwardens of Littleton Parish to bind out her "mulattoe" children Nathaniel, Ansel, and Elizabeth Rodgers to Jesse Thomas [Orders 1758-62, 185, 315; Orders 1774-8, 321]. She was taxable in the northern district of Campbell County on a horse in 1787 and 1789 and taxable on a free male aged 16-21 in 1791 [PPTL, 1785-1814, frames 57, 113, 196]. She purchased for 20 pounds 50 acres on Jumping Run of Button Creek in Campbell County bounded by lands of the **Jenkins** family on 26 October 1789 with the provision that it pass to her son Ansel at her death. And she sold this land on 20 November 1793 [DB 2:490; 3:207]. She was the mother of

2.   i. Sarah, born say 1757.
3.   ii. Ann, born say 1759.
   iii. Jane, born say 1761, probably identical to James(?) Rogers, the mother of a "mulatto" son John Rodgers who was bound to Edward Clements in Cumberland County on 25 October 1779 [Orders 1779-84, 76].
   iv. Nathaniel, born say 1763, taxable in the southern district of Campbell County in 1786 and from 1791 to 1794: listed with 3 slaves and 2 horses in 1793, 4 slaves in 1794 [PPTL, 1785-1814, frames 28, 176, 258, 293].
   v. Ansel, born say 1765, taxable in Campbell County in 1792 [PPTL, 1785-1814, frame 240], taxable in Henry County from 1797 to 1814, in the list of "free Negroes & Mulattoes" in 1813 and 1814, listed in 1813 next to Fanny Rogers, no relationship stated [PPTL, 1782-1830, frames 442, 469, 495, 641, 656].
   vi. Elizabeth, born say 1767.

2. Sarah Rogers, born say 1757, was bound to Job Thomas in Southam Parish on 27 April 1775. She was the mother of
   i. Molly, born say 1775, bound to John Johnson by the churchwardens of Southam Parish in Cumberland County on 25 March 1776, called Mary Rodgers, a poor orphan, on 26 October 1776 when she was ordered bound by the churchwardens of Littleton Parish to John Montague. She complained to the court on 26 March 1781 and the court cancelled the indenture [Orders 1774-8, 364; 1779-84, 154, 158].
   ii. ?David, born say 1782, a "mulattoe" orphan ordered bound to Jesse Thomas on 25 November 1782, no parent named [Orders 1779-84, 293].

3. Ann Rogers, born say 1759, was bound by the churchwardens of Southam Parish to Job Thomas on 27 April 1761. She was the mother of
   i. Absalom, son of Ann Rogers bound to Joel Meggs in Cumberland County on 25 February 1782 [Orders 1779-84, 173].
   ii. Isham, son of Naney Rogers, ordered bound to Martin Richardson in Cumberland County on 23 February 1784 [Orders 1779-84, 500].
   iii. ?Stephen, orphan of Nancy Rogers, bound to William Sanderson in Littleton Parish on 24 January 1785 [Orders 1784-6, 195].

ROLLINS FAMILY

1. Elizabeth Floid, alias Rollins, born say 1738, servant of John Brown, confessed in Prince George's County, Maryland court on 22 November 1757 that she had a "Mulatto" child. The court ordered her sold for seven years and bound her seven-month-old daughter Jane to her master until the age of thirty-one [Court Record 1754-8, 540]. She was the mother of

    2   i.   Jane, born April 1757.

2. Jane Rollins, born April 1757 in Prince George County, Maryland, registered in Petersburg, Virginia, on 8 June 1810: *a dark brown Mulatto woman, five feet one and a half inches high, fifty two years old, born free in Fredericksburg* [Register of Free Negroes 1794-1819, no. 578]. She may have been the mother of

    i.   Lucy, born about 1774, registered in Petersburg on 9 June 1810: *a dark brown free Mulatto woman, five feet one inches high, thirty six years old, born free p. cert. of Registry of Fredericksburg* [Register of Free Negroes 1794-1819, no. 577]. She (called Lucy Rawlings) was head of a Petersburg household of 3 "other free" in 1810 [VA:119b]. She may have been identical to Lucy Rawlings who was head of a Fredericksburg, Spotsylvania County household of 5 "other free" in 1810 [VA:110b].

    3   ii. Benjamin, born say 1777.

    iii. Charlotte, born about 1779, registered in Petersburg on 6 June 1816: *a free woman of colour, five feet one half inches high, dark brown, near black, supposed thirty seven years old, born free in Essex County* [Register of Free Negroes 1794-1819, no. 809]. She (called Charlotte Rollings) was head of a Petersburg Town household of 3 "other free" in 1810 [VA:120b].

    iv. Betsy **Jarratt**, born about 1782, registered in Petersburg on 8 June 1810: *Betsy Jarratt, a light brown Mulatto woman, five feet four and a half inches high, twenty eight years old, born free p. cert. of Registry from the Clerk of Fredericksburg, her name Betsy Rollins* [Register of Free Negroes 1794-1819, no. 569]. She may have been the wife of Richard **Jarratt** who registered in Petersburg on 11 December 1809: *a dark brown Mulatto man, five feet seven 3/4 inches high, thirty years old, born free and raised in the County of Chesterfield* [Register of Free Negroes 1794-1819, no. 500]. He was head of a Petersburg Town household of 6 "other free" in 1810 [VA:119a].

3. Benjamin Rollins, born say 1777, was taxable in St. Ann's Parish, Essex County, in 1800 and was listed there as a "free Negro" in 1813 [PPTL, 1782-1819, frame 510]. He was head of an Essex County household of 7 "other free" in 1810 [VA:198]. He was probably the husband of Jane Rollins who registered as a free Negro in Essex County on 8 December 1810: *daughter of Mary Soleleather by statement of Thomas Brockenbrough always passed as a free born person, 25 years of age, five feet 2-1/4 inches, bright Mulattoe* [Register of Free Negroes 1810-43, p.14, no. 30]. She was the mother of

    i.   Polly, born about 1809, registered in Essex County on 8 December 1810: *by statement of Thos. Brockenbrough daughter of Jenny Rollins who always passed as a free born person, 1-3/4 years of age* [Register of Free Negroes 1810-43, p.14, no.31].

ROSARIO FAMILY

1. Philip[1] Rosario, born say 1700, was an Indian living in Northampton County, Virginia, had an account with John Abdell, ordinary keeper, in 1722. In July 1724 the court ordered him to pay 4 barrels of corn which he had lost in a card game to David Stott. In November 1730 the court ordered the sheriff to arrest him until he provided security to appear in court to answer the suit of Andrew Walls, merchant, for a debt of 4 pounds. Philip sued William Vawter for 1 pound, 12 shillings in February 1730/1 [Orders 1729-32, 70; Mihalyka, *Loose Papers, 1628-1731*, 59, 90, 232]. He was taxable in Northampton County from 1722 to 1729 [Bell, *Northampton County Tithables*, 31, 44, 110, 124, 166, 189]. He died before 16 July 1752 possessed of an estate so small in value that the court ordered its sale by the sheriff [Orders 1751-3, 143]. He was probably the ancestor of

   2   i.   Philip[2], born say 1740, an Indian bound by the Northampton County court to Thomas Barlow on 12 January 1762 [Minutes 1761-5, 4].
      ii.   Elizabeth Rozario, listed in the town of Williamsburg with 3 "Black" persons in her household in 1782 [VA:45], probably the mother of Caroline and Suckey Rosara who were counted in a list of "Free Negroes and mulattoes" in Williamsburg in 1813. They were in the same list as Kizza **Sunket** who was probably from Northampton County [Waldrep, *1813 Tax List*]. See also the De Rosario family.

2. Philip[2] Rosario, born say 1740, was an Indian bound by the Northampton County court to Thomas Barlow on 12 January 1762 [Minutes 1761-5, 4]. He may have had children by a slave since a number of manumitted slaves in Accomack County used the name Rosario. He may have been the ancestor of

      i.   Cyrus Rosarrous, registered in Accomack County: *Born about the year 1762, a light Black inclining to yellow, Emancipated by a deed of manumission from Mary Griffin recorded in Accomack County Court* [Register of Free Negroes, 1785-1863, no. 192].
      ii.   Sarah Roseairy, registered in Accomack County: *born in June 1776, a very dark yellow approaching to a light black, 5-4-3/4", Emancipated by Robertson Rodgers by a deed of Manumission of Record in Accomack County Court* [Register of Free Negroes, 1785-1863, no. 90].

ROSS FAMILY

1. Jane[1] Ros, born say 1717, was living in Caroline County, Virginia, on 9 May 1735 when she was presented by the grand jury for having a "mulatto" child at William Oliver's house. The presentment was dismissed on 13 February 1735/6 [Orders 1732-40, 291, 326]. She was probably the grandmother of

      i.   Reuben, born say 1755, a soldier from Culpeper County who served in the Revolutionary War [Jackson, *Virginia Negro Soldiers*, 42]. He married Sally Terrel, 25 October 1791 Culpeper County bond. He was a "Ma." taxable on a horse in Culpeper County in 1800 [*Virginia Genealogist* 16:277] and a "F. Mo." head of a Culpeper County household of 9 "other free" and one white woman in 1810 [VA:68]. They were probably the parents of George Ross who registered as a free Negro in the Corporation of Staunton: *A bright mulatto man said to be 20 years of age the 10th day of May last. About 6 feet high, free born of a white woman in the county of Culpeper* [Free Negro Register, no.28, http://jefferson.village.virginia.edu/vshadow2].
      ii.   David, born say 1760, a soldier from Culpeper County who served in the Revolutionary War.
      iii.   Jane[2], head of a New Kent County household of 2 "other free" in 1810 [VA:766].

iv. Jonathan, a "Ma." taxable on a horse in Culpeper County in 1800.

ROUSE FAMILY

Members of the Rouse family were
1   i.   Peter[1], born say 1738.
     ii. John[1], purchased 100 acres on Panther Branch in Bladen County, North
          Carolina, on 31 May 1762 with Peter Rouse as witness (signing) [DB
          23:87]. He was a "Molato" taxable in Bladen County, North Carolina,
          with (his brother?) Neil Rouse in 1771 [Byrd, *Bladen County Tax Lists*,
          I:61]. He died before 8 June 1790 when Neal Rouse was granted
          administration on his Marlboro County, South Carolina estate [Minutes
          1785-1808, n.p.].
2   iii. Cornelius, born say 1740.
     iv. Nancy, born about 1775, registered in Petersburg on 13 February
          1798: *a dark brown Mulatto woman, five feet high, twenty three years
          old, born free in the County of Dinwiddie & raised in the Town of
          Petersburg. Feb. 27, 1817: Reentered by name of Nancy Johnson
          alledged to have been married* [Register of Free Negroes 1794-1819,
          no. 135].
     v.   Samuel, a "free" taxable in Dinwiddie County in 1792, 1796, 1797 and
          1798 [PPTL, 1791-9 (1792 B, p.11), (1796 A, p.12), (1797 A, p.13),
          (1798 B, p.13)].

1. Peter[1] Rouse, born say 1738, was listed in the muster of Captain Paul
    Demere's Company of Independent Foot on duty in South Carolina and
    Georgia, "stationed on the spot," from 25 August 1756 to 24 October 1756
    [Clark, *Colonial Soldiers of the South*, 989]. He was head of a South
    Orangeburgh, South Carolina household of 11 "other free" in 1790 [SC:99].
    Perhaps his widow was Charity Rouse, head of a Barnwell District household
    of 6 "other free" in 1800 [SC:65]. Charity was taxable on 150 acres in
    Winton, South Carolina, in 1800. He may have been the father of
3   i.   Peter[2], born say 1760.
     ii. Tristram, taxable on one "free Negro" in Winton, South Carolina, in
          1800 [S.C. Tax Returns 1783-1800, frame 301, 313].

2. Cornelius Rouse, born say 1740, was a "Molato" taxable in Bladen County,
    North Carolina, with (his brother?) John Rouse in 1771 [Byrd, *Bladen County
    Tax Lists*, I:61]. He was a "Negroe" head of a Cheraw District, South
    Carolina household of 2 "other free" males above the age of 16, 2 "other free"
    males under 16, and 7 "other free" females in 1790 [SC:358], 15 "other free"
    in Barnwell District in 1800 [SC:62], and 9 in Abbeville District in 1810
    [SC:84]. He was called Neale Rous when he received pay for thirty days duty
    in the militia in 1782 [S.C. Archives Accounts Audited For Revolutionary War
    Services, AA6636, frame 466, roll #128]. He was granted administration on
    the Marlboro County, South Carolina estate of John Rous on 8 June 1790
    [Minutes 1785-1808, n.p.]. He may have been the Cornelius Ross (born before
    1776) who was head of an Abbeville District household of 5 "free colored" in
    1820 [SC:5a]. He may have been the father of
     i.   Edmond Rouce, head of an Abbeville District household of 8 "other
          free" in 1810 [SC:82].
     ii. John[2], head of an Abbeville District, South Carolina household of 6
          "other free" in 1810 [SC:82].
     iii. Charles, born before 1776, head of an Abbeville District household of
          6 "free colored" in 1820 [SC:5a].

3. Peter[2] Rouse, born 22 December 1760, enlisted in the 2nd Virginia Regiment
    under Captain William Campbell in Dinwiddie County according to his

application for a pension in Greene County, Pennsylvania, on 10 September 1832 [M805-706, frame 0545]. He was taxable in Brunswick County, Virginia, in 1787 [Schreiner-Yantis, *1787 Census*, 241] and married Sarah **Lawrence**, daughter of Robert **Lawrence**, deceased, 19 October 1786 Brunswick County bond, Woody **Lawrence** bondsman. He was head of a Northampton County, North Carolina household of 9 "other free" in 1800 [NC:473]. He was probably the ancestor of

 i. Isaac, a "free boy of Colour," who was bound to William Moore to be a farmer by the 2 September 1822 Northampton County court [Minutes 1821-25, 123].

ROWE FAMILY

1. Patty Rowe, born say 1736, was living in Nottoway Parish, Amelia County, on 28 April 1755 when the court ordered her daughter Lucy bound to Robert Mumford. She had two children who were ordered bound to Jonas Vasser: Moll on 22 January 1756 and Tabitha on 24 March 1757. On 24 November 1763 the Amelia County court presented Nathaniel Robertson for not listing her as his "Mulatto" tithable in Nottoway Parish [Orders 1763, fol. 232]. She was probably identical to "Patt a Free Mulatto" of Nottoway Parish who was presented on 22 May 1766 for not listing herself as a tithable. On 23 March 1769 the court ordered the churchwardens of Nottoway Parish to bind out her children Randall White Roe and Dinny Roe to William Wilson. She was probably the mother of Tabb and Jack Roe, "Free Mulattoes," who were ordered bound by the churchwardens of Nottoway Parish to Colonel Richard Jones on 24 October 1771. They were probably identical to Jack and Tabb (no last names), "Free Mulattoes," who were ordered bound by the churchwardens of Nottoway Parish to William and Mary Vasser on 25 September 1767 [Orders 1754-8, n.p.; 1765-7, 90, 95; 1767-8, 83; 1768-9, 88; 1769-72, n.p.]. Patty was living in Bute County, North Carolina, on 15 February 1775 when the court bound her children Charles Randolph and Dinney Randolph to William Toulson to read and write and learn "the planters business" [Minutes 1767-76, 322]. Her children were

 i. Lucy, born before 28 April 1755.
 ii. Moll, born before 22 January 1756.
 iii. Charles Randolph, born about 1759 in Virginia, one of the Continental soldiers who volunteered in Bute County in 1779 (abstracted as Charles Kons[?] in *NCGSJ*): *5'8" tall, dark hair and dark eyes* [*NCGSJ* XV:109 & *The North Carolinian* VI:727]. He was called "Charles Roe a poor boy" on 24 November 1763 when the Amelia County court ordered the churchwardens of Nottoway Parish to bind him out [Orders 1763, 237]. He was called Randolph Rowe when he married Susannah **Stewart**, 17 December 1793 Warren County bond with Richard **Evans** bondsman, and he was called Charles Rowe when he married, second, Elizabeth **Taborn**, 11 December 1797 Granville County bond, Solomon **Harris** bondsman. He was sued for a 2 pound debt in Mecklenburg County, Virginia, on 13 October 1794 [Orders 1792-5, 351]. He was taxable in Warren County, North Carolina, from 1796 to 1800 [Tax List 1781-1801, 318, 344, 366, 404] and head of a Wake County household of 2 "other free" in 1800 [NC:793], 5 in Chatham County in 1810 (called Randolf Roe) [NC:201], and 2 "free colored" in 1820 [NC:209]. He received a pension in 1832 when he was seventy-eight years old [M804-2072].
 iv. John[1], born about 1760, a "free man of Colour," about sixty-one years old on 8 August 1820 when he made a declaration in Botetourt County court to obtain a pension for his services in the Revolution. He stated that he enlisted in 1778 with Colonel Fabeger in the 2nd Regiment in New Jersey [M804-2072, frame 0209]. He was head of a Fluvanna

County, Virginia household of 1 "other free" in 1810 [VA:478]. He registered in Nottoway County on 5 November 1818 and again in Botetourt County on 13 March 1820: *58 years, Black Colour, 5 feet 8 inches* [Free Negroes Registered in the Clerks Office of Botetourt County, no.29].

   v.   Tabitha, born say 1764.

   vi. Dinney Randolph, born say 1765.

Other members of the family were

   i.   Frederick, "F.N.", head of a 96 District, Laurens County, South Carolina household of one "other free" in 1790 [SC:71].

   ii.   James[1], born say 1760, granted land for service in the Revolution [Franklin County, North Carolina DB 6:780].

   iii. James[2], born about 1770, bound to Edmund Denny in Wilkes County, North Carolina, on 7 September 1779 [Absher, *Wilkes County Court Minutes 1778-1788*, I:11].

   iv. Sarah **Baltrip**, alias Roe, born about 1778, bound in Wilkes County to Charles Gordon on 28 October 1790 [Absher, *Wilkes County Court Minutes 1789-1797*, III:19] and to Edmund Denny on 3 August 1792 [Absher, *Wilkes County, N.C. Will Books One & Two 1778-1811*, 33].

   v.   John[2], born 12 September 1780, a "Molatto boy" bound to P. R. Walker in Person County on 19 March 1793 [Minutes 1792-96], head of a Person County household of 3 "other free" in 1810 [NC:632], 3 "free colored" in 1820 [NC:498], and a "Negro" head of a Guilford County household of 3 in 1830. He married Tamer **Bass**, 2 December 1801 Granville County bond, George **Pettiford** bondsman, and second, Sally **Pendergrass**, 2 March 1802 Person County bond.

   vi. Polly, born about 1799, registered as a free Negro in the Corporation of Staunton, Virginia, on 14 June 1832: *(alias Polly Harris) a free woman of colour aged about 33 years, of a dark yellow complexion, 5 feet 7-1/4 inches high...as appears from the certificate of M.W. Norvell Clerk of Lynchburg Hustings Court dated 14th June 1825* [Register of Free Negroes, no.119].

   vii. Samuel, Polly, and William, "children of colour" bound apprentice in Warren County on 31 August 1804 [WB 12:242 by Kerr, *Abstract of Warren County Will Books*].

ROWLAND FAMILY

1.   Ann Rowland, born say 1700, was living in Surry County, Virginia, on 20 May 1719 when the court presented her for having a "molatto" bastard [DW 7:188]. She was probably the mother of

   i.   Simon, born about 1719, a servant bound to Peter Bagly until the age of thirty-one. By Bagly's 15 November 1735 Surry County will he ordered his executors to give Simon his freedom at the age of twenty-eight. Simon was probably the "Molleto boy" with eleven years to serve who was listed in the 17 March 1735/6 inventory of Peter Bagly's estate [DW 8:547, 576].

   ii.   Mary, born say 1721, presented by the court in Surry County on 21 May 1740 for having a "Negro Bastard" [DW 9:172].

RUFFS FAMILY

1.   Margaret Ruffs, born say 1725, was living in Southwarke Parish, Surry County, Virginia, on 21 November 1752 when her daughter Lucy was brought to court and adjudged to be the "Mulatto" child of a "white woman" [Orders, 1751-53, 503]. She was apparently the mother of

2   i.   Deley, born say 1743.

ii. Lucy, born say 1752, a "poor orphan" daughter of Margaret Ruff bound out by the Surry County court on 20 April 1756 [Orders 1753-7, 378].

2. Deley/ Dilce Ruffs, born say 1743, was a "Mullatto" girl (no parent named) who was bound out by the Henrico County court in July 1743. She was the mother of Jeffrey, John and Joseph Ruff who were ordered bound out by the Henrico County court on 3 February 1783. She died before 1 December 1788 when the court ordered the churchwardens of the lower district of Henrico County to bind her son Joseph Rough to Arthur Giles, carpenter [Orders 1737-46, 225; 1781-4, 183; 1787-9, 493]. She was the mother of

i. Jeffry.

ii. John, head of a Fluvanna County, Virginia household of 2 "other free" in 1810 [VA:492].

iii. Joseph, born say 1778, bound to Arthur Giles in Henrico County on 1 December 1788, a "free Black" head of a Bedford County, Virginia household of 6 "other free" in 1810 [VA:480]. He was living in Bedford County on 9 December 1833 when he petitioned the Virginia Legislature to allow him to own a gun since it was required for hunting wild fowl and protecting the crop on the small farm he owned in the mountains [Johnston, *Race Relations*, 59].

iv. ?Sally, married Abram **Goff**, 25 July 1798 Bedford County bond, John **Mann** and Richard **Moss** bondsmen.

Other descendants were

i. Winifred, born 20 August 1765, a "Free Negroe Girl" bound to Thomas Silgreaves until the age of eighteen years in Craven County, North Carolina, on 8 October 1766 [Minutes 1764-66, 50d].

ii. Britton, a "melatto" taxable in the northern district of Campbell County from 1788 to 1810 [PPTL, 1785-1814, frames 88, 113, 157, 197, 241, 277, 307, 702, 664, 773], head of a Campbell County household of 1 "other free" in 1810 [VA:881].

iii. Step, a "f. negroe" or "melatto" taxable in Campbell County in 1790 and 1791 [PPTL, 1785-1814, frames 155, 196].

iv. Rebecca, born about 1792, registered in Southampton County on 4 December 1817: *age 25, 5 feet 4-1/2 inches, Mulatto woman free born (in) Prince George County* [Register of Free Negroes 1794-1832, no. 1129].

v. James, born say 1800, married Betsy **Blizzard**, 23 May 1823 Surry County bond. He was head of a Surry County household of 4 "free colored" in 1830.

RUFFIN FAMILY

Members of the Ruffin family were

i. Dilcy, head of a Richmond City household of 5 "other free" and a slave in 1810 [VA:345].

ii. Thomas, head of a Southampton County household of 5 "other free" in 1810.

iii. Polly, head of a Richmond City household of 3 "other free" in 1810 [VA:361].

iv. Joe, head of a Richmond City household of 2 "other free" in 1810 [VA:369].

v. James, married Betsy **Bird**, 20 January 1810 Surry County bond, Wright **Walden** surety.

RUSSELL FAMILY

1. Eleanor Russell, born before 1723, was over eighteen years of age on 27 April 1741 when she appeared as a witness against Jack, "a mulatto Slave" convicted by the Craven County, North Carolina court of killing his master, Robert Pitts. She helped to convict him by testifying that he tried to convince her to do it for him. The court ruled that he be

    hangd by the neck till he is Dead & then his head to be Severed from his body & stuck upon a pole [Haun, *Craven County Court Minutes*, II:275-6].

    The Craven County records do not mention Eleanor's fate, but apparently she was also convicted since she petitioned the General Assembly on 5 May 1742 for reprieve from her death sentence. Eleanor's "Mixtd Blood" daughter Hannah Russell was indentured later that year on 21 September [Saunders, *Colonial Records of North Carolina*, III:339, 617, 653]. Her children were

    2   i.   ?John, a "Mulatto" born about 1736.
        ii. Hannah, daughter of Eleanor Russell, ordered bound out to Nicholas Rutledge by the Craven court on 25 September 1742 [Haun, *Craven County Court Minutes*, III: 339], perhaps identical to Ann Russell, head of a Craven County household of 1 "other free" in 1790 [NC:131].

2. John[1] Russell, born about 1736, a "Mulatto," no parent named, was six years old on 21 September 1742 when the Craven County court bound him to David Lewis. Lewis promised to teach him, "to Read & Write a Ledgable hand & to teach him or cause to be taught the Shoemakers trade." However, Lewis gave him to his brother, John Lewis of Chowan County, and he sold him to Captain Hews of Suffolk County, Virginia [Haun, *Craven County Court Minutes*, III:328, 653]. He may have been the John Russell who was a "Mulato" taxable in Bladen County in 1769 [Byrd, *Bladen County Tax Lists*, I:16]. He may have been the father of

    i.   Thomas, a taxable "Mulato" in Bladen County in 1768 and 1776 [Byrd, *Bladen County Tax Lists*, I:7; II:68, 92], head of a Georgetown District, Prince Fredericks Parish, South Carolina household of 6 "other free" in 1790.
    ii. Polly, head of a Barnwell District, South Carolina household of 3 "other free" in 1800 [SC:65].

Loudoun County, Virginia
1. Anne Russell, born say 1737, was the mother of a "Mulatto" daughter who the churchwardens of Cameron Parish, Loudoun County, were ordered to bind out on 13 September 1757 [Orders 1757-62, 17]. She was the mother of
    i.   Jane, born say 1757.

Other members of the Russell family were
    i.   John[2], "a Negro poor person" who was assigned counsel by the Goochland County court in January 1759 to sue the executors of Thomas Drumwright who were detaining him as a slave [Orders 8:175].
    2   ii. Amy, born say 1747.
    3   iii. George, born say 1756.

2. Amy Russell, born say 1747, was a "free Negro" living in Norfolk County on 16 January 1767 when the churchwardens of Elizabeth River were ordered to bind her children James and Frank as apprentice bakers to Paul Heriter. She complained to the court against John Halstead, Jr., in February 1774 [Orders 1766-68, 69; 1773-5, 27]. Her children were

    i.   James¹, born say 1764, bound to Paul Heriter on 16 January 1767 and a "free negro" bound to John Runsberg on 17 December 1773 [Orders 1773-5, 8].

    ii.   Frank, born say 1766.

    iii.   ?Lewis, head of a Richmond City household of 2 "other free" in 1810 [VA:316].

    iv.   ?Molly, head of a Norfolk County household of 2 "other free" in 1810 [VA:917].

3.   George Russell, born say 1756, enlisted in the Revolution while resident in Brunswick County, Virginia [Jackson, *Virginia Negro Soldiers*, 42]. He was head of a Wake County household of 11 "other free" in 1790 [NC:103] and 4 in 1800 [NC:791]. He sold 75 acres, and James Russell sold an adjoining tract of 60 acres in Wake County about 1800 [DB Q:415]. He applied for a pension while resident in Smith County, Tennessee. Perhaps George's children were

    i.   James², head of a Wake County household of 3 "other free" in 1790 [NC:103], 9 in 1800, and 7 "free colored" in Richmond County in 1820 [NC:200].

    ii.   Matthew, head of a Montgomery County household of 3 "other free" in 1790 [NC:166].

SAMPLE FAMILY

1.   Dorothy¹ Sample, born say 1690, was living in Accomack County, Virginia, on 15 November 1792 when her mother Mary Sample, a widow, bound her to John and Dorothy Washbourne until the age of eighteen [Orders 1690-7, 78a]. She was in adjoining Northampton County in May 1710 when the court bound her eighteen-month-old son Jacob as an apprentice. On 15 June 1714 she successfully sued Rebecca Maddux, administratrix of the estate of Thomas Maddux, for 405 pounds of tobacco [O&W 1698-1710, 536; Orders 1710-16, 165]. She was called a "white Christian Single Woman" when she was presented by the churchwardens of Accomack County on 6 April 1715 and 2 May 1721 for having illegitimate children by "one Negro Slave named Black Daniel" [Orders 1714-7, 7-7a; 1719-24, 30]. On 4 November 1718 she bound her three-year-old daughter Tabitha to Benjamin Wattson [Orders 1717-9, 23a]. Her children were

2   i.   Jacob, born about December 1708.

    ii.   Tabitha, born 12 January 1715.

2.   Jacob Sample, born about December 1708, eighteen-month-old son of Dorothy Sample, was bound apprentice in Northampton County, Virginia, in May 1710 [O&W 1693-1710, 536]. He was taxable in Richard Smith's Northampton County household in the list of Thomas Marshall in 1725 and in the Tobacco List of Daniel Luke and Jonathan Bell in 1728 [L.P. 1725, 1728]. He probably left the county that year since he was not taxable in 1729 or the following years. Jacob may have been the father of

    i.   Eliza Simbler, born 6 January 1733, a "Mulatto girl" bound to William Waddill in St. Peter's Parish, New Kent County [NSCDA, *Parish Register of St. Peter's,* 117].

3   ii.   Daniel¹, born say 1740.

3.   Daniel¹ Sample, born say 1740, was tithable with (his wife?) Mary Sample in Thomas John Marshall's list for Northampton County in 1765 [Bell, *Northampton County Tithables,* 371]. He sued a member of the **Stephens** family for a debt of 1 pound, 9 shillings on 16 September 1773 [Minutes 1771-7, 177, 189]. The Accomack County court presented him on 30 May 1775 for failing to list himself as a tithable in 1774. The case was dismissed at the next

court [Orders 1774-7, 349, 365]. He was a "free Negro" taxable in Accomack County from 1787 to 1789: taxable on 2 tithes in 1789 [PPTL 1782-1814, frames 239, 304], head of a St. George Parish, Accomack County household of 4 "other free" in 1800 [*Virginia Genealogist* 2:162] and 4 in 1810 [VA:60]. He was head of a Northampton County, Virginia household of 3 "free colored" in 1820 [VA:216]. He may have been the father of

    i.   Thomas, born say 1765, "free Negro" taxable in Accomack County in 1787 [PPTL 1782-1814, frame 239] and head of a St. George Parish, Accomack County household of 1 "other free" and 4 slaves in 1800 [*Virginia Genealogist* 2:161].

    ii.   Daniel[3], a "fn" taxable in Accomack County in 1798 [PPTL, 1782-1814, frame 365], registered in Accomack County: *born about 1767, a Black, 5 feet 3-1/4 inches, Born free in Accomack County* [Register of Free Negroes, 1785-1863, no. 481].

    iii.   Solomon, a "fn" taxable in Accomack County from 1798 to 1800 [PPTL, 1782-1814, frames 365, 404, 441].

Members of the family in Accomack and Northampton County, Virginia, were

    i.   Comfort, registered in Accomack County: *born about 1766, a Black, 5'1", born free in Accomack County* [Register of Free Negroes, 1785-1863, no. 681].

    ii.   Francis, born say 1768, taxable in Northampton County from 1789 to 1796 [PPTL, 1782-1823, frames 103, 147, 198]. He was sued in Northampton County court for 5 pounds on 14 September 1790, registered as a "free Negro" in Northampton County on 13 June 1794 [Orders 1789-95, 83, 107, 364], head of an Accomack Parish, Accomack County household of 1 "other free" in 1800 [*Virginia Genealogist* 2:14].

    iii.   Sinah, born say 1770, married Charles **Webb**, "Free Negroes," 7 June 1791 Northampton County bond, William Satchell security.

    iv.   Tince, head of a St. George Parish, Accomack County household of 5 "other free" in 1800 [*Virginia Genealogist* 2:163], perhaps the same person as Finney Sample, head of an Accomack County household of 7 "other free" in 1810 [VA:61].

    v.   William, taxable in Northampton County in 1795 [PPTL, 1782-1823, frame 199].

    vi.   Betty, head of an Accomack County household of 9 "other free" in 1810 [VA:60], married in 1813 to Isaac, a slave freed by Ames [PPTL 1782-1814, frame 833].

    vii.   Lisha, head of a St. George Parish, Accomack County household of 6 "other free" in 1800 [*Virginia Genealogist* 2:163], perhaps the same person as Eliha Sample, head of an Accomack County household of 4 "other free" in 1810 [VA:59].

    viii.   Sarah, head of a St. George Parish, Accomack County household of 3 "other free" and a slave in 1800 [*Virginia Genealogist* 2:161] and 5 "other free" in 1810 [VA:59].

    ix.   Littleton, a "free Negro" bound by the churchwardens of St. George's Parish to Thomas Jacob to be a farmer on 27 August 1776 [Orders 1774-7, 460].

    x.   Saul, head of a St. George Parish, Accomack County household of 2 "other free" in 1800 [*Virginia Genealogist* 2:163].

    xi.   Sabra, registered in Accomack County about 1832: *born about 1780, Black, born free in Accomack County* [Register of Free Negroes, 1785-1863, no. 592].

    xii.   Peggy, registered in Accomack County about 1832: *born about 1782, Black, 5'3", born free in Accomack County* [Register of Free Negroes, 1785-1863, no. 597].

xiii. Ader, head of an Accomack County household of 4 "other free" in 1810 [VA:60].

xiv. Scarburgh, head of an Accomack County household of 3 "other free" in 1810 [VA:61].

xv. John, married Kesiah **Beavans**, 13 February 1810 Accomack County bond, Isaiah **Carter** security.

xvi. Emmerson, born in April 1785, registered in Accomack County on 29 September 1807: *Dark Mulatto, 5 feet 6-1/8 Inches, a little pitted by the smallpox on his face, Born free* [Register, no. 1].

xvii. Fanny, born about 1785, registered in Accomack County: *born about 1785, a light Black, 5'1" high, born free in Accomack County* [Register of Free Negroes, 1785-1863, no. 502].

xviii. Molly, married Nathaniel **Collins**, 16 August 1810 Northampton County bond, Isaiah **Carter** security.

xix. Billy, registered as a "free Negro" in Northampton County on 13 June 1794 [Orders 1789-95, 364], married Christina **Weeks** 26 November 1817 Northampton County bond, Frank Sample security.

xx. Edy, bound by the Accomack County court to Elijah Handcock on 25 September 1793 [Orders 1793-6, 1].

xxi. Dingledy, bound by the Accomack County court to Elijah Handcock on 25 September 1793 [Orders 1793-6, 1].

Members of the family on the Southside of Virginia were

3   i. Dorothy[2], born say 1750.

ii. Ezekiel, born 10 December 1754, a seven-year-old "Mullatto" bound to Benjamin Dingly Gray by the Princess Anne County court on 18 March 1761 to learn to read and write [Minutes 1753-62, 420]. He was in a "free Negro" taxable in St. Bride's Parish of Norfolk County in 1816 and 1817 [PPTL, 1813-24, frames 187, 226].

iii. Hannah, born 7 August 1757, a four-year-old "Mullatto" bound to Benjamin Dingly Gray by the Princess Anne County court on 18 March 1761 to learn to read, sew and spin [Minutes 1753-62, 420]. She registered as a "free Negro" in Northampton County on 10 June 1794 [Orders 1789-95, 354].

4   iv. Charity, born about 1764.

v. Daniel[2], born say 1766, a "F.N." tithable in Isle of Wight County in 1797 and from 1804 to 1809: taxable on 4 slaves and a horse in 1804, 6 slaves and 2 horses in 1805, 5 slaves and 3 horses in 1806, 6 slaves and 5 horses in 1807, 3 slaves and 4 horses in 1809 [PPTL 1782-1810, frames 412, 641, 703, 742, 761, 819].

vi. Randall, born say 1774, a "F.N." tithable in Isle of Wight County in 1797 [PPTL 1782-1810, frames 412].

vii. Henry, born say 1776, married Dinah **Bevans** 17 November 1797 Norfolk County bond, Francis Drake security. He was a "F.N." taxable in Isle of Wight County from 1806 to 1809 [PPTL 1782-1810, frames 742, 761, 819].

3. Dorothy[2] Sample, born say 1750, was sued by Teackle Robins in Accomack County court on 27 July 1774. The suit was abated by the death of the plaintiff [Orders 1774-7, 226, 254]. She may have been the Dorothy Sample who was living in Princess Anne County on 8 July 1779 when her "free Mulatto" children Christopher and Dorothy were bound by the court to William Hancock [Minutes 1773-82, 401]. She married James **Whitehurst**, 4 October 1786 Princess Anne County bond, George Smyth surety. Dorothy was the mother of

i. Christopher, born say 1775, in a list of "Free Negroes and Mulattoes" in St. Bride's Parish, Norfolk County in 1812 and 1814 [PPTL, 1791-1812, frame 802; 1813-24, frame 67].

    ii.   Dorothy³, born say 1777.

    iii. Sebria, daughter of Dorothy Sample, bound to Richard and Hannah Sparrow by the Princess Anne County court on 15 February 1782 [Minutes 1782-4, 43].

4.   Charity Sample, born about 1764, married Jacob **Carter**, 6 December 1787 Princess Anne County bond, James **Whitehurst** security. Jacob **Carter** was head of a Petersburg Town household of 6 "other free" in 1810 [VA:119b]. She was still called Charity Sample when she registered in Norfolk County on 19 July 1814: *5-3 inches, 50 years of age, of a light complexion* [Register of Free Negros & Mulattos, no.94]. She may have been the mother of

    i.   Caesar, born about 1782, registered in Norfolk County on 14 July 1810: *5 feet 2 Inches, Twenty eight years of age of a dark Complexion* [Register, no 8].

    ii. Ned, born about 1789, registered in Norfolk County on 20 July 1812: *5 feet 6 Inc., 23 years of age of a Yellowish Complexion, Born free by the affidavit of Matt Halstead* [Register, no. 74].

    iii. Mary, born about 1790, registered in Norfolk County on 22 September 1812: *4 ft. 9 Inc., 22 Years of age of a Yellowish Complexion, Born free* [Register, no. 87].

SAMPSON FAMILY

1.   John¹ Sampson, born say 1690, was sued by Edward Myhill of Elizabeth City County for 300 pounds of tobacco on 21 September 1715. Myhill was security for the payment of a 20 pounds sterling debt John owed William Armistead, Jr. The court ordered him held in custody on 17 November 1715 when he appeared and denied he owed the plaintiff anything. The case was dismissed on 17 May 1716 when the parties reached agreement. He apparently bound himself as a servant to Samuel Sweny sometime that year because the following January the court ordered him to serve Sweny another 60 days for being absent thirty days. The court also ordered him to serve Sweny another two months in exchange for Sweny paying his levy for the year. Edward Mihill testified for John at his trial. On 20 March 1716/7 he sued Robert Armistead for 1000 pounds of tobacco damages for a house John had built for Armistead [Orders 1715-21, 9, 16, 23, 27, 42, 55, 59, 78]. He was called "a Molatto man named John Sampson belonging to Samuel Swinney" on 17 April 1718 when John Berry produced a certificate in Middlesex County court for taking him up as a runaway [Middlesex County Orders 1710-21, 370]. He testified in Elizabeth City County in May 1724 that Joshua Myhill had sworn or cursed profanely. Francis Mallory sued him in January 1724/5 but failed to prosecute. He sued Joshua Myhill for trespass and 50 pounds damages in May 1725, but the court found against him. He paid Humphrey and Matthew Ward as his evidences and William **Cattilla** testified for Myhill. On 20 January 1725/6 he bound himself to serve Philip Mallory for a year in exchange for 1,000 pounds of tobacco, apparently to pay his debts. On 6 May 1726 he was granted a certificate for taking up a runaway servant named Sawney belonging to William Tapley of Essex County [Elizabeth City County Orders 1724-30, 13, 74, 103, 146, 148, 164]. Ten days later on 16 May 1726 John Mundell presented a claim to the York County court for taking up a "free runaway Mulatto man servant named John Sampson belonging to Francis Mallory of Elizabeth City County above ten miles distance from his said master's habitation." He brought an action of trespass upon the case against Sarah **Hobson** which was dismissed by the York County court on 16 August 1742 when both parties reached agreement, and he brought a case against Rebecca **Hulet** which was dismissed on 15 November 1742. Sarah Pegram testified for him, and Sarah **Hobson** testified for Rebecca **Hulet** [York OW 16, pt. 2, 383; W&I 19:121, 131, 132]. He may have been the ancestor of

2 i. John², born say 1740.

3 ii. Sylvia, born say 1745.

  iii. Nanny, born say 1752, a "negro" tithable in James Atchinson's household in Elizabeth River Parish, Norfolk County in 1768 [Wingo, *Norfolk County Tithables, 1766-80,* 80].

  iv. James, head of a Guilford County, North Carolina household of 4 "other free" in 1790 [NC:153].

  v. Joshua, head of a Pasquotank County, North Carolina household of 1 "other free" in 1790 [NC:29].

  vi. Lovey, "a Free woman of Colour," purchased her husband David from Jeremiah Symons and petitioned the Pasquotank County court in June 1797 for permission to manumit him, saying that she had "some years agoe took to Husband a Mulatto man Slave named David late the property of a certain Jeremiah Symons" [Byrd, *In Full Force and Virtue,* 198].

2. John² Sampson, born say 1740, was a Pamunkey Indian who attended William and Mary College in 1764 [Rountree, *Pocahontas's People,* p. 336, note 304]. He may have been the ancestor of

  i. Charles, registered in Petersburg on 2 April 1817: *a free man of Colour, five feet nine and a half inches high, dark brown complection, born free in King William County, Registered at Request of his mother Sall Major* [Register of Free Negroes 1794-1819, no. 843].

  ii. John³, born about 1798, registered in Petersburg on 18 October 1817: *a lad of Colour (son of Sally Major, a free woman) about nineteen years old, five feet nine inches high, of a light yellow brown Complection, has strait hair, cow lick in his hair, born free in King William County, said to be of Indian descent & by trade a shoemaker. Registered by desire of his mother* [Register of Free Negroes 1794-1819, no. 877].

3. Sylvia Sampson, born say 1745, was a "free negro Woman" living in Carteret County, North Carolina, on 17 September 1771 when her unnamed two-year-old son, a "Negro boy," was bound to Reuben Benthall [Minutes X:403]. Perhaps her children were

  i. Isaac, head of a Carteret County household of 6 "other free" in 1800, received a discharge for twelve months service in the North Carolina Infantry in Captain Brevard's Company on 1 May 1782 [*NCGSJ* XV:231].

  ii. Polly, head of a Carteret County household of 4 "other free" in 1800 and 6 in 1810 [NC:447].

  iii. Frances, married Anthony **Brown**, 23 September 1808 Craven County bond with Peter **George** bondsman. Anthony was head of a Craven County household of 5 "free colored" in 1820 [NC:67].

  iv. Esther, married Asa **Spelman**, 6 June 1819 Craven County bond, Aaron **Spelman** bondsman.

SANDERLIN FAMILY

1. James Sanderlin and his wife Sarah were living in Bertie County on 9 November 1731 when Susannah Clements claimed in Bertie court that they brought their female infant child to her for support but refused to bind the child to her. Susannah appeared in court again on 8 February 1732 when the court agreed to bind "Nany, a Molatto child mentioned in the last court order" to her [Haun, *Bertie County Court Minutes,* I:39, 46]. James and Sarah's child was

2 i. Nany, born about 1731.

2. Ann Sanderlin, born say 1731, was a "free Mullatta Woman" living in Bertie
    County when several of her children were bound apprentices. They were
3   i.   Mariah, born about 1748.
4   ii. Diana, born about 1750.
5   iii. Hecuba(?)/ Hunba(?), born about 1751.
        iv. Amiah, born about 1753, three years old on 29 April 1756 when she
             was bound an apprentice to Elizabeth Lockhart [Haun, *Bertie County
             Court Minutes*, II:167-8].
        v.   ?Lazarus Summerlin, born say 1760, a taxable "free molattor" in
             Jonathan Standley's 1764 Bertie tax list [CR 10.702.1].

3. Mariah Sanderlin, born about 1748, was eight years old on 29 April 1756
    when she was bound an apprentice to Elizabeth Lockhart [CR 010.101.7 by
    NCGSJ XIII:169]. Her children were
        i.   Prince, born in August 1779, "___ son of Mariah" ordered bound to
             Thomas Sutton to be a cooper in August 1783, discharged from his
             indenture in August 1790 [Haun, *Bertie County Court Minutes*, V:458;
             VI:833].
        ii. ?King, born 7 August 1780, no parent named, ordered by the
             November 1790 Bertie court bound to Parrott Hardy to be a hatter, and
             then bound to William Ashburn to be a blacksmith [Haun, *Bertie
             County Court Minutes*, VI:828, 837]. He married Rachel **Brantley**, 21
             December 1805 Bertie County bond with Richard **Demsey** bondsman.
        iii. ?Caesar, no parent named, ordered bound by the August 1786 Bertie
             court to Frederick Lawrence to be a house carpenter [Haun, *Bertie
             County Court Minutes*, V:596].
        iv. ?Patt Sanderlin, no parent named, ordered by the February 1787 Bertie
             court bound to Frederick Lawrence [Haun, *Bertie County Court
             Minutes*, V:631].

4. Diana Sanderlin, born about 1750, was six years old on 29 April 1756 when
    she was bound an apprentice to Elizabeth Lockhart [*NCGSJ* XIII:168]. She
    was mentioned in the 1754 Bertie County will of Thomas Allday, probably the
    "Free Mulatto, Dianah" taxed in the 1775 Bertie Tax Lists of Ann Lawrence
    and her son Frederick Lawrence in the list of George Lockhart. Her "Mulatto"
    children bound out by the court were
        i.   Mariah, daughter of Dinah, born circa 1780, ordered bound to
             Humphrey Nichols by the May 1786 Bertie court. However, the same
             court issued a citation to Nichols to show cause why the child should
             not be bound to Frederick Lawrence who had raised the child and had
             the mother's consent and desire that she be bound to him. The
             November Bertie court bound her to Frederick Lawrence [Haun, *Bertie
             County Court Minutes*, V:580, 585, 617]. She was head of a Bertie
             County household of 2 "other free" in 1800 [NC:75].
        ii. Jack, born about 1775, bastard of Dianah, bound to Thomas Baker to
             be a mariner by the August 1781 Bertie court [Haun, *Bertie County
             Court Minutes*, V:393].
        iii. Conweth(?), "bastard Mulatto of Diannah" born about December 1773
             [Haun, *Bertie County Court Minutes*, IV:91].

5. Hunba Sanderlin, born about 1751, was five years old on 29 April 1756 when
    she was bound an apprentice to Elizabeth Lockhart [Haun, *Bertie County Court
    Minutes*, II:170]. She was not mentioned in the Bertie Tax Lists, but her
    "Mulatto" children were bound out by the court:
        i.   Moses, born about 1772, "bastard Mulatto of Hunba Sanderlan,"
             ordered bound to Aaron Boulton by the August 1774 Bertie court
             [Haun, *Bertie County Court Minutes*, IV:91]. He married Mourning

Demsey 13 July 1805 Bertie County bond with William Sanderlin bondsman.

ii. Milley, born 1775, ordered bound to Aaron Boulton by the May 1784 Bertie court [Haun, *Bertie County Court Minutes*, V:486].

iii. ?Jenny, born circa 1775, no parent named, ordered bound to Aaron Boulton by the November 1779 Bertie court [Haun, *Bertie County Court Minutes*, IV:334], head of a Edenton household of 2 "free colored" in 1820 [NC:130].

iv. ?Harry, born 1779, no parent named, ordered bound to Aaron Boulton by the November 1779 Bertie court [Haun, *Bertie County Court Minutes*, IV:334]. He was bound out a year later on 17 August 1780 to Jeremiah Fleetwood [*NCGSJ* XIV:36]. He was head of a Bertie County household of 1 "other free" in 1800 [NC:75].

v. ?David, born about 1778, no parent named, bound to Jeremiah Fleetwood to be a shoemaker on 17 August 1780 [*NCGSJ* XIV:36].

vi. ?William, born 1783, no parent named, ordered bound to Aaron Boulton by the November 1784 Bertie court [Haun, *Bertie County Court Minutes*, V:509] and bound out a second time on 14 November 1796 to Hardy Fleetwood to be a cooper [*NCGSJ* XV:34]. He married Betsy **Dempsey**, 13 July 1805 Bertie County bond with (his brother?) Moses Sanderlin bondsman. He was head of an Edgecombe County household of 8 "free colored" in 1820 [NC:129].

SANTEE FAMILY

1. Samuel Sante, born say 1670, was one of Robert Caufield's "negro slaves." By his 2 January 1691 Surry County, Virginia will, Caufield directed that Samuel was to be free after four years of service. On 11 January 1695/6 Elizabeth Caufield confirmed his manumission in Surry County court [DW 1694-1709, 84]. He may have been the ancestor of

    i. Caesar, born say 1760, enlisted in the 2nd North Carolina Regiment. He was granted a land warrant for 640 acres in 1783 [Crow, *Black Experience*, 102].

2   ii. John, born say 1765.

   iii. William, married Mazy **Blizzard**, 7 February 1786 Sussex County, Virginia bond. He was taxable in St. Andrew's Parish, Greensville County, from 1792 to 1794 [PPTL, 1782-1830, frames 149, 156, 172].

2. John[1] Santee, born say 1765, was head of a Northampton County, Pennsylvania household of 4 "other free" in 1790. He was head of a Bladen County, North Carolina household of 7 "other free" in 1800, 5 in 1810 (called John, Sr.) [NC:191], perhaps the John Santee who was head of a Bladen County household of 11 "free colored" in 1820 [NC:154]. He may have been the father of

    i. John[2], Jr., head of a Bladen County household of 4 "other free" in 1810 [NC:191].

SAUNDERS FAMILY

1. Elizabeth Saunders, born say 1717, appeared before the Caroline County, Virginia court on 12 September 1735 and identified Thomas **Lantor** as the father of her illegitimate child. The court ordered the child bound to Samuel Coleman. The 8 October 1736 Caroline County court ordered her to serve her master Samuel Coleman additional time for having an illegitimate "mulatto" child [Orders 1732-40, 307, 378]. She may have been the ancestor of

    i. John[1], born about 1734, a twenty-three-year-old "Mulatto" who ran away from William Pickett of Prince William County, Virginia, on 27

March 1757 according to the 2 September 1757 issue of the *Virginia Gazette* [Headley, *18th Century Newspapers*, 299].

ii.   John[2], a free man of color born in Hanover County who served in the Revolution from Henrico County [NSDAR, *African American Patriots*, 153]. He was head of a Henrico County household of 3 "other free" in 1810 [VA:980].

iii.   Sam, head of a Fluvanna County household of 5 "other free" in 1810 [VA:474].

Norfolk County

1.   Hannah Saunders, born say 1745, was the mother of a "free Negro" boy named Saunders Saunders who was bound apprentice in Norfolk County on 21 March 1771. She was the mother of

i.   Saunders, a "free Negro" son of Hannah Saunders bound to James Jollif by the churchwardens of St. Brides Parish by order of the Norfolk County on 21 March 1771 and bound instead to Scarbrough Tankard with the consent of Jollif on 21 November 1771 [Orders 1768-71, 233; 1771-3, 38].

SAVEE/ SAVOY FAMILY

1.   Abraham[1] Savoy, born say 1613, was called Abraham Saby, a "negro," when the Elizabeth City County court granted his petition to be levy free on 29 September 1693 on consideration of his great age, claiming that he was one hundred years old. He may have been identical to Abraham Savoy who a few years later on 18 August 1696 brought suit in Elizabeth City County against Lewis Burell and Thomas Goddin, executors of Col. John Lear, for 5 pounds currency and 600 pounds of tobacco by account. On 18 May 1698 the court ordered that Abraham Savoy be levy-free by reason of his extreme old age [Orders 1692-9, 18, 97, 132]. He may have been the ancestor of

i.   Francis Savoy, born say 1675, sued in Elizabeth City County court before 18 February 1694/5 when his attorney William Mallory confessed judgment for 400 pounds of tobacco he owed Major William Wilson. He brought a successful suit against Michael Brittonell for a mare on 19 June 1699 [Orders 1692-99, 53, 151]. He appointed Charles Mallory as his attorney to sell land on the north side of the Mattaponi River in King and Queen County which he bought from Michael Bartlett of New Poquoson in York County (no date indicated) [DW 1688-1702, original p. 256, restored p.171]. He left 50 acres on the Poquosin River bounded by the land of Thomas Wythe and John George to his three sisters by his Elizabeth City County estate. His sister Hannah **Francis** exchanged her third part of the land on 7 March 1740/1 [DW 1737-56, 101].

2   ii.   John, born say 1677.

2.   John Savoy, born say 1677, was married to Patience on 2 May 1695 when the birth of their son Abraham was recorded in Charles Parish, York County [Bell, *Charles Parish Registers*, 171]. Patience Savey petitioned the York County court on 20 August 1744 for relief from paying taxes. The court rejected her petition [W&I 19:301]. They were the parents of

i.   Abraham[2], born 2 May 1695.

3   ii.   Mary[1], born say 1696.

4   iii.   ?John[2], born say 1700.

3.   Mary[1] Savoy, born say 1696, sued Michael Pierce in Elizabeth City County court for 3 pounds on 18 July 1717. On 15 June 1720 she confessed in Elizabeth City County court that she had a bastard child [Orders 1715-21, 94]. She may have been the mother of

i. Tomerson, born say 1730, presented by the York County court on 20 May 1754 for having a bastard child (no race indicated) [Judgments & Orders 1752-4, 419, 451].

4. John[2] Savee, born say 1700, had a child by Ann **Combs** in Charles Parish on 24 February 1724 [Bell, *Charles Parish Registers*, 171]. On 21 February 1738/9 Anne was called Anne Savoy, "the Mother of Jane Savoy," when she complained to the Elizabeth City County court against Nehemiah Nichols [Orders 1731-47, 200]. John and Anne's children were

5 i. Mary[2], born 30 March 1721.
   ii. Jane, born 24 February 1724, baptized 3 October 1725. The York County court presented her on 20 November 1749 for failing to list herself as a tithable [Judgments & Orders 1746-52, 256, 277].

5. Mary[2] Savoy, born 30 March 1721, "daughter of Ann Combs a bastard child," was baptized in Charles Parish, York County, on 6 May 1721 [Bell, *Charles Parish Registers*, 171]. She was presented by the grand jury of Elizabeth City County for having a bastard child, but the case was dismissed because the child was born in another county. On 4 September 1751 she was sued for slander by Thomas and Anne Pinnell in Elizabeth City County [Orders 1747-55, 260]. Anne Pinnell was apparently identical to Ann Pannel who was paid by the vestry of Elizabeth City Parish paid for keeping Sary **Combs** from 14 December 1756 to 18 December 1758. On 11 October 1753 the vestry paid Mary **Combs** for keeping Mary Savoy [von Doenhoff, *Vestry Book of Elizabeth City Parish*, 23, 66, 75]. She may have been the mother of

i. Martha, born say 1748, still a child on 9 October 1755 when the vestry of Elizabeth City Parish paid Thomas Jennings for keeping her [von Doenhoff, *Vestry Book of Elizabeth City Parish*, 46].

SAWYER FAMILY

1. Joanna Sawyer, born say 1745, was the mother of six unnamed children bound to David George in August 1777 when he posted 1,000 pounds bond in Granville County, North Carolina court to appear in court in Ninety-Six District, South Carolina, to answer the charge that he had "disposed of her children" [Granville County Minutes 1773-83, August 1777 dockets]. She was a "M°" or "FN" taxable on a horse in the lower district of Halifax County, Virginia, from 1792 to 1813: called Hannah Sawyer in 1799, 1801, and from 1809 to 1811 [PPTL 1782-99, frames 424, 833, 925; 1800-12, frames 159, 207, 818, 868, 965, 1042]. She may have been the mother of

i. Susanna, born say 1772, married Thomas **Good**, 24 June 1793 Halifax County, Virginia bond. Thomas was emancipated by a February 1785 Halifax County bill of freedom from Charles Kennon [Pleas 1783-6, 243].

ii. Job, taxable in Halifax County, Virginia, in 1798 [PPTL 1782-99, frame 833], head of a Chatham County household of 1 "other free" in 1800.

iii. Charles, born say 1785, a "FN" taxable in the lower district of Halifax County, Virginia, in 1801 and 1802, a "Mulatto" taxable in 1805 [PPTL 1800-12, frames 159, 207, 537].

iv. Polly, married Jesse **Hood**, 18 May 1807 Caswell County bond, Henry **Curtis** security.

v. Edmund, born about 1802, registered in Halifax County, Virginia, on 22 November 1830: *a dark mulatto man, about 28 years of age last spring, with black hair a little inclined to be straight, born free.* His wife was probably Frances Sawyer who registered the same day: *otherwise Frances Wilson, a bright mulatto who was born free, 29 years of age, 5 feet 6 inches high with straight black hair* [Register of Free Negroes, nos. 93, 126, 137].

Other members of a Sawyer family were

    i.   William, born March 1776, a "Free Negro Boy" living in Craven County, North Carolina, on 17 September 1784 when the court ordered him bound to Sylvester Pendleton to be a seaman [Minutes 1784-6, p.5d].

    ii. Robert, born before 1776, head of a Newbern, Craven County household of 6 "free colored" in 1820 [NC:78].

    iii. Sarah, born before 1776, head of a Gates County, North Carolina household of 9 "free colored" in 1820 [NC:154].

SCOTT FAMILY

Lancaster County, Virginia

1. Catherine Scott, born say 1675, a "Molattoe Woman," was the servant of Elizabeth Spencer, widow of George Spencer. Elizabeth Spencer had married William Man by 8 September 1697 when Catherine petitioned the Lancaster County court for her freedom. Catherine claimed that John Beaching had purchased her and her son Daniel from Elizabeth Spencer with the intention of marrying her but had died about a year after the purchase. The jury found in Catherine's favor [Orders 1696-1702, 26, 27, 42-4]. She was the mother of

    i.   Daniel, born say 1695.

Henrico County

The Scott family of Henrico County may have descended from Joane Scott who entered bond on 2 December 1695 for her appearance in Henrico County court [Orders 1694-9, 81]. She may have been the ancestor of John, James, and Nicholas (no family name) who were "Mulatto" servants of John Woodson, Jr., in August 1724 when they were ordered to serve him additional time for running away [Minutes 1719-24, 352]. Two members of the Scott family owned adjoining land in Henrico County in 1735. They were

1   i.   Anne[1], born say 1685.
2   ii. Jane[1], born say 1690.

1. Anne[1] Scott, born say 1685, made a deed of gift of fifty acres in Henrico County adjoining John Scott, Abram Childers and Jane Scott to her son Benjamin Scott on 4 August 1735. This was the lower half of 100 acres which she had purchased from John Price. She had already given the other half to her son John Scott [Miscellaneous Court Records, Vol. 3, 1727-37, 757]. She was the mother of

3   i.   John[1], born say 1712.
    ii. Benjamin[1], born say 1714, perhaps the Benjamin Scott who was taxable in the Lunenburg County household of Thomas **Maclin** in 1752 [Bell, *Sunlight on the Southside*, 192].
4   iii. ?Elizabeth[1], born say 1720.

2. Jane[1] Scott, born say 1690, sold 100 acres on the north side of the James River in Henrico Parish, Henrico County, adjoining Benjamin Scott to John Pleasants, Jr., on 10 April 1747 [DB 1744-8, 331]. She sued five men in Henrico County court on 3 October 1752 for chasing and driving away her horse. The court awarded her ten pounds damages. She was presented by the court on 6 November 1752 for failing to list herself as a tithable but was acquitted after "being heard." Perhaps she was excused due to old age. She may have been identical to Joana Scott who was security for Pat Scott in the suit brought against her by the churchwardens on 2 April 1753. She was called Jane Scott the following day on 3 April when she pleaded not guilty to

Benjamin Burton's suit against her for dealing with his slaves. The court ordered that she remain in prison for a month and then find security of 10 pounds for her good behavior for a year [Minutes 1752-5, 7, 19, 27, 51, 67, 102]. She may have been the ancestor of

5 i. Betty/ Elizabeth², born say 1722.

6 ii. Pat, born say 1725.

  iii. Lucy¹, born say 1730, presented by the Henrico County court on 6 November 1752 for failing to list herself as a tithable. She was fined 500 pounds of tobacco. On 21 January 1764 she was ordered to appear at the General Court in Williamsburg to give testimony against David Scott who was tried for breaking into Isaac Youngblood's warehouse and stealing goods valued at 8 pounds. Jacob Burton posted her bond of 20 pounds [Minutes 1752-5, 19, 27; 1763-7, 176].

7 iv. Sarah, born say 1731.

8 v. Agnes, born say 1735.

9 vi. Ann², born say 1736.

  vii. Joseph¹, born say 1738, bound out by the churchwardens of Henrico Parish in February 1744/5 [Orders 1737-46, 295].

10 viii. Susannah, born say 1739.

  ix. Betty/ Elizabeth³, born say 1740, a "Mulatto" ordered bound out by the churchwardens of Henrico Parish in February 1744/5 [Orders 1737-46, 295], perhaps the Elizabeth Scott who married William **Lansford**, "Mulattoes, he in this parish (Goochland County) and she in Hanover," on 24 December 1761 [Jones, *The Douglas Register*, 347].

11 x. Phebe, born say 1742.

12 xi. Molly, born say 1747.

3. John¹ Scott, born say 1712, may have been identical to John (no family name), the "Mulatto" servant of John Woodson, Jr., in August 1724 when the Henrico County court ordered him to serve additional time for running away [Minutes 1719-24, 352]. He received 50 acres in Henrico County from his mother Anne Scott before 4 August 1735. His suit against Miliner Redford, executor of John Redford, was dismissed by the court on 6 November 1752. On 6 November 1752 he was presented for not listing his "Mulatto" wife Hannah as a tithable and was fined 500 pounds of tobacco. Perhaps Hannah was the Hannah Scot who entered a petition in court against John Redford in December 1743. On 2 December 1754 the court ordered the churchwardens to bind out John Scott's children Ezekiel and Sarah Scott (no race indicated). He may have been the father of Sarah, Jane and Kizia Scott, "Mulatto's," who the court ordered bound out on 3 February 1755 [Minutes 1752-5, 19, 20, 28, 237; 1737-46, 241, 244; Orders 1755-62, 239]. He was the father of

13 i. ?Robert, born say 1735.

  ii. Ezekiel¹, born say 1748.

  iii. Sarah, born say 1750, daughter of John Scott bound out on 2 December 1754, perhaps the Sarah Scott, a "Mulatto" bound apprentice on 3 February 1755.

14 iv. ?Jane², born say 1752.

15 v. ?William, born about 1753.

  vi. ?Kesiah, born say 1754, a "Mulatto" bound apprentice on 3 February 1755, perhaps the Kesy Scott who was the parent of James Scott, a "Mulatto" who was bound to Didier Colin in Richmond City to become a barber on 4 April 1791 [Hustings Court Deeds 1782-92, 506-7 cited by Gill, *Apprentices of Virginia*, 223].

4. Elizabeth¹ Scott, born say 1720, was living in Henrico County in February 1743/4 when the court ordered the churchwardens of Henrico Parish to bind out her children Harry and Jenny Scott (no race indicated) [Orders 1737-46, 246]. She was presented by the court on 6 November 1752 for failing to list

herself as a tithable and fined 500 pounds of tobacco [Minutes 1752-5, 19, 27]. She was the mother of

    i.   Harry, bound apprentice in February 1743/4.

    ii. Jane²/ Jenny, daughter of Elizabeth bound apprentice in February 1743/4 (no race indicated).

5.   Betty/ Elizabeth² Scott, born say 1722, was living in Henrico County in June 1744 when the court ordered the churchwardens of Henrico Parish to bind out her son Jack (no race indicated). He was a seven-year-old "Mulatto Boy" ordered bound to John Coles in August the same year [Orders 1737-46, 264, 276]. She was presented by the court on 6 November 1752 for failing to list herself as a tithable and fined 500 pounds of tobacco [Minutes 1752-5, 19, 27]. She was the mother of

    i.   Jack/ John², born about 1737, a seven-year-old "Mulatto" boy ordered bound apprentice in August 1744.

6.   Pat Scott, born say 1725, was presented by the court on 6 November 1752 for failing to list herself as a tithable and fined 500 pounds of tobacco. She was sued by the churchwardens for debt on 2 April 1753, probably for having an illegitimate child [Minutes 1752-5, 19, 27, 51, 112]. She may have been the mother of

16   i.   Elizabeth⁴, born say 1750.

    ii. Frances, born say 1752, a "Mulatto" (no parent named) ordered bound out by the churchwardens of Henrico Parish on 7 April 1755 [Minutes 1752-55, 286].

    iii. John³, born say 1753, a "Mulatto" bound out by the court on 6 January 1755 [Minutes 1752-5, 238]. He was taxable in Henrico County from 1783 to 1713: taxable on 2 horses and 3 cattle in 1783; listed as a "free Negro" starting in 1806; listed as a "Mulatto" in 1809 and 1810; taxable on a horse in 1814 but exempt from personal tax [PPTL 1782-1814, frames 39, 185, 243, 436, 518, 622, 689, 707, 775, 793]. He and John Scott, Jr., were among the hands ordered by the Henrico County court to keep in repair the road from Cornelius's to Four Mile Creek bridge on 3 August 1789 [Orders 1789-91, 35]. He refused administration of the estate of Ann Scott, deceased, before 5 September 1791 when Francis Scott provided security of 200 pounds for John James's administration of the estate [Orders 1787-9, 430, 583; 1789-91, 35, 608]. He was taxable on 50 acres in the lower district of Henrico County in 1801 and 1802; taxable on 50 acres and another 140 acres which had been transferred to him by Goodin in 1803; taxable on 90 acres after he and his unnamed wife transferred 55-1/2 acres to Jesse Frayser in 1804; taxable on 90 acres from 1805 to 1809, called John Scott, Sr., in 1809; a "Mulatto" taxable on 80 acres in 1811; taxable on 50 acres near Talman's Tavern in 1815 [Land Tax List, 1799-1816].

17   iv. Zachariah, born say 1754.

7.   Sarah¹ Scott, born say 1731, was presented by the Henrico County court on 6 November 1752 for failing to list herself as a tithable. She was fined 500 pounds of tobacco [Minutes 1752-5, 19, 27]. On 7 November 1757 the court ordered the churchwardens to bind out her sons Pompey and Sampson Scott. The court ordered her son Isaac bound out on 4 April 1765 and her daughter Milley on 2 February 1767 [Orders 1755-62, 207; 1763-67, 441, 463, 646]. She was said to have been deceased on 7 July 1788 when the court ordered her son Archer bound out [Orders 1787-9, 347]. Her children were

    i.   Pompey, born say 1754, ordered bound out on 7 November 1757 and on 3 June 1765.

    ii. Sampson, born say 1756.

18   iii.   Benjamin², born say 1758.

      iv.   Isaac, born say 1760, son of Sarah Scott bound out on 4 April 1765.

      v.   Milley, born say 1764, "Mulatto child of Sarah Scott" ordered bound out by the Henrico County court on 2 February 1767 [Orders 1763-67, 646].

      vi.   James/ Jemmy, born say 1765, child of Sarah Scott (no race mentioned), ordered bound out by the Henrico County court on 7 August 1769 [Orders 1767-69, 491]. He petitioned the court on 1 December 1788 against his master Alexander Young for misusage. The court ruled that he was above the age of twenty-one and was therefore free and should be paid 3 pounds, 11 shillings (his freedom dues). He was one of the hands ordered by the Henrico County court to keep in repair the road from Cornelius's to Four Mile Creek bridge [Orders 1787-9, 496; 1789-91, 20, 35]. His Henrico County tax was charged to Zachariah Valentine in 1789 and he was charged with his own tax in 1790 [PPTL 1782-1814, frames 185, 243]. He married Betsey **Clarke**, 14 December 1790 Henrico County bond, surety Thomas **Clarke**.

      vii.   Fatha, born say 1766, child of Sarah Scott (no race mentioned), ordered bound out by the Henrico County court on 7 August 1769 [Orders 1767-69, 491].

      viii.   Archer, born say 1778, orphan of Sarah Scott ordered bound out on 7 July 1788, ordered bound to Daniel Vanderval on 5 January 1789 [Orders 1787-9, 347, 508]. He may have been the Archer Scott who was taxable in the upper district of Goochland County in 1792, 1797 and 1798 [PPTL, 1782-1809, frame 303, 471, 487]. He was a "free Negro" taxable in Henrico County from 1799 to 1814, called Archibald in 1802 [PPTL 1782-1814, frames 380, 411, 436, 519, 560, 579, 622, 689, 708, 793; Land Tax List, 1799-1816 (includes Personal Property Tax lists)].

      ix.   William, orphan of Sarah Scott, ordered bound apprentice in Henrico County on 6 May 1783 [Orders 1781-4, 280].

8.   Agnes Scott, born say 1735, may have been identical to "Aggy, a poor orphans girl," who was bound out by the churchwardens of Dale Parish, Henrico County, in March 1738 [Orders 1737-46, 76]. She was sued by the churchwardens for debt on 7 May 1753, probably for having an illegitimate child [Minutes 1752-5, 76, 114]. Her "Mulatto" son Jacob Scott was bound out in Henrico County in May 1759 [Orders 1755-62, 324]. Her children were

      i.   Jacob, born say 1756, a "Mulatto" son of Agnes Scott ordered bound out by the churchwardens of Henrico Parish in May 1759 and again on 5 May 1760 [Orders 1755-62, 324, 420].

      ii.   Sarah, born say 1758, a "Mulatto" child of Agnes Scott ordered bound out by the churchwardens of Henrico Parish on 7 April 1760 and on 7 May 1764, perhaps the Sarah Scott, an orphan girl, who was bound to Elizabeth Woodson until the age of twenty-one on 4 July 1764 [Orders 1755-62, 324, 409; 1763-7, 239].

9.   Ann² Scott, born say 1736, was a "Mulatto" ordered bound out by the churchwardens of Henrico Parish, Henrico County in February 1744/5 [Orders 1737-46, 295]. She may have been the Nanny Scott whose "Negro" son Thomas complained to the Cumberland County court on 24 November 1760 against his master John Burch [Orders 1758-62, 285]. And she may have been the Ann Scott whose children Joseph and Sarah (no race mentioned) were ordered bound out by the churchwardens of Henrico County about fourteen years later on 4 July 1765. On 3 August 1767 the Henrico County court bound out her children Benjamin and Squire Scott [Orders 1763-7, 474; 1767-9, 93]. Nanny Scott was living in Cumberland County on 27 April 1767 when the

court ordered the churchwardens of Southam Parish to bind her "mulattoe" children Drury and John Scott to Robert Moore. On 3 August 1767 the Cumberland County court bound her "mulattoe" daughter Charity Scott to Edward Clements, and on 27 February 1769 the court summoned Robert Moore to court to answer a complaint regarding his usage of orphan children John and Drury Scott who were bound to him [Orders 1764-7, 459; 1767-70, 62, 307]. She may have been the Nanny Scott who testified with Andrew Scott in Henrico County on 4 February 1788 that Axom (Exum) Scott was the legal representative of John Scott, a soldier who died in the service of the state [Orders 1787-91, 169]. Her children were

   i.   ?Jesse, born 11 September 1747, registered in Petersburg on 26 January 1798: *a dark brown Mulatto man, five feet seven inches high, stout well made, short thin black hair & rather inclined to be a little bald on top of his head, was born free, age fifty years 11 September 1797* [Register of Free Negroes 1794-1819, no. 129]. He was the administrator of Ann Scott, deceased, on 7 July 1783 when William Scott sued him in Henrico County court [Orders 1781-4, 308].
   ii. Thomas, "Negro" son of Nanny Scott.
19 iii. ?Francis, born say 1750.
   iv. Joseph[2], born say 1755, son of Ann Scott, ordered bound out by the Henrico County court on 7 November 1757 (no race mentioned) [Orders 1755-62, 207] and bound out again with his sister Sarah by the court on 4 July 1765 [Orders 1763-67, 474]. He was taxable in Henrico County from 1783 to 1801 [PPTL 1782-1814, frames 21, 82, 111, 168, 185, 243, 260, 297, 309, 322, 335, 347, 359, 391, 436].
   v.   Sarah, born say 1757, ordered bound out by the Henrico County court on 7 November 1757 and on 4 July 1765 [Orders 1755-62, 207].
   vi. Benjamin[3], born say 1759, son of Ann Scott ordered bound out by the Henrico County court on 3 August 1767 [Orders 1767-9, 93]. He may have been the Benjamin Scott who was security for the 18 November 1796 Henrico County marriage of Mary Scott and Adam **Armstrong**. He was taxable in Henrico County from 1794 to 1796 [PPTL 1782-1814, frames 78, 95, 111, 168, 185, 322, 336, 347] and head of a Buckingham County household of 11 "other free" in 1810 [VA:835].
   vii. Squire, born say 1761, son of Ann Scott ordered bound out by the Henrico County court on 3 August 1767.
   viii. John, born say 1762, "mulattoe" son of Nanny Scott, bound as an apprentice blacksmith to Robert Moore in Cumberland County on 27 April 1767 [Orders 1764-7, 459]. He may have been the John Scott who was a soldier that died in the service of the state according to testimony of (his mother?) Nanny Scott and (brother?) Andrew Scott in Henrico County court on 4 February 1788 [Orders 1787-9, 169].
   ix. Drury, born say 1763, "mulattoe" son of Nanny Scott bound as an apprentice blacksmith to Robert Moore on 27 April 1767 [Orders 1764-7, 459]. He was called Andrew Scott when he married Milender Scott, "daughter of Robert Scott and Mary Scott," 14 August 1787 Henrico County bond, Edward **Bowman** and John Scott sureties. Andrew was taxable in Henrico County from 1784 to 1799 [PPTL 1782-1814, frames 81, 111, 168, 185, 243, 261, 296, 309, 322, 336, 347, 358, 392]. He and Nanny Scott testified on 4 February 1788 that Axom Scott was the legal representative of John Scott, a soldier who died in the service of the state. Andrew's suit against Francis Scott was dismissed by the court on 3 March 1790 on agreement of the parties. His suit against Claiborne **Evans** was dismissed by the Henrico County court on 8 February 1791 because his attorney was not prepared to prosecute [Orders 1787-9, 169; 1789-91, 184, 417, 430]. He may have been the Andrew Scott who married Lucy Scott, 10 July 1810 Goochland County bond, Samuel **Martin** surety, 19 November return

[Ministers' Returns, 301]. He was a "Mulatto" farmer living with his wife Lucy on Ben Sadlers land in Goochland County in 1813 and 1814 [PPTL, 1810-32, frames 108, 174, 207].

x. Charity, born say 1767, "mulattoe" daughter of Ann Scott bound out in Cumberland County on 23 November 1767.

xi. Lewis, born say 1764, orphan of Nanny Scott, ordered bound out by the Henrico County court on 7 October 1782 [Orders 1781-4, 103]. He was taxable in Henrico County in 1789 [PPTL 1782-1814, frame 186].

xii. ?Tempy, born say 1776, married John **Jones**, 1 June 1797 Henrico County bond, John Scott surety.

10. Susannah Scott, born say 1739, was the mother of "orphan" children Ezekiah and Milner Scott who were in Prince Edward County on 15 March 1773 when the court ordered the churchwardens of St. Patrick's Parish to bind them out [Orders 1771-81, part 1, 218]. They were probably identical to Ezekiel and Milner Scott, "Melatto" boys named in the 7 January 1774 Chesterfield County will of Daniel Stone [WB 2:342]. Susannah was the mother of

i. ?Priscilla, born say 1758, an apprentice bound to Daniel Stone by the Henrico County court until the age of twenty one and serving him when he made his 7 January 1774 Chesterfield County will by which he left her remaining time and service to his daughter Charity Stone [WB 2:342].

ii. Ezekiel[2], born say 1760, a "Mellato boy" bound to Daniel Stone by the Henrico County court until the age of twenty one and serving him when he made his 7 January 1774 Chesterfield County will by which he left Ezekiel's remaining time to his son Daniel Stone [WB 2:342]. He was a "Mulatto" taxable in Chesterfield County from 1792 to 1807 [PPTL, 1786-1811, frames 125, 491, 644, 689], counted as a "FB" in Powhatan County in 1813 [PPTL, 1787-1825, frame 444].

iii. Milner, born say 1762, a "mellatto boy" bound to Daniel Stone by the Henrico County court until the age of twenty one and serving him when he made his 7 January 1774 Chesterfield County will [WB 2:342].

11. Phebe Scott, born say 1742, was a "Mulatto" ordered bound out by the churchwardens of Henrico Parish in February 1744/5 [Orders 1737-46, 295]. She was the mother of

i. Elizabeth[5]/Betty, born say 1763, daughter of Phebe Scott, bound out by the churchwardens of Henrico Parish on 7 October 1765 (no race indicated) [Orders 1763-67, 525]. She was taxable on 2 horses and Anderson Scott's tithe and 2 horses in the lower district of Henrico County in 1803 [Land Tax List, 1799-1816 (includes Personal Property Tax lists)].

12. Molly Scott, born say 1747, was living in Henrico Parish on 2 May 1768 when her "Mulatto" children were bound out by the court. Her children were

i. Walter, born say 1766, a "Mulatto" child of Molly Scott ordered bound out by the Henrico County court on 2 May 1768. On 7 June 1790 Richard Timberlake recorded a certificate in Henrico County court which he had written for Walter on 6 October 1787: *This is to certify that Walter Scott is free and that he has been a good and faithful servant and whoever employs him will find him so* [Orders 1767-69, 237; 1789-91, 296; DB 3:220]. He married Sarah **Nichols** who consented, 23 July 1790 Henrico County bond, surety Peter Hay.

ii. Lucy[3], born say 1766, a "Mulatto" child of Molly Scott ordered bound out by the Henrico County court on 2 May 1768 [Orders 1767-69, 237]. She married James **Baker**, 7 April 1787 Henrico County bond.

13.   Robert Scott, born say 1735, mortgaged 100 acres in Henrico County adjoining Hayse Whitlow, Robert Pleasants and William Frazier on 19 June 1756 to secure a 30 pound debt he owed William Frazier. The land was sold to Frazier for 35 pounds on 26 April 1765 [Miscellaneous Court Records 6:1949-50]. He was taxable with (his brother?) John Scott, "Mulattos," in Norfolk County in the district of Portsmouth and Southern Branch in 1767, living near (their sister?) Betty Scott, a "negro" tithable in David Cross's household [Wingo, *Norfolk County Tithables 1766-80*, 45, 47]. Esther Mayo's suit against him for debt was dismissed by the Henrico County court on 6 October 1788 at his costs [Orders 1787-9, 430]. He was taxable in Henrico County from 1786 to 1794: taxable on his own tithe, a free male 16-21, 2 horses and 4 cattle in 1786; taxable on his own tithe, John Scott and 3 horses in 1788 [PPTL 1782-1814, frames 82, 168, 243, 260, 297, 309, 322]. He married Martha Scott who consented, 23 October 1793 Henrico County bond, Edward **Bowman** surety. He was probably over the age of sixty on 6 July 1795 when the Henrico County court excused him from paying taxes [Orders 1794-6, 394]. Robert was the father of
    i.   Catherine, "daughter of Robert and Mary Scott," married Edward **Bowman**, 28 December 1786 Henrico County bond, John and Andrew Scott sureties.
    ii.   Milender, "daughter of Robert Scott and Mary Scott," married Andrew Scott, 14 August 1787 Henrico County bond, Edward **Bowman** and John Scott sureties.
    iii.   John, born say 1767, married Charity Scott, with the consent of their parents Robert Scott and Sarah Scott, 4 January 1788 Henrico County bond.
    iv.   Mary, married Edward B. **Edwards**, 14 February 1789 Henrico County bond, John Scott and Edward **Bowman** sureties.
    v.   Abby, born about 1787, a poor orphan of Robert Scott, deceased, bound out by the overseers of the poor of the lower district of Henrico County to Francis and Mildred Williams on 12 May 1798 [Orders 1798-9, 97]. She registered in Henrico County on 11 November 1831: *age 44, a mullatto woman, 5 feet 1 inch, Born free per register of the Richmond Hustings Court* [Register of Free Negroes and Mulattoes, 1831-1844, p.4, no.635].

14.   Jane Scott, born say 1752, was a "Mulatto" bound out in Henrico County on 3 February 1755. Her grandson Samuel Scott proved to the Davidson County court that she was a "dark complected woman" (also referred to as a "girl") who was brought to North Carolina from Henrico County by James Alley about 1771. Alley bound Jane out to a man named Creson and Jane "married one of Creson's negro fellows and had several children" including a daughter named Jemima. The Surry County, North Carolina court ordered Jane's unnamed children bound out in 1779. Jemima was bound to Joseph Williams, Sr., in Surry County, North Carolina, in 1789. She was the mother of
    i.   Jemima, born say 1775, indentured to Joseph Williams, Sr., in Surry County, North Carolina, in 1789. She was the mother of Samuel Scott who sued for his freedom from Joseph Williams, Jr., in Davidson County, North Carolina Superior Court in Spring Term 1828 [Minutes vol. 1, n.p.]. The case was appealed to the North Carolina Supreme Court [North Carolina Supreme Court 12 NC 376].

15.   William Scott, born about 1753, was a "yellow" complexioned soldier listed in the size roll of troops who enlisted at Chesterfield Courthouse [The Chesterfield Supplement cited by NSDAR, *African American Patriots*, 153]. He sued Jesse Scott, administrator of Ann Scott, deceased, on 7 July 1783 in Henrico County court [Orders 1781-4, 308]. He registered in Petersburg on 16 August 1794: *a light Mulatto man five feet six inches high, about forty one*

years old, who served in the American Army during the Revolution [Register of Free Negroes 1794-1819, no. 10]. His wife Sarah (born about 1762) registered in Petersburg on 13 August 1800: *a bright yellow Mulatto woman, five feet three inches high, thirty eight years old, bushy hair, born free by the name of Spruce & raised in York County, had afterwards married to William Scott* [Register of Free Negroes 1794-1819, no. 154]. He was taxable in the lower district of Henrico County from 1783 to 1810: taxable on a slave from 1789 to 1791; called William Scott, Sr., from 1792 to 1795; taxable on his son Jack in 1801; taxable on his sons Jack and William Scott, Jr., from 1802 to 1804, called a "Mulatto" in 1803 and 1804. He was taxable on 25 acres in the lower district of Henrico County on the Four Mile Creek near Talman's tavern from 1799 to 1816; called William Scott, Senr., in 1800; a "Mulatto" in 1809, 1810, and 1812 [PPTL 1782-1814, frames 32, 62, 77, 111, 186, 243, 260, 309, 322, 424, 436, 468, 518, 560, 579, 622; Land Tax List, 1799-1816 (includes Personal Property Tax lists)]. He was head of a Henrico County household of 9 "other free" in 1810 [VA:989]. He was the father of

i.   John/ Jack, born say 1783, taxable in Henrico County from 1801 to 1812: listed as a "Mulatto" in 1809 and 1810 [PPTL 1782-1812, frames 518, 580, 623, 689, 707], head of Henrico County household of 2 "other free" in 1810 [VA:992].

ii.   William, Jr., born say 1785, taxable in Henrico County from 1802 to 1813: [PPTL 1782-1814, frames 468, 518, 560, 580, 623, 689, 707, 775], perhaps the Billy Scott who was head of a Henrico County household of 8 "other free" in 1810 [VA:992]. He may have been the William Scott whose seven children registered in Henrico County on 6 July 1840. The oldest was Ellen **Charity**: *late Ellen Scott (daughter of W^m and Frances Scott), age 17, a woman of very light complexion, has long straight hair, 4 feet 11-1/2 inches, Born free as appears from evidence of Ro: H. B. Taylor* [Register of Free Negroes and Mulattoes, 1831-1844, p.35, nos. 956-62].

16. Betty/Elizabeth[4] Scott, born say 1750, was a "Mulatto" bound out by the Henrico County court on 6 January 1755 [Minutes 1752-5, 238]. She was a "Mulatto" living in Henrico County on 2 January 1769 when the court ordered her daughters Caroline and Lucretia bound out [Orders 1767-69, 377]. She may have been the Betsy Scott whose son Arvey Scott was bound out in Mecklenburg County, Virginia, on 15 April 1788 [Orders 1787-92, 176]. She was probably related to Francis Scott, a "Mulatto" taxable in Mecklenburg County from 1784 to 1792 [PPTL, 1782-1805, frames 64, 330, 383, 451]. She was the mother of

i.   Caroline, born say 1765, ordered bound out on 2 January court 1769.

ii.   Lucretia, born say 1767, "Mulatto" daughter of Betty Scott bound out in Henrico County on 2 January 1769.

iii. Phebe, born say 1780, daughter of Betsey Scott, married Jacob **Chavous**, 24 December 1800 Charlotte County bond and 8 December 1800 Mecklenburg County bond, Thomas A. Jones & James Wilson security, with a note from James Wayne.

iv.   Arvey, born say 1787, called "Avory Scott a bastard child at John Cox's Senr" on 15 May 1787 when the Mecklenburg County court ordered the overseers of the poor to bind him out and called "bastard of Betty Scott, deced" on 15 April 1788 when the court ordered the overseers of the poor to bind him out. He was bound to Lewis Burwell on 9 December 1799 and to Thomas Rowlett on 8 December 1800 [Orders 1787-92, 29, 176; 1798-1801, 283, 472]. He was to marry Elizabeth **Chavous**, 9 January 1809 Mecklenburg County bond, with the permission of Elizabeth **Chavous** (widow of Jacob) but married her sister Martha instead. He and his wife Martha Scott released their rights to land due to her from the estate of her father Jacob **Chavis**,

Sr., to her brother Jacob **Chavis**, Jr., of Charlotte County by deed proved in Mecklenburg County on 10 July 1809 [DB 14-107, 308].

17. Zachariah Scott, born say 1754, was a "Mulatto" (no parent named) living in Henrico Parish on 7 August 1758 when the court ordered the churchwardens to bind him out [Orders 1755-62, 273]. On 7 August 1788 he purchased 10 acres in Henrico County adjoining William Young and Jackson Fraser from Samuel **Red** who stated in the deed that he had purchased the land from Francis Scott. Actually, **Red**'s 2 June 1783 deed says it is from Jackson Frayser, so perhaps the land at one time belonged to Francis Scott [DB 2:113, 649-50]. Zachariah was one of the hands ordered to keep the road in repair from Cornelius's to Four Mile Creek bridge on 3 August 1789 [Orders 1787-9, 430; 1789-91, 35]. He was taxable in Henrico County from 1783 to 1802: taxable on 2 horses and 3 cattle in 1783; taxable on James Scott in 1789; taxable on son Peter and 3 horses in 1801 and 1802; taxable on a slave and 3 horses in 1803 and 1804; taxable on 10 acres in the lower district from 1799 to 1804. In 1804 he was taxable on an additional 50 acres which had been transferred to him by John Scott. His estate was taxable on the 10 and 50 acre tracts from 1805 to 1807. In 1809 John Scott, Jr., "Mulatto," was taxable on the two tracts [PPTL 1782-1814, frames 76, 111, 168, 185, 243, 260, 297, 309, 322, 335, 391, 437, 468; Land Tax List 1799-1816]. His 7 March 1805 Henrico County will was proved on 2 September 1805. He left his wife Lucy and daughters Fanny, Polly, Kesiah, and Eliza Scott his land during their single lives, and at the death or marriage of his wife the land was to go to his son John **Lansford** Scott. His son John L. Scott was to pay his son Harrad Scott ten pounds on his twenty-first birthday. He named his son Elijah Scott and Jesse Frayser executors and asked that they relinquish a proper right to the land he had sold William Young by his paying $6 per acre and that they get a right for the lands he had purchased from Edward **Bowman** and relinquish the same to his son John L. Scott [WB 3:196-7]. He was the father of

i. Peter, born say 1784, taxable in Henrico County from 1801 to 1814: listed as a "Mulatto" in 1803 and from 1812 to 1814 [PPTL 1782-1814, frames 518, 560, 580, 708, 775, 794; Land Tax List 1799-1816], head of a Henrico County household of 6 "other free" in 1810 [VA:1009].

ii. ?John, called John **Lansford** Scott when he was taxable in the lower district of Henrico County in 1797 and 1799, called John Scott, Jr., a "Mulatto," when he was taxable in 1809 on tracts of 50 and 10 acres in Henrico County which had been charged to the estate of Zachariah Scott from 1805 to 1807 [PPTL 1782-1814, frames 358, 391; Land Tax List, 1799-1816]. He and his wife Lucinda mortgaged 10 acres adjoining William Randolph Bottom's land in Henrico County for $49 on 7 December 1807 [DB 8:161]. He was taxable on 50 acres from 1810 to 1813 and his estate was taxable on 50 acres near Hith's Mill in 1814 and 1815 [Land Tax List, 1799-1816].

iii. Elijah, born say 1784, a "free Negro" taxable in Henrico County from 1800 to 1809; taxable in Bowler Cocke's household in 1801 and 1802, called a "free Mulatto" in 1804 [PPTL 1782-1814, frames 424, 461, 518, 560, 579; Land Tax List, 1799-1816].

iv. Harrad, not yet twenty-one in March 1805.

18. Benjamin[2] Scott, born say 1758, was ordered bound out by the churchwardens of Henrico Parish in March 1759, no parent or race mentioned [Orders 1755-62, 319], called son of Sarah Scott (no race mentioned) when he was ordered bound out by the court in March 1767 [Orders 1763-67, 715]. He taxable in Henrico County from 1785 to 1789 [PPTL, 1782-1814, frames 78, 95, 111, 168, 185]. He was one of the hands ordered by the Henrico County court to keep the road in repair from Cornelius's to Four Mile Creek bridge on 3

August 1789 [Orders 1787-9, 430; 1789-91, 35]. His orphans John and Elisha Scott were bound out by the Henrico County court to Joseph Goode, farmer, on 5 October 1795 [Orders 1794-6, 496]. He was the father of
  i.   John, born say 1785.
  ii. Elisha, born about 1787, registered in Petersburg on 20 May 1818: *a free man of Colour, dark brown Complection, five feet seven and a half inches high, thirty one years old, born free p. certificate of the City of Richmond* [Register of Free Negroes 1794-1819, no. 909].

19. Francis Scott, born say 1750, was ordered bound to a trade by the Chesterfield County court on 7 September 1764 [Orders 1759-67, 580]. He and his wife Elizabeth of Henrico County sold 33 acres in Henrico County adjoining John Depriest, Peyton Randolph and William Young on 6 March 1786 [DB 2:293-4]. He was taxable in the lower district of Henrico County from 1783 to 1800: taxable on 2 horses and 4 cattle in 1783; taxable on slaves Lucy, Mark, Jupiter and Phillis in 1784; charged with Andrew Scott's tithe in 1784 and with Anderson Scott's tithe from 1786 to 1788 [PPTL, 1782-1814, frames 21, 68, 82, 111, 111, 168, 185, 243, 261, 296, 309, 322, 335, 347, 358, 392, 436]. Joseph Bailey sued him in Henrico County court on 8 April 1789 for 4 pounds due by note. He, Andrew and Anderson Scott were among the hands ordered to keep the road in repair from Cornelius's to Four Mile Creek bridge on 3 August 1789. On 5 September 1791 he provided security of 200 pounds for John James's administration of the estate of Ann Scott, deceased, after John Scott refused to administer it [Orders 1787-9, 430, 583; 1789-91, 35, 608]. He married Rachel Scott, "widow," with the consent of her sister Patience Scott, 25 February 1792 Henrico County bond, Andrew Scott security. Rachel was taxable on a horse in Henrico County in 1790, perhaps the Rachel Scott who was counted in the list of "Blacks free above the age of sixteen" in the upper district of Henrico County with her unnamed daughter in 1813 [PPTL 1782-1814, frames 243, 760]. Francis was probably the father of
  i.   Anderson, born say 1769, taxable in the lower district of Henrico County from 1786 to 1810: his tax charged to Francis Scott from 1786 to 1788; his tax charged to Elizabeth Scott in 1803; called "free" when he was taxable on a horse in 1804; listed as a "free Negro" starting in 1806 [PPTL 1782-1814, frames 82, 111, 168, 185, 261, 309, 322, 335, 347, 358, 391, 436, 518, 579, 622]. The Henrico County court awarded him 30 pounds in his suit against Francis Gaddy on 10 March 1791 [Orders 1789-91, 484].

Other members of the Scott family in Henrico and the surrounding area were
  i.   Nicholas, born say 1715, a "free Mulatto man" living in Halifax County, Virginia, on 6 May 1758 when he was tried for having shot and killed John Herring with Jacob Cogar as his accomplice. He was sent to Williamsburg for further trial where he was reprieved by the Governor but ordered to leave Virginia. The Halifax County court bound out his children John, Mary, and Elizabeth to William Wright of Antrim Parish. In July 1759 Scott was accused of being frequently in Virginia and threatening the life of William Wright because he still held Scott's children. In August 1759 his suit against James Collings was dismissed by the court because he was not a resident of Virginia [Pleas 2:330, 336, 452, 471].
20 ii. James, born about 1738.
  iii. Nicholas, born say 1748, a "yellow" complexioned soldier born in Henrico County but living in Charles City County when he was listed in the size roll of troops who enlisted at Chesterfield Courthouse [The Chesterfield Supplement cited by NSDAR, *African American Patriots*, 153]. He may have been the Nicholas Scott who was living in Henrico

County on 6 March 1769 when the court ordered the churchwardens to bind out his son Exum Scott [Orders 1767-9, 384].

iv.   Lucy[2], born say 1753, a "Mulatto" (no parent named) ordered bound out by the churchwardens of Henrico Parish on 4 February 1754 [Minutes 1752-55, 161] and again on 7 November 1757 [Orders 1755-62, 207]. She may have been the Lucy Scott who was a "free Negro" taxable on 3 horses in the lower district of Henrico County in 1806 [PPTL 1782-1814, frame 518].

v.   William, born say 1760, an "Indian," taxable on 2 horses in the lower district of Henrico County in 1783, 1786, and from 1802 to 1804: taxable on a slave and 2 horses in 1803; taxable on his own tithe in 1804 [PPTL 1782-1814, frames 21, 82, 468; Land Tax List 1799-1816].

vi.   Jesse, born about 1760, registered in Petersburg on 16 August 1794: *a light Mulatto man five feet six & 1/2 inches high who served as a Soldier & a free man during the American Revolution about thirty four years old* [Register of Free Negroes 1794-1819, no. 9]. He was taxable in Henrico County in 1786 [PPTL 1782-1814, frames 93]. He acknowledged a debt of 5 pounds to James Stevens in Henrico County court on 2 August 1790 [Orders 1789-91, 321].

vii.   Littleberry, born about 1761, registered in Petersburg on 2 June 1801: *a light brown Mulatto man, five feet four inches high, forty years old, born free & raised in Charles City County* [Register of Free Negroes 1794-1819, no. 256]. He was a "yellow" complexioned soldier born in Charles City County who served in the Revolution from Henrico County [NSDAR, *African American Patriots*, 153].

viii.   Polly (Mrs.), married Samuel **Redd**, 20 July 1798 Henrico County bond. Samuel was emancipated by deed of Robert Pleasant acknowledged in Henrico County court on 4 November 1782 [Orders 1781-4, 114].

21   ix.   Hannah, born about 1763.

x.   Abby[2], born say 1765, married Isaac **Wood**, 18 December 1789 Henrico County bond. Isaac was a "Negro slave" emancipated by John Orr's deed proved in Henrico County court on 7 July 1788 [Orders 1787-9, 346].

xi.   Mary, born say 1765, married Thomas **Gilliat**, 12 November 1789 Henrico County bond. She may have been the Mary Scott whose orphan "Mulatto" children Anthony and James were ordered bound by the Henrico County court to Edward Clarke on 3 September 1787 and again on 6 July 1789 [Orders 1787-9, 135; 1789-91, 20]. Anthony was taxable in Henrico County in Edward Clarke's household in 1799 [PPTL 1782-1814, frame 387].

xii.   Priscilla, born about 1766, registered in Petersburg on September 1, 1794: *a brown Mulatto woman, five feet two and a half inches high, twenty eight years old, born free & raised in the Town of Petersburg* [Register of Free Negroes 1794-1819, no. 90].

xiii.   Anne, born say 1766, married Johnson **Smith**, 10 August 1787 Henrico County bond.

xiv.   Jeffrey, born say 1767, taxable in the lower district of Henrico County in 1788, 1791, 1806, and 1807 [PPTL 1782-1814, frames 168, 260, 518, 560].

xv.   Joshua, born about 1770, registered in Petersburg on 27 August 1800: *a dark brown Mulatto man, five feet six and a half inches high, thirty years old, born free & raised in the Town of Petersburg* [Register of Free Negroes 1794-1819, no. 197].

xvi.   Nancy, born say 1771, married David **Cooper**, 11 August 1792 Henrico County bond, surety Robin **Smith**. David **Cooper** was a "free

Negro" taxable in Henrico County in 1790 [PPTL 1782-1814, frame 213].

xvii. Charles, born say 1774, a poor orphan bound out in Henrico County to William Woodfin on 4 September 1786 [Orders 1784-7, 569]. He married Betsy **Howell**, "daughter of Isaac Howell," 3 June 1800 Goochland County bond, consent for Betsy by Judith **Howell**, Junior **Howell** surety. Charles was taxable in the lower district of Henrico County from 1789 to 1814: his tax charged to George Williamson in 1792 and 1793; called a Mulatto" in 1803, "free" in 1804; listed as a "free Negro" starting in 1806, a "Mulatto" in 1810 [PPTL 1782-1814, frames 185, 261, 310, 347, 436, 518, 579, 689, 775, 793]. His suit against Andrew Scott for trespass, assault and battery was dismissed by the Henrico County court on 5 March 1798 when his attorney stated that he had not been instructed by his client [Orders 1796-8, 594]. He was head of a Henrico County household of 2 "other free" in 1810 [VA:989].

xviii. James, born say 1775, his Henrico County tax charged to Alexander Young in 1792; charged to Andrew Frayser in 1793 and 1794 [PPTL 1782-1814, frames 299, 303, 316].

xix. Jephtha, born say 1776, taxable in Henrico County in 1792 [PPTL 1782-1814, frame 297].

xx. Nicholas, born about 1777, registered in Petersburg on 9 July 1798: *a dark brown Mulatto man, five feet five and a half inches high, bushy hair, twenty one years old, born free & raised in Dinwiddie County near the Town of Petersburg* [Register of Free Negroes 1794-1819, no. 141]. He purchased 2 acres in Petersburg from John Lee and was taxable on the land in 1799 [1799 Land Tax List A, p.12]. He was a "free Negro" shoemaker in Dinwiddie County n 1802 and 1803 [PPTL, 1802 B, p.20; 1803 A, p.22].

xxi. Ned, born say 1778, bound apprentice to Joseph Goode on 2 October 1786 [Orders 1784-7, 580], a "free Negro" taxable in the lower district of Henrico County from 1794 to 1814: listed with Samuel **Red** in 1794; charged with his own tax in 1806 and 1807; listed with his unnamed wife in the upper district of Henrico County in 1813 [PPTL 1782-1814, frames 321, 518, 560, 759, 824].

xxii. Abraham, born say 1780, bound apprentice to Arthur Giles on 2 October 1786, paid by the sheriff of Henrico County on 6 February 1797 for digging a grave and burying "Negro Harry, an old negro who died in jail" [Orders 1784-7, 580; 1796-8, 232].

xxiii. Ritter, head of a Henrico County household of 5 "other free" in 1810 [VA:998].

xxiv. Susan, a "free Negro" taxable on a slave and a horse in the lower district of Henrico County in 1807 [PPTL 1782-1812, frame 560].

xxv. Griffin, born 25 May 1780, registered in Petersburg on 30 December 1805: *a dark brown free Negro man, five feet eight inches high, twenty four years old the 25th May last, born free & raised in the Town of Petersburg* [Register of Free Negroes 1794-1819, no. 370]. He married Lavina Ash, 21 June 1817 Petersburg Hustings Court marriage.

xxvi. Polly, born about 1782, registered in Petersburg on 7 June 1810: *a yellow brown Mulatto woman, five feet three inches high, twenty eight years old, born free and raised in the County of Chesterfield* [Register of Free Negroes 1794-1819, no. 521].

xxvii. Daniel, born say 1785, a "F.N." taxable in the upper district of Henrico County from 1801 to 1807 [PPTL 1782-1814, frames 452, 495, 540].

xxviii. Isaac, born about 1785, registered in Petersburg on 29 July 1807: *a dark brown free Negro man, five feet seven 3/4 inches high, twenty two years old, brought up in the tanners business, born free & raised in the*

Town of Petersburg [Register of Free Negroes 1794-1819, no. 414]. He was head of a Petersburg household of 3 "other free" in 1810 [VA:121b].

xxix. Buck, born say 1790, a "free Negro" taxable in the lower district of Henrico County from 1807 to 1814: his tax charged to Miles Turpin in 1807 [PPTL 1782-1814, frames 560, 579, 622, 707, 751, 775, 793].

xxx. Lenn, born say 1792, a "free Negro" taxable in the lower district of Henrico County in 1809, 1813 and 1814: his tax charged to Bowler Cocke in 1813 [PPTL 1782-1814, frames 579, 767, 794].

xxxi. Aaron, born say 1793, a "Mulatto" taxable in Henrico County from 1810 to 1814 [PPTL 1782-1814, frames 623, 689, 708, 775, 794], head of a Henrico County household of 4 "other free" in 1810 [VA:998]. He was taxable on a lot in Port Mayo near Rockett's from 1812 to 1816 [Land Tax List, 1799-1816].

20. James Scott, born about 1738, registered in Petersburg on 23 August 1794: *a dark brown Mulatto man, five feet seven inches high, fifty six, born free & raised in James City* [Register of Free Negroes 1794-1819, no. 81]. He may have been the father of

i. Harriet, born about 1776, registered in Petersburg on 28 August 1804: *a light brown Mulatto woman, five feet five inches high, twenty eight years old, short bushy hair & holes in her ears, born free in James City* [Register of Free Negroes 1794-1819, no. 280]. She was head of a Petersburg household of 1 "other free" in 1810 [VA:121a].

21. Hannah Scott, born about 1763, registered in Petersburg on 14 August 1800: *a stout, thick made brown Mulatto woman, five feet three inches high, thick bushy hair, thirty seven years old, born free & raised in the Town of Petersburg* [Register of Free Negroes 1794-1819, no. 168]. She was the mother of

i. Rebecca, born about 1778, registered in Petersburg on 27 September 1797: *a dark brown Mulatto woman, five feet two inches high, nineteen years old, short bushy hair, straight & well made, born free daughter of Hannah Scott of the Town of Petersburg & raised in the sd. Town* [Register of Free Negroes 1794-1819, no. 124].

ii. Christian, born 15 August 1783, registered in Petersburg on 2 June 1801: *(son of Hannah Scott, a free woman) a brown Mulatto lad, seventeen years old 15 Aug. last, five feet three inches high, short bushy hair* [Register of Free Negroes 1794-1819, no. 216].

iii. ?Christian, born 15 August 1783, registered in Petersburg on 28 June 1806: *a brown Mulatto woman, five feet six inches high, twenty two years old 15 August last, born free & raised in the Town of Petersburg* [Register of Free Negroes 1794-1819, no. 384]. She was head of a Petersburg household of 5 "other free" in 1810 [VA:122b].

Goochland County
Members of the Scott family in Goochland County were

i. Stephen, born say 1752, married Molly **Ferrar**, "Molattoes," on 10 November 1773 in Goochland County [Jones, *The Douglas Register*, 347]. He may have been the Stephen Scott who was head of a Northampton County, North Carolina household of 5 "other free" in 1790 [NC:72].

ii. Abbie[1], born say 1754, married Charles **Howell**, "Mulattoes both," on 18 June 1775 in Goochland County [Jones, *The Douglas Register*, 347].

1   iii. Elizabeth, born say 1755.
2   iv. Joseph, born say 1756.

1. Elizabeth Scott, born say 1755, was living in Goochland County on 11 March 1790 when her daughter Barbara married Elisha **Sims**. She was the mother of
   v. Barbara, born say 1774, "daughter of Elizabeth Scott," married Elisha **Sims**, 11 March 1790 Goochland County bond, George Payne surety, 27 March marriage [DB 15:452]. Elisha was head of a Goochland County household of 4 "other free" in 1810 [VA:715].
   vi. Fanny, born say 1775, "daughter of Elizabeth Scott," married John **Lile**, 18 February 1791 Goochland County bond, Elisha **Sims** surety, 26 February marriage [DB 16:34].
   vii. ?Sally, married Francis **Tyler**, 15 January 1802 Goochland County bond, Henry **Cockrun** surety, 18 February marriage.

2. Joseph Scott, born say 1756, was a "Mulattoe" taxable in Goochland County from 1787 to 1790 and from 1796 to 1816: charged with Isham **Smith**'s tithe and 2 horses in 1787; charged with Lewis Scott's tithe in 1789; charged with Meredith and Royal Scott's tithe in 1798; a "Free Born Ditcher" living on Thomas Stratton's land in 1805; charged with Joel Scott's tithe in 1806 and 1809 and 1810; charged with Grief Scott's tithe in 1812; living with his wife Jenny on William Bolling's land in 1813 and 1814 [PPTL, 1782-1809, frames 156, 183, 227, 245, 429, 487, 535, 554, 677, 750, 791, 834, 876; 1810-32, frames 85, 110, 174, 208, 293]. He was head of a Goochland County household of 6 "other free" in 1810 [VA:715]. He was the father of
   viii. ?Riley, born say 1778, married Nancy **Johns**, 18 October 1799 Goochland County bond, Joseph Scott surety, 19 October marriage [Ministers' Returns, 287]. He was taxable in Goochland County from 1804 to 1816, a "Mulatto" shoemaker at Joseph Scott's in 1813 [PPTL, 1782-1809, frames 697, 751, 792; 1810-32, frames 17, 84, 174, 293]. Riley was head of a Goochland County household of 2 "other free" in 1810 [VA:714].
   ix. ?Joel, taxable in Goochland County from 1806 to 1811, listed as a "Mulatto water man" or ditcher at Joseph Scott's from 1811 to 1813, a "Mulatto" shoemaker at Rily Scott's in 1814 [PPTL, 1782-1809, frames 791, 876; 1810-32, frames 85, 110, 175, 207].
   x. ?Grief, taxable in Goochland County in Joseph Scott's household in 1812, listed with Joseph R. Royster in 1813 [PPTL, 1810-32, frames 110, 173].
   xi. ?Joshua, born about 1783, head of a Goochland County household of 1 "other free" in 1810 [VA:715]. He obtained a certificate of freedom in Chesterfield County on 13 March 1823: *forty years old, bright yellow complexion, blue eyes, straight hair, born free* [Register of Free Negroes 1804-53, no. 480, 598].
   xii. Nancy, born say 1788, "daughter of Joseph Scott," married Harris **Nichols**, 24 May 1804 Goochland County bond, Edward **Morris** surety, 29 May marriage [Ministers' Returns, 93].
   xiii. ?Morris, married Charity **Jenkins**, 7 July 1806 Goochland County bond, Harris **Nichols** surety, 8 July marriage.
   xiv. ?Patsy, born say 1777, married Orange **Freeman**, 19 September 1800 Goochland County bond, Riley Scott surety, 20 September marriage. Orange **Freeman** was head of a Goochland County household of 7 "other free" in 1810 [VA:692].

Caroline County, Virginia
1. Mary Scott, born say 1720, was living in Caroline County on 13 May 1748 when the court ordered the churchwardens of Saint Margaret's Parish to bind out her "mulatto" children Sarah, Nicholas and James Scott to Thomas Wild, Gent. On 10 March 1748/9 the court ordered her son Tom (no race indicated) bound to Thomas Wild [Orders 1746-54, 81, 131]. She was the mother of
   i. Sarah, born say 1743.

2   ii.   Nicholas, born say 1745.
       iii. James, born say 1747.
       iv.   Tom, born say 1748, son of Mary Scott ordered bound to Thomas Wild
             on 10 March 1748/9.

2.   Nicholas[1] Scott, born say 1745, was a resident of Prince George County on 22
       October 1776 when he purchased 60 acres in Surry County, Virginia,
       adjoining Simmons [DB 10:492].[182] He was head of a Surry County
       household of 9 persons in 1782 [VA:43], 11 in 1784 [VA:78] and 6 "other
       free" in 1810 [VA:616]. He was taxable in Cabin Point district of Surry
       County from 1782 to 1815: taxable on 2 horses and 8 cattle in 1782; charged
       with Drury **Walden**'s tithe in 1790; taxable on slave George in 1798; taxable
       on John Scott's tithe and slave George in 1800; taxable on John and Graham
       Scott's tithes in 1803 and 1804; free from personal tax in 1815 [PPTL, 1782-
       90, frames 351, 379, 398, 558, 605; 1791-1816, frames 116, 167, 346, 424,
       500, 543, 617, 657, 675, 695, 829]. He was called a "mulatto" in Surry
       County on 21 June 1814 when he made an affidavit as to Elizabeth **Peters**' age
       and was surety for her marriage bond to Randolph **Valentine**. His will was
       proved in Surry County in 1816 [Wills, Etc. 3:111-2]. He was the father of
       i.   ?William, born say 1766, taxable in Surry County from 1787 to 1814:
             taxable on Alexander **Charity**'s tithe in 1795; taxable on John
             Charity's tithe from 1799 to 1802; taxable on 2 slaves from 1805 to
             1807; listed with 1 "free Negro & Mulatto above the age of 16" in
             1813 [PPTL, 1782-90, frames 481, 605; 1791-1816, frames 117, 243,
             271, 346, 385, 426, 463, 575, 599, 617, 714, 755]. He married Edy
             Charity, 28 December 1792 Surry County bond, Major **Debrix** surety,
             30 December marriage [Ministers' Returns, 35]. John **Charity** was
             taxable in William's Surry County household in 1800 [PPTL 1791-
             1816]. Edy Scott, born before 1776, was a "free colored" woman
             living alone in Surry County in 1830.
       ii.   ?Judah, married Caesar **Parham**, 13 November 1788 Sussex County
             marriage by Reverend Jesse Lee [Ministers' Returns, 261]. Caesar was
             head of a Sussex County household of 11 "other free" in 1810,
             probably the "free negro" Cezar (no last name), born about 1762, who
             obtained a certificate in Sussex County on 9 June 1810: *dark brown
             complexion, 5'4-1/4", freed by July 1784 deed of Steth Parham* [Sussex
             County "Certificates granted to Free negroes & mulattoes," no.84].
       iii. ?Nicholas[2], born about 1773, registered in Surry County on 12 August
             1812: *a mulattoe man of Surry County who was born of free parents of
             said County of a bright complexion aged about 39 years...is 5'6-1/4"
             hight...and has rather a thin visage* [Hudgins, *Surry County Register
             of Free Negroes*, 48]. He may have been identical to Nicholas G. Scott
             who was taxable in Surry County from 1810 to 1816 [PPTL 1791-
             1816, 676, 714, 867].
       iv.   Hannah, born say 1773, "daughter of Nicholas Scott," married Drewry
             Walden, 29 July 1790 Surry County bond, Armstead **Peters** surety, 1
             August marriage in Southwark Parish [Ministers' Returns, 29].
       v.   ?Milley, married Aaron **Taylor**, 24 December 1793 Surry County
             bond, Armstead **Peters** surety, 29 December marriage [Ministers'
             Returns, 37].
       vi.   ?Tabitha, married Joseph **Canada**, 23 December 1797 Surry County
             bond, William Scott surety.

---

[182]A "Mulatto" servant named Nicholas (no last name indicated) was brought before the Henrico
County Court in August 1724 by his master John Woodson, Jr., and ordered to serve additional time for
running away for nine days [Minutes 1719-24, 352].

vii. ?Fanny, married Jones **Cannada** /**Cannady**, 20 February 1799 Surry County bond, William Scott surety.

viii. Polly, "daughter of Nicholas Scott," married David **Johns** 23 January 1802 Surry County bond, Drewry **Walden** surety, William Simmons witness.

ix. ?Nancy, married David **Debrix**, 25 December 1802 Surry County bond, William Scott surety, 26 December marriage.

x. ?Lucy, married Samuel **Stewart**, 11 October 1808 Surry County bond, David **Charity** surety.

xi. Grayham, born about 1786, married Patsey **Andrews**, daughter of Beckey **Andrews**, 20 April 1810 Surry County bond, David **Charity** surety. He registered in Surry County on 28 July 1807: *a free Mulatto Man who is the Son of Nicholas Scott aged 21 years or there abouts, tolerable bright Complexion...5'11" high* [Hudgins, *Surry County Register of Free Negroes*, 35].

xii. ?John, taxable in Surry County from 1801 to 1808 and from 1810 to 1816: his tax charged to Nicholas Scott in 1801 and 1803; listed with 1 "free Negro & Mulatto above the age of 16" in 1813 [PPTL, 1791-1816, frames 463, 543, 676, 759, 829, 867]. He was a "Molatto" taxable in Sussex County in 1809 [PPTL 1782-1812, frame 758].

xiii. ?James, a "Molatto" taxable in Sussex County from 1806 to 1809 [PPTL 1782-1812, frames 686, 710, 758].

North Carolina

The Scott family of North Carolina may have originated in Henrico County, Virginia. A Francis Scott was sued for trespass in Henrico County court on 2 September 1708 by Bartholomew **Chavis** who was sued by Thomas **Evans** for debt in October that year [Orders 1707-9, 74, 92]. Francis and Abraham Scott were listed (consecutively) in the Edgecombe County, North Carolina muster of militia with members of the **Chavis** and **Evans** families in the 1750s: Willm Allen, Francess Scoot, James Evens, Benjamine Cheavers, Abraham Scoot [N.C. Archives Militia Troop Returns, box 1, folder 12, last page]. Members of the Scott family were

1 i. John, born say 1700.
2 ii. Abraham, born say 1710.
3 iii. Francis, born say 1720.

1. John^1 Scott, born say 1700, was a "free Negro" living in Berkeley County, South Carolina, when he sent an affidavit to the Orange County, North Carolina court on 12 March 1754:

> *Joseph Deevit Wm. Deevit & Zachariah Martin, entered by force, the house of his daughter, Amy Hawley, and carried her off, by force, with her six children, and he thinks they are taking them north to sell as slaves.*

One of the children, "a mulatto boy Busby, alias John Scott," was recovered in Orange County, and on 12 March 1754 the court appointed Thomas **Chavis** to return the child to South Carolina [Haun, *Orange County Court Minutes*, I:70, 71]. John purchased land from John **Chavous** by deed proved in South Carolina in 1753 [DB N-N:446]. He was granted 200 acres in Berkeley County on 7 May 1767 [S.C. Archives series S213019, vol. 14:357]. One of his children was

i. Amy **Hawley**, who was probably the wife of William **Hawley** of Northampton and Granville counties, North Carolina.

Perhaps John Scott's other descendants were those living in or near South Carolina:

    i.   James, head of a St. Bartholomew's Parish, Charleston District household of 13 "other free" in 1790.

    ii.   John[3], a "Mixt Blood/ Free Negro" taxable in Bladen County, North Carolina, in 1776 [Byrd, *Bladen County Tax Lists*, II:94].

4   iii.   Israel, born say 1755.

    iv.   Abraham, head of a South Orangeburg District household of 9 "other free" in 1790. He was a man of color who served in the Revolution [Moss, *Roster of South Carolina Patriots*, 1849; NSDAR, *African American Patriots*, 183].

    v.   Moses, head of a Beaufort District household of 8 "other free" in 1790 [SC:11].

    vi.   William, head of a South Orangeburg District household of 2 "other free" in 1790.

    vii.   William, head of a St. Bartholomew's Parish, Charleston District, household of 6 "other free" in 1790.

    viii.   Winney, "Negro" head of a Cheraw District household of 2 "other free" males under 16 and 2 "other free" females in 1790 [SC:369].

2.   Abraham[1] Scott, born say 1710, bought land on 26 September 1738 on Bear Branch in North West Parish of Bertie County. Northampton County was formed from this part of Bertie County in 1741. He gave 100 acres of this land to Martha Bray, wife of Peter Bray, for "love and affection" on 22 September 1747, 100 acres on the north side of Falling Run near Abrams Branch and the river to his son Abraham, Jr., on 30 December 1755, 100 acres to his son George Scott, near his sister Martha Bray, on 3 August 1761, and 75 acres near Abraham's line to his son David Scott on 27 August 1761. This land had been deeded to Highland Scott in 1738 [DB 1:330; 2:240; 3:134, 145]. On 29 October 1773 Cordall Norfleet was paid by the churchwardens of St. George Parish for finding and maintaining him [CR 071.927.1, fols. 1, 2]. His children were

    i.   Martha Bray, born say 1730, wife of Peter Bray, a white man.

5   ii.   Abraham[2] Jr., born say 1735.

    iii.   George, who sold the 100 acres deeded to him by his father on 19 July 1766 [DB 3:452].

6   iv.   David[1], born say 1740.

    v.   ?Randall, a Northampton County taxable on an assessment of 100 pounds in 1780 [GA 46.1], head of a Northampton County household of 7 "other free" in 1790 [NC:72] and 11 in Martin County in 1800 [NC:410].

    vi.   John[2], born say 1750. He and his wife Nancy sold 100 acres in Northampton County on 11 October 1774 "that Arthur Oneal bought of Edward Earp 14 Feby 1756" [DB 6:3]. This was land given to Nancy before her marriage by her father Arthur O'Neill by deed of 22 February 1758 to take effect after his death [DB 2:447]. John and Nancy bought 100 acres in Halifax County adjacent to Jonathan Carpenter 10 days later on 21 October 1774. On 19 November 1781 he bought a further 100 acres adjacent to "Jenitoe" Swamp, and he and Nancy sold this land on 9 June 1783 [DB 13:202; 14:552; 15:65]. He was head of a Halifax County household of 7 "other free" in 1790 [NC:65], 6 in 1800 [NC:338], and 6 in 1810 [NC:50].

    vii.   ?Sterling, head of a Northampton County household of 6 "other free" in 1790 [NC:72].

3.   Francis Scott, born say 1720, purchased 200 acres on the north side of the Tar River joining Burnt Coat Swamp in Edgecombe County on 19 February 1747 [DB 3:269]. And on 4 November 1757 he purchased another 9 acres on the

south side of Burnt Coat Swamp which is the part of Edgecombe County from which Halifax County was formed in 1758 [DB 6:320]. He was charged in Edgecombe County in November 1756 with concealing his tithables, probably failing to pay tax on his wife and daughters [Haun, *Edgecombe County Court Minutes*, I:133, 135]. Samuel Jones sued him in Halifax County court in May 1770 and the court issued a subpoena to Margaret Scott (his wife?) [Gammon, *Record of Estates* II:13]. His 10 August 1771 Halifax County will, proved May 1774, lent land between the Spring branch and Horessen(?) Branch to his wife Sarah, and then to "Acsom" with 5 shillings each to his other unnamed children [WB 1:339]. His children were

    i. Exum, born say 1754, received his fathers land after the death of his mother. On 15 March 1775 he sold 10 acres on both sides of Burnt Coat Swamp in Halifax County joining "Scott's Mill Place" for 10 pounds [DB 13:548]. He was taxable on 158 acres in District 10 of Halifax County in 1782 and 140 acres and one free poll in 1790. He was head of a Halifax county household of 9 "other free" in 1790 [NC:63], and in 1800 he was called "Axiom" in Cumberland County, head of a household of 9 "other free." He testified in Wake County in 1818 in support of Allen **Sweat**'s application for a Revolutionary War pension, stating that he was acquainted with him from his infancy when **Sweat** was living on his plantation in Roanoke [M804-2332].

    ii. ?Emanuel, born say 1758, taxable on an assessment of 100 pounds in Northampton County in 1780 [GA 46.1] and taxable on one free poll in District 4 of Halifax County in 1782. He made a deposition in Halifax County court on 22 August 1789 that he was a twelve months soldier in the Continental Line [*NCGSJ* XV:232]. He was head of a Halifax County household of 7 "other free" in 1790, 2 in 1800 [NC:342], and 6 in Cumberland County in 1810 [NC:599].

    iii. ?Isham[2], born about 1763, head of a Halifax County household of 8 "other free" in 1800 [NC:342] and 8 in 1810 [NC:49]. He married Rebecca **James**, widow of Jeremiah **James**, according to her application for Jeremiah's Revolutionary War pension. Isham Scott made a declaration in order to obtain a Revolutionary War pension before the Halifax County court at the age of sixty on 19 May 1823. He stated that he was a servant to Major Hogg and was at the skirmish at Halifax. He rented one third of 60 acres and had a wife and two children, one girl twenty-one years of age and a son who was of age and self supporting. James **Jones** testified that he was in the service with him. He died 19 March 1837 [M804-2136, frame 0433].

    iv. ?James, taxable on one free poll in District 4 of Halifax County in 1782 and head of a Halifax County household of 5 "other free" in 1790 [NC:61].

    v. ?Priscilla, born before 1776, head of a Halifax County household of 3 in 1800 [NC:340], 4 in 1810 [NC:49], and 6 "free colored" in 1820 [NC:164].

4. Israel[1] Scott, born say 1755, was a "Mixt Blood/ Free Negro" taxable in Bladen County in 1776 [Byrd, *Bladen County Tax Lists*, II:94]. He was head of an Edgecombe County household of 7 "other free" in 1790 [NC:55], 6 in 1800 (called "Free Negro"), 5 in 1810 [NC:776], and 2 "free colored" in 1820 [NC:94]. He owned 100 acres on both sides of Mercer's Mill in Edgecombe County when he died on 22 September 1825, leaving a wife Elizabeth and heirs (children?): Israel, Betsy, Creasy, Priscilla, and Maalsy Lowrie Scott, a minor [Gammon, *Record of Estates Edgecombe County*, 85]. He may have been the father of

    i. William[1], born say 1778, head of an Edgecombe County household of 2 "other free" in 1800, called "Free Negro" [NC:241], and 5 in 1810 [NC:775].

      ii.   Israel², married Sally **Lomack**, 26 April 1820 Cumberland County bond, Berry Lucas bondsman.

     iii.   Betsy.

     iv.   Creasy.

     v.   Maalsy **Lowrie**, a minor in 1825.

5.   Abraham² Scott Jr., born say 1735, received 100 acres on the north side of Falling Run at the mouth of Abrams Branch in Northampton County from his father on 30 December 1755 and sold this land for 100 pounds on 19 February 1784 [DB 2:240; 7:219]. About a year later he moved to Halifax County where he bought 200 acres joining Barrot for 100 pounds on 10 May 1785 [DB 15:382]. He sold this land to William Burt on 2 March 1797 and purchased 200 acres between Buck and Beaverdam Swamp on the south side of Little Swamp later that month on 28 March 1797 from Richard Burt [DB 18:144, 149]. He was head of a Halifax County household of 6 "other free" in 1790 [NC:61] and 7 in 1800 [NC:344]. His 13 June 1799 Halifax County will, proved in February 1803, mentioned his wife Sally and children [WB 3:400]:

     i.   Sally.

     ii.   Hardemon, executor of his father's will. He was head of a Northampton County household of 8 "other free" in 1790 (Hardy Scott) [NC:73] and 12 in 1800 [NC:479]. Mary Hucks, a single woman, charged him in the 20 February 1800 Halifax County court with begetting her bastard child [Minutes 1799-1802, 95]. On 4 March 1800 he purchased 231 acres in Northampton County near Occoneechee Swamp and mortgaged this land on 25 December 1804 [DB 10:490; 11:154].

     iii. Judea, perhaps the Judy Scott, born before 1775, head of a Halifax County household of two "free colored" in 1830.

     iv. Tabitha.

     v.   Saul, head of a Northampton County household of one "other free" in 1790 [NC:72].

     vi. Rhody, head of a Halifax County household of "3 "other free" in 1810 [NC:50].

     vii. Lydia, head of a Northampton County household of 4 "other free in 1800 [NC:479].

     viii. Dicey.

     ix. Abigail, called Abigail **Richardson**, formerly Abigail Scott, when she charged Samuel **Hawkins** in Halifax County court on 24 November 1796 with being the father of her unnamed base born child [Minutes 1784-87].

     x.   Mary.

     xi. Simon, who received the "land that lies on north side of the branch that divides the two fields" by his father's will.

6.   David¹ Scott, born say 1740, received 75 acres near Abraham's line in Northampton County from his father Abraham¹ Scott on 27 August 1761 [DB 3:145]. He was head of a Northampton County household of one male 21-60 years old, 2 males less than 20 or more than 60, and one female in Captain Williams' District for the 1786 State Census, 8 "other free" in 1790 [NC:72], and 3 in 1800 [NC:477]. His children may have been

     i.   Isaac, born say 1761, received a grant for 48 acres on the side of Licking Branch in Northampton County on 29 October 1782 [DB 7:180]. He purchased 72 acres adjoining Robert Finny on 28 May 1797 and sold this land on 12 January 1799 [DB 10:312, 446]. He was head of a Northampton County household of 9 "other free" in 1790 [NC:73] and 4 in 1800 [NC:479].

ii. David², Jr., born say 1770, head of a Northampton County household of 3 "other free" in 1800 [NC:479], 7 in 1810 [NC:747], and 10 "free colored" in Halifax County in 1820 [NC:166].

7. Isham¹ Scott, born say 1760, was head of an Edgecombe County household of 7 "other free" in 1790 [NC:55] and an insolvent taxpayer in Edgecombe County in 1798 [Minutes 1797-1800, August 1799 court]. His children were

    i. Isham³, born about 1783, the "son of Isham" ordered bound an apprentice in Edgecombe County by the Wednesday session of the August 1799 court [Minutes 1797-1800]. He was head of an Edgecombe County household of 5 "other free" in 1810 [NC:741].

    ii. Abraham³, born about 1787, the "son of Isham Scott," twelve years old in August 1799 when he was ordered bound an apprentice to David Davidson to be a farmer and shoemaker by the Edgecombe County court. He may have been the Abraham Scott who married Lucinda **Walden**, 22 October 1822 Wake County bond, Zachariah Scott bondsman. He moved to Cumberland County where he was mentioned in the court minutes in the 1830s and 1840s. He was the grandfather of Julia **Jasper**, a ten-year-old free girl of colour, who was bound to him on 3 June 1840. He was issued a permit to carry his gun in Cumberland County on 4 March 1841. He posted security bond for Sewell **Pettiford** in a 6 June 1842 case against him in Cumberland County court. Since **Pettiford** did not appear, Abram had to pay the judgment against him [Minutes 1842-44]. He also posted bond in a famous case against Elijah **Newsom** who was charged with carrying his gun without a license. **Newsom** was found guilty, but the judgment was arrested on the grounds that the law requiring free persons of color to obtain licenses was unconstitutional. However, on appeal the State Supreme Court ruled the law constitutional [Franklin, *Free Negro in North Carolina*, 77-78].

    iii. William², born about 1791, eight-year-old "son of Isham Scott" bound an apprentice by the August 1799 Edgecombe County court. He was granted free papers in Fayetteville on 6 February 1844, signed by (his brother?) Abram Scott, and recorded them in Logan County, Ohio. They described him as: *aged about 52 years, 5 feet 6 inches, common laborer, was free living in Edgecomb County* [Turpin, *Register of Black, Mulatto, and Poor Persons*, 13].

SELDON FAMILY

1. Mary Sildom, born say 1738, was the mother of a poor orphan "Mulatto" named Milly Sildom who was bound out by the Charles City County court on 5 July 1758 [Orders 1758-62, 24]. She was the ancestor of

    i. Milly, born say 1757.

2   ii. Molly, born about 1759.

    iii. ?Robert¹, born say 1760, taxable in St. Paul's Parish, Hanover County, from 1789 to 1812: listed with 4 slaves and 2 horses in 1789; a "Malato" taxable on 2 free tithes, a slave and 2 horses in 1791, 2 free and 4 slaves in 1794; 2 free, 7 slaves and 4 horses in 1798; 1 free and 3 slaves in 1812 [PPTL 1782-91, pp. 224, 267; 1792-1803, pp. 16, 29, 49, 100, 154, 215, 226; 1804-24].

    iv. ?Elizabeth, head of a Charles City County household of 2 "other free" in 1810 [VA:959]. She was called Elizabeth **Syldom** in the 11 July 1789 Charles City County will of Abraham **Brown** by which he allowed her the use of the house and garden on his land during her life [WB 1:16-17].

2.   Molly Selden, born about 1759, registered in Bedford County on 26 July 1803: *aged 44, Light Mulatto, 5 feet 2 inches high, Born free* [Register of Free Negroes 1803-20, p.3]. She may have been the mother of

    i.   Jacob, born about 1781, registered in Bedford County on 26 July 1803: *aged 22, Mulatto, 5 feet 3 inches high, Born free* [Register of Free Negroes 1803-20, p.3]. He was a "F.B." head of a Bedford County household of 8 "other free" in 1810 [VA:489].

    ii. Sally, born about 1783, registered in Bedford County on 26 July 1803: *aged 20, dark Mulatto, 5-1/4", Born free* [Register of Free Negroes 1803-20, p.3].

    iii. Robert[2], born about 1794, registered in Bedford County on 24 October 1831: *5'3" high, bright mulattoe, aged 37, Born free* [Register of Free Negroes 1820-60, p.16].

SEXTON FAMILY

1.   Hagai Sexton, born about 1749, indentured herself to William and Ann Smith in Spotsylvania County on 5 March 1770 [Orders 1768-74, 96]. She ran away from her master, and he placed an ad in the 31 October 1771 issue of the *Virginia Gazette* for her return:

> *RUN away from the Subscriber, in April last, dark Mulatto Woman named HANKEY, alias HAGAI SEXTON, between two and three and twenty Years of Age, about five Feet high, has long black curled Hair tied behind, remarkable bow Legs, and is very talkative; she had on, when she went away, a cross barred Pompadour Ground Stuff Gown, an Osnabrug Shift and Petticoat, and an old dressed Gauze Cap. She was born in Caroline County, is well known about Port Royal, at which Place she has several Times been seen since her Elopement, and in July last was entertained at the Plantation of Mr. John Macon in that County, but has since left that Place, and is supposed to be gone towards Williamsburg* [*Virginia Gazette*, Purdie & Dixon edition].

Smith recovered her by 21 May 1772 when the Spotsylvania County court ordered her to serve him an additional twenty-six months [Orders 1768-74, 192]. She may have been identical to Agnes Sexton who was head of a Charlotte County household of 2 free persons in 1782 [VA:15]. And she may have been the mother of

    i.   Ransom, head of a Warren County, North Carolina household of 4 "other free" in 1810 [NC:758].

SHAW FAMILY

1.   Margaret Shaw, born say 1665, was taxable in the Surry County household of Anthony **Cornish** in 1698 [*Magazine of Virginia Genealogy*, vol. 24, no.2, p.73], perhaps the Margaret **Cornish** who was taxable in John Hencock's Lawns Creek Parish household in 1703 [DW 5:291]. She may have been the mother of

    i.   Mary, born say 1685, a "malato wife to a negro man of Mr. Thomas Howlett" who indentured herself in Henrico County to William Soane for two years starting 3 March 1707 for 600 pounds of tobacco per year. She was apparently in debt to the churchwardens for having an illegitimate child. The indenture specified that she would have to serve additional time at the same rate if she incurred any more debts during her service [Deeds, Wills, Etc. 1697-1704, 115]. She may have been identical to Mary Shaw, "a Mollatto," who died on 9 April 1746 in

Stafford County [Overwharton Parish, Stafford County, Register, 1724-1776, 123].

SHEPHERD FAMILY

1. Ann Shepherd, born say 1703, was a "Christian white woman" who was presented by the Accomack County, Virginia court for having an illegitimate child. When required to identify the father of her child on 6 June 1721, she told the Accomack County court that it was "Indian Edmund," but on 6 July 1721 she admitted that it was Henry **Jackson**, "a Mullatto." The court ordered that she be sold for five years [Orders 1719-24, 33]. She may have been the ancestor of

    i. George, head of an Accomack County household of 8 "other free" in 1810 [VA:60].

2. James[1] Shepherd, born say 1730, (no race indicated) complained to the Granville County, North Carolina court that Robert Chandler unlawfully detained him as a servant sometime between 1749 and 1759 [CR 044.101.2, undated 1749-1759 indenture bond]. He may have been the father of

    i. William, born before 1776, head of a Stokes County, North Carolina household of 3 "free colored" in 1820 [NC:370].

    ii. Byrd, married Mavel **Stewart**, 20 April 1815 Person County bond. She was the daughter of Thomas **Stewart**, who mentioned her in his May 1818 Person County, North Carolina will [WB 8:77].

Other members of a Shepherd family were
2   i. James[1], born say 1730.
    ii. James[2], a "free Negro" taxable in Nansemond County in 1815.
    iii. Richard, born about 1750, a "Mullatto Boy" living in Truro Parish, Fairfax County, on 21 August 1752 when the court ordered the churchwardens to bind him to Henry Collem until the age of thirty-one [Orders 1749-54, 234].
    iv. Francis, a "melatto" taxable in Campbell County in 1792 [PPTL 1785-1814, frame 242], a "free Mulatto" charged in Cumberland County, Virginia, on 26 August 1796 with stealing from Woodson's warehouse in the town of Cartersville [Orders 1792-7, 561, 564, 581], head of a Richmond City household of 2 "other free" in 1810 [VA:317].

SHOECRAFT FAMILY

1. William[1] Shoecraft, born say 1640, was tithable in Lancaster County, Virginia, from 1697 to 1700 but was declared tax-free in April 1701, probably due to old age [Orders 1696-1702, 32, 93, 129, 134]. Lancaster County records give no indication of his race, but many of his descendants were mixed-race. He was probably the ancestor of

    i. William[2], born say 1700, a tithable in Norfolk County from 1732 to 1734 in the household adjoining Johnson **Driggers**, Sr., and Johnson **Driggers**, Jr., in the district from Suggs Mill to the Great Bridge [Wingo, *Norfolk County Tithables, 1730-50*, 54, 81, 131]. Perhaps he was the William Shewcraft who left a Princess Anne County will on 25 April 1768 leaving his land to Dorcas Franklin, a widow [DB 10:252].

    ii. Abraham[1], born say 1702, acknowledged in Northumberland County court on 18 July 1723 that he was indebted to Edward **Nickens** [Orders 1719-29, 109]. He was taxable in his own household in Norfolk County in the district above Great Bridge from 1734 to 1735 [Wingo, *Norfolk County Tithables, 1730-50*, 127, 160, 172].

2   iii. Simon[1], born say 1708.
3   iv. Ann, born say 1710.

2. Simon[1] Shoecraft, born say 1708, was a witness (with Richard and Elizabeth
    Weaver) to the Lancaster County will of Edward Nicken in 1735 [D&W
    12:355]. He was in North Carolina in the 1750s when he and Richard **Nickens**
    were listed in the Muster Roll of Captain Thomas Davis' Company in the
    Currituck County Militia [Clark, *Colonial Soldiers of the South*, 657-8].
    Members of the Shoecraft family were counted as "other free" persons near
    the **Nickens** and **Weaver** families in Hertford County from 1790 to 1810.
    Simon was taxable in the Edmund Bridge District of Norfolk County in 1759
    [Wingo, *Norfolk County Tithables, 1751-65*, 154]. His 29 December 1760
    Norfolk County will, proved in November 1763, mentioned his wife Lucy and
    children: William, Abraham, Rodha, Mary, and Martha Shewcraft. William
    Shewcraft, his oldest son, was named as executor and was to raise his children
    after his wife's decease [WB 2, fol.187, 220]. Lucy was a taxable head of a
    Norfolk County, Virginia household in St. Brides Parish: taxable with her son
    Abraham in 1765, taxable on one tithe in 1768, taxable for John **Archer**'s tithe
    in 1770 on the Northside of Western Branch, taxable for (her grandson?) Cary
    Shewcraft's tithe in 1773 and taxable for (her grandson) Kinner Shoecraft's
    tithe in 1774 [Wingo, *Norfolk County Tithables, 1751-65*, 196; 1766-1780, 55,
    132, 195, 225]. Simon and Lucy were the parents of
    4   i.   William[3], born say 1732.
           ii.   Rodha, born say 1744.
          iii.   Abraham[2], born say 1745, taxable in the Edmonds Bridge District
                 household of his mother Lucy Shewcraft in 1765 [Wingo, *Norfolk
                 County Tithables, 1751-65*, 196], counted as white in 1790, head of a
                 Hertford County household of 2 males over 16 and 3 females in 1790
                 [NC:26], and head of a Hertford County household of 6 "other free"
                 in 1800. His wife Elizabeth Shewcraft was the sister of William **Butler**
                 of Bertie County whose 16 November 1802 estate division records that
                 she first married James Craft, had two children, but she and Craft had
                 "parted about twenty or twenty-five years ago," and she had married
                 second to Abraham Shewcraft [Gammon, *Record of Estates, Bertie
                 County* II, 18].
           iv.   Mary, born say 1748.
            v.   Martha, born say 1750.

3. Ann Shoecraft, born say 1710, perhaps a sister of Simon Shoecraft, was called
    Anne Suecraft of Christ Church Parish on 8 May 1728 when she was accused
    in Lancaster County court of having a bastard child. The charge was dismissed
    later that year on 14 August 1728 [Orders 1721-29, 270, 287]. She was called
    Ann **Mitchell** in Bertie County, North Carolina court on 24 October 1758
    when her "free Mulattoe" son William Shoecraft was bound an apprentice
    [Haun, *Bertie County Court Minutes*, II:452]. Her son was
    5   i.   William[5], born about 1749.

4. William[3] Shoecraft, born say 1732, was tithable in his own Norfolk County
    household in the district from Edmund's Bridge to the Upper Inhabitants from
    1753 to 1757 [Wingo, *Norfolk County Tithables, 1751-65*, 46, 76, 98, 111]
    and head of a Blackwater Precinct, Princess Anne County household of 5
    persons in 1783 and 5 in 1785 [VA:60, 103]. His 30 December 1792 Princess
    Anne County will was proved on 1 April 1793. He named his wife Mary to
    whom he left all the household goods that she brought to the marriage. He also
    named his daughter Lucy **Turner** and her son **John**. Lucy was probably the
    wife of one of Sampson **Turner**'s sons. Sampson was a "F.N." taxable in
    Great Bridge District of Norfolk County from 1761 to 1765 and taxable in
    Blackwater Precinct, Princess Anne County, in 1784. He also named his son-
    in-law James **Harmon** who was a "Mulatto" bound apprentice to George
    Chappel in Princess Anne County on 17 July 1759 [Minutes 1753-62, 357].
    He left his land to his son William and timber to his son Kinner Shewcrafts

Collons and also stipulated that Kinner was to have half of what fell to him from his own father's estate [WB 1:210]. William was the father of

   i.   Lucy, probably the wife of Pormenus, Nicholas, or Butler **Turner**.

   ii.   William[4], born say 1755, called brother to Lucy.

   iii. ?Cary, born say 1757, taxable in the household of Malachi Wilson in Edmonds Bridge District in 1772 and in Lucy Shoecraft's household in 1773 [Wingo, *Norfolk County Tithables, 1751-65*, 185, 195]. The inventory of Cary's estate was proved in Princess Anne County in March 1786 [WB 1:87].

   iv.   a daughter who married James **Harmon**. Their son James received a heifer from his grandfather. He was probably related to Craftshoe **Harmon**, head of a Liberty County, South Carolina household of 3 "other free" in 1800 [SC:806].

   v.   Kinner, born say 1758, taxable in the Norfolk County household of (his grandmother) Lucy Shoecraft in 1774 and head of a household in 1778 and 1780 [Wingo, *Norfolk County Tithables, 1751-65*, 225, 250, 282]. He was taxable in Norfolk County from 1782 to 1787 [PPTL, 1782-91, frames 392, 417, 452, 497, 597].

   vi.   Simon[2].

   vii. Abraham[3].

   viii. Elizabeth.

5.   William[5] Shoecraft, born about 1749, son of Ann **Mitchell**, "a free Mulattoe," was about nine years old on 24 October 1758 when he was bound an apprentice to James Boon by the Bertie County court [Haun, *Bertie County Court Minutes*, II:452]. He was probably living in the part of Bertie County which became Hertford County since James Boon signed a petition to form Hertford County from Bertie County in 1759 [*Journal of N.C. Genealogy*, 2167]. William was taxable on one poll in Hertford County in Captain Harrell's Company in 1784 [LP 64.1]. He was head of a Hertford County household of 8 "other free" in 1790 [NC:26], 6 in 1810 [NC:101], 4 "free colored" in Orange County in 1820 [NC:336], and a "Negro" head of a Guilford County household of 2 "free colored" in 1830. William's grandson Jeremiah made an application for Cherokee Indian benefits in 1908 in which he stated that his grandfather "Billy Shocraft" died about 1836 in Guilford County (when Jeremiah, born about 1821, was about fifteen or sixteen years old). His claim was rejected, but it identifies William's wife as Bicey **Nickens** and names their children: Silas, James, Sarah **Milton**, and Tabitha **Robbins**. Their children were

   i.   James, born about 1766, head of a Hertford County household of 4 "other free" in 1810 [NC:101], an Orange County household of 8 "free colored" in 1820 [NC:336] and a "Negro" head of a Guilford County household of 9 "free colored" in 1830. He was a "Mulatto" counted in New Garden Township, Wayne County, Indiana, in the 1850 census with Anna Shoecraft who was born about 1785. He married Mary Anna **Milton**, sister of Mills **Milton**, according to the testimony of his grandson Samuel Shoecraft in 1908.

   ii.   Silas E., born about 1783, head of an Orange County household of 10 "free colored" in 1820 [NC:336] and a "Negro" head of a Guilford County household of 9 "free colored" in 1830. He was living in Green Township, Wayne County, Indiana, in 1850 with Polly Shoecraft who was also a "Mulatto" born in North Carolina about 1783.

   iii. Sarah **Milton**, probably the wife of Miles **Milton**.

   iv. Tabitha **Robbins**, the wife of Josiah **Robbins** who was head of an Orange County, North Carolina household of 5 "free colored" in 1820 [NC:336]. She was head of a Guilford County household of 7 "free colored" in 1830. Their grandson Philander **Weaver** applied for Cherokee benefits.

SHOEMAKER FAMILY

1. Sarah Shoemaker, born say 1730, was living in Craven County, North
    Carolina, in May 1754 when the court issued a summons for her to show
    cause why her child John **Bowers** should not be bound out [Haun, *Craven
    County Court Minutes*, IV:231]. She was the mother of
    i.   John **Bowers**, born before May 1754.
    ii. ?Saul **Bowers**, born say 1760, head of a Craven County household of
         3 "other free" in 1790 [NC:131].

2. James Shoemaker, born say 1740, and his wife Mary were "Black" taxables
    in Fishing Creek District, Granville County, North Carolina, in 1762 [CR
    044.701.19], and he was an insolvent taxpayer in Samuel Benton's 1764 list.
    He was among the "Black" members of the undated colonial muster roll of
    Captain James Fason's Northampton County militia [Mil. T.R. 1-3] and was
    head of a Georgetown District, Prince George's Parish, South Carolina
    household of 7 "other free" in 1790. Perhaps his children were
    i.   Sampson, sued for a debt of 32 pounds in Marlboro County, South
         Carolina, on 5 March 1788 [Court Minutes 1785-1808, n.p.]. He
         recorded a plat for 100 acres in Craven on the southwest side of
         Catfish Swamp in Georgetown District on 16 November 1787 [S.C.
         Archives Series S213190, vol. 22:152]. He was head of a Prince
         George Parish household of 6 "other free" in 1790 and 1 in Liberty
         County in 1800 [SC:806]. John Shoemaker recorded a plat for 997
         acres on Catfish Swamp adjoining Sampson's land in Marion District
         on 19 October 1819 [S.C. Archives series S213190, vol. 39:171].
    ii. James Jr., head of a Georgetown District, Prince George's Parish
         household of 4 "other free" in 1790 and 4 in Liberty County in 1800
         [SC:806].
    iii. Solomon, born say 1765, head of a Georgetown District, Prince
         George's Parish household of 4 "other free" in 1790 [SC:56], 1 in
         Liberty County in 1800 [SC:806], and 5 in Darlington District in 1810
         [SC:669]. His land on Black Creek near the Pee Dee River was
         mentioned in the 4 August 1817 Darlington deed of land to John and
         William Shoemaker and a 8 June 1822 plat for land in Darlington on
         Black Creek and the Pee Dee River [DB G:347-8; S.C. Archives Series
         S213192, vol. 47:40]. According to the Cherokee Claim of his
         grandson Samuel **Evans**, Solomon's wife was named Betty and they
         had a child named Elizabeth who was born on the Pee Dee River. His
         other grandparents were Henry and Molly **Evans** of North Carolina
         [Application to Eastern Cherokees of the United States, Court of
         Claims, 1806-1809 microfilm, nos. 28545 and 24480].
    iv. John, born about 1766 in South Carolina, a "Mulatto" counted in the
         1850 Jackson County, Alabama census, worth $3,000. His daughter
         Elizabeth was born in Tennessee about 1808 [AL:50a].

SILVA/ SILVER FAMILY

1. Edward Silver, born say 1745, purchased land in Granville County, North
    Carolina, adjoining William **Chavis**, Jr., on 19 October 1767 (called Edward
    Silvey) and sold this land on 1 October 1768 (called Edward Silva) [DB
    L:306, 327]. Perhaps he was identical to or related to the Edward Silva who
    purchased land by deed proved in Amelia County, Virginia, in June 1749
    [Orders 2:151]. He may have married Milly, the daughter of Richard and
    Susannah **Chavis**. Milly was taxable in her parents' household in 1767 in the
    list of Stephen Jett, adjoining the household of William **Chavis**, Jr. [CR
    44.701.19]. Edward Silver was taxable on married-man poll tax in Granville

County in 1780, and counted as white in Wake County in 1800, head of a household of two males over 16, 2 under 16, and 4 females [NC:104]. Milly Silver was head of a Halifax County, North Carolina household of 5 "other free" in 1800 [NC:342]. They may have been the parents of

2   i.   Susannah[1]/ Sukey, born before 1776.

2. Sukey Silver, born before 1776, was head of a Halifax County, North Carolina household of 4 "free colored" in 1820 [NC:164]. She was probably the mother of

    i.   Susan[2], born about 1790, called "Sukey" when she was head of a Halifax County household of 1 "free colored" in 1830, a "Mulatto" living in household no. 1370, Halifax County in 1860.
   ii. Henry, born about 1795, a "Mulattto" living in household no. 878 in 1860.
  iii. Rose Silvey, born about 1817, ordered bound out by the Halifax County court on 16 August 1824.

SIMMONS FAMILY

Members of the Simmons family were

1   i.   Margaret[1], born say 1700.
   ii. Anne Simmonds, born say 1712, a servant (no race indicated) of Thomas Stanton. She confessed to the churchwardens of St. George Parish, Spotsylvania County, Virginia, on 1 December 1730 that she had a "Mulatto bastard by a Negro man" [Orders 1730-32, 9].

1. Margaret[1] Simmons, born say 1700, was a "free Mulatto Woman" who came into King George County, Virginia court on 4 September 1730 and bound her daughters Rachel and Betty Simmons to serve William Strother, Gent., until the age of twenty-one [Orders 1721-34, pt.3, 526]. She was the mother of

    i.   Rachel, born in October 1717, twelve years old on 4 September 1730 when she was bound apprentice to William Strother.
   ii. Betty, born in July 1720, ten years old on 4 September when she was bound apprentice to William Strother.

Their descendants may have been

2   i.   William[1], born say 1732.
   ii. William[2], head of an Essex County, Virginia household of 6 "other free" in 1810 [VA:198].
  iii. Margaret[2] (Peggy), head of an Essex County household of 4 "other free" in 1810 [VA:198].
  iv. Samuel, born say 1753, head of a Craven County, North Carolina household of 5 "other free" and a slave in 1790 [NC:130]. His children were probably Backhouse Simmons, head of a Craven County household of 4 "free colored" in 1820 [NC:77] and Larry Simmons, head of a Craven County household of 2 "free colored" and 7 slaves in 1820 [NC:77].

2. William[1] Simmons, born say 1732, died before September 1766 when his children Phereby and James (no race indicated) were bound out by the Bertie County, North Carolina court [Haun, *Bertie County Court Minutes*, III:748]. William's children were

3   i.   ?Sarah[1], born say 1755.
4   ii. Phereby[1], born about 1757.
  iii. James[1], born about 1759, the seven-year-old orphan of William Simmons, ordered bound as an apprentice cooper to Thomas Collins by the September 1766 Bertie County court. In 1775 he was an under-sixteen-year-old taxable "molatto," called Jem Simmons, in John

Hyman's household in David Standly's Bertie County list [CR 10.702.1, box 3].

3.   Sarah[1] Simmons, born say 1755, was living in Bertie County in November 1787 when her daughter Hannah was bound apprentice. Sarah was the mother of

5   i.   ?Phereby[2], born say 1772.

        ii.   ?Charity, born say 1781, no age, race, or parent named when she was bound to Elizabeth Rascoe in Bertie County on 8 August 1785 [*NCGSJ* XIV:161].

       iii.   Hannah[1], born say 1783, "Daughter of Sarah Simmons" (no age or race mentioned), ordered bound apprentice to William Bentley in Bertie County by the November 1787 court [Haun, *Bertie County Court Minutes*, V:676].

        iv.   Amy, born say 1786, "daughter of Sarah Simmons," ordered bound to Mary Seals by the November 1788 Bertie County court [Haun, *Bertie County Court Minutes*, VI:719].

         v.   ?Polly, born about 1788, about eleven years old when she was bound to David Ryan in Bertie County [*NCGSJ* XV:170]. Perhaps she was the Mary Simons who was a 26-45 year-old head of a Washington County household of 5 "free colored" in 1820 [NC:410].

        vi.   ?Andrew, born about 1796, six years old (no race mentioned) when he was bound to William Swain to be a shoemaker in Bertie County on 9 August 1802 [*NCGSJ* XVI:39]. He was called "an orphan of color, 14 years old last November" when he was bound to Daniel Young to be a block maker on 14 May 1810 [*NCGSJ* XVII:41].

       vii.   ?James[2], born about 1804, a five-year-old "orphan of color" bound to John Bond to be a shoemaker on 16 August 1809. On 18 November the same year he was bound instead to Peter Kirkham to be a carpenter [*NCGSJ* XVII:41].

4.   Phereby[1] Simmons, born about 1757, was the nine-year-old orphan of William Simmons (no race mentioned), bound apprentice on 30 September 1766 in Bertie County, North Carolina [*NCGSJ* XIV:31]. She may have been the mother of

         i.   Sarah[3], born about 1777, a twelve and one-half year-old child (no parent or race mentioned) bound apprentice to Zedekiah Stone in Bertie County on 17 August 1789 [*NCGSJ* XIV:163].

        ii.   Henry, born in February 1778, "14 years old next February," ordered bound to William Armstead as an apprentice blacksmith and corker by the May 1791 Bertie County court [Haun, *Bertie County Court Minutes*, VI:868].

       iii.   Charles[2], born about 1781, a four-year-old child (no parent or race mentioned) bound an apprentice shoemaker to Luke Warburton in Bertie County in May 1785 [Haun, *Bertie County Court Minutes*, V:631].

        iv.   Levi, born say 1790, head of a Hertford County household of 5 "free colored" in 1820 [NC:190].

5.   Phereby[2] Simmons, born say 1772, was not mentioned in Bertie County records. However, in a 1 June 1853 Wayne County deposition, Winney Huff deposed that she had been acquainted with Phereby for seventy to seventy-five years and that Phereby's mother was a "Colored Woman" who lived in Bertie County when Phereby was bound apprentice to William Burnham. Phereby moved with Burnham to Duplin County where her children were apprenticed to him. One daughter named Hannah was apprenticed to Burnham's daughter, Elizabeth (married Simpson), when he moved to Georgia [2 June 1853 Wayne County Deposition of Winney Huff]. Other Wayne County residents, Charity

Bryant and Mary Wiggs, deposed that they were acquainted with Phereby for sixty to sixty-five years and that she had been William Burnham's apprentice [3 July & 1 June 1853 Wayne County Depositions]. Phereby was probably the "other free" person counted in William Burnham's Duplin County household in 1790 [NC:191]. According to the 2 June 1853 deposition of Winney Huff and Charity Bryant, Phereby was the mother of

    i.   Hannah^2, born about 1794, a "free born negro" about one year old when she was bound to Betsy Burnham in Wayne County on 21 January 1795.

SIMMS FAMILY

1. Margaret Syms, born say 1681, the servant of Robert Dudley, Gent., was presented by the Middlesex County court on 7 July 1701 for having a "mulatto bastard Childe." She confessed to the fact when she appeared in court on 6 April 1702. She may have been the mother of "William, a Mullato boy," who was bound to Major Robert Dudley by the Middlesex County court on 4 March 1699/1700 [Orders 1694-1705, 323, 424, 461]. And she may have been the ancestor of

    i.   Lewis, born about 1745, a "black man" listed in the militia returns for Granville County, North Carolina, in 1778 [N.C. Archives Troop Returns 4-40; *The North Carolinian*, 1960, p.727].

    ii. Humpy, "free Negro" head of a Fairfax County household of 4 "other free" and 5 slaves in 1810 [VA:301].

    iii. Lee, "free Negro" head of a Fairfax County household of 2 "other free" and a white woman in 1810 [VA:299].

    iv. Elisha, married Rebecca **Scott**, 11 March 1790 Goochland County bond. He was head of a Goochland County household of 4 "other free" in 1810 [VA:715].

SIMON FAMILY

1. Thomas Simon, born say 1730, was among fourteen free African Americans presented by the Surry County, Virginia court on 21 November 1758:

Against...Wm Walden...Thomas Simon... for each and every of them not listing their wife's according to law supposing the said persons to be Mulattoes...[Orders 1757-64, 135].

On 19 February 1760 he purchased 50 acres in Southwark Parish on Horsemeadow Branch in Surry County. He probably died before 4 June 1787 when (his wife & daughter?) Nanny and Sarah Simon sold his 50 acres in Southwark Parish adjoining William **Walden** [DB 7:495; 12:268]. He was taxable in Surry County from 1782 to 1787 [PPTL, 1782-90, frames; 351, 367, 459]. He may have been the father of

    i.   Sarah, born say 1762, sold her father's Surry County land on 4 June 1787.

SIMPSON FAMILY

1. Ann Simpson, born say 1709, was presented by the King George County, Virginia court on 3 November 1727 for having a "Mulatto Child." She was the servant of John Farguson on 8 March 1728/9 when she was again presented for having an illegitimate child [Orders 1721-34, 384, 391, 443]. She may have been the ancestor of

    i.   Archable, born before 1755, a "Free Mulattor" taxable in John Smith's household in the 1766 Bertie County, North Carolina tax list of John Crickett [CR 10.702.1, box 3].

2   ii.   Sarah, born say 1760.

        iii.   Reddin, born say 1760, "free colored" head of a Tyrrell County, North Carolina household of one male and 3 females in 1790 [NC:34].

        iv.   Jacob, born say 1765, "free colored" head of a Tyrrell County household of one male over 16, one under 16 and one female in 1790 [NC:34].

        v.   Molly, a "Mullato" child bound to James Patterson in Augusta County, Virginia, on 18 March 1772 [Orders 1769-73, 331].

        vi.   Charon, head of a Tyrrell County household of 4 "other free" in 1810 [NC:785].

        vii. Milly, head of a Martin County, North Carolina household of 5 "other free" in 1810 [NC:452].

        viii. Isaac, head of a Hyde County, North Carolina household of 4 "other free" in 1810 [NC:119] and 7 "free colored" in 1820 [NC:240].

2.   Sarah Simpson, born say 1760, was head of a Washington County, North Carolina household of 4 "other free" at Stewart's Mill in 1800 [NC:710]. She may have been the mother of

        i.   Jemima, bound an apprentice in Tyrrell County on 26 April 1792 [CR 96.102.1, box 1].

SISCO FAMILY

1.   John[1] Francisco, born say 1630, was the slave of Stephen Charlton for whom Charlton claimed a headright in Northampton County, Virginia, in August 1647 [DW 1645-51, 97 by Deal, *Race and Class*]. In July 1648 Charlton made a deed of manumission to free him ten years later in November 1658: *and then the said Negro is to bee a free man* [DW 1645-51, 150-2]. He was called "Black Jack" in Charlton's October 1654 will by which he received his freedom. Charlton also agreed to free John's wife Christian, a "Negro woman," three years after his death or within six months if she paid 2,500 pounds of tobacco [DW 1654-55, fol.57]. John and Christian were tithable in their own household in Northampton County from 1665 to 1671. Grace Susanna (Sebastian **Cane**'s wife?) was in their household in 1667. In 1668 the court agreed to have the "Negro" child of Thomas **Driggers**, then living with him, bound to him until the age of twenty-one [Orders 1657-64, 198; 1664-74, fol.14, p.42, 53, fol.54, fol.115]. He was called "John Francisco Negroe" on 7 July 1685 when the Accomack County court ordered him to pay his debt of 5,090 pounds of tobacco to Colonel William Kendall [W&cO 1682-97, 66a]. He was taxable in Accomack County from 1674 to 1695, called a "negro" in 1676 and 1686. In 1684 one of his three tithables was identified as his unnamed wife [Orders 1676-78, 33, 57; 1678-82, 18, 99; W&cO 1682-97, 191, 258; Nottingham, *Accomack Tithables*, 12, 16, 18, 19, 22, 23, 25, 27, 28, 31, 33, 35, 37, 40, 42, 44, 47, 50, 52, 54, 60]. John was probably the ancestor of

2   i.   Daniel[1], born say 1680.

3   ii.   Elizabeth, born say 1695.

        iii.   Thomas[1] Frisco, born say 1700, a Northampton County taxable with Ann Frisco in 1724 and called Thom Frica when he was tithable without Ann in the household of Nathaniel Andress in 1725 [Bell, *Northampton County Tithables*, 64, 89].

2.   Daniel[1] Francisco, born say 1680, was sued for debt in Northampton County, Virginia, on 28 November 1706. The case was dismissed because neither part appeared [Orders, Wills, Etc., 1698-1710, 308]. He was the father of an illegitimate child which Mary Winslow had in Somerset County in March 1707. Daniel was probably living in the same community as William **Driggers** because Mary Winslow had a child by William **Driggers** in Somerset County

in 1708. Daniel admitted to being the father of her child when he appeared in court seven years later in March 1713/4 [Judicial Records 1707-11, 95-6, 103; 1713-5, 5, 26]. He was living in Accomack County on 6 July 1715 when the court ordered that he, John Smith, John Martiall, and Richard Rowle/ Rowlin be summoned to the next court for disobeying Constable Hill Drummond while he was trying to break up a fight. The other parties were fined when they appeared at the next court on 4 October, but there was no further mention of Daniel [Orders 1714-17, 10a, 11]. He died before 22 September 1732 when the inventory of his Kent County, Delaware estate was taken.[183] He may have married the daughter of Thomas **Consellor** who mentioned his daughter Elizabeth Francisco in his 26 September 1739 Kent County will. "Elisabeth Siscom" was head of a household in Little Creek Hundred, Kent County in 1738, taxable on (her son?) Thomas. They may have been the parents of

4   i.   Daniel^2, born say 1700.
5   ii.   Thomas^2, born say 1721.
6   iii.   John^2, born say 1723.

3.   Elizabeth Francisco, born say 1695, a "negro," bound out her daughter Rachel to Robert Nottingham in Northampton County on 17 March 1717/18 and bound her daughter Sabra, a "Negro child," to Abraham Bowker on 18 August 1719. On 10 October 1720 Bowker sued her for 20 bushels of Indian corn, and on 13 September 1722 Bowker and his wife were examined when she was acquitted of murdering her child [Orders 1716-18, 84; 1719-22, 31, 95, 183]. In November 1722 Bowker sued her to recover his costs for looking after her during her childbirth. She may have left the county since Ralph Pigot forfeited the bail he posted for her appearance in court to answer Bowker [Orders 1719-22, 95; Milhalyka, *Loose Papers 1628-1731*, 37, 42]. Her children were

7   i.   Rachel^1, born say 1715.
      ii.   Sabra, born say 1717.

4.   Daniel^2 Francisco, born say 1700, was sued by Evan Jones in Kent County, Delaware court in November 1724 and by Nicholas Greenway in May 1725 [General Court Records 1722-5, 68, fol. 75]. He was taxable in Little Creek Hundred, Kent County from 1727 to 1748. Since he is not mentioned in the tax lists after 1748, he may have been the brother of John Francisco who petitioned the Kent County Orphans Court on 26 February 1756 stating that his brother had died "some years ago," as had his brother's wife Catherine leaving an infant [Estate Accounts, by Heite]. And he may have been the father of

8   i.   Ephraim Sisco, born say 1745.

5.   Thomas^2 Francisco, born say 1721, was taxable in the Little Creek Hundred, Kent County household of (his mother?) Elisabeth Siscom in 1738 and taxable in his own household from 1740 to 1745. He died before 16 July 1748 when his widow Patience Sisco was granted administration on his Kent County estate [WB I-1, fol. 231]. The 29 November 1750 account of his estate mentions Daniel **Durham** and Elizabeth Francisco [Estate Accounts, by Heite]. Thomas and Patience may have been the parents of

9   i.   Benjamin, born say 1735.

6.   John^2 Francisco, born say 1723, was taxable in Little Creek Hundred from 1743 to 1758 [1743 to 1767 Levy Assessments, frame nos. 16, 24, 43, 51, 107, 136, 143, 187, 226]. On 26 February 1756 he petitioned the Kent County Orphans Court stating that his brother (Daniel?) had died "some years ago,"

---

[183]He is called David Francisco in the inventory. It is not the original, but a copy made by the clerk in 1752. He probably wrote David for Daniel.

as had his brother's wife Catherine leaving an infant in the care of John Swaney who was unable to care for it. The court placed the child in his care [Estate Accounts, by Heite]. He died before 18 December 1798 when administration of his Kent County estate was granted to (his wife?) Elizabeth Francisco [WB N-1, fol. 221]. The inventory of his estate totalled over 942 pounds. On 10 November 1800 the estate was divided among Charles, Lydia, and Esther Francisco [Estate Accounts, by Heite]. His children were most likely

	i.	John³, Jr., born say 1738, taxable in Little Creek Hundred from 1758.
10	ii.	Charles, born say 1745.
11	iii.	Lydia, born say 1747.
	iv.	James², born say 1749, taxable in Little Creek Hundred in 1770.
	v.	William, born say 1750, taxable in Little Creek Hundred in 1770 and 1771.
	vi.	Esther, born say 1752, left an 11 February 1815 Kent County will in which she left 4-1/4 acres and her personal estate to Gelica **Lockerman** and Susan **Derham**, wife of George **Derham** (**Durham**) [WB P-1:69].

7. Rachel¹ Sisco, born say 1715, was bound apprentice by her mother Elizabeth Francisco in Northampton County, Virginia, on 17 March 1717/18. She was presented on 15 May 1734 and 9 November 1736 for bastard bearing [Orders 1732-42, 113, 117, 246, 255]. She was tithable in Ann Batson's Northampton County household in 1738 and 1739 [Bell, *Northampton County Tithables*, 282, 309]. She was apparently identical to "Negro Siss" who was living at Ann Batson's on 13 November 1739 when she was presented for bastard bearing [Orders 1732-42, 372, 378]. Her children were

12	i.	Phillis¹, born in March 1736/7.
	ii.	Bridget, born in September 1739, daughter of Rachel Sisco, bound apprentice to Major Brickhouse on 11 May 1742 [Orders 1732-42, 484].
	iii.	?James¹, born say 1745, a "free Negro," petitioned the Northampton County court for his freedom from William Roan on 12 November 1766. The court ruled on 11 February 1767 that his indenture was illegal and ordered him discharged from further service [Minutes 1765-71, 76, 79, 98].

8. Ephraim Sisco, born say 1745, was taxable in Little Creek Hundred, Kent County from 1765 to 1772 and head of a Little Creek Hundred household of 11 "other free" in 1800 [DE:36]. He was the father of

	i.	John⁵, born say 1768, called "son of Ephr." in 1788 and 1789 when he was taxable in Little Creek Hundred. He was head of a Little Creek Hundred, Kent County household of 7 "other free" in 1800 [DE:33].
	ii.	?Amelia² Cisco, born say 1770, married Jeremiah **Shad**, July 1790. Jeremiah was head of a New Castle County household of 8 "other free" in 1800 [DE:161].

9. Benjamin Sisco, born say 1735, was taxable in Little Creek Hundred from 1754 to 1756, taxable in Duck Creek Hundred, Kent County, Delaware from 1761 to 1764 and taxable in Little Creek Hundred in 1768. He may have been the father of

	i.	Amelia¹, born say 1755, married **Hanser**, perhaps Nehemiah² **Hanser** who was taxable in Dover Hundred from 1785 to 1788. Amelia died before 9 December 1814 when administration on her Kent County estate was granted to John Francisco [WB P-1:61].
	ii.	George, born say 1765, taxable in Little Creek Hundred from 1785 to 1789, a taxable "Mulattoe" in 1797 and 1798. By his 10 November 1814 Kent County will, proved two weeks later on 26 November, he divided his estate between his sister Emela (Amelia) **Hanser** and his

brother William Sisco. Abraham **Allee** was surety in the sum of one thousand dollars [WB P-1:59].

10. Charles Sisco, born say 1745, was taxable in Little Creek Hundred from 1765 to 1785. He was granted administration on the estate of (his father?) John Francisco on 24 October 1791 [WB N-1, fol. 5]. His 20 January 1798 Little Creek Neck, Kent County will, proved 9 February 1798, named his sister Lydia Francisco and niece nephew Elizabeth (daughter of Lydia) [WB N-1, fol. 195-6]. Charles was the father of
    i. John⁴, born say 1767, taxable in Little Creek Hundred in 1785 and called "son of Chrls." in the list for 1787, perhaps the John Francisco who died before 24 October 1791 when Charles Francisco was granted administration on his Kent County estate [WB N-1, fol. 5].

11. Lydia Francisco, born say 1747, was named in her brother Charles' 20 January 1798 Kent County will. Her 7 November 1798 Little Creek Neck, Kent County will, proved 18 December 1798, named her daughter Elizabeth [WB N-1, fol. 221-2]. She was the mother of
    i. Elizabeth, born say 1770.

12. Phillis¹ Sisco, born in March 1736/7, daughter of Rachel Sisco, was bound apprentice to John Roberts in Northampton County on 11 May 1742. She was presented on 11 September 1753, 11 June 1755, and 14 June 1763 for bastard bearing [Orders 1732-42, 484; Orders 1751-3, 325; Orders 1753-8, 218-9; Minutes 1761-5, 71, 82]. She may have been the mother of
    13 i. Phillis², born in December 1758.
       ii. Rachel², born about 1760, nine years old on 8 July 1769 when she was bound apprentice to Elizabeth Scott [Minutes 1765-71, 306]. Rachel, Betty, Cellar, Sarah, and Moses Scisco registered as "free Negroes" in Northampton County on 13 June 1794 [Orders 1789-95, 364]. She was taxable on a free male tithable in Northampton County in 1798, 1800 and 1803 [PPTL, 1782-1823, frames 253, 293, 356].
      iii. Sarah, taxable on a free male tithable in Northampton County from 1798, 2 free males in 1802 and 1803 [PPTL, 1782-1823, frames 253, 335, 356].

13. Phillis² Sisco, born in December 1758, was a five-year-old "Negro" bound apprentice to Baily Scott in Northampton County on 10 April 1764 and bound to David and Leah Stott on 12 May 1772. She was presented on 13 May 1777 for bastard bearing [Minutes 1761-65, 111; 1771-7, 52, 370; 1777-83, 4]. She was the mother of
    i. Isaiah, born about 1776, son of Phillis Sisco, nine years old when he was bound apprentice by the Northampton County court on 1 May 1785 [Orders 1783-87, 284]. He was taxable in Northampton County in 1799 [PPTL, 1782-1823, frame 271].
   ii. ?James³, born in July 1767, bound apprentice to Robert Henderson in Northampton County on 14 April 1772 [Minutes 1771-77, 44].
  iii. ?Daniel³, born on 19 August 1771, bound apprentice to William Roberts, Jr., in Northampton County on 10 June 1777 and bound to Abel Garrison on 8 February 1780 [Minutes 1771-77, 372; 1777-83, 220]. He registered as a "free Negro" in Northampton County on 11 June 1794 [Orders 1789-95, 354]. He married Betsy West, 9 December 1794 Northampton County bond, William Roberts, Jr., security. He was taxable in Northampton County from 1795 to 1797 [PPTL 1782-1823, frames 193, 234] and head of an Accomack Parish, Accomack County household of 3 "other free" in 1800 [*Virginia Genealogist* 2:14].

iv.   ?Samuel, a "free Negro" taxable in Northampton County from 1797 to
      1800 [PPTL, 1782-1823, frames 234, 292].

SKIPPER FAMILY

The Skipper/Scipper family may have descended from Francis Skiper, a white
man, whose "Negro" wife Ann was tithable in Norfolk County, Virginia, in 1671
[Orders 1666-75, 73, 73a, 84a, 89, 92 by Morgan, *American Slavery-American
Freedom*, 335]. She was still living there in 1691 [Deeds 1686-95, 130].

1.   George¹ Skiper, born say 1685, was sued in Bertie court by George Allen who
     accused him of having detained his servant, Mary Bailey, between 17
     December 1719 and 13 August 1722 [Saunders, *Colonial Records of North
     Carolina*, V]. Mary Bailey may have been related to Wat Bailey, one of the
     "Chief men of the Nottoway Indians" who sold their land in Southampton
     County on 2 February 1749/50 [DB 1:98]. George was called George Skeper,
     Sen., when he purchased 120 acres in Bertie County in Urahaw Woods on the
     northeast side of Quarter Swamp (present-day Northampton County) from
     James Skeper on 6 August 1725. He and his wife Mary sold this land on 11
     January 1728. On 14 March 1729 he sold 615 acres in this same area on the
     south side of Potecasie Creek which he had patented on 1 January 1725 [DB
     B:184; C:118, 230]. He received a patent for 200 acres on the north side of
     the Neuse River on 21 March 1742/3 which was probably the land he sold by
     deed proved in Johnston County between 1 November 1746 and April 1750
     [DB 1:20].[184] He may have been the father of
2   i.   George², born say 1720.

2.   George² Skiper, born say 1720, was one of the "Chief men of the Nottoway
     Indian Nation" who sold their land in Southampton County, Virginia, on 2
     February 1749 [DB 1:98, 131, 144]. He may have been the George Skipper
     who the previous day, 1 February 1749/50, purchased 200 acres in Anson
     County, North Carolina, on the north side of the Pee Dee River [DB A:92].
     He sold 50 acres of this land and eight horses to (his son?) Barnabas Skipper
     on 15 February 1765 [DB 3:188, 192]. He was called George Skipper, Sr., in
     the 1763 list of taxables for Anson County where he was taxable on five tithes
     [Holcolm, *Anson County, North Carolina*, 122]. His sons were most likely
     i.   Barnabas, born say 1744, taxable on one tithe in Anson County in
          1763.
     ii. Benjamin, born say 1745, taxable on one tithe in Anson County in
          1763.

Some of their likely descendants were
     i.   Moses Skipper/ Scipper, a "Mulato" taxable in Bladen County in 1768
           [Byrd, *Bladen County Tax Lists*, I:9] and taxable in Brunswick County
           on one "white poll" in 1772 [GA 11.1], head of a Brunswick County
           household of 4 males and 2 females in 1790 [NC:189] and 5 "other
           free" in 1800 [NC:14].
     ii.   Isom, a "Mulato" taxable in Bladen County in 1768 [Byrd, *Bladen
           County Tax Lists*, I:4].
     iii. Clemonds, taxed in Brunswick County on one "white poll" in 1772
           [GA 11.1].
     iv.   Urias Scipper, head of a Brunswick County household of 8 "other free"
           in 1800 [NC:14].
     v.   Isaac Scipper, head of a Brunswick County household of 3 white males
           in 1790 (abstracted as "Supper" [NC:189] and 8 "other free" in 1800

---

[184]Only the index entry has survived for George Skipper's Johnston County deed.

[NC:14].[185] He entered 125 acres on Rattlesnake Branch on 7 December 1704 [Pruitt, *Land Entries: Brunswick County*, 91].

vi. Jesse Scipper, head of a Brunswick County household of 2 males and one female in 1790 (abstracted as "Supper") [NC:189] and 3 "other free" in 1800 [NC:14].

vii. John Scipper, head of a Brunswick County household of 1 male and 3 females in 1790 [NC:189] and 5 white females in 1800 [NC:14]. He entered 50 acres in Brunswick County on 13 December 1800 [Pruitt, *Land Entries: Brunswick County*, 67].

viii. Abram Scipper, head of a Brunswick County household of 3 males and 3 females in 1790 [NC:189] and 4 white females in 1800 [NC:14]. He entered 100 acres bordering his land and John Hogg's on Town Creek on 24 September 1807 [Pruitt, *Land Entries: Brunswick County*, 106].

ix. John Skipper, Jr., head of a Brunswick County household of 3 "other free" in 1810 [NC:228].

x. Nancy Skipper, married John **Tann**, 3 October 1756 Chowan County bond, Joseph Price bondsman.

SLAXTON/ THAXTON FAMILY

1. Judith Slaxton, born say 1730, was called Judy (no last name) a "Molatto" servant of George Walker when the Prince Edward County court bound her daughter Merah to her master in September 1755 and in April 1761 when the court bound her daughter Bennaba to Walker. She was called Judith Slaxton in September 1761 when she sued Walker for her freedom. In May 1767 her children Cyrus, Nancy, and Polly Slaxton complained to the court that Walker was mistreating them, but the case was dismissed after a hearing [Orders 1754-8, 59; 1759-65, fol. 83, 106; 1767-70, 5, 17]. By March 1776 Judith had moved to Charlotte County, where the court ordered Christopher Isbell to post bond for her good behavior. She was called Judith Slaxtone on 1 May 1780 when she complained to the Charlotte County court that Thomas Epperson had taken from her a "mulatto" child named Lucy, the daughter of Nancy Slaxon [Orders 1774-80, 78, 215]. Her children were

i. Merah, born say 1748, a "Molatto Girl" bound to George Walker in September 1755, perhaps identical to Polly Slaxton who successfully sued George Walker in Prince Edward County for discharge from her apprenticeship on 18 September 1769 [Orders 1767-70, 230, 233].

2 ii. Nancy, born say 1753.

iii. Bennaba, born say 1755, daughter of "Judith a Molatto" bound until the age of thirty-one to George Walker in Prince Edward County in April 1761 [Orders 1759-65, fol. 83].

iv. Cyrus[1], born say 1757.

2. Nancy Slaxton, born say 1753, was the mother of Cyrus and Peter Slaxton who were ordered bound to James Mullings in Charlotte County court on 4 July 1778 [Orders 1774-80, 142]. She was probably identical to Nancy Slack, a mulattoe" whose three children were ordered bound to Miller Woodson in Cumberland County on 23 November 1778 [Orders 1774-8, 526]. In June 1778 the Prince Edward County court ordered Miller Woodson to release her from her apprenticeship. The court called her Ann Slaxton on 15 February 1779 when it reversed its decision after Woodson produced her indentures by which he held her until the age of thirty-one [Orders 1771-81, part 2, 2, 13, 16]. She was called Nancy Thaxton when she married Thomas **Chavus**, 27

---

[185]There were no persons counted as "other free" in the 1790 census for Brunswick County. The Skipper family, John **Hays**, and James **Potter** were counted as white in 1790 [NC:189] and "other free" in 1800 [NC:14].

January 1786 Charlotte County bond, William Dabbs surety, 3 February
marriage [Ministers Returns, 90]. Her children born before her marriage were

   i.   Cyrus[2], born about 1775, ordered bound to James Mullings in Charlotte
        County on 4 July 1778 and "a mulatto boy" bound to Hugh Frazier on
        1 August 1791 [Orders 1789-92, 164]. He was an eighteen-year-old
        "mulatto" called Saras Thaxton who ran away from Hugh Frazer of
        Charlotte County according to the 2 January 1793 issue of the *Virginia
        Gazette and General Advertiser* [Headley, *18th Century Newspapers*,
        334].
   ii. Peter, born say 1777, ordered bound to James Mullings in Charlotte
        County on 4 July 1778.
   iii. Lucy, born say 1778, a "mulatto" daughter of Nancy Slaxon, taken by
        Thomas Epperson according to the complaint of her grandmother in
        Charlotte County on 1 May 1780 [Orders 1774-80, 215].

SMITH FAMILY

Northumberland County, Virginia
1. Hester Smyth, born say 1659, the servant of William Jones, confessed to the
   Northumberland County court on 19 February 1678/9 that she had a child by
   a "Negro belonging to Mr. Thomas Haines" [Orders 1678-1698, 21].

Middlesex County, Virginia
1. Joan Smith, born say 1685, confessed in Middlesex County court on 5
   December 1704 that she had a "mulatto" bastard child. The court ordered that
   she receive twenty lashes [Orders 1694-1705, 597].

Virginia and North Carolina
1. John Smith, born say 1690, was a "free negro" taxed on 300 acres in
   Currituck County in 1715 [Jones, *Records of Currituck and Dare Counties*].
   He may have been the father of
2   i.   Ann, born say 1720.
3   ii. Permenos/ Meanes, born say 1730.

2. Ann[1] Smith, born say 1720, was presented by the Norfolk County, Virginia
   court on 16 November 1744 for not giving in her list of tithables [Orders
   1742-46, 108]. She was a "Free Negro" living in Norfolk County on 18
   October 1759 when the churchwardens of Elizabeth River Parish were ordered
   to bind out her daughter Nanny Smith [Orders 1759-63, 2]. She was a tithable
   in the 1767 Norfolk County household of "free negroes" Sarah and Mary
   Cuffee in the district from Great Bridge to Edmond's Bridge and New Mill
   Creek and tithable in her own household in 1768 [Wingo, *Norfolk County
   Tithables, 1766-80*, 23, 55]. She was the mother of
   i.   ?Elizabeth, born say 1737, a taxable in Benjamin Miller's household
        in the upper district of Norfolk County in 1753 [Wingo, *Norfolk
        County Tithables, 1751-65*, 46].
   ii. Ann[2], born say 1756, daughter of "free Negro" Nanny Smith, bound
        to Josiah Randolph in Norfolk County on 18 October 1759 [Orders
        1759-63, 2], perhaps the Ann Smith who was taxable in St. Bride's
        Parish, Norfolk County, from 1792 to 1799: taxable on slave and 2
        horses in 1792, a free male tithable in 1795 and 1799 [PPTL, 1791-
        1812, frames 57, 127, 162, 197, 212, 327].
4 iii. Sarah, born free about 1758.
   iv. ?John, a "M°" taxable in Norfolk County in 1782 [PPTL, 1782-1791,
        frame 392].
   v.   Elijah, born say 1762, bound apprentice to Benjamin Britt by the
        churchwardens of St. Brides Parish in Norfolk County on 19 February
        1767 [Orders 1766-68, 73]. He was described as a "Black Indian" who

was a substitute from Norfolk County in a register of soldiers who enlisted in the Revolution [NSDAR, *African American Patriots*, 154]. He was taxable in St. Bride's Parish, Norfolk County, from 1788 to 1794 and was included in the "List of Free Negroes and Mulattoes" from 1801 to 1814 [PPTL, 1782-1791, frame 614; 1791-1812, frames 11, 127, 400, 456, 548; 1813-24, frame 67]. He was head of a Norfolk County household of 7 "other free" in 1810 [VA:793], perhaps the same Elijah Smith who was counted as a "Free Black" head of a household of 8 "other free" in 1810 in neighboring Princess Anne County [VA:475]. He registered in Norfolk County on 19 June 1815: *5 feet 6 1/4 inches of a light complexion...Born free* (no age noted) [Register of Free Negros & Mulattos, no.99].

   vi. Dinah, born say 1764, "Daughter of Ann Smith a free Negro" bound apprentice on 19 February 1767 [Orders 1766-68, 72].

3. Permenos /Meanes Smith, born say 1730, and his wife Sarah were "Molatto" Currituck County taxables in 1755 [SS 837]. He was a witness to the 17 August 1749 Currituck County will of David Linsey [Grimes, *North Carolina Wills*, 217]. He sold 23-1/2 acres in Currituck County adjoining Hardy Woodhouse on 21 January 1784 [DB 4:214]. Perhaps his wife was the Sarah Smith who was an "other free" woman living alone in Currituck County in 1800 [NC:138]. Their children may have been

5   i. James, born about 1760.
   ii. William, head of a Hertford County household of 4 "other free" in 1810 [NC:101].

4. Sarah Smith, born free about 1758, a child of Ann Smith, was bound apprentice to Benjamin Britt by the churchwardens of St. Bridges Parish in Norfolk County on 19 February 1767 [Orders 1766-68, 73]. She registered as a "free Negro" in Norfolk County on 17 July 1810: *5 feet 2 Inches, fifty two years* [Register of Free Negros & Mulattos, no.21]. She was the mother of several children who also registered. They were

   i. William, born about 1787, registered on 16 July 1810: *son of Sally, 5 feet 6 1/2 Inc., Twenty three years of age, of a dark Complexion with long hair* [Register, no.9].
   ii. Sally, born about 1794, registered on 16 July 1810: *daughter of Sally Smith, 5 feet 1-1/4 Inc., Sixteen years of age, of a light Complexion* [Register, no.10].
   iii. Edward, born about 1796, registered on 16 July 1810: *son of Sally, 5 feet 2 1/2 In, fourteen years of age, light complexion* [Register, no.11].
   iv. Caleb, born about 1808, registered on 16 July 1810: *son of Sally Smith, Two years of age, of a dark Complexion* [Register, no.12].

5. James Smith, born about 1760, was head of a Hertford County household of 6 "other free" in 1790 [NC:25], 4 in Captain Moore's District in 1800, and 11 "free colored" in 1820. He enlisted in the 10th North Carolina Regiment for three years and reenlisted for twelve more months in December 1781 [Crow, *Black Experience in Revolutionary North Carolina*, 102]. He testified for Malachi **Nickens** and John **Weaver** in Hertford County court saying he was a soldier with them. He was one of the "Sundry persons of Colour of Hertford County" who petitioned the General Assembly in 1822 to repeal the act which declared slaves to be competent witnesses against free African Americans [*NCGSJ* XI:252]. He died in July 1830 according to a deposition made in Hertford County court that same month by his executor, Pleasant Jordan. He named James Smith's heirs: Andrew, Obed, and Jacob Smith and Mary **Wiat** [*NCGSJ* XVII:31]. His children were probably

   i. Andrew, head of a Hertford County household of 6 "free colored" in 1830.

    ii.   Obed.

   iii.   Jacob.

   iv.   Mary **Wyatt**. She may have been the wife of Nathan **Wyatt**, born 1794-1806, head of a Hertford County household of 4 "free colored" in 1830. He was probably the son of Orrin **Wiott**, head of a Hertford County household of 16 "free colored" in 1820 [NC:182] and 9 in 1830. Orrin **Wiott** was one of the "Sundry persons of Colour of Hertford County" who petitioned the General Assembly in November-December 1822 to repeal the act which declared slaves to be competent witnesses against free African Americans [*NCGSJ* XI:252]. The family probably originated in Prince William County, Virginia, where Ann **Wyatt**, a "mulatto," was bound apprentice on 9 February 1779 [Historic Humphries, *Dettingen Parish Vestry*, 82].

Other members of the Smith family living in or near Norfolk County were

    i.   Philip, head of a Norfolk County household of 10 "other free" in 1810 [VA:796].

    ii.   George, "free Black" head of a Princess Anne County household of 7 "other free" in 1810 [VA:475].

   iii.   Neal, head of a Norfolk County household of 5 "other free" in 1810 [VA:795].

   iv.   Betsy, head of a Norfolk County household of 4 "other free" in 1810 [VA:804].

Prince Edward County

1.   Sarah Smith, born say 1730, was living in Prince Edward County in October 1757 when the court ordered Abner Nash and Philemon Holcomb to bring her children's indentures to court. In February 1758 the court cancelled the indentures of her children Jane, John, and James Smith to Nash and bound them instead to William Boyd and Henry Caldwell who posted bond of 200 pounds currency not to remove the children out of the colony. In the same court Philemon Holcolm produced the indentures binding her unnamed children to him, and the court ordered that the words "taught to write" be inserted [Orders 1754-8, 132, 142]. She was the mother of

    i.   Jane, bound apprentice to William Boyd in February 1758.

    ii.   John, bound apprentice to William Boyd in February 1758, perhaps the John Smith who was head of a Charlotte County household of 8 "other free" in 1810 [VA:64].

   iii.   James, son of Sarah bound to Henry Caldwell in February 1758, a "Mulato" ordered bound to Thomas Wild by the churchwardens of St. Patrick's Parish in Prince Edward County in June 1767 [Orders 1754-8, 142; 1767-70, 28].

   iv.   ?Shadrick, head of a Prince Edward County household of 1 "other free" in 1810 [VA:585]

Henrico County, Virginia

Members of the Smith family in Henrico County were

    i.   Jammy[1], born say 1740, a "free Mulatto" who was charged with stealing a pair of "Calimanco" shoes at a court of Oyer and Terminer in Henrico County on 3 October 1761. He agreed to receive 30 lashes to avoid being charged at the General Court [Orders 1755-62, 527].

1   ii.   Jenny, born say 1742.

2   iii.   Lucy, born say 1748.

1.   Jenny Smith, born say 1742, was a "Mulatto" living in Henrico County on 5 August 1752 when the court ordered the churchwardens of Henrico Parish to bind her out. And on 1 December 1766 the court ordered her "Mulatto" child

Jammy bound out [Minutes 1752-5, 222; Orders 1763-67, 645]. Her children were

    i.   ?Susannah, born say 1759, a "Mulatto" (no parent named) ordered bound out by the churchwardens of Henrico Parish in December 1760 [Orders 1755-62, 481].

    ii.   Jammy², born say 1764, "Mulatto" child of Jenny Smith ordered bound out on 1 December 1766 [Orders 1763-67, 645].

    iii.   Betsy, "Mulatto" child of Jenny Smith bound out in Henrico County on 3 April 1769 [Orders 1767-9, 429]. She was head of a Chesterfield County household of 4 "other free" in 1810 [VA:1062].

    iv.   London, "Mulatto" child of Jenny Smith bound out in Henrico County on 3 April 1769 [Orders 1767-9, 429].

    v.   ?Jack, born say 1770, head of a Henrico County household of 9 "other free" in 1810 [VA:992].

    vi.   ?Joseph, head of a Henrico County household of 4 "other free" in 1810 [VA:1009].

    vii.   ?Patty, head of a Henrico County household of 5 "other free" in 1810 [VA:998].

2.   Lucy Smith, born say 1748, was a "Mulatto" (no parent named) living in Henrico County on 5 August 1754 when the court ordered the churchwardens of Henrico Parish to bind her out [Orders 1752-55, 222]. On 2 February 1767 the court ordered the churchwardens of Henrico Parish to bind out her "Mulatto" child Bob [Orders 1763-67, 646]. She was a "free Negroe" taxed on a slave in Henrico County in 1800 [*Virginia Genealogist* 31:251]. Her children were

3   i.   Robert/Bob, born say 1766.

    ii.   ?Peter, a "free Negroe" taxable on a horse in Henrico County in 1800 [*Virginia Genealogist* 31:251].

3.   Robert Smith, born say 1766, was ordered bound out by the Henrico County court on 2 February 1767. He was head of a Chesterfield County household of 11 "other free" in 1810 [VA:1062]. He may have been the father of

    i.   Nancy, born about 1777, obtained a certificate of freedom in Chesterfield County on 14 February 1814: *thirty seven years old, brown complexion, born free* [Register of Free Negroes 1804-53, no. 205].

    ii.   Polly, born about 1787, obtained a certificate of freedom in Chesterfield County on 14 February 1814: *twenty seven years old, brown complexion, born free* [Register of Free Negroes 1804-53, no. 204].

    iii.   Fanny, born about 1791, obtained a certificate of freedom in Chesterfield County on 14 February 1814: *twenty three years old, brown complexion, born free* [Register of Free Negroes 1804-53, no. 206].

Members of the Smith family in Charles City County were

    i.   William, fined by the court on 6 September 1758 for failing to list his wife as a tithable.

    ii.   Arthur, a "mulatto" poor orphan ordered bound out by the churchwardens to Theodorick Carter in August 1758.

    iii.   Thomas, a "mulatto" ordered bound out to Theodorick Carter on 2 July 1760 [Orders 1758-62, 33, 57, 197].

    iv.   William, born about 1769, registered in Petersburg on 18 August 1794: *a light Mulatto man, five feet seven inches high, twenty five years old, born free & raised in Charles City County* [Register of Free Negroes 1794-1819, no. 38].

Members of the Smith family in Prince George and Dinwiddie counties were

    i.   Joseph, a "yellow" complexioned soldier from Dinwiddie County who enlisted as a substitute in the Revolution [NSDAR, *African American Patriots*, 154].

    ii.   Lewis, a man of color born in Prince George County who was living in Dinwiddie County when he enlisted as a substitute in the Revolution [National Archives pension file S6112 cited by NSDAR, *African American Patriots*, 154].

    iii.   James, a man of color born in Prince George County who enlisted as a substitute in the Revolution from Bedford County [NSDAR, *African American Patriots*, 154].

    iv.   John, born about 1768, registered in Petersburg on 18 August 1794: *a dark brown Mulatto man, six feet one inches high, about twenty six years old, born free & raised in the Town of Petersburg* [Register of Free Negroes 1794-1819, no. 42].

    v.   Polly, born about 1775, registered in Petersburg on 8 September 1795: *a likely brown Mulatto woman, five feet four inches high, twenty years old born free & raised in the Town of Petersburg* [Register of Free Negroes 1794-1819, no. 105].

    vi.   Thomas, born about 1783, registered in Petersburg on 12 December 1800: *a dark brown Mulatto man, five feet one and a half inches high, seventeen years old, stout & thick made, born free & raised in the Town of Petersburg* [Register of Free Negroes 1794-1819, no. 210].

Members of the Smith family in Cumberland County, Virginia, were

    i.   Robert, born say 1752, a "Mulatto" sued by Robert Pleasants, executor of John Pleasants, deceased, on 24 March 1773 in Cumberland County court [Orders 1772-4, 145-6].

1   ii.   Betty, born say 1750.

1.   Betty Smith, born say 1750, was living in Cumberland County on 22 April 1771 when the court ordered the churchwardens of Southam Parish to bind her "mulattoe" daughter Catey to William Fretwell. The same order was repeated to the churchwardens of Littleton Parish on 27 July 1772 [Orders 1770-2, 224, 506]. She was the mother of

    i.   Catey, born say 1770.

Greensville County

1.   Mary Smith, born about 1761, registered as a "free Negro" in Greensville County on 2 April 1821: *free born of a yellow Complexion, aged Sixty, 5 feet 1 inches & 1/8 high in shoes...a weaver* [Register, no.83]. Her children were

    i.   Lucy, born about 1792, registered in Greensville County on 3 February 1817: *(Daughter of Mary Smith) free born, light Yellow complexion, about twenty five years old, five feet high (in shoes)...a weaver* [Register, no.63].

    ii.   ?John, born about 1798, registered on 25 January 1820: *a free born black Complexion twenty one years old about five feet Seven Inches high* [Register, no.77].

    iii.   ?Berry, born about 1799, registered in Greensville County on 7 September 1824: *free Born of a Yellow Complexion supposed to be twenty five years old, 5' 10-3/4 inches high...a planter* [Register, no.114].

    iv.   Polly, born in February 1804, registered on 25 November 1824: *(commonly Called Polly Main) daughter of Mary Smith, free born of a yellow Complexion, 5 feet 1/2 inch high in Shoes, aged 20 years last February...a weaver* [Register, no.121]. She may have been related to John **Main**, head of a Southampton County household of 4 "other free" in 1810.

Granville County, North Carolina
1. Sarah Smith, born say 1750, was a "Molatto" taxable in the Granville County list of Len Henry Bullock in 1768 [CR 44.701]. She was probably related to Betty Smith who was one of George **Anderson**'s children mentioned in his May 1771 Granville County will [Original in Granville County, not recorded]. Perhaps she was related to Sallie Smith, wife of John Smith, who made an undated request to the Granville County court to bind out as apprentices her children, "all colored," to her father Aaron Alston. They were Corrina, Molly, and Rosa Frances Smith [CR 44.101.2].

SMITHERS/ SMOTHERS FAMILY

The Smothers family of Virginia may have been related to Sarah Smither, a "free Mullatto Woman" who had a child called "Mullatto Nanny" by a white man. In August 1743 Nanny brought a successful suit for her freedom against Mrs. Holland, widow of Col. William Holland, in Anne Arundel County, Maryland court [Judgment Record 1743-4, 170]. Members of the family in Virginia were

    i.   Godfrey Smithers, born about 1713, a twenty-one-year-old "Mulatto" who ran away from Abraham Nicholas of James City County according to the 26 September 1734 issue of the *AWM* [Headley, *18th Century Virginia Newspapers*, 317].

1   ii. Nell, born say 1740.

1. Nell Smothers, born say 1740, was the mother of Thomas Smothers who was called a "Molatto" on 24 February 1780 when the Henry County court ordered him bound to John Stokes and called orphan of Nell Smurthers alias Evans on 25 August 1785 when the court ordered him bound to John Stokes [Orders 1778-82, 72; 1785-8, 46]. She was the mother of

    i.   ?William[1], born say 1760, a man of color born in Albemarle County, Virginia, who enlisted in the Revolution from Powhatan County [NSDAR, *African American Patriots*, 154]. He was taxable in Powhatan County from 1793 to 1804, called a "M°" in 1793 and 1803 [PPTL, 1787-1825, frames 98, 123, 111, 138, 170, 193, 230, 266, 282]. He married Nancy **Brown**, 17 September 1795 Powhatan County bond.

    ii. ?Elizabeth, born before 1776, head of a Rockingham County, North Carolina household of a white woman and a white male under 16 years of age in 1790 [NC:169], 5 whites in 1810 [NC:177] and 4 "free colored" in 1820 [NC:584].

    iii. ?Charles, born 1775-1796, head of a Rockingham County, North Carolina household of 6 "free colored in 1820 [NC:602] and 9 "free colored" in Guilford County in 1830.

    iv. ?William[2], born 1775-1796, head of a Guilford County household of 1 "free colored" in 1820 [NC:115]. He married Mason **Melton**, 6 December 1823 Guilford County bond and Mary Ann **Newby**, both "colored," 21 November 1825 Guilford County bond, no bondsman listed.[186] William (born about 1787) with Mason Smuthers (born about 1804) was counted as a "Mulatto" laborer in Hertford County in 1850 [NC:648].

    v. John, married Fanny **Kersey**, 25 September 1825 Guilford County bond, Aaron **Nuby** bondsman.

---

[186]Moses **Newby**, born about 1782, was apprenticed as a potter to John Bullock of Orange County, North Carolina, in 1798. In 1805 the Guilford County Court ruled that he was free because his parents had been emancipated by Quakers. George **Newby**, born about 1786, was apprenticed as a potter to William Dennis of Randolph County in 1813 [*NCGSJ* XI:93].

vi.   Thomas, born say 1775, taxable in Patrick County from 1801 to 1805 [PPTL 1791-1823, frames 326, 380, 439], head of a Stokes County, North Carolina household of 6 "free colored" in 1820 [NC:371]. He may have been the Thomas Smothers who married Rebecca **John**, 12 September 1799 Washington County, Virginia bond.

vii. ?Amealey, counted in the list of "Free negros & Malatters" in Patrick County, Virginia, in 1813 [PPTL 1791-1823, frame 598].

SNEED FAMILY

1. Jane Sneed, born say 1753, was the mother of a "Mulatta" girl who the Lunenburg County court ordered bound by the churchwardens of Cornwall Parish to Sherwood and Anne Walton on 14 July 1763 [Orders 1762-3, 87]. She may have been the ancestor of

    i.   the wife of John **Vier**. On 5 April 1838 he sold for $5 a mare, a yoke of oxen, three cows, two calves, seventeen hogs and household furniture to William **Going** in Amherst County in consideration for his friendship with Martha Jane Snead, his wife's daughter [DB W:274].

2   ii. Susan, born say 1800.

2. Susan Sneed, born say 1800, was the mother of

    i.   Betsy, born about 1821, registered in Amherst County on 17 March 1851: *a free woman daughter of Susan Sneed, 5 feet 3-1/2 Inches high, bright mulatto...born in Nelson County of parents free prior to the 1st of May 1806.*

    ii. Adaline Frances, born about 1824, registered in Amherst County on 11 November 1842: *daughter of Susan Snead, eighteen years of age, a bright mulatto 5 ft & 3 inches high .. born free* [McLeRoy, *Strangers in Their Midst*, 63, 80].

SNELLING FAMILY

1. Aquilla Snelling, "son of Aquilla & Mary Snelling," was born 28 June and baptized 14 July 1723 in Christ Church Parish, Middlesex County, Virginia [NSCDA, *Parish Register of Christ Church*, 113]. He was taxable in Stephen Jett's Granville County tax list for 1755: one "Black" tithe in the household of William **Chavis** [CR 44.701.23]. By 1761 he was head of a household in Fishing Creek District, taxable on 3 black tithes for himself, his wife Lettice, and hired woman Amey. His wife was most likely Lettice **Chavis**, born about 1742, taxable in the 1754 Granville County household of her father William **Chavis** in Edward Moore's list. By 1767 he owned one slave in the list of Stephen Jett and purchased a woman slave and her two children at the sale of the estate of William **Chavis** on 7 May 1778 [WB 1:178]. On 5 May 1767 he made a deed of gift to his brother Alexander of 100 acres on Long Creek adjoining John Smith whereon Alexander then lived [DB:337]. He entered 640 acres on Little Creek bordering his own land and **Chavis'** in an undated 1778-85 land entry [Pruitt, *Land Entries: Granville County*, 10]. The inventory of his Granville County estate, recorded May 1779, including a slave, 4 horses, and 22 cattle, totalled 3,789 pounds [WB 1:232, 235].

His wife Lettice was taxable in 1782 in Fishing Creek District of Granville County on 100 acres, 4 slaves, and 5 cattle. In the 1786 state census she was head of a Granville County household of 4 free females, 1 free male, and 4 slaves. She and her son Hugh sold three tracts of land in Granville County where they were then living on 30 August 1788 [DB O:599]. In 1801 she was given a lifetime right to remain on 180 acres of land on the east side of Mine Creek adjacent to her son-in-law Jordan **Chavis** in Wake County by a deed from Hugh Snelling to Curtis Snelling [DB Q:520]. Her 2 April 1814 Wake County will, proved August 1814, named their children:

i. Hugh, born say 1762, made provision for Lettice in his 1801 Wake County deed. He married Ann Snelling, 30 August 1779 Granville County bond with Bartlet **Tyler** bondsman. In 1780 his Epping Forest, Granville County property was assessed at 4,108 pounds. He purchased land in Granville County from Philip **Chavis** on 20 November 1778 [DB O:3], purchased 800 acres from Benjamin Sewell for 1,000 pounds in ten yearly payments on 20 February 1781 [WB 1:324], and was taxable in 1785 on 940 acres. In 1800 he was head of a Granville County household of 11 "other free," one white woman over forty-five years old, and 11 slaves, and 7 "other free," one white woman, and 23 slaves in 1810 [NC:881]. He was still in Granville County in 1818, taxable on 402 acres and 9 slaves.

ii. Tabathy, married Wright **Bass**, 12 November 1781 Granville County bond, Drury **Pettiford** bondsman.

iii. Curtis, born say 1770, head of a Wake County household of 2 "other free" and 2 slaves in 1800 [NC:795]. On 8 January 1801 he bought 180 acres from his brother Hugh on the east side of Mine Creek [DB Q:520]. He married Levina (Silvanius) **Evans**, 7 February 1811 Wake County bond. His children mentioned in his mother's will were Lemuel and Calvin Snelling. His 28 May 1829 Wake County will, proved November 1829, named his children: Lemuel, Calvin, William, John, Emsley, and Sidney Hugh.

iv. a daughter, married Jordan **Chavis**.

SOLELEATHER FAMILY

1. Mary Soleleather, born about 1771, registered as a free Negro in Essex County on 8 December 1810: *free born by the statement of Thomas Brockenbrough in person that she has always passed as a free born person, colour a shade lighter than black, about 39 years of age, four feet 11 inches* [Register of Free Negroes 1810-43, p. 10, no. 19]. She was head of an Essex County household of 5 "other free" in 1810 [VA:208]. Mary, Betsey, Thomas and Billy Soleleather were listed as "free Negroes" above the age of sixteen in South Farnham Parish, Essex County, in 1813 [PPTL, 1782-1819, frame 522]. Mary was the mother of

i. Jenny **Rollins**, born about 1785, registered in Essex County on 8 December 1810: *by statement of Thomas Brockenbrough daughter of Mary Soleleather, always passed as a free born person, 25 years of age, bright Mulattoe, 5 feet 2-1/4 Inches* [Register of Free Negroes 1810-43, p.14, no.30].

ii. William, born about 1789, registered in Essex County on 14 April 1812: *son of Mary Soleleather, free born by statement of Thomas Brockenbrough, dark Mulattoe, 23 years of age, 5 feet 5-3/4 Inches.* He may have been the husband of Betty Soleleather who registered in Essex County on 8 December 1810: *formerly Betty McGuy by certificate of the clerk of Richmond County to be born free, bright Mulattoe, about 21 years of age, five feet 5-3/4 inches* [Register of Free Negroes 1810-43, p.9, no. 18; p.21, no. 52].

iii. Philip, born about 1792, registered in Essex County on 8 December 1810: *son of Mary Soleleather, born free by statement of Thomas Brockenbrough, dark Mulattoe, 18 years of age, five feet 7 inches* [Register of Free Negroes 1810-43, p.10, no.21]. He was head of an Essex County household of 2 "other free" in 1810 [VA:208].

iv. Thomas, born about 1795, registered in Essex County on 8 December 1810: *son of Mary Soleleather by statement of Thomas Brockenbrough,*

>l

15 years of age, five feet 3/4 inches [Register of Free Negroes 1810-43, no.20].
</blockquote>

    v.   Mary, born about 1801, registered in Essex County on 8 December 1810: *daughter of Mary Soleleather, dark Mulattoe, 9 years of age, five feet 3-3/4 inches* [Register of Free Negroes 1810-43, p.11, no. 22].

    vi. Nancy, born about 1803, registered in Essex County on 8 December 1810: *daughter of Mary Soleleather, dark Mulattoe, about 7 years of age* [Register of Free Negroes 1810-43, p.11, no. 23].

    vii. Charlotte, born about 1805, registered in Essex County on 8 December 1810: *daughter of Mary Soleleather, dark Mulattoe, about 5 years of age* [Register of Free Negroes 1810-43, p.11, no. 24].

SORRELL FAMILY

1. Judith Serell, born say 1720, had a "Molato" son, Thomas Serell, born 15 October 1738 in Northumberland County, Virginia [Fleet, *Northumberland County Record of Births*, 82]. Her children were

    i.   Thomas[1], born 15 October 1738.

2   ii. ?James[1], born say 1750.

3   iii. ?Edward[1], born about 1753.

    iv. ?Jesse, born say 1755, head of a Northumberland County household of 4 "Black" persons in 1782 [VA:37] and "free mulatto" head of a Northumberland County household of 8 "other free" in 1810 [VA:996].

4   v.   ?Thomas[2] Sorrell, born about 1758.

2. James[1] Sorrell, born say 1750, was head of a Northumberland County household of 6 "Black" persons in 1782 [VA:37], was taxable on one tithe, a horse, and 6 cattle in Northumberland County in 1787 [Schreiner-Yantis, *1787 Census*, 1269], and was a "free mulatto" head of a Northumberland County household of 8 "other free" in 1810 [VA:996]. During the Revolution he served as a gunner's mate aboard the *Hero* and the *Larter* [Jackson, *Virginia Negro Soldiers*, 43]. His children were

    i.   Nancy, born say 1796, "daughter of James Sorrell, Sr.," married John **Thomas**, 7 April 1812 Northumberland County bond, James Sorrell, Jr., security.

    ii. ?Thomas[3], married Polly **Credit**, 22 October 1816 Northumberland County bond, John **Credit** security.[187] He was called a widower when he married, second, Elizabeth **Simple** 14 May 1821 Northumberland County bond, Thomas **Credit** security.

3. Edward[1] Sorrell, born about 1753, was seventy-nine years old when he applied for a Revolutionary War pension in Northumberland County court on 14 August 1832 [M804-2246, frame 0911]. He married Judith **Kesterson**, 13 April 1789 Northumberland County bond, Charles Curtis security. He was a "free mulatto" head of a Northumberland County household of 10 "other free" in 1810 [VA:996]. He married Dorcas **Lewin** on 15 December 1814 in Lancaster County. He died 7 July 1839, and his will was proved in August 1840. His widow Dorcas, born about 1791, moved to Baltimore about 1846 where she applied for and received a survivor's pension on 21 November 1853 [M804-2246, frame 0927]. His children were

    i.   James[2], born about 1790, married Polly **Luen** (**Lewin**), 13 November 1815 Northumberland County bond, Edward Sorrell security. Molly and Charles **Lewin** were heads of "other free" Lancaster County

---

[187]John **Credit** was "free mulatto" head of a Northumberland County household of 5 "other free" in 1810 [VA:976]. Moses **Credit** was a soldier in the Revolution from Northumberland County [Jackson, *Virginia Negro Soldiers*, 33].

households in 1810 [VA:352]. He was called James Sorrel of Edward on 2 March 1835 when he mortgaged his household goods for $216 in Northumberland County [DB 29:416]. He married, second, Judith **Causey** 13 May 1837 Northumberland County bond and was listed with her and their four children in the 1850 Northumberland County census.

ii. Cambia, born say 1808, "daughter of Edward Sorrell," married Holland **Evans**, 4 February 1824 Northumberland County bond, Moses **Blundon** security.[188]

iii. ?Edward[2], Jr., born about 1797, married Betsy **Harriman**, 1 January 1817 Northumberland County bond, Edward Sorrell security. He was listed in the 1850 Northumberland County census with six children.

iv. Steptoe, married Miranda **Lewis**, 10 September 1827 Northumberland County bond, Edward Sorrell security, with the consent of Miranda's mother Rebecca **Weaver**.

v. Delia, married William **Toulson**, 10 February 1827 Northumberland County bond, Steptoe Sorrell, "son of Edward Soreall, father of Dealy Soreall" security.

vi. Mary, married John **Edwards** with the consent of her father Edward Sorell, 20 November 1833 Northumberland County bond, James Sorrell security.

vii. Emily, "daughter of Edward Sorrell," married Samuel **Green**, 13 February 1837 Northumberland County bond, Edward Sorrell security.

viii. Walter, who testified on behalf of (his mother?) Dorcas Sorrell when she applied for her husband's pension [M804-2246, frame 0927].

4. Thomas[2] Sorrell, born about 1758, married Elizabeth **Lucas**, 3 December 1794 Westmoreland County bond. He was listed among the "Free Molattoes" living on Thomas Rowand's land in Westmoreland County in 1801 with his wife Elizabeth and children William and Libby Sorrell [*Virginia Genealogist* 31:41].[189] He was a sixty-two-year-old resident of Westmoreland County living with his forty-five-year-old wife and eleven-year-old daughter in 1820 when he applied for a Revolutionary War pension [M804-2246, frame 0992]. He was probably the father of

i. Sukey, born say 1770, married Spencer **Thomas**, "widower," 11 June 1792 Northumberland County bond.

ii. Fannah, born say 1771, married John **Evins**, 23 November 1792 Northumberland County bond, Thomas Pollard security.

iii. Grace, born say 1774, married Augustin **Boyd**, 24 July 1795 Northumberland County bond, Thomas Pollard security.

iv. William, a "free Molatto" living with Thomas Sorrell in 1801.

v. Libby, a "free Molatto" living with Thomas Sorrell in 1801.

SPARROW FAMILY

1. Elizabeth[1] Sparrow, born say 1673, was the indentured servant of Roger Rise on 15 September 1690 when the Norfolk County court ordered her to serve another two years for bearing a bastard child named Mary who was "begotten by a negro." The court ordered Mary bound to Rise until the age of twenty-one [Deeds 5, pt. 2, 190]. She was the mother of

2   i. Mary[1], born about 1690.

---

[188]Moses **Blundel** was head of a Northumberland County household of 6 "other free" in 1810 [VA:973].

[189]The name was abstracted as So*n*ell [*Virginia Genealogist* 31:41].

2. Mary[1] Sparrow, born about 1690, was called "a Molato woman" on 18
    September 1713 when she claimed in Norfolk County court that she had fully
    served her time as an indentured servant to Mrs. Ann Furlong. The court
    agreed that she had served her time but imposed a fine of 500 pounds of
    tobacco for each of two illegitimate "Molato" children she had during her
    service. She agreed to serve Samuel Boush two years in exchange for his
    paying her fine. On 15 February 1713/4 the Norfolk County court ordered her
    daughter Betty bound to Mrs. Ann Furlong because Mary had left the child
    with her [Orders 1710-17, 69, 77]. Mary was the mother of

3   i.   Elizabeth[2], born say 1713.

3. Elizabeth[2] Sparrow, born say 1713, was bound to Mrs. Ann Furlong on 18
    February 1713/4 by the Norfolk County court. She was probably the mother
    of

4   i.   Margaret[1], born say 1728.
5   ii.   Mary[2], born say 1730.
6   iii. Anne, born say 1738.

4. Margaret[1] Sparrow, born say 1728, was a "Negro" living in Norfolk County
    on 20 June 1754 when the court ordered the churchwardens of Elizabeth River
    Parish to bind her son John Sparrow as an apprentice to John Hamilton
    [Orders 1753-5, 53]. She was a taxable head of a household in Norfolk County
    in the district from Tanners Creek to Great Bridge in 1759 [Wingo, *Norfolk
    County Tithables, 1751-65*, 147]. Her children were

      i.   John[1]/ Jack, born 20 December 1748, ordered bound apprentice to John
    Hamilton by the Norfolk County court on 20 June 1754, perhaps
    identical to Jack Sparrow, a "Mullatto" bound for fifteen years by the
    Princess Anne County court to Thomas Walke on 16 July 1754 to learn
    to read and write and the trade of sawyer [Minutes 1753-62, 120].

      ii.   ?Sarah, mother of Penelope Sparrow (no race indicated) who was
    bound to Wright Brickell of Elizabeth River Parish by order of the
    Norfolk County court on 18 June 1773 [Orders 1771-3, 181].

7   iii. John[2]/ Jack, born September 1760.

      iv.   Roger, son of Peggy Sparrow, bound to George Veale, Jr., on 18
    August 1768. He was called a "free negro" on 21 April 1774 when the
    court ordered him bound to James Nicholson [Orders 1768-71, 11;
    1773-5, 38].

      v.   ?Alexander Guthery, a "free Negro" bound by the Norfolk County
    court to Bartholomew Thompson on 20 June 1771 [Orders 1771-3, 1].

      vi.   Betty, born say 1770, "daughter of Peggy Sparrow, a free Molatto,"
    ordered bound by the churchwardens of Portsmouth Parish to William
    North on 18 June 1778 [Orders 1776-9, n.p.].

5. Mary[2] Sparrow, born say 1730, was a "Negro Woman" who complained to the
    Princess Anne County court on 15 June 1762 that she was entitled to her
    freedom but kept in slavery by Tully Robinson, Gentleman. The court
    appointed James Holt, Gentleman, as her attorney, and he called John
    Williams, Alice Ivy, Mary Hurt, and Margaret Langley as her witnesses. On
    17 July 1764 the court found Robinson guilty and ordered him to pay her forty
    shillings and the costs of the suit [Minutes 1753-62, 501, 505, 519; 1762-9,
    21, 78, 109]. She was a taxable head of a household in Norfolk County in the
    district from Tanners Creek to Great Bridge in 1759 [Wingo, *Norfolk County
    Tithables, 1751-65*, 147]. She may have been the mother of

      i.   Lettice, a "Mullatto" bound until the age of eighteen by the Princess
    Anne County court to Mrs. Frances Smyth on 16 April 1755 to be
    taught to read, sew, knit and spin [Minutes 1753-62, 168].

      ii.   Dinah, born say 1755, a "Mullatto" bound to Mary Burgess until the
    age of eighteen by the Princess Anne County court on 20 January 1756

to be taught to read, sew, knit and spin [Minutes 1753-62, 213]. She married George **Valentine**, "mulattoes," 14 November 1787 Norfolk County bond.

   iii. Margaret², born say 1760, a "free Negro" ordered bound to Richard Cheshire by the churchwardens of Elizabeth River Parish, Norfolk County, on 21 April 1763 [Orders 1763-65, 5] and an infant "free Negroe" ordered bound to Robert Ballard by the Princess Anne County court on 22 August 1764 [Minutes 1762-9, 127].

8   iv. America, born about 1762.

9   v. Bash¹, born about 1763.

   vi. Nancy, born about 1768, counted in a list of "free Negroes and Mulattoes" in St. Bride's Parish, Norfolk County, in 1803 [PPTL, 1791-1812, frame 456], registered in Norfolk County on 22 September 1812: *5 ft. 7 In., 44 years of age dark Complexion pitted with the Small Pox, Born free* [Register of Free Negroes, no.83]. She was head of a "Free Black" Princess Anne County household of 4 "other free" in 1810 [VA:474].

6. Nanny Sparrow, born say 1738, was apparently identical to "Nanny a free Molatto" (no last name mentioned) whose daughters Bridget and Betty were ordered bound by the Princess Anne County court to Robert Dearmore until the age of twenty-one on 15 December 1761. She was called Nanny Sparrow, a "free Mulatto," on 4 April 1771 when the court bound her son George and daughter Bridget as apprentices and called Anne Sparrow on 13 April 1775 when the court bound her daughter Betty [Minutes 1753-62, 460; 1770-3, 116]. She was the mother of

   i. Bridget, born in 1756, ordered bound by the Princess Anne County court to Robert Dearmore on 15 December 1761 and bound apprentice to William and Mary Whitehurst on 4 April 1771 [Minutes 1753-62, 460; 1770-3, 116]. She was a "Free Black" head of a Princess Anne County household of 6 "other free" in 1810 [VA:474].

   ii. Elizabeth³/ Betty, born in 1759, ordered bound by the Princess Anne County court to Robert Dearmore on 15 December 1761 and an infant daughter of Anne Sparrow, a free ___tto, bound to Katherine Anne Broughton by the Princess Anne County court on 13 April 1775 [Minutes 1753-62, 460; 1773-82, 92 and index].

   iii. George, bound to Robert Burley to learn the trade of ship carpenter on 4 April 1771. He was a "Free Black" head of a Princess Anne County household of 4 "other free" in 1810 [VA:474].

   iv. Amy, born say 1774, daughter of Nanny Sparrow, ordered bound to William Whitehurst by the Princess Anne County court on 23 April 1774 [Minutes 1773-82, 45].

7. John²/ Jack Sparrow, born September 1760, was called a "free Negro" when he was bound apprentice in Norfolk County on 18 April 1765 and called the nine-year-old son of "free Molatto" Margaret Sparrow on 15 June 1769 when the court ordered the churchwardens of Portsmouth Parish to bind him to John Carr [Orders 1763-65, 196-7; 1768-71, 91]. He was taxable in Portsmouth and Elizabeth River Parishes in 1792 and from 1800 to 1809: in a list of "free Negroes and Mulattoes" in 1801, a carpenter living near Norfolk with a boy named Jesse and a female named Jenny Sparrow in his household [PPTL, 1791-1812, frame 42, 361, 384, 436, 469, 567, 652, 696]. He may have been the John Sparrow who was head of a Nelson County household of 12 "other free" in 1810 [VA:728]. His descendants may have been

   i. Elizabeth⁴, born about 1771, registered in Petersburg on 4 August 1807: *a dark Mulatto woman, five feet five and a half inches high, thirty six years old, born free in Princess Anne p. Cert. of Register from Norfolk Boro* [Register of Free Negroes 1794-1819, no. 416].

1076   *Sparrow Family*

    ii.   Anthony, head of a "Free Black" Princess Anne County household of 4 "other free" in 1810 [VA:474].
    iii.   Billy, head of a "Free Black" Princess Anne County household of 6 "other free" in 1810 [VA:474].

8.   America Sparrow, born about 1762, probably identical to America, "a free Negro" living in Norfolk County on 19 November 1778 when the court ordered the churchwardens of St. Bride's Parish to bind him to John Whitehouse [Orders 1776-9, n.p.]. He was taxable in St. Bride's Parish in 1787 and from 1796 to 1811, in the lists of "free Negroes and Mulattoes" which start in 1804 [PPTL, 1782-91, frame 597; 1791-1812, 195, 285, 548, 636, 674]. He married Fanny **Rudd**, 5 May 1804 Norfolk County bond, Lemuel **Bailey** security. He registered in Norfolk County on 4 May 1811: *5 feet 11 In. 49 years of a yellowish Complexion and Pitted with the Small Pox* [Register of Free Negros & Mulattos, no.51]. He may have been the father of

    i.   Charity, born about 1787, registered in Norfolk County on 21 September 1812: *5 ft. 4 1/2 In., 25 years of age light Complexion, born Free* [Register of Free Negroes, no.82].
    ii.   Caty, born about 1788, registered in Norfolk County on 22 September 1812: *5 ft. 1 1/2 Inc., 24 years of age light Complexion, Born free* [Register of Free Negroes, no.84].
    iii.   Chany, born about 1792, registered in Norfolk County on 22 September 1812: *5 feet 2 1/2 In., 20 years of age of a Yellowish Complexion with two Scars on the right cheek* [Register of Free Negroes, no.86].
    iv.   Keziah, born about 1795, registered in Norfolk County on 19 July 1814: *5 feet 2 Inches, 19 years of age of a Light Complexion, born Free* [Register of Free Negroes, no.92].
    v.   Sarah, born about 1798, registered in Norfolk County on 19 July 1814: *5 feet 4 Inc., 16 years of age of a Light Complexion, born Free* [Register of Free Negroes, no.93].

9.   Bash[1] Sparrow, born about 1763, probably identical to Bash, "a free Negro" living in Norfolk County on 19 November 1778 when the court ordered the churchwardens of St. Bride's Parish to bind him to William Whitehouse [Orders 1776-9, n.p.]. He was taxable on a horse in St. Bride's Parish from 1789 to 1817: taxable on 2 tithes in 1791, in the lists of "free Negroes and Mulattoes" starting in 1801, called Bash Sparrow, Sr., starting in 1804 [PPTL, 1782-91, frames 613, 668; 1791-1812, frames 10, 400, 456, 548, 636, 716, 802; 1813-24]. He registered in Norfolk County on 22 September 1812: *5 ft. 7 Inc., 49 years of age of a Yellowish complexion, born Free* [Register of Free Negroes, no.88]. His children may have been

    i.   Elizabeth[5]/ Betty, born about 1788, registered in Norfolk County on 21 September 1812: *5 ft. 1 Inch, 24 years of age dark Complexion, born Free* [Register of Free Negroes, no.81].
    ii.   Jonas, born about 1788, registered in Norfolk County on 25 December 1809: *5 feet 8 Inches and a half, Twenty one years of age of a Dark Complexion, Born free* [Register of Free Negroes, no.1].
    iii.   Rose, born about 1791, registered in Norfolk County on 22 September 1812: *5 feet 2 In., 21 years of age of a dark Complexion, born Free* [Register of Free Negroes, no.85].
    iv.   Ned, born about 1793, registered in Norfolk County on 19 July 1814: *5 feet 3 1/2 In., 21 years of age of a dark Complexion with a Scar on his right cheek, born Free* [Register of Free Negroes, no.91].
    v.   Bash[2], Jr., born say 1789, taxable in St. Bride's Parish from 1804 to 1811 [PPTL, 1791-1812, frames 548, 674].

SPELMAN FAMILY

1. Sarah **Spelman**, born say 1730, was called a "free Negro wench" on 10 October 1760 when her two-year-old son Tony was bound to Joseph Leech in Craven County [CR 028.101.1]. She was sued for debt about a year later in the July 1761 Craven County court, but the jury ruled in her favor [Minutes 1761-2, 32a]. On 10 January 1762 she was called a "Negors or Mollato Wench" in the service of Mrs. Ann Bryan when the court ordered that Ann Bryan keep Sarah's children in her household until Sarah's suit against her was settled [Minutes 1758-61, 104b]. Sarah's children: Lydia, Asa, Aaron, and David were bound to Ann Bryan in April that year [Minutes 1761-2, 73a]. Her children were

    i. Lydia, born about 1749, thirteen years old when she was bound an apprentice by the April 1762 Craven County court, and ordered by the 11 April 1767 court to serve Christopher Dawson an additional year for having borne a child during her indenture [Minutes 1767-75]. She may have been the Lydia Spelman who was head of a Camden County household of 4 "other free" in 1790 [NC:16].

    ii. Asa, born about 1751, eleven years old when he was bound an apprentice in the April 1762 Craven County court. George Kernegy had a suit against him in Craven County court on 9 April 1767, but Kernegy failed to appear [Minutes 1767-75]. Asa was head of a Craven County household of 5 "other free" in 1790 [NC:134] and 4 "free colored" in 1820 [NC:72]. He purchased land by deed proved in Craven County in 1781. On 1 January 1796 he sold 65 acres on the north side of the Neuse River between Trent and Smiths Creek in Craven County [DB 24:191; 32:873]. He married Esther **Sampson**, 6 June 1819 Craven County bond, Aaron Spelman bondsman. He was called Asa Spelmore alias Spelman on 13 September 1820 when he made a declaration in Craven County court to obtain a pension for service with Captain Quinn in the tenth North Carolina Regiment. He stated that during his nine months service he was engaged in a skirmish at West Point and at Kings Ferry in Jersey. Isaac **Perkins** testified that he had seen Asa while they were both on duty in White Plains, New York. John **Carter** testified that Asa and he were in the same regiment. Asa was a cooper with no family but his unnamed brother (Aaron?) who he was living with in 1820 [Craven County Minutes, September 1820, 136-8; 1821, 185; and May 1822, 16 by *NCGSJ* XVII:33].

2   iii. Aaron, born about 1753.

    iv. David, born about 1755, seven years old in April 1762 when he was bound an apprentice in Craven County court. He was head of a Craven County household of 1 "other free" in 1790 [NC:134]. He married Lethe **Brown**, 16 June 1798 Craven County bond. She was probably the daughter of Samuel **Brown**, head of a Craven County household of 4 "other free" in 1790 [NC:134].

    v. Jacob, born about 1756, the four-year-and-nine-month-old son of Sarah ordered bound by the October 1760 Craven County court [Minutes 1758-61, 85a]. A 5 May 1800 Fayetteville newspaper warned that a runaway slave might have changed his name to Jacob Spelman in order to pass as free [Fouts, *Newspapers of Edenton, Fayetteville, & Hillsborough*, 10].

    vi. Tony, born about 1758, the two-year-old son of Sarah bound apprentice on 10 October 1760 [CR 028.101.1].

    vii. ?Sarah, born in April 1760, bound an apprentice to Benjamin Fordham by the 14 September 1768 Craven County court [Minutes 1766-75, 89a]. She was freed by the court from this indenture on 10 March 1779 [Minutes 1772-78, 2:4b].

    viii. ?Simon, born about July 1764, a "free Negro" bound apprentice to Christopher Dawson on 13 March 1770 [Minutes 1766-75, 137].

    ix. Kent, born in May 1768, a "Free born Negroe Boy" bound an apprentice house carpenter to Sampson Leath by the 15 June 1774 Craven County court [Minutes 1772-84, 1:16d].

    x. ?Jenny, born say 1770, head of a Craven County household of 3 "other free" in 1790 [NC:132].

2. Aaron[1] Spelman, born about 1753, was about nine years old when he was bound out by the April 1762 Craven County court [Minutes 1761-62, 104b]. He was head of Craven County household of 3 "other free" in 1790 [NC:134], called Aaron Spelmore on 18 January 1791 when he assigned his right to his final settlement for services in the "Twelve Months Draftees" in the Revolution [T&C, Box 22, by *NCGSJ* XVI:234]. The September 1807 Craven County court ordered his two twin boys, aged seven years, and his daughter, aged fourteen years, bound out. He was called Aaron Spelmore on 12 September 1820 when he made a declaration in Craven County court to obtain a pension for his service under Captain Sharpe in the Tenth North Carolina Regiment. He stated that he was a caulker and was living with his twenty-year-old daughter Betty Spelmore [Minutes 1820 and 1821, 125-6, 262-3, by *NCGSJ* XV:33]. One of his children was

    i. Betty, born about 1800 according to her father's pension application.

Other members of the Spelman family were

    i. Aaron[2], head of a Camden County household of 1 "other free" in 1790 [NC:16].

    ii. Timothy, head of a Camden County household of 1 "other free" in 1790 [NC:16].

    iii. Seney, married Marshall **Mitchell**, 1 July 1806 Craven County bond, Lewis Cavans bondsman.

    iv. Ferebe, married William **Mitchell**, 14 July 1806 Craven County bond, Joab **Mitchell** bondsman.

    v. Courtney, head of a Pasquotank County household of 4 "other free" in 1810 [NC:928].

    vi. Nancy, head of a Pasquotank County household of 3 "other free" in 1810 [NC:928].

    vii. Rachel, head of a Pasquotank County household of 3 "other free" in 1810 [NC:928].

    viii. David[2], born about 1804, listed among "Sundry Free Born Colored persons...needy of proper persons" (to be bound to) on 10 March 1818.

    ix. Church, born about 1808, listed among "Sundry Free Born Colored persons...needy of proper persons" on 10 March 1818 [CR 28.101.1].

SPILLER FAMILY

1. Judith Spiller, born say 1720, was a "Mullatto Woman" living in Carteret County on 8 December 1742 when George Read brought her daughter Tamer, "begotten by a Negro man," into court to have her bound to him until the age of thirty-one years. She may have been the "Judy a Mulatto formerly belonging unto the estate of Mr. James Winright decd" whose daughter Katherine, "a child of Mixt blood," was bound to Neill Puriell nineteen years later in December 1761 [Minutes 1747-64, fol.54a, 187].[190] The name Spiller does not appear in the 1790-1820 North Carolina census, so perhaps her descendants used a different surname. Her children were

2   i. Tamer, born 22 January 1738.

---

[190]James Winright owned land on the north side of the Newport River in 1752 [ibid., f.21b].

    ii.   Katherine, born in 1748.

   iii.   Tom, born about 1750, the "one year old boy child of Mixt blood born of one Judy a Mulatto" bound to Thomas Lovick.

   iv.   Rose, born about 1758, the five-year-old child of "Molato Judy" bound to Cornelius Canady in February 1764.

    v.   George, born about 1760, the three-year-old child of "Molato Judy" bound an apprentice cooper to Cornelius Canady [Minutes 1747-64, 297].

2.   Tamer (no last name), born 22 January 1738, was living in Carteret County on 9 December 1757 when her daughter Rachel, "of a Negroe Wench named Thamer now a Servant to Mrs. Anne Read," was bound to Frances Read [Minutes 1747-64, 42]. Her children were

    i.   Rachel, perhaps 1756.

   ii.   Rodey, born about 1758, "Mulato Daughter of Mulatto Tamer" bound apprentice in November 1763 to Thomas Oglesby.

   iii.   Nan, born about 1762, one-year-old sister of Rodey bound apprentice in November 1763 [Minutes 1747-64, 294].

SPRIDDLE FAMILY

1.   Spencer Spradley, born 9 January 1735, was a "molato" whose birth was registered in Northumberland County. He may have been the father of

2   i.   Elizabeth Sprittle, born say 1753.

2.   Elizabeth Sprittle, born say 1753, had an illegitimate son Philip Sprittle by William **Causey** on 29 December 1770 [Fleet, *Northumberland County Record of Births*, 107]. She was a "free mulatto" head of a Northumberland County household in 1810 [VA:994]. She was the mother of

    i.   Philip, born 29 December 1770.

3   ii.   Nancy, born 26 April 1775 [Fleet, *Northumberland County Record of Births*, 87].

3.   Nancy Spriddle, born 26 April 1775, was head of a Northumberland County household of 7 "other free" in 1810 [VA:996]. She was the mother of

    i.   James, born say 1795, security for the 15 December marriage of Mary Spriddle and Samuel **Cassidy**.

   ii.   Mary, born say 1798, married Samuel **Cassidy**, 15 December 1819 Lancaster County bond, James Spriddle security.

   iii.   Thomas, married Elizabeth **Nickens**, 11 August 1817 Northumberland County bond, Joseph **Weaver** security.

   iv.   Jesse, married Elizabeth **Evans**, 11 November 1818 Northumberland County bond, Moses **Blundon** security.

SPRUCE FAMILY

The Spruce family may have been related to Elizabeth Sproson who had "lately come out of New Kent County" in November 1712 when the Henrico County court reported that she had delivered a bastard child at the house of Edward Heathcot [Orders 1710-4, 198]. Members of the Spruce family were

    i.   Mary Sproose/ Spruce, born say 1731, a "Mulatto" presented by the Warwick County court on 6 April 1749 for having a bastard child [Minutes 1748-62, 17].

1   ii.   Martha Spruce, born say 1734.

2   iii.   William, born say 1736.

1. Martha Spruce, born say 1734, was the mother of David Spruce, a "Molatto" boy bound apprentice in Isle of Wight County on 6 February 1752. She was the mother of

    i. David, born say 1751, a "Molatto" son of Martha, bound apprentice in Isle of Wight County to Andrew Sikes [Orders 1746-52, 393], taxable in Eliza beth City County in 1782 [Fothergill, *Virginia Tax Payers*, 119] and taxable in York County from 1784 to 1789 [PPTL, 1782-1841, frames 89, 95, 144, 155].

2. William Spruce, born say 1736, was presented by the York County court on 20 May 1765 for not attending Yorkhampton Parish Church and presented on 15 November 1773 for absenting himself from church and not listing himself as a tithable [Judgments & Orders 1763-5, 374, 448; 1772-4, 437-8]. He and his wife Rebecca had a daughter named Sally who was baptized in Charles Parish, York County, on 3 November 1765, but he was married to Betty by 25 September 1768 when their son John was baptized there [Bell, *Charles Parish Register*]. The York County court bound out (his daughters) Sarah and Mary Spruce on 21 August 1775, and on 19 April 1784 the court ordered the churchwardens to bind out his daughter Mary because he had left no estate to maintain her [Orders 1774-84, 104, 473]. His children were

    i.   ?James, a poor orphan bound out in York County on 15 August 1774 [Orders 1774-84, 54].
    ii. Mary, probably identical to Polly Spruce, the "free Mulatto" mother of Elizabeth Spruce who was born 1 May 1791 and baptized 4 March 1792 in Bristol Parish [Chamberlayne, *Register of Bristol Parish*, 370].
    iii. Sally **Scott**, born 1 September, baptized 3 November 1765 [Bell, *Charles Parish Register*], registered in Petersburg on 13 August 1800: *a bright yellow Mulatto woman, five feet three inches high, thirty eight years old, bushy hair, born free by the name of Spruce & raised in York County, had afterwards married to William Scott* [Register of Free Negroes 1794-1819, no. 154].
    iv. John, born __ August, baptized 25 September 1768 [Bell, *Charles Parish Register*]. He was a "free Negro" taxable in Norfolk County in 1813, 1814 and 1816 [PPTL, 1813-24, frames 67, 188].

SPURLOCK FAMILY

Members of the Spurlock family in Virginia were

1   i.   John[1]/ Jack, born say 1728.
    ii. John Whitloe, born about 1735, an eighteen-year-old "Mulato" who bound himself for six years as an apprentice to learn carpentry from John Richardson in York County on 21 August 1753 [DB 5:558-9; Judgments & Orders 1752-4, 320]. He may have been the John Spurlock who sued Henry Mann for 4 pounds, 1 shilling in York County court on 18 June 1764 [Judgments & Orders 1763-5, 226].
    iii. John[2], head of a Norfolk County household of 9 "other free" in 1810 [VA:920].
    iv. Robert, a "free Negro" listed with his wife Hannah in Hanover County in 1813 [PPTL, 1804-24].

1. John[1]/ Jack Spurlock, born say 1728, a "Virginia born Negro" ran away from Thomas Dansie of King William County according to the 15 March 1749 issue of the Maryland Gazette [Headley, *18th Century Virginia Newspapers*, 319]. He may have had children by a woman who was a slave of the Neale family. Former slaves Harry and Billy were enumerated in the tax list for King William County after members of the white Neale family in 1805: "Billey fr[d] by N." and "Harry do." A Francis Neale was taxable on 6 slaves in 1804 but only 1 slave in 1805. Henry, Billy and Jane Spurlock were each taxable on a

slave in 1809 [PPTL 1782-1811; 1812-50]. John Spurlock may have been the father of

    i.   Harry, born say 1780, taxable in King William County from 1807 to 1820: taxable on a slave above the age of sixteen but not taxable on a free tithe from 1807 to 1812, also taxable on a horse in 1810, listed as a "free Negro" taxable from 1813 to 1820, aged 16-45 in 1815 when he was taxable on 5 cattle, taxable on 2 free males in 1820 [PPTL 1782-1811; 1812-50].

    ii.   Billy, taxable in King William County on a slave above the age of sixteen but not on a free tithe from 1807 to 1810 [PPTL 1782-1811].

    iii.   John[3]/ Jack, taxable in King William County from 1807 to 1819: taxable on a slave above the age of sixteen but not on a free tithe from 1807 to 1812, a "free Negro" taxable from 1813 to 1819 [PPTL 1782-1811; 1812-50].

    iv.   Jane, taxable in King William County from 1807 to 1819: taxable on a slave above the age of sixteen but not on a free tithe from 1807 to 1812, a "free Negro" taxable in 1813 and 1814 [PPTL 1782-1811; 1812-50].

    v.   Edward, counted in James City County as a "free Person of Colour above the age of 16" who was not tithable in 1813 [PPTL 1800-15].

STAFFORD FAMILY

Members of the Stafford family were

    i.   Henry, taxable in Norfolk County in 1767, a "free negro" taxable on the south side of Western Branch District in 1768, and taxable there in 1770 [*Norfolk County Virginia Tithables, 1766-1780*, 15, 72, 88, 106].

    ii.   John, head of a Martin County, North Carolina household of 5 "other free" in 1790 [NC:68].

    iii.   Anna, head of a Hertford County household of 5 "free colored" in 1820 [NC:186].

    iv.   Cortne, head of a Hertford County household of 4 "free colored" in 1820 [NC:186].

    v.   Evey/ Emey(?), head of a Hertford County household of 9 "free colored" in 1820 [NC:190].

STEPHENS FAMILY

1.   Rebecca Stephens, born say 1676, was living in York County, Virginia, on 24 September 1706 when she was sold for five years to pay her fine of fifteen pounds for "having a mulato Bastard male Child lately born of her body & Confessing the Father to be a negro" [DOW 13:19]. She may have been the mother of

2   i.   Mary[1], born say 1692.

2.   Mary[1] Stephens, born say 1692, was living in Northampton County, Virginia, in 1715 when her four-year-old son Henry and two-year-old son Jonathan were bound apprentices [Orders 1710-6, 197]. She was a tithable head of her own household in Northampton County in 1728 and in 1729, a "malatto" living near Matthew Harmonson. She was called Mary Powell, "negro," in Michael Christian's list of tithables for 1729 and 1731, living near Matthew Harmonson [L.P. 1728, 1729; Bell, *Northampton County Tithables*, 166, 179, 198, 225]. Mary Powell died before 11 March 1731/2 when Captain Matthew Harmonson informed the court that she left so small an estate that no one would administer it. On 11 April 1732 the sheriff recorded the account of her estate, which included lumber, hogs, corn, flax, bacon, a wheel, sifters, and a tub. The court ordered the sheriff to sell the estate and ordered her children Southy, Daniel, James, Mason and Littleton bound out to Harmonson. And on 12 June

1733 Captain Harmonson asked the court whether Mason, Daniel, Tamer and Southy, children of Mary Powell deceased, were entitled to the benefit of the orphan's law. The court ruled that they were entitled [Orders 1729-32, 138; 1732-42, 51; Deeds & Wills 1725-33, 297]. Mary's children, who all used the name Stephens, were

3   i.   Henry[1], born on 31 July 1711.
4   ii.   Jonathan, born on 4 August 1713.
5   iii. ?Abigail, born say 1715.
      iv. James, born say 1722, bound to Matthew Harmonson on 11 March 1731/2.
      v.   Mason, born say 1724, taxable in the household of (his brother) Henry Stephens in 1744.
      vi. Southy[1], born say 1726, taxable in the Northampton County household of (his brother) Jonathan Stephens in 1742.
6   vii. Daniel[1], born say 1728.
     viii. Tamer[1], born say 1730, presented by the grand jury of Northampton County on 13 May 1766 for bastard bearing [Minutes 1765-71, 39]. Her suit against Isaac **Reed** for slander was agreed to at **Reed**'s costs in Northampton County court on 13 June 1794 [Orders 1789-95, 363].
      ix. Littleton[1], born say 1731, bound to Matthew Harmonson on 11 March 1731/2.

3. Henry[1] Stephens, born on 31 July 1711, the four-year-old son of Mary Stephens, was bound apprentice in Northampton County in 1715 [Orders 1710-16, 197]. He was a "Molatto" head of a Northampton County, Virginia household with his wife Esther Stephens in Peter Bowdoin's lists for 1737 to 1739 [L.P. 1737-9] and in the 1744 list of Thomas Preeson with Esther and Mason Stephens [L.P. 1744]. His wife was probably Esther **Mongon**, a tithable in the household of their neighbor John **Drighouse** in 1731. He was called Henry Stephens ("Negro") on 12 February 1754 when he acknowledged that he owed John Custis Matthews a debt of 3 pounds, 16 shillings [Orders 1753-8, 51]. He was taxable in Nathaniel Stratton's household in 1769 [L.P. 1769]. He may have been the father of
      i.   Mary[2], born say 1742, paid a fine in Northampton County on 8 June 1762 for bastard bearing [Minutes 1761-5, 23, 30].

4. Jonathan[1] Stephens, born on 4 August 1713, the two-year-old son of Mary Stephens, was bound apprentice in Northampton County in 1715 [Orders 1710-6, 197]. He was taxable with Margaret Stevens in the Northampton County list of Peter Bowdoin for 1738, adjacent to Henry Stephens and Thomas **Drighouse**, and was a "negro" in the 1742 list of Thomas Preeson with his wife Margaret Stephens "negro" and (his brother) Southy Stephens [L.P. 1738, 1742]. He may have been the father of
      i.   Henry[2]/ Harry, born about 1760, a five-year-old "negro" bound out in Northampton County on 10 October 1765 to learn the trade of shoemaker from Richard Hewett's slave [Minutes 1765-71, 26]. He registered as a "free Negro" in Northampton County on 12 June 1794 [Orders 1789-95, 358].

5. Abigail[1] Stephens, born say 1715, received twenty-five lashes on 13 May 1735 and on 13 February 1738/9 for having bastard children. On 13 February 1739/40 she acknowledged an indenture to serve Matthew Harmonson, Gent., for twelve years on condition that he allow her to marry his "Negroe fellow" Cudgeo" [Orders 1732-42, 155, 164, 342, 387]. She was the mother of
7   i.   ?Amy, born about 1737.
8   ii.   Southy[2], born 4 August 1738.

6. Daniel[1] Stephens, born say 1728, was bound apprentice on 11 March 1731/2 to Captain Matthew Harmonson. He was sued by Comfort **Morris**, administrator of Jacob **Morris**, for a 3 pound, 1 shilling debt on 15 April 1752 [Orders 1751-3, 89]. He may have married Comfort because he was allowed 30 shillings for maintaining the orphans of Jacob **Morris**, "Negro," deceased, on 10 September 1754 [Orders 1753-8, 129]. He was taxable in Northampton County with (his son?) Daniel Stephens, Jr., in 1766 and taxable with (his wife?) Comfort Stephens in 1769 [L.P. 1769; Bell, *Northampton County Tithables*, 380, 401]. He may have been the father of
   i.   Daniel[2], born say 1750, taxable in 1766.

7. Amy Stephens, born in May 1737, was an orphan bound as an apprentice in Northampton County in February 1742/3. She was presented for bastard bearing on 13 November 1750. She was called a "Negro" on 14 January 1755 when she was ordered to serve her master Henry Gascoyne for two years commencing 1 March 1755, probably for having an illegitimate child [Orders 1742-8, 58; 1748-51, 281, 332, 363, 404]. She was presented for bastard bearing again on 13 May 1772 and fined 20 shillings [Minutes 1771-7, 58, 70]. She registered as a "free Negro" in Northampton County on 11 June 1794 [Orders 1789-95, 354]. She was the mother of
   i.   Anthony, born in December 1755, two-year-old "Negro" son of Amy Stephens, bound apprentice to Daniel Luke on 12 September 1758. He was bound to Jane Luke on 10 April 1764 [Minutes 1754-61, 168; 1761-5, 110].
   ii. Ephraim, born say 1760, son of Amey Stephens, bound apprentice to John Tankard on 10 January 1775 [Minutes 1771-7, 277]. He was presented on 13 November 1787 and 11 November 1788 for tending crops on the Indians' land in Northampton County. The Commonwealth discontinued the case on 14 March 1792 for unstated reasons. He registered as a "free Negro" in Northampton County on 11 June 1794. Perhaps his wife was the Lear (Leah) Stevens who registered with him [Orders 1787-9, 64; 1789-95, 193, 354]. He was taxable in Northampton County from 1784 to 1796: taxable on 5 horses and 13 cattle in 1785 and 1786; taxable on a slave and 5 horses in 1788 [PPTL, 1782-1823, frames 31, 45, 54, 88, 147, 199]. His suit against Lighty **Collins** was dismissed on agreement of the parties on 13 May 1794, and in July 1794 the court ordered the overseers of the poor to bind Abraham **Beckett**, son of Comfort **Beckett**, as an apprentice to him [Orders 1789-95, 346, 369].
9 iii. ?Isaac[1], born in July 1763.
   iv. Littleton[2], born in the Spring of 1773, six-year-old son of Amy, bound apprentice to Hezekiah Belote on 12 October 1779 [Minutes 1777-83, 200]. He registered as a "free Negro" in Northampton County on 12 June 1794 [Orders 1789-95, 358] and was taxable in Northampton County from 1791 to 1797 [PPTL, 1782-1823, frames 133, 184]. He was head of a Northampton County, Virginia household of 5 "free colored" in 1820 [VA:216].
   v.   Abigai' registered as a "free Negro" in Northampton County on 11 June 1794 [Orders 1789-95]. She married Abel **Gusties**, 6 September 1806 Northampton County bond, York **Stepney** security. He was called Stepney **York** on 6 June 1807 when he married Peggy **Lewis**, 6 June 1807 Northampton bond, Jacob **Morris** security.
10 vi. Ritter, born say 1763.

8. Southy[2] Stephens, born 4 August 1738, was a "Negroe" child bound to Matthew Harmonson, Gent., on 13 February 1739/40. He was apparently the son of Abigail Stephens and Matthew Harmonson's slave Cudgeo [Orders 1732-42, 387]. He was taxable in Northampton County from 1783 to 1792:

taxable on John Stephens' tithe and 2 horses in 1787 [PPTL, 1782-1823, frames 16, 75, 132]. He registered as a "free Negro" in Northampton County on 12 June 1794 [Orders 1789-95, 358]. He was probably the father of

  i. John, born say 1762, a "Mulatto" taxable in Northampton County from 1783 to 1794: a 16-21 year-old taxable in Southy Stephens' household in 1787 [PPTL, 1782-1823, frames 16, 75, 82, 133, 184]. He married Betsey **Thompson**, 7 August 1798 Northampton County bond, Ben Lewis security.

9. Isaac[1] Stephens, born in July 1763, was bound apprentice to William Gascoigne in Northampton County on 15 February 1770 [Minutes 1765-71, 365]. He served as a soldier in the Revolution [Jackson, *Virginia Negro Soldiers*, 43] and married Rachel **Thompson**, 22 January 1791 Northampton County bond, Coventon Simkins security. He registered as a "free Negro" in Northampton County on 12 June 1794 [Orders 1789-95, 358] and was taxable in Northampton County from 1794 to 1800 [PPTL, 1782-1823, frames 176, 216]. He may have been the father of

  i. Isaac[2], married Sabra **Nutts**, 16 August 1809 Northampton County bond, Isaac Stevens, Sr., security. He was head of a Northampton County household of 9 "free colored" in 1820, called Isaac Steavens, Senr. [VA:215A].

10. Ritter Stephens, born say 1763, complained to the Northampton County court on 11 January 1791 about the treatment of her son Jonathan Stevens by his master Curtis Haslop. The court ordered that he be removed from Haslop's service. She registered as a "free Negro" in Northampton County on 11 June 1794 [Orders 1789-95, 81, 108, 354]. She was the mother of

  i. ?Tobias, born say 1782, ordered bound out by the overseers of the poor to learn the business of planter on 11 September 1789 [Orders 1787-9, 229]. He married Bridget **Nutts**, 7 September 1804 Northampton County bond, Ben Dunton security. He was head of a Northampton County, Virginia household of 3 "free colored" in 1820 [VA:216].

  ii. Jonathan[2], born say 1783, bound out by the overseers of the poor to learn the business of a planter on 11 February 1789. He was called the son of Ritter Stevens when he was bound to Curtis Haslop on 14 September 1790 [Orders 1787-9, 229; 1789-95, 81].

  iii. ?Henry[3]/ Harry, an orphan bound out to Robert Rodgers to learn the trade of wheelwright on 11 January 1791 [Orders 1789-95, 98].

Their descendants in Virginia were

  i. Patience, born say 1750, presented by the grand jury of Northampton County on 8 May 1770 for bastard bearing [Minutes 1765-71, 365].

  ii. Jacob, about 1758, a three-year-old "Negro" bound apprentice to John Thomas on 12 January 1762 [Minutes 1761-5, 4].

  iii. Thomas, a "free Negro" taxable in Northampton County from 1788 to 1795 [PPTL, 1782-1823, frames 89, 183, 199], registered in Accomack County: *born about 1761, Born free in Accomack County, a Black, 5'9"* [Register of Free Negroes, 1785-1863, no. 464], head of a St. George Parish, Accomack County household of 3 "other free" in 1800 [*Virginia Genealogist* 2:161] and 9 in 1810 [VA:59].

  iv. Simon, a resident of Accomack County who was a cook aboard the *Accomac* during the Revolution.

  v. Stephen, a resident of Accomack County who served as a regular seaman aboard the *Accomac* [Jackson, *Virginia Negro Soldiers*, 43].

  vi. Mary[3], .ead of an Accomack County household of 9 "other free" in 1810 [VA:57]. She received bounty land scrip as the only heir of (brothers?) Simon and Stephen Stephens [*Virginia Genealogist* 2:86].

vii. Mary[4], born say 1764, married George **Morris**, 19 October 1785 Northampton County, Virginia bond, David Jones security.

viii. William, born about 1766, sued by Myer Derhaim in Northampton County court on 11 February 1795 for a debt of 2 pounds, 6 shillings [Orders 1789-95, 436], registered as a "free Negro" in York County on 19 September 1831: *a black man 5 feet 7 inches high about 67 years of age very high forehead, pitted with the small pox, large full eyes, pouting thick lips, long thin visage & grey thin hair. Born free in Northampton County, Virg[a], as appeared by satisfactory evidence & has been residing in York County upwards of 30 years* [Free Negroes Registe., 1831-50, no.288].

ix. Matthew, head of a York County household of 5 "other free" in 1810 [VA:883].

x. Leah, born say 1771, married Isaac **Thompson**, 22 September 1792 Northampton County bond, Jacob Frost security. Isaac was head of a Northampton County household of 12 "free colored" in 1820 [VA:215].

xi. Betty, born say 1772, married Isaac **Reed**, 2 July 1793 Northampton County bond, Ralph **Collins** security.

xii. Tamer[2], married Jacob **Thompson**, 26 September 1800 Northampton County bond, Johannes Johnson security.

xiii. Jane, born before 1776, head of a Northampton County household of 3 "free colored" in 1820 [VA:216].

xiv. Cugis (Cudjo), married Betsy **Pool**, 20 December 1806 Northampton County bond, Charles **Pool** security.

xv. Esther, registered as a "free Negro" in Northampton County on 11 June 1794 [Orders 1789-95, 354]. She was head of a St. George Parish, Accomack County household of 5 "other free" in 1800 [*Virginia Genealogist* 2:163].

xvi. Bello, head of a St. George Parish, Accomack County household of 2 "other free" in 1800 [*Virginia Genealogist* 2:163], perhaps the Annabella Stephens who was an Accomack County taxpayer in 1787 [Fothergill, *Virginia Tax Payers*, 119].

xvii. Susannah, head of an Accomack County household of 6 "other free" in 1810 [VA:59].

xviii. Mary, head of a King George County household of 8 "other free" and one white woman in 1810 [VA:218].

xix. Thomas, head of a King George County household of 3 "other free" and a white woman in 1810 [VA:218].

Surry County, Virginia

1. Lucy Stephens, born say 1759, was taxable in Surry County, Virginia, on a horse in 1803, taxable on "free Simon" in 1804, and taxable on 2 slaves in 1805 and 1806 [PPTL, 1791-1816, 543, 576, 599, 617]. Her children were

i. ?Thomas, born about 1777, taxable in Surry County from 1797 to 1807: listed as David **Charity**'s tithable in 1797 and 1798, charged with hi own tax in 1803 [PPTL, 1791-1816, frames 287, 323, 542, 599, 616, 637]. He registered in Petersburg on 29 October 1817: *a free man of colour, yellow brown complection, five feet seven inches high, forty years old, born free in Surry County* [Register of Free Negroes 1794-1819, no. 878].

ii. Alexander, born 10 November 1780, registered as a "free Negro" in Surry County, Virginia, on 31 May 1800: *son of Lucy Stephens a resident of this county aged 20 years the 10th of November next pretty stout and well made of a yellowish complexion, 5'3-1/4' high, short hair, by profession a water-man - was born of a free parent* [Back of Guardian Accounts Book 1783-1804, no.59]. He registered in Petersburg on 6 January 1809 [Register of Free Negroes 1794-1819, no. 448]

iii.   Isham, born 24 December 1782, registered as a "free Negro" in Surry
County on 2 October 1800: *son of Lucy Stephens a free woman of this
county aged 17 years on the 24th day of December last, of a bright
complexion stout made and 5' high* [Back of Guardian Accounts Book,
1783-1804, no.66].

iv.   ?Sarah, married Benjamin **Charity**, 5 September 1803 Surry County
bond, William **Scott** surety.

Another member of the Stephens family was
i.   John, born say 1745, head of an Edgecombe County, North Carolina
household of 9 "other free" in 1790 [NC:54].

STEWART FAMILY

The Stewart family probably originated near present-day Dinwiddie County since
there were at least a dozen members of the family in that general area by 1730. No
evidence has yet been located to indicate whether or not they were all related.
There were several Stewart to Stewart marriages. William ("Sonkey") Stewart
married Nancy, the daughter of Dr. Thomas Stewart of Dinwiddie County, about
1770, Doctor Stewart's brother James married Priscilla Stewart in Mecklenburg
County in 1791, and a Thomas Stewart married the daughter of Peter Stewart
before 1801 when he named her in his Chesterfield County will.
Dinwiddie was formed in 1752 from Prince George County which was formed in
1702 from Charles City County. All three are burned-record counties. However,
the register of Bristol Parish from 1720-1789 contains records for Dinwiddie and
Prince George counties, and the Prince George County court order books for the
years 1710-1714 and 1737-1740 as well as wills and inventories for the years 1713-
1728 have survived. These contain a number of references to mixed-race members
of the Stewart family, but they also contain over thirty references to free, mixed-
race people whose full names are not provided.[191] One mixed-race child was
called "a Moll. Boy named Wm" in 1725 when William Eaton petitioned the
churchwardens of Bristol Parish to bind the child to him. He may have been
identical to the "Mulatto Boy" William Stewart who was bound to Eaton by the
churchwardens of Bristol Parish in 1739 [Chamberlayne, *Bristol Parish Register*,
24; Prince George County Orders 1737-40, 241].

Members of the Stewart family were
1   i.   Elizabeth, born say 1695.
2   ii.   John[1], born say 1715.
3   iii.   Rebecca[1], born say 1717.

---

[191]The year 1721: *Three Mallattos not slaves.* 1722: *One Mallatto Woman and four children valued
at 20 pounds.* 1725: *Three Mallatto Children...Dureing their time.* 1727: *One Mallatto girl named Sue
to serve till 22 years. Mallatto Girl if a slave 13 pounds if Born free then valued to 8 pounds* [Prince
George County Deeds, Etc. 1713-1728, 15, 428-9, 498-9, 669, 802, 972-4, 1049]. 1722: *Bind out three
Moll. Children their Mother a Mollatto the names of the Children Peter, Dick, & Nan, To serve James
Williams.* 1724: *Hen. Royall petitioneth that two Moll. Children born in his house Wm. & hannah may
be bound to him...granted.* 1725: *Godfry Radgsdale doth petition that a Moll. girll born in his house may
be bound to him. Wm. Eaton prays a Moll. Boy name Wm. be bound unto ye sd Eaton.* 1727: *Bind to
Godfrey Ragsdail two Mullatto Children Dol and bidde.* 1728: *Peter a mulatt Boy Bound to Edward
Colwell.* 1729: *Two Mulotto Children peter & tom be Bound to Henry Royall. Betty and Jno. Mullattoes
bound to Saml Harwell, Jr.* 1730: *A Mulatto Child Ned bound to Godfrey Rags Dail.* 1731: *Two Melettos
Tom & Will bound to Capt Peter Wynn. Maletto Child Tom be bound to Eliza Ragsdale.* 1732: *Two
Mellattos Patt aged three year Griffen aged Nine Months be bound to Philip Morgan* [Chamberlayne,
Bristol Parish Register, 11, 18-9, 24, 45, 47, 50, 58-9, 63]. 1739: *Robin and Dick two Mulato Boys
Sons of Amy a Mulato Woman be bound by the Churchwardens of Bristol Parish to William Coleman
until the age of twenty one* [Prince George County Orders 1737-40, 378].

4   iv.   Ann, born say 1722.
5   v.   Elizabeth², born say 1724.
6   vi.   Thomas¹, born say 1727.
7   vii.   Peter¹, born say 1729.
8   viii. James¹, born say 1734.

1. Elizabeth¹ Stewart, born say 1695, was the mother of "Mulatto" children: Ned,
    Matthew, Mary, and Martha whose births, indentures, and baptisms were
    registered in Bi:stol Parish (Henrico, Prince George, and Dinwiddie Counties).
    Her "Moll." son Ned was born in the household of Mrs. Frances Wynn
    sometime before 28 June 1725 when Mrs. Wynn petitioned the Bristol Parish
    Vestry to have the boy bound to her. She may have also been the mother of
    William, a "Moll. boy," who was bound to William Eaton in Bristol Parish in
    1725 [Chamberlayne, *Bristol Parish Register*, 24, 27, 362, 366, 368]. Her
    children were
            i.   ?Joshua¹, born say 1719, a "Mulatto" taxable in Chesterfield County
                  in 1747 [Tax List 1747-1821, 4].
9   ii.   Edward¹/ Ned, born 19 August 1721.
10   iii. ?William¹, born say 1723.
11   iv.   Matthew¹, born 6 January 1726.
12   v.   Mary, born 19 September 1732.
13   vi.   Martha, born 3 October 1741.

2. John¹ Stewart, born say 1715, owed a debt of about 6 pounds currency to
    William McLain in December 1747 when the Lunenburg County court ordered
    the sheriff to sell items held by his security, Redman Fallen [Orders 1746-8,
    353]. He was ¿ "mulatto" taxable in Lunenburg County in the list of William
    Caldwell in 1749 [Bell, *Sunlight on the Southside*, 94]. He had married Martha
    Harris sometime before 13 October 1763 when the Lunenburg County court
    bound Patty Steward's son Isham **Harris** to Amos Tims, Jr. John died before
    14 February 1765 when the Lunenburg County court ordered the
    churchwardens of St. James Parish to bind his orphan daughter Eleanor
    Steward to William Taylor [Orders 1763-4, 257; 1764-5, 2, 203].
    Mecklenburg County was formed from St. James Parish later that year, and
    in September 1772 the Mecklenburg County court bound Eleanor to Molly
    Taylor [Orders 1771-73, 318]. On 27 April 1777 Martha's son Moses
    purchased 100 acres from Henry Jackson in Mecklenburg County on the south
    side of Allen's Creek adjoining Stephen Mallett, with Stephen and Zachariah
    Mallett as witnesses [DB 5:56]. She apparently purchased this land in his name
    since he was only eleven years old at the time. Her 17 January 1779
    Mecklenburg County, Virginia will, witnessed by Zachariah Mallett, was
    proved 9 October 1780 on motion of her executor, Henry Jackson.[192] By her
    will she left her land to her son Moses and left livestock and money to her
    children Isham, Nelly, Edy, Fanny, Moses, Sinai, and Disea [WB 1:341]. She
    was counted aͻ head of a Mecklenburg County household of 7 persons in
    1782, but this was probably the listing for her estate [VA:32]. Her estate
    included 54 acres of land which was sold for taxes in 1793 [DB 8:407-8]. John
    was the father of
14   i.   ?Thomas², born about 1742.
15   ii.   Nelly¹, born say 1760.
            iii. Edy, born say 1762, ordered bound by the churchwardens of
                  Cumberland Parish, Lunenburg County, to John Blaxton on 11 October
                  1764 (no parent named) and called "Daughter of Martha Stewart" on

---

[192]Henry have been identical to or related to the Henry Jackson whose daughter Hannah was
mentioned in the 15 January 1744 Brunswick County will of Ralph Jackson. Ralph Jackson's 3 June 1745
inventory included "2 Mullatto Apprentice Boys" [WB 2:100-2].

8 March 1770 when the court ordered her bound by the churchwardens of Cumberland Parish to Sarah Blaxton [Orders 1763-64, 171; 1769-77, 27]. She married William **Harris** before 11 September 1780 when the Mecklenburg County court ordered Zachariah Mallett to deliver up the will of Patty Stewart, deceased, on the motion of William **Harris** and his wife Eady. She was called "Edith Stewart now Harris" on 9 August 1784 when the court ordered her son Jerry Stewart bound out [Orders 1779-84, 76; 1784-7, 103].

    iv.   Fanny[2], born say 1764.

Martha was the mother of

    i.   Isham **Harris**, born say 1756, called "Isham Harris, Son of Patty Stewart" on 13 October 1763 when he was ordered bound to Amos Tims, Jr., by the Lunenburg County court. On 13 April 1769 the court ordered Isham bound instead to John **Evans** (alias **Eppes**) [Orders 1763-64, 257; 1766-69, folio 202]. He was taxable in John Evans' Lunenburg County household in 1772 [Bell, *Sunlight on the Southside*, 304]. He applied for a pension for services in the Revolution at the age of eighty-four years on 8 August 1843 in Rutherford County, North Carolina, stating that he was born in Charlotte County, Virginia, in 1759 and that he was drafted in Lunenburg County.

16   ii.   Moses[1], born 18 November 1766.

    iii.   Sinai, orphan of Martha Stewart, ordered bound apprentice in Mecklenburg County on 9 October 1780 [Orders 1779-84, 81], married Samuel **Chandler**, 23 December 1793 Mecklenburg County bond, William **Chandler** bondsman.

    iv.   Disea/ Dicey, born 27 January 1770 according to her mother's will, married Isaac **Evans**, 24 December 1792 Mecklenburg County bond.

3.   Rebecca[1] Stewart, born say 1717, sued Charles Hix in Brunswick County, Virginia court in September 1738 for her freedom and a certificate for the same, but the court dismissed the case in February 1738/9 when she failed to appear. Hix was ordered to pay Douglas Irby as an evidence for one day and for coming and going fifty miles [Orders 1732-41, 203, 223]. She was living in Surry County, Virginia, on 17 July 1750 when the court ordered the churchwardens of Albemarle Parish to bind out her children: Moggy, Tom, Jack, Nan, Peter, and James [Orders 1749-51, 110]. Joseph Walker sued her in Brunswick County court on 22 June 1756. The jury found her not guilty on 23 February 1757 and ordered Walker to pay costs. She sued Daniel Clarke and Sylvanus Stanton for trespass, but both suits were dismissed by agreement of the parties on 28 February 1759. And her suit against William Evans was dismissed on 28 May 1760 by agreement of the parties [Orders 1756-7, 65, 128, 201-2; 1757-9, 300; 1760-84, 65]. She purchased 50 acres in Brunswick County on the south side of the Meherrin River and the north side of the Great Road from John Parham for 25 pounds on 26 September 1763, and she purchased 70 acres on Fox Branch from Kirby Moody on 16 April 1764 and sold this 70 acres to Moody on 6 June 1766. She purchased 200 acres near the Rocky Run in Meherrin Parish, Brunswick County, on 23 September 1776. Her land adjoined Drury **Going** and the **Pompey** family according to **Going**'s deed of sale for land on the south side of the Meherrin River in Brunswick County on 10 October 1787 [DB 4:215; 7:384; 8:311; 12:84-5; 14:366]. She was called the executrix of Peter Moggy on 23 January 1783 when the Greensville County court dismissed a suit against her for debt brought by Batt Peterson, assignee of Ephraim Peebles, because she was not residing in the county [Orders 1781-9, 56]. She was called administratrix of the estate of Peter Moggy, deceased, on 27 March 1787 when Peterson sued her in Brunswick County court [Orders 1784-8, 463]. She was probably the unnamed mother of Thomas Stewart who provided for her maintenance by his 24

February 1791 Greensville County will [WB 1:181-3]. Rebecca was the mother of
- i. Moggy, born say 1740.
- 17 ii. Thomas[3], born say 1743.
- 18 iii. John[2]/ Jack, born say 1745.
- iv. Ann[1], born say 1746, perhaps the Nanny **Pompey** who, with husband Littleberry **Pompey** and (brother?) James Stewart, sold 135 acres adjoining Steward's Branch in Meherrin Parish, Brunswick County, on 26 January 1778 [DB 13:45].
- 19 v. Peter[2], born say 1748.
- 20 vi. James[2], born say 1750.
- 21 vii. ?Barnett[1], born say 1760.
- 22 viii. ?William[4], born say 1761.

4. Ann Steward, born say 1720, was the mother of Fanny Stewart (no race indicated) whose 1 August 1740 birth was registered in Bristol Parish [Chamberlayne, *Bristol Parish Register*, 367]. She may have been the same Ann Stewart whose children Billy, Matthew, Peyton, Abram, Woody, and Lucretia Stewart (no race indicated) were bound out to the Rev. Arch. McRoberts by the Chesterfield County court on 7 May 1763 [Orders 1759-63, 410]. Peyton (Patron), Abram and Woody Stuard were taxable in Manchester Parish, Chesterfield County, in 1777 [Tax List 1747-1821, frame 131]. Ann was the mother of
- i. Fanny, born 1 August 1740.
- ii. William born say 1749.
- iii. Matthew, born say 1751.
- iv. Peyton[1], born say 1753.
- v. Woody, born say 1757, taxable in Chesterfield County from 1793 to 1796 [PPTL, 1786-1811, frames 188, 220, 286].
- vi. Lucretia, born say 1759.
- vii. Abram, born about 1761, bound apprentice in Chesterfield County on 7 May 1763. He was a "Mulatto" taxable in Chesterfield County on a tithe and a horse from 1788 to 1810, taxable on a slave in 1809 [PPTL, 1786-1811, frames 72, 109, 147, 220, 286, 545, 622, 717, 753, 802]. He obtained a certificate of freedom in Chesterfield County on 13 March 1809: *forty eight years old, black complexion, born free* [Register of Free Negroes 1804-53, no. 113]. He was taxable on 10 acres in Chesterfield County from 1811 to 1816 [Land Tax List 1791-1822, B lists].

5. Elizabeth[2] Stewart, born say 1724, was the "free mulatta" mother of Thomas Stuart who was baptized in Bruton Parish, James City County, on 3 April 1748 [Bruton Parish Register, 8]. She was the ancestor of
- i. Thomas[4], born say 1748, baptized on 3 April 1748.
- ii. ?Sarah, born about 1750, registered in Petersburg on 15 August 1800: *a light Coloured Malatto woman, five feet four inches high, fifty years old, born free & raised in Charles City County* [Register of Free Negroes 1794-1819, no. 175].
- iii. ?Tomison, born about 1769, registered in Petersburg on 21 December 1809: *a dark brown woman of Colour, five feet two inches high, forty years old, born free & raised in Wmsburg* [Register of Free Negroes 1794-1819, no. 516].
- iv. ?John[7], born say 1775, taxable in Charles City County from 1805 to 1814: listed with 2 tithables in 1807 and 1809, listed as a "Mulattoe" in 1813 and 1814 [PPTL 1788-1814]. He was head of a Charles City County household of 8 "other free" in 1810 [VA:958].
- v. ?William, born say 1780, head of a Charles City County household of 3 "other free" in 1810 [VA:958], taxable in Charles City County from

1805 to 1813, listed as a "Mulattoe" in 1813 [PPTL 1788-1814]. He
was the father of Sarah who registered in Charles City County on 19
January 1832: *Sarah Evans, wife of Thomas Evans, who was Sarah
Stewart, daughter of Wm Stewart, a light mulato, twenty four years of
age* [Minutes 1830-9, 89]. On 19 March 1835 the overseers of the poor
bound to him William Stewart (born April 1827), orphan of Sally
Stewart [Minutes 1830-9, 227].

23   vi.   ?Henry, born say 1785.

6.   Thomas[1] Stewart, born say 1727, was taxable in Dinwiddie County on a free
tithable, 17 slaves and 874 acres in 1782 [PPTL, 1782-90; Land Tax List
1782-1814]. The land tax records of Mecklenburg County, Virginia, list a
grant of 362 acres to Thomas Stewart [Land Tax List, 1782-1814, 1782 Land
Office Grants]. This was apparently the land office grant he received on 15
May 1784 as assignee of Jacob **Chavous** for 362 acres on Sandy Creek [Grants
L:614]. He was called Thomas Stewart of Dinwiddie County when he was
taxable on 720 acres in Mecklenburg County from 1782 to 1793 [Land Tax
List 1782-1811A, A lists]. He was called Doctor Thomas Stewart in the
Dinwiddie County tax records in 1787 and thereafter. He was called Dr.
Thomas Stewart when he was taxable in Dinwiddie County on 874 acres on
Walker's Road from 1787 to 1789 and on 845 acres from 1790 to 1807 [Land
Tax List 1782-1814, B lists]. James Crook owed him 109 pounds on 27 March
1788 when Crook mortgaged three slaves in Brunswick County to secure the
debt [DB 14:439]. The February 1789 session of the Dinwiddie County court
granted him permission to keep an ordinary in his house. Between March 1789
and March 1790 he sued four persons for debt in Dinwiddie County court
[Orders 1789-91, 4, 8, 177, 180]. While resident in Dinwiddie County he was
taxable in Mecklenburg County on slaves Berry, Patty and Lewis in 1787,
taxable on Frederick **Gowen** and slaves Berry, Judy, Patty and Lewis in 1788,
taxable on his son Charles and four slaves in 1790, taxable on his sons Charles
and Joseph and four slaves in 1791, taxable on son Joseph and five slaves in
1793, but not taxable thereafter in Mecklenburg County [PPTL 1782-1805,
frames 177, 223, 276, 329, 383, 451, 470]. He was called Thomas Stewart of
Dinwiddie County on 5 December 1792 when he made a deed of gift (signing)
to his son James Stewart for 150 acres in Mecklenburg County adjoining the
land of his brother James Stewart [DB 8:306]. His grandson John **Day**
described him as:

*a coloured man of Dinwiddie County, Virginia whose name was Thomas
Stewart, a medical doctor* [Rev. John Day to Rev. J.B. Taylor by Sneed
& Westfall, *History of Thomas Day*, 6].

He was called Thomas Stewart, Sr., of Dinwiddie County on 10 November
1799 when he sold 102 acres on Butcher's Creek in Mecklenburg County to
(his son-in-law) Humphrey **Wilson** for 30 pounds, and the same day Thomas
and his wife Mildred Stewart of Dinwiddie County sold 162 acres adjoining
Wilson's line on Sandy Creek to (their son-in-law) William Stewart for 60
pounds [DB 10:267, 268]. Thomas married, second, Winnifred **Atkins**, 5
February 1795 Sussex County bond. He died about 1810 when his estate was
taxable on 13 slaves. His widow Winnie was taxable on 5 slaves in Dinwiddie
County in 1811 [PPTL, 1810-14]. The Mecklenburg County chancery suit of
his granddaughter Hannah Stewart described him as a "black man but a great
doctor" and stated that he was married twice and that his second wife died
about 1812 [Chancery Causes, 1872-008, LVA]. His will survived because it
was included in a 24 April 1832 to 4 September 1832 Dinwiddie County
chancery court suit which also named his children and their heirs. The will
was dated 18 May 1808 and proved in January 1810. He divided the land
where he was living among his sons Charles, Joseph and Armstead; lent half

his land, four slaves, his "mantion house" and stage wagon to his wife Winnie during her natural life; divided another eighteen slaves among his children Charles, Joseph, Armstead, Mary Stewart, Nancy Stewart (of Mecklenburg), grandson Henry Armstead Stewart, grandson John **Day**, grandchildren Eliza and Richard **Deen** (**Aberdeen**) (children of his daughter Sophy), and Tempy Boyd wife of Capt. Boyd of Portsmouth. He noted that his sons Charles and Joseph had moved to the "Western Country" and might never return, in which case their share was to go to his grandson Henry Armstead Stewart when he reached the age of twenty-one. The July 1810 court were of opinion that it ought not be admitted to record because he was not of sound mind and for other reasons it was not his true last will [Chancery Orders 1832-52, 1, 12, 13]. He was the father of

- i. Nancy, born say 1755, married William ("Sonkey") Stewart.
24 - ii. James[3], born say 1757.
- iii. Charles[1], born say 1763, taxable on 233 acres on Cox's Road in Dinwiddie County which was transferred to him by William Sallard between October 1783 and November 1784. He was taxable on this land until 1806, taxable on 185-1/2 acres from 1807 to 1814, and taxable from 1811 to 1814 on 80 acres which he inherited from his father Doctor Thomas Stewart [Land Tax List 1782-1814, B lists]. He was tithable in Dinwiddie County in the same district as Dr. Thomas Stewart from 1784 to 1820: in his own household from 1784 to 1788, listed in Dr. Thomas Stewart's household in 1789 and 1793, taxable on 2 slaves in 1801, and taxable on about 3 slaves until 1820 [PPTL, 1782-90; 1791-9; 1800-9; 1810-14; 1814-19, B lists]. He was living on his father's Mecklenburg County land in 1790 and 1791 [PPTL, 1782-1805, frames 329, 383].
- iv. Mourning, born about 1766, married John **Day** [Chancery Orders 1832-52, 1]. She was counted as an eighty-four-year-old woman in the 1850 census for Caswell County.
- v. William, father of William, Herbert and Lucy Stewart. Lucy was married to Stephen **Hall** by 1832 [Chancery Orders 1832-52, 12]. Herbert and Polly Stewart were bound by the Mecklenburg County court to Thomas **Spence** and his wife on 11 September 1809 [Orders 1809-11, 53]. Herbert, born 1794-1806, was head of a Mecklenburg County household of 1 "free colored" in 1820 [VA:144b].
- vi. John[5], born about 1772, taxable in his father's Dinwiddie County household from 1788 to 1792 and in 1798 [PPTL, 1782-90; 1791-9, B list]. His son John S. Stewart was named in the September 1832 Dinwiddie County chancery suit brought by the heirs of Dr. Thomas Stewart [Chancery Orders 1832-52, 13].
- vii. Mary, born say 1774, married Edmund **Gowan** (**Gowen**). Edmund was taxable in his father-in-law's Dinwiddie County household in 1788. He purchased 200 acres in Mecklenburg County on Sandy Creek adjoining William Stewart's line from his father-in-law on 5 November 1799 [DB 10:176]. Edmund and Mary's heirs Henry, Lemon and Thomas **Gowan** were plaintiffs in a 4 September 1832 Dinwiddie County chancery suit [Chancery Orders 1832-52, 12].
- viii. Joseph[1], born about 1775, a sixteen-year-old taxable in Mecklenburg County in 1791 [PPTL, 1782-1805, frame 383]. He was taxable in the Dinwiddie County household of his father from 1796 to 1805 [PPTL, 1791-9; 1800-9].
- ix. Thomas[6], born say 1776, taxable in the Dinwiddie County household of his brother Charles in 1797 [PPTL, 1791-9, B list].
- x. Tabitha, born say 1777, married ___ **Eppes** [Chancery Orders 1832-52, 13], the Joel **Epps** who purchased 200 acres on Sandy Creek in Mecklenburg County from his father-in-law on 5 November 1799 [DB 10:177].

xi.   Sally, born say 1779, married Humphrey **Wilson** [Chancery Orders 1832-52, 1]. Humphrey purchased land in Mecklenburg County from his father-in-law by deed recorded in 1800 [DB 10:268].

xii. Elizabeth[2], married Moses **Brown** [Chancery Orders 1832-52, 1], head of a Southampton County household of 5 "other free" in 1810.

xiii. Soffee, married Henry **Aberdeen** [Chancery Orders 1832-52, 13], head of a Norfolk County household of 4 "other free" and 4 slaves in 1810 [VA:826]. He was administrator of his father-in-law's Dinwiddie County estate [Chancery Orders 1832-52, 1]. Henry purchased a lot at Dinwiddie and Glasgow Streets and a half lot in Westminster Square in Portsmouth, Norfolk County, from Willis Culpeper on 1 October 1790 [DB 32:140]. He was taxable in Norfolk County from 1794 to 1817: taxable on 2 slaves over 16 and 2 horses but not charged with his own tithe in 1794; called a seaman from 1798 to 1803 when he was taxable on 2 slaves over 16; a mariner living in Portsmouth when he was in a list of "free Negroes and Mulattoes" with males Richard and Henry, and females Tempy, Corn, Sophia and Elizabeth Aberdeen in his household in 1801 [PPTL, 1791-1812, frames 94, 167, 241; 1813-24, frames 11, 56, 94, 121, 238, 350, 460]. Their heirs Henry, Soffee and Richard **Aberdeen** were named in the September 1832 Dinwiddie County chancery suit brought by the heirs of Dr. Thomas Stewart [Chancery Orders 1832-52, 13].

xiv. Armstead, born say 1783, over sixteen years old when he was listed in John **Day**'s Dinwiddie County household in 1800 (with his brother Henry Stewart). He was taxable in the household of his father in 1807 and taxable in his own household with a slave in 1809 [PPTL, 1782-99; 1800-9; 1810-14]. He was head of a Dinwiddie County household of 5 "other free" in 1810 [VA:161]. He was called Armstead Stewart of Dinwiddie County when he married Flora **Crook**, 10 October 1806 Brunswick County bond, Robert **Crook** security. Robert **Crook** was a "free negro" head of a Brunswick County household of 4 "other free" in 1810 [VA:708]. Armstead was taxable in Dinwiddie County on 3 slaves in 1811, 2 in 1812 and his estate was taxable on 2 slaves and 3 horses in 1813. (His widow) Flora Stewart was taxable on 2 slaves from 1815 to 1819 [PPTL 1810-14; 1815-19]. His heirs Theophilus H., Edward R., Henry A., Julian, and Robert (still an infant) were named in a chancery suit in Dinwiddie County on 4 September 1832 [Chancery Orders 1832-52, 13].

7. Peter[1] Stewart, born say 1729, purchased 100 acres in Northampton County, North Carolina, joining Robert Duke, the road, and Seymore Somersall for 5 shillings from Humphrey Revell and his wife Margaret on 19 February 1751.[193] This was probably a deed of gift from his wife's parents. He and his wife Celia sold this land back to Humphrey Revell three and one-half years later on 26 August 1755 for one pound, ten shillings. On 20 November 1760 he purchased 335 acres near Wiccacon Swamp and Bridger's line and sold it on 15 March 1765 without a dower release [DB 2:161, 229; 3:368]. He voted for Joseph Sikes in the Northampton County election of 1762 [SS 837 by *NCGSJ* XII:170]. On 5 September 1775 he purchased 165 acres from Charles Gregory, and he and his wife Jean sold this land to Francis Stewart of Greensville County, Virginia, on 26 March 1795 with the proviso that he live on it rent free [DB 6:127; 10:162; 11:149]. He was head of a Northampton County household of 2 "other free" and 5 slaves in 1790 [NC:73] and 4 "other free" in 1800 [NC:477]. His 30 December 1794 Northampton County will was

---

[193]Some members of the Revell family were free African Americans, but Humphrey Revell and other members of the Northampton County branch of the family were counted as white.

proved in December 1805. He left his land to his wife, to be divided among his unnamed children at her death. He mentioned Jane **Evans** and his grandchild James Stewart [WB 2:309]. Perhaps he was the father of

25   i.   Francis[2], born say 1760.
        ii. Christopher, born say 1775, head of a Northampton County, North Carolina household of 3 "other free" in 1790 [NC:76]. According to his grandson Samuel T. Stewart's application for Cherokee compensation in 1908, his wife's name was Clara and they were the parents of John Stewart who was born in Henry County, Virginia, about 1784 and married Virginia **Fendley**, daughter of Thomas **Fendley** and Priscilla **Rickman** [Jordan, *Cherokee by Blood*, Cherokee Roll of 1909, application no. 19117]. Christopher's widow Clara Stewart was head of a Stokes County, North Carolina household of a "free colored" woman aged 26-45 and 2 females under age 14 in 1820 [NC:371] and a "free colored" woman aged 36-55 in 1830 [NC:237]. Their son John was a "M" taxable in Patrick County, Virginia, in 1819 and 1820 [PPTL, 1791-1823, frames 700, 717] and head of a Patrick County household of 6 "free colored" in 1830.

8. James[1] Stewart, born say 1734, may have been the James Stewart of Brunswick County who leased land on Flat Rock Creek in Cumberland Parish, Lunenburg County, from Agnes Freeman (widow of Arthur Freeman) for twelve years on 10 December 1754 for the yearly rent of 20 pounds currency. The lease included the use of a grist mill and a slave named Tony [DB 4:131]. He was taxable on 100 acres, 3 horses, and about 10 cattle in Dinwiddie County from 1782 to 1788 [PPTL, 1782-90; Land Tax List 1782-1814, B lists]. He was called James Stewart, Sr., of Dinwiddie County when he purchased 225 acres in Mecklenburg County, Virginia, at the head of Little Creek adjoining Stith and Munford from William and Mary Stewart for 100 pounds on 11 February 1788 [DB 7:253]. That same day he was security for the 11 February 1788 Mecklenburg County, Virginia, marriage bond of (his nephew) James Stewart, Jr. He was a "Mulatto" taxable in Mecklenburg County on his own tithe, a slave named Isham, and two horses in 1790 [PPTL 1782-1805, frame 356]. He married Priscilla Stewart, 14 November 1791 Mecklenburg County bond, John (**Chavis**) **Walden** security. He was called brother of Doctor Thomas Stewart of Dinwiddie County on 5 December 1792 when Thomas made a Mecklenburg County deed of gift to his son James [DB 8:306]. He was an exempt taxable in Mecklenburg County in 1795, taxable in 1796 on a slave named Judy, adjacent to James Stewart, Jr. [PPTL, 1782-1805, frames 558, 622]. He was called a blacksmith on 10 June 1799 William Stewart, shoemaker, sued him for a 3 pound debt due by account [Orders 1798-1801, 192]. He was taxable in Mecklenburg County on 242 acres in 1804 [DB 16:272]. He head of a Mecklenburg County household of 2 "free colored" in 1820 [VA:148b]. He sold 45 acres in Mecklenburg County on Mill Creek adjoining William Stewart to Elizabeth **Brandun** on 10 September 1811 [DB 14:461]. On 26 July 1816 James **Drew** paid the taxes which were due for the years 1804 and 1805 on 170 acres of James Stewart, Sr.'s land [DB 16:277]. His 22 March 1804 Mecklenburg County will, proved 20 May 1816 by William Stewart, left 125 acres to his "housekeeper Priscilla Stewart" and her eight children Polly, James, Amey, Peter, Joseph, Patty, Anny and William [WB 8:237]. He was the father of

        i.   Thomas, born say 1773, over the age of sixteen in 1791 when he was taxable in his father's Mecklenburg County household [PPTL, 1782-1805, frame 383].
        ii. John, born say 1775, over the age of sixteen in 1791 when he was taxable in his father's Mecklenburg County household [PPTL, 1782-1805, frame 383].
        iii. Polly, married James **Drew**, 1817 Mecklenburg County bond.

iv.   James[6], born say 1785.

v.   Amey, married Robin (Robert) **Evans**, 13 February 1809 Mecklenburg County bond, James **Chavous** security.

vi.   Peter[6], born in 1789, not yet twenty-one years old in 1804 when James Stewart made his will. He and his brother Joseph were to live with Elison Crew and receive tuition until the age of twenty-one. He received a certificate in Mecklenburg County on 20 May 1812 signed by Christopher Blackburn, Alexander S. Field, J.B. Jones, and Jo. B. Clausel: *a free man born and raised in the County of Mecklenburg and State of Virginia...five feet ten Inches and three quarters, a bright mulatto born some time in the year one thousand Seven hundred and eighty nine...resided in the County and State above mentioned, since his birth to the present period and has generally supported a good Character* [Free Person of Color, no.3, p.2].

vii. Joseph[2], born say 1790, head of a Mecklenburg County household of 5 "free colored" in 1820. On 21 November 1828 he sold 125 acres adjoining the lands of William Stewart, deceased, to Henry **Avery** [DB 23:512].

viii. Patty, born say 1792.

ix.   Anney[3], born say 1794.

x.   William[8], born say 1796.

9.   Edward[1]/ Ned Stewart, born 19 August 1721, son of Elizabeth Stuard, was baptized in Bristol Parish on 29 October 1721. On 28 June 1725 Mrs. Frances Wynn petitioned the Bristol Parish Vestry to have a "Moll. boy named Ned son of Eliz. Stuard born in ye house of Mrs. Wynne" bound to her as an apprentice. And on 6 March 1725/6 Captain Buller Herbert petitioned the Vestry to have "A Mollatto boy named Ned son of Elizabeth Stuard born in his house" bound to him [Chamberlayne, *Bristol Parish Register*, 24, 27, 362]. He was a "Mulatto" taxable in Chesterfield County in 1747 [Tax List 1747-1821], was taxable in Chesterfield County on a tithe, 2 horses, and 3 cattle in 1786, on 2 tithes in 1794, taxable on a slave over the age of 16 and a horse in 1795 but not taxable himself, called Edward Stewart, Sr., in 1796 when he was taxable on 2 tithes and was last taxable in 1801 [PPTL, 1786-1811, frames 19, 88, 92, 125, 165, 205, 237, 305, 343, 377, 453]. Edward may have been the father of

26   i.   John[3], born say 1757.

      ii.   James[3], born say 1760, taxable in Powhatan County in 1787, a "Mul°" taxable on a horse in 1788 and 1789 but not listed again in Powhatan County [PPTL, 1787-1825, frames 10, 24, 38]. He may have been the James Stewart who was a "freed Negroe" taxable in the lower district of adjoining Goochland County in 1793 and 1794, called an "Indian" in 1795 [PPTL, 1782-1809, frames 332, 380, 411].

27   iii. Edward[2], born about 1762.

      iv.   William, a "M°" taxable on a horse in Powhatan County in 1789 [PPTL, 1787-1825, frame 38].

      v.   Daniel, born say 1770, taxable in Chesterfield County on one tithe and a horse from 1791 to 1797, two tithes from 1798 to 1801, one tithe and a horse in from 1802 to 1805, and a "Mulatto" taxable in 1806 and 1807 [PPTL, 1786-1811, frames 91, 125, 165, 206, 272, 305, 343, 377, 453, 488, 529, 604, 642, 689].

      vi.   Nathaniel[1], born about 1774, obtained a certificate of freedom in Chesterfield County on 9 January 1809: *thirty five years old, yellow complexion, born free* [Register of Free Negroes 1804-53, no. 94]. He was taxable in Chesterfield County from 1797 to 1811, a "Mulatto" laborer living with his wife and six children on the land of Samuel Davis in 1811 [PPTL, 1786-1811, frames 305, 453, 530, 604, 642, 689, 738, 824].

vii. Pleasant, born about 1778, obtained a certificate of freedom in Chesterfield County on 8 October 1810: *thirty two years old, yellow complexion, born free* [Register of Free Negroes 1804-53, no. 142]. He was taxable in Chesterfield County from 1801 to 1811, a farmer living on John W. Gilly's land in 1809, living with his wife and child in 1811 [PPTL, 1786-1811, frames 453, 529, 604, 689, 738, 824] and a "Free Negrow of Colour" living on William Roulett's land in 1813 [Waldrep, *1813 Tax List*].

viii. Joshua[2], born about 1779, registered in Petersburg on 22 May 1802: *a light brown Mulatto man, five feet eight and a half inches high, twenty three years old, short knotty hair, has holes in his ears, born free and raised in the County of Chesterfield & now a resident of the sd. County. Renewed in 1809 - a shoemaker.* His wife Darkey registered on 21 December 1809: *a light brown Mulatto woman, wife of Joshua Steward, five feet three 3/4 inches high, twenty seven years old, born free & raised in Lancaster County* [Register of Free Negroes 1794-1819, nos. 223, 502]. He was taxable in Chesterfield County in 1801 [1801 PPTL A, p.13] and head of a Petersburg Town household of 6 "other free" in 1810 [VA:122a].

ix. William[5], born about 1779, registered in Petersburg on 8 September 1804: *a light brown Mulatto man, five feet seven and a half inches high, twenty five years old, born free and raised in the County of Chesterfield* [Register of Free Negroes 1794-1819, no. 284].

x. William[6]/ Billy, born about 1779, registered in Petersburg on 21 December 1809: *a yellow brown Mulatto man, five feet six inches high, thirty years old, born free and raised in the County of Chesterfield* [Register of Free Negroes 1794-1819, no. 519]. He was a "Free Negrow of Colour" living on William Roulett's land in Chesterfield County in 1813 [Waldrep, *1813 Tax List*].

xi. Lucy, born about 1784, obtained a certificate of freedom in Chesterfield County on 9 January 1809: *twenty five years old, yellow complexion, born free* [Register of Free Negroes 1804-53, no. 89].

xii. Jesse, born about 1789, obtained a certificate of freedom in Chesterfield County on 8 October 1810: *twenty one years old, yellow complexion, born free* [Register of Free Negroes 1804-53, no. 144].

xiii. John[10], born about 1791, obtained a certificate of freedom in Chesterfield County on 14 February 1814: *twenty three years old, bright yellow complexion, born free* [Register of Free Negroes 1804-53, no. 196]. He was head of a Chesterfield County household of 2 "other free" in 1810 [VA:70/1062].

10. William[1] Stewart, born say 1723, was called the "Moll. boy named William who formerly lived with William Standback" by William Eaton in 1725 when he petitioned the churchwardens of Bristol Parish to have William bound to him [Chamberlayne, *Bristol Parish Register*, 24]. On 13 March 1738/9 the churchwardens of Bristol Parish in Prince George County ordered William Stewart, a "Mulatto Boy" (no parent or age indicated), bound an apprentice to William Eaton [Orders 1737-40, 241]. He was a taxable head of household in Lunenburg County, Virginia, with Ephraim **Drew** in 1772 [Bell, *Sunlight on the Southside*, 299, 351]. He purchased 200 acres on the head branches of Little Creek in Mecklenburg County from Jacob **Chaves** on 8 March 1779 [DB 5:399]. He was head of a Mecklenburg County household of 6 free persons and 2 slaves in 1782 [VA:33] and was taxable in Mecklenburg County on slaves Edward and Charles, 6 cattle and 4 horses in 1782; taxable on Anselm Cunningham's tithe and a slave named Ned in 1784, called "William Stewart B. Smith" (blacksmith) in 1785 when he was taxable on slaves Bob and Charles. He was taxable on slave Ned from 1786 to 1788 but not taxable thereafter in Mecklenburg County [PPTL, 1782-1805, frames 12, 27, 85, 126,

223]. William (signing) and his wife Mary sold their 200 acres on Little Creek to James Steward, Sr., of Dinwiddie County, on 11 February 1788 [DB 7:253]. Mary may have been identical to "Mary Haris now Stuart" whose son Isham **Harris** was ordered bound out by the churchwardens of St. James Parish in Mecklenburg County court on 8 November 1766 [Orders 1765-8, 231]. Isham was head of a Wake County household of 7 "other free" in 1800 [NC:769]. William was head of a Wake County household of 11 "other free" in 1790 [NC:105] and 11 "other free" and 2 slaves in 1800 [NC:798]. He had undertaken to pay Thomas **Evans'** costs on 13 February 1786 when Jacob **Chavis** sued **Evans** in Mecklenburg County court, but William left the county without paying **Chavis**. On 13 September 1790 **Chavis** obtained an attachment against William's estate and recovered part of the debt from a number of persons including Henry **Chavis**, Henry **Chavis**, Jr., and James Stewart who testified that they owed William money [Orders 1784-87, 461; 1787-92, 536, 540]. William was residing in North Carolina on 11 July 1806 when Jacob **Chavis** of Mecklenburg County, Virginia, gave John **Chavis** power of attorney to recover a debt from him [Mecklenburg DB 13:1, 2]. Perhaps he was the father of

28   i.   William², born say 1745.
29   ii.   John⁴, born say 1761.
       iii.   Benjamin, born say 1769, a "Mulatto" taxable in Mecklenburg County in 1790 (adjacent to Moses Stewart) [PPTL, 1782-1805, frame 357].
       iv.   Prissey, born say 1777, married Frederick **Ivy**, 14 December 1795 Mecklenburg County bond, William Willis security.
       v.   John Ginnet, born say 1778, married Polley **Manning**, 9 December 1794 Mecklenburg County bond, Earbe **Chavous** security, with a note from Polly's mother Susanna **Chavous**. He may have been the John Stewart who obtained a certificate in Mecklenburg County from W. Birdett on 22 November 1809: *John Stewart, is a free man, and an Inhabitant of the County of Mecklenburg, he came down with my waggon, and not going home as he expected by the return of the waggon, has made application to me for this Certificate being fearful of molestation* [Free Person of Color, no.1, p.1].

11. Matt/ Matthew¹ Steward, born 6 January 1726, "Son of Eliza Stuard" (no race indicated), was living in Bristol Parish on 22 December 1750 when the birth of his son Charles **Toney** by Mary **Toney** was recorded [Chamberlayne, *Register of Bristol Parish*, 364, 369]. He may have been the Matthew Stewart who was a taxable head of a Lunenburg County household with Titus Stewart in 1772 and taxable with Titus and Francis Stewart in 1773 and 1774 [Bell, *Sunlight on the Southside*, 302, 313, 343]. He was taxable in Mecklenburg County on his own tithe and a horse in 1782 and 1783 [PPTL, 1782-1805, frames 11, 27]. He sued Abram Morris in Mecklenburg County court on 9 December 1783 for a debt of 7 pounds [Orders 1779-84, 483]. He may have been the father of

30   i.   Titus, born say 1753.
       ii.   Francis¹, born say 1756, taxable in Lunenburg County with Matthew and Titus Stewart in 1773 and 1774 [Bell, *Sunlight on the Southside*, 313, 343]. He was head of a Mecklenburg County, Virginia household of two persons in 1782 [VA:33] and taxable there from 1783 to 1785 [PPTL, 1782-1805, frames 77, 90, 101]. He was taxable on 157 acres in the lower district of Mecklenburg County in 1787 and 1788 but taxable on no land in 1789 [Land Tax List 1782-1811A, B list].

12. Mary Stewart, born 19 September 1732, was the "Mullatto girl of Elizabeth Stuart" who was baptized in Bristol Parish, Virginia, on 4 February 1733 [Chamberlayne, *Bristol Parish Register*, 366]. She died before December 1778 court in Northampton County, North Carolina, when her 13 September 1778

will was proved. Arthur Williams and William Stuart were named executors. She left ten shillings to her daughter Rebecca, made a bequest of six pounds to Sarah **Mitchell**, and divided the remainder of her estate among her children when they came of age: Deme, Tempta, James, Thomas, and Bitha [WB 1:309]. Her children were

    i.   Rebecca[2], born say 1756.

31   ii. Deme (Dempsey), born say 1758.

   iii. Tempta.

   iv. James[4], born say 1761.

    v. Thomas[5], born say 1770, bound by the Greensville County court as an apprentice to Thomas Stewart on 26 October 1786 [Orders 1781-9, 294]. He was taxable in Greensville County in 1795 [PPTL 1782-1850, frame 192].

   vi. Bitha, perhaps the Tabitha Stewart who was head of a Mecklenburg County, Virginia household of 7 "free colored" in 1820.

13. Martha Stewart, born 30 October 1741, the daughter of Elizabeth Stewart (no race indicated), was baptized in Bristol Parish, Virginia, on 4 July 1742 [Chamberlayne, *Bristol Parish Register*, 368]. She may have been the ancestor of

    i.   Jane, born about 1757, registered in Petersburg on 24 January 1803: *a brown Mulatto woman, five feet three inches high, forty six years old, born free & raised in the County of Prince George* [Register of Free Negroes 1794-1819, no. 246].

    ii. Arey, born about 1765, registered in Petersburg on 19 August 1794: *a dark brown Mulatto woman, five feet high, twenty nine years old, born free & raised in the County of Prince George* [Register of Free Negroes 1794-1819, no. 63].

   iii. Nancy, born about 1765, registered in Petersburg on 12 September 1805: *a dark brown, rather black free Negro woman, five feet four inches high, forty years old, short black hair, born free & raised in the County of Prince George* [Register of Free Negroes 1794-1819, no. 362].

   iv. Frank, born about 1771, registered in Petersburg on 18 August 1794: *a dark Mulatto man, five feet eight & a half inches high, twenty three years old, born free & raised in the town of Brandford, Prince George County* [Register of Free Negroes 1794-1819, no. 29].

    v. David, born about 1771, registered in Petersburg on 24 August 1796: *a black Mulatto man, five feet ten inches high, large lips & bushy head of hair, twenty five, born free in County of Prince George* [Register of Free Negroes 1794-1819, no. 113].

   vi. Betsy, born about 1786, registered in Petersburg on 9 July 1805: *a dark brown Mulatto woman, five feet inches high, nineteen years old, holes in her ears, born free & raised in the County of Prince George* [Register of Free Negroes 1794-1819, no. 314].

14. Thomas[2] Stewart, born about 1742 in Mecklenburg County, Virginia, enlisted in Captain Dawson's Company in Lunenburg County under General Gibson and was at Valley Forge and Guilford Courthouse. He may have been the Thomas Stewart who had an illegitimate child named Tempy by Keziah Matthews before 14 June 1784 [Orders 1784-87, 51,]. He was taxable in Mecklenburg County in 1790 (with the initials "B.S." after his name) [PPTL, 1782-1805, frame 330]. He and his wife Sarah were married by James Yancey of Granville County, North Carolina, in the fall of the year 1791 [M805-772, frame 69]. He was called "Thomas Stewart a Dark Man" by the 17 September 1792 Person County court when the court exempted him from payment of poll tax [Minutes 1792-6]. He was head of a Person County household of 7 "other free" in 1800 [NC:598] and 11 in 1810 [NC:632]. His 30 January 1818 Person

County will, proved in May 1818, named his wife Sarah and children: Nathaniel, Mavel **Sheppard**, Nancy, Joseph, John, David, and Thomas [WB 8:77]. He died on 15 February 1818 leaving seven children. His wife Sarah Stewart, formerly Sarah Drummond, born about 1769, was living in Person County on 4 March 1843 when she received a pension for his services [M805-772, frame 69]. Their children were

   i. Nathaniel[2], head of a Person County household of 7 "free colored" in 1820 [NC:498].

   ii. Mavel, married Byrd **Shepherd**, 20 April 1815 Person County bond.

   iii. Nancy Stewart.

   iv. Joseph[3], born say 1792.

   v. John[11], born say 1795.

   vi. David.

   vii. Thomas[9], perhaps the Thomas Stewart, born about 1804, who obtained "free papers" in Halifax County, Virginia, on 29 November 1831, and registered them in Ross County, Ohio: *a man of color, aged about 27 years, 5 ft 9 1/4 in., was born free* [Turpin, *Register of Black, Mulatto, and Poor Persons*, 34].

15. Nelly[1] Stewart, born say 1760, was called "Eleanor Steward orphan of John Stewart, deceased," on 14 February 1765 when the Lunenburg County court ordered the churchwardens of Cumberland Parish to bind her to William Taylor [Orders 1764-5, 205]. She was living in Mecklenburg County, Virginia, in September 1772 when the court ordered her bound to Molly Taylor, and on 8 July 1782 she was called Milley Steward when the court ordered her children Elizabeth and Bartley Steward bound to Robert Taylor. She was called Nelly Stewart on 12 June 1786 and 8 February 1790 when the court ordered her bastard children Betsy and Bartlett Stewart bound out by the overseers of the poor [Orders 1771-3, 318; 1779-84, 176; 1787-92, 470, 511, 524]. Nelly was head of a Warren County, North Carolina household of 7 "other free" in 1810 [NC:756]. Her children were

   i. ?Matthew, born say 1776, son of Thomas **Evans**, bound out by the Mecklenburg County court to Charles **Evans** on 10 March 1789 [Orders 1787-92, 363]. He was probably identical to twelve-year-old Matthew Stewart, "orphan of Matthew Stewart," who was bound out by the Warren County court to John Moseley on 27 February 1788 [Minutes 1787-93, 39; WB 5:6]. He married Siller **Walden**, 25 February 1799 Mecklenburg County bond, William **Chandler** security.

   ii. Betsy, born say 1780, bastard of Nelly Stewart bound out on 8 July 1782 and bound to Martha Coleman in Mecklenburg County on 12 June 1786 [Orders 1779-84, 176; 1787-92, 524]. She was head of a Mecklenburg County household of 7 "free colored" in 1820.

   iii. Bartlett, born say 1782, bound out to Robert Taylor in Mecklenburg County on 8 July 1782, bound out again on 8 February 1790, and bound to John White on 9 October 1797 [Orders 1779-84, 176; 1787-92, 470; 1795-8]. He married Elizabeth **Drew**, 21 October 1807 Mecklenburg County, Virginia bond, George **Guy** security. He was taxable on 100 acres and 1 poll in Nutbush District of Warren County in 1815 [Tax List Papers, Vols TC 8, 1795-1815].

   iv. Mahalah, "bastard of Nelley Stewart," ordered bound out by the overseers of the poor on 12 July 1790 [Orders 1787-92, 511].

16. Moses[1] Stewart, born 18 November 1766 according to his mother's will, purchased 100 acres in Mecklenburg County, Virginia, on the south side of Allen's Creek adjoining Stephen Mallett from Henry Jackson on 27 April 1777, Stephen and Zachariah Mallett witnesses [DB 5:56]. Since he was only ten years old at the time, his mother probably purchased the land in his name. He was taxable on a 16-21 year old tithe, 3 horses, and 8 cattle in

Mecklenburg County from 1787 to 1798 [PPTL, 1782-1805, frames 202, 304, 486, 698]. He married Polly **Walden**, 20 December 1788 Mecklenburg County bond, and moved to Randolph County, North Carolina, near his wife's family. He was head of a Randolph County household of 10 "other free" in 1800 [NC:341] and 11 in 1810 [NC:65]. He obtained a certificate of freedom in Randolph County on 20 November 1829 for himself and his son Shadrack Stuart, "a man of colour," which stated that Moses had been known as free in Randolph County for over thirty years and wished to move to Indiana or Illinois. He was described as a "large mulatto man" when he recorded the certificate in Madison County, Illinois, on 17 October 1838, and testified that his family consisted of his seventy-year-old "mulatto" wife Mary, thirty-seven-year-old daughter Winnie (wife of Turner Stewart), and thirty-nine-year-old daughter Queentina (wife of George Barton) [Madison County Emancipation Register 1830-60, 17, 29-30]. His grandson Dalton Stewart applied for Cherokee benefits (rejected) in 1908 and named Moses Stewart's children: Griffin, Shadrick, George, Allen, Machack, Walden, Quiny, Darcus, Winnie, Clara, and Mary [Jordan, *Cherokee by Blood*, III:42-3]. Moses was the father of

i. Griffin[2].
ii. Shadrack.
iii. George.
iv. Allen.
v. Meshack.
vi. Walden, born 24 January 1795 in Mecklenburg County, Virginia, according to his son Dalton. He was head of a Rockingham County, North Carolina household of 3 "other free" in 1830.
vii. Queentina, born about 1799, married George **Barton** in Madison County, Illinois, on 9 March 1831 [Marriage Register 6:21, license #21; Emancipation Register 1830-60, 39].
viii. Darcus.
ix. Winnie, born about 1801, called Winny **Chavers** when she married Turner **Stewart** on 1 October 1834 in Madison County, Illinois [Madison County marriage license no. 117; Emancipation Register 1830-60, 19, 21, 23].
x. Clara.
xi. Mary.

17. Thomas[3] Stewart, born say 1743, son of Rebecca Stewart, was ordered bound by the churchwardens of Albemarle Parish in Surry County, Virginia, on 17 July 1750 [Orders 1749-51, 110]. He sued Chisland and Henry Morris in Brunswick County, Virginia court for trespass, assault and battery on 25 July 1769, and he sued Joseph Wright for debt on 24 November 1783 [Orders 1768-72, 125; 1760-84, 289]. He purchased 114 acres on the southside of Meherrin Branch in Brunswick County for 75 pounds in January 1778 [DB 13:28]. He won a case against Robert Hicks for a debt of 100 pounds in Brunswick County court on 26 April 1785 and sued several other persons for debt on 23 March 1786, 26 March 1787, and on 28 July 1788. On 22 September 1788 James Crook acknowledged a Brunswick County deed of trust to satisfy a debt he owed Thomas Stewart [Orders 1784-8, 130, 265, 344, 436, 448; 1788-92, 41, 74, 81]. He was taxable in Meherrin Parish, Greensville County, from 1782 to 1790: taxable on 6 horses and 12 cattle in 1782, 6 slaves in 1786, 5 in 1787, 3 slaves and 5 horses in 1790 [PPTL 1782-1850, frames 3, 21, 28, 46, 68, 87]. On 29 May 1782 the Greensville County court credited him for 325 pounds of beef and 4 bushels of oats which was impressed during the war, and on 26 October 1786 the court ordered the overseers of the poor to bind Henry and Thomas Stewart to him [Orders 1781-9, 29, 294]. His 14 October 1790 Greensville County will was proved 24 February 1791. He left his land and his two slaves Solomon and Anaky to his

wife Crecy and allowed 5 pounds a year for the maintenance of his unnamed mother. He directed that his slaves be treated well and freed after six years and that his children receive schooling. He named his children: Rebecca, Henry, Sally, Peyton, and Nancy. His sons Henry (who was under twenty-one years of age) and Peyton were to divide his land between them after his wife's death. He left 10 pounds to Aaron **Newsom**. He left a fairly large estate of 437 pounds, excluding his land. His estate record indicates that he died from drowning and that a total of 88 pounds cash was found in his house and pockets. Dempsey and Francis Stewart were renting part of his land in 1792 [WB 1:181-3, 262]. On 22 September 1791 his wife Lucretia Stewart renounced all benefit from the will and petitioned the Greensville County court to lay out and assign her dower land. On 23 October 1794 the court appointed Peyton Harwell guardian to Sally, Henry, Peyton and Nancy Stewart, orphans of Thomas Stewart, and on 28 November 1795 Lucretia returned an account of their estates. She sued William Vincent for trespass on 24 March 1796 and was awarded 10 pounds. On 27 November 1798 one of Vincent's slaves named Phebe was accused of stealing Lucretia's shoats, but the case was dismissed when Phebe's counsel argued "the want of due form and regularity in the warrant" [Orders 1790-9, 97, 241, 299, 316, 411, 455, 520, 539, 549, 582]. Lucretia was taxable in Greensville County from 1791 to 1802: taxable on William Stewart's tithe and 3 slaves in 1791, taxable on 2 slaves from 1794 to 1797, taxable on a slave and 2 horses from 1798 to 1802 [PPTL 1782-1850, frames 129, 141, 164, 181]. She sold 100 acres in Greensville County to (their daughter?) Rebecca Stewart on 23 May 1799. She married Asa **Byrd** before 10 October 1806 when she and her children Henry and Peyton Stewart sold 114 acres in Greensville County which they had received by their father's will [DB 2:552; 3:520]. Lucretia died shortly before 16 January 1808 when Asa **Byrd** was examined in court but found not guilty of having murdered her [Orders 1799-1806, 204]. On 13 March 1809 the court divided 244 acres of Lucretia's land among her heirs: 50 acres to Viney G. Stewart, 57 acres to Rebecca **Dimmery**, 22 acres to Nancy **Banks**, 55 acres to Henry Stewart, 30 acres to Peyton Stewart and 30 acres to Sally **Watkins**. On 11 September 1809 Lucretia's last will was presented in court but set aside since it was revoked by her intermarriage with Asa **Byrd** [Orders 1806-10, 279, 340, 398; DB 4:117]. Thomas's emancipated slave Solomon Scott registered in Greensville County on 12 March 1807: *Set free by the last Will of Thomas Stewart, Decd., Dark complexion, aged thirty two years* [Register of Free Negroes, no. 18]. Thomas and Lucretia's children were

   i.   Rebecca[4], born say 1778, orphan of Thomas Stewart, chose Francis Stewart as her guardian in Greensville County court on 28 February 1792 [Orders 1790-9, 178]. She purchased 100 acres in Greensville County from (her mother) Lucretia Stewart on 23 May 1799 [DB 2:552]. She mortgaged 100 acres in Brunswick County (bounded on the west by Barney Stewart, on the south by Nanny **Pompey** and on the north by Daniel Hammmons) to William Stewart on 12 April 1800 for 30 pounds to secure a debt of 20 pounds she owed him [DB 18:36]. She married John **Demery**, 10 February 1806 Greensville County bond, Frederick Shelton surety. She and her husband were living in Northampton County, North Carolina, on 8 November 1806 when they sold 91 acres in Greensville County to (her brother) Henry Stewart with Benjamin Gowing as witness [DB 3:523].

  ii. Viney G., received 50 acres by the distribution of her mother Lucretia **Byrd**'s estate on 13 March 1809 [Orders 1799-1806, 340]. Asa **Byrd** made a deed of gift to her which was proved in Greensville County court on 9 May 1808 [Orders 1806-10, 231].

 iii. Henry[1], born about 1781, taxable in Greensville County from 1802 to 1820: listed as a "Mulatto" with his unnamed wife in 1813 [PPTL 1782-1850, frames 289, 325, 449, 465, 488, 609]. He registered as a

"Free Negro" in Greensville County on 7 October 1805: *born free of a darkish complexion...aged about 24 years. 5 feet 7-3/4 Inc. high* [Free Negro Register, no.3]. His wife was Celia Stewart who registered in Greensville County on 26 August 1824: *a free Woman of Colour & the wife of Henry Stewart, of a black Complexion supposed to be about 33 years old, 5'4 inches high...by occupation a Spinstress* [Free Negro Register, no. 109]. He and his wife Celia, Peyton Stewart and their mother Lucretia **Byrd** sold 114 acres in Greensville County which their father Thomas Stewart left them by his will. On 20 December 1804 he purchased from Nancy **Jones** all her rights to the Greensville County estate of Jesse **Jones**, with Rebecca Stewart as witness [DB 3:412]. On 14 January 1805 he provided security for the payment of 10 pounds per year for seven years to maintain Lindsey Stewart, an illegitimate child Joseph **Holley** (**Hawley**) begot by Jane Stewart. In exchange, **Holley** bound himself to serve Henry for seven years. On 10 February 1806 Henry complained to the court that Joseph had left his service and was living with his father Jacob **Holley**. The court ordered Joseph to return to Henry's service, serve four months for absenting himself, and then serve until the illegitimate child was bound out by the overseers of the poor [Orders 1799-1806, 540, 541; DB 3:402]. He purchased 53 acres in Greensville County from David Haithcock for 53 pounds on 16 January 1807 [DB 3:412, 520; 4:49]. On 12 January 1807 he sued Peyton Stewart on an attachment and the court granted him a commission to take the deposition of Rebecca Stewart who was about to move out of the state. Asa and Lurcetia **Byrd** were Peyton's witnesses in the suit [Orders 1806-10, 71-2]. He was head of a Greensville County household of 6 "free colored" in 1820 [VA:265].

iv. Sally, born say 1782, married James **Watkins** by 8 May 1809 when they sold 30 acres on the south side of Fountain Creek and both sides of Jordan's Road in Greensville County. This was their allotment of the estate of Lucretia **Byrd**, widow of Thomas Stewart [DB 4:117]

v. Peyton[3], born about 1784, registered as a "Free Negro" in Greensville County on 25 January 1805: *born free of a darkish complexion, aged Twenty one or upwards, is about five feet nine Inches high...*[Free Negro Register, no.2]. He married ____, 12 May 1806 Greensville County bond. Asa **Byrd** gave his consent for the bride and was security. Peyton and his wife Vicey, his brother Henry Stewart, and his mother sold 114 acres in Greensville County on 10 October 1806 which was land they received by their father's will. On 18 September 1806 he sold Asa **Byrd** a crop of corn and peas, a bed, furniture, and two hogs in Greensville County for 16 pounds. He was taxable in Greensville County in 1804 and 1805 [PPTL 1782-1850, frames 317, 333]. On 13 October 1806 his mother Lucretia **Byrd** (formerly Stewart) came into court and made oath that her son Peyton Stewart was 21 years of age on the day of October 1806 to the best of her knowledge [Orders 1806-10, 44]. He was living in Sumner County, Tennessee on 12 December 1807 when he sold 30 acres on Jordan's Road in Greensville County to Anthony **Banks**. This was land he received at the death of his mother Lucretia [DB 3:511, 520; 4:282].

vi. Nancy, born say 1789, chose John Robinson as her guardian in Greensville County court on 13 February 1804 [Orders 1799-1806, 366]. She married Anthony **Banks** "of Sussex County" before 8 May 1809 when they were identified as heirs of Lucretia **Byrd** in a deed by which 244 acres of her land was divided among her heirs. Anthony and Sally purchased 30 acres on the south side of Fountain Creek which was James and Sally **Watkins**' part of the estate [DB 4:117].

18. John[2]/ Jack Stewart, born say 1745, may have been identical to Jack Stewart, a "mulatto," who was listed among seven deserters, drafted out of Prince George County, for whom a reward was offered in the 28 November 1777 issue of the *Virginia Gazette* [Purdie edition, p. 3, col. 3]. He was a "Mulatto" taxable in Chesterfield County on a tithe and three horses from 1788 to 1807 [PPTL, 1786-1811, frames 73, 91, 148, 166, 206, 253, 286, 360, 508, 545, 585, 622, 717]. He was a "Mulattoe" taxable on 79-1/4 acres in 1809, 61-1/4 acres in 1811, and 52 acres in 1815. He transferred 9 acres to Ezekiel Stewart in 1814 [Land Tax List 1791-1822, B lists]. He was probably the father of

   i.   Ezekiel, born about 1785, obtained a certificate of freedom in Chesterfield County on 8 August 1814: *twenty nine years old, light brown complexion, born free* [Register of Free Negroes 1804-53, no. 223]. He was head of a Petersburg Town household of 3 "other free" in 1810 [VA:123a] and taxable in Chesterfield County from 1814 to 1816 on 9 acres which had been transferred to him by John Stewart in 1814 and taxable on 57 acres from 1820 to 1822 [Land Tax List 1791-1822, B lists].

19. Peter[2] Stewart, born say 1748, son of Rebecca Stewart of Brunswick County, may have been the Peter Stewart (born about 1751) who obtained a certificate of freedom in Chesterfield County on 13 October 1807: *fifty five years old, bright mulatto complexion, born free* [Register of Free Negroes 1804-53, no. 39]. He was taxable in Chesterfield County on a tithe and a horse from 1791 to 1802, 2 tithes and 2-3 horses from 1803 to 1810, and living on Roger Atkinson's land from 1809 to 1811 when he had 8 persons in his family [PPTL, 1786-1811, frames 91, 125, 165, 205, 262, 305, 343, 529, 566, 605, 689, 782, 824]. He died in 1827 and left a will which divided his property among his children Peter, Archibald, John, Jane (wife of William **Harris**), Berry and Joseph and his grandchildren Nancy, Polly (wife of Silas **Hill**) and James Stewart. In 1831 his estate was distributed to the legatees after they brought a Chesterfield County suit in chancery against the administrator of the estate, sheriff William Fendley [LVA chancery suit 1831-035]. His children were

   i.   Peter, born say 1775. He may have been the Peter Stewart who was head of a Dinwiddie County household of 3 "other free" in 1810 [VA:161].

   ii.   Archibald, born say 1777.

   iii. Peggy, not named in her father's will but named in the 21 September 1801 Chesterfield County will of Thomas Stewart by which he left all his estate to his wife Peggy and appointed her and her father Peter Stewart his executors [WB 5:491-2].

   iv.   John[7], born about 1779, registered in Petersburg on 21 December 1809: *a light Coloured free Mulatto man, with grey eyes, five feet six inches high, thirty years old, a Blacksmith, born free in Chesterfield County & raised in the Town of Petersburg* [Register of Free Negroes 1794-1819, no. 504]. He was head of a Petersburg Town household of 5 "other free" in 1810 [VA:122a].

   v.   Jane, wife of William **Harris**. William registered in Petersburg on 24 June 1805: *a brown Mulatto man, five feet five inches high, twenty two years old, born free in Chesterfield County* [Register of Free Negroes 1794-1819, no. 293].

   vi.   Berry, born about 1781, taxable in Chesterfield County from 1802 to 1805 [PPTL, 1786-1811, frames 492, 530, 566, 605]. He died unmarried before 1831 when his father's estate was distributed among the heirs. Administration on his estate was granted to James Britton by order of the Hustings Court of Petersburg.

   vii. Joseph, born about 1786, a laborer taxable in Chesterfield County in 1811 [PPTL, 1786-1811, frame 824]. He obtained a certificate of freedom in Chesterfield County on 8 October 1810: *twenty four years old, yellow complexion, born free* [Register of Free Negroes 1804-53, no. 143]. He died intestate before 1831 leaving a widow Dolly Stewart and infant children Lizzy and Anderson.

20. James² Stewart, born say 1750, was living in Brunswick County, Virginia, on 11 January 1774 when he and Littleberry **Pompey** of Sussex County purchased 270 acres in Meherrin Parish, to be equally divided between them as if two separate deeds had been made. He purchased 50 acres on the north side of the Maherrin River in Brunswick County adjoining Richard Branscomb and Thomas Evans on 23 November 1778 [DB 11:251-3; 13:280]. He was taxable in Meherrin Parish, Brunswick County, from 1782 to 1796 [PPTL 1782-98, frames 19, 206, 271, 325, 401, 497, 543]. On 26 January 1778 he and Littleberry **Pompey** and wife Nanny **Pompey** (James's sister?) sold 135 acres in Meherrin Parish, Brunswick County, adjoining Steward's Branch. And on 15 August 1792 James and his wife Sarah sold for 50 pounds 137 acres on Buckwater Creek in Meherrin Parish, Brunswick County, adjoining Dempsey Stewart's land [DB 13:45; 15:498]. He may have been the James Stewart who married Sally **Evans**, 2 May 1791 Warren County, North Carolina bond, Eaton **Walden** bondsman. He was head of a Wake County household of 6 "other free" in 1800 [NC:798]. By his Wake County will, proved in November 1824, he left his land to his children: Evans, Beedy (married James **Walden**), Mackey (married Joel Stuart), Tazewell, Dickson, Elijah, and Elisha [WB 19:130]. His children were
    i.   Evans, married Milly Stuart, 15 November 1817 Wake County bond, Joel Stuart bondsman.
    ii.   Beedy, married James **Walden**.
    iii. Mackey, married Joel Stuart, 2 January 1821 Wake County bond.
    iv.   Tazewell.
    v.   Dickson.
    vi.   Elijah.
    vii. Elisha.

21. Barnett¹ Stewart, born say 1760, was taxable in Meherrin Parish, Brunswick County, Virginia, from 1782 to 1792: taxable on 2 horses and 2 cattle from 1782 to 1796, taxable on a free tithe and a slave in 1799, taxable on 2 free tithes and a slave in 1801, 2 free tithes from 1803 to 1805, 1 in 1806 [PPTL 1782-1798, frames 19, 206, 271, 364, 437, 592; 1799-1815, frames 43, 92, 259, 349, 394, 439]. On 23 September 1784 a Greensville County jury awarded him 5 pounds in his suit for trespass against Hayley Dupree. John Chapman and John Robinson were his witnesses [Orders 1781-9, 36, 138, 163]. He owned land on the south bank of the Meherrin River near Buckwater Run in Brunswick County before 4 January 1787 [DB 14:321]. He may have been the brother of Thomas Stewart of Greensville County since he gave his consent for the 12 May 1806 Greensville County marriage bond of Thomas' son Peyton Stewart. He and his wife Lucy sold 200 acres on the Meherrin River in Brunswick County to Benjamin Wyche for $800 on 5 August 1806. (Lucy signed her name to the deed) [DB 19:484]. Francis Sterling was awarded a judgment against him for $25 in Greensville County court on 12 November 1805. He filed a motion for an injunction against Sterling for which Francis Stewart was required to post security on 8 February 1808 since Barnett was not an inhabitant of the state. The case was decided in Barnett's favor on 17 November 1809 [Orders 1799-1806, 520, 532, 1806-10, 201, 207, 311-2]. Perhaps he was identical to Barnabus Stewart, head of a Chatham County, North Carolina household of 5 "other free" in 1810 [NC:200]. He left a 1 March 1832 Sumner County, Tennessee will, proved March 1840, which named his wife Lucy and children: Sally, Mumfre, Naney, Virey, Peterson, Barnet, Woody, Patsy, and Dollison. He directed that his land be sold after his

wife's death and that his son Peterson receive one hundred dollars [WO:315].
His children were

 i. Sally.

 ii. Mumfort, born about 1783, registered as a "Free Negro" in Brunswick County on 3 October 1805: *a black man about 22 years of age about 5 feet 11 1/2 Inches high rather slender made...free born and has been raised in the County* [Wynne, *Register of Free Negroes*, 4]. He was taxable on a horse in Meherrin Parish, Brunswick County, in 1806 [PPTL 1799-1815, frame 394].

 iii. Naney.

 iv. Virey.

 v. Peterson.

 vi. Barney/ Barnett[2], born say 1785, registered as a "Free Negro" in Brunswick County on 2 October 1806: *a tall black man...has a very droning speech when he talks, he is free born as I have always understood and verily believe as he has lived in the county for a number of years* [Wynne, *Register of Free Negroes*, 6]. He was probably the Barnes Stewart who was head of a Northampton County household of 7 "free colored" in 1820 [NC:260].

 vii. Woody.

 viii. Patsy.

 ix. Dollison.

22. William[4] Stewart, born say 1761, purchased 100 acres in Brunswick County, Virginia, adjoining James Steward, William Fergason, Branscom and Thomas Evans on 23 September 1778 [DB 13:281]. He was taxable in Meherrin Parish, Brunswick County, from 1782 to 1815: taxable on a slave and 3 horses in 1797 and 1798, taxable on 2 persons from 1806 to 1809, taxable on 3 "persons of colour" in 1810 and 1811, listed as a "Free Negro" from 1813 to 1815 [PPTL 1782-98, frames 20, 54, 166, 206, 237, 271, 325, 364, 401, 437, 448, 543, 592, 642; 1799-1815, frames 43, 92, 139, 197, 259, 295, 349, 394, 439, 478, 520, 559, 637, 675, 733]. He married Kissey **Corn**, undated Mecklenburg County bond, Robert **Corn** security.[194] Rebecca Stewart mortgaged 100 acres to him in Brunswick County adjoining Barney Stewart, Nanny **Pompey** and Daniel Hammons for 30 pounds on 12 April 1800. He and his wife Keziah sold 100 acres adjoining Barney Stewart, Nanny **Pompey** and Richard Harrison for $300 on 6 September 1805 [DB 18:36; 19:322]. He was head of a Free Town, Brunswick County household of 10 "other free" in 1810 [VA:770], 9 "free colored" in 1820 [VA:670] and 9 in 1830 [VA:249]. He died before 15 February 1839 when his Brunswick County estate was appraised [WB 14:384]. His children can be identified from the deeds by which they sold the land they received from his estate. They were

 i. John[9], born about 1787, head of a Brunswick County household of 6 "free colored" in 1820 [VA:670], 11 in 1830 [VA:249], and 12 in 1840. He registered as a "Free Negro" in Brunswick County on 23 November 1813: *a black of a yellow complexion five feet nine or ten inches high about Twenty five or six years old...has a stoppage in his Speech when spoken to, his hair rather inclined to be Straight was freeborn in this county* [Wynne, *Register of Free Negroes*, 18]. Dempsey Stewart left him land by his 11 December 1848 Brunswick County will [WB 15:231]. John's Brunswick County estate was appraised on 5 January 1860 and included 144 acres he had from Dempsey, land he inherited from his father, as well as land he had purchased in 1835 [WB 18:96-7].

---

[194]William Stewart's marriage to Kissy **Corn** probably took place prior to 1790 when Robert **Corn** moved to Wake County where he was head of a household of 3 "other free" [NC:106].

ii. William⁷, born about 1793, head of a Brunswick County household of 1 "free colored" in 1820, called Wm B. [VA:670], registered on 28 August 1823: *a free man of black complexion six feet & an half Inch high about thirty Years of age...born free as appears from the evidence of Phil Claiborne and by Occupation a carpenter* [Wynne, *Register of Free Negroes*, 67]. He was living in Greene County, Ohio, on 2 January 1840 when he sold his interest in his father's Brunswick County estate [DB 32:72].

iii. Rebecca⁵, born about 1794, registered on 23 September 1839: *a free person of color yellow complexion about forty five years of age five feet six Inches high...born free as appears from the evidence of George Stone* [Wynne, *Register*, 152]. On 4 March 1840 she sold 37 acres of land in Brunswick County which she had received from her father's estate [DB 32:75].

iv. Julius, born about 1798, head of a Brunswick County household of 1 "free colored" in 1820 [VA:670], registered in May 1837: *a free man of Color Dark complexion five feet eleven Inches and three quarters high, thirty nine years of age... born free as appears from the Evidence of R H H Wallton* [Wynne, *Register*, 139].

v. Jincey, born about 1802, registered on 24 February 1840: *a free woman of color Dark complexion about 38 years of age five feet three Inches high...born free as appears from the evidence of F. W. Green* [Wynne, *Register*, 154]. On 29 November 1841 she sold 40 acres of her father's Brunswick County land to her brother Julius Stewart [DB 32:297].

vi. Littleton, born about 1804, head of a Brunswick County household of 5 "free colored" in 1830 [VA:249] and 6 in 1840, registered on 24 February 1840: *a free person of color Dark complexion about thirty six years of age six feet two Inches high...born free as appears from the evidence of F. W. Green* [Wynne, *Register*, 154]. On 2 February 1839 he executed a Brunswick County deed of trust for the land he inherited from his father [DB 31:509].

vii. Wyatt, born about 1807, registered on 22 September 1828: *a free man of colour, dark complexion, five feet nine & a half inches high twenty one years Old...was born free as appears by the evidence of John Wyche & R.H.H. Wallton & by occupation a ditcher* [Wynne, *Register*, 100]. He was living in Ohio when he sold his part of his father's land to his brother Julius [DB 33:53].

viii. Thomas¹⁰, born about 1809, registered on 23 May 1836: *a free man of Colour dark complexion twenty seven years old six feet high...born free...from the evidence of R H H Wallton* [Wynne, *Register*, 135]. He was living in Ohio in 1842 when he sold his part of his father's land by Brunswick County deed [DB 32:335].

23. Henry Stewart, born say 1785, was taxable in Charles City County from 1805 to 1813, listed as a "Mulattoe" in 1813 [PPTL 1788-1814]. He died before 16 April 1835 when the Charles County court ordered the overseers of the poor to bind out his orphans Peter and William Steward to Micajah **Brown** until the age of twenty-one [Minutes 1830-7, 231]. His widow Maria Stewart registered with four of their children in Henrico County on 5 February 1838: *wife of Henry Stuart, about 51 years of age, a bright mulatto woman, 5 feet 3 inches, Born free as appears by a certificate from the clerk of Charles City County* [Register of Free Negroes and Mulattoes, 1831-1844, p.28, no.871]. They were the parents of

i. Thomas, born 22 October 1816, registered in Charles City County on 18 June 1835: *son of Henry Steward, brown complexion, age 18 the 22 October 1834* [Minutes 1830-7, 237]. He registered in Henrico County on 5 February 1838: *age about 22 years, son of Henry Steward, a man of brown complexion, 5 feet 8-1/4 inches, born free as appears by a certificate from the clerk of Charles City County* [Register of Free Negroes and Mulattoes, 1831-1844, p.28, no.870].

ii. Isaiah, born 30 December 1814, registered in Charles City County on 18 June 1835: *son of Henry Steward, brown complexion, age 20 the 30 December 1834* [Minutes 1830-7, 237].

iii. John, born 12 October 1818, registered in Charles City County on 18 June 1835: *son of Henry Steward, brown complexion, age 16 the 12 October 1834* [Minutes 1830-7, 237].

iv. Peter, born 12 December 1820, registered in Charles City County on 18 June 1835: *son of Henry Steward, bright mulatto, age 14 the 12 December 1834* [Minutes 1830-7, 237]. He registered in Henrico County on 5 February 1838: *age 17 years the 12 December 1837, a mulatto man, 5 feet 4 inches, born free as appears by a certificate from the clerk of Charles City County* [Register of Free Negroes and Mulattoes, 1831-1844, p.28, no. 869].

v.   Lockey, born 22 March 1822, registered in Charles City County on 18 June 1835: *daughter of Henry Steward, bright mulatto girl, age 13 the 22 March 1835* [Minutes 1830-7, 237]. She registered in Henrico County on 5 February 1838: *about 14 years of age, a girl of light complexion, 5 feet 1/2 inch, born free as appears by the evidence of James Binford* [Register of Free Negroes and Mulattoes, 1831-1844, p.28, no. 871].

vi. William, born 29 September 1824, registered in Charles City County on 18 June 1835: *son of Henry Steward, bright complexion, age 10 the 19 September 1834* [Minutes 1830-7, 237]. He registered in Henrico County on 5 February 1838: *about 13 years of age, a boy of very light complexion, 4 feet 8 inches, born free as appears by the evidence of James Binford* [Register of Free Negroes and Mulattoes, 1831-1844, p.28, no.873].

24. James[3] Stewart, born say 1757, was taxable in Dinwiddie County on a horse and 3 cattle in 1782, taxable on a horse in 1787, and taxable on a horse in 1788 when he was listed the same day as (his father) Dr. Thomas Stewart [PPTL, 1782-90 (1787B, p.13)]. He married Ryte **Chavous**, 11 February 1788 Mecklenburg County bond, James Stewart, Sr., security.[195] He received a deed of gift of 150 acres in Mecklenburg County from his father Thomas Stewart on 5 December 1792. On 14 April 1793 the Mecklenburg County court granted him a license to keep an ordinary at his house [Orders 1792-5, 430]. He, called James Stewart, Junr., and his wife Ritter Stewart (both signing) sold 50 acres of land adjoining Durham, Munford, and Doctor Thomas Stewart to William Stewart on 12 September 1796, and they sold the remaining 100 acres where they were then living on 10 November 1796 to Benjamin Edmundson for 5 shillings [DB 8:306; 9:153, 164]. He was a "mulatto" insolvent taxpayer in Mecklenburg County in 1789, taxable on himself and a horse [*Virginia Genealogist* 22:49]. He was "B. Smith" (blacksmith) taxable on a slave named Winny in 1795, called James Stewart, Jun., in 1796 when he was taxable on his son Thomas and an ordinary license. He was living in the lower district of Mecklenburg County when he was taxable on his own tithe and an ordinary license in 1798 and taxable on slave Peter in 1799 but was not taxable thereafter in Mecklenburg County [PPTL, 1782-1805, frames 558, 622, 698, 779]. He was taxable in Lunenburg County from 1802 to 1805, taxable on a slave in 1804 [PPTL 1782-1806]. He was a blacksmith living on Beaver Pond, counted in a "List of all free Negroes &

---

[195]Ryte **Chavous** may have been identical to Kitty **Chavous** who married James Steward, 16 February 1788 Brunswick County bond.

Mulattoes in the lower District of Lunenburg County" in March 1802 and April 1803 with his wife Ritter and children: Drury, Nelly, Aggy, Henry, Jordan, and Rebecca and Allen **Norton** [Lunenburg County Free Negro & Slave Records, 1802-1803, p.1]. He may have been the James Stewart who was a "Free Black" head of a Bedford County household of 9 "other free" in 1810 [VA:482] and a "f. negro" taxable in Bedford County with (his sons?) Henry and Drury [Waldrep, *1813 Tax List*]. According to the Mecklenburg County, Virginia chancery suit of Hannah Stewart (daughter of Nancy Stewart and William Sonkey Stewart), James was Doctor Thomas Stewart's oldest son, and he died in Tennessee about 1820. He was head of a Smith County, Tennessee household of 4 "free colored" in 1820, living near Thomas, Drury, and Henry Stewart [TN:87]. James was the father of

    i.   Thomas⁷, born say 1779, married Sary **Cattiler (Cuttillo)**, 15 July 1800 Mecklenburg County, Virginia bond, Richerson Farrar bondsman. He was a farmer on Bears Element Creek in Lunenburg County living with his wife Salley and child Haily in March 1802 but not listed there in 1803 [Lunenburg County Free Negro & Slave Records, 1802-1803, LVA]. He was head of a Smith County, Tennessee household of 7 "free colored" in 1820 [TN:87]. He was the oldest son of James Stewart according to the Mecklenburg County chancery suit of Hannah Stewart. He died in Lunenburg County about 1830 leaving six children: Hailey, Anderson, Branch, James, and Delila, wife of William **Chapman**. Hailey died about 1831 [Chancery Causes, 1872-008, LVA].

    ii. Drury, born say 1781, taxable in Lunenburg County in 1804 and 1806 [PPTL 1782-1806]. He was head of a Smith County, Tennessee household of 9 "free colored" in 1820 [TN:87] and 8 in 1830 [TN:42].

    iii. Nelly².

    iv. Aggy.

    v. Henry³, born 1794-1806, head of a Smith County, Tennessee household of 5 "free colored" in 1820 [TN:87].

    vi. Jordan², born 1794-1806, head of a Smith County household of 6 "free colored" in 1830 [TN:109].

    vii. Rebecca, probably born 1802-1803, not listed in her parents' household in 1802.

25. Francis² Stewart, born say 1760, was taxable in Greensville County in 1782, 1785 and from 1787 to 1815: taxable on a horse in 1782, taxable on 3 horses and 3 cattle in 1787, taxable on a free tithable aged 16-21 in 1796, taxable on a slave in 1799, taxed on an ordinary license in 1800, taxable on (his son) Peter Stewart's tithe in 1801, taxable on his son Francis's tithe in 1812, a "Mulatto" listed with his unnamed wife and daughter in 1813 [PPTL 1782-1850, frames 4, 28, 46, 69, 87, 112, 129, 141, 164, 181, 192, 206, 222, 235, 248, 262, 277, 289, 306, 325, 339, 356, 375, 389, 404, 417, 435, 449, 465, 488]. On 26 March 1790 Kitt, "a free man," sued him for debt in Greensville County court [Orders 1790-9, 12, 79]. He purchased 100 acres in Brunswick County, Virginia, on 22 November 1790 for 15 pounds, and he and his wife Patience, "of Greensville County," sold this land about fifteen months later on 11 February 1792 for 22 pounds [DB 15:5, 179]. He rented land in Greensville County from Thomas Stewart in 1792 [WB 1:262] and was called Francis Stewart of Greensville County when he purchased 165 acres in Northampton County, North Carolina, from Peter Stewart on 26 March 1795 [DB 10:162]. The Greensville County court presented him on 24 March 1796 for retailing liquor without a license, and on 27 June 1799 the court granted him a license to keep an ordinary at his house. The court presented him for the same charge on 8 June 1801 and renewed his license for a year on 10 May 1802 [Orders 1790-9, 410, 594, 621; 1799-1806, 132, 220]. He was executor of Peter Stewart's 30 December 1794 Northampton County will, proved in

December 1805 [WB 2:309]. On 17 November 1808 he provided security for the Greensville County suit of Barnett Stewart since Barnett was not an inhabitant of the state, and he was assignee of Barnett Stewart in a Greensville County suit against John Wyche on 12 June 1809 [Orders 1806-10, 207, 367]. His 27 January 1816 Greensville County will was proved on 8 December 1817. He left his Greensville County land to his wife Patience, left his land in Northampton County, North Carolina, to his son Peter, a horse and cattle to his son Nevison, land to son Francis after his wife's death, land to daughters Patsey and Rebecca Stewart after his wife's death, and a cow, calf, and furniture to his daughters Seley Stewart and Jane **Hathcock**. His wife Patience and son Nevison were executors [WB 3:41]. Patience made a deed to Allen Deberry which was proved in Northampton County court by her son Peter on 5 June 1820 [Minutes 1817-21, 271]. Patience Stewart, born about 1764, was head of a Greensville County household of 10 "free colored" in 1820 [VA:265]. She registered in Greensville County on 26 August 1824: *a free Woman of Colour of a black Complexion supposed to be Sixty years old, 5' 3-3/4 inches high in shoes...by occupation a Spinstress* [Free Negro Register, no.108]. She was probably living with her son Peter in the 1830 census for Northampton County. Francis was the father of

   i.   Neverson, born about 1789, married Anna **Jones**, 18 May 1809 Greensville County bond, Asa **Byrd** security, registered as a "Free Negro" in Greensville County on 8 November 1813: *born free of a black Complexion, aged twenty four years last May, about six feet high* [Free Negro Register, no.33]. He was taxable in Greensville County in 1812 and a "Mulatto" taxable with his unnamed wife in 1813 [PPTL 1782-1850, frames 435, 449]. He was head of a Caswell County, North Carolina household of 7 "free colored" in 1820 [NC:87] and listed a second time as Everson Stewart [NC:92].

   ii.   Peter[5], born say 1780, a plaintiff in a suit for trespass in Northampton County against Hezekiel and Wheeler, judged in his favor for $30 on 2 March 1819. He and Stephen **Walden** were assessed damages of $13 in another suit on the same day [Minutes 1817-21, 167]. He was head of a Northampton County household of 8 "other free" in 1810 [NC:746] and 13 "free colored" in 1830, with a woman born before 1776 (his mother Patience?).

   iii. Seley.

   iv. Patsey, born say 1784, left a 13 October 1824 Greensville County will, proved 6 December the same year. She devised her land to her daughters Tabitha and Eliza Stewart. William and John **Walden** (of Northampton County, North Carolina) were witnesses to the will [WB 3:378].

   v.   Jane **Hathcock**.

   vi. Francis[3], born about 1794, registered as a "Free Negro" in Greensville County on 14 December 1819: *free born, black Complexion, twenty five years old, about five feet 8 inches high (in shoes) by profession a planter* [Register of Free Negroes, 1805-32, no.73], head of a Greensville County household of 6 "free colored" in 1820 [VA:265]. His wife Dolly registered on 3 January 1826: *of a dark yellow Complexion free born Thirty years old five feet three & three quarter inches high (in shoes)*, and they registered their children the same day: *Mariah (about 14 years old), Warren (about 8 or 9), Dick (7 or 8), Betsy (6), Mary Jane (4)* [Register of Free Negroes, 1805-32, nos. 152, 154].

26. John[3] Stewart, born say 1758, was head of a Powhatan County household with no whites and a slave in 1783 [VA:59]. He was a "Mul°" taxable in Powhatan County from 1787 to 1810: taxable on 2 slaves in 1787, 3 in 1788, 5 in 1798; taxable on Thomas Stewart's tithe from 1796 to 1800; taxable on James

Stewart's tithe from 1799 to 1802; taxable on 4 slaves, 4 horses and a stud horse in 1802 [PPTL, 1787-1825, frames 10, 38, 68, 97, 124, 151, 193, 245, 283, 351, 370, 386]. He married (second?) Frances **Dungey**, 20 April 1797 Powhatan County bond, Wade Woodson, Sr., surety [Powhatan County Marriage Register, 34]. He was a "Free Black" head of a Powhatan County household of 26 "other free" and 3 slaves in 1810 [VA:2]. He made a 25 March 1817 White County, Tennessee will by which he left his plantation, his two "servants" Dafney and Randal, and his farm animals, wagon and household effects to his wife Frances Stewart during her lifetime and named his children Thomas, James, Elisha, John, Elizabeth **Coker**, William, Richard, Littleberry, Rebecca and Mariah Stewart. He also named his wife's daughter Susanna **Dungy**. He appointed Joseph Upchurch, Thomas Stewart and Elisha Stewart executors [WB A:78-9]. He was the father of

    i. James[6], born say 1777, a "Mul°" taxable in Powhatan County from 1799 to 1811 [PPTL, 1787-1825, frames 193, 266, 283, 305, 369, 386, 406]. He married Frances **Dungey** (twenty-one years of age), 8 January 1801 Powhatan County marriage, John **Moss** surety [Powhatan County Marriage Register, 44].

    ii. Thomas[8], born say 1780, a "M°" taxable in Powhatan County from 1796 to 1815: charged with his own tax from 1802; taxable on 2 slaves in 1811, 3 in 1813 [PPTL, 1787-1825, frames 138, 193, 245, 351, 386, 406, 428, 446, 466, 493]. He married Page (Peg) **Crowder**, 3 January 1804 Powhatan County marriage, John **Moss** surety, Elisha Steward and Samuel **Branch** witnesses [Marriage Register, p.51]. He died before 20 July 1818 when his White County, Tennessee inventory was taken. The administrators were (his brother) Elisha Stewart and (widow) Margaret Stewart [WB A:95-6].

    iii. Elisha, born say 1783, a "M°" taxable in Powhatan County on 3 horses in 1807 [PPTL, 1787-1825, frames 351, 369, 386]. He married Lucy Crecy, daughter of Elizabeth Crecy, 19 January 1803 Powhatan County bond, James Steward surety. He died before 25 March 1822 when his White County inventory was recorded [WB A:162].

    iv. John[8], born say 1786, a "M°" taxable on a horse in Powhatan County from 1809 [PPTL, 1787-1825, frames 370, 386].

    v. Elizabeth, born say 1792, married Peter **Coker**.

    vi. William, born say 1795.

    vii. Richard[3], born 10 January 1800, married Barbara Creacy, who was born 7 May 1799 in Powhatan County. They moved to White County, Tennessee, in 1810 and travelled by wagon train to Cass County, Michigan, with William **Chavous** and his family. Richard died in Cass County on 6 May 1885 with an estate valued at $12,000 [Cass County Probate Court Liber 33:196; 37:107 cited in personal communication by his descendant E.P. Stewart].

    viii. Littleberry.

    ix. Rebecca.

    x. Mariah, born about 1807-1810.

27. Edward[2] Stewart, born about 1762, was a "yellow" complexioned man born in Chesterfield County who was living in Dinwiddie County when he was listed as a substitute in the Revolution [NSDAR, *African American Patriots*, 154]. He was a "Mulatto" taxable on a tithe and 2-3 horses in Chesterfield County from 1791 to 1811: called "Edward Stewart, Jr." from 1796 to 1801, a farmer taxable on 2 tithes and 4 horses in 1809 when he was living at Booker's shop, and living on Jones's land with 3 in his family in 1811 [PPTL, 1786-1811, frames 92, 205, 272, 343, 488, 529, 604, 642, 689, 738, 824]. He obtained a certificate of freedom in Chesterfield County on 11 June 1810: *forty eight years old, yellow complexion, born free* [Register of Free Negroes 1804-53, no. 131]. His wife Sally Stewart (born about 1764) registered in

Petersburg on 9 June 1810: *a brown Mulatto woman, wife of Edward Stewart, five feet three inches high, forty six years old, emancipated by Edward Stewart in the Town of Petersburg* [Register of Free Negroes 1794-1819, no. 589]. They may have been the parents of

    i.   Henry, born about 1781, registered in Petersburg on 8 July 1802: *a light brown Mulatto man, five feet eight inches high, twenty one years old, short knotty hair, born free and raised in the County of Chesterfield* [Register of Free Negroes 1794-1819, no. 239].

28. William[2] ("Sonkey") Stewart, born say 1745, was married to Nancy Stewart ("of Mecklenburg"), daughter of Dr. Thomas Stewart, on 18 May 1808 when Doctor Stewart left her a slave woman named Daus [Dinwiddie County Chancery Orders 1832-52, 13]. William was taxable in Mecklenburg County, Virginia, on a slave named Dorman in 1782, taxable on 12 head of cattle and 2 horses in 1783 (called William Stewart, Jr.), adjacent to William Stewart), called a shoemaker in 1785 when he was taxable on slaves Daws and Len, taxable on slaves Daws, Len and Jenny in 1786 and 1787, taxable on slave Daws in 1789, and taxable with his son Jordan and slave Daws in 1790 and 1791. His son Jordan Stewart and Robert **Cole** were taxable in his household in 1792. He was taxable on slaves Daws, Fan and Len in 1795 and 1796 but taxable on only his own tithe from 1797 until 1802 when he was taxable on his son William [PPTL, 1782-1805, frames 13, 27, 101, 125, 178, 276, 329, 383, 451, 558, 622, 645, 743, 880, 902]. He purchased 50 acres in Mecklenburg County adjoining the land of Doctor Thomas Stewart from James Stewart, Jr., and wife Ritter on 12 September 1796. And he purchased 162 acres on Sandy Creek adjoining **Wilson**'s line from Thomas and Mildred Stewart of Dinwiddie County for 60 pounds on 10 November 1799 [DB 9:153; 10:267]. He was called a shoemaker on 10 June 1799 when he sued James Stewart, blacksmith, for a 3 pound debt due by account [Orders 1798-1801, 192]. He was taxable in Mecklenburg County on 242 acres in 1804 [DB 16:272] and head of a Mecklenburg County household of 2 "free colored" in 1820 [VA:148b]. He sold 60 acres adjoining Frederick **Ivey**'s land on 21 August 1815 [DB 16:212]. He died intestate in Mecklenburg County before 7 December 1820 when the coroner viewed his body. His estate included a slave named Nelson who was valued at $500. The administrator of his estate sold 144 acres of his land and sold 41 acres to (his son-in-law) Thomas **Spence**. His estate was settled in 1821, and a Mecklenburg County chancery suit gives many details of his descendants [WB 9:163; 10:243; DB 19:33; Chancery suit 1872-008, LVA]. William and Nancy's children were

    i.   Jordan[1], born about 1765 in Dinwiddie County, taxable in his father's Mecklenburg County household in 1790 [PPTL, 1782-1805, frame 329], head of a Chatham County household of 8 "other free" in 1810 [NC:193]. He was in Wake County in 1849 when he applied for a pension for his services in the Revolution.

   ii. Griffin[1], never married and died intestate.

  iii. Peter[4], lived in Richmond, never married and died in Nashville, Tennessee.

   iv. Rebecca[3], born say 1775, married Anthony **Chavous**, 10 September 1792 Mecklenburg County bond.

    v. William, born about 1785, over the age of sixteen when he was taxable in his father's Mecklenburg County household in 1802 and 1803, called son of William when he was taxable in his own household in 1804 [PPTL, 1782-1805, frames 902, 982, 1007].

   vi. Charles[2], born about 1787, over the age of sixteen when he was taxable in his father's Mecklenburg County household in 1806 [PPTL, 1806-28, frame 17]. He married Sabra **Elam**, 14 March 1808 Mecklenburg County bond, Frederick **Ivey** security. He received a certificate in Mecklenburg County on 16 September 1814: *born free, & raised in the*

County of Mecklenburg...of a yellow Complection and good Stature, he is five feet nine inches high, about Twenty Seven years old [Free Person of Color, no.8, p.5]. He was head of a Mecklenburg County household of 6 "free colored" in 1820. His bond was mentioned in the account of his father's estate [WB 10:243]. He and Sabra had four children: Margaret, William, Joel, and Thomas Stuart [Mecklenburg County chancery suit, 1872-008, LVA].

vii. Nancy, born about 1788, married Thomas **Spence**, called Thomas Spain when they married, 14 September 1801 Mecklenburg County bond, Frederick **Ivy** security. Thomas **Spence**, born before 1776, was head of a Mecklenburg County, Virginia household of 5 "free colored" in 1820. His Mecklenburg County registration states that he was born free in Amelia County. His wife Nancy **Spence** registered as a free Person of Color in Mecklenburg County on 20 October 1828: *yellow complexion, about forty five years of age...born of a free woman in the county of Dinwiddie* [Free Person of Color no.54, p.41]. Thomas may have been a descendant of John **Spence**, a "Mulatto man" who was freed by the 20 July 1720 Northumberland County of Elizabeth Banks [RB 1718-26, 128, 148 by W. Preston Haynie, *Bulletin of the Northumberland County Historical Society* XXXIII:61].

viii. Hannah, born about 1790, a sixty-year-old "Black" woman counted in the 1850 Mecklenburg County census [VA:138]. She was still living on her parents land in February 1858.

ix. Dicey, married Mat Stuart.

x. Elizabeth[3], lived on her parents land and died in December 1853. She never married but left five children: Susan, Viney, Cresa, Sally **Mayo**, and Franky Stuart. James and Priscilla Stewart charged Susanna with stealing 16 yards of cloth from their home in Mecklenburg County on 1 August 1811. Susanna's sister Cresy testified that Susanna "striped" herself, went down James and Priscilla's chimney, rolled away a mortar in the fire place, and cut out the cloth [Orders 1811-13, 14].

29. John[4] **Stewart**, born say 1761, purchased 303 acres in Mecklenburg County in 1786 and was a "Mulatto" taxable on 303 acres in the lower district of Mecklenburg County in 1787 and 1788, taxable on 199 acres in 1790, but not taxable on any land in 1791 [Land Tax List 1782-1811A, B lists]. He was taxable on personal property in 1787, 1789, 1794, and 1797-1802 [PPTL, 1782-1805, frames 202, 304, 507, 698, 778, 807, 929]. On 27 January 1797 he purchased 100 acres in Mecklenburg County on Allen's Creek adjoining Mallett from Henry Jackson [DB 9:299] and was taxable on 100 acres in the lower district of Mecklenburg County until 1810 [Land Tax List 1782-1811A, B lists]. His wife Ann was apparently a white woman. On 10 January 1809 Ann Stewart was called "widow of John Stewart formerly Ann Jackson" in a Mecklenburg County chancery suit by which she and Patsy Jackson, Peter Jones and Sally his wife (formerly Sally Jackson), and Augustine Smith sued Isaac Jackson, Jeremiah Claunch and Prudence his wife (formerly Prudence Jackson), William Jones and his wife Charity (formerly Charity Jackson), to sell 296 acres which had belonged to Henry Jackson, deceased. The land was sold to Roderick Coleman who distributed 17 pounds, 14 shillings to each litigant on 11 July 1809 [Orders 1809-11, 5]. On the same date Ann Stewart bought 23 acres adjoining her land and Mrs. Boyd's from Roderick Coleman for 17 pounds, 5 shillings [DB 14:109-10]. She was called Nancy Stewart when she was taxable on 23 acres from 1809 to 1816 [Land Tax List 1811B-1824A]. And she was called Nancy Stewart when she was taxable on a horse in 1810 and taxable on 2 "Mulattoes over the age of 16" and a horse in 1813 [PPTL 1806-28, frames 173, 362]. She died before January court 1817 when the court ordered the commissioners to sell land which was late the property of John Stewart. His son Archibald was the buyer of the land on 13 March

1817. Later that year on 18 August Archibald sold to Roderick Coleman the timber on 23 acres which had belonged to Nancy Stewart, deceased widow of John Stewart [DB 9:299; 14:109; 17:87, 201]. A May 1817 chancery suit divided John's estate among his heirs who were probably his children [LVA chancery case 1824-039]:

  i. Elizabeth/ Betsy, married John **Walden**, 21 April 1804 Mecklenburg County bond, Kinchin **Chavis** security.
  ii. Henrietta, married John **Harris**, 27 December 1802 Mecklenburg County bond, Jere **Harris** security.
  iii. Archibald/ Archer, born say 1785, married Jincy **Chavos**, 14 August 1809 Mecklenburg County bond, Edward **Brandon** security, and second, Elizabeth **Brandon**, 19 December 1818, Mecklenburg County bond, 22 December marriage, Ned **Brandon** surety. He was head of a Mecklenburg County household of 8 "free colored" in 1820 with a woman in his household over forty-five years old. He died before 23 January 1826 when his estate was appraised at $96 [WB 11:151].
  iv. Abel.
  v. Henry²/ Harry, born say 1798, a "Mulatto" Mecklenburg County taxable in 1814, 1818 and 1820 [PPTL 1806-28, frames 405, 659, 709], head of a Mecklenburg County household of 1 "free colored" in 1820. His estate consisted of a gun, skillet and saddle when it was appraised at Archer Stewart's house on 1 February 1825 [WB 10:396].
  vi. John.
  vii. Sally.
  viii. Franky.
  ix. Jane, born about 1798, married Luke **Burkes**.

30. Titus Stewart, born say 1753, taxable in Lunenburg County in Matthew Stewart's household from 1772 to 1774 and taxable in his own household from 1782 to 1784 [Bell, *Sunlight on the Southside*, 302, 313, 343; PPTL 1782-1806]. He and Matthew Stewart were sued for debt in Mecklenburg County court on 13 December 1784 [Orders 1784-7, 188, 204]. Daniel Durham sued him and his securities Frederick **Ivey** and Thomas **Spence** for a bond of 18 pounds on 9 June 1806, and he made a deed of trust with Birchett & Company which was acknowledged in court on 14 July 1806 [Orders 1805-6, 209, 225]. He was taxable in Mecklenburg County in Ephraim **Drew**'s household in 1785 and taxable in his own household from 1786 to 1815. He was a "free Negro" taxable with his unnamed wife in 1813. He was not listed in 1816 and was deceased by 1817 when his estate was taxable on a horse [PPTL, 1782-1805, frames 99, 125, 224, 329, 558, 721, 902; 1806-28, frames 17, 95, 118, 197, 221, 314, 425, 582]. He was the father of

  i. Matthew, born say 1784, over the age of sixteen when he was taxable in his father's household in 1802 and taxable in his own household from 1803 to 1811 [PPTL, 1782-1805, frame 902; 1805-28]. He married Eliza Stewart, 8 February 1802 Mecklenburg County bond, Miles **Dunston** surety. And married second, Kesiah **Drew**, 20 June 1804 Warren County bond, Standfield **Drew** security. Kesiah was named in the 8 May 1827 Warren County, North Carolina will of her father John **Drew**.
  ii. John, born about 1791, over the age of sixteen when he was taxable in his father's household in 1807 [PPTL, 1806-28, frame 95].

31. Dempsey Stewart, born about 1764, enlisted in the 1st North Carolina Regiment for eighteen months while residing in Northampton County, North Carolina. He married Lucy **Berry**, 4 February 1786 Greensville County, Virginia bond, Cannon **Cumbo** bondsman, Thomas and Barney Steward witnesses. They were married 10 February 1786 [Greensville County Marriage Bonds & Ministers Returns, 6]. He was taxable on a tithe and 2 horses in St.

Andrew's Parish, Greensville County, from 1787 to 1792 [PPTL 1782-1850, frames 55, 74, 94, 102, 123, 149] and taxable in Meherrin Parish, Brunswick County, from 1793 to 1815: listed as a "Free Person of Colour" in 1810 and 1811, a "Free Negro" from 1813 to 1815 [PPTL 1782-1798, frames 401, 497, 543; 1799-1815, frames 197, 259, 295, 349, 394, 478, 520, 559, 637, 675, 733]. He rented land in Greensville County on the south side of Fountain Creek from Thomas Stewart from 1790 to 1792 [WB 1:181-3, 262]. He purchased property by deed proved in Brunswick County court on 26 March 1792, and he and his wife Lucy sold 40 acres in Brunswick County on the south side of the Meherrin River for 30 pounds on 2 October 1795 [Orders 1788-92, 636; DB 16:178]. He registered in Petersburg on 9 November 1805: *a brown Free Negro man, five feet ten inches high, thin made, about forty one years old, Born free p. register from the Clk of Brunswick County* [Register of Free Negroes 1794-1819, no. 368]. He purchased 60 acres on Buck Water Creek in Brunswick County by deed proved in 1806 and another 84 acres in 1827 [DB 16:178; 17:486; 27:224]. He was head of a Free Town, Brunswick County household of 4 "other free" in 1810 [VA:770], 2 "free colored" over forty-five years old in 1820 [VA:670], and 5 in 1830 [VA:249]. He was about fifty-seven years old on 27 January 1823 when he made a declaration in Brunswick County court, stating that he had entered the service in 1782, that his property included 60 acres of land, and that his family consisted of his wife who was about fifty-six [M804-2290, frame 0162]. His 11 December 1848 Brunswick County will, proved January 1849, left five dollars each to his daughters who were living in Indiana: Lucy **Cary** and Holly **Anderson**, and left the balance of his estate (including his land) to John Stewart, no relationship stated, who was to support his wife Lucy [WB 15:231]. She was head of a household in Freetown, Brunswick County, in 1850 (born about 1767) with (her son?) Murfree. She was a resident of Petersburg on 17 March 1853 when she applied for a widow's pension based on Dempsey's service for eighteen months in the 1st Regiment of North Carolina. Murphy Stewart testified that he was present when Dempsey died in January 1849 and that Lucy had lived with him since her husband's death [M804-2290, frame 0162]. Dempsey and Lucy's children were

    i.   ?Murfree B.T., born about 1806, registered on 7 September 1832: *a free man of yellow complexion about twenty six years of age, six feet one inch and a half high...was born free as appears by the evidence of John Wyche* [Wynne, *Register*, 122].

    ii.   Lucy, in a list of "Free Negroes and Mulattoes" over the age of sixteen in Meherrin Parish, Brunswick County, in 1813 [PPTL 1799-1815, frame 637], married ___ **Cary**.

    iii. Holly, in a list of "Free Negroes and Mulattoes" over the age of sixteen in Meherrin Parish, Brunswick County, in 1813 [PPTL 1799-1815, frame 637], married ___ **Anderson**.

Other members of the Stewart family were

    i.   Thomas, born say 1750, a "mulatto" runaway jailed in Rowan County, North Carolina, on 8 February 1772 when the court ordered the sheriff to hire him out [Minutes 1769-72, original p.56, abstract p.233].

    ii.   Samuel, born about 1758, taxable in Surry County from 1783 to 1816: called a "FN" in 1809, listed with 2 "free Negroes & Mulattoes above the age of 16" in 1813 [PPTL, 1782-90, frames 368, 398; 1791-1816, 17, 169, 271, 384, 462, 574, 616, 657, 757, 866]. He first married Celia **Bell**, 27 January 1791 Surry County bond; and second, Lucy **Scott**, 11 October 1808 Surry County bond, David **Charity** surety. He was head of a Surry County household of 6 "free colored" in 1830. He enlisted in the Revolution in Brunswick County, Virginia, in 1777 and was granted a pension while resident in Surry County, Virginia, in

    1832. His widow Lucy received a grant for 160 acres in 1855 [Jackson, *Virginia Negro Soldiers*, 44].

 iii. William³, "a Colored man...free born" about 1759 in Brunswick County, Virginia, according to his Revolutionary War pension file. He enlisted in 1777 under Major Hardy Murphy in Northampton County, North Carolina, and marched to West Point and Valley Forge. After the war he returned to Northampton County. He married Mary **Artis**, 3 January 1792 Greensville County, Virginia bond, 5 January marriage, John Jeter, Sr., surety [Ministers' Returns, 25]. He was taxable in Greensville County in Lucretia Stewart's household in 1791 and taxable on a horse in his own household from 1793 to 1799 [PPTL 1782-1850, frames 129, 164, 181, 193, 206, 220, 248]. He was head of a Northampton County, North Carolina household of 7 "other free" in 1800 [NC:479], perhaps the William Stuart who was witness to Mary Stuart's September 1778 Northampton County will [WB 1:309]. He moved with his family to Westmoreland County, Pennsylvania, where he had been living from 1814 until 19 May 1835 when he made his pension application. Nancy **Scott**, a "Colored woman," who came to Pennsylvania with the Stewart family, testified on his behalf [M805-773, frame 400].

 iv. Reps, born say 1763, taxable in Brunswick County on his own tithe and a horse in 1784 [PPTL 1799-1815, frame 93], taxable in Meherrin Parish, Greensville County, from 1787 to 1792 [PPTL 1782-1850, frames 46, 68, 87, 112, 129, 141] and taxable in Warren County, North Carolina, in 1793 and 1795 [Tax List 1781-1801, 249, 294]. He was surety for the 23 June 1791 Greensville County marriage of Nathan **Jeffries** to Clary **Norton** and bondsman for the 21 February 1800 Orange County, North Carolina marriage of William **Jeffries** and Penelope **Evans**. He was head of an Orange County household of 2 "other free" in 1800 [NC:530].

 v. William, born say 1770, a "free man" living with his wife Betsy in Henrico County on 25 January 1797 when Sam "a Negro man slave the property of Samuel Pleasants" was acquitted of entering their house and robbing them of a red cloak and sundry other articles of clothing valued at 10 dollars [Orders 1796-8, 227].

 vi. Thomas, taxable on a tithe and a horse in Chesterfield County from 1791 to 1797, 2 tithes and a horse in 1798 and 1799, and 1 tithe in 1801 [PPTL, 1786-1811, frames 91, 125, 166, 205, 237, 305, 377, 453]. He left a 21 September 1801 Chesterfield County will by which he gave all his estate to his wife Peggy and appointed her and her father Peter Stewart his executors [WB 5:491-2].

32 vii. Molly, born about 1772.

 viii. Nancy, born about 1773, registered in Petersburg on 8 December 1795: *a light brown Mulatto woman, five feet two inches high, twenty two years old, born free & raised in Dinwiddie County* [Register of Free Negroes 1794-1819, no. 106].

 ix. George, born say 1774, married Jean **Chandler**, 27 December 1797 Mecklenburg County bond, Moses Stewart security, with a note from Zacharias Mallett that he had "sold George (commonly of late called George Stewart) to Moses Stewart and therefore have no further claim or title on him whatsoever."¹⁹⁶ George was head of a Cumberland County, North Carolina household of 3 "free colored" in 1820 [NC:194].

 x. Betsy, head of a Petersburg Town household of 7 "other free" in 1810 [VA:125a].

---

¹⁹⁶Zachariah Mallett was witness to Martha Stewart's 17 January 1779 Mecklenburg County will.

xi. Ann[2], born about 1775, registered in Petersburg on 27 September 1800: *a very light Mulatto woman, five feet three inches high, light grey eyes, twenty five years old, born free & raised in Dinwiddie County* [Register of Free Negroes 1794-1819, no. 209]. She was head of a Dinwiddie County household of 3 "other free" in 1810 [VA:161].

xii. Richard/Dick, born about 1776, registered in Petersburg on 27 January 1797: *a dark brown Mulatto man, five feet eleven inches high, short hair, twenty one years old the beginning of the present month, born free & brought up in the business of a Blacksmith in the Town of Petersburg* [Register of Free Negroes 1794-1819, no. 120].

xiii. Pheaby, head of a Petersburg Town household of 3 "other free" and 7 slaves in 1810 [VA:120a]. A Phobe Stewart was the mother of illegitimate children Nancy and Polly who were bound to Thomas Cartelon and his wife in Mecklenburg County on 12 February 1787 [Orders 1784-7, 652].

xiv. Peyton[2], born about 1779, registered in Petersburg on 14 August 1800: *a light brown Mulatto man, five feet seven inches high, thin made, twenty one years old, born free & raised in the Town of Petersburg* [Register of Free Negroes 1794-1819, no. 163].

xv. Nancy, born say 1781, married Miles **Dunstan**, 18 February 1802 Mecklenburg County bond, Thomas **Spence** security.

xvi. Jarrald, born about 1782, registered in Petersburg on 8 August 1808: *a brown free Negro man five feet six and a half inches high, twenty six years old, born free and raised in the County of Chesterfield* [Register of Free Negroes 1794-1819, no. 430]. He was a "Mulatto" taxable in Chesterfield County from 1802 to 1806 [PPTL, 1786-1811, frames 492, 605, 642].

xvii. Jane, born say 1784, had a child by Joseph **Holley (Hawley)** in Greensville County before 14 January 1805 he was charged with bastardy. Henry and Peyton Stewart were security for his maintenance of the child [Orders 1799-1806, 439]. In return, **Holley** bound himself to serve Henry for the period of seven years [DB 3:402]. On 13 January 1806 the court ordered her son Lindsey bound to Francis Stewart but rescinded the order the following month on 10 February for reasons appearing to the court [Orders 1799-1806, 532, 533].

xviii. Nancy, born about 1784, registered in Petersburg on 21 December 1809: *a dark brown Mulatto woman, five feet four inches high, twenty five years old, born free & raised in Dinwiddie County. 22 March 1820: now wife of Geo. Valentine* [Register of Free Negroes 1794-1819, no. 529].

xix. Henry, born about 1787, registered in Petersburg on 25 February 1809: *a light yellow brown free Negro man, five feet five inches high, twenty one years old, born free & raised in the Town of Petersburg* [Register of Free Negroes 1794-1819, no. 458].

xx. Moses[2], born say 1789, head of a Randolph County, North Carolina household of 7 "other free" in 1810 [NC:64].

xxi. Richard/ Dick, born about 1790, registered in Petersburg on 9 May 1809: *a light Mulatto man, five feet eight and a half inches high, nineteen years old, born free & raised in the Town of Petersburg* [Register of Free Negroes 1794-1819, no. 466].

xxii. Edward[3], born say 1792, head of a Randolph County, North Carolina household of 4 "other free" in 1810 [NC:64].

xxiii. Peter[7], born about 1792, registered in Petersburg on 1 May 1816: *a brown man of colour, five feet nine and a half inches high, twenty four, born free & raised in Mecklenburg County* [Register of Free Negroes 1794-1819, no. 806].

xxiv. Robert, born say 1793, married Polly **Jones**, 8 December 1814 Greensville County bond, Nevison Stewart surety.

32. Molly Stewart, born about 1772, charged Aaron **Newsom** in Greensville
County court with breach of the peace, but the case was dismissed on 10 May
1802 [Orders 1799-1806, 217]. She was listed as a "Mulatto" in Greensville
County in 1813 [PPTL 1782-1850, frame 449]. She was head of a Greensville
County household of 6 "free colored" in 1820 [VA:265]. She registered as a
"Free Negro" in Brunswick County on 26 February 1827: *Molly Stewart a free
woman of color about 5 feet 2 1/2 Inches high about 55 years of age...of a
yellow complexion was born of free parents as appears from the evidence of
Phil Claiborne* [Wynne, *Register of Free Negroes*, 87]. She was the mother of
i. Siddy, born about 1805, registered on 26 February 1827: *a free woman
of yellow complexion about 21 or 23 years of age five feet high...is the
daughter of Molly Stewart a free woman as appears from the evidence
of Phil Claiborne* [Wynne, *Register of Free Negroes*, 86].

STRINGER FAMILY

1. Elizabeth Stringer, born say 1673, was a (white) servant who was convicted
by the Charles City County court in January 1690 of "having a bastard by a
Negroe." Her master Edmund Irby agreed to pay her fine, and she was
ordered to serve him an additional two years after her term of service was
completed [Orders 1687-95, 322]. She was probably the mother or
grandmother of

2   i. Dorothy, born say 1715.

2. Dorothy Stringer, born say 1715, was excused from paying tax by the 29
August 1755 Craven County, North Carolina court:

> *moved that Dorothy Stringer ____ Negro be excused from paying levies
> on account of their? Infirmity, It was ordered that she have a Certificate
> thereof to recommend to the Assembly accordingly* [Haun, *Craven County
> Court Minutes*, IV:289].[197]

She and (her daughter?) Jane Stringer were committed to jail under suspicion
of petty larceny but released by the Craven County court in October 1760
[Minutes 1758-61, 88b]. On 10 October 1761 she asked the court to bind her
two young children Sall and Mingo as apprentices [Minutes 1761-62, 50a]. She
was probably the "Free Doll of Handcocks Creek" who was ordered by the 17
March 1775 Craven County court to produce her children at the next court so
they could be bound out as apprentices [Minutes 1772-84, 31c]. The court
gave the same order twelve years later on 16 June 1787 when it called her
Doll Stringer [Minutes 1786-87, 55a]. She was head of a Craven County
household of 4 "other free" in 1790 [NC:130]. Her children were
i. ?Jane, born say 1740, jailed in 1760 and taxed in 1769 as a "Black"
female in Craven County [SS 837].

3   ii. ?Hezekiah[1], born say 1757.
iii. Sall, born about 1758, three years old in 1761 when her mother bound
her as an apprentice.

4   iv. Mingo, born July 1761.
v. ?Thomas, born say 1770, head of a Craven County household of 2
"other free" in 1790.

5   vi. Keziah, born say 1770.

---

[197]She may have been the "Mullato Doll free Woman" who was bound with her children Jean (9
years old), Sang__ (5 years old), and Patience (3 years old) to Mr. Hunter in Pasquotank County on 12
July 1738 [Minutes 1737-46, 32].

3. Hezekiah[1] Stringer, born say 1757, was in Craven County on 20 March 1787 when he registered his furlough papers before the Justice of the Peace. His papers, dated 26 May 1783, granted him a leave of absence from the 1st North Carolina Regiment until his final discharge [*NCGSJ* XVI:238]. He was called Kiah Stringer in 1800, head of a New Hanover County household of 5 "other free" [NC:316]. The September 1807 Craven County court bound out his children:
    i.   John, born about 1798.
    ii. Dale, born about 1799.

4. Mingo Stringer, born about July 1761, was brought to the Craven County court by his mother to be bound an apprentice in October 1761 [Minutes, 1761-62, 50a]. He served in Sharp's Company of the 10th North Carolina Regiment between 5 May 1781 and 5 April 1782 [Clark, *State Records*, XVI:1166]. He purchased 100 acres on the south side of the Neuse River near Long Creek in 1782 [DB 24:284] and was head of a Craven County household of 2 "other free" in 1790 [NC:131]. Perhaps he was the father of
    i.   William, born circa 1790, head of a Craven County household of 3 "free colored" in 1820 [NC:77]. He described himself as a "colored man" in his 12 July 1847 Craven County will, proved in March 1857. He left his house in New Bern to his aunt Keziah and mentioned his brother George and Keziah's grandchildren Caroline and Judy [WB D:275].
    ii. George, born circa 1790, head of a Craven County household of 2 "free colored" in 1820 [NC:77].

5. Keziah Stringer, born say 1770, received the New Bern house of her nephew William Stringer by his 12 July 1847 Craven County will [WB D:275]. She was living in Craven County in September 1807 when the court bound out her child,
    i.   Hezekiah[2], born about 1800.

SUNKET FAMILY

1. Elishe Sunket, born say 1735, was the mother of several children bound out by the Northampton County, Virginia court. They were
    i.   Fanny, born in January 1757, bound to Laban Belote by the court on 10 August 1762, no race indicated, called a "Negro" when she was bound to Anne Belote on 10 April 1764 [Minutes 1761-5, 37, 110].
    ii. Tabitha, born in May 1759, an Indian bound to Reubin Giddings on 9 November 1762, no parent named [Minutes 1761-5, 44].
    iii. ?Sarah, born say 1760, presented by the court for bastard bearing on 9 November 1779. She may have been the mother of Richard Sunket, born in January 1781, who was bound to John Stott on 11 January 1792 [Minutes 1777-83, 207; Orders 1789-95, 184].
    iv. Brit, born in January 1762, Indian son of Elishe Sunket, bound by the court to Benjamin Dixon on 12 August 1766 and bound to Sarah Dixon on 13 January 1772 [Minutes 1765-71, 27; 1771-7, 54].
    v.   Nanny, daughter of Elishe Sunket, bound to John Stott on 13 January 1772 [Minutes 1771-7, 29].
    vi. ?Kizza, counted in a list of "Free Negroes and mulattoes" above the age of sixteen in Williamsburg in 1813 [Waldrep, *1813 Tax List*].

SWAN FAMILY

1. Ann Wall, born say 1670, an English woman, was presented by the Elizabeth City County court on 29 September 1693 for "keeping company with the negro man under pretense of marriage," and on 18 May 1694 she was presented for

"having a bastard child begotten (by a) Negro." On 19 August 1695 she was presented for having a "Mulatto" child "begotten by a Negro," and on 30 December 1695 the court bound her for five years and her two "mulatto" children until the age of thirty years to Peter Hobson (of Norfolk County). The court also ordered that she be banished to Barbados if she ever returned to Elizabeth City County [Orders 1692-99, 19, 38, 69, 70, 72, 78]. She was called Ann Wall alias Swann on 19 June 1713 when William Roe sued her in Norfolk County court. And she was called Ann Swann in Norfolk County court in October 1711 when she sued John Holowell because he planned to transport her "Molato" son Thomas Swann to North Carolina where Thomas' master, Lyonell Reding, was then living. Ann was worried that he would be sold as a slave. In February 1713 the court ordered that Thomas be hired out until Reding gave security that he would not remove the boy from Norfolk County. But on 16 October 1713 the court allowed Reding to take Thomas to North Carolina after he posted bond that he would release him from his indenture when he reached the age of thirty years. On 15 May 1713 Ann sued John Corprew in Norfolk County court claiming that her son John Swan had been bound apprentice before passage of the law (in 1691) which bound mixed-race children of white women to the age of thirty years. However, the court ruled that he serve the full 30 years after viewing a copy of the Elizabeth City County order [Norfolk County Orders 1710-17, 20, 46, 48, 56, 62, 71]. Ann's children were

    i.   John Swan, born about 1692, about twenty-one years old on 20 November 1713 when he petitioned the Norfolk County court for his freedom from John Corprew. On 20 July 1722 he and "Ann Wall his mother" successfully sued for his freedom. On 13 June 1725 the court ordered that he be whipped for hog stealing, on 15 May 1730 he was presented by the grand jury for not attending church, and in 1730 he was taxable in Norfolk County in the precinct from Sugg's Mill to Great Bridge but did not appear again in Norfolk County records [Orders 1710-17, 74; 1719-22, 47-8; 1723-34, 39, 109; Wingo, *Norfolk County Tithables*, 1730-50, 2].

    ii.   Thomas Swan, born say 1695.

SWEAT FAMILY

1.   Robert[1] Sweat, born say 1610, was made to do public penance during divine service at James City Church, James City Parish, Virginia, on 17 October 1640 because he

> *hath begotten with Child a negro woman servant belonging unto Lieutenant Sheppard* [Minutes of the Council (Robinson's Notes), 30, Virginia Historical Society Mss 5:9R5613].

He may have been identical to or the son of Robert Sweete, Gentleman, who was a member of the Virginia House of Burgesses [McIlwaine, *Journals of the House of Burgesses*, I:ix, 51]. And the "negro woman servant" may not have been a slave. The courts also referred to indentured white servants as belonging to their masters. She may have been Margaret **Cornish**. See further the **Cornish** History. Perhaps their children were

    i.   Robert **Cornish**, born say 1640.

2   ii.   William[1], born about 1642.

2.   William[1] Sweat, born about 1642, was about twenty-five years old on 3 March 1667/8 when he made a deposition in Surry County court about two horses which belonged to his master, Thomas Binns. He testified that he had seen one of these horses at James City while travelling with Captain John Groves. He claimed payment in court in March 1671 for looking after Susan Robinson's

horses [Haun, *Surry Court Records* II:305; III:2]. He was taxable in Francis Mason's Surry County household in Lower Chipoakes, Lawnes Creek Parish, in 1674 and 1675, taxable from 1680 to 1684 in Thomas Binns' household, and taxable in his own household from 1685 to 1703: with (his son?) Robert Sweat in 1694 and with (his son?) William, Jr., in Southwarke Parish from 1698 to 1703 [*Magazine of Virginia Genealogy*, vol. 22, no.2, 43, 47; no.4, 49, 51, 56; vol.23, no.1, 42, 49; no.2, 61, 64; no.3, 56, 60, 65; no.4, 64, 69; DW 5:289]. He was not listed from 1676 to 1679, perhaps one of seven unnamed "Negroes" listed with Thomas Binns in Francis Mason's household in 1677 and one of five unnamed "Negroes" in Thomas Binns' household in 1679 [*Magazine of Virginia Genealogy*, vol.22, no.3, 59, 66]. His wife was probably Margaret Swett who made a claim for wages of 375 pounds of tobacco against the estate of John Whitson on 6 May 1679. This claim was granted to William Swett on 5 September 1679. He was granted 842 pounds of tobacco as judgment in a suit against John Phillips, Jr., on 5 January 1685/6, granted 365 pounds of tobacco in his suit against Thomas Binns on 2 March 1685/6, granted 415 pounds of tobacco in his suit against the estate of Joseph Malden on 5 January 1688/9, and granted a cow and a calf in his suit against Thomas Deerhim on 7 November 1691. He was ordered to pay Robert Caufield 772 pounds of tobacco in December 1687 and 1,131 pounds of tobacco on 5 July 1692. In July 1694 the Surry court ruled that his unnamed, free born "Mallatto" daughter was not tithable. In September 1696 he and Anthony **Cornish** were security for Margaret Sweat's administration on the estate of Robert Sweat. In December 1711 he was exempted from payment of public tax because of old age [Haun, *Surry Court Records*, III: 250, 278; IV:504, 510, 691; V:15; IV:589; V:43, 108, 168; VI:176]. William's children were probably

3   i.   Robert², born say 1670.
4   ii. William², Jr., born say 1676.
5   iii. Eve, born say 1678.

3.   Robert² Sweat, born say 1670, was taxable in Francis Mason's household from 1686 to 1693. He and John **Warwick** were called "Jno & Robt. Mula[ttos]" in Mason's household in 1687 and he was listed as one of Francis Mason's "negroes" in 1692. He was tithable in his own household in 1695 adjacent to William Sweat [*Magazine of Virginia Genealogy*, vol.23, no.2, 60; no.3, 56, 61, 66, 69; no.4, 64, 68]. He was listed in a 3 January 1687/8 Surry County muster. He died before September 1696 when William Sweat and Anthony **Cornish** were security for Margaret Sweat's administration on his estate [Haun, *Surry Court Records* V:621, 168]. Margaret was probably his widow. She was called Margaret Swett, the younger, in 1696 when she was presented by the churchwardens of Southwarke Parish for fornication [DW 5:94]. By May 1697 Margaret was married to John **Kicotan** when they were ordered to present an account of the estate of Robert Sweat's orphan, Cornish Sweat [Haun, *Surry Court Records*, V:185, 192, 196]. They presented the account, totalling 2,930 pounds of tobacco, on 6 July 1697 [DW 5:128]. See the **Tann** history. Robert²'s child was

6   i.   Cornish, born say 1690.

4.   William² Sweat, born say 1676, was taxable in Surry County from 1698 to 1703 in William Sweat, Sr.'s household. He produced an account against the public for 50 pounds of tobacco in Surry County court on 21 October 1713 [Orders 1713-18, 14]. In December 1722 he was paid 9 shillings and Margaret **Jeffries** was paid 17 shillings by the estate of Samuel Thompson, deceased. William paid the estate four barrels and two bushels of corn as his rent [DW 7:456-8]. He was sued for a debt in Surry County in February 1744/45, and the court attached his household items when it was reported that he had left the county [Orders 1744-49, 24]. In September 1746 James Johnson sued him for

a 34 shilling debt in Charles City County, and in December 1746 he and Edward Broadnax each posted a 20 pound bond that he would keep the peace towards William Snukes. He confessed in August 1747 that he owed Francis Dancy 5 pounds [Orders 1737-51, 425, 429, 445, 450]. On 9 June 1748 the Isle of Wight County court ordered that he be exempt from paying levies because of his great age and infirmity [Orders 1746-52, 106]. He was married to Margaret **Jeffries** by 8 November 1753 when they, Margaret's daughter Margaret **Jeffries**, and Francis **Locus** and his wife Hannah lost their right to 190 acres on the north side of the Meherrin River in Southampton County in a dispute with Arthur Taylor heard at the Council of Virginia [Hall, *Executive Journals of the Council*, V:448]. Margaret Sweat was living in Southampton County on 12 June 1755 when the court exempted her from paying levies [Orders 1754-9, 94]. He may have been the father of

  7   i.   William³, born say 1700.
  8   ii. Robert³, born say 1707.

5.   Eve Sweat, born say 1678, may have been the unnamed "Mulatto" daughter of William Sweat who the court ruled was not tithable in 1694. Eve was reported to have left the county when the Surry County grand jury presented her in July 1705 for bearing a bastard child. She appeared before the court in March 1705/6, confessed her crime, but refused to pay the fine and received "correction" (a whipping). She was apparently the common-law wife of a slave since she was presented for the same crime again on 2 May 1710 and admitted in February 1710/11 that the father of her child was Dick, the slave of William Harris [Haun, *Surry Court Records* VI:268, 276, 342, 357; DW&c 6:15]. Her descendants may have been

  9   i.   Sarah, born say 1730.
         ii. John¹, born say 1735, purchased a lot of books and an old table from the Brunswick County, Virginia estate of Matthew Parham, deceased, before 24 January 1758 [DB 3:235]. He was a "Mulato" taxable in Aaron Odam's Bladen County household in 1769 [Byrd, *Bladen County Tax Lists*, I:15]. He was head of a Beaufort District, South Carolina household of one male over 16, one under 16, and two females in 1790 [SC:11], perhaps the John Sweat who was head of a Richland District, South Carolina household of 6 "other free" in 1810 [SC:176].
        iii. Barnet, born say 1740, listed in the 8 October 1759 to 10 January 1760 muster roll of Captain James McGirrt's Company in the South Carolina Regiment in the Cherokee Expedition [Clark, *Colonial Soldiers of the South*, 883]. He may have been the same Barney Sweat who was listed among the "Black" members of the undated colonial muster roll of Captain James Fason's Company of Northampton County, North Carolina [N.C. Archives Troop Returns, 1-3]. He was counted as white in Camden District, Richland County, South Carolina, in 1790: head of a household of one male over 16, two under 16, and four females [SC:26].
        iv. Hannah, the common-law wife of William **Brooks** who mentioned her and his son William **Swett** in his 9 May 1788 Southampton County will [WB 4:276].
        v. Elizabeth, born say 1770, married Lewis **Pettiford**, 2 January 1788 Granville County bond, Elias **Pettiford** bondsman.

6.   Cornish Sweat, born say 1690, was called Corney Sweet in Isle of Wight County on 17 July 1740 when he and his wife Lucy recorded the birth of their son Robert Sweet [*Old Parish Register of Newport Parish*, 183]. On 11 August 1748 he was one of the freeholders of Isle of Wight County who were ordered to work on the road from Days's Neck Road near Thomas Day's over Wakefield Run to Hogpen Point. On 3 July 1760 he confessed that he owed James Ridley, executor of William Hogsden, 9 pounds, 11 shillings [Orders

1746-52, 115, 158]. Administration of his Isle of Wight County estate was granted to William Sweat on 7 May 1767 [Orders 1764-8, 402]. His children were

10   i. ?William⁴, born say 1721.
       ii. Robert⁴, born 17 July 1740.

7.   William³ Sweat, born say 1700, was married to Martha Cawze by 11 December 1735 when the baptism of their three-year-old "Natural Son" William Sweat was recorded in the register of the Parish of Prince Frederick Winyaw in South Carolina [NSCDA, *Register Book For Parish of Prince Frederick Winyaw*, 42]. Their children were

11   i. William⁶, born about 1732.
       ii. ?Thomas, born say 1738, listed in the Muster Roll of Captain Alexander McKintosh's Company of Colonel Gabriel Powell's Battalion in the expedition against the Cherokees from 11 October 1759 to 15 January 1760, in the same list as Winslow **Driggers** [Clark, *Colonial Soldiers of the South*, 929]. He was a "Mulato" taxable in his own household in Bladen County, North Carolina, in 1768 and 1769 and taxable in the household of Ann **Perkins** in 1771 [Byrd, *Bladen County Tax Lists*, I:8, 17, 60]. He was granted 150 acres on the north side of the Pee Dee River in Craven County, South Carolina, on 28 July 1775. He was in the list of Captain Robert Lide's Company of Volunteer Militia who signed a petition to the Council of Safety of South Carolina on 9 October 1775.
      iii. ?Anthony¹, born say 1741, probably named for Anthony **Cornish**. He was listed in the Muster Roll of Captain John McCant's Company of Colonel Gabriel Powell's Battalion of South Carolina Militia from 11 October 1759 to 15 January 1760 in the Cherokee Expedition [Clark, *Colonial Soldiers of the South*, 895, 925]. He purchased land by deed proved in South Carolina between 1766 and 1767 and sold land in South Carolina by deed proved between 1771 and 1772 [Lucas, *Index to Deeds of South Carolina*, F-3:305, Y-3:418]. He may have been the father of Anthony Sweat whose 29 October 1813 Marion County will was proved 27 November the same year. He left land, slaves, and $1,000 worth of cattle to his children [WB 1:90-1].

8.   Robert³ Sweat, born say 1707, was sued in Goochland County for trespass by James Taylor in June 1729 [Orders 1728-30, 114, 123] and was living on the north east side of the Black River in South Carolina on 19 July 1736 when Alexander Nesbitt recorded a plat for land adjoining his [S.C. Archives series S213184, vol. 3:333]. He was granted 100 acres on Wilkerson Swamp near the Little Pee Dee River on 23 December 1754 on the South Carolina line in what was called Anson County but was later part of Bladen County, North Carolina, and became Robeson County in 1787 [Hoffman, *Land Patents*, I:340]. This land adjoined land of Joshua **Perkins** and was sold by Philip **Chavis** on 21 November 1768 [Bladen DB 23:104-5, 424-5]. Robert may have been the father of

12   i. Margaret, born say 1728.
13   ii. William⁵, born say 1730.

9.   Sarah Swett, born say 1730, was a taxable "Molato" in Bladen County, North Carolina, in 1770 with (her son?) James Sweet [Byrd, *Bladen County Tax Lists*, I:35]. She was taxable on 50 acres in District 10 of Halifax County, North Carolina, in 1782. She may have been the Sarah Schot who gave a cow, a calf, and household furniture to Abraham Sevett (Swett?) and Bay Moore on 16 August (no year) for maintaining her for the rest of her life by deed proved

in November 1793 Halifax County court [DB 17:593].[198]   She may have
been the mother of

    i.   James[2], born say 1757, a "Molato" taxable in Sarah Sweet's household
in Bladen County in 1770 and a "Mulato" taxable in Aaron Odam's
household in 1772 [Byrd, *Bladen County Tax Lists*, I:35, 80]. He was
head of an Onslow County household of 6 "other free" in 1790
[NC:197], perhaps the J. Swett who was head of a Brunswick County,
North Carolina household of 10 "other free" in 1810 [NC:238].

14   ii.   William[7], born say 1756.

    iii.   Abraham, born say 1758, served in Raiford's Company of the 10th
North Carolina Regiment between 25 April 1781 and 25 April 1782
[Clark, *State Records*, XVI:1162]. He purchased 246 acres in Halifax
County by deeds of 5 August 1782, 3 September 1782, and 31 May
1784 [DB 15:70, 75, 222]. He was head of a Halifax County household
of 3 male and 5 female free persons in the 1786 state census for district
8 and was taxable on 250 acres and 4 free polls in Halifax County in
1790. He was head of a Halifax County household of 5 "other free" in
1790 [NC:62], 6 in 1800 [NC:344], and 4 in 1810 [NC:50]. His 10
December 1819 Halifax County will was proved in May 1820. He gave
his friend, Richard H. Crowell, 273 acres and mentioned his grandchild
John Langston of Virginia and the heirs of Lucy Cook [WB 3:653].

15   iv.   George[2], born say 1760.

16   v.   Allen, born about 1765.

10. William[4] Sweat, born say 1721, was granted administration of the Isle of
Wight County estate of Cornish Sweat on 6 August 1767. He may have been
the father of

    i.   Anthony[2], born say 1757, purchased 140 acres in Meherrin Parish,
Brunswick County, Virginia, on 25 July 1777 [DB 13:63]. He was
taxable in Meherrin Parish from 1782 to 1787 [PPTL 1782-98, frames
24, 63, 93, 136, 206] and taxable in Greensville County from 1788 to
1801 [PPTL 1782-1850, frames 68, 112, 141, 181, 206, 235, 262,
277]. He voted in Greensville County on 26 April 1792. He and his
wife Peggy sold 50 acres in Greensville County on the south side of
Jordan's Road on the Halifax Road to William Sweat on 13 October
1800, and they sold 91 acres in Greensville County for 91 pounds on
10 October 1801 [DB 1:451; 2:632; 3:63].

17   ii.   William[9], born say 1760.

    iii.   James[3], born say 1765, living alone in Dupree's District, Northampton
County, North Carolina, in 1786, counted as a "black" person 12-50
years old. He married Patience **Read**, "daughter of John and Sarah
Reed," 3 March 1790 Southampton County bond, David **Reed** surety,
and was the executor of the 23 August 1790 Southampton County will
of her father John **Read** [WB 5:58]. He was taxable in Southampton
County from 1788 to 1814: listed in John Francis's household in 1788,
taxable on a horse in 1790 and 1793, listed in Willie Francis's
household in 1794, taxable on a horse in 1798 and 1799, a "Mulatto"
taxable from 1805 to 1812, not listed with a wife in 1813 and 1814
[PPTL 1782-92, frames 659, 768, 884; 1792-1806, frames 62, 79,
170, 203, 279, 329, 391, 819, 852; 1807-21, frames 78, 176, 201,
299, 326, 425].

---

[198]The deed was witnessed by Elisha Elliott and Shadrach Merritt, two of Abraham Sweat's
neighbors in the 1790 Halifax County Census [NC:62]. The original deed book no longer exists. This
is the abstract of a copy made about 1896 [*The Deeds of Halifax County, North Carolina*, abstracted by
Dr. Stephen E. Bradley, Jr.].

11. William[6] Sweat, born about 1732, was baptized in Prince Frederick Winyaw Parish in South Carolina on 11 December 1735. He purchased land by deed recorded in South Carolina between 1757 and 1758 and sold this land by deed recorded during the same period [Lucas, *Index to Deeds of South Carolina*, S-S:343, 346]. He married Lucy Turbeville before 23 July 1763 when he was named as executor and son-in-law of John Turbeville who mentioned his daughter Lucy Sweat and grandson Nathan Sweat in his Craven County, South Carolina will (which was proved 3 August the same year) [WB RR:55]. According to the Rev. Alexander Gregg, Rector of St. David's Church in Cheraw, South Carolina, William was the father of Nathan, James and William Sweat [Gregg, *History of the Old Cheraws*, 101, 311, 312]. William's children were

    i.   Nathan, born say 1753, listed in Captain Robert Lide's Company of Volunteer Militia who signed a petition to the Council of Safety of South Carolina on 9 October 1775. He was counted as white in 1790, head of a Beaufort District, South Carolina household of one male over 16, one under 16, and four females [SC:11].

    ii. James[1], born say 1755, counted as white in 1790, head of a Beaufort District, South Carolina household of four males over 16, three under 16, three females, and a slave [SC:11].

    iii. William[8], born say 1757, received a grant for 150 acres on Three Creeks in Craven County, South Carolina, on 16 July 1772. He was listed in Captain Robert Lide's Company of Volunteer Militia who signed a petition to the Council of Safety of South Carolina on 9 October 1775. He was counted as white in 1790, head of a Beaufort District, South Carolina household of one male over 16, three under 16, and two females [SC:11].

12. Margaret/ Peggy Sweat, born say 1728, was living in Chesterfield County, Virginia, on 6 December 1751 when the court ordered the churchwardens to bind out her unnamed son [Orders 1749-54, 159]. She was head of a Williamsburg City household of 4 persons in 1782 [VA:46]. She may have been the ancestor of

    i.   William, taxable in King William County from 1788 to 1815: taxable on 2 horses in 1793, taxable on his own tithe and 2 horses while living on the Pamunkey Indian Reservation from 1797 to 1800, not listed in 1801 and 1802, taxable on 3 horses in 1803, a "Mulatto" taxable on 2 horses in 1813 and 1814 [PPTL 1782-1811; 1812-50]. He may have been the father of Judy Sweat, wife of Gideon **Langston**. William, Abram and Allen Sweat were among twenty-eight Pamunkey Indians who signed a petition to the governor in 1836 [Rountree, *Pocahontas's People*, 193-4, 337, 344].

13. William[5] Sweat, born say 1730, was a "Mulato" taxable in Bladen County, North Carolina, on himself and son Benjamin in 1768 and taxable on himself and son George in 1772 [Byrd, *Bladen County Tax Lists*, I:7, 82]. He was one of the "free Negors and Mullatus living upon the Kings Land" in "A List of the Mob Raitously Assembled together in Bladen County" on 13 October 1773: Ephraim, William, George, and Benjamin Sweat [G.A. 1773, Box 7]. He received a patent for 100 acres "in Bladen or Anson County" on the northeast of Leith's Creek on 6 March 1775 [Hoffman, *Land Patents*, II:212], perhaps the William Sweat who was head of a Greenville County, South Carolina household of 5 "other free" in 1800 [SC:275]. He was the father of

    i.   Benjamin, born say 1750, taxable in his father's household in 1768, taxable in 1772 in the Bladen County household of Benjamin **Dees** (who was counted as white) [Byrd, *Bladen County Tax Lists*, I:7, 78]. He was taxable on one poll in Bladen County in Captain John Cades' District in 1784 and counted as white in Orangeburgh District, South

Carolina, in 1790: head of a household of one male over 16, four
under 16, and seven females in 1790 [SC:96]. He was living near
Richard **Groom** and William **Groom**, also counted as white, who were
listed with Benjamin as "free Negors and Mullatus" in Bladen County
in 1773 [G.A. 1773, Box 7].

ii. George[1], born say 1753, a Bute County, North Carolina taxable in
1771 in the list of William Person in John Coggin's household, and
taxable in his father's Bladen County household in 1772 [Byrd, *Bladen
County Tax Lists*, I:82]. He was probably one of two George Sweats
who were heads of "other free" households in Halifax County, North
Carolina, in 1790 [NC:62, 66].

18   iii. ?Ephraim, born say 1755.

iv. ?Gilbert, born about 1756, taxable in Washington County, Tennessee,
in 1788 [*Tennessee Ancestors* 5:37]. He was counted as white in the
1790 census for Burke County, North Carolina: head of a household of
one male over 16, one under 16, and 2 females [NC:108]. On 7 June
1797 he purchased 313 acres in Greenville County, South Carolina, on
a branch of the Saluda River. On 12 August 1799 he sold 50 acres in
Greenville on Brush Creek of Reedy River and on 13 February 1800
sold 213 acres on both sides of Reedy Creek including Laughenties
Shoals for $430 [DB D:388; E:331; F:311]. He was counted as white
in Greenville County in 1800, head of a household of one male 16-26,
one male 26-45, two females 10-16 and one female 26-45 [SC:264]. By
1806 he was involved in a lawsuit in Opelousas, St. Landry Parish,
Louisiana. He was head of a Opelousas household of 3 "other free" and
a slave in 1810 [LA:325] and 5 "free colored" in 1820. On 20 January
1817 he and Peter McDaniel recorded a survey for 1,354 acres on the
waters of Bayou Chicot in St. Landry Parish. He recorded patent
certificate no.504 on 27 April 1830 in St. Landry Parish for a tract of
508 acres on the right bank of the Bayou Chicot based on a survey
which he had filed 9 July 1811 [Wise, *Sweat Families of the South*, 12-
17]. The story of his travels was recorded in a 21 August 1829 St.
Landry Parish court case in which his wife's daughter by a previous
marriage sued him for her share of his deceased wife's estate. Joshua
Perkins, testifying on his behalf, deposed that Gilbert was born in what
was by then Marion County, South Carolina, about 1756 (seventy-three
or seventy-four years old on 25 May 1830). About the year 1777
Joshua helped him to run away with Frances Smith, the wife of John
Barney Taylor, who left her husband because he was mistreating her.
Gilbert moved from South Carolina to Tennessee, to North Carolina,
to Big Black River, Mississippi, and arrived in Louisiana about 1804
with a slave named Dick and a mare. Another deponent, George
Nelson, testified that he knew Gilbert on Reedy River near the iron
works in Greenville County, South Carolina, went with him to
Tennessee, and lived in the same house or neighborhood with him for
thirty years. Aaron **Dial** deposed that he remembered seeing him and
his brother Ephraim Sweat at the iron works, moved with him to
Tennessee, and that James **Graves** lived with him until he married
[Parish of St. Landry, case no.1533]. Gilbert died on 25 May 1830
according to the petition to the St. Landry Parish Probate Court of his
brother Ephraim who stated that he was the only heir of Gilbert who
died leaving a considerable amount of property which consisted of
lands, slaves, horses and cattle [Wise, *Sweat Families of the South*, 15-
17].

14. William[7] Sweat, born say 1756, was taxable in District 10 of Halifax County,
North Carolina, in 1782 and head of a household of 1 free male and 3 females
in District 8 of Halifax County for the 1786 state census. He received a 640

acre grant for his services in the Revolution [mentioned in Franklin County DB 6:89]. He was the father of

    i.   Nancy, born December 1792, called the orphan of William Sweat, deceased, on 20 May 1799 when she was bound to James Conner in Halifax County court [Minutes 1799-1802, 23].

15. George[2] Sweat, born say 1760, received army pay for service to the Revolution [Clark, *State Records*, XVII:250]. He was taxable on one free poll in Halifax County, North Carolina, in 1790 and head of a Halifax County household of 4 "other free" in 1790 [NC:62]. He was deceased by 18 November 1799 when the Halifax County court ordered two of his children bound to (his brother?) Abram Sweat [Minutes 1799-1802, 62]. Perhaps his widow was Delilah Sweat, head of a Halifax County household of 4 "other free" in 1810 [NC:50]. George's children bound out in 1799 were

    i.   Nancy, born about 1788.
    ii. George[3], born about 1791.

16. Allen Sweat, born about 1766, was head of a household of a free male and 2 free females in the state census in District 10 of Halifax County, North Carolina, in 1786. He married Nancy **Evans**, 7 January 1792 Wake County bond, Reuben **Evans** bondsman. He was taxable in Henry King's list for Wake County on 100 acres in 1794 and 1 poll in 1799 and 1802 [MFCR 099.701.1, frames 151, 228, 254]. He was about fifty-two years old on 7 June 1818 when he made a declaration in Wake County court to obtain a pension. He stated that he enlisted in Halifax County about 1782. Exum **Scott** testified that he had known him since his infancy while living on **Scott**'s plantation in Roanoke. And Francis **Jones** testified on his behalf. He later moved to McNairy County, Tennessee, where his wife received a survivor's pension. She testified that they were married on 28 January 1792 and her husband died 29 March 1844 [M804-2332]. His children living with him in Wake County in 1820 were

    i.   John[2], born about 1802.
    ii. Hezekiah, born about 1806.
    iii. Terrell, born about 1808.
    iv. Cary, born about 1810.
    v. Aggy, born about 1813.
    vi. Candis, born about 1815.
    vii. Hillsmon, born about 1818.

17. William[9] Sweat, born say 1760, was taxable in Meherrin Parish, Brunswick County, Virginia, from 1782 to 1787 [PPTL 1782-98, frames 24, 63, 93, 136, 206] and taxable in Greensville County from 1788 to 1801: taxable on a slave in 1789, 1791 and 1792, taxable on a free tithable over the age of sixteen from 1794 to 1797, taxable on his son Levi Sweat's tithe from 1798 to 1801 [PPTL 1782-1850, frames 69, 87, 112, 129, 141, 164, 193, 206, 222, 235, 248, 262, 277]. He purchased land on Rocky Run in Brunswick County which he and his wife Sarah sold on 21 May 1784 [WB 2:442]. On 26 August 1791 he was paid for attending as a witness for George Collier in Greensville County court, and he voted in Greensville County on 26 April 1792. He and his wife Sally sold 50 acres for 55 pounds in Greensville County on 12 October 1801 [DB 1:451; 3:62; Orders 1790-9, 94]. He was head of Northampton County, North Carolina household of 5 "other free" in 1800 [NC:477], 6 in 1810 [NC:746], 9 "free colored" in 1820, and 8 in 1830. He was the father of

    i.   Levi, born say 1778, taxable in the Greensville County household of William Sweat from 1798 to 1801 [PPTL 1782-1850, frames 235, 248, 262, 277].
    ii. ?James[4], born say 1800, married Maron **Roberts**, 5 December 1825 Northampton County bond, William Finney bondsman.

    iii.   ?Elizabeth, born about 1810, married Madison **Tann**, 11 September 1838 Northampton County bond, Drewry **Bass** bondsman, counted with Madison in household no. 632 of the 1850 census for Northampton County.

18. Ephraim Sweat, born say 1755, was counted as white in the 1790 census for Burke County, North Carolina: head of a household of one male over 16, two under 16, and 3 females, adjacent to Gilbert Sweat [NC:108] and counted as white in Greenville District, South Carolina, in 1800, head of a household of one male over 45, two males 16-26, two males under 10 years of age, one female 26-45, two 10-16, and four under 10 [SC:264]. Ephraim married Olive **Perkins** according to the 18 April 1811 Opelousas, St. Landry Parish, Louisiana marriage bond of their son Gideon [marriage license no.6].[199] Ephraim was head of an Opelousas, St. Landry Parish household of 7 "other free" in 1810 [LA:325] and 4 "free colored" in 1820. He petitioned the St. Landry Parish Probate Court as the only heir of his brother Gilbert who died on or about 25 May 1830. His children were

    i.   Robert[4], born say 1780, called the brother of Gideon Sweat in a St. Landry Parish court case in which he was charged with stealing a horse and mule. He was found not guilty of the charge but had fled the parish before the ruling [Wise, *Sweat Families of the South*, 31-2]. Perhaps his widow was Betsy Sweat who married George **Nelson** in Opelousas on 26 August 1811 [Opelousas marriage license no.11]. George **Nelson**, born about 1772, and his wife Mrs. Nelson made depositions for the 21 August 1829 St. Landry court case against Gilbert Sweat in which they stated that George's wife had been married to one of Ephraim Sweat's sons who died on 29 May 1809 [St. Landry Parish Case no.1533]. Their daughter Eleanor **Nelson** was called the daughter of Betsy Corder and George **Nelson** when she married in Opelousas on 28 June 1828 [Marriage license no.29].

    ii. Sarah, born 5 May 1785, married Amos **Avery**, 25 January 1819 Wilkinson County, Mississippi bond [Book B:137].

    iii. Gideon, born 1776-94, son of Ephraim Sweat and Olive **Perkins**, married Letty **Johnson**, daughter of Francis **Johnson** and Sarah **Gibson**, on 18 April 1811 [Opelousas marriage license no.6]. Letty **Johnson** was head of an Opelousas Parish household of 4 "other free" in 1810 [LA:325]. Gideon was head of a St. Landry Parish household of 5 "free colored" in 1830 [LA:45].

    iv. Mary, daughter of Ephraim and Olive Sweat, married Isaac **Perkins** on 23 September 1811 [Opelousas marriage license no.12].

    v. Olive, daughter of Ephraim Sweat, married William **Perkins** on 1 August 1818 [Opelousas marriage license no.11].

SWEETIN(G) FAMILY

1. Elisha Sweetin(g), born say 1740, was living in Anson County, North Carolina, on 10 March 1769 when he purchased 100 acres on Shoe Heel Creek, northeast of Drowning Creek, in Bladen County [DB 23:22]. He was taxable in Bladen County as white with a slave named Peg in 1771, taxable on Peg and a boy slave in 1772, a "Mix Blood" taxable on himself, his unnamed son, and two female slaves in 1774, and taxable on a "Mixt Blood/ Free Negro" male and female in 1776 [Byrd, *Bladen County Tax Lists*, I:60, 77, 124, 136; II:64, 94]. He was probably the father of

---

[199]The Opelousas Court House marriage licenses are listed in *Sweat Families of the South*, pp.97-99, copied from *Southwest Louisiana Records*, by Rev. Donald J. Hebert].

i. Charles, born say 1762, head of a Wilkes County, North Carolina household of one white male over 16, one under 16, and two white females in 1790 [NC:125], 3 "other free" and a white woman 16-26 years of age in 1810 [NC:900] and 4 "free colored" in 1820 [NC:496].

SYMONS FAMILY

1. Damarius/Damaris Symons, born 7 May 1724, was the white daughter of John Symons, a wealthy Pasquotank County Quaker, and Priscilla (Tomes) Nicholson Kinsey. She was disowned by the Pasquotank Monthly Meeting of 6 of 2 Month 1749 [Haun, *Pasquotank County Births, Marriages*, 26 and the Symons Genealogy, in *N.C. Genealogy* XV:2296-7]. In July 1748 the Pasquotank County court bound her "Mullatto" daughter Rachel to Peter Symons until she was thirty-one years old [Minutes 1747-53, 47-8]. Damaris' brothers, Thomas and Peter Symons, were her securities. Her child was
2   i. Rachel, born before July court 1748.

2. Rachel Symons, born about 1748, may have been the mother of
    i. Benjamin, born say 1779, head of a Pasquotank County household of 1 "other free" and one slave in 1800 [NC:625]. He purchased 9-1/2 acres in Pasquotank County on the north east side of the Little River from William Trueblood and sold Trueblood 6-1/4 acres in Pasquotank County on 1 December 1807 [DB R:208-9].
    ii. Isaac, born say 1782, head of a Pasquotank County household of 5 "other free" in 1810 [NC:928].
    iii. Tony Simmons, born say 1785, head of a Pasquotank County household of 3 "other free" in 1810 [NC:926].

Another, probably unrelated branch of the family
1. Amaritha Symons, born say 1750, was a taxable slave in Jeremiah Symons' Pasquotank County household in 1769: *Negrs. Isaac & Ammerica* [*N.C. Genealogy* IX:1207]. He applied for permission to emancipate her, and the bill authorizing the emancipation passed in the North Carolina Senate on 13 November 1790. Also emancipated with her were Davy, Joan, and Abbey, "negro and mulatto slaves" [Clark, *State Records of North Carolina*, XXI:749]. Jeremiah Symons called her "my Negro Woman by name Amereto who hath served me in the Station of House Servant" in March 1798 when the Pasquotank County court granted his request to manumit her [Byrd, *In Full Force and Virtue*, 200]. Her 24 February 1825 Pasquotank County will named her grandchildren: Aby, Jeremiah, Thomas, Elizabeth, Peninah, and Jesse **Sylvester**, David **Nixon** and Mary **Bow**.[200] Her grandson Jeremiah **Sylvester** was the executor. She was the mother of
    i. David, born say 1765, head of a Pasquotank County household of 3 "other free" and 3 slaves in 1800 [NC:636]. David's wife Lovey **Sampson**, "a Free woman of Colour," petitioned the Pasquotank County court in June 1797 saying that she had "some years agoe took to Husband a Mulatto man Slave named David, late the property of a certain Jeremiah Symons," and that she had purchased him from Symons [Byrd, *In Full Force and Virtue*, 198].
    ii. Johanna/ Joan, born say 1770, married Thomas **Sylvester**, head of a Pasquotank County household of 4 "other free" in 1790, 6 in 1800 [NC:633] and 18 "free colored" in 1820 [NC:275]. Thomas was called "a freeman of Colour" in June 1797 when he petitioned the Pasquotank County court for permission to manumit his "Wife a Negroe Woman

---

[200]David **Nixon** was probably related to Isaac **Nixon**, head of a Pasquotank County household of 3 "other free" in 1810 [NC:916].

Slave by the Name of Joan the property of a certain Jeremiah Symons"
and their four children: Abba, Nancy, Jerry, and Annaretta [Byrd, *In
Full Force and Virtue*, 198]. They apparently had a common-law
marriage until 21 December 1822 when Johanna made a deed of
jointure in which they were legally married, and she transferred to him
the land her brother David Symons had given her. She died before
December 1829 when her lands were divided between Jeremiah,
Thomas, and Jesse **Sylvester**, Nancy **Nixon**'s heirs, Abigail Symons,
Elizabeth **Relfe**, Sarah **Bow**'s heirs, and Penelope **Leonard** [Division
B:61].

TABORN FAMILY

1.   Thomas¹ Taborn, born say 1705, received a patent for 135 acres on the north
side of the Meherrin River by the side of the Miry Branch in Isle of Wight
County on 16 June 1744 [Patents 23:707; 29:304]. This part of Isle of Wight
County became Southampton County in 1749. He and William Tabers were
charged with trespass by Francis **Locus** in Southampton County court on 14
September 1749 [Orders 1749-54, 17]. He received a patent for 275 acres in
Isle of Wight County on the south side of the Nottoway River and northeast
side of Cockes Swamp on 3 November 1750 [Patents 29:304] and purchased
goods at the sale of the 5 December 1751 Isle of Wight County estate of
Joseph **Allen** [WB 5:391-2]. He was sued for debt in Southampton County on
14 May and 9 July 1752, but the cases were dismissed on agreement between
the parties. He and William Bynum were sued for a 2 pound, 10 shilling debt
on 15 May 1752. He sued John **Roberts** on 12 September 1752 and he was
sued by Exum Scott on 22 September the same year when the case was
dismissed on agreement between the parties. Scott brought suit against him
again on 14 December 1752, but the sheriff reported that he had either left the
county or was avoiding a summons. The court ordered his goods, which were
in the hands of garnishee William Barnes, sold to pay a debt he owed Scott of
11 pounds, 14 shillings. His goods included a parcel of tobacco, two stocks of
fodder, an iron pot and hooks, three hides, two plates, one porringer, a
tankard, plates, a rug blanket, spinning wheel, frying pan and other household
effects [Orders 1749-54, 224, 225, 249, 266, 280, 286, 319, 323, 354]. He
and his wife Mary were living in Brunswick County, Virginia, on 21 January
1754 when they sold their land on the north side of Cock's Swamp adjoining
Stephen **Powell** by Southampton County deed [DB 2:17-19]. On 13 May 1762
he sued James **Brooks** in Southampton County for trespass, assault and battery
and was awarded 20 shillings [Orders 1759-63, 219]. He died before 13 March
1770 when his son William sold by Brunswick County deed 100 acres on
Fountain's Creek in present-day Greensville County adjoining the North
Carolina line, being land that fell to him by the death of Thomas Taybor [DB
9:596]. Thomas was the father of

2   i.   William¹, born say 1730.
        ii.   ?Thomas², born say 1753, called Tom Tabor and living on Joseph
              Delk's land in Southampton County on 8 November 1770 when Delk
              was presented for not listing him as a tithable [Orders 1759-63, 219,
              284]. He was head of a Chatham County, North Carolina household of
              3 "other free" and a white woman in 1790 [NC:84]. He purchased land
              in Wake County by deed proved in December 1787 and sold land to
              Peter **Hedgpeth** by deed proved in Wake County court in September
              1791 (called Thomas Tabour) [Haun, *Wake County Court Minutes*,
              II:535]. He also purchased land by deed proved in May 1791 session
              of the Chatham County court (called Thomas Tabert) [Minutes 1790-
              92, 83]. His 1798 Chatham County will named his children Amos,
              Philip, Delilah, and Collier.
3   iii. ?Henry¹, born say 1750.

4   iv.   ?Burrell, born about 1760.

      v.   ?Dempsey, born say 1760, head of a Wake County household of 5 "other free" in 1790 [NC:105] and 8 in 1800 [NC:801].

     vi.   ?Joel, born about 1761, living in Nash County, North Carolina, in 1776 when he enlisted in the company of Captain Tarrent under Colonel Lytle. "Being a very young person of color" he was first employed as a servant to the officers before being placed in the ranks a short time after his arrival in Charleston. He was discharged in Charleston in 1783. He was taxable in Meherrin Parish, Greensville County, Virginia, in 1788 [PPTL 1782-1807; 1809-50, frame 68] and taxable in St. Luke's Parish, Southampton County, from 1790 to 1805: his tax charged to Jonas Bryant from 1790 to 1795, listed in his own household after 1797, a "M"(ullato) taxable on 2 free tithes, himself and "Surrel," in 1805 [PPTL 1782-92, frames 756, 826, 870, 885; 1792-1806, frames 51, 74, 155, 181, 280, 330, 392]. He assigned his right to a 100 acre land warrant to William Cheatham in Northampton County, North Carolina, on 29 May 1797. He was surety for the 19 May 1808 Southampton County marriage of Sarah Tabor and Cordall Newsum. He was a resident of Wake County on 10 February 1821 when he made his declaration in Granville County court in order to obtain a pension [M804-2335, frame 0772].

    vii.   ___, born say 1762, the mother of Labon Taborn, the two-year-old "Free Malater" son of Jesse **Hawley**, who was bound to David Bradford by the 3 November 1784 Granville County court [Owen, *Granville County Notes*, vol. 6]. He was called a "free Mulatto" by the February 1794 Orange County court when he was jailed as a runaway apprentice. The court ordered him hired out to the highest bidder to pay for his prison charges. The August 1794 court concluded that he was bound by the Granville County court to David Bradford who left him when he moved to Rowan County "being alleged his mother had used him ill." He married Anna **Tyner**, 5 August 1799 Granville County bond with Zachariah **Mitchell** bondsman.

   viii.   ?James, born say 1765, taxable in Wake County on 50 acres in 1793 and 21 acres in 1802 [MF CR 099.701.1, frames 71, 250], head of a Wake County household of 3 "other free" in 1790 [NC:106], 10 in 1800 [NC:802], perhaps the James Taburn who was a "free colored" head of a Northampton County household in 1820.

    ix.   ?Avory, a "free Mulatto" taxable in the lower district of Henrico County on a horse in 1804 and taxable on a horse and a retail license in 1805 [Land Tax List, 1799-1816 (includes Personal Property tax lists)].

2.   William[1] Taborn, born say 1730, married Judy **Allen** in Northampton County, North Carolina, according to the pension application of his son William [M804-2335, frame 0798]. Judy Tabour, late **Allen**, was mentioned in the account of the 5 December 1751 Isle of Wight County estate of Joseph **Allen** [WB 5:391-2]. He was charged with trespass by Francis **Locus** in Southampton County court on 14 September 1749. On 13 June 1754 he was one of fourteen heads of household who were sued in Southampton County court for failing to pay the discriminatory tax on free African American and Indian women.[201] He pled not guilty at first but withdrew his plea and confessed when Francis **Locust**, James **Brooks**, James **Brooks**, Jr., John **Byrd** and John **Byrd**, Jr., were found guilty. He was fined 1,000 pounds of tobacco,

---

[201]The other householders were John **Porteus**, John **Demery**, Isaac **Young**, Thomas **Wilkins**, Francis **Locust**, James **Brooks**, Jr. and Sr., John **Byrd**, Jr. and Sr., Abraham **Artis**, Lewis **Artis**, William **Brooks**, and Ann **Brooks**.

the fine for concealing two tithables, so he probably had two women in his household over the age of sixteen [Orders 1749-54, 17, 501, 513; 1754-9, 25, 39-40]. He was living in Northampton County on 13 March 1770 when he and his wife Judith sold 100 acres in Brunswick County, Virginia, for 27 pounds, explaining in the deed that the land fell to him by the death of his father Thomas Taybor and that it adjoined Fountain' Creek and the North Carolina line [DB 9:596]. His children were

5   i.   William[2], born in Northampton County about 1758.
6   ii.   ?Nathan, born say 1760, died about March 1833.
7   iii.   ?Allen[1], born say 1763.
8   iv.   ?Isaac, born say 1768.
     v.   Elizabeth, born say 1770, married Abram **Artis**, 11 October 1788 Greensville County, Virginia bond, with the consent of her mother Judy Tabour, Tempy Tabour and Peter Pelham witnesses.
     vi.   ?Wyatt, born say 1775, purchased land in Northampton County by a deed filed 29 April 1805, sold land by deed filed 29 September 1811, and purchased land by deed filed 10 October 1811 [DB 13:15; 15:214, 216]. He was head of a Northampton County household of 2 "other free" and one slave in 1810 [NC:748] and two "free colored" in 1820 [NC:262]. He successfully sued John Wood for a five pound debt in the 10 March 1814 Northampton County court. The sheriff sold his land for a debt by a deed filed 30 June 1820 [DB 20:385]. Rhody Taborn, Allen Taborn, and Wyatt obtained free papers in Northampton County on 22 March 1831 and registered them in Logan County, Ohio [Turpin, *Register of Black, Mulatto, and Poor Persons*, 10].

3.   Henry[1] Taborn, born say 1750, died before April 1778 when his son Henry was bound apprentice to Jesse **Booth** by the Nash County court [Bradley, *Nash County, North Carolina, Court Minutes* I:5]. He was the father of
     i.   Henry[2], head of a Nash County household of 2 "other free" in 1800 [NC:123] and 6 in Franklin County in 1810 [NC:826].
     ii.   ?Solomon, born say 1776, head of a Nash County household of 3 "other free" in 1800 [NC:122] and 3 in 1810 [NC:668].

4.   Burrell Taborn, born about 1760, was a resident of Nash County in 1781 when he enlisted in Captain Lytle's Company for twelve months. He was head of a Nash County household of 7 "other free" in 1800 [NC:122], 10 in 1810 [NC:668], and 6 "free colored" in 1820 [NC:445]. He died on 9 January 1842. His children were mentioned in the survivor's pension application of his son Hardimon [M804-2335, frame 744]. His children were
     i.   Hardimon, born about 1795, head of a Nash County household of 5 "free colored" in 1820 [NC:445]. He purchased land in Nash County adjoining Jesse **Booth** from Pheraby **Tann** on 28 January 1822 [DB 10:391].
     ii.   Larkin, born about 1797, purchased 120 acres on Turkey Creek in Nash County on 8 February 1817 [DB 7:414] and was taxed on this land in 1820.
     iii.   Caleb, born about 1809.
     iv.   Beady, born about 1812, married Berry **Locust**.
     v.   Elizabeth, born about 1814.
     vi.   Boling, born about 1816.

5.   William[2] Taborn, born about 1758, married Nelly **Evans**, 1 January 1778 Northampton County bond, John Watson bondsman [M804-2335, frame 0798]. He was living in Granville County in 1778 when Colonel William Taylor and Captain James Saunders requisitioned his wagon and team of horses for use as a baggage wagon for the soldiers. He made an agreement with John Davis to look after his crop in exchange for Davis looking after his wagon. He was

later drafted as a soldier and received a pension. He served in South Carolina under Colonel Lytle, who placed him under guard for getting drunk and cursing him. Fowler Jones, Sr., one of the witnesses for his pension application, testified that William served for a while as cook to General Butler. Another witness, Zachariah Hester, testified that he was a "Brother Soldier" with him in the expedition to the Savannah River. Jacob **Anderson** testified that he lived near him in Granville County when his wagon was requisitioned [M804-2335, frame 0798]. He was listed in Captain Satterwhite's Company in the Granville County Militia Returns for 1778: *19 years old, 5 feet 8 inches high, Darkish coloured hair & complexion, planter* [Mil. TR 4-40 by Granville County Genealogical Society, *Granville Connections*, vol.1, no.1, 15]. He entered 150 acres on Fishing Creek in Granville County on 29 May 1778 [Pruitt, *Land Entries: Granville County*, 13]. He was taxed in Fishing Creek on an assessment of 345 pounds in 1780, and on 149 acres, 2 horses, and 3 cattle in 1782. He was charged with trespass, assault, and battery in Granville County in February 1785 but was acquitted of the charge [Minutes 1773-83, November 178_ Dockets]. He was head of a Granville County household of 8 "other free" in 1810 [NC:898]. According to his pension record, he died 4 February 1835. The February 1835 Granville County court recorded the receipt for cash by his son Littleton Taborn for his support for six months, "but he only lived 1 mo. 16 days, 8 Nov. 1834" [Gwynn, *Granville County Guardian Accounts 1810-56*, 142]. William's wife Nelly, born about 1760, was living in Warren County on 26 May 1845 when she applied for a survivor's pension. William and Nelly were the parents of

    i.   ?Delilah, born say 1780, married James **Hedsbeth** 15 July 1797 Granville County bond with William **Mitchell** bondsman.

    ii.   ?William³, Jr., head of a Granville County household of 2 "other free" in 1810 [NC:898] and 6 "free colored" in 1820 [NC:34].

    iii.   ?Burton, head of a Granville County household of 2 "other free" in 1810 [NC:908].

    iv.   Littleton, born before 1776, head of a Granville County household of 5 "free colored" in 1820 [NC:32].

    v.   ?Edmond, born 1776-94, head of a Granville County household of 1 "free colored" in 1820 [NC:45].

    vi.   ?Elisha, neglected to give in his list of tithables in Wake County in 1794 [MFCR 099.701.1, frame 212], a "Mul°" taxable in Halifax County, Virginia, in 1794 [PPTL, 1782-1799, frame 546], married Mary **Allen**, 11 September 1795 Person County bond, Matthew **Allen** bondsman.

    vii.   ?Nancy, married Charles **Chavis**, 4 November 1795 Granville County bond, Benjamin **Bass** bondsman.

    viii.   ?Elizabeth, married Charles **Roe**, 11 December 1797 Granville County bond, Solomon **Harris** bondsman.

    ix.   ?Pomphrey/ Pomfrett, born about 1778, taxable in Oxford District of Granville County in 1799 [Tax List, 1796-1802, 177], married Patty **Hedspeth**, 24 December 1801 Wake County bond, Peter **Hedspeth** bondsman.

6.   Nathan Taborn, born say 1760, purchased 320 acres in Northampton County on 28 November 1782. He sold 100 acres to (his brother?) Isaac Taburn for 20 pounds on 24 August 1802, 100 acres to (his brother?) Allen Taburn for 20 pounds on 24 August 1802, and 100 acres on 1 January 1814 [DB 7:118; 12:97, 99; 16:355]. This last deed was cosigned by Mary Taborn, Sarah **Byrd**, and Ann Taborn who may have been his wife and daughters. Wyatt Taborn and Sterling **Haithcock** were witnesses (signing). He was head of a Northampton County household of 3 "other free" in 1790 [NC:73], 15 in 1800 [NC:481], 6 in 1810 [NC:748], and 4 "free colored" in 1820 [NC:262]. His

20 August 1830 Northampton County will, proved in March 1833, left his land
to his nephew Eli Taburn [WB 4:97]. His children were probably
  i.   Sally **Byrd**.
  ii. Ann.

7. Allen[1] Taborn, born say 1763, enlisted in Baker's Company in the 10th
    Regiment on 20 July 1778 but deserted three days later [Saunders, *Colonial
    and State Records* XVI:1173]. He was head of a Northampton County
    household of 7 "other free" in 1790 [NC:73] and 8 in 1810 [NC:748]. He
    purchased 100 acres in Northampton County from Nathan Taborn on 24
    August 1802 and purchased land by a deed filed in Northampton County on
    5 November 1804 [DB 12:99, 353]. He was sued by the State in Northampton
    County court and Halifax County Superior Court, and he had an unsuccessful
    suit in Northampton County court against James **Bass** on 5 September 1822
    [Northampton County court Minutes 1817-21, 318; 1821-25, 10, 140]. He sold
    his land by a deed filed 8 April 1828 [DB 24:92]. He obtained his free papers
    in Northampton County on 22 March 1831 and registered them in Logan
    County, Ohio [Turpin, *Register of Black, Mulatto, and Poor Persons*, 10].
    Perhaps his children were
      i.   Eli, born about 1804, received land in Northampton County from his
           uncle Nathan Taborn by his March 1833 will. He was head of Logan
           County, Ohio household in 1860 with one-year old William Tabor who
           was born in Ohio [Census, p.38].
      ii. Allen[2], born about 1790, married Charlotte **Tann**, 20 August 1814
           Franklin County bond. He was taxable on one poll in Franklin county
           in 1815 [*NCGSJ* XIV:237]. He was living in Monroe Township, Logan
           County, Ohio, in 1850 [Census p.13] and in household no. 279 with
           Ely Taborn in 1860 [p.38].
      iii. Exum, born 1776-94, head of a Northampton County household of 2
           "free colored" in 1820 [NC:262], sold land by a Northampton County
           deed filed in 1839 [DB 28:338].

8. Isaac Taborn, born say 1768, was head of a Northampton County household
    of 3 "other free" in 1790 [NC:73]. He purchased 100 acres in Northampton
    County from Nathan Taborn on 24 August 1802 [DB 12:97]. Perhaps his son
    was
      i.   Arthur, who sold land in Northampton County by deed proved on 27
           June 1823 [DB 21:279].

TALBOT FAMILY

1. Patt, born say 1729, was a "Melatto woman" who was bound by the
    Lunenburg County court to Matthew Talbot, Gentleman, in July 1750 [Orders
    1748-52, 298]. The eastern part of Halifax County was formed from
    Lunenburg County. Pat may have been the mother of
2   i.   Sally Talbot, born say 1760.

2. Salley Talbott, born say 1760, married Robert **Wilson**, 27 April 1789 Halifax
    County, Virginia bond, Richard Walne surety. Prior to her marriage, Sally had
      i.   Judith, born about 1782, married Sam **Beech**, 31 August 1831 Halifax
           County bond. Sam registered in Halifax County on 29 March 1803:
           *aged about forty-five years...black colour, Emancipated in Halifax
           County Court by the last will and Testament of Thomas Beech*. Judith
           may have been the mother of Joel Talbot who registered in Halifax
           County on 21 May 1831: *a ~~bright~~ dark Mulatto man, about 27 years
           of age, 5 feet 9-1/4 inches high, born free*. Judith registered in 1832
           [Registers of Free Negroes, 1802-1831, nos. 19, 137].
      ii. Susannah, married John **Hatten**, 1 January 1802 Halifax County bond.

iii. Betsey, married Bartlett **Chavis**, 11 July 1803 Halifax County bond.

TANN FAMILY

1. John[1] Kecatan, born about 1636, had been the slave of the Hoe family of Charles City County, Virginia, for about twenty-nine years on 14 October 1665 when he appealed to the Governor and Council of Virginia for his freedom. He was called "John a Negro" when he presented a note written on 26 November 1653 by his master, Rice Hoe, Sr., deceased, that he should be free after serving eleven years, "provided that he the sd Negro doth carefully and honestly performe his labour." Hoe's son, Rice Hoe, Jr., refused to release him, claiming that he had not lived up to the agreement. The General Court ruled that he should be free but referred the case back to the local court to determine if John had kept his half of the agreement. Hoe testified before the Charles City County court that his servant had been "refractory and disobedient" and presented the deposition of a former servant, Margaret Barker, who swore that

   the sd Hoe had never a serv't maid but the sd Jack the Negro lay with her or got her w'th child.

   But five other neighbors deposed that

   John Kecatan Mr Howes Negro have done Mr Hoe true and good service,

   and the court ordered him set free in February 1665/6 [DWO 1655-65, 601, 604, 605, 617, 618]. He was probably the "Jack negro" who was taxable on two persons in Surry County in 1670 [*Magazine of Virginia Genealogy*, vol.22, no.1, 23]. He was apparently the father of

   2 i. John[2], born about 1670.

2. John[2] Kiketan/ Kicotan, born about 1670, was a seven-year-old "Mollato boy" bound until the age of twenty-four on 3 November 1677 when Stephen Lewis sold the remainder of his indenture to William Edwards by Surry County deed for 2,500 pounds of tobacco [DW 2:157]. He was called a "Molatto boy Named Jno. Kikeson(?)" when he was named in a 7 May 1678 Surry County court suit between William Edwards and Stephen Luies [Haun, *Surry County Court Records*, III:381].[202] John Kickotan was taxable in William Edwards' household from 1687 to 1694.[203] He was head of his own household in 1695 and 1696 and lived adjacent to the **Cornish** family in Lawnes Creek Parish on Hog Island from 1697 to 1702. John Blackshire was taxable in his household in 1700 [*Magazine of Virginia Genealogy*, vol.23, no.2, 63; no.3, 56, 60, 65; no.4, 68, 71 vol.24, no.1, 69, 74, 76; no.2, 73, 77, 81; no.3, 71, 75]. He married Margaret **Sweat** before September 1697 when they were ordered by the Surry County court to present an account of the estate of Cornish **Sweat**, orphan of her first husband Robert **Sweat**. Anthony **Cornish** was Margaret's security. John Kecotan and Evan Humphreys were witnesses in the May 1705 Surry County court case between Roger **Case** and John Sugar [Haun, *Surry County Court Records*, V:168; VI:57]. In 1717 he sued Roger Delk for assault and battery in Surry County court [Orders 1713-18, 128]. He was paid 7 shillings by the Surry County estate of Edward Portice on 17 December 1723 [DW 1715-30, 496]. His children were most likely

---

[202]Likewise, "Black Dick," a slave freed in Lancaster County, chose the name Dick Yoconohancon which was later shortened to Nicken [See the Nickens History].

[203]John Kicotan's descendants owned land next to the Edwards family.

        i.   William[1] Kicatan, paid 1 shilling by the Surry County estate of John Ogburn on 25 May 1721 [DW 1715-30, 378].

3   ii.   Anthony[1] Tann, born say 1697.

3.   Anthony[1] Tann, born say 1697, was one of the residents of Brunswick, Virginia, who were paid for one old wolf's scalp on 2 December 1737. He was involved in a Brunswick County court case for debt on 3 May 1739 and 4 September 1740, and on 3 September 1741 he was one of the freeholders who were ordered to keep the road from Flat Creek to the Meherrin River in repair [Orders 1732-41, 182, 243, 348]. His son Benjamin Tann was called an "orphan" on 20 February 1744 when the Surry County, Virginia court ordered the churchwardens of Albemarle Parish to bind him out [Orders 1744-9, 11, 22]. Anthony was married to the unnamed daughter of John **Jeffries**, Sr., of Albemarle Parish whose 3 November 1746 Surry County will, recorded on 16 June 1752, mentioned his grandson Benjamin Tann [DW 1738-54, 798]. He may have been identical to the Anthony Tann who was granted 550 acres of land on Jeffreys Creek and the Pee Dee River for himself, his wife, and nine children on 6 June 1749 [Holcomb, *Petitions for Land from the South Carolina Council Journals*, I:266]. He recorded a plat for this land in Craven County, South Carolina, on 7 June 1749 [Plats 5:306]. Anthony's children were

4   i.   ?Thomas[1], born say 1721.

        ii.   ?Joseph, born say 1726, living in Southampton County when the court dismissed a suit against him by Matthew Revel on 9 November 1752 [Orders 1749-54, 286]. His heirs received 640 acres for his services in the North Carolina Continental Line [Clark, *State Records of North Carolina*, XVI:1173].

5   iii.   ?John[3], born say 1730.

      iv.   William[2], born say 1732, named in a memorial of 13 November 1771 as having title to 550 acres on Jeffrey's Creek in Craven County (apparently the land which belonged to Anthony Tann in 1749) [S.C. Archives series S2111001, vol. 10:238].

6   v.   ?Anthony[2], born say 1734.
7   vi.   Benjamin[1], born about 1735.

4.   Thomas[1] Tann, born say 1721, was paid 7 shillings by the Isle of Wight County estate of Joseph Bridger on 25 September 1742 [Guardian Accounts 1741-66, 3]. He purchased 100 acres adjoining Allen and Newitt Edwards in Surry County on 14 September 1745 and sold 20 acres of it on 18 March 1748 [DB 1741-6, 341; 1746-9, 388]. On 21 November 1758 he and thirteen other "Mulatto" residents of Surry County were presented by the court for failing to pay tax on their wives [Orders 1744-64, 135].[204] He and his wife Sarah Tan were "free mulattos" who recorded the birth of their son Thomas in Bruton Parish, James City County, in 1766 [Bruton Parish Register, 28]. He left no will, but his oldest son was probably Jacob since he sold part of Thomas's land in 1777. His children were

8   i.   Jacob[1], born say 1755, died circa 1780.

       ii.   Thomas[2], born in 1766 [Bruton Parish Register, 28].

5.   John[3] Tann, born say 1730, was mentioned in a 26 February 1754 Surry County suit for debt he brought against Chambers Humphries. Humphries failed to appear on 26 February the following year, so John was awarded 2 pounds and 12 shillings [DB 1753-7, 114, 191]. He and his wife Susannah "of

---

[204]"Against Joseph Barkley, John Banks, John Banks Jr., Jas. Barlow, John Eley, Thomas Thorn, John Deverix, Wm Walden, Thomas Charity, Thomas Simon, Thomas Tann, David Walden, Thomas Wilson, Edward Peters, for each and every of them not listing their wife's according to law supposing the said persons to be Mulattoes..."

Southampton County" sold 400 acres in Brunswick County, Virginia, on both sides of Little Creek which he had purchased by deed recorded in the General Court on 11 October 1757 [DB 8:220-1]. Sue was paid 12 shillings by the Isle of Wight County estate of Martha Fiveash, orphan of Peter Fiveash, for seven yards of Virginia cloth before 7 August 1766 [Guardian Accounts 1741-66, 356]. John and Susannah Tan, "Both free Mulattas Now Living in Southampton County," had their son John baptized in Bruton Parish, James City County on 30 May 1768 [Bruton Parish Register, 32]. He purchased 65 acres near Beetree Branch adjoining Edwards and Thomas Pritlow in Nottoway Parish, Southampton County, on 9 March 1771 and sold this land on 13 October 1789 [DB 4:341; 7:332]. He was taxable in Southampton County from 1782 to 1792: taxable on a horse and 5 cattle in 1782, on 2 tithes, a horse, and 4 cattle in 1787, 2 tithes in 1789, called John, Sr., in 1791 and 1792, listed next to John, Jr. [PPTL 1782-92, frames 503, 526, 542, 576, 598, 625, 696, 745, 857; 1792-1806, frame 18]. He and his wife Susannah gave their consent for their daughter Elizabeth to marry by 27 December 1786 Southampton County bond. He was exempted from further payment of taxes by the Southampton County court on 13 June 1793 [Minutes 1793-9, 18]. Nelson Peirce, orphan of Peter Peirce, chose him as his guardian in Isle of Wight County court on 4 January 1796 [Orders 1795-7, 269]. John's children were

    i.   ?Susannah, married Matthew **Williams**, both of Isle of Wight County, 22 December 1783 Southampton County bond.

    ii.   John[4], Jr., born 26 October 1767, baptized 30 May 1768 [Bruton Parish Register, 32], taxable in Southampton County from 1791 to 1800 [PPTL 1792-1806, frames 18, 251, 301, 358, 459]. He registered in Southampton County on 6 January 1795: *aged 26, 5 feet 6-3/4 inches, Free born* and on 28 June 1797: *aged 31, Mulatto, 5 feet 7 inches, Free born* [Register of Free Negroes 1794-1832, nos. 96, 115]. He was a "F.N." taxable in Isle of Wight County in 1802 and 1803 [PPTL 1782-1810, frames 587, 607].

    iii.   Elizabeth, "daughter of John and Susannah Tan," married John **Cannady**, 27 December 1786 Southampton County bond, John Tann surety, Thomas Tann witness. The bond said her name was Susannah, but the Minister's return said Elizabeth.

    iv.   Thomas[3], born about 1770, registered in Southampton County on 28 September 1794: *a free mulatto abt 24 years of age 5 feet 7-1/2 inches high born of free parents in Southampton* [Register of Free Negroes 1794-1832, no. 91].

    v.   ?Isham, presented by the Southampton County court on 9 November 1786 for living in fornication with Sarah Crocker (a white woman) [Orders 1784-9, 217, 270].

    vi.   Sarah, born about 1778, twenty-five years old when she married Lewis **Bazden**, 27 October 1803 Southampton County bond, Mat **Williams** surety, 28 October marriage. Sally registered in Surry County on 15 February 1812: *Sally Bazden late Sally Tann a daughter of John and Susanna Tann decd. free mulattoes of Southampton county, of a bright complexion, aged about thirty four years of age...is 4'11-1/4" high* [Hudgins, *Surry County Register of Free Negroes*, 47].

    vii.   ?Ann, mother of a poor child named Betsy **Thomas** living in the upper district of Nottoway Parish when the Southampton County court ordered the overseers of the poor to bind her out [Minutes 1799-1803, 104].

6.   Anthony[2] Tann, born say 1734, was a "Free Mulattoe" taxable in Colleton, St. Bartholomew's Parish, South Carolina, in 1786 [S.C. Tax Returns 1783-1800, frame 138]. He purchased land by lease and release recorded in South Carolina between 1800 & 1801 [Lucas, *Index to Deeds of South Carolina*, D-7:277]. He was counted as white in 1800: head of a St. James Goose Creek household

of one male aged 45 or older, one female 26-45 years, and one male and two females 10-16 years old [SC:66]. He and his wife Margaret sold 100 acres in St. James Goose Creek Parish, Charleston District, on 21 October 1801 [Register of Mesne Conveyance Book, Charleston, E7:450]. He was listed in the 1807 census for Knox County, Indiana [IN:50]. He was living on the east bank of the Wabash in July 1808 when he was visited by Shaker missionaries. He and his family were members of the Shaker Village in West Union, Knox County, by May 1810. According to Shaker records, he was a "coloured man" man who died on 17 June 1811. His wife Peggy, a "real white woman," was "near fifty" when she died on 28 December 1814 [MacLean, *Shakers of Ohio*, 279-80, 286, 312]. His 17 June 1811 Knox County, Indiana will was proved in July 1811. He left his wife Margaret all his estate which was to be equally divided among his unnamed children at her death [Original Knox County will, box 3; recorded p.35]. His children were

9   i.   ?Jacob[2], born say 1760.

    ii.   ?Barney, census entry blank in St. Bartholomew Parish, South Carolina in 1790.

    iii. ?George, counted in the 1820 census for Knox County, Indiana census: entry blank with one "free colored" female 14-25 [IN:90].

    iv.   William[4], born September 1794, left the Shaker Village of Pleasant Hill, Kentucky, on 10 October 1828 [Shaker Village Roll Book, p.208].

    v.   Polly, born on the Santee River in South Carolina on 13 March 1797, died 1 April 1883 according to the records of Shaker Village, Pleasant Hill, Kentucky [Roll Book, p.65]. She was counted in the Mercer County, Kentucky census in Shaker Village in 1850: born in South Carolina about 1799 [MERC:281].

    vi.   Charlotte, born 1 August 1799 in Charleston, South Carolina, joined the Shaker Village in West Union, Knox County, Indiana, in May 1810, moved to the Shaker Village at Pleasant Hill on 30 March 1827 (after the Shaker Village at West Union closed), and died 15 March 1875 according to the records of Shaker Village in Pleasant Hill, Kentucky [Record Book C, p.77, Harrodsburg, Kentucky, Historical Society; Pleasant Hill Roll Book, p.62]. She was counted in the Mercer County, Kentucky census in 1850: born in South Carolina about 1802 [MERC:280].

7.   Benjamin[1] Tann, born say 1735, orphan of Anthony Tann, was ordered bound out by the churchwardens of Albemarle Parish in Surry County on 19 December 1744. In 1754 he was an insolvent Sussex County taxpayer [*Southside Virginian* 6:48]. He moved to Northampton County, North Carolina, where he was listed among the "Black" members of the undated colonial muster roll of Captain James Fason [Mil. T.R. 1-3]. He was occupying land adjacent to James Morgan when Morgan made his 24 November 1774 Nash County will [WB 1:19]. He was taxed in Nash County on 260 acres, a mule, and 5 cattle in 1782. He received 9 pounds payment on certificate number 1859 from the North Carolina Army Accounts on 10 June 1783 and a further 14 pounds, 18 shillings on undated certificate no. 238 [T&C, Rev. War Accounts, Vol I:45 folio 2; XI:48, folio 2]. On 15 October 1787 he purchased 200 acres on the south side of the Tar River on Cooper's Creek in Nash County [DB 4:42]. He was head of a Nash County household of 5 "other free" in 1790 [NC:71] and 8 in 1800 [NC:122]. He sold 10 acres of his land to his neighbor and executor of his will, Jesse **Booth**, on 10 February 1804 [DB 7:215]. His 11 September 1806 Nash County will, proved November 1806, mentioned his wife Priscilla and two of his children, Benjamin Tann and Amy **Locus** [WB 4:42]. Priscilla was probably identical to Priscilla **Booth** whose illegitimate children Jesse and Sylvia **Booth** were indentured by the Nash County court in April 1778 [Bradley, *Nash County*

Court Minutes I:5]. On 28 September 1807 there was a judgment levied on Benjamin's land for a \$35 note in favor of John Lewis [Estates Records 1770-1909, 1807]. The account of sale of his estate on 5 June 1813 mentioned \$129.94 divided among six unnamed heirs [DB 9:265]. His children were

    vii. ?Ephraim, a private in Baker's Company, enlisted on 20 July 1778 for nine months. His heirs received 640 acres for his services in the North Carolina Continental Line [Clark, *State Records of North Carolina*, XVI:1173; T&C Rev. War Army Accts. Vol III:73, folio 3 & VII:108, folio 3].

    viii. ?James, a soldier who died in the service in Philadelphia during the Revolutionary War. He enlisted on 20 July 1778 and was omitted in 1779 [Clark, *State Records of North Carolina*, XVI:1173]. Jesse **Boothe**, executor of Benjamin Tann's Nash County will, deposed on 20 June 1821 that James' rightful heir was Hannah Tann, daughter of his brother Jesse Tann [S.S. 460.1]. She received a land warrant for 640 acres for her uncle's service [S.S. 460.1, 460.2, 460.3, 460.12].

    ix. ?Jesse, died before 20 June 1821, father of Hannah Tann.

10   x. ?Drury, born about 1760.

11   xi. Benjamin[2], born say 1765.

    xii. Amy **Locus**.

    xiii. Pheraby, living in Franklin County on 28 January 1822 when she sold land in Nash County adjoining Jesse **Booth** to Hardemon **Taborn** [DB 10:391].

8.   Jacob[1] Tann, born say 1755, was listed as a buyer in the 21 December 1775 account of the sale of the Halifax County, North Carolina estate of James Barnes [Gammon, *Record of Estates* II:25]. He sold 30 acres adjoining Ethelred Edwards and William Allen in Surry County, Virginia, on 19 July 1777 [DB 1769-78, 531]. His 1 December 1780 Surry County will was recorded 26 June 1780. He mentioned his unnamed wife, and underage children. He divided his land between his sons Thomas and Jacob [Wills 1778-83, 187]. His wife was Jemima Tann who was taxable on property tax for this land from 1787 until 1795 when Thomas reached maturity. The transfer of the land from Jemima to Thomas Tann was recorded in the Surry County Property Tax Alterations for that year. On 3 December 1801 Jemima was described as "a white woman late of this county" in her son's registration paper as a "free Negro." When her son Thomas married on 27 March 1804, he was called "alias Thomas Price," so perhaps this was her maiden name. Jacob and Jemima's children were

    i. Thomas[4], born say 1774, taxable in Surry County from 1791 to 1812, listed with Janson Edwards in 1794 [PPTL, 1791-1816, frames 46, 182, 224, 274, 305, 546, 577, 617, 658, 696, 715]. He was taxable on his father's 70 acres in Surry County in 1795 [Land Tax List 1782-1820]. He brought suit against his brother Jacob, still "an infant," in Surry County court on 28 February 1795, perhaps over payment of the taxes. The suit was continued until 28 May 1799 [DB 1795-1803, 309, 337, 367]. He sold the 35 acre portion of his inheritance in Surry County on 22 June 1795 [DB 1792-9, 272]. He married Selah **Cofer**, 27 March 1804 Surry County bond and marriage. He was head of a Surry County household of 2 "other free" in 1810 [VA:617].

    ii. Martha, born say 1778, chose Jeremiah **Banks** as her guardian on 28 February 1795 to represent her interests in her father's will. She registered as a "free Negro" in Surry County on 18 June 1810: *a mulattoe woman born of free parents late of the county of Surry deceased, of a bright complexion, aged about 26 years, has long straight hair...5'1-1/4" high* [Surry County Register, p.41]. She registered in Petersburg on 18 October 1810: *a light coloured Mulatto woman, five feet one inches high, twenty six years old, long straight*

hair, *born free in Surry p. certificate* [Register of Free Negroes 1794-
1819].

iii.   Jacob[3], born about 1777, taxable in Surry County from 1797 to 1810,
his tax charged to John **Banks** in 1797 [PPTL, 1791-1816, frames 284,
504, 546, 639, 658, 676] and taxable in Surry County on his 35 acres
inheritance in 1798, sold his land on 27 June 1803 [Land Tax List
1782-1820; DB 1800-4, 387].

iv.   William[3], born September 1780, not mentioned in his father's will,
registered as a "free Negro" in Surry County on 3 December 1801: *a
Mulatto man and son of Jemima Tan a white woman late of this county
- he is of a bright complexion, has straight & black hair, pretty stout
and straight made, aged 21 last September* [Back of Guardian
Accounts, 1783-1804, no.136].

9.   Jacob[2] Tann, born say 1760, was head of a Charleston District, Bartholomew
Parish, South Carolina household of 5 "other free" in 1790 [SC:36]. His
children may have been

i.   Sarah, born say 1785, married Peter **Graves** 15 September 1801 in
South Carolina [Bryan Journal].

ii.   William, fled from South Carolina to Georgia about 1835 after Simon
Verdier posted his bond on charges he had killed a "Negro" on John's
Island in Colleton District. Upon the court's determination of his race
as "colored," Verdier captured him, and he was tried and executed
[S.C. Archives series S165015, item 5164].

iii.   Jacob[4], living in St. Bartholomew's Parish, South Carolina, in 1840
[COLL:268].

iv.   Jonathan C., living in Spartanburg, South Carolina, in 1840
[SPAR:268].

10.   Drury Tann, born about 1760, enlisted as a private in Hadley's Company of
the 10th Regiment of the North Carolina Continental Line on 1 August 1782,
but there was no record of his service [Clark, *State Records of North Carolina*,
XVI:1175]. He was head of a Northampton County, North Carolina household
of 3 "Black" persons 12-50 years old and 2 "Black" persons less than 12 or
over 50 years old in Dupree's District for the 1786 state census. He was head
of household of 4 "other free" in Northampton County in 1790 [NC:74], 3 in
Hertford County in 1800 [NC:722], and 2 "free colored" in Southampton
County, Virginia, in 1820: a man and woman over 45 years of age. He was
taxable in Southampton County as a "free Negro" laborer in 1813 and 1814,
living on Arthur Carr's land in 1820. In 1830 he was listed as a "F.N." on
Samuel Williams' land [PPTL 1807-21, frames 326, 426]. He was probably
the "free colored" man over 55 years of age counted in Hamilton Tann's
household in the 1830 Southampton County census. He made an application
for a Revolutionary War pension in Southampton County court on 7 March
1834 in which he told about his early years in North Carolina:

he was stolen from his parents when a small boy by persons unknown to
him, who were carrying him to sell him into Slavery, and had gotten with
him and other stolen property as far as the Mountains on their way, that
his parents made complaint to a Mr. Tanner Alford who was Then a
magistrate in the county of Wake State of North Carolina to get me back
from Those who had stolen me and he did pursue the Rogues & overtook
Them at the mountains and took me from Them.

He may have been the son of Benjamin[1] Tann since Benjamin was listed in the
1782 Nash County Tax list as a neighbor of Tanner Alford. Drury did not
name his children, but they may have been

i.   Nancy, born before 1776, head of a Hertford County household of 4
"free colored" in 1820 [NC:198] and 3 in 1830.

ii. Jincy, born 1776-94, head of a Northampton County household of 3 "free colored" in 1820 [NC:262], married James **Boon**, 5 June 1826 Northampton County bond.

iii. Britton, born about 1800, head of a Northampton County household of 3 "free colored" in 1820 [NC:264], taxable on one poll in District 10 of Northampton County in 1823 and District 6 in 1824. He married Mitetto **Jones**, 24 March 1828 Halifax County bond, and was head of a Halifax County household of 2 "free colored" in 1830.

iv. Randall/Randolph Tann, born about 1807, married Betsy **Banks**, 5 July 1816 Northampton County bond, John Predens bondsman. He was taxable on one poll in District 9 of Northampton County in 1825.

v. Anney, married Acre **Johnson**, 27 February 1826 Northampton County bond.

12 vi. Patsey, born say 1793.
13 vii. Cherry, born about 1796.

viii. Exum, born 1794-1806, head of a Northampton County household of 1 "free colored" in 1830.

ix. William^5, born about 1800, indentured to John Priden to be a shoemaker in Northampton County in 1812.

x. Hamilton, born about 1803, taxed in 1819 as a "free Mulatto" over sixteen years old in Southampton County, Virginia. He married Jane **Gardner** in Southampton County on 28 December 1824, and he was taxed on one horse in Southampton in 1826. He was counted as white in 1830 with 2 "free colored" in his household, probably Drury Tann and his wife. On 21 November 1831 he (called "fn.") and his wife Jincy Tan sold 160 acres adjoining Seacock Swamp in Southampton County for $150 [DB 22:107].

11. Benjamin^2 Tann, born about 1765, was head of a Nash County household of 4 "other free" in 1800 [NC:122]. He received land by his father's 10 February 1804 Nash County will. On 14 August 1809 the Nash County court bound John and Susanna **Locus** to him as apprentices [Rackley, *Nash County North Carolina Court Minutes* VI:71]. Perhaps his children were

i. Benjamin^3, born about 1795, "Negro," purchased land in Cincinnati District, Indiana, on 21 April 1837 [Land Entries, Vol I, SE 1/4 - SE 1/4 - SE 1]. He was head of a Randolph County, Indiana household of 3 "free colored" in 1840 [Census p.108]. He was counted in the 1870 census for Porter Township, Cassapolis, Michigan: a seventy-five year-old born in North Carolina living with seventy-five-year-old Mary Tan who was born in Virginia [household no.221].

ii. Leroy, purchased one acre on the north side of Tar River and Fox Swamp in Franklin County on 15 March 1824 and sold this land to Elizabeth Tan on 3 January 1831 [DB, p.319]. He married Margaret **Pettiford**, 15 March 1831 Franklin County bond.

iii. Amy, purchased 3 acres on Driving Branch joining John Predens in Northampton County on 5 January 1818 [DB 20:164].

12. Patsey Tann, born say 1793, was the mother of Newsom Tann who was ordered bound an apprentice carpenter to Nathaniel Ingram by the Northampton County court on 5 June 1822 [Minutes 1821-25, 104]. Patsy married Winborne **Manly**, 27 February 1826 Northampton County bond. Her children were

14 i. Newsom, born about 1810.

ii. ?Cordy, born about 1813, may have been Newsom's brother since he was living near him in Ohio. He was head of a Jefferson Township, Logan County, Ohio household of 4 "free colored" in 1840 [Census p.77]. In 1850, still in Jefferson Township, he was counted as a

"Mulatto" with Eliza Tan, born 1820 in North Carolina, with five children born in Ohio, the oldest born in 1838 [Census p.288].

13. Cherry Tann, born about 1796, was head of a Northampton County household of 4 "free colored" in 1820 [NC:264] and was living in household no. 1038 in Northampton County in 1850. On 6 December 1853 when she was about fifty-seven years old, she married Everett **Banks**, Northampton County bond. Her children may have been

   i.   Madison, born about 1812, paid $2.60 as a witness in the State against Anthony Deberry on 8 June 1824 in Northampton County court. James Daughtrey received the money for him [Minutes 1821-25, 288]. The December 1826 court presented him for being without a guardian. He was bound an apprentice to William R. Taylor on 6 December 1826, no parent named, and was bound to Alfred Aldridge to be a farmer a year later on 4 December 1827 [CR 71.101]. His poll tax was charged to Herod Faison in District 6 in 1835, to Drewry **Bass** in District 3 in 1838, and to Diley Kee in District 3 in 1843. In 1837 he had a child by Tissie, a slave of the Kee family. Their son James Tann Kee named his father and mother in his marriage license when he married for the second time in Northampton County on 5 March 1894. Madison married Elizabeth **Sweat**, 11 September 1838 Northampton County bond. He was head of a Northampton County household of 4 "free colored" in 1840 and was counted in the Northampton County census for 1850, 1860, and 1880 with their nine children. His oldest daughter Louisa married Hardy **Artis**.
   ii. Joseph, born about 1831, living in Cherry's household in 1850.
   iii. Benjamin, born about 1838, living in Cherry's household in 1850.
   iv. Winnifred, born about 1837, living near Cherry in household no. 1040 in 1850.

14. Newsom Tann, born about 1810, was bound to Nathaniel Ingram "to read and write" on 6 June 1822 in Northampton County, North Carolina [CR 71.101.1]. In 1840 he was living in Monroe Township, Logan County, Ohio: head of a household of 4 "free colored" [Census, p.19]. By 1850 he had moved to Cass County, Michigan, where he was listed as a "Mulatto" farmer, married with a $400 estate, unable to read or write. Catherine, born about 1815 in North Carolina, living in his household, was probably his wife [Census, p.576]. By 1870 he was married to Rachel, born about 1830 in Indiana [Census p.21]. He had real estate in Cass County worth $3,000 in 1860 [household no.750]. His 28 March 1873 Cassapolis, Michigan will, recorded 26 September 1879, lent his farm in Calvin Township to his wife Rachel, and at her death to Levi **Hathcock**. He mentioned his daughter Margaret **Roberts**. His daughter was

   i.   Margaret, born about 1836 in Ohio, living with her parents in Cass County, Michigan, in 1850. She married first, Andrew **Shavers** in Cass County on 31 December 1854, recorded 18 January 1855; and second, Exum A. **Roberts** (born about 1826) on 23 September 1855 at Allen Hill's house, Jefferson Township, Cass County.

TATE FAMILY

1. James[1] Tate, born say 1660, "a Negro slave to Mr. Patrick Spence," was married to Hester Tate, an English woman servant of James Westcomb. Their son James was bound an apprentice to James Westcomb in Westmoreland County, Virginia, in 1691, and that same year three more of their children were bound apprentices. Her children were probably the "two mulatto servants" who belonged to the orphans of Patrick Spence, Jr., in December 1703 [Orders 1690-98, 40-41; 1698-1705, 210a]. James and Hester's children were

    i.   James^2, born say 1685, bound to James Westcomb in 1691. On 30 August 1716 John Chilton sued Joseph Moxley, claiming that he was detaining James who he claimed as his servant. The court ruled that James was a free person [Orders 1705-21, 261a].

    ii. Jane^1, born say 1687, bound apprentice to Patrick Spence in 1691.

    iii. Elizabeth, born say 1688, bound to Patrick Spence in 1691. She was presented by the churchwardens of Cople Parish, Westmoreland County, in September 1714 for having a "Mulatto" bastard child. On 27 April 1715 her attorney George Eskridge argued that she was not within the purview of the law against having illegitimate children because she was a "Mulatto." He posted bond to appeal the case to the general court. On 30 August 1716 the court ordered that John Chilton, Gentleman, pay her 1,160 pounds of tobacco for attending court for nine days in the suit which he brought against Joseph Moxley for detaining his servant James Tate [Orders 1705-21, 261a, 293].

    iv. William^1, born say 1690, bound to Patrick Spence in 1691.

Their descendants were

2   i.   William^2, born say 1726.

3   ii. Joyce, born say 1730.

4   iii. Penelope, born say 1732.

5   iv. Winnie, born say 1750.

6   v. Nancy, born say 1758.

    vi. Jesse^1, born say 1758, a seaman in the Revolution aboard the *Dragon* from 1777 to 1779 [Jackson, *Virginia Negro Soldiers*, 44] and head of a Richmond County household of 8 "other free" in 1810 [VA:395].

7   vii. William^3, born say 1766.

    viii. James^4, married Charity **Grimes**, 22 August 1804 Westmoreland County bond, Nathaniel Brewer security. James Teet, Jr., was head of a Westmoreland County household of 3 "other free" in 1810 [VA:787].

    ix. Fanny, born say 1775, a "free Negro" farmer living with children George, Elliner, James, and Jenney Tate, on William Edward's land in Westmoreland County in 1801 [*Virginia Genealogist* 31:45].

8   x. Peggy, born say 1780.

    xi. Peter, born say 1780, a "Molatto" farmer living with (his wife?) Phillis Tate in Westmoreland County on William Hutt's land in 1801 [*Virginia Genealogist* 31:45]. Phillis Tate was in a "List of Free Negroes and Mulattoes over the age of 16" in Northumberland County in 1813 [PPTL, frame 22].

    xii. Jane^2, head of a Stafford County household of 3 "other free" in 1810 [VA:128].

2.   William^2 Tate, born say 1726, was a "Mullatto" boy who still had 17 years to serve when he was listed in the inventory of the Westmoreland County estate of Captain Patrick Spence taken on 10 April 1740 [Estate Settlements, Records, Inventories 1723-46, 230]. He was taxable in the upper district of Westmoreland County 1783 to 1791: taxable on William Tate, Jr.'s tithe in 1787 and 1789 [PPTL, 1782-1815, frames 263, 311, 335, 343, 343, 355]. Perhaps his widow was Judy Tate who was taxable on 2 horses in the upper district of Westmoreland County from 1792 to 1797 [PPTL, 1782-1815, frames 395, 419, 444, 469]. She was listed as a farmer in Westmoreland County in 1801 with children: Elfried, Molley and Yewell Tate and Mimea **Locus**. She married Dick **Young**, 3 June 1805 Westmoreland County bond, John Watts and Jesse Tate security. William may have been the father of

    i.   William^4, born say 1771, taxable in the upper district of Westmoreland County from 1787 to 1798, called William, Jr., in 1790 and 1791 [PPTL, 1782-1815, frames 395, 419, 469, 485], listed as a "free

Mulatto" in 1801 when his place of abode was Louisa County [*Virginia Genealogist* 31:42].

   ii. Elfried.

   iii. Molley.

   iv. Yewell.

3. Joice Teet (Joyce Tate), born say 1730, was an "Old woman" in 1801 when she was a "free Molatto" living on William Fitzhugh's land in Westmoreland County, listed next to James Teet [*Virginia Genealogist* 31:42]. She may have been the mother of

   i. James³, born say 1760, taxable on 2 horses and 3 cattle in Westmoreland County in 1782 [PPTL, 1782-1815, frame 249]. He was a "Molatto" farmer living with (his wife?) Sarah Teet and children: Lovell, Betsey, Mauening, Sary, Laurence, and Lucey Teet on Henry Lee's land in Westmoreland County in 1801. Perhaps John and Ann **Locus**, two children living in their household, were his wife's relatives [*Virginia Genealogist* 31:42].

   ii. Samuel, born about 1779, married Hannah **Lucas**, 30 December 1809 Westmoreland County bond, Lawrence **Ashton** security. Samuel Teet was head of a Westmoreland County household of 4 "other free" in 1810 [VA:788]. He registered in Westmoreland County in May 1843: light complexion, 5 feet 6-1/2 inches high, about 64 years of age, Born free [Register of Free Negroes, 1828-1849, no.349].

   iii. Joseph, born say 1781, a "free Molatto" farmer living with Felicia Tate and children Sophia and Delphia on William Fitzhugh's land in Westmoreland County in 1801 [*Virginia Genealogist* 31:47]. He was head of a Westmoreland County 8 "other free" in 1810 [VA:787]. Felicia registered in Westmoreland County in May 1833: *a mulatto woman, 5 feet 4-1/2 inches high, 50 years of age, born free* [Register of Free Negroes, 1828-1849, no.180].

   iv. Ann, listed with children Nacy and Willis(?) Tate in Westmoreland County on William Fitzhugh's land in 1801 [*Virginia Genealogist* 31:47], head of a Westmoreland County household of 4 "other free" in 1810 [VA:787]. Perhaps Willis(?) was the William Tate who married _ **Pumroy**, 1805 Westmoreland County bond. William Teet was head of a Westmoreland County household of 4 "other free" in 1810 [VA:787].

4. Penelope Tate, born say 1732, brought complaint to the Westmoreland County court against (her master) James Clayton on 29 January 1756. The suit was dismissed in February 1757 [Orders 1755-8, 34, 123a]. She was living in Richmond County on 6 April 1767 when the court ordered the churchwardens of Lunenburg Parish to bind her son Charles to William Dekins. On 5 June 1786 the parish of Lunenburg allotted 280 pounds of tobacco to (her son?) Matthew Tait for her support [Orders 1765-9, 237; 1784-6, 335]. She was the mother of

   i. ?Matthew, born say 1760, allowed 280 pounds of tobacco for the support of (his mother?) Penelope Tait on 5 June 1786. He was a "free Molatto" farmer living with children: John, Lucy, Rodham, Alcey, and Presley Teet on Lusetty Smith's land in Westmoreland County in 1801 [*Virginia Genealogist* 31:42].

   ii. Charles, born say 1765, a "free Molatto" farmer living with (his wife?) Abby Teet and children James, Betsey, John, and Campbell Teet on John Neal's land in Westmoreland County in 1801 [*Virginia Genealogist* 31:42].

5. Winnie Tate, born say 1750, was living in Westmoreland County on 26 August 1777 when the court ordered that she appear at the next session to

show cause why her daughter Judith should not be bound out [Orders 1776-86, 46]. And on 22 February 1785 she was summoned to appear at the next court to show cause why her son Henry should not be bound out. On 26 March 1793 the court ordered her children Jesse and William bound out but rescinded the order the following day [Orders 1776-86, 46, 262; Orders 1790-5, 236, 239, 253]. She was the mother of

   i. Judith, born say 1770, married John **Evins**, 28 April 1795 Westmoreland County bond, Hugh Quinton, security. John and Judy **Evins** and child Rockey Tate were "free Negro" farmers living on William Fitzhugh's land in Westmoreland County in 1801 [*Virginia Genealogist* 31:47].

   ii. Henry, born say 1780, married John **Johnson**, 25 December 1809 Westmoreland County bond, Edmond Tate security.

   iii. Jesse[2], born say 1782

   iv. William, born say 1784.

6. Peggy Tate, born say 1780, was head of a Westmoreland County household of 4 "other free" in 1810 [VA:787]. She was the mother of

   i. Henry, born about 1800, registered in Westmoreland County in September 1821: *a Black Boy about 5 feet 6 or 7 inches high about 21 years of age and son of Peggy Teete who was free born* [Free Negro Register 1819-1826, p.7].

7. William[3] Tate, born say 1766, married Ann **West**, 28 January 1787 Culpeper County bond. He was taxable in Madison County from 1793 to 1817: taxable on his unnamed son in 1803, taxable on 2 sons in 1809, a F.N." listed with unnamed wife and son in 1813 [PPTL, 1793-1818]. He was head of a Madison County household of 14 "other free" in 1810 [VA:409]. He was apparently the father of

   i. Beverly, born about 1789, taxable in Madison County on John Tate's tithe and 2 horses in 1811 [PPTL, 1793-1818], registered in the Corporation of Staunton, Virginia, on 14 August 1820: *a yellow man (now) aged about 31 years, five feet 7-3/4 inches high, who was born free; is registered...upon the certificate of Benjamin Cave, Clerk of Madison County Court dated 10 October 1812* [Register of Free Negroes, no.53].

   ii. John, taxable in Madison County in 1811, listed as a "F.N." in 1813 [PPTL, 1793-1818].

   iii. Reuben, a "F.N." listed with his unnamed wife in Madison County in 1813 [PPTL, 1793-1818].

   iv. Coleman, a "Free Negro" taxable in Madison County in 1815 [PPTL, 1793-1818].

8. Nancy Tate, born say 1758, living in Westmoreland County on 26 March 1793 when the court ordered the overseers of the poor in Cople Parish to bind out her children Edmond and Eliza. The court rescinded its order the following day [Orders 1790-5, 236, 239, 253]. She was a "free Negro" farmer on William Edward's land in Westmoreland County in 1801 with children Edmond, Jesive(?), Lewis, Haney, and Simon Tate [*Virginia Genealogist* 31:44]. Her children were

   i. Jesive(?).

   ii. Lewis, born about 1775, perhaps identical to James Lewis alias Tate who registered in Westmoreland County on 16 May 1835: *light complexion, about 60 years old, 5 feet 4-1/2 inches, Born free* [Register of Free Negroes, 1828-1849, no. 215].

   iii. Edmond, born about 1779, married Peggy **Aston** (**Ashton**), 12 December 1806 Westmoreland County bond, Joseph Tate security. He registered in Westmoreland County in October 1828: *a black man, 5'6"* *high, about 49 years of age, free born* [Register of Free Negroes, 1828-1849, no.24].

iv. Haney, listed in Nancy Tate's Westmoreland County household in 1801, perhaps identical to Haraway Tate (born about 1786) who registered in Westmoreland County in April 1846: *a Mulatto woman, 5 feet 2-1/2 inches high, about 60 years of age, Born free* [Register of Free Negroes, 1828-1849, no.415].

v. Simon.

TAYLOR FAMILY

1. Susannah **Pickett**, born say 1718, was called Susannah Pickett alias Taylor when her children: Sarah, Edward, Lydia, and James were bound out by the Surry County, Virginia court in January 1745/6 [Orders 1744-9, 108]. She was the mother of

     i. Sarah, born say 1739.

2   ii. Edward, born say 1741.

3   iii. Lydia, born say 1743.

     iv. James, born say 1745.

2. Edward **Pickett**, born say 1741, complained to the Surry County court on 16 January 1754 against his master Joseph Eelbeck. The court noted that Eelbeck had moved to North Carolina and ordered the churchwardens of Southwarke Parish to take him under their care [Orders 1753-7, 43]. He may have been the Edward Taylor whose son Aaron Taylor registered as a "free Negro" in Surry County in 1796. He was a "free" taxable in Prince George County in 1802, 1803, 1805 and 1810 [PPTL, 1782-1811, frames 565, 613, 637, 730]. His children were

     i. Aaron Taylor, born say 1770, taxable in Surry County from 1786 to 1816: called Aaron **Peters** in 1789 and 1790; listed in Armstead **Peters**' household in 1791; called a "M"(ulatto) in 1811; listed with 2 "free Negroes & Mulattoes above the age of 16" in 1813 [PPTL, 1782-90, frames 399, 461, 482, 557, 603; 1791-1816, frames 15, 68, 118, 245, 577, 601, 639, 676, 696, 728, 869]. He married Milly **Scott**, 24 December 1793 Surry County, Virginia bond, Armstead **Peters** surety, 29 December marriage. On 23 January 1796 he registered as a "free Negro" in Surry County: *son of Edward Taylor, resident of this County, a bright mulattoe man aged about 26 years, straight & well made, 6'1/2" high - born of free parents* [Back of Guardian Accounts Book 1783-1804, no.18]. He married, second, Elsey **Charity**, 23 December 1799 Surry County bond and was head of a Surry County household of 9 "other free" in 1810 [VA:617].

     ii. ?John Taylor, married Arry **Williams**, 25 December 1797 Southampton County bond. John apparently died before 19 February 1803 when his widow Aira **Taylor** married Aaron **Byrd**, Southampton County bond, Burwell **Gardner** surety.

3. Lydia Taylor, born say 1750, was a "Mulatto" living in Surry County, Virginia, on 19 June 1753 when the court ordered the churchwardens of Albemarle Parish to bind her out [Orders 1751-3, 443]. She may have been the mother of

     i. James, born about 1783, registered in Surry County on 26 August 1805: *a negro man aged about 22 years, 5'7-1/4" high, of a complexion more bright than otherwise...born of a free woman late of this county* [Hudgins, *Register of Free Negroes*, 27]. He registered in Petersburg on 23 July 1806: *a dark brown Negro man, five feet seven inches high, twenty three years old, born free & raised in Surry County by Cert* [Register of Free Negroes 1794-1819, no. 389]. His Surry

County tax was charged to Armstead **Peters** in 1801 and 1802 [PPTL, 1791-1816, frames 459, 496].

Other members of the Taylor family in Virginia were

    i.   John, born say 1740, in jail for eighteen months in Norfolk County and in the public jail in Williamsburg but freed in May 1762 when no one appeared to claim him [McIlwaine, *Executive Journals*, VI:220]. He may have been the John Taylor who was head of a Norfolk County household of 3 "other free" in 1810 [VA:923].

    ii. Prince, born say 1745, head of an Essex County household of 6 "Blacks" in 1783 [VA:52]. He was probably the Peirce Taylor who was head of an Essex County household of 8 "other free" in 1810 [VA:197].

    iii. Thomas, head of a Petersburg Town household of 8 "other free" in 1810 [VA:127a].

    iv. Dick, head of a Southampton County household of 3 "other free" in 1810 [VA:54].

    v.   Phil, head of a Southampton County household of 2 "other free" in 1810 [VA:60]. He was living on Ben Jordan's land in Southampton County with his wife Patty and with Bitha & Lisha **Artis** in 1813 [PPTL 1807-21, frame 326].

    vi. Dicey, wife of David **Bird** of Southampton County.

    vii. John, head of a Prince George County household of 1 "other free" and 5 slaves in 1810 [VA:541].

    viii. Charles, born about 1794, registered in Sussex County on 12 October 1816: *light complexion, 5'3-1/2", free born, 22 years old* [Register, no.89].

Members of the family in North Carolina were

    i.   Burwell, head of a Nash County household of 6 "other free" in 1790 [NC:71].

    ii. Keziah, head of a Halifax County household of 6 "other free" in 1800 [NC:346] and 4 in 1810 [NC:52].

    iii. Malachi, head of a Halifax County household of 7 "other free" in 1810 [NC:52].

    iv. Margaret, head of a Halifax County household of 2 "other free" in 1810 [NC:52].

    v.   George, born before 1776, head of a Cumberland County household of 10 "free colored" in 1820 [NC:216].

    vi. Harry, born before 1776, head of a Cumberland County household of 4 "free colored" in 1820 [NC:158].

TEAGUE FAMILY

1. John Teage, born say 1700, was called an Indian in Accomack County court on 8 September 1725 when the land he was renting was the subject of a court case between John Goodright and Thomas Thrustout [Orders 1724-31, 37]. His likely descendants were

    i.   Robert, born say 1750, a "Mulato" taxable on a horse in Northampton County, Virginia, in 1787 [PPTL, 1782-1823, frame 75].

    ii. Peter, born about 1751, a "Mulatto" bound apprentice in Northampton County in July 1753 [Orders 1751-53, 322].

    iii. Mason Teague **Toby**, born about 1756, "a neg° Girl aged 2 years," bound apprentice to Thomas Marshall in Northampton County on 12 December 1758 [Minutes 1754-61, 174].

2   iv. Jacob, born say 1760.

> v.   Abraham, head of a St. George's Parish, Accomack County household in 1800 [*Virginia Genealogist* 2:163]. He married Martha ___, July 1791 Northampton County bond.
> vi. Nelly Tigue, head of an Accomack County household of 7 "other free" in 1810 [VA:65].

2. Jacob Teague, born say 1760, was a resident of Accomack County who served in the Revolution [Jackson, *Virginia Negro Soldiers*, 44]. He was head of an Accomack County household of 7 "other free" in St. George's Parish in 1800 [*Virginia Genealogist* 2:164] and 6 "other free" in 1810 [VA:65]. He may have been the father of

> i.   Liliah, head of a St. George's Parish, Accomack County household of 3 "other free" in 1800 [*Virginia Genealogist* 2:164].
> ii.   Rachel, born say 1781, married Daniel **Moses**, 25 September 1802 Northampton County bond, Levin **Morris** security.
> iii. Armistead, registered in Accomack County: *born about 1781, a dark yellow, 5'4-1/4", born free in Accomack County* [Register of Free Negroes, 1785-1863, no. 657].
> iv.   Sacker, registered as a "free Negro" in Accomack County: *born in July 1785, a light Black, 5 feet 10-1/2 Inches, Born free* [Register of Free Negroes, 1785-1863, no.3].
> v.   Levin, registered in Accomack County: *born about 1797, a light Black, 5' 6-1/2" high, Born free* [Register of Free Negroes, 1785-1863, no.267].

TEAMER FAMILY

1. Sarah[1] Teemo, born say 1690, a "malato," bound her son James to William and Elizabeth **Brooks** in Elizabeth City County court on 15 June 1720 [Orders 1715-21, 189]. She was the mother of

> 2   i.   ?Mary, born say 1710.
>   ii.   James[1], born say 1719.
>   iii. ?William[1], born say 1721, ordered to pay John Webb 25 pounds of tobacco for appearing as a witness for him against Charles **Hopson** in Elizabeth City County on 20 July 1743 [Orders 1731-47, 341]. William was taxable in Jeremiah Creech's household in the Western Branch District of Norfolk County in 1761 and taxable in his own Norfolk County household in 1765 [Wingo, *Norfolk County Tithables 1751-66*, p.134, 171, 191].
> 3   iv.   ?Sarah[2], born say 1723.
> 4   v.   ?Ann, born say 1727.

2. Mary Temo, born say 1710, was presented by the Elizabeth City County court on 15 December 1731 for having two bastard children (no race indicated) [Orders 1731-47, 15]. She may have been the mother of

> i.   ?John/Jack, born say 1730, won a suit in Elizabeth City County court on 22 September 1743 against his master William Bayley for not supplying him with sufficient clothing and misusing him [Orders 1731-47, 352]. He was taxable in Norfolk Borough, Norfolk County, in 1767 [Wingo, *Norfolk County Tithables 1766-80*, 35].

3. Sarah[2] Teamer, born say 1722, was living in Elizabeth City County on 7 February 1748/9 when her son William (no race indicated) was ordered to be bound out. On 4 February 1755 the court ordered her "Molatto" son Sam bound out [Orders 1747-55, 68, 467]. She was a taxable head of household in Norfolk Borough, Norfolk County, in 1767 [Wingo, *Norfolk County Tithables 1766-80*, 35]. Her children were

    i. ?Edward, born say 1743, no parent or race indicated, ordered bound to George Barbee in Elizabeth City County on 21 September 1743 [Orders 1731-47, 348]. He was taxable in Norfolk Borough, Norfolk County, in 1767 and in Elizabeth River Parish in 1768 [Wingo, *Norfolk County Tithables 1766-80*, 35, 83].

    ii. William², born say 1748, ordered bound out in Elizabeth City County on 7 February 1748/9. He was taxable in Norfolk County in 1770 [Wingo, *Norfolk County Tithables 1766-80*, 119].

    iii. Samuel, born say 1754, ordered bound out in 1755.

    iv. ?Jeremiah, born say 1760, "Mulatto" head of a Nansemond County household in 1784 [VA:74]. He was over 45 years of age in 1815 when he and his two unnamed sons (16-45 years of age) were taxable in Nansemond County. He was probably the father of William Teamer (16-45 years of age) who was also taxable in Nansemond County in 1815 [Waldrep, *1813 Tax List*].

4. Ann Teamer, born say 1727, no race indicated, was living in Elizabeth City County on 7 February 1748/9 when the court ordered her daughter Bess bound to Ann Hawkins [Orders 1747-55, 69]. On 22 March 1756 her son James was bound to Robert Miller on the condition he give security not to carry him out of the colony [Orders 1755-57, 47]. On 5 October 1756 she complained to the court that her son Thomas had been bound to Charles Neilson but was then in the possession of Archibald White who was not teaching him any trade. On 5 April 1757 the court ordered her children Bess and Thomas bound to Ann Pattison, on 3 April 1759 the court ordered her daughter Sarah bound out, and on 25 June 1767 the court ordered the churchwardens to bind out her son Sam [Orders 1755-57, 81, 85, 106; Minutes 1756-60; Court Records 1760-9, 461]. Her children were

    i. Bess, born say 1748, ordered bound to Ann Hawkins on 7 February 1748/9 and then to Ann Pattison on 5 April 1757 [Orders 1755-57, 106].

    ii. James², born say 1755, "son of Ann Teemer," ordered bound to Robert Miller to learn the trade of "Barber and Perry Wigg Maker" by the Elizabeth City County court on 22 March 1756 [Orders 1755-57, 47].

    iii. Thomas, born say 1750, bound to Charles Neilson in Elizabeth City County on 5 April 1757, called "Thomas Teemare a free negro" on 21 May 1772 when the Norfolk County court ordered the churchwardens of Elizabeth River Parish to bind him to Francis **Jordan** [Orders 1771-3, 68]. He taxable in Francis **Jordan**'s Norfolk County household in 1771 and in his own household in 1772 [Wingo, *Norfolk County Tithables 1766-80*, 167]. On 19 August 1773 the Norfolk County court ordered Amos Etheridge, George Bowness, and Thomas Temar to audit the estate of Hardress Lamount [Orders 1771-3, 192]. He was a "free Negro" taxable in Isle of Wight County from 1783 to 1803: taxable on slave Nancy and a horse in 1785, taxable on slave Suck and a horse in 1786 [PPTL 1782-1810, frames 37, 70, 83, 94, 154, 189, 236, 252, 280, 341, 355, 400, 424, 438, 482, 501, 532, 587, 607]. Perhaps his widow was Sally Teamer who was listed as a "free Negro" in Isle of Wight County with her unnamed daughter in 1813 [Waldrep, *1813 Tax List*].

    iv. Sarah, ordered bound out on 3 April 1759.

    v. Sam, ordered bound out on 25 June 1767.

THOMAS FAMILY

1. Ann Thomas, born say 1720, was the servant of Mrs. Clark Hobson on 14 October 1740 when she admitted in Northumberland County, Virginia court that she had a "mulatto" child. The court ordered that she serve her mistress

an additional year after the completion of her indenture and then be sold for five years. She was convicted of having a second "mulatto" child on 13 June 1743 [Orders 1737-43, 169, 345]. She was probably the ancestor of

    i.   Milly[1], born say 1743, a servant who was bound until the age of thirty-one years to Joseph Ball. On 14 April 1778 the Northumberland County court denied his petition that she serve him an additional three years for having three children during her time of service [Orders 1773-83, 319].

2   ii.   Spencer, born about 1750.

3   iii.   James, born say 1760.

2.   **Spencer Thomas**, born about 1750, was a soldier in the Revolution from Northumberland County [Jackson, *Virginia Negro Soldiers*, 44]. He was a widower when he married Sukey **Sorrell**, 11 June 1792 Northumberland County bond, Thomas Pollard security. He married, third, Salley **Hogins**, widow, 11 October 1817 Northumberland County bond, John **Credit** security. He registered in the District of Columbia court in Alexandria on 1 April 1803: *a yellow man about 53 years of age was free born in the family of the grandfather of the deponent and that he served in Northumberland County until he became thirty-one years of age. William Lewis, Justice of the Peace* [Arlington County Register of Free Negroes, 1797-1861, p. 4]. He was a "free mulatto" head of a Northumberland County household of 7 "other free" in 1810 [VA:996]. His children were

    i.   ?Raleigh, born say 1784, head of a Northumberland County household of 7 "other free" in 1810 [VA:997].

    ii.   Nancy, born say 1790, "daughter of Spencer Thomas," married John **Wood**, 13 January 1807 Northumberland County bond, Spencer Thomas security.

    iii.   ?George, married Fanny **Marsh**, 25 March 1808 Northumberland County bond, Spencer Thomas security.

    iv.   ?Sukey, "free mulatto" head of Northumberland County household of 5 "other free" in 1810 [VA:997].

    v.   ?Amy, "free mulatto" head of Northumberland County household in 1810 [VA:997]. She was a "free mulatto" whose son Bill Thomas was bound as an apprentice cooper to Bridgar Haynie by the Northumberland County court on 11 September 1809 [Orders 1807-11, 124].

3.   **James Thomas**, born say 1760, enlisted in Norfolk County and served for three years as a seaman in the Revolution. James Barron, Jr., later a commodore in the U.S. Navy, described him as: *a fellow of daring and though a man of color was respected by all the officers who served with him.* In 1813 Nancy **Bell**, his sole heir, received two land warrants of 1,333 acres each for his services [Jackson, *Virginia Negro Soldiers*, 44]. Perhaps his widow was Rosa Thomas, head of a Norfolk County household of 2 "other free" in 1810 [VA:829]. His children were

    i.   Nancy, married _____ **Bell**, perhaps the John **Bell**, born about 1777, who registered in Norfolk County on 20 July 1812: *5 feet 6 inches 35 years of age. light complexion, Born free* [Register of Free Negros & Mulattos, no.79].

    ii.   ?John, head of a Norfolk County household of 2 "other free" in 1810 [VA:922].

Elizabeth City, Charles City, Prince George and Dinwiddie counties

1.   **Hannah Thomas**, born say 1705, was a "free Negro" presented by the court in Elizabeth City County on 16 May 1728 for having a bastard child [DWO 1724-30, 244]. She may have been the ancestor of

    i.   Philip, born say 1737, a "molatto Boy" indentured to serve until the age of thirty one and valued at 10 pounds in the 1 September 1747 inventory of the Charles City County estate of John Yuille of Henrico County [Henrico County Miscellaneous Court Records 5:1443-4]. He was a "servant Mulatto" of Thomas Yuille on 1 February 1765 when the Chesterfield County court found him guilty of petty theft. He was given twenty-five lashes because he could not pay his fine of 10 pounds currency [Orders 1763-7, 626].

    ii.   John, born say 1740, married Sarah **Lawrence**, widow of Robin **Lawrence**, 14 October 1786 Brunswick County, Virginia bond. Sarah was called Sarah Thomas on the 7 March 1796 Charlotte County marriage bond of her daughter Mason **Lawrence**. The **Lawrence** family was from Prince George, Dinwiddie, and Brunswick counties.

2   iii.   Robert, born about 1749.

3   iv.   William, born say 1760.

    v.   John, a "yellow" complexioned man born in Prince George County who was living in Caroline County when he was listed in a register of soldiers who enlisted in the Revolution [The Chesterfield Supplement cited by NSDAR, *African American Patriots*, 154].

    vi.   Abraham Thomas (alias **Cumbo**), born say 1769, married Mary **Brown**, "daughter of Abram Brown deceased," by marriage agreement of 13 April 1791 proved in Charles City County court on 15 December 1791 by which he recognized her right to slaves Isaac and Jane, two feather beds, and some stock of cattle and hogs which were in her possession [DB 4:66]. He was taxable in Charles City County as Abraham **Cumbo** alias Thomas from 1790 to 1799 and called Abraham Thomas in 1800 and thereafter, taxable on 2 slaves and a horse in 1800 and a "Mulatto" taxable on 2 slaves in 1813 and 1814 [PPTL, 1788-1814]. He (called Abraham **Cumbo**) was taxable on 30 acres in Charles City County from 1794 to 1801 [Land Tax List, 1782-1830]. He purchased 20 acres in Charles City County on the dividing line between the land of William **Brown** and John **Brown** from William **Brown** for 30 pounds on 17 July 1800 and he and his wife Mary sold 30 acres of land called Currabunga(?) on 21 November 1801. He purchased 41-1/2 acres from William **Brown** for 65 pounds on 20 February 1806 and he made a deed of trust for 50 acres on 23 April 1811. He purchased 40 acres for $240 in July 1816, and he and his wife Mary sold 40 acres to George **Jones** for $259 on 6 November 1816. He and his wife Mary made a deed of trust for a tract of 40 acres, a tract of 35-1/3 acres, a mare, seven cattle and two featherbeds on 15 May 1818 to secure a debt he owed Edward B. Colgin [DB 4:520, 600; 5:118, 384, 625; 6:47, 143]. He was head of a Charles City County household of 4 "free colored" in 1820 [VA:7]. Administration on his wife Mary's estate was granted to Abraham **Brown** on 17 March 1836 with Morris **Harris** providing $90 security [Minutes 1830-7, 270].

    vii.   David, born about 1766, registered in Petersburg on 16 August 1794: *a dark Mulatto man near five feet eleven inches high, twenty eight years old, born & raised in Prince George & Dinwiddie County's* [Register of Free Negroes 1794-1819, no. 14]

    viii.   Benjamin, born say 1767, taxable in Charles City County in 1788, a "Mulattoe" taxable in 1813 and 1814 [PPTL, 1788-1814].

    ix.   Sarah, born in August 1770, registered in Petersburg on 1 January 1799: *a Brown Mulatto woman, twenty eight in August last, five feet two and a half inches high, dark bushy hair, born free in Prince George County & raised in the Town of Petersburg* [Register of Free Negroes 1794-1819, no. 143].

    x.   William², born say 1772.

xi.   Willis, born about 1772, registered in Petersburg on 15 August 1800: *a light brown Mulatto man, five feet nine inches high, twenty eight years old, born free & raised in Dinwiddie County* [Register of Free Negroes 1794-1819, no. 178].

2.   Robert Thomas, born about 1749, registered in Petersburg on 5 May 1795: *a brown Mulatto man, six feet one inches high, forty six years old, born free & raised in the County of Prince George* [Register of Free Negroes 1794-1819, no. 100]. His widow Hannah Thomas, born about 1760, registered in Petersburg on 18 August 1800: *a dark brown Mulatto woman, widow of Robert Thomas, deced., four feet eleven inches high, forty years old, born free* [Register of Free Negroes 1794-1819, no. 187]. They were the parents of

i.   Susannah, born about 1778, registered in Petersburg on 14 August 1800: *a brown Mulatto woman, five feet six inches high, twenty two years old, thick bushy hair, being a daughter of Robert Thomas, born free & raised in the County of Dinwiddie* [Register of Free Negroes 1794-1819, no. 164].

ii.   ?John, born about 1781, registered in Petersburg on 4 August 1803: *a dark mulatto man, five feet five inches high, twenty two years old, born free & raised in the Town of Petersburg* [Register of Free Negroes 1794-1819, no. 255].

iii.   ?Frederick, born about 1784, registered in Petersburg on 13 January 1809: *yellowish brown free ~~Negro~~ man, five feet four inches high, twenty five years old, born free & raised in the Town of Petersburg, a shoe maker* [Register of Free Negroes 1794-1819, no. 451].

iv.   Nancy, born about 1791, registered in Petersburg on 13 January 1809: *a yellowish brown free Negro, daughter of Hannah Thomas, five feet one inches high, eighteen years old, born free & raised in the Town of Petersburg* [Register of Free Negroes 1794-1819, no. 452].

3.   William[1] Thomas, born say 1760, was a "yellow" complexioned soldier from Charles City County listed in the size roll of troops who enlisted at Chesterfield Courthouse [The Chesterfield Supplement; National Archives pension file S38435 cited by NSDAR, *African American Patriots*, 154]. He was taxable in Upper Westover Precinct of Charles City County in 1784, taxable on 2 horses from 1788 to 1793, a "Mulattoe" taxable in 1813 and 1814 [PPTL, 1788-1814] and head of a household of 4 "free colored" in 1820 [VA:11]. He made a deed of trust for 140 acres bounded by land of Peter Crews and the road leading to Westover on 29 December 1818 to secure a debt of $150 he owed Samuel Ladd, and he and his wife Lisey made a deed of trust for 50 acres adjoining Peter Crews and the road leading from the Long Bridges to Westover on 15 June 1820 [DB 6:281, 368]. He was called William Thomas, Sr., in his 22 February 1824 Charles City County will, proved 19 August 1824. He gave Hannah **Fields** her first choice of bed, cow and household items and five barrels of corn, left his granddaughter Elizabeth Thomas a bed and furniture, left his son Claiborn Thomas $6 cash and divided the balance between his daughter Elizabeth Thomas, son Claiborn and granddaughter Elizabeth Thomas. His estate paid Benjamin Harrison $10 for rent. Bolling and Smallwood **Bradby** purchased items at the sale of the estate [WB 3:28, 99, 158]. He was the father of

i.   Claiborn.

ii.   Elizabeth, born 23 March 1808, married to Littleberry **Fields** by 16 February 1826 when he received the legacy due her from her father's estate [WB 3:158]. She obtained a certificate of freedom in Charles City County on 17 November 1831: *(testimony of Peter Crew) wife of Littleberry Fields who was Elizabeth Thomas, bright mulatto, was twenty three years old 23 March last* [Minutes 1830-7, 84].

4. William[2] Thomas, born say 1772, was taxable in Charles City County in 1802 (called William, Jr.), a "Mulattoe" taxable in 1813 and 1814 [PPTL, 1788-1814] and head of a Charles City County household of 7 "free colored" in 1820 [VA:3]. He purchased 50 acres in Charles City County adjoining Abraham Binford's, Benjamin Harrison's and Herren Creek for $200 on 15 June 1820. He and his wife Elizabeth sold this land on 27 November 1820 [DB 6:369, 430]. He made a 22 March 1835 Charles County will (signing), proved 18 June 1835, by which he left $1 to his son Barnett, $10 to his daughter Elizabeth **Field**, $10 to his son James. He left his land to his wife Elizabeth and after her death left his "mill pond tract" of 50 acres to his son William on condition he pay $40 to his daughter Susannah **Miles**, and left his daughter Judith 50 acres on the east side of Herring Creek. And he named his wife Elizabeth and son William executors [WB 4:126]. He was the father of

    i. Barnett, born say 1793, called Barrot Thomas when he was a taxable "Mulatto" in Charles City County in 1814 [PPTL, 1788-1814].
    ii. Elizabeth **Fields**.
    iii. Susannah **Miles**.
    iv. James.
    v. William, born 17 July 1815, obtained a certificate of freedom in Charles City County on 17 September 1835: *son of William Thomas, a mulatto man, aged twenty years 17 July last* [Minutes 1830-7, 248].
    vi. Judith.

Other members of the Thomas family in Virginia were

    i. John/ Jack, born say 1760, served in the Revolution from Northampton County, Virginia [Jackson, *Virginia Negro Soldiers*, 44], perhaps the John Thomas who first married Nancy **Credit**, 12 July 1805 Northumberland County bond, Raleigh Thomas security; and second, Nancy **Sorrell**, "daughter of James Sorrell, Sr.," 7 April 1812 Northumberland County bond, James Sorrell, Jr., security.
    ii. Buckner, born say 1760, a man of color from Dinwiddie County who served in the Revolution [NSDAR, *African American Patriots*, 154].
    iii. Milly, born about March 1775, "a mulatto bastard girl," about two and one-half years old when she was bound to Fanny Melton in Dettingen Parish, Prince William County on 2 September 1777 [Historic Dumfries, *Records of Dettingen Parish*, 119].
    iv. Grace, head of a Prince William County household of 4 "other free" in 1810 [VA:499].
    v. Ralph, "Free Negroe" head of a Fauquier County household of 9 "other free" in 1810 [VA:370].
    vi. Samuel, "Free Negroe" head of a Fauquier County household of 6 "other free" in 1810 [VA:370].
    vii. Moses, head of a Botetourt County household of 9 "other free" in 1810 [VA:661].
    viii. Susanna Thomas, alias **Humbles**, born about 1790, married John **Redcross**, in 1807 in Amherst County.

North Carolina

1. James Thomas, born say 1755, was assessed 4 pounds tax in Currituck County in 1779. He was head of a Currituck County household of 8 "other free" and 1 slave in 1790 [NC:21] and 9 "other free" in 1800 [NC:150]. His 27 June 1811 Currituck County will, proved in 1812, named his wife Jane and children: James, Joseph, Aaron, John, Sam, William, and Seney Thomas.

2. Hillery Thomas was head of a Wake County household of 2 "other free" in 1790 [NC:105]. He may have been the father of those counted as "other free" in Franklin County, North Carolina, in 1810:
    i. Lettice, head of a household of 5 [NC:826].

ii.   Eliza, head of a household of 3 [NC:826].
iii.   Basdil, head of a household of 2 [NC:825].

THOMPSON FAMILY

1.   Joshua Thompson, born say 1690, and his wife Sarah bound their daughter Martha to John Sorrell until the age of twenty-one. On 25 March 1732 Martha petitioned the Westmoreland County court for freedom from John Footman, Gentleman, who then held the indenture. She testified that she was twenty-one years old on 22 June 1731 and the daughter of Sarah Thompson, a free "Mulatto" who was married to Joshua Thompson by whom she had several children [Orders 1731-9, 15]. Joshua and Sarah were the ancestors of

2   i.   Martha, born 22 June 1710.

2.   Martha Thompson, born 22 June 1710, was twenty-one years old on 25 March 1732 when she successfully petitioned the Westmoreland County court for her freedom. She may have been the mother of

i.   Thomas, born say 1731, a "Free Mulatto" who bound himself as an apprentice carpenter and joiner for six years to John Ariss of Cople Parish by Westmoreland County indenture on 31 January 1748/9 [Records & Inventories 1746-52, 81].
ii.   William, born say 1735, a "Mallato boy" listed in the 4 June 1751 Westmoreland County inventory of the estate of Thomas Collensworth.
iii.   John, born say 1737, a "Mallato boy" listed in the 4 June 1751 Westmoreland County inventory of the estate of Thomas Collensworth [Records & Inventories 1746-52, 156b].

They may have been the ancestors of some of the members of the Thompson family in Virginia and North Carolina:

i.   John[1], born say 1730, and his wife Hannah, "Mulatto" taxables in the Fishing Creek District list of Daniel Harris in Granville County, North Carolina, in 1761 [CR 44.701.19].
ii.   William[1], born say 1735, taxable with his wife Eliza in John Brickell's Bertie County tax list in 1757 [CR 10.702.1, box 1].

3   iii.   Mary, born say 1747.
iv.   Nicholas, born about 1747, registered in Petersburg on 20 August 1794: *a dark brown Man, five feet two and a half inches high, forty seven years old, born free in Hampshire County* [Register of Free Negroes 1794-1819, no. 69].

4   v.   Lazarus, born say 1750.
5   vi.   John[2], born say 1750.
6   vii.   Amy, born say 1752.
viii.   Henry, born say 1768, married Catherine **McGuy**, 29 September 1789 Westmoreland County bond, Bennett **McGuy** security. Catherine may have been the Kitty Thompson who was a "free Negro" farmer in Westmoreland County in 1801 [*Virginia Genealogist* 31:46].
ix.   William, born about 1770, registered in Petersburg on 18 August 1794: *a light brown Mulatto man five feet three and a half inches high, twenty four years old, born free in Charles City County* [Register of Free Negroes 1794-1819, no. 34].
x.   Reuben, born about 1774, registered in Petersburg on 3 July 1799: *a light brown, strait well made Mulatto man, five feet ten inches high, long bushy hair, twenty five years old, born free in Charles City on testimony of Travis Harwood* [Register of Free Negroes 1794-1819, no. 145]. He was head of a Charles City County household of 7 "other free" in 1810 [VA:943].
xi.   Joshua, born about 1781, registered in Petersburg on 8 June 1810: *a light brown Mulatto man, five feet eight and a half inches high, twenty*

nine years old, born free in Charles City County [Register of Free Negroes 1794-1819, no. 560]. He was head of a Petersburg household of 5 "other free" in 1810 [VA:119a].

xii. George, head of a Charles City County household of 4 "other free" in 1810 [VA:940].

xiii. John, head of a Charles City County household of 3 "other free" in 1810 [VA:958].

xiv. Samuel[2], born say 1775, a "free Negro" carpenter living with (his wife?) Alcey Thompson and (their?) children Christian and Cortney Thompson in Forrest Quarter of Westmoreland County in 1801 [*Virginia Genealogist* 31:46]. He was head of a Westmoreland County household of 6 "other free" in 1810 [VA:788].

xv. Hanabell, a "free Negro" farmer living with Sarah Thompson and (their?) children Felicia and Anney Thompson in Forrest Quarter of Westmoreland County in 1801 [*Virginia Genealogist* 31:46].

xvi. Robert, a "free Negro" farmer living alone in Forrest Quarter of Westmoreland County in 1801 [*Virginia Genealogist* 31:46], head of a Westmoreland County household of 7 "other free" in 1810 [VA:788].

xvii. William[2], a "free Negro" farmer living in Forrest Quarter of Westmoreland County in 1801 [*Virginia Genealogist* 31:46]. He was probably the Willoughby Thompson who was head of a Westmoreland County household of 8 "other free" in 1810 [VA:788].

xviii. Moore, head of a Westmoreland County household of 9 "other free" in 1810 [VA:788].

3. Mary Thompson, born say 1747, had been a resident of Surry County, Virginia, sometime before 19 August 1822 when her son Samuel registered there as a "free Negro." Mary was the mother of

7 i. Samuel[1], born 12 February 1765.

ii. ?William[3], born about 1777, registered as a "free Negro" in Brunswick County on 25 October 1830: *a free man of Colour about fifty three years of age, five feet seven inches high... born free as appears from the evidence of Robert Hicks* [Wynne, *Register of Free Negroes*, 108].

4. Lazarus Thompson, born say 1750, was a "Mulatto" taxable in Northampton County, Virginia, from 1787 to 1799 [PPTL, 1782-1823, frames 75, 98, 216, 273]. He was probably related to Kesiah, Tamer, Mary and Betsy Thompson who registered as "free Negroes" in Northampton County on 12 June 1794 [Orders 1789-95, 358]. He may have been the ancestor of

i. Peter, born about 1767, a "Mulatto" taxable in Northampton County from 1788 to 1799 [PPTL, 1782-1823, frames 82, 112, 217, 273], registered in Accomack County: *born about 1767, a light black, 5'8" high, born free in Accomack County* [Register of Free Negroes, 1785-1863, no. 739].

ii. Rachel, born say 1770, married Isaac **Stevens**, 22 January 1791 Northampton County bond, Coventon Simkins security.

iii. Isaac, born say 1771, married Leah **Stevens**, 22 September 1792 Northampton County bond, Jacob Frost security. He was taxable in Northampton County from 1796 to 1800 [PPTL, 1782-1823, frames 217, 294].

iv. Jacob[1], born say 1774, a "Negro" taxable in Northampton County from 1788 to 1799 [PPTL, 1782-1823, frames 89, 273]. He married Sukey **Morris**, 26 May 1795 Northampton County bond, Thomas Lewis security. He registered as a "free Negro" in Northampton County on 11 June 1794 [Orders 1789-95, 354] and was head of a Northampton County household of 3 "free colored" in 1820 [VA:215].

v. Sarah, born say 1776, registered as a "free Negro" in Northampton County on 12 June 1794 [Orders 1789-95, 358], married Abraham

Beckett, 26 October 1797 Northampton County bond, Jacob Thompson
security.
vi.   Jacob², Jr., taxable in Northampton County from 1798 to 1800 [PPTL,
1782-1823, frames 256, 294], married Tamar **Stevens**, 26 September
1800 Northampton County bond, Johannes Johnson security.

5.   John² Thompson, born say 1750, was a "Free Negro" farmer living with (his
wife?) Haney Thompson and children on Henry Lee's land in Westmoreland
County in 1801 [*Virginia Genealogist* 31:45]. He was head of a Westmoreland
County household of 13 "other free" in 1810 [VA:788]. Their children living
with them in 1801 were
   i.   James, born say 1773.
   ii.   Priscilla, born say 1775.
   iii. Bennett, born say 1777, married Barbara **Bell**, 28 December 1807
         Westmoreland County bond, William Thornton **Peirce** security. Bennett
         was head of a Westmoreland County household of 5 "other free" in
         1810 [VA:788]. William T. **Peirce** and Fanny and Barbara **Bell** were
         "Free Molattoes" listed in Samuel **Day**'s Westmoreland County
         household in 1801 [*Virginia Genealogist* 31:40].
   iv.   Nancy, born say 1779.
   v.   Joseph, born say 1781.
   vi.   Meriah, born say 1783, married John **Smith**, 13 February 1804
         Westmoreland County bond, William Thompson, Jr., security. John
         Smith was a "Free Negro" farmer living with Rose **Smith** in
         Westmoreland County in 1801 [*Virginia Genealogist* 31:45].
   vii. William⁴.
   viii. Gerard, called Jarrat Thompson on 21 May 1822 when he married
         Betsy **McKoy**, 21 May 1822 Westmoreland County bond.

6.   Amy Thompson, born say 1752, was living in Mecklenburg County, Virginia,
on 25 January 1798 when she consented to the marriage of her daughter
Suckey Thompson to Boling Chavous (**Chavis**). She was the mother of
   i.   Susan, born say 1770, married Boling **Chavis**, 25 January 1798
         Mecklenburg County bond.
   ii.   John, born say 1775, called "S. Amy" in the 1790 Mecklenburg
         County tax list [PPTL, p.44].
   iii. ?William, born say 1784, married Thrudy **Stewart**, 1805 Mecklenburg
         County bond, and second, Mary **Hailestock** (**Ailstock**), 19 February
         1808 Mecklenburg County bond, Abel **Stewart** bondsman. He was
         head of a Mecklenburg County household of 10 "free colored" in 1820.

7.   Samuel¹ Thompson, born 12 February 1765, married Edy **Debrix**, 18
September 1790 Surry County, Virginia bond, Howell **Debrix** surety. He was
taxable in Surry county from 1789 to 1812: taxable on a slave named Daphne
in 1790; taxable on 2 tithes in 1812 [PPTL, 1782-90, frames 538, 585; 1791-
1816, frames 196, 545, 638]. He was counted in the 1803 census of "Free
Negroes and Mulattos" in Surry County with his wife Eady and children:
Edwin Thompson (a sailor), Polly, Betsy, Rebekah, Nancy, and Averilla. He
was head of a Surry County household of 9 "other free" in 1810 [VA:617]. He
registered in Surry County on 19 August 1822: *a Mulatto Man, free born, the
Son of Mary Thompson formerly of Surry County, who is 5'6-1/4" high, a
pretty bright Mulatto...by profession a Black-smith, aged 57 years the 12th
Feby last pass'd* [Hudgins, *Surry County Register of Free Negroes*, 75]. His
children were
   i.   Edwin, born about 1791, registered in Surry County on 26 August
         1826: *a Mulattoe man of a bright complexion, his left Shoulder out of
         place...aged about 35 years and is 5'6-3/4" high, a black Smith by
         trade* [Hudgins, *Register*, 82].

   ii. Mary Whiten, born about 1794, registered in Surry County on 19 September 1817: *a mulattoe woman, the daughter of Samuel and Edith Thompson free persons, of this County aged about 23 years, is 5' high, of bright complexion, has long bushy hair* [Hudgins, *Register*, 67].

   iii. Betsey Atkins, born about 1796, registered in Surry County on 19 September 1817: *a Mulattoe Woman the daughter of Samuel and Edith Thompson...about 21 years of bright complexion, long bushy hair...is 5'2-1/4" high* [Hudgins, *Register*, 67].

   iv. Rebecca, born about 1799, registered in Surry County on 26 August 1822: *daughter of Samuel and Edy Thompson...aged 23 years, is 5'2-1/8" high...is a bright Mulattoe* [Hudgins, *Register*, 75].

   v. Nancy.

   vi. Averilla.

Members of the family in North Carolina were

   i. Ann, born before 1776, head of a Halifax County household of 5 "free colored" in 1820 [NC:167].

   ii. Zac(?), born before 1776, head of a Craven County household of 14 "free colored" in 1820 [NC:67].

   iii. Samuel[3], head of a Chatham County household of 4 "other free" in 1810 [NC:208].

An unrelated member of the Thompson family was:

1. Talbot/Talbert Thompson, born say 1735, entered into an agreement with Benjamin Waller to purchase his freedom after his master Alexander McKensie moved to England. He paid Waller sixty pounds and then petitioned the governor and Council of Virginia for his freedom in November 1761. Eight years later he purchased his wife Jenny from the estate of Robert Tucker of Norfolk County and then successfully petitioned for her freedom [McIlwaine, *Executive Journals*, VI:200; VI:320]. He was a taxable "free negro" on the east side of the borough of Norfolk in 1767 with his slave Joseph, and in 1774 he was taxable on "negroes" (slaves): Peter, Murray and Joe [Wingo, *Norfolk County Tithables 1766-80*, 39, 243]. He sued John Mallett in Norfolk County court for a 5 pound debt on 22 December 1769. The court found in his favor and ordered the sheriff to give Mallett 39 lashes if he failed to pay immediately. He was ordered to pay James Cooper for 13 days attendance as a witness for him in his suit against Christopher Bustin which was heard between 1769 and 1773. On 18 August 1774 the court ordered the churchwardens of Elizabeth River Parish to bind Jacob, "a free negro," as an apprentice to him [Orders 1768-71, 145, 147; 1773-5, 9, 60]. He may have been the father of

   i. Samuel, "free negro" head of a Norfolk County household in 1773 [Wingo, *Norfolk County Tithables 1766-80*, 206].

TIMBER(S) FAMILY

1. Sarah Timber, born say 1736, was the mother of a "mollato" girl named Priscilla whose birth was registered in Overwharton Parish, Stafford County [Overwharton Parish Register, 1724-1774, 189]. She was the ancestor of

   i. Priscilla, born 19 March 1757 [Overwharton Parish Register, 1724-1774, 189]. On 3 July 1805 a Mrs. Mary McCalanahan appeared in Greenville County, South Carolina court and testified that Sarah Timbers and her daughter Priscilla had lived with her in Virginia and that Priscilla was the mother of David, Thomas, Lewis, James, John, Patsy, and Charlotte **Burden/ Burdin** [DB R:162].

ii.   Thomas, "F.N." head of a Culpeper County household of 9 "other free" in 1810 [VA:82], and a "Free Negroe" taxable in 1813 [Waldrep, *1813 Tax List*].

iii.   John, "Free Negroe" taxable in Culpeper County in 1813 [Waldrep, *1813 Tax List*].

iv.   Susanna, "Free Negroe" listed in Culpeper County in 1813 [Waldrep, *1813 Tax List*].

TONEY FAMILY

1.   James Tony, born say 1698, was a "mulatto man Servant" of Thomas Jefferson (grandfather of the president). In February 1719/20 James confessed to the Henrico County court that he had been absent from his master's service for eighteen days without permission, and a year later confessed to another thirteen days absence [Minutes 1719-24, 7, 61]. He may have been the father of

2   i.   Elizabeth[1], born say 1716.
3   ii.   Mary[1], born say 1732.
       iii.   ?William[1], born say 1737, a taxable "Mulatto" in Wood Jones' list for Raleigh Parish, Amelia County, in 1753. He appeared in Granville County, North Carolina, on 8 March 1755 and bound himself an apprentice: *William Toney late of Colony of Virginia Molatto bound himself apprentice to Wm Eaton & unto Mary his wife 7 years* [CR 044.101.2]. A few years later William was taken up as a runaway in Prince Edward County, Virginia, and accused of burning down the county's prison while in jail. He was acquitted of the arson charge, but the court ordered that he be given thirty-nine lashes because he "appeared to be a great Imposture by appearing in womans cloaths and by often changing his name." And the court ordered that he be returned to his master William Eaton in North Carolina [Orders 1754-8, 66, 67].

2.   Elizabeth[1] Toney, born say 1716, was summoned before the Prince George County court on 13 March 1738 to answer for her "Misbehavior to the Gentlemen of the Court," and the same court ordered the churchwardens of Martin Brandon Parish to bind out her children Margaret and Elizabeth (no race mentioned). On 9 May 1739 the complaint against her was dismissed [Orders 1737-40, 244, 280]. Her children were

4   i.   Margaret[1], born say 1733.
       ii.   Elizabeth[2], born say 1738.
5   iii.   ?Mary[2], born about 1745.

3.   Mary[1] Toney, born say 1732, was living in Bristol Parish, Virginia, on 22 December 1750 when the birth of her son Charles by Matt **Steward (Stewart)** was recorded [Chamberlayne, *Register of Bristol Parish*, 369]. Mary was the mother of

       i.   Charles[2], born 22 December 1750.
       ii.   ?Lucy, born about 1758, registered in Petersburg on 20 August 1794: *a dark brown Mulatto woman, five feet two and a half inches high, thirty six years old, born free & raised in County of Prince George* [Register of Free Negroes 1794-1819, no. 66].
       iii.   ?Susannah, born about 1762, registered in Petersburg on 20 August 1794: *a dark brown Mulatto woman, much pitted with the small pocks, five feet one and a half inches high, thirty two years old, born free & raised in County of Prince George* [Register of Free Negroes 1794-1819, no. 67].
       iv.   ?Anthony[2], born say 1767, head of a Bertie County, North Carolina household of 4 "other free" in 1790 [NC:15].

v. ?Peter, a "free Negro" or "Melatto" taxable in the northern district of Campbell County from 1790 to 1793 [PPTL, 1785-1814, frames 160, 199, 243, 279], head of a Buckingham County, Virginia household of 14 "other free" in 1810 [VA:835].

4. Margaret[1] Toney, born say 1733, was living in Amelia County on 25 March 1756 when the court ordered the churchwardens of Raleigh Parish to bind out her children Charles, Jack, and Margaret Toney to Charles Hamlin. She was called a "poor Mulatto" on 28 January 1768 when the court ordered the churchwardens of Raleigh Parish to bind out her unnamed children to John Hamlin [Orders 1754-8, n.p.; 1767-8, 132; 1766-9, 123, 175]. She was the mother of

    i. Charles[1], born say 1749, a "Free Mulatto" added to Wood Jones' list of tithables for Amelia County on 27 November 1766 [Orders 1766-9, 24].

6   ii. John[1], born say 1750.
7   iii. Margaret[2]/ Peg, born say 1752.
    iv. Arthur[1], born about 1764 in Dinwiddie County, Virginia. He lived there until he was ten years old when he moved to Halifax County, North Carolina. He took the place of his brother John Toney in the Revolutionary War in Warren County and marched to Bacon's Bridge in South Carolina where he reenlisted. He was not involved in any battles since he was assigned to the baggage wagon. When he returned in 1782, he moved to Caswell County and made his declaration to obtain a pension in Caswell County court fifty years later on 9 October 1832. He was in Halifax County on 1 April 1847 when he made another declaration for a pension. His widow, formerly Elizabeth **Edwell**, born about 1780, was living in Caswell County on 10 November 1854 when she appeared before the Hustings Court in Virginia to obtain a survivor's pension. She stated that they were married in December 1799 in Caswell County, and her husband died there in his own house on 19 July 1847 [M805-807, frame 582]. Elizabeth **Edwell** was the five-year-old daughter of Winnie **Edwell** (not identified by race) who was bound to John Williams of Caswell County on 20 December 1780.[205] Winnie **Edwell** was probably the "free Winnie" who was counted as a "Mulatto" in the 1786 State Census for the Caswell District of Caswell County adjacent to "Mulattoes" Arthur Toney, William **Hood**, and John **Wright**. Arthur was a Caswell County taxpayer in 1790 [NC:79], an insolvent taxpayer in 1802 [Court Minutes E:38], and head of a Caswell County household of 10 "free colored" in 1820 [NC:90].

5. Mary Toney, born about 1745, registered in Petersburg on 10 July 1805: *a yellow brown Mulatto woman, five feet four and a half inches high, about sixty years old, born free in Dinwiddie County* [Register of Free Negroes 1794-1819, no. 315]. She may have been the mother of

8   i. John[2], born say 1763.
    ii. Mat/ Matthew[1], born say 1768, taxable in Dinwiddie County in 1800, counted in the "List of Free Negroes" at the end of the tax list from

---

[205]Other children of Winnie **Edwell** bound out in 1780 were Sarah, Jonathan, Judith, Joseph, and Robert **Edwell** [CR 020.101.1]. They were probably related to Dick **Edwell**, head of a Caswell County household of 4 "other free" in 1810 [NC:473]. Eady **Edwell**, born perhaps 1790, married William **Long**, 22 September 1807 Caswell County bond, Isaac Wright bondsman. William **Long** was head of a Caswell County household of 5 "other free" in 1810 [NC:488]. He was a resident of Caswell County on 5 October 1788 when he made a declaration in Orange County court to obtain a pension for his services in the Revolution [*NCGSJ* XII:102].

1801 to 1819 [PPTL, 1800-19, (1800 A, p.18)], head of a Dinwiddie County household of 8 "other free" in 1810 [VA:154].

iii.   Charles[4], born about 1775, taxable in Dinwiddie County in 1800, counted as a sawyer or carpenter in the "List of Free Negroes" at the end of the tax list from 1801 to 1817 [PPTL, 1800-19, (1800 A, p.18)]. He registered in Petersburg on 16 June 1809: *a light brown free Negro, five feet nine inches high, thirty four years old, short bushy hair, a sawyer, born free & raised in Dinwiddie County* [Register of Free Negroes 1794-1819, no. 480].

iv.   Becky, born about 1783, registered in Petersburg on 10 July 1805: *a light Mulatto woman, five feet five and a half inches high, twenty two years old, holes in her ears, born free & raised in the County of Dinwiddie* [Register of Free Negroes 1794-1819, no. 316].

v.   Kezia, born about 1783, registered in Petersburg on 30 April 1806: *a dark brown Mulatto woman, five feet six and a half inches high, twenty three years old January last, spare & straight made, holes in her ears, born free in the County of Dinwiddie* [Register of Free Negroes 1794-1819, no. 375].

6.   John[1] Toney, born say 1750, was a "Free Mulatto" added to Wood Jones' list of tithables for Amelia County on 27 November 1766 [Orders 1766-9, 24]. He married in May 1777 Martha **Carpenter** who was born about 1753 according to Winney Holly of Halifax, North Carolina, who testified for Martha's 14 August 1838 application for John's Revolutionary War pension.[206] Winney stated that she attended the same school as John's children. John enlisted in the 10th Regiment of the North Carolina Continental Line. He fought at the battle of Guilford Courthouse and "ran home and was taken and made to serve to the end of the war." He died in November 1823 [M805, reel 807, frame 623]. He was taxable on one free poll in District 6 of Halifax County in 1782 and 1790, and was listed in Halifax County in the 1786 North Carolina state census with 3 free males and 3 free females in his household. He was head of a Halifax County household of 7 "other free" in 1790 [NC:62], 16 in 1800 [NC:344], 11 in 1810 [NC:51], and 11 "free colored" in 1820 [NC:167]. On 28 September 1801 he was living on the land of Archibald Sledge when Sledge sold it [DB 18:817]. His 20 August 1823 Halifax County will was proved in February 1825 [WB 4:1]. His will mentioned his unnamed wife and children:

i.   Charles[3], born before 1775, head of a Halifax County household of 6 "free colored" in 1820.

ii.   Kinchen, born about 1775, head of a Halifax County household of 8 "free colored" in 1820 [NC:167] and 9 in 1830. He was charged in Halifax County court for a variety of petty offenses between 1833 and 1841. He was fined $10 on 20 February 1833, $20 on 19 February 1834, acquitted of a charge on 16 May 1836, placed in the stocks for two hours and fined $25 for "keeping a disorderly house" on 21 November 1837, and fined $10 the same day for assault and battery. On 19 November 1837 he was indicted along with (his wife?) Maria Toney [Minutes 1832-46].

iii. Matthew[2], born about 1787, head of a Halifax County household of 9 "free colored" in 1820 [NC:167]. He married Celia **Evans**, 22 December 1808 Warren County bond with Allen **Green** bondsman. He was living in Wilson County, Tennessee, when he was counted in the 1850 census: a sixty-three-year-old Black laborer, born in North

---

[206]Martha **Carpenter** may have been related to Sarah **Carpenter**, head of a Northumberland County household of 5 "Blacks" in 1782 [VA:37] and James **Carpenter**, "free mulatto" head of a Northumberland County household in 1810 [VA:974]. Winney Holly also testified to the marriage of Drury **Walden** in his son's application for his pension.

Carolina, living with Catherine, thirty years old, and six children born in Tennessee [Census p.267].

    iv. William[3], head of a Halifax County household of 4 "free colored" in 1830.

    v. Nancy **Cart[er]**, perhaps the wife of Samuel **Carter**.

    vi. a daughter or perhaps two, names obliterated from the will.

    vii. Martha, born before 1775, head of a Halifax County household of 3 "free colored" in 1830.

    viii. Israel, who had a suit in Halifax County court against William B. Toney (his brother?) on 20 November 1835. The court gave him permission to use his gun in the county on 16 August 1841 and renewed his license on 24 August 1843.

    ix. Arthur[2], born about 1802, registered in Mecklenburg County, Virginia, on 21 July 1828: *a man of dark complexion, five feet eleven and three quarter inches high about 26 years of age who it appears was born of a free woman in the County of Halifax and State of North Carolina* [Free Person of Color, no.51, p.40]. He was found guilty in the Halifax County court of a minor offence on 20 August 1833. On 18 February 1836 he and John Fulder were charged with larceny, for which he paid $100 bail. And the next day, 19 February 1836, he brought a suit against Thomas Scuggins.

7. Margaret[2]/ Peg Toney, born say 1752, was the "free Mulatto" wife of an unnamed slave of John Hamilton of Prince George County. He was described in the 28 January 1775 issue of the *Virginia Gazette* as: *a likely Virginia born Negro Fellow, about 25 years of age, of yellowish Complexion, lisps a little, and plays on the Fiddle.* He, Peg, and their two-year-old boy were headed towards her relatives in Charles City [Dixon's edition, p. 3, col. 2]. She was the mother of

    i. George, born about 1771, registered in Petersburg on 15 November 1796: *a dark brown Mulatto man, five feet six and a half inches high with short knotty hair, twenty five years old, son of Peggy Toney a Free woman, & raised in the Town of Petersburg* [Register of Free Negroes 1794-1819, no. 116].

8. John[2] Toney, born say 1763, was head of a household of 3 free males and 2 free females in District 5 of Halifax County, North Carolina, in 1786 for the state census (called John Toney, Jr.) and was head of a Fayetteville, Cumberland County household of 5 "other free" in 1790 [NC:42]. He sold 50 acres by deed proved in the July 1792 session of Richmond County, North Carolina court [Minutes 1779-92, 231]. Perhaps he was the father of

    i. Malachi, head of a Cumberland County household of 1 "other free" in 1810 [NC:570] and 5 "free colored" in 1820 [NC:191], married Russia **Hammons**, 1 February 1810 Cumberland County bond.

TOOTLE FAMILY

1. Dorcas Tootle, nee Letchworth, born say 1738, was the wife of Absalom Tootle when she had a "Molatto Girl" by her father's "Negro fellow" Caesar [Byrd, *In Full Force and Virtue*, 2]. She was the mother of

2   i. Elizabeth, born about 1758-1763.

2. Elizabeth Tootle, born about 1759, was a "Molatto Girl" who lived with Doctor James Seay in the upper part of Bertie County near Norflet's ferry. Seay died before December court 1772 when the account of his estate was recorded in Bertie County court. In May 1787 her son William was bound by the court to Thomas Rhodes. Sometime before February 1788 she and her children petitioned the Bertie County court for their freedom from Joel Brown

[Haun, *Bertie County Court Minutes* IV:87; VI:691, 750]. One of the deponents at the trial testified that two of her children were with (bound to) Thomas White, one with Thomas Rhodes, and two with Jesse Brown [Byrd, *In Full Force and Virtue*, 3]. She was head of a Bertie County household of 4 "other free" in 1800 [NC:82]. She was the mother of

i.   Eady, born about June 1779, ten years old "last June" in May 1790 when she was bound by the Bertie County court to John Johnston.
ii. ?Celia, head of a Tyrrell County household of 4 "other free" in 1810 [NC:796].
iii. William, born 3 March 1785, bound to Thomas Rhodes by the Bertie County court in May 1787, called Wylie Tootle in May 1790 when the court bound him to John Johnston [Haun, *Bertie County Court Minutes* V:649; VI:812].
iv. David, born 4 October 1787, bound to John Johnston in May 1790.
v.   ?Jonathan, born say 1776-1794, head of a Halifax County, North Carolina household of 5 "free colored" in 1820 [NC:166].
vi. ?Janasal, born 1776-1794, head of an Edgecombe County household of 5 "free colored" in 1820 [NC:125].
vii. ?Thomas, born 1794-1806, head of a Halifax County household of 4 "free colored" in 1820 [NC:166].

TOULSON FAMILY

Several members of the Toulson family, born about 1750, were living in Northumberland County in the 1770s. They were

1   i.   Patrick, born say 1750.
2   ii. Sarah[1], born say 1752.

1. Patrick Toulson, born say 1750, was head of a Northumberland County household of 8 "blacks" in 1782 [VA:37], no whites and a dwelling in 1784 [VA:75], and a "free Mulatto" head of a Northumberland County household of 5 "other free" in 1810 [VA:997]. He and his wife Elinder were the parents of

i.   Elizabeth, born 31 August 1772, "Daughter of Patrick Toleson," [Fleet, *Northumberland County Record of Births*, 88]. She registered as a "free Negro" on 11 November 1811: *black woman, about 37 years, Born of free parents in North[d] County* [Register no.57, Northumberland County Courthouse], and she was in the 1813 list of "free negroes and mulattoes" in Northumberland County [PPTL, frame 24].
ii. ?Isaac Tolson, born say 1773, head of Perquimans County, North Carolina household of 3 "other free" in 1800 [NC:647] and 7 in 1810 [NC:970].
iii. Sarah[2], born 20 November 1775, "Daughter of Patrick & Elinder his wife" [Fleet, *Northumberland County Record of Births*, 88].
iv. ?William[2] Tolson, born say 1777, head of a Perquimans County household of one "other free" in 1800 [NC:647], and 2 "other free" and a white woman in 1810 [NC:970].
v.   ?Polly, born about 1791, married William **Boyd**, 13 March 1809 Northumberland County bond, Jerry Toulson security.
vi. ?Jerry, bondsman for the 13 March 1809 Northumberland County marriage of (his sister?) Polly Toulson.

2. Sarah[1] Toulson, born say 1752, was the "free mulatto" mother of William and James Toulson whose births were recorded in Northumberland County [Fleet, *Northumberland County Record of Births*, 107]. Her children were

i.   William[1], born 22 February 1771, "Son of Sary Toulson," a "free mulatto" head of a Northumberland County household of 8 "other free" in 1810 [VA:998]. He married Sally **Boyd**, 22 February 1802 Northumberland County marriage, Joseph **Boyd** security, with the consent of her father Augustine **Boyd**.

ii.   James, born 15 July 1773, "son of Sary Toulson," a "free mulatto" head of a Northumberland County household of 7 "other free" in 1810 [VA:998].

iii. ?Nelly, born say 1781, married Gabriel **Bee**, 29 September 1802 Northumberland County bond, James Toulson security.

TOYER FAMILY

1.   Anne[1] Toyer, born say 1678, was the mother of a "Mulatto" child named Anne Toyer who was bound out by the churchwardens of Kingston Parish, Gloucester County, to Robert Johnson until the age of thirty years on 3 October 1699. She identified Peter, a "Negro" slave belonging to Captain John Gwyn of Gwyn's Island, as the father of her child. On 10 May 1733 James Callis of Kingston Parish deposed before three of the justices of Northampton County, Virginia, that Anne alias Judah was the daughter of a white woman owned by his father. His father gave the younger Anne to Robert Johnson who carried her to Middlesex County where he sold her to John Jacob of Northampton County when she was about twelve years old [Mihalyka, *Loose Papers II:*19]. Ann and Peter were the parents of

2   i.   Ann[2], born 28 August 1698.

2.   Ann[2] Toyer, born 28 August 1698, was bound to Robert Johnson in Gloucester County on 3 October 1699 and sold by him to John Jacob of Northampton Count about 1710. She was called "Nanny Bandy alias Judea Mulatto" on 12 July 1732 when she petitioned the Northampton County court saying she was detained as a slave by Clark Nottingham. Her petition was rejected at first based on insufficient evidence. However, the court allowed Elias Roberts to examine witnesses in Gloucester County on behalf of "Nanny Bandy, alias Toyer," and freed her on 12 June 1733 based on the new evidence [Orders 1732-42, 15, 17, 26, 35, 47, 53]. She was probably married to Bandy, a "negro" slave who was tithable in William Jacob's Northampton County household from 1723 to 1737. Nanny may have been identical to Nan, a tithable in John Jacob's household from 1726 to 1727 in the same district as William Jacob and Bandy [Bell, *Northampton County Tithables*, 45, 63, 109, 123-4, 142, 187, 267]. On 10 July 1733 she petitioned the court against William Jacob for detaining her son Solomon, against Addison Smaw for detaining her daughter Jane Toyer, and Clark Nottingham for detaining her daughter Rhodea in slavery. The court released Solomon and Jane, but ordered Rhody to continue in slavery until the age of thirty years. Ann was presented for bastard bearing on 14 May 1734 [Orders 1732-42, 59, 60, 67, 70, 71, 107, 114]. She was the mother of

     i.   Solomon[1], born on 22 January 1720/1, thirteen-year-old "son of Ann Toyer" freed by the Northampton County court from the service of William Jacob and bound as an apprentice turner to Elias Roberts on 11 September 1733. He was sued for debt by Nathaniel Brown on 12 April 1780 [Orders 1732-42, 70-1; Minutes 1777-83, 233].

2   ii.   Jane, born about 1722.
3   iii. Rhody, born say 1726.
4   iv.   Dido, born about 1734.

2.   Jane Toyer, born 20 November 1722, was bound apprentice to Elias Roberts by the Northampton County court on 11 September 1733. Her petition to the court against John Roberts was dismissed on 15 November 1749 [Orders 1732-42, 71; 1748-51, 151]. Her son was

      i.   Peter[1], born in March 1748, "son of Jane Toyer," bound to Henry Tomlinson in Northampton County on 10 August 1756 [Orders 1753-58, 354]. He was eleven years old on 12 December 1759 when the court bound him to John Holland to be a blacksmith [Minutes 1754-61, 210]. He was taxable in Northampton County from 1789 to 1800: called a blacksmith from 1795 to 1798, taxable on a free male aged 16-21 in 1797 [PPTL, 1782-1823, frames 104, 200, 217, 234] and was security for the 7 December 1803 Northampton County marriage of Thomas **Carter** and Sophia **Jeffries**.

3.   Rhody Toyer, born about 1725, was a "Negro slave girl called Rhodie of 11 years of age" who came into the possession of Esau Jacob by the distribution of the Northampton County estate of his father John Jacob on 14 December 1736. He sued the other heirs in December 1737 asking that they pay for his loss because she and her mother Ann Toyer were freed by the court [W&I 18:191-3; Mihalyka, *Loose Papers II:*87-8]. She brought suit against George Holt for her freedom on 8 December 1747 and was freed the following month. She was presented for bastardy on 8 May 1750 and 8 May 1753 [Orders 1742-8, 484-5, 491; 1748-51, 207, 230, 265, 324]. She was the mother of

5   i.   Peg, born about 1750.

      ii.   ?Jacob[2], born in May 1765, bound to William Floyd on 14 February 1769 [Minutes 1766-71, 277]. He was taxable in Northampton County from 1787 to 1793 [PPTL, 1782-1823, frames 69, 165].

      iii.   Peter[3], taxable in Northampton County from 1793 to 1813: called "son of Rhody" in 1793 and 1796 [PPTL, 1782-1823, frames 165, 200, 217, 497, 548].

4.   Dido Toyer, born about 1734, a two-year-old "Negroe," was bound apprentice in Northampton County to Hannah Roberts on 12 May 1736 with the consent of her mother Ann Toyer [Orders 1732-42, 213]. She was presented for bastardy on 8 May 1753, on 11 June 1755, on 11 May 1756 and on 14 November 1758 [Orders 1751-3, 265; 1753-8, 218, 315, 330; Minutes 1754-61, 170]. She registered as a "free Negro" in Northampton County on 13 June 1794 [Orders 1789-95, 364]. She was the mother of

      i.   Solomon[2], born August 1752, son of Dido Toyer, bound to Samuel Williams on 12 May 1756 [Orders 1753-8, 320].

      ii.   Jacob[1], born in April 1757, child of "free Negro" Dido Toyer, bound to John Parkerson on 10 April 1759. He was sued by John Swift for a 50 pound debt on 12 April 1780 [Minutes 1754-61, 187; 1777-83, 186, 202, 233].

      iii. ?Peter[2], born in December 1760, bound to Walter Hyslop on 14 January 1768 [Minutes 1765-71, 162]. He enlisted as a substitute in the Revolution in Gloucester County [NSDAR, *African American Patriots*, 154].

      iv. ?John, born about 1764, a five-year-old "Negro" bound to Edmund Glanville on 15 June 1769 [Minutes 1765-71, 300].

5.   Peg Toyer, born about 1750, "free Negro daughter of Rhody Toyer," was bound apprentice to Josiah Dowty on 12 May 1762. She was called as a witness for John Daniel (Indian) against a member of the Jacob family on 16 September 1773 but failed to appear [Minutes 1761-5, 28; 1771-7, 177]. She may have been the mother of

      i.   Daniel, bound to Samuel Atchison on 13 January 1773 [Minutes 1771-7, 117].

      ii.   Adah, born in September 1771, bound to Richard Savage on 8 September 1778 [Minutes 1777-83, 102]. She was head of a Northampton County household of 1 "free colored" in 1820 [VA:215].

iii. George, registered as a "free Negro" in Northampton County on 13 June 1794 [Orders 1789-95, 364], a "Negro" taxable in Northampton County from 1798 to 1813 [PPTL 1782-1823, frames 256, 549].

iv. Zerobabel, "free Negro" taxable in Northampton County in 1797 [PPTL, 1782-1823, frame 235].

TRAVIS FAMILY

1. Ann Travis, born say 1744, was living in Isle of Wight County on 4 April 1764 when the court bound her "Molatto orphan" daughter Nan bound out and on 4 July 1765 when the court ordered the churchwardens of Newport Parish to bind out her illegitimate child Jane Travis [Orders 1764-8, 11, 195]. She was the mother of

2 i. Nan, born say 1762.

ii. Jane, born say 1764, bound out in Isle of Wight County on 4 July 1765 and called a "poore child" when she was ordered bound out again on 2 December 1774 [Orders 1772-80, 218].

iii. ?William, born say 1768, a "free Negro" ordered bound out to Till **Williams** of Elizabeth River Parish by the Norfolk County court on 20 July 1770 [Orders 1768-71, 185].

2. Nan/ Nancy Travis, born say 1762, was the mother of

i. Thomas, born say 1790, a "poor child of Nancy Travis," bound out by the Isle of Wight County court on 2 February 1795 [Orders 1795-7, 11]. He was a "free negro" above the age of 16 in Isle of Wight County in 1813 [Waldrep, *1813 Tax List*].

ii. ?Jow, a "free negro" above the age of 16 in Isle of Wight County in 1813 [Waldrep, *1813 Tax List*].

iii. ?Peter, a free Negro apprentice in Isle of Wight County in 1813 [Waldrep, *1813 Tax List*].

TURNER FAMILY

Thomas Turner was the servant of Captain Daniel Parke of York County on 26 October 1657 when the court ordered him to do open penance at the next public meeting of St. Martin Church because it appeared by the report of a "Negro woman" as well as by circumstantial evidence that he was the father of her child [DWO 3:2].

Members of the Turner family were

1 i. James, born say 1715.

2 ii. Sampson[1] Turner, born say 1740.

iii. Moses, born say 1750, a "Mulato" taxable in Bladen County in 1772 [Byrd, *Bladen County Tax Lists*, I:78]. He was head of a Richmond County, North Carolina household of 7 "other free" and a slave in 1790 [NC:47] and was taxable in Richmond County on 150 acres and two polls in 1795.

iv. Charles, born about 1759, made a declaration in Pasquotank County court on 4 March 1834 to obtain a pension for his service in the North Carolina Continental Line [*NCGSJ* XVII:160]. He was head of a Pasquotank County household of 4 "other free" in 1790 [NC:29] and 9 in 1810 [NC:933].

v. Sylvanus, "free negro" head of a Pasquotank County household of 4 "other free" in 1790 [NC:29].

vi. Dempsey, head of a Pasquotank County household of 4 "other free" in 1790 [NC:29]. He was called Demsey Turner of Pasquotank County when he married Sarah **Reid**, 19 May 1801 Gates County bond.

3 vii. Simon[1], born say 1770.

1. James Turner, born say 1715, and his wife Mary were taxable "mollatoes" in the Granville County, North Carolina list of William Person in 1750 and 1751 with their children David and Moll and two slaves [CR 044.701.19]. Their children were

    i.   David, born before 1739 since he was taxable in 1751.
    ii. Moll, born before 1739 since she was taxable in 1751.
4   iii. ?John, born say 1740.

2. Sampson[1] Turner, born say 1740, was taxable in Edmunds Bridge District of Norfolk County in 1761 and a "F.N." taxable there with his wife Sebra in 1765 [Wingo, *Norfolk County Tithables, 1751-65*, 159, 196]. He was taxable with his son Butler in Blackwater Precinct of Princess Anne County, Virginia, in 1784 [*Virginia Genealogical Society Quarterly* 28:31]. He was head of a Currituck County, North Carolina household of 6 "other free" in 1790 [NC:22]. His January 1792 Currituck County, North Carolina will was proved 30 July 1792 [WB 2:2]. He named his wife Sabarey as executor and mentioned his children:

    i.   Pormenus, head of a head of a Currituck County household of 8 "other free" in 1800 [NC:147] and a Norfolk County household of 7 "other free" in 1810 [VA:794]. He was probably named for Permenos **Smith**, a "Molatto" Currituck County taxable in 1755 [SS 837]. He was in a "List of free Negroes and Mulattoes" in St. Bride's Parish, Norfolk County, from to 1812 to 1817, listed with 2 tithables in 1812 and 1814 [PPTL, 1782-1791, frames ; 1791-1812, frames 802; 1813-24, frames 67, 227].
5   ii. Nicholas, born about 1763.
6   iii. Butler, born say 1765.
    iv. Sampson[2], "F.B." head of a Princess Anne County household of 10 "other free" in 1810 [VA:477].
    v.   Frances.
    vi. Sabra.
    vii. Sinia.
    viii. Molley.
    ix. Lisha.

3. Simon[1] Turner, born say 1770, was head of a Northampton County, North Carolina household of 5 "other free" in 1800 [NC:481], 8 in 1810 [NC:748], and 10 "free colored" in 1820 [NC:264]. Perhaps his descendants were

    i.   Winny, born 1775-94, head of a Northampton County household of 3 "free colored" in 1820 [NC:262].
    ii. Jerry, born 1775-94, head of a Halifax County household of 4 "free colored" in 1830.
    iii. Simon[2], born 1794-1806, head of a Halifax County household of 5 "free colored" in 1830.
    iv. Burton, born 1794-1806, head of a Halifax County household of 3 "free colored" in 1830. He married Poly **Hawkins**, 22 December 1820 Halifax County bond.
    v.   Bedford, born 1794-1806, head of a Halifax County household of 2 "free colored" in 1830.

4. John Turner, born say 1740, was head of a Georgetown District, Prince Georges Parish, South Carolina household of 10 "other free" in 1790 [SC:56] and a Liberty County, South Carolina household of 3 "other free" in 1800 [SC:803]. He may have been the father of

    i.   Amy, head of a Marlboro County, South Carolina household of 9 "other free" in 1800 [SC:60].
    ii. Rhoday, head of a Marlboro County household of 7 "other free" in 1800 [SC:59].

iii. Reuben, head of a Liberty County household of 6 "other free" in 1800 [SC:806].

iv. John, Jr., head of a Liberty County household of 4 "other free" in 1800 [SC:806].

5. Nicholas Turner, born about 1763, was a "F.B." head of a Princess Anne County household of 3 "other free" in 1810 [VA:477]. He registered in Norfolk County on 20 May 1811: *five feet 10 1/2 In. 48 years of age of a light Complexion, Born free* [Register of Free Negros & Mulattos, no.55]. He was in a list of "free Negroes and Mulattoes" in St. Bride's Parish, Norfolk County, from 1812 to 1816 [PPTL, 1791-1812, frame 802; 1813-24, frames 67, 189]. He married Alice **Collins**, 7 June 1814 Norfolk County bond, Aaron **Rogers** security. Aaron **Rogers** married Ann **Stewart**, "a free woman of colour," 17 March 1814 Norfolk County bond, John **Jasper** security. Aaron was a cobbler living near Norfolk in a "List of Free Negroes and Mulattoes" in 1801 [PPTL, 1791-1812, frame 384]. Nicholas may have been the father of

i. William, born about 1786, registered in Norfolk County on 30 June 1812: *5 feet 9 inches 26 years of age, a yellowish complexion...Born free* [Register of Free Negros & Mulattos, no.72]. He married Mrs. Amy **Singleton**, 15 June 1814 Norfolk County bond, Nicholas Turner security. Amy was probably the widow of Samuel **Singleton**, head of a Norfolk County household of 6 "other free" in 1810 [VA:921].

ii. Ann, born say 1790, married Pleasant **Stewart**, 27 June 1811 Norfolk County bond, Nicholas Turner security.

6. Butler Turner, born say 1765, was taxable in his father's 1784 Princess Anne County household, and called "Bellar Turner" when he was head of a Currituck County, North Carolina household of 5 "other free" in 1790 [NC:22]. He was a labourer in Portsmouth, Norfolk County, in 1801 when he was in a "List of Free Negroes and Mulattoes" with males George and Thomas Turner and females Ascilla (his wife?), Limy and Mary Turner [PPTL, 1791-1812, frame 383]. He was probably the father of

i. George.

ii. Limy.

iii. Thomas.

iv. Mary.

Others members of the Turner family in Pasquotank County in 1810 were

i. Winny, head of a household of 7 "other free" [NC:933].

ii. Caleb, head of a household of 6 "other free" [NC:933].

iii. Lovey, head of a household of 8 "other free" [NC:934].

iv. Mary, head of a household of 7 "other free" [NC:933, 934].

v. Patsy, head of a household of 3 "other free" [NC:933].

Other members of the family in Virginia were

i. Peter, head of a Southampton County household of 8 "other free" in 1810 [VA:59].

ii. John, head of a Westmoreland County household of 8 "other free" in 1810.

iii. Olive, head of a Southampton County household of 4 "other free" in 1810 [VA:77].

iv. Lewis, head of a Sussex County household of 3 "other free" in 1810 [VA:666].

v. Andrew, born about 1795, registered in Sussex County on 10 November 1817: *light complexion, 5'6-1/2", free born, 22 years old* [Register, no.316].

vi. Willie, born about 1795, registered in Sussex County on 27 April
1818: *brown complexion, 5'10-1/2", free born, 23 years old* [Register,
no.325].

TYLER FAMILY

1. Barbara Tyler, born say 1725, was living in Granville County on 12 April
1758 when her orphan children were bound apprentices to Robert Priddy, Jr.,
to learn to read and write [Owens, *Granville County Notes*, vol. III].[207] Her
children were

2   i.   Bartlet[1], born 18 June 1744.
3   ii.   Elizabeth, born 12 April 1746.
        iii. ?William, born say 1747, taxable on two tithes in the Granville County
summary list for 1766 and a taxable "free Negro" with his wife
Frankey in 1767 [CR 44.701.19].
        iv.   Jane, born say 1752, called "mulatto Jane" in 1762, a taxable in
Gilliam Harris' Granville County household and a "black female"
taxable in Harris' household in 1764 (called Jean Taylor) [CR
44.701.19]. She was taxable in the Granville County household of her
brother Bartlet in 1768 and married David **Mitchell** about the same
time. She was probably the Jean Tylor who was sued by Olive **Bass** in
March 1770 [WB 1:73].

2. Bartlet[1] Tyler, born say 1742, was bound to Robert Priddy, Jr., to learn to
read and write on 12 April 1758 [Owen, *Granville County Notes*, vol. I]. He
was probably the "Bartlet" who was one of the "negros & mulattos" taxable
in the 1762 Granville County household of Robert Priddy's widow Eleanor
[CR 44.701.19]. Bartlet was taxed in his own household in the Granville
County summary on two tithes in 1766 [CR 44.701.20]. On 13 January 1767
he was charged in Granville County court with having a bastard child by
Lovey **Bass** [Camin, *N.C. Bastardy Bonds*, 87]. In 1768 he was taxable in the
list of Robert Harris, head of a household with his unnamed wife and sister
Jane, and taxable on only one tithe in 1771. On 5 August 1774 Uriah Smith,
alias Huckey Smith, was charged with kidnapping several of his children. On
5 August 1778 he complained to the Granville County court that he was forced
into Revolutionary War service on the pretence that he was a vagrant [Owen,
Granville County Notes, vol. V]. He was taxed on an assessment of 2,210
pounds in 1780 and 600 acres and one poll in 1785. Perhaps his wife was
Sarah **Anderson**, called Sarah Tyler in the May 1785 will of her father Lewis
Anderson. Bartlet sold 325 acres by deed proved in Granville County court
on 8 November 1786, and he proved a deed from Hugh **Snelling** to Samuel
Jones on 10 November 1786 [Minutes 1786-87]. He was involved in numerous
Granville County court cases, both as defendant and plaintiff:

- November 1777   - charged with trespass, assault, and battery, but no
decision recorded.
- May 1780   - charged with false swearing and stealing but was
discharged.
- November 1782   - presented for horse racing with Thomas Newby.
- 5 May 1786   - with Drury **Pettiford** ordered to pay Samuel
Walker 16 pounds.
- 8 August 1796   - awarded one penny and costs in his suit against
Isaac Ralph.
- 7 November 1786   - Court ruled in his favor in John Dock's suit
against him.

---

[207]The family name was written Taylor instead of Tyler in the minutes.

- 11 May 1787   - suit against him and Hugh **Snelling** withdrawn.
- November 1789   - ordered to pay George White 5 pounds on appeal.
- 7 May 1790   - ordered to pay John Cooper 15 pounds, 9 shillings on appeal.
- 8 February 1791   - awarded one penny and costs for his suit against Jesse Garret.

Bartlet was head of a household of 6 free males, five free females, and one female slave for the 1786 state census. He was taxed on 338 acres and one poll in Fishing Creek District of Granville County in 1796 [Tax List 1796-1802, 14], but he had moved to Warren County by 1800 when he was head of a household of 5 "other free," one white woman 26-45 years, and one white boy under ten years of age [NC:836]. In February 1803 he sued the administrator of Thomas Person's estate in Warren County court [Gammon, *Record of Estates, Warren County*, I:83]. In 1810 he was head of a Warren County household of 5 "other free" and one white woman over forty-five years old [NC:738]. Perhaps his children were

     i. Dicey **Bass**, born about 1766, "base born mulatto child of Lovey Bass," bound to Mary **Anderson**, wife of George **Anderson**, on 18 July 1770. This was probably the child of Lovey **Bass** for which Bartlet posted bastardy bond in Granville County in January 1767 with Lewis **Anderson**, Jr., and Reuben **Bass** bondsmen.

     ii. Pink, born 1776-94, taxed on one white (free) tithe and one black tithe in Oxford District of Granville County in 1802 and 1803 [Tax List 1796-1802, 339; 1802-09, 33]. He married Lucy **Bass**, 25 September 1797 Granville County bond. He was head of a Chatham County household of 5 "free colored" in 1820 [NC:192].

3.   Elizabeth Tyler, born 12 April 1746, was bound apprentice to Robert Priddy, Jr., on 12 April 1758 [Owen, *Granville County Notes*, vol. III]. She was probably the "Betty" who was one of the "negros & mulattos" taxable with her brother Bartlett in the 1762 Granville County household of Robert Priddy's widow Eleanor [CR 44.701.19]. She was living in Granville County on 9 August 1766 when her son John was indentured to Samuel Benton [CR 44.101.2]. In 1800 she was in Lenoir County with her son Moses where she was head of a household of 2 "other free" [NC:22]. Her children were

     i. John[2], born about January 1765, eighteen months old when he was indentured to Samuel Benton on 9 August 1766. He was called Tobias (but christened John) and was five years old on 18 July 1770 when the court ordered him bound to Frances Benton.

     ii. Simon, born about 1768, two-year-old "son of Elizabeth" bound to Frances Benton on 18 July 1770.

     iii. Moses, born say 1769, "base born Mulatto child of Elizabeth Tyler bound to Frances Benton on 18 July 1770. He was head of a Lenoir County household of 6 "other free" in 1810 [NC:286] and 10 "free colored" in 1820 [NC:290].

Barbara Tyler may have moved to Goochland County, Virginia, soon after her children were bound out in Granville County on 12 April 1758. She may have been the Barbery Tyler (no race mentioned) who was living in Goochland County on 17 July 1759 when Bouth Napier brought a suit against her and William Tylor. The suit abated against William because he was no longer an inhabitant of the county, and the court found against her for 5 pounds damages. John Pewit provided her bail, and John Boswell and James Cawthen of Hanover County were witnesses for her. Her son Arthur Tyler was bound to William Pledge in Goochland County in July 1761 [Orders 1757-61, 227, 252, 324, 352-3, 369, 422]. Other members of the Tyler family in Goochland and surrounding counties were

i.   George, born about 1757, taxable in the upper district of Goochland County from 1787 to 1815: a "Mulatto" planter near Charles Watkins' Shop in 1804, living on Joseph Woodson's land in 1811, exempt in 1815 [PPTL, 1782-1809, frames 157, 184, 227, 349, 367, 626, 698; 1810-32, frames 87, 270]. He was head of a Goochland County household of 3 "other free" in 1810 [VA:717]. He registered as a free Negro in Goochland County on 16 December 1814: *a free man of color about Sixty years old, about five feet six inches high, yellow complexion, short curled hair intermixed with grey...free born* [Register of Free Negroes, p.84, no.159]. He was about sixty-one years old on 20 July 1818 when he applied for a pension in Goochland County for eighteen months service in 1781, stating that he was farming on rented land with his 100 year-old wife Nancy **Cooper** [M804-2432, frame 0669]. He was a "yellow" complexioned soldier who was born in Louisa County, lived in Goochland County, and was listed in the size roll of troops who joined at Chesterfield Courthouse after 1 September 1780 [NSDAR, *African American Patriots*, 154].

ii. Richard[1], born say 1760, taxable in the upper district of Goochland County from 1788 to 1813: taxable on a slave over the age of sixteen and a horse in 1788, 1791, 1792, 1794, 1795, 1800, 1802, 1803; a "Mulatto" planter living on David Ross's land from 1804 to 1811; on William Galt's land in 1812, on John Minor's land with his wife Aggy in 1813 [PPTL, 1782-1809, frames 183, 227, 288, 303, 349, 367, 398, 430, 472, 489, 535, 555, 626, 678, 698, 752, 793; 1810-32, frames 19, 87, 111, 176]. He was head of a Goochland County household of 4 "other free" in 1810 [VA:717].

iii. Francis, born say 1769, taxable in the upper district of Goochland County in 1790, 1796, 1797, 1798, 1803, a "Mulatto" planter on Booker Carroll's land in 1804, listed with wife Sally on John Minor's land in 1813 and 1814, taxable on a horse in 1816 [PPTL, 1782-1809, frames 245, 430, 472, 678; 1810-32, frames 176, 209, 295]. He married Sally **Scott**, 15 January 1802 Goochland County bond, Henry **Cockrum (Cockran)** surety, 18 February marriage [Ministers Returns, 88]. He was head of a Goochland County household of 3 "other free" in 1810 [VA:717].

iv. John[2], born about 1771, married Polly **Banks**, daughter of Jacob **Banks**, 23 December 1797 Goochland County bond, Francis Tiler surety. He was taxable in the upper district of Goochland County from 1803 to 1814: a "Mulatto" planter living on Booker Carroll's land in 1804, on William Richardson's land in 1806 and 1807, with wife Polly on John Minor's land in 1813 and 1814 [PPTL, 1782-1809, frames 678, 698, 751, 792; 1810-32, frames 19, 110, 176, 209]. He was head of a Goochland County household of 10 "other free" in 1810 [VA:717]. He registered as a free Negro in Goochland County on 18 November 1822: *about fifty one years old, about five feet seven & an half inches high of a yellow complexion...free born*, and his wife registered on 18 September 1829: *yellowish complexion, about forty four years of age, about five feet three & an half inches high* [Register of Free Negroes, pp.136, 204].

v.   Phil, born say 1785, a "Mulatto" planter living on John Thurston's land in Goochland County in 1804 and 1806, living on Wright Moreland's land in 1807 [PPTL, 1782-1809, frames 698, 793, 835].

vi. John[3], head of a Henrico County household of 5 "other free" in 1810 [VA:994].

vii. Richard[2], a "F.N." taxable in the upper district of Henrico County from 1801 to 1807 and in 1811 [PPTL 1782-1814, frames 453, 496, 541, 673].

Another member of the Tyler family in Virginia was

    i.   Ann, born say 1756, a "free Molatto" whose "free Molatto" daughter Ann **Cross** was bound by indenture to Richard Blake by the Norfolk County court on 21 August 1778 [Orders 1776-9, n.p.]. Ann Tyler was head of a Norfolk County household of 6 "other free" in 1810 [VA:922] and Ann **Cross** was head of a Norfolk County household of 2 "other free" in 1810 [VA:892].

Indian ancestry

1.   Priss, born about 1718, was a fifteen or sixteen-year-old Catawba Indian who was induced by an Indian trader named Captain Robert Hicks to come to Virginia with him about 1733 according to depositions taken in 1768 for her son Joe's trial for his freedom in Louisa County. Hicks sold her as a slave and after changing owners several times, she became the slave of John Thompson of Hanover County. She may have had a relationship with a member of the **Tyree** and/or **Tyler** family because she was called Priss **Tyree** by one deponent, and her son Joseph used the name **Tyler** [Abercrombie, *Louisa County Judgments*, 11-14]. She was the mother of

    i.   Joseph, born about 1745, a slave called "Indian Joe" when he sued for his freedom from Charles Hutcherson, executor of John Thomson, in Louisa County court on 13 July 1767. The court took depositions from Eleanor Stanley and Samuel Clark and ruled in Joseph's favor on 13 March 1769. He was called "Joseph Tyler alias Indian Joe" on 12 October 1772 when he was charged with stealing a 5 shilling bill from the house of Richard Johnson. George **Gibson** was his security. On 9 October 1775 he complained to the court that Walter Overton was mistreating Bartlett Tyler, and the court ordered Bartlett bound instead to George Sharp [Orders 1766-72, 50, 74, 122, 196, 214, 248, 249, 260, 265; 1766-74, 60; 1774-82, 132, 136]. He was described as a "Mulatto, or Indian Man" in Gabriel Jones' company of marines in Culpeper County on 2 September 1776 when Jones advertised in the *Virginia Gazette* that he had recovered a silver spoon which Joseph "had (stolen) from a Negro Boy belonging to Major Carr of Louisa County" [*Virginia Gazette*, Dixon's edition, p. 3, col. 2].

    ii.   Nan, born say 1752, an infant under the age of twenty-one in 1770 when she sued for her freedom. She was called "Indian Nan" on 9 April 1771 when she and her sisters "Indian Betty," Indian Priss," and "Indian Bartlett" sued for their freedom from the executors of John Thomson, deceased, in Louisa County court with the assistance of their "next friend Indian Joe." Witnesses on her behalf were James Johnson, William and Jemima Cockerham, and Mary Brown and Ann Smith who travelled about thirty miles to testify in her favor [Orders 1766-72, 389, 431, 451-2].

    iii. Betty, born say 1754.

    iv. Priss, born say 1756.

    v.   Bartlett[2], born say 1760, ordered bound apprentice by the churchwardens of Trinity Parish, Louisa County, on 13 July 1772 [Orders 1766-74, 38]. He may have been the Bartlett Tyler who was deceased on 28 December 1790 when his orphan Jones Tyler was bound to George Jude by the overseers of the poor in the upper district of Henrico County [Orders 1789-91, 378]. Jones Tyler was counted as white in Henrico County.

TYNER FAMILY

1.   Lovi Tiner, born say 1728, was the mother of a four-year-old "melato garl," Olif?, who was bound apprentice to Nathan Grimes by the October 1762

Johnston County, North Carolina court [Haun, *Johnston County Court Minutes*, I:132]. She was the mother of

2   i.   ?Asa, born about 1744.
      ii. Oliff?, born about 1758.

2. Asa Tyner, born about 1744, was taxable with his unnamed wife in Bute County in 1771 [CR 015.70001]. She was Keziah **Chavis**, born about 1742, still taxable in the Granville County household of her father William **Chavis** in 1764 but not in 1766 [CR 44.701.19]. Asa and his wife "Cuzzah" sold 700 acres adjoining William **Chavis**, deceased, on the county line between Granville and Bute counties on 11 August 1777 [Warren County DB 6:198]. On 10 May 1770 William **Chavis** appeared in Bute County court complaining that he was afraid Asa planned to do him some bodily harm or damage his estate. Asa had to post 50 pounds bond for his good behavior [Minutes 1767-76, 128]. This was the start of a long series of court cases between him and William **Chavis**, a wealthy slave owner of Granville County. On 26 April 1775 he was ordered to be put in jail when he was found to be in possession of a slave named Dick who belonged to William **Chavis** [CR 044.928.25]. This was probably the charge he was acquitted of in May 1775 Granville County court [Minutes 1773-83, August 1775 dockets]. Asa was a buyer at the sale of William **Chavis'** estate, recorded in February 1778 Granville County court [WB 1:178]. On 10 November 1778 he was brought into Granville County court as a vagrant and "delivered to a Continental Officer and to serve as the Law directs" [Minutes 1773-83, 142]. He was listed among the volunteers for nine months service as a Continental soldier from Bute County on 3 September 1778:

> *Asea Tyner, Place of Abode Bute County, born N.C., 5'8", 34 years of Age, Dark Fair, Dark Eyes* [*NCGSJ* XV:109 (N.C. Archives Troop Returns, Box 4)].

His wife Keziah was head of a Granville County household of 4 "other free" in 1800. He was probably the father of

3   i.   John, born after 1759 since he was not taxed in 1771.
      ii. Uriah, born about 1774, bondsman for John Tyner's Granville County marriage, head of a Petersburg Town household of 4 "other free" and 2 slaves in 1810 [VA:118b]. He and Major **Elbeck**, who was said to have been originally from Pennsylvania, had married and were living in Petersburg for over ten years when the magistrates ordered them to leave the state in accordance with the law which prohibited the emigration of "free Negroes." On 15 December 1810 they submitted petitions to the Dinwiddie County court endorsed by over 100 residents, including the mayor and other officials of the city, that they be allowed to remain in the city since they owned homes and lots there [Johnston, *Race Relations in Virginia*, 55-56]. Major **Eelbeck** was the "mulattoe" slave of Henry Eelbeck who petitioned the Chowan County, North Carolina court in September 1801 for permission to manumit him [Byrd, *In Full Force and Virtue*, 14]. Major **Elbeck** was head of a Petersburg household of 8 "other free" and a slave in 1810 [VA:120a]. Uriah registered in Petersburg on 14 September 1811: *a dark brown free Mulatto man, five feet six 1/4 inches high, thirty seven years old, Imigrated into this state as a free man, permitted to remain by act of assembly 26 Jany(?) 1811* [Register of Free Negroes 1794-1819, no. 676]. He married Phebe **Kennon**, 4 May 1816 Petersburg Hustings Court marriage.
     iii. Anna, married Labon **Taborn**, 5 August 1799 Granville County bond with Zachariah **Mitchell** bondsman.

3. John Tyner, born say 1760, married Betsy **Bass**, 5 July 1796 Granville County bond with Uriah Tyner bondsman. John was taxed on 50 acres and one poll in Fishing Creek District, Granville County, from 1796 to 1808 [Tax List 1796-1802, 14, 65, 112, 163, 214, 268, 323; 1803-09, 15, 219, 275]. He was head of a Granville County household of 4 "other free" in 1800 and 2 "free colored" in Stokes County in 1820 [NC:371]. He died before 3 June 1831 when his Stokes County estate papers were filed [CR 090.508.108]. He may have been the father of

   i. Jonathan, born say 1783, married Pheby **Bass**, 9 July 1804 Granville County bond, Arthur Tyner bondsman. He was taxed on 100 acres and one poll in Fishing Creek District from 1801-07 [Tax List 1796-1802, 268, 323; 1803-09, 15, 219]. He was head of a Stokes County household of 2 "free colored" in 1820 [NC:372].

   ii. Patsy, married Thomas **Pettiford**, 1 September 1807 Granville County bond with Jonathan Tyner bondsman.

   iii. James, married Betsy **Bass**, 5 January 1805 Granville County bond, perhaps the James Tinor who was head of a Caroline County, Maryland household of 2 "other free" in 1790.

   iv. Hannah Tinor, head of a Caroline County, Maryland household of 2 "other free" in 1790.

TYRE FAMILY

1. Jane[1] Tyre, born say 1702, was living in Christ Church Parish, Middlesex County, on 25 February 1719/20 when her "Mulatto" daughter Rachel was born [NSCDA, *Parish Register of Christ Church*, 105]. She was the mother of

2   i. Rachel, born 25 February 1719/20, baptized 3 April 1720.

   ii. ?William, born say 1730, a "black" taxable in James Muckelroy's Beaufort County, North Carolina household in 1755 [SS 837].

2. Rachel Tyre, born 25 February 1719/20, "a Mulatto" born in Christ Church Parish, Middlesex County, was probably the ancestor of

   i. Barnet, "free mulatto" tithable in Caroline County in 1800 [*Virginia Genealogist*, 14:113].

   ii. Micajah, "free Negro" taxable in Hanover County in 1800, living with William D. Taylor in 1814 [PPTL, 1792-1803, p. 182; 1804-24].

3   iii. Jonathan, born say 1765.

   iv. Winney, born December 1771 according to Mary Hackett, a witness to her 9 October 1793 Albemarle County marriage to Jesse Middlebrook, Jonathan Tyree bondsman.

   v. James, born say 1780, taxable in Fredericksville Parish, Albemarle County, from 1797 to 1813: called a "Mulatto" from 1811 to 1813 [PPTL, 1782-1799, frames; 1800-1813, frames 261, 445, 488, 531, 576]. He married Caty **Gowen**, 21 December 1807 Albemarle County bond, head of an Albemarle County household of 4 "other free" in 1810 [VA:210].

   vi. Milly, taxable in Fredericksville Parish, Albemarle County, on 5 cattle in 1787 taxable on a horse in 1788 [PPTL, 1782-1799, frames 127, 162].

   vii. Anderson, taxable in Fredericksville Parish, Albemarle County, with the initials "P.S" (P.'s son) in 1809 [PPTL, 1800-1813, frame 399].

   viii. Richard, born say 1770, taxable in Fredericksville Parish, Albemarle County, in 1788 and from 1797 to 1800 [PPTL, 1782-1799, frame 162, 522, 562, 599; 1800-13, frame 37].

   ix. Betty, taxable on a horse in Fredericksville Parish, Albemarle County, in 1803 [PPTL, 1800-1813, frame 169].

4   x. Sam, born say 1785.

3. Jonathan Tyre, born say 1765, married Usly **Gowing**, 21 October 1786 Albemarle County, Virginia bond, Shadrack **Battles** bondsman. He was taxable in Fredericksville Parish, Albemarle County, from 1786 to 1813: listed with 2 tithables from 1803 to 1805; called a "Mulatto" in 1811 and 1813 [PPTL, 1782-1799, frames 84, 212, 391, 455, 522, 599; 1800-1813, frames 37, 169, 261, 445, 530, 576] and head of an Albemarle County household of 4 "other free" in 1810 [VA:210]. He may have been the father of

    i. Milly, married William **Brock**, 5 January 1807 Albemarle County bond, with the consent of Jonathan Tyree, Martin Tyree witness.

    ii. Nancy, married John **Brock**, 6 January 1807 Albemarle County bond, William **Brock** bondsman.

    iii. Martin, taxable in Fredericksville Parish, Albemarle County, in 1810 [PPTL, 1800-1813, frame 445].

    iv. Jane²/ Jinney, listed as a "Mulatto" in Fredericksville Parish, Albemarle County, in 1813 [PPTL, 1800-1813, frame 576].

4. Sam Tyree, born say 1785, was living in Louisa County on 13 December 1830 and married to Nancy Tyree when his son James registered as a free Negro. He may have been deceased by 11 February 1843 when (their son?) William Tyree was called son of Nancy Tyree. He and his wife Nancy were the parents of

    i. James, born about 1810, registered in Louisa County on 13 December 1830: *son of Sam and Nancy Tyre who was born free, rather a yellowish complexion, 5'8" high about 20 years of age.*

    ii. ?William, born about 1815, registered in Louisa County on 11 February 1843: *free man of color heretofore registered in the clerks office of Hustings Court of Town of Lynchburg...very dark yellow complexion* [Abercrombie, *Free Blacks of Louisa County*, 35, 63].

UNDERWOOD FAMILY

1. Christopher Underwood, born say 1720, was a runaway "Mollatto" servant of Henry Nixon of Orange County, Virginia, before 24 August 1744 when Francis Whittle proved his claim in Louisa County for taking him up [Orders 1742-8, 117]. He was probably the ancestor of

    i. Lewis, born say 1751, head of a Wilkes County, North Carolina household of 9 "other free" in 1800 [NC:66] and 10 in 1810 [NC:856]. He entered 200 acres in Wilkes County on Moravian Creek on 27 February 1808 [Pruitt, *Land Entries: Wilkes County*, 2:42]. Perhaps his widow was Nancy Underwood, head of a Wilkes County household of 5 "free colored" in 1820 [NC:528].

    ii. William, born say 1755, head of a Wilkes County household of 4 persons in the 1787 census for North Carolina and 9 "other free" in 1800 [NC:66]. Perhaps his widow was Ann Underwood, head of a Buncombe County household of 6 "free colored" in 1820 [NC:73].

    iii. Edy, born say 1760, mother of Micajah **Chavis** alias Underwood, a seven-year-old "mulatto" orphan boy bound to William Tatham, Esq., in Cumberland County, North Carolina, on 27 July 1787 [Minutes 1784-87], perhaps also the mother of Daniel Underwood, a fifteen-year-old "boy of Colour" bound to Alexander McDaniel in Cumberland County on 16 September 1808 [Minutes 1808-10]. Daniel was charged with carrying firearms without a license in Cumberland County, North Carolina, on Thursday, 8 March 1844 [Minutes 1842-44].

    iv. Sally, born say 1770, mother of George Underwood, a base born child (no race indicated) who was two months old on 30 October 1788 when the Cumberland County court bound him apprentice to John Winslow [Minutes 1787-91].

v. Isham, born say 1778, a "Mulatto" head of an Edgecombe County household of 2 "other free" in 1800 [NC:249]. He owned 99 acres when he died in March 1807 leaving a wife Bishop Underwood, and (son?) Silas Underwood [Gammon, *Record of Estates Edgecombe County*, 97]. Bishop was head of an Edgecombe County household of 2 "other free" and 3 slaves in 1810 [NC:743].

vi. Mary, born say 1785, head of a Halifax County, North Carolina household of 4 "other free" in 1810 [NC:52], perhaps the Mary Underwood who was head of a Richmond County, North Carolina household of 3 "other free" in 1810 [NC:206].

VALENTINE FAMILY

Members of the Valentine family born during the colonial period were

1   i.   Edward[1], born say 1715.
2   ii.   Charles[1], born say 1718.
3   iii. John[1], born say 1721.
4   iv.   Sarah[1], born say 1722.
5   v.   Mary[1], born say 1729.
6   vi.   Lucy[1], born say 1730.
7   vii. Elizabeth[1], born say 1733.
    viii. Terry, a "Mullatto Boy" indentured to Ephraim Garthwright when he left the remainder of Terry's indentured time to his son Ephraim by his undated Henrico County will, proved December 1750 [DW 1750-7, 39-40].
8   ix.   Amy[1], born say 1745.
9   x.   Mary[2], born say 1748.
10 xi.   Sarah[5], born about 1750.
11 xii. Lucy[3], born about 1758.
12 xiii. Jenny[1], born about 1763.

1. Edward[1] Valentine, born say 1715, was taxable in Chesterfield County in 1752 and 1756 [Tax List 1747-1821, frames 6, 24]. On 2 March 1753 his suit in Chesterfield County against William Glascock for trespass, assault, and battery was dismissed by consent of both parties. On 5 October 1753 Augustine Claiborne won a suit against him for 30 shillings, and the court ordered the churchwardens of Dale Parish to bind out his children Charles, Peter, Sarah, Elizabeth, Edward, and Susanna Valentine (no race indicated and no reason for the order stated). The sheriff reported that he was not an inhabitant of the county on 7 December 1753 when Claiborne's suit against him came to trial [Orders 1749-54, 315, 404, 428]. He may have been the Edward Valentine, husband of Ann Valentine, whose son Zachariah (no race indicated) was born a year later on 8 October 1754 in New Kent County [NSCDA, *Parish Register of St. Peter's*, 182]. In August 1758 David Sims testified in Chesterfield County court that Edward had administered poisonous medicines to him, and the court ordered Edward to post bond for his good behavior for a year. On 17 August 1763 he was charged with horse stealing and sent to Williamsburg for trial. Peter Matthews, John Kimbles, Thomas Brentlow, Lewis Andrews, and Moses Granger testified against him. On 6 February 1767 Stephen Dance sued him for a 1 pound, 7 shilling debt, and on 3 July 1767 the court ordered the churchwardens of Dale Parish to bind out his children Matthew and Nanny [Orders 1754-9, 461-2; 1759-63, 440; 1763-7, 62]. His children were

13 i.   Charles[2], born say 1742.
14 ii.   Peter[1], born say 1744.
15 iii. Sarah[2], born say 1746.
    iv.   Elizabeth[2], born say 1748.

     v.   Edward[3], born say 1750, perhaps the Edward Valentine who was living in Dinwiddie County when he applied for a pension for Revolutionary War service [Jackson, *Virginia Negro Soldiers*, 45].

     vi.   Susanna, born say 1752.

    vii. Zachariah[1], born 8 October 1754 in New Kent County, may have been the father of Richard Valentine who registered in King George County on 4 April 1822: *a dark Mulatto, about 34 years of age, 5' 1 Inch high...was born free in the County of New Kent* [Register of Free Persons, no.64].

   viii. Matthew, born say 1756.

    ix. Ann/ Nanny, born say 1758.

2.   Charles[1] Valentine, born say 1718, sued John **Pompey** for a one pound, six shilling debt in Brunswick County, Virginia, in October 1741. The case was dismissed in May 1742 because Charles did not prosecute. He was sued for debt in Brunswick County in July 1758 [1737-41, 443; 1741-2, 45; 1757-9, 228; 1760-84, 21]. He may have been the father of

16   i.   Howard, born say 1743.
17   ii.   John[2], born say 1745.
18   iii. Isham[1], born say 1755.

3.   John[1] Vollentine, born say 1721, complained to the Amelia County court in May 1743 that "he being a free person is kept a slave by Charles Irby." The court ordered that depositions be taken from Ann Hunt and Elizabeth Mallory in the adjacent county of Prince George. The suit was dismissed in 1744 when both parties were in agreement [Orders 1735-46, 232, 235, 238, 244, 250, 262, 269, 273, 286, 295]. He was a tithable head of household in the lower part of Nottoway Parish, Amelia County, from 1748 to 1750 [Amelia County Tithables, 1748, 1749, 1750]. He may have been the father of "poor Mulattos" Sarah, Will, Sam, Amy, Vall, Charles, Dorcas, Martha, and Ann Valentine of Nottoway Parish who were ordered bound out by the Amelia County court on 27 January 1763 [Orders 7:5]. His children may have been

19   i.   Sarah[3], born say 1746.
     ii.   William[1], born say 1748, called William, son of ____ Valentine, in Chesterfield County on 5 November 1756 when the court ordered the churchwardens of Dale Parish to bind him out to a trade [Orders 1754-9, 237]. He may have been the Will Valentine who was bound out in Amelia County on 27 January 1763 [Orders 7:5].
    iii. Sam, taxable in Wm Totty's Dinwiddie County household in 1792 [PPTL, 1782-90 (1792 A, p.16)], a "Black" complexioned soldier who was enlisted as a substitute in the Revolution from Dinwiddie County [NSDAR, *African American Patriots*, 154].
    iv. Amy[2], born say 1752, called a "free Mulatto" on 27 April 1767 when the Amelia County court ordered the churchwardens to bind her and Pat Valentine to Henrietta Irby [Orders 8A:44].
     v.   Vall, perhaps identical to Vaul Valentine who was a "FN" taxable in Nottoway County in 1813 [Waldrep, *1813 Tax List*].
    vi. Charles[4], born say 1756, married Nancy **Chavous**, 28 November 1785 Mecklenburg County, Virginia bond, Thomas **McLin** security. He was sued for a 4 pound debt in Mecklenburg County on 8 April 1799 [Orders 1798-1801, 163]. He was taxable on his own tithe and a horse in the lower District of Mecklenburg County from 1795 to 1800 and taxable on his son Henry in 1801 [PPTL, 1782-1805, frames 583, 670, 702, 811, 860].
   vii. Dorcas.
  viii. Martha[1], called Pat Valentine on 27 December 1764 when the Amelia County court ordered the churchwardens of Nottoway Parish to bind her out and called a "free Mulatto" on 27 April 1767 when the court

ordered the churchwardens to bind her and Amey Valentine to Henrietta Irby [Orders 8:325; 8A:44].
   ix. Ann.

4. Sarah[1] Valentine, born say 1722, was living in Charles City County, Virginia, in August 1746 when her "mulatto" son Caesar Valentine was bound to Edmund Eppes [Orders 1737-51, 420]. Her children were
    i. Caesar[1], born say 1739, a "Mullatto" indentured to John Wayles on 2 March 1757 when the Charles City County court ordered that he serve additional time for running away for six months [Orders 1751-7, 444]. He was charged with felony in Brunswick County, Virginia court on 23 July 1759 and sent to Williamsburg for trial [Orders 1757-9, 383]. He was a "free Negro" executed near Williamsburg according to the 30 November 1759 edition of the *Virginia Gazette* [Headley, *18th Century Virginia Newspapers*, 347].
    ii. ?Anthony, born about 1747, a thirty-three-year- old "Black" complexioned soldier who was born in Charles City County and residing there when he was listed in the size roll of troops who enlisted after 1 September 1780 [The Chesterfield Supplement cited by NSDAR, *African American Patriots*, 154; *Virginia Genealogical Society Bulletin* 6:76].
20   iii. ?Charles[3], born about 1751.
21   iv. ?Martha[2], born say 1758.
22   v. ?Lucy[5], born say 1761.
23   vi. ?Phebe, born say 1763.

5. Mary[1] Valentine, born say 1729, was living in Charles City County in June 1748 when the churchwardens were ordered to bind her son Edward Valentine (no race mentioned) to Thomas Coley [Orders 1737-51, 477], and she was living in Chesterfield County on 6 April 1753 when the churchwardens of Dale Parish were ordered to bind out her daughter Betty Valentine (no race mentioned) [Orders 1749-54, 333]. Her children were
    i. Edward[2], born say 1747.
24   ii. Elizabeth[3], born say 1752.

6. Lucy[1] Valentine, born say 1730, was living in Lunenburg County, Virginia, in October 1751 when the court ordered the churchwardens of Cumberland Parish to bind out her children Lucy and Sarah. The same October court called her a late servant of Matox Mayes when it granted her a certificate proving her freedom [Orders 1748-52, 466, 485]. On 22 November 1753 she was in Halifax County, Virginia, when the churchwardens of Antrim Parish were ordered to bind out her children Nanny and Sarah to George Abney [Pleas 1:324]. In February 1754 the Lunenburg County court ordered the churchwardens to bind out her daughter Cloe [Orders 1753-4, 541]. In February 1761 the Halifax County, Virginia court confirmed the indenture of Sarah and Ann to George Abney [Pleas 3:181, 194]. She was the mother of
25   i. Lucy[2], born say 1746.
26   ii. Sarah[4], born say 1748.
    iii. Ann, born say 1750, bound apprentice to George Abney in Halifax County on 22 November 1753.
27   iv. Chloe, born say 1752.
28   v. ?Luke[1], born about 1754.

7. Elizabeth[1] Valentine, born say 1733, was living in Chesterfield County on 7 December 1753 when the churchwardens of Dale Parish were ordered to bind out her daughter Nanny Valentine. She was the mother of
29   i. Ann/ Nanny, born say 1753.

ii.   ?Abraham, born say 1766, taxable in Dinwiddie County in 1787, 1789, 1790, 1793, 1795, and a "free" tithable in 1796 and 1797 [PPTL, 1782-90 (1787 A, p.14), (1789 A, p.13), (1790 A, p.12), (1793 A, p.13), (1795 A, p.15), (1796 B, p.15), (1797 A, p.16)].

iii. ?William², born say 1772, over sixteen years of age when he was listed in the Dinwiddie County household of James Valentine in 1790. He was taxable in his own household in 1795 and 1796 [PPTL, 1782-90 (1790 B, p.18), (1795 B, p.16), (1796 B, p.20)]. He was taxable on 20 acres in Dinwiddie County on Whipponock Creek from 1801 to 1814 [Land Tax List 1782-1814, B lists]. He was counted in the list of "free Negroes & Mollattoes" in Dinwiddie County from 1802 to 1819, listed as a sawyer most years, but called a planter in 1813 when he was listed with his wife Polley [PPTL 1800-9; 1810-14; 1814-19, B lists].

iv.   ?Archibald, born about 1774, taxable in Dinwiddie County in the household of James Valentine in 1796 and taxable in his own household from 1797 to 1800 [PPTL, 1782-90 (1795 B, p.20), (1796 B, p.20), (1797 B, p.19), (1798 A, p.17) (1799 A, p.17), (1800 A, p.19)]. He registered in Petersburg on 15 August 1800: *a dark brown Mulatto man, five feet ten inches high, twenty six years old, born free & raised in Dinwiddie County* [Register of Free Negroes 1794-1819, no. 183]. He was head of a Petersburg Town household of 7 "other free" and a slave in 1810 [VA:122a].

8.   Amy¹ Valentine, born say 1745, was a taxable head of a household in Norfolk Borough in 1768 [Wingo, *Norfolk County Tithables, 1766-80*, 86]. She travelled to Cumberland County, North Carolina, in October 1784 to secure the freedom of her daughter Sally who was held there as a slave. About eight years later in August 1792 the Governor of Virginia was asked to help bring to justice Jacob Abrahams, James Bishop and a man named Skinner who had been involved with stealing Sally from Norfolk and selling her in Fayetteville [*Calendar of Virginia State Papers* 6:185-6]. She was the mother of

i.   Sally, born about 1761, a "free Negro girl" bound to Samuel Blue of Elizabeth River Parish by order of the Norfolk County court on 20 June 1771 [Orders 1771-3, 1]. She was a "Negro woman" who was sold by Nathaniel Folsom to James McCracking by 11 October 1792 when she sued for her freedom in Cumberland County, North Carolina. The court ordered her released [Minutes 1791-7]. She was a thirty-year-old free-born "Black Woman" who registered in Norfolk Borough on 18 August 1794 and produced her papers in the District of Columbia court in Alexandria in 1805 [Arlington County Register of Free Negroes, 1797-1861, p.14].

ii.   ?George, born say 1765, taxable in Princess Anne County in 1787, his tax charged to Anne Campbell [Schreiner-Yantis, *1787 Census*, 1157]. He married Dinah **Sparrow**, "mulattoes," 14 November 1787 Norfolk County bond, and was a "F.B." head of Princess Anne County household of 3 "other free" and 2 slaves in 1810 [VA:477].

9.   Mary² Valentine, born say 1748, was the mother of Boatswain Valentine, an illegitimate child bound to Batt Crowder by the Mecklenburg County court on 13 March 1769. On 14 April 1777 the court bound her son Isham Valentine to Edward Waller [Orders 1768-71, 151; 1773-9, 358]. She was the mother of

i.   Boatswain, bound out on 13 March 1769.

30   ii.   Isham², born say 1774.

10.   Sarah⁵ Valentine, born about 1750, was a "Mulatto" living in Henrico County on 4 December 1752 when the court ordered the churchwardens of Henrico Parish to bind her out [Minutes 1752-5, 23]. On 7 September 1770 the

Chesterfield County court ordered the churchwardens of Dale Parish to bind out her daughter Winny. On 13 March 1789 she brought suit in Chesterfield County court against William Tolly for trespass, assault and battery, but the suit abated when the sheriff reported that Tolly was not found in the county The court bound out her sons Jeffrey and John Valentine on 16 May 1789, and she may have been the mother of Sally, Polly and Nancy Valentine who were bound out by the court on 12 October 1786 [Orders 1767-71, 449; 1784-7, 399; 1787-91, 231, 257]. She was taxable on a free male tithe and a horse in Chesterfield County in 1793 and 1794 [PPTL, 1786-1811, frames 167, 207]. She obtained a certificate of freedom in Chesterfield County on 10 July 1810: *sixty years old, brown complexioned, born free* [Register of Free Negroes 1804-53, no. 135]. She was the mother of

  i. Winny, born say 1770, bound out in Chesterfield County on 7 September 1770.
  ii. ?Mann/ Manuel, born about 1772, head of a Chesterfield County, Virginia household of 2 "other free" in 1810 [VA:70/1062]. He married Nancy **Cox** (free persons of colour), 13 September 1813 Chesterfield County bond, Jeremiah **Ligon** security [Marriage Register, 122]. He obtained a certificate of freedom in Chesterfield County on 15 August 1821: *forty nine years old, black complexioned, born free* [Register of Free Negroes 1804-53, no. 412].
  iii. Jeffrey, born say 1780, bound out on 16 May 1789.
  iv. John[6], born about 1782, orphan of Sarah Valentine, bound out by the Chesterfield County court on 16 May 1789. He registered in Petersburg on 9 October 1805: *a dark Free Negro man, five feet five inches high, twenty three years old, born free and raised in the County of Chesterfield* [Register of Free Negroes 1794-1819, no. 366].
  v. ?Nancy[5], born about 1785, bound out by the Chesterfield County court on 12 October 1786, no parent named [Orders 1784-7, 399]. She obtained a certificate of freedom in Chesterfield County on 10 July 1810: *twenty five years old, brown complexioned, born free* [Register of Free Negroes 1804-53].
  vi. ?Polly, born about 1785, registered in Petersburg on 30 December 1808: *a brown free Negro woman, five feet one inches high, twenty three years old, born free & raised in the Town of Petersburg* [Register of Free Negroes 1794-1819, no. 437].
  vii. ?Sally, born about 1787, bound out by the Chesterfield County court on 12 October 1786, no parent named [Orders 1784-7, 399]. She obtained a certificate of freedom in Chesterfield County on 10 July 1810: *twenty three years old, brown complexioned, born free* [Register of Free Negroes 1804-53, no. 139].
  viii. ?William, born about 1789, obtained a certificate of freedom in Chesterfield County on 10 July 1810: *twenty one years old, brown complexioned, born free* [Register of Free Negroes 1804-53, no. 240].

11. Lucy[3] Valentine, born about 1758, registered in Petersburg on 11 July 1805: *a brown Mulatto woman, rather above five feet, about forty seven years old, born free and raised in the County of Chesterfield* [Register of Free Negroes 1794-1819, no. 330]. She was head of a Petersburg household of 7 "other free" in 1810 [VA:122b]. She may have been the mother of
  i. Thomas, born 21 October 1785, registered in Petersburg on 23 July 1806: *a dark brown free Negro man, twenty one Oct. next, born free & raised in the Town of Petersburg* [Register of Free Negroes 1794-1819, no. 388].

12. Jenny[1] Valentine, born about 1763, registered in Petersburg on 9 July 1805: *yellow brown Mulatto woman, five feet and a half inches high, forty two years*

old, born free and raised in the County of Chesterfield [Register of Free Negroes 1794-1819, no. 313]. She may have been the mother of

    i.   Molly, born about 1778, registered in Petersburg on 11 July 1805: *a yellowish brown Mulatto woman, five feet four inches high, twenty seven years old, born free & raised in the Town of Petersburg* [Register of Free Negroes 1794-1819, no. 331].

    ii. Patsey, born about 1780, registered in Petersburg on 10 July 1805: *a yellow brown Mulatto woman, five feet two and a half inches high, twenty five years old, born free & raised in the Town of Petersburg* [Register of Free Negroes 1794-1819, no. 319].

13. Charles[2] Valentine, born say 1742, the son of Edward Valentine, was bound apprentice in Chesterfield County in October 1753 [Orders 1749-54, 404]. He may have been the Charles Valentine who was a "free Negroe" taxable in Bladen County, North Carolina, in 1768 and a chain carrier with Thomas **Lowry** for a 9 August 1786 Robeson County survey for James **Lowry**'s 150 acres on the north side of Drowning Creek [Byrd, *Bladen County Tax Lists*, I:6; 70:396, envelope 4,469], and head of a Robeson County household of 5 "other free" in 1790 [NC:48]. He may have been the father of

    i.   J., head of a Brunswick County, North Carolina household of 7 "other free" in 1810 [NC:232].

    ii. Nancy[3] Vollintine, born say 1775, head of an Abbeville District, South Carolina household of 4 "other free" in 1810 [SC:35].

14. Peter[1] Valentine, born say 1744, purchased 50 acres in Southwark Parish, Surry County, Virginia, from Henry **Charity** and his wife Sacugoth **Charity** on 12 January 1768 [DB 8:374]. Peter was taxable on this 50 acres in Surry County in 1784 [Land Tax List 1782-1820]. He was taxable on his personal property from 1782 to 1785 [PPTL, 1782-90, frames 359, 380, 388]. His 21 December 1785 Surry County will was proved on 23 October 1791 [Wills 1792-1804, 13-14]. However, his death was recorded earlier in 1785 [Surry County Property Tax Alterations]. He left his wife Priscilla the use of his plantation during her life and named his sons James and Frederick and his six daughters. Priscilla was taxed on their land from 1786 to 1814 and taxable on personal property from 1786 to 1792: taxable on 2 horses and 5 cattle in 1786; taxable on Frederick Valentine's tithe in 1791 and 1792 [PPTL, 1782-90, frames 398, 461, 559; 1791-1816, frame 18, 68]. Peter was the father of

    i.   James[2], born say 1766.

    ii. Mary[4], born say 1768, married Benjamin **Banks**, 12 December 1788 Surry County bond.

    iii. Mason, born say 1770.

    iv. Mildred, born say 1772, married John **Banks**, 29 May 1789 Surry County bond, Sampson **Walden** security.

    v. Frederick, born about 1775, taxable in Surry County from 1791 to 1793 [PPTL, 1791-1816, frames 18, 68, 118].

    vi. Charlotte, born about 1780, registered in Surry County on 23 June 1810: *a mulattoe woman born of free parents of Surry county, rather of a bright complexion aged about 30 years, of a thin visage, and delicate features...and is 5'1/2" high* [Hudgins, *Surry County Register of Free Negroes*, 41].

    vii. Sarah[8].

    viii. Hannah.

15. Sarah[2] Valentine, born say 1746, daughter of Edward Valentine, was bound apprentice by the churchwardens of Dale Parish, Chesterfield County, in October 1753. She may have been the mother of

    i.   Peter[2], born say 1756, a "Mulatto" taxable in Chesterfield County from 1792 to 1807 (called Peter, Sr.) [PPTL, 1786-1811, frames 127, 238,

273, 306, 344, 379, 531] and taxable on 8 acres from 1804 to 1814 [Land Tax List 1791-1822, A lists]. He served in the Revolution and received a warrant for bounty land according to the application for a survivor's pension which his nephews Daniel and Sarah made while living in Halifax County, North Carolina [M805-820, frame 0119].

    ii. Daniel[1], born say 1760, ordered bound apprentice in Chesterfield County in August 1763 (no parent or race mentioned) [Orders 1759-67, 459], the brother of Peter and Polly Valentine according to the declaration of Polly's children on 21 May 1835 in Halifax County, North Carolina court. A military land warrant was issued on 3 November 1834 for his service as a soldier under Captain Bradley in the Tenth North Carolina Regiment [M805-820, frame 0119].

31   iii. Mary[3]/ Polly, born say 1762.

16. Howard Valentine, born say 1743, was taxable in Dinwiddie County on 2 horses and 7 cattle in 1783, taxable on a slave named Bibiana in 1786, a slave over the age of 16 in 1792, 1794 and 1795, taxable on a slave in 1798 and taxable on 2 horses in 1799 [PPTL, 1782-90, (1783 B, p.53), (1786, p.4); 1791-99 (1792 A, p.17), (1794 A, p.20), (1797 B, p.19), (1798 A, p.17), (1799 A, p.17)]. He died before June 1809 when his 29 December 1807 Dinwiddie County will was proved. He left his whole estate to his wife Winney Valentine and named his children Mimy **Scott**, Nancy Valentine, Jimmy Valentine and grandchildren John Valentine and Betsy **Bibby** [*Virginia Genealogist* 18:95; 16:170-171]. He was the father of

32   i. ?Jemima, born about 1764.

    ii. James[1], ("of Dinwiddie County"), married Anne **Owins**, 10 December 1785 Petersburg Hustings Court bond, William **Cypress** surety, 11 December 1785 marriage. Sarah **Owins**, mother of the bride, gave her consent. He was taxable in Dinwiddie County in 1787, 1790, 1795, 1796 [PPTL, 1782-90, (1787 B, p.11); 1791-9 (1790 B, p.18), (1795 B, p.20), (1796 B, p.20)]. He registered in Petersburg on 1 May 1799: *a brown Mulatto man, five feet seven inches high, twenty eight in August last, strait & well made with a Bushy head of hair, born free in Dinwiddie County upon the evidence of his mother Winny Volentine & Wm Scott, inspector* [Register of Free Negroes 1794-1819, no. 144].

    iii. Nancy[1], born say 1774.

17. John[2] Valentine, born say 1745, was tithable in Cumberland Parish, Lunenburg County, in 1764, 1769, 1773, and 1774 [Bell, *Sunlight on the Southside*, 233, 276, 322, 344], and tithable in Lunenburg County from 1785 to 1806: taxable on 2 horses and 7 cattle in 1785, taxable on 3 tithables most years from 1795 to 1805 [PPTL 1782-1806] and taxable on 70 acres in 1802 [Land Tax List, 1802, by *VMHB* 92:65]. He was sued in Lunenburg County by Matthew Parham for a debt of 20 pounds on 9 July 1772, and he sold property by deed proved in court on 10 June 1802 [Orders 1769-77, 217; 1802-5, 252]. He was counted in a "List of free Negroes & Mulattoes" in Lunenburg County in 1802 and 1803 with his wife Betty and their children: Nancy, Betsy, John, Polly, Jinsy, Charles, Henry, Tommy, and Patsy [LVA, Lunenburg County, Free Negro & Slave Records, 1802-1803]. He was taxable in the lower district of Mecklenburg County on 2 taxables in 1812, 3 "Mulattos above the age of 16" in 1813, and 2 in 1814 [PPTL, 1806-28, frames 274, 370, 407]. He was the father of

    i. Nancy[2], born about 1773, counted in her parent's household in a list of "free Negroes & Mulattoes" in Lunenburg County in 1802, counted with her children Bob and Polly in 1803 [LVA, Lunenburg County, Free Negro & Slave Records, 1802-1803] and counted with Polly, Jordan, Elizabeth and Eliza-Ann at the head of Kettlestick Creek in 1814 [*Magazine of Virginia Genealogy* 33:268]. She registered in

Lunenburg County on 11 June 1827: *about 54 years of age, dark brown Complexion, about 5 feet 5 inches high.* Her son Robert Harrison Valentine, born about 1799, registered on 11 January 1827 [WB 5, after page 89, no.49, 50].

ii. Elizabeth[4], born say 1775, perhaps the Lizzy Valentine who was head of a Mecklenburg County household of 5 "free colored" in 1820.

iii. John[5], born say 1776, married Mary **McLin**, 4 January 1797 Mecklenburg County, Virginia marriage bond, Earby **Chavous** security. He was taxable in Lunenburg County in 1797 and 1798 [PPTL 1782-1806] and was a "Mulatto" taxable in Mecklenburg County from 1813 to 1816 [PPTL, 1806-28, frames 370, 407, 524, 550].

iv. Polly.

v. Jane, born say 1785, head of a Lunenburg County household of 4 "other free" in 1810 [VA:363].

vi. Charles[5], born about 1796, registered in Lunenburg County on 8 March 1824: *yellow Complexion, his hair rather straight, about 5 feet 10 inches high...about 28 years of age.*

vii. Henry.

viii. Thomas[2], born about 1796, received a certificate in Mecklenburg County on 13 September 1817: *born free and raised in the County of Lunenburg & Mecklenburg & Commonwealth of Virginia of a bright Yellow Complexion, five feet nine inches & three quarters high about Twenty one years old* [Free Person of Color, no.13, p.7]. He married Sally **Stewart**, 18 May 1818 Mecklenburg County bond, Randolph **Chavous** surety, 21 May marriage by Milton Robertson. He was a "Free" taxable in Mecklenburg County in 1815 and 1818 [PPTL, 1782-1805, frames 524, 660] and head of a Brunswick County, Virginia household of 3 "free colored" in 1820 [VA:672].

ix. Patsy.

18. Isham[1] Valentine, born say 1755, was mentioned in *William Cabell's Commonplace Book* (of Amherst and Buckingham Counties) on 9 March 1780: *Sent by Isham Valentine a free Negro, 1 pr. Silver mounted Pistols and Bullet Moulds to Col. Sam. J. Cabell. Also all his Clothes, etc., Consisting of one Blue Broad Cloth Coat, one white ditto Vest & Pr. Breeches with Silver oval buttons, 1 pr. mosquito Curtains Seven shirts 5 of which ruffled at the Hands, 1 pr. Sheets, 2 Towels* [McLeRoy, *Strangers in Their Midst*, 210]. He was taxable in Dinwiddie County on 2 horses and 2 cattle in 1787 and 1788 [PPTL, 1782-90 (1787 A, p.16), (1787 B, p.14), (1788 A, p.8)] and taxable in Surry County, Virginia, from 1790 to 1800 [PPTL, 1782-90, frames 606; 1791-1816, 68, 170, 275, 349, 428]. He was living in Dinwiddie County when he applied for a pension for Revolutionary War service [Jackson, *Virginia Negro Soldiers*, 45]. He and his wife Caty were the parents of

i. Nancy[4], born about 1781, registered in Surry County on 25 May 1818: *daughter of Isham Valentine & Caty his wife of Surry County free people of Colour the said Nancy Valentine is about 37 years old of a bright Complexion tolerable straight made...is 5'3-1/2" high* [Hudgins, Surry County Register of Free Negroes, 68].

ii. ?Elizabeth[5], born about 1787, registered in Surry County on 12 August 1812: *a mulattoe woman who was born of free parents of Surry County, of a bright complexion aged about 25 years...long bushy hair straight and delicately formd and is 5'5-1/4" high* [Hudgins, *Register*, 48]. She registered in Petersburg on 15 August 1812: *Elizabeth Shepherd alias Valentine, a brown Mulatto woman, five feet five inches high, twenty five years old, born free & raised in Surry County, is the wife of Jos. Shepherd of this town Registered in Surry 12 Jany. by name of Valentine* [Register of Free Negroes 1794-1819, no. 725].

19. Sarah[3] Valentine, born say 1746, was living in Brunswick County, Virginia, on 25 September 1775 when the court ordered the churchwardens of St. Andrew's Parish to bind out her "Bastard" daughter Lucy Valentine [Orders 1774-82, 91]. She was the mother of
   i. Lucy[6], born say 1774, bound apprentice in Brunswick County on 25 September 1775. She married Isaac **Seward**, 25 October 1803 Mecklenburg County, Virginia bond, Isham Valentine security. Isaac, born before 1776, was head of a Mecklenburg County household of 10 "free colored" in 1820 [VA:161a]. He registered in Brunswick County, Virginia, on 23 October 1810: *Isaac, a black man of a yellowish Complection, about forty two years of age, about five feet three inches high...appears to have been emancipated by John Seward agreeable to the within deed.* He registered again in Brunswick County on 28 July 1828 when he was about sixty years of age [Wynne, *Register of Free Negroes*, 10, 95].

20. Charles[3] Valentine, born about 1751, was listed in a 13 March 1779 offer of a reward in the *Virginia Gazette* for deserters from the infantry of the Virginia State Garrison Regiment stationed near Williamsburg. The advertisement described him as: *a mulatto, born in Surry County, Virginia, 28 years old, 5 feet 9 inches high, well made* [Dixon's edition, p. 2, col. 2]. He enlisted in Chesterfield County and was living in Sussex County after 1 September 1780 [*Virginia Genealogical Society Bulletin*, 6:58 (Chesterfield Supplement at Va. Lib.]. He was head of a Brunswick County, Virginia household of a "free colored" man over forty-five years of age in 1820 [VA:672]. He may have been the father of
   i. James[3], born about 1786, registered in Petersburg on 25 June 1807: *a dark brown free Negro man, five feet nine inches high, twenty one years old, a carpenter, born free in Sussex County* [Register of Free Negroes 1794-1819, no. 427]. He was head of a Brunswick County, Virginia household of 3 "free colored" in 1830 [VA:272].
   ii. William, head of a Brunswick County, Virginia household of 5 "free colored" in 1840.
   iii. Patsey, born 1804-16, head of a Brunswick County, Virginia household of 8 "free colored" in 1840.

21. Martha[2] Valentine, born say 1758, was living in Surry County, Virginia, on 7 October 1800 when her son John registered as a "free Negro" [Back of Guardian Accounts Book, 1783-1804, no.78]. She may have been the Patsy Valentine who was head of a Richmond City household of 2 "other free" and 2 slaves in 1810 [VA:365]. Her children were
   i. ?Nicholas, born say 1774, taxable in Cabin Point district of Surry County from 1794 to 1798 and from 1809 to 1816: listed with Hartwell Carseley in 1794; charged with his own tax in 1795; called Nicholas **Scott** Valentine starting in 1812; listed with 2 "free Negroes & Mulattoes above the age of 16" in 1813 [PPTL, 1791-1816, frames 158, 245, 308, 349, 639, 677, 697, 715, 761, 832, 869] and taxable in Prince George County in 1805 and 1806 [PPTL, 1782-1811, frames 637, 663]. He was called Nicholas **Scott** Valentine when he married Keziah **Charity**, the twenty-four-year-old daughter of Judith **Charity**, 28 May 1804 Surry County bond, Wright **Walden** security.
   ii. John[3], born 25 December 1777, registered as a "free Negro" in Surry County, Virginia, on 7 October 1800: *son of Martha Valentine a free Woman of Surry County, he is of a bright complexion, 5'7" high, straight and well made, aged 23 years old next Xmass* [Back of Guardian Accounts Book, 1783-1804, no.78]. He was taxable in Surry County from 1793 to 1800: listed with James Bishop in 1793; with Hartwell Carsely in 1795; with James Oney in 1797; charged with his

own tithe in 1799 and 1800 [PPTL, 1791-1816, frames 104, 234, 302, 388, 428] and a "Mulatto" taxable in Prince George County from 1801 to 1811 [PPTL, 1782-1811, frames 542, 566, 589, 614, 637, 663, 711, 753].

iii.   Randolph, born about 1789, registered in Surry County on 16 June 1809: *a Mulatto man son of Martha Valentine, a free mulatto woman of Surry County, has long bushy hair, yellow complexion, thick upper lip, aged about 20 years and is 5'8-1/4" high* [Hudgins, *Surry County Register of Free Negroes*, 39]. He married Elizabeth **Peters**, 21 June 1814 Surry County bond. Nicholas **Scott**, "Mulatto," testified as to Elizabeth's age and was surety.

22. Lucy[4] Valentine, born say 1761, was living in Surry County on 25 January 1785 when the churchwardens ordered her "natural child" Jeremiah bound out [Minutes 1775-85, 392]. She was taxable on a free male tithable in adjoining Prince George County in 1799 [PPTL, 1782-1811, frame 498]. She was the mother of

i.   ?Isaac, born say 1778, taxable in Prince George County in 1799 and 1800 [PPTL, 1782-1811, frame 498, 519].

ii. Jeremiah, born about 1781, bound apprentice in Surry County on 25 January 1785 [Minutes 1775-85, 392]. He was listed as one of James Kee's tithables in Cabin Point district of Surry County from 1794 to 1798 [PPTL, 1791-1816, 164, 298, 336]. He registered in Surry County on 24 September 1811: *a mulattoe man, a son of Lucy Valentine late of Surry County aged about 30 years, has long hair, flat Nose, is 5'1-3/4" hight of a very bright complexion* [Hudgins, *Surry County Register of Free Negroes*, 47].

23. Phebe Valentine, born say 1763, was the mother of Martha Valentine who registered as a "free Negro" in Surry County:

i.   Martha[3], born about 1790, registered in Surry County on 22 February 1836: *(daughter of Phoebe Valentine) aged 46 years dark yellowish complexion 5'6" high born free in the County of Dinwiddie as appears by the certificate of the Clerk of Dinwiddie Court by occupation a spinner* [Hudgins, *Surry County Register of Free Negroes*, 123].

24. Elizabeth[3] Valentine, born say 1752, daughter of Mary Valentine, was living in Chesterfield County on 6 April 1753 when the court ordered the churchwardens to bind her out. She was the mother of

i.   ?Joshua, born about 1768, a "Mulatto" taxable in Prince George County from 1799 to 1804: taxable on a slave in 1802, a horse in 1804 and taxable from 1809 to 1811: taxable on a horse in 1809 and 1810 and taxable on 3 free males in 1811 [PPTL, 1782-1811, frame 498, 519, 542, 566, 568, 614, 711, 731, 753]. He registered in Petersburg on 31 May 1808: *a dark brown Negro man, five feet six inches high, forty years old, short bushy hair, born free & raised in the Town of Petersburg* [Register of Free Negroes 1794-1819, no. 425].

ii. William/ Billy, born about 1785, registered in Petersburg on 17 February 1802: *a dark brown free Mulatto boy, five feet one inches high, seventeen years old, short hair, now in the service of David Alexander of Petersburg, son of Betty Valentine a free woman of sd. town* [Register of Free Negroes 1794-1819, no. 224].

iii. ?Sally, born about 1787, registered in Petersburg on 30 December 1808: *a brown free Negro woman, five feet two inches high, twenty one years old, born free & raised in the Town of Petersburg* [Register of Free Negroes 1794-1819, no. 438].

25. Lucy[2] Valentine, born say 1746, daughter of Lucy Valentine, was bound out by the churchwardens in Lunenburg County, Virginia, in October 1751 [Orders 1748-52, 466]. She was a "free Negro" living in Bedford County on 25 May 1773 when the court ordered the churchwardens to bind her ten-year-old daughter Lucy to Mrs. Martha Gilbert [Orders 1772-4, 113]. She was taxable in Campbell County on 2 cattle in 1785 [PPTL, 1785-1814, frame 9]. She was the mother of

    33   i.   Lucy[5], born in November 1762.

          ii.   Sarah[7], daughter of Lucy Valentine bound to Mrs. Lucy Stith in Bedford County on 29 February 1780 [Orders 1774-82, 273].

26. Sarah[4] Valentine, born say 1748, was bound apprentice in Cumberland Parish, Lunenburg County, in October 1751 [Orders 1748-52, 466]. She was head of a Lunenburg County household of 11 "white" (free) persons, none of whom were tithable in 1783 [Bell, *Sunlight on the Southside*, 390]. She was taxable in Lunenburg County on 3 horses and 10 cattle in 1783, taxable on Didimus Valentine in 1786, taxable on a male tithable 16-21, 3 horses, and 10 cattle in 1787, 2 males in 1788, and 1 male in 1803 [PPTL 1782-1806]. She was head of a household in a list of "Free Negroes and Mulattos" on Kettlestick Creek in the lower district of Lunenburg County in 1802 with (her children?) Zachariah and Jane in 1802 and with Zachariah, Jane, and Molly in 1803 [LVA, Lunenburg County, Free Negro & Slave Records, 1802-1803]. She was the mother of

          i.   Zachariah[2], born about 1767, perhaps identical to Didimus Valentine who was taxable in Sarah's household in 1786. He was taxable in Lunenburg County in 1793 to 1806 [PPTL 1782-1806]. He was a shoemaker living at the head of Kettlestick in a list of "Free Negroes and Mulattos" in the lower district of Lunenburg County in Sarah Valentine's household in 1802 and 1803 [LVA, Lunenburg County, Free Negro & Slave Records, 1802-1803] and was head of a Lunenburg County household of 8 "other free" in 1810 [VA:363]. In 1814 he was head of a household with Ritter **Lester**, Dolly **Cordle**, and Eddins **Cordle** [*Magazine of Virginia Genealogy* 33:268]. He registered as a free Negro in Lunenburg County in 1841: *aged about 74 years of age, dark brown complexion, the hair in his head & his beard Grey, 5 feet Ten inches & three quarters high* [WB 5, after page 89, no. 109].

          ii.   ?Elizabeth Jones Volentine, born say 1768, married Isam **Lester**, 11 December 1789 Lunenburg County bond, Zachariah Valentine surety.

         iii.   ?Buckner, born about 1772, taxable in Lunenburg County on his own tithe and a horse from 1801 to 1806 [PPTL 1782-1806]. He married Sina **Chavous**, 21 December 1802 Mecklenburg County bond, Boling **Chavous** security. He and his wife Cinna were counted as "free Negroes and Mulattos" in the lower district of Lunenburg County in 1803 [LVA, Lunenburg County, Free Negro & Slave Records, 1802-1803]. He made a deed of trust to Thomas Adams which was proved in Lunenburg County on 12 September 1805 [Orders 1802-5, fol. 221]. He registered as a free Negro in Lunenburg County on 8 March 1824: *Brown Complexion, hair nearly Straight, some grey hairs in his head, about 52 years of age, 5 feet 10 or 11 inches high* [WB 5, after page 89, no. 24]. He was head of a Surry County, North Carolina household of 4 "free colored" in 1830.

         iv.   Jane, listed in Sarah Valentine's household in Lunenburg County in 1802 and 1803 [LVA, Lunenburg County, Free Negro & Slave Records, 1802-1803], taxable on a horse in 1806 [PPTL 1782-1806].

         v.   Molly, born say 1776, listed with her children Lively, Biddy, and Polly Valentine in her own household on the Lunenburg County "List of free Negroes & Mulattoes" in 1802 and listed with her children in Sarah

Valentines' household in 1803 [LVA, Lunenburg County, Free Negro
& Slave Records, 1802-1803], taxable on 2 horses in 1802 [PPTL
1782-1806].

vi.   ?Sukey, born about 1780, registered in Lunenburg County on 5
December 1818: *about 38, black Complexion, about 4 feet 8 inches
high* [WB 5, after page 89, no.8].

vii. ?William, taxable in Lunenburg County from 1801 to 1804 [PPTL
1782-1806], counted in the "List of free Negroes & Mulattoes" in
Lunenburg County in 1802 and 1803, a hireling for Charles Irby
[LVA, Lunenburg County, Free Negro & Slave Records, 1802-1803].

27. Chloe Valentine, born say 1752, daughter of Lucy Valentine, was ordered
bound out by the churchwardens of Cumberland Parish, Lunenburg County,
in February 1754 [Orders 1753-4, 541]. She was a "free Negroe" living in
Bedford County in September 1774 when the court ordered her son Thomas
Stewart Valentine bound to Richard Stith, Gentleman. She may have been
identical to "free Negro" Chloe **Stewart** whose daughter Lucy **Stewart** was
ordered bound to Harry Terrill on 23 January 1775 [Orders 1774-82]. She was
the mother of

i.   Thomas **Stewart**, born say 1772.
ii.   ?Lucy **Stewart**, born say 1774.
iii. Augustine, bastard child of Chloe Valentine, a "free Negroe," bound
to John Clayton in Bedford County on 9 May 1776 [Orders 1774-82].
iv.   ?Harry **Stewart**, a "Mulattoe" child of Chloe **Stewart** bound to Samuel
Clayton in Bedford County on 28 August 1781 [Orders 1774-82, 324].
Henry **Stewart** was a "f. negroe" taxable in Bedford County in 1813
with (his brothers?) Drury and James **Stewart** [Waldrep, *1813 Tax
List*].

28. Luke[1] Valentine, born about 1754, was called a "free man of Colour" on 13
November 1832 when he made a declaration in Campbell County in order to
obtain a pension for his services in the Revolution. He stated that he was born
on or about Christmas day 1754 or 1753 on Fedlay River in Bedford County
and lived in Russell Parish, Campbell County, which was formed from
Bedford. His discharge papers were burned when his mother's house was
destroyed by a fire [M804-2438]. He was called a "free Black Man" on 3
November 1785 when he was charged in Campbell County with stealing a
horse, the property of John Harvey. He chose to receive 39 lashes rather than
be tried at the District Court [Orders 1785-6, 193, 210, 211]. He was taxable
in the southern district of Campbell County from 1785 to 1812: called Luke
M. Valentine in 1787; charged with Thomas **Stewart**'s tithe in 1794; taxed on
2 free males in 1795 [PPTL, 1785-1814, frames 9, 46, 295, 323, 646, 843].
He was head of a Campbell County household of 10 "other free" in 1810
[VA:848]. He was called Luke M. Valentine on 29 August 1825 when he and
Mildred Valentine consented to the marriage of her daughter Jane **Jackson** to
John **Jackson**. They also consented to the marriage of her daughter Nancy
Jackson to Hezekiah **Jackson** by 27 June 1727 Campbell County bond
[Marriage Bonds and Consents, 1782-1853]. Luke was probably the father of

i.   David, taxable in the southern district of Campbell County in 1795
[PPTL, 1785-1814, frame 323, 372, 447, 479, 537, 560, 641].
ii.   Winnie, born say 1785, married Harry **Moss**, "free negroes," 15 June
1806 Campbell County bond, Benjamin **Armstrong** and Harry **Moss**
bondsmen.
iii. Austin, born in September 1804, registered in Campbell County on 8
January 1839: *born Septr. 1804; 5 ft 4-1/2 Inches high, bright
Mullattoe...Born free in Campbell* [Register of Free Negroes, p.16].
He was probably identical to Gus Valentine who was taxable in the

northern district of Campbell County in 1809 [PPTL, 1785-1814, frame 738].

29. Ann/ Nanny Valentine, born say 1753, daughter of Elizabeth Valentine, was ordered bound apprentice in Chesterfield County in December 1753 [Orders 1749-54, 429]. She may have been the mother of

    i. Fanny, born about 1772, obtained a certificate of freedom in Chesterfield County on 14 May 1810: *thirty eight years old, Mulatto complexion, born free* [Register of Free Negroes 1804-53, no. 130].

    ii. Peter³, Jr., born about 1773, a "Mulatto" taxable in Chesterfield County from 1796 to 1811, living on his own land in 1809 [PPTL, 1786-1811, frames 273, 306, 344, 379, 531, 737]. He obtained a certificate of freedom in Chesterfield County on 10 November 1816: *forty three years old, brown complexioned, born free* [Register of Free Negroes 1804-53, no. 308]. He was head of a Chesterfield County household of 7 "other free" in 1810 [VA:70/1062].

    iii. John⁵, born say 1778, taxable in Chesterfield County from 1799 to 1805 [PPTL, 1786-1811, frames 379, 455, 493, 531, 607].

    iv. Samuel, born say 1780, a "Mulatto" taxable in Chesterfield County from 1801 to 1803 [PPTL, 1786-1811, frames 455, 493, 531].

    v. William, born say 1780, a "Mulatto" taxable in Chesterfield County from 1801 to 1811, a shoemaker living on Thomas Jones's land in 1809 [PPTL, 1786-1811, frames 568, 607, 738, 824].

30. Isham² Valentine, born say 1774, son of Mary Valentine, was ordered bound apprentice to Edward Waller by the Mecklenburg County court on 14 April 1777 [Orders 1773-9, 358]. He was taxable in the lower district of Mecklenburg County in the household of Edward Waller from 1790 to 1792, taxable in his own household from 1802 to 1820, called a "Mulatto" in 1805, 1810 and from 1813 to 1820 [PPTL 1782-1805, frames 360, 416, 434, 931, 960, 1040, 1071; 1806-28, frames 47, 148, 175, 245, 274, 370, 407, 660], counted with his wife Peggy in the "List of free Negroes & Mulattoes" in Lunenburg County in 1802 [LVA, Lunenburg County, Free Negro & Slave Records, 1802-1803] and taxable in Lunenburg County in 1802 [PPTL 1782-1806]. Peggy was head of a Mecklenburg County household of 5 "free colored" in 1820 [VA:157a]. He was apparently the father of Polly and Wiltshire Valentine who were bound to Tilman Elder by the Mecklenburg County court on 15 March 1813 (no parent named). He petitioned the court on 17 October 1815 setting forth that he was the father of two children bound to Tilman Elder who intended to remove them from the county and commonwealth [Orders 1813-15, 440, 499]. He was the father of

    i. Polly, born about 1802, registered in Mecklenburg County on 18 June 1827: *a woman of yellow complexion, about twenty five years of age, five feet four inches and a half hight...born of a free woman* [Register of Free Negroes, p.35, no.41].

    ii. Wiltshire, born about 1804, registered in Mecklenburg County on 17 December 1827: *a man of yellow complexion, about six feet one inch high, about twenty three years of age...born of a free woman in this County* [Register of Free Negroes, p.39, no.47].

31. Mary³ Valentine, born say 1762, was taxable in Chesterfield County on a horse in 1795 [PPTL, 1786-1811, frame 239]. Polly was the sister of Daniel and Peter Valentine according to the 21 May 1835 pension application of her children in Halifax County, North Carolina court. According to the application, her children were

    i. Daniel², born 1775-94, head of a Halifax County household of 8 "free colored" in 1830.

    ii. Sarah⁹, born say 1784.

32. Jemima Valentine, born about 1764, registered in Petersburg on 31 January 1801: *a light Mulatto woman, five feet four inches, thirty seven years old, born free & raised in Dinwiddie County* [Register of Free Negroes 1794-1819, no. 211]. She apparently married a member of the **Scott** family since she was called Mimy **Scott** in her father's 29 December 1807 Dinwiddie County will. She was the mother of

    i.   Betsy **Stewart**, born about 1782, registered in Petersburg on 31 January 1801: *(daughter of Jemima Valentine, a free Mulatto woman) a light Coloured Mulatto woman, five feet three and a half inches high, nineteen years old, long bushy hair* [Register of Free Negroes 1794-1819, no. 212]

    ii. Sally **Bibby**, born about 1784, registered in Petersburg on 31 January 1801: *(daughter of Jemima Valentine, a free Mulatto woman) a brown Mulatto woman, five feet two inches high, seventeen years old, bushy hair, holes in her ears, born free & raised in Dinwiddie County* [Register of Free Negroes 1794-1819, no. 213].

33. Lucy[5] Valentine, born in November 1762, was called young Lucy Valentine on 7 November 1782 when the Campbell County court ordered the churchwardens of Russell Parish to bind out her "Mulattoe Bastard" son Luke Valentine to Jones Wynne and called Lucy Valentine, Jr., on 3 February 1791 when the court ordered the overseers of the poor to bind out her children [Orders 1782-5, 113; 1786-91, 333]. She was the mother of

    i.   Luke[2], Jr., born about 1780, a "F.N." taxable in the northern district of Campbell County from 1805 to 1809 [PPTL, 1785-1814, frames 627, 666, 738], registered as a "Free Negro" in Campbell County on 18 November 1806: *Age: 26; 5 feet 11 In., Dark Complexion, Born free in this County* [Register of Free Negroes, p.5].

    ii. John[7], born about 1786, "son of free Lucy" bound out by the Campbell County court to George Cock, Jr., on 7 April 1791 [Orders 1786-91, 351], registered in Campbell County on 25 September 1810: *Age: 24; 5 feet 9 In.; Yellowish Complexion, born free* [Register of Free Negroes, p.5].

    iii. Lucy[7], born about 1807, registered as a "Free Negro" in Campbell County on 24 April 1848: *Age: 41; 5' 3-7/8"; Bright Mulatto; Born free of Lucy Valentine* [Register of Free Negroes and Mulattoes, p.22].

Other members of the Valentine family were

    i.   Jenny[2], born say 1772, a "mulatto girl" who ran away from Thomas Brown in Fredericksburg and was lurking around Hannah **Maclin**'s house in Richmond City according to the 12 June 1788 issue of the *Virginia Gazette and Weekly Advertiser*. The article said her mother was living in Williamsburg [Headley, *18th Century Virginia Newspapers*, 347].

    ii. Rebecca, born before 1776, a "Negro" head of a Guilford County, North Carolina household of 5 "free colored" in 1830.

    iii. Elijah, born say 1780, married Polly **Bass**, 28 June 1806 Granville County, North Carolina bond. He was head of a Granville County household of 3 "free colored" in 1820 [NC:10].

    iv. William/ Billy, born about 1784, registered in Petersburg on 4 December 1805: *a dark brown free Negro man, five feet seven inches high, twenty one years old the 20 March last, very short knotty hair, born free & raised in the Town of Petersburg* [Register of Free Negroes 1794-1819, no. 369]. He may have been the Will Valentine who was head of a Petersburg Town household of 5 "other free" and a slave in 1810 [VA:123a], perhaps the Bill Valentine who was head of a Rowan County, North Carolina household of 8 "free colored" in 1820 [NC:334].

v. Isham[3], born about 1795, obtained a certificate of freedom in Chesterfield County on 10 November 1816: *twenty one years old, mulatto complexioned, born free* [Register of Free Negroes 1804-53, no. 309].

vi. John[8], born about 1801, registered in Mecklenburg County on 20 November 1826: *alias Claiborne Volentine a Free Mulatto about 25 Years of age five feet seven inches high...Short black hair...born of a Free Woman in this County* [Free Person of Color, no.19, p.22].

vii. Billy **Brogden** Valentine, born about 1804, registered in Mecklenburg County in 1826: *a Free Mulatto about 22 years of age six feet one Inch high* [Register, no.18, p.21]. He was probably named for William **Brogdon**, head of a Mecklenburg County household in 1782 [VA:34] and a "Free Negro" head of a Charlotte County household of 6 "other free" in 1810 [VA:1019]. Mary **Brogden** was listed as a midwife in "A list of Free Negroes and Mulattoes for the Year 1802" in Lunenburg County."

viii. Betsy, born about 1806, registered in Lunenburg County on 12 August 1828: *22 years of age, dark mulatto Complexion, about 5 feet 7 or 8 inches high, tolerable long hair* [WB 5, after page 89, no. 26].

ix. Betsy Washington Valentine, born 7 March 1807, registered in Mecklenburg County on 17 October 1825: *a woman of Colour, five feet nine Inches and one quarter high...who it appears was born of a free woman in said County on the 7th day of March 1807...registered as a free mulattoe* [Free Person of Color, no.14, p.19].

VAUGHAN FAMILY

1. Stephen Vawhon, born say 1688, (a white man) was living in Surry County, Virginia in January 1709/10 when Mary, the "Mulatto" servant of William Thomas, swore that he was the father of her illegitimate child. He posted bond for the maintenance of the child in July 1710 [Haun, Surry County Records VI:124, 129, 139]. They may have been the ancestors of

  2   i. Elizabeth, born say 1746.

      ii. Isaac, born say 1752, one of the "free Negors and Mullatus living upon the Kings Land" who were in Bladen County, North Carolina, on 13 October 1773 [G.A. 1773, Box 7].

      iii. William, born about 1753, registered in Petersburg on 18 August 1794: *a dark brown Mulatto man five feet eight inches high, forty one years old, born free & raised in the Town of Petersburg* [Register of Free Negroes 1794-1819, no. 45].

      iv. Sarah, born say 1770, head of a Petersburg Town household of 6 "other free" & 7 slaves in 1810 [VA:126a].

      v. John, born say 1775, a "Mulatto" taxable in St. Paul's Parish, New Hanover County, on 2 horses from 1796 to 1800 [Cocke, *Hanover County Tax Payers*, 135].

2. Elizabeth Vaughan, born say 1746, was the mother of Faithy, a "base born child" (no race mentioned) who was twelve years old when she was bound out by the Edgecombe County, North Carolina court on 26 August 1776. She was the mother of

      i. Faithy, born about 1764, a twelve-year-old child bound out in Edgecombe County in 1776.

  3   ii. ?Cherry, born say 1765.

      iii. ?William, born say 1780, head of a Northampton County, North Carolina household of 5 "other free" in 1810 [NC:749].

3. Cherry Vaughan, born say 1765, was the mother of an "orphan" child Amey who was bound apprentice to James Burk by the Warren County, North

Carolina court in July 1784. Cherry was head of Halifax County, North Carolina household of 2 "free colored" women in 1820 [NC:168]. She was the mother of

    i.   Amey, born in June 1782, bound apprentice in Warren County to James Burk and his wife Sarah in July 1784 and bound out again in November 1793 [Minutes 1783-7, 48; 1787-93, 259].

    ii. ?Henry, born 1794-1806, head of a Halifax County, North Carolina household of 6 "free colored" in 1830.

    iii. ?Tempy, born 1794-1806, head of a Halifax County, North Carolina household of one "free colored" in 1830. She may have been the mother of Elijah Vaughan, a "colored boy" bound to Elie Lewis by the Halifax County, North Carolina court on 17 November 1823.

Halifax County, Virginia
1.   Ann Vaughan, born say 1740, (not identified by race) was living in Halifax County, Virginia, in August 1759 when the county court ordered the churchwardens to prosecute her for living in adultery with James Winford, an Indian slave who belonged to Joseph Mays. He was called a servant or slave of Mays in May 1758 when the court ordered Mays to allow him to attend court in his case against Mays for false imprisonment. Winford lost his case in September 1759. Ann was presented by the grand jury again in November 1760 but the case was dismissed [Pleas 2:333, 478, 502; 3:174, 195].

VENA/ VENNER/ VENY FAMILY

1.   William Venners, born say 1701, petitioned the Richmond County, Virginia court in September 1732 stating that, "he is a Mulatto born of a white woman named Elizabeth Venners who at the time of his birth was a Servt. in Northumberland County, That he is now kept in Servitude by one Arjalon Price." The court ordered him set free [Orders 9:652, 658]. He was probably the brother of Richard[1] Venie/ Veny who was permitted by the Richmond County court to sue for his freedom in forma pauperis on 6 July 1747. The court assigned Charles Beale as his attorney. He had a suit against William Hammond for trespass, assault and battery which was dismissed in April 1749 [Orders 1746-52, 61, 75, 117, 138, 176]. William and Richard were probably the ancestors of the Vena family counted as "other free" in the Richmond County census for 1810 [VA:413]:

    i.   Hannah, head of a household of 10.

    ii.   Judy, head of a household of 10.

    iii.   Joseph, Sr., head of a household of 1, perhaps the Joseph Venea who was taxable in the upper district of Henrico County in 1787 [PPTL 1782-1814, frames 132].

    iv.   Joseph, Jr., head of a household of 9.

2   v.   Molly, born say 1760.

    vi.   Hannah, Jr., head of a household of 6.

    vii. Judy, Jr. head of a household of 5.

    viii. Dorcas, head of a household of 5.

    ix.   Humphrey, head of a household of 2 and 3 slaves.

    x.   Samuel[2], head of a household of 3.

    xi.   George, head of a household of 2.

    xii. Richard[2], head of a household of 2.

    xiii. James, head of a household of 1.

2.   Molly Veny, born say 1760, was head of a Richmond County household of 8 "other free" in 1810 [VA:413]. She was the mother of

    i.   Sally, born about 1787, registered as a "free Negro" in Madison County on 10 November 1812 and again on 28 October 1823 in Augusta County: *Sally Veny (daughter of Molly Veny) a yellow woman, with straight black har, now about thirty six years of age five feet three inches high, and born free.* Her daughter Charlotte registered the same day: *(daughter of Sally Veny) a very bright yellow complexion, fourteen years of age the 27th day of February 1823* [Register of Augusta County, nos. 57, 58, http://jefferson.village.virginia.edu/vshadow2/].

Other members of the family were

3   i. Edward, born say 1760.

ii. Samuel[1], born in December 1764, taxable in the upper district of Henrico County from 1788 [PPTL 1782-1814, frames 152], registered as a free Negro in Rockingham County, Virginia, on 9 April 1801: *Samuel Viney, a black man...about five feet 7-1/4...36 years old in December last* [Register of Free Negroes, no.10].

iii. Daniel, taxable in the upper district of Henrico County from 1787 to 1809, listed as a "free Negro" starting in 1799 [PPTL 1782-1814, frames 132, 205, 280, 453, 542, 604].

iv. Lucy, taxable on a horse in the upper district of Henrico County in 1788 [PPTL 1782-1814, frame 152].

4   v. Mary, born say 1775.

5   vi. Rachel, born say 1785.

3. Edward Vena, born say 1760, was a "free black man" living in Culpeper County on 20 January 1801 when the court ordered the overseers of the poor to bind his daughter Pleasant Vena to Fisher Michell [Minutes 1798-1800, 282]. He was the father of

i. ?Andrew, born say 1784, an apprentice to Edward Voss in September 1802 when the Culpeper County court rescinded the indenture and instead bound Andrew to Peter Vaughan to be a farmer [Minutes 1798-1802, 43, 73]. Andrew was called a "free negro man" on 15 April 1805 when he was charged with attempting to break into a storehouse in the town of Stevensburg. He was ordered to give security of $100 for his good behavior for a year [Minutes 1803-5, 350].

ii. Pleasant, born say 1795.

4. Mary Vena, born say 1775, was living in Culpeper County on 17 June 1800 when the Culpeper County court ordered the overseers of the poor to bind out her "Mulatto" child Beverly [Minutes 1798-1800, 211]. She was the mother of

i. Beverly, born say 1799, an illegitimate "Mulatto" child of Mary Vena bound to Thomas Eldridge in Culpeper County on 17 June 1800 [Minutes 1798-1802, 211].

ii. ?Joseph Veney, a "free Mulatto" bound out by the overseers of the poor in the district south of "Mo. Run" in Culpeper County in September 1801 [Minutes 1798-1802, 364].

5. Rachel Vena/ Veney, born say 1785, was living in Louisa County when her children registered as free Negroes. Her children were

i. Edmund, born about 1806, registered in Louisa County in March 1827: *son of Rachel Veney who was born free, dark complexion, about 21 years of age.*

ii. Joseph, born about 1808, registered in Louisa County on 10 March 1829: *son of Rachel Veney who was born free, dark complexion, 5'9" about 21 years of age.*

iii. Esther, born about 1825, registered on 14 July 1829: *daughter of Rachael Veney who was born free, girl of dark complexion, about 3' high, about 4 years old.*

iv.   Polly, born about 1811, registered in Louisa County on 14 July 1829: *daughter of Rachel Veney who was born free, dark complexion about 5'1" high, about 18 years old.*

v.   Rhoda, born about 1816, registered in [Abercrombie, *Free Blacks of Louisa County*, 32-4].

VERTY FAMILY

1.   Ann Verty/ Virtue, born say 1725, servant of Marquis Calmes, Gentleman, was ordered to pay 15 pounds or be sold for five years on 1 December 1747 for having a "Mulatto" child. She was the mother of an eight-year-old "Mulatto" boy named James Virtue who was bound to William Calmes on 6 July 1756 [Orders 1745-8, 354; 1748-51, 18; 1755-8, 85]. She was the mother of

i.   James, born 1 October 1747, a "Mulatto" son of Ann Virtue bound to William Calmes on 6 July 1756, perhaps identical to James Vardy, head of a Frederick County household of 5 "other free" in 1810 [VA:577].

VICKORY FAMILY

1.   Indian Moll, born say 1700, was the slave of Captain Humphrey Marshall of Isle of Wight County. She had a daughter named Sarah according to depositions taken in Sarah's suit for freedom in Southampton County in 1757. Two of the deponents said that Moll was from Cape Fear (North Carolina). She was the mother of

2   i.   Sarah, born say 1725.

2.   Indian Sarah, born say 1725, was the slave of Captain Marshall of Nansemond County when she was given by will to Sarah Clark [Byrd, *In Full Force and Virtue*, 151-3]. Indian Sarah petitioned the court in Southampton County for her freedom from Sarah Clark, and on 11 March 1756 the court appointed Miles Cary as her attorney. The court allowed her to take depositions from witnesses in Nansemond County, Isle of Wight County, and North Carolina. On 11 February 1757 the jury considered the depositions of Mary Hayes, Cornelius Ratcliff, Rachel Norworthy and John Sawyer, but the defendant asked that the jurors be discharged from giving their verdict and the action be quashed. The court ruled against Indian Sarah on 10 March that year [Orders 1754-9, 207, 219, 236, 265-6, 276, 291, 333, 345]. According to a suit heard in Granville County, North Carolina, she was the mother of

3   i.   Ben, born say 1760.

3.   Ben Vickory, born say 1760, was still a boy when he was sold by John Clark to John Potter. He sued Potter's executors for his freedom and won his case in Granville County on 7 August 1782. He proved his ancestry by the Southampton County court papers in the suit brought by his mother Sarah [Byrd, *In Full Force and Virtue*, 151-3]. He was head of a Chowan County household of 8 "other free" in 1810 [NC:535]. He may have been the father of

i.   Nancy, married Henry **Harman**, 18 December 1818 Chowan County bond.

VIERS FAMILY

1.   Mary Via, born say 1734, had a "Mulatto" son named Benjamin who was bound by the churchwardens of Fredericksville Parish, Louisa County, to Andrew Ray on 27 November 1754. She was the mother of

2   i.   Benjamin Viers, born 4 June 1754.

ii. ?John Vier, sold for $5 a mare, a yoke of oxen, three cows, two calves, seventeen hogs and household furniture to William **Going** in Amherst County on 5 April 1838 in consideration for his friendship with Martha Jane **Snead**, his wife's daughter [DB W:274]. She was probably related to Jane **Snead** whose unnamed "Mulatta" daughter was bound to Sherwood Walton and his wife in Lunenburg County on 14 July 1763 [Orders 1762-1763, 87].

2. Benjamin Viers, born 4 June 1754, was bound to Andrew Ray on 27 November 1754 [Fredericksville Parish Vestry Indentures & Processing 1742-87, p. 64 cited by Gill, *Apprentices of Virginia*, 257]. He voluntarily bound himself to Andrew Ray in Pittsylvania County on 25 May 1775 [Court Records 1772-5, 431]. He was taxable in Amherst County from 1786 to 1795 [PPTL 1782-1803, frames 68, 188, 317, 342]. He was a "free coloured man" who enlisted in Revolutionary War service in Henry County, Virginia, in October 1775. He married Betsy **Long** in Amherst County and lived there for five years before moving to Gallia County, Ohio, in September 1827. His pension application states that he was born on 3 September 1752 in Charlotte County, Virginia, but Charlotte was not formed until after 1764 [M804-2459, frame 2]. He was counted in the list of "Free Negroes and Mulattoes" for Botetourt County with three women over the age of sixteen in 1813: Polly, Patsy, and (his wife?) Betty Vires [Waldrep, *1813 Tax List*]. He was probably the father of
    i. Polly.
    ii. Patsy.

WALDEN FAMILY

The Waldens may have descended from the family of William Walden, a tithable in Surry County, Virginia in 1687 [DW 3:5]. The origin of the family is probably lost in the order books for Surry County which are missing for the years 1719 to 1741. One early ancestor of the family probably married a descendant of William Chivers (**Chavis**), a tithable in Surry County in 1679 [DW 2:422].

Members of the family living in Southside Virginia about 1750 were
    i. Matthew[1], born say 1718, a defendant in Surry County court in May 1750 [Orders 1749-51, 91] and a defendant in Brunswick County, Virginia court in April 1755. He sued William Randle in Brunswick County court in June 1758 for 2 pounds, 4 shillings. John Walden (his brother?) was his witness [Orders 1753-6, 396; 1757-9, 203]. He died before 26 April 1762 when the inventory of his Brunswick County estate totalled 22 pounds and included a horse, 3 head of cattle, 14 hogs, and carpenter's tools [WB 4:383].

1   ii. John **Chavis**[1] Walden, born say 1720.
2   iii. William[1], born say 1727.
3   iv. Elizabeth, born say 1728.
4   v. David, born say 1735.

1. John **Chavis**[1] Walden, born say 1720, was called John Charvis in July 1745 when John Meally sued him in Surry County, Virginia court. He was called John Chevas alias Walden when the case was dismissed because he had left the county [Orders 1744-8, 71, 130]. He was living in Southampton County, Virginia, on 9 November 1749 when the churchwardens bound out his unnamed son, "a mulatto of John Walden a poor child according to law" [Orders 1749-54, 22]. He was in Brunswick County, Virginia, in June 1758 when he gave testimony in the suit of (his brother?) Matthew Walden against William Randle [Orders 1757-59, 203]. The inventory of John **Chavis** Walden's estate, presented in Brunswick County on 25 September 1761,

totalled 10 pounds and included a mare, a colt, hogs, and carpenter's tools
[WB 4:265]. His children may have been

5   i.   John **Chavis**[2] Walden, born say 1742.

       ii.   Bartholomew **Chavis** Walden, born say 1748, called Batt C. Walden in 1782 when he was taxable on 60 acres in Dinwiddie County and called Batt **Chavis** when he sold this land in 1787 [Land Tax List 1782-1814, 1787 Alterations]. He was taxable in Dinwiddie County on 3 horses and 2 cattle in 1783 and 1787 (called Batt **Chavies**). In 1788 he was called Batt **Chavis** when he was taxable on 2 horses in Wood Tucker's district, and on 23 May 1788 he was called Batt Walden when he and Isham Walden listed their taxable property in William Watts' district, but the entry was crossed out and the same property was listed in Watts' district for Batt **Chavis** (2 horses), Isham **Chavis** (a horse) and Robert **Chavis** three days later on 26 May. He was taxable as Batt Walden in 1791, Batt **Chavis** in 1793 and Bartholomew Walden from 1795 to 1799 [PPTL, 1782-90, (1783, p.41), (1787 A, p.4; B, p.16) (1788 A, p.4, B, pp.5, 17); 1791-9, (1791 A, p.20), (1793 B, p.4), (1794 A, p.21), (1795 B, p.21), (1796 B, p.21), (1797 B, p.20), (1798 A, p.18), (1799 A, p.18)]. He was called Batt Waldane when he sued Micajah Harris for trespass, assault and battery in Dinwiddie County court in March 1790 [Orders 1789-91, 187].

6   iii.   Isham, born say 1750.

      iv.   Robert[1], born say 1760, a "yellow" complexioned soldier from Dinwiddie County who enlisted as a substitute in the Revolution [NSDAR, *African American Patriots*, 154], called Robert **Chavis** when he was listed as a tithable in Dinwiddie County with Batt and Isham **Chavis** in 1788, called Robert Walden in 1789 [PPTL, 1782-90 (1788 B, p.5), (1789 A, p.21)].

2.   William[1] Walden, born say 1727, was called a "Mulatto" on 17 November 1747 when he was presented by the Surry County court for "Profane Swearing" [Orders 1744-53, 391]. He was sued for a 2 pound debt in the Surry County court on 17 September 1755 [Orders 1751-57, 287]. He was married before 21 November 1758 when he was presented by the court:

> *Against...Wm Walden...David Walden...for each and every of them not listing their wife's according to law supposing the said persons to be Mulattoes...*[Orders 1757-64, 135].

He received a patent for 43 acres on the south side of Cypress Swamp in Surry County on 11 July 1761 and a patent for 27 acres on 7 August 1761 [Patents 33:1040; 34:924]. On 14 June 1762 he sold the 43 acres to David **Debrix** and the following day, 15 June 1762, his wife Sarah relinquished her dower rights to this land in the Surry County court. He was called William Walden, carpenter, on 21 December 1762 when he purchased 194 acres adjoining his land [DB 8:129, 151]. His 8 February 1775 will, proved 27 June 1775 in Surry County, left 221 acres of land to his wife Sarah, and at her death to his three sons: William, Michael, and Drury. It also named his son John and daughters Priscilla and Elender [WB 10:405-7].[208]

Sarah Walden was taxable in Surry County from 1782 to 1787: taxable on a slave named Glasgow in 1782; taxable on slaves Sarah and Nanny in 1788; taxable on slave Aggy in 1791; taxable on a horse from 1792 to 1798 [PPTL, 1782-90, frames 359, 380, 390, 482; 1791-1816, frames 69, 275, 308]. She

---

[208]William Walden's name was written as "William Woleing" in the will. However, the 27 June 1775 court order to appraise the estate calls him William Walden [Orders 1775-85, 9].

was taxable on 147 acres from 1782 to 1787. She was deceased by 1814 when her estate was taxable [Land Tax List 1782-1820]. On 27 March 1783 the Surry court released her from paying taxes on "Betty, her Negro slave" [Orders 1775-85, 225]. She was probably the Sarah Walden whose estate was settled in Northampton County, North Carolina, in 1808. Drury[1] Walden, executor, paid Harwood Walden for keeping Dorothy and John Walden, orphans of Sarah [CR 71.508.24]. William[1] and Sarah Walden had

7   i.   William[2], born say 1755.

       ii.   Micajah[1], born say 1757, married Martha **Franklin**. She was the heir of Charles and Ambrose **Franklin** who died in the service during the Revolutionary War [*NCGSJ* III]. Micajah's will was proved in December 1806 in Northampton County. He left 94 acres of land in Northampton County to his wife Martha and William[3] Walden and left land in Surry County, Virginia, to his brother Drury [WB 2:575]. Martha's Northampton County will, proved in March 1808, mentioned her son Noah **Franklin** and cousins Martha and Margaret **James** [WB 2:597].

8   iii.   John[1], born say 1758.

9   iv.   Dolly, born December 1761.

10   v.   Drury[1], born about 1762.

       vi.   Priscilla, born say 1764, perhaps the Siller Walden who married Matthew **Stewart**, 25 February 1799 Mecklenburg County bond, William Chandler security.

      vii.   Elender, born say 1767.

     viii.   Rebecca, born say 1769, "daughter of William Walden," married William **Cypress**, Surry County, Virginia bond of 30 December 1785.

3.   Elizabeth Walding, born say 1728, was living in Surry County on 16 April 1746 when she and James **Evans** were presented by the churchwardens for living in adultery. On 18 June 1746 the court ordered the churchwardens of Albemarle Parish to bind out her "base born child" Mary (no race indicated) as an apprentice to William Thompson [Orders 1744-49, 166, 175]. By 22 July 1747 the sheriff reported to the court that she was not to be found in the county [Orders 1744-49, 354]. She may have moved to Isle of Wight County where a month later on 13 August 1747 the court ordered the churchwardens of Nottoway Parish to bind out (her daughter?) Elizabeth Walden [Orders 1746-52, 37]. Elizabeth may have been the ancestor of

       i.   Mary, born say 1745.

      ii.   Elizabeth, born say 1747.

11   iii.   Milly, born say 1758.

12   iv.   Martha[1], born say 1762.

       v.   Lewis, an illegitimate "Molatto" child living in Orange County, Virginia, on 26 January 1775 when the court ordered the churchwardens of St. Thomas's Parish to bind him out [Orders 1769-77, 348].

4.   David Walden, born say 1735, a "Mulatto," was married before 21 November 1758 when he was presented by the Surry County court for failing to pay tax on his wife [Orders 1757-64, 135]. His children may have been

       i.   Stephen[1], born say 1758, head of a Surry County household of one person in 1782 [VA:43]. He was taxable in Surry County from 1782 to 1787 [PPTL, 1782-90, frames 354, 370, 398, 461]. He married Ann **Bartel** of Sussex County, 5 December 1784 Surry County bond, David **Debrix** surety. He was probably deceased by 1788 when Ann Walding was taxable on a horse in Surry County [PPTL, 1782-90, frame 482]. He may have been the Stephen Walden who died before 14 May 1791 when the Warren County court granted administration on his estate to John **Harris** in right of his unnamed wife. John (**Chavis**?) Walden was a buyer at the sale of the estate which totalled 38 pounds [WB 5:257; 6:82; Minutes 1787-93, 176]. John **Harris** was head of a Warren County household of 6 "other free" in 1790 [NC:77].

13   ii.   Drury², born about 1765.
14   iii.   Sampson, born say 1765.
      iv.   Abel, born say 1770, a "poor infant" ordered bound apprentice in Surry County on 23 May 1775 [Orders 1775-85, 8].

5.   John **Chavis**² Walden, born say 1742, was taxable on 125 acres in Dinwiddie County in 1782 [Land Tax List 1782-1814]. He purchased 70 acres in Warren County, North Carolina, on the east side of Causeway Branch adjoining Worrell on 23 April 1782 and purchased 125 acres on the west side of Smith's Creek in Warren County for 40 pounds on 27 February 1783. He sold (signing) the 125 acres for 50 pounds on 1 November 1785 [DB 8:13, 93, 347]. He was taxable on 460 acres and 1 poll in Warren County in 1784 and taxable on 75 acres and no polls in 1786 [Tax List 1781-1801, 81, 119]. He purchased three tracts of land in Mecklenburg County, Virginia: 400 acres joining the Warren County line on 26 December 1785 for 120 pounds; a 1-1/5 acre lot on the south bank of the Roanoke River on the west side of the road leading to Christopher Haskins' ferry, about 400 yards from the ferry on 9 July 1792 for 12 pounds; and 110 acres on the Warren County line and the head branches of Cotton Creek for 55 pounds on 8 January 1795 [DB 6:529; 8:149, 485]. He was taxable on 3 horses and 9 cattle in Mecklenburg County in 1787; taxable on himself and William **Kersey** in 1788; taxable on himself and slaves Pompey and Tiller in 1790; and on himself and John Walden, Jr., in another list for 1790; on himself, John Walden, and Robert **Corn** in 1791; on himself and son Jarrell in 1795 and 1796; and taxable on himself, son John and slaves Patty, Milly, Amy, Mary & Hannah in 1805 and 1806 [PPTL 1782-1805, frames 255, 333, 360, 416, 584, 604, 1095; 1806-28, frame 20]. He was called John C. Walden in August 1793 when the Warren County court ordered the Collector to pay him 67 pounds for building and keeping in repair the bridge across Palmer's Mill Pond, and on 27 August 1793 he was called John Walden of Mecklenburg County, Virginia, when he and John Birchett of Warren County posted a bond for 200 pounds to insure their keeping the bridge in repair for seven years [Warren County Minutes 1793-1800, 15; WB 6:252]. He (signing) and his wife Rebecca sold 400 acres where he was then living in Mecklenburg County on 3 February 1797, sold 60 acres at the head of Cotton Creek on 11 March 1797, and sold 50 acres on the county line to Susanna **Mayo** on 25 December 1797 with Moses **Stewart** and Charles **Durham** as witnesses [DB 9:218, 219, 431-2]. His sons Eaton and John were counted in the 1800 Warren County census [NC:837].²⁰⁹ He owned land in Chatham County before May 1785 when he was among the freeholders ordered by the court to work on one of the county roads [Minutes 1781-85, 109b]. On 20 July 1800 he was called John C. Walden of Chatham County when he purchased 172 acres in Randolph County on Brush Creek, and on 27 February 1805 he bought another 170 acres on Flat Creek in Randolph County which he sold to his son William on 1 September 1810 [DB 8:174; 11:110; 12:97]. In the Tuesday, November 1819 session of the Chatham County court, a bond from him and John Farrar for building a bridge and keeping it in repair for seven years was returned, and the court ordered the County Treasurer to pay him 33 dollars for building the bridge across Hughs' Creek on the road leading from Ramsey's Mills on Deep River to Fayetteville. He was head of a Warren County household of 10 "other free" in 1800 [NC:837] (perhaps the same John Walden who was head of a Chatham County household of 12 "other

---

²⁰⁹And a Nancy **Walden** was head of a Warren County household of 10 "other free" in 1800 [NC:837].

free" in 1800), 4 "other free" and a slave in 1810 [NC:747] and 6 "free colored" in Chatham County in 1820 [NC:202]. head of a Chatham County household of 12 "other free" in 1800. He transferred 100 acres to his son Bartley Walden by deed proved in Chatham County court on Tuesday, November 1819 and to (his son-in-law) Wiley **Jean** by deed proved in Chatham County court on Tuesday, February 1821. His 12 September 1829 Chatham County will, recorded November 1829, mentioned his wife Rebecca and thirteen children to whom he left 514 acres in Chatham and Randolph counties [WB B:170]. The will also mentioned a granddaughter Lucy **Scott**, probably the Lucy Walden who married Abraham **Scott**, 22 October 1822 Wake County bond. John **Chavis** Walden's children were

15   i.   Eaton, born say 1768.
      ii.   Mary/Polly, born say 1769, married Moses **Stewart**, 20 December 1788 Mecklenburg County bond with a note from the bride's father "John Cha. Walden." Her brother Eaton was security. Moses was head of a Randolph County, North Carolina household of 10 "other free" in 1800 [NC:341].

16   iii.   John², born say 1774.
     iv.   ?Robert², born say 1775, (not mentioned in John **Chavis** Walden's will, perhaps he predeceased him), sued for a debt of 3 pounds due by account in Mecklenburg County on 8 June 1795 [Orders 1792-5, 465], taxable in Mecklenburg County, Virginia, adjacent to John, Jarrell, and Eaton Walden in 1796 and 1799 [PPTL 1782-1805, frame 593]. He was probably one of John Chavis Walden's tithables since the Mecklenburg County court ordered that he work on the road from Burton's road to Haskins Ferry on 8 April 1799 [Orders 1798-1801, 151]. He married Elizabeth **Evans**, 15 February 1813 Wake County bond, Andrew Peddy bondsman. Jesse Walden was charged with Robert's Wake County tax in 1820 [CR 99.252], and a Robert Walden was also counted in Chatham County, head of a household of 10 "free colored" in 1820, born before 1776, living next to Jarrel Walden [NC:211].

17   v.   James¹, born say 1773.
     vi. Richard¹, born say 1774, called son of John Walden when he was listed in his Mecklenburg County household from 1800 to 1804 [PPTL, 1782-1805, frame 834, 883, 905, 984, 1009].

18   vii. Jarrel, born say 1777.
   viii. Rhoda, born say 1779, married ____ **Chavis**.
19   ix. William⁴, born say 1784.
     x.   Lucy, born say 1785, called the "consort of Willie Jean" in her father's will. Willie **Jean** was probably related to John **Jean**, born before 1776, a "Negro" head of a Guilford County household of 4 "free colored" in 1830.
     xi. Bartley, born before 1799, listed as an insolvent taxpayer in Chatham County in the Tuesday, August 1819 session. He received 100 acres from his father by deed proved in Chatham County in the Tuesday, February 1821 court session. He married Matilda McBain, 10 December 1829 Orange County, North Carolina bond, posting his own bond. He sold land by deed proved in the Tuesday, November 1835 session of the Chatham County court and moved to Owen County, Indiana, by 19 May 1836 when he married Lucy Walden [Book B:35]. He was head of a Washington Township, Owen County, Indiana household of 4 "free colored" in 1840 [OWEN:33].
    xii. Stephen³, born say 1787, one of the freeholders of Chatham County ordered by the court to work on the road from Little Lick Creek to the Moore County line in the Tuesday, August 1823 session. The Thursday, May 1829 session of the Chatham County court ordered that he be paid $30 for building the bridge across Lick Creek near William

Hinton's, and the Tuesday, November 1829 session ordered that he be paid $60 when he returned his bond for building the bridge. A deed of trust between him and Isham Rosser and Thompson Lawrence was proved in Chatham County in the Tuesday, May 1832 session, and he purchased land by deed proved in the Tuesday, May 1833 session. He was named as executor of the Chatham County will of Anthony **Evans**, but he was living in Indiana when the will was probated by John **Dungill** on Wednesday, August 1835 session.

xiii.   Elizabeth, married ____ **Simpson**.

xiv.   Sarah, married ____ **Stewart**.

xv.   Anna, perhaps the Ann Walden who was head of a Chatham County household of 4 "other free" in 1810 [NC:209].

6. Isham **Chavis** Walden, born say 1750, was taxable on a horse in Dinwiddie County from 1782 to 1799: called Isham Walding in 1782 and 1784, called Isham **Chavis** in 1787 and 1788, called Isham Walden from 1789 to 1800 and in 1801 when he was counted as a "free Negro" and called "free" Isham **Chavis** when he was taxable in 1804 [PPTL, 1782-90 (1782 A, p.18), (1784, p.25), (1787 B, p.2) (1788 B, p.5), (1789 A, p.21); 1791-9, (1791 A, pp. 4, 20), (1795 B, p.21), (1797 B, p.20), (1798 A, p.18), (1799 A, p.19); 1800-9, (1800 B, p.23), (1801 B, p.25), (1804 a, p.4)]. He may have been the father of

i.   Martha^2/ Patty, born say 1768, mother of Anna Waldane who was bound out by the Dinwiddie County court in July 1789. Ann may have been identical to "free" Ann **Chavis** who was taxable on a slave in Dinwiddie County in 1804. Martha may have also been the mother of Stephen Waldane who was ordered bound out in Dinwiddie County in June 1789 [Orders 1789-91, 48, 55]. Stephen and Boswell Walden were "free Negro" taxables in Dinwiddie County in 1815 [PPTL, 1800-9; 1815-19, list A, p.16].

ii.   William, born say 1780, over the age of sixteen when he was listed in Isham Walden's Dinwiddie County household in 1800 and 1801. He may have been the "free" William **Chavis** who was called the "school master" when he was taxable in 1804 [PPTL, 1800-19 (1800 A, p.21)].

iii. Harbert^1, born say 1782, over the age of sixteen when he was listed in Isham Walden's Dinwiddie County household in 1800 and 1801 [PPTL 1800-19 (1800 A, p.21)].

7. William^2 Walden (William^1), born say 1755, married Priscilla **Banks**, daughter of John **Banks**, Surry County bond of 2 February 1778. He was also taxable in Surry County in 1782 on 74 acres, the land he was to inherit upon the death of his mother. He was taxable in Surry County from 1783 to 1796. His wife Priscilla was listed in his stead in 1797, taxable for Wright Walden who was probably their oldest son [PPTL, 1782-90, frames 367, 380, 390, 461, 482, 560, 607; 1791-1816, frames 19, 119, 171, 245, 275, 308, 349, 388, 428, 466, 504, 546, 578, 602, 618, 640, 659]. He died about 1797 when the Surry County Property Tax Alterations recorded the transfer of 74 acres from William Walden, deceased, to Sarah Walden. Priscilla was listed as living on her own land in an 1803 census of "Free Negroes" in Surry County with (her sister-in-law) Dolly Walden, (her son) John Walden, and "Children of P. Walden" living with her: Polly, Nancy, and Claiborn. She was last mentioned in the 1820 Surry County Tax list, taxable on a free tithe. William and Priscilla had

20   i.   Wright, born about 1780.

21   ii.   William^3, born about 1782.

22   iii. John^3, born about 1783.

23   iv.   Jesse^1, born say 1787.

v. Polly, born say 1790, married Major **Debrix**, 18 March 1814 Surry County bond, Nicholas **Scott**, surety. Her illegitimate child Elizabeth Walden, born before her marriage to Major, registered as a "free Negro" in Surry County on 23 April 1827: *daughter of Polly Debereaux who was formerly Polly Walden...is upwards of 21 years old as appears from a certificate from Mary Deboreax, well made...5'6" high* [Surry County Register, p.148].

vi. Nancy, born about 1791, registered as a "free Negro" in Surry County on 3 June 1817: *a Mulattoe Woman about 26 year old is 5'5-3/8" high...long bushy hair, is the daughter of Priscilla Walden* [Surry County Register, p.105].

vii. Claiborne (apparently an illegitimate son of Priscilla), born in April 1800, registered as a "free Negro" on 25 November 1822: *Willis Claiborne Walden, son of Priscilla Walden of this County aged 21 years last April is 5'7-1/2" high, of yellow complexion* [Surry County Register, p.126].

8. John[1] Walden (William[1]), born say 1758, may have been identical to John Waldon who was a taxable "Molato" in John Hutson's Bladen County household in 1770 [Byrd, *Bladen County Tax Lists*, I:34]. He was head of a household of 7 in Captain Winborne's District, Northampton County, North Carolina, for the 1786 state census and head of a Northampton County household of 7 "other free" and a slave in 1790 [NC:73]. On 19 February 1791 he purchased household items from Elisha Daughtry in Northampton County for a 1,000 weight of tobacco [DB 9:145]. Winnifred Walden (his wife) was granted administration on his Northampton County estate on 7 June 1796 [Minutes 1792-6, 240]. By 6 February 1802 she had married Moses **Newsom** who was named as the representative for the estate in the account of sales [CR 71.508.24]. Winnifred **Newsom**'s 4 November 1807 Northampton County will, proved in December 1807, named her son Harwood Walding, granddaughter Winna Walding, daughter Penny **Newsom**, and granddaughter Lucy **Newsom** [WB 2:353]. One of John and Winnie Walden's children was

i. Harwood, born before 1776, head of a Northampton County household of 7 "other free" in 1800, 8 "other free" and a white woman in 1810 [NC:751], 6 "free colored" in 1820 [NC:266], and 11 "free colored" in 1830. He was executor of the estate of Philip **Byrd** who mentioned Harriet Walden, perhaps Harwood's wife, in his will [WB 2:363].

9. Dolly Walden, born in December 1761, registered as a "Free Negro" in Surry County on 22 May 1800: *a Mulatto Woman a daughter of William Walden late of this county is of a bright Complexion...5'4" high aged about 38 last December* [Surry County Register, p.117]. Her child was

i. Matilda, born in November 1803, registered as a "free Negro" on 22 May 1820: *a Mulatto Woman of rather a dark Complexion for a Mulatto a daughter of Dolly Walden...5'2-3/4" high, aged about 17 years last November* [Register, 118].

10. Drury[1] Walden (William[1]), born about 1762, was a Revolutionary War pensioner. He made a declaration in Northampton County court to obtain a pension on 4 September 1832. He stated that he was living in Bute County in 1779 when he was called into the service. Drury served three tours as a musician and private, the last one in 1781. He marched to Augusta on his first tour and on his second tour made gun carriages for the cannon and canteens for the soldiers, so he was probably a carpenter like his father. He married Elizabeth **Harris** in 1780 in Northampton County. William Hardee, Clergyman, testified that Drury "was for years a preacher of the Gospel of Jesus Christ." Charles R. Kee, executor of Drury's will, testified that:

1198   *Walden Family*

... *no man; no, not Jas K. Polk himself, is of better moral character* [National Archives File R11014].

He was also in the Third Company detached from the Northampton County Regiment in the War of 1812 [N.C. Adjutant General, *Muster Rolls of the War of 1812*, 20]. He was taxable in Warren County in the same district as John **Chavis** Walden in 1786 [Tax List 1781-1801, 119]. He was head of a Northampton County household of 8 other free in 1790 [NC:73], 9 in 1800 [NC:483], 12 in 1810 [NC:752], 11 "free colored" in 1820 [NC:266], and 4 "free colored" in 1830. He purchased 173 acres in Northampton County on the south side of Occoneechee Swamp on 27 August 1794, sold 3 acres of this land on 1 September 1797 [DB 10:204, 316], and was taxable on 288 acres in all the extant Northampton County Tax lists from 1823 to 1834. On 2 March 1818 the court appointed him guardian to David **Byrd** on 250 pounds bond [Minutes 1817-21, 84]. His 9 October 1834 Northampton County will, proved December 1834, named his wife Elizabeth and his children [WB 4:117]. On 2 September 1844 his son Armstead made a declaration in Northampton County court to obtain a survivor's pension in which he provided the whereabouts of each member of the family. He stated that Drury died 22 December 1834, and his wife Elizabeth died in the fall of the year 1840. Their children were

    i.   Stephen[2], born say 1782, purchased 77-1/4 acres of land in Northampton County from Drury Walden by a deed registered 9 February 1819. He was head of a Northampton County household of 9 "free colored" in 1830. He died in July 1842. Bryant (his son?) received Stephen's share of Drury's estate with instructions to support Stephen and his family. Bryant was head of a household of 7 "free colored" in Ripley Township, Rush County, Indiana, in 1840: aged 24-36 with a woman aged 55-100.

    ii. Matthew[2], head of a Northampton County household of 3 "other free" in 1810 [NC:753] and 5 "free colored" in 1820, taxable on one poll in Northampton County in 1826. He was deceased when Drury made his 9 October 1834 will.

    iii. Drury[3], born about 1786, "went to Tennessee" according to Armstead's pension application. He was listed in the Northampton County muster of soldiers in the War of 1812 [N.C. Adjutant General, *Muster Rolls of the War of 1812*, 20]. He was counted in the 1820 census in Halifax, North Carolina, the 1840 Tennessee census, and the 1850 Nashville, Tennessee census: 74 years of age, with Priscilla, 75 years, both born in Virginia, owning $1,000 in real estate.

    iv. John[4], born say 1790, went to Ohio according to Armstead.

    v. Micajah[2], born about 1799, "went to Indiana" where he was head of a household in Jackson Township, Hamilton County, with wife Mary and children, owning $1,200 real estate [HAMI 141].

    vi. Armstead, born 1795, remained in Northampton County, taxable on one poll in Northampton County in 1824, and head of a Northampton County household of 9 "free colored" in 1840.

    vii. Polly, died 1835.

    viii. Nancy, married Asey **Byrd**, 13 August 1821 Northampton County bond. She went to Ohio and died before 1834. In 1850 Asa **Byrd** was counted in the Jefferson Township, Logan County, Ohio census.

    ix. Patsy, "went to the Red River."

11. Milly Walden, born say 1758, married Jacob **Hatter**, 14 June 1806 Petersburg Hustings Court marriage. She was the mother of

    i. ?Amy, born in November 1775, registered in Petersburg on 23 July 1798: *a yellow brown Mulatto woman, twenty two years old in November last, five feet one and 1/2 inches high, Bushy Hair, born free*

& raised in the County of Dinwiddie [Register of Free Negroes 1794-1819, no. 142]. She was head of a Petersburg Town household of 2 "other free" in 1810 [VA:123b].

ii. Freeman **Kelly**, born about 1779, registered in Petersburg on 5 August 1800: *Freeman Kelly, a brown Mulatto man, five feet ten and a half inches high, spare & strait made, twenty one years old April last, son of Milly Walden a free woman & born free in the County of Dinwiddie* [Register of Free Negroes 1794-1819, no. 152].

iii. ?Betsy, born about 1791, registered in Petersburg on 10 May 1809: *a light brown Mulatto woman, five feet three inches high, eighteen years old, long black hair, holes in her ears, born free & raised in Dinwiddie County* [Register of Free Negroes 1794-1819, no. 469]. She was head of a Petersburg Town household of 1 "other free" in 1810 [VA:118a].

iv. Boswell, born about 1794, registered in Petersburg on 5 July 1810: *a brown Mulatto boy, sixteen years old, four feet eleven inches high, son of Milly Walden, now Milly Hatter, a free woman & born in Dinwiddie County* [Register of Free Negroes 1794-1819, no. 632].

12. Martha[1] Walden, born say 1762, was the mother of James and Thomas Walden, orphans who were ordered bound to William Headen to be wagon makers by the Chatham County court in February 1792. The court rescinded the order during the same session and ordered them bound instead to Thomas Glover [Minutes 1790-4, 126, 134, 312]. Martha was probably the common-law wife of Thomas Glover who divided his land between her sons James and Thomas Walding and left his household goods, a cow and a mare to Martha and her daughters Elizabeth and Mary by his 18 October 1799 Chatham County will, proved in February 1800 [WB A:25]. Martha was the mother of

    i. James[2], born about 1783, nine years old in February 1792 when he was bound as an apprentice.

    ii. Thomas, born say 1785, about seven when he was bound apprentice in February 1792.

    iii. Mary, born about 1787, a thirteen-year-old "Girl of Colour" (no parent named), ordered bound to Mary Welch by the Chatham County court in May 1800 [Minutes 1794-1800, 269].

    iv. Elizabeth.

13. Drury[2] Walden (David), born about 1765, was a "poor infant" ordered to be bound apprentice in Surry County on 26 March 1776 [Orders 1775-85, 21]. He married Hannah **Scott**, 29 July 1790 Surry County bond, Armstead **Peters** surety, 1 August marriage by Rev. Samuel Butler [Ministers' Returns, 29]. He registered as a "free Negro" in Surry County on 5 January 1796: *a bright mulattoe man aged about 30 years, pretty square made bushy hair, 5'7" high, born of free parents* [Back of Guardian Accounts Book 1783-1804, no.13]. He purchased 35 acres in Surry County in 1794, and he was taxable on this land from 1796 through 1814 [Property Tax Lists and Alterations]. He was taxed on his personal property from 1787 to 1816: listed with Armstead **Peters** in 1787; charged with his own tax in 1790; taxable on slave Clary in 1803; taxable on 3 free males from 1814 to 1816 [PPTL, 1782-90, frames 479; 1791-1816, frames 19, 118, 428, 602, 698, 795, 869]. He was listed in Surry County in 1803 with his wife and children Nora, Faithy, Edwin, and Jack in John Bartle's 1803 list of "Free Negroes" [p.205]. Drury was head of a Surry County household of 15 "other free" in 1810 [VA:619]. Hannah was head of a Surry County household of 5 "free colored" in 1830. Her 2 May 1842 Surry County will, proved 27 June the same year, named her son Drury executor and named her son Turner and his wife Nancy, formerly Nancy **Debrix**, and their children Elizabeth, John, Sam, and Martha Walden [WB 8:283]. Drury was the father of

    i. Nora, born say 1792.

    ii.   Faithy, born say 1794, "daughter of Drew Walden," married Thomas **Andrews**, 20 February 1815 Surry County bond, 22 February marriage by Rev. James Warren, Methodist [Ministers' Returns, 97].

    iii. Edwin, born say 1796.

    iv. John[6], born say 1798.

    v.   Turner, born say 1805, married Nancy **Debrix**.

    vi. Drury[4], born about 1812, registered as a "free Negro" in Surry County on 24 February 1833: *a Mulatto Man aged about 21 Years, is the son of Drury and Hannah Walden...long bushy hair...5'6-1/2" high* [Surry County Register, p.234].

14. Sampson Walden (David), born say 1765, was taxable in Surry County from 1786 to 1810, listed with James **Bruce** in 1787 [PPTL, 1782-90, frames 403, 409, 560; 1791-1816, frames 19, 119, 308, 466, 602, 677]. He married Scillar **Porter**, twenty-one-year-old daughter of Edward **Porter**, 6 April 1793 Surry County bond, Howell **Debrix** surety, 7 April marriage by Rev. Berriman [Ministers' Returns, 36]. He purchased 75 acres in Surry County in 1794, and he and his wife Priscilla (both signing) sold this land to Matthew **Banks** on 1 February 1796 [Property Tax Alterations; DB 1792-99, 296-7]. He purchased 45 acres in 1799, and he was taxable on this land until his death in 1810 when his wife Priscilla was taxed on it [Land Tax List 1782-1820]. His 6 March 1810 Surry County will, proved 24 April 1810, left all to his wife Priscilla [WB 2:343]. Priscilla was head of a Surry County household of 6 "other free" in 1810 [VA:619]. Her 9 September 1828 Surry County will, proved 24 October 1828, named their children [WB 6:196-7]:

    i.   Susannah, born say 1794, received her mother's plantation.

    ii. John[5], born say 1796.

    iii. Silas.

    iv. Allen Porter.

    v.   Elizabeth, married David **Cypress**, 28 July 1812 Surry County bond, David Sebrell surety, Sillar Walden witness, 6 August marriage by Rev. James Hill [Ministers' Returns, 89].

    vi. Rebecca **Elliott**, formerly Rebecca **Johns**. She married Reuben **Johns**, 9 February 1818 Surry County bond, John Walden surety.

15. Eaton Walden (John Chavis[2], John Chavis[1]), born say 1768, was taxable in the Mecklenburg County household of his father in 1788. He was taxable in his own household in 1789, taxable on himself and 2 horses in 1795, and taxable on himself and a horse in 1796 [PPTL 1782-1805, frame 255, 308, 584, 604]. He married Nanney **Evans**, daughter of Charles **Evans**, 20 December 1788 Mecklenburg County bond. He was taxable in adjoining Warren County, North Carolina, on 75 acres and a free poll in 1790 and taxable on a free poll in 1792, 1797, 1798, 1800 and 1801 [Tax List 1781-1801, 187, 243, 337, 362, 407, 419]. He was head of a Warren County, North Carolina household of 3 "other free" in 1790 [NC:78] and 6 in 1800 [NC:837]. He was bondsman for the 24 June 1793 Mecklenburg County marriage of Boling **Chavous** and Nancy **Thomerson**. He was taxable in Randolph County in 1815, and he was head of a Randolph County household of 8 "free Colored" in 1830 [NC:12]. By 1840 he had moved to Lafayette Township, Owen County, Indiana, where he was head of a household of 5 "free Colored" [OWEN:31]. On 7 April 1842 he was called "my father" (no name mentioned) in the Owen County will of his son Richard. In 1850 he was living with Morgan Walden in Washington Township, District 83, Owen County, counted as an eighty-three-year-old Black man born in Virginia. Eaton's children were

    i.   Richard[2], born say 1790, an insolvent taxpayer in 1822, listed in the Wednesday, August 1823 session of the Chatham County court. He was in Owen County, Indiana, by 31 August 1826 when he purchased

Lot no. 119 in the town of Spencer [DB 2:14]. He purchased Lot no. 175 on 18 August 1827 and sold Lots no. 105 and 109 in November 1826 to Pardon Boen **Roberts**. He was head of an Owen County household of 1 "free colored" in 1830 and 14 in 1840, with a man and woman over fifty-five years of age [OWEN:18, 33]. He received a license to sell groceries and liquor in Owen County on 6 March 1833, in November 1834, January 1837, and March 1838 [County Commissioner's Record Book 2:29, 110, 259, 340]. He purchased 40 acres in Washington Township on 17 October 1836 and made a deed of gift of 1/4 acre of this land to (his brothers) Jesse and Morgan Walden as a "burying ground for myself and all my colored friends and relations forever" on 7 April 1842. His mother was already buried there [DB 5:97; 7:344]. By his 7 April 1842 Owen County will, proved five days later, he left land in Owen County to his brother Jesse and sisters Winney and Elizabeth Walden, and he mentioned but did not name his father [WB 1:57].

ii.   Winney, mentioned in her brother Richard's will.
iii. Elizabeth, mentioned in her brother Richard's will.
iv.   Jesse[2], born about 1795, one of the freeholders of Chatham County who were ordered by the court to work on the road from Bell's Cross Roads to the County line near Goodwins by the Monday, February 1825 session. He married Martha **Turner**, 16 October 1828 Mecklenburg County, Virginia bond. He obtained "free papers" in Randolph County on 1 October 1834 and recorded them in Owen County, Indiana, on 2 February 1835. They stated that he was a "young man of colour," a laborer, "moving to some of the western states" [DB 4:244]. He was head of an Owen County, Indiana, household of 5 "free colored" in 1840 [OWEN:37] and counted in the 1850 Owen County census: 55 years old, Black, born in Va., $250 estate, with Patsy, 35, Black, born in N.C., and nine children born in Indiana after 1834 [OWEN 089].
v.   ?Morgan, married Clary Walden 20 October 1829 Randolph County bond. He was head of an Owen County, Indiana, household of 9 "free colored" and one 70-80 year old white woman in 1840 (his light-skinned mother?) [OWEN:32]. Eaton (his father?) was living in his Owen County household in 1850. He was counted in the census as having an estate worth $600 and being deaf and dumb. Also listed were Morgan's wife Polly, born in North Carolina, and his five children who were all born in Indiana [OWEN 090].
vi.   ?Nancy, born about 1801, living nearby Eaton Walden in the 1850 Owen County census.

16. John[2] Walden (John **Chavis**[2], John **Chavis**[1]), born say 1774, was taxable in Mecklenburg County in his father's household from 1790 to 1794 (called John Walden, Junr., in 1790), taxable in his father's household in 1805 and 1806, and a "Mulatto" taxable in his own household from 1810 to 1827: listed with two "Mulattoes" over the age of 16 in 1813, probably himself and his wife [PPTL 1782-1805, frames 360, 360, 434, 509, 1095; 1806-1828, 20, 177, 374, 410, 526, 609, 711, 911]. He purchased 252 acres in Mecklenburg County for 230 pounds on 18 February 1800 and he and his wife Sarah sold this land to Ray Moss by deed proved in Mecklenburg County court on 12 October 1801 [DB 10:389; Orders 1801-3, 86]. He was taxable on 75 acres and 1 poll in Nutbush District of Warren County in 1808 and 1815 [C.R. 100.702.1; Tax List Papers, Vols. TC 8, 1795-1815]. He married Betsy **Stewart**, 6 April 1804 Mecklenburg County bond, Kinchin **Chavis** security, and was head of a Mecklenburg County household of 10 "free colored" in 1820 [VA:150b]. One of his children may have been

    i.   Milly, married Banister **Chavis**, 29 December 1819 Mecklenburg County bond. Banister **Chavis** was living in the household next to John Walden in the 1820 Mecklenburg County census.

17. James[1] Walden (John **Chavis**[2], John **Chavis**[1]), born say 1773, was head of a Chatham County household of 5 "other free" in 1810 [NC:195]. He married Beedy **Stewart** according to the 1824 Wake County will of her father Thomas **Stewart**. He was one of the freeholders in Chatham County who were ordered to work on the road from Lick Creek to the Moore County line by the May 1816 and August 1822 session of the Chatham County court [Orders 1811-18, 266]. He may have been the father of

    i.   Edward/ Edmund, born about 1797, listed as an insolvent taxpayer for 1823 in the Wednesday, August 1824 session of the Chatham County court. Farrar and Sanders had a suit against him in the Tuesday, May 1827 session of the court, but it was ruled a non-suit. He and (his brother?) William Walden were ordered to work on the road from Gums Spring Meeting House to the Deep River Bridge at Haywood by the Wednesday, February 1832 session, and he was ordered to work on the road from Boylan's Mill to Stinking Creek by the Monday, November 1832 session. He was listed as a fifty-three-year-old farmer with $300 estate living with Lucy, forty-eight years old, and their children in the 1850 Chatham County census [NC:457].

    ii. William[5], born say 1800, listed as an insolvent taxpayer for 1823 in the Wednesday, August 1824 session of the Chatham County court. The Wednesday, August 1826 session of the court ordered seven persons paid for being witnesses in a State case against him in the Superior court.

18. Jarrel Walden (John **Chavis**[2], John **Chavis**[1]), born say 1777, was taxable in his father's Mecklenburg County household from 1793 to 1796 [PPTL 1782-1805, frames 492, 509, 584, 604]. He married Mourning **Jackson**, 16 September 1801 Mecklenburg County marriage bond. He purchased 150 acres in Chatham County on Shaddox Creek on 9 March 1810. He was living in Wake County on 14 November 1812 when he sold 75 acres of this land and was living in Chatham County on 12 February 1816 when he sold the remaining 75 acres [DB U:181, 123; W:169]. He was head of a Chatham County household of 11 "free Colored" in 1820 [NC:211]. He received land in Chatham County from his father by deed proved in the Tuesday, February 1828 session, and he sold land by deed proved in the Monday, November 1829 session. On 1 September 1828 he paid $250 for 162 acres on the south side of Deep River in Randolph County [DB 20:102], and he headed a Randolph County household of 13 "free colored" in 1830 [NC:5]. By 1840 he was in Lafayette Township, Owen County, Indiana, head of a household of 16 "free colored" [OWEN:19]. His 17 February 1843 Owen County will, recorded 5 March 1844, mentioned a lot in the town of Vandaley and named his wife Rebecca and children [WB 1:77]:

    i.   Harbard[2], born about 1803 in Virginia, married Jane **Scott**, 27 February 1824 Wake County bond. The Thursday, August 1826 session of the Chatham County court listed him as an insolvent taxpayer for the year 1825. He obtained free papers in Wake County on 23 March 1841 and recorded them in Owen County, Indiana, on 14 February 1846: *a free man of color, thirty five years of age, five foot eleven inches high, light complected prety strait hair, Yellow eyes…with a five and seven children…his father and mother was respectable coloured people Also his wife's father and mother who is and have been Citizens of this neighborhood* [DB 8:518 by Peterson, *Owen County Records*, 30]. He was counted near Eaton Walden in the 1850 Owen County census

without a wife but with his children. He had a personal estate worth $800 [OWEN 090].
   ii. Sally.
   iii. Clara.
   iv. Lucy.
   v. Amos.
   vi. Beverly.
   vii. Leanah.
   viii. Larken H.
   ix. Betsey, married Farrow **Powell**, 02 April 1829 Randolph County bond. He was head of an Owen County household of 7 "free colored" in 1840, living near the Walden family [OWEN:35]. He married, second, Rebecca **Bass**, on 17 September 1844 in Owen County, Indiana [DB B:239]. He entered the NE:SW part of Section 28 in Marion Township of Owen County on 1 June 1849 [Land Entry Book 1].

19.   William⁴ Walden (John **Chavis**², John **Chavis**¹), born say 1784, bought land from his father John **Chavis**² Walden in Randolph County on 1 September 1810 [DB 12:97] and was taxable in Randolph County in 1815. He married (second?) Elizabeth **Lytle**, 6 February 1819 Randolph County bond. Elizabeth died on 12 March 1830 [*NCAAHGS* vol. V, no.1, 1-8]. He was head of a Randolph County household of 7 "free colored" in 1830 [NC:43] and 7 in 1840 [NC:56]. In February 1842 the Randolph County court accepted a petition signed by William, his four sons Anderson, John C., William D., and Stanford B., and numerous neighbors stating that, "as Mulattoes or free persons of Colour...of good moral character," they be allowed to carry firearms. He died before 3 May 1842 when his Randolph County estate papers were filed and his wife Levina received her widow's portion [CR 081.508.141]. His children were
   i. Anderson, born about 1800, married Sally Walden, 30 September 1830 Randolph County bond. He was head of a Randolph County household of 6 "free colored" in 1840 [NC:56], counted in the household next to William Walden in the 1850 Randolph County census [NC:88].
   ii. John C., married Martha **Evans**, 4 January 1836 Wake County bond, counted in the 1850 Randolph County census in the household next to William [NC:80].
   iii. William D.
   iv. Stanford B.

20.   Wright Walden (William², William¹), born about 1780, was taxable in Surry County from 1797 to 1816: listed with (his mother) Priscilla Walden in 1797, 1799 and 1800; with Sterling **Charity** in 1798; charged with his own tax starting in 1802 [PPTL, 1791-1816, frames 308, 325, 388, 506, 618, 659, 698, 797, 871]. He married Sally **Byrd**, daughter of Joseph, on 30 March 1804, Surry County bond. He was head of a Surry County household of 6 "other free" in 1810 [VA:619]. He registered as a "free Negro" in Surry County on 22 February 1834: *bright mulatto man aged about 50 years was born of free parents...is a little grey...is 5'9" high* [Surry County Register, p.250]. He was counted in the 1850 Surry County census: 72 years old with Sally, 65 years old, and $400 estate. They had
   i. Reuben, born about 1807, registered in Surry County on 22 February 1834: *bright mulatto man, son of Wright Walden and Sally his wife...about 27 years of age...5'5-3/4" high* [Surry County Register, p.251].
   ii. Eliza Ann, born about 1809, registered on 22 May 1831: *daughter of Wright Walden and Sally his wife...bright complexion about 22 years of age...5'1-1/2" high* [Register, 173].

21. William[3] Walden (William[2], William[1]), born about 1782, was taxable in Surry County in 1800. He probably moved to Northampton County, North Carolina, about 1803 since he was not taxed in Surry County after 1802. His uncle Micajah left him 94 acres of land in Northampton County in 1806. Micajah referred to him as "Neffu William Walden son of William Walden" [WB 2:575]. He may have been the William Walden who married Katy Rowell 1 April 1815, Northampton County bond with Matthew Walden bondsman. He was security for the apprentice indenture of John and Fanny **Dungill**, "children of color," who were bound to Beverly **Brown** in Northampton County, North Carolina, on 7 June 1813 [Minutes 1813-21], and he was witness to the 13 October 1824 Greensville County, Virginia will of Patsey **Stewart** [WB 3:378]. He was counted in the 1850 Northampton County census: a 78 year old "Mulatto" in the same household with Squire Walden, 38 years old, and in 1860: 90 years old, still living with Squire. He was also listed in the Northampton County Tax List in district 9 from 1824-38. In a deed registered on 29 March 1843 he purchased an additional 70 acres adjoining his land from John B. Odom [DB p.329]. However, he lost all his land when he defaulted on a debt for $224.07 to Odom in March 1853 [DB pp. 374-5]. William[3]'s name does not appear in the 1870 census so he probably died between 1860 and 1870 at the age of 80-90 years. His son was

24   i.   Squire, born about 1815.

22. John[3] Walden (William[2], William[1]), born about 1783, married Eady **Cannada**, 9 August 1809 Surry County bond. He was taxable in Surry County from 1803 to 1809, his tax charged to (his mother) Priscilla Walden from 1803 to 1805. He probably died before 1813 when Eady Walden was listed as a "free Negro & Mulatto above the age of 16" [PPTL, 1791-1816, frames 546, 578, 659, 762]. They were the parents of
        i.   John[7], born about 1809, registered as a "free Negro" in Surry County on 28 November 1831: *a bright mulatto man aged about 22 years...son of Edy Walden...is 5'-1/2" high* [Surry County Register, p.215].

23. Jesse[1] Walden (William[2], William[1]), born say 1787, married Milley **Stewart**, 6 April 1805 Mecklenburg County, Virginia bond, Frederick **Ivy** security. He was taxable in Mecklenburg County in 1806 [PPTL, 1782-1805, frame 21] and taxable in Surry County from 1809 to 1816: called a "M"(ullato) in 1810; listed with 3 "free Negroes & Mulattoes above the age of 16" in 1813, 2 of whom were free males [PPTL, 1791-1816, frames 659, 678, 716, 761]. He was head of a Surry County household of 4 "other free" in 1810 [VA:619]. He may have been the Jesse Walden whose will was proved 20 November 1838 in Putnam County, Indiana [WB PA:574]. He left 80 acres of land valued at $750 to his wife Elizabeth and their children: William M., Rachel Ann, Elizabeth Jane, John S, Palmilea E., and an infant.

24. Squire Walden (William[3], William[2], William[1]), born about 1815, married Tempy **James**, 28 March 1832, Halifax County, North Carolina bond. Squire was named as surety for the bond which William[3] Walden defaulted on in 1853 [DB p. 27]. Squire was taxable in Northampton County in 1836, his free poll charged to William[3] Walden. In 1849 Squire was charged with his own free poll. He and his wife Tempy were listed with their children in the Northampton County census for 1850, 1860 and 1870 [NC:649]. He was listed as a ditcher who could read and write. He probably worked on his father's farm. Tempy, "Mulatto," eighty-four years old, born August 1816, was living with their youngest son Benjamin in dwelling no.176 in Rich Square, Northampton County in 1900. Squire's youngest child Molly Walden **Markham**, as an elderly woman, told a tale to the WPA Writer's Project how her mother Tempy was a white woman and her father Squire Walden was a slave on her father's plantation. Tempy fell in love with Squire, her father

found out about it, and sold Squire to another slave owner in another state. Tempy bought Squire's freedom and then drank the blood from a cut in his finger so she could honestly tell the Justice of the Peace that she had Negro blood in her [WPA Project vol. XI, part 2, 106-8]. Tempy was actually the daughter of Benjamin **James**, a light-skinned free African American who lived in Halifax County, North Carolina. Molly **Markham** said that she was the youngest of fifteen children, but only twelve were listed in Squire's household in the 1850-1870 census. Squire and Tempy's children were

  i. ?John Felson, born about 1832, not listed in Squire's household, married first, Rebecca **Haithcock**, 20 April 1853 Northampton County license, and second Henrietta **Clark**, 5 September 1856 Northampton County bond.
  ii. ?Bryant, born about 1834, not listed in Squire's household.
  iii. Samuel, born about 1836.
  iv. William[6], born about 1837, married Elizabeth F. **Jones**, 1856 Northampton County bond.
  v. Amanda, born about 1838, married James **Artis** 28 December 1859, Northampton County bond.
  vi. Martha, born about 1839.
  vii. James, born about 1841.
  viii. Hester, born about 1842.
  ix. Peyton, born about 1845.
  x. Whitand, born about 1849, living in Halifax County in 1870.
  xi. Patsy, born about 1851.
  xii. Betsy, born about 1853.
  xiii. Benjamin, born about 1855, died 6 February 1930 in Rich Square.
  xiv. Mary/Molly Walden **Markham**, born 20 August 1857, died 19 February 1941. She met the Reverend Edian **Markham** while he was on a missionary tour of Rich Square and married him in her parents' home. Reverend **Markham** founded the St. Joseph African Methodist Episcopal Church [*NCAAHGS* IV, no.4, 36]. Their son William Benjamin **Markum** published a booklet about his father and the founding of the church in which he wrote that tradition said his great grandfather *Billy Walden rode horseback at 100 and one years old and only gave it up because he thought it unseemly.* The booklet contains a photo of Molly and her three children: William Benjamin, Maggie, and Robert [Markum, *The Life of a Great Man*, 26-7]. They were counted in the 1900 North Carolina census [23/26/11/23].

WALKER FAMILY

1. Sarah Walker, born say 1704, was the mother of "a Mulatto Boy named Daniel, Son of Sarah Walker a Mulatto Woman, aged six years last February," who was brought before the King George County, Virginia court on 7 September 1733 by Mary Brocke who asked the court to bind him to her. The court ordered the churchwardens of Hanover Parish to bind Daniel as an apprentice until the age of twenty-one [Orders 1721-34, pt.3, 649]. Sarah was the ancestor of

2 i. ?Moses, born about 1724.
  ii. Daniel, born in February 1727.
  iii. ?Samuel, born about 1752, an eight-year-old "Mulatto Bastard Child" bound out in Frederick County, Virginia, on 3 September 1760 [Orders 1760-2, 159].
  iv. ?Thomas, head of a Westmoreland County, Virginia household of 8 "other free" in 1810.
  v. ?George, taxable in Prince William County from 1795 to 1810 [PPTL, 1782-1810, frames 277, 371, 462, 670, 740], head of a Prince William County household of 4 "other free" in 1810 [VA:506].

      vi.   ?David, taxable in Prince William County from 1792 to 1807, described as "y" (yellow) in 1807 [PPTL, 1782-1810, frames 205, 411, 513, 601, 671].

2.   Moses Walker, born about 1724, was a sixteen-year-old "mulatto" boy who was listed in the Stafford County estate of Edward Derrick on 13 May 1740 [WB Liber M, 1729-48, 295]. He and his wife were taxable "Mulatoes" in Bladen County in 1768, taxable "free Negroes" in 1770 and 1771, "Mixt Blood" taxables in 1774, and taxable in 1775. His wife was probably Mary Walker, a "free Negro" head of a household of one Black from 12-50 and one over 50 or under 12 years of age in 1786 [Byrd, *Bladen County Tax Lists*, I:7, 26, 67, 124; II:39, 175]. Mary was head of a Fayetteville, Cumberland County household of 1 "other free" in 1790 [NC:42] and 3 in 1800. Moses and Mary may have been the parents of

3   i.   Elizabeth, born say 1765.

3.   Elizabeth Walker, born say 1765, was head of a Fayetteville Town, North Carolina household of 1 "other free" in 1790 [NC:42]. She may have been the mother of

4   i.   David, born 28 September 1785.

      ii.   James, born say 1788, a "free Black boy," who was mentioned in the 29 December 1798 Bladen County will of Joseph Cain [Campbell, *Abstracts of Wills, Bladen County*, 20]

4.   David Walker, born 28 September 1785 in Wilmington, North Carolina, was the son of a free African American woman and a slave father. He travelled widely throughout the United States and settled in Boston where he owned a used clothing shop near the wharves. He was one of the most militant of the abolitionists, encouraging slaves to fight for their freedom whatever the cost in blood. He was also a militant leader of the Massachusetts General Colored Association, which was fighting for better education and employment for those who were already free as well as the freedom of slaves. This association was one of the forerunners of the Boston anti-slavery movement [Horton, *Black Bostonians*, 81, 93]. In 1829 he wrote and published at his own expense, "An Appeal to the Colored Citizens of the World." Walker distributed his pamphlet by placing it in the pockets of the clothes he sold to sailors. One of his pamphlets was found by the mayor of Richmond in 1830 in the house of a free African American [*Richmond Enquirer*, January 28, 1830]. Governor Floyd of Virginia was referring to this incident when he appealed for the passage of additional restrictions against "free Negroes" since they were allowed to go at liberty and "distribute incendiary pamphlets and papers" [House Journal, 1831-32, 10, cited by Russell, *Free Negro in Virginia*]. Warned that his life was in danger, he refused to flee to Canada. A price was placed on his head, and in 1830 he was found dead in the doorway of his shop [*New Encyclopedia Britannica, Micropedia*, X:521]. His only son was

      i.   Edwin G. Walker, elected to the Massachusetts legislature in 1866.

WALLACE FAMILY

1.   Martha Wallace, born say 1720, was living in Charles City County, Virginia, in November 1745 when the court ordered the churchwardens to bind out her children Philip and Lucy (no race indicated) and ordered that she be discharged from the service of Thomas Ballard [Orders 1737-51, 388]. She was the mother of

2   i.   ?Elizabeth, born say 1738.

      ii.   Philip[1], born say 1740, taxable in New Kent County from 1782 to 1803. He may have been the father of Benjamin Wallis, a "Mulatto" taxable in Gerard Ellyson's household in 1788 and a "Negroe" taxable in his own household in 1792 [PPTL 1782-1800, frames 8, 17, 44, 86, 101, 112, 154, 197, 221; 1791-1828, frames 362, 374, 387].

    iii. Lucy, born say 1742, probably the Lucy Wallace who was called the indentured servant of James Major in June 1761 when the Charles City County court ruled that she had served her time and set her at liberty [Orders 1758-62, 290].

3   iv. ?James[1], born say 1755.

    v. ?Joseph, a man of color who served in the Revolution from Bedford County [NSDAR, *African American Patriots*, 154].

2. Elizabeth Wallace, born say 1738, was a "Free Negro" whose daughter Elizabeth was baptized in Bruton Parish, James City County, on 4 January 1762 [Bruton Parish Register, 20]. She was probably the unnamed "free Negro" living in York County on 19 March 1759 when the court ordered the churchwardens of Bruton Parish to bind her children Mary and James Wallace to Fleming Bates [Judgments & Orders 1759-63, 16]. She was a "free" head of a Williamsburg City household of 4 "Blacks" in 1782 [VA:45]. She was the mother of

    i. Mary, born say 1756.

4   ii. James[2], born about 1757.

    iii. ?John, born say 1760, taxable in James City County from 1785 to 1813: a Mulatto" taxable on a horse and 5 cattle in the upper precinct of Bruton Parish in 1785, taxable on 2 tithes in 1806 and 1809, listed as a "Mulatto" in 1805 and 1806, a "col[d]" man" listed with a tithable and 2 "free persons of colour" (probably himself and his wife) in 1813 [PPTL 1782-99; 1800-15].

    iv. ?Elizabeth, baptized 4 January 1762, a "mulato" head of a James City County household of 2 "free persons of colour above the age of 16" in 1813 Her son Henry obtained a certificate of freedom in James City County and registered it in York County on 15 July 1833: *son of Betty Wallace* (remainder of certificate not copied by the York County clerk) [Free Negroes Register 1831-1850, no. 349].

5   v. ?Lylla, born say 1764.

    vi. ?Rebecca[1], born say 1765, "Free Mulatto" mother of Rebecca[2] Wallace who was baptized 13 March 1783 in Bruton Parish [Bruton Parish Register, 35].

    vii. ?William, taxable in James City County in 1786, 1794, from 1800 to 1803 and listed as a "Mulatto" taxable in 1805 [PPTL 1782-99; 1800-15].

6   viii. ?Edward[1], born say 1771.

3. James[1] Wallace, born say 1755, was taxable in Charles City County from 1792 to 1805 [PPTL, 1788-1814], taxable on 30 acres in 1800 [Land Tax List, 1782-1830], head of a Charles City County household of 7 "other free" in 1810 [VA:957] and 13 "free colored" in 1820 [VA:7]. He leased 30 acres from Nicholas Holt of Charles City County for seven years on 21 August 1799 and leased 10 acres on Oldman's Run on the path from the courthouse to Samuel Hargrave's for twenty-one years on 21 January 1802 [DB 4:484, 587]. On 24 December 1811 the Charles City County estate of William H. Lightfoot, deceased, paid him $43 for clover seed [WB 2:214]. He purchased 31-1/2 acres in Charles City County adjoining Edward Wallace and the "roling road" for $126 on 16 January 1812, and he and his wife Martha (making their mark) made a deed of trust to sell this land for a debt of $76 he owed Samuel Ladd [DB 5:410, 432]. He and his wife transferred 30 acres to (his son?) Peter Wallis by deed acknowledged in court on 20 April 1837 [Minutes 1830-9, 317]. He registered as a free Negro in Charles City County about 1806 (no details provided) and "removed to Ohio" sometime after 1835 [Register of Free Negroes, 1835-64, no.1]. He was the father of

     i.   ?Edward², born say 1780, called Edward Wallis, Jr., when he was taxable in Charles City County from 1801 to 1805 [PPTL, 1788-1814].

    ii.   ?Philip², born say 1784, taxable in Charles City County in 1805 [PPTL, 1788-1814], registered as a free Negro in Charles City County about 1806 (no details provided) [Register of Free Negroes, 1835-64, no. 26] and was head of a Charles City County household of 4 "other free" in 1810 [VA:959]. He married Elvy **Morris**, daughter of James **Morris**, 24 March 1815 Charles City County bond [*Wm & Mary Quarterly Historical Papers* Vol. 8, No.3, p.195].

    iii.   ?Peter, born about 1808, obtained a certificate of freedom in Charles City County on 17 March 1831: *certificate of Emancipation from the clerk of Henrico, Peter Gwin, alias Peter Wallis, a man of dark brown Complexion and 23 years was born free* [Minutes 1830-9, 43].

    iv.   James⁴, Jr., born about 1809, obtained a certificate of freedom in Charles City County on 21 September 1826: *(by testimony of Nelson New) son of James Wallace, a black boy, aged seventeen years, 5 feet 7 inches, born free in this county* [Minutes 1823-9, 189].

4.   James² Wallace, born about 1757 in New Kent County, made a declaration in James City County on 13 August 1832 to obtain a pension for his services in the Revolution. "Being a Coloured man," he acted as a cook for Colonel Porterfield and guarded prisoners. He enlisted in James City County and returned there after the war [M804-2479, frame 0558; The Chesterfield Supplement cited by NSDAR, *African American Patriots*, 154]. He was taxable in James City County from 1786 to 1813: listed as a "Mulatto" in 1805 and 1806, taxable on 2 tithables in 1806, 3 in 1809, 2 in 1810, taxable on 2 tithables and a "free person of colour" (probably his wife) in 1813 [PPTL 1782-99; 1800-15]. He may have been the father of

     i.   Joseph D., taxable in James City County from 1806 to 1814: taxable on a tithe and a "free person of colour" (probably his wife) in 1813 [PPTL 1800-15].

    ii.   Nathaniel¹, taxable in James City County from 1806 to 1810, a "col^d man" taxable on a tithe and a "free person of colour" (probably his wife) in 1813 [PPTL 1800-15].

    iii.   James³, Jr., a "col^d man" taxable in James City County in 1813 [PPTL 1800-15]. perhaps the James Wallace who was head of a Warwick County household of 6 "free colored" in 1830.

    iv.   Jasper, taxable on a tithe in James City County in 1813 [PPTL 1800-15].

5.   Lylla Wallace, born say 1764, was the "Free Mulatto" mother of Matthew Wallace who was baptized in Bruton Parish on 2 March 1783 [Bruton Parish Register, 35]. She was the mother of

     i.   Matthew, baptized 2 March 1783, head of a Norfolk County household of 4 "other free" in 1810 [VA:926].

    ii.   ?Mahlon, born 1776-1794, head of a Guilford County, North Carolina household of 6 "free colored" in 1830.

    iii.   ?Polly, born about 1798, registered in York County on 16 December 1822: *a Mulatto about 24 years of age...has short hair...Born free* [Register of Free Negroes 1798-1831, no. 170].

6.   Edward¹ Wallace, born say 1771, was taxable in Charles City County from 1792 to 1801 [PPTL, 1788-1814]. He was a resident of Henrico County on 16 January 1812 when he purchased 31-1/2 acres adjoining the land of James Wallace in Charles City County [DB 5:408]. He was head of a Charles City County household of 3 "free colored" in 1820 [VA:7]. His widow Rhoda Wallis obtained a certificate of freedom in Charles City County on 18 June

1835: *widow of Ned Wallis, a black woman, thirty eight years of age* [Minutes 1830-9, 237]. He was the father of

   i. Nathaniel[2], born about 1816, registered in Charles City County on 20 April 1837: *son of late Ned Wallis, a black man, twenty one years of age* [Minutes 1830-9, 316].

   ii. Alexander, born 14 July 1818, obtained a certificate of freedom in Charles City County on 16 June 1836: *son of late Ned Wallis, aged seventeen years 14 July last, black lad* [Minutes 1830-9, 280].

A member of the Wallace family may have had a child by a slave:

   i. James[3], born about 1760, registered in York County on 18 June 1810: *James als. James Wallace, a bright Mulo. about 49 or 50 years of age, 5 feet 9-1/2 Inches high...long hair which seems inclined to curl - Liberated by deed from Sam. L. Goodson & Wm. G. Goodson by deed recorded in York Ct.* [Register of Free Negroes 1798-1831, no. 43]. He was head of a Williamsburg, York County household of 4 "other free" in 1810 [VA:886].

WARBURTON FAMILY

1. "John Wabbleton, a Molatto fellow," born say 1750, and his wife Beck were taxables in Sarah Smithwick's household in the Bertie tax list of Joseph Jordan in 1772 [CR 10.702.1, box 3]. He and Beck were taxables in Luke Smithwick's household in the 1775 list of David Standly, and he was called John "Wharburton" in 1790, head of a Bertie County household of 4 "other free" [NC:15]. He may have been related to Richard Wattleton, "free negro" head of a Norfolk County household in Elizabeth River Parish in 1768 [Wingo, *Norfolk County Tithables, 1766-80*, 83].

WARRICK/ WARWICK FAMILY

1. Hannah Warwick, born say 1647, was convicted of an unspecified offence, but the General Court of Virginia ruled on 23 April 1669 that the case against her was "extenuated because she was overseen by a negro overseer" [*VMHB* VIII:243 (General Court Judgments and Orders 1664-1670)]. She may have been the mother of

2   i. John, born say 1668.

2. John Warrick, born say 1668, was called "Jack Orrick a Mollato" in May 1686 when Mary Arsbrook, a servant of Francis Mason, confessed in Surry County court that Jack was the father of her bastard child [Haun, *Surry County Court Records*, IV:567]. On 7 September 1687 Mary's daughter, Mary Arsbrooke, was bound as an apprentice to Thomas Drew [DW&c 4:39]. He was called "Jno. Warwick" when he was taxable in Mason's household in 1690 and called "Orick" when he was taxable in Mason's household in 1695 [*Magazine of Virginia Genealogy*, v.23, no.3, p.61; v. 24, no.1, p.71]. He purchased 80 acres at Upper Chipoakes adjoining the county line on 6 September 1698. He and his wife Mary sold this land on 2 February 1723 and sold another 95 acres in the same area adjoining Charles City County on 14 May 1723 [DW&c 5:161; 7:470, 472]. He was the father of

   i. Mary Arsbrooke, born about 1686.

3   ii. ?Job, born say 1705.

3. Job Warrick, born say 1705, sued Solomon Borakin in Brunswick County, Virginia court on 24 May 1757 [Orders 1757-9, 20]. He sold 10 acres in Northampton County, North Carolina, on the state line with Brunswick County, Virginia, to (his son?) Jacob Warrick on 23 April 1772. He was deceased by 10 January 1776 when a deed of sale from his son Jacob

mentioned land belonging to the heirs of Job Warrick [Northampton DB 5:205; 6:86]. He may have been the father of

4   i.   Jacob, born about 1721.

       ii.   Moses, born say 1740, listed among the "Black" members of the undated colonial muster of Captain James Fason's Company of Northampton County militia [Mil. T.R. 1-3].[210] He may have been the Moses Warwick who was counted as white in Robeson County in 1790, head of a household of 3 males and one female [NC:49].

     iii.   Henry, head of a household of one "Black" person 12-50 years old and 2 "Black" persons less than 12 or over 50 years old in Elisha Webb's District of Northampton County for the 1786 state census.

4.   Jacob Warwick/ Warrick, born about 1721 in Surry County, Virginia, was listed among the soldiers in King George's War who failed to report to their camp at Williamsburg in July 1746: *a whitish mulatto, age 25, 5'10"* [*Magazine of Virginia Genealogy* 31:92]. He was called Jacob Warrick, Junr., in July 1746 when he sued John Mons in Surry County court [Orders 1744-9, 195]. He was a resident of Isle of Wight County when he purchased 100 acres in Northampton County, North Carolina, joining the county line and Thomas Jordan on 21 February 1746/7 [DB 1:288]. On 24 September 1754 the Brunswick County, Virginia court ordered Jacob and Job Warwick to clear the road from Longs Road to the country line across Fountain Creek on the southside [Orders 1753-6, 286]. He was sued for debt in Sussex County in September 1754 [Orders 1754-56, 68]. The sheriff sold 50 acres of his Northampton County land on 26 November 1755 and sold another 100 acres of his land on 10 May 1757. Jacob purchased 10 acres at "Country Line" adjoining Arthur Hart from Job Warrick on 23 April 1772 [DB 2:262, 404; 5:205]. He, Job, and Moses Warrick were "Black" members of the undated colonial muster of Captain James Fason's Company of Northampton County Militia [Mil. T.R. 1-3]. He was called Jacob Warrick of Brunswick County, Virginia, blacksmith, on 20 January 1776 when he sold 100 acres "lying in Brunswick and Northampton Counties...by Fountain Creek...by the land belonging to the heirs of Job Warrick...being all the land he now owns." Perhaps it was this land belonging to the heirs of Job Warrick, "90 acres bounded by the land Jacob Warwick formerly possessed," which he sold two years later on 23 April 1778 [Northampton County DB 6:86, 230]. He may have been the Jacob Warrick who was counted as white in Wayne County in 1790, head of a household of 2 males and one female [NC:149]. His children may have been

     i.   James, born before 1776, perhaps the James Warwik who was in the Third Company detached from the Northampton County Regiment in the War of 1812 [N.C. Adjutant General, *Muster Rolls of the War of 1812,* 20]. He was head of an Anson County household of 7 "free colored" in 1820 [NC:13].

     ii.   Riley, head of an Anson County household of 6 "free colored" and 2 white women in 1820 [NC:13].

WALTERS/ WATERS FAMILY

1.   Joseph Walters, born say 1670, complained to the Lieutenant Governor of Virginia that the child born to his wife while she was the slave of Isaac Collyer was held by Collyer as his slave. The case was referred to the York County court which decided that the child was born while Joseph's wife was still a slave. He and his wife Mary, "free Negroes," were arrested for assault

---

[210]Only John **Newsom** had "Black" written next to his name, but all those persons listed below him were counted as "other free" in the census.

and battery in York County on 24 August 1693. His wife Mary was convicted of assaulting Elizabeth Samson, and there was also a "general complaint against her...of threats...of dangerous consequence," so the court ordered her transportation out of the colony. Joseph was probably identical to Joseph Waters, a "free Negroe," who the grand jury of York County presented on 25 February 1694/5 for "keeping company with an English woman & constantly lying with her." The court also presented the unnamed English woman for having a "Molotto Child" [DOW 9:173, 240, 255, 270; 10:106].

WATKINS FAMILY

1. Catherine[1] Watkins, born say 1720, was listed in the inventory of the Northumberland County, Virginia estate of John Coppedge between 1743 and 1749, valued at 4 pounds currency. Also listed were (her?) "Molatto" children Robert, Jeane and Michael Watkins, valued at 15 pounds, 13 pounds and 11 pounds respectively [RB 1743-9, 131]. She may have been the mother of
    i.   Robert[1], born say 1737, may have been the Robert Watkins who brought a petition against Seymour Powell in Brunswick County, Virginia court. The court dismissed the suit on 27 June 1758 after hearing both sides [Orders 1757-9, 202].
    ii. Jean/ Jane[1], born say 1739, perhaps the ancestor of the member of the Watkins family who married Judy **Nickens** of Lancaster and Northumberland counties.
1   iii. Michael, born say 1741.
    iv. Catherine[2], born say 1743.

1. Michael Watkins, born say 1741, was living in Lancaster County, Virginia, on 21 October 1765 when the court ordered his daughter Kate Watkins bound to Robert Watkins [Orders 1764-7, 168]. He was in Brunswick County, Virginia, on 25 January 1779 when the court ordered the churchwardens of St. Andrew's Parish to bind out his "poor Children" William and Robert Watkins. His wife was apparently Ann Watkins who was living in Brunswick County on 22 April 1771 when the court ordered her children William, Robert, and Mary Watkins, "(Mulattoes) poor Children," bound out by the churchwardens of St. Andrew's Parish [Orders 1768-72, 346; 1774-82, 242]. He was taxable in St. Andrew's Parish, Greensville County, Virginia, from 1787 to 1820: taxable on a horse and 4 cattle in 1787, taxable on a free male tithable 16-21 years of age in 1790, 1795 and 1796; taxable on James Watkins' tithe in 1804 and 1805, listed in 1813 with Ann Watkins ("Mulattos") [PPTL 1782-1850, frames 57, 124, 149, 157, 195, 207, 236, 271, 299, 317, 334, 350, 369, 384, 399, 413, 430, 444, 460, 503, 599]. He was head of a Greensville County household of 5 "free colored" in 1820 [VA:266]. Michael and Ann were the parents of
2   i.   Catherine[3], born say 1763.
    ii. William, born say 1768.
3   iii. Robert[2], born about 1770.
4   iv. Mary, born say 1771.
    v.   ?John[1], born before 1776, taxable in Greensville County from 1797 to 1820, listed with (his wife) Sally, "Mulattos," in 1813 [PPTL 1809-50, frames 225, 236, 250, 290, 307, 317, 341, 375, 450, 466, 538, 610]. He was head of a Greensville County household of 12 "free colored" in 1820 [VA:266].
    vi. ?Daniel[1], born before 1776, taxable in Greensville County in 1795, 1799 and 1800 [PPTL 1782-1850, frames 195, 249, 257], head of a household of 6 "free colored" in 1820 [VA:266].
5   vii. ?David, born say 1780.
    viii. ?James, born say 1782, married to Sally on 8 May 1809 when they sold 30 acres on the south side of Fountain Creek and both sides of

Jordan's Road in Greensville County. This was their allotment of the
estate of Lucretia **Byrd**, widow of Thomas **Stewart** [DB 4:117]. He
was taxable in Michael Watkins' household in 1804 and 1805, in his
own household from 1807 to 1811, probably deceased by 1812 since
Sally Watkins was taxable on a horse in 1812 and listed by herself as
a "Mulatto" in 1813 [PPTL 1782-1850, frames 369, 399, 384, 403,
417, 430, 444].

  ix. ?Frederick, born in 1785, registered in Greensville County on 10
November 1806: *aged 21 years the 24 December 1806 is free born, of
a yellowish complexion...about 5 feet 8-1/2 Inches high* [Register of
Free Negroes, no.6].

2. Catherine[3] Watkins, born say 1763, was bound to (her uncle?) Robert Watkins
in Lancaster County in 1765. She was living in Greensville County, Virginia,
on 26 June 1783 when the court ordered the churchwardens of St. Andrew's
Parish to bind out her illegitimate children Moses and Cherry Watkins [Orders
1781-9, 73]. She was the mother of

  i. Moses, born 1776-94, head of a Warren County, North Carolina
household of 1 "other free" and 3 slaves in 1810 [NC:756], and 3 "free
colored" in 1820. His estate was ordered settled in Warren County in
November 1828 [Gammon, *Record of Estates Warren County*, vol. II,
no. 566].

  ii. Cherry.

3. Robert[2] Watkins, born about 1770, was taxable in Greensville County from
1792 to 1815: in the same household with John Deen in 1792 when they were
taxable on a slave, taxable on 2 horses in 1793, his tax charged to George
Harwell in 1799, taxable on a slave and 2 horses in 1812, listed in 1813 with
Nancy ("Mulattos") [PPTL 1782-1850, frames 149, 157, 207, 244, 264, 278,
299, 317, 334, 350, 384, 417, 436, 450, 489]. He married Nancy **Jones**,
daughter of Thomas and Rebecca **Jones**, 10 February 1796 Greensville County
bond, Abraham **Artis** surety [Marriage Bonds, 34]. Robert and his wife Nancy
and Mark **Gowen** and his wife Sally sold 9 acres in Greensville County on 23
September 1799. This was part of the land their wives inherited from their
father Thomas **Jones** [DB 2:577]. Robert registered as a "free Negro" in
Greensville County on 1 September 1824: *a free Man of Colour of a Yellow
Complexion supposed to be 54 years old, 5'9-1/4 inches high (in shoes)...a
farmer* [Register of Free Negroes, no.113]. He was head of a Greensville
County household of 5 "free colored" in 1820 [VA:266]. He may have been
the father of

  i. Daniel[2], born about 1798, registered on 29 April 1817: *free born of a
black complexion, nineteen years of age the 28th May next, five feet 9-
3/4 inches high (in Shoes)...a planter* [Register of Free Negroes,
no.66], married Fanny **Dungill**, 10 February 1824 Greensville County
bond, David Wadkins surety, 12 February marriage by Rev. Nathaniel
Chambliss [Ministers' Returns, 93].

  ii. Sterling, born about 1807, registered in Greensville County on 1 April
1825: *free born of a yellowish Complexion about Eighteen years old,
5 feet 10-1/2 inches high in shoes...a planter* [Register of Free
Negroes, no.141].

4. Mary Watkins, born say 1771, "Mulato" daughter of Ann Watkins, was bound
apprentice in Brunswick County on 22 April 1771 [Orders 1768-72, 346]. Her
children were

  i. John[2], born about 1802, registered in Greensville County on 17 July
1822: *(son of Mary Watkins a free Mulatto Woman) free born of a
black complexion, about 20 years of age, five feet 7 inches high
(barefoot)...a sawyer* [Register of Free Negroes, no.100].

ii. Jesse, born about 1804, registered in Greensville County on 3 January 1826: *son of Mary Watkins, free born 22 years of a yellow Complexion, 5'8-1/8 inches high (in shoes)...a ditcher* [Register of Free Negroes, no.151]. He was head of a Halifax County, North Carolina household of 5 "free colored" in 1820.

5. David Watkins, born say 1780, was taxable in Greensville County from 1798 to 1820: taxable on a horse in 1805, his tax charged to John Blanks in 1806 and 1807, taxable on a slave in 1809, 5 slaves in 1811 and 4 slaves and 3 horses in 1812, listed in 1813 with (wife) Jemima ("Mulattos") [PPTL 1782-1850, frames 235, 249, 257, 299, 317, 334, 347, 367, 367, 384, 413, 430, 444, 459, 478, 503, 551, 575, 599]. He married Mima, "a mulatto woman freed by Mr. John Wickham," 25 December 1805 Greensville County bond, James Watkins surety. He was head of a Greensville County household of 12 "free colored" and 7 slaves in 1820 [VA:266] and 21 "free colored" and 12 slaves in 1830 [VA:41]. He was the father of

   i. Mary Ann, born say 1804, "daughter of David Watkins," married Thomas **King**, "people of color," 29 January 1822 Greensville County bond.

Other members of the family in North Carolina and Virginia were

   i. Clarkey, born before 1776, head of a Caswell County household of 5 "free colored" in 1820 [NC:93].
   ii. Sarah, born before 1776, head of a Guilford County household of 8 "free colored" in 1830.
   iii. Robert⁴, born about 1786, *obtained a certificate of freedom in Chesterfield County, Virginia, on 8 January 1811: twenty five years old, yellow complexion, born free* [Register of Free Negroes 1804-53, no. 152].
   iv. Isaac, born 1776-94, head of a Caswell County household of 3 "other free" in 1810 [NC:512] and 7 "free colored" in 1820 [NC:93], married Jenny **Jones**, 23 February 1816 Caswell County bond.
   v. Jane², born say 1780, living in Caswell County on 22 February 1805 when the court ordered her unnamed children bound apprentices. Her children were probably Betsy, "child of colour," and Lewis Watkins, a five-year-old, both bound to Christopher Dameron on 30 July 1806 [CR 20.101.1]. Jane was a "Negro" head of a Guilford County household of 4 "free colored" in 1830.
   vi. Nathan, born 1776-94, head of a Gates County household of 1 "free colored" in 1820 [NC:145].
   vii. Joseph, born say 1765, married Sally **Porter**, daughter of Edward **Porter** who consents and is surety, 28 October 1788 Surry County, Virginia bond, Elizabeth **Porter** witness.

WEAVER FAMILY

1. Richard¹ Weaver, born say 1675, and (his wife?) Elizabeth Weaver were witnesses to the 21 November 1735 Lancaster County will of Edward **Nicken** [WB 12:355]. He was called "an ancient poor man of Wiccocomoco Parish" on 12 September 1739 when the Lancaster County court excused him from paying taxes in the future [Orders 1729-43, 251]. His son Isaac Weaver was a tithable in his household in 1745 [Lancaster County Tithables 1745-95, 2]. Richard and Elizabeth Weaver were the parents of

2   i. ?William¹, born say 1710.
   ii. ?Elizabeth, born say 1714, living in Bertie County, North Carolina, on 12 August 1735 when the county court nullified the indenture of "Elizh. Weaver Setting forth that being a Free woman she is detained by Edmd. Wiggons as a servant by indenture illegally obtained...from

the Petnrs. mother." And on 13 August 1740 the court read the petition of Charles Horne "Shewing that he has bound to him by ye Cts. of ye N W Par & two Majestrates O. & Elizabeth Weavers a Mallatto Boy wch Allex. Cotton refuses to Deliver ye sd. Boy" [Haun, *Bertie County Court Minutes*, I:152, 293].

3   iii.   ?James[1], born say 1719.
4   iv.   Isaac[1], born say 1720.
5   v.   Aaron[1], born say 1722
     vi.   Ann[1], born say 1725, a sister of Isaac, wife of Thomas **Nicken**, named in Isaac Weaver's will.
6   vii.   ?Elijah[1], born about 1737.

2.   William[1] Weaver, born say 1710, was taxed in Norfolk County, Virginia, in 1732 in Thomas **Archer**'s household. Three years later on 10 June 1735 he was head of a household in Thomas Wright's Norfolk County list, taxed on himself and James Weaver [Wingo, *Norfolk County Tithables, 1730-50*, 158, 167]. In February 1741 he paid 70 pounds for 300 acres adjoining Alexander Cotton and Jonathan Clift in the part of Bertie County, North Carolina, which became Hertford County after 1759 with Thomas **Archer** as witness [DB F:319]. In 1751 William and Elizabeth were taxed in Bertie County as "free Mulattos" [CCR 190]. He purchased 100 acres on Potecasi Creek joining John **Carter**'s Mill on 27 August 1753 [DB H:4]. In 1757 he was taxed in the list of John Brickell with wife Elizabeth and James Weaver [CR 10.702.1, Box 1]. Most early Hertford County records were destroyed in courthouse fires, but William was taxable on two persons in 1770 and his taxable property was recorded in a 1779 Hertford Tax list for District 3 filed with the state government: 300 acres, 2 horses, 16 cattle, and 143 pounds money. James and Carter **Nickens** and Abel and Baker **Archer** were taxed in the same district [Fouts, *Tax Receipt Book*, 66; GA 30.1]. William's children may have been

7   i.   Amey, born say 1730.
     ii.   Charles[1], born before 1748, taxed in 1759 in the household of Peter Jones in John Brickell's Bertie County tax list and taxable on 2 persons in Hertford County from 1768 to 1770 [Fouts, *Tax Receipt Book*, 13]. He was head of a Hertford County household of 4 "other free" in 1800 [NC:350], 6 in 1810 [NC:106], and 13 "free colored" in 1820 [NC:182].
8   iii.   Jesse[1], born before 1759.
9   iv.   Edward (Ned), born say 1760.
     v.   James[3], born say 1762, purchased 160 acres on the south side of Conway Creek in Halifax County, North Carolina, on 13 October 1784 and sold this land on 3 May 1792 [DB 15:467; 17:746]. He was head of a Halifax County household of 4 "other free" in 1790 [NC:63], 5 in 1800 [NC:350], 9 in 1810 [NC:54], and 10 "free colored" in 1820 [NC:170]. He was charged with bastardy by Martha **Lynch** in Halifax County court on 24 May 1798. Their son was probably two-month-old Charles **Lynch** who was ordered bound to James Weaver on the same day to learn the trade of cooper [Minutes 1796-8].

3.   James[1] Weaver, born say 1719, was taxable in the Norfolk County household of (his brother?) William[1] Weaver in 1735. He was also taxable in William's household in the Bertie County list of John Brickell in 1757. Perhaps his widow was Sarah Weaver who was taxed on 300 acres and 5 cattle in District 4 of Hertford County in 1779 [GA 30.1]. Their children may have been

10   i.   James[2], born say 1749.
      ii.   Charles[2], head of a Hertford County household of 1 "other free" in Captain Langston's District in 1800.
      iii.   Mary, head of a Hertford County household of 6 "other free" in Captain Lewis' District in 1800.

4. Isaac[1] Weaver, born say 1720, was taxable in the Lancaster County household of his father Richard Weaver in 1745 and taxable in John Longworth's household in 1775 and 1777 [Tithables 1745-95, 2, 14, 22, 35]. The churchwardens were ordered to bind out his children in Lancaster County on 17 April 1764. He brought a successful suit in Lancaster County against William Steptoe on 21 May 1764. His suit against Joseph McAdams was dismissed on 19 November 1764, and on 15 July 1765 he was sued by David Galloway [Orders 1764-67, 32, 39, 78, 144]. His children were probably the "Mulatto" boys and girls listed in the 17 June 1765 inventory of the Lancaster County estate of William Haydon: Darcus Weaver (25 pounds currency), John Weaver (20 pounds), William Weaver (18 pounds), Thomas Weaver (15 pounds) and Betty Weaver (10 pounds) [DW 1764-70, 38]. Isaac's 30 November 1777 Lancaster County will, proved 19 March 1778, named his brother Aaron Weaver and his brother-in-law Thomas **Nicken** [WB 20:120]. His children may have been

    i.   Dorcas, born say 1755, mother of Wilson Weaver who was bound to Thomas Lovelace in Halifax County, Virginia, on 19 September 1776 [Pleas 1774-9, 172]. She may have been identical to Dorcas Hamilton who sued Thomas Lovelace in court for her freedom on 19 August 1773 [Pleas 1773-4, 194; 1774-9, 172, 192]. Wilson registered in Halifax County on 30 August 1802: *aged about twenty five years, five feet seven inches and three quarters high, yellow colour... born free...registered as a free Negro* [Register of Free Negroes 1802-31, no. 21]. He may have been the son of a member of the **Wilson** family of Halifax County.

    ii. John[2], born about 1760, married Dorcas **Bell**, 10 June 1789 Lancaster County bond. He was taxable in Lancaster County from 1788 to 1813 [PPTL, 1782-1839, frames 54, 86, 291, 322, 385]. He registered as a "free Negro" in Lancaster County on 19 September 1808: *Age 48, Color yellow, Height 5'3-1/4*. His wife Dorcas, born about 1754, registered on 18 July 1803: *w/o John, Age 49, Color dark, Height 4'11, Served till 31 years of age* [Burkett, *Lancaster County Register of Free Negroes*, 1]. He left a 6 November 1809 Lancaster County will, proved 20 February 1815 which named his wife Darkey Weaver and grandsons: John, James, and Samuel **Bell**. Betsy **Bell** was one of the witnesses to the will [WB 28:162]. He was a Revolutionary war veteran who died before 19 May 1834 when his only heir Betty Weaver was named in Lancaster County court [Orders 1834-41, 7]. Dorcas left a 23 July 1820 Lancaster County will, proved 21 August the same year, naming her son Spencer **Bell** and grandchildren John Weaver **Bell**, James **Bell**, and Nancy **Bell** [WB 28:208].

    iii. William[2], born say 1760, taxable in Mary Haydon's Wicomico Parish, Lancaster County household in 1781 [Tithables 1745-95, 38].

    iv. Thomas, born say 1762, married Eliza **Lawes/Laws**, 7 July 1794 Lancaster County bond. Thomas was taxable in Lancaster County in 1795 [Tithables 1745-95, 58] and a "free mulatto" head of a Northumberland County household of 6 "other free" in 1810 [VA:998]. Perhaps his wife was the Betty Weaver who was listed as a "free Negro" in Northumberland County in 1813 with a male over sixteen years of age and 2 slaves over sixteen [A list of Free Negroes and Mulattoes in 1813 [PPTL, p.13].

    v.   Elizabeth, born say 1763.

5. Aaron[1] Weaver, born say 1722, was mentioned in the 30 November 1777 Lancaster will of his brother Isaac Weaver [WB 20:120]. He was taxable in Lancaster County in 1775 in the list of John Longworth on himself and slave Phebe, on himself in 1776, one of Betty Brady's tithables in 1777, a tithable head of a household with slave Sarah in 1779, and tithable on himself and

slave Lucy in 1781 [Tithables 1745-95, 14, 18, 22, 35, 42]. In 1782 he was taxable on 5 cattle in Northumberland County [PPTL 1782-1812, frame 232] and head of a Northumberland County household of 9 "Black" persons (called "Free Aaron Weaver") [VA:37]. He was taxable in Lancaster County from 1783 to 1785 [PPTL, 1782-1839, frames 18, 32]. Aaron may have been the father of

    i.   Joseph[1], born say 1750, head of a Northumberland County household of 6 "Black" persons in 1782 [VA:37], taxable on 2 tithes, 18 cattle, and a horse in 1782 [PPTL, frame 232] and on 10 cattle in 1787 [Schreiner-Yantis, *1787 Census*, 1276]. He was listed as a "free Negro" in Northumberland County with a female over sixteen years of age in his household in 1813 [PPTL, p. 23].

    ii.   Richard[2], born about 1752, an indentured servant who ran away from Robert Dudley of King and Queen County who offered a reward for his return in the 21 March 1771 *Virginia Gazette*, describing him as: *a young Negro fellow...about 19 years of age, of a yellow complexion, and very spare, had on when he went off a grey serge coat and waistcoat, lined with red, and a pair of leather breeches* [*Virginia Gazette*, Rine edition, p. 4, col. 3]. He was taxable in Lancaster County in 1787, perhaps identical to Richard B. Weaver who was taxable there from 1797 to 1813 [PPTL, 1782-1839, frames 46, 157, 178, 191, 206, 219, 232, 385]. On 13 October 1794 he was administrator of the Northumberland County estate of Rebecca Weaver [Orders 1790-95, 471].

11   iii. Aaron[2], born say 1758.

    iv. Benjamin[1], born say 1765, taxable in Northumberland County in 1787, his tax charged to Joseph Weaver [Schreiner-Yantis, *1787 Census*, 1276] and in 1788 he was taxable on himself and Joseph Weaver [PPTL B, p.7]. He purchased 100 acres in Lancaster County on 3 May 1796 and another 10 acres on 19 November 1803 [DB 23:89; 25:20]. He was head of a Lancaster County household of 6 "other free" and 2 slaves in 1810 [VA:364]. His 13 July 1812 Lancaster County will, proved 17 November the same year, named his niece Elizabeth, left a bible to his niece Jenny Weaver, and left his land to Jenny's male issue [WB 28:137].

    v.   Ann[2], born say 1778, married Henry **Johnson**, 13 February 1795 Lancaster County bond.

    vi. Nanny, head of a Lancaster County household of 8 "other free" in 1810 [VA:363].

    vii. Anthony, born about 1780, married Susan **Causey**, 30 May 1807 Northumberland County bond, James **Toulson** security. Anthony was "a free mulatto" head of a Northumberland County household of 3 "other free" in 1810 [VA:998]. He registered as a "free Negro" on 13 May 1811: *Mulatto, about 31 years, 6 feet 1-3/4 Inches high* [Northumberland County Courthouse, Register no.52].

    viii. Henry, married Jenny Weaver, 28 November 1811 Lancaster County bond.

    ix. Joseph[2], married Nancy **Causey**, 6 May 1810 Northumberland County bond, Amos **Nicken** security.

    x.   Lucy, "a free mulatto" head of a Northumberland County household of 4 "other free" in 1810 [VA:999].

    xi. S., head of a Lancaster County household of 4 "other free" in 1810 [VA:364].

    xii. Moses, born about 1785, registered as a "free Negro" in Lancaster County on 17 February 1807: *Age 22, Color mulatto...born free* [Burkett, *Lancaster County Register of Free Negroes*, 3]. He married Janette **Smith**, "daughter of Sally Mactear," 31 December 1816 Lancaster County bond. Sally **McTyre** registered on 15 May 1829: *Age*

42, Color bright...born free [Burkett, *Lancaster County Register of Free Negroes*, 9]. Sally was head of a Lancaster County household of 6 "other free" in 1810 [VA:354].

6. Elijah[1] Weaver, born about 1737, was a defendant in a case which was dismissed in Lancaster County on 17 February 1764 [Orders 1764-67, 15]. He was administrator of the estate of John **Kelly** in Northumberland County in 1778 [Orders 1773-83, 362, 371, 374]. He complained to the 22 March 1782 Lancaster County court that Jesse **Waddy** carried away his son Spencer [Orders 1778-83, 93]. He was taxable in Lancaster County in 1781 [Tithables 1745-95, 41] and taxable there from 1783 to 1791 [PPTL 1782-1839, frames 18, 23, 64, 86]. He registered as a "free Negro" in Lancaster County on 18 July 1803: *Age 66, Color dark...born free*. His wife Dorcas Weaver registered the same day: *w/o Elijah, Age 62, Color mulatto...born free* [Burkett, *Lancaster County Register of Free Negroes*, 1]. He was a Revolutionary War veteran who died intestate in Lancaster County before 15 September 1834 when his heirs Spencer Weaver, Elijah Weaver, Mary **Pinn**, Agatha **Bell**, Betsy Weaver, and Polly the wife of Armstead **Nicken** were named in court [Orders 1834-41, p.37]. His children were most likely

    i. Spencer, born about 1773, taxable in Lancaster County from 1794 to 1810 [PPTL 1782-1839, frames 124, 206, 277, 338]. He registered as a "free Negro" in Lancaster County on 16 January 1804: *Age 31, Color mulatto* [Burkett, *Lancaster County Register of Free Negroes*, 2].

    ii. Elijah[2], married Elizabeth **Frary**, 8 April 1796 Westmoreland County bond, Tracy Richard Clayton security.

    iii. Mary **Pinn**, perhaps the Mary Weaver who was bound apprentice in Northumberland County court on 9 June 1772 by the churchwardens of Wicomico Parish [Orders 1770-73, 378]. Mary **Kelly** Weaver married Aaron **Pinn**, 3 March 1794 Lancaster County bond.

    iv. Agatha, born about 1785, registered as a "free Negro" in Lancaster County on 18 July 1803: *Age 18, Color bright mulatto...born free* [Burkett, *Lancaster County Register of Free Negroes*, 1]. She married Coleman **Bell**, 26 December 1806 Lancaster County marriage.

    v. Betsy.

    vi. Polly, married Armstead **Nicken**, 21 January 1819 Lancaster County bond.

7. Amey Weaver, born say 1730, "a Free Mullattoe," was taxable in the Bertie County household of Margaret **Bynus** (also a taxable) in William Wynn's list for 1757. Her children bound apprentices in Bertie County were

    i. Lucy, born about 1746.

    ii. Peter, born about 1750, bound to John Campbell to be a seaman on 28 January 1757 [*NCGSJ* XIII:168].

    iii. John[1], born about 1753, a six-year-old son of "Free Mullattoe" Amey Weaver bound to William Witherington to learn the trade of shoe making in July 1759 [Haun, *Bertie County Court Minutes*, II:491]. He was taxable in Portsmouth and Elizabeth River Parishes in Norfolk County, Virginia, in 1788 and 1789 and from 1796 to 1806: called a "Mulatto" in 1798, 1800 and 1804; a labourer in Western Branch Precinct in a "List of Free Negroes and Mulattoes" in 1801 [PPTL, 1782-1791, frames 633, 652; 1791-1812, frames 180, 235, 261, 306, 364, 384, 569, 584]. He purchased 11 acres in Norfolk County on 1 February 1798 [DB 37:136]. He was head of a Northampton County, North Carolina household of 3 "other free" in 1810 [NC:750], 5 "free colored" in Hertford County in 1820 [NC:206] and 3 "free colored" in Hertford County in 1830. On 28 November 1823 he testified in Hertford County court for Evans **Archer** saying that he was in the same regiment with him during the Revolution, stationed in South

Carolina. He made a declaration in Hertford County court for his own
pension on 13 October 1828, stating that he was born about 1752.
James **Smith** testified for him [M805-845, frame 272].

  iv.   Bridgett, born about 1756, three-year-old daughter of "Free Mullattoe"
Amey Weaver, bound to William Witherington to learn household
business [Haun, *Bertie County Court Minutes*, II:491]. She was head
of a Hertford County household of 2 "free colored" in 1820 [NC:206].

  v.   ?James[4], born say 1770, head of a Hertford County household of 6
"other free" in Captain Lewis' District in 1800.

8.   Jesse[1] Weaver, born before 1759, was taxable on 1 poll in District 3 of
Hertford County in 1779 [GA 30.1] and taxable on 230 acres and 1 poll in
Hertford County in 1784 [L.P. 64.1]. He was head of a Hertford County
household of 6 "other free" in 1790 [NC:26], 5 in Captain Lewis' District in
1800, 3 in 1810 [NC:102], 13 "free colored" in 1820 [NC:182], and 6 "free
colored" in 1830 [NC:404]. His 14 January 1834 Hertford County will was
proved in February 1834. He mentioned but did not name his wife and named
his sons William and Jesse who were "keeping the Mill" and daughters Fanny
Cotton, Phebe **Cotton**, Nany, and Martha Weaver [WB A:65]. His children
were

  i.   William[3], born before 1776, head of a Hertford County household of
17 "free colored" in 1820 [NC:186] and 9 "free colored" in 1830
[407]. William, Elias, Lawrence, Jesse, Charles, Thomas and John
Weaver as well as Micajah, Wiley, and Richard **Cotton** were among
the "Sundry persons of Colour of Hertford County" who petitioned the
General Assembly in 1822 to repeal the act which declared slaves to be
competent witnesses against free persons of Colour [*NCGSJ* XI:252].

  ii.   Jesse[3], born 1776-94, head of a Hertford County household of 6 "free
colored" in 1820 [NC:206] and 3 "free colored" in 1830.

  iii.   Fanny **Cotton**.

  iv.   Phebe **Cotton**.

  v.   Nan.

  vi.   Martha.

9.   Edward (Ned) Weaver, born say 1760, was head of a Hertford County
household of 7 "other free" in 1790 [NC:25] and 7 in Captain Moore's District
in 1800. His 8 April 1816 Hertford County will was proved in May 1816. He
left land in the "middle of little wood yard" to his wife and then to his
granddaughter Polly Weaver and named his daughters Anga(?) Auga(?)
Weaver and Helen **Newton**, mother of Allen **Newton**. He also gave 5 pounds
each to grandson Benjamin Weaver and son John. Margaret **Hall** was a witness
to the will [WB A:188]. His children were

  i.   John[3], head of a Hertford County household of 3 "free colored" in
1830 [NC:403].

  ii.   Anga or Auga.

  iii.   Helen, married ___ **Newton**.

10.   James[2] Weaver, born say 1749, was taxable in Norfolk County, Virginia, in
1765 in St. Brides Parish [Wingo, *Norfolk County Tithables 1751-65*, 211]. He
was head of a Gates County household of 6 "other free" in 1790 [NC:23] and
4 in 1800 [NC:280]. The Gates County court ordered Benjamin Weaver,
"Molatto" son of Lucy Weaver, bound to him as an apprentice shoemaker in
August 1793 [Fouts, *Minutes of County Court 1787-93*, 133]. His children
Carter and Joel Weaver were called orphans of James Weaver when they were
bound out in Gates County in 1802 [Black Craftsmen in North Carolina,
NCGSJ XI:95]. Perhaps his widow was Jane Weaver, a "free Negro" taxable
on a slave and a horse in St. Bride's Parish, Norfolk County, from 1801 to
1803 [PPTL, 1791-1812, frames 400, 416, 456]. James was the father of

    i. ?Lucy, born say 1770, mother of Benjamin Weaver who was bound to James Weaver in August 1793.

    ii. ?Willoughby, born say 1780, a labourer heading a household in Western Branch District of Norfolk County in a "List of Free Negroes and Mulattoes" in 1801 and included in Josiah **Flood**'s household in the same list [PPTL, 1791-1812, frame 383]. Perhaps his widow was Mrs. Mary Ann Weaver who married John **Robbins**, "free persons of colour," 1816 Norfolk County bond, Robert Barrett security.

    iii. ?Jesse², born say 1782, a "M"(ulatto) taxable in Portsmouth and Elizabeth River Parish District of Norfolk County from 1803 to 1817 [PPTL, 1791-1812, frames 471, 585, 653, 698, 750; 1813-24, frames 115, 257] and head of a Norfolk County household of 8 "other free" in 1810 [VA:819]. He acquired land from Thomas **Archer** by deed proved in Norfolk County in 1817. Perhaps he was the husband of Elizabeth Weaver who was called the daughter of Thomas **Archer** in the Norfolk County deed by which he gave her all his personal estate [DB 47:168; 48:85].

    iv. Carter, born about 1790, bound to Richard Rawls of Gates County to be a house carpenter.

    v. Joel, born about 1792, bound to Richard Rawls of Gates County to be a house carpenter.

    vi. ?Jemima, born about 1794, registered in Norfolk County on 19 December 1815: *5 feet 2 In. 21 Years of age of a Yellowish Complexion...Born free in the County of Norfolk* [Register of Free Negros & Mulattos, no.105].

11. Aaron² Weaver, born say 1758, was head of a Lancaster County household of 3 free persons and a slave in 1783 [VA:55]. He was a Lancaster County seaman in the Revolutionary War who made application for a pension while resident in Princess Anne County [Jackson, *Virginia Negro Soldiers*, 45]. He was a "F.B." head of a Princess Anne County household of 4 "other free" in 1810 [VA:479]. One of his children was

    i. Betsy, "daughter of Aaron Weaver," married Demce **Anderson**, Jr., 4 January 1796 Princess Anne County bond, Thomas Weaver surety.

12. Lucy Weaver, born about 1746, the eleven-year-old daughter of "Amiah Wever a free Mullattoe," was bound to John Campbell by the Bertie County court on 28 January 1757 [*NCGSJ* XIII:168]. She was called "Negroe Lucy Weaver" on 29 January 1767 when the Chowan County court bound her four-month-old "Free Negroe" son Lewis to Richard Brownrigg, Esq., until the age of twenty-one [Minutes 1766-72, 318]. In August 1793 the Gates County court ordered her fourteen-year-old "Molatto" son Benjamin Weaver bound as an apprentice shoemaker to James Weaver [Fouts, *Minutes of County Court of Pleas and Quarter Sessions 1787-93*, 133]. She was the mother of

    i. Lewis, born about October 1768, four months old on 29 January 1767 when he was bound to Richard Brownrigg. He was head of a Hertford County household of 2 "other free" in 1810 [NC:102] and 1 "free colored" in 1830 [NC:398].

    ii. Benjamin², born about 1779, bound apprentice in 1793.

Other members of the family in Virginia were

    i. William L., born about 1795, registered in Petersburg on 9 November 1818: *a free man of colour, five feet six inches high, twenty three years old, born free in Lancaster County, a barber* [Register of Free Negroes 1794-1819, no. 936].

Those counted as "other free" in Orange County, North Carolina, in 1800 were
    i.   Penny, head of a household of 7 "other free" [NC:605].
    ii. Zadock, head of a household of 6 "other free" [NC:605].

Those counted as "other free" in South Carolina were
    i.   Bett, (free) head of a household of 4 "other free" and a slave in St. Philip's & Michael's Parish in 1790.
    ii. John, head of a Liberty County, South Carolina household of 5 "other free" in 1800 [SC:804].

WEBB FAMILY

1. Daniel¹ Webb, born say 1646, was a tithable slave in the Northampton County, Virginia household of Captain John Custis from 1664 to 1677, called Daniel Negro from 1664 to 1671 and called Daniel Webb when he was listed with Isbell Webb } Negroes in 1677 [Orders 1657-64, fol.198; 1664-74, p.15, fol.42, p.55, fol.114; OW&c 1674-79, 191]. He was witness to the 6 February 1677 Northampton County will of "King Tony Negro" [Orders, Wills 1674-9, 247]. Daniel was probably the father of several children born to Ann Williams, a white indentured servant. Two of their children, Jane and Ann, were listed in 1693 in the Northampton County will of Henry Warren, a neighbor of Captain Custis [OW 1689-98, 261-2; OW&c 1674-79, 191]. Warren's widow Susanna married Hamond Firkette, and Ann's "Maletto" daughter Anne Williams was bound apprentice to him on 30 November 1699. The indenture required Firkette to pay Henry Warren's daughter Esther 1,000 pounds of tobacco at the expiration of the indenture when Anne reached the age of eighteen years [OW&c 1698-1710, 30]. Daniel was the father of
2   i.   ?Daniel², born about 1666.
3   ii. Jane, born about 1682.
        iii. Ann¹, born in September or October 1686, named in Henry Warren's Northampton County will, a thirteen-year-old "Maletto childe" called Anne Williams when she was bound to Hamond Firkette of Northampton County on 30 November 1699 [OW&c 1698-1710, 30].

2. Daniel² Webb, born about 1666, was a "molatto" son of an English woman and had attained the age of twenty-one on 5 October 1687 when the Northumberland County, Virginia court released him from his service to the orphans of Major John Mottram. He may have had a child by Mary Day, an indentured white servant, who had a "molatto child" Samuel Webb alias Day who was apprenticed in Northumberland County on 23 November 1694. On 16 July 1701 another English woman named Margaret Lawson confessed in court that "a Negro called Daniell Webb" was the father of her illegitimate child. The court ordered the churchwardens to dispose of her according to law at the expiration of her service to Sarah Dawson [Orders 1678-98, 405, 412, 681; 1699-1713, part 1, 167, 272]. Daniel was the father of
        i.   ?Samuel¹ Webb, alias Day, born say 1694, son of Mary Day, apprenticed in Northumberland County on 23 November 1694. See the Day history.
        ii. Robert¹ Lawson, born say 1701. See the Lawson history.

3. Jane Webb, born about 1682, was called a "muletto Girle named Jane" in the Northampton County will of Henry Warren in 1693. She agreed to indenture herself for seven years to Thomas Savage in exchange for permission to marry his slave Left. On 17 April 1711 the court bound her children Diana, Daniel and Frances to her master, and on 20 June 1716 the court bound to Savage her two "Malatto" children Ann and Elizabeth, "Born of ye body of Jane Webb ye wife of a Negro man belonging to Captain Thomas Savage" [Orders 1711-6, 225]. On 16 August 1722 Jane was called "Jane Webb, formerly Jane

Williams, the daughter of a white woman," when she petitioned the court to release her children Diana (then eighteen), Daniel and Frances from their indenture to Savage, asking the court not to adjudge her children in servitude since they were born in lawful wedlock. Savage delayed the case until 10 January 1722/3 when the court ruled that her petition was frivolous [Orders 1719-22, 185, 191; 1722-9, 11, 46; Deal, *Race and Class*, 466-71; Mihalyka, *Loose Papers II:*41-2]. She sued Benjamin Barth for 3-1/2 yards of Virginia linen in November 1723 [Mihalyka, *Loose Papers II:*60]. Jane was head of her own Northampton County household in 1724, called Jane Webb in one list and "Jane Left mulatto" in the list of tobacco planters. In February 1724/5 the court dismissed her petition for release of her daughter Diana from servitude, but it released her two months later when Diana produced evidence from the parish register that she was twenty-one. In February 1725/6 Savage petitioned the court to have her children Lisha and Abimeleck bound to him because their mother "has no visible means of support" [Mihalyka, *Loose Papers II:*125]. She brought a suit in chancery against Savage maintaining that as part of her original indenture he had agreed to free her husband Left and had agreed not to make any claim on her children born after her servitude was completed. And she said that Savage had taken the written indenture and would not allow her to see it [Mihalyka, *Loose Papers II:*147]. On 12 July 1726 two of Savage's neighbors, Colonel George Harmonson and Mrs. Margaret Forse, testified that they had seen an indenture by which Jane agreed to serve Savage seven years and that any children born in the lifetime of her husband Left should serve Savage in exchange for his permission to allow her to marry his slave Left. Savage failed to produce the indenture in court, but testified that he had never agreed to free her husband Left. When asked for what term the children were to serve him by the indenture, he answered that he could not say. His witnesses Colonel Harmonson and Philip Jacob testified that they had heard Jane declare, "if all Negros had as good a heart as she had they would all be Free," for which she received ten lashes. The case was discontinued on 14 December 1726 while the court considered whether to allow the evidence of "Free Negros." Jane failed to make her court appearance shortly after the court decided not to allow her evidence, and the case was dismissed on 11 July 1727 [Orders 1722-32, 247, 248, 258, 260, 265, 278, 287, 297]. She was called Jane Webb, alias Left, in September 1727 when she petitioned to have her name added to the list of tithables. Jane was head of a household with son Daniel and daughter Dinah in 1728, and Jane was in the household of her daughter Dinah **Manly** in 1730 and 1731. Dinah left the county before 1735, and Jane was tithable as Jeane Webb in Thomas Savage's household in 1737 [Bell, *Northampton County Tithables*, 53, 67, 102, 149, 167, 206, 214, 221, 265, 284]. On 14 June 1732 she informed the court that Sophia Savage had not listed her overseer as a tithable and that Major James Forse had not listed her daughter Elizabeth as a tithable, but the court dismissed her evidence as insufficient and did not pay her the usual informer's fee [Orders 1732-42, 6]. On 12 August 1740 the court excused her from paying taxes because of her old age [Orders 1732-42, 409]. Jane and Left's children were

    i.   Dinah, born 14 February 1703/4, eighteen years old in 1722 when her mother petitioned the court for her release from indenture. When she was twenty-one years old, Dinah petitioned the court herself with a note from the parish certifying her birth date, and the court released her on 14 April 1725 [Orders 1722-9, 17, 46, 179; Mihalyka, *Loose Papers II:*100]. She married Gabriel **Manly** and was called Dinah **Manly** on 1 September 1727 when she petitioned to have her name added to the list of tithables [Orders 1722-9, 206].

4   ii. Daniel[3], born 25 August 1706.

    iii. Frances, born 14 January 1708/9 [Mihalyka, *Loose Papers II:*100].

    iv. Ann[2], born about 1711, "a malatto...Born of ye body of Jane Webb ye wife of a Negro man," was bound to Thomas Savage on 20 June 1716.

She had four more years to serve when she was listed in the inventory of estate of Thomas Savage who died in 1728 [Orders 1711-16, 255; DW 1725-33, 229-30]. On 9 May 1732 she was presented for bastard bearing and the same day petitioned the court against Sophia Savage who was detaining her children Daniel and Abraham in servitude on the pretense that Ann owed her three years of service for having three bastard children during her servitude. The court ordered that she be set free and ordered Mrs. Savage to deliver her clothes and bedding to her [Orders 1729-32, 143-5; 1732-42, 7, 8, 14]. On 12 February 1733/4 she was called "Nanny Week, late Nanny Webb," when the court bound out her three-year-old "free Negroe" son Daniel to William Scott with her consent [Orders 1732-42, 92]. She and her descendants were called **Weeks** thereafter. See the **Weeks** history.

5   v.   Elizabeth[1], born about 1713.
        vi. Lisha/ Elishe[1], born about 1716, bound to Thomas Savage on 17 July 1726 [Orders 1722-9, 247]. She had nine more years to serve when she was listed in the inventory of the estate of Thomas Savage who died in 1728 [DW 1725-33, 229-30]. She was presented by the grand jury on 12 March 1733/4 for having a bastard child which she charged to William **Beckett** [Orders 1732-42, 97, 103, 107].
6   vii. Abimileck, born about 1720.

4.   Daniel[3] Webb, born 25 August 1706 in Northampton County, was "the son of Left and Jane" according to the petition of his sister Dinah Webb in April 1725 [OW 1698-1710, 397; Mihalyka, *Loose Papers II:*100]. He was probably identical to Daniel, a "negro" tithable in the household of Thomas Savage from 1723 to 1726, tithable in the household of his mother "Jane Web malato" in 1728, in Daniel **Jacob**'s household in 1729, in the household of his sister Dinah **Manly** in 1730, and with his wife Frances **Jacob** in Daniel **Jacob**'s household in 1731. Frances was Daniel **Jacob**'s daughter who was listed in his household as Frances **Jacob** from 1724 to 1729 and called Frances Web in 1731 [Bell, *Northampton County Tithables*, 47, 92, 116, 149, 190, 214, 229]. He was called a "Negroe" on 14 August 1733 when he admitted in Northampton County court that he owed Peter Mifflin a debt of 18 bushels of corn due by obligation [Orders 1732-42, 67]. And he was called "free Negro" on 1 October 1764 in a New Hanover County, North Carolina deed, proved on 2 September 1766, by which he purchased 100 acres on the east side of the mouth of Nichols Creek and the sound from Joshua **Pavey** (**Peavey**), "a Mullato" [DB E:274; Minutes 1738-69, 274]. Daniel's 18 July 1769 New Hanover County will was proved on 5 October the same year with his sons Isaac and Samuel Webb qualifying as executors. He left 64 pounds and his land to his children William, Solomon, Jacob, Samuel, and Isaac and his grandchildren John and Elizabeth Webb [Original, NC Archives; Minutes 1738-69, 418, 420]. His children were

7   i.   _____, born say 1730.
8   ii. William, born say 1738.
        iii. Solomon, received only "one shilling and no more" by his father's will.
        iv. Jacob, received only "one shilling and no more" by his father's will. He may have been the Jacob Webb who was taxable in Alex McDowgal's household in Bladen County, North Carolina, in 1763.
        v.   Samuel[2], born say 1742, one of the executors of his father's will.
        vi. Isaac[1], born in August 1743, an eighteen-year-old "Negro" bound by the Northampton County, Virginia court to John Ellegood on 12 May 1762 [Minutes 1761-5, 28]. He was one of the executors of his father's 18 July 1769 Hanover County, North Carolina will.

5.   Elizabeth[1] Webb, born about 1713, "a malatto...Born of ye body of Jane Webb ye wife of a Negro man belonging to Captain Thomas Savage," was bound to

Savage in Northampton County, Virginia, on 20 June 1716 [Orders 1711-16, 255]. She was about nineteen on 14 June 1732 when her mother Jane Webb informed the court that Major James Forse had failed to list her as a tithable. On 11 December 1733 she was presented for having a bastard child, and on 9 January 1733/4 agreed to serve Major James Forse and his wife Margaret for three years for the trouble of his house and fine for having the child. She was called "Betty Webb Mulatto" on 9 May 1738 when she was again presented for having a bastard child [Orders 1732-42, 6, 87, 89, 312, 321; Mihalyka, *Loose Papers II:*5]. She was a taxable "negro" in John Ellgood's household from 1737 to 1739 [Bell, *Northampton County Tithables*, 255, 276, 292]. She may have been identical to Elizabeth **Laylor**, otherwise Webb, who was presented for bastardy on 11 May 1756, perhaps the wife of "William **Ailor** (Negro)" who was sued by Arthur Robins on 12 February 1754 [Orders 1753-8, 67, 315]. Elizabeth Webb was the mother of

9   i.   Katherine, born on 26 January 1732/3.

6. Abimileck Webb, born about 1720, was bound to Thomas Savage in Northampton County on 17 July 1726 [Orders 1722-9, 247]. He was a "mulatto boy" with thirteen more years to serve when he was listed in the estate inventory of Thomas Savage who died in 1728 [DW 1725-33, 229-30]. He was probably the "Ebemilech" listed among Norly Ellgood's tithables from 1737 to 1740. He was called Bemalidg Web when he was tithable in George Winget's household in 1744 [Bell, *Northampton County Tithables*, 264, 284, 358]. On 11 September 1750 he was accused of "combining with sundry Negros in a conspiracy against the white People of this county." His companion, Barbary White, a white hired laborer, deposed that he had told her that:

> *they (Negroes) would be free...with their one indeavour [an]d godalmightys assistance or blessing, for what would it be for the Negroes to go through this County in one nights time.*

He received thirty-nine lashes and was ordered to give security of 100 pounds for his good behavior for a year [L.P. #36 (1750), cited by Deal, *Race and Class*, 470; Orders 1748-51, 271-2]. He was tithable in Thomas Speakman's household in 1765 and head of his own household with (his wife?) Susanna Webb in 1769 [Bell, *Northampton County Tithables*, 374, 388]. Perhaps she was the Susannah Webb who was taxable on 2 horses and 4 cattle in Northumberland County in 1787 [Schreiner-Yantis, *1787 Census*, 1276]. They may have been the parents of

    i.   Charles, born about 1760, a "Mulattoe" delinquent tithable in Northampton County in 1786 [*Virginia Genealogist* 20:269]. He was taxable in Northampton County from 1786 to 1792 [PPTL, 1782-1823, frames 54, 119, 149]. He married Sinah **Sample** ("Free Negroes"), 7 June 1791 Northampton County bond, William Satchell security. On 9 July 1793 the Northampton County court bound Aaron Webb, son of Leah Webb, to him as an apprentice. He registered as a "free Negro" in Northampton County on 14 May 1794 [Orders 1789-95, 296, 349]. He was a "fn" taxable in Accomack County from 1800 to 1813, listed with wife Sinah and son Henry at Sleek Neck in 1813 [PPTL, 1782-1814, frames 437, 601, 835], head of a St. George Parish, Accomack County household of 6 "other free" in 1800 [*Virginia Genealogist* 2:165] and 9 in 1810 [VA:69]. He registered in Accomack County about 1832: *born about 1760, a Black, 5'8-3/4", born free in Accomack County.* His wife Sinah Webb registered about the same time: *born about 1762, a light black, 5'3-3/4" high, born free in Accomack County* [Register of Free Negroes, 1785-1863, nos. 623, 626].

ii.   Leah, mother of Aaron Webb (born Christmas 1785) who was bound
as an apprentice to (his uncle?) Charles Webb on 9 July 1793 [Orders
1789-95, 296]. Aaron married Catherine **Drighouse**, 31 December
1811 Northampton County bond, James **Carter** security. He was
taxable in Northampton County from 1809 to 1813 [PPTL, 1782-1823,
frames 459, 553]. Perhaps his widow was the Catherine Webb who
was head of a Northampton County, Virginia household of 7 "free
colored" in 1820 [VA:214A].

7.   _____ Webb, born say 1730, child of Daniel Webb, was the parent of Daniel's
grandchildren John and Elizabeth Webb who he gave a total of 34 pounds by
his 18 July 1769 New Hanover County will [Original, NC Archives].
Children:

i.   John, born say 1750, received twenty pounds by his grandfather's will.
He was taxable in Bladen County on one male and two female "Mixt
Bloods" in 1774, taxable on one "Black" male and two "Black" females
in 1776, taxable on 100 acres, four horses and three cattle in 1779,
taxable on 150 acres and one black poll in Captain Dupree's District
of Bladen County in 1784, taxable on four "Blacks" from 12-50 years
old and five under 12 or over 60 in 1786 and taxable on 200 acres in
1789 [Byrd, *Bladen County Tax Lists*, I:124; II:48, 97, 141, 169, 204;
Bladen Co. Historical Society, *1784 Tax List*, 13]. He was head of a
Bladen County household of 8 "other free" in 1800. His farm animals
and household goods were sold for a debt in Bladen County on 28
February 1797 [DB 12:51]. In 1810 he was in South Carolina, head of
a Richland District household of 6 "other free" [SC:176].

ii.   Elizabeth², head of a Bladen County household of 6 "other free" in
1800.

8.   William Webb, born say 1738, was taxable on a horse in Bladen County,
North Carolina, in 1779, taxable on 150 acres and one black poll in Captain
Dupree's District of Bladen County in 1784 and taxable on one "Black" male
from 12 to 50 years old in 1786 [Byrd, *Bladen County Tax Lists*, II:141, 173,
202; Bladen Co. Historical Society, *1784 Tax List,* 13]. He purchased 50 acres
in Bladen County on 3 October 1786 between Fryar and Slapass and another
50 acres on 30 October 1786 [DB 1:302; 25:243]. He was head of a Bladen
County household of 7 "other free" in 1800, 2 in 1810 [NC:204], and 4 "free
colored" in 1820 [NC:150]. His children may have been

i.   Daniel⁴, born say 1770, head of Brunswick County household of 8
"other free" in 1810 [NC:230] and 8 "free colored" in Cumberland
County in 1820 [NC:152]. He may have been the father of William²
Webb, born after 1776, head of a Cumberland County household of 5
"free colored" in 1820 [NC:153].

ii.   Pegg, a "Malatto," bound to William Rutlege by the 10 July 1790 New
Hanover County court [Minutes 1779-92, 388].

iii.   Benjamin, married Chloe Webb, "Blacks," on 13 June 1806 in St.
Philip's Parish, Charleston, South Carolina.

iv.   Matthew, petitioned the South Carolina State Legislature on 1 January
1791 to repeal the discriminatory laws against free African Americans
[Berlin, *Slaves Without Masters*, 65-66].

9.   Katherine Webb, born on 26 January 1732/3, one-year-old daughter of
Elizabeth Webb, was bound apprentice to Major James Forse and his wife
Margaret in Northampton County, Virginia, on 26 January 1733/4 [Minutes
1732-42, 89]. She was presented for bastard bearing on 8 May 1750, 10 July
1753, and on 8 June 1756. She petitioned the court on 13 August 1755 saying
she had been bound to John Ellegood and completed her servitude while
serving his son by the same name. However, he sold her to George Scott for

a further five years. The court ordered that she be discharged and paid her freedom dues [Orders 1748-51, 207, 228, 241; Orders 1751-3, 293, 316; 1753-8, 243, 248, 330]. She was awarded 2 pounds by the court on 11 July 1786 in her suit against Charles Floyd for debt. Her suit for trespass against Peter Warren was dismissed by the court on 13 March 1793. She and Grace Webb registered as "free Negroes" in Northampton County on 13 June 1794 [Orders 1783-7, 501; 1789-95, 276, 364]. She was the mother of

i. ?Elishe², born about 1748, bound to Stratton Caple on 11 June 1755 [Orders 1753-8, 219].

ii. ?Bridget, born in August 1750, bound to Stratton Caple on 11 June 1755 [Orders 1753-8, 219].

iii. Isaac², born in September 1752, the three-year-old son of Catherine Webb (no race mentioned), bound apprentice to George Scott on 9 September 1755. He was eleven years old when he was bound to John Wilkins, Sr., Gent., on 10 January 1764 [Orders 1754-61, 251; Minutes 1761-5, 95]. He was living with his wife Margaret on 20 March 1778 when he was charged with felony in Northampton County court and sent for further trial. He was awarded 12 pounds on 9 June 1784 in his suit against Kendall Goodwin for trespass [Minutes 1777-83, 43; Orders 1783-7, 126]. He was taxable in Northampton County from 1783 to 1789: taxable on a free male tithable in 1789 [PPTL, 1782-1823, frames 16, 29, 54, 105]. He and (his wife) Peggy Webb registered as "free Negroes" in Northampton County on 11 June 1794 [Orders 1789-95]. He was head of an Accomack Parish, Accomack County household of 3 "other free" in 1800 [*Virginia Genealogist* 2:83] and 3 in 1810 [VA:69].

iv. ?Susanna, born in August 1756, bound apprentice to James Ellot in Northampton County on 8 October 1765 [Minutes 1765-71, 19].

v. ?Grace, registered as a "free Negro" in Northampton County on 13 June 1794. She died before 16 September 1795 when the court ordered the Overseers of the Poor of the second district to bind her sons John and James Webb to (their uncle?) Isaac Webb [Orders 1789-95, 296, 507].

Other members of the Webb family in Virginia were

i. Aaron, born say 1760, a "Negro" bound to John Stripe, Jr., by the Northampton County court on 10 May 1763 [Minutes 1761-5, 65]. He was taxable in Northumberland County in 1787.

ii. Armstead, born 1 March 1762, a ten-year-old "negro" bound apprentice in Northampton County on 11 August 1772 [Minutes 1771-77, 77]. He was taxable in York County from 1791 to 1812, head of a household of 4 "free Negroes and mulattoes above 16," two of whom were tithable in 1813 [PPTL, 1782-1841, frames 175, 185, 196, 214, 248, 259, 280, 320, 357, 397, 413] and head of a York County household of 5 "other free" in 1810 [VA:886].

iii. Mark, born 11 June 1769, bound to William **Roberts**, Sr., by the Northampton County court on 14 April 1779 [Minutes 1777-83, 148]. He was taxable in Northampton County from 1790 to 1792 [PPTL, 1782-1823, frames 119, 142, 149] and taxable in Western Branch Precinct of Norfolk County from 1796 to 1814: called a "M"(ulatto) in 1801 when he and William Webb were labourers [PPTL, 1791-1812, frames 181, 382, 384, 491, 585, 698, 750; 1813-24, frames 16].

iv. Levin, born in February 1771, a three-year-old "negro" bound apprentice to Mark **Beckett** in Northampton County on 10 May 1774 [Minutes 1771-77, 251]. He was taxable in Northampton from 1794 to 1800 [PPTL, 1782-1823, frames 184, 295] and head of a Northampton County, Virginia household of 9 "free colored" in 1820 [VA:215].

    v.   Southy, born say 1774, an orphan who complained to the Northampton County court against Thomas Speakman on 13 November 1781. He was bound to Major Brickhouse on 12 June 1782 [Minutes 1777-83, 331, 364]. He married Ann **Miles**, 26 October 1795 Northampton County bond, John Carpenter security. He was taxable in Northampton County from 1795 to 1812 [PPTL, 1782-1823, frames 201, 294, 520].

    vi.   William, a "free Negro" taxable in Northampton County in 1796 [PPTL, 1782-1823, frame 219].

Spotsylvania County, Virginia

1.   Frances Webb, born say 1705, was called "Francis Tibbo a Mullato" in Spotsylvania County court on 3 October 1733 when her master, James Roy, petitioned to have her son George bound to him. The court ruled that the case was "not properly coming before this Court." On 1 July 1735 she petitioned the court for her freedom from Roy, stating that she had been bound until the age of thirty-one and that her time had expired. She was called "Frances Webb alias Tibbo" in December 1735 when the court ruled that she should be free on 22 April 1736 according to a letter from Mrs. Frances Smith, widow of William Bird, Gent., who sold her to David Darnell. On 2 March 1735/6 James Roy petitioned the court for an additional year of service from her for having a bastard child, but the court ruled that the law did not apply to her because she was a "Mullatto." She was probably the mother of the "Mulatto girl," about eleven or twelve years old and bound until the age of thirty-one, who was listed in the estate of David Darnell on 2 February 1742/3 [Orders 1735-8, 401, 412, 423; 1740-2, 204]. She was living in adjoining King George County on 5 September 1740 when the court ordered that she serve Peter Lee twelve months for having a bastard child and that the child be bound to Lee by the churchwardens of Brunswick Parish until the age of eighteen. A suit brought by the churchwardens of Brunswick Parish was dismissed on 5 June 1741 and another dismissed on 6 August 1742 because it had not been executed [King George Orders 1735-51, 240, 254, 296]. On 5 December 1758 the Spotsylvania County court bound her illegitimate "Mullatto" sons John and Richard Tibbo, who were born after her servitude, to John Carter, Gent., until the age of twenty-one [Orders 1755-65, 127]. She was the mother of

    i.   Catherine Webb alias Tibbo, born about 1729, probably the "Mulatto girl," about eleven or twelve years old and bound until the age of thirty-one, who was listed in the Spotsylvania County estate of David Darnell on 2 February 1742/3. She sued her master Thomas Roy for her freedom in Spotsylvania County court on 7 December 1756, but the court ruled that she serve him another three years from 3 March 1757. It also ruled that he provide her with warm clothing [Orders 1755-65, 59, 64].

    ii.   George, born before 3 October 1733, perhaps the George Web who was head of a New Kent County household of one "other free" and two slaves in 1810 [VA:772].

    iii.   John, born say 1748.

    iv.   Richard Webb, born about 1750, a 25-30 year old "mulatto" servant who ran away from Hunter's Forge near Falmouth according to the 13 November 1778 edition of the *Virginia Gazette* [Headley, *18th Century Newspapers*, 360].

Other members of the family in Virginia were

    i.   Betsy, head of a Richmond City household of 4 "other free" and 2 slaves in 1810 [VA:317].

    ii.   William, head of a Norfolk County household of 6 "other free" in 1810 [VA:815]. He married Sally **Bailey**, 18 December 1792 Norfolk County bond, James Williams surety.

iii. General, head of an Essex County household of 5 "other free" in 1810 [VA:208].

WEBSTER FAMILY

Members of the Webster family were
  i. Thomas, born say 1745, presented by the Charles County, Maryland court in August 1772 for failing to list as a tithable his wife who was a slave hired to him. He was fined 500 pounds for the offense in November 1772 [Court Records 1772-3, 2, 171]. He was a "Mulatto" head of a Charles County household of 3 "other free" in 1790.
  ii. Daniel, born about 1752, head of a Prince William County, Virginia household of 6 "other free" in 1810 [VA:501], a sixty-year-old "free Negro" living in Prince William County in 1812 when he petitioned the legislature to allow him to free his wife and children who were his slaves [Petitions, Prince William County, 1812, cited by Russell, *The Free Negro in Virginia*, 92]. He and his wife Lucy were residing at Accoquan Mills in Prince William County on 28 September 1821 when their son William **Armstead** Webster registered in the Court of the District of Columbia in Alexandria: *free born, twenty-three years of age, a bright mulatto* [Arlington County Register of Free Negroes, 1797-1861, no. 89, p.65].
  iii. John, head of a Talbot County household of 8 "other free" in 1800 [MD:549].
  iv. Joseph, head of a Baltimore City household of 6 "other free" in 1800 [MD:391].

WEEKS FAMILY

1. Ann **Webb**, born about 1713, "a malatto...Born of ye body of Jane Webb ye wife of a Negro man belonging to Captain Thomas Savage," was bound to Savage by the Northampton County, Virginia court on 20 June 1716. She had four more years to serve when she was listed in the inventory of Thomas Savage's estate which was recorded on 12 May 1730 [Orders 1711-16, 255; DW 1725-33, 229-30]. On 9 May 1732 she was presented for bastard bearing and the same day petitioned the court against Sophia Savage who was detaining her children Daniel and Abraham in servitude on the pretense that Ann owed her three years of service for having three bastard children during her servitude. The court ordered that she be set free and ordered Mrs. Savage to deliver her clothes and bedding to her [Orders 1729-32, 143-5; 1732-42, 7, 8, 14]. She may have married or had children by John Weeks, a taxable in Gawton Hunt's household in the Northampton County list of John Forse from 1723 to 1731. He was listed separately from Hunt's "negroes": Eliza, Sarah, and Daniel and called "Weeks" only in 1726, 1728 and 1729 [L.P. 1723; Bell, *Northampton County Tithables*, 48, 65, 92, 116, 129, 146, 161, 172, 228]. On 12 February 1733/4 she was called Nanny Week, late Nanny Webb, when the court bound out her three-year-old "free Negroe" son Daniel to William Scott with her consent [Orders 1732-42, 92]. She was called Ann Weeks thereafter. She was taxable in Jacob Smith's household in the Northampton County list of John Robins for 1737, taxable in her own household in Captain Ralph Pigot's list for the lower precinct in 1739, taxable in Philip Jacob's household in 1740 and 1742, and taxable in her own household in the list of P. Norly Ellegood for 1744 [L.P. 1737, 1744; Bell, *Northampton County Tithables*, 254, 295, 305, 342, 361]. She won a suit against Stephen Whitehead for 50 bushels of corn on 14 November 1738 for one year's service. She was called "Anne Weaks, Negro" on 9 October 1739 when Edmund Custis, storekeeper, won a suit against her for payment of 1 pound/ 11 shillings for five yards of material, a gown, and a handkerchief [Orders 1732-42, 338, 371; Mihalyka,

Loose Papers, 101, 115]. The court bound her "orphan" son Peter Weeks to John Millard on 28 July 1750 but bound him instead to Alexander Kemp six months later based on her complaint. Her suit against John Frazer was dismissed on 11 February 1757 when the parties agreed [Orders 1748-51, 270, 339, 384]. She was the mother of the following members of the Weeks family:

    i.   Abraham, born about August 1728, called Abraham Webb, a "poor Negroe child" when he was bound apprentice to Benjamin Johnson by the Northampton County court with the consent of his mother Nanny Webb in June 1733 [Orders 1732-42, 57]. He was called Abraham Weeks Negro" when he was sued in Northampton County court by Samuel Grafton on 15 November 1749 [Orders 1748-51, 148; Orders 1751-3, 89]. He sued Caleb Weeks for trespass, assault and battery on 14 December 1757 and was sued by Hemphill for debt on 14 December 1757. On 14 November 1770 the court presented Isaac Clegg for not listing him as a tithable. He was sued for 8 pounds, 8 shillings on 8 March 1774 [Orders 1753-8, 471; Minutes 1761-5, 159; 1765-71, 399; 1771-7, 231]. He was taxable in Northampton County from 1782 to 1787: called a "Mulatto" in 1787 [PPTL, 1782-1823, frames 7, 12, 75] and head of an Accomack County household of 3 "other free" in 1800 [*Virginia Genealogist* 2:84].

    ii.   Daniel[1], born 4 May 1731, a "free Negroe" bound to William Scott by the Northampton County court on 12 February 1733/4 with the consent of his mother Nanny **Week**, late Nanny Webb [Minutes 1732-42, 92]. He was called "Daniel Weeks Negro" when he was awarded his freedom dues based on his suit against Benjamin Scott and John Ellegood in Northampton County on 14 August 1751. And he was called "Daniel Weeks Negro" when he was sued by Peter Hog on 11 July 1753, when he sued Thomas Speakman for trespass, assault and battery on 11 September 1754, and when he sued John Smaw for the same on 15 September 1756 [Orders 1748-51, 425; 1751-3, 8; 1753-8, 138, 361, 373].

2   iii.   Esther, born 4 July 1733.

    iv.   Leah[1], born 15 July 1735, two-year-old daughter of Ann Weeks (no race mentioned), bound apprentice to Thomas Church with the consent of her mother on 12 July 1737 [Minutes 1732-42, 270].

    v.   ?Peggy, born say 1739, presented in Northampton County on 13 July 1757 for bastard bearing [Orders 1753-8, 415, 431-2].

    vi.   Jerome, born in April 1741, nine-year-old "orphan of Ann," bound apprentice to John Millard on 28 July 1750 [Minutes 1748-51, 270], taxable Northampton County in Josias Willes household in 1765, in Jacob Freshwater's in 1769, and taxable from 1783 to 1800 [PPTL, 1782-1823, frames 16, 54, 177, 201, 296]. He registered as a "free Negro" in Northampton County on 10 June 1794 [Orders 1789-95, 354].

3   vii.   Jane, born 28 July 1745.

4   viii.   Peter[1], born 27 November 1746.

5   ix.   ?Dido, born say 1750.

6   x.   ?Ann[2], born about 1752.

    xi.   Daniel[2], born say 1754, "negro son of Anne Weeks," ordered bound to Azariah Hunt on 9 October 1759 [Minutes 1754-61, 202]. He was a "negro" taxable in Northampton County from 1785 to 1800: taxable on 5 slaves and a horse in 1787 [PPTL, 1782-1823, frames 47, 69, 178, 201, 296].

7   xii.   ?Barbara, born say 1756.

    xiii.   Jacob, born 23 March 1758, orphan of Ann Weeks, ordered bound apprentice to Nathaniel Stratton on 11 September 1759, a three-year-old called "Job Weeks Negro" when he was ordered bound to Thomas Widgeon on 11 August 1761 [Minutes 1754-61, 201, 265]. He

registered as a "free Negro" in Northampton County on 10 June 1794
[Orders 1789-95, 354]. He was taxable in Northampton County from
1790 to 1800 [PPTL, 1782-1823, frames 119, 149, 201, 295] and head
of a Northampton County, Virginia household of 8 "free colored" in
1820 [VA:214A].

    xiv.   ?William, taxable in Northampton

2.   Esther Weeks, born 4 July 1733, four-year-old daughter of Anne Weeks, was
bound apprentice by the Northampton County court to Joseph Toleman with
the consent of her mother on 12 July 1737 and bound to Ebenezer Toleman on
12 February 1744/5 [Orders 1732-42, 270; 1742-8]. On 11 December 1750 the
court presented her, a "Mulatto," for bastard bearing, but two months later on
13 February the sheriff reported that she was not found in the county [Orders
1748-51, 306, 333-4, 365-6]. She was called "Easter Weeks a Mullatto Servant
woman" on 15 May 1753 when the Princess Anne County court ordered that
she serve her master Thomas Garvis an additional year for having a child born
during her indenture [Minutes 1753-62, 15]. She registered as a "free Negro"
in Northampton County on 12 June 1794 [Orders 1789-95, 358]. She may
have been the mother of

    i.   Juda, born say 1744, taxable in Norfolk County in 1761 in the district
between the west side of Church Street and Town Bridge, called Judith
Wicks, free negro" in 1765, and taxable on the west side of Church
Street in Norfolk Borough in Edmund Bruce's household in 1767 and
1768 [Wingo, *Norfolk County Tithables 1751-65*, 183, 214; *1766-80*,
32, 80].

3.   Jane Weeks, born 28 July 1745, the five-year-old "orphan of Ann Weeks,"
was bound apprentice to John Millard on 28 July 1750. The court ordered her
whipped for bastardy on 14 September 1763, and on 14 November 1775 the
grand jury presented her for entertaining "slave Negros" in her house [Orders
1748-51, 270; Minutes 1761-5, 85; 1771-7, 298]. She registered as a "free
Negro" in Northampton County on 12 June 1794 [Orders 1789-95, 358]. She
may have been the mother of

8   i.   James[1], born say 1763.
    ii.   Gabriel, born 1 June 1765, three years old when he was bound to
William Floyd on 14 February 1769 [Minutes 1765-71, 277].
    iii.   Ann[3], born 11 October 1766, a "free Negro" bound to Luke Smaw on
11 March 1777 [Minutes 1771-7, 357].
    iv.   Bob, born 1 November 1780, son of Jenny Weeks, bound to John
Graves, Sr., on 14 May 1788 [Orders 1787-9, 143].

4.   Peter[1] Weeks, born 27 November 1746, the three-year-old "orphan of Ann
Weeks," was ordered bound apprentice to John Millard on 28 July 1750,
bound to Alexander Kemp on 13 February 1750/1, and bound to Robinson
Savage, Jr., on 11 July 1758 [Minutes 1748-51, 270, 339; 1753-8, 158]. He
was a "free Negro" taxable in Northampton County in 1769 [L.P. 1769]. He
was sued for debt on 11 August 1773 and was sued for a debt of 2 pounds, 15
shillings by a member of the **Jeffery** family on 13 April 1774 [Minutes 1771-
7, p.165, 247]. On 10 February 1779 the court ordered his son Daniel bound
out. He was the father of

    i.   Daniel[3], born say 1775, son of Peter Weeks, bound apprentice to Mr.
Christian on 10 February 1779 [Minutes 1777-83, 144]. He married
Nancy **Morris**, 6 July 1803 Northampton County bond, Abraham **Lang**
security.

5.   Dido Weeks, born say 1750, was a "free negro" mother of a child who had
contracted smallpox on 23 July 1777 when the magistrates of Northampton
County met at the courthouse to approve inoculation of the remainder of her

family by Doctor William Foushee. On 14 April 1784 Colonel John Robins received 10 Shillings which was allowed to Dido by the Northampton County court for nursing a man who had smallpox [Minutes 1777-83, 5; Orders 1783-7, 88]. She was the mother of

  i.   Susanna, daughter of Dida Weeks, bound to Peter Bowdoin on 11 December 1787 [Orders 1787-9, 79].

6. Ann[2] Weeks, born say 1752, was presented by the grand jury of Northampton County on 14 November 1775 for entertaining "slave Negros" in her house [Minutes 1771-7, 298]. She was the mother of

  i.   Betty, born in September 1775, four-year-old daughter of Ann Weeks bound apprentice to William Cable in Northampton County on 11 July 1780 [Minutes 1777-83, 254]. She registered as a "free Negro" in Northampton County on 12 June 1794 [Orders 1789-95, 358].

  ii. Littleton, born about 1785, son of Nanny Weeks, bound to John Graves, Sr., on 14 May 1788 [Orders 1787-9, 143].

7. Barbara Weeks, born say 1756, was the mother of

  i.   Zerobabel, born in August 1772, son of Barbara Weeks, bound apprentice to Thomas Bullock in Northampton County on 13 December 1780 [Minutes 1777-83, 298]. He married Nancy **Beavens**, 3 January 1793 Northampton County bond, Reubin **Reed** security. He registered as a "free Negro" in Northampton County on 12 June 1794 and his wife may have been the Nancy Weeks who registered on 10 June 1794 [Orders 1789-95, 358, 354]. He was taxable in Northampton County from 1794 to 1800 [PPTL, 1782-1823, frames 177, 201, 295].

8. James[1] Weeks, born say 1763, was a "negro" bound to Savage Cowdry by the Northampton County court on 14 August 1765 [Minutes 1765-71, 8]. He was taxable in Northampton County from 1788 to 1800 [PPTL, 1782-1823, frames 90, 119, 148, 296]. He and (his wife?) Rachel Weeks registered as "free Negroes" in Northampton County on 12 June 1794 [Orders 1789-95, 358]. He was head of a Northampton County, Virginia household of 7 "free colored" in 1820, called James Weeks, Sr. [VA:215]. He was the father of

  i.   Jacob, taxable in Northampton County from 1806 to 1815: called "son of James" in 1806 [PPTL, 1782-1823, frames 459, 552].

  ii. Eli, taxable in Northampton County from 1806 to 1808: called "son of James" in 1808 and 1812 [PPTL, 1782-1823, frames 420, 438, 459, 521], head of a York County household of 2 "free Negroes and mulattoes above 16" (probably himself and his wife) from 1813 to 1815 [PPTL, 1782-1841, frames 397, 413, 428].

Other members of the family in Northampton County were

  i.   John, born say 1765, taxable in Northampton County from 1786 to 1800: a "Negro" taxable in 1800 [PPTL, 1782-1823, frames 54, 119, 177, 201, 296], head of a Northampton County, Virginia household of 13 "free colored" in 1820 [VA:214A].

  ii. Leah[2], born 23 March 1769, a four-year-old (no parent or race mentioned) bound apprentice to Isabella Dunton on 23 May 1773 [Minutes 1771-7, 142].

  iii. William, taxable in Northampton County from 1790 to 1792 [PPTL, 1782-1823, frames 119, 149, 177].

  iv. Edmund, born about 1774, a seven-year-old (no parent or race mentioned) bound apprentice in Northampton County in December 1781 [Minutes 1777-83, 336].

  v.   Thomas, taxable in Northampton County from 1792 to 1795 [PPTL, 1782-1823, frames 148, 201].

vi. Jeremiah, born before 1776, head of a Northampton County, Virginia household of 5 "free colored" in 1820 [VA:215A].

vii. Meriah, born before 1776, head of a Northampton County, Virginia household of 6 "free colored" in 1820 [VA:214A].

viii. James[2], born in September 1775, a four-year-old (no parent or race mentioned) bound apprentice to James Smith on 15 September 1779 to learn the shoemaker's trade [Minutes 1777-83, 196]. He registered as a "free Negro" in Northampton County on 13 June 1794 [Orders 1789-95, 364]. He was taxable in Northampton County from 1800 to 1815 [PPTL, 1782-1823, frames 295, 553]. He married Peggy **Stephens**, 8 May 1810 Northampton County bond, Richard Johnson security. He was head of a Northampton County, Virginia household of 5 "free colored" in 1820 [VA:214A].

ix. Lucy, married Peter **Wakefield**, 7 September 1794 Northampton County bond, Nathaniel Holland security. Peter may have been related to Mary **Wakefield**, head of a Petersburg household of 2 "other free" in 1810 [VA:125b].

x. Comfort, married George **Pool**, 10 May 1793 Northampton County bond, Abraham **Lang** security.

xi. Levi, married Peggy **Stephens**, 6 January 1809 Northampton County bond, James Travis security.

Other members of the family were

i. Peter[2], born say 1758, a "mulatto lad" who said he belonged to John Parker of Accomack County when he was jailed as a runaway in York County according to the 7 July 1775 edition of the *Virginia Gazette* [Headley, *18th Century Newspapers*, 360].

ii. Haley, head of a Dinwiddie County household of 3 "other free" in 1810 [VA:166].

WELCH FAMILY

1. Mary[1] Welsh, born say 1690, was a convict servant from Baltimore County, Maryland, who married a slave named Bankka. They had four daughters: Mary, Katherine, Esther, and Jemima. Some of her children adopted the name **Banneker** [Barnes, *Baltimore County Families, 1659-1759*; Bedini, *Life of Benjamin Banneker*, 19]. They were the parents of

2   i. Mary, born say 1710.

2. Mary[2] Welch, born say 1710, was the servant of Thomas Harwood on 13 November 1728 when she admitted to the Prince George's County, Maryland court that she had a "Malatto" child. The court bound her for an additional seven years and bound her two-month-old son Henry to her master until the age of thirty-one [Court Records 1728-9, 346-7]. She was married to a former slave named Robert and they were using the name **Banneker** by March 1736 when the Baltimore County court declared that they were levy free during the lifetime of their "crippled mulatto" daughter Julian [Barnes, *Baltimore County Families, 1659-1759*]. On 10 March 1737 Robert purchased 100 acres in Patapsco Upper Hundred, Baltimore County, called "Stout," for 7,000 pounds of tobacco, listing his six-year-old son Benjamin as co-owner [Land Records HWS #IA, ff. 58-9]. He had also acquired 25 acres, called "Timber Point," before 1737 when he was taxable on both tracts [Debt Book, Baltimore County, Calvert Papers No. 904, p.69 in the Maryland Historical Society by Bedini, *Life of Benjamin Banneker*, 29, 347]. Robert was called "Robert Banakey, a Negro free," on 1 November 1743 when the Baltimore County court ordered that his daughters be levy free for the future [Proceedings 1743-6, 78]. Robert died on 10 July 1759 according to the entry in his family Bible. He had daughters Molly, who married a member of the **Morten** family, and

Minta who married a member of the **Black** family [Bedini, *Life of Benjamin Banneker*, 46-7]. Mary, widow of Robert **Bannaker**, was still living on 19 April 1774 when she deposed that Benjamin was the true and lawful son of Robert **Banneker**, deceased [Baltimore Chattel Records 4:98]. Mary and Robert were the parents of

3   i.   ?Henry **Welch**, born 28 September 1728.

ii.   Molly, born say 1730, married a member of the **Morton** family, perhaps identical to Samuel **Morton** who was listed in the Ledger of Ellicott & Company between September 1774 and July 1775. They were the parents of Greenbury **Morten** who was employed at Ellicott's Lower Mills [Bedini, *Life of Benjamin Banneker*, 62]. Greenbury was head of a Patapsco Hundred, Baltimore County household of 7 "other free" in 1810 [MD:644]. Another member of the **Morton** family was Deb. **Morton**, head of a Baltimore City household of 6 "other free" in 1810 [MD:280], perhaps identical to the Deb **Morton** who was counted in Baltimore City with 8 "other free" in 1810 [MD:300].

iii.   Benjamin **Banneker**, born 9 November 1731, taxable as a bachelor owning 100-300 pounds in St. Paul's Parish, Baltimore, sometime between 1756 and 1762 [Wright, *Inhabitants of Baltimore County 1692-1763*, 75]. He sold 20 acres of his land to Greenbury **Morten** on 20 December 1785, and 10 acres to his neighbor, John **Barton** on 2 April 1792 [Land Records WQ# Y, ff. 653-4; WG #HH. ff. 341-2]. This was land his father had purchased in 1737. John **Barton** was head of a Patapsco Upper Hundred, Baltimore County household of 5 "other free" in 1810 [MD:639]. He also sold two acres to Edward **Shugar** on 10 December 1794 [Land Records WG #PP:606-8]. Edward was head of a Patapsco Upper Hundred household of 5 "other free" in 1810 [MD:641].

iv.   Julian, born say 1733, the "crippled" daughter of Robert and Mary **Banneker**.

v.   a daughter, married a member of the **Black** family.

vi.   a daughter, perhaps Ursula Banninger who was presented by the Prince George's County court in 1768 for having a "Malatto" child on information of the constable of Rock Creek Hundred [Court Records 1766-8, 574; 1768-70, 477]. She may have been the wife of William **Hubbard/ Hubert**, head of a Patapsco Upper Hundred, Baltimore County household of 5 "other free" in 1810 [MD:639]. William was the father of Henry and Charles **Hubbard** who obtained certificates of freedom in Loudoun County on 24 December 1795: *son of a free woman and grandson of Robert Banneker, whose wife was also a free woman. Robert Banneker lived in Baltimore County about two and a half miles from Ellicott's Mills* [Certificates of Freedom in Loudoun County Courthouse, cited by *Journal of the AAHGS* 11:123].

3.   Henry[1] **Welch**, born 28 September 1728, son of Mary Welch, may have been the father of

i.   Henry[2], a "yellow" complexioned soldier born in King George County, Virginia, who was living in Culpeper County between 1777 and 1783 when he enlisted in the Revolution as a substitute [NSDAR, *African American Patriots*, 154].

Other members of the family were

i.   Dan **Welsh**, a "Mulatta boy" listed in the 3 February 1748/9 inventory of the King George County, Virginia estate of Thomas Bartlett [Inventories 1745-65, 36].

ii.   Sarah **Welsh**, a "Mulatta girl" listed in the 3 February 1748/9 inventory of the King George County, Virginia estate of Thomas Bartlett [Inventories 1745-65, 36].

iii. Rebecca, head of a Loudoun County, Virginia household of 3 "other free" in 1810 [VA:291].
iv. Clary, head of a Stafford County, Virginia household of 2 "other free" in 1810 [VA:127].

WELLS FAMILY

1. Ann Wells, born say 1750, was a Northampton County, North Carolina taxable on an assessment of 105 pounds in 1780. She received a grant for 128 acres in Northampton County on Corduroy Swamp on 9 October 1783 [DB 7:274]. She was head of a Northampton County household of 1 "Black" person 12-50 years old and 3 "Black" persons less than 12 or over 50 years old in Elisha Webb's District in 1786 for the state census, 6 "other free" in 1790 [NC:75], 5 in 1800 [NC:483], 6 in 1810 [NC:753], and 4 "free colored" in 1820 [NC:266]. She was the mother of
   i. King, born 1776-94, head of a Northampton County household of 3 "free colored" in 1820 [NC:266].
   ii. Anthony, charged with bastardy in Northampton County court by Amey **Allen**, on 7 June 1820 [Minutes 1817-21, 281]. He may have been the Anson Wells of Columbia County, Ohio, who gave Henry Deberry his power of attorney to sell 79 acres in Northampton County to King Deberry on 12 February 1838 [DB 28:257, 258].

WEST FAMILY

1. Mary West, born say 1690, left Accomack County before 7 July 1718 when William Wise petitioned the court to bind to him a "Mullatto boy" named William West, six-year-old son of Mary West who had left the boy with him [Orders 1717-9, 15a]. She was in York County on 15 January 1721/2 when the court presented her for having an illegitimate "Mullatto" child. She failed to appear at the next session of the court in March, and in August 1722 the court directed John Holloway, Esq., and Henry Tyler, Gent., to examine witnesses relating to the cause. The case was decided against her on 21 January 1722/3 when the court ordered her to pay the churchwardens 15 pounds sterling for having a "Mullatto" child. On 17 May 1736 the court presented her for having a bastard child by a "Molatto" [OW 15, pt. 2, 10, 120, 134, 153, 179; W&I 18:279]. She was the mother of
2 i. ?Martha, born say 1710.
   ii. William[1], born about 1712.

2. Martha West, born say 1710, was a "Mollato" woman living in Yorkhampton Parish, York County, on 17 July 1732 when the court ordered the churchwardens to bind her two "Mollato" boys Charles and James to her mistress Sarah Walker until the age of thirty-one, "being the time their mother was bound for" [OW 17:295]. She was the mother of
   i. Charles, born say 1730.
   ii. James[1], born say 1732, perhaps the James West who was head of a Fredericksburg household of 9 "other free" and a slave in 1810 [VA:111a]. He was a soldier in the Revolution [Jackson, *Virginia Negro Soldiers*, 46].
   iii. ?Sarah, living in York County on 16 November 1761 when (her employer?) Thomas Craig was presented by the court for not listing her as a tithable. The case was dismissed when he paid her levy [Judgments & Orders 1759-63, 298, 312].

Other members of the West family were
   i. Will[2], born say 1765, head of a Bladen County, North Carolina household of 3 "other free" in 1790.

ii.   James[2], born say 1767, head of a Spotsylvania County household of 10 "other free" in 1810 [VA:102a].
iii. Benjamin, head of a Middlesex County household of 2 "other free" in 1810.
iv.   Susanna, head of a Nelson County household of one "other free" in 1810.
v.   Peter, head of a Nelson County household of one "other free" in 1810.

Brunswick County, Virginia
1.   Anne West, born say 1729, (a white woman?) was living in Brunswick County, Virginia, in April 1747 when the churchwardens of St. Andrew's Parish were ordered to bind her "Mulatto" daughter Frances West to Richard Berry [Orders 1745-49, 156]. Her child was
i.   Frances, born say 1747.

WHARTON FAMILY

Members of the Wharton family of North Carolina were
1   i.   Daniel, born say 1730.
     ii. Jacob, born say 1750, a free "Mulatto" taxable in Bertie County in Martha Hinton's household in the list of Josiah Harrell in 1769 [CR 10.702.1, box 2].

1.   Daniel[1] Wharton, born say 1730, was a "Mulato" taxable in Bladen County with his wife and son Richard in 1768 and with his wife and son Daniel in 1771 [Byrd, *Bladen County Tax Lists*, I:7, 17, 36, 58]. He was the father of
i.   Richard, born say 1750, a "Molato" taxable in Bladen County in his father's household in 1768 and taxable with his wife and Jacob **Braveboy** in 1771 [Byrd, *Bladen County Tax Lists*, I:7, 62].
ii.   Daniel[2], born say 1755, a "Molato" taxable in Bladen County in his father's household in 1771 [Byrd, *Bladen County Tax Lists*, I:58].

WHISTLER FAMILY

1.   Mary[1] Whistler, born say 1697, was fined 500 pounds of tobacco by the Middlesex County court on 2 June 1719 for having a bastard child (no race indicated) [Orders 1710-21, 427]. She was the mother of Anne, "an illegitimate mulatto daughter," born in Christ Church Parish, Middlesex County, on 12 April 1715. On 2 May ___ (1720?) Mary was called a "mulatto in ye Service of John Price" when the birth of her daughter Betty was recorded in Christ Church Parish. Mary died on 14 December and was buried on 19 December 1720 [NSCDA, *Parish Register of Christ Church Parish, Middlesex County*, 92, 310, 177]. She was the mother of
2   i.   Anne, born 12 April 1715.
     ii. Betty, born 2 May ___ (1718?).
     iii. Will, born 26 April___ (1720?) son of Mary Whistler a mulatto in ye Service of John Price."[212]

2.   Anne Whistler, born 12 April 1715, "mulatto" daughter of Mary Whistler, was baptized in Christ Church Parish, Middlesex County on 4 November 1715. She was the mother of
3   i.   Mary[2]/ Molly, born 18 December 1736.

3.   Mary[2] Whistler was born 18 December 1736 in Christ Church Parish, Middlesex County [NSCDA, *Parish Register of Christ Church Parish,*

---

[212]The year is missing from the register, but the entries before and after this are 1720.

Middlesex County, 144]. She was living in Essex County on 16 June 1789 when John Clarke complained to the court that he was deprived of the indenture of Mary's children Milly and Tom by a former order of the court. The court ordered Mary to appear at the next court to show cause why they should not be bound to Clarke [Orders 1788-90, 198]. She registered in Middlesex County on 27 May 1801: born free; *60 years of age; 5'1-1/2"; Dark complexion* [Register of Free Negroes 1800-60, p.15]. She may have been the Molly Whistler who was head of a Richmond City household of 6 "other free" in 1810 [VA:365]. She was the mother of

    i. ?Alexander/ Sawney, born free in Middlesex County in 1762, a man of dark complexion who served in the Revolution for three years and received a warrant for 200 acres which he assigned to Richard Smith on 30 July 179_. He served in the Revolution from Middlesex County as a substitute [M804-2549, frame 0028; NSDAR, *African American Patriots*, 154; Jackson, *Virginia Negro Soldiers*, 46]. He was a "Black" taxable in the lower district of King and Queen County in 1801 [PPTL, 1782-1803]. He registered in Middlesex County on 26 June 1805: born free; *40 years of age; Black complexion* [Register of Free Negroes 1800-60, p.15].

    ii. ?Philip, born about 1770, registered in Middlesex County on 2 June 1802: *born free; 32 years of age; 5'7"; Black complexion* [Register of Free Negroes 1800-60, p.15].

    iii. Thomas, born about 1780, registered in Middlesex County on 27 May 1801: *born free; 21 years of age; 5'2"; Dark complexion* [Register of Free Negroes 1800-60, p.15].

    iv. Millie, born about 1780, registered in Middlesex County on 27 May 1801: *born free; 21 years of age; 4'11"; Dark complexion* [Register of Free Negroes 1800-60, p.15].

WHITE FAMILY

1. Eleanor White, born say 1695, was living in Princess Anne County on 1 June 1715 when the court ordered the churchwardens to sell her for five years as punishment for having a "Molatto" child [Minutes 1709-17, 186]. She was probably the mother of

2   i. Jane, born say 1715.

2. Janney White, born say 1715, was among nine persons who were presented by the Norfolk County, Virginia court on 16 November 1744 for not paying the discriminatory tax on free African American and Indian women [Orders 1742-46, 108]. She was probably the mother of

    i. John[1], born say 1744, taxable with (his wife?) Lucy White in the Borough of Norfolk in 1765 [Wingo, *Norfolk County Tithables, 1751-65*, 218].

<u>York County</u>
1. Mary White, born say 1696, was a "free Mulatto Woman" living in York Hampton Parish, York County, on 20 August 1716 when the grand jury presented her for having a bastard child. She was ordered to pay 500 pounds of tobacco or suffer corporal punishment. She paid the fine on 16 September 1717 and Charles Haynes was her security for indemnifying the parish for the child's support [OW 15, pt. 1, 23, 30, 162]. She may have been the ancestor of

    i. Ben, head of a York County household of 5 "other free" in 1810 [VA:886].

Stafford County
1.   Moll White, born say 1680, was the servant of Mr. Hart of Stafford County
     in 1700 when the court presented her for having a "Mulatto" child [WB Liber
     Z:51]. She may have been the ancestor of
     i.   David, a "Molato Bastard" bound to George McCormuck by order of
           the Fairfax County court on 17 June 1772 [Orders 1772-4, 85].
     ii.   Harvey, "F.Negroe" head of a Fauquier County household of 2 "other
           free" in 1810 [VA:417].
     iii. Juday, "F. Negroe" head of a Fauquier County household of 1 "other
           free" in 1810 [VA:420].
     iv.   Milly, head of a Fredericksburg, Spotsylvania County household of 2
           "other free" in 1810 [VA:111b].

North Carolina
1.   _____ White, born say 1726, was the unnamed mother of Susannah White, the
     "Mulatto" child of a white woman, who was bound apprentice in New
     Hanover County, North Carolina court to Moses John Derosset on 5
     September 1756 [Minutes 1738-69, 166, 185]. She was the mother of
2   i.   ?Cato, born say 1750.
           ii.   Susannah, born about 1756.

2.   Cato White, born say 1750, was head of a Craven County, North Carolina
     household of 7 "other free" in 1790 [NC:130], 5 "other free" in the town of
     Washington, Beaufort County, in 1800 [NC:23], and head of a Beaufort
     County household in 1810 [NC:141]. He may have been the father of
     i.   Mona, whose four-year-old "Mullattoe" child Polly was bound
           apprentice to Daniel L. Woolard by the June 1810 Beaufort County
           court. She was called Moning White in June 1812 when Polly was
           bound to Alligood Woolard [Minutes 1809-14, n.p.].
     ii.   William, whose son William, a free boy of Color, was bound to John
           Wolfkencon to be a mariner in June 1813 Beaufort County court
           [Minutes 1809-14, n.p.].

Other members of the White family were
     i.   Jesse, head of a Robeson County household of 6 "other free" in 1810
           [NC:241].
     ii.   Dick, head of a Pasquotank County household of 7 "other free" in 1810
           [NC:939].
     iii. Randolph, head of a Norfolk County household of 1 "other free" in
           1810 [VA:814].
     iv.   John[2], born circa 1790, head of an Edgecombe County household of 6
           "other free" in 1810 [NC:715] and 4 "free colored" in Halifax County
           in 1830. On 17 May 1841 the Halifax County court permitted him to
           carry a gun in the county.

WHITEHURST FAMILY

1.   Sarah Whitehurst, born say 1722, was a "free" head of a Princess Anne
     County household of 3 "Black" persons in 1783 [VA:61]. She may have been
     the mother of
     i.   James, born say 1740, a "Mulatto" taxable with his wife Violet in the
           Norfolk County district from Ferry Point to Great Bridge from 1761
           to 1771, the year he was called a free Indian [Wingo, *Norfolk County
           Tithables, 1751-65*, 181, 204; *1766-80*, 43, 63, 102, 140]. He sued
           Marshall **Anderson** in Princess Anne County court for four pounds on
           10 May 1782. Isaac **Anderson** testified in his favor [Minutes 1782-4,
           67]. He was a "free negro" head of a Princess Anne County household
           of 7 "Black" persons in 1783 [VA:61]. He married, second, Dorothy

Sample, 4 October 1786 Princess Anne County bond, George Smyth surety.

ii. Jesse, born say 1745, was a "free negro" head of a Princess Anne County household of 6 "Black" persons in 1783 [VA:61] and a "F.B." head of a Princess Anne County household of 8 in 1810 [VA:480]. He married (second?) Mrs. **Lavery**, "a free mulatto," 7 December 1815 Norfolk County bond, Armistead Willis security, married the same day by Thomas T. Jones, Methodist Elder. Mrs. **Lavery** may have been related to the **Munlavery** family. See the **Mongon** history.

iii. Joseph, born say 1758, a "free Negro" taxable in his own household in Princess Anne County in 1784 [*Virginia Genealogical Society Quarterly* 27:267].

iv. Charles, born say 1760, head of a household of 4 "whites" in Upper Precinct of the Eastern Shore District of Princess Anne County in 1783 and 1785 [VA:61, 104], married Sally **Anderson**, 8 February 1788 Princess Anne County bond, Joseph Whitehurst surety.

v. Nancy, born say 1763, married Marvel **Anderson**, 7 January 1791 Princess Anne County bond, Charles Whitehurst surety.

vi. Nathaniel, born say 1765, married Anne **Weaver**, 1 April 1789 Princess Anne County bond, Charles Whitehurst surety, 4 April 1789 marriage.

WIGGINS FAMILY

1. Anne[1] Wiggins, born say 1682, was the servant of the estate of Captain Spencer Mottrom on 20 January 1702/3 when she was convicted by the Northumberland County court for having an illegitimate child by a "Negroe." According to testimony at her trial, her "Mulatto" son was begotten by a one of Mottrom's slaves named Billy about December 1700. On 6 July 1708 she bound her three-year-old son John (no race indicated) to Richard Tulles of St. Stephen's Parish until the age of twenty-two. Tulles agreed to pay James Magow eight hundred pounds of tobacco for keeping the boy for fourteen months. Ann recorded the indenture in court five years later on 16 September 1713 [Orders 1699-1713, pt. 1, 231, 235, 236, 238; pt. 2, 841; Record Book 1706-20, 204]. She was the ancestor of

   i. John, 25 February 1705, bound as an apprentice cooper to Richard Tulles on 6 July 1708. He was a "Molatto" of St. Stephens Parish who was presented in Northumberland County court on 10 November 1746 for being a "common swearer" [Orders 1743-49, 133].

2 ii. ?Sarah[1], born say 1725.

3 iii. ?Violet, born say 1726.

2. Sarah[1] Wiggins, born say 1725, was a "free Mulatto" taxable in James Morris' household in the 1764 Bertie County list of Thomas Pugh and in the household of her son Edward in the 1766 list of Arthur Brown [CR 10.702.1, box 1]. She was head of a Hertford County household of 8 "other free" in 1790 [NC:26], 7 in 1800, and 8 in 1810 [NC:106]. Her children were

4 i. Edward, born say 1745.

   ii. ?Judah, born say 1748, mother of Sarah[2], a ten-year-old child bound an apprentice in Bertie County in 1774. Sarah[2] Wiggins was head of a Bertie County household of 9 "free colored" in 1820 [NC:116].

   iii. ?Samuel, born say 1750, head of a Bertie County household of 13 "other free" in 1790 [NC:15]. He may have been living in the part of Bertie County which became Hertford County after 1759 since he was not taxed in the colonial Bertie County lists. He was head of a Hertford County household of 6 "other free" in 1800 and 11 "free colored" in 1820 [NC:182].

iv.   ?Charles, born about 1753, a taxable "molato" in Bertie County in 1769 in Cullen Pollock's list, a taxable "Molattow" in 1772 in the household of Jethro Kitterell in James Churchwell's list, and taxable with his unnamed wife in the list of Samuel Granberry in 1774.

v.   ?Ann², born about 1757, a taxable "molattow" in the Bertie County list of Jonathan Standley in 1769.

vi.   ?Matthew, born about 1757, a "free Mulatto" taxable in the Bertie County list of Cullen Pollock in 1769 and taxable as Matthias in the 1774 list of Samuel Granberry. He was called Mathias Wiggins (a Mulatto) when he married Prissey **Tabert (Taborn**?), 3 January 1786 Bertie County bond. Matthew was head of an Edgecombe County household of 4 "other free" in 1790 [NC:55]. He died before 13 February 1833 when his brother Arthur applied for a pension in Bertie County court. His widow Prissey was probably identical to Prisey Wiggins who married Robert **Corn**, 12 December 1802 Wake County bond.

vii.   ?Arthur, born in Bertie County about 1758 but not listed in the tax records. He was living in Bertie County in 1779 when he was drafted in the town of Winton, Hertford County. In his pension application in Bertie County court on 13 February 1833 he mentioned his brother Matthew [M804-2572, frame 0377]. He was head of a Bertie household of 5 "other free" in 1800 [NC:86], 4 in 1810 [NC:163], and 3 "free colored" in 1820 [NC:114].

viii.   ?James, born about 1760, a taxable "free Molatto" in Solomon Pender's Bertie County tax list in 1772.

ix.   ?Major, born say 1761, a "Molato" taxable (with Bud **Chavers**) in the Bladen County household of Archibald McKissak, Jr., in 1776 [Byrd, *Bladen County Tax Lists*, I:68].

x.   ?Michael, born about 1762, a taxable in the list of Samuel Granberry in Derias(?) Brimage's Bertie County household in 1774. He was head of a Bertie County household of 4 "other free" in 1790 [NC:15].

xi.   ?Jean, born about 1763, a taxable "molatto" in the list of David Standly in Luke Smithwick's Bertie County household in 1775.

xii.   William, born about 1764, orphan of Sarah bound to Josiah Goddens by the June 1769 Bertie court [Haun, *Bertie County Court Minutes*, III:864].

3.   Violet Wiggens, born say 1726, was a "Free Mullo Woman" whose children were ordered bound to Peter Matthews of Craven County, North Carolina, by the March 1750 court [Haun, *Craven County Court Minutes*, IV:26]. Her children were

i.   Dolphin, born April 1745.
ii.   Flora, born October 1747.

4.   Edward Wiggins, born say 1745, was a "free Mulatto" taxable in James Moore's household in the 1763 Bertie County, North Carolina tax list of John Hill [CR 10.702.1, box 1]. By 1766 he was head of his own household with his "Wife Sarah" and "Mother Sarah Wiggins" in the 1768 list of Arthur Brown. In 1774 he was head of a Bertie County household with his wife and (his brother-in-law?) James **Price**, a "Molato," in the list of Samuel Granberry [CR 10.702.1, box 3]. The November 1774 Bertie County court of Pleas and Quarter Sessions ordered Jemima Wiggins, eight years old, and Mary Beth Wiggins, ten years old, "bastard Mulattos of Sarah Wiggins," bound to John Skinner. However, this order was reversed in the May 1775 court session when Edward Wiggins, the children's father, convinced the court "of the said Skinners ill & deceitful Behavior procuring sd Order" [Haun, *Bertie County Court Minutes*, III:113; IV:157]. Edward was head of a Northampton County

household of 3 "other free" in 1800 [NC:483] and 4 in 1810 [NC:751]. Their children were

    i.   Mary Beth, born about 1764, ordered bound an apprentice by the Bertie court in November 1774 [Haun, *Bertie County Court Minutes*, III:113], perhaps the Mary Wiggins who was head of a Sampson County household of 6 "other free" in 1790, listed near Patty Wiggins, head of a Sampson County household of 5 "other free" [NC:53].

    ii.   Jemima, born about 1766, ordered bound an apprentice by the Bertie court in November 1774 [Haun, *Bertie County Court Minutes*, III:113].

WILKINS FAMILY

1.   Thomas Wilkins, born say 1720, may have been the husband of Olive Wilkins who was living in Southampton County on 8 November 1750 when she was charged with having a bastard child. The case was dismissed for want of prosecution. Thomas was one of fourteen people sued for tax evasion in Southampton County by William Bynum (quitam) on 13 June 1754, apparently for not listing their wives as tithables. The case against him was dismissed [Orders 1749-54, 96, 111; 1754-9, 500]. Thomas may have been the father of

2   i.   Jonas, born say 1745.

    ii.   James, born say 1748, grandfather of Robert Wilkins who was born about 1799 according to his 17 October 1818 Dinwiddie County free papers which he recorded 27 March 1821 in Ross County, Ohio: *grandson of James Wilkins, aged about 19 years, black complexion, 5 ft, 9 in., occupation waggoner, was born free* [Turpin, *Register of Black, Mulatto, and Poor Persons*, 23].

    iii.   William, born say 1750, a "Mulato" taxable in Bladen County, North Carolina, in the household of Benjamin Odoms from 1768 to 1770 and a taxable with his wife Constant in Daniel Mills' household in 1776 [Byrd, *Bladen County Tax Lists*, I:4, 16, 35, 78; II:68]. He was head of a Bladen County household of 2 "other free" in 1800.

2.   Jonas Wilkins, born say 1745, was granted 400 acres of land in Halifax County, North Carolina, adjoining Benjamin and William **Richardson** on 7 October 1783 and sold this land on 11 June 1788 [DB 16:272; 17:442].[213] He moved to Robeson County where he entered 150 acres on the south side of Jacobs Swamp including the plantation then occupied by James **Moore** on 5 September 1787 [Pruitt, *Land Entries: Robeson County, 1787-1795*, 7]. He was head of a Robeson County household of 6 "other free" in 1800 [NC:428] and 4 in 1810 [NC:234]. He sold two tracts of land in Robeson by deeds proved on 6 October 1801 [Minutes I:171] and sold personal property to Solomon **Locklear** by Robeson County deed proved in 1808 [DB P:46]. Perhaps his children were

3   i.   Matthew, born say 1765.

4   ii.   Tamer, born say 1767.

    iii.   Nancy, born say 1770, head of a Northampton County household of 6 "other free" in 1810 [NC:750].

    iv.   Nancy, born say 1770.

    v.   John, born before 1776, head of a Halifax County household of 3 "other free" in 1800 [NC:350], 7 in 1810 [NC:54], and 12 "free colored" in 1820.

    vi.   David, born before 1776, head of a Halifax County household of 5 "other free" in 1810 [NC:58] and 8 "free colored" in 1820.

---

[213]The date of this sale of Jonas Wilkins' Halifax County land was abstracted as 11 June 1778, but this land was still called Jonas Wilkins' line in a 19 June 1787 deed [DB 16:405] and was located near Haw Swamp [DB 18:540].

    vii.   Priscilla, head of a Halifax County household of 4 "other free" in 1810 [NC:58].

    viii. Sophia, head of a Halifax County household of 4 "other free" in 1810 [NC:58].

    ix.   Mildred, head of a Halifax County household of 2 "other free" in 1810 [NC:58].

3.   Matthew Wilkins, born say 1765, was head of a Robeson County household of 7 "other free" in 1800 [NC:429]. He sold land to Elijah **Hammons** by deed proved in Robeson County on 6 April 1801 [Minutes I:142]. He may have been the father of

    i.   Jesse, head of a Robeson County household of 4 "other free" in 1800 [NC:428].

4.   Tamer Wilkins, born say 1767, was the mother of Eli Wilkins who was bound as an apprentice to John Edwards of Bertie County. His indenture was transferred to John Acrey of Cumberland County from whom he ran away in 1802. He was taken up in Edenton Town and was bound for his appearance in Chowan County court to be sold as a slave until his mother Tamer and her surety, E. Slade of Martin County, certified that Tamer was free born and the mother of Eli [Byrd, *In Full Force and Virtue*, 31-2]. She married William **Demmery**, 31 January 1816 Northampton County marriage bond with Wright **Demmery** bondsman. William and Tamer were found dead six years later on 5 March 1822 when a coroner's jury was appointed by the Northampton County court to determine the cause of death [Minutes 1821-25, 84]. She was the mother of

    i.   Eli, born 7 July 1785 according to his mother's testimony, obtained free papers in Northampton County on 8 March 1834 and registered in Logan County, Ohio: *yellow complexion, 6 feet tall* [Turpin, *Register of Black, Mulatto, and Poor Persons*, 12].

WILKINSON/ WILKERSON FAMILY

Members of the Wilkinson/ Wilkerson family were

    i.   John Wilkinson, born say 1760, head of a Northampton County, North Carolina household of 6 "other free" in 1800 [NC:485] and head of a Halifax County household of 6 "free colored" in 1820 [NC:169]. Perhaps he was the John Wilkinson of Northampton County who gave Presly Prichard his power of attorney to receive his final settlement certificate for his services in the Revolution [*NCGSJ* XVIII:99].

    ii. Edward Wilkerson, born say 1760, a soldier from Chesterfield County in the Revolution [Jackson, *Virginia Negro Soldiers*, 46].

1   iii. Miles, born before 1776.

2   iv. Peggy, born about 1782.

1.   Miles Wilkinson, born before 1776, was head of a Halifax County, North Carolina household of 8 "free colored" in 1820 [NC:169]. Perhaps his child was

    i.   John, born about 1800, married Ann **Peters**, 7 February 1820 Halifax County bond, Jeremiah **James** bondsman. He was head of a Halifax county household of 4 "free colored" in 1830.

2.   Peggy Wilkerson, born about 1782, registered as a free Negro in Louisa County on 7 September 1832: *a mulatto woman who was free born, yellowish complexion, 5'2-1/2" high, about 50 years old, hair inclined to be straight.* She was the mother of

    i.   Maria Wilkinson, born about 1798, registered in Louisa County on 7 September 1832: *daughter of Peggy Wilkinson who was free born, dark mulatto woman about 34 years old, 5'2-1/2" high, low forehead, bushy head of hair.*

ii. ?Cyrus, born about 1804, registered in Louisa County on 7 December 1832: *a free man of colour, 5'8-1/2" high, light complexion, good countenance, age 28 years.*

iii. ?Peggy[2], registered in Louisa County on 7 September 1832: *free born, mulatto woman about 24 years old, 5'3-1/2" high, hair inclined to be straight...light complexion, thick lips.*

iv. Tom, born about 1814, registered in Louisa County on 25 July 1837: *(son of Peggy Wilkerson, persons of colour born free) stout made man, 5'8" high, age 23, copper colour.*

v. Edward, born about 1821, registered in Louisa County on 7 December 1844: *son of Peggy Wilkersons (both mother and son were born free), dark mulatto man aged 23 years.*

vi. Henry, born about 1816, registered in Louisa County on 11 January 1839: *son of Peggy Wilkerson who was free born a man of darkish complexion, regular features, age 23* [Abercrombie, *Free Blacks of Louisa County*, 41-3, 53, 56, 66]

WILLIAMS FAMILY

1. John Williams, born say 1654, was the "Molatto" servant of Mr. Martin Gardner on 26 April 1675 when the York County court ordered that he receive thirty lashes for stealing a hog. The court also prohibited his master from furnishing him with powder and shot or allowing him to carry a gun [DWO 5:110]. He may have been the ancestor of

    i. Faith, born say 1720, presented by the Surry County, Virginia court on 18 May 1739 for having a "Malato bastard Child" by information of Capt. John Ruffin [Deeds, Wills #9:54].

2   ii. William[1], born about 1723.

3   iii. Mary, born say 1725.

    iv. Hannah[1], born say 1734, a "free negro" taxable in Norfolk County from 1752 to 1765, taxable in her own household in 1752, in Ann **James**'s household in 1757, in her own household in 1759, and taxable with (her husband?) Till/ Tully Williams from 1765 to 1767 and with Tell and (their daughter?) Mary Williams in 1768 [Wingo, *Norfolk County Tithables, 1751-66*, 33, 120, 147, 165, 213; 1766-80, 39, 86]. Hannah may have been the mother of Fanny Williams, a "free Mullatto" bound by the Princess Anne County court to Anthony Walke on 17 June 1760 to learn to read, sew and knit [Minutes 1753-62, 384].

    v. Polly, born about 1785, registered in York County on 18 March 1833: *a bright Mulatto about 48 years of age...light gray Eyes, long hair which is a little gray...Born free* [Free Negroes Register 1831-50, no. 345].

2. William[1] Williams, born about 1723, was a thirty-three-year-old, 5'6" Virginia "Negro" planter who was listed in the 13 July 1756 roll of Captain Henry Harrison's Company, drafted in Surry County, Virginia [Clark, *Colonial Soldiers of the South*, 390]. He may have been the father of

    i. William[2], born say 1758, called "Billy Williams a Mulatto" on 15 April 1760 when the Surry County court ordered the churchwardens of Southwarke Parish to bind him out [Orders 1757-63, 236]. He was taxable in Surry County in 1783 [PPTL, 1782-90, frame 367].

4   ii. James[2], born about 1762.

3. Mary Williams, born say 1725, was living in Warwick County on 1 May 1760 when the court ordered the churchwardens of Warwick Parish to bind out her children Davy, James, Godfrey, Matt, Sarah, Jack, Mary and Will "for

reasons appearing to the court." Her children were described as "Mulattoes" when the indentures were certified in court on 3 July 1760. On 7 August 1760 the churchwardens charged her with bearing a bastard child, but the case was dismissed at the next session of the court on 4 September [Minutes 1748-62, 322, 325, 334, 337]. She was the mother of

- i. David, born say 1743, bound to Harwood Jones in Warwick County on 3 July 1760. At the next session of the court on 7 August, Moses Collikin testified that David had absented himself from the service of Jones for twenty eight days. And on 4 September Jones reported that David had absented himself another nine days [Minutes 1748-62, 325, 334, 335]. He was probably the David Williams who died before 15 April 1793 when John Williams was granted administration on his York County estate with John Wright and Edward **Cuttillo** as his securities [Orders 1788-95, 548].

5   ii.   James[1], born say 1745.
6   iii. Godfrey, born say 1747.
     iv.   Sarah, born say 1752.
7   v.   John, born say 1754.
8   vi.   Matthew, born about 1755.
     vii. Mary, born say 1756.
9   viii. William[3], born say 1759.

4.   James[2] Williams, born about 1762, was taxable in Surry County from 1783 to 1816: charged with Solomon Williams' tithe from 1801 to 1803; called a "Man of Color" in 1805; a "Mulatto" from 1806 to 1812; listed with 2 "free Negroes & Mulattoes above the age of 16" in 1813 [PPTL, 1782-90, frames 373, 398, 606; 1791-1816, 18, 170, 275, 349, 429, 466, 504, 546, 602, 618, 659, 677, 716, 762, 871]. He registered as a "free Negro" in Surry County, Virginia, on 17 February 1797: *a mulattoe man pretty dark complexion born of free parents resident of this County, aged about 35, thin visage and rather slender made - 5'10-1/2"* [Back of Guardians Accounts Book, no.22]. He was counted in the 1803 census of "Free Negroes and Mulattos" in Surry County with his wife Molly and their children: Sollomon, (a labourer), Caty, Samuel, James, Hannah, and Elijah on Mrs. Marston's land. He married, second, Pamelia **Debrix**, thirty-five years old, 6 November 1813 Surry County bond, Nicholas **Scott**, surety. His children were

- i.   Solomon, born about 1782, registered in Surry County on 24 October 1804: *a mulatto man of complexion more bright than otherwise, short hair, aged 21 years the 31 day of December, 1803, 5'6-1/2" high...by occupation a Laborer, was born of free parents, residents of Surry county to wit James Williams and Mary his wife* [Hudgins, *Surry County Register of Free Negroes*, 24].
- ii. Caty, born say 1791, "daughter of James Williams," married Samuel **Blizzard**, 28 December 1807 Surry County bond, David **Charity** surety, 7 January 1808 marriage.
- iii. Samuel.
- iv. James[3], Jr., born say 1795, married Keziah **Blizzard**, 25 October 1819 Surry County bond, James Williams, Sr., surety, 28 October marriage.
- v.   Hannah[2].
- vi. Elijah, born about 1801, registered in Surry County on 23 June 1823: *a mulatto man, the son of Jas. Williams and Polly, his wife, he was born free supposed to be 22 years old, is of a bright complexion, pretty stout made, 5'5-3/4" high...has a large flat Nose* [Hudgins, *Surry County Register of Free Negroes*, 77].

5.   James[1] Williams, born say 1745, a "Mulatto," was bound to William Harwood, Gent., in Warwick County on 3 July 1760 [Minutes 1748-62, 325]. He was taxable in York County from 1782 to 1810: on 2 free tithes in 1790,

1796, and 1797. Perhaps his widow was Faith Williams who was taxable on 2 free tithes in 1811 [PPTL, 1782-1841, frames 69, 166, 186, 224, 259, 300, 344, 357, 368] and head of a York County household of 7 "other free" in 1810 [VA:886]. James may have been the father of

   i.   William⁵, born say 1783, called "William Williams, Jr." when he was taxable in York County from 1804 to 1813: called a "free Negro" in 1805 and head of a household of 2 "free Negroes & mulattoes over 16" in 1813 [PPTL, 1782-1841, frames 300, 310, 331, 357, 368, 397].

   ii. Henry, born about 1791, taxable in York County in 1812 and head of a household of 2 "free Negroes & mulattoes over 16" in 1813 (probably himself and his wife) [PPTL, 1782-1841, frames 379, 397]. He registered in York County on 17 September 1810: *about 19 years of age, 5 feet 8-1/2 Inches high, fine hair, tawny complexion (rather dark), flat nose, long visage and pleasant countenance...born free* [Register of Free Negroes 1798-1831, no. 51].

   iii. Sarah, born about 1793, registered in York County on 17 September 1810: *a dark mulatto, about 17 years of age, 5 feet 5 Inches high...born of free parents* [Register of Free Negroes 1798-1831, no. 49].

6. Godfrey Williams, born say 1747, was head of a Warwick County household of 5 persons in 1782 [VA:45], a "Mulat" taxable in Warwick County in 1789 [1789 PPTL, p.4], taxable in York County from 1790 to 1812 and head of a household of 2 "free Negroes & mulattoes over 16" in 1813 [PPTL, 1782-1841, frames 166, 186, 214, 224, 259, 290, 397]. He may have been the father of

   i.   Polly, born about 1785, registered in York County on 18 March 1833: *a bright Mulatto about 48 years of age, 5 feet 6-1/2 Inches high, has light grey Eyes, long hair which is a little grey. Born free* [Free Negroes Register 1831-1850, no. 346].

   ii. Hannah, born about 1790, registered in York County on 17 September 1810: *a bright mulatto, about 20 years of age, 5 feet 4 Inches high...long hair. Born of free parents* [Register of Free Negroes 1798-1831, no. 48].

   iii. Maria, born about 1791, registered in York County on 17 September 1810: *a tolerably bright mulatto, about 19 years of age, 5 feet 2-12 Inches high...she is very freckled. Born of free parents* [Register of Free Negroes 1798-1831, no. 49].

7. John Williams, born say 1754, was a "Mulatto" bound to William Harwood, Gent., in Warwick County on 3 July 1760. He was taxable in Nottoway Parish, Southampton County, from 1784 to 1800: charged with Jesse **Ash**'s tithe, 2 horses and 6 cattle in 1784, called a "black" in 1788 when he was taxable on 3 free persons over the age of 16, a "free Negro" with 3 persons over 16 and 3 horses in 1795 and 1800, 1 person in 1801 and 1802, and 3 free tithables, 2 slaves and 2 horses in 1803, 2 free persons and 2 slaves in 1804, perhaps identical to John Williams "Preacher" who was taxable on 3 tithes in 1791 [PPTL 1782-92, frames 554, 697, 860; 1792-1806, frames 149, 461, 497, 603, 674, 745]. His estate was administered in Southampton County before 1808 when his daughter Aira **Byrd** sued his son-in-law and executor Lemuel **Clark** over her part of the estate [LVA, Southampton County chancery suit 1814-017]. His widow may have been the Mary Williams who was a "F.N." taxable on a horse in Nottoway Parish, Southampton County, from 1805 to 1811, a free male tithable in 1811 [PPTL 1792-1806, frames 787, 896; 1807-21, frames 35, 117, 153, 235] and head of a Southampton County household of 8 "other free" in 1810 [VA:78]. His children were

   i.   ?Jerry, born about 1782, registered in Southampton County on 14 May 1828: *age 46, Yellow Bright, 5 feet 4-1/4 inches, free born* [Register of Free Negroes 1794-1832, no. 1721]. He was a "F.N." taxable in Nottoway Parish, Southampton County, in 1805, 1806 and 1810 [PPTL 1792-1806, frames 787, 896; 1807-21, frame 154].

    ii.   Arry/ Aira, married John **Taylor**, 25 December 1797 Southampton County bond and second, Aaron **Byrd**, 19 February 1803 Southampton County bond.

   iii.   Mary, married Lemuel **Clark**, 29 January 1795 Isle of Wight County bond, David Jones surety.

8.   Matthew Williams, born about 1755, was a "Mulatto" bound to Servant Jones by the Warwick County court on 3 July 1760. He was a man of color who served in the Revolution from Southampton County [National Archives pension file S6414 cited by NSDAR, *African American Patriots*, 155]. He was probably the Matthew Williams who married Susannah **Tan**, "both of Isle of Wight County," 22 December 1783 Southampton County bond. He registered in Southampton County on 12 July 1810: *age 55, Blk, 5 feet 7-1/2 inches, free born*. His wife was probably the Sally Williams who registered the same day: *age 40, Blk., 5 feet 5 inches, free born* [Register of Free Negroes 1794-1832, nos. 589, 590]. He was taxable in Nottoway Parish, Southampton County, from 1787 to 1800: called a "Black" in 1787, a "free Negro" from 1789 to 1802, listed with 3 free male tithables from 1802 to 1804, 2 male tithables in 1805, 1810 and 1811, listed with his wife Sally, daughter Sally and son Jack in 1813, taxable on his son Jack in 1814 [PPTL 1782-92, frames 627, 698, 747; 1792-1806, frames 19, 38, 149, 253, 361, 479, 604, 747, 787, 896; 1807-21, frames 35, 154, 238, 404]. He was called a "free person of colour" on 16 November 1818 when he made a declaration in Southampton County court setting forth that he was a soldier in the Revolutionary War by voluntary enlistment [Minutes 1816-9, unpaged]. He was the father of

    i.   John, born about 1785, registered in Southampton County on 30 June 1806: *age 21, Blk., 5 feet 9-1/2 inches, free born in York* [Register of Free Negroes 1794-1832, no. 389, 413]. He was head of a Southampton County household of 4 "other free" in 1810 [VA:78]. He was a "F.N." taxable in Nottoway Parish from 1807 to 1812 [PPTL 1807-21, frames 35, 117, 153, 235, 277].

    ii.   Sally.

9.   William[3] Williams, born say 1762, and his wife Rachel, "Free Mulattoes," registered the birth of their daughter Lydia in Bruton Parish, James City and York counties [Bruton Parish Register, 35]. He was taxable in York County from 1792 to 1806: called "William Williams, Sr." in 1804 and thereafter, called "free Negro" in 1805. In 1813 (his widow?) Rachel Williams was counted in a York County list of "free Negroes & mulattoes over 16," taxable on a horse [PPTL, 1782-1841, frames 186, 214, 280, 300, 320, 397]. William and Rachel were the parents of

    i.   Lydia, born 5 January 1783 [Bruton Parish Register, 35].

Other members of the Williams family were

    i.   William[4], born say 1765, a "Mulatto" taxable in Warwick County on a tithe in 1789, 2 tithes and 2 horses in 1798 [1789 PPTL, p.4; 1798, p.6], head of an Elizabeth City County household of 6 "other free" in 1810 [VA:185], and 2 "Free negroes & mulattoes 16 yrs. old" in Elizabeth City County in 1813 [Waldrep, *1813 Tax List*].

    ii.   William[7], born about 1792, obtained a certificate of freedom in Gloucester County on 7 December 1822: *a free tawny Coloured man about 30 years of age, 5 feet 8 inches high...born of free parents*, and registered it in York County on 17 October 1831 [Register of Free Negroes 1798-1831, no. 326].

iii. William[6], a "F.N." taxable in York County in 1807 [PPTL, 1782-1841, frame 331]. He may have been the Billy Williams who registered in York County on 21 February 1814: *of dark complexion, about (blot) of age, 5 feet 6-3/4 Inches high, has high cheek bones, very short wooly hair. Born free.* He renewed his registration in 1822 and 1826 [Register of Free Negroes, 1798-1831, no. 75].

Middlesex County, Virginia

1. Mary Williams, born say 1660, a "Negroe Wooman," was sued in Middlesex County court by Christopher Robinson on 3 September 1688 for a debt of 3,866 pounds of tobacco [Orders 1680-94, 371].

Westmoreland County, Virginia

1. Mary Williams, born say 1685, was the white servant of Willoughby Allerton, Gent., of the Parish of Copely, on 25 April 1705 when she was convicted by the Westmoreland County court of having a "mulatto" child by a "Negro man" [Orders 1698-1705, 256a]. She was probably the mother of

2   i. William[1], born say 1704.

2. William Williams, born say 1704, was a "free Mulato" who petitioned the Westmoreland County, Virginia court for his freedom from Isaac Allerton on 31 July 1733. On 27 March 1753 the court ordered "his several Children" bound out as apprentices. And on 25 March 1755 he sued John and Spencer Ayris for detaining his children, but the court stood by its original order [Orders 1731-9, 99a; 1752-5, 60, 227, 249]. He may have been the father of

   i. George, born about 1731, a soldier from Richmond County in the French and Indian War, *age 26, a mulatto, 6'1"*, when he was listed as a deserter on 2 September 1757 [*Magazine of Virginia Genealogy* 31:95].

Northampton County

1. Anne Williams, born in September or October 1686, was the child of Daniel **Webb**, a Northampton County, Virginia slave, and Ann Williams, a white servant woman. See further the **Webb** History. She was called a thirteen-year-old "maletto childe" on 29 November 1699 when she was bound to Hamond Firkette until the age of eighteen years in Northampton County, Virginia [OW&c 1698-1710, 30].

Richmond County, Virginia

1. Hannah Charlton, born say 1685, was released from servitude and "given" her daughter Ann by Francis Williams, Sr., of Sittenbyrne Parish in Richmond County. She recorded the document in court on 6 December 1710. She was called "Hannah, a Mulato belonging to Francis Williams" on 6 March 1711/2 when she appeared in Richmond County court on the complaint of her master's wife, Alice Williams, that Hannah was threatening and abusing her. Hannah was ordered to give security for her good behavior for one year. On 7 July 1715 Francis Williams was presented by the Richmond County court for living in adultery with "a Mulatto Woman." And on 1 August 1716 he recorded a paper in court which set free her children: Catherine, Mary, and John Charlton [Orders 1708-11, 220; 1711-6, 8; 1716-7, 28]. Hannah was the mother of

   i. Ann Williams, born say 1710, ordered to be given twenty-five lashes in March 1735/6 by the Orange County, Virginia court [Orders 1734-9, 61].

   ii. Catherine Charlton, born say 1712, called Catherine Carleton alias Williams in November 1735 when the churchwardens of Orange County, Virginia, presented her for having a bastard child. John Becket agreed to pay her fine, and Francis Williams and John Haddocks provided security for the child. In March 1738 John Becket was

accused in Orange County court of failing to pay tax on "Kate Williams, a Mulattoe woman" [Orders 1734-9, 42, 290].
iii.   Mary Charlton, born say 1714.
iv.   John Charlton, born say 1716.

Lunenburg County
1.   Zedekiah Williams, born say 1775, was living with his wife Anna, daughter Lucy and (wife's niece?) Ritter **Lester** on Bears Element Creek in the lower district of Lunenburg County in 1802 and 1803 when they were counted in a "List of all free Negroes & Mulattoes" [LVA, Lunenburg County, Free Negro & Slave Records, 1802-1803]. Zedekiah and Anna were the parents of
i.   Lucy, born 1795-1800, registered in Lunenburg County on 10 October 1825: *aged about twenty five or thirty years, yellow complexion, very corpulent...born free* [WB 5, after page 89, no. 40].

Members of the Williams family in North Carolina were
1   i.   James[1], born about 1748.
ii.   William, head of a Beaufort County household of 2 "other free" in 1800 [NC:20], 4 in 1810 [NC:113], and 5 "free colored" in 1820 [NC:42].
2   iii.   Charles, born before 1776.

1.   James[1] Williams, born about 1748, was a thirteen-year-old "Mullatto Boy" ordered bound an apprentice to William Armstrong in Cumberland County, North Carolina, on 19 August 1761 [Minutes 1759-65, 70]. Perhaps his children were
i.   Joseph, head of a Sampson County household of 4 "other free" in 1790 [NC:53].
ii.   Crecy, head of a Sampson County household of 3 "other free" in 1790 [NC:53] and may have been the C. Williams, head of a Cumberland County household of 1 "other free" in 1810 [NC:627].
iii.   Hannah[2], head of a Sampson County household of 2 "other free" in 1790 [NC:53], perhaps the H. Williams who was head of a Cumberland County household of 2 "other free" in 1810 [NC:623].

2.   Charles Williams, born before 1776, was head of an Ashe County household of 12 "free colored" in 1820 [NC:3]. He may have been the father of
i.   Charles Williams Loyd, born about 1787, registered in Petersburg on 11 March 1817: *a free man of colour, five feet three and a half inches high, thirty years old, a waggoner, born free & raised in the Town of Petersburg* [Register of Free Negroes 1794-1819, no. 837].
ii.   James Williams Loyd, born 1810, son of Charles Williams and Sally Lloyd, resided in Chillicothe, Ross County, Ohio, on 28 September 1818 [Turpin, *Register of Black, Mulatto, and Poor Persons*, 25]. Sally Lloyd may have been related to "Indian" Robin Loyd, a "person of color" residing in Jennings County, Indiana, about the age of eighty on 12 February 1838 when he made a declaration to obtain a pension for his services in the Revolution. He stated that he enlisted at Dinwiddie County courthouse and had resided in Dinwiddie for many years after the war, went to North Carolina for a few years, and had been living in Indiana for more than twenty years. John Grimes of Ripley County, Indiana, testified for him that Indian Robin, "a negro man," had served as a footman and also as a soldier in the light horse service. Bartholomew Turner of Jennings County testified that he had seen a "Negro man" named Indian Robin as a soldier on horseback and armed for battle [M804-1596, frame 0594].

WILLIS FAMILY

1. Edith Willis, born say 1730, was taxable in Charles City County on a horse
    in 1788 [PPTL, 1788-1814] and taxable with Betty Willis on 110 acres near
    the Quaker Meeting House from 1788 to 1799 [Land Tax List, 1782-1830].
    She left a 24 November 1791 Charles City County will, proved 18 December
    1794, by which she left a shilling to each of her children Rodger, London,
    David, Limos, Doctor, and Billy Willis and left her children Jesse and Betty
    Willis the use of her land during the life of her son Jesse, and then all of it to
    go to Betty [WB 1:197-8]. She was the mother of
    i.   Betty, taxable in New Kent County on 2 horses in 1788 and 2 horses
         and a slave in 1789 [PPTL 1782-1800, frames 121, 135], taxable in
         Charles City County with Eady Willis on 110 acres from 1788 to 1799,
         taxable with Jesse Willis on 110 acres from 1800 to 1815 [Land Tax
         List, 1782-1830] and taxable on a tithe in 1804 and 1805 [PPTL, 1788-
         1814]. On 14 April 1813 she was living in Henrico County when she
         and Jesse Willis of Charles City County made a deed of trust for 56
         acres adjoining Joseph Crew, Francis Dixon and John Crew's estate to
         secure a debt of $34 they owed Ann Ladd, and on 21 April 1815 they
         made a deed of trust for the same land to secure a debt of $77 they
         owed George Hubbard. On 27 September 1815 Elizabeth sold 53 acres
         adjoining the land of John Crew, deceased, to Jesse Willis for $125,
         explaining in the deed that this was land devised to her by the wills of
         Thomas Ladd and Edith Willis, deceased [DB 5:568, 594]. She was
         head of a Richmond City household of 8 "other free" in 1810
         [VA:364].
    ii. Roger.
    iii. London.
    iv. David, born say 1758, taxable in Lower Westover District of Charles
         City County in 1784, taxable on slaves Nanny, David and Charles in
         1785, taxable on a horse in 1788, 2 tithes in 1789 and 1 in 1792
         [PPTL, 1788-1814]. He was a "free Negro" taxable in the lower
         district of Henrico County from to 1807 to 1814: taxable on son James
         Willis from 1809 to 1811 [PPTL 1782-1814, frames 562, 582, 625,
         691, 710, 777, 795]. He was head of a Henrico County household of
         10 "other free" in 1810 [VA:1010] and 1 "free colored in Charles City
         County in 1820 [VA:3].
    v.   Limos.
    vi. Jesse, born say 1762, taxable in Charles City County from 1785 to
         1805 [PPTL, 1788-1814] and taxed with Betty Willis on 110 acres in
         Charles City County in 1800 [Land Tax List, p.13]. He was taxable in
         the lower district of Henrico County in 1802 and taxable on his son
         Jesse Willis, Jr., in 1807 [PPTL 1782-1814, frames 470, 562]. On 28
         September 1815 he made a Charles City County deed of trust for 53
         acres adjoining John Crew's estate to secure a debt of $125 he owed
         George Hubbard [DB 5:607]. And on 20 December 1817 he sold 56
         acres which had been devised by Thomas Ladd to the Willises
         excepting his and his wife Letty's right to live on a certain part during
         their natural lives. (The account of Thomas Ladd's Charles City
         County estate includes a payment to John Evans in 1786 for digging his
         grave, but Ladd's will has not survived [WB 1:563]). Jesse was called
         a "free man of colour" on 20 April 1820 when he manumitted his wife
         Letty whom he had purchased from Henry Dick of Caroline County for
         $100 [DB 6:175, 351]. He was head of a Charles City County
         household of 2 "free colored" in 1820 [VA:15].
    vii. Doctor, born about 1756, taxable in Charles City County in 1784
         [PPTL, 1788-1814], taxable in New Kent County in 1785 [PPTL 1782-
         1800, frame 78], a "FN" taxable in the northern district of Campbell

County from 1797 to 1813 [PPTL, 1785-1814, frames 427, 465, 892].
He registered in Campbell County on 18 August 1812: *age 56, 5 feet 9 inches, Black Complexion, set free by Thomas Ladd in Charles City County* [Register of Free Negroes and Mulattoes, p.6].

    viii. Billy.

Other members of the family were

    i. Moses, a "free Negro" taxable in the lower district of Henrico County from 1801 to 1813 [PPTL 1782-1814, frames 470, 562, 581, 624, 690, 709, 776], head of a Henrico County household of 3 "other free" in 1810 [VA:1009].

    ii. Nancy, born before 1776, head of a Charles City County household of 3 "other free" in 1810 [VA:959] and 3 "free colored" in 1820 [VA:14]. She was the mother of William Willis who obtained a certificate of freedom in Charles City County on 18 October 1827: *son of Nancy Willis, a bright mulatto man, born free in this county* [Minutes 1823-9, 255].

    iii. Samuel, a "free Negro" taxable in Henrico County in 1813 [PPTL 1782-1814, frame 777] allowed to keep a gun in Charles City County on 20 May 1824 [Minutes 1823-9, 52].

WILSON FAMILY

1. Mary[1] Wilson, born say 1673, the servant of Captain Thomas Thorpe, was convicted by the York County court on 24 March 1692/3 of having a "molatto" child on information of the churchwardens of Bruton Parish [DOW 9:200, 209]. She may have been the ancestor of

2   i. Samuel[1], born say 1693.
3   ii. Mary[2], born say 1724.
4   iii. Mary[3], born say 1725.
5   iv. Isaac[1], born say 1730.

    v. Stephen, born say 1732, purchased property by indenture proved in Halifax County, Virginia, on 15 March 1781 [Pleas 1779-83, 181]. He left a 4 October 1780 Halifax County will, proved 20 June 1782, in which he named his wife Elizabeth as his executrix. Peter Wilson, David **Going**, and Shadrack **Going** were witnesses [WB:1:404].

    vi. John, born say 1733, jailed in King William County with Zachariah Johns (a white man) on suspicion of murder. They made their escape from the sheriff when he was transporting them to Williamsburg for trial. Lieutenant Governor Robert Dinwiddie issued a proclamation on 31 October 1754 offering a reward for their capture, describing John as: *a Mulattoe, about Six feet high, and speaks good English; had on when he made his Escape, a blue double-breasted wastecoat with Metal Buttons, an old yellow Wig, old Shoes and Worstead Hose* [Hillman, *Journals of the Council*, VI:586].

    vii. Edward[2], born say 1755, a "Mulatto" living in Henrico County on 3 August 1767 when the court ordered the churchwardens to bind him out as an apprentice [Orders 1767-9, 93], perhaps the same Edward Wilson who was a "Mulatto" apprenticed to Philip Mallory of Mecklenburg County, Virginia, when he ran away according to the 5 September 1771 *Virginia Gazette*. Mallory described him as "an apprentice lad named Wilson, a clear mulatto, a carpenter and joiner by trade" when he offered to hire him out. He may have been the Edward Wilson who was head of a Norfolk County household of 9 "other free" in 1810 [VA:837].

2. Samuel[1] Wilson, born say 1693, was a "Mulatto" servant indentured to Charles Chiswell of York County on 24 July 1708 when the court ordered that he

serve additional time for running away. Chiswell asked that the court also add a penalty for Samuel's riding three of his horses in his absence, but the court ruled that there was no law "that relates to or gives any penalty for unlucky boys rideing horses but that they are subject to their master's correction." He may have been the father of

6   i.   William[1], born say 1713.

3.   Mary[2], born say 1724, was the mother of an illegitimate child named Anne Wilson who was born 14 January and baptized 5 May 1745 in Charles Parish, York County [Bell, *Charles Parish Registers*, 195]. She was called a "Molatto" on 20 May 1745 when the York County court presented her for having an illegitimate child and fined her 500 pounds of tobacco [W&I 19:365, 372, 381, 398]. She may have been the Mary Wilson who was living in Elizabeth City County when she was accused of concealing the death of her bastard child by secretly burying it on 13 January 1757 [Orders 1755-7, 86]. She was the mother of

7   ii.   Anne, born 14 January 1744/5.

4.   Mary[3] Wilson, born say 1725, was the "free Mulatto" mother of Charles, Peter, and Samuel Wilson who were bound apprentices in Halifax County, Virginia, on 20 August 1754 [Pleas 1:388]. She was head of a Halifax County, Virginia household of 2 "white" (free) persons in 1782 [VA:24]. She was taxable in Halifax County on 2 horses and 8 cattle in 1783 and was charged with Robert Wilson's tithe in 1786, taxable on a horse in 1788 [PPTL, 1782-1799, frames 26, 71, 86, 210]. She sold property by deed proved in Halifax County on 21 September 1786 [Pleas 1786-8, 3]. Her children were

    i.   Charles, born say 1747, taxable in Halifax County in 1786, taxable on Martin Wilson's tithe in 1790, taxable on 2 horses in 1798 [PPTL, 1782-1799, frames 86, 358, 381, 713, 843], perhaps the Charles Wilson, born before 1776, who was head of a Stokes County household of 2 "free colored" males and a white woman in 1820 [NC:377].

8   ii.   ?Milly, born say 1748.

    iii.   Peter, born say 1750, witness to Stephen Wilson's 4 October 1780 Halifax County, Virginia will [WB:1:404]. He was head of a Halifax County, Virginia household of 4 "white" (free) persons in 1782 [VA:24]. He was taxable in Halifax County from 1782 to 1799: listed with 2 tithables in 1785, called a "M°" from 1792 to 1799 [PPTL, 1782-1799, frames 7, 58, 79, 202, 427, 614, 686, 711, 931]. In 1810 he was a "F.B." head of a Nottoway County household of 8 "other free" and a Giles County household of 10 "other free" and a white woman [VA:643, 1021].

    iv.   Samuel[2], born say 1752.

9   v.   Robert[2], born about 1762.

5.   Isaac[1] Wilson, born say 1730, was head of a Halifax County, Virginia household of 1 "white" (free) person in 1782 [VA:23]. He married (second?) Susanna **Matthews**, 18 August 1785 Halifax County bond. He was taxable in Halifax County from 1785 to 1799, called a "Mul°" from 1792 to 1799 [PPTL, 1782-1799, frames 71, 86, 149, 202, 427, 453, 549, 614, 686, 931]. He left an undated Halifax County, Virginia will, proved 27 December 1802 on $2,000 security. He left his property to his wife Susanna and named his sixteen children [WB 6:422]. They were

    i.   Sary.

    ii.   Judy.

    iii.   Billy (Betty?), perhaps the William Wilson who married Milly Wilson, 18 April 1812 Halifax County bond, Robert Wilson surety.

    iv.   Samuel[3].

v.   Solliman (Solomon), born about 1787, registered as a "free Negro" in Halifax County on 26 October 1812: *aged 25 years about 5 11-1/2 of a yellow Colour* [Register of Free Negroes 1802-31, no.35]. He married Rhoda Wilson, 18 April 1812 Halifax County bond, Robert Wilson surety.

vi.   Vina.

vii.   Polly.

viii.   Richard².

ix.   Mathaw, perhaps the Martha Wilson who married Pleasant Wilson, 29 August 1812 Halifax County bond, surety Martin Wilson. Pleasant, born about 1786, registered as a free Negro in Halifax County on 24 August 1812: *aged twenty Six years, about five feet, Seven inches and a quarter high, of a dark mulatto Colour* [Register of Free Negroes 1802-31, no.33]. Martha, born about 1793, registered as in Halifax County in 1831.

x.   Isack².

xi.   Susanna.

xii.   Mastan, apparently identical to Martin Wilson, born about 1766, registered as a "free Negro" in Halifax County, Virginia, on 28 January 1806: *aged about forty years, five feet seven Inches high, yellow complexion* [Register of Free Negroes 1802-31, no.25]. He married Syller **Matthis**, 10 January 1804 Halifax County bond, John Wilson surety. The Halifax County court awarded him 15 pounds in his suit against Luke Williams for false imprisonment on 17 November 1787 [Pleas 1786-8]. He was taxable in Halifax County from 1788 to 1799: called a "Mulº" in 1792 and 1793 [PPTL, 1782-99, frames 210, 284, 427, 453, 614, 931].

xiii.   Elasabeth/ Betty, married James Wilson, 31 January 1818 Halifax County bond, Richard **Matthews** surety. He may have been the James R. Wilson, born about 1796, who registered in Halifax County on 26 February 1827 and 22 November 1830: *born free, dark Mulatto man about 31 years old, 5 feet 8 inches and a half high, long wooly hair* [Registers of Free Negroes, 1802-1831, no. 95, 124].

xiv.   Luke, born about 1799, registered as a "free Negro" in Halifax County on 23 November 1829: *a bright Mulatto man about thirty years old, five feet 11 inches, long straight hair, born of a free woman* [Registers of Free Negroes, 1802-1831, no. 122].

xv.   Luzereous (Lazarus), born about 1799, registered in Halifax County on 22 December 1823: *aged about 24 years, five feet nine and a half inches high, of a bright complexion...born of a free woman of Colour* [Registers of Free Negroes, 1802-1831, no. 72]. He was called the minor son of Isaac in Halifax County court in 1809 [Pleas 26:421]. He married Catherine **Goen**, 27 December 1829 Surry County, North Carolina bond, Willis Wilson bondsman.

xvi.   Franky, born about 1800, registered as a "free Negro" in Halifax County in 1832.

6.   William¹ Wilson, born say 1713, may have been the husband of Margaret Wilson who was named in the 19 September 1749 York County will of her mother Mary **Roberts** [DOW 13:151; W&I 20:163-4]. He was living in Elizabeth City County on 13 January 1757 when the court ordered his children bound out because he was neglecting to educate them and bring them up in a Christian-like manner [Orders 1755-7, 87]. He was living in Bruton Parish on 16 January 1764 when the York County court ordered the churchwardens to bind out his children because he was neglecting to maintain and educate them. On 18 March 1765 he was a witness for John **Poe** in his York County suit against Anthony and Jasper **Peters**. On the same day Anthony **Peters** sued William for a 31 shilling debt he owed by account proved in court [Judgments

& Orders 1762-5, 137, 358, 361]. On 15 July 1771 the court presented him for failing to list himself as a tithable [Orders 1770-2, 337]. He may have been the father of

 i. John, born say 1750, presented by the York County court on 15 July 1771 for failing to list himself as a tithable [Orders 1770-2, 337]. He was head of a York County household of 7 "other free" and a slave in 1810 [VA:885].

 ii. Robert[1], born say 1760, taxable in Petsworth Parish, Gloucester County, on his own tithe and 3 cattle in 1783, a "mulatto" taxable from 1801 to 1816, over forty five years of age in 1815 [PPTL, 1800-20], head of a household of 9 "other free" in 1810 [VA:677]. He may have been the father of Robert Wilson, Jr., who was a "mulatto" taxable from 1814 to 1820 [PPTL, 1800-20].

 iii. Cary, born say 1769, called Wilson Wilson when he was taxable in Gloucester County from 1790 to 1801, a "mulatto" taxable called "Wilson C. Wilson" in 1802 and 1803, and a "mulatto" called Cary Wilson from 1804 to 1820, over forty-five years of age in 1815 [PPTL, 1782-99; 1800-20]. He was head of a Gloucester County household of 8 "other free" in 1810 [VA:677].

7. Anne Wilson, born 14 January 1744/5, was baptized 5 May 1745 in Charles Parish, York County. She was the common-law wife of Thomas **Combs** on 10 October 1766 when he was presented by the York County court for not listing her as a tithable [Orders 1765-68, 161]. Thomas left a 29 June 1777 York County will, proved 15 September 1777, which left a heifer to each of his "old" children: William, Thomas, Edmund, and George Combs and left Ann Wilson and her children "had by me" the remainder of his estate [W&I 22:374-5]. Ann died before 15 September 1777 when Mead Wood was granted administration on the estate [Orders 1774-84, 151]. Thomas and Anne were the parents of

 i. Sally Wilson, born 24 June, baptized 28 July 1765, daughter of Thomas Combs and Anne Wilson.

 ii. Anne **Combs**, born 22 April 1769, baptized 25 June, daughter of Thomas and Anne Combs.

 iii. Martha **Combs**, daughter of Thomas and Anne, born 17 February, baptized 22 March 1772.

 iv. Willis **Combs**, son of Thomas and Anne born 4 May 1774, baptized 12 June.

 v. Frances **Combs**, daughter of Thomas and Anne, born 17 March 1776, baptized 14 April [Bell, *Charles Parish Registers*, 67, 68, 195].

8. Milly Wilson, born say 1748, was living in Halifax County, Virginia, in January 1769 when the court bound out her children Richard and Mary [Pleas 6:270]. She was head of a Halifax County, Virginia household of 5 "white" (free) persons in 1782 [VA:24]. She was taxable in Halifax County from 1783 to 1799: charged with David Wilson's tithe in 1786, a "Mul°" taxable on a free male tithe and a horse from 1794 to 1798 [PPTL, 1782-1799, frames 26, 71, 86, 210, 549, 614, 711, 841, 931]. Her children were

 i. Richard[1], born say 1766.

 ii. Mary[3], born say 1768.

 iii. ?David, taxable in Halifax County in 1787, a "Mul°" taxable from 1792 to 1799 [PPTL, 1782-1799, frames 86, 149, 427, 453, 548, 614, 686, 931].

 iv. John, born about 1777, illegitimate son of Milley Wilson, bound by the Halifax County court to Henry Hopson on 23 February 1789 [Pleas 1788-9, 103]. He registered as a "free Negro" in Halifax County, Virginia, on 15 March 1812: *aged about 35 years, 5 feet 11-1/2 inches high - of a yellow complexion - Straight haire* [Register of Free

Negroes 1802-31, no.31]. He was head of a Stokes County household
of 6 "free colored" in 1820 [NC:376].

v.   Tabitha, born say 1778, illegitimate daughter of Milley Wilson, bound
by the Halifax County court to Dudley Glass on 23 February 1789
[Pleas 1788-9, 103]. She married Obadiah Wilson, 30 December 1811
Halifax County bond, Martin Wilson surety.

vi. Henry, born say 1780, bound out by the Halifax County court in 1789
[Pleas 13:128], head of a Monroe County, Virginia household of 5
"other free" in 1810 [VA:583].

9. Robert[2] Wilson, born about 1762, was head of a Halifax County, Virginia
household of 1 "white" (free) person in 1782 [VA:23]. He was taxable in
Halifax County from 1783 to 1799: listed as Mary Wilson's tithe in 1786,
called a "Mul°" from 1794 to 1796, a "FN" in 1799 [PPTL, 1782-1799,
frames 26, 71, 79, 149, 210, 358, 548, 615, 686, 933]. He married Patience
Cumbo, 16 April 1787 Halifax County, Virginia bond, Robert Smith surety;
and married, second, Salley **Talbott**, 27 April 1789 Halifax County bond,
surety Richard Walne. He registered as a "free Negro" in Halifax County on
24 September 1802: *aged about forty years, five feet nine inches and three
quarters high, black colour, - who it appears was born free.* He registered
again on 26 September 1814 at the age of fifty-two [Register of Free Negroes
1802-31, nos.17, 46]. He was head of a Stokes County, North Carolina
household of 7 "other free" in 1810 [NC:602]. He may have been the father
of

i.   Jeremiah, head of a Stokes County household of 8 "free colored" in
1820 [NC:376].

ii.   Willis, born about 1790, registered as a "free Negro" in Halifax
County, Virginia, on 23 November 1813: *aged twenty three years, five
feet 8 inches high, of a bright yellow complexion* [Register of Free
Negroes 1802-31, no.39]. He was head of a Stokes County household
of 3 "free colored" in 1820 [NC:376].

iii. Rhoda, married Solomon Wilson, 18 April 1812 Halifax County bond,
Robert Wilson surety.

iv.   Milly, married William Wilson, 18 April 1812 Halifax County bond,
Robert Wilson surety.

Members of the Wilson family in Mecklenburg County, Virginia, were

i.   Humphrey, born say 1778, married Sally **Stewart** of Dinwiddie County
[Chancery Orders 1832-52, 1], purchased land in Mecklenburg County,
Virginia, from his father-in-law Thomas **Stewart** by deed proved in
Mecklenburg County in 1800 [DB 10:268]. He and his wife Sarah sold
their land by deed proved in Mecklenburg County court on 11 February
1805 [Orders 1803-5, 320]. He was head of a Chatham County
household of 7 "other free" in 1810 [NC:203].

ii.   Drury, born say 1788, a Mecklenburg County taxable from 1809 to
1817, counted with his unnamed wife as "free Negroes and Mulattoes
over 16" in 1813 [PPTL, 1806-28, frames 123, 224, 317, 584, 628,
694]. He married Ann **Chavis**, daughter of James **Chavis**
[Mecklenburg County chancery suit 1832-026, LVA].

Westmoreland County, Virginia

1. Ann Wilson, born say 1675, an English servant woman, appeared in
Westmoreland County, Virginia court on 26 July 1693 and "made confession
she was lately delivered of a bastard mulatto child begott on her body by Jack
a Negro slave to Youel." On 26 May 1697 she petitioned the court for her
freedom, but the court ruled that she still had considerable time to serve for
having bastard children. In February 1699/1700 she confessed to having an

illegitimate child by a white man [Orders 1690-8, 102, 242; 1698-1705, 71, 73a].

Bertie County, North Carolina

1. Thomas[1] Wilson, born say 1715, purchased 183 acres on the north side of the Cashie River in Bertie County, North Carolina, from William **Leviner** on 26 April 1756 [DB H:326]. He was called a shoe maker when he sold 80 acres of this land to (his son?) Edward Wilson on 10 July 1759 for 1 pound 10 shillings [DB I:364]. He died before August court 1783 when the Bertie court assigned Edward Wilson administrator of his estate on a bond of 50 pounds [Haun, *Bertie County Court Minutes*, V:462]. Perhaps his children were

    i. Edward[1], born say 1738, purchased 80 acres in Bertie County at the mouth of Plumtree Branch of Cashie Swamp from Thomas Wilson by deed of 10 July 1759 witnessed by Embry **Bunch** [DB I:364]. He was a "free male molattor" in Jonathan Standley's 1764 Bertie tax list, taxed with his "Molattor Servant" John **Cobb** [CR 10.702], and taxed with (his brother?) James Wilson in Jonathan Standley's 1767 list. Embry **Bunch** was also taxed in Standley's list in a household nearby. He purchased 20 acres on the north side of the Cashie Swamp between his own line and **Bunch**'s from David Standley on 22 May 1786 and another 56 acres between Connaritsa Swamp and Mill Branch in Bertie near Jonathan Standley on 8 September 1795 [DB N:333; Q:454]. He was counted as white in 1790, head of a Bertie County household of 5 males and 5 females [NC:15].

Surry and Isle of Wight counties

1. Thomas[2] Wilson, born say 1737, was among fourteen free African Americans who were presented by the Surry County, Virginia court on 21 November 1758 for failing to pay tax on their wives [Orders 1757-64, 135]. He may have been the Thomas Wilson, Jr., who purchased 200 acres on the south side of Cypress Swamp bounded by Spratleys Branch and Great Branch in Surry County on 20 November 1759 and sold this land on 19 January 1762 [DB 7:483; 8:96]. He was taxable in Surry County on a horse in 1785 but not subject to personal tax [PPTL, 1782-90, frame, 391]. His children were

    i. ?Armstead, born about 1762, registered as a "free Negro" in Surry County on 29 October 1795: *a free man of a pretty dark cast, born of free parents aged about 33 years, about 5'5 or 6" and pretty stout made* [Back of Guardian Accounts Book 1783-1804, no.11]. He was taxable in Surry County from 1787 to 1790 [PPTL, 1782-90, frames 436, 510, 586].

    ii. Thomas[3], born about 1768, registered as a "free Negro" in Surry County on 5 January 1796: *son of Thomas Wilson a Mulattoe man aged about 28 years, pretty well made, 5'9" high, born of free parents* [Back of Guardian Accounts Book 1783-1804, no.13]. He was taxable listed as Nicholas Faulcon's Surry County tithable in 1788 and 1789 and charged with his own tax in 1791 [PPTL, 1782-90, frames 495, 525, 607; 1791-1816, frame 49]. He may have been the Thomas Wilson who was head of a Granville County, North Carolina household of 2 "other free" in 1810 [NC:861] and 4 "free colored" in Stokes County in 1820 [NC:376].

    iii. ?James[1], born say 1765, a "poor mulatto" ordered bound apprentice in Isle of Wight County on 4 December 1777 [Orders 1772-80, 408]. He married Faithy **Banks**, "daughter of John Banks," 31 May 1786 Surry County bond, Joseph **Roberts** surety, 1 June 1786 Isle of Wight marriage. He was taxable in Surry County from 1786 to 1793 (called a free Negro in 1792), 1800, 1805 (called a "Mulatto" in 1805 and in 1806 when he was crossed off the list) [PPTL, 1782-90, frames 404, 436, 510, 541, 586; 1791-1816, 97, 603, 619]. He was a "F.N."

taxable in Isle of Wight County in 1794 and 1795, called James Wilson, Sr., in 1801, 1802, 1803, 1806, 1809 and 1810, 1813 [PPTL 1782-1810, frames 325, 370, 469, 551, 569, 627, 741, 820, 838].

Members of the Wilson family in Isle of Wight County were

   i.   William[3], born say 1769, a "F.N." taxable in Isle of Wight County from 1790 to 1810 [PPTL 1782-1810, frames 203, 219, 370, 627, 643, 744, 823, 838]. He married Sarah **Blizzard**, 29 July 1797 Surry County bond, Peter **Blizzard** surety.

   ii.   Randolph, born say 1769, a "F.N." taxable in Isle of Wight County from 1790 to 1810: taxable on a slave in 1803 [PPTL 1782-1810, frames 203, 219, 267, 325, 370, 384, 413, 453, 517, 627, 643, 741, 765, 838]. He married Milly **Charity**, October 1809 Isle of Wight County bond, Hartwell **Charity** bondsman.

   iii.   Angelina, born say 1773, mother of "free negroes" Thomas and Edy Wilson who had been bound apprentices to William Hardy, deceased, and were bound instead to George Hardy in Isle of Wight County on 2 February 1795 [Orders 1795-97, 7].

   iv.   Judith, born say 1774, a "poor mulatto" ordered bound apprentice in Isle of Wight County on 7 October 1779 [Orders 1772-80, 490].

   v.   Simon, born say 1775, a "poor mulatto" ordered bound apprentice in Isle of Wight County on 7 October 1779 [Orders 1772-80, 490]. He was a "F.N." taxable in Isle of Wight County from 1793 to 1810 [PPTL 1782-1810, frames 266, 304, 325, 413, 469, 517, 567, 627, 764, 821, 839].

   vi.   Michael, born say 1776, a "poor Mulatoe" ordered bound apprentice in Isle of Wight County on 3 February 1780 [Orders 1772-80, 506]. He was a "F.N." taxable in Isle of Wight County from 1793 to 1802 [PPTL 1782-1810, frames 304, 384, 413, 567, 627].

   vii.   Willis, born say 1785, a "F.N." taxable in Isle of Wight County from 1802 to 1810 [PPTL 1782-1810, frames 568, 627, 643, 741, 821, 839].

   viii.   James, Jr., born say 1785, a "F.N" taxable in Isle of Wight County in 1801 and 1806, listed as Henry Harrison's tithable in 1807 [PPTL 1782-1810, frames 551, 569, 756].

Members of the family in Granville County, North Carolina, were

   i.   Lucy, born say 1740, a "black" taxable in 1762 in the Granville County household of "black" taxable John **Portee**, Sr., in the list of Phil Pryor. Portee's other taxables were John, Jr., Uriah, Rachel, and Milley **Portee** [CR 44.701].

   ii.   John, born say 1745, a "Mulattoe" taxable in Michael **Gowen**'s Granville County, North Carolina household in 1759 and 1761 in the list of John Pope [CR 44.701.19]. He was a "Mulato" taxable in Bladen County from 1768 to 1772 [Byrd, *Bladen County Tax Lists*, I:7, 16, 79].

   iii.   Sarah, born say 1746, a "black" taxable in 1762 in the Granville County household of "black" taxable John **Portee**, Sr., in the list of Phil Pryor [CR 44.701].

   iv.   William[2], born say 1747, a "Mulattoe" taxable in Michael **Gowen**'s 1771 Bute County household in the list of Philemon Hawkins [CR 15.70001, p.11]. Michael **Gowen** moved to Prince George Parish, Craven County, South Carolina, before 3 June 1778 [Granville Co., N.C., WB 1:193], and William may have moved there with him. William was head of a Charleston District, St. Bartholomew's Parish, South Carolina household of 6 "other free" in 1790 and an Abbeville District household of 8 "other free" in 1810 [NC:12]. His neighbor, William **Bryan/ Bryant**, head of a St. Bartholomew's Parish household of 5 "other free" in 1790, was a taxable "free Mulatto" neighbor of the Wilsons in the 1769 and 1770 Bertie County list of Jonathan Standly [CR 10.702.1].

v.   Basil, born say 1750, a "black" taxable in the 1762 Granville County list of Phil Pryor in the household of "black" taxable John **Portee**, Sr. [CR 44.701], perhaps identical to Brazwel Wilson and wife, "free negroes" taxable in the district between Broad and Catawba Rivers in South Carolina in 1784 [South Carolina Tax Returns 1783-1800, frame 37]. Edey Wilson, Elizabeth Wilson, Rachel **Portie** and Sarah **Portie** were residents of Richland District in 1806 when they petitioned the South Carolina legislature to be exempted from the tax on free Negro women [S.C. Archives, General Assembly Petitions ND 1796, frames 786-92].

Other members of the Wilson family in Virginia were

i.   Forrister, a "Mulatto" child bound apprentice to Charles Littleton in Frederick County on 4 March 1761 [Orders 1760-2, 269].
ii.   Mary, born say 1776, "a free Mulato girl" brought to Surry County, North Carolina, by John Martin. On 14 May 1782 the court ordered her delivered to Elizabeth **Chavis** so she could return her to her parents [Absher, *Surry County, North Carolina, Court Minutes*, 38]. She may have been the Mary Wilson who was head of a Rockingham County, North Carolina household of 1 "free colored" in 1820 [NC:652].
iii. Isbell, head of a Petersburg Town household of 12 "other free" in 1810 [VA:127b].
iv.   John, born about 1786, registered in York County on 17 September 1810: a *dark Mulatto about 24 years of age...wooly Hair...born free* [Free Negro Register 1798-1831, no. 52]. He was head of a York County household of 7 "other free" and a slave in 1810 [VA:885].
v.   Samuel, head of a Norfolk County household of 8(?) "other free" in 1810 [VA:837].
vi.   Sally, head of a Petersburg Town household of 4 "other free" in 1810 [VA:125a].
vii. Sally, head of a Richmond City household of 4 "other free" in 1810 [VA:370].

South Carolina

1.   Jenney Wilson, born say 1770, was living with Henry Glencamp, State Superintendent of the Santee Canal, on 13 December 1823 when he made his St. Stephen's Parish, Berkeley County, South Carolina will, proved 2 March 1824. He called her a "free Woman of Colour" and left his plantation called Pine Hill to her and her six children: Isaac, Christiana, Nanny, Henry, Mary, and Harriet. He named her son Isaac his executor [WB 36:985-7]. Henry Glencamp was head of a St. Stephen's Parish household of 1 "other free" and 4 slaves in 1810, and there was also a Mustafa **Glencamp** who was head of a St. Stephen's Parish, Berkeley County household of 3 "other free" in 1810 [SC:464]. Henry and Jenney's children were

i.   Isaac, born say 1800.
ii.   Christiana, born say 1802.
iii. Nanny, born say 1804.
iv.   Henry, born say 1806, not yet twenty-one years old when Henry Glencamp made his will.
v.   Mary, born say 1808.
vi.   Harriet, born say 1810.

WINBORN FAMILY

1. Thomas[1] Winborn, born say 1750, was head of a Halifax County household of 3 "other free" in 1790 [NC:65], and 2 in 1800 [NC:354]. He was probably the same person as Thomas Winmon who was head of a household with his wife Patience, counted as "free molattows" in the Bertie County list of Josiah Harrell for William Vann's District adjacent to Benjamin **James** in 1770 and 1771 and in the list of Samuel Granberry adjacent to Benjamin **James** in 1774 [CR 10.702.1, box 2]. Thomas Winborn was counted in the 1790 census for Halifax County living in a household nearby Benjamin **James** [NC:65]. Thomas' 15 March 1829 Halifax County will, proved August 1829, left 148 acres in Halifax to his heirs who were his wife Easter, his brother David, his grandnephew John Henry Winborn (son of Thomas, Jr.) and Willie Winborne (son of Nancy Winborne) [WB 4:52]. His children may have been

    i. William, born before 1776, head of a Halifax County household of 6 "free colored" in 1820 [NC:170].

    ii. Benjamin, born say 1785, married Sarah **Jones**, 26 May 1804 Bertie County bond with Frederick **James** bondsman. He was head of a Bertie County household of 5 "other free" in 1810 [NC:142].

2. David Winborn, born before 1776, was head of a Halifax County household of 11 "other free" in 1810 [NC:56] and 9 "free colored" in 1820 [NC:170]. He received 50 acres by the 15 November 1815 Halifax County will of (his mother-in-law?) Lucy **Murray**, proved in August 1816 [WB 3:587]. He may have been the father of

    i. Thomas[2], father of John Henry Winborne who was mentioned in the will of Thomas[1] Winborn.

The family moved to Ripley township, Rush County, Indiana, where John, Lewis, David, Hardy, and Benjamin B. Winborn were heads of "free colored" households in 1840.

WYNN/ WINN FAMILY

Members of the Wynn/ Winn family were

1   i. George[1], born say 1720.
2   ii. Gloucester, born say 1740.

1. George[1] Wynne, born say 1720, was the "Mulatto Man Servant" of Colonel Benjamin Harrison before 4 September 1740 when he was taken up as a runaway in Brunswick County, Virginia [Orders 1732-41, 351]. On 4 May 1759 the Chesterfield County court ordered the churchwardens of Dale Parish to bind out his daughter Sarah [Orders 1754-9, 516]. He was the father of

3   i. Sarah, born say 1750.
4   ii. ?Mary Caroline, born about 1763.

2. Gloucester Winn, born say 1740, was taxable in King William County from 1782 to 1788: taxable on 200 acres from 1782 to 1787; taxable on 2 free tithes and 11 slaves in 1782; taxable on a free tithe, 3 slaves over 16 (named Wagg, Siller and Bett), 8 slaves aged 12-16, and 11 "white" (free) souls in 1783; taxable on 4 slaves over 16 (named Wog, Silla, Bet, and Rachel) and 6 slaves aged 12-16 (named Lewis, Randol, Suck, Bernard, Frank and Silloho) in 1784 and 1785; 12 slaves, 2 horses and 14 cattle in 1787; and 2 free tithables and 7 slaves in 1788 and 1789 [Land Tax List 1782-1832; PPTL 1782-1811]. He died before 1791 when his land was surveyed in order to divide it among his wife and sons Seaton, Curtis and George Winn [Record Book 3:441]. "Gloucester Winn's orphans" were taxable in King William County on 77-1/2 acres from 1792 to 1799. Sarah Winn, apparently his widow, was taxable in

King William County from 1790 to 1811: taxable on 5 slaves in 1790, 8 in 1791, 4 slaves from 1792 to 1810 but not listed in 1811, taxable on 179-1/2 acres (which had been transferred to her by Gloster Winn) from 1792 to 1811 and also taxable on 46-1/2 acres as guardian to Nancy, Charity and Hamm Winn in 1800 [PPTL 1782-1811; Land Tax List 1782-1832]. Gloucester was the father of

   i.   William, born say 1763, taxable in King William County from 1784 to 1817: taxable on his own tithe and a slave under the age of 16 in 1784, taxable on his own tithe in 1791, taxable on 4 slaves over the age of 16 in 1797, taxable on 4 slaves in 1809, 3 in 1810, 6 in 1811, listed as a "Mulatto" in 1813 and taxable on 25 acres in 1798, 15-1/2 acres in 1800 and 1801 [PPTL, 1787, p.30; 1797, p.16; Land Tax List 1782-1832]. On 3 December 1798 he purchased from Curtis Winn 15-1/2 acres in the parish of Saint David in King William County as well as Curtis's rights to his mother's dower land for 15 pounds [Record Book 3:441].

   ii.   Seaton, born say 1768, taxable in King William County from 1784 to 1814: listed in Gloster Winn's household in 1784, taxable on his own tithe and a slave in 1794; taxable on 4 slaves in 1797, a "Mulatto" taxable in 1813. He was taxable on 15-1/2 acres in 1800, 1801, and from 1804 to 1811 [PPTL 1782-1811; 1812-50; Land Tax List 1782-1832].

   iii.   Armstead, born say 1773, taxable in King William County on 1-3 slaves from 1794 to 1807, taxable on his own tithe in 1809 [PPTL, 1782-1811] and taxable on 15-1/2 acres from 1800 to 1811 [Land Tax List 1782-1832].

   iv.   George[2], born say 1774, taxable in King William County on his own tithe and a slave in 1795 and 1796. He owned a tract of land in King William County on 3 December 1798 which he received by division of the land of his father Gloucester Winn [Record Book 3:441]. He was taxable on 15-1/2 acres from 1800 to 1811 [Land Tax List 1782-1832].

   v.   Oney, taxable on 31 acres in King William County from 1800 to 1810, taxable on 46-1/2 acres in 1811, taxable on a horse from 1809 to 1811, taxable on a slave in 1811, listed as a "Mulatto" in 1813 [PPTL 1812-50]. She married a Pamunkey Indian [Rountree, *Pocahantas's People*, 343].

   vi.   Polly, taxable in King William County on 15-1/2 acres from 1800 to 1811, taxable on a horse in 1809 and 1810, taxable on a slave in 1811, listed as a "Mulatto" in 1813 [Land Tax List 1782-1832; PPTL 1782-1811; 1812-50].

   vii.   Curtis, born say 1777, taxable in King William County from 1800 to 1820: taxable on a slave from 1800 to 1811, listed as a "Mulatto" taxable in 1813 [Land Tax List 1782-1832; PPTL 1812-50]. On 3 December 1798 he and his wife Clary Winn sold to William Winn for 15 pounds 15-1/2 acres of land in Saint David's Parish, King William County, which he had received by the division his the estate of his father Gloucester Winn's as well as his rights to a third of his mother's dower land. This land adjoined the lots drawn by (his brothers) Seaton Winn and George Winn [Record Book 3:441].

   viii.   Betty, taxable in King William County on 15-1/2 from 1802 to 1811, taxable on a slave and 3 horses from 1809 to 1811, listed as a "Mulatto" in 1813 [Land Tax List 1782-1832; PPTL 1782-1811; 1812-50].

   ix.   Nancy, taxable in King William County on 15-1/2 acres from 1802 to 1811, taxable on a slave in 1811 [Land Tax List 1782-1832]. She married a Pamunkey Indian [Rountree, *Pocahantas's People*, 343].

   x.   Charity, taxable on 15-1/2 acres in King William County from 1802 to 1811 [Land Tax List 1782-1832].

      xi.   Hamm, taxable in King William County on 15-1/2 acres from 1802 to 1811 [Land Tax List 1782-1832].

3.   Sarah Winn, born say 1750, was bound apprentice in Chesterfield County on 4 May 1759. In August 1782 the court ordered the churchwardens of Dale Parish to bind out her son Lewis [Orders 1754-9, 516; 1774-84, 369]. She was the mother of

      i.   ?Jincy, born about 1774, registered in Petersburg on 25 August 1794: *a brown Mulatto woman, five feet seven inches high, twenty one years old, born free & raised in the Town of Petersburg*. She was married to a member of the **Elliott** family by 8 June 1810 when she registered again: *Jane Elliott a light brown Mulatto woman formerly registered as Jiney Winn, five feet seven inches high, thirty seven years old, born free & raised in the Town of Petersburg* [Register of Free Negroes 1794-1819, nos. 83, 550]. She was head of a Petersburg Town household of 5 "other free" in 1810 [VA:125a].

      ii.   Lewis, born say 1780.

      iii.   ?Anna, born about 1778, registered in Petersburg on 25 June 1810: *a light brown Mulatto woman, five feet three inches high, thirty two years old, long strait black hair, born free and raised in the County of Chesterfield* [Register of Free Negroes 1794-1819, no. 628].

      iv.   ?Patience, born about 1782, registered in Petersburg on 30 June 1804: *a brown Mulatto woman, five feet five and a half inches high, twenty two years old, straight & rather spare made with short wooly hair, born free and raised in the County of Chesterfield* [Register of Free Negroes 1794-1819, no. 277]. She was head of a Petersburg Town household of 2 "other free" in 1810 [VA:124a].

      v.   ?Sally, born about 1783, registered in Petersburg on 15 August 1800: *a brown Mulatto girl, five feet five inches high, seventeen years old, short thick hair, born free and raised in the County of Chesterfield* [Register of Free Negroes 1794-1819, no. 182].

4.   Mary Caroline Wynn, born about 1763, was living in Chesterfield County on 9 January 1809 when she obtained a certificate of freedom: *forty six years old, yellow complexion, born free* [Register of Free Negroes 1804-53, no. 102]. She was head of a Petersburg household of 6 "other free" and 3 slaves in 1810 [VA:118a]. She was probably the mother of

      i.   Elizabeth, born about 1783, obtained a certificate of freedom in Chesterfield County on 9 January 1809: *twenty six years old, brown complexion, born free* [Register of Free Negroes 1804-53, no. 99].

      ii.   Peggy, born about 1786, obtained a certificate of freedom in Chesterfield County on 9 January 1809: *twenty three years old, yellow complexion, born free* [Register of Free Negroes 1804-53, no. 99].

North and South Carolina

1.   Martha Winn, born say 1750, was living in Anson County, North Carolina, on 12 January 1769 when her eight-year-old son Zachariah Winn was bound apprentice to Solomon Gross. On 21 March 1806 Daniel McDaniel testified in Darlington District, South Carolina, that Zachariah's mother was a free white woman [DB G:209]. She was the mother of

2   i.   Zachariah, born about 1761.

2.   Zachariah Winn, born about 1761, was eight years old on 12 January 1769 when he was bound apprentice until the age of twenty-one. He was head of an Anson County household of 1 "other free" in 1790 [NC:35] and was counted as white in 1800: head of a Darlington District, South Carolina household of 1 male 26-45, 2 males under 10, 2 females 26-45, and 3 females under 10. He was granted 77 acres in Darlington District on 2 September 1805 and

purchased another 95 acres there on 11 March 1807. He recorded his indenture papers with the deed to prove that he was free. On 13 May 1820 he used his land as security for a loan of $413 from Alexander Sparks [DB G:207-9, 386-8]. He was head of a Darlington District household of 9 "other free" in 1810 [SC:654] and 7 "free colored" in 1830. He and his wife Lucy were the parents of

    i.   Letitia, married Isaac Weatherford, head of a Darlington District household of 4 "free colored" in 1820. In 1859 their son James Weatherford of Marlboro District sued the tax collector and sheriff to avoid paying the capitation tax on free persons of color. Deponents from Darlington District testified that James was the grandson of Zachariah Wynn and his wife Lucy who had a son David and a daughter Letitia. Letitia and her husband Isaac Weatherford were said to have been members of the Methodist Church at Society Hill where they sat with whites and were visited by the ministers. Isaac was considered to be a white man, Letitia a "Coloured" woman, but she was buried in the white cemetery [South Carolina Archives, Marlboro County, Mixed Provenance Papers, circa 1800-1860, L-35247, Weatherford vs. Stanton, by *The Darlington Flag*, Fall 1999, 131-7].

    ii.   David D., born 1794-1806, head of a Darlington District household of 4 "free colored" in 1830.

    iii.   ____, married first a white man and second, a member of the **Mumford** family according to testimony in James Weatherford's case in 1859.

WINTERS FAMILY

Members of the Winters family in Virginia and Maryland were

    i.   Henry, head of a Baltimore City household of 5 "other free" in 1800 [MD:396].

    ii.   James, head of a Loudoun County household of 12 "other free" in 1810 [VA:293].

    iii.   Lydia, head of a Baltimore City household of 5 "other free" in 1810 [MD:396].

    iv.   Rachel, head of an Anne Arundel County household of 6 "other free" in 1810 [MD:73].

1   v.   William, born say 1770.

1.   William Winters, born say 1770, was living in Amherst County, Virginia, and married to Nancy when she registered on 15 November 1843: *wife of William Winters bright coloured mulatto 71 years old 5 feet 5 inches high...born free.* They were the parents of

    i.   ?Thomas, born about 1792, registered in Amherst County on 18 March 1844: *a free man of colour 5 feet nine inches high, dark complexion 52 years old .. born free.* He married Elvira Ann **Arnold** in Amherst County in 1833. His wife Elvira registered the same day: *wife of Thomas Winters, free woman of colour 29 years old bright mulatto, born free.*

    ii.   Lucy, born about 1802, registered in Amherst County on 15 November 1843: *daughter of William and Nancy Winters...about 41 dark complexion...born free.*

    iii.   Jane, born about 1812, registered in Amherst County on 15 November 1843: *daughter of William & Nancy Winters dark complexion...about 31 years of age...born free.*

    iv.   Edward, born about 1808-1818, registered in Amherst County on 18 November 1843: *about 25 years old of black complexion...son of William & Nancy Winters...born free.* He married Elizabeth **Arnold**, daughter of Robert **Arnold**, in Amherst County in 1839. His wife

Elizabeth registered the same day: *wife of Edward Winters bright mulatto...24 years old...born free.* Edward registered again in January 1851: *born in the County of Nelson...age 43 years* [McLeroy, *Strangers in their Midst*, 65, 67, 112].

WISE FAMILY

1. Mary Wise, born say 1714, was the servant of Robert Wells on 21 August 1732 when she appeared in Prince George's County, Maryland court and admitted that she had given birth to an illegitimate "Malatto" child. The court bound her nine-week-old child Becky to serve for thirty-one years and sold her and the child to her master for 1,500 pounds of tobacco [Court Records 1732-4, 14]. She was the mother of
    i. Becky, born in June 1732.

They may have been the ancestors of
    i. Agnes, head of an Accomack County, Virginia household of 4 "other free" and 2 slaves in 1800 and 11 "other free" in 1810 [VA:35].
    ii. Thomas, head of an Elizabeth City County, Virginia household of 5 "other free" and a slave in 1810 [VA:185].
    iii. Peter, head of a Norfolk County household of 6 "other free" in 1810 [VA:839], perhaps the Peter Wise, born before 1776, who was head of a Dagsboro Hundred, Sussex County, Delaware household of 4 "free colored" in 1820 [DE:380].

WOMBLE FAMILY

1. John Womble, born about 1755, was a carpenter who enlisted in the 10th North Carolina Regiment on 1 June 1779 in Halifax County.[214] He was captured in the siege of Charleston and remained on parole for the remainder of the war. He married his wife Catherine in Edgecombe County in 1798 [M805, reel 883, frame 836]. He purchased land in Edgecombe County by deed proved on 30 May 1799 and sold land there by deed proved in February court 1800 [Minutes 1797-1800, n.p.]. His wife Catherine was one of the siblings of Jacob Greene, deceased, who petitioned the Edgecombe County court to divide 91 acres of his land in November 1804 [Gammon, *Record of Estates Edgecombe County*, 85]. John was head of an Edgecombe County household of 1 "other free" in 1790 and 11 "free colored" in 1820 [NC:112]. He owned 75 acres on 25 August 1818 when he made his pension application in Edgecombe County court, listing his family then living with him: wife Catherine (forty-one years old), Nathaniel (eighteen), Finnety (fourteen), twins Jacob and Ajax (ten), Benjamin (eight and one-half), Enos (seven), John Washington (five and one-half), and Catherine (two and one-half). He was granted a pension of $96 per year but died soon afterwards, about 1820 [M805, reel 883, frame 836]. In 1835 his wife Catherine petitioned the Edgecombe County court for dower, stating that her husband died in 1821 and listing their children: Doctor Warren Womble, Nathaniel G. Womble, Mary Ann Proctor, Celia P. Sorey, and Jacob, Benjamin, Enos, John, and Catherine Womble [Gammon, *Record of Estates Edgecombe County*, 105]. Catherine moved to Fayette County, Tennessee, and died on 2 February 1843 according to the 19 October 1853 survivor's pension application of her son Benjamin in Carroll County, Tennessee [M805, reel 883, frame 836]. According to his pension and estate files, his children were
    i. Warren.

---

[214]He may have been related to Celia Wumble, a base born child bound to John Brown, Jr., by the 11 February 1773 Bute County Court [Minutes 1767-76, 259].

   ii.   Nathaniel G., born about 1800, perhaps the Nathaniel G. Womble who married Celia Sorrell, 9 January 1823 Edgecombe County bond and Martha Frier, 3 December 1823 Edgecombe County bond.

   iii. Mary Ann Proctor, died before 1835.

   iv. Finneyty, born about 1804.

   v.   Cealy Pollard Sorey, born about 1806.

   vi. Jacob Y., born about 1808.

   vii. Ajax, born about 1808, Jacob's twin brother.

   viii. Benjamin F., born about 1810, living in Carroll County, Tennessee, on 19 October 1853 when he applied for a survivor's pension for his father's services.

   ix. Enos G., born about 1811.

   x.   John Washington, born about 1813.

   xi. Catherine, born about 1816.

WOOD FAMILY

1.   Rebecca Wood, born say 1686, was the white servant of Mingo Ingles on 24 June 1707 when the York County court convicted her for having a "mulata female child." The court ordered that she serve her master an additional year and that she be sold by the churchwardens of Bruton Parish at the completion of her indenture for five years. On 4 May 1708 and 24 January 1709/10 she was convicted for having other "Mulatto" children [DOW 13:72, 115, 127, 137, 216, 235, 263]. She may have been the ancestor of

   i.   Frank, born say 1707, a "malatto" taxable in Northampton County, Virginia, in 1728 in Ralph Pigot's list for the Lower Precinct [L.P. 1728].

   ii. Ann, born say 1730, sued for debt on 15 May 1752 by the churchwardens of Nottoway Parish, Southampton County (for having a bastard child). On 22 September 1752 and 13 December 1753 the court ordered the churchwardens of Nottoway Parish to bind out her unnamed "Mulatto" child [Orders 1749-54, 239, 250, 278, 430].

2   iii. Esther, born say 1737.

   iv. Philip, born say 1756, a seaman from Lancaster County who served in the Revolution [Jackson, *Virginia Negro Soldiers*, 46].

3   v.   Thomas[1], born say 1758.

   vi. Charles, taxable in Lancaster County from 1795 to 1814 [PPTL, 1782-1839, frames 134, 192, 385, 399].

2.   Esther Wood, born say 1737, was a "mulatto girl" bound out by the churchwardens of Henrico County in October 1741 [Orders 1737-61, 158]. She may have been the mother of

   i.   Jesse, born about 1760 in Hanover County, a "yellow" complexioned soldier who enlisted for three years service in the Revolutionary War while resident in King William County in 1778. He lived in Fluvanna County for more than fifty years [National Archives pension file S7962; The Chesterfield Supplement cited by NSDAR, *African American Patriots*, 154; Jackson, *Virginia Negro Soldiers*, 45]. He was a "Mulatto" taxable in the upper district of Goochland County from 1804 to 1813: a groom at George Holman's in 1804, a farmer on David Ross's land in 1810, charged with Jack Wood's tithe in 1812, a carpenter at James **Cockran**'s in 1813 [PPTL, 1782-1809, frames 698; 1810-32, frames 20, 88, 112, 177]. He was head of a Goochland County household of 6 "other free" in 1810 [VA:722].

3.   Thomas[1] Wood, born say 1758, was a seaman from Lancaster County who served in the Revolution [Jackson, *Virginia Negro Soldiers*, 46]. He and Abel **Spriggs** were "mulattoes" listed among the deserters from the ship *Dragon*

who were allowed until 20 July 1779 to return without punishment according to the 3 July 1779 issue of the *Virginia Gazette* [Dixon's edition, p. 3, col. 2]. Spriggs was probably related to Aaron **Sprigg**, a black labourer living with his wife in Alexandria in 1799 [*Virginia Genealogist* 4:169], and James **Sprigg**, head of a Washington, D.C. household of 1 "other free" in 1800. Thomas married Sally **Bee**, 20 January 1813 Lancaster County bond. He may have been the ancestor of

   i.   Holland, born say 1800, married Jane **Haw**, 15 October 1821 Lancaster County bond.
   ii.   Polly, married Robert **Rich**, November 1813 Lancaster County bond.
   iii.   Charlotte, "free mulatto," head of a Northumberland County household of 5 "other free" in 1810 [VA:1000], perhaps the Charlotte Wood who was head of a Richmond County household of 4 "other free" in 1810 [VA:407].
   iv.   John, married Nancy **Thomas**, "daughter of Spencer **Thomas**, 13 January 1807 Northumberland County bond, Spencer **Thomas** security. John was a "free mulatto" head of a Northumberland County household of 4 "other free" in 1810 [VA:1000].

Frederick County
1.   Elizabeth Wood, born say 1726, was presented by the churchwardens of Frederick Parish, Frederick County, on 5 November 1746 for having a "Mulatto" child [Orders 1745-8, 195, 253]. She may have been the mother of
   i.   Agnes, mother of Betsey **Bell**, a "mullatoe" child bound out by the Frederick County court on 15 February 1785 [Orders 1783-5, 350].

Warwick County
1.   Anne Wood, born say 1730, a widow, was presented by the Warwick County court on 1 May 1760 for having a "Mulatto" bastard child. On 3 July the jury found her guilty and ordered her to pay a fine of 15 pounds currency [Minutes 1748-62, 330].

WOOTEN FAMILY

1.   Tom Wooten, born say 1700, a "mulatto boy," ran away from Cutbert Hubberd of Warwick County, before 26 July 1715 when Philip Lightfoot preferred his claim in York County court for taking him up [OW 14:404]. He may have been the ancestor of
2   i.   Lucy, born say 1750.
   ii.   Stephen, taxable in Meherrin Parish, Greensville County, in 1791, 1800 and 1802 [PPTL 1782-1850, frames 130, 263, 290].
   iii.   Benjamin, born before 1776, taxable in Meherrin Parish, Greensville County, from 1792 to 1820: listed in 1813 with (wife) Frances, "Mulattos" [PPTL 1782-1850, frames 143, 165, 195, 207, 225, 250, 263, 290, 341, 376, 417, 450, 466, 489, 610] and head of a Greensville County household of 2 "free colored" in 1820 [VA:266].
   iv.   Abner, born before 1776, head of a Wilkes County, North Carolina household of 3 "other free" in 1800 [NC:67], 6 in 1810 [NC:859] and 9 "free colored in 1820 [NC:491].
   v.   Elizabeth, head of a Wilkes County household of 3 "other free" in 1800 [NC:67].
   vi.   Fanny, head of a Northampton County, North Carolina household of 5 "other free" in 1810 [NC:753].
   vii.   Tilley, married Edmund **Guy**, 8 September 1813 Orange County, North Carolina bond, Jesse and Buckner **Guy** bondsmen.
   viii.   Icy, head of a Wilkes County household of 3 "other free" in 1810 [NC:859] and 2 "free colored" in 1820 [NC:506]. She married Isaac **Harris**, 22 September 1832 Wilkes County bond.

    ix. Polly, born 1776-1794, head of a Wilkes County household of 4 "free colored" in 1820 [NC:529].

2. Lucy Wooton, born say 1750, was the mother of an illegitimate "Mulattoe" boy named Reuben Wooton who was bound out by the Orange County, Virginia court on 25 October 1770. She was the mother of
    i. Reuben, born say 1770.

WORRELL FAMILY

1. Martha Worrell, born say 1735, was living in Southampton County on 10 December 1756 when the churchwardens sued her for 15 pounds for having an illegitimate child and the court ordered the churchwardens to bind out her unnamed "mullatto" child. Sarah Turner and Christopher Wade were witnesses for the churchwardens. The court issued the same order two years later on 14 December 1758 [Orders 1754-9, 316, 323, 474]. She was probably the ancestor of
    i. Sally, born 1794-1806, head of a Halifax County, North Carolina household of 5 "free colored" in 1830.
    ii. Lucy, born 1806-1820, head of a Halifax County, North Carolina household of 3 "free colored" in 1830.

WRIGHT FAMILY

1. Jane Wright, born say 1732, the servant of Richard Vernon, confessed to the Orange County, Virginia court on 22 November 1752 that she had a "Mullato bastard Child begot by a Negro" [Orders 1747-54, 392]. She may have been the ancestor of
    i. Henry, head of a New Hanover County, North Carolina household of 1 "other free" in 1800 [NC:311].
    ii. Caroline, born before 1776, head of a Cumberland County, North Carolina household of 1 "other free" in 1820 [NC:222].
    iii. Silvy, head of a Campbell County, Virginia household of 4 "other free" in 1810 [VA:871].

A member of another Wright family in Virginia was
    i. Sawney, born say 1728, a "mulatto servant man" who was bound to Anthony Sydnor, Gent., in April 1749 when the Richmond County, Virginia court ordered that he serve another four months for running away [Orders 12:162].

YOUNG FAMILY

1. Mary Young, born say 1668, was the servant of Mrs. Ann Farmer of Northumberland County on 17 April 1689 when the court ordered her to serve her mistress additional time for having a child by a "negro" [Orders 1678-98, pt. 2, 461]. She may have been the mother of
2   i. Elizabeth, born say 1700.

2. Elizabeth Young, born say 1700, was a "free Mulatto" woman of Norfolk County who purchased her husband Abraham **Newton**, a "Mulatto." She died in November 1743 and left a will (not recorded) which gave him his freedom. The Council of Virginia ordered him set free [McIlwaine, *Executive Journals, Council of Colonial Virginia,* V:196, 215]. She may have been the ancestor of
3   i. Isaac, born say 1730.
4   ii. Jane, born say 1736.

3. Isaac Young, born say 1730, was living in Southampton County on 13 June 1754 when he was one of fourteen heads of household who were sued by William Bynum (informer) for failing to pay the discriminatory tax on free African American and Indian women.[215] He was found not guilty. On 14 August 1755 the court ordered the churchwardens of Nottoway Parish to bind out his children [1749-54, 500, 512; 1754-9, 24, 33, 121]. He may have been the Isaac Young who was head of a Nansemond County household of 5 persons in 1783 [VA:57] and 4 "other free" in Norfolk County in 1810 [VA:816]. He may have been the father of

    i.   Aaron, born say 1762, head of a Nansemond County household of one "white" (free) person in 1783 and a "Mulatto" listed in Buxton's List for Nansemond County in 1783 [VA:57].
    ii. Jacob, head of a Nansemond County household of 4 persons in 1783 [VA:57].
    iii. Peggy, born say 1764, a "free Negro" who married Peter **Elliott** on 20 August 1785 in Norfolk County.

4. Jane Young, born say 1736, was the mother of a "mulatoe orphan," William Young, bound as an apprentice bricklayer to Samuel Milburn in Bertie County, North Carolina, on 28 December 1769 [*NCGSJ* XIV:34]. Perhaps she had the child by a member of the **Demery** family since Wiley and Micajah **Demery** sometimes used the name Young. She may have been the Jane Young who purchased 50 acres in Northampton County, North Carolina, jointly with Philip **Byrd** on 16 March 1778 [DB 6:262]. Jane was the mother of

    i.   William, born about 1755, fourteen years old when he was bound apprentice on 28 December 1769, perhaps the same person as Wiley **Demery**, head of an Anson County household of 3 "other free" in 1800 [NC:207], and counted a second time in 1800 as Wiley **Young** [NC:203], called William **Demery** in 1810, head of a Marion District, South Carolina household of 3 "other free" in [SC:80].
    ii. ?Robert, born say 1759, purchased 150 acres in Franklin County, North Carolina on 2 November 1780 [DB 5:14]. He was head of a Franklin County household of 5 "other free" in 1810 [VA:825].
    iii. ?Charity, born say 1768, married Solomon **Bibby**, 25 December 1789 Franklin County bond.
    iv. ?Micajah[1] **Demery**, born say 1770, a "Black" person 12-50 years old living alone in Captain Dupree's District of Northampton County, North Carolina, in 1786 for the state census. He called himself Micajah Young on 30 April 1794 when he married Elizabeth **Evans**, Wake County bond. He was head of a Wake County household of 2 "other free" in 1790 (abstracted as Micajah Dempsey) [NC:106]. He was head of an Anson County household of 5 "other free" in 1800, counted as Micajah Young [NC:203] and counted a second time as Micajah **Demery** [NC:207], 7 in 1810 (as Micajah **Demery**) [NC:44], and 11 "free colored" in 1820, called "Micajah Demery alias Young" [NC:12].

Other members of the Young family were
    i.   Nancy, born about 1756, registered in Middlesex County on 23 August 1801: *born free; 45 years of age; 5'2-1/4"; Dark complexion* [Register of Free Negroes 1800-60, p.15].
    ii. Tony, "Free Negro" head of a Charlotte County household of 7 "other free" in 1810 [VA:69].

---

[215]The other householders were John **Porteus**, John **Demery**, Thomas **Wilkins**, Francis **Locust**, James **Brooks**, Jr. and Sr., John **Byrd**, Jr. and Sr., Abraham **Artis**, Lewis **Artis**, William **Brooks**, Ann **Brooks**, and William **Tabor**.

iii. David, head of a Charles City household of 3 "other free" in 1810 [VA:939].

iv. Powers, head of a Charles City household of 3 "other free" in 1810 [VA:939].

v. Lucy, head of a Charlotte County household of 4 "other free" in 1810 [VA:67].

vi. Sall, head of a Westmoreland County household of 2 "other free" in 1810.

Accomack County

1. Catherine Young, born say 1698, was a "Free Negro Woman" who complained to the Accomack County court on 5 March 1728 that John McAlester was detaining her against her will as a slave. The court ordered her released [Orders 1724-31, 148, 154]. In 1731 she was a taxable "negro" in Richard Haise's Northampton County, Virginia household in the list of Thomas Marshall [L.P. 1731]. She may have been the ancestor of

    i. Ned, head of an Accomack Parish, Accomack County household of 2 "other free" in 1800 [*Virginia Genealogist* 2:85].

Augusta County

1. Lodowick Young, born say 1730, was a "Negro slave" who had a son named James Young by Jane Colligen in Augusta County about 1755. He was the father of

    i. James, born about 1755, a two-year-old "Mulato" boy living in Augusta County on 17 August 1757 when the court ordered the churchwardens of Augusta Parish to bind him out [Orders 1753-5, 428].

    ii. ?Julia, born say 1758, "Molatto" mother of Kitty Young who was ordered bound to Jacob Doran by the Augusta County court on 20 February 1781. She may have been identical to Julia (no last name), the "Mulattoe" mother of James Charles who was bound out by the court on 13 June 1782 [Orders 1779-83, 325, 414].

SOURCES

NORTH CAROLINA COUNTIES

Albemarle

Haun, Weynette Parks. 1982. *Old Albemarle County, North Carolina, Miscellaneous Records, 1678 to ca 1737.* Durham, N.C.

Haun, Weynette Parks. 1980. *Old Albemarle County, North Carolina, Perquimans Precinct, Births, Marriages, Deaths & Flesh Marks 1659 thru 1820.*

Anson

MS County Court Minutes 1771-1777; Record of Deeds. Books 1, 6, 7, A, B, C-1. N.C. Archives microfilms C.005.3001; C.005.4002 & C.005.40001.

MS Tax Lists. N.C. Archives Treasurer and Controller's Papers.

Holcolm, Brent, Howard. *Anson County, North Carolina, Deed Abstracts, 1749-1766, Abstracts of Wills & Estates, 1749-1795.* Columbia, S.C.

Beaufort

MS Tax Lists. N.C. Archives Secretary of State Papers (SS 837).

MS Beaufort County Minute, Appearance, Prosecution, & Trial Dockets, County Court of Pleas & Quarter Sessions, 1756-1761, N.C. Archives Microfilm # C.009.30001.

MS Beaufort County Court Minutes 1785-1786, 1809-1814, 1824-1829, N.C. Archives Microfilm # C.009.3002.

Beaufort County Genealogical Society. 1990. *Beaufort County, North Carolina, Will Abstracts, 1720-1868.* Washington, NC.

Camin, Betty J. 1984. *Beaufort Orphans Book A 1808-1828 (Wills and Estate Record of Beaufort County, North Carolina.* Raleigh, N.C.

Bertie

MS Apprentice Indentures prior to 1750. N.C. Archives stack file no. CR 10.101.

MS Real Estate Conveyances, 1722-1784, Vols. A-M. N.C. Archives Microfilms C.010.40001-5.

MS Tax Lists. N.C. Archives stack file no. CR 10.702.

MS Tax Lists, Secretary of State. SS 837.

MS Colonial Court Records, Taxes & Accounts, 1679-1754, stack file number CCR.190.

Dunstan, Edythe Smith. 1966. *The Bertie Index for Courthouse Records of Bertie County, North Carolina, 1720-1875.* privately printed.

Gammon, David B. 1986. *Records of Estates Bertie County, North Carolina Volume I, 1728-1744, 1762-1790.* Raleigh, N.C.

Gammon, David B. 1993. *Records of Estates Bertie County, North Carolina Volume II, 1734-1788.* Raleigh, N.C.

Haun, Weynette Parks. 1976-1984. *Bertie County North Carolina County Court Minutes (Court of Pleas & Quarter Sessions).* Durham, N.C.

Book I	*1724-1739*	*Book II*	*1740-1762*
Book III	*1763-1771*	*Book IV*	*1772-1780*
Book V	*1781-1787*	*Book VI*	*1788-1792*

Bladen

MS Tax Lists, Secretary of State [SS 837].

MS Deeds and Wills photocopied by the Court Clerk of Bladen County.

Bladen County Historical Society. *1784 Tax List Bladen County N.C.* Elizabethtown, N.C.

Byrd, William L. 1998. *Bladen County, North Carolina Tax Lists, 1768 through 1774, Volume I.* Privately printed.

Byrd, William L. 1998. *Bladen County, North Carolina Tax Lists, 1775 through 1789, Volume II.* Heritage Books, Inc. Maryland.

Philbeck, Miles S. 1985. *Surviving Land Warrants and Surveys 1735-1749 and Surviving Land Entries 1743-1761.*
Pruitt, A.B. 1989. *Abstracts of Land Entries: Bladen County, NC, 1778-1781.* Cary, N.C.

Brunswick
MS Tax Lists, General Assembly [GA 11.1], Secretary of State [SS 837].

Pruitt, A.B. 1989. *Abstracts of Land Entries: Brunswick County, NC, 1794-1820.* Cary, N.C.

Buncombe
MS County Court Minutes, 1792-1812, N.C. Archives microfilm reel CR.013.30001.

Bute
MS List of Taxables. 2 pamphlets, 1771. N.C. Archives Microfilm CR.015.70001.

Holcolm, Brent Howard. 1988. *Court of Pleas and Quarter Sessions, Minutes 1767-1779.* Columbia, S.C.

Carteret
MS County Court Minutes 1723-1747, 1747-1777. N.C. Archives Microfilms C.019.30001-2.

Caswell
MS Tax Lists, N.C. Archives stack file no. CR 020.701.10, Secretary of State SS 837.

Pruitt, A.B. 1990. *Abstracts of Land Entries: Caswell Co, NC 1778-1795, 1841-1863, and Person Co, NC 1792-1795.* Cary, N.C.

Chatham
MS County Court Minutes, 1774-1841. N.C. Archives Microfilms C.022.30001-3.

Chowan
Minutes, Court of Pleas and Quarter Sessions, 1755-1772, N.C. Archives Microfilm C.024.30001.
MS Record of Deeds Vol. W-1. N.C. Archives Microfilm C.024.40001.
MS Tithables, 1717-1769. N.C. Archives stack file no. CR 024.701.2.
MS General Court Docket, 1742-1745, Vols. 36-43. N.C. Archives Microfilm *Y.1.10011.

Fouts, Raymond Parker. 1983. *Vestry Minutes of St. Paul's Parish, Chowan County, North Carolina, 1701-1776.* Cocoa, Fl.
Haun, Weynette Parks. 1983. *Chowan County, North Carolina, County Court Minutes (Court of Pleas & Quarter Sessions), Book I (1730-1745), Book II (1735-1738: 1746-1748), Book III, 1749-1754.* Durham, N.C.
Hoffman, Margaret M. 1972. *Chowan Precinct North Carolina 1696 to 1723. Genealogical Abstracts of Deed Books.* Weldon, N.C.: The Roanoke News Company.

Craven
MS Apprentice Indentures, County. N.C. Archives stack file no. CR 28.101.1.
MS County Court Minutes, 1758-1766, 1764-1775, 1772-1784, 1784-87. N.C. Archives Microfilms C.028.30004-7.
MS Deeds, photocopied by Ms. Becky Thompson, Register of Deeds, Craven County, New Bern, North Carolina.

Haun, Weynette Parks. 1978-1987. *Craven County, North Carolina, County Court Minutes (Court of Pleas & Quarter Sessions):*
   Book I   1712-1715   Book II 1730-1741
   Book III   1742-1748   Book IV   1749-1756. Durham, N.C.

Cumberland
MS County Court Minutes, Minutes 1755-1844. N.C. Archives Microfilms C.029.30001-5.

MS Tax Lists. N.C. Archives Treasurer and Controller's Papers.

Currituck

MS Tax Lists, Treasurer and Controller's Papers.

MS Deeds and Wills photocopied by the Court Clerk of Currituck County.

Bates, Jo Anna Heath. 1985. *The Heritage of Currituck County, North Carolina*. Currituck, NC.

Bennett, William Doub. 1994. *Currituck County, North Carolina, Eighteenth Century Tax & Militia Records*. Baltimore.

Jones, Gordon C. 1982. *Abstract of Land Grants, Tax Lists, Orphans Dockets, Inventories and Other Records Currituck and Dare Counties North Carolina*.

Dobbs

MS Grantee Index to Deeds 1746-1880, Lenoir, Johnston, Dobbs Co. N.C. Archives Microfilm MF.95.

Edgecombe

MS County Court Minutes, 1757-1800. N.C. Archives Microfilm reels 1&2.

Gammon, David B. 1992. *Abstract of Wills Edgecombe County, North Carolina Volume I, 1732-1792*. Raleigh, N.C.

Gammon, David B. 1989. *Records of Estates Edgecombe County, North Carolina Volume I, 1761-1825*. Raleigh, N.C.

Haun, Weynette Parks. 1985. *Edgecombe County North Carolina County Court Minutes, 1744 thru 1762, Book I (Fee Docket 1745-1746) Edgecombe County, Northampton County (Crown Docket 1755-1763) Edgecombe County*. Durham, N.C.

Hoffman, Margaret M. 1969. *Abstracts of Deeds, Edgecombe Precinct, Edgecombe County, North Carolina 1732 through 1758 as found in Halifax County, North Carolina Public Registry Deed Books 1-2-3-4-5-6*. Weldon, N.C.: The Roanoke News Co. repr. 1987.

Watson, Joseph W. 1966. *Abstracts of Early Deeds of Edgecombe County, North Carolina, 1759-1772*.

Watson, Joseph W. 1970. *Estate Records of Edgecombe County, North Carolina*. Rocky Mount, N.C.

Franklin

Watson, Joseph W. 1984. *Abstracts of The Early Deeds of Franklin County, North Carolina 1779-1797*. Rocky Mount, N.C.

Bradley, Stephen E. 1996. *Franklin County, North Carolina Original Wills, vol. 1: 1780-1861*. Privately printed.

Gates

Fouts, Raymond Parker. *Minutes of County Court of Pleas and Quarter Sessions, Gates County, N.C. 1779-1786; 1787-1793; Vols. I-IV: 1794-1799, 1800-1805, 1806-1811, 1812-1817*. Cocoa, Fl.

Taylor, Mona Armstrong. 1987. *Abstracts of Deeds Books A-5, Gates County, North Carolina 1776-1803*.

Granville

MS Apprentice Indentures. N.C. Archives stack file no. CR 044.101.2-7.

MS Record of Deeds, 1746-1778, Vol. A., B, C-1, C-2, D-L. N.C. Archives Microfilm reels 28-33.

MS Wills, Vols. 1-5. N.C. Archives Microfilms C.044.8002-3.

MS County Court Minutes, 1754-1770 & 1766-1795. N.C. Archives Microfilm reels 2 & 3.

MS Granville County Marriage Bonds. N.C. Archives microfilm.

MS Tax Lists, 1755, 1769, 1771, 1780, 1782, 1785, 1786, 1786-1791, 1796-1802, 1803-1809. N.C. Archives Microfilm C.044.70012.

MS Tax Lists, 1767-1823. N.C. Archives Microfilm reel 162.

MS Tax Lists. N.C. Archives stack file no. CR 44.701.19-20.

MS Criminal and Civil Action Papers Concerning Slaves and Free Persons of Color [CR 044.928.15 & CR 44.289.19].

Gwynn, Zae Hargett. 1978. *Granville County Guardian Accounts, 1810-1856.* Rocky Mount, N.C.

Owen, Thomas McAdory. 190_. *Granville County, North Carolina, Notes.* Montgomery, Alabama. Library of Congress Microfilm Shelf No. 28037, call no. F262.G85087. (Minutes 1746-1759, 1767-1772, transcribed in 1895 - now missing).

Pruitt, A.B. 1988. *Abstracts of Land Entries: Granville Co., N.C. 1778-1877.* Cary, N.C.

Halifax

MS Record of Wills, Vols. 1-6, N.C. Archives Microfilms C.047.80001, 2.

MS Minutes, Court of Pleas and Quarter Sessions 1784-87, 1796-98, 1799-1802, 1822-1824, 1832-1846, 6 Vols. N.C. Archives Microfilm Reels 1 & 2.

MS The Roanoke Advocate, 5 January 1832 - February 1856. N.C. Archives Microfilm HaRA-2.

Bradley, Stephen E., Jr. 1989-1991. *The Deeds of Halifax County, North Carolina, 1758-1771, 1771-1786, 1786-1796.*

Gammon, David B., 1996. *Records of Estates, Halifax County, North Carolina, Volume II, Revised Edition, 1759-1805.*

Hertford

Tax Lists. N.C. Archives General Assembly Papers GA 30.1 and L.P. 64.1.

Fouts, Raymond Parker. 1993. *William Murfree Tax Receipt Book, Hertford County, North Carolina.* Cocoa, Fl.

Hyde

MS Tax Lists. N.C. Archives Treasurer and Controller's Papers.

Haun, Weynette Parks. 1985. *Hyde County, North Carolina County Court Minutes (Court of Pleas & Quarter Sessions) 1736-1756, Book I (1736-1756), Book II (1757-1785).* Durham, N.C.

Johnston

MS Tax Lists. N.C. Archives General Assembly Papers GA 64.1.

Haun, Weynette Parks. 1980-1988. *Johnston County, North Carolina, County Court Minutes (Court of Pleas & Quarter Sessions), Book I (1759-1766), Book II (1767-1777), Book III (1778-1786), Book IV (1787-1792).* Durham, N.C.

Haun, Weynette Parks. 1980-1988. *Johnston County, North Carolina, Deed Abstracts*

Vol. I   1759-1771   Vol. II 1764-1791
Vol. III   1771-1782   Vol. IV 1779-1794

Haun, Weynette Parks. 1980. *Johnston County, North Carolina, Land Entries 1778-1805.* Durham, N.C.

Martin

MS Tax Lists. N.C. Archives General Assembly Papers GA 30.1.

Mecklenburg

MS Tax Lists. N.C. Archives stack file no. CR 065.928.5.

Nash

MS Wills 1778-1897, Vol 1-5. N.C. Archives Microfilm C.069.80001.

Watson, Joseph W. 1963. *Abstracts of Early Records of Nash County, North Carolina 1777-1859.* Rocky Mount, N.C.

New Hanover

> MS Court of Pleas & Quarter Sessions Minutes 1738-1769, 1771-1798. N.C. Archives Microfilm reel 1.
>
> MS Tax Lists. N.C. Archives Treasurer and Controllers Papers.
>
> MS Deeds & Wills, Vols. AB, A-C. N.C. Archives Microfilm reels 26, 27.
>
> Pruitt, A.B. 1990 *Abstracts of Land Entries: New Hanover County.* Cary, N.C.

Northampton

> MS Court of Pleas and Quarter Sessions Minutes 1792-96, 1813-21, 1821-25. N.C. Archives Microfilm Reels 2 & 3.
>
> MS Real Estate Conveyances Vols. 1-11, 28. N.C. Archives Microfilm reels C.071.40001-3, reels 21-22.
>
> MS Tax Lists. N.C. Archives General Assembly Papers GA 46.1.
>
> MS Record of Wills, Vols 1-6. N.C. Archives Microfilm Reels 125-6.
>
> MS St. George's Parish Warden Records, 1773-1814. N.C. Archives stack file no. CR 71.927.1.
>
> MS Troop Returns. N.C. Archives file no. TR 1-3.
>
> Gammon, David B. *Records of Estates Northampton County, North Carolina,* Volume I.
>
> Hoffman, Margaret M. 1974. *1741-1759, Abstracts of Deeds, Northampton County, North Carolina Deeds, Public Registry Deed Book One and Deed Book Two.* Privately printed.

Onslow

> MS Court of Pleas and Quarter Sessions Minutes 1734-1778, 1779-1794. N.C. Archives Microfilms C.072.30001-2.
>
> MS Tax Lists. N.C. Archives stack file CR 72.703.1, General Assembly Papers GA 11.1, Secretary of State Papers SS 837.

Orange

> MS Record of Deeds, Vol. 1, 2. N.C. Archives Microfilm C.073.40001.
>
> MS Tax Lists. N.C. Archives Treasurer and Controllers Papers T&C 1.
>
> Haun, Weynette Parks. *Orange County, North Carolina, Court Minutes, Volume I, 1752-1761; Volume II, 1762-1766.* Durham, N.C.

Pasquotank

> County Court Minutes 1737-1785, N.C. Archives microfilm no. C.075.30001.
>
> MS Tax Lists. N.C. Archives stack file no. CR.075.701. Secretary of State Papers SS 837.
>
> Haun, Weynette Parks. 1981. *Pasquotank County, North Carolina, Births, Marriages, Deaths, Brands & Flesh Marks, & County Claims 1691-1833.* Durham, N.C.
>
> Haun, Weynette Parks. 1983, 1990. *Pasquotank County, North Carolina, County Court Minutes 1737-1746 (I), 1747-53 (II).* Durham, N.C.

Perquimans

> Minutes, Precinct Court, 1688-1693, 1688-1706, 1735-1738; Minutes County Court 1738-1742, 1752-1755, 1759-1761, 1774, 1755-1761, 1784-1789, N.C. Archives microfilm no. C.077.30002.
>
> MS Apprentice Indentures. N.C. Archives stack file no. CR 077.101.6.
>
> MS Tax Lists. N.C. Archives stack file no. CR 077.701.1.
>
> Haun, Weynette Parks. 1987. *Perquimans County, North Carolina County Court Minutes.* 1638 thru 1754, Books I & II. Durham, N.C.

Person

> MS Court of Pleas & Quarter Sessions Minutes 1792-1802. N.C. Archives Microfilm C.078.30001.

Pruitt, A.B. 1990. *Abstracts of Land Entries: Caswell Co, NC 1778-1795, 1841-1863, and Person Co, NC 1792-1795.* Cary, N.C.

Pitt

MS Tax Lists. N.C. Archives Secretary of State Papers SS 837.

Richmond

MS Minutes, County Court of Pleas & Quarter Sessions 1779-1808, 5 vols. N.C. Archives Microfilm C.082.30001-2.

Pruitt, A. B. *Abstracts of Land Entries: Richmond County, North Carolina: 1780-1795.* Cary, N.C.

Robeson

MS Court of Pleas & Quarter Sessions Minutes 1797-1843, 1843-1860. N.C. Archives Microfilm C.038.30001-2.

MS Wills and Deeds photocopied by the Court Clerk of Robeson County.

Pruitt, A.B. *Abstracts of Land Entries: Robeson County, N.C., 1787-1795.* Cary, N.C.

Rowan

Minutes, Court of Pleas and Quarter Sessions (Abstracts), 1753-1795, Vols. 1, 2. N.C. Archives microfilm no. C.085.30001.

MS Tax Lists. N.C. Archives stack file no. CR 085.701.6.

Sampson

Bizzell. *Sampson County Court Minutes 1784-1800.*

Surry

Absher, Mrs. W. O.. 1985. *Surry County, North Carolina, Court Minutes, Volume I & II, 1768-1789.* Southern Historical Press.

Tyrrell

MS Apprentice Indentures. N.C. Archives stack file no. CR 96.102.1.

MS Tax Lists. N.C. Archives Treasurer and Controllers Papers T&C 105, box 1.

Wake

MS Apprentice Indentures. N.C. Archives stack file no. CR 099.101. 1; Microfilm of MS Tax Lists, MF CR 99.701.1.

Haun, Weynette Parks. 1978. *Wake County, North Carolina, County Court Minutes (Minutes of Pleas & Quarter Session),* Vol. A1, I & II. Durham, N.C.

Warren

MS Record of Deeds, Warren County 1764-1787, Vols. A-8; Tax List 1779-1808; Minutes of Pleas and Quarter Sessions 1777-1800. N.C. Archives microfilms C.100.40001-5, C.100.7001; C.100.30001.

Gammon, David B. 1988. *Records of Estates, Warren County, North Carolina, Volume I, Estates Found in Court Records 1780-1805.* Raleigh.

Kerr, Mary Hinton. 1967. *Warren County, North Carolina records. Abstracted, indexed and compiled.* Warrenton, N.C.

Wilkes

Absher, Mrs. W.O. 1989. *Wilkes County, N.C. Will Books One & Two 1778-1811.* Easley, S.C.: Southern Historical Press, Inc.

Absher, Mrs. W.O. 1988. *Wilkes County Court Minutes 1778-1788, Volumes I & II, Volumes III & IV.* Easley S.C.: Southern Historical Press, Inc.

Absher, Mrs. W.O. 1989. *Some Pioneers from Wilkes County, North Carolina.* Easley S.C.: Southern Historical Press, Inc.

Pruitt, A.B. *Abstracts of Land Entries: Wilkes County.* Cary, N.C.

VIRGINIA COUNTIES

Accomack

MS Accomack County Court Orders 1663-1777; 1790-6; Register of Free Negroes 1785-1863. LVA microfilms 1-9, 79-85, 88, 316. PPTL 1782-1814. LVA microfilm reel no. 1.

Nottingham, Stratton, comp. 1931. *Accomack Tithables (Tax Lists) 1663-1695.* Onancock, Va.

Albemarle

MS Wills and Deeds No. 1, 1748-1752; Court Orders 1744-48; 1783-1801. LVA microfilm reels 33, 46-8.

PPTL, 1782-1813. LVA microfilm reel 5 and 6.

Weisiger, Benjamin B. 1987. *Albemarle County, Virginia, Court Papers, 1744-1783.* Richmond.

Amelia

MS Court Orders 1735-1782, Latter Day Saints Family History Department microfilm no. 30459. LVA microfilm reels 40-43.

MS List of Tithables, LVA microfilm reel 55.

Register of Free Negroes, 1804-1855, microfilm reel no. 84.

Amherst

MS Court Orders 1766-1820; Marriage Register 1763-1852. LVA microfilm reels 27-30, 37, 59. PPTL 1782-1823. LVA microfilm reels 18, 19.

Houck, Peter, W. 1984. *Indian Island in Amherst County.* Lynchburg, Virginia: Progress Printing Co., Inc.

McLeRoy, Sherrie S. & William R. 1993. *Strangers in Their Midst, The Free Black Population of Amherst County, Virginia.* Heritage Books, Inc.

Sweeny, William Montgomery. 1973. *Marriage Bonds and Other Marriage Records of Amherst County, Virginia 1763-1800.* Baltimore: Genealogical Publishing Company.

Sweeny, Lenora Higginbottom. 1951. *Amherst County, Virginia, in the Revolution, Including Extracts from the "Lost Order Book" 1773-1782.* Lynchburg, Virginia.

Arlington County

MS Free Negro Register, 1797-1861, LVA microfilm reel 62. (District of Columbia, Alexandria)

Provine, Dorothy S. 1996. *District of Columbia Free Negro Registers* 1821-1861. 2 vols. Heritage Books. Bowie, Maryland.

Augusta

MS Orders 1743-85. LVA microfilm reels 62-67.

Bath

Free Negro Register, 1794-1841. LVA microfilm reel 141.

Bedford

MS Orders 1754-1782; Register of Free Negroes 1803-1860. LVA microfilm reels 39-40, 120a.

T.L.C. Genealogy. 2000. *Bedford County, Virginia Order Book 1, 1754-1761.* Miami Beach, Florida.

Botetourt
>   MS Order Books 1770-1776. LVA microfilm reel 27.
>
>   MS A List of Free Negroes & Mulattoes 1802-1804 [Orders 1800-1804, Loose Papers] photocopied by the Clerk of Botetourt County.
>
>   MS Free Negroes &c Registered in the Clerks office of Botetourt County photocopied by the Clerk of Botetourt County.

Brunswick
>   MS Orders 1732-1792, Deed Books 1-21, Will Books 2-7. LVA microfilm nos. 1-10, 20-22, 29-34.
>
>   Wynne, Frances Holloway. 1983. *Register of Free Negroes and also Dower Slaves: Brunswick County, Virginia 1803-1850.* Fairfax, Virginia.
>
>   Knorr, Catherine Lindsay. 1953. *Marriage Bonds & Ministers' Returns of Brunswick county, Virginia, 1750-1810.*
>
>   Hopkins, William Lindsay. 1989. *Bath Parish Register 1827-1897 of Dinwiddie County and St. Andrew Parish Vestry Book, 1732-1797, of Brunswick County, Virginia.* Richmond, Virginia.

Buckingham
>   MS PPTL 1782-1809. LVA microfilm reel 60.
>
>   Ward, Roger G. *Buckingham County Virginia Records, Land Tax Summaries & Implied Deeds, 1782-1814*, Volume 1. Athens, Georgia.

Campbell
>   MS Court Orders 1782-1792. LVA reel no. 25. PPTL 1785-1814. LVA reel no. 66. MS Marriage Bonds, 1782-1853. LVA reel no. 44. MS List of Free Negroes. Campbell County Courthouse photocopied by Duke University Library.

Caroline
>   MS Court Orders 1732-1763, LVA microfilm reels 13-16, 19.
>
>   Dorman, John Frederick. 1965-1990. *Caroline County, Virginia Order Book 1732-40, 1740-46, 1746-54; 1755-8, 1759-63, 1765-7.* Washington, D.C.
>
>   Sparacio, Ruth and Sam. 1989. *Order Book Abstracts of Caroline County, Virginia 1765-1778.* McLean, Va.: The Ancient Press.

Charles City
>   MS Deeds, Wills, Orders 1655-1665, 1689-90, 1724/5-1731, 1763-64, 1766-74; Deed Book 4-7; Will Book 1-4; PPTL 1783, 1788-1807, 1809-23; Land Tax List 1782-1830. LVA microfilm reels 1, 2, 3, 8, 9, 23, 78.
>
>   MS Court Orders 1650, 1672-73, 1677-79, 1680, 1685, 1687-95, 1737-51, 1751-7, 1758-62; Minutes 1769, 1788-9, 1823-9, 1830-7. LVA reels 13-16.
>
>   Ayres, Margaret McNeill. 1968. *Charles City County, Virginia Order Book 1676-1679.* Privately printed.
>
>   Weisiger, Benjamin B. III. 1986. *Charles City County, Virginia Records 1737-1774. With Several 17th Century Fragments.* Privately printed.

Charlotte
>   MS Court Orders 1765-1792. LVA microfilm reels 22-25. PPTL 1782-1813, LVA microfilm no. 80.
>
>   Knorr, Catherine Lindsay. 1957. *Marriage Bonds and Ministers' Returns of Charlotte County, Virginia, 1764-1815.*
>
>   Ailsworth, Timothy, et. al. 1979. *Charlotte County--Rich Indeed.* Charlotte County Courthouse.

Chesterfield
> MS Court Orders 1749-1791; Will Book 1, 1749-1765; Will Book 2, 1765-1774; Tithables 1747-1821; PPTL 1786-1811; Land Tax List 1791-1822; Register of Free Negroes 1804-1830. LVA microfilm reels 26, 38-41, 74, 84, 330, 351.
>
> Knorr, Catherine Lindsay. 1958. *Marriage Bonds and Ministers' Returns of Chesterfield County, Virginia, form 1771-1815.*

Culpeper
> MS Court Minute Book 1763-1764; 1798-1802; 1802-1803; 1803-1805; Will Book A & B, 1749-1783. LVA microfilm reels 31, 40.
>
> Knorr, Catherine Lindsay. 1954. *Marriages of Culpeper County, Virginia, 1771-1815.*

Cumberland
> MS Order Books 1749-1801. Will Book 1, 1749-69; Will Book 2, 1769-1792. Virginia State Archive Microfilm Reels, nos. 17, 23-28. PPTL 1782-1816, LVA microfilm no. 93.

Dinwiddie
> MS Order Book 1789-91, Latter Day Saints Family History Department microfilm #31090. PPTL 1782-1819; Land Tax List 1782-1814. LVA microfilms nos. 85, 96, 97.
>
> Hughes, *Land Records, Dinwiddie County.*

Elizabeth City
> MS Court Orders 1692-99, 1715-57; Minutes 1756-60; Court Records 1760-1769. Deeds, Wills, Inventories, 1684-1699, 1715-21, 1723-30; 1737-71. LVA microfilm reels 1-6, 17, 18.
>
> Neal, Rosemary Corley. 1988. *Deeds, Wills, Court Orders 1715-1721.* Heritage Books, Inc.
> Neal, Rosemary Corley. 1986. *Deeds, Wills, Court Orders, Etc. 1634, 1659, 1688-1701.* Heritage Books, Inc.
> von Doenhoff, Marion Ruth. 1957. *The Vestry Book of Elizabeth City Parish, 1751-1784.* A thesis presented to the faculty of the Department of History of the College of William and Mary.

Essex
> MS Orders 1685-1783; Deeds, Wills 1699-1702; Wills, Inventories 1717-1730; Register of Free Negroes 1810-1843. LVA microfilm nos. 1-3, 40, 65-82, 119. PPTL 1782-1819. LVA microfilm no. 103.
>
> Dorman, John Frederick. 1961. *Essex County, Virginia Wills, Bonds, Inventories, etc. 1722-1730.* Washington, D.C.
> Sparacio, Ruth and Sam. 1989-1991. *Essex County Order Book Abstracts 1695-1729.* McLean, Va.: The Ancient Press.

Fairfax
> MS Minutes 1749-65; Orders 1768-74; 1783-88. LVA microfilm reels 37, 38, 38a, 39, 39a.
> Sparacio, Ruth and Sam. 1988. *Land Records of Long Standing, Fairfax County, Virginia (1742-1770).* McLean, Va.: The Ancient Press.

Fauquier
> Sparacio, Sam & Ruth. 1993-1996. *Minute Book Abstracts of Fauquier County, Virginia 1759-1775.* The Antient Press. McLean, Virginia.

Fluvanna
> List of Free Negroes photocopied by the Court Clerk of Fluvanna County.
> PPTL 1782-1826. LVA microfilm no. 118.

Frederick
MS Orders 1743-81. LVA microfilm nos. 66-73.

Fredericksburg
Knorr, Catherine Lindsay. 1954. *Marriage Bonds & Ministers' Returns of Fredericksburg, Virginia 1782-1850.*

Gloucester
MS PPTL 1782-1820. Gloucester County Tax Accounts 1770-1771; Land Tax Books 1782-1820. LVA microfilm nos. 7, 117, 132, 133.

Mason, Polly Cary. 1946. Reprint 1965. *Records of Colonial Gloucester County Virginia. A Collection of abstracts from original documents concerning the lands and people of Colonial Gloucester County.* vol. I. Berryville, Va.

Goochland
MS Court Orders 1728-1779; Register of Free Negroes 1804-1857. LVA microfilm reels 21-25, 43. PPTL 1782-1832. LVA microfilm reels 136-7.

Williams, Kathleen Booth. 1960. *Marriages of Goochland County, Virginia 1733-1815.*

Greensville
MS Deed Books 1, 2; Will Books 1-5, Court Orders 1781-1810, LVA microfilm reels 1, 2, 7, 8, 12, 13.
MS Registry of Free Negroes photocopied by the Court Clerk of Greensville County (LVA microfilm reel 25).

Knorr, Catherine Lindsay. 1955. *Marriage Bonds and Ministers' Returns of Greensville County Virginia 1781-1825.* Pine Bluff, Arkansas.
Vogt, John and T. William Kethley, Jr. eds. 1989. *Greensville County Marriages 1781-1853.* Athens, Ga., Iberian Publishing Co.

Halifax
MS Pleas [Court Orders] Nos. 7-14, 1770-1790; Will Books 1753-1792. Registers of Free Negroes 1802-1831; 1831-1853. LVA microfilm reels 36, 57-9, 83a, 147. PPTL, 1782-1812. LVA reels 147, 148.

Knorr, Catherine Lindsay. 1957. *Marriage Bonds & Ministers' Returns of Halifax County, Virginia, 1753-1800.*
T.L.C. Genealogy. 1998-2000. *Halifax County, Virginia Court Orders (Pleas) 1755-1773.* Miami Beach, Florida.

Hanover
MS Court Records [Wills, Deeds, Etc.] 1733-1735. LVA microfilm reel 2. PPTL, 1782-1816; LVA microfilm reels 159, 160.
Cocke, William Ronald, 1956. *Hanover County Taxpayers, Saint Paul's Parish, 1782-1815.*

Henrico
MS Court Orders 1678-93, 1694-1701, 1707-9, 1710-4; Minutes 1719-24; Orders 1737-46, 1752-69, 1781-91, 1791-99; Deeds, Wills, Etc. 1677-1718; 1725-1737; 1744-1748; 1748-50; 1750-67; DB 1-7; WB 1-4; Miscellaneous Court Records Vols. 1-7 [Deeds, Wills, Etc. 1650-1807]; Orphans Court 1677-1739; Register of Free Negroes 1831-1844. LVA microfilm reels 1-14, 53, 55-6, 65-72, 91, 113.
PPTL 1782-1814; Land Tax List 1799-1816. LVA microfilm nos. 171, 143.

Lindsay, Joyce H. 1960. *Marriages of Henrico County, Virginia, 1680-1808.*
Weisiger, Benjamin B. 1977. *Colonial Wills of Henrico County, Virginia. Part Two, 1737-1781.* Richmond, Va., Privately Printed.

Henry
MS Court Orders 1777-97; Will Book 1-3; Deed Book 1-3. LVA reels no. 1, 15, 20. PPTL, 1782-1830, LVA reel no. 175.

Isle of Wight
MS Court Orders 1693-1695, 1746-1780; Record of Deeds, Wills, Etc. 1661-1719; Deeds, Wills, Guardian Accounts Book, 1636-1767. Deeds 1688-1704, 1704-1715; Deeds & Wills 1715-1726; A, 1741-1766. LVA microfilm reels 1, 2, 3, 8, 22-6, 34 and 35. PPTL 1782-1810. LVA film 178.
MS List of Free Negroes photocopied by the Clerk of Court of Isle of Wight County.
Boddie, John Bennett. 1973 [1938]. *Seventeenth Century Isle of Wight County Virginia.* Genealogical Publishing.
Chapman, Blanche Adams. 1976. *Marriages of Isle of Wight County, Virginia, 1628-1800.*

James City
PPTL 1782-1824, LVA microfilm no. 183.

Duvall, Lindsay O. 1979. *Virginia Colonial Abstracts Series 2, Volume 4, James City County, Virginia 1634-1904.* Easley, S.C.: Southern Historical Press, Inc.

King George
MS Court Orders 1721-1790; Register of Free Person 1785-1799; Inventories 1721-1744; 1745-1765. LVA microfilm reels 5, 16, 22, 24, 25, 26, 58. PPTL 1782-1830. LVA reel no. 196.

Sparacio, Sam & Ruth. 1992. *Order Book Abstracts of King George County, Virginia 1721-1728.* The Antient Press. McLean, Virginia.

King & Queen County
PPTL, 1782-1823. LVA microfilm reels 192 and 193.

King William
MS Records Book 1, 1702-1707; Book 2, 1702-6, 1721-2, 1785-6; Book 3, 1793-1800. LVA microfilm reel nos. 1-2. PPTL 1782-1832; Land Tax List 1782-1811. LVA microfilm reel nos. 164, 198.

Lancaster
MS Court Orders 1696-1783. LVA microfilm nos. 26-30.
MS List of Tithables, 1745-1795. LVA microfilm.
MS Wills 1690-1835. LVA microfilm nos. 3-6; 18-21.

Burkett, Brigette. 1999. *Lancaster County, Virginia, Register of Free Negroes.* Iberian Publishing.
Lee, Ida J. 1972. *Lancaster County, Virginia Marriage Bonds, 1652-1850.*
Sparacio, Sam & Ruth. 1995-1999. *Lancaster County, Virginia Order Book, 1678-1706.* The Antient Press. McLean, Virginia.

Loudoun County
MS Court Orders 1765-83. LVA microfilm reels 71 & 72.

Sparacio, Sam & Ruth. 1997. *Loudoun County, Virginia Order Book, 1757-1764.* The Antient Press. McLean, Virginia.
Sparacio, Sam & Ruth. 1998. *Loudoun County, Virginia Tithable Lists, 1770-1774.* The Antient Press. McLean, Virginia.

Louisa
MS Orders 1742-48, 1766-82. LVA microfilm no. 29.
MS PPTL, 1782-1814, LVA microfilm no. 213.
Abercrombie, Janice. 1994. *Free Blacks of Louisa County, Virginia.* Iberian Publishing. Athens, Georgia.

Davis, Rosalie Edith. 1981. *Louisa County, Virginia, Tithables and Census 1743-1785.* Manchester, Mo., Heritage Trails.
Davis, Rosalie Edith. 1980. *Louisa County, Virginia, 1743-1814: Where Have All the Children Gone?* Manchester, Mo.: Heritage Trails.

Lunenburg
MS Court Orders 1746-84; 1796-1805; Will Book 1-5; List of Free Negroes 1815-1820. LVA microfilm reels 19-20, 25-30, 32.
MS Tax List 1748-1752, LVA Accession no.20094.
Free Negro & Slave Records, 1802-1803 ("Free Negro" census), LVA.
PPTL 1782-1807. LVA microfilm no. 217.

Bell, Landon C. 1974. *Sunlight on the Southside; List of Tithes, Lunenburg County, Virginia 1748-1783.* Baltimore: Genealogical Publishing.
TLC Genealogy. *Lunenburg County Deeds 1746-1790.* TLC Genealogy.

Madison
PPTL 1793-1818. LVA microfilm reel no. 220.

Mecklenburg
MS Orders 1765-1815; Deed Book 1-10; Will Book 1-3. LVA microfilm reels 1-5, 23, 34-40. MS Personal Property Tax Lists, 1782-1828. LVA reel 230-1. Land Tax Lists 1782-1824A. LVA reel 188-9.
MS "Free Person of Color" Registry 1809-1835 photocopied by the Clerk of Mecklenburg County.

T.L.C. Genealogy. *Mecklenburg County Deeds 1765-1776.* Miami Beach.

Middlesex County
MS Court Orders 1721-26; 1732-82; PPTL 1782-1850; Register of Free Negroes 1800-60. LVA microfilm reels 4, 23, 38-40, 74. PPTL reel 235.

Sparacio, Sam & Ruth. 1994-1998. *Middlesex County, Virginia Order Book Abstracts, 1673-1721.* The Antient Press. McLean, Virginia.
T.L.C. Genealogy. 1997. *Middlesex County, Virginia Court Orders 1711-1713.* Miami Beach, Fl.

Montgomery County
MS Court Orders 1773-1790. LVA microfilm reel 20.

New Kent
PPTL 1782-1800; 1791-1828. LVA microfilm reel nos. 246, 246A.

NSCDA, 1904. *The Parish Register of St. Peter's, New Kent County, Virginia, 1680-1787.* Richmond.
T.L.C. Genealogy. 1992. *New Kent County, Virginia Land Tax Lists, 1782-1790.* Miami Beach.

Norfolk
MS Orders 1675-1783; DB 5-8, 11-22, 25-6, 30-8, 45-48; WB F-H. LVA microfilm reels 2-9, 11, 13-5, 19-20, 46-7, 53-6. PPTL 1813-24. LVA microfilm reels 247, 249, 250.
MS Norfolk County Register of Free Negroes & Mulattos photocopied by the Court Clerk of Norfolk County.

McIntosh, Charles Fleming. 1914. *Brief Abstracts of Norfolk County Wills, 1637-1710.*
Wingo, Elizabeth B. 1961. *Marriages of Norfolk County, Virginia, 1706-1792.*
Wingo, Elizabeth B. and W. Bruce Wingo. 1979-1985. *Norfolk County, Virginia, Tithables 1730-1750, 1751-1765, 1766-1780.*

Northampton
MS Order Books: 1645-51, 1651-54, 1657-64, 1664-74; Deeds, Wills 1654-1666; Orders, Wills 1674-1710; Orders 1710-1758; Minutes 1754-1783; Orders 1783-1795. Wills & Inventories 1733-1740; Parish Record (Hungar's Parish) 1758-82. LVA microfilm reels 4-5, 27, 27a, 28-30, 46-52, 66. PPTL 1782-1823. LVA reel no. 254. Tithables 1720-23, 1727, 1737, 1744, 1769 in the loose papers at the county courthouse, photocopied by the court clerk.

Bell, John B. 1993. *Northampton County, Virginia Tithables, 1720-1769.* Heritage Books, Bowie, Maryland.
Mihalyka, Jean M. 1997. *Loose Papers and Sundry Court Cases 1628-1731, Volume I.* Hickory House, Eastville, Virginia.
Mihalyka, Jean M. 2000. *Loose Papers and Sundry Court Cases 1732-1744/5, Volume II.* Hickory House, Eastville, Virginia.
Nottingham, Stratton. 1974. *The Marriage Bonds of Northampton County, Virginia, from 1706-1854.*

Northumberland
MS Court Order Books, 1678-1783. LVA microfilm reels 48-56.
MS Personal Property Taxes 1782-1813. LVA microfilm reel 256.

Fleet, Beverley. 1961. *Virginia Colonial Abstracts, Northumberland County Record of Births 1661-1810.* Washington, D.C.
Nottingham, Stratton. 1976. *The Marriage Bonds of Northumberland County, Virginia, from 1783-1850.*
Sparacio, Sam & Ruth. 1995-1999. *Northumberland County, Virginia Order Book Abstracts 1669-1686.* McLean, Virginia.

Orange
MS Court Orders 1734-77; 1801-3; Will Book 1 (1735-1744), 2 (1744-1778). LVA microfilm reels 23, 30-33.

Little, Barbara Vines. 1988. *Orange County, Virginia Tithables 1734-1782.* Orange, Virginia.
Little, Barbara Vines. 1990. *Orange County, Virginia Order Book One 1734-1739, Part One 1734-1736.* Orange, Virginia.
Sparacio, Sam & Ruth. 1997-1998. *Orange County, Virginia Order Book, 1747-1756.* McLean, Virginia.
T.L.C. Genealogy. 1994. *Orange County, Virginia, Court Orders, 1734-1741: An Every Name Index.* Miami Beach, Fl.

Patrick
Orders 1791-1831; Will Book 1-3. LVA microfilm nos. 14, 18. PPTL, 1791-1823. LVA reel 267.

Petersburg
Register of Free Negroes & Mulattos, 1794-1819; Marriages 1785-1850. LVA microfilm no. 337.

Pittsylvania
MS Court Records 1767-1791. LVA microfilm reel 47.

Powhatan
MS Deeds & Wills 1809-1898; Deed Books 1 & 2; Register of Free Negroes 1820-65. LVA microfilm reels 1, 45. PPTL 1787-1825. LVA microfilm reel 278.

Knorr, Catherine Lindsay. 1957. *Marriage Bonds & Ministers' Returns of Powhatan County, Virginia 1777-1830.*

Prince Edward
MS Orders 1754-85. LVA microfilm nos. 21 & 22.

1280   *Sources*

Prince George
    MS Court Orders 1714-1720; 1737-40; 1811-14; Deeds, Etc. 1713-1728; Deed Book 1759-60; Deed Book 1787-92; LVA microfilm reels 1-3, 7-9. PPTL 1782-1811. LVA reel 283.

Princess Anne
    MS Court Orders/ Minutes 1691-1784. LVA Microfilm reels 38-41.

    Wingo, Elizabeth B. 1961. Reprint 1978. *Marriages of Princess Anne County, Virginia 1749-1821.*

Prince William
    MS Court Orders 1761-3; 1766-9; 1804-6; 1812-4; Will Book C, 1734-1744. LVA microfilm reel nos. 18 & 26. PPTL, 1782-1810. LVA microfilm reel 288.

    Sparacio, Ruth & Sam. 1988. *Prince William County, Virginia Order Book Abstracts 1752-1767.* McLean, Virginia.

Richmond
    MS Orders 1721-32, 1732-39, 1739-46, 1746-52. Will Book 4, 1717-25. Latter Day Saints Family History Department microfilm #33708-33710. Orders 1692-1704, 1752-84; Wills & Inventories 1699-1717; Will Book 4, 1717-25. LVA microfilm reels 22, 23, 30, 31, 36-39.

    King, George Harrison Sanford. 1966. *The Register of North Farnham Parish, 1663-1814, and Lunenburg Parish, 1783-1800, Richmond County, Virginia.* Fredericksburg, Virginia.
    Sparacio, Ruth & Sam. 1996-1997. *Richmond County, Virginia Order Book, 1704-1721.* McLean, Virginia.
    TLC Genealogy. *Richmond County, Virginia Court Orders, 1721-1752: An Every-name Index.* TLC Genealogy.

Southampton
    MS Orders 1749-89; Minutes 1775-8; 1786-1811. County Court Papers 1741-1784. Will Book 1-3. Chancery Court Papers 1750-1770. Register of Free Negroes 1794-1832. LVA microfilm reels 16, 25-7, 32, 73, 90, 91. MS Personal Property Taxes 1782-1830. LVA reels 320-3.

    Knorr, Catherine Lindsay. 1955. *Marriage Bonds & Ministers' Returns of Southampton County, Virginia 1758-1800.*

Spotsylvania
    MS Court Orders 1722-4; 1738-82; Will Book A & B 1722-59. LVA microfilm reels 26, 44 and 45.
    Sparacio, Ruth & Sam. 1987-8. *Spotsylvania County Court Orders 1724-1730; 1730-1746.* McLean, Virginia.
    T.L.C. Genealogy. 1999. *Spotsylvania County Court Orders 1746-48; 1748-50.* Miami Beach, Florida.

Stafford
    MS Will Book Liber Z, 1699-1709; Liber M, 1729-48; Liber O, 1748-63 LVA microfilm no. 6.
    Sparacio, Ruth & Sam. 1987-8. *Stafford County, Virginia Order Book Abstracts 1691-1692, 1664-1668, 1689-1690, 1691-1692, 1692-1693.* McLean, Virginia.

Surry
    MS Orders 1671-1800; Deeds, Wills, 1652-1783. LVA microfilms 1-7, 28-34.
    MS PPTL, 1782-1790; 1791-1816, LVA microfilms 329, 331.
    MS Property Tax Alterations 1782-1810, LVA microfilm.
    MS Guardian Accounts Book, 1783-1804. Registry of Free Negroes at back of book. LVA Microfilm.
    MS Registry of Free Negroes, 1804-1840. Abstracted by Mrs. Doris Stone at the Surry County Court House.

Haun, Weynette Parks. 1986-1992. *Surry County, Virginia Court Records, Book I (1652-1663), Book II (1664-1671), Book III (1672-1682), Book IV (1682-1691), Book V (1691-1700), Book VI (1700-1711).* Durham, N.C.
Hudgins, Dennis. 1995. *Surry County, Virginia Register of Free Negroes.* Virginia Genealogical Society.
Knorr, Catherine Lindsay. 1960. *Marriage Bonds and Ministers' Returns of Surry County, Virginia, 1768-1825.*

Sussex
MS Court Orders 1754-1794. LVA microfilm reels 21-23.
MS PPTL 1782-1812. LVA microfilm no. 333.
MS Certificates granted to Free negroes & mulattoes from October 1800 in conformity of an act of December 1793 photocopied by the Court Clerk of Sussex County.

Haun, Weynette Parks. 1993. *Sussex County, Virginia Court Records 1754-1801, Book I, Court of Oyer & Terminer, 1754-1801; Order Book 1754-56.* Durham, N.C.
Knorr, 1952. *Marriage Bonds and Ministers' Returns of Sussex County, Virginia, 1754-1810.*

Warwick
MS Court Orders 1713-1714, Minute Book 1748-1762, LVA microfilm reel no. 1.

Westmoreland
MS Court Orders 1690-1797; Records, Inventories, 1723-1746, 1746-52, 1752-56, 1756-67; Deeds & Wills 1653-1748; 1756-61; 1773-1799; Free Negro Register, 1819-1826; 1828-1849. LVA microfilm reels 1-6, 9, 12, 14-15, 29-32, 52-62, 100. PPTL, 1782-1815. LVA reel no. 344.

Dorman, John Frederick. 1962-1988. *Westmoreland County, Virginia, Order Books 1675-1689, 1690-1698, 1698-1705.* Washington, D.C.: J.F. Dorman.
Nottingham, Stratton. 1928. Reprint 1975. *The Marriage License Bonds of Westmoreland County, Virginia, 1786 to 1850.*

York
MS Deeds, Wills, Orders 1633-1787; Deeds 1729-54; Orders 1788-1803. LVA microfilm reels 1-11, 14, 29-34, 38. PPTL 1782-1841. LVA reel 353.
MS Register of Free Negroes 1798-1831; Free Negroes Register 1831-1850 photocopied by the clerk of York County.

Dorman, John Frederick. 1974-1980. *York County, Virginia, Deeds, Orders, Wills, etc., 1687-1697.* Washington, D.C.: J.F. Dorman.
Duvall, Lindsay O. 1978. *Virginia Colonial Abstracts Series 2, Vol. 5, Wills, Deeds, Orders of York County, Virginia 1657-1659.* Easley, S.C.: Southern Historical Press.

SOUTH CAROLINA

Journal of the South Carolina Court of General Sessions, 1769-1776. South Carolina Archives microfilm SC-AR-M-14, AD721.
MS South Carolina Tax Returns 1783-1800, South Carolina Archives microfilm AD-941 and AD-942.
MS Marlboro County, South Carolina, Clerk of Court Minutes of the County; Intermediate; Common Pleas; and Gen Sessions Court. South Carolina Archives Microfilm C258.
MS Fairfield County, South Carolina County Court Minutes of the County Court, 1785-86; 1791-99. South Carolina Archives microfilm C348.
MS Parochial Register of the Parishes of St. Thomas & St. Denis, 1693-1794. Latter Day Saints Microfilm no. 22742.

The Combined Alphabetical Index. South Carolina Department of Archives and History, Columbia, South Carolina. http://www.archivesindex.sc.gov
Accelerated Indexing Systems. 1973. *South Carolina 1800 Census.* Accelerated Indexing Systems.

Brown, Richard Maxwell. 1963. *The South Carolina Regulators*. Cambridge: Belknap Press of Harvard University.
Gregg, Right Rev. Alexander. 1867. *History of the Old Cheraws*. New York.
Henry, H.M. 1968. *The Police Control of the Slave in South Carolina*. New York: Negro Universities Press.
Holcolm, Brent Howard. 1980. *South Carolina Marriages, 1688-1799*. Genealogical Press.
_____. 1996. *Petitions for Land from the South Carolina Council Journals, Volume I (1734-1748) Volume III (1752-1753)*. Columbia, S.C.
Lucas, Silas Emmett, Jr. 1977. *An Index to Deeds of the Province and State of South Carolina 1719-1785 and Charleston District 1785-1800*. Easley, S.C.: Southern Historical Press.
NSCDA. 1916. *The Register Book for the Parish Prince Frederick Winyaw*. Baltimore.
Salley, A.S., Jr., ed. 1904. Reprint 1971. *Register of St. Philips Parish, Charles Town, South Carolina, 1720-1758*. University of S.C. Press.
Smith, D.E. Hugger and Salley, A.S., Jr., ed. 1927. Reprint 1971. *Register of St. Philips Parish, Charles Town, or Charlestown, South Carolina, 1754-1810*. University of S.C. Press.
Warren, Mary Bondurant. 1988. *South Carolina Newspapers*, Heritage Papers.

CENSUS RECORDS

MS North Carolina Governor's Office Census of 1784-87. N.C. Archives Microfilm S.51.567.
MS North Carolina Census: 1800, 1810, 1820, and 1830. Microfilms M32:29-34; M252:38-43; M33:80-85; M19:121,123.
MS Virginia Census: 1810 and 1820. M252:66-71; M33:130, 140.
MS South Carolina Census: 1790, 1800, 1810, and 1820. Microfilms M637-11; M32:47-50; M252:60-62.

Bradley, Stephen E., Jr. 1987. *The 1860 Federal Census Halifax County, North Carolina*. South Boston, Va.: Privately printed.
Bureau of the Census. 1966 [1908]. *Heads of Families at the First Census of the United States Taken in the Year 1790 - Records of the State Enumerations: 1782 to 1785, Virginia*. Baltimore.
Bureau of the Census. 1990 [1908]. *Heads of Families at the First Census of the United States Taken in the Year 1790: North Carolina*. Athens, Ga.: Iberian Publishing Co.
Bureau of the Census. 1978 [1908]. *Heads of Families at the First Census of the United States Taken in the Year 1790: South Carolina*. Baltimore.
Bureau of the Census. 1965 [1908]. *Heads of Families at the First Census of the United States Taken in the Year 1790: Maryland*. Baltimore.
Bureau of the Census. *Pennsylvania, First Census 1790*.
Schreiner-Yantis, Netti and Florene Speakman Love. 1987. *The 1787 Census of Virginia. An Accounting of the Name of Every White Male Tithable Over 21 Years; the Number of Slaves Over 16 & those Under 16 Years; together with a Listing of their Horses, cattle & Carriages; and also the Names of all Persons to whom Ordinary Licenses and Physician's Licenses were Issued*. Springfield, Virginia, Genealogical Books in Print.
Fothergill, Augusta B. and John Mark Naugle. 1986. *Virginia Tax Payers 1782-87 Other Than Those Published by the United States Census Bureau*. Baltimore.
Yantis, Netti Schreiner. 1971. *A Supplement to the 1810 Census of Virginia*.

VIRGINIA PARISH REGISTERS AND VESTRY BOOKS

MS Overwharton Parish, Stafford County, Register 1724-1774. LVA Accession No. 25593.
MS Bruton Parish, James City and York County Register and Baptisms 1739-1797, Burials 1662-1761. LVA Miscellaneous Microfilm Reel 448a.
MS Abingdon Parish, Gloucester County, Register.
MS Albemarle Parish, Surry and Sussex County Parish Register, 1739-1778, Latter Day Saints Family History Department microfilm no. 0030161.
MS St. Paul's Parish, King George County, Virginia, Parish Register, 1716-1793. Latter Day Saints Family History Department microfilm no. 0033859.

Bell, Landon C. 1932. *Charles Parish, York County, Virginia, History and Registers, Births 1648-1789, Deaths 1665-1787.* Richmond: VSLB.

Chamberlayne, Churchill G. 1898. *The Vestry Book and Register of Bristol Parish, Virginia, 1720-1789.* Richmond, Va.: William Ellis Jones Steam Book and Job Printer.

Chamberlayne, Churchill G.ˊ 1931. *The Vestry Book of Stratton Major Parish, King & Queen County, Virginia, 1729-1783.* Richmond.

Chamberlayne, Churchill G. 1935. *The Vestry Book of Blisland Parish, New Kent and James City Counties, Virginia, 1721-1786.* Richmond: Virginia State Library Board.

Chamberlayne, Churchill G. 1937. *The Vestry Book & Register of St. Peter's Parish, New Kent & James City Counties, Virginia 1684-1786.*

Chamberlayne, Churchill G. 1940. *The Vestry Book of St. Paul's Parish Hanover County Virginia.* Richmond, Va.: Library Board.

Davis, Rosalie Edith. 1981. *Fredericksville Parish Vestry Book, Indentures and Processioning Returns 1742-1787.* Manchester, Mo.: Heritage Trails.

Historic Dumfries Virginia, Inc. 1976. *The Records of Dettingen Parish, Prince William County, Virginia, Vestry Book 1745-1785, Minutes of Meetings of the Overseers of the Poor 1788-1802, Indentures 1749-1782.* Dumfries.

Jones, W. Mac. 1966. *The Douglas Register, Being a Detailed Record of Births Marriages and Deaths, Kept by Rev. William Douglas 1750-1797.* Baltimore.

Matheny, Emma R. and Helen K. Yates. *Kingston Parish Register, Gloucester and Mathews Counties, 1749-1827.* privately printed.

National Society of the Colonial Dames of America. 1964. *The Parish Register of Christ Church, Middlesex County, Virginia from 1653 to 1812.* Baltimore.

Richards, Gertrude, R.B. 1958. *Register of Albemarle Parish, Surry & Sussex Counties, Virginia, 1739-1778.*

GENERAL

MS *The Virginia Gazette*, photocopied by Prince William County Genealogical Society, Manassas, Virginia 22110-0812.

Runaway Slave advertisements from 18th-century Virginia newspapers. Compiled by Professor Thomas Costa, Associate Professor of History, University of Virginia's College at Wise. http://etext.lib.virginia.edu/subjects/runaways/allrecords.html

MS Revolutionary War Pension Files. National Archives microfilm series M805.

Adjutant General of North Carolina. 1976. *Muster Rolls of the Soldiers of the War of 1812 Detached from the Militia of North Carolina in 1812 and 1814*, Genealogical Publishing, Baltimore.

Bockstruck, Lloyd DeWitt. *Virginia's Colonial Soldiers.*

Byrd, William L. 1999. *In Full Force and Virtue: North Carolina Emancipation Records, 1713-1860.* Heritage Books, Inc. Bowie, Maryland.

Clark, Murtie June. 1983. *Colonial Soldiers of the South, 1732-1774.* Baltimore, Md.: Genealogical Publishing Co., Inc.

Clark, Walter, ed. 1895-1907. *The State Records of North Carolina.* 16 vols. numbered XI-XXVI. Winston and Goldsboro, N.C.: State of North Carolina.

Creekmore, Pollyanna. 1980. *Early East Tennessee Taxpayers.* Easley, S.C.: Southern Historical Press.

des Cognets, Louis, Jr., ed. 1958. *English Duplicates of Lost Virginia Records.* Princeton.

Dorman, Frederick. 1958-1995. *Virginia Revolutionary Pension Applications*, Volumes 1-45. Washington, D.C.

Dumont, William H. *Some Virginia Revolutionary Veterans and Their Heirs.* Washington, D.C.: Fiscal Section of the National Archives.

Fouts, Raymond Parker. 1984. *Abstracts from Newspapers of Edenton, Fayetteville, & Hillsborough, North Carolina 1785-1800.* Cocoa, Fl.

Fouts, Raymond Parker. 1983. *Abstracts from the North Carolina Gazette of New Bern, North Carolina 1751-1759 and 1768-1790 Volume I.* Cocoa, Fl.

Fouts, Raymond Parker. *Abstracts from the North Carolina Journal, Halifax, North Carolina. 1792-1794, Vol. I.* Cocoa, Fl.

Gray, Gertrude Entz. 1987. *Virginia Northern Neck Land Grants 1694-1742.* Baltimore: Genealogical Publishing Co., Inc.

Gill, Harold B. 1989. *Apprentices of Virginia, 1623-1800.* Ancestry.

Grimes, Bryan J. 1967. *Abstract of North Carolina Wills. Compiled from Original Wills Recorded in the Office of the Secretary of State.* Baltimore.

Hall, Wilmer L., ed. 1945. *Executive Journals of the Council of Colonial Virginia, Vol. V, November 1739 - May 7, 1754.* Virginia State Library.

Haun, Weynette Parks. 1990. *North Carolina Revolutionary Army Accounts Secretary of State Treasurer's & Comptroller's Papers, Vol. I & II, Part II.* Durham, N.C.

Haun, Weynette Parks. 1989. *North Carolina Revolutionary Army Accounts Secretary of State Treasurer's & Comptroller's Papers, Journal "A", (Public Accounts) 1775-1776.* Durham, N.C.

Hening, William W., ed. 1809-23. *The Statutes at Large: Being a Collection of all the Laws of Virginia.* Richmond.

Hillman, Benjamin J., ed. 1966. *Executive Journals of the Council of Colonial Virginia, Vol. VI., June 20, 1754 - May 3, 1775.* Virginia State Library.

Historical & Genealogical Society of Randolph County (Indiana) 1882. *History of Randolph County.*

Hoffman, Margaret M. 1979. *Province of North Carolina, 1663-1729, Abstracts of Land Patents.* Roanoke Rapids, N.C.

Hoffman, Margaret M. *Colony of North Carolina (1735-1764), Abstracts of Land Patents, Volume I.* Roanoke Rapids, N.C.

Hoffman, Margaret M. 1984. *Colony of North Carolina (1765-1775), Abstracts of Land Patents, Volume II.* Roanoke Rapids, N.C.

Hoffman, Margaret M. 1986. *The Granville District of North Carolina 1748-1763: Abstracts of Land Grants.* Roanoke Rapids, N.C.

Hopkins, William Lindsay. 1988. *Suffolk Parish Vestry Book, 1749-1784, Nansemond County, Virginia, and Newport Parish Vestry Book, 1724-1772, Isle of Wight County, Virginia.* Richmond, Va.

Hopkins, William Lindsay. 1988. *Virginia Revolutionary War Land Grant Claims, 1783-1850 (Rejected).* Richmond.

Joyner, Peggy Shomo. 1986. *Abstracts of Virginia's Northern Neck Warrants & Surveys, Dunmore, Shenandoah, Culpeper, Prince William, Fauquier & Stafford Counties 1710-1780.* Volume III. Portsmouth, Va.: Privately printed.

Kent, Henriette Thorne. 1991. *Swampers, Free Blacks and The Great Dismal Swamp.* Privately printed.

Leary, Helen F.M., and Maurice R. Stirewalt, eds. 1980. *North Carolina Research, Genealogy and Local History.* Raleigh: North Carolina Genealogical Society.

McBride, Ransom. *Revolutionary War Service Records and Settlements*, published in the *North Carolina Genealogical Society Journal.*

MacLean, J. P. 1907 (1975 reprint). *Shakers of Ohio: Fugitive Papers Concerning the Shakers of Ohio, with Unpublished Manuscripts.* Philadelphia: Porcupine Press.

McIlwaine, H. B., ed. 1925. *Executive Journals of the Council of Colonial Virginia, Vol. I, June 11, 1680 - June 22, 1699...Vol. IV.* Virginia State Library.

McIlwaine, H. B., ed. 1908. *Journals of the House of Burgesses of Virginia, 1619-1658/9...1761-1765.* Richmond.

McIlwaine, H.B., ed. 1979 (second edition). *Minutes of the Council and General Court of Virginia,* Richmond: Virginia State Library.

North Carolina Daughters of the American Revolution. *Roster of Soldiers from North Carolina in the American Revolution.* Durham: North Carolina DAR, 1932. reprinted: Baltimore: Genealogical Publishing Co., 1984.

North Carolina Genealogical Society Journal. Raleigh: North Carolina Genealogical Society. 1975-

North Carolinian. 20 volumes (Raleigh, 1955-74).

North Carolina Historical & Genealogical Register (Hathaway's Register). 1970-1971. Baltimore: Genealogical Publishing.

Nugent, Nell Marion. 1934-1980. *Cavaliers and Pioneers: Abstracts of Virginia Land Patents and Grants, 1623-1732.* 3 Vols. Richmond.

Puetz, C.J. 1983. *North Carolina County Maps.* Lyndon Station, Wisconsin.

Schweninger, Loren, *Race, Slavery and Free Black Petitions to Southern Legislatures, Race And Slavery Petitions Project*, http://library.uncg.edu/slavery_petitions

Saunders, William L., et. al., eds. 1886-1890. *The Colonial Records of North Carolina*, vols. I-IX. Raleigh, N.C.: Josephus Daniels.

Smith, Annie Laurie Wright, comp. 1975. *The Quit Rents of Virginia, 1704*. Baltimore: Genealogical Publishing Co., Inc.

Southern Historical Press. 1978. *Virginia Colonial Abstracts Series 2, Vol. 5. Wills, Deeds, Orders of York County, Virginia 1657-1659*. Easley, S.C: Southern Historical Press, Inc.

Torrence, Clayton. 1965. *Virginia Wills and Administrations 1632-1800*.

Torrence, Clayton. 1973 [1935]. *Old Somerset on the Eastern Shore of Maryland: A Study in Foundations and Founders*. Baltimore: Regional Publishing Company.

Turner, C.H.B. 1909. *Some Records of Sussex County, Delaware*. Philadelphia: Allen, Lane & Scott.

Turpin, Joan. 1985. *Register of Black, Mulatto, and Poor Persons in Four Ohio Counties 1791-1861*. Heritage Books, Inc.

Virginia Genealogist, Volumes 1-33. Washington D.C.

Whitelaw, Ralph T. 1951. *Virginia's Eastern Shore*. Virginia Historical Society.

Woodson, Robert F. and Isobel B. 1970. *Virginia Tithables from Burned Record Counties*. Richmond.

BOOKS AND ARTICLES

Bell, Albert D. 1961. *Bass Families of the South, A collection of historical and genealogical source materials from public and private records*. Rocky Mount, N.C.: Privately printed.

Berlin, Ira. 1976. *Slaves Without Masters: The Free Negro in the Antebellum South*. New York: Vintage Books.

Blu, Karen. 1980. *The Lumbee Problem*. Cambridge University Press.

Bockstruck, Lloyd DeWitt. 1988. *Virginia's Colonial Soldiers*. Baltimore.

Brown, Kathleen M. 1996. *Good Wives, Nasty Wenches, and Anxious Patriarchs*. University of North Carolina Press, Chapel Hill.

Butler, Reginald Dennin. 1989. *Evolution of a rural free black community: Goochland County, Virginia, 1728-1832*. Ph.D. Diss. The Johns Hopkins University.

Catterall, Helen Honor Tunnicliff. 1926. *Judicial Cases Concerning American Slavery and the Negro*. Carnegie Institute of Washington; repr. New York: Negro Universities Press, a Division of Greenwood Publishing Corp., 1968.

Crow, Jeffrey J. 1983. *The Black Experience in Revolutionary North Carolina*. Raleigh.

Davidson, Thomas E. "Free Blacks in Old Somerset County, 1745-1755," *Maryland Historical Magazine*, Vol. 80, no.2, 151-156.

Deal, Joseph Douglas, III. 1981. *Race and Class in Colonial Virginia: Indians, Englishmen and Africans on the Eastern Shore during the Seventeenth Century*. Ph.D. Diss., Univ. of Rochester.

Franklin, John Hope. *The Free Negro in North Carolina, 1790-1860*. Chapel Hill: University of North Carolina Press.

Horton, James Oliver and Lois E. 1979. *Black Bostonians*. New York.

Jackson, Luther Porter. 1944. *Virginia Negro Soldiers and Seamen in the Revolutionary War*. Norfolk, Virginia.

Johnston, James Hugo. 1970. *Race Relations in Virginia and Miscegenation in the South 1776-1860*. Amherst.

Jordan, Winthrop D. 1977. *White over Black: American Attitudes Toward the Negro, 1550-1812*. New York: W.W. Norton & Co.

Kimmel, Ross M. "Free Blacks in Seventeenth Century Maryland," *Maryland Historical Magazine*, vol. 71, No. 1, 19-25.

Koger, Larry. 1995. *Black Slaveowners: Free Black Masters in South Carolina, 1790-1860*. University of South Carolina Press.

Madden, T.O. 1993. *We Were Always Free*. Vintage Books.

Minton, Henry M. *Early History of Negroes in Business in Philadelphia (read before the American Negro Historical Society, March 1913)*. Nashville, Tennessee: A.M.E.S.S. Union.

Mordecai, Samuel. 1860. 1975 reprint. *Virginia, Especially Richmond in By-gone Days*. New York: Arno Press.

Morgan, Edmund S. 1975. *American Slavery American Freedom, The Ordeal of Colonial Virginia*. New York.

National Society Daughters of the American Revolution. 2001. *African American and American Indian Patriots of the Revolutionary War*. Washington, D.C.

Nicholls, Michael, L., "Passing Through This Troublesome World, Free Blacks in the Early Southside," *Virginia Magazine of History and Biography*, 92(1984), 50-70.

Norment, Mrs. Mary C. 1895. *The Lowrie History*. Weldon, N.C.: Harrell's Printing House.

Richter, Caroline Julia. 1992. *A Community and its Neighborhoods: Charles Parish, York County, Virginia, 1630-1740*. PhD. Dissertation, College of William and Mary.

Rountree, Helen C. "The Termination and Dispersal of the Nottoway Indians of Virginia," *Virginia Magazine of History and Biography*, Vol. 95 No.2 (1987), 193-214.

Rountree, Helen C. 1990. *Pocahantas's People. The Powhatan Indians of Virginia through four centuries*. Norman: University of Oklahoma Press.

Rountree, Helen C. & Thomas E. Davidson. 1997. *Eastern Shore Indians of Virginia and Maryland*. Charlottesville: University Press of Virginia.

Russell, John H. 1913. *The Free Negro in Virginia 1619-1865*. Baltimore.

Sneed, Laurel C. & Christine Westfall. 1995. *Uncovering the Hidden History of Thomas Day: Findings and Methodology*. Thomas Day Education Project of the Communications Resources Foundations, Inc. of North Carolina.

Taylor, R. H. 1920. *The Free Negro in North Carolina* (James Sprunt Historical Publications). Chapel Hill.

Swanton, John R. 1979. *The Indian Tribes of North America*. Smithsonian Institute Press.

Wiley, Bell I., ed. 1980. *Slaves No More: Letters From Liberia, 1833-1869*. Lexington: University Press of Kentucky.

Wise, Erbon, W. 1983. *Sweat Families of the South*. Sulphur, La.: Privately printed.

Workers of the Writers' Program of the Work Projects Administration in the State of Virginia. 1994. *The Negro in Virginia*. Winston Salem, North Carolina.

INDEX